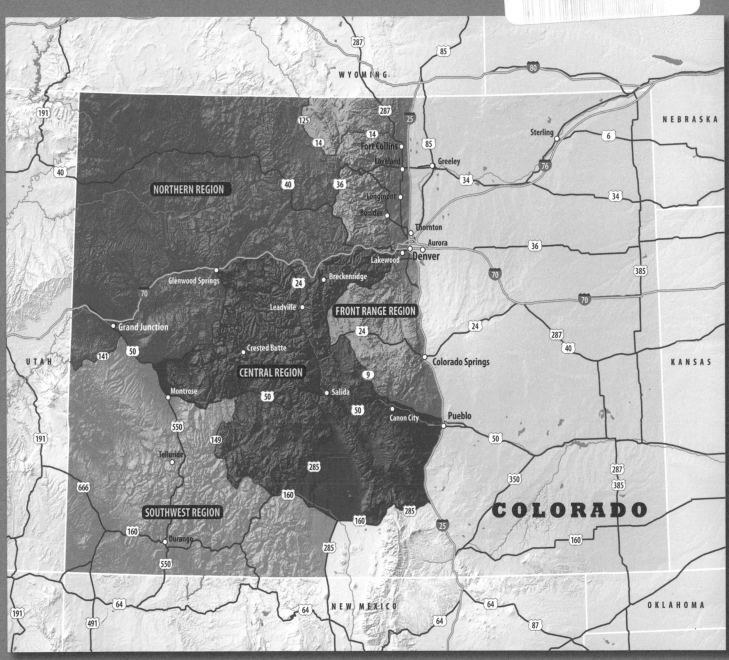

COLORADO MAP
Showing Regional Boundaries

BACKCOUNTRY ADVENTURES
COLORADO

Publisher's Cataloging-in-Publication
(Provided by Quality Books, Inc.)

    Massey, Peter,
        Backcountry adventures. Colorado / Peter Massey,
        Jeanne Wilson, Angela Titus.
        p. cm.
        Includes bibliographical references and index.
        ISBN-13: 978-1-930193-06-2
        ISBN-10: 1-930193-06-8

        1. Automobile travel--Colorado--Guidebooks.
    2. Four-wheel drive vehicles. 3. Ghost towns--Colorado--
Guidebooks. 4. Plants--Colorado--Identification.
5. Animals--Colorado--Identification. 6. Colorado--
Guidebooks. I. Wilson, Jeanne. II. Titus, Angela.
III. Title.

GV1024.M37 2008   917.8804'34
                      QBI08-600152

BACKCOUNTRY ADVENTURES
COLORADO

**PETER MASSEY
JEANNE WILSON
ANGELA TITUS**

ADLER
PUBLISHING

Adler Publishing Company, Inc.
P.O. Box 519, Castle Rock, CO 80104
Phone: (303) 660-2158
Toll-free: (800) 660-5107
Fax: (303) 660-4300
www.4WDbooks.com

Contents

Introduction

Four-wheel driving spells freedom and adventure. A four-wheel drive vehicle, whether a sport utility vehicle or a pickup truck, is vastly superior to a normal family sedan when it comes to exploring the sights of Colorado because many of the best sights require you to leave the pavement.

Yet most of the millions of sport utility vehicle owners do not take full advantage of the opportunities their vehicles can provide. If you would like to make more of the off-highway capabilities of your vehicle, then this book is for you.

Four-wheeling helps you to make the most of Colorado's backcountry, opening up a multitude of opportunities:

- explore the grandeur of the Rocky Mountains
- visit ghost towns straight out of the Wild West
- step back in history to the remote silver-mining camps of the 1800s
- cross mountain passes used by the American Indians for centuries
- view Colorado's wild animals in their own habitats
- marvel at peaceful alpine meadows, ablaze with spring wildflowers
- enjoy backcountry locations, far from the maddening crowds
- access the best locations for other activities—backcountry camping, hiking, mountain-bike and trail-bike riding, hunting, and fishing

We have selected 143 trails to let you escape into the magical Colorado backcountry. All the trails are within the scope of stock, high-clearance sport utility vehicles. They range in difficulty from trails that are suitable for those who have never driven off-highway to trails that provide more of a challenge to drivers accustomed to off-highway touring.

The rewards of touring Colorado's scenic backroads and 4x4 trails are immense. We hope all readers are rewarded with as much enjoyment as we have had as they travel to the most spectacular, interesting, and historic locations in Colorado.

Before You Go

Why a 4WD Does It Better

The design and engineering of 4WD sport utility vehicles provide them with many advantages over normal cars when you head off the paved road:

■ improved distribution of power to all four wheels;

■ a transmission transfer case, which provides low-range gear selection for greater pulling power and for crawling over difficult terrain;

■ high ground clearance;

■ less overhang of the vehicle's body past the wheels, which provides better front- and rear-clearance when crossing gullies and ridges;

■ large-lug, wide-tread tires;

■ rugged construction (including underbody skid plates on many models).

If you plan to do off-highway touring, all of these considerations are important whether you are evaluating the capabilities of your current sport utility vehicle (SUV) or are looking to buy one; each is considered in detail in this chapter.

To explore the most difficult trails described in this book, you will need a SUV that is well rated in each of the above features. If you own a 2WD sport utility vehicle, a lighter car-type SUV, or a low-clearance 2WD pickup truck, your ability to explore the more difficult trails will depend on conditions and your level of experience.

A word of caution: Whatever type of 4WD vehicle you drive, understand that it is not invincible or indestructible. Nor can it go everywhere. A SUV has a much higher center of gravity and weighs more than a car, and so has its own consequent limitations.

Experience is the only way to learn what your vehicle can and cannot do. Therefore, if you are inexperienced, we strongly recommend that you start with trails that have lower difficulty ratings. As you develop an understanding of your vehicle and of your own taste for adventure, you can safely tackle the more challenging trails.

One way to beef up your knowledge quickly, while avoiding the costly and sometimes dangerous lessons learned from on-the-road mistakes, is to undertake a 4WD driving course taught by a professional. Look in the Yellow Pages for courses in your area.

Using This Book

Route Planning

Regional maps at the beginning of each chapter provide a convenient overview of the trails in that portion of the state. Each trail is highlighted in a different color, and major highways and towns are indicated, to help you plan various routes by connecting a series of trails and paved roads.

As you plan your overall route, you will probably want to utilize as many backroads and 4x4 trails as possible. However, check the difficulty rating and time required for each trail before finalizing your plans. You don't want to be stuck 50 miles from the highway—at sunset and without camping gear, since your trip was supposed to be over hours ago—when you discover that your vehicle can't handle a certain difficult passage.

You can calculate the distances between Colorado towns by turning to the Colorado Distance Chart inside the back cover of this book.

Difficulty Ratings

We utilize a point system to rate the difficulty of each backroad and 4x4 trail. Any such system is subjective, and your experience of the trails will vary depending on your skill and the road conditions at the time. Indeed, any amount of rain may make the trails much more difficult, if not completely impassable.

We have rated the trails on a scale of 1 to 10—1 being passable for a normal passenger vehicle in good conditions and 10 requiring a heavily modified vehicle and an experienced driver who expects to encounter vehicle damage. Because this book is designed for owners of unmodified, high-clearance 4WD vehicles—who we assume do not want to damage their vehicles—most of the trails are rated 5 or lower. A few trails are included that rate as high as 7, while those rated 8 to 10 are beyond the scope of this book.

This is not to say that the moderate-rated trails are easy. We strongly recommend that inexperienced drivers not tackle trails rated at 4 or higher until they have undertaken a number of the lower-rated ones, so that they can gauge their skill level and prepare for the difficulty of the higher-rated trails.

In assessing the backroads and 4x4 trails, we have always assumed good road conditions (dry road surface, good visibility, and so on). The factors influencing our ratings are as follows:

■ obstacles such as rocks, mud, ruts, sand, slickrock, and stream crossings;

■ the stability of the road surface;

■ the width of the road and the vehicle clearance between trees or rocks;

■ the steepness of the road;

■ the margin for driver error (for example, a very high, open shelf road would be rated more difficult even if it was not very steep and had a stable surface).

The following is a guide to the ratings.

Rating 1: The trail is graded dirt but suitable for a normal passenger vehicle. It usually has gentle grades, is fairly wide, and has very shallow water crossings (if any).

Rating 2: High-clearance vehicles are preferred but not necessary. These trails are dirt roads, but they may have rocks, grades, water crossings, or ruts that make clearance a concern in a normal passenger vehicle. The trails are fairly wide, making passing possible at almost any point along the trail. Mud is not a concern under normal weather conditions.

Rating 3: High-clearance 4WDs are preferred, but any high-clearance vehicle is acceptable. Expect a rough road surface; mud and sand are possible but will be easily passable. You may encounter rocks up to 6 inches in diameter, a loose road surface, and shelf roads, though these will be wide enough for passing or will have adequate pull-offs.

Rating 4: High-clearance is required, 4WD is preferred, though some stock SUVs are acceptable. Expect a rough road surface with rocks larger than 6 inches, but there will be a reasonable driving line available. Patches of mud are possible but can be readily negotiated; sand may be deep and require lower tire pressures. There may be stream crossings up to 12 inches deep, substantial sections of single-lane shelf road, moderate grades, and sections of moderately loose road surface.

Rating 5: High-clearance 4WDs are required. These trails have either a rough, rutted surface, rocks up to 9 inches, mud and deep sand that may be impassable for inexperienced drivers, or stream crossings up to 18 inches deep. Certain sections may be steep enough to cause traction problems, and you may encounter very narrow shelf roads with steep drop-offs and tight clearance between rocks or trees.

Rating 6: These trails are for experienced four-wheel drivers only. They are potentially dangerous, with large rocks, ruts, or terraces that may need to be negotiated. They may also have stream crossings at least 18 inches deep, involve rapid currents, unstable stream bottoms, or difficult access; steep slopes, loose surfaces, and narrow clearances; or very narrow sections of shelf road with steep drop-offs and possibly challenging road surfaces.

Rating 7: Skilled, experienced four-wheel drivers only. These trails include very challenging sections with extremely steep grades, loose surfaces, large rocks, deep ruts, and/or tight clearances. Mud or sand may necessitate winching.

Rating 8 and above: Stock vehicles are likely to be damaged and may find the trail impassable. Highly skilled, experienced four-wheel drivers only.

Scenic Ratings

If rating the degree of difficulty is subjective, rating scenic beauty is guaranteed to lead to arguments. Despite the subjectivity of attempting a comparative rating of diverse scenery, we have tried to provide a guide to the relative scenic quality of the various trails. The ratings are based on a scale of 1 to 10, with 10 being the most attractive.

Estimated Driving Times

In calculating driving times, we have not allowed for stops. Your actual travel time may be considerably longer depending on the number and duration of the stops you make. Add more time for stops and if you prefer to drive more slowly than good conditions allow.

Current Road Information

All the 4WD trails described in this book may become impassable in poor weather conditions. Storms can alter roads, remove tracks, and create impassable washes. Most of the trails described, even easy backroads, can quickly become impassable even to 4WD vehicles after only a small amount of rain. For each trail, we have provided a phone number for obtaining current information about conditions.

Abbreviations

The route directions for the 4WD trails use a series of abbreviations as follows:

SO	CONTINUE STRAIGHT ON
TL	TURN LEFT
TR	TURN RIGHT
BL	BEAR LEFT
BR	BEAR RIGHT
UT	U-TURN

Using Route Directions

For every trail, we describe and pinpoint (by odometer reading) nearly every significant feature along the route—such as intersections, streams, washes, gates, cattle guards, and so on—and provide directions from these landmarks. Odometer readings will vary from vehicle to vehicle, so you should allow for slight variations. Be aware that trail conditions can quickly change. A new trail may be cut around a washout, a faint trail can be graded by the county, or a well-used trail may fall into disuse. All these factors will affect the accuracy of the given directions.

If you diverge from the route, zero your trip meter upon your return and continue along the route, making the necessary adjustment to the point-to-point odometer readings. In the directions, we regularly reset the odometer readings—at significant landmarks or popular lookouts and spur trails—so that you won't have to recalculate for too long.

Most of the trails can be started from either end, and the route directions include both directions of travel; reverse directions are printed in blue below the main directions. When traveling in reverse, read from the bottom of the table and work up.

Route directions include cross-references whenever two trails included in this book connect; these cross-references allow for an easy change of route or destination.

Each trail includes periodic latitude and longitude readings to facilitate using a global positioning system (GPS) receiver. These readings may also assist you in finding your location on the maps. The GPS coordinates were taken using the WGS 84 datum and are in the format dd°mm.mm'. To save time when loading coordinates into your GPS receiver, you may wish to include only one decimal place, since in Colorado, the first decimal place equals about 165 yards and the second only about 16 yards.

Map References

We recommend that you supplement the information in this book with more-detailed maps. For each trail, we list the sheet maps and road atlases that provide the best detail for the area. Typically, the following references are given:
- Bureau of Land Management Maps
- U.S. Forest Service Maps
- *Colorado Road & Recreation Atlas,* 1st ed. (Medford, Oregon: Benchmark Maps, 2007)—Scale 1:400,000
- *Colorado Atlas & Gazetteer,* 7th ed. (Yarmouth, Maine: DeLorme Mapping, 2004)—Scale 1:260,000
- *The Roads of Colorado* (Addison, Texas: Mapsco, Inc., 2007)—Scale 1:160,000
- Maptech-Terrain Navigator Topo Maps—Scale 1:100,000 and 1:24,000
- *Trails Illustrated* Topo Maps; National Geographic Maps —Various scales, but all contain good detail

We recommend Benchmark's *Road & Recreation Atlas* series. The maps provide excellent overall coverage with page-to-page overlap, large type, topographical relief, and they are field checked for accuracy. These atlases provide United States, regional, and state maps for orientation, as well as enlarged "Metro Maps" for navigating urban areas. The Recreation Guide section, which provides information on local attractions and recreation, is also handy for trip planning. It is particularly useful if you wish to explore the hundreds of side roads that you will encounter when driving the backroads and 4x4 trails in this book.

The *Trails Illustrated* series of maps is reliable, easy to read, and printed on nearly indestructible plastic paper. However, the series does not cover all of the backroads and 4x4 trails described in this book.

The DeLorme *Colorado Atlas & Gazetteer* is useful and provides you with maps of the entire state at a reasonable price.

U.S. Forest Service maps lack the topographic detail of the other sheet maps and, in our experience, are occasionally out of date. They have the advantage of covering a broad area and are useful in identifying land use and travel restrictions. These maps are most useful for the longer trails.

The Terrain Navigator series of maps published on CD by Maptech are also very useful. These CDs contain an amazing level of detail because they include the entire set of U.S. Geological Survey topographical maps of Colorado at both the 1:24,000 scale and the 1:100,000 scale. These maps offer many advantages over normal maps:
- GPS coordinates for any location can be found and loaded into your GPS receiver. Conversely, if you have your GPS coordinates, your location on the map can be pinpointed instantly.
- Towns, rivers, passes, mountains, and many other sites are indexed by name so that they can be located quickly.
- 4WD trails can be marked and profiled for elevation changes and distances from point to point.
- Customized maps can be printed out.

The CDs can be used with a laptop computer and a GPS receiver in your vehicle to monitor your location on the map and navigate directly from the display.

All these maps should be available through good map stores.

Backcountry Driving Rules and Permits

Four-wheel driving involves special techniques and road rules. This section outlines information all backcountry drivers should know.

4WD Road Rules

To help ensure that these trails remain open and available for all four-wheel drivers to enjoy, it is important to minimize your impact on the environment and not be a safety risk to yourself or anyone else. Remember that the 4WD clubs fight a constant battle with the government and various lobby groups to retain the access that currently exists.

The fundamental rule when traversing the backroads and 4x4 trails described in this book is to use common sense. In addition, special road rules for 4x4 trails apply:
- Vehicles traveling uphill have the right of way.
- If you are moving more slowly than the vehicle behind you, pull over to let the other vehicle by.
- Park out of the way in a safe place. Blocking a track may restrict access for emergency vehicles as well as for other recreationalists. Set the parking brake—don't rely on leaving the transmission in park. Manual transmissions should be left in the lowest gear.

Tread Lightly!

Remember the rules of the Tread Lightly! program:
- Be informed. Obtain maps, regulations, and other information from the forest service or from other public land agencies. Learn the rules and follow them.
- Resist the urge to pioneer a new road or trail or to cut across a switchback. Stay on constructed tracks and avoid running over young trees, shrubs, and grasses, damaging or killing them. Don't drive across alpine tundra; this fragile environment can take years to recover.
- Stay off soft, wet backroads and 4x4 trails readily torn up by vehicles. Repairing the damage is expensive, and quite often authorities find it easier to close the road rather than repair it.
- Travel around meadows, steep hillsides, stream banks, and lake shores that are easily scarred by churning wheels.
- Stay away from wild animals that are rearing young or suffering from a food shortage. Do not camp close to the water sources of domestic or wild animals.
- Obey gate closures and regulatory signs.
- Preserve America's heritage by not disturbing old mining camps, ghost towns, or other historical features. Leave historic sites, Native American rock art, ruins, and artifacts in place and untouched.
- Carry out all your trash, and even that of others.
- Stay out of designated wilderness areas. They are closed to all vehicles. It is your responsibility to know where the boundaries are.
- Get permission to cross private land. Leave livestock alone. Respect landowners' rights.

Report violations of these rules to help keep these trails open and to ensure that others will have the opportunity to visit these backcountry sites. Many groups are actively seeking to close these public lands to vehicles, thereby denying access to those who are unable, or perhaps merely unwilling, to hike long distances. This magnificent countryside is owned by, and should be available to, all Americans.

Assessing Your Vehicle's Off-Road Ability

Many issues come into play when evaluating your SUV, although all of the high-clearance 4WDs with high- and low-range gearing are suitable for even the roughest trails described in this book. Engine power will be adequate in even the least-powerful modern vehicle. However, some vehicles are less suited to off-highway driving than others, and some of the newest, carlike sport utility vehicles simply are not designed for off-highway touring. The following information should allow you to identify the good, the bad, and the ugly.

Differing 4WD Systems

All 4WD systems have one thing in common: The engine provides power to all four wheels rather than to only two, as is typical in most standard cars. However, there are a number of differences in the way power is applied to the wheels.

The other feature that distinguishes nearly all 4WDs from normal passenger vehicles is that the gearboxes have high and low ratios that effectively double the number of gears. The high range is comparable to the range on a passenger car. The low range provides lower speed and more power, which is useful when towing heavy loads, driving up steep hills, or crawling over rocks. When driving downhill, the 4WD's low range increases engine braking.

Various makes and models of SUVs offer different drive systems, but these differences center on two issues: the way power is applied to the other wheels if one or more wheels slip, and the ability to select between 2WD and 4WD.

Normal driving requires that all four wheels be able to turn at different speeds; this allows the vehicle to turn without scrubbing its tires. In a 2WD vehicle, the front wheels (or rear wheels in a front-wheel-drive vehicle) are not powered by the engine and thus are free to turn individually at any speed. The rear wheels, powered by the engine, are only able to turn at different speeds because of the differential, which applies power to the faster-turning wheel.

This standard method of applying traction has certain weaknesses. First, when power is applied to only one set of wheels, the other set cannot help the vehicle gain traction. Second, when one powered wheel loses traction, it spins, but the other powered wheel doesn't turn. This happens because the differential applies all the engine power to the faster-turning wheel and no power to the other wheels, which still have traction. All 4WD systems are designed to overcome these two weaknesses. However, different 4WDs address this common objective in different ways.

Full-Time 4WD

For a vehicle to remain in 4WD all the time without scrubbing the tires, all the wheels must be able to rotate at different speeds. A full-time 4WD system allows this to happen by using three differentials. One is located between the rear wheels, as in a normal passenger car, to allow the rear wheels to rotate at different speeds. The second is located between the front wheels in exactly the same way. The third differential is located between the front and rear wheels to allow different rotational speeds between the front and rear sets of wheels. In nearly all vehicles with full-time 4WD, the center differential operates only in high range. In low range, it is completely locked. This is not a disadvantage because when using low range the additional traction is normally desired and the deterioration of steering response will be less noticeable due to the vehicle traveling at a slower speed.

Part-Time 4WD

A part-time 4WD system does not have the center differential located between the front and rear wheels. Consequently, the front and rear drive shafts are both driven at the same speed and with the same power at all times when in 4WD.

This system provides improved traction because when one or both of the front or rear wheels slips, the engine continues to provide power to the other set. However, because such a system doesn't allow a difference in speed between the front and rear sets of wheels, the tires scrub when turning, placing additional strain on the whole drive system. Therefore, such a system can be used only in slippery conditions; otherwise, the ability to steer the vehicle will deteriorate and the tires will quickly wear out.

Some vehicles offer both full-time and part-time 4WD in high range.

Manual Systems to Switch Between 2WD and 4WD

There are three manual systems for switching between 2WD and 4WD. The most basic requires stopping and getting out of the vehicle to lock the front hubs manually before selecting 4WD. The second requires you to stop, but you change to 4WD by merely throwing a lever inside the vehicle (the hubs lock automatically). The third allows shifting between 2WD and 4WD high range while the vehicle is moving. Any 4WD that does not offer the option of driving in 2WD must have a full-time 4WD system.

Automated Switching Between 2WD and 4WD

Advances in technology have led to greater automation in the selection of two- or four-wheel drive. When operating in high range, these high-tech systems use sensors to monitor the rotation of each wheel. When any slippage is detected, the vehicle switches the proportion of power from the wheel(s) that is slipping to the wheels that retain grip. The proportion of power supplied to each wheel is therefore infinitely variable as opposed to the original systems where the vehicle was either in two-wheel drive or four-wheel drive.

Manufacturers of these higher-priced SUVs have led the way in introducing sophisticated computer-controlled 4WD systems. Although each of the manufacturers has its own approach to this issue, all the systems automatically vary the allocation of power between the wheels within milliseconds of the sensor detecting wheel slippage.

Limiting Wheel Slippage

All 4WDs employ various systems to limit wheel slippage and transfer power to the wheels that still have traction. These systems may completely lock the differentials or they may allow limited slippage before transferring power back to the wheels that retain traction.

Lockers completely eliminate the operation of one or more differentials. A locker on the center differential switches between full-time and part-time 4WD. Lockers on the front or rear differentials ensure that power remains equally applied to each set of wheels regardless of whether both have traction. Lockers may be controlled manually, by a switch or a lever in the vehicle, or they may be automatic.

Some SUVs offer the option of having manual lockers on all three differentials, while others offer manual lockers on the center and rear differential. Manual lockers are the most controllable and effective devices for ensuring that power is provided to the wheels with traction. However, because they allow absolutely no slippage, they must be used only on slippery surfaces.

An alternative method for getting power to the wheels that have traction is to allow limited wheel slippage. Systems that work this way may be called limited-slip differentials, positraction systems, or in the center differential, viscous couplings. The advantage of these systems is that the limited difference they allow in rotational speed between wheels enables such systems to be used when driving on a dry surface. All full-time 4WD systems allow limited slippage in the center differential.

For off-highway use, a manually locking differential is the best of the above systems, but it is the most expensive. Limited-slip differentials are the cheapest but also the least satisfactory, as they require one wheel to be slipping at 2 to 3 mph before power is transferred to the other wheel. For the center differential, the best system combines a locking differential and, to enable full-time use, a viscous coupling.

Tires

The tires that came with your vehicle may be satisfactory, but many SUVs are factory-fitted with passenger-car tires. These are unlikely to be the best choice because they are less rugged and more likely to puncture on rocky trails. They are particularly prone to sidewall damage as well. Passenger vehicle tires also have a less aggressive tread pattern than specialized off road tires, providing less traction in mud.

For information on purchasing tires better suited to off-highway conditions, see Special Equipment below.

Clearance

Road clearances vary considerably among different SUVs—from less than 7 inches to more than 10 inches. Special vehicles may have far greater clearance. For instance, the first consumer Hummer, modelled on the military vehicle, had a 16-inch ground clearance. High ground clearance is particularly advantageous on the rockier or more rutted 4x4 trails in this book.

When evaluating the ground clearance of your vehicle, you need to take into account the clearance of the bodywork between the wheels on each side of the vehicle. This is particularly relevant for crawling over larger rocks. Vehicles with side-steps have significantly lower clearance than those without.

Another factor affecting clearance is the approach and departure angles of your vehicle—that is, the maximum angle the ground can slope without the front of the vehicle hitting the ridge on approach or the rear of the vehicle hitting on departure. Mounting a winch or tow hitch to your vehicle is likely to reduce your angle of approach or departure.

If you do a lot of driving on rocky trails, you will inevitably hit the bottom of the vehicle. When this happens, you will be far less likely to damage vulnerable areas such as the oil pan and gas tank if your vehicle is fitted with skid plates. Most manufacturers offer skid plates as an option. They are worth every penny.

Maneuverability

When you tackle tight switchbacks, you will quickly appreciate that maneuverability is an important criterion when assessing SUVs. Where a full-size vehicle may be forced to go back and forth a number of times to get around a sharp turn, a small SUV might go straight around. This is not only easier, it's safer.

If you have a full-size vehicle, all is not lost. We have traveled hundreds of trails in a Suburban. That is not to say that some of these trails wouldn't have been easier to negotiate in a smaller vehicle! We have noted in the route descriptions if a trail is not suitable for larger vehicles.

In Summary

Using the criteria above, you can evaluate how well your SUV will handle off-road touring, and if you haven't yet purchased your vehicle, you can use these criteria to help select one. Choosing the best 4WD system is, at least partly, subjective. It is also a matter of your budget. However, for the type of off-highway driving covered in this book, we make the following recommendations:

■ Select a 4WD system that offers low range and, at a minimum, has some form of limited slip differential on the rear axle.

■ Use light truck, all-terrain tires as the standard tires on your vehicle. For sand and slickrock, these will be the ideal choice. If conditions are likely to be muddy, or traction will be improved by a tread pattern that will give more bite, consider an additional set of mud tires.

- For maximum clearance, select a vehicle with 16-inch wheels or at least choose the tallest tires that your vehicle can accommodate. Note that if you install tires with a diameter greater than standard, the speedometer and odometer will undercalculate speed and the distance you have traveled. Your engine braking and gear ratios will also be affected.

- If you are going to try the rockier 4x4 trails, don't install a sidestep or low-hanging front bar. If you have the option, have underbody skid plates mounted.

- Remember that many of the obstacles you encounter on backcountry trails are more difficult to navigate in a full-size vehicle than in a compact SUV.

Four-Wheel Driving Techniques

Safe four-wheel driving requires that you observe certain golden rules:

- Size up the situation in advance.
- Be careful and take your time.
- Maintain smooth, steady power and momentum.
- Engage 4WD and low-range gears before you get into a tight situation.
- Steer toward high spots, trying to put the wheel over large rocks.
- Straddle ruts.
- Use gears and not just the brakes to hold the vehicle when driving downhill. On very steep slopes, chock the wheels if you park your vehicle.
- Watch for logging and mining trucks and smaller recreational vehicles, such as all-terrain vehicles (ATVs).
- Wear your seat belt and secure all luggage, especially heavy items such as tool boxes or coolers. Heavy items should be secured by ratchet tie-down straps rather than elastic-type straps, which are not strong enough to hold heavy items if the vehicle rolls.

Colorado's backroads and 4x4 trails have a number of common obstacles, and the following provides an introduction to the techniques required to surmount them.

Rocks

Tire selection is important in negotiating rocks. Select a multiple-ply, tough sidewall, light-truck tire with a large-lug tread.

As you approach a rocky stretch, get into 4WD low range to give yourself maximum slow-speed control. Speed is rarely necessary, since traction on a rocky surface is usually good. Plan ahead and select the line you wish to take. If a rock appears to be larger than the clearance of your vehicle, don't try to straddle it. Check to see that it is not higher than the frame of your vehicle once you get a wheel over it. Put a wheel up on the rock and slowly climb it, then gently drop over the other side using the brake to ensure a smooth landing. Bouncing the car over rocks increases the likelihood of damage, as the body's clearance is reduced by the suspension compressing. Running boards also significantly reduce your clearance in this respect. It is often helpful to use a "spotter" outside the vehicle to assist you with the best wheel placement.

Steep Uphill Grades

Consider walking the trail to ensure that the steep hill before you is passable, especially if it is clear that backtracking is going to be a problem.

Select 4WD low range to ensure that you have adequate power to pull up the hill. If the wheels begin to lose traction, turn the steering wheel gently from side to side to give the wheels a chance to regain traction.

If you lose momentum, but the car is not in danger of sliding, use the foot brake, switch off the ignition, leave the vehicle in gear (if manual transmission) or park (if automatic), engage the parking brake, and get out to examine the situation. See if you can remove any obstacles, and figure out the line you need to take. Reversing a couple of yards and starting again may allow you to get better traction and momentum.

If halfway up, you decide a stretch of road is impassably steep, back down the trail. Trying to turn the vehicle around on a steep hill is extremely dangerous; you will very likely cause it to roll over.

Steep Downhill Grades

Again, consider walking the trail to ensure that a steep downhill is passable, especially if it is clear that backtracking uphill is going to be a problem.

Select 4WD low range and use first gear to maximize braking assistance from the engine. If the surface is loose and you are losing traction, change up to second or third gear. Do not use the brakes if you can avoid it, but don't let the vehicle's speed get out of control. Feather (lightly pump) the brakes if you slip under braking. For vehicles fitted with ABS, apply even pressure if you start to slip; the ABS helps keep vehicles on line.

Travel very slowly over rock ledges or ruts. Attempt to tackle these diagonally, letting one wheel down at a time.

If the back of the vehicle begins to slide around, gently apply the throttle and correct the steering. If the rear of the vehicle starts to slide sideways, do not apply the brakes.

Sand

As with most off-highway situations, your tires are the key to your ability to cross sand. It is difficult to tell how well a particular tire will handle in sand just by looking at it, so be guided by the manufacturer and your dealer.

The key to driving in soft sand is floatation, which is achieved by a combination of low tire pressure and momentum. Before crossing a stretch of sand, reduce your tire pressure to between 15 and 20 pounds. If necessary, you can safely go to as low as 12 pounds. As you cross, maintain momentum so that your vehicle rides on the top of the soft sand without digging in or stalling. This may require plenty of engine power. Avoid using the brakes if possible; removing your foot from the accelerator alone is normally enough to slow or stop. Using the brakes digs the vehicle deep in the sand.

Air the tires back up as soon as you are out of the sand to avoid damage to the tires and the rims. Airing back up requires a high-quality air compressor. Even then, it is a slow process.

Slickrock

When you encounter slickrock, first assess the correct direction of the trail. It is easy to lose sight of the trail on slickrock, as there are seldom any developed edges. Often the way is marked with small cairns, which are simply rocks stacked high enough to make a landmark.

All-terrain tires with tighter tread are more suited to slickrock than the more open, luggier type tires. As with rocks, a multiple-ply sidewall is important. In dry conditions, slickrock offers pavement-type grip. In rain or snow, you will soon learn how it got its name. Even the best tires may not get an adequate grip. Walk steep sections first; if you are slipping on foot, chances are your vehicle will slip too.

Slickrock is characterized by ledges and long sections of "pavement." Follow the guidelines for travel over rocks. Refrain from speeding over flat-looking sections, as you may hit an unexpected crevice or water pocket, and vehicles bend easier than slickrock! Turns and ledges can be tight, and vehicles with smaller overhangs and better maneuverability are at a distinct advantage—hence the popularity of the compacts in the slickrock mecca of Moab, Utah.

On the steepest sections, engage low range and pick a straight line up or down the slope. Do not attempt to traverse a steep slope sideways.

Mud

Muddy trails are easily damaged, so they should be avoided if possible. But if you must traverse a section of mud, your success will depend heavily on whether you have open-lugged mud tires or chains. Thick mud fills the tighter tread on normal tires, leaving the tire with no more grip than if it were bald. If the muddy stretch is only a few yards long, the momentum of your vehicle may allow you to get through regardless.

If the muddy track is very steep, uphill or downhill, or off camber, do not attempt it. Your vehicle is likely to skid in such conditions, and you may roll or slip off the edge of the road. Also, check to see that the mud has a reasonably firm base. Tackling deep mud is definitely not recommended unless you have a vehicle-mounted winch—and even then, be cautious, because the winch may not get you out. Finally, check to see that no ruts are too deep for the ground clearance of your vehicle.

When you decide you can get through and have selected the best route, use the following techniques to cross through the mud:

■ Avoid making detours off existing tracks to minimize environmental damage.

■ Select 4WD low range and a suitable gear; momentum is the key to success, so use a high enough gear to build up sufficient speed.

■ Avoid accelerating heavily, so as to minimize wheel spinning and to provide maximum traction.

■ Follow existing wheel ruts, unless they are too deep for the clearance of your vehicle.

■ To correct slides, turn the steering wheel in the direction that the rear wheels are skidding, but don't be too aggressive or you'll overcorrect and lose control again.

■ If the vehicle comes to a stop, don't continue to accelerate, as you will only spin your wheels and dig yourself into a rut. Try backing out and having another go.

■ Be prepared to turn back before reaching the point of no return.

Stream Crossings

By crossing a stream that is too deep, drivers risk far more than water flowing in and ruining the interior of their vehicles. Water sucked into the engine's air intake will seriously damage the engine. Likewise, water that seeps into the air vent on the transmission or differential will mix with the lubricant and may lead to serious problems in due course.

Even worse, if the water is deep or fast flowing, it could easily carry your vehicle downstream, endangering the lives of everyone in the vehicle.

Some SUV user manuals tell you what fording depth the vehicle can negotiate safely. If your vehicle's owner's manual does not include this information, your local dealer may be able to assist. If you don't know, then avoid crossing through water that is more than a foot or so deep.

The first rule for crossing a stream is to know what you are getting into. You need to ascertain how deep the water is, whether there are any large rocks or holes, if the bottom is solid enough to avoid bogging down the vehicle, and whether the entry and exit points are negotiable. This may take some time and involve getting wet, but you take a great risk by crossing a stream without first properly assessing the situation.

The secret to water crossings is to keep moving, but not too fast. If you go too fast, you may drown the electrics, causing the vehicle to stall midstream. In shallow water (where the surface of the water is below the bumper), your primary concern is to safely negotiate the bottom of the stream, avoiding any rock damage and maintaining momentum if there is a danger of getting stuck or of slipping on the exit.

In deeper water (between 18 and 30 inches), the objective is to create a small bow wave in front of the moving vehicle. This requires a speed that is approximately walking pace. The bow wave reduces the depth of the water around the engine compartment. If the water's surface reaches your tailpipe, select a gear that will maintain moderate engine revs to avoid water backing up into the exhaust; and do not change gears midstream.

Crossing water deeper than 25 to 30 inches requires more extensive preparation of the vehicle and should be attempted only by experienced drivers.

Snow

The trails in this book that receive heavy snowfall are closed in winter. Therefore, the snow conditions that you are most likely to encounter are an occasional snowdrift that has not yet melted or fresh snow from an unexpected storm. Getting through such conditions depends on the depth of the snow, its consistency, the stability of the underlying surface, and your vehicle.

If the snow is no deeper than about 9 inches and there is solid ground beneath it, crossing the snow should not be a problem. In deeper snow that seems solid enough to support your vehicle, be extremely cautious: If you break through a drift, you are likely to be stuck, and if conditions are bad, you may have a long wait.

The tires you use for off-highway driving, with a wide tread pattern, are probably suitable for these snow conditions. Nonetheless, it is wise to carry chains (preferably for all four wheels), and if you have a vehicle-mounted winch, even better.

Vehicle Recovery Methods

If you do enough four-wheel driving, you are sure to get stuck sooner or later. The following techniques will help you get back on the go. The most suitable method will depend on the equipment available and the situation you are in—whether you are stuck in sand, mud, or snow, or are high-centered or unable to negotiate a hill.

Towing

Use a nylon yank strap of the type discussed in the Special 4WD Equipment section below. This type of strap will stretch 15 to 25 percent, and the elasticity will assist in extracting the vehicle.

Attach the strap only to a frame-mounted tow point. Ensure that the driver of the stuck vehicle is ready, take up all but about 6 feet of slack, then move the towing vehicle away at a moderate speed (in most circumstances this means using 4WD low range in second gear) so that the elasticity of the strap is employed in the way it is meant to be. Don't take off like a bat out of hell or you risk breaking the strap or damaging a vehicle.

Never join two yank straps together with a shackle. If one strap breaks, the shackle will become a lethal missile aimed at one of the vehicles (and anyone inside). For the same reason, never attach a yank strap to the tow ball on either vehicle.

Jacking

Jacking the vehicle allows you to pack under the wheel (with rocks, dirt, or logs) or use your shovel to remove an obstacle. However, the standard vehicle jack is unlikely to be of as much assistance as a high-lift jack. We highly recommend purchasing a good high-lift jack as a basic accessory if you decide that you are going to do a lot of serious, off-highway four-wheel driving. Remember a high-lift jack is of limited use if your vehicle does not have an appropriate jacking point. Some brush bars have two built-in forward jacking points.

Tire Chains

Tire chains can be of assistance in both mud and snow. Cable-type chains provide much less grip than link-type chains. There are also dedicated mud chains with larger, heavier links than on normal snow chains. It is best to have chains fitted to all four wheels.

Once you are bogged down is not the best time to try to fit the chains; if at all possible, try to predict their need and have them on the tires before trouble arises. An easy way to affix chains is to place two small cubes of wood under the center of the stretched-out chain. When you drive your tires up on the blocks of wood, it is easier to stretch the chains over the tires because the pressure is off.

Winching

Most recreational four-wheel drivers do not have a winch. But if you get serious about four-wheel driving, this is probably the first major accessory you should consider buying.

Under normal circumstances, a winch would be warranted only for the more difficult 4x4 trails in this book. Having a winch is certainly comforting when you see a difficult section of road ahead and have to decide whether to risk it or turn back. Also, major obstacles can appear when you least expect them, even on trails that are otherwise easy.

Owning a winch is not a panacea to all your recovery problems. Winching depends on the availability of a good anchor point, and electric winches may not work if they are submerged in a stream. Despite these constraints, no accessory is more useful than a high-quality, powerful winch when you get into a difficult situation.

If you acquire a winch, learn to use it properly; take the time to study your owner's manual. Incorrect operation can be extremely dangerous and may cause damage to the winch or to your anchor points, which are usually trees.

Navigation by the Global Positioning System (GPS)

Although this book is designed so that each trail can be navigated simply by following the detailed directions provided, nothing makes navigation easier than a GPS receiver.

The global positioning system (GPS) consists of a network of 24 active satellites, nearly 13,000 miles in space, in six different orbital paths. The satellites are constantly moving at about 8,500 miles per hour, making two complete orbits around the earth every 24 hours.

Each satellite is constantly transmitting data, including its identification number, its operational health, and the date and time. It also transmits its location and the location of every other satellite in the network.

By comparing the time the signal was transmitted to the time it is received, a GPS receiver calculates how far away each satellite is. With a sufficient number of signals, the receiver can then triangulate its location. With three or more satellites, the receiver can determine latitude and longitude coordinates. With four or more, it can calculate altitude. By constantly making these calculations, it can determine speed and direction. To facilitate these calculations, the time data broadcast by GPS is accurate to within 40 billionths of a second.

The U.S. military uses the system to provide positions accurate to within half an inch. When the system was first established, civilian receivers were deliberately fed slightly erroneous information in order to effectively deny military applications to hostile countries or terrorists—a practice called selective availability (SA). However on May 1, 2000, in response to the growing importance of the system for civilian applications, the U.S. government stopped intentionally downgrading GPS data. The military gave its support to this change once new technology made it possible to selectively degrade the system within any defined geographical area on demand. This new feature of the system has made it safe to have higher-quality signals available for civilian use. Now, instead of the civilian-use signal having a margin of error being between 20 and 70 yards, it is only about one-tenth of that.

A GPS receiver offers the four-wheeler numerous benefits:

■ You can track to any point for which you know the longitude and latitude coordinates with no chance of heading in the wrong direction or getting lost. Most receivers provide an extremely easy-to-understand graphic display to keep you on track.

■ It works in all weather conditions.

■ It automatically records your route for easy backtracking.

■ You can record and name any location, so that you can relocate it with ease. This may include your campsite, a fishing spot, or even a silver mine you discover!

■ It displays your position, allowing you to pinpoint your location on a map.

■ By interfacing the GPS receiver directly to a portable computer, you can monitor and record your location as you travel (using the appropriate map software) or print the route you took.

However, remember that GPS units can fail, batteries can go flat, and tree cover and narrow canyons can block the signals. Never rely entirely on GPS for navigation. Always carry a compass for backup.

Special 4WD Equipment

Tires

When 4WD touring, you will likely encounter a wide variety of terrain: rocks, mud, talus, slickrock, sand, gravel, dirt, and bitumen. The immense variety of tires on the market includes many specifically targeted at one or another of these types of terrain, as well as tires designed to adequately handle a range of terrain.

Every four-wheel driver seems to have a preference when it comes to tire selection, but most people undertaking the backroads and 4x4 trails in this book will need tires that can handle all of the above types of terrain adequately.

The first requirement is to select rugged, light-truck tires rather than passenger-vehicle tires. Check the size data on the sidewall: it should have "LT" rather than "P" before the number. Among light-truck tires, you must choose between tires that are designated "all-terrain" and more-aggressive, wider-tread mud tires. Either type will be adequate, especially on rocks, gravel, talus, or dirt. Although mud tires have an advantage in muddy conditions and soft snow, all-terrain tires perform better on slickrock, in sand, and particularly on ice and paved roads.

When selecting tires, remember that they affect not just traction but also cornering ability, braking distances, fuel consumption, and noise levels. It pays to get good advice before making your decision.

Global Positioning System Receivers

GPS receivers have come down in price considerably in the past few years and are rapidly becoming indispensable navigational tools. Many higher-priced cars now offer integrated GPS receivers, and within the next few years, receivers will become available on most models.

Battery-powered, hand-held units that meet the needs of off-highway driving currently range from less than $100 to a little over $300 and continue to come down in price. Some high-end units feature maps that are incorporated in the display, either from a built-in database or from interchangeable memory cards. Currently, only a few of these maps include 4WD trails.

If you are considering purchasing a GPS unit, keep the following in mind:

■ Price. The very cheapest units are likely outdated and very limited in their display features. Expect to pay from $125 to $300.

■ The display. Compare the graphic display of one unit with another. Some are much easier to decipher or offer more alternative displays.

■ The controls. GPS receivers have many functions, and they need to have good, simple controls.

■ Vehicle mounting. To be useful, the unit needs to be placed where it can be read easily by both the driver and the navigator. Check that the unit can be conveniently located in your vehicle. Different units have different shapes and different mounting systems.

■ Map data. More and more units have map data built in. Some have the ability to download maps from a computer. Such maps are normally sold on a DVD. GPS units have a finite storage capacity and having the ability to download maps covering a narrower geographical region means that the amount of data relating to that specific region can be greater.

■ The number of routes and the number of sites (or "waypoints") per route that can be stored in memory. For off-highway use, it is important to be able to store plenty of waypoints so that you do not have to load coordinates into the machine as frequently. Having plenty of memory also ensures that you can automatically store your present location without fear that the memory is full.

■ Waypoint storage. The better units store up to 500 waypoints and 20 reversible routes of up to 30 waypoints each. Also consider the number of characters a GPS receiver allows you to use to name waypoints. When you try to recall a waypoint, you may have difficulty recognizing names restricted to only a few characters.

■ Automatic route storing. Most units automatically store your route as you go along and enable you to display it in reverse to make backtracking easy.

After you have selected a unit, a number of optional extras are also worth considering:

■ A cigarette lighter electrical adapter. Despite GPS units becoming more power efficient, protracted in-vehicle use still makes this accessory a necessity.

■ A vehicle-mounted antenna, which will improve reception under difficult conditions. (The GPS unit can only "see" through the windows of your vehicle; it cannot monitor satellites through a metal roof.) Having a vehicle-mounted antenna also means that you do not have to consider reception when locating the receiver in your vehicle.

■ An in-car mounting system. If you are going to do a lot of touring using the GPS, consider attaching a bracket on the dash rather than relying on a Velcro mount.

■ A computer-link cable and digital maps. Data from your GPS receiver can be downloaded to your PC; maps and waypoints can be downloaded from your PC; or if you have a laptop computer, you can monitor your route as you go along, using one of a number of inexpensive map software products on the market.

Yank Straps

Yank straps are industrial-strength versions of the flimsy tow straps carried by the local discount store. They are 20 to 30 feet long and 2 to 3 inches wide, made of heavy nylon, rated to at least 20,000 pounds, and have looped ends.

Do not use tow straps with metal hooks in the ends (the hooks can become missiles in the event the strap breaks free). Likewise, never join two yank straps together using a shackle.

Cell Phones and CB Radios

Each year the reception of cell phones in remote areas becomes better. Many times we have found we have cell phone reception in locations where we would never have expected it. However, the difference between cell phone companies can be considerable and one company can be superior in one location and not in another. The topography is also a major contributor to variances in reception. We highly recommend you take your cell phone with you; better yet take two if you have them and they have different service providers.

A citizen's band (CB) radio can also be invaluable. CB radios are relatively inexpensive and do not require an FCC license. Their range is limited, especially in very hilly country, as their transmission patterns basically follow lines of sight. Range can be improved using single sideband (SSB) transmission, an option on more expensive units. Range is even better on vehicle-mounted units that have been professionally fitted to ensure that the antenna and cabling are matched appropriately.

Winches

There are three main options when it comes to winches: manual winches, removable electric winches, and vehicle-mounted electric winches.

If you have a full-size SUV—which can weigh in excess of 7,000 pounds when loaded—a manual winch is of limited use without a lot of effort and considerable time. However, a manual winch is a very handy and inexpensive accessory if you have a small SUV. Typically, manual winches are rated to pull about 5,500 pounds.

Electric winches can be mounted to your vehicle's trailer hitch to enable them to be removed, relocated to the front of your vehicle (if you have a hitch installed), or moved to another vehicle. Although this is a very useful feature, a winch is heavy, so relocating one can be a two-person job. Consider that 5,000-pound-rated winches weigh only about 55 pounds, while 12,000-pound-rated models weigh around 140 pounds. Therefore, the larger models are best permanently front-mounted. Unfortunately, this position limits their ability to winch the vehicle backward.

When choosing between electric winches, be aware that they are rated for their maximum capacity on the first wind of the cable around the drum. As layers of cable wind onto the drum, they increase its diameter and thus decrease the maximum load the winch can handle. This decrease is significant: A winch rated to pull 8,000 pounds on a bare drum may only handle 6,500 pounds on the second layer, 5,750 pounds on the third layer, and 5,000 pounds on the fourth. Electric winches also draw a high level of current and may necessitate upgrading the battery in your 4WD or adding a second battery.

There is a wide range of mounting options—from a simple, body-mounted frame that holds the winch to heavy-duty winch bars that replace the original bumper and incorporate brush bars and mounts for auxiliary lights.

If you buy a winch, either electric or manual, you will also need quite a range of additional equipment so that you can operate it correctly:

■ at least one choker chain with hooks on each end,
■ winch extension straps or cables,
■ shackles,
■ a receiver shackle,
■ a snatch block,
■ a tree protector,
■ gloves.

Grill/Brush Bars and Winch Bars

Brush bars protect the front of the vehicle from scratches and minor bumps; they also provide a solid mount for auxiliary lights and offer high-lift jacking points. The level of protection they provide depends on how solid they are and whether they are securely mounted onto the frame of the vehicle. Lighter models attach in front of the standard bumper, but the more substantial units replace the bumper. Prices range from about $150 to $450.

Winch bars replace the bumper and usually integrate a solid brush bar with a heavy-duty winch mount. Some have the brush bar as an optional extra to the winch bar component. Manufacturers such as Warn, ARB, and TJM offer a wide range of integrated winch bars. These are significantly more expensive, starting at about $650.

Portable Air Compressors

Many portable air compressors on the market are flimsy models that plug into the cigarette lighter and are sold at the local discount store. These are of very limited use for four-wheel driving. They are very slow to inflate the large tires of a SUV vehicle; for instance, to reinflate from 15 to 35 pounds typically takes about 10 minutes for each tire. They are also unlikely to be rated for continuous use, which means that they will overheat and cut off before completing the job. If you're lucky, they will start up again when they have cooled down, but this means that you are unlikely to reinflate your tires in less than an hour.

The easiest way to identify a useful air compressor is by the price—good ones cost $200 or more. All such pumps draw between 15 and 20 amps and thus should not be plugged into the cigarette lighter socket but attached to the vehicle's battery with clips. Some units can be permanently mounted under the hood.

Auxiliary Driving Lights

There is a vast array of auxiliary lights on the market today, and selecting the best lights for your purpose can be a confusing process.

Auxiliary lights greatly improve visibility in adverse weather conditions. Rear-mounted auxiliary lights provide greatly improved visibility for backing up.

For off-highway use, you will need quality lights with strong mounting brackets. Some high-powered off-highway lights are not approved by the Department of Transportation for use on public roads.

Roof Racks

Roof racks can be excellent for storing gear, as well as providing easy access for certain weatherproof items. However, they raise the center of gravity on the vehicle, which can substantially alter the rollover angle. A roof rack is best used for lightweight objects that are well strapped down. Heavy recovery gear and other bulky items should be packed low in the vehicle's interior to lower the center of gravity and stabilize the vehicle.

A roof rack should allow for safe and secure packing of items and be sturdy enough to withstand knocks.

Packing Checklist

Before embarking on any 4WD adventure, whether a lazy Sunday drive on an easy trail or a challenging climb over rugged terrain, be prepared. The following checklist will help you gather the items you need.

Essential

❒ Cell phone
❒ Rain gear
❒ Small shovel or multipurpose ax, pick, and sledge-hammer
❒ Heavy-duty yank strap
❒ Spare tire that matches the other tires on the vehicle
❒ Working jack and base plate for soft ground
❒ Maps
❒ Emergency medical kit, including sun protection and insect repellent
❒ Bottled water
❒ Blankets or space blankets
❒ Parka, gloves, and boots
❒ Spare vehicle key
❒ Jumper leads
❒ Heavy-duty flashlight
❒ Multipurpose tool, such as a Leatherman
❒ Emergency food—high-energy bars or similar

Worth Considering

❒ Global Positioning System (GPS) receiver
❒ A set of light-truck, off-highway tires and matching spare
❒ High-lift jack
❒ Additional tool kit
❒ CB radio
❒ Portable air compressor
❒ Tire gauge
❒ Tire-sealing kit
❒ Tire chains
❒ Handsaw and ax
❒ Binoculars
❒ Firearms
❒ Whistle
❒ Flares
❒ Vehicle fire extinguisher
❒ Gasoline, engine oil, and other vehicle fluids
❒ Portable hand winch
❒ Electric cooler

If Your Credit Cards Aren't Maxed Out

❒ Electric, vehicle-mounted winch and associated recovery straps, shackles, and snatch blocks
❒ Auxiliary lights
❒ Locking differential(s)

Along the Trail

Towns, Ghost Towns, and Interesting Places

Alma

The community of Alma was established in 1872. When silver strikes became common in the area and prospectors began traveling over Mosquito Pass from Leadville to seek new claims, Alma became a desirable place to live. Not only silver, but also gold, copper, and lead were to be found in abundance in nearby Mount Bross and Mount Lincoln. A smelter was built as a division of the Boston and Colorado Smelting Works to process the ores from the surrounding mines. Alma became an important smelting center.

In the early days, locals were terrorized by a gang called "The Bloody Espinozas," who hated the Anglos. The Espinozas killed 32 victims, six of them from the Alma area. It is not known exactly why the Espinozas felt such hostility, but some people say it was because whites killed their parents. Others say it was because white men stole their land. Alma authorities placed a bounty on the heads of the Espinozas, but somehow the gang managed to evade even the most competent of posses. Finally, an organized party of miners was able to surround and kill all the Espinozas in a surprise attack. They cut off and carried one gang member's head back to Fort Garland to prove victory.

In 1937, the town's main street was nearly destroyed when a fire started in one of Alma's saloons and high winds spread it to a dozen buildings. Alma had no fire department to extinguish the flames. In the smoldering ruins was a local garage that had housed most of the town's automobiles. Most of the buildings you see on Alma's main street today were reconstructed after this fire.

Alma has seen high and low times, but it has never been completely deserted. It is alive today as a small town, still home to many local miners.

GPS COORDINATES: 39°17.03'N 106°03.72'W
TRAIL REFERENCE: Central #21: Mosquito Pass Trail

Alpine Station and Tunnel

Two railroads waged a battle to be the first to connect the Gunnison area to Denver. The Denver & Rio Grande Railroad chose Marshall Pass as its route, so the owner of the Denver, South Park & Pacific Railroad, ex–Governor John Evans, financed a project to tunnel through the Sawatch Range.

A tunnel through the Continental Divide seemed a shorter and more strategic route. Bids were opened to build the Alpine Tunnel in 1879. The bore through the mountain was to be 1,800 feet long. However, the railroad underestimated the severity of the weather, the geologic rock formations at the site, and the difficulty of working at the 11,600-foot altitude,

Train exiting the Alpine Tunnel, circa 1900

with wind gusts to 50 miles per hour and temperatures at 40 degrees below zero.

In 1880, work began, and 500 laborers worked day and night. Work camps were established at each end of the tunnel. Severe weather conditions and poor working conditions created and exacerbated gigantic labor problems. Workers walked off the site in droves when they experienced the high winds and freezing temperatures they were expected to endure. The railroad recruited workers from the East and Midwest by offering free transportation to Colorado. More than 100,000 men were employed, and many worked only a day or two before leaving. Sometimes the entire crew threatened to quit en masse.

The tunnel was bored by July 1881, almost a year behind schedule (which had allowed only six months to complete the project). When the competing Denver & Rio Grande reached Gunnison in early August, the discouraged Denver, South

A long snowshed that was located near Alpine Station, circa 1882

Inside the Alpine Tunnel in 1975

Park & Pacific Railroad Company halted the Alpine Tunnel project for about six months. Finally, work continued, and the first train passed through the tunnel in December 1881.

The Alpine Station was developed at the west, or Pacific, end of the tunnel, with a bunkhouse where track workers lived, a storehouse, and a section house. The section house included a kitchen, dining room, pantry, and several bedrooms. A large stone engine house was built at the station in 1881. Aside from holding six engines, the engine house also contained a large coal bin and a water tank with a 9,516-gallon capacity, a turntable, and a locomotive service area. In 1883, a telegraph office was added.

Snowsheds were erected at each end of the tunnel bore to protect the rails. The shed on the Atlantic side was 150 feet in length, and the one on the Pacific side was 650 feet.

Train service through the Alpine Tunnel began in June 1882. The completed project was considered an engineering marvel. At 16 places on the western descent, walls were laid to provide a shelf for rail construction. The most spectacular shelf is at the Palisades, a mile below the tunnel, where a stone wall 450 feet long, 30 feet high, and 2 feet thick was built from hand-cut stones without mortar. You can see this wall along the drive to the Alpine Tunnel. Over 500,000 feet of California redwood were used to reinforce the tunnel, as workers found loose rock and decomposed granite instead of self-supporting granite. The total cost of the tunnel was more than $250,000.

Alpine Station, circa 1885

Many problems plagued the Alpine Tunnel during its period of operation. In March 1884, a train whistle caused a severe snow slide that swept away the town of Woodstock and killed many of its residents. In 1906, a fire destroyed the wood buildings at Alpine Station; even the stone buildings were demolished when they collapsed from the intense heat of the blaze. In 1910, several people lost their lives when the tunnel caved in. The tunnel was never reopened.

The first rails were removed in November 1918; however, the rails in the tunnel itself remain in place. Eventually the railroad property was sold.

You can drive to the Alpine Station only from the west side. The telegraph station has been restored, and you can see the ruins of the stone engine house and section house. Volunteers have reconstructed the station platform and relaid 120 feet of the original Denver, South Park & Pacific rails.

GPS COORDINATES: 38°38.44'N 106°24.44'W
TRAIL REFERENCE: Central #33: Hancock Pass Trail, Central #36: Alpine Tunnel Road

Alta

Alta was a company town for the Gold King Mine, which was discovered in 1878 and operated as recently as the 1940s. Gold, silver, copper, and lead were mined and transported in aerial tramcars from the Gold King and other mines to the Ophir Loop, 2 miles farther down the mountain.

Alta's Gold King was a very rich mine, but it was expensive to operate because of its high elevation. Fortunately, L. L. Nunn found a way to reduce expenses by bringing electrical power to the mine. In 1881, he organized a contract with the Westinghouse company to construct an electrical plant in Ames, less than 3 miles away. The plant harnessed the San Miguel River's power, transmitting 3,000 volts of alternating current back up to the Gold King Mine. Encouraged by the success of this first alternating current power transmission plant in America, Nunn expanded his venture to supply the city of Telluride, as well as many nearby mines, and installed transmission lines across Imogene Pass. Subsequently, electricity became widely used in Colorado and the world.

There were three mills at Alta, all of which have burned down. The last one burned in 1945 while seven men were underground. The superintendent ordered the portal to be dynamited in order to cut

View of Alta, circa 1895

Ames power station in 1933, built in 1881 to service the Alta Mine

A view of Animas Forks in 1875

off the draft that was feeding the fire, even though his son was one of the men inside.

Due to the longevity of the Gold King Mine, Alta thrived longer than most high-country mining towns. Visitors can still see quite a few well-preserved old buildings, including a boardinghouse, cabins, and some more substantial homes. Alta never had a church or a post office.

GPS COORDINATES: 37°53.16'N 107°51.15'W
TRAIL REFERENCE: Southwest #20: Alta Ghost Town Trail

Animas Forks

Animas Forks, originally called La Plata City, experienced its first silver strike in 1875. As an enticement to live near timberline and brave the harsh winters, the government offered settlers free lots and aid for building homes.

Within a year, settlers had erected 30 cabins, a post office, saloon, general store, hotel, and two mills; the town boasted a population of 200. All the buildings were well constructed, with finished lumber and shingled roofs. The jailhouse, a rough, boxlike structure made of two-by-six lumber and consisting of two cells and a jailer's office in front, was a rare exception to the building standard.

In 1877, Otto Mears constructed a wagon road to Eureka, extending it from Silverton to Lake City as a toll road. Animas Forks became an important junction for the roads that headed in all directions to the area's many mining camps. Much of the town's other activity centered on its mill, which treated ore from Red Cloud Mine in Mineral Point.

Snow presented a huge problem for Animas Forks. Although the town was consid-

Animas Forks today

ered a year-round mining community, the population dropped in the wintertime. In 1884, the population reached 400 in the summer but dropped to a dozen men, three women, and 20 dogs in the winter. A winter storm that same year lasted for 23 days.

During the 1880s, telephone lines were installed, running from Lake City and passing over the 12,500-foot Continental Divide near Engineer Pass. Stagecoaches ran daily from Lake City to Silverton via Engineer Pass.

Mrs. Eckard, the first woman in Animas Forks, ran an extremely popular boardinghouse. Eckard won the favor of the local miners by extending them credit. When one freeloader slipped out of town without settling his account for three months' lodging, a vigilante committee set out after him. They caught him in Silverton and threatened to lynch him. He paid up, and no more bad debts were reported!

At its peak, Animas Forks was home to about 1,500 residents. Located at an elevation of 11,584 feet, it once boasted that it was the largest city in the world at this elevation.

Although its prosperity began to wane by the 1890s and the town was nearly deserted by 1901, Animas Forks experienced a resurgence of activity between 1904 and 1916. Otto

The famous Walsh house in Animas Forks, one of many buildings still standing in the ghost town

The rocky dirt Main Street of Animas Forks, circa 1880

Mears extended the railroad in 1904 and planned an elaborate system of seven snowsheds to permit the line to operate from Lake City to Silverton. Snowdrifts in the area sometimes piled over 25 feet high. When the first big snow slide of the season destroyed the first of Mears's sheds, his idea was abandoned. The remains of this shed are clearly visible along Southwest Trail #6.

The Gold Prince Mill, constructed in 1904, operated until 1910 and was moved to Eureka in 1917. Animas Forks rapidly declined once more.

In 1942, the railroad tracks were removed and scrapped. The railroad bed became a road again after the tracks were removed.

Today, Animas Forks is a fascinating ghost town, consisting of about a dozen houses. The Columbus Mill still stands, as do several other structures, including an elaborate house with a bay window. The foundations of the Gold Prince Mill remain at the southern end of town.

GPS COORDINATES: 37°55.89'N 107°34.23'W

TRAIL REFERENCE: Southwest #6: Silverton to Animas Forks Ghost Town, Southwest #12: California Gulch Trail, Southwest #5: North Fork Cutoff, Southwest #3: Cinnamon Pass Trail

Ashcroft

After silver strikes in 1879, this site was first settled as Castle Forks. Soon renamed Ashcroft, in its early days the town served as the gateway to Aspen for travelers coming over Tay-

A row of buildings in Ashroft ghost town

lor Pass or Cottonwood Pass. Established at about the same period as Aspen, Ashcroft seemed likely to become the more successful of the two.

The Ashcroft Post Office was established in 1880. The town had five hotels, a newspaper, a school, a jail, a doctor, a bowling alley, several stores, and many saloons.

In 1881, Horace Tabor (of Leadville) purchased a part share in the Tam O'Shanter silver mine near Ashcroft. It was never a profitable investment, because transport-

Ashcroft from the Hotel View

ing ore from an elevation of over 13,500 feet proved too difficult and expensive. Tabor and his wife, Baby Doe, enjoyed a lavish home in Ashcroft that served as a pleasant summer retreat and a haven from the Leadville gossip. Baby Doe enjoyed Ashcroft because she was a popular figure there.

Two factors led to the decline of Ashcroft. One was the completion of Independence Pass, which opened accessibility to nearby Aspen. Then, in 1887, the Denver & Rio Grande completed a railway line into Aspen, which encouraged Ashcroft's residents to migrate to Aspen.

One man remained for years after Ashcroft was deserted. If Aspen gossip can be trusted, Jack Leahy (nicknamed "the hermit of Ashcroft") didn't move away until 1935, four years before his death.

In 1974, the Aspen Historical Society leased Ashcroft's town site from the U.S. Forest Service in order to preserve the historic remains. While some of the buildings you see there today are original, others were

Blue Mirror Saloon in Ashcroft

moved there to replace deteriorated ones so that tourists can safely walk around and explore the resurrected ghost town.

GPS COORDINATES: 39°03.22'N 106°47.94'W

TRAIL REFERENCE: Central #26: Taylor Pass Trail

Aspen

The area in which the town of Aspen is now found was originally home to many Ute Indians. Fear of these tribes kept settlers out of the region until miners spreading out from Leadville found silver veins in the surrounding mountains. Originally named Ute, the city now known as Aspen formed as a mining camp in 1879.

B. Clark Wheeler arrived and platted the town in 1880, naming it Aspen. He had big plans for the town. At that time, the town site was a mix of log cabins, frame structures, and tents. The "business district" consisted of a hotel, a restaurant, an assay office, a few stores, and several saloons.

Aspen quickly began to flourish and prosper with the discovery of mines such as the Smuggler. Other important mines were the Durant, Mollie Gibson, Aspen, and Midnight.

An early prospector sold a half interest in the Smuggler Mine for a burro and $50. The burro soon died, but the Smuggler went on to produce millions, including the largest silver nugget in the world. The nugget weighed 2,060 pounds and had to be cut down to 1,840 pounds in order to fit through the mine shaft.

The first road into Aspen came across Taylor Pass from Buena Vista. In 1881, Independence Pass opened, connecting Aspen and Leadville and making Aspen much more accessible.

Jerome B. Wheeler (no relation to B. Clark Wheeler), founder of Macy's department stores, is credited with bringing prosperity to Aspen in 1884 with the development of mining interests. He invested much money in Aspen, opened

Hotel Jerome, circa 1900

a bank, and purchased a smelter to provide a local market for silver ore. He also established and edited the *Aspen Daily Times* newspaper.

Wheeler backed the construction of the Hotel Jerome (330 East Main Street), which had its grand opening in 1889. He outfitted the lavish three-story hotel with fine European furnishings, electricity, a barber shop, a billiard parlor, and an elegant dining hall. The hotel even had its own greenhouse, where staff gardeners cultivated vegetables and flowers during the winter. A water-powered elevator, which brought guests to the second and third floors, operated until 1952 when it was replaced by an electric one.

Jerome Wheeler financed the construction of the Wheeler Grand Opera House (320 East Hyman Avenue). The building, with its exquisite woodwork, brass trim, and plush upholstery and curtains, suffered from two fires in 1912 but was refurbished in 1947. It is still in operation today showing movies and hosting live events.

In 1885, Aspen became the first Colorado city to have electric lights. By 1887, two railroads were servicing the community, and

during the first month of rail operations more than $1 million worth of ore was shipped out of the state. The first of the two railroad lines was a spur of the Denver & Rio Grande narrow gauge from Glenwood Springs. The other, the Colorado Midland, was a standard gauge railway and reached Aspen from Leadville through the Hagerman Tunnel. Both railways were a huge benefit to the miners, who had previously paid about $50 to $100 per ton to transport ore; with the arrival of the railroad, costs were reduced to $10 to $15 per ton.

One merchant, H. P. Cowenhoven, was a popular and good-hearted man who was a "soft touch" for the less fortunate miners. He justified a number of worthless accounts on his books by his theory "The boys have to eat!" One miner with an outstanding tab of $400 finally settled his bill by paying Cowenhoven with a half share of his Aspen Mine, which he thought was worthless. Needless to say, the mine became extremely successful, and Cowenhoven was made a very rich man.

By 1890, the town reached a population of about 12,000 residents, making it the third largest city in Colorado. Aspen had four schools, four newspapers, eight churches, three banks, a hospital, nine hotels, five drugstores, six bakeries, nine restaurants, 31 saloons, and its own brewery. By 1892, one-sixth of all silver in the United States was mined from the Aspen area.

The silver crash of 1893 had a devastating outcome for Aspen. Over 1,800 workers lost their jobs, and within one month, all the mines shut down. The crash dealt a terrible blow to the town's economy, and the population began to plummet. Some of the remaining miners agreed to take pay cuts. The miners who stayed on eventually discovered gold, lead, and copper, but the town did not recover. Aspen came so close to dying with its lack of population in the 1920s that it almost became another of Colorado's ghost towns.

Aspen's first ski resort was established and opened in 1936. Further development of the slopes was abandoned during World War II due to lack of funds. In 1946, a group of developers formed the Aspen Skiing Corporation in order to raise capital and expand development. A 3.5-mile chair lift (the longest in the world at the time) was erected, and over 4 miles of trails were cleared.

Aspen is currently a world-famous playground for the wealthy. A modern town, it maintains its nineteenth-century Victorian appeal through the numerous buildings and sites listed on the National Register of Historic Places. The ski area continues to be one of the most popular in the world.

GPS COORDINATES: 39°11.44'N 106°49.13'W
TRAIL REFERENCE: Central #24: Aspen Mountain Trail

Basalt

First known as Frying Pan City, this community was a wild railroad construction town along the Colorado Midland line to Aspen. The name was derived from the phrase "The fishing was so good, the trout jumped out of the river and into the frying pan!"

Frying Pan City became known as Aspen Junction when it became a station stop. It consisted of several saloons, restaurants, stores, and a boardinghouse. Even after the crews moved on to other sites, Aspen Junction remained riotous and was known for its gamblers and seductive ladies.

In 1891, two trains collided just outside of Aspen Junction. A steam valve on one engine broke, and passengers were sprayed with steam and boiling water. Ten died and many others were badly burned in this tragic accident.

Fires throughout the years have taken their toll on the town. In 1892, the train depot was completely destroyed in a fire. Six years later, a kerosene lantern in a boardinghouse exploded, and high winds spread the flames throughout the town. In 1900, a kerosene lamp in a restaurant exploded, and the blaze consumed several buildings.

According to town lore, President Theodore Roosevelt once snubbed Aspen Junction because he felt it did not merit his attention. When he was touring, the town anticipated his arrival by decorating the train station and gathering to cheer him on. Roosevelt, in turn, did not even bother to show himself to the crowd.

Because Aspen Junction was so often confused with Aspen and Grand Junction, in 1894 the town took the name Basalt, after the nearby Basalt Peaks.

Basalt today is a small transportation and ranching town in an attractive setting.

GPS COORDINATES: 39°22.15'N 107°01.96'W
TRAIL REFERENCE: Central #22: Hagerman Pass Trail

Boreas
Named for the Greek god of the north wind, Boreas was originally established as a wagon stop for travelers between Breckenridge and Como.

The narrow gauge Denver, South Park & Pacific Railroad crossed through this route in 1884. A depot, section house, engine house, and other buildings were constructed, as well as a 600-foot snowshed, later extended by another 350 feet. For a while, this railroad run was the highest in America. The steep inclines, sharp curves, and abrupt drop-offs were constantly swept by storms and wind. There were 11 snowsheds along the route, and the grades were so steep that engines were allowed to pull a maximum of only three cars. When the Barnum circus traveled the Boreas route, the engines couldn't pull the heavy cars up the steep grade. The circus was stalled until someone had the brilliant idea to unload the elephants and have them tow the engines to the top.

Snow was a big problem on Boreas Pass. Winter storms began early, and by November, there was often 10 feet of snow to contend with. In 1899, a severe winter snowstorm isolated Boreas for one and a half months. No trains ran that year between February and April. Supplies ran short, so two men set out for Como on snowshoes. It was just too cold and too far— their frozen bodies were found buried in the snow.

Even without snow, the Boreas route was treacherous. In 1901, during perfectly fine weather, a runaway train with 13 cars of ore derailed and crashed. The brakeman was killed.

By 1905, Boreas Station was deserted except for the railroad workers who remained at the pass to keep the tracks clear of snow so the trains could keep operating.

In 1936, two locomotives were descending from the pass at about 20 miles per hour when they hit a frozen snowdrift and plunged down the mountain at Catastrophe Curve. One engine slid 200 feet from the track, and the other 50 feet. Temporary tracks had to be built to retrieve the train. A series of cables, ropes, pulleys, and chains were used to stand the trains upright and haul them back up the mountain.

In 1937, the railroad was shut down in South Park and over Boreas Pass. In 1952, the railroad bed was converted to an automobile road on the Breckenridge side; and four years later, it was converted to an automobile road on the Como side.

The walls of a two-story house and a partially roofed shed remain standing atop the pass. In 1996, the section house was rebuilt. When walking around you can also see boards and rotting logs that were once part of the snowsheds. Many other historic items can be found along Boreas Pass between Breckenridge and Como.

GPS COORDINATES: 39°24.64'N 105°58.07'W
TRAIL REFERENCE: Central #16: Boreas Pass Trail

Boulder
Boulder was originally home to the Arapaho Indians and other nomadic tribes. The first European settlers arrived in the Boulder area in 1858. Less than a year later, A. A. Brookfield, president of the Boulder City Town Company, offered 44 lots for sale for $1,000 apiece. Boulder was named for the numerous rocks found in the area, and its economy developed as a supply center for the nearby mining camps.

Although Boulder was originally part of the Nebraska Territory, it became part of the Colorado Territory by an act of Congress in 1861. Boulder incorporated in 1871, and two years later the railroad arrived, which helped put Boulder officially on the map. The town developed a fairly extensive infrastructure early on. The Boulder Post Office was established in 1860, a hospital built in 1873, and in 1874 the water system was developed and the first bank opened.

Around the turn of the century, the major force in Boulder's economy was still the mining industry, but to a lesser degree than when the town was founded. To diversify, Boulder turned increasingly to tourism and education to drive the economy. In 1909, the Hotel Boulderado opened and attracted tourists from across the nation and abroad. In 1967, the

A view of Boulder, circa 1888

Hotel Boulderado would be the first place alcohol would be legally served since the year 1907, when Boulder adopted an anti-saloon ordinance.

Students also came to Boulder when the University of Colorado (CU) first opened its doors in 1876. The university received a boost in enrollment during World War II when the Navy located its Japanese language school at CU. Following the war, a number of veterans who were taking advantage of the G.I. bill studied at the university.

Boulder continued to expand, and the new turnpike from Boulder to downtown Denver, which opened in 1952, fueled this growth. The local Boulder government has tried to manage the effects of significant growth by purchasing thousands of acres of open space beginning in 1967 and passing laws restricting building height and regulating residential growth. Today Boulder has a diversified economy, widely known as a launching pad and home for natural/organic ideas and businesses, and a vibrant cultural scene. It also is considered a very fit and active community, with many miles of hiking and biking trails throughout the city and surrounding foothills. The town has been consistently voted as one of the best places to live in the United States by a number of publications.

GPS COORDINATES: 40°00.90'N 105°16.20'W

TRAIL REFERENCE: Front Range #13: Gross Reservoir Trail

Bowerman

Originally named Nugget City, the camp was laid out in 1903 by J. C. Bowerman, who claimed to have found extremely rich gold deposits nearby. It was incorporated as Bowerman in 1904.

Bowerman, an unlucky prospector, had for years depended on his wife's odd jobs to bring in enough money so they could eat and he could search for minerals. Then, one day, it seemed his luck had changed. Bowerman told his wife that he had struck rich ore, but he wished to keep the find a tight secret in an effort to secure it for himself. His wife, excited by the new discovery, simply could not keep her mouth shut. She boasted to all who would listen that she would soon be rich. Before long, word spread like wildfire, and some 500 miners rushed to the area and swarmed all over her husband's property.

Newspapers announced far and wide that Bowerman had the potential to become the greatest gold camp of the twentieth century. The town sprang up as a result, and contained two hotels, a newspaper, five saloons, five gambling halls, and several other businesses.

In addition to J. C. Bowerman's Independent Mine, several other claims were established, but they produced only low-grade ore. Meanwhile, despite his original declaration that he had found rich gold, Bowerman failed to ship out any ore. He became more secretive, fenced off the property, and would not show the mine to anyone. He came up with all kinds of excuses for his failure to produce.

The 500 townspeople who had been lured to the area by Bowerman's rich find were bitterly disappointed by their below-average finds. Although some ore was shipped out, even from Bowerman's mine, people began drifting away. By 1910, the mining ended and the town was abandoned.

The site of Bowerman is about 3 miles north of Waunita Hot Springs. The buildings have been reduced to ruins, some of which are visible from the road but are on private property.

GPS COORDINATES: 38°33.75'N 106°30.69'W

TRAIL REFERENCE: Central #32: Waunita Pass Road

Breckenridge

Breckenridge was settled after the discovery of placer gold in 1859 and named for President James Buchanan's vice president, John C. Breckinridge. This political maneuver helped speed the establishment of a post office in 1860. However, when the vice president later fell out of favor with the American public, the spelling of the town's name was changed to Breckenridge.

From the beginning, Breckenridge grew quickly and became a convenient center for commerce. Supply wagons constantly rolled in and out of town. Stores, hotels, and saloons sprang up, and the population was soon estimated at 9,000. The first stagecoach entered Breckenridge in 1860.

When the residents decided they wanted to make Breckenridge the county seat of Summit County instead of nearby Parkville, their methods weren't entirely aboveboard. One night in 1862, Breckenridge townsfolk held a secretive raid on the Parkville City Hall, after which all the county records went missing. Some time later, the records were conveniently "discovered" in the new county seat of Breckenridge.

The boom in placer mining lasted only about three years. As in many of Colorado's mining towns, when the gold began to play out, so did the number of residents. By 1866, the population dropped to fewer than 500.

It is rumored that the ensuing silver discoveries in the late 1870s in Breckenridge were completely serendipitous. Supposedly, a gold miner was getting his hair cut one afternoon and chatting with his barber about the massive silver rush in

A snow tunnel in Breckenridge on Main Street during the winter of the big snow in 1898–99

Breckenridge Main Street, circa 1888

Leadville. It was then that the barber looked down and noticed large amounts of silver dust in his customer's hair.

In the 1880s, Breckenridge underwent a second gold boom when prospectors discovered new mines and new techniques for extracting ore from fissures and veins. Dozens of new mines were established in the mountains and gulches near Breckenridge. This helped the population climb back to around 2,000 by 1885. The boom was also helped along when the Denver, South Park & Pacific Railroad constructed a Breckenridge depot in 1882.

The town took on a much more permanent look, as log cabins were replaced with attractive Victorian-style homes with gingerbread trim, false-fronted stores, and other commercial buildings styled with elaborate wood trim and attractive architectural detail.

Breckenridge had its share of brothels, but it is interesting to note that most of the prostitutes lived in their own community across the river to the west of town. When miners said they were going "over the Blue," they meant that they were heading to the prostitute district on the other side of the Blue River. Considering that the ratio of men to women in Breckenridge was about 30 to 1, the brothels were a welcome outlet for the miners.

Thanks to the railroad and the good roads over Hoosier, Loveland, Argentine, Webster, and Boreas Passes, Breckenridge never suffered from transportation problems that plagued many Colorado mountain towns.

Breckenridge's third gold boom occurred in 1898, with the discovery of dredge mining. This type of mining utilized dredge boats, or barges, floated along the rivers and gulches. The residents tolerated the deafening noise caused by the boats because dredge mining provided a number of jobs at a time when mines all over Colorado were going out of business.

One evening in 1898, Pug Ryan and his gang held up the patrons of Breckenridge's elaborate Denver Hotel. Ryan's gang quickly stole the cash from the barroom and were intent on stealing the hotel safe, but one of their guns accidentally discharged, creating havoc. They were tracked to a cabin in Kokomo (between Breckenridge and Leadville), and a bloody shoot-out ensued. Two members of the posse were killed, as were two of Pug Ryan's gang. Ryan escaped and was not captured until four years later, when the tattoo "Pug" on his arm gave him away in Seattle. He was convicted and died in prison in 1931.

Surprisingly, some schoolchildren on a picnic discovered the loot from the robbery 10 years later. Included in the goods found was a watch belonging to the manager of the Denver Hotel. When he heard of the discovery, he took the first train to Kokomo and dug around in the dirt until he found his stolen diamond stickpin, too.

Winter snowstorms later that same year were particularly difficult for Breckenridge. The railroad tracks were buried so deeply that trains couldn't reach the town for 79 days. Supplies and food ran so low that when the train finally arrived in April with supplies and 50 bags of overdue mail, the townspeople greeted it in wild celebration.

After the third gold boom, the population of Breckenridge fell into decline again. In 1900, the population was listed as down to fewer than 1,000. During World War II, Breckenridge looked very much like a ghost town.

Today, Breckenridge is alive and prospering. The town found new gold in a ski area, developed in 1962. It has since evolved as a world-class resort. While the town still retains much of its Victorian styling and charm, it is now mixed with the towering condos and "Victorianesque" homes of more modern times. The only real telltale sign of the town's rich mining history lies in the countless gravel piles left from the many years of dredging.

GPS COORDINATES: 39°28.93'N 106°02.74'W
TRAIL REFERENCE: Central #12: Middle Fork of the Swan Trail, Central #16: Boreas Pass Trail

Bridal Veil Falls

Just off Black Bear Pass, east of Telluride, is a 365-foot-high waterfall—the highest in Colorado. On the canyon rim above the falls is a restored hydroelectric plant, built in 1904. Now a national historic landmark, it once generated power for nearby mines.

GPS COORDINATES: 37°55.15'N 107°46.16'W
TRAIL REFERENCE: Southwest #21: Black Bear Pass Trail, Overlooked from Southwest #18: Imogene Pass Trail

Buckskin Joe

Buckskin Joe mining camp was founded in 1859 by a group of prospectors led by a trapper named Joe Higgenbottom, nicknamed "Buckskin" because of the deerskin clothing he wore.

It is rumored that a hunter first discovered gold in the area when he shot at his prey and hit a rich gold vein instead, but it is more probable that the find was made by more conventional methods.

The area's best mine was the Phillips, later renamed the Buckskin Joe Mine. News of the Phillips discovery caused miners to pour over the mountains from Leadville with hopes of finding riches in Buckskin Joe. The thriving little town reached its peak in the 1860s with a population of 1,000. Saloons, hotels, and gambling halls provided employment for at least half of the residents, many of whom were women.

Horace and Augusta Tabor were the first managers of the first post office in Buckskin Joe, opened in 1861. The Tabors also ran the general store.

Also in 1861, a devastating outbreak of smallpox hit Buckskin Joe. According to legend, a beautiful dancer named Silverheels—so named because of the silver heels on her dancing shoes—nursed the afflicted miners. Silverheels remained when many others fled town so that she could cook and clean for the suffering miners. When she eventually caught the virus herself, her beautiful face was disfigured by scars. With her beauty ravaged, she disappeared. The miners later raised about $5,000 to show their gratitude, but Silverheels could not be found. Eventually all funds were returned to the donors. It is rumored that a black-veiled woman occasionally turned up at the Buckskin Joe Cemetery to visit the graves of the smallpox victims. Perhaps this was the mysterious Silverheels, visiting the graves of her friends, with her veil in place to cover her disfigured face. No one ever knew, because the woman disappeared before anyone could approach her. Majestic Mount Silverheels was named in her honor.

Although a dozen mills operated in the area during Buckskin Joe's peak years, the high times were short-lived. By 1866, the mines played out. The population dropped, and the county seat moved to Fairplay that same year. The post office remained open until 1873.

Little evidence of the town remains at the original site of Buckskin Joe, because most of the buildings were moved to a tourist park in Fairplay.

GPS COORDINATES: 39°17.48'N 106°05.16'W

TRAIL REFERENCE: Central #21: Mosquito Pass Trail

Burrows Park, Tellurium, Sterling, Whitecross

Between Lake City and Cinnamon Pass, a cluster of mining camps sprouted up in the alpine meadow of Burrows Park between 1877 and 1880. The park was 5 miles long and 0.5 miles wide. The exact locations of the camps are disputed, but the general area is about 10 miles southwest of Lake City, at the western end of the valley.

Burrows Park was the name of one of the camps, founded in 1877.

About a mile south of Burrows Park, there was a community named Tellurium. This very small camp had only about a dozen people, who hoped to find tellurium there. The highly optimistic group built an expensive mill. Unfortunately, Tellurium never became prosperous, and it soon was deserted.

Sterling was located a short distance beyond Tellurium, toward Animas Forks.

Nearer the Continental Divide toward Cinnamon Pass, Whitecross was the largest of the settlements and served as the center of activity for the other camps. Whitecross's post office, established in 1880, was first called Burrows Park, after the region. Two years later it was renamed Whitecross.

Many men who lived in this area worked at the Tabasco Mine and Mill, which operated from 1901 to 1904 and was one of the first to use electric alternating current. Tabasco, the Louisiana hot sauce manufacturing company, owned both the mine and the mill. Ruins of the mine are scattered around the summit of Cinnamon Pass.

GPS COORDINATES: 37°56.24'N 107°27.63'W

TRAIL REFERENCE: Southwest #3: Cinnamon Pass Trail

Camp Bird

In 1896, Thomas Walsh, an Irishman, discovered very rich gold in Imogene Basin. He immediately purchased more than 100 claims in the area and consolidated them under the name Camp Bird.

Camp Bird, a company town that grew up around the Camp Bird Mine, soon became the second largest gold producer in Colorado, turning out over $1 million per year. The camp had its own post office, which was established in 1898 and discontinued in 1918.

Walsh furnished a boardinghouse for his employees with marble-topped lavatories, electric lights, steam heat, and even a piano. Meals were deliciously prepared and served on china plates.

Camp Bird Mine in 1911

Winter and snow were always problems for the community. The men often had to tunnel out of their quarters to reach the mine. Snow slides killed several men over the years. It was necessary to construct a 2-mile aerial tramway from the mines to the mill. Camp Bird and the Tomboy Mine were linked together by underground tunnels.

Six years after discovering the prosperous mine, millionaire Walsh sold the properties to an English company for $3.5 million cash, a half million in shares of stock, and royalties on fu-

The miners' dining room at the Camp Bird Mine, circa 1900

Camp Bird Mine today

ture profits. Upon selling the mine, Walsh showed his appreciation to his employees by issuing bonus checks of up to $5,000.

With profits from Camp Bird, Walsh bought a mansion in Washington, D.C., and his wife and daughter hobnobbed with international society. They became "jet-setters" of their era. Walsh's daughter, Evalyn, married Edward B. McLean, whose family owned the *Washington Post* newspaper. As wedding gifts, each family gave the couple $100,000, which they supposedly spent before the honeymoon was over. Evalyn Walsh McLean later purchased the famed Hope Diamond, which is now on display at the Smithsonian Institution.

GPS COORDINATES: 37°58.28'N 107°43.59'W
TRAIL REFERENCE: Southwest #17: Yankee Boy Basin Trail, Southwest Trail #18: Imogene Pass Trail

Cañon City

Cañon City is situated in a mountain bowl along the Arkansas River valley. In 1859, during the Pikes Peak gold rush, prospectors settled the area, which Ute Indians formerly used as a camping ground. It has functioned as the seat of Fremont County since 1861. In its early years, Cañon City was primarily a commercial center for the nearby mining camps of Leadville and Cripple Creek. A number of railroads including the Denver & Rio Grande, the Cañon City & Cripple Creek, and the Cañon City & San Juan serviced the city and made it an important hub for transporting gold.

Although silver had been king in Colorado for much of the 1880s, the silver crash of 1893 reduced the value of silver and caused many boomtowns in Colorado to go bust. Neighboring Cripple Creek, however, prospered as the "world's greatest gold camp." A lot of this wealth trickled into Cañon City, as men from the camps sought places to display their newfound riches. Much of downtown Cañon City was built between 1899 and 1910, during a peak period of gold production at Cripple Creek.

Colorado State Penitentiary, Cañon City, circa 1920

In addition to its more illustrious residents, Cañon City has housed numerous inmates, as it has been home to the Colorado State Penitentiary since 1871. Thomas Macon, a Cañon City attorney elected to the state legislature, pushed hard for the prison to be located in Cañon City. The Territorial Legislature declared on January 7, 1868, that such an institution should be established in Cañon City, and the prison received its first inmate, John Shepler, convicted of larceny, in 1871.

One of the prison's most famous inmates was the notorious cannibal Alfred Packer. Packer was found guilty of five counts of manslaughter and sentenced to 40 years in the Colorado State Penitentiary. He served only 15 years when Governor Charles S. Thompson pardoned him in 1901. Today Cañon City is home to nine state prisons and four federal prisons. The highest security prison in the nation is located just a few miles from Cañon City in neighboring Florence. It houses or has housed such infamous prisoners as the Unabomber Theodore Kaczynski, the Oklahoma City bombers Timothy McVeigh and Terry Nichols, the shoe bomber Richard Reid, and various members of al-Qaeda.

While the gold mines are mostly gone, a number of original buildings remain. Cañon City has about 16,000 residents, and an average of nearly half a million tourists travel to the vicinity annually to visit the neighboring Royal Gorge. The city is home to the Royal Gorge Route Railroad, which takes tourists on a historic train ride along the most famous portion of the former Denver & Rio Grande Railroad.

GPS COORDINATES: 38°26.53'N 105°14.08'W
TRAIL REFERENCE: Front Range #35: The Shelf Road, Front Range #34: Phantom Canyon Road

Capitol City

Rich silver discoveries in 1877 about 10 miles west of Lake City brought prospectors to the area. The town of Galena City began as a tent city, but the tents were soon replaced by more permanent structures.

George S. Lee, a miner with grand plans, had the town's name changed to Capitol City because he was certain that Colorado would move its capital to the San Juan Mountains and he would live in the governor's mansion. To aid in the

The house built to be the Colorado governor's mansion, circa 1930

construction of Capitol City, Lee built a sawmill and planing mill. He also erected the Henson Creek Smelter, 1 mile below the town, to process ore from the many mines nearby. Additionally, he took over another mill at the other end of town. He seemed to play a part in virtually everything that went on in Capitol City.

A town site of 200 acres was laid out, and a schoolhouse was built, though the population never exceeded 400, with only a handful of students.

Lee built himself a large and elegant house at the edge of town to be the governor's mansion, where he and his wife entertained lavishly. Their home even had a ballroom and orchestra pit. Bricks imported from Pueblo were estimated to have cost a dollar apiece!

However, Lee's efforts did not work out the way he had planned. Capitol City never even became the county seat. His expectations were far too grand, and the ore played out too soon. The town declined in the 1880s and 1890s. The silver crash seemed to signal the end, but the discovery of gold in 1900 revived hopes. These hopes were short-lived though, as the gold proved limited.

GPS COORDINATES: 38°00.47'N 107°27.93'W
TRAIL REFERENCE: Southwest #1: Engineer Pass Trail

Carson

There were actually two towns named Carson about 2 miles from each other that were active at different times. The newer one is lower in elevation and was a gold camp. The older one rests atop the Continental Divide and was a silver camp.

The original Carson was one of the most inaccessible mining camps in Colorado and was completely exposed to Colorado's harsh winters. It was first settled in 1882 and named for Christopher Carson, who staked out the Bonanza King Mine, the first claim in the area. During the late 1880s, approximately 100 miners were working 150 claims. The town is believed to have met its demise in the 1893 silver crash, although some gold discoveries may have kept it going a while longer. Little or no evidence of the town remains on this site.

In 1896, the discovery of ores rich in gold spurred the growth and development of "New Carson" on the north side of the Divide. The town became increasingly active throughout the decade, with its population peaking at about 500. Much of the activity centered on the Bachelor Mine.

Miners reached Carson from Lake City on the northern side of the Continental Divide by a difficult wagon road up Wager Gulch. In 1887, a road following Lost Creek into town was completed from Creede on the south side.

By 1909, only six prospectors were still working in Carson. The remains of "New Carson" are well preserved, with several buildings still standing today.

GPS COORDINATES: 37°52.13'N 107°21.72'W
TRAIL REFERENCE: Southwest #4: Carson Ghost Town Trail

Clark

Clark was dependent upon the nearby Greenville Mine, which produced gold, silver, and copper. In addition to mining, some lumbering was carried out in the area. The post office was established in 1889.

It is not clear whether Clark was named for Rufus Clark, the first postmaster, or Worthington Clark, a property owner with local stagecoach operations.

GPS COORDINATES: 40°42.33'N 106°55.08'W
TRAIL REFERENCE: Northern #19: Farwell Mountain Trail

Colorado Springs

Colorado Springs was the vision of William Jackson Palmer. In 1871, Palmer founded the Denver & Rio Grande Railway Company (D&RG) and bought 10,000 acres of land east of Colorado City, a mining town built at the base of Pikes Peak that had been incorporated in 1859. Jackson planned a utopian community for the land that would be open to the wealthy, and he advertised the community throughout Britain and America. To join the community a membership fee of a $100 land certificate plus the additional cost of buying a plot of land with a permanent building was required. Members were also required to have strict morals with teetotaling habits.

The utopian settlement of Colorado Springs grew quickly, numbering 800 residents within just six months of the

Pikes Peak Avenue, Colorado Springs, with Antlers Hotel in the background, circa 1895

groundbreaking. The town lived up to Palmer's vision initially, boasting wide streets, quality shops and restaurants, and professional landscaping. By 1873, Palmer opened the Antlers Hotel, and residents as well as tourists from around the world flocked to Palmer's community called Colorado Springs. The town gained the nickname "Little London" because of the many English residents and visitors.

Although the resort community had golf courses and polo fields, there were no saloons or gambling houses to be found. Palmer intended for Colorado Springs to be a dry community and, in fact, it remained illegal to produce or sell alcohol until 1933 when prohibition was lifted. If residents or visitors wanted alcohol, they often went to the neighboring Manitou Springs or Colorado City.

In its early days, the neighboring town of Colorado City, now known as Old Colorado City, served as a major hub for supplying mining camps. Many who made money from mining during the gold rush built large homes in the undeveloped downtown area of Colorado Springs. Large stone civic structures, such as the library, county courthouse, and Colorado College, were also built before Colorado Springs had a large population, which was unique during this period. The expense was justified, however, as the El Paso County seat moved from Colorado City to Colorado Springs in 1873.

Winfield Scott Stratton, who had discovered one of richest gold mines in the world—Independence Mine, left the majority of his estate to establish the Myron Stratton House in Colorado Springs. Stratton built the foundation as a place for "the aged poor and dependent children." Throughout his life, Stratton helped to improve Colorado Springs, donating land for public use and expanding the city's trolley car system. Another millionaire from the gold mines, Spencer Penrose, was also a benefactor to Colorado Springs. He financed construction of the Broadmoor Hotel, the Cheyenne Mountain Zoo, the Will Rogers Shrine of the Sun, and the Pikes Peak Highway.

As the gold mines dried up, Colorado Springs's economy shifted to the health tourism industry. With its natural beauty, dry climate, and mineral springs, Colorado Springs became a primary destination for tuberculosis patients looking for rest and recuperation. To the delight of dentists everywhere, in 1909, Dr. Frederick McKay discovered that the fluoride in Colorado Springs's water could help prevent cavities.

Colorado Springs is a well-known tourist destination today. Visitors flock to such landmarks as Garden of the Gods and Pikes Peak. In addition to tourism, Colorado Springs's economy centers largely on the military. The U.S. Army established Camp Carson in 1942 to train troops for World War II, and at the same time began using Colorado Springs Municipal Airport (later named Peterson Field) as a training base for heavy bombers. After the Korean War, Peterson Field became Peterson Air Force Base, and Camp Carson became Fort Carson, which was Colorado Springs's first Army post. President Eisenhower then selected Colorado Springs as home to the Air Force Academy in 1954. Numerous other military installations, including NORAD (North American Aerospace Defense Command), Schriever Air Force Base, and Air Force Space Command, increased Colorado Springs' ties with the U.S. military.

GPS COORDINATES: 38°50.03'N 104°49.26'W
TRAIL REFERENCE: Front Range #31: Old Stage Road to Gold Camp Road, Front Range #21: Rampart Range Road, Front Range #30: Pikes Peak Highway

Columbine

Columbine was settled in 1897, after the Royal Flush Mine was discovered 2 miles to the east. The town is nestled in a grove of aspen about 4 miles north of Hahns Peak and was named for Colorado's state flower.

Columbine's primary industry was centered on the Royal Flush Mine, which operated sporadically over the years. After the Royal Flush Mill closed down in 1918, the town went into decline.

Logging and sheep herding in the area helped support the town for a while. A sheepherder once gambled away his wages and those of two herders who worked for him. Rather than fess up to his men, he killed them and roasted their bodies over a campfire!

Today, a store and a few seasonal cabins and other buildings remain in Columbine. The town functions mainly as a stop for tourists traveling along the forest route.

GPS COORDINATES: 40°51.23'N 106°57.90'W
TRAIL REFERENCE: Northern #17: Ellis Jeep Trail, Northern #18: Elkhorn Mountain and Stock Trail, Northern #19: Farwell Mountain Trail

Como

Originally Stubbs Ranch, a stage stop for wagons crossing over Boreas Pass into Breckenridge, Como eventually developed and became more diversified. Established in 1873, the town of Como started as a tent community, built by the railroad to house the thousands of workers constructing the Denver, South Park & Pacific Railroad. The many Italian immigrants working on the railroad had named their community after Lake Como in Italy.

Aside from the railroad activity, there was also some coal mining in Como and the surrounding area, which increased as the railroad was being built. In 1893, a huge explosion in the King Cole coal mine killed 16 miners.

Como was rowdy, with its share of fights and racial bigotry. In 1879, some Chinese miners were brought in to work the coal mines. This incensed the Italians, who beat up the man responsible for offering the employment and then chased the Chinese out of town.

In 1864, a group of outlaws known as the Reynolds Gang, robbed a stagecoach of its gold box near Como. One of the bandits was killed by an ensuing posse, and the other five were later shot on their way to jail, evidently for not revealing where the treasure was hidden. As the story goes, the gold was never found, and people still search for the missing fortune.

Although thousands of people passed through Como on their way over Boreas Pass in search of silver and gold riches, the town had an estimated population of only about 500 permanent residents.

Como experienced a number of fires through the years. In 1896, a fire destroyed the 43-room Pacific Hotel. A blaze in 1909 burned down a number of railroad buildings, which were never rebuilt. In 1935, a fire destroyed the wooden section of the railroad's huge roundhouse. The stone portion remains and is listed on the National Register of Historic Places.

The Denver, South Park & Pacific Railroad stopped running in 1937. In 1956, the railroad bed was converted to an automobile road.

GPS COORDINATES: 39°18.64'N 105°53.15'W
TRAIL REFERENCE: Central #16: Boreas Pass Trail

Creede

Creede was named for Nicholas C. Creede, a hard-luck prospector who was exploring the mountains near Wagon Wheel Gap in 1889. Picking at some rocks as he ate his lunch one afternoon, he looked closely at the ore he found and exclaimed, "Holy Moses!" This became the name of the mine that he established. The area saw a real boom after that, when word got out that David Moffat, president of the Denver & Rio Grande Railroad, and some other investors purchased the rich claim for $70,000. After Moffat's term as president of the railroad ended, the rail company refused to extend the line to Creede. Anxious for the railroad reach his mine in order to transport ore more efficiently, Moffat personally financed the construction of an extension of the rail line from Wagon Wheel Gap, 10 miles from Creede. The spur was completed in 1891.

After the railroad reached Creede, the town saw upwards of 200 people arriving each day. In the first few months, there were more than 10,000 men, women, and children scouring the mountains in search of a rich claim.

The men mined by day and sought entertainment at night; flimsy tents became saloons, with boards laid across boxes to constitute drinking bars. Because property on the outskirts of town cost a fraction of the price for real estate in the center of town, some drinking establishments were even set up on poles straddling the creek. The canyon was so narrow, it could facilitate only one main street.

Because of the narrow, deep gorge, Creede was a dangerous place to live. Heavy rains and melting snows often caused water levels to run high. Dangerous flows of water have been known to roar through the area annually. Over the years, numerous floods have washed away buildings and sections of the town. Consequently, many miners built their cabins and pitched their tents as far up the sides of the canyon as possible.

While many people made money on mining claims, an equal number made their fortunes on property claims. They would buy lots and then (with the soaring real estate market) unload them for a beefy profit.

There are some colorful characters associated with Creede. Bob Ford moved to Creede several years after killing Jesse James in Missouri in 1882. A man with a reputation, who considered himself the "boss," Ford was not a popular man. He opened the biggest tent-saloon and gambling house in town called the Exchange. In June 1892, Edward "Red" O'Kelly ambled into Ford's saloon and gunned him down. Some say that

Top: Creede in 1890, before the fire
Bottom: After the fire on June 5, 1892

O'Kelly was seeking revenge as a relation of Jesse James, and some say he was settling a gambling debt. The underworld of Creede paid for Ford's funeral; although the service was not much, the wake afterward became a real party. The revelry lasted for days: Copious quantities of whiskey were served, and people danced on Ford's grave. O'Kelly fled but was arrested and tried for murder in Pueblo. He was sentenced to life in jail at the Cañon City penitentiary but was released early in 1900. However, he could not stay out of trouble and was killed three years later by an Oklahoma City police officer.

Bat Masterson managed a saloon in town on behalf of a Denver firm. Since the usual way to settle differences in Creede was with guns, when one day a drunk slapped Bat, the hushed saloon ceased drinking to watch the gunman take revenge. Luckily for the drunk, Masterson merely laughed and told him to try again when he was sober.

When the branch of the Denver & Rio Grande came through town. People of all walks of life flooded into the town on every train to the overcrowded region. A melting pot of unique and interesting people, Creede was a fiery town that reached a population of about 10,000.

More than once, fire took a devastating toll on Creede. In 1892, a saloon fire raged so out of control it burned down the entire business district. Due to the big fire in 1892 and the silver crash of the following year, people began an exodus from Creede in massive numbers. Another fire in 1936 destroyed about one third of the rebuilt business district. Ten years later, a fire burned down the courthouse.

Three hundred people currently live in Creede year-round, but the population swells to about 3,000 in the summer. Creede's last mine closed down in the late 1980s, and these days the economy is sustained by tourism. According to the Creede Chamber of Commerce, data indicates a flow of 8,000 to 10,000 tourists in Creede from May to September every summer season.

GPS COORDINATES: 37°50.99'N 106°55.54'W

Crested Butte

Before the first miners, this area and the surrounding Elk Mountains were inhabited by the Ute Indians and used as summer hunting grounds. Seven years after the 1873 Brunot Treaty was signed, the town of Crested Butte was laid out and incorporated.

In 1880, Crested Butte already had a population of 250, as well as 50 businesses and dwellings. The town also had two-story outhouses that were unique to Crested Butte. The upper level proved functional during the deep winter snows, and since both levels were offset from each other, the outhouses could accommodate two people at the same time.

Although gold discoveries first attracted miners to the area, the town soon flourished as a way station for coaches traveling between Gunnison and Aspen. In 1882, the Denver & Rio Grande laid narrow gauge railway tracks from Gunnison, and Crested Butte diversified as a supply and railroad center for the area.

A road over Pearl Pass to Aspen was established that same year, but the road was said to have been so rough that wagons occasionally had to be disassembled and lowered down the steep cliffs.

The discovery of coal saw Crested Butte emerge as one of the foremost producers of bituminous coal in the West. Some of the mines were taken over by the Colorado Fuel and Iron Company in 1882. A huge economic boost for Crested Butte, coal mining kept the town going for 70 years.

Crested Butte saw its share of disasters. The Jokerville was an early, ill-fated coal mine owned by the Colorado Fuel and Iron Company. Tragedy struck when a powerful underground explosion claimed the lives of 58 miners. Fire ravaged Crested Butte in 1890, wiping out 15 of the town's businesses. Damage was high and warranted the establishment of local fire companies and fire hydrants. Another fire broke out three years later; but the water system was frozen, and firefighters had to resort to dynamiting some buildings in order to control the blaze. While this effectively snuffed the fire, the force of the explosions managed to blow out every window in town and blast a gaping hole in the town hall.

When the coal played out, Crested Butte's economy dwindled. In the early 1960s, about 10 years after the last mine was closed, things picked up again when enterprising entrepreneurs purchased property on the outskirts of town and developed it into a successful winter ski resort.

In 1974, the entire town of Crested Butte was listed on the National Register of Historic Places. Although Crested Butte has expanded with more modern architecture further up the mountain near the ski resort, the old town continues to thrive and successfully maintains the Victorian charm and appearance it had nearly 100 years ago.

GPS COORDINATES: 38°52.18'N 106°59.13'W
TRAIL REFERENCE: Central #28: Schofield Pass and Devils Punchbowl Trail

Cripple Creek

Once a gold mining camp located about 44 miles southwest of Colorado Springs, Cripple Creek is the seat of Teller County. The town allegedly received its name when a cattleman frightened a calf by accidentally firing his gun. The startled animal jumped over the creek and broke its leg, causing the cattleman to refer to the creek as "Cripple Creek."

For several years, the high valley in which Cripple Creek is situated was passed over by gold prospectors due to the Mount Pisgah hoax of 1884. Unscrupulous sellers in the area "salted" a claim by planting small amounts of gold in the rock in order to entice investors. Miners avoided the area after the hoax, but in 1891 rich veins of gold were discovered on the south side of Pikes Peak, and thousands flocked to the region again to try their luck. On July 4, 1891, W. S. Stratton staked claims on Battle Mountain for the Independence and the Washington Mines, naming them in honor of the July Fourth holiday. After mining operations began, one single boulder from the Independence Mine yielded $60,000 of ore. Stratton quickly invested the money back into his mining operations to unearth more gold. Between late 1893 and April 1899, roughly 200,000 ounces of gold were extracted from the Independence Mine. Stratton became Cripple Creek District's first millionaire. The region produced so much wealth, 29 more men struck it rich to the tune of millions.

As for those who did not become millionaires, many joined the miners' union, the Western Federation of Miners (WFM),

Panic erupts as fire breaks out in Cripple Creek in 1896

during the 1890s. When the mine owners attempted to extend the workday to 10 hours without offering further compensation, the union went on strike. Eventually the mine owners agreed to the union's demands. Increasing tension between the claim owners and workers erupted again in 1903 when miners called a sympathy strike to support the actions of the mill workers of Colorado City. Governor James Peabody sent the Colorado militia to handle the striking laborers, and the two groups clashed on numerous occasions. The WMF lost sympathy when Harry Orchard, a union-sponsored terrorist, bombed the Independence Mine railroad station, killing 13 strikebreakers in the blast. The strike finally ended in 1904, and nonunion laborers took over working the mines.

Although today the underground mines of the Cripple Creek district are exhausted, an open pit mine, operated by the Cripple Creek & Victor Gold Mining Company and known as the Cresson Project, has operated since 1994 just east of Cripple Creek in Victor. The population of Cripple Creek dropped to only a few hundred during the 1970s and 1980s but has climbed to about 1,500 residents since Colorado voters allowed Cripple Creek to establish legalized gambling in the early 1990s. Much of the economy now centers around the casinos and the tourist trade.

GPS COORDINATES: 38°44.80'N 105°10.66'W°

TRAIL REFERENCE: Front Range #35: The Shelf Road

Crystal

Originally called Crystal City, Crystal began as a silver mining camp in 1880. Early prospectors named the town after the crystal-like quartz they found along the creek.

The trail to Crystal was arduous, leading from Crested Butte over Schofield Pass. The difficulty of traversing this trail made it economically impossible to transport anything but the richest ores in or out of Crystal. Eventually, a better road was constructed, connecting the town with Carbondale.

In the mid-1880s, Crystal had a population of about 500. It had a newspaper, a general store, many private homes, several saloons, and the Crystal Club (a men's club), which still stands in town.

Crystal Mill in 1893

Crystal Mill today

The Lead King was the principal mine of the region and continued to produce until 1913. Silver from the Black Queen Mine was exhibited at the Chicago World's Fair in 1893.

Although Crystal survived the silver crash of 1893 by mining other minerals (copper, lead, and zinc) until World War I, its population was reduced to a small number of residents.

The beauty of its location ensured the town's survival. Many of the original cabins have been converted to summer homes, although they still appear much as they did in years past. The much-photographed Crystal Mill remains standing on the outskirts of town, along the Crystal River.

GPS COORDINATES: 39°03.56'N 107°06.14'W

TRAIL REFERENCE: Central #28: Schofield Pass and Devils Punchbowl Trail, Central #29: Lead King Basin Trail

De Beque

Located in Mesa County, De Beque is a small town that sits on the north side of the Colorado River. Originally inhabited by Indian tribes for thousands of years, De Beque was later a hunting ground for the Ute Indians. White settlers began encroaching on their territory in 1880. The town's namesake, Dr. W.A.E. de Beque, explored the area in 1884 while searching for suitable ranchland. The post office was established under the name De Beque in 1888.

Hotel McDowell in De Beque, circa 1895

Herds of wild horses roamed the surrounding lands, and De Beque was a central location for rounding up and selling the horses. To commemorate this important aspect of the town's history, a mustang statue sits in the town square. De Beque is one of only three certified wild horse sanctuary cities in the United States. In cooperation with the Bureau of Land Management and other private organizations, De Beque participates in programs to help protect wild horses and burros, including the construction of a public corral to house injured horses awaiting adoption. The patient wildlife viewer can still spot the protected herds of wild horses in the area today.

GPS COORDINATES: 39°20.06'N 108°12.86'W

TRAIL REFERENCE: Northern #4: Little Bookcliffs Wild Horse Trail

Delta

Delta is located about 30 miles southeast of Grand Junction at the confluence of the Gunnison and Uncompahgre Rivers. Juan María Antonio Rivera, one of southwest Colorado's first explorers, traveled through the region in 1761. About 5 miles west of Delta, the Frenchman Antoine Robidoux established a fur trading post known as Fort Uncompahgre in 1828. The fort remained there for 18 years and then relocated to what is considered modern-day Delta. The town site itself was first platted in 1882 and was called Uncompahgre. The name changed later to Delta because of its location on the delta of the Gunnison and Uncompahgre Rivers.

In addition to trade between the Ute Indians and white fur traders, raising livestock was one of the earliest industries in Delta, and ranching and agriculture remain the primary industries today. Ranching has such a strong history in Delta that some cattle brands existing prior to 1900 can still be

Delta, circa 1925

found in use. Delta has retained its close links to the land and serves as the gateway into the Uncompahgre and Grand Mesa National Forests. The town also has celebrated its historic relationship with the Ute by designating an 85-foot cottonwood tree at the entrance of the town a Colorado landmark. The tree, which dates back to around 1802, was once a gathering place and tribal council area for the Ute. The tree was dedicated to Chief Ouray and his wife, Chipeta, who both worked throughout their lives to achieve peace between Indians and settlers.

GPS COORDINATES: 38°44.53'N 108°04.10'W

TRAIL REFERENCE: Southwest #41: Escalante Rim Trail,
Southwest #40: Dry Mesa Jeep Road,
Southwest #39: Escalante Canyon Road

Denver

In July 1858, William G. Russell discovered gold on the South Platte River, triggering the 1859 gold rush. Prospectors streamed into the Rocky Mountains with the slogan "Pikes Peak or Bust." Russell established the town of Auraria along the South Platte River and Cherry Creek, naming it after his hometown in Georgia. Just across the river, William Larimer, a town promoter from Kansas, started the settlement of Denver City, named after James Denver, the former governor of the Kansas Territory, because the location was originally a part of the territory. A fierce rivalry developed between the two towns that were established within weeks of one another. Competition ceased in April 1860 when the towns merged.

Denver served as a supply center for the mining camps in the nearby mountains. Although Denver experienced solid growth in its early years, its path to development was not entirely smooth. The town experienced a devastating fire in 1863, then severe flooding only a year later. Attacks by the Cheyenne and Arapaho tribes, which increased after the Sand Creek Massacre in 1864, were also troublesome to Denver. One of the greatest setbacks to the growth of the town was the Union Pacific Railroad's decision to circumvent Denver and build its line through Cheyenne, Wyoming, to the north.

By 1870, however, Denver had managed to reverse its fortunes. The Colorado Territory was created in 1861, and Governor John Evans banded together with local investors to build the Denver Pacific Railway, which linked Denver to the Union Pacific Railroad in Cheyenne. Denver became a significant railway hub in the West, helping to cement the town's industrial as well as its political dominance. Denver served as the de facto capital of the Colorado Territory from 1871 to 1876. Later it became the first temporary capital and finally the permanent capital of Colorado when the territory became a state in 1876. In the 1870s and 1880s, gold and silver mines boomed, and those who became wealthy through mining and ranching built several mansions in the Capitol Hill district.

Brown Palace shortly after it opened in 1892

15th Street, Denver, circa 1895

With Denver's fortunes closely tied to the mining industry, the silver crash of 1893 damaged the city's economy. To overcome the ill effects of the silver crash, Denver started to heavily promote itself as a tourist destination. Local businessmen developed the Festival of Mountain and Plain, which was held annually from 1895 to 1912, to showcase the state's agricultural, industrial, mineral, and mercantile enterprises. A concerted effort was made to clean up the city's image, perceived as rough and tumble since its inception as a frontier town. Robert Speer, elected mayor in 1904, made improvements to Denver's infrastructure and added a number of parks and civic buildings, earning Denver the nickname "Queen City of the Plains."

During the Great Depression, Denver again suffered when drought ruined crops and mineral exploration that had been fueled by World War I slackened. However, New Deal projects brought improvement and growth to Denver, as federal money flowed into the state to help build schools, government buildings, highways, Red Rocks Amphitheater, and other structures.

After World War II, the population of metropolitan Denver exploded and the suburbs expanded significantly. Dozens of skyscrapers sprung up downtown in the 1950s, including the Mile High Center, designed by I. M. Pei. The Denver Urban Renewal Authority further altered the landscape of the downtown area when it tore down a number of buildings to make room for the Auraria Higher Education Complex in the 1970s.

Today Denver is a thriving city and a popular tourist destination. Many federal agencies have offices in Denver, and the city is the commercial transportation hub for the region. A number of industries, including communications, aerospace, defense, bioscience, manufacturing, and energy research, support Denver's diversified economy. The city is home to a number of museums and boasts eight professional sports teams. The opening of Denver International Airport in 1995 made access to the city easier than ever before, bringing more tourists to the gateway to the mountains.
GPS COORDINATES: 39°44.36'N 104°59.05'W

Doyleville

Doyleville was originally a 160-acre ranch homestead, owned by Henry Doyle, at the junction of Tomichi and Hot Springs Creek. It was established in 1879 and functioned as a stage stop and supply center on the route from Salida to Gunnison.

The Denver & Rio Grande Railroad began running through Doyleville in 1881. Between then and 1885, over 400 railway cars of hay and sheep were loaded out of Doyleville each year.

Doyleville was active until the 1950s with a post office, school, train depot, and community hall. Today, there is virtually no evidence of Doyleville's former existence, and the site has reverted to ranchland.
GPS COORDINATES: 38°27.08'N 106°36.47'W
TRAIL REFERENCE: Central #32: Waunita Pass Road

Durango

Durango was founded in 1880, when the Denver & Rio Grande Railroad platted the site 1.5 miles south of Animas City. The depot at this new site attracted most of the population of Animas City to a new home in Durango. Durango was, and is still, a railroad and smelting center.

By 1881, Durango was growing at a rapid rate and boasted 20 saloons, a red-light district, and 134 businesses. Newspaper advertisements declared Durango to be the "Denver of the Southwest," effectively luring about 2,000 pioneers to the area.

Durango saw its share of rowdiness and Wild West violence. Brawls and shoot-outs were common, sometimes injuring or killing innocent victims. The members of the Stockton gang were notorious gunslingers who did as they pleased in Durango. They frequently clashed with a rival gang from nearby Farmington. One Christmas season, the Stocktons rode into Farmington all fired up and ready for blood from the Simmons gang. They crashed a local Christmas party, shooting up the place and killing an innocent guest with a stray bullet. The Stockton gang escaped, followed by more bloodshed and shoot-outs.

The people of Durango did what they could to maintain a semblance of law and order. Justice was usually so speedy that sometimes the guilty party would be hanged on the same day he had committed his crime. When the grand opening of the West End Hotel in 1881 had to be delayed because two feuding cowboys shot up the hotel, one of the brawlers was lynched that afternoon. In 1883, citizens thwarted an at-

Durango's Main Street, circa 1900

tempt to rob the Bank of San Juan (1st National Bank today). The town promptly formed a posse, and the culprit was soon captured.

H.A.W. Tabor owned a livery stable and stage line in Durango. It was here that Tabor filed secret divorce papers against his wife so that he could marry Baby Doe. After he had married Baby Doe, his divorce was declared invalid; but because Tabor was both exceedingly rich and a U.S. senator, he was able to keep his reputation intact.

There is much preserved history in Durango, such as the 100-year-old Durango & Silverton Narrow Gauge Railroad, which is listed on the National Register of Historic Places. Two historic districts in Durango are recognized by the National Register: Main Avenue Historic District and the East Third Avenue Historic Residential District.

Durango and its surrounding areas have been the settings for a few of Hollywood's memorable scenes. For instance, about 12 miles north of town, crossing the Animas River, is "Bakers Bridge." The chasm provided the setting for Paul Newman and Robert Redford as they made their leap from the cliff into the river in *Butch Cassidy and the Sundance Kid.* Another movie that used the same area for some scenes was *The Naked Spur.*

GPS COORDINATES: 37°16.74'N 107°52.69'W
TRAIL REFERENCE: Southwest #30: Junction Creek Trail

Engineer City

Engineer City originated around 1874, when H. A. Woods staked the first claim in the area and named it the Annie Woods Lode. By 1875, the population of prospectors grew to about 400.

For a short while, Engineer City prided itself on being the largest city in the state without a saloon. The prospectors were simply too busy looking for silver to spend time in a bar.

In 1875, when Woods overheard some men from Howardsville discussing another claim in the area, he sneaked out and beat them to the area by several hours. He marked the claim and named it the Polar Star, after the cold night air he endured as he traveled through the night to beat the other party. The Polar Star became the best producer in the area.

In 1882, the Frank Hough Mine was discovered. A camp of about 50 men operated it in American Flats on the eastern side of Engineer Mountain. It was closed in 1900, and the ruins of the mine remain.

GPS COORDINATES: 37°58.43'N 107°34.71'W
TRAIL REFERENCE: Southwest #1: Engineer Pass Trail

Estes Park

Estes Park has a long history of human inhabitants. Earliest evidence dates back to the Clovis culture, whose people are the first to have crossed the Bering Strait from Asia to North America roughly 13,000 years ago. Following the Clovis people, the Ute and Arapaho Indians located their summer camps in Estes Park. Part of the trail they used to cross the Continental Divide is still visible in Rocky Mountain National Park.

Joel Estes, a man who made his fortune mining in California, moved his wife and 13 children to the Estes Park area in

The Stanley Hotel while still under construction in 1909

1859 and set up a homestead. A visitor who stayed with the family, William Byers, owner and editor of the *Rocky Mountain News,* named the locality Estes Park in 1864. Estes Park received further publicity when Isabella Bird, a traveler from England, wrote of her trip to Estes Park in letters home, which were later published as *A Lady's Life in the Rocky Mountains.* An Irish nobleman, the Earl of Dunraven, also visited and fell in love with the area in the 1860s when he decided to purchase more than 15,000 acres of land for his personal hunting grounds. Pressure from settlers desirous of the valuable ranching land around Estes Park eventually forced Dunraven to lease large tracts of his land.

By 1900, ranching and tourism fueled the Estes Park economy. The town had its first long-distance telephone connection, and in the summers mail arrived daily by stagecoach. "The Grand Old Man of Estes Park," F. O. Stanley, helped the town grow by funding road improvements, establishing a bank, and donating property for civic buildings. In 1909, he opened the Stanley Hotel, which he built as a luxury travel stop. The Stanley was an inspiration for the Overlook Hotel in Stephen King's 1977 novel *The Shining.* Today the hotel is listed on the National Register of Historic Places.

In 1915, President Woodrow Wilson signed the Rocky Mountain National Park Act, which officially established the park as a national treasure. The park's scenery, abundant wildlife, and hiking trails have continued to draw visitors to Estes Park. Over the years, the town has hosted many famous guests, including Pope John Paul II, the Japan's Emperor Hirohito, and President George W. Bush. Estes Park suffered an extensive flood in 1982 when a man-made earthen dam burst in Rocky Mountain National Park. The subsequent renewal of the downtown area earned Estes Park the nickname "Gutsiest Little Town in Colorado."

GPS COORDINATES: 40°22.62'N 105°31.26'W
TRAIL REFERENCE: Front Range #7: Pole Hill Road, Front Range #6: Old Fall River Road

Eureka

Eureka was founded in the early 1870s. Although not a boom town, it grew slowly and steadily.

The Sunnyside Mine was located in 1873 and became one of the best producers in the area. Sunnyside Mill was built in

The Sunnyside Mill, circa 1920

The foundations of the Sunnyside Mill in Eureka today

1899, with a 3-mile cable tramway connecting the mine to the new mill. The Sunnyside Mill was easily the leading producer of income for the town.

Eureka flourished and boasted a population of 2,000 and many stores, meat markets, saloons, and a restaurant. It was incorporated in 1883, making it one of only two incorporated towns in San Juan County (Silverton was the other). Eureka had its own post office, and the monthly newspaper, the *San Juan Expositor,* was published there. Otto Mears routed the Silverton Northern Railroad through the town in 1896, further strengthening Eureka's economy.

The Gold Prince Mill was moved to Eureka from Animas Forks in 1917 but did not begin operation until 1918, because it was damaged by fire and had to be rebuilt. Eureka also served the Toltec, the Golden Fleece, the Tom Moore, the Silver Wing, and the Sound Democrat Mines. The Sunnyside Mine operated continuously until 1931, when it shut down for a few years and then reopened in 1937. Two years later the miners went on strike, and since an agreement could not be reached, the mine was shut down again.

Toward the end of the Silverton Northern Railroad's operation, its steam engines were replaced by a combination of auto and locomotive parts called the Casey Jones, which could speed down the tracks between Silverton and Eureka in just 20 minutes. To clear snow off the tracks,

the Casey Jones carried brooms strapped behind its cowcatcher. Service between Silverton and Eureka ended in 1939 and the railroad was sold and junked in 1942.

In 1976, the state of Colorado decided that the town had had no municipal government for the past five years and declared Eureka formally abandoned. Today, only a reconstructed two-story building stands on what was Eureka's flat town site. You also can still see the enormous skeleton of the Sunnyside Mill.

GPS COORDINATES: 37°52.76'N 107°33.88'N
TRAIL REFERENCE: Southwest #11: Eureka Gulch Trail

Fairplay

Fairplay was first established in 1862 as Fair Play. Prospectors, who had just moved on from Tarryall (dubbed "Grab-All" because of greedy miners and claim jumping there), wanted a more civilized and fair-minded mining camp.

The town fell short of its literal name, and people sometimes took justice into their own hands. For instance, in 1879, a judge sentenced a convicted murderer to eight years in jail for getting drunk and shooting a local. The residents were so outraged by the light penalty, they took it upon themselves to seize the killer that night and hang him from the courthouse window until he was dead. When the judge turned up for work the next day, he faced the lifeless body strung up from the second-story window

A view of Eureka and the Sunnyside Mill in 1929

The Casey Jones

Fort Collins, circa 1900

and then discovered an extra noose beside the gavel on his desk. Shrewdly realizing that his services were no longer required in Fair Play, the judge promptly caught the first ride out of town.

Fairplay has been the county seat of South Park County since 1867. In 1924, the post office officially changed the city's name from Fair Play to Fairplay.

Fairplay today is an agricultural and ranching community, also serving as a mecca for fishermen, hunters, and tourists. The courthouse, built in 1874, is the oldest still standing in Colorado and is now a library. The town's South Park City Museum is home to 30 old buildings that were moved from Alma, Garo, Leavick, and other places, intermingled with original buildings from Fairplay. They have been restored and filled with thousands of artifacts and furnishings to represent the look and feel of an authentic 1880s Colorado mining town.

GPS COORDINATES: 39°13.48'N 106°0.08'W

TRAIL REFERENCE: Central #21: Mosquito Pass Trail, Central #19: Weston Pass Trail, Central #20: Breakneck Pass and Browns Pass Trail

Fort Collins

Erected in 1862 to protect the Overland Trail mail route during the Indian Wars, Camp Collins did not remain for long at its original location on the Cache La Poudre River near what is now Laporte. A flood in 1864 wiped out most of the camp, and it was relocated several miles farther down the river to the present-day location of Fort Collins. The new post became known as Fort Collins, although there seems to be no official order for the name change. For almost two years Fort Collins remained a military post until 1866 when it was decommissioned.

Although the fort was abandoned, a sizable number of people had already settled in the area. The first school and church were established in 1866, and the town was platted in 1867. Joseph Mason, a local businessman, lobbied to relocate the seat of Larimer County from Laporte to Fort Collins, and he succeeded in 1868.

Around the time the government opened the land on the military settlement, an agricultural colony developed, modeled after nearby Greeley's Union Colony. The Colorado Agricultural College opened in the fall of 1879 and helped develop new methods and innovations in agriculture. The harvesting of beet tops, an abundant food source for sheep, was an industry supported by the college, and by the early 1900s Fort Collins earned the reputation as the "Lamb Feeding Capital of the World." The arrival of the Colorado Central Railroad in 1877 allowed for livestock and produce to be shipped more easily and helped boost Fort Collins's economy.

In the decade after World War II, Fort Collins's population doubled, and the 1960s saw an immense growth in enrollment to Colorado State University (CSU), which would become the city's primary economic force by 2000. With the help of CSU students, the prohibition on the sale of alcohol—in place since the 1890s—was lifted in 1969, long after the national repeal in 1933. Concerned citizens also organized to preserve the historic buildings in town and protect Fort Collins's heritage. Today Fort Collins continues to grow, but it has managed to retain its small-town atmosphere. In 2006, *Money* magazine ranked Fort Collins as the country's best small city to live in.

GPS COORDINATES: 40°35.11'N 105°50.02'W

TRAIL REFERENCE: Front Range #2: Old Flowers Road, Front Range #3: Moody Hill Trail, Front Range #4: Crystal Mountain Trail

Georgetown

Georgetown began as a gold settlement in 1859, when George Griffith from Kentucky found gold there. He brought his brother, their father, George's wife, and a couple of prospectors to the area. They called it George's Town, in honor of George Griffith. The group worked hard to live on the modest amounts of gold they found, despite the large amounts of seemingly worthless (at the time) silver-bearing ore in their lode.

In 1864, plentiful veins of quartz were discovered, creating a boom that brought prospectors pouring into the area. The resulting settlement was called Elizabethtown, in honor of George's wife, Elizabeth. Before long, George's Town and Elizabethtown combined under the name Georgetown, and a post office was established in 1866.

The following year brought the silver explosion. Houses and businesses were erected at a dizzying rate, the streets buzzed with activity, merchants did brisk business, and lots of people were on the verge of becoming very wealthy. Georgetown was known as "the Silver Queen of the Rockies." As it grew, the town acquired an attractive mix of Victorian cottages

The Georgetown Railroad Loop, circa 1890

and a substantial brick business district. Georgetown became the home of many rich men with rich tastes. Large, ornate residences grew in size and ostentation as their owners prospered.

While Georgetown had a wild side—with more than 30 saloons and plenty of red-light houses and gambling dens—it was also a mining town with culture and refinement. Citizens enjoyed two opera houses, met in public halls and a Masonic lodge, and attended society events. Unlike in most other mining camps, families were an integral part of Georgetown. Schools and churches were constructed from the early days, and homes were built with an air of permanence.

Georgetown is home to many interesting old buildings with their own histories. The Hotel de Paris (now a museum operated by the National Society of Colonial Dames) was a luxurious French inn of outstanding quality that used to accommodate businessmen from the East and Europe while they speculated over mining investments. President Ulysses S. Grant stayed there and was very fond of it. The Hotel de Paris was richly furnished and served exotic foods. The owners bottled their own wine and kept an extensive wine cellar. Fresh fish were kept in an indoor fountain so they could be selected by

A view of High Bridge on the Georgetown Loop, circa 1920

and prepared for the guests. The Hammill House (now a museum at Argentine and Third Streets) was once a modest home built by mining investor and politician William A. Hammill. As Hammill grew wealthier, his house became more opulent. He added bay windows, a solarium with curved glass panels, a stable, an office, and a six-seat outhouse (with three walnut seats for the family and three pine ones for the servants). The Maxwell House is another immaculately kept Victorian home that was quite modest in its original state and took on a much more lavish appearance as the owner prospered.

In 1884, railroad workers accomplished a true feat of engineering when they completed the Georgetown Loop narrow gauge railway between Georgetown and Silver Plume (2 miles west). A series of curves constructed in a spiral fashion helped trains gain momentum for the steep grades on the straightaways; in one spot, the railroad actually crossed over itself on a 300-foot trestle. The trip, popular with tourists who wanted to observe the beautiful scenery and experience the thrilling ride, was similar to a roller coaster ride.

After the silver crash of 1893, Georgetown became a sleepy mountain town, although it continued to produce gold and other metals. The railroad was abandoned in 1939; the trestle was dismantled, and the rails were scrapped. However, the entire narrow gauge railway route between Georgetown and Silver Plume has been reconstructed. Thousands of tourists ride the Georgetown Loop Railroad across the 95-foot Devil's Gate High Bridge between Silver Plume and Georgetown during Colorado's milder months.

Georgetown today is a charming community with interesting architecture and lots of history to observe. The town has been a National Historic Landmark since 1966. In 1970, residents formed the Georgetown Society, which has made an ongoing effort to restore and preserve many of Georgetown's Victorian buildings (including the Hammill House) to their original states.

GPS COORDINATES: 39°42.37'N 105°41.81'W

TRAIL REFERENCE: Central #1: Saxon Mountain Road, Central #2: Guanella Pass Trail; Central #3: Waldorf and Santiago Ghost Town Trail

Golden

The Arapaho, Ute, and Cheyenne Indians first inhabited the Golden area. Gold fever caused a surge of pioneers to travel west, and many settled in the valley near the location of modern-day Golden. As important as gold was to the town's economy, Golden City was not named for the precious metal but rather for Thomas L. Golden, a miner who established a base camp near the mouth of Clear Creek Canyon in 1858.

Golden City itself was actually established in 1859 by the Boston Company, a group of prospectors headed by George West. By the end of 1859, Golden City boasted more than 700 residents. The first schools and churches were organized in 1859 and 1860. A mountain road system was built in 1860 to link the mining communities with Golden City at about the same time a weekly mail service arrived in the town.

While prospectors did not have much luck fulfilling their gold lust in the vicinity of Golden City, rich coal deposits were discovered just north of the town. These coal mines provided

Washington Avenue, Golden, circa 1880

employment for many locals, and Golden City evolved into an industrial town, as well as a supply center for miners. Local clay deposits provided materials for brickmaking, as wood was hard to come by.

Golden City was an innovative place and the site of numerous historical firsts. In 1859, David K. Wall established the county's first commercial garden when he began selling his crops to miners. George Pullman built the first railway sleeper cars in Golden. Colorado's first railroad, the Colorado Central and Pacific, was headquartered in Golden City and served Idaho Springs, Georgetown, Central City, and Black Hawk.

A fierce rivalry existed between Golden City and Denver for railroad supremacy during the 1870s. Although Golden City initially took the lead as Colorado's primary railway hub, by the late 1800s Denver supplanted Golden City as the most important rail terminus in the state.

In politics as well as in railroads, Denver overtook Golden. In 1861, the Colorado Territory and Jefferson County were legally formed, and Golden City became both the county seat of Jefferson County and the territorial capital of Colorado. When Colorado achieved statehood in 1867, the capital officially moved from Golden (which had changed its name in 1872) to Denver.

Even after the capital moved, Golden continued to prosper. The Colorado School of Mines was founded in 1874 and has continued to operate since. The U.S. Geological Survey Earthquake Hazards Program is currently housed on the school's campus. Coors Brewery opened in 1874 and attracts roughly 300,000 visitors each year with its brewery tours. Golden remains the seat of Jefferson County, and a new courthouse that was built in 1993 dominates the southeast ridge of the town.

GPS COORDINATES: 39°45.33'N 105°13.23'W

Gothic

Named for Gothic Mountain, the town was established in 1879, with the discovery of gold and silver ores in the area. Within four months, nearly 200 buildings had been erected, including a hotel, three stores, a butcher shop, a barber shop, and a saloon. Millions of dollars' worth of gold and silver ores were extracted from the hills. At its peak, the bustling mining city had a population of around 8,000.

Gothic gained a reputation as a very wild town with lots of drinking, gambling, and prostitution. When Ulysses S. Grant

Gothic, circa 1885

wanted to see a wild mining town in 1880, he went to Gothic. He reportedly drove his own stage into town and arrived to a riotous celebration.

Gothic's first mayor was elected by a roll of dice between two men. The winner, Garwood Judd, was a saloonkeeper who later earned the reputation of "the man who stayed." He was proud of his title and even nailed a plaque engraved with the phrase over his door.

After gold and silver played out, fortunes receded quickly; by 1884, most of the residents had left town. The city faded as quickly as it had formed. As the last resident of Gothic, Garwood Judd remained all by himself until his death in 1930. His ashes were scattered around the town.

Gothic is now the home of the Rocky Mountain Biological Survey, which studies the wide variety of regional flora and fauna.

A few well-preserved old buildings still stand in Gothic. Set in a beautiful area, the town is experiencing a revival as a summer tourist and residential area.

GPS COORDINATES: 38°57.53'N 106°59.34'W
TRAIL REFERENCE: Central #28: Schofield Pass and Devil's
                       Punchbowl Trail

Grand Junction

Fremont Indians first inhabited the Grand Valley area from about A.D. 1300 to A.D. 250, at which time they mysteriously disappeared. The Ute Indians occupied the valley after that. The U.S. government formalized the Ute's ties to the land in an 1868 treaty that designated the Grand Valley a Ute reservation. However, pressure from the increasing influx of gold

Grand Junction's Main Street in 1890

rushers and other white settlers led to conflicts with the Ute, and in 1880 the government relocated the tribe to reservations in northeast Utah and the southwest corner of Colorado.

Congress declared the Ute lands public and open for white settlement in June 1882, although many white migrants had already staked claims before the official declaration. Led by George A. Crawford, a group of men laid out the town of Ute. They later changed the name to West Denver and finally to Grand Junction when the town was incorporated in June 1882. The name is derived from the town's location at the junction of the Gunnison and Grand Rivers. The Grand River was later renamed the Colorado River.

Not long after the establishment of Grand Junction, the Denver & Rio Grande Railroad (D&RG) laid down tracks for a narrow gauge line through the city, connecting it to the cities of Gunnison and Denver. The following year, 1883, Mesa County was carved out of Gunnison County, and Grand Junction became the county seat. With the railroad and its new status as county seat, Grand Junction became a central transportation hub for the Western Slope.

In the 1880s, Grand Junction saw the establishment of a volunteer fire department, a National Guard unit, and the Teller Institute and Indian School, which taught Ute and other Indian children practical trades. In 1901, Andrew Carnegie helped build the public library.

Today, public lands managed by the Bureau of Land Management and the U.S. Forest Service surround Grand Junction. The city is located among three geologically remarkable areas: the Bookcliffs to the northwest, Grand Mesa to the east, and Colorado National Monument to the southwest. A number of wineries have been built in recent years, earning the area the reputation as "Colorado's Wine Country."

GPS COORDINATES: 39°03.83'N 108°33.00'W

TRAIL REFERENCE: Northern #5: Rattlesnake Canyon Trail

Gunnison

Gunnison was named after Captain John W. Gunnison, an army explorer who passed through the area in 1853, leading a group of government engineers in search of the safest and best transcontinental railroad route.

Gold and silver seekers arrived in the 1870s. Valuable ores were found in all directions encompassing Gunnison. With all the mining activity, the town soon became a shipping and supply center. Fortune seekers would stock up in Gunnison before setting out into the mountains.

In 1880, the town became incorporated and was a robust frontier town with a population of 10,000. As the miners arrived, Gunnison became a wild place. Once, an Alpine Tunnel railway laborer was accused of killing some contractors. He was arrested and taken to his cell, but at midnight a group of vigilantes took him out and lynched him on the main street.

Also in 1880, H.A.W. Tabor established the Bank of Gunnison. He put up capital of $30,000 and served as president. The Tabor family members were stockholders in the bank until 1898.

The Denver & Rio Grande Railroad arrived in Gunnison in the summer of 1881. The line was soon extended to Grand Junction.

Alferd Packer (the admitted cannibal) had his second trial in Gunnison in 1886. He was found guilty of manslaughter and sentenced to 40 years in the Cañon City state penitentiary.

After gold and silver miners exhausted the metals, the town dwindled but did not die. Ranchers moved in, and Gunnison became a cattle and ranching area. The population is not as high as it was during the mining boom, but the town is very much alive. Gunnison is currently the county seat of Gunnison County.

GPS COORDINATES: 38°32.67'N 106°55.58'W

Hahns Peak

The story of Hahns Peak begins in 1862, the year Joseph Hahn found traces of gold at the base of a volcanic peak. He returned the following year with partners to form a new mining company.

In 1866, there were at least 50 men working the mining district, an estimated 47 of whom returned to civilization when the harsh winter set in. Three who kept going were Hahn and his two partners, Doyle and Way. Unfortunately for them, supplies were waning, so Way set out to bring back more provisions. He never returned, and although he lived on for many years, he never explained why he disappeared. Hahn and Doyle nearly starved to death but managed to survive the winter; in April they set out for Empire. Hahn never completed the trip; he died of hunger and exhaustion along the way. A mile later, Doyle, snow-blind and delirious, stumbled into a camp of strangers.

The town of Columbine grew up around Hahns Peak; but mining in the area was never very profitable, and the town faded.

GPS COORDINATES: 40°48.42'N 106°56.61'W

TRAIL REFERENCE: Northern #18: Elkhorn Mountain and Stock Driveway, Northern #19: Farwell Mountain Trail, Northern #17: Ellis Jeep Trail

Hancock

Hancock was named for the Hancock Placer, the first claim in the area. The Denver, South Park & Pacific Railroad established the town in 1880 to support the construction of the Alpine Tunnel. Most of the hundreds of workers employed to build the

A train at Hancock in 1881

The former railroad bed and a water tank at Hancock in 1940

tunnel lived in Hancock. With five general stores, a hotel, several saloons and restaurants, and two sawmills cutting lumber for the tunnel and railroad, the town supported a population of close to 1,000.

After the Alpine Tunnel was completed in 1881, Hancock became a station on the line to Pitkin, and its Main Street faced the railroad tracks. The population saw a substantial decline with the tunnel's completion, but many workers were still needed to keep the tracks clear of heavy snow. Large crews labored constantly throughout winter months.

Hancock's population continued to dwindle when many of the area mines closed down, but the big decline occurred after the collapse of the Alpine Tunnel in 1910. Hancock became a true ghost town. All the buildings have now collapsed, although the structures and foundations are clearly visible in the meadow. The last to fall away was a saloon.

GPS COORDINATES: 38°38.40'N 106°21.64'W

TRAIL REFERENCE: Central #33: Hancock Pass Trail

Henson

Henson was a small camp laid out midway between Lake City and Capitol City, near the Ute-Ulay veins. Little was done to develop claims until after the signing of the Brunot Treaty in 1873.

Named for Henry Henson, the camp became one of the most prosperous in the area after the Henson Creek and Uncompahgre toll road was completed in 1877. Settlers pitched in to extend the road to connect with the Animas Forks road to Ouray and Silverton. This well-traveled route traversed the Continental Divide at 12,200 feet.

Henson was a rough town. It was never very large, but it was filled with troubles. Shootings and mine accidents were common. The eight doctors in town frequently stayed busy around the clock. A miscalculation in tunneling once caused a terrible gas explosion when mine tunnels of the Ute-Ulay and Hidden Treasure accidentally met, killing 36 miners.

Henson also saw a long, bitter, and violent miners' strike. Reportedly, the strike started because the mine owners insisted that all single men board at the company boardinghouse. To protest, miners went on strike. When the owners hired non-union labor to replace the striking miners, violent fights erupted and some scabs were run out of town. The volatility of the situation prompted the governor of Colorado to send

four companies of cavalry and two companies of infantry to settle the dispute. The dispute eventually went to trial, and all the miners were forced to leave camp.

Henson's post office, established in May 1883, was closed in November 1913. The buildings still standing in Henson are privately owned, and many are still in use.

GPS COORDINATES: 38°01.23'N 107°22.58'W

TRAIL REFERENCE: Southwest #1: Engineer Pass Trail

Highland Mary

Highland Mary was actually a town near the Highland Mary Mill and Highland Mary Mine in Cunningham Gulch.

Highland Mary was founded by two enterprising brothers from New York City who decided to go into mining. To figure out where they should begin prospecting, the Ennis brothers consulted a fortune-teller who pointed to a map, marking the area where the two would find treasure. The brothers named the area the Highland Mary and continued to visit the spiritualist for advice. Her instructions regarding where and how to find ore led the brothers on a peculiar and unsuccessful search through the mountains, in which they must have crossed over some rich gold veins without knowing it! Occasionally they made some lucky discoveries, but all too rarely. The Ennises had invested about $1 million in the mine by 1885, and gave another $50,000 to the spiritualist. The pair ended up bankrupt; they sold the mine and their elaborate house nearby and returned to New York.

The new owners of the mine prospected using more conventional methods, and Highland Mary immediately began to pay off. It became one of the best mines in Cunningham Gulch. Despite the harsh winters at the mine's elevation of 12,000 feet, the Highland Mary proved quite worthwhile to the new owners.

All that remains in modern days are ruins of the mill.

GPS COORDINATES: 37°47.37'N 107°34.68'W

TRAIL REFERENCE: Southwest #24: Cunningham Gulch and Stony Pass Trail

Howardsville

Howardsville was originally named Bullion City for the Bullion City Company, which laid out the town as a promotional settlement in late 1872. However, the following year the residents changed the name to Howardsville, after the individual who built the first cabin on the site in 1872.

Because Howardsville was growing at the same time as nearby Silverton, the two towns became rivals. Howardsville was named the first county seat in Colorado in 1874, but a vote the following year moved the county seat to Silverton.

Howardsville consisted of about 30 buildings and at its peak had about 150 residents.

Howardsville, circa 1873

Howardsville today

The post office that served Howardsville was claimed to have been the first post office in western Colorado, serving the community from 1874 to 1939.

Some of the old mines in the area included the Pride of the West, the Highland Mary, the Little Nation, and the Old Hundred. The Pride of the West Mill has operated intermittently over recent years under various owners. The Old Hundred Mine is privately owned and open for daily tours.

Most of the early buildings of Howardsville are gone today, but a few residents still live in the gulch.

GPS COORDINATES: 37°50.17'N 107°35.64'W
TRAIL REFERENCE: Southwest #6: Silverton to Animas Forks Ghost Town, Southwest #24: Cunningham Gulch and Stony Pass Trail

Idaho Springs

George Jackson discovered the hot springs around which the town of Idaho Springs grew up when he was scouting for gold and spotted smoke in the distance. Suspecting the smoke came from an Indian campfire, Jackson crept forward to get a closer look and found that it was actually steam rising from a natural hot spring in the frozen ground. Upon closer inspection of the area, Jackson found promising traces of gold in the nearby stream.

Jackson marked his placer discovery and then left it for several months until the ground thawed. In the meantime, he organized a group of miners from Chicago and quietly established the Chicago Mining Company. Upon his return, Jackson and his men found more rich ore. When news of their success got out, other prospectors poured into the area.

In 1859, the town formed a short distance from the original strike and was successively called Jackson's Diggings, Sacramento City, Idahoe City, Idaho Bar, Payne's Bar, and finally, Idaho Springs. It grew so quickly that within just a few months there were 10 saloons, 150 homes, a handful of shops, and a boardinghouse.

Horace Tabor, his wife, Augusta, and their baby son came to Idaho Springs in the early days. Augusta set up a bakery to earn money while Horace prospected. One old prospector advised Horace to take Augusta to Denver for the winter, where she'd be safe from the inevitable avalanches. When Horace returned to Idaho Springs, he found that the old prospector had jumped his claim. Also living in Idaho Springs at the time were newlyweds Harvey and Baby Doe. They were working the Dictator Mine, which Harvey's father, William, had staked out before he went on to become a banker and a state legislator. Baby Doe later became Tabor's second wife.

The medicinal benefits of the hot springs were recognized early on, and by 1866 two bathhouses had opened to the public. Idaho Springs became a renowned health resort that attracted invalids and tourists alike.

In 1868, stagecoaches began carrying passengers and mail between Idaho Springs and Georgetown. Ten years later, the Colorado Central Railroad completed a narrow gauge line from Golden to Georgetown, and Idaho Springs became an important stop on the run.

Idaho Springs never did collapse when mining declined, as did many other mining towns. In fact, the town is still very much alive. Because of its good location, accessibility, and diversity of businesses, the town has survived through the years.

GPS COORDINATES: 39°44.56'N 105°31.12'W
TRAIL REFERENCE: Front Range #18: Oh My God Road

Ironton

After the mining craze around Red Mountain, Ironton was formed in 1883 as a tent colony. At the time, the camp was also called Copper Glen, but that name quickly fell out of use.

Ironton developed into a somewhat refined town. Some merchants of the better stores in Ouray and Silverton opened branches in Ironton. Ironton served as the residential center for workers in the nearby mines, such as the Yankee Girl and the Guston.

Ironton also served as an important stage and supply center for the region. Wagons arrived at regular intervals, and ore wagons headed out from the city continuously. When Otto Mears opened the Rainbow Route, extending his railroad from Silverton, over Red Mountain Pass, through to Ironton in 1889, the town had a grand celebration to welcome it.

Prospectors found gold in nearby mountains, which helped create another rush. New mine shafts were drilled deeper into the mountains. Digging deep mine shafts entailed finding underground water; and unfortunately the water was found to contain deadly sulfuric acid. It often ate through machinery, making equipment maintenance a constant and expensive endeavor.

The mines all closed after the silver crash of 1893, and though most of Ironton's residents moved on to other areas, Ironton remained inhabited until the early 1930s. Some old buildings are left in the area.

GPS COORDINATES: 37°56.13'N 107°40.59'W
TRAIL REFERENCE: Southwest #16: Corkscrew Gulch Trail

Ironton, circa 1908

Jefferson

Jefferson was originally a tent colony that grew up when the Denver, South Park & Pacific Railroad arrived in 1879.

Like Fairplay, Jefferson was first settled by prospectors who were disgusted by the greedy miners and claim jumpers in Tarryall (dubbed "Grab-All"). However, Jefferson did not last long as a gold camp, although some prospectors carried out modest mining activity along the Michigan and Jefferson Creeks.

Located at the junction of Georgia Pass (some very rich strikes were made in Georgia Gulch) and the road from Denver to Fairplay, Jefferson was a convenient place for miners to send their ore for shipping via the Denver, South Park & Pacific. It was also a handy supply depot.

The railroad tracks were torn up in the 1930s, but the station still exists, as does a modest little town.

GPS COORDINATES: 39°22.65'N 105°47.97'W

TRAIL REFERENCE: Central #14: Georgia Pass Trail

Kenosha

Kenosha was a railroad stop and post office on the summit of Kenosha Pass. Kenosha is likely to have been named after a tribe of Chippewa Indians.

GPS COORDINATES: 39°24.69'N 105°45.56'W

TRAIL REFERENCE: Central #14: Georgia Pass Trail, Central #5: Handcart Gulch Trail

Keystone

Keystone Mountain saw some mining activity in the early 1880s, but Keystone's main role was as a significant transportation center for the mining industry.

The Denver, South Park & Pacific Railroad route from Como, over Boreas Pass, and through Breckenridge terminated in Keystone. A number of wagon roads and mountain passes (Loveland and Argentine) also led to Keystone, allowing miners to ship their ore from the many regional mining camps to connect with the railroad in Keystone. In addition, Keystone loggers were able to ship a significant amount of lumber to the surrounding mining camps.

The railroad company's plans to extend the railroad east over the Continental Divide were never carried out, and Keystone remained the terminus of the line until the tracks were removed in 1937.

Keystone ski area was built some 30 years later, near the old town. Today the resort is one of the most popular in Colorado.

GPS COORDINATES: 39°36.34'N 105°58.47'W

TRAIL REFERENCE: Central #11: Saints John and Glacier Ridge Trail, Central #9: Deer Creek Trail, Central #4: Peru Creek Trail

Lake City

In 1871, Henry Henson discovered the Ute-Ulay Mine; but the land belonged to the Indians, who did not take kindly to white trespassers. Henson was unable to develop the property until well after the Brunot Treaty of 1873, as violence with the Indians continued for several years. White settlers clashed violently with the native Indians near Lake City as late as 1879.

Looking south on Silver Street, Lake City in 1894

In 1874, the Golden Fleece Mine was located; originally named the Hotchkiss Mine, it soon became the best producer in the area. Many other strikes followed, and the development of Lake City was underway. In 1875, Lake City was registered. It was named for nearby Lake San Cristobal, which was formed by two massive mud and rock slides: the first around the year 1270 A.D. and the second about 350 years later.

Also in 1875, the first stagecoach arrived and began making three trips a week to Saguache. That same year, Harry M. Woods published Lake City's first newspaper, the *Silver World*.

Lake City began to take on a permanent look by its second year. Substantial buildings constructed of attractive frames with gingerbread trim outnumbered log cabins. An influx of women signaled the arrival of families and a civilizing influence. Schools and churches went up; and social activities such as balls, suppers, raffles, and skating parties became popular entertainment. The post office opened with a mail stage to Del Norte.

Lake City was one of the first towns in Colorado to have telephone service. In 1876, Western Union initiated telephone service; and by 1881, service had been extended to Silverton, Ouray, Capitol City, Rose's Cabin, Mineral Point, and Animas Forks. Musicians utilized the telephone service to perform popular telephone concerts for listeners along the various lines!

At its high point, Lake City had around 2,500 residents. Since the town was platted at the junction of two toll roads—Saguache to Silverton and Antelope Springs to Lake City—hundreds of people passed through the community each week. Stagecoaches continued to stop in the city daily.

The wild red-light district on the west of town was known as Hell's Acres. Gambling dens and dance halls were interspersed among the many brothels. Lake City had its rough side: Many of

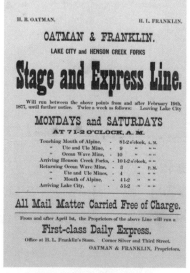
A schedule for the stage that ran between Lake City and Henson

its residents were killed in mine accidents, snow slides, and shoot-outs.

In 1882, Sheriff E. N. Campbell and a posse attempted to arrest George Betts and James Browning, two saloonkeepers who moonlighted as burglars. In an ensuing gunfight, the sheriff was killed and others in the posse were wounded. Nonetheless, surviving members of the posse were able to recognize and pursue Betts and Browning. Soon after, the burglars were captured and jailed. Two hundred people met at the murdered sheriff's home and formed a lynch mob. They stormed the jail and strung up Betts and Browning from the Ocean Wave Bridge. The mob left the corpses dangling as a lesson to any others contemplating theft. Both are buried in the Lake City cemetery.

The Denver & Rio Grande Railroad arrived in 1889. There were two trains daily in the 1890s, and ore shipments left regularly.

Lake City experienced a series of economic fluctuations. It suffered greatly after the silver crash of 1893 and went into a long decline, relieved only by subsequent gold and lead production.

After the turn of the century, Lake City was on the decline; but camping, fishing, and hunting helped revive it as a summer community. In 1933, the railroad tracks were sold for scrap.

Lake City never became a ghost town, although its population dwindled and it is currently a sleepy little community. Many buildings were made of stone and still survive. The large stone schoolhouse was built in 1882. The courthouse was built in 1877 and is still used.

One of the best-known stories about Lake City took place in 1874 and revolves around the infamous Alferd Packer. The activities of this unique cannibalistic scout are described in the section of this book entitled "People".

GPS COORDINATES: 38°01.76'N 107°18.98'W

TRAIL REFERENCE: Southwest #1: Engineer Pass Trail,
Southwest #3: Cinnamon Pass Trail

Harrison Street, Leadville, circa 1892

Tabor Opera House in 1882

Leadville

As early as 1860, prospectors staked claims in the California Gulch, which yielded gold for the following six years. The camp was then called Oro City. The miner H.A.W. (Horace) Tabor, along with his wife, Augusta, arrived during a food shortage. Tabor sacrificed his oxen to feed the miners and hence made many friends.

The gold soon played out but was followed by rich discoveries of silver. In 1877, the area's silver boom took flight, and the town began to evolve. Hundreds of prospectors arrived on a daily basis and slept wherever they could. Some slept in alleyways, some in tents, and one saloon even rented out floor space (the owner is said to have saved the tabletops for regular customers). Still, others could not find room in the saloons, and hundreds died of exposure.

Officially named Leadville in January 1878, the town was incorporated the following month. Later that year, two prospectors asked Tabor to lend them $17 worth of mining supplies in exchange for a one-third interest in their findings. The two prospectors discovered a mine about a mile up East 7th Street, which they called the Little Pittsburg. It turned out to be one of the richest silver lodes in Colorado and promptly made all three men millionaires. Tabor became Leadville's first mayor that same year.

By the summer of 1879, Leadville's architects and builders had endowed the town with a sophisticated air. The town was quickly blossoming with its 19 hotels, 82 saloons, 38 restaurants, 13 liquor houses, 10 lumber yards, 7 smelting and reductions works, 2 works for ore testing, 12 blacksmith shops, 6 jewelry stores, 3 undertakers, 21 gambling houses, and 36 brothels. The town grew so prosperous that not only miners but also merchants, business owners, and artisans could earn a comfortable living.

Leadville became a place where countless fortunes could be made. Even seemingly barren mines produced. Leadville claimed that in a 10-year period it had created more millionaires than any city in the world. And there were many places for rich men to spend their money. The red-light district along State Street was a notorious haunt for the most infamous of

The stage of the Tabor Opera House, Leadville, circa 1879

Leadville's early gamblers. It was considered to be one of the most wicked and rowdy areas in the entire West. Easy money inevitably encouraged lawlessness lurking everywhere. Violence, murder, and thievery were prevalent in Leadville. Anyone who flashed a wad of cash could be staked out as prey. It was dangerous to walk the streets at night.

Leadville saw some interesting characters and fortunes come and go. Doc Holliday had a famed dispute with a Leadville bartender. The bartender, who had previously lent Holliday $5, demanded to be repaid. He followed Holliday into a saloon and threatened to "lick" him if he did not get his money back right away. Holliday drew his pistol and fired a shot that wounded the bartender in his arm. Holliday was taken into custody, tried, and acquitted.

"Broken Nose Scotty" sold his mining claim for $30,000 while he was in jail for drunkenness. With the proceeds he paid bail for all the other inmates, bought everyone new clothes, and then took them out on the town. Needless to say, before the night was over the group was back in jail for disturbing the peace!

Once, a group of men were digging a grave for their friend when they struck a fortune. Their poor "friend" ended up buried in a snowbank.

Young Margaret Tobin was 19 years old when she married J. J. Brown. After Brown struck it rich on the Little Jonny Mine, the couple moved to Denver. Mrs. Brown later became famous as a survivor of the *Titanic* and was subsequently known as the Unsinkable Molly Brown.

During Leadville's boom years, its population swelled to somewhere between 20,000 and 40,000. It was the second largest city in Colorado.

The Tabor Opera House (308 Harrison Avenue) was opened in 1879 with the financial assistance of Horace Tabor.

The Great Houdini, poet Oscar Wilde, and John Philip Sousa's Marine Band are among the famous performers who made appearances there. (It is rumored that Wilde drank the miners under the table at local saloons.)

Tabor was also responsible for construction of the Tabor Grand Hotel, which opened in 1885. Its famous lobby floor was embedded with silver dollars, and its bar was known as the best-stocked bar in the state. (Renamed the Hotel Vendome in 1894, it still stands at 701 Harrison Avenue.)

Tabor and his wife began to drift apart. A woman of simple taste, Augusta frowned on her husband's free spending and did not enjoy the lavish life the two led after striking it rich. In 1881, Tabor met and romanced beautiful divorcee Elizabeth McCourt Doe (Baby Doe). Their relationship became an open secret, and Tabor and Augusta were divorced the following year. Tabor and Baby Doe were married in an elaborate wedding in Washington, D.C., in 1883.

Ten years later Tabor lost everything in the silver crash, as all his money was tied up in silver investments. Baby Doe remained a devoted wife as Tabor was forced to sell everything—except the Matchless Mine (2 miles east on 7th Street), which Tabor strongly believed would once again become valuable. After Tabor's death in 1899, Baby Doe moved into a small shack on the premises. She became a recluse and destitute woman. Thirty-six years later, in March 1935, her lifeless body, dressed in rags, frozen in the shape of a cross, was found at the mine. Surrounding her were scrapbooks with yellowed pages and mementos of the elegant life she had once known.

Businessmen attempting to bring tourists to the community built the Leadville Ice Palace between 6th and 8th Streets during the winter of 1895. The palace covered five acres and cost $40,000. It looked like a castle but was constructed with 5,000 tons of ice. Up to 250 men cut the ice and constructed the palace. Inside its five-foot-thick walls were a large skating rink, a ballroom, and a dining room. Leadville held a huge celebration and parade to commemorate the opening day. The railroads even added extra passenger cars to accommodate the flocks of tourists who came to visit the structure. Unfortunately, a mild winter forced the ice to melt early, and the palace was closed after only three months of operation.

After the turn of the century, Leadville's economy was in shambles. Mine production had dropped to a fraction of what it had been, and houses were torn down for firewood. Leadville became a source of illicit whiskey, the county's major source of income during prohibition.

Today Leadville is home to a few thousand residents, but it never did revive. Although it is not an especially pretty town, with a little imagination one can still glimpse the faded splendor of a long-gone era.

GPS COORDINATES: 39°14.91'N 106°17.48'W
TRAIL REFERENCE: Central #21: Mosquito Pass Trail, Central #22: Hagerman Pass Trail, Central #19: Weston Pass Trail

London Junction

London Junction was also called Alma Junction and Alma Station. Located at the intersection of Mosquito Pass and the road between Alma and Fairplay, the settlement served as a stop for travelers to and from Leadville and Fairplay, as well as a home to those who worked in the nearby London Mines. The McLaughlin stagecoach line ran between Alma and Fairplay, providing transfers at London Junction for travelers heading west.

In 1882, a spur of the London, South Park & Leadville Railroad was completed—a 6-mile segment leading from London Junction, through Park City, to the London Mountain mining area. Used for hauling ore from the London Mine, the spur was abandoned two years later when the mine closed down.

Although London Junction was never incorporated, in 1884 there were 150 people living there. At its peak, the population reached 300.

Some ruins of the original cabins still remain, and a few residents occupy the area today.

GPS COORDINATES: 39°16.02'N 106°02.68'W

TRAIL REFERENCE: Central #21: Mosquito Pass Trail

The London Mines
(North London and South London)

The London Mines were established in the 1870s by London Mines, Inc., a British syndicate. Small settlements grew up in the area to house the miners. A concentration works was constructed at London Junction in 1883 to process ore.

The South London Mine, which opened in 1874, lies on the eastern slope of Mosquito Pass. It was the terminus of the London, South Park & Leadville spur up Mosquito Gulch.

The North London Mine was high on London Mountain (12,280 feet). The mine had its own boardinghouses and an aerial tram, with wooden tram towers that are still visible among the trees. The tram was constructed to span the 3,300-foot distance between the North London Mine and its mill because a conventional chute was not sufficient. Buildings that remain in evidence at the site include some ruins of cabins and the bunkhouse.

The North London and South London Mines merge via a tunnel beneath them on the interior of London Mountain. Over 100 miles of tunnels burrow through London Mountain in all directions and have yielded millions of dollars' worth of ore.

GPS COORDINATES: 39°16.93'N 106°09.96'W

TRAIL REFERENCE: Central #21: Mosquito Pass Trail

The block of marble that was used for the Tomb of the Unknowns in Arlington National Cemetery, ready for shipment east in 1931

Marble

Marble began as a silver and gold mining camp in the 1870s. The ores were of poor grade, and the mines never became very popular. The area went mostly ignored until the discovery of a huge mountain of pure white, high-grade stone in 1882.

The marble was said to have been of the best quality and in the most plentiful supply in the world. Contractors from Italy traveled to Colorado to lend their knowledge of mining marble quarries.

Transporting the marble presented a major problem. Miners shipped marble to Carbondale by way of wagons and pack trains in summer and horse-drawn sleds in winter. The marble was heavy and the trip was difficult and slow; thus, the cost was high. To counteract these problems, the Colorado Yule Marble Company built the Crystal River and San Juan Railroad into Placita in 1907.

High-quality stone from Marble was used in both the Lincoln Memorial and the Washington Monument. However, the most remarkable stone ever produced was reserved for the Tomb of the Unknown Soldier in Arlington, Virginia. The largest single block of marble ever quarried—it weighed over 100 tons raw and almost 56 tons dressed—took a year to excavate.

The town of Marble has seen a number of fires, avalanches, and mud slides. In 1941, a huge cloudburst sent mud sliding down through the valley like a tidal wave, destroying much of the business district and many homes. In just a few minutes, deep mud and debris filled street after street. The damage was so extensive that the mill was rendered inoperable. Many of the residents left town.

There is still plenty of marble left in the area, but demand for marble has tapered off over the years. Genuine marble is used less frequently than it once was, because of the many synthetics, veneers, and other alternatives available. The mill is currently open and operates during summer months under the direction of the Colorado Yule Marble Company.

GPS COORDINATES: 39°04.30'N 107°11.37'W

TRAIL REFERENCE: Central #28: Schofield Pass and Devil's Punchbowl Trail

Marshall Pass

Marshall Pass, a small railroad town with a post office, sat at the top of Marshall Pass. At 10,846 feet, it was the highest railroad pass and the highest railroad town on the Continental Divide in the 1930s, before the railroad abandoned the run.

GPS COORDINATES: 38°23.50'N 106°14.85'W

TRAIL REFERENCE: Central #43: Marshall Pass Poncha Creek Trail, Central #44: Marshall Pass Railway Grade Road

Middleton

Two men, named Gotlieb and Konneker, made the first strike in 1893, and the town formed the following year. The site was named for neither of these men; rather, it was named for nearby Middle Mountain, presumably because it was halfway between Howardsville and Eureka.

Middleton was located 2 miles above Howardsville, where Maggie Gulch enters the Animas Valley. Because the town was too close to other residential towns (such as Silverton, Eureka, and Howardsville), Middleton never really became a permanent community, despite some very well-paying mines there. Middleton was abandoned by the early 1900s.

GPS COORDINATES: 37°51.30'N 107°34.32'W
TRAIL REFERENCE: Southwest #9: Maggie Gulch Trail

Mineral Point

Mineral Point mining camp was founded by prospectors Abe Burrows and Charles McIntyre in 1873. It was located below the crest of Engineer Pass, at an elevation of 11,500 feet.

The discovery of large composites of quartz and other minerals gave the area its name and spurred the influx of numerous miners in search of riches. To generate interest in the camp, promoters of Mineral Point circulated far-fetched advertisements with unrealistic claims and pictures to raise capital. One advertisement depicted a steamship running up the Animas River and streetcars running from Mineral Point to Animas Forks!

In truth, only very mediocre transportation was available, and miners had to use cumbersome wagons or burros to transport their ore. Most was sent either to Silverton via Animas Forks or to Lake City.

The Old Lout was a regional mine that was considered worthless. The mining company sank a 300-foot shaft without finding anything profitable. The mine was on the verge of being abandoned when the miners took one last shot and uncovered a rich body of ore. The mine produced a staggering $85,000 the following month.

Due to the inhospitable winters, the lack of transportation, and the silver crash of 1893, by the mid-1890s Mineral Point was on its way to becoming a ghost camp.

GPS COORDINATES: 37°57.28'N 107°35.80'W
TRAIL REFERENCE: Southwest #1: Engineer Pass Trail

Monarch

Camp Monarch was established in 1879 after the discovery of numerous local mines, some of which were discovered by Nicholas Creede. Residents of the fledgling community boasted that there were over 20 productive mines within half a mile of the town. The town was located along the Old Monarch Pass, down in a valley about a mile from the current Monarch Pass, or US 50.

In 1880, the tent city began to develop into a town with log cabins and dressed lumber buildings; its name was changed from Camp Monarch to Chaffee City, in honor of Senator Jerome Chaffee. In 1884, the town was renamed Monarch. Monarch's population peaked between 2,000 and 3,000.

In the beginning, miners hauled ore to Cañon City in wagons, but in 1881, the railroad reached Monarch.

The town fell victim to the silver crash in 1893. People began leaving Monarch, and those who stayed dismantled the buildings for firewood. Later, an avalanche swept away everything that remained.

GPS COORDINATES: 38°32.44'N 106°18.75'W
TRAIL REFERENCE: Central #30: Old Monarch Pass Road,
Central #34: Tomichi Pass Trail

Montezuma

Mining strikes in 1865 led to the founding of the Montezuma silver camp, named after the Aztec chief in Mexico. The camp grew slowly, mainly because of its poor accessibility and transportation problems. When the Argentine and Webster Passes were built, Montezuma began to expand. Montezuma became a hospitable area, something of a social center for local miners, offering dances, sports, and poker games—which are said to have gone on 24 hours a day.

Montezuma reached its peak population of about 800 residents around 1880. The town had the normal mining town amenities by this point, including a post office. The following year, the city was incorporated.

A story is told about two miners who loved the same girl back in Missouri. The two were friendly rivals, each endeavoring to be the first to earn enough money to return home and take her hand in marriage. One night around the campfire, one of the men suddenly realized that he could kill the other and thus double the fortune he could take home. He killed his fellow prospector and set out for Missouri. But by the time he reached there, his crime had been discovered and he was extradited back to Montezuma. En route, he hired a lawyer. When they reached Montezuma, the wedding ceremony had been replaced with a hanging scaffold, and the execution papers were all prepared. While the lawyer presented his case to the town officials, the murderer made his escape and was never heard from again.

Montezuma suffered greatly from the silver crash of 1893, but some residents stayed on and waited for better times to come.

In 1958, a fire started at the Summit House hotel and blazed through town, completely destroying the hotel, the town hall, houses, garages, and other buildings. Almost half of the 75 residents were rendered homeless—a week before Christmas.

Montezuma never did totally become a ghost town and today is a pretty mountain town with a few residents. The one-room schoolhouse, which operated from 1884 to 1958, still stands on a slope east of Main Street.

GPS COORDINATES: 39°34.86'N 105°52.04'W
TRAIL REFERENCE: Central #9: Deer Creek Trail, Central #11:
Saints John and Glacier Ridge Trail,
Central #8: Santa Fe Peak Trail

Mosquito

Mosquito was formed after gold was discovered high in the mountains between Leadville and South Park. In 1861, when early settlers met to decide on a name, they supposedly chose the name "Musquito" (originally misspelled) because a mosquito had landed on their pages of notes. While there is some confusion of what area actually constituted Mosquito, it seems that it was the name of the gulch, creek, road, peak, pass, and mining district.

That first year was a busy one for the Mosquito District. The Newland Lode was the first discovery, followed by the Sterling Lode a few months later, then the Lulu and the Orphan Boy. Soon, miners worked about 50 claims in the area, and there was much hope for Mosquito. By September, the town of Sterling was laid out in the Mosquito District near the Orphan Boy Mine. In its time, Sterling was alternatively called Sterling City and Mosquito. In 1862, a post office was established to serve the 250 residents. In this law-abiding community (rare in Colorado at the time), there were no lynchings, no murders, and no gambling.

Mosquito Pass, constructed in the late 1870s, was one of the most important passes in the state and served as the main route to the Leadville boom area. It was nicknamed the Highway of Frozen Death because of the ill-prepared prospectors and travelers too cheap to pay stagecoach fares who met their deaths trekking in subzero temperature and blizzards along the precarious route. A halfway house was built in 1879 as a stage stop and a saloon, where the "ladies" would often await male travelers.

It is not clear why Sterling met its demise. Some speculate that men began leaving for mines in other areas or heading east to fight in the Civil War. The population steadily declined, and by the mid-1870s, fewer than 30 residents remained. Stagecoach service across the pass was discontinued; the pass fell completely into disuse and was closed by 1910.

Mosquito Pass is now open to 4WD traffic, and there is very little evidence of the activity seen in days gone past. The forest has reclaimed much of the area.

GPS COORDINATES: 39°17.95'N 106°09.25'W

TRAIL REFERENCE: Central #21: Mosquito Pass Trail

Nathrop

Originally called Chalk Creek, Nathrop came into existence in 1880 as a stage stop and supply center for the area mines. Not a mining community itself, Nathrop developed as a farming town, where the first grist mill (for processing grain) in the Arkansas Valley was constructed.

The Denver & Rio Grande Railroad junction with the Denver, South Park & Pacific was established nearby in 1880. To be closer to the station, the whole town moved 1.5 miles.

The town is named for entrepreneur Charles Nachtrieb, part owner in the town site, who also built the town's Gothic Hotel. Nachtrieb met his death in 1881 at the age of 48, when a cowboy gunned him down over a wage dispute.

GPS COORDINATES: 38°44.72'N 106°04.61'W

TRAIL REFERENCE: Central #38: Mount Antero Trail, Central #39: Browns Lake Trail, Central #40: Baldwin Lakes Trail

Nederland

A town with many names, Nederland was first known as Dayton, then Brownsville, then, with the establishment of the post office in 1871, Middle Boulder. That same year Abel Breed bought the silver-rich Caribou Mine and decided to locate the mill in Middle Boulder. Dutch investors bought the mine two years later and renamed it Nederland, meaning "lowlands." The town elected to change its name to Nederland after the name of the mine.

Not long after the Dutch company purchased the mine, output began to decline and the company pulled out. By 1890 only a few families lived in Nederland year-round. The town experienced a revival just after the turn of the twentieth century, as Sam Conger, who had discovered the Caribou Mine, also found deposits of tungsten to the north and east of Nederland. The old silver mill was converted to processing tungsten, a valuable part of the steelmaking process. By 1916, Nederland had roughly 3,000 residents, about double the present-day population. A small town named Tungsten even sprang up near the deposits. Today you can look down from Boulder Canyon and see the remains of the once bustling town.

Although the demand for tungsten during both world wars briefly reanimated Nederland's mining industry, the town became known more as a gateway to outdoor recreation because of its proximity to the Indian Peaks and the James Peak Wilderness Areas. It also serves as a quiet retreat from nearby Boulder.

Nederland made international news in 1994 after a Norwegian, Trygve Bauge, moved the corpse of his grandfather, Bredo Morstol, to Nederland in 1993 and had him cryogenically frozen in a shed in his mother's backyard. When town officials learned of the situation, they passed an ordinance making it illegal to keep human body parts on one's property. However, because laws can't be passed after the fact, an exception was made for Bauge. Today the town holds an annual Frozen Dead Guy Days celebration each winter.

GPS COORDINATES: 39° 57.69'N 105°30.62'W

TRAIL REFERENCE: Front Range #29: Rollins Pass Trail, Front Range #33: Central City to Rollinsville Trail

North Star

Originally called Lake's Camp, the site was founded in 1878 as a camp for the miners at the North Star Mine. Owned by the May-Mazeppa Company, it was considered a "suburb" of Whitepine. The camp, renamed North Star, became its own town and prospered from the mining of galena ore.

After the silver crash in 1893, before the town was properly developed, miners abandoned North Star for areas with the promise of gold. However, the North Star Mine reopened a few years later and experienced a new boom. During 1901, men worked the mines day and night. Buildings continued to be erected, including the Leadville House and a post office. Mining declined again, although there has been some resurgence in the twenty-first century.

Several buildings are still standing today. The mine is situated on the May-Mazeppa Company's property and may be visited only by special permission.

GPS COORDINATES: 38°32.47'N 106°23.06'W

TRAIL REFERENCE: Central #34: Tomichi Pass Trail

Ohio City

In 1880, the town was officially founded as Eagle City at the junction of Gold and Quartz Creeks. It was a silver camp with about 50 tents and log cabins. Later that year, the name was changed to Ohio City, and the population expanded to over 250.

Ohio City's first murder occurred in 1880, when two men had a shoot-out. It seems they had previously engaged in a bitter dispute in Leadville and some months later eyed each other on the street in Ohio City. The two drew their guns, firing off many shots as they approached each other. Both men's aim was so hopeless that bullets sprayed everywhere. All at once, they fired shots that struck each other in the heart. Witnesses reported that the two men were so close when they finally fell, they almost hit each other on the way down!

A stage line connected Ohio City with Pitkin. The Denver, South Park & Pacific Railroad arrived in Ohio City in 1882. It later continued on to Parlin and Gunnison. While the community benefited from the railroad's arrival, Ohio City's economy was already in trouble because ore was beginning to dwindle.

The silver crash of 1893 was a severe blow to the community, and miners left town. However, Ohio City was able to survive by switching to gold production in 1896, which continued until 1943.

Today Ohio City has several full-time residents, a post office, a general store, a restaurant, and a hunting lodge. Excellent hunting and fishing in the area have helped the town's survival.

GPS COORDINATES: 38°34.10'N 106°36.61'W

TRAIL REFERENCE: Central #35: Cumberland Pass Trail

Ophir and Ophir Loop

Throughout the mining period, the name Ophir referred to two areas near each other. Early settlers named the town after an Old Testament reference to a region rich in gold, in hopes that the nearby mines would bring similar fortunes.

Located at the foot of Ophir Pass, Old Ophir, or just Ophir, was established shortly before Ophir Loop, in 1870. The first claims were staked in 1875, after which time prospectors worked the area sporadically.

By 1885, the population of Ophir grew to 200. In three years, it blossomed to 500. Ophir had five saloons, several churches, a school, and its own electricity and waterworks.

The town was often snowbound because of avalanches. In December 1883, a mail carrier named Swen Nilson left Silverton to deliver 60 pounds of Christmas packages and letters to Ophir and was never seen or heard from again. While some people believed he had stolen the mail and fled the county, Swen's brother set out searching. He searched for two years, fi-

Ophir Loop, circa 1890

Ophir Loop, circa 1940

nally discovering Swen's skeleton with his mail sack still around his neck.

New Ophir, or Ophir Loop, was 2 miles away from Ophir and founded in the mid-1870s. Although having a railway in this area seemed inconceivable, Otto Mears did not know the word impossible. Getting trains started up the steep grade to Lizard Head Pass was a true feat of railroad engineering. Mears oversaw the construction of three tiers of tracks with loops crossing above and below each other and trestles as much as 100 feet high. This difficult project enabled the railroad to run from Telluride to Durango. Two cars of ore were shipped from Ophir Loop each day, and the town accumulated a small population as a few of Ophir's residents moved to be closer to the railroad.

The population of Ophir dwindled after the turn of the century, and the area was close to being a ghost town by 1929. In 1960, it was listed as one of four incorporated towns in the United States with no residents. However, today the town is home again to a number of summer residents.

GPS COORDINATES: Ophir Loop–37°51.56'N 107°51.96'W;
Ophir–37°51.38'N 107°49.89'W

TRAIL REFERENCE: Southwest #19: Ophir Pass Trail

Ouray

Ouray is located in a beautiful box canyon at the base of steep and colorful mountains. When miners first came to the area in the early 1870s, the land belonged to the Ute Indians. The first mining camp was called Uncompahgre City.

Ute leader Chief Ouray functioned as a peace ambassador between the Indians and the white prospectors. Realizing that the influx of white men was inevitable, Ouray continued his peaceful arbitration between the whites and Utes, saving countless lives. Chief Ouray signed the Brunot Treaty of 1873, giving the San Juan Mountains to the United States. The town's name was changed to honor Chief Ouray in 1876.

In its early days, the town was quite isolated. Roads were so poor that there was little transportation into or out of Ouray. Food was scarce, particularly in winter months. Supplies were hard to get and expensive. The postal service had such difficulties negotiating the roads that mail carriers often arrived behind a team of sled dogs. Since local mines

Main Street, Ouray, circa 1889

could not afford to ship out all of their ore, they transported only their high-grade ore and had to scrap the lower-grade commodity. Mining implements freighted in were outrageously priced.

By 1877, the town reached a population of 800. Two newspapers were published in Ouray. The printing presses had to be carried over the mountains by wagon train. The people of Ouray used their saloons in more ways than one. Early in the town's history, residents held church services in saloons and used kegs of beer for seating. When Ouray became the county seat a few years later, the Star Saloon was renovated as the first courthouse. The bar was removed, the first floor functioned as city hall, and the second-floor rooms were changed into county offices.

Otto Mears earned his nickname, "Pathfinder of the San Juans," by constructing a toll road in 1881. His ambitious 12-mile road from Ouray to Red Mountain cost $10,000 per mile to construct. Some sections cost $1,000 per foot! However, improved accessibility boosted Ouray and its economy. The toll road enabled the mining companies to ship their lower-grade ore at reasonable expense instead of

A stagecoach in front of the famous Beaumont Hotel in Ouray, circa 1888

throwing it away. This road was the beginning of Mears's Million Dollar Highway from Silverton to Ouray. He later followed the route with his railroad but could go only as far north as Ironton. Supplies from Ouray reached the northern end of the railroad by wagon. Because Mears still wanted to reach Ouray by train, he began building the Rio Grande Southern from Durango, through Ophir and Ridgway, and into Ouray. This line was completed in 1887.

By the 1890s, much of Ouray's downtown area had been replaced with brick and stone buildings. Ouray became one of the most elegant mining towns in the San Juans. The remarkable Beaumont Hotel at Main and 5th Streets, with its three-story rotunda and divided stairway, displayed French architectural influences. The furnishings came from Marshall Fields in Chicago, and the dining room staff was trained at the Brown Palace Hotel in Denver. Its interior was lush and luxurious. Many prominent people stayed there, including Herbert Hoover. The Beaumont closed in 1965, but went up for auction in 1998. After undergoing five years of extensive restoration to restore the Beaumont to its original grandure, the hotel reopened and remains open today.

Thomas Walsh, owner of the Camp Bird Mine, was a miner who struck it rich and became famous. Walsh gave Ouray a 7,500-volume library, although it has been said he was illiterate. The Walsh family became so rich from the Camp Bird Mine that Walsh's daughter, Evalyn, purchased the Hope Diamond. Later, Harry Winston bought the diamond from her and donated it to the Smithsonian Institution.

Today, Ouray is an attractive Victorian town prospering by tourism, particularly during summer months. Its population peaked at around 6,500 in 1890; for the past 50 years it has stabilized at around 2,500. As virtually all of Ouray's major public buildings and commercial structures were constructed over 100 years ago, the town's appearance is largely unchanged. Some popular vacation activities in the area include hiking, bathing in the Ouray Hot Springs Pool, and exploring countless 4WD routes.

GPS COORDINATES: 38°01.30'N 107°40.29'W

TRAIL REFERENCE: Southwest #1: Engineer Pass Trail,
Southwest #17: Yankee Boy Basin Trail

Parkville

Parkville, on the South Fork of the Swan River, was established after placer gold was found in Georgia Gulch in 1859. It quickly evolved as a mining center, supply town, and hub for social activities. It became *the* mining camp of Summit County.

It is estimated that in the early 1860s as many as 100,000 people lived in Parkville. The post office opened in 1861. There was also a county courthouse, hotels, restaurants, saloons, various stores, a newspaper, and a popular playhouse. The town had a mint that produced gold pieces in denominations of $2.50, $5.00, and $10.00.

Parkville was the county seat of Summit County from 1860 until 1862, when Breckenridge townsfolk decided they wanted to make Breckenridge the county seat. One night a secret raid took place on the Parkville courthouse during which all the county records disappeared. After a number of weeks, the records mysteriously surfaced in the newly constructed county courthouse in Breckenridge. From then on, Breckenridge was the county seat. Because Parkville had already begun to experience its decline, no legal action was taken to have the records or county seat returned.

The post office closed its doors in 1866, after the placer gold played out. Subsequent dredge mining in the area during the 1880s produced massive amounts of tailings, which buried the remains of Parkville in rubble.

GPS COORDINATES: 39°29.86'N 105°57.01'W
TRAIL REFERENCE: Central #14: Georgia Pass Trail

Pearl

The brothers Luke, Bill, and Bob Wheeler settled this area in 1884 and founded the Phantom Valley Ranch. A post office was established in 1889. Located in Jackson County, Pearl is a very small town located in a rather desolate, treeless meadow near the Wyoming border. It is unclear whether the town was named for its first postmistress, Pearl Ann Wheeler, or for a daughter of Benjamin Franklin Burnett, a developer.

Copper was discovered nearby in 1894. In the early 1900s, Charles Knapp founded the Pearl Mining and Smelting Company. He bought Pearl, Elms Ranch, and other valuable properties for $5 million; and Pearl became a company town. Among the businesses in town were two saloons, three hotels, a general store, a blacksmith shop, a printer, and a meat market. Further mining in the area produced silver and gold. The Big Horn Lode was a prominent producer, and the best-known mine was the Zirkel. After mining waned, Pearl developed its livestock and lumber industries, which it continues today.

GPS COORDINATES: 40°59.12'N 106°32.81'W
TRAIL REFERENCE: Northern #17: Ellis Jeep Trail

Pitkin

Before Pitkin became a town, early prospectors braved the Indian territory to search for silver and gold. Miner Karl Warenski found about $50,000 worth of gold in 1862. The Ute killed one of his miners and chased the terrified party out of the area. Warenski, who had buried his gold, returned 18 years later to retrieve it.

The first recorded inhabitants arrived in 1878 and set up a gold camp. Originally called Quartzville, the camp was renamed Pitkin in 1879 to honor Governor Frederick Pitkin. It claims to be the first incorporated town on the Western Slope of Colorado.

Pitkin experienced rapid growth; within two years of its founding, its population had ballooned to 1,500, making it the twelfth largest city in Colorado. There were nearly 200 houses, 4 hotels, 8 restaurants, a dozen saloons, and a bank in Pitkin, as well as a very busy jail. Two stagecoach lines served the town. Gold and silver generated early wealth for the town, with some ore assayed at as much as $20,000 per ton.

The Denver, South Park & Pacific Railroad came to town in 1882; but its arrival was anticlimactic, as it had lost its race to be the first to service the area, and most of the freight carriers and passengers were using the Denver & Rio Grande over Marshall Pass. The Denver, South Park & Pacific's late arrival was caused partly by complications in constructing the Alpine Tunnel.

That same year, Pitkin's mines were starting to face serious problems, too. Gold and silver were playing out and did not justify further development. Frustrated with the low-grade ore, many miners began to leave town for areas of more promise.

Pitkin enjoyed a short silver revival in 1891, but that ended after the crash in 1893. Gold production continued sporadically, but silver mining went into an eclipse.

Pitkin was hit by several disastrous fires, one of which occurred in 1898 and reduced the business section to ashes. The fire was fueled as it spread by illegally stored blasting powder in a general store. Five years later, another fire took out one square block when a drunkard accidentally set the fire with a candle.

By the 1920s, Pitkin was totally dependent on revenue from the timber industry. In 1927, over 150 men worked in the business, shipping over 800 railroad cars out via the Denver, South Park & Pacific Railroad. When the Great Depression hit in 1929, the timber business in Pitkin was seriously affected and ceased operation for several decades.

Today, fewer than 100 permanent residents live in Pitkin, although the summer population swells to around 400. Its principal industries are the state fish hatchery and tourism. Pitkin is a quiet town in a beautiful setting.

GPS COORDINATES: 38°36.53'N 106°31.07'W
TRAIL REFERENCE: Central #32: Waunita Pass Road, Central #35: Cumberland Pass Trail

Placerville

Prospectors panning in the San Miguel River in 1876 found placer deposits in the area, which resulted in the establishment of a tent colony originally called Dry Diggings. By 1877, prospectors had built several cabins, and the area was officially named Placerville.

Placerville's gold deposits were quickly exhausted, and the town went into decline until the Rio Grande Southern laid tracks for its route from Telluride to Ridgway. The depot was about a mile from the original town of Placerville. A general store and saloon sprung up near the depot, and eventually the population of Placerville actually moved the town nearer to the station.

Placerville never was a very successful mining town. Instead, the town became a ranching town with cattle first and then sheep. Western cattlemen hated sheepherders, so the area saw a violent range war; and several sheep ranchers were killed before the ranchers learned to coexist peacefully. Placerville became a major transportation center for livestock.

In 1919, a fire swept through the town, and many of the buildings were destroyed. The town was subsequently rebuilt with sturdier materials. These days, Placerville is a very small town with only a few residents.

GPS COORDINATES: 38°00.96'N 108°03.13'W
TRAIL REFERENCE: Southwest #18: Imogene Pass Trail, Southwest #21: Black Bear Pass Trail

Poncha Springs

American Indians discovered and used the numerous medicinal hot springs in the region now called Poncha Springs long

Jackson Hotel, Poncha Springs in 1878

before white men settled in the area.

Originally called South Arkansas, Poncha Springs was founded in 1879 and incorporated in 1880. The town's founder, James True, traveled to the area and set up shop when he saw the potential of the area. He laid out Poncha Springs and set up a bank.

Shortly after a dispute between True and his business partners, True's bank caught fire. When True found one of his partners at the scene fighting flames, he immediately presumed him to be an arsonist and shot the fellow on the spot. The town marshal later found an oil-soaked rag among the charred remains, so there was no doubt that the fire had been intentionally set; but the burning question was, Who set it? Some suspected True had set the fire himself to cover up bad management. Nevertheless, True was put on trial and was acquitted of murder.

The town saw the arrival of the Denver & Rio Grande Railroad in 1880. The railroad designated the town Poncha Junction. At that time, the population was around 5,000 people, but that figure included a large number of railroad construction workers who continued to labor on Marshall Pass.

Poncha Springs served as a supply center for camps in all directions during the mining boom. It was also an agricultural village. The town's economy was aided by businesses that capitalized on the local hot springs. Entrepreneurs built hotels to create a resort community, drawing in customers for the springs' medicinal and soothing effects.

Poncha Pass Road, which travels south of Poncha Springs, was the first toll road Otto Mears ever built. Although this first attempt was not a huge financial success, it launched Mears into his road-building career.

While Poncha Springs was in danger of being abandoned after 1900 and into the 1930s, residents acted to reverse the decline and today the town is a crossroads center. Poncha Springs is a small and pleasant town with a population of about 200.

GPS COORDINATES: 38°30.88'N 106°04.56'W

TRAIL REFERENCE: Central #43: Marshall Pass Poncha Creek
Trail, Central #44: Marshall Pass Railway
Grade Road

Poughkeepsie

Poughkeepsie was high in the Uncompahgre Mountains, about 7 miles south of Ouray. The town's remote location and the poor quality of the roads leading to it hindered development. The winters were so harsh that miners could work only two or three months of the year.

Despite the hardships Poughkeepsie residents had to endure, the town was surprisingly well planned. It had a post office established in 1880, a newspaper called the *Poughkeepsie Telegraph,* stores, restaurants, saloons, and other businesses.

Miners usually sent ore to Lake City or Silverton via rough roads by burro. Transporting the ore in this manner was so difficult and expensive that eventually mine owners decided it wasn't worth it and ceased operations.

GPS COORDINATES: 37°56.02'N 107°37.35'W

TRAIL REFERENCE: Southwest #1: Engineer Pass Trail,
Southwest #12: California Gulch Trail

Pueblo

Located on the Arkansas River along the Front Range of the Rockies, Pueblo was an important cultural crossroads of the Southwest. In 1806, Zebulon Pike traveled through Pueblo before setting out to explore Pikes Peak. Around 1842, Fort Pueblo, or El Pueblo, was established on the north side of the Arkansas River, along the old border between Mexico and the United States. Anglo, French, and African American trappers and traders, Mexican settlers, and Indians traded, farmed, and ranched here. The settlement existed peacefully until Christmas of 1854 when members of the Ute and Apache tribes attacked and killed the majority of the residents at Fort Pueblo.

Fort Pueblo remained largely deserted until 1858, when the discovery of gold and silver along the Arkansas River drew prospectors to the area. In 1870, Pueblo incorporated as a town. The current city of Pueblo represents the consolidation of four towns: Pueblo, South Pueblo, Central Pueblo, and Bessemer. The consolidation was complete by 1894, when Bessemer became the last to join with Pueblo.

The Denver & Rio Grande Railroad reached Pueblo in 1872. The town's central location between the gold and silver mines in the north and the coal mines in the south made Pueblo the ideal spot to construct a workshop for the mines.

The Federal Building (foreground) and the Grand Opera House, Main Street, Pueblo, circa 1900

The Colorado Coal & Iron Company, later named the Colorado Fuel & Iron Company (CF&I), became the primary employer in Pueblo. In 1908, John D. Rockefeller took over CF&I. Deteriorating working and living conditions led to the Colorado Coalfield War of 1913–1914, a bloody conflict between the coal miners and owners. CF&I continued to represent a large stake of Pueblo's economy until the steel market crash of 1982 led to the company's decline.

Pueblo had faced adversity before the declining fortunes of CF&I. On June 3, 1921, the Arkansas River flooded Pueblo, destroying 600 houses and an estimated $19 million worth of property, as well as taking a number of lives.

Since both the flood and, in particular, the decline of the steel industry, Pueblo has attempted to diversify its economy, and it is now home to a number of electronics and aviation companies. It has earned the nickname "Colorado's Second City," not because of its size but because it is considered by many to be the economic hub of southern Colorado and northern New Mexico. Pueblo is also known as the "Home of Heroes," as it is the hometown of four recipients of the Medal of Honor—the highest military award that can be bestowed on someone in the U.S. armed services.

GPS COORDINATES: 38°15.26'N 104°36.50'W

Quartz

Quartz was established in 1879 as Quartz Town Company with the discovery of carbonate in the area. Although nearby Pitkin was also originally named Quartz, they were always two separate towns.

In 1882, the Denver, South Park & Pacific Railroad arrived, and the town was given a post office. At the time, there were about 100 residents. Two boxcars served as a jail.

Quartz was about 2.5 miles above Pitkin at the Alpine Tunnel turnoff. The town site is now a grazing range, marked by a U.S. Forest Service sign.

GPS COORDINATES: 38°37.38'N 106°28.56'W
TRAIL REFERENCE: Central #35: Cumberland Pass Trail, Central #36: Alpine Tunnel Road

Redcliff

Redcliff was established during the Leadville boom, when prospectors sought to find ore in the surrounding areas. Miners discovered gold on Battle and Horn Mountains.

The Meeker Massacre in 1879 terrified new settlers across Colorado. Redcliff residents quickly built a blockhouse where women and children could seek refuge while the men guarded the camp. The Indians, however, never did come to Redcliff.

Redcliff's development was greatly enhanced by the arrival of the Denver & Rio Grande Railroad in the early 1880s. During the construction of the railroad, Redcliff evolved as a commercial center when during the surveying procedure, more local mines were discovered, thus generating new towns. The railroad not only made Redcliff an accessible destination but also provided a reasonable method for receiving supplies and shipping out ore.

The largest camp in the area, Redcliff assumed the role of county seat of Eagle County, which it held for nearly 40 years.

Redcliff had its own newspaper, an opera house, numerous businesses, saloons, and hotels.

Not long after the Redcliff cemetery was established, two men who killed each other in a gunfight were brought to town for burial. The locals refused to put murderers alongside the respectable townspeople, so the pair were buried along the roadside.

Mining activity continued until as recently as the late 1970s, when the last mine closed. Today, Redcliff is a modest residential community.

GPS COORDINATES: 39°30.78'N 106°22.03'W
TRAIL REFERENCE: Central #17: Shrine Pass Trail, Central #18: Ptarmigan Pass and McAllister Gulch Loop

Rico

Gold was discovered in Rico as early as 1866; but because the Ute Indians were not inclined to share their land, prospectors could not safely search for gold until a few years after the Brunot Treaty was signed in 1873. Rico's boom era officially began in 1878, when some very rich ores were found in the area and the riches warranted braving the miner's fear of the Ute.

Rico (the Spanish word for "rich") was appropriately named: The land provided millions of dollars' worth of minerals and metals over the years.

During 1879, miners poured into Rico, and in a single month more than 100 cabins and 30 commercial buildings—25 percent of them saloons—were constructed. The population was approximately 600.

Later that same year, rumor spread that the Ute were about to attack Rico. The men of the town gathered the women and children and sent them to hide in one of the buildings while the men went on sentry duty around the town. Some men took the task of "guarding" Lovejoy's Saloon and proceeded to barricade it with bales of hay and kegs of beer. Though the Ute never did attack, when a pack train arrived in town during the night, one inebriated guard from the saloon was so startled by the sound of hooves that he shot one of the burros. The only human injury suffered that night belonged to the guard, who was severely beaten by the packer.

Miners lived in continuous fear of the Indians. In 1881, the Ute burned a ranch outside of town, killing all the occupants. The following year, the government sent in troops to eradicate the Indians from the region.

In January 1880, Rico faced a famine because of heavy snow. The town was snowbound; and food, whiskey, tobacco, and other supplies became desperately scarce. When a pack train finally reached town four months later, the driver was able to sell his 100-pound sacks of flour for $35 to $50 dollars each. He disposed of every one of them as quickly as he could unload them.

Rico has remained somewhat isolated because of poor roads and lack of railroad transportation into the town. Shipping ore was so expensive that it consumed a huge percentage of mining profits. Whenever supplies arrived in town via wagon or pack trains, townspeople found reason to celebrate.

In 1891, Otto Mears brought his railroad to Rico, inciting a four-day celebration. Because the railway opened Rico up to the rest of the world, Rico truly began to flourish and has continued to thrive.

Locals tell an interesting story about one of the largest producing mines in Rico, the Enterprise. A man named Swickhimer, who was either a sheriff or handyman, owned the mine. He was convinced that there was ore to be found at the Enterprise, but he and his wife had spent all their savings to purchase the claim. They had no option but to put the mine up for sale. However, Mrs. Swickhimer bought a lottery ticket with the last of their coins, and her winning ticket paid out $5,000! The Swickhimers spent the money on further developing the mine until they struck silver, and their efforts paid off. They sold the Enterprise in 1891 for $1.25 million.

Rico is not a ghost town in modern times, although it has few residents and many businesses have been boarded up. It has survived because its residents have mined different minerals as the markets fluctuate. Many mines continue to operate in the area, and some optimists claim that Rico's best days are yet to come.

GPS COORDINATES: 37°41.68'N 108°01.85'W
TRAIL REFERENCE: Southwest #19: Ophir Pass Trail

Ridgway

Ridgway was founded in 1890 as a transportation center, named for R. M. Ridgway, a railroad official.

The Denver & Rio Grande's railway line ran between Ouray and Montrose, with Ridgway located between them. The Rio Grande Southern's Telluride route also passed by Ridgway.

The town attracted swarms of gamblers and con men. Swindlers encouraged bets on fixed horse races and lion hunts. Reportedly, an unfortunate mountain lion was kept tied behind one of Ridgway's saloons. Once a week the lion was released as the subject of a hunt, in which he would be captured and promptly hauled back to the saloon—only to be tethered and forced to await the next week's hunt.

Ridgway became a prosperous town; attractive stone and brick buildings, Victorian-style houses, stores, saloons, and pool halls adorned its streets. Its post office was established in the year the town was founded and still exists.

Bank president C. M. Stanwood pulled off a noteworthy fraud in Ridgway in 1931. He "borrowed" the deposits and

View of Romley, circa 1915

contents of customers' security boxes and invested them in the stock market; but the market dropped and most everything was lost. The bank's patrons were wiped out. Some depositors were able to recoup some of their money, but those who lost their securities were unable to retrieve them.

When mining tapered off, the railroad began to suffer economic problems, although it continued to operate. In an effort to cut costs, the railroad introduced the Galloping Goose, a relatively inexpensive construction—part car, part train, with a cowcatcher on the front. The Galloping Goose operated until the early 1950s, and then the train and tracks were disposed of for scrap.

Much of the John Wayne movie *True Grit* was filmed in locations around Ridgway.

Ridgway is alive and well today. The town now consists of a number of homes, modern stores, and other businesses.
GPS COORDINATES: 38°09.09'N 107°45.57'W
TRAIL REFERENCE: Southwest #35: Owl Creek and Chimney Rock Trail

Romley

The Mary Murphy and Pat Murphy Mines led to the founding of the town of Romley in the late 1870s. Originally called Morley and also Murphy's Switch, the town changed its name

The Galloping Goose, Ridgway

Romley town site today

to Romley in 1897. One book theorizes that the name Romley may have originated as a typographical error—an inversion of the first three letters of the name Morley. Colonel B. F. Morley had operated the Murphy mines through the 1890s with great success.

The Mary Murphy Mine was by far the biggest mine in the Alpine District. It was named after a kind nurse in Denver who once cared for the prospector who discovered the mine. The Mary Murphy grew so large that it supported Romley, St. Elmo, and Hancock, making the region quite prosperous.

The Denver, South Park & Pacific Railroad came through town in 1881. A 5,000-foot tramway was built to transfer ore to the railroad cars.

In 1908, tragedy struck when sparks from a train engine kindled a fire that reduced most of Romley to ashes. When the town was rebuilt, the buildings were painted bright red with white trim, although nobody knows why!

In 1912, five men from the Mary Murphy boardinghouse died of food poisoning. Canned spinach was thought to be the culprit, because after the leavings were thrown out into the garbage heap, five burros died.

The Murphy mines continued to produce until 1926, when the ore ran out. Hundreds of workers had been employed in the mines during Romley's boom time, and the town had a population of nearly 1,000.

The buildings of Romley stood until 1990, when bulldozers leveled the dilapidated remains.

GPS COORDINATES: 38°40.72'N 106°22.00'W
TRAIL REFERENCE: Central #33: Hancock Pass Trail

Rose's Cabin

Rose's Cabin was once a lively inn offering food, lodging, and entertainment to miners and travelers.

Corydon Rose was one of the first pioneers to explore the San Juans after a treaty was signed with the Utes in 1873. Rose decided to build an inn to serve the area, locating it about halfway between Ouray and Lake City to provide a convenient stopover for travelers along the route.

In 1877, Otto Mears constructed a toll road between Ouray, Animas Forks, and Lake City, which passed right in front of Rose's Cabin. This increased the inn's business substantially, particularly when the road became the main stage route.

Inside the cabin were 22 partitioned bedrooms. Road-weary travelers, exhausted from the rough coach trip, would scurry inside to secure their lodgings. Rose often greeted them heartily at the door in his high hat and long coat. Rose's guests could dine, socialize, quench their thirst at the bar, or perhaps take in a game of poker before retiring for the evening.

The area around the cabin began to grow in population as miners settled there. They built cabins nearby and worked mines in the surrounding hills. It is estimated that about 50 people settled in the vicinity. Rose's Cabin served the community as its local bar, restaurant, hotel, general store, and post office. Rose even kept 60 burros in a stable to ship supplies to the miners and carry their ore down to his cabin. The cabin was the hive of activity in the region.

With the silver crash of 1893, activity at Rose's Cabin gradually trickled off. By about the turn of the century, need for the lively inn ceased entirely. Only a few traces of the cabin remain. The structure still standing is the old stable; the cabin was situated to the left.

GPS COORDINATES: 37°58.58'N 107°32.20'W
TRAIL REFERENCE: Southwest #1: Engineer Pass Trail

Saints John

Saints John was originally named Coleyville, after John Coley, who located the first ore in 1863. A slightly more colorful story tells of hunters in the area before Coley who ran out of bullets and resorted to using pieces of rock in their guns instead. Several years later the hunters were in Nevada and noticed a great similarity between the rich ore they saw there and the rocks that they had used as ammunition. They contacted Coley, who set up camp in the area and subsequently located silver ore.

The town was renamed Saints John by Freemasons who gave it the biblical name after John the Baptist and John the Evangelist.

A prospector named Bob Epsey once made an unusual strike. Suffering from a hangover one day, Epsey laid down to sleep it off under a shady tree. When he awoke, he steadied himself by grasping a rock as he stood. When the rock broke off in Epsey's hand, he discovered in it a big chunk of solid ore.

Saints John became a company town when it was taken over by the Boston Silver Mining Association, an East Coast company, in 1872. At great expense, the company erected a sophisticated milling and smelter work, complete with bricks imported from Europe. A few years later it was taken over by the Boston Mining Company. For such a remote mining town, Saints John was exceptionally well endowed, with a 350-volume library (complete with regularly stocked newspapers from Boston and Europe), a boardinghouse, a dining hall, a company store, an assay office, various cabins, and a beautiful superintendent's house with elegant furnishings from Europe and the eastern United States. However, Saints John had no saloon, so the miners regularly traveled down the mountain to Montezuma, where they indulged to their hearts' content in brothels, saloons, and poker dens.

Poor access, harsh winters, and waning silver finds caused the decline of Saints John. The Argentine and Webster Passes were impassable due to snow in the winter and at other times suffered from rock slides. The post office was closed by 1881.

GPS COORDINATES: 39°34.26'N 105°52.86'W
TRAIL REFERENCE: Central #11: Saints John and Glacier Ridge Trail

Salida

When the Denver & Rio Grande Railroad decided to construct a main junction 2 miles away from the small town of Cleora, residents were devastated because the train would not travel through their town; they unsuccessfully protested the action. A new town, developed at the site of the junction, was to be named South Arkansas. But the postal department rejected that name because it had been given three years earlier to the post office at nearby Poncha Springs. According to town lore, it took two elections and a bribe from the railroad to provide trees for the city streets before residents agreed to incorporate as Salida.

Salida, circa 1895

Salida grew quickly, and the residents wanted it to become Colorado's state capital. However, when nearby Buena Vista was named county seat, Salida soon abandoned its capital ambitions.

Colonel Thomas Fauntleroy led U.S. troops in a famous battle against the Ute Indians near Salida in 1885. The troops killed 40 Indians and captured many others, thus helping open the territory for white settlement.

Salida's downtown historic district lies off the main highway. The interstate was designed to bypass the downtown area. For a pleasant diversion, drive through town to see some of Salida's turn-of-the-century architecture.

Ranching and farming have always been important to Salida's economy. The town also relies on the trade of passing motorists and travelers, who find it a convenient place to stop and eat or stay overnight. Year-round tourist trade includes sightseeing, river rafting, hunting, and skiing.

GPS COORDINATES: 38°32.18'N 105°59.48'W
TRAIL REFERENCE: Central #30: Old Monarch Pass Road, Central #43: Marshall Pass Poncha Creek Trail, Central #44: Marshall Pass Railway Grade Road

Schofield

Prospectors discovered silver in the area as early as 1872, but their fear of Indians deferred permanent settlement for several years. Located 8 miles northwest of Gothic, Schofield was platted in August 1879 by B. F. Schofield and his party.

A smelter was built in 1880, and a mill in 1881. By 1882, the town had a population of about 400 and the usual amenities of a hotel, a restaurant (whose staff had trouble cooking because of the altitude), a general store, a blacksmith shop, and a barbershop.

Schofield, located at the base of Schofield Pass, served as a stagecoach station for people traveling over the pass. Because the pass was so rough and dangerous, few people made the journey unless it was absolutely necessary.

In 1880, former President Ulysses S. Grant and ex–Governor Routt visited Schofield. Grant reportedly rode into town atop a white mule. The residents of Schofield thought that if they could sell shares in one of the local mines to Grant, they could boast that the president owned a mine in Schofield. When that failed, they tried to unsuccessfully "lose" shares to Grant in a poker game—to no avail. Finally, they brought out a big barrel of whiskey, hoping to get Grant drunk and just give him the mining shares! Needless to say, Grant was impressed with Schofield's hospitality, but it is unclear whether he ended up with any claim.

Old Lady Jack was a character who wore a gunnysack as a shawl and claimed to be the niece of Indian scout Jim Bridger. No one could fault Old Lady Jack for uncleanliness: She washed everything—including her firewood and even her multitude of cats, hanging them out to dry by the napes of their necks.

Unfortunately, the ore found around Schofield was poor in quality. Although miners did find some good galena, the inaccessible location and high transportation costs drained off their profits. These factors, coupled with the immense problems of eight-month winters dumping as much as 40 feet of snow, led to the demise of Schofield. The post office closed in 1885. Some residents moved down the valley to Crystal, while others left to seek fortunes elsewhere in the state.

The town is now gone, and the lovely area is visited primarily by summer tourists.

GPS COORDINATES: 39°02.49'N 107°03.87'W
TRAIL REFERENCE: Central #28: Schofield Pass and Devils Punchbowl Trail

Sherman

Sherman was founded in 1877 and named for an early pioneer. The town grew slowly at first, then expanded quickly in the 1880s. Although several mines in the area yielded large amounts of gold, silver, copper, and lead, the principal mine was the Black Wonder. Located on the north side of town, the Black Wonder produced primarily silver. Sherman's population and prosperity fluctuated with the fortunes of the Black Wonder Mine, which continued to produce into the turn of the century. Most of the mine's ore was transported to smelters in Lake City.

Otto Mears's toll road passed by Sherman. To travel between Sherman and Lake City cost $2.50 and between Sherman and Animas Forks cost $2.00 in either direction. The town was a convenient stagecoach stop since it was located halfway between Animas Forks and Lake City.

Sherman peaked in the mid-1880s, when the summer population reached about 300. Because winters were harsh, few stayed in town during those months. After the snow melted in the spring, miners would return to Sherman, repair any damages from the winter snowstorms, and resume their work.

The town had frequent problems with flooding, especially during the spring runoff. Sherman's location—in a valley at the intersection of Cottonwood Creek and the Lake Fork of the Gunnison River—made it particularly susceptible to floods. Around 1900, an ambitious 150-foot dam was constructed upstream to hold back the waters. However, only a few days after the dam's completion, runoff from torrential rains flooded the mountainside, ripped the dam to pieces, and swept away much of the town of Sherman.

Like many Colorado mining towns, Sherman was devastated by the silver crash of 1893. The silver devaluation, combined with the wreckage from the big flood, led to Sherman's demise.

By 1925, Sherman was deserted. Travelers to the area can still see some ruins of scattered cabins throughout the lush wooded valley. Because these are on private property, it is necessary to view them from the road only.

GPS COORDINATES: 37°54.17'N 107°25.38'W

TRAIL REFERENCE: Southwest #3: Cinnamon Pass Trail

Sherrod

Also called Camp Sherrod and Sherrod Switch, Sherrod was a mining camp named for W. H. Sherrod, a gold and silver miner who found some rich gold and silver ore in the late summer of 1903. Almost immediately after this discovery, the rush to Sherrod was on.

By 1904, Sherrod had two hotels, two stores, a loading station, several log cabins, numerous tents, a depot, and even the *Sherrod News*. The town was a stop on the Denver, South Park & Pacific Railroad and a terminus for the Whitepine stagecoach route over Tomichi Pass.

The tough winters in Sherrod contributed to the demise of the camp. At 12,000 feet, miners were in perpetual danger of snow slides, and the heavy snows prohibited work for long periods of time.

The area's ores soon played out, and Sherrod was a ghost town by 1906. The depot was subsequently moved to Ohio City.

GPS COORDINATES: 38°36.82'N 106°23.40'W

TRAIL REFERENCE: Central #33: Hancock Pass Trail, Central #36: Alpine Tunnel Road

Shirley

Shirley was originally a tollgate station on Mears's toll road. It later functioned as a railroad station on the Marshall Pass route. There was some mining in the area, and a 7.5-mile aerial tram carried the ore to Bonanza for treatment.

GPS COORDINATES: 38°25.35'N 106°7.67'W

TRAIL REFERENCE: Central #43: Marshall Pass Poncha Creek Trail, Central #44: Marshall Pass Railway Grade Road

Silverton

In July 1860, before the Brunot Treaty, Charles Baker (a native Virginian) and a party of six men explored Ute Indian territory in search of gold. They crossed the peaks of the San Juan Mountain ranges and set up camp in an area they called Baker City or Baker's Park. The miners lived in almost constant dread of the Ute, who were fierce fighters and the original occupants of the land.

When the Brunot Treaty was signed in 1873, the land was opened for settlement to white men. At this time, 12 houses were recorded in Baker City, and the settlement's name was changed to Silverton. It is rumored that the town earned its name when a prospector exclaimed there was not much gold in the area, but there was "silver by the ton."

Prospectors discovered an enormous number of rich silver properties in the surrounding area, and miners began flooding in from all over.

Greene Street, Silverton with the Grand Hotel in the foreground, circa 1892

La Plata Miner, Silverton's first newspaper, was published in 1875. Some of the other early businesses established at the same time were the Greene & Company general store, a general merchandise store, a meat market, a drugstore, an attorney's office, an assay office, a doctor's office, and a post office. There was no jail at this time, and it has been reported that the first lawbreaker was actually chained to the floor of a cabin.

While Greene Street was considered the main commercial district, Blair Street was alive with numerous saloons and the red lights of prostitutes' bordellos. Blair Street became one of the West's most notorious hell-raising areas, 24 hours a day, seven days a week. Silverton's 37 saloons and numerous whorehouses lined the several block stretch. It is also reported that the underworld settled in on Blair Street and began to control Silverton. Wyatt Earp ran the gambling rooms for a while at the Arlington, a fancy saloon and gaming hall. Crime was so rampant that local vigilantes could not settle the town, so they hired Bat Masterson from Dodge City to take charge of the Silverton Police Department. He was able to calm things down a bit but did not close down Blair Street completely because he enjoyed what it had to offer a bit too much.

Up until 1880, Silverton's buildings consisted mainly of all-wood frames. From that time onward, brick and stone con-

Burros in Silverton loaded with iron track for the local mines in 1887

struction became commonplace, and many of the buildings from that era remain. One of Silverton's most elegant establishments, the Grand Hotel at the corner of 12th and Green Streets, opened in 1882. The name of the hotel later changed to the Grand Imperial Hotel. It was a lavish, grandly decorated, three-story showplace.

Because Silverton was situated in a mountain valley, like Ouray it had a problem with transportation over the San Juan ranges. Only the richest gold and silver ores were worth shipping out by pack trains of burros, which brought supplies on the return trip. Because the mountain passes were navigable only in summer, residents had to haul in enough supplies to last the snowy winter months.

Mid-1882 saw the arrival of the Denver & Rio Grande Railroad from Durango. Otto Mears established three other narrow gauge lines from Silverton, making a total of four railway lines serving Silverton. This solved Silverton's transportation problems and opened it up economically and geographically to the rest of the world. To this day, the Denver & Rio Grande narrow gauge railway still makes trips between Durango and Silverton during warm months.

The railroad did not guarantee comfortable living in the San Juan Mountains. During the winter of 1884, avalanches blocked the railroad for 73 continuous days, leaving Silverton desperate for supplies. Crews of men eventually dug from both directions to clear an 84-foot snow slide. When the train finally reached Silverton, it was met by a cheering crowd of townspeople, many of whom were down to their last morsels of food.

Several wealthy characters lived in Silverton. Thomas Walsh of the Camp Bird Mine had interests there. The Guggenheims accumulated a sizable portion of their fortune from the Silverton area. Lena Stoiber, married to the owner of the Silver Lake Mine, was a rich woman who shared her wealth by piling gifts into her sleigh at Christmastime and delivering toys to the town's children.

Silverton never did become a ghost town. It survived the silver crash of 1893, primarily because gold was discovered in the region. Also, copper and lead were mined locally. The Du-

rango-Silverton narrow gauge railway attracts tourists to the area and accounts for a major part of Silverton's economy today. Hollywood also discovered Silverton—with its authentic Victorian storefronts still intact and its nineteenth-century train—an ideal site for filming. Such films as *Ticket to Tomahawk, Around the World in Eighty Days,* and *The Naked Spur* were filmed in Silverton.

GPS COORDINATES: 37°48.70'N 107°39.83'W

TRAIL REFERENCE: Southwest #6: Silverton to Animas Forks Ghost Town

Sneffels

During the winter of 1874, several prospectors built a cabin in the region of Sneffels and endured the harsh, snowy winter. As the snow thawed, it was clear they had chosen a very successful locale for mining; so they founded the camp in 1875 and called it Porters. This was before Ouray was founded and several years prior to the first strikes at Camp Bird.

During its peak, as many as 3,000 men worked the area's silver and gold mines. Sneffels served as the headquarters for local mines, although some smaller camps were situated around the more distant mines. Some of the profitable mines included the Yankee Boy, the Ruby Trust, the Wheel of Fortune, and the best producer of all, the Virginius Mine.

A shelf road was cut down the mountain to Ouray, passing by the future site of Camp Bird. The narrow ledges and steep grades were dangerous; rock and snow slides were frequent.

In 1884, the Revenue Tunnel was bored 3 miles into the side of Mount Sneffels, nearly 3,000 feet below the original shaft of the Virginius Mine. This venture further enhanced new mining prospects and developed into one of the best mines in the state, known as the Revenue-Virginius. The Revenue Mill was powered by electricity furnished by the stream. When the stream froze in the wintertime, a boiler engine powered the mill.

While the silver crash of 1893 saw the end of some local mines, rich ore and good management kept the Virginius open. Prospectors discovered additional gold veins. Operations were suspended in 1905 for some improvements to the mining works; but in 1906, a fire badly damaged the mine.

View of Silverton in 1909 looking down 12th Street

Sneffels, circa 1900

In 1909, operations resumed as normal; but the activity was short-lived. When miners began sending their ores to the more economical Tomboy Mill on Imogene Pass, the Revenue Mill ceased operations. Ten years later, the mill was destroyed by fire.

The Sneffels Post Office closed down in 1930. The town experienced a brief revival during the late 1940s when some enterprising folks rehabilitated several of the town's buildings and attempted to get the Revenue Tunnel operating again, but the town was never the same. The Revenue-Virginius properties later became property of Camp Bird.

GPS COORDINATES: 37°58.53'N 107°44.97'W

TRAIL REFERENCE: Southwest #17: Yankee Boy Basin Trail

St. Elmo

The town site was established in 1880 and incorporated under the name of Forest City. The post office soon insisted that the name be changed to St. Elmo, because other towns had been named Forest City.

St. Elmo grew with the success of the Mary Murphy Mine and several other mines in the vicinity. It became a major supply center within the district and served as a convenient stopover for travelers to Tincup, Alpine, and various other mountain passes nearby. Before the railroad's arrival, St. Elmo was a stage stop. With the opening of the Alpine Tunnel by the Denver, South Park & Pacific Railroad in 1882, St. Elmo became a main station on the line.

In its heyday, St. Elmo was a thriving town with a population of about 1,500. It had five hotels, a newspaper, and many other businesses. Although nearby towns had saloons, St. Elmo was considered the best place to spend a Saturday night. The construction workers on the Alpine Tunnel came to St. Elmo for their weekend sprees.

Fire swept through the town in 1890, causing much damage. Two blocks in the business district burned and were never rebuilt.

By 1910, a cave-in and lack of freight caused the closure of the Alpine Tunnel. By 1926, it was no longer profitable to continue rail service to St. Elmo. A few residents continued to live in the area, hoping that mining would revive.

By the mid-1950s only two residents remained in the town: Tony and Annabelle Stark, who grew up in St. Elmo and op-

St. Elmo today

St. Elmo's main street around 1880

erated a general store (which still stands) from the boom years. They stayed on long after the town faded, living in isolation during the long winters and opening their store to tourists in the summer. After the Starks passed away, St. Elmo assumed the role of a true ghost town.

St. Elmo is one of the best-preserved mining towns in Colorado, with most of the buildings along its main street looking much the same as they did a hundred years ago. It is listed on the National Register of Historic Places and has been the subject of a Historic American Building survey. St. Elmo is a must-see for visitors who want to step back into a Wild West mining town of the 1800s.

GPS COORDINATES: 38°42.23'N 106°20.65'W

TRAIL REFERENCE: Central #33: Hancock Pass Trail, Central #37: Tincup Pass Trail

Steamboat Springs

Named for a nearby spring that once made puffing noises that sounded much like the hoots of a steam train, Steamboat Springs was established in 1875 and incorporated in 1907. The spring was destroyed during the building of the Moffat Railroad in 1908.

Steamboat Springs is very much alive today and is the county seat of Routt County. The biggest industry in Steamboat Springs is the ski resort, which attracts large numbers of tourists to the area each winter.

GPS COORDINATES: 40°29.17'N 106°50.04'W

TRAIL REFERENCE: Northern #16: Buffalo Pass Trail

Stunner

Although little is known about Stunner, it is suspected that the first construction occurred in 1882. Both gold and silver were mined in the vicinity, but the remoteness of the camp prevented proper development. No railroad came through Stunner, but the LeDuc and Sanchez Toll Road Company built a road to the area.

Between 100 and 150 people lived in Stunner in its best days. A post office was established in 1890, but the town lasted only a few more years. Stunner's decline began with the high costs of transporting ore from the area's mines and was speeded by the lack of good ores to justify these costs. Because nearby Summitville (on the other side of the range) offered better ore and lower transportation costs, Stunner's population began to dwindle.

There is now nothing left of Stunner. A U.S. Forest Service ranger station and the Stunner Campground are on the site of the old town.

GPS COORDINATES: 37°22.66'N 106°34.44'W

TRAIL REFERENCE: Southwest #34: Summitville Ghost Town Trail

Summitville

Summitville, on South Mountain, was once the highest of Colorado's major gold camps.

In 1870, miner John Esmund discovered rich ore in abundance near the area that years later would become the Summitville mining camp. After Esmund's initial discovery, he returned to his location several times to extract ore, during which time he failed to file proper paperwork to make the claim legally his. When he showed up at the site in 1873, he found that someone else had established a mine on his spot. The mine, the Little Annie, became the best gold-producing mine in the area. Esmund was discouraged, but he knew there was more gold to be found nearby, so he scoured the hills and located two other sites rich in gold; but this time he filed the paperwork to make the claims lawfully his.

As it turned out, numerous other gold strikes made all of South Mountain practically one giant gold mine. Summitville became a bustling gold camp.

By 1882, Summitville had swelled to a population of over 600; there were several hotels, the *Summitville Nugget* newspaper, saloons, stores, and nine mills at which to process the ore. One of the mining companies set up a pool hall to entertain the men during their free time, especially over the long winter months. This attracted pool sharks from all over the state, who came to match skills with the miners.

Del Norte, about 24 miles northeast of Summitville, was an important shipping point, supply center, and stagecoach junction. One of its residents, Tom Bowen, struck it rich with his Little Ida Mine in Summitville. Suave and colorful, Bowen wore many hats; and his skill and luck were legendary. Over the course of his life, Bowen was a judge, an entrepreneur, a lawyer, the governor of Idaho Territory, brigadier general for the Union Army, a U.S. senator, and a very big gambler. Bowen once lost shares of a mining company in a poker game, only to have the winner decide he didn't want the shares. Bowen redeemed the stock for a nominal purchase; and the mine, the Little Ida, later made him very rich. He purchased many other mining properties, including the Little Annie.

In 1885, some of the mines in the area began having financial difficulties, and even the Little Annie could not pay its workers' salaries. Other mines were playing out, so the population of Summitville rapidly declined. By 1889, only about 25 residents remained in town.

There were a few short revivals in mining: one in the late 1890s and another in the late 1930s. In recent years, mining started up again with Galactic Resources Ltd. They suffered heavy losses through 1991 and sold the balance of their mining interests. In 1993, the *Wall Street Journal* reported that Galactic had filed for bankruptcy.

Current operations near Summitville are restricted to the environmental restoration of the area. The U.S. Environmental Protection Agency has ordered a cleanup of high concentrations of copper and minerals distributed in the local water sources through mining procedures. This problem could date back to the earliest mining operations in the 1870s.

Although some of the ghost town's buildings have been torn down to make room for modern-day mining, a number of well-preserved buildings still stand in Summitville. It is an interesting ghost town to explore and photograph.

GPS COORDINATES: 37°25.84'N 106°35.50'W

TRAIL REFERENCE: Southwest #34: Summitville Ghost Town Trail

Swandyke

Swandyke had its boom in the late 1890s, considerably later than most other Colorado mining camps. The gold camp was actually divided into two sections called Swandyke and Upper Swandyke, about a mile apart, near the Middle Fork of the Swan River.

Stagecoach service connected the camp to Breckenridge and Jefferson; and from there, railroad service ran regularly to Denver.

The population peaked at about 500 in 1899, when the post office was set up. Many of the camp's families were summer habitants who would move away to avoid the harsh, bitter winters. Some miners, however, chose to remain and work their claims during the cold months. In the winter of 1898, snow began falling one morning and was soon five feet deep on Swandyke. Additional snow fell every day until mid-February. The huge quantities of snow caused a number of avalanches and snow slides, some of which destroyed buildings in the town. One avalanche carried Swandyke's mill from one side of the mountain across a deep gulch, leaving the wreckage on the opposite mountainside.

Swandyke's life span was rather short, partly due to the town's remote location and difficult transportation. Furthermore, mining in Colorado began to decline after the turn of the century, except in extraordinary areas like Creede or Cripple Creek. Swandyke's post office was closed in 1910.

Today, Swandyke is a crumbling Colorado ghost town with a couple of wasted cabins remaining. It is a beautiful location in a remote setting.

GPS COORDINATES: 39°30.50'N 105°53.50'W

TRAIL REFERENCE: Central #12: Middle Fork of the Swan Trail

Tarryall

The gold camp of Tarryall was established along Tarryall Creek in July 1859, following the discovery of gold flakes "as big as watermelon seeds." The early prospectors found abandoned log cabins presumed to have belonged to miners a decade earlier, who had been killed by Indians. Hamilton, a sister town, was set up next door.

When word got out about Tarryall's rich placer gold finds, prospectors flocked to the area, and the banks of Tarryall

Colorado Avenue in Telluride after a flood, circa 1914

Creek were soon lined with tents. Meanwhile, the original settlers furiously grabbed up all the best sites and became jealous of any newcomers, aggressively running them off. This earned Tarryall a reputation as an inhospitable and greedy place. Prospectors left in disgust, dubbing the camp "Grab-All."

The city was platted in 1861 and became the county seat of Park County for a short while. A private mint was established in the mid-1860s to stamp out $2.50 and $5.00 pieces.

After producing nearly $2 million in gold, the mine played out, and miners moved on. By 1875, both Tarryall and Hamilton were totally deserted. Much of Tarryall and Hamilton were buried under rock prior to World War II as a result of dredging operations along Tarryall Creek.

GPS COORDINATES: 39°07.32'N 105°28.45'W

TRAIL REFERENCE: Front Range #19: La Salle Pass Trail

Telluride

Telluride began as a small mining camp along the San Miguel River in 1878. The first residents there called it Columbia. Because the post office sometimes confused Columbia with other towns of the same name, the town was renamed in 1881.

The Wild Bunch pose for a photo in Fort Worth, Texas, in 1900

Telluride, derived from tellurium (a metallic substance that is often attached to silver and gold in their natural states), was an apt name, since tellurium was widespread in the region.

In 1881, business sites in Telluride were being sold for $25, and residential lots went for 75¢. At this time, Telluride had a population of around a thousand people to patronize two grocery stores and a whopping 13 saloons! Two newspapers were established, and a school district was organized, with classes held in private homes. The following year, the townspeople raised funds to erect the first schoolhouse. The building still stands, but now it serves as Telluride's city hall. The first church was built in 1889, which was followed by a number of others. One unconventional pastor even held services in a local saloon!

Telluride's mountains held fortunes in silver and gold. Zinc, copper, and lead were also mined in the area, but transporting the ores presented a major difficulty. At the Liberty Bell, miners tried to send ore from the mine to the mill downhill on sleds. This failed, because the ore kept falling off the sleds. The miners tried to steady the toboggans by constructing and adding wings, but too many sleds practically flew off the mountainside!

Telluride was isolated, so the townspeople often had trouble obtaining supplies and food. Lack of transportation also made shipping ore to Ouray on burros an arduous task. From Ouray, teams of oxen towed the ore to Alamosa. Finally, the ore traveled on to Denver by rail to reach the smelter.

When Otto Mears brought the Rio Grande Southern Railroad to Telluride in 1890, population growth was colossal, but little did people know what lay ahead of them. "To hell you ride!" the conductor would yell to passengers headed for Telluride.

Telluride was a wild and crazy place, where guns and tempers often got out of hand. The town's three dozen saloons and gambling halls never shut their doors. Telluride's saloon patrons seemed prone to drunken brawls and fights, and gun battles and murders were common. "The Law" itself committed much of the lawlessness. Prostitutes were plentiful, especially along Pacific Avenue. The residents of town tolerated the prostitutes because the bordello madams paid all the town's taxes in regular installments on their behalf.

Butch Cassidy robbed his first bank in Telluride in 1889. Cassidy and two other men held up a bank at the corner of

The destroyed car from the real Wild Bunch train robbery that was depicted in the 1969 movie, *Butch Cassidy and the Sundance Kid*

First and Colorado in broad daylight. Although they had three fresh horses waiting for them outside of town, they had no time to make the exchange as they rode for their lives toward Rico with the posse on their tails. Cassidy and his cohorts never were caught for the robbery, but several weeks later three dead horses were found still tied to the tree.

Although Telluride in its early days certainly was not for the faint of heart, it did offer more than saloon fights and gun-slinging bank robbers. The townspeople enjoyed dances, concerts, and various social clubs.

Set magnificently in a box canyon surrounded by snowy mountains and breathtaking waterfalls, Telluride has suffered problems from the elements. Historically, snow piling up in the mountain bowls has presented the greatest threat. In 1902, several men were swept away in an avalanche that also took out the Liberty Bell's tramway. More were killed when a slide buried the rescue party recovering the first bodies. The following day a third slide hit, bringing the death toll to 19. It took months to locate all the bodies. Two years later, nearly 100 people lost their lives in snow slides.

Floodwaters once washed out a dam on the San Miguel River, depositing up to eight feet of mud on the streets and isolating the town for weeks. To counteract this problem, residents constructed a flume leading from the town to the creek so that mud would wash into the creek, sometimes assisted by fire hoses.

Largely because of numerous complicated disputes between labor unions and mining companies, Telluride's economy declined dramatically in the early part of this century. One by one, the mines ceased operation. The most recent to close its doors was the Smuggler Union, renamed the Idarado in the 1970s.

Today, Telluride's gold is the ski industry, which started in the 1970s and has boomed ever since. Thanks to successful efforts at architectural preservation of Victorian houses and other buildings, the town looks much as it did a century ago. Telluride's community is currently prosperous and thriving with year-round resort activities.

GPS COORDINATES: 37°56.26'N 107°48.71'W

TRAIL REFERENCE: Southwest #18: Imogene Pass Trail, Southwest #19: Ophir Pass Trail, Southwest #20: Alta Ghost Town Trail, Southwest #21: Black Bear Pass Trail

Tincup

Established and laid out after the Gold Cup Mine was discovered in 1879, the town was first named Virginia City. Because other towns had that same name, the post office encouraged the town to change its name. In 1882, it was reincorporated as Tincup.

People flooded into Tincup—one of the wildest and roughest mining camps in Colorado. Its saloons and gambling parlors operated night and day. Drunkenness and shootings were casual occurrences. Tincup was a controlled town, meaning it was ruled by the underworld. Organized crime took charge of all city offices, many saloons, gaming halls, and houses of ill repute. When the first marshal started work in 1880, he was told to see nothing, hear nothing, and do nothing; his first arrest would be his last. He lasted only a few months, because when

Tincup in 1906

he went unpaid, he quit. The second marshal occasionally rounded up a few drunks, put them in jail, and then released them. The third marshal decided to harass a saloon owner one night and didn't live long enough to regret it. The fourth marshal went insane and killed himself. The fifth marshal was shot and killed. Quite a record of accomplishment for the lively little town, isn't it?

By 1882, Tincup had several thousand residents and was the biggest silver producer in the Gunnison area. It was a supply center and social center for the area, despite lacking a railroad. The absence of good transportation forced miners to cart out their ore by pack train. Eventually, construction of the Alpine Tunnel brought the railroad to nearby Pitkin.

By 1884, Tincup suffered a mild recession, partially due to high transportation costs. Tincup strengthened again and even managed to survive through the silver crash of 1893 with its gold and silver production.

The town's good fortunes continued into the twentieth century, only to end dramatically in a fire that burned the town to the ground in 1906. The fire started in a store that sold kerosene. As it spread, the flames destroyed everything for one city block. The town was rebuilt, but it never fully recovered. Another fire in 1913 started at a saloon and went on to heavily damage several other buildings.

After the Gold Cup Mine closed in 1917, Tincup declined rapidly. All the working mines in the area shut down, and in 1918 Tincup's post office closed.

The Tincup cemetery has four sections, on separate knolls. One section is for Protestants, another for Catholics, and another for

Tincup Town Hall, built in 1906

Jews. By far the largest is Boot Hill, where those who had no religion and died with their guns blazing and boots on were buried.

Today the town is supported by tourism and offers many fine opportunities for fishing and backcountry camping. It is a summer resort community with many buildings restored as residences and businesses.

GPS COORDINATES: 38°45.27'N 106°28.77'W

TRAIL REFERENCE: Central #35: Cumberland Pass Trail, Central #37: Tincup Pass Trail

Tomboy

The Tomboy Mine, located in 1880 by Otis C. Thomas, was situated high above Telluride. The mine was named Tomboy because it was Thomas's nickname.

For several years there was little activity at Tomboy because it was so difficult to reach. However, after the silver crash in 1893, prospectors struck gold at the Tomboy, and the mine began to produce handsomely.

At its peak, the mining camp supported about 900 people. Although Tomboy's residents relied on Telluride for supplies,

A view of Tomboy as it once was; the remains of many of the structures are still in evidence today

they did not necessarily turn to Telluride for entertainment. About halfway between the Tomboy Mine and the Smuggler Mine was a renegade district called The Jungle, offering a mix of brothels, poker dens, and saloons.

In 1897, the Tomboy Mine was sold to the Rothschilds of London for $2 million. At this time, the mining camp was booming. It continued to produce for several years but began to decline around the turn of the century. Mining operations ceased entirely in 1928.

There is still much to see at the Tomboy site. The area is littered with ruins of many old buildings and evidence of mining activity, with beautiful views and spectacular scenery all around.

GPS COORDINATES: 37°56.18'N 107°45.23'W

TRAIL REFERENCE: Southwest #18: Imogene Pass Trail

Tomichi

First called Argenta, Tomichi Camp was laid out because of silver finds in the area in 1880. The town of Tomichi de-

veloped around the successful Magna Charta Tunnel, which was the best-producing silver mine in the area. Before long, the town's population swelled to nearly 1,500. A smelter was constructed to serve the Magna Charta Tunnel and the other local mines. Unfortunately, it was destroyed by fire in 1883.

The silver crash in 1893 drastically reduced the town's population. All the nearby mines were closed except the Eureka, which operated until 1895.

In 1899, a huge avalanche struck the town, destroying all the buildings and mine machinery. Five or six people were killed, and all the survivors left the town.

Only a few foundations remain at the town site, about 2 miles north of Whitepine. A large metal sign marks the site.

GPS COORDINATES: 38°34.26'N 106°22.17'W

TRAIL REFERENCE: Central #34: Tomichi Pass Trail

Waunita Hot Springs

Ute Indians were the first to enjoy this region's many hot springs (there are nearly 100 springs in the area).

First named Tomichi (meaning boiling) Hot Springs, the lower springs were later called Elgin in 1882. The settlement had a post office and a two-story hotel with a mineral bath that was reported to relieve rheumatism, arthritis, and other illnesses.

The upper springs were called Waunita and developed by Colonel Moore in 1879 to include a hotel, a restaurant, and a post office. The town was named for an Indian maiden: According to a Shoshoni legend, the beautiful Indian maiden Waunita roamed the valley for days, weeping and grieving the death of her love, a Shoshoni warrior who had been killed in battle. After Waunita died of a broken heart, the hot springs appeared wherever her tears had fallen.

In 1916, Dr. Charles Gilbert from Chicago started a hot springs resort that became world famous. He built cottages and a large hotel. Guests arrived from all over the world to seek relief from various diseases in the hot springs. The resort boomed until Gilbert died in 1927, but went into decline soon after. It never recovered, although several attempts were made. Today Waunita Hot Springs operates as a private dude ranch.

GPS COORDINATES: 38°30.85'N 106°30.41'W

TRAIL REFERENCE: Central #32: Waunita Pass Road

Webster

Located near the foot of the Kenosha and Webster Passes, Webster was established in 1877 and named for William Emerson Webster. William Webster, along with the Montezuma Silver Mining Company, was responsible for the construction of Webster Pass from Handcart Gulch to Montezuma.

By 1879, the Denver, South Park & Pacific Railroad reached Webster, and the town became a shipping point. At that time, the railroad did not venture over Kenosha Pass (only 9,950 feet), so Webster was the end of the line. Supplies and passengers intending to go farther south had to terminate and find another method of transportation.

Miners, railroad workers, prostitutes, con men, and fortune seekers all poured through Webster. It became a rough, violent town where disorder and shootings were commonplace. The cemetery had two sections; one was a crowded "boot hill."

Although thousands of people flooded through Webster, it had only one hotel. The proprietor rented floor space and blankets when he ran out of beds. When customers outnumbered blankets, the proprietor collected blankets from snoring patrons and reissued them numerous times during the night.

Webster met its demise for two reasons. First, better routes than Webster Pass were established through the mountains. Second, the railroad eventually made it over Kenosha Pass, thus allowing travelers to reach their destinations conveniently by train.

GPS COORDINATES: 39°27.39'N 105°43.23'W

TRAIL REFERENCE: Central #5: Handcart Gulch Trail, Central #6: Red Cone Peak Trail

Weston

Originally a well-used Ute Indian trail, Weston Pass quickly became a busy wagon road used by prospectors when gold was discovered south of Leadville. Early miners called it the California Gulch toll road.

In 1859, Philo M. Weston arrived in Colorado and purchased a 480-acre ranch that straddled the California Gulch toll road—soon to become Weston Pass toll road. By 1862, Weston and his wife had set up a roadside hotel.

During Leadville's heyday, Weston Pass may have been the busiest road in Colorado. Reportedly, a steady flow of wagons, stages, and animals over the pass stirred up a permanent cloud of dust that resembled a dense fog.

The actual town of Weston was established as the Denver, South Park & Pacific Railroad extended toward Leadville in 1879. Weston was a tent town for the railroad, and it served as a shipping point on the east end of the road for cargo to be picked up and hauled over the pass to Leadville. During the boom, piles of freight were always waiting to be transported. Colonel Robert J. Spotswood controlled the flow of traffic and freight traversing the pass. Three forwarding and commission houses held a monopoly on wagons, horses, and burros crossing the pass.

At its peak, the busy little town had 11 restaurants that catered to the many travelers. Several saloons operated day and night. In 1879, the county issued liquor licenses to establishments along the road. One of these was known as Park Place, or simply Clara's kitchen. It served up cooked meals to hungry passengers making the laborious trip over Weston Pass. One notable customer was Charles Dow, a wealthy New Yorker who later established the Dow-Jones Stock Market Index. He described his meal as excellent—lacking style but with great variety and quality.

The road over the pass was so busy that in the narrow sections traffic jams and even bloody stage crashes were commonplace. The poor animals that towed heavy wagons for miles, sometimes with loads of up to 6,000 pounds, lived a brutal existence. Carcasses of the beasts of burden littered the side of the road.

After the railroad reached Buena Vista and Leadville, the need for Weston passed. Today nothing remains at the site of Weston, which is approximately 3.5 miles southeast of the intersection of Weston Pass Road and US 285.

GPS COORDINATES: 39°02.69'N 105°55.20'W

TRAIL REFERENCE: Central #19: Weston Pass Trail

Whiskey Park/Elkhorn

The discovery of gold around Hahns Peak led to the settlement of a mining camp called Elkhorn, also known as Whiskey Park, in the 1890s. Reports heralded rich lodes of precious metals in the area, and a population of about 100 sprang up around the Elkhorn Mine. Although the mine produced some good ore, most was lower grade. The boom was very short-lived.

For a while Elkhorn survived on other industries such as lumber, agriculture, and dairy farming, but today there is little or nothing left of Elkhorn.

GPS COORDINATES: 40°58.29'N 106°55.03'W

TRAIL REFERENCE: Northern #18: Elkhorn Mountain and Stock Driveway

Whitepine

Prospectors began arriving in Whitepine in 1879, and the town was founded in 1880. The primary mines in the area were the North Star and the May-Mazeppa.

The Whitepine and Tomichi stagecoach service to Sargents started in 1881. That same year, the Denver & Rio Grande Railroad service commenced.

The town thrived throughout the 1880s and was considered a sociable, bustling place. The population of Whitepine reached about 3,000.

Despite high expectations, none of the area mines produced much, and with the silver crash of 1893, the town was doomed. By the following year, Whitepine was virtually deserted. The town saw a brief resurgence of activity in 1901.

Whitepine experienced a comeback when lead, zinc, and copper were mined during World Wars I and II, mainly at the Akron Mine. The Akron Mine hit a high point in 1948, when it reached production of 100 tons per day. By then the North Star and May-Mazeppa Mines were back in production with some lead and zinc mining.

Whitepine opened a ski area in 1946 with an 1,800-foot rope tow. After just two years, the tow was dismantled and moved.

Whitepine is now primarily a summer residence, with many reconstructed miners' cabins.

GPS COORDINATES: 38°32.55'N 106°23.59'W

TRAIL REFERENCE: Central #34: Tomichi Pass Trail

Wild Irishman

The Wild Irishman was a silver-producing mine in the late 1870s. It remained a camp and never did formally incorporate as a town. The camp had no church or school. Several cabins were situated around the mine so that the miners could be close to their work. The Wild Irishman camp is typical of a number of camps where men and their families worked during the mining boom.

The ruins of the Wild Irishman Mine are still in evidence in a beautiful timberline meadow along the Saints John and Glacier Ridge road.

Woodstock

Woodstock was initially established as a silver mining camp in 1881. It is a mysterious town with a tragic end.

Located below the Palisades of the Denver, South Park & Pacific Railroad, Woodstock reached its peak population of 17 in 1881, the same year the train came to town.

In the spring of 1884, a giant avalanche, perhaps caused by a train whistle, destroyed the town and killed 14 people. Six of those who died were children. A rescue party traveled from Pitkin in temperatures near 40 degrees below zero. The rescue party dug up what bodies they could find and brought them back to Pitkin on sleds. Woodstock was never rebuilt.

GPS COORDINATES: 38°37.09'N 106°23.53'W
TRAIL REFERENCE: Central #36: Alpine Tunnel Road

Railroads

Colorado's First Railroads

In the 1850s when miners struck gold in the Rocky Mountains, people flocked to Colorado. Front Range settlers counted on the planned transcontinental railroad to stop in Denver and run through the mineral-rich mountains in order to sustain new settlement and mining operations. As fate would have it, an unexpected snowstorm in the spring of 1866 caught Union Pacific Railroad surveyors in western Colorado where they were planning a route for the railway to cross the Continental Divide. The blizzard convinced them to build the railway to the north, through Wyoming.

Union Pacific Railway Company—Eastern Division had begun building a railway from Kansas City to Denver, but construction stalled in western Kansas due to lack of funds. With settlers deserting and property values plunging, town leaders and entrepreneurs scrambled to plan and procure financing for railroads that would connect Denver to the rest of the nation. The resulting rail network allowed Colorado to export its mineral wealth and import much-needed supplies as well as new settlers. During the first decade of railroad development alone, Colorado's population jumped 500 percent as

A Denver & Rio Grande Western locomotive pulls into Moffat in 1951

Union Station and the Denver City Cable Railway Company streetcar stables in 1884

support industries flourished in tandem with mining. The rails truly transformed the state from a sparsely settled territory into a viable state rich in agriculture, tourism, and raw materials.

In 1867, a group of entrepreneurs led by John Evans and William Byers incorporated the Denver Pacific Railway & Telegraph Company with aid from the Union Pacific. The group succeeded in connecting Denver with the transcontinental tracks through Cheyenne, Wyoming, on June 22, 1870. The journey from Denver to Cheyenne took five hours and cost $10. Kansas Pacific Railway Company bought the line in 1872.

Also answering the call for new rail networks was William A. H. Loveland, who in 1869 incorporated the Colorado Central Rail Road Company with the help of Edward L. Berthoud. Theirs was the first railway chartered in Colorado Territory. The two businessmen built a line from Loveland's hometown of Golden to the Union Pacific's transcontinental hub in Cheyenne via Boulder, Longmont, Fort Collins, Berthoud,

General William J. Pamer, circa 1870

and Loveland. Later they added a branch to Denver. The Colorado Central also constructed a narrow gauge railroad following Clear Creek into Central City and the surrounding gold region and then to Georgetown and surrounding silver mines. In 1881, a short line from Julesburg to La Salle was added and named Omaha and Denver Short Line. On April 1, 1890, the Colorado Central was reorganized under the name Union Pacific, Denver & Gulf Railway Company.

Formerly known as the Union Pacific Railway Company—Eastern Division, Kansas Pacific Railway Company completed its rail line from Kansas City to Denver in the summer of 1870 under the able leadership of General William Jackson Palmer. In 1880, the Kansas Pacific was consolidated into Union Pacific Railway Company. Palmer resigned from the Kansas Pacific to pursue his vision of creating a slim-gauge line joining Denver and Mexico City. The line's 3-foot width would be less costly and allow trains to negotiate steep grades and tight turns.

Palmer incorporated the Denver & Rio Grande Railway Company (D&RG) in 1870 and broke ground on July 28, 1871. Running through the new towns of Castle Rock and Palmer Lake, the rail line reached Colorado Springs in less than three months. Next Palmer extended the line to El Moro, near present-day Trinidad, to tap the rich commerce moving along the Santa Fe Trail. Torn between his vision to reach Mexico and the lure of tapping the rich business of new mountain mining ventures, Palmer extended his railroad instead to Cañon City and the San Luis Valley via La Veta Pass. To reach the mines high in the Rockies to the west, he faced an expensive and difficult endeavor of laying rail through the 2,000-foot-deep and extremely narrow Royal Gorge.

Lack of funds and competition from a new railroad in the south, the Atchison, Topeka & Santa Fe (AT&SF), distracted the general from his western push through the narrow gorge. The AT&SF had expanded along the Arkansas River, developing the towns of Lamar, Las Animas, and La Junta. Encroaching deep into Denver & Rio Grande territory, it branched off to both Trinidad and Pueblo. The two rail companies raced to occupy the only route into New Mexico, the narrow Raton Pass. The AT&SF narrowly beat the D&RG, shutting Palmer out of trade south of Colorado.

A battle ensued between the two railroads in 1878 when vast quantities of silver were discovered in the mines near Leadville. General Palmer shifted resources back to extending his railroad through Royal Gorge with AT&SF hot on his heels. The rival companies reached the gorge nearly simultaneously and armed their workers to help defend and advance their causes. When a tenuous truce fell through, it is said that Bat Masterson barricaded himself in a roundhouse in Pueblo and opened fire on D&RG forces with a Gatling gun. The

Otto Mears standing in front of a locomotive operated by his Silverton Northern Railroad, circa 1900

An elegant Colorado & Southern Railway dining car in 1907

two armies entrenched themselves in forts at opposite ends of the Royal Gorge, and Palmer instructed his workers to sabotage AT&SF operations.

In 1880, the federal courts finally awarded D&RG the right to complete its line through the gorge and beyond to Leadville. The settlement, known as the Treaty of Boston, stipulated that for 10 years the D&RG could not build a line south over Raton Pass or to the east. The AT&SF was required to give up ambitions to build rails to Leadville or farther to the north. Though defeated in the "Royal Gorge War," the AT&SF expanded south and east and became successful transporting agricultural goods and tourists.

The D&RG expanded west, eventually encompassing nearly 1,700 miles of narrow gauge rails, connecting the remote towns of Aspen, Ouray, and Silverton. The company even laid 772 miles of continuous narrow gauge rails between Denver and Ogden, Utah. D&RG began converting to standard gauge tracks in 1890 to link to the national rail system. In 1920, the D&RG was incorporated as the Denver & Rio Grande Western Railroad Company (D&RGW). Although much of the company's long-distance passenger service ceased operations in 1970, one famous line operates to this day. The Durango & Silverton Narrow Gauge Railroad is a popular 45-mile historic pleasure-ride from Durango to Silverton through scenic Animas River canyon.

While D&RG and AT&SF were deadlocked over the Royal Gorge route, the Denver, South Park & Pacific Railway Company (DSP&P) was busy laying tracks toward the rich mountain mines. The narrow gauge line emerged in 1872, originating in Denver and bound for the Pacific Ocean. DSP&P's line followed the South Platte River through Grant and Como, southwest of Denver. Extending the line through Breckenridge and Leadville via Boreas Pass, the company built another branch through Fairplay to Buena Vista, constructing the Alpine Tunnel and reaching Gunnison in September 1882.

The amazing Alpine Tunnel was constructed at 11,600 feet, making it the highest in the United States. Its 1,805-foot length also made it the longest tunnel ever constructed for a Colorado narrow gauge line. Because the DSP&P anticipated

The Colorado Midland passenger train behind a stagecoach, circa 1890

boring the shaft through solid granite but instead encountered underground streams and loose stone, the tunnel required reinforcement by California redwood timbers.

Construction delays resulted in the D&RG advancing south and west ahead of the DSP&P, preempting the line from further westward expansion. Hardships plagued the South Park line, which extended beyond Gunnison about 17 miles northwest to Baldwin and finally another 4 miles farther to the northwest in the direction of Ohio Pass. Massive avalanches destroyed entire stations and major tunnel cave-ins made operating the line unprofitable. The DSP&P first lapsed into foreclosure in 1888 and was reorganized several times until its final incarnation under control of the Colorado & Southern Railway Company (C&S) in 1899. The C&S repeatedly attempted to close the costly narrow gauge line partially or completely, but it was not until 1910 that C&S abandoned the line through to Gunnison because of a collapse in the Alpine Tunnel. Amazingly the narrow gauge line continued to operate, at least in part, until August 25, 1943.

The legendary Rio Grande Southern Railroad Company overcame incredible obstacles to construct a railroad servicing the remote, high-elevation silver mines of Telluride. Visionary Otto Mears, with aid from the Denver & Rio Grande, broke ground in fall 1889 and completed the 162-mile track in December 1891. Most of the road climbs at an impressive four percent grade over Lizard Head Pass (10,250 feet) and zigzags through hairpin Ophir loops on rickety wooden trestles. The railroad prospered only through the silver crash in 1893. Although it went into receivership for the second time in 1929, it operated 172 miles of rails until its complete abandonment on December 31, 1951.

Reorganization and Era of Big Railroads

With nearly 175 companies having laid rails throughout Colorado, the task of totaling and defining the state's railroads is daunting and difficult. These companies commonly constructed branches and extensions under completely different names, multiplying the number. Further complicating Colorado railroad history, the Pacific Railway Act, the silver crash, the Depression, and the advent of automobiles caused buy-

outs, mergers, and name changes among the state's original railroads. These factors combined would change Colorado's rail system dramatically for years to come.

Abraham Lincoln signed the Pacific Railway Act in 1862, and Congress chartered the Union Pacific, underwriting the cost for a transcontinental railroad. In the 1870s, Jay Gould seized control of the Union Pacific and began assuming Colorado railroads. When the line reached Colorado in the 1880s, the Union Pacific overtook the Denver Pacific, Kansas Pacific, Colorado Central, and Denver, South Park & Pacific. In 1881, Gould also financed the construction of Denver's Union Station.

Industrious businessmen in Colorado Springs incorporated Colorado Midland Railway in 1883. The line became the first standard gauge railroad to cross the Rockies and featured incredible climbs, trestles, and tunnels. The rails were protected by 10 snowsheds, totaling nearly 2,000 feet in length, and 17 tunnels. The impossible railroad operated as a subsidiary of the Atchison, Topeka & Santa Fe from 1892 to 1897 when it became leased as a subsidiary of the Colorado & Southern Railway Company. Underfinancing forced the company to abandon the rails in 1918, the first major railroad failure in the West. The portion from the Midland Terminal in Colorado Springs to Cripple Creek functioned until 1948.

The Colorado & Southern Railway merged several older lines in 1898, including the Colorado Central and Denver, South Park & Pacific, and began servicing coal mines along the Front Range and the agricultural center in north-central Colorado. In 1908, the Colorado & Southern officially merged with the Chicago, Burlington & Quincy but maintained independent operations and management until 1982.

Colorado's largest rail network, the Denver & Rio Grande, became the Denver & Rio Grande Western (D&RGW) in a 1921 reorganization but continued to function independently even after Philip Anschutz bought Southern Pacific Railroad in the 1980s. It wasn't until the 1990s that Southern Pacific cars began replacing D&RGW trains when they started to be referred to as "Dangerous and Rapidly Growing Worse."

In 1903, David A. Moffat began construction of the Denver Northwestern & Pacific Railway, also known as Moffat Road. The railroad, which became known as the Denver &

Salt Lake Railroad Company, became the first to cross the Continental Divide due west of Denver. In 1928, the company completed an impressive 6.2-mile tunnel under the Continental Divide. At the time it was the longest tunnel of its kind in the United States. In all, the rail company used 54 tunnels totaling 23,800 feet and helped reduce the line's maximum elevation to 9,239 feet. Moffat Road expanded to Craig in northwest Colorado, but never beyond. The Denver & Rio Grande Western Railroad Company absorbed the road in 1947.

People

Explorers, Mountain Men, and Surveyors

The Bent Brothers

Fur traders and businessmen, the four Bent brothers—Charles, William, Robert, and George—left their home in St. Louis, Missouri, and traveled west where they saw an opportunity in the fur trade. In 1830, Charles Bent partnered with Ceran St. Vrain, a Taos trader and trapper, forming Bent, St. Vrain and Company, a trading company that would become one of the largest operations in the Southwest. In particular, the company dominated the buffalo robe trade.

The partners built Bent's Fort in 1833 on the Arkansas River in what is today southeast Colorado. It served both the mountain fur trappers and the Plains Indians in its centralized location between present-day La Junta and Las Animas. William largely managed the fort and helped supervise its construction; to many it became known as William's Fort. The brothers further expanded their operations from their initial trading post, building Fort St. Vrain on the South Platte in 1837 and a post on the Canadian River in 1842.

Charles Bent

The eldest brother, Charles, moved to Taos, New Mexico, in the 1830s and married Maria Ignacia Jaramillo. As one of the most prominent Anglo-Saxon residents of the area, Charles was appointed governor of the New Mexico Territory after the Americans gained control during the Mexican War. Over the years, Charles managed to accrue a number of enemies among the Taos Indians and native residents. Their animosity resulted in the Taos Rebellion of 1847, during which Charles was scalped and killed.

In 1849, St. Vrain left the firm and William became sole owner. His brother George likely died of consumption the same year Charles was killed. Robert, the youngest brother, was attacked by Comanche Indians and died in 1841.

It is believed that the government's refusal to meet William's purchase price for Bent's Fort in 1849 resulted in William blowing up the fort and building a new post farther

Reconstruction of Bent's Fort

downstream. By 1849, the fur trade had largely collapsed and increasing traffic from settlers moving west signaled the end of the frontier age. In 1857, William gathered a number of settlers and built what was essentially Colorado's first Anglo-American settlement on the Purgatoire River.

William epitomized the frontier man. He married three Indian women over his lifetime and worked in both a public and private capacity to keep the peace between Indians and settlers. He had such a strong alliance to the Indians that before the Sand Creek Massacre, officers had to prevent William from warning the Cheyenne about the impending attack. William settled in his final years in Westport, Kansas, near the famous mountain men James Bridger and Louis Vasquez.

James Bridger

On March 17, 1804, two months before Meriwether Lewis and William Clark set off on their journey to the Pacific Northwest, James Bridger was born in Richmond, Virginia. With little formal schooling, he became a blacksmith's apprentice in St. Louis, Missouri, at the age of 14. In 1822, Bridger joined William H. Ashley, founder of the group that became the Rocky Mountain Fur Company, on his initial expedition to the Rocky Mountains. He was the youngest member of the group.

While on a trapping expedition in 1824, he and several companions became the first white men to follow the Bear River to its end, discovering the Great Salt Lake. Bridger is attributed with exclaiming, "Hell, we are on the shores of the Pacific," after tasting the water.

In 1830, after working as a trapper for Ashley's fur company, Bridger and several others in the trade purchased the firm. Bridger continued trapping in the Rocky Mountains despite being injured with an arrowhead in 1832 during the battle of Pierre's Hole with the Gros Ventre Indians. The company faced fierce com-

James Bridger

petition, in particular from John Jacob Aster's American Fur Company, which forced Rocky Mountain Fur Company to dissolve in 1834.

Bridger joined the American Fur Company in 1838, at which time he met Pierre Louis Vasquez, a fellow mountain man and trader. Together they constructed Fort Bridger. The fort, which was located on the Green River in southwest Wyoming, became an important stop along the Oregon Trail, a base for military operations, and a Pony Express station. Dwindling beaver populations and immigrants streaming into and settling in trapping territory accelerated Bridger's 1843 retirement from trapping, widely regarded as the end of the fur trade era in the American West.

An authority on western geography and Indian sign language, Bridger was a highly sought expedition guide. From 1854 to 1857, Bridger guided Irish nobleman Sir St. George Gore on possibly the most massive hunting expedition in western history. (Sir St. George Gore was also known as Sir George Gore; it is said that he dropped "St." from his name for his trip to America.) Bridger, along with the avid sportsman and a sizable and extravagantly outfitted entourage, roamed the Arkansas and South Platte Rivers into the Yampa Valley and finally northward to the region of present-day Yellowstone National Park.

Numbering more than 40 men, the hunting party included Gore's valet, a dog handler, a fly-tying specialist, a supervisor for Gore's massive gun collection, and other attendants, servants, guides, and scouts. Gore's troop traveled in a wagon train of as many as 26 wagons, 16 of which carried his personal luggage. With his 32 greyhounds and 18 foxhounds—along with his collection of 75 rifles, a dozen or more shotguns, and many pistols—Gore's hunting party killed as many as 2,000 buffalo, 1,500 elk and deer, and 100 bears. He wreaked havoc on the animal population, incensing the local Plains Indian tribes.

Bridger's employer, Sir St. George Gore, left his mark on Colorado with such locations as Gore Pass, the Gore Mountain Range, and the Gore Wilderness Area, which bears his name today. Although Bridger is remembered for being a member of Gore's infamous hunting expedition, he had other more well-known achievements. Some of his accomplishments include locating Bridger's Pass, which helped to shorten the Oregon Trail, guiding the Powder River Indian Expedition of 1865–66, and assisting in the survey for the Union Pacific Railroad.

Over his lifetime, Bridger married three times to women from different Indian tribes: Flathead, Ute, and Shoshone. With his wives he had six children, all of whom he sent east for their education. In his later years, Bridger began spending more and more time at his farm in Westport, Missouri, until he finally settled there permanently in 1866. In 1873, his health began to fail and he became blind. He passed away on July 17, 1881, and was buried in the Mount Washington Cemetery in Independence, Missouri. He is honored throughout the West, where his name lives on in many different locations, a fitting memorial to one of the greatest frontiersmen in American history.

John Frémont

John Charles Frémont

A native of Savannah, Georgia, John Charles Frémont was born in 1813 to French and American parents. He grew up primarily in Charleston, South Carolina, where he attended the College of Charleston's Scientific Department before being expelled in 1831. After teaching math to midshipmen in the Navy for a few years, Frémont joined the U.S. Corps of Topographical Engineers as a second lieutenant. He traveled in 1838 with Joseph N. Nicollet on multiple reconnaissance missions and received invaluable training in cartography.

It was during this time that Frémont met Missouri senator Thomas Hart Benton, a man who would have a great influence in the young explorer's life. Frémont also met and fell deeply in love with Benton's 16-year-old daughter, Jessie Benton. Despite the couple's 11-year age difference, they happily eloped and were married in October 1841.

With Benton's sponsorship, Frémont set out on his first expedition: to survey the Oregon Trail. From Washington, D.C., he traveled to St. Louis, Missouri, where he spent several months preparing to proceed up the Platte River to South Pass in Wyoming. Frémont needed an experienced guide for his trip, so he hired Kit Carson, who would become a life long friend.

In his second expedition in 1843–44, Frémont explored a massive circle of the least-known parts of the West: from the Colorado Rockies north to South Pass, northwest to the Columbia River, south along the Cascade and Sierra Nevada mountain ranges into California, east across the Great Salt Desert, and finally back to the Colorado Rockies. The U.S. Congress as well as commercial printers across the United States and Europe printed the map he created from his famous expedition.

Nicknamed "The Pathfinder" for his western expeditions, Frémont headed west a third time in 1845, again with Kit Carson leading the way. The group spent one month exploring the Utah Valley and Great Salt Lake, conducting scientific research on the area. The explorer was the first to accurately measure the elevation of the Great Salt Lake at 4,200 feet above sea level, as well as the first to map the region. Frémont's accounts of the Salt Lake region are credited with influencing Brigham Young's decision to settle his Mormon followers in the area.

This same expedition led Frémont to California, where he participated with the Americans in the Bear Flag Rebellion against Mexico. After refusing to side with the commander-in-chief of California, Brigadier General Stephen Watts Kearney, he was court-martialed for insubordination and removed from the Army. Although President James K. Polk reversed the decision, Frémont resigned his commission.

Despite leaving the military, Frémont led his fourth excursion in 1848 through the San Juan Mountains of Colorado in order to establish a central railroad route. This ambitious project led to the death of 10 men and the loss of all his equipment when they became trapped by heavy snow. In 1853, Frémont led his fifth and last expedition, crossing the Rockies in midwinter to California in search of a viable railroad pass.

Frémont participated in politics, serving as a U.S. senator from the new state of California in 1851. He ran for president in 1856 as the first candidate of the Republican Party but lost to James Buchanan. Frémont remains best known for his western explorations and for completing the first comprehensive map of the American West with accurate astronomical readings. Congress finally recognized Frémont's contributions and granted him a pension for his explorations only three months before his death; however, as a result of several poor business ventures, he died a virtual pauper in 1890.

John Gunnison

John Williams Gunnison was born in Goshen, New Hampshire, in 1812. He attended West Point and graduated second in his class of 50 in 1837. Upon completion of his education, Gunnison served as an ordnance officer during the Seminole War in Florida. When the Seminole and white settlers began peace talks, Gunnison was ordered to explore unknown water routes in central Florida.

Unable to withstand the hot and humid weather of the southern U.S., he was reassigned to the U.S. Corps of Topographical Engineers in 1838. After his transfer, Gunnison married Martha Delony in 1841, and the same year the couple moved to the Great Lakes region. Gunnison surveyed unexplored land of modern-day Wisconsin and Michigan and mapped a large portion of the shores of Lake Michigan.

In the spring of 1849, the corps reassigned Gunnison to Howard Stansbury's expedition surveying the Great Salt Lake valley. The team spent months exploring and mapping the Great Salt Lake and its tributaries. As winter set in, massive amounts of snow isolated Gunnison's survey team from the outside world. During this time, Gunnison studied the Mormons and wrote a book entitled *The Mormons, or Latter-Day Saints, in the Valley of the Great Salt Lake.*

John Gunnison

In 1853, after John Frémont's expedition failed to locate a suitable pass through the San Juan Mountains, Gunnison was chosen to survey possible railroad routes from the Kansas-Nebraska border west to the Pacific. During the expedition, Gunnison traversed the Great Plains, the Rocky Mountains, and the Gunnison River Valley to the location of the eponymously named Colorado town.

By October 1853, Gunnison's 37-man party with its 18 wagons of supplies had explored the northern end of the San Luis Valley, threaded Cochetopa Pass (near Saguache, Colorado), and followed the Gunnison River to the mighty barrier of the Black Canyon, the spectacular geographic formation now designated as a national park. In his reports on the region, which became the first official account of the Black Canyon, he described the landscape as "the roughest, most hilly and most cut up" he had ever witnessed. His survey proceeded to the site of modern-day Grand Junction and finally crossed into Utah to reach the Sevier River.

Only days prior to Gunnison's arrival, white pioneers had killed several members of the local Paiute Indian tribe. The angry tribe sought revenge and massacred Gunnison along with seven of his men on the banks of the Sevier River on October 26, 1853. Although many easterners blamed the Mormons for instigating the attack, there is little proof to support their accusation.

In 1862, a group of Mormon settlers named their community "Gunnison" in memory of the slain explorer. A monument lies 5 miles west of present-day Delta, Utah, where several of Gunnison's men are buried. Gunnison, who died at age 41, was buried in nearby Fillmore, Utah. He was the last official explorer before Colorado's gold rush period.

Ferdinand Hayden

Ferdinand Vandeveer Hayden was born in Westfield, Massachusetts, on September 7, 1828, and raised on a farm near Rochester, New York, before graduating in medicine from Albany Medical College in New York.

On his first expedition, Hayden accompanied F. B. Meek to the Dakota Badlands in 1853. During the next three years, he made a series of expeditions of the upper Missouri River into Montana. In 1858 he undertook the geological exploration of Kansas, and in the following year he returned to Montana for a similar geological survey.

Following Civil War service as a surgeon in the Union Army, Hayden was appointed a professor at the University of Pennsylvania; but he continued his exploration of the American West, undertaking a geological survey of Nebraska in 1867.

In 1869, Hayden was placed in charge of the forerunner of the U.S. Geological Survey and made his first expedition to Colorado. During the next eight years, he was responsible for the systematic, scientific investigation of Colorado west of the Continental Divide. He directed parties of surveyors, artists, and scientists who made a detailed record of the topography of the region, including a great number of the routes that are contained in this book. He published this record in *The Geological and Geographical Atlas of Colorado and Portions of Adja-*

Hayden's survey party, 1872; Ferdinand Hayden is third from left (seated)

cent Territory in 1877. The information was instrumental to the settlement of Colorado and the development of railroad and mining activity.

The establishment of Yellowstone National Park in 1872 followed Hayden's survey of the area the previous year and his support for the proposal upon his return.

Hayden was an initial appointee to the U.S. Geological Survey when it was established in 1879, but was forced to retire due to ill health in 1886. He died the following year, aged 59.

Stephen H. Long

Born in 1784 in Hopkinton, New Hampshire, Stephen H. Long was a prominent explorer of the West, leading several of the first official expeditions into the Louisiana Purchase. After graduating from Dartmouth in 1809, he taught school briefly and then joined the Army in 1814 as a second lieutenant of engineers. He continued teaching, this time at West Point, when in 1816 he became a major in the Corps of Topographical Engineers. At this time, Long began his first explorations by surveying the Fox, Wisconsin, and upper Mississippi Rivers, as well as helping to establish Fort Smith in Arkansas.

In 1819, Long was commissioned to lead a scientific expedition of the West via its rivers. He supervised the construction of a steamboat named the *Western Engineer*, which was elaborately decorated as a dragon in order to frighten and awe hostile frontier Indians. The party is credited with traveling farther than any previous explorers on the Missouri River into the territory of the Louisiana Purchase. The expedition camped for the winter at "Engineer Cantonment" near Council Bluffs in present-day Iowa, where a number of men died due to an outbreak of scurvy. The project was abandoned and Long returned to the East Coast.

The following spring, under orders from the U.S. government, Long led a new expedition west with the goal of locating the source of the Platte and Red Rivers. In June 1820, Long and 19 men moved west along the Platte River and its south fork to the Rocky Mountains. Although Zebulon Pike and his party had previously explored the Rocky Mountains, Long and his team were conducting the first official reconnaissance of the area in search of anything that could prove of value to the United States. Long and his party followed the Platte River and then the South Platte to the Rocky Mountains. The expedition named Longs Peak, which is the highest peak in modern Rocky Mountain National Park. Three of the explorers are also attributed with the first successful summit of Pikes Peak in July 1820.

Stephen Long

Proceeding south to the Arkansas River, the party came to a notable geographical obstacle, the Royal Gorge. The men divided into two groups; one group explored the Arkansas River while Long and his group moved south with the intent to survey the Red River. Long mistook the Canadian River for the Red River, and his group followed the Canadian River east onto the plains and across the present-day Texas Panhandle, encountering many hardships along the way. The official report of the expedition included Long's map, which labeled the area east of the Rockies the "Great American Desert." He claimed the area "wholly unfit for cultivation" as a result of his difficulties finding fresh water sources. The idea of the high plains as a large desert was perpetuated for generations.

Long continued to conduct exploratory surveys of the West, traveling as many as 26,000 miles during his five surveys. In later years, he was promoted to lieutenant colonel and became a consulting engineer for several railroads. In 1829, his experiences led him to publish the *Railroad Manual*, the first volume of its kind to be published in the United States. Promoted to colonel in 1861, Long served as commander of the topographical engineers until his retirement in 1863. He died in 1864 at the age of 80 at his home in Alton, Illinois.

Zebulon Pike

Zebulon Montgomery Pike was the first official explorer of Colorado. When the United States purchased the Louisiana Territory in 1803, the eastern boundary was not established. France and the United States considered the territory to include everything east of the Continental Divide, but Spain contended that its land extended north to the Arkansas River. This dispute was not settled until 1819.

Zebulon Pike

The lack of knowledge about the land the United States had purchased led to the formation of the Lewis and Clark Expedition. The following year, Pike was sent to explore the source of the Mississippi. He returned, having incorrectly concluded that Lake Cass was the source of the great river.

In 1806, Pike was sent with a party of 22 men to examine the extent of the southwestern part of the Louisiana Purchase. During the course of this expedition, he discovered Pikes Peak but failed in his attempt to climb it. He did not name the peak; John Frémont named it, following what had become common usage. Pike also discovered the Royal Gorge, the upper waters of the South Platte, South Park, and several important passes, including Medano Pass.

Pike served as brigadier-general in the War of 1812. He won a brilliant victory at the Battle of York when the United States besieged Toronto, only to be killed when an abandoned

British powder magazine exploded. He was 34 years old when he died.

John Wesley Powell

John Wesley Powell was born in Mount Morris, New York, in 1834. He left home at age 16 to study natural science, and by 1858 he had gained recognition in the science community for his work. A passionate abolitionist, Powell felt compelled to join the Union forces in the Civil War. He became an officer after attracting the attention of Ulysses S. Grant. Powell lost the lower section of his right arm at the Battle of Shiloh, but this would not stop him from becoming one of the most influential explorers in the history of the West.

John Wesley Powell

After the war, Powell served as a professor of geology at Illinois Wesleyan University in Bloomington, as well as a museum curator. He left Illinois for the Rocky Mountains in 1867 where he combined a survey of the region with fieldwork for some of his higher-level students. While in the Rockies on August 23, 1868, Powell and six companions achieved the first recorded summit of Longs Peak (14,255 feet). Later that year, with authorization from Congress, he explored the Grand (later Colorado) and Green Rivers, which inspired his future famous survey of the Colorado River that took him through the Grand Canyon.

In 1869, along with 10 other men aboard four boats loaded with provisions, Powell rode the Green and Colorado Rivers 1,000 miles to the Grand Canyon. One man quit the expedition early; three others, refusing to risk the danger of the rapids through the final stretch of the canyon, climbed the canyon walls, only to be slain by Indians. The remainder of the party reached the quieter lower Colorado River in safety.

Impressed by the expedition, Congress agreed to give Powell $10,000 for a second trip in 1871. The explorer used this opportunity to conduct serious scientific research. Powell hired men to help map the region as well as to photograph the phenomenal scenery. This group eventually became the U.S. Geological and Geographical Survey, operating under the Smithsonian Institution.

John Wesley Powell on his horse

During the 1870s, Powell focused much of his energy on researching the geography of the West and on studying the American Indians (which led to his classification of their languages). He presented his geological findings in the 1879 publication "Reports on the Lands of the Arid Regions of the United States," and that same year, with the support of a $20,000 grant from the federal government, he founded the U.S. Bureau of Ethnology. Powell was appointed the first director of the bureau in 1879 and served as director of the U.S. Geological Survey from 1881 to 1894.

His work had profound implications for development in Colorado and other areas in the West. He demanded a reform of land laws so that corporations could not monopolize resources, and he put forward proposals to irrigate arid lands and make them fruitful. Although Congress and special interests initially blocked Powell's plans, the Newlands Reclamation Act was passed in 1902, authorizing government irrigation and reclamation projects. Powell died the same year the act was passed and was buried at Arlington National Cemetery.

Antoine Robidoux

Antoine Robidoux was born on September 24, 1794, in Florissant, Missouri. His father, a fur trader, moved his family to St. Louis, where the family business flourished. It did not take long, however, until the young Antoine Robidoux ventured west to find his own fortune in the trading and trapping business.

In 1825, Robidoux traveled to Santa Fe, where he established himself as a prominent trader and where, in 1828, he met and married Carmel Benevides, the adopted daughter of the governor of Mexico. Like many men in the business, Robidoux soon became a Mexican citizen in order to continue trading in Mexico; otherwise he would have been subject to stiff fines and penalties for illegal trading. He even changed his name to Don Antonio Robidoux and briefly served in the Mexican government.

Antoine Robidoux

In 1828, Robidoux also established the first of his trading posts, Fort Uncompahgre, on the Gunnison River near present-day Delta, Colorado. Robidoux preferred the permanent trading post to the rendezvous system, in which trappers and traders met annually at an ever-changing location to exchange goods. By 1833, Robidoux had a number of trappers working for him in the region and had managed to significantly build the business. The Ute Indians encouraged the establishment of a trading post in their territory so they could more easily obtain arms, yet increasing hostilities between the Ute and traders resulted in an attack on the fort in 1844 that killed most of its occupants. Local Ute destroyed the vacant fort two years later.

After Robidoux had established Fort Uncompahgre, he traveled to Utah and in 1832 purchased the Reed Trading Post, renaming it Fort Robidoux (also referred to as Fort Uintah). In addition to trading with settlers, Robidoux dabbled in trading horses, illegal guns, and liquor with the local Ute Indians. Some evidence exists that Robidoux, often considered an unscrupulous businessman, may even have sold Ute Indian women and children into prostitution and slavery.

Although there was much competition between other trading posts, Fort Robidoux dominated the trade in the northern Utah region. Antoine, along with his brothers, also managed to maintain a strong supply line along the Western Slope of the Rocky Mountains. Competition from Fort Laramie and Bent's Fort would eventually push Antoine out of this area.

In 1846, Robidoux fought in the Mexican War, serving as an interpreter for General Stephen W. Kearney. He received serious injuries during the Battle of San Pascual in San Diego, California, and returned to St. Louis in 1857. He died there on August 29, 1860, after years of ill health that left him blind. His obituary described him as "tall, slender, athletic, and agile," a man "whose life was one of great activity and public usefulness."

William Green Russell

William Green Russell was born in Georgia in 1818. He worked as a miner in Georgia, until he left to search for gold in California. Unsuccessful, he returned to Georgia determined to organize a mining party to search for gold in the Rocky Mountains. Russell was married to a Cherokee woman and, through members of her tribe in what is now Oklahoma, he heard about deposits of gold in the foothills of the Rockies.

In 1858, Russell, along with his two brothers and six other companions, made their way west, meeting up with the Cherokee along the Arkansas River as planned. As the party continued following the Santa Fe Trail, more hopeful prospectors joined the Russell brothers until their party numbered more than 100.

At Bent's Fort the party headed northwest, stopping at the confluence of Cherry Creek and the South Platte River. After panning for gold unsuccessfully for weeks, a number of members of the party returned home. The Russell brothers and 10 other men remained, and in July 1858 they managed to pan several hundred dollars' worth of gold. It was not a particularly significant find, yet news of their discovery spread quickly, and thousands joined them in what would become the Pikes Peak gold rush.

Russell established the town of Auraria in 1858 at the site of his original discovery. Only a few weeks later, the town of Denver sprung up across the river. Although the two towns originally were fierce rivals, Auraria merged with Denver in 1860. Russell's discovery of gold occurred in what is now Denver's Confluence Park. The man who sparked the rush to the Rocky Mountains died in 1887.

Prospectors, Miners, and Road Builders

Nicholas C. Creede

Nicholas Creede was born William Harvey in Fort Wayne, Indiana, in 1842. He changed his name and headed west after his girlfriend married his brother.

Creede worked at odd jobs as he traveled across Illinois to Iowa, where he joined the Union Army as a scout in the Civil

Nicholas Creede

War. As a scout, Creede trained his eyes to observe small details on his long treks into the wilderness; he trained his body to endure all sorts of weather, surviving on only small rations of food. The experience proved to be good preparation for the man whose next occupation was scouting the countryside in search of riches in the earth.

Creede spent the next decade as a less-than-successful prospector. In 1878, he turned up a little silver float in what later became Monarch, west of Salida; and another strike a few months later netted him a quickly spent $13,000. These mines are speculated to have been the Monarch and the Madonna. Creede continued to search for riches and was not discouraged. He traveled southward from Salida, prospecting until he came to Wagon Wheel Gap, where he accepted a job as a ranch hand. He was determined to find pay dirt in his spare time. In 1889, when Creede was 47 years old, he found specks of silver floating along Willow Creek. It was enough to cause him to follow the creek for another mile or so upstream into a steep and narrow canyon where the silver particles appeared to concentrate. Creede scaled the sheer canyon wall with great difficulty, until he reached a small ledge where he stopped to catch his breath and have a bite to eat. As his sharp eyes surveyed the rock around him, he chipped into a section and hollered, "Holy Moses! Chloride of silver!"

The Holy Moses lode was a vein of silver ore five feet wide; and with three hired men, Creede worked it until winter set in. Back at the ranch bunkhouse, Creede realized that he needed capital and a railroad to get the ore to the smelter as cheaply as possible. Creede decided to visit David Moffat, president of the Denver & Rio Grande Railroad in Denver, to discuss both issues.

Moffat was impressed with Creede's findings. After investigating the facts, Moffat bought the Holy Moses for $70,000 and put Creede on the payroll as a prospector, with a guaranteed salary and a one-third interest in future discoveries.

Nicholas Creede wasted no time getting back to prospecting in the mountains. He soon found another lode, whereupon he immediately sent a letter of resignation to Moffat. Creede hired miners, dug shafts, and in December, when Moffat's Denver & Rio Grande Railroad reached the junction of Willow Creek, sent wagonloads of his ore off to the smelter. This time, when Moffat volunteered to buy him out, Creede refused. Creede knew he was onto a good thing, and he was right; in the first year, he took $2 million out of his Amethyst Mine.

The silver crash of 1893 did not affect Nicholas Creede at all. He had already made his fortune by selling his investments the previous year. Unfortunately, the cowboy millionaire only had five years to enjoy his wealth. In the

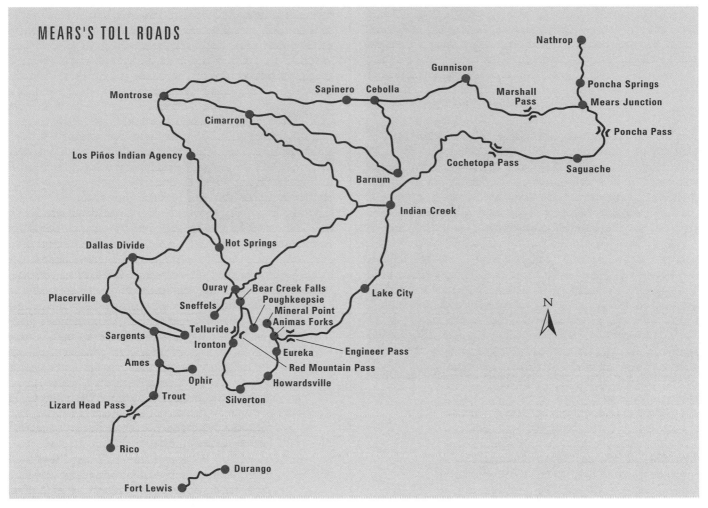

MEARS'S TOLL ROADS

Nathrop
Poncha Springs
Mears Junction
Marshall Pass
Poncha Pass
Gunnison
Sapinero
Cebolla
Montrose
Cimarron
Cochetopa Pass
Saguache
Los Piños Indian Agency
Barnum
Indian Creek
Dallas Divide
Hot Springs
Placerville
Ouray
Bear Creek Falls
Poughkeepsie
Mineral Point
Animas Forks
Lake City
Sneffels
Telluride
Sargents
Ironton
Engineer Pass
Ames
Eureka
Red Mountain Pass
Ophir
Howardsville
Lizard Head Pass
Trout
Silverton
Rico
Durango
Fort Lewis

N

late fall of 1892, Creede, upon advice from his doctors, was forced to leave his home in Colorado and move to Los Angeles.

Creede's retirement was not completely easy, as he and his wife decided to divorce after years of bickering. In late 1896, Creede gave his wife $20,000 and moved her back to her family home in Alabama for what he hoped would be the last of her. She was back in six months, hounding him for more money. Creede became increasingly depressed, and in 1897 a servant found him dead of a morphine overdose.

Otto Mears

Otto Mears was born in Russia in 1840 and was orphaned at the age of four. Various relatives took care of him, first in Russia, then in England, then in New York, and finally in San Francisco when he was 12. When he arrived in San Francisco to live with an uncle, he found

Otto Mears

that the uncle had left for the gold rush in Australia; Mears was on his own.

He drifted through the mining camps of Nevada before serving in the First California Volunteers in the Civil War. In 1863–64, he served under Kit Carson in the Indian campaign against the Navajo.

After the war, Mears first went to Santa Fe before moving to Colorado, where he opened a store in Saguache. He prospered and expanded his business interests. He farmed in the San Luis Valley and operated a sawmill and a grain mill.

To expand market access for his wheat, Mears constructed a road over Poncha Pass. The government gave permission for this road to become a toll road. This was the beginning of Mears's reputation as the "Pathfinder of the San Juans."

By the time he was finished, Mears had built 450

Mears with Chief Ouray in 1880

A stagecoach on Mears's narrow toll road that became the Million Dollar Highway in 1909

miles of roads in the region. His most famous road is what has become known as the Million Dollar Highway, US Highway 550 between Silverton and Ouray.

As the railroads expanded in Colorado, Mears naturally expanded his interests into railroad construction. In partnership with the Denver & Rio Grande Railroad, he built a network of four narrow gauge rail lines. In 1887, he built the main line from Durango to Rico, over Lizard Head Pass on what is now Colorado Highway 145, descending with the aid of the Ophir Loop and proceeding to Placerville, Ridgway, and south to Ouray.

Mears learned the Ute language and was friendly with Chief Ouray. He served as an interpreter in the Brunot Treaty negotiations. Following the Meeker Massacre, he assisted Chief Ouray in freeing the women captives. This led Mears to work with Ouray to negotiate the resulting Washington Treaty, which was signed in March 1880. In June, Mears was chosen by President Rutherford B. Hayes as one of five commissioners to implement the treaty. In 1884, he was elected to the Colorado legislature and became influential in the Republican Party.

Mears suffered heavily in the silver crash of 1893, with many of his enterprises being jeopardized or bankrupted. In 1907, Mears returned to Silverton and remained there until his retirement to Pasadena, California, in 1917. He died there on June 24, 1931, at the age of 91.

Horace Tabor, Augusta Tabor, and Baby Doe

Horace Austin Warner Tabor was born in Vermont in 1830. He rose to enormous riches and became an inspiration to every gold and silver seeker in the West. Unfortunately, he sank back to poverty before his life was over.

Horace Tabor

The son of a tenant farmer and a mother obsessed with religion, H.A.W. Tabor found his first job as a stonemason. He married his boss's homely, no-nonsense daughter, Augusta Pierce. In 1859, they set off together to find a fortune in the Colorado gold rush.

Horace, Augusta, and their son spent the next 19 years traveling and prospecting between various mining camps in Colorado, from Idaho Springs to Oro City, trying to make enough money to survive. The Tabors operated a succession of shops, run by Augusta, who also sold her bakery goods and took in boarders to support Horace while he prospected.

By 1878, Tabor had made money from his shops and had become mayor of Leadville. At that time, he occasionally grub-staked other prospectors (provided supplies in return for a share in their profits), which brought him instant wealth when two men whom he had given $17 worth of provisions in exchange for a one-third interest in their strikes discovered a silver lode. Tabor immediately bought all shares of the Little Pittsburgh and in six months netted half a million dollars.

For a while, everything Tabor touched seemed to turn to silver; even his seemingly worthless or overpriced investments, such as the Matchless Mine, made him increasingly richer. He felt the urge to splurge and spent his money on everything from opera houses in Leadville and Denver to silk nightshirts with huge diamond buttons. He loved dining on oysters and drinking champagne at Leadville's Saddle River Café, which was where he met and fell in love at first sight with Baby Doe.

Born Elizabeth Nellis McCourt in Oshkosh, Wisconsin, Elizabeth was nicknamed Baby by her brother, James. In 1877, beautiful, blonde Elizabeth abandoned her dreams of becoming an actress to marry Harvey Doe, a good-looking mama's boy who was also son of the mayor. Because of Harvey's possessive mother, the marriage seemed doomed from the beginning, as Harvey's mother faked heart attacks and pretended she was dying in order to get his attention. Since "Papa" Doe owned some mining interests near Idaho Springs, Baby persuaded her husband to seek their fortunes in the West.

Baby was so intent on getting rich, she even donned miner's pants and dug for ore alongside Harvey when his efforts were ineffective. She didn't care what people who

Baby Doe

Baby Doe's cabin at the Matchless Mine

talked about her "lewd" behavior thought of her. Their mine made them money for a while, but then failed to produce. They had money problems, and Harvey began to drink heavily.

Baby met another man named Jake Sandelowski and bore a stillborn baby that was believed to have been his. She divorced Harvey in 1880 and went to Leadville in pursuit of a new life. In Leadville, she met up again with Sandelowski, who had money to show her the best restaurants and entertainment spots in town. He became a good friend to her.

Baby Doe's strong desire for riches drove her to pursue Horace Tabor, then 49, married, and worth millions of dollars. On the night they met at the Saddle River Café, Tabor fell hard for her; and within five days, she became his mistress. Tabor's millions hypnotized Baby Doe, but over time she fell deeply in love with him.

Augusta was left out of Horace's new rich life and began to feel lonely, unwanted, and bitter. She resented being ignored after she had lovingly stayed with him through their lean years, and she wanted to live a simple life with her husband in Leadville.

Tabor entered politics and became lieutenant governor of Colorado from 1879 to 1883. In 1883, he was named to fill a 30-day term in the U.S. Senate. It was rumored that Tabor was viewed as a vulgar, uncouth, and low-class man and tolerated in Washington only because of his great wealth.

The interior of Baby Doe's cabin today

Horace Tabor married Baby Doe while in Washington, D.C., in one of the most flamboyant weddings of all time. Even President Chester Arthur attended, along with many other prominent men whose wives snubbed Baby Doe and stayed away. Tabor's divorce from faithful Augusta to marry Baby Doe was a scandal that tarnished Tabor's reputation in both Washington and Colorado.

The next 10 years were full of riches and happiness for Baby Doe and Horace Tabor, although they were scorned by Denver society. They spent money on every whim they had.

Tabor, by some accounts, was an incompetent man in his business dealings; despite his amassed fortunes, his gullibility and wild spending caused him to steadily lose everything. Tabor thought he owned overseas holdings, but in fact, his money had been swindled. The silver crash of 1893 saw

Augusta Tabor

Tabor lose the last of his investments, except for the Matchless Mine, which by that time was full of water and worthless.

In 1898, Tabor became a postmaster in Denver and lived on a small salary. He became ill and was destined to die the following year in utter poverty. Before he died, he told his wife to hold on to the Matchless Mine and never sell it. She lived in exile in a cabin at the mine and was deserted by her family.

In 1935, Baby Doe was found frozen to death at age 81. She was dressed in rags, penniless among the many mementos of her wealthy years.

Winfield Scott Stratton

Winfield Scott Stratton was born on July 22, 1848, in Jeffersonville, Indiana. His father was a shipbuilder, and young Stratton grew up studying carpentry in his father's shipyards. After the Civil War, Stratton moved west to serve an apprenticeship with one of his father's friends. Once he finished his apprenticeship, Stratton started his own carpentry firm in Colorado Springs, Colorado. Stratton was briefly married but sent his wife back to her parents, claiming her baby was not his.

Although Stratton initially found contentment with the carpentry business, he soon caught gold fever and set off for the mountains. Over the years, Stratton stopped over in many prominent mining areas including Leadville, Red Cliff, Chalk Creek, and Aspen. In an effort to learn more about metallurgy, Stratton took courses at the Colorado School of Mines in Golden.

For years Stratton had little luck prospecting, until he wandered into the Cripple Creek District. When Stratton first arrived in the Cripple Creek area, it was not known as a productive mining area due to the Mount Pisgah hoax. As part of the hoax, gold had been falsely planted on the land in order to attract investors. The area's reputation changed dramatically when Stratton made a rich gold strike on July 4, 1981, near

Victor, Colorado. He named his claim the Independence Mine in honor of the Fourth of July holiday.

When the owners of the nearby Portland Mine, Jimmy Burns and Jimmy Doyle, discovered a rich vein of gold, they offered Stratton one-third of the claim in return for legal assistance. Typically, when a vein was discovered, owners of neighboring claims would sue for possession, as the law stated that the true owner of a vein was the person on whose property it surfaced. Stratton agreed and eventually became one of the largest shareholders of the incorporated Portland Company. The company's two mines, the Portland and the Independence, were some of the largest ore producers in the Cripple Creek District. Stratton became the first of Cripple Creek's many millionaires. In 1900, Stratton sold the Independence Mine to the British Venture Corporation for $10 million.

Stratton was exceedingly generous with his wealth. When a fire destroyed a large percentage of the town of Cripple Creek, Stratton donated funds to those who had lost their homes. He also helped miners who had a bad turn of luck, including "Crazy Bob" Womack, who made the first discovery of gold in Cripple Creek, and Horace Tabor, who had made and lost a silver fortune in Leadville.

Stratton became a patron of sorts to the town of Colorado Springs, the first town in which he settled when he moved to the West. He helped fund the construction of civic buildings, including the post office, city hall, courthouse, and mining exchange. After making his fortune, instead of building a mansion like many newly minted millionaires, Stratton returned to Colorado Springs to live in the house he had built as a carpenter.

Stratton became rather eccentric and withdrawn in his later years. His health started to deteriorate in 1900, and he passed away September 14, 1902. Stratton left the majority of his money to charity. He willed a large portion of his fortune to the establishment and maintenance of a foundation for the poor named after his father, Myron Stratton. The Myron Stratton Home opened in 1913 and has operated continuously to this day.

Thomas Walsh

Thomas Walsh was born in Ireland and came to America in 1869 at the age of 19. He was a carpenter who worked his

away across America by building bridges.

Walsh spent some time prospecting in the Black Hills of South Dakota. By 1878, he had moved on to Leadville and made some money in mining and even more from owning the Grand Hotel.

In Leadville, Walsh married Carrie Bell Reed, a schoolteacher. She was a charming woman, who as a youngster had taught herself to have a graceful, gliding walk by practicing with a glass of water balanced on her head.

Thomas Walsh

The silver crash of 1893 wiped out everything the Walshes had, so they packed up and moved to Ouray, where most of the silver mines had recently been abandoned.

Walsh, convinced there was gold to be mined in the San Juans, began exploring the deserted mines. In 1896, he found that samples from mine dumps in the Imogene Basin had strong gold showings, so he quietly purchased more than 100 claims in the area for next to nothing.

Walsh consolidated his properties as Camp Bird (supposedly named after a jay that stole his lunch one day), reinvesting the first mining profits straight back into further development. Walsh built a smelter and a 2-mile tram to bring ores down from the mines.

Camp Bird grew up as a company town. Walsh provided unusual luxury for his miners. They ate from china plates, slept in enameled iron beds, and enjoyed electric lights, steam heat, modern plumbing, and marble-topped lavatories! Walsh also supplied a reading room and stocked it with magazines and newspapers.

By 1900, Walsh's 103 mining claims were producing between $3 million and $4 million annually. By 1902, Walsh had accumulated claims covering 1,200 acres. He was netting about $95,000 a month from the mines.

Later that year, Walsh sold Camp Bird to the Rothschilds of London for $3.5 million in cash, $0.5 million in stock, and 25 percent royalty on future profits (excluding thenproven reserves).

Walsh moved to Washington, D.C., where he and his family became popular and prominent society figures. President William McKinley appointed Walsh as commissioner to the Paris Exposition, and the family sailed to Europe, where they became friends with King Leopold of Belgium.

Back in Washington, Walsh built a 60-room mansion at 2020 Massachusetts Avenue, where he and Carrie entertained with elaborate dinners, receptions, and soirees. His daughter, Evalyn, married wealthy Edward B. McLean, whose family owned the *Washington Post* and *Cincinnati Enquirer* newspapers.

Evalyn's father told her to choose a wedding present (in addition to the cash gifts he had given her), and she opted for the 92.5-carat Star of the East Diamond for $120,000. She later purchased the famous Hope Diamond, which is now on display at the Smithsonian.

Walsh died in 1910 after making $10 million from his mining interests.

Lawmen, Gunfighters, and Outlaws

Wyatt Earp

The controversial emblem of the West, Wyatt Berry Stapp Earp, was born on March 19, 1848, in Illinois. His father, Nicholas Porter Earp, had served in the Mexican War under Wyatt Berry Stapp, and young Wyatt was named in honor of his father's revered commander. When the Civil War broke out in 1861, Wyatt ran off in hopes of joining, but his father caught up to him and brought him home.

He was the middle boy among his five rough-and-tumble brothers who were dubbed "the Fighting Earps." His siblings were James C., Virgil W., Morgan, and Warren B., in order from oldest to youngest. They had an older half-brother, Newton Jasper, and a younger sister, Adelia. Two other sisters, Virginia and Martha, died when very young.

Wyatt Earp

Wyatt worked on his father's farm but soon learned to hate the backbreaking labor. Upon Virgil's return from the Civil War, Wyatt left with him and took such jobs as loading freight wagons and working on the Union Pacific Railroad. For a time, the Earp sons, including Wyatt and Virgil, settled down on their father's farm in Lamar, Missouri. Wyatt married Urilla Sutherland there in 1870 and got his first taste of dispensing law and order when he was elected the local constable. Urilla died suddenly of typhoid just a year later. Grief-stricken and fleeing accusations of fraud, Wyatt left Lamar.

Wyatt continued to drift from one frontier town to the next. In 1875, he became a policeman in Wichita, Kansas, where he gained a reputation as an excellent lawman. He rarely smiled, had nerves of steel, and never killed unless he had to. Yet Wyatt was by no means a saint, and he often let his fists do the talking.

In 1876, Wyatt joined the police force in the wild and morally destitute Dodge City, Kansas—the Babylon of the West. He frequently chased criminals and tracked them over the countryside. One such case led Wyatt to Fort Griffin, Texas. Once there, Wyatt met a slender, gambling dentist by the name of Doc Holliday, and the two developed a strong friendship.

Bat Masterson (standing) with Wyatt Earp

In April 1877, Wyatt followed the gold rush to the Black Hills of South Dakota but was back in Dodge City before the end of summer. Wyatt left Dodge City for good on September 9, 1879, and moved to Tombstone, Arizona, followed by his brothers Morgan and Virgil, Doc Holliday, and their families. Wyatt worked as a shotgun guard for Wells Fargo until July 1880, when he became the deputy sheriff of Tombstone. During this period, the Earps met the Clanton family and the McLaury brothers, and from the start, a feud developed between the families.

The brewing conflict exploded at the shoot-out at the O.K. Corral on October 26, 1881. During the skirmish both the McLaury brothers and one of the Clantons were killed and Morgan and Virgil Earp and Doc Holliday were wounded. The vendetta continued and within the year Virgil was wounded and Morgan was fatally shot. In retribution, Wyatt, who had been deputized as a U.S. marshal after Virgil's shooting, tracked and gunned down two Clanton supporters. But Tombstone had finally had enough of the shooting and Wyatt was forced to leave.

He began drifting from town to town throughout the West. He roamed through Colorado, catching up with Holliday, and eventually following the gold rush to Idaho, where he bought a couple of saloons. He was on the move again by 1887, this time to California, where he was elected marshal of Colton. From 1889 to 1890, Wyatt owned saloons in San Diego. Raising thoroughbreds in San Francisco was his next venture. Also in California, he refereed the Bob Fitzsimmons–Tom Sharkey prizefight. After naming Sharkey the winner, he was branded a cheater by the press.

He returned to Arizona briefly but left with his third wife for the Alaska gold rush and opened a saloon in Nome in 1877. Leaving Alaska during the Nevada silver boom, Wyatt finally settled down in Los Angeles in 1906. After trying unsuccessfully to attract the attention of the burgeoning Hollywood film industry, he endeavored to publish his adventures. In 1928, Stuart N. Larke took an interest in the project, but the fanciful account of Wyatt's life did not appear until after he died on January 13, 1929, at the age of 80.

Bob Ford

Born in Virginia in 1861, Bob Ford became an outlaw and Jesse James's assassin, for which he earned the sobriquet "that dirty little coward who killed Mr. Howard."

In 1882, Bob Ford had only just joined Frank and Jesse James's gang when he shot Jesse James in the back of the head in order to collect the reward money offered by the governor of Missouri. He was convicted and then pardoned for the murder. The shooting was so unpopular with the people of Missouri that Ford was forced to leave town.

He settled in Creede, Colorado, where he opened a dance hall and saloon called the Denver Exchange, which he financed with part of his reward money. One day, Ed O'Kelly

Bob Ford's saloon in Creede, where he was shot to death

Bob Ford

wandered into the bar, leveled his shotgun, and fired a fatal shot at Ford.

Little is known about O'Kelly except that he was a native of Missouri; it is suspected that he was a distant relation to Jesse James or that James was his hero.

Ford was not especially popular in Creede—particularly because he acted as if he were boss of the town, when he was generally considered a repulsive criminal. According to Creede town lore, the townspeople celebrated for three days and three nights after Ford's funeral, with plenty of whiskey and dancing on Ford's grave.

O'Kelly's sentence for killing Ford was life in jail. However, he was paroled after only eight years and released in 1900. Three years after his release, he was shot to death by an Oklahoma City police officer.

Doc Holliday

John Henry Holliday was born in Georgia in 1851. Relations between Holliday and his father were strained, especially after his mother's death from tuberculosis when the young Holliday was 15. As a teenager, Holliday was supposedly involved in an attempt to blow up the county courthouse, after which he left town and enrolled in the Pennsylvania College of Dental Surgery, founded by his cousin. He graduated with a Doctor of Dental Surgery degree in 1872 and began practicing in Atlanta. When he developed a bad case of tuberculosis (possibly from his mother), he decided to move to the American West, hoping the drier climate would improve his health problems. This was the onset of Holliday's transition from a respectable citizen into a notorious, hard-drinking gunfighter, gambler, and con man.

In Dallas, Texas, Holliday continued to practice dentistry but became increasingly involved in gambling. Although it was rumored that he shot one of his irate patients, he was, for a fact, arrested for the first time in Dallas when he and a saloon keeper exchanged a couple of shots. In 1875, he left Dallas and began drifting across the West, leaving behind a trail of suspected shootings. As Holliday got sicker, he became progressively more quarrelsome and continued to drink heavily. He was a feisty, hot-tempered man who never backed away from a fight. Few people were silly enough to challenge him; he had killed many men, several of them lawmen.

Doc Holliday

Holliday became particularly well known for his friendship with Wyatt Earp. Holliday reportedly saved Earp's life in Dodge City, Kansas, by coming to his rescue during a confrontation between Earp and some cowhands. In the late 1870s, Holliday moved to Las Vegas, Nevada, and opened a saloon. He soon had to leave town after killing Mike Gordon, who had attempted to wreck his saloon. After leaving Las Vegas, Holliday participated in the Colorado Railroad Wars, a battle between the Denver & Rio Grande Railroad and the Atchison, Topeka, & Santa Fe Railroad for land on which to lay track. Around the same time, Holliday reputedly robbed the Santa Fe–Las Vegas stage, as well as a train.

In 1880, Holliday followed Earp to Tombstone, Arizona. Kate Elder, a close long-time companion of Holliday, implicated him in the 1881 stagecoach robbery that resulted in the deaths of two men. Although Holliday caused trouble for Earp, who had become deputy sheriff in Tombstone, the two remained friends. Holliday stood by the Earp brothers during the notorious shooting at the O.K. Corral. Holliday killed Frank Stilwell during the Earp Vendetta Ride, which was sparked by killings at the O.K. Corral. After killing Stilwell, Holliday never returned to Arizona, the scene of the crime. Instead, he spent the rest of his life in Colorado. Friends of Earp, in particular Bat Masterson, worked behind the scenes to ensure Holliday was not extradited back to Arizona. Masterson charged Holliday with a nominal offense but saw to it that the case was continued indefinitely, preventing Holliday from being extradited.

In 1887, Holliday moved to Glenwood Springs, hoping the mineral springs would help cure the tuberculosis that was slowly killing him. His health was so bad that he died in bed later that year at age 35. Holliday is buried in the Glenwood Springs cemetery on the hill overlooking the town, and his ornate tombstone is decorated with engravings of six-shooters and playing cards.

Bat Masterson

Blue-eyed William Barclay "Bat" Masterson was known as a dapper lawman. Born November 1853 in Quebec, he was originally christened with the name Bartholomiew. He later changed it to William Barclay Masterson and used the nickname "Bat."

When he was 18, Masterson moved to Wichita, Kansas, and then to Dodge City the next year, along with his brothers. He tried several professions, from railroad construction worker to buffalo hunter, from Indian fighter to civilian scout.

In 1877, Masterson operated a saloon in Dodge City while also serving as an assistant sheriff to Charles Bassett. In September of that year, Masterson was appointed a city policeman. He later succeeded to the position of sheriff and held this office from January 1878 to January 1880.

In 1879, while still sheriff of Dodge City, Masterson was recruited by the Atchison, Topeka, & Santa Fe Railroad in its fight with the Denver & Rio Grande Railroad over the right of way through the Royal Gorge of the Arkansas River. He recruited 30 heavily armed men to assist him in this endeavor, but the dispute was settled without bloodshed and Masterson returned to Kansas.

Masterson ventured back to Colorado to investigate mining opportunities, but disappointedly returned to Dodge City

Bat Masterson

a few months later. After that, he spent time in Tombstone, Arizona, before returning to Dodge to assist his brother in a dispute with Al Updegraff and A. J. Peacock, which led to one of Dodge City's more famous gunfights.

Masterson was recruited from Dodge to become town marshal of Silverton in an effort to restore order to the town after two outlaws murdered a marshal on Blair Street. The town had become notoriously rowdy, and and someone needed to take control.

Under Masterson's rule, shoot-outs, drunken brawls, and the undesirable element disappeared from Silverton. However, Masterson did not close down the red-light district of Blair Street, since he was known to enjoy district's saloons, gambling, and girls.

In 1882, Masterson served as the marshal at Trinidad. In 1884, he was appointed marshal of La Junta, but served for only five weeks. He then returned to Dodge City, where he first tried his hand as a sportswriter, then briefly served as deputy sheriff, and refereed a prize fight. In 1886, when the saloons in Dodge were closed down, Masterson moved to Denver. He was married in 1891.

Masterson arrived in Creede, Colorado, in 1892, during the early days of the town, to manage the Denver Exchange, a high-class drinking and gambling establishment. Masterson tolerated no troublemakers and allowed no gunplay inside. The ex-lawman was good at setting the rules and being in command.

Masterson was always known for being well groomed and dressing well; he was considered a dandy, though no one is recorded to have told him so! When he was running the Denver Exchange, he usually wore an impeccable ensemble—such as a lavender corduroy suit, white shirt, and black string tie. A style of hat named after Masterson is still sold.

In 1902, Masterson moved to New York City, where Theodore Roosevelt appointed him deputy U.S. marshal. He became interested in writing and published a series of his articles, *Famous Gunfighters of the Western Frontier*. He became a sportswriter for the *Morning Telegraph* and eventually served as the sports editor. For the next few years, he drank heavily. His fiery temper occasionally got him into trouble. He died at his desk of a heart attack in 1921.

Ed O'Kelly

Born in 1858, Ed O'Kelly is best known for killing Robert Ford, the man who murdered the outlaw Jesse James. In 1882, Robert Ford joined Jesse James's gang and then shot him to collect reward money offered by the governor of Missouri. Ford was convicted of murder but then pardoned. The shooting was so unpopular with the people of Missouri that Ford

fled. With his reward money, he moved to Creede, Colorado, and set up a saloon and dance hall called the Denver Exchange.

About 10 years after Jesse James's death on June 8, 1892, O'Kelly walked into the Denver Exchange and killed Ford by shooting him in the neck. O'Kelly remained mum about his motivation for avenging the murder of Jesse James, and his reason for shooting Ford remains a mystery to this day. It is rumored that the con artist Soapy Smith convinced O'Kelly that he would become famous if he killed the unpopular Ford. O'Kelly spent 10 years in prison for Ford's murder but was released on October 14, 1902, for health reasons.

O'Kelly traveled to Oklahoma City upon his release. The following year, he was arrested by police officer Joe Burnett as a "suspicious character." O'Kelly fostered a serious grudge against the officer after his arrest. About a month after the incident, he encountered Burnett while on duty and, unprovoked, drew his revolver on the police officer. The two struggled and Burnett finally fired two shots, killing his attacker. Ed O'Kelly died on January 13, 1904, and was buried at Fairlawn Cemetery in Oklahoma City.

Alferd Packer

Alferd Packer was born in Pennsylvania. He served for a short time in the Union Army during the Civil War and was discharged due to "disability."

Packer, like many other men of his era, migrated westward with hopes of finding fabulous riches at the end of his arduous journey. He never made a fortune; he simply bummed around the mining camps, prospecting on occasion.

In November 1873, Packer led a party of 21 men from Provo, Utah, to prospect in the San Juan Mountains of Colorado.

Two months later, the group reached Ute chief Ouray's winter camp at the junction of the Uncompahgre and Gunnison Rivers, near Montrose. Chief Ouray was friendly to the men and tried to warn them of the severe blizzards that regularly bombarded the mountains in the wintertime. Ouray tried to persuade the men to stay with him and his people to wait out the season. After a few days, Packer and five men decided they would continue their journey in search of gold, departing on February 9. The other 16 men remained with Chief Ouray.

Alferd Packer

According to Packer, for some unknown reason, his group left camp with rations of only seven days' worth of food for one man. It did not take the six men long to go through such a small supply, so after nearly a week, Packer separated from the group and ventured off in search of food.

In April, Packer arrived alone at the Los Piños Indian Agency on Cochetopa Creek, carrying with him money and possessions from the other men in his party. The authorities' suspicions were aroused, and they questioned Packer about the fate of his five companions.

Packer claimed his companions had deserted him. He told the authorities that when he returned to camp after his fruitless search for food, he found one man sitting near the fire roasting a piece of meat cut from the leg of another man. Another three corpses lay near the fire; the head of each one had been bashed by a hatchet. Packer claimed that when the man saw him, he stood with his hatchet in hand, and Packer shot him through the belly.

In time, Packer finally admitted to killing the men and eating their bodies. He escorted a search party to recover the remains, but he quit the search before locating the bodies.

Packer was arrested and jailed in Saguache but escaped before he could be tried. Nine years later, he was arrested in Wyoming, where he had been living under another name.

In April 1883, following a trial in Lake City, Packer was found guilty and sentenced to hang the following month. An angry mob wanted to lynch him immediately, so he was moved to Gunnison for safekeeping.

Packer won a retrial, and his sentence was reduced to 40 years at the state prison in Cañon City for manslaughter. He had served almost 15 years when Governor Charles Thomas pardoned him in 1901. As part of the pardon agreement, Packer moved to Denver, where for a while he worked as a doorman at the *Denver Post*'s offices.

In April 1907, Packer died and was buried in Littleton Cemetery. A memorial plaque marking the site of the murders overlooks Lake San Cristobal on Cannibal Plateau.

Jefferson Randolph "Soapy" Smith

Jefferson Randolph Smith was born in 1860 into a life of wealth and privilege. His family, residents of Georgia during the Civil War, fell on financial hard times. In 1876, the Smiths moved to Texas for a fresh start. It was in Texas that Smith began his life as a con man, swindling people out of their money with such scams as the shell game, three-card monte, and other games of chance.

Starting in the late 1870s, Smith set up similar operations in Denver. His activities during this time period would earn him his nickname. Smith wrapped bars of soap in money, ranging in value from $1 to $100. Then he would stand on a busy street corner where a member of his gang who was planted in the crowd would buy the soap and proclaim to the crowd that he had won money. Starting at $1 a bar, Smith would auction off the soap. As his stock dwindled, he raised his prices with promises that the $100 bill remained. Smith soon became known across the western United States as "Soapy Smith."

By 1879, Smith had begun building his first of three criminal empires. Smith used the money from his cons to bribe city officials in Denver, after which they rarely bothered him. In the mid-1880s, Smith opened a gambling hall called the Tivoli Club and located his offices just down the street from the club. From these locations, Smith ran a number of small- and large-scale cons. Although Smith fleeced money with impunity, he also gave generously, donating to a number of local charities and causes.

In 1892, as Denver officials began cracking down on crime, Smith left Denver for the silver town of Creede, Colorado. There he opened the Orleans Club, a gambling hall much like the Tivoli. In one of his most outrageous schemes, Smith supposedly purchased a figure of a man made of cement. He had the "man" buried close to a nearby mine, and it was later "discovered" by one of his associates. He then charged visitors 25 cents to view the petrified man. Not long after Smith arrived in Creede, he heard that Denver was once again safe for con men. He sold his gambling hall just before a fire destroyed much of the downtown area.

Back in Denver, Smith set up several new con operations. A showdown of sorts quickly developed between Smith and the newly elected governor, David Waite, who had run on the platform of cleaning up Denver. When Waite called out the state militia to remove corrupt officials he had fired, Smith and his men went to city hall with weapons, prepared to fight off the militia. In doing so, Smith won points with Denver's political bosses who did not want to see the city's bureaucracy reformed. Once the "City Hall War" cooled down, the case went to the Colorado Supreme Court, which ruled in favor of the governor. Not long after, Smith's empire began to crumble and he was forced to flee Colorado a wanted man. He was accused of attempted murder of a rival saloon owner.

Relocating to Skagway, Alaska, in 1897, Smith opened a saloon named Jeff Smith's Parlor, out of which he resumed his swindling operations. His establishment soon became known as "the real city hall," because Smith ruled the town as the "Sultan of Skagway." When a group of vigilantes called "the Committee of 101" threatened to have Smith run out of town, he responded by forming his own powerful society.

Smith ran into trouble for the final time when he attempted to enter a meeting of the Committee of 101. The group had convened to discuss taking action against one of Smith's men, who had stolen a sack of gold from a local miner. At the entrance to the meeting, Smith began arguing with the guard and a fight escalated. Shots rang out from both sides. Smith died from a bullet to the heart on July 8, 1898, and was buried in Skagway.

Leaders, Ranchers, Settlers, and Other Colorful Characters

Black Kettle

Black Kettle, or Moketaveto, was born in the Black Hills of South Dakota in 1803. Details of his life are not well documented, but it is known that he moved to Colorado in 1832 and joined the Southern Cheyenne. By 1854, he served as a chief on the Council of Forty-Four, the Cheyenne's governing body. Before Black Kettle became chief, the Cheyenne had signed the 1851 Treaty of Fort Laramie, which granted them a wide swath of territory. However, the 1859 Pikes Peak gold rush brought numerous prospectors and settlers through Cheyenne lands, disrupting their traditional hunting grounds.

The U.S. government, acceding to pressure from the settlers, persuaded Black Kettle and his tribe, as well as the Arapaho, to sign the 1861 Treaty of Fort Wise, in which the tribes

Top row: White Antelope, Bull Bear, Neva; Bottom row: Bosse, Left Hand, White Wolf, Black Kettle; Chiefs of Arapahoe, Sioux, Cheyenne, and Kiowa tribes, circa 1865

relinquished to the government much of the land granted to them in the earlier Treaty of Fort Laramie. The land left to them was in eastern Colorado between the Arkansas River and Sand Creek. Black Kettle feared that if his tribe did not agree to the treaty provisions, they would receive even less favorable terms. He tried hard to keep the peace between his tribe and the white settlers, but some Cheyenne braves refused to stay on the reservation, as the land could not provide enough sustenance for those living there.

Some of the Cheyenne joined with Kiowa and Arapaho warriors to attack new settlements. These attacks and counterattacks escalated into the Cheyenne-Arapaho War. One of the greatest atrocities in this conflict occurred when John M. Chivington led the 1st Regiment of Colorado Volunteers in a massacre of Black Kettle's people at Sand Creek. Black Kettle had believed he was under government protection at the Sand Creek Reservation and was flying a flag of peace, yet the Cheyenne were attacked regardless, and more than 200 were killed.

Even after the Sand Creek Massacre, Black Kettle counseled peace. He signed a new treaty relocating the Cheyenne to a reservation in southwestern Kansas. Many braves refused to follow; some joined the Northern Cheyenne, while others banded together under Cheyenne warrior Roman Nose to defend and continue to attack the white settlements popping up on their traditional land. Not long after the Cheyenne under Black Kettle reached Kansas, the government sought to move them again. Under the Medicine Lodge Treaty of 1867, the government promised the Cheyenne annual provisions if they would agree to move to reservation land in present-day Oklahoma. Black Kettle was again among the leaders who signed the treaty.

The new treaty caused more braves to join Roman Nose's band of rebels, which further enraged the government. General Philip H. Sheridan was authorized to lead a campaign against Cheyenne settlements. In 1868, it was George Armstrong Custer who attacked Black Kettle's peaceful settlement on the Washita River, an Indian Reservation in Oklahoma. Tragically, Black Kettle and his wife, along with about 150 others, died in the attack. He is remembered today for his ex-

traordinary efforts to maintain a way of life for his people while living in peace with white settlers. Black Kettle is buried in Colony Indian Cemetery in Colony, Oklahoma.

Margaret Tobin Brown aka "Molly Brown"

Born on July 19, 1870, Margaret Tobin was one of six children. Her father insisted that his children be educated, and Margaret attended school until about the age of 13. Upon turning 18, she joined her brother in Leadville, Colorado. Although Margaret had intended to marry a rich man in order to help her family, in Leadville she met and fell in love with James Joseph ("J.J.") Brown. The two were married in 1886.

After the marriage, the couple lived in a small cabin near the mines. J.J was in charge of operations for the Ibex Company and became exceed-

Molly Brown in 1927

ingly wealthy when a rich vein of gold was discovered in the Little Johnny Mine. The vein of gold was said to be so wide and pure that it was deemed the world's richest gold strike.

Both before and after acquiring riches, Margaret occupied herself with philanthropic activities. She also became a strong advocate for women's rights and helped establish the Colorado chapter of the National American Women's Suffrage Association. In 1894, Margaret and J.J. moved to Denver, where Margaret continued to pursue her causes. The same year, she joined the Denver Woman's Club, which sought to improve women's daily lives through education. Margaret believed strongly in education, and she herself attended the Carnegie Institute in New York in 1901 as one of its first students. She enriched her education by traveling the world and learning to speak five languages.

Putting her belief in women's rights to practice, Margaret ran for Congress in 1909 and 1914. Although not elected, she helped revolutionize the justice system. Margaret worked with Denver judge Ben Lindsey to help create the nation's first juvenile court system. In addition to her reformist zeal, Margaret was quite a successful fundraiser. She held numerous events to raise money for building Denver's Cathedral of the Immaculate Conception, which was completed in 1912.

Margaret thoroughly enjoyed life as a philanthropist and socialite; however, J.J. did not appreciate the spotlight, and the couple formally separated in 1909. Margaret continued to travel extensively after her separation. It was during one of her trips to Europe, upon hearing of her grandson's illness, that she booked passage on the first ship returning to the United States, the *RMS Titanic*.

When the *Titanic* began sinking after hitting an iceberg, Margaret helped fellow passengers onto lifeboats until someone finally forced her into one. Once aboard the rescue boat *Carpathia*, Margaret made lists of survivors, served as an interpreter, and collected funds for those who lost everything. Back on shore, when asked about her survival, she attributed it to "typical Brown luck . . . we're unsinkable." In the 1960s, a stage musical and popular movie called *The Unsinkable Molly Brown* made Margaret famous for another generation. The 1997 blockbuster movie *Titanic* again brought Molly Brown to the attention of the public.

Surviving the *Titanic* disaster, Margaret continued her humanitarian pursuits. She organized nurses for the Red Cross of Colorado to help at the frontlines of the Mexican-American War. Immediately following the Ludlow Massacre of 1914, during which the Colorado National Guard opened fire on a tent colony of striking coal miners and their families, killing 25, Margaret sent medical assistance and supplies to the area. When World War II erupted in Europe, Margaret traveled to France and helped form the American Committee for Devastated France. For her help, Margaret was awarded the French Legion of Honor.

Later in her life, Margaret adopted many conservation projects. In Denver she helped preserve the home of children's poet Eugene Field. Denver's Art Museum and the Museum of Natural History also benefited from Margaret's generosity when she donated to the organizations a number of artifacts she had purchased during her travels around Europe.

Margaret died on October 26, 1932, from a brain tumor. Although she had been wealthy most of her life, she died during the Great Depression, and her heirs were only able to get $5,000 for the sale of her grand Denver home. The mansion passed through several owners until Historic Denver, Inc., purchased it in 1970. Fittingly, the house has been restored to its former splendor. It now houses the Molly Brown House Museum and is a popular tourist attraction located in the prestigious Capitol Hill neighborhood of Denver.

John M. Chivington

John M. Chivington was born in Lebanon, Ohio, in 1821. He became an ordained Methodist minister in 1844 and began preaching throughout the Midwest, accepting assignments from the church in Illinois in 1848 and then in Missouri the following year.

In 1856, he encountered trouble within his congregation in Missouri because of his outspoken opinions against slavery and succession. In an intimidating letter, Confederate-minded church members instructed Chivington to leave the church. The group planned to tar and feather the minister if he showed up the following Sunday. Undeterred, Chivington allegedly took his place at the head of the church that Sunday, armed not only with his Bible but also two pistols. He announced, "By the grace of God and these two revolvers, I am going to preach here today." It was from these events that he became known as the "Fighting Parson."

The church relocated Chivington to Omaha, Nebraska, as a result of the episode. Assigned to the lead position of the Rocky Mountain District of the Methodist Church, he settled in Denver in 1860 to establish a new church. While in Colorado, Chivington also traveled to the nearby mining camps where he would preach to residents.

When the Civil War began, Chivington was offered a chaplaincy by Colorado's territorial governor, William Gilpin, but he declined, choosing instead to fight in the 1st Colorado Volunteers. Chivington led a surprise attack against the rear guard of the Confederate forces at La Glorieta Pass in New Mexico. The Confederates were forced to retreat from the area and Chivington became something of a hero.

John Chivington

Chivington spent the remainder of his military career fighting Indians. On November 29, 1864, Chivington led the 3rd Colorado Volunteers in a brutal attack against a peaceful camp of Cheyenne and Arapaho Indians in southeastern Colorado, which became known as the Sand Creek Massacre. Chivington and his men slaughtered more than 200 Indians and further escalated tensions between Indians and settlers.

News of the Sand Creek Massacre was met with both praise and condemnation and prompted military and congressional inquiries into Chivington's actions. Congress issued a scathing condemnation of Chivington, yet he had resigned from the military soon after the massacre, putting himself out of reach of military justice. Although Chivington escaped punishment, the scandal of the Sand Creek Massacre plagued him for the rest of his life.

In 1865, he relocated to Nebraska, where he tried his hand unsuccessfully for several years in freight hauling. Leaving Nebraska, he made a brief stop in California and then went back to Ohio where he became a farmer and editor of a local newspaper. It was in Ohio that Chivington campaigned for a seat in state government, but the sordid events of the Sand Creek Massacre forced his withdrawal from the race and from the state. He took a job as a deputy sheriff in Denver where he died of cancer in 1892.

William Frederick "Buffalo Bill" Cody

William Frederick Cody was born in 1846 in Iowa, though his family relocated to Kansas after the death of his older brother when Cody was seven. At the age of 11, Cody left home and began a series of jobs that would lead him across the West and back numerous times. He started herding cattle but moved on to fur trapping and gold mining. News of the Pikes Peak gold rush gave Cody gold fever, and he went to Colorado in 1858 to prospect. He worked the goldfields of Black Hawk but achieved little for his efforts.

Buffalo Bill Cody

Unsuccessful at prospecting, Cody joined the Pony Express from 1860 to 1861. He stayed with the Pony Express until his mother's illness drew him back to Kansas. With the eruption of the Civil War, Cody joined multiple irregular militias before enlisting with the Union Army's 7th Kansas Volunteer Cavalry in 1864. He fought with the Union Army for the remainder of the war. After being mustered out of the Army in 1865, Cody served as a scout for hire for such notable U.S. Army officers as William Tecumseh Sherman, Philip H. Sheridan, and George Armstrong Custer. Cody received his nickname "Buffalo Bill" around 1867 while displaying his prodigious hunting skills to a group of army officers. Based on his reputation, the Union Pacific Railroad hired Cody to provide buffalo for its construction crews. According to legend, Cody killed over 4,000 buffalo for the company.

Cody received great praise for his participation in the 1869 Battle of Summit Springs. The skirmish occurred between the U.S. Army and a group of Cheyenne Dog Soldiers under the leadership of Tall Bull. Cody is generally credited with killing Tall Bull, helping to ensure a victory for the U.S. Army. In one year, Cody had participated in more Indian fights than any other serviceman at the time. Cody met dime novel author E.Z.C. Judson (Ned Buntline) in 1869, and Buntline went on to write a series for the *New York Weekly* based on Cody's life— "Buffalo Bill, King of the Border Men." Cody became even more well known when he began guiding hunting expeditions on the plains. One of these parties included General Philip H. Sheridan and Grand Duke Alexis of Russia.

On December 17, 1872, Cody starred in a drama by Buntline entitled *The Scouts of the Plains*, which kick-started his career as a showman. Soon after, he organized his own troupe of actors, the Buffalo Bill Combination, which included his friends "Texas Jack" Omohundro and "Wild Bill" Hickok. For the next 10 years, Cody spent his summers as a scout and the remainder of his time touring with his show.

Cody conceived his show, "Buffalo Bill's Wild West," in 1882, and over the next 20 years he crisscrossed the country, performing in Colorado on at least 35 occasions. Buffalo Bill's Wild West show featured horse parades, races, shooting exhibitions, and re-enactments. A number of famous figures from the West participated in the show, including Annie Oakley and Sitting Bull. Despite his reputation as a rough frontiersman, Cody believed in equal rights for woman and paid them the same amount as he paid men. He also had a strong respect for Indians and used his show to educate people about Indian culture. Cody was even made a "special Indian agent" by the government to properly allow Indians to participate in his show.

At its peak, Buffalo Bill's Wild West included more than 1,200 performers. In 1887, Cody traveled with his show to London to perform for Queen Victoria's Golden Jubilee. Two years later, he and his troupe returned to Europe for a continental tour. In 1893, Cody took his show to the Chicago World's Columbian Exposition. Although the fair organizers turned down Cody's request to perform, he set up his show near the perimeter of the exposition and enjoyed great crowds. Apart from helping to develop Wyoming's Big Horn Basin and founding the town of Cody, Wyoming, few of Cody's investments outside of his show met with success.

In 1912, Cody asked for and received a $20,000 loan from Denver businessman Harry Tammen to continue performing and touring. The following year at a Denver staging of Buffalo Bill's Wild West, Tammen demanded payment for the balance of the loan. Cody was unable to repay the loan, so the businessman sold off the show's assets at auction. Tammen then required Cody to work in his circus to pay off his debt.

Leaving Tammen's circus in 1915, Cody performed in various Wild West shows until his death in 1917. While in Denver visiting his sister, he died of kidney failure, and at his request was buried just outside of Golden, Colorado, on Lookout Mountain overlooking the Rocky Mountains and the Great Plains. In 1921, Cody's close friend Johnny Baker founded the Buffalo Bill Memorial Museum near his grave. Since the memorial opened its doors, millions have visited the iconic Buffalo Bill's grave. The site continues to be a noteworthy tourist attraction to this day.

Father Dyer

Reverend John L. Dyer preached from the pulpit of various Midwestern churches. He was a 40-year-old widower when John M. Chivington, a Methodist minister from Kansas, recruited him to carry the word of God to men in the Colorado gold rush.

In 1860, with only $15 in his pockets, determined Father Dyer departed on his journey to preach the gospel to the prospectors and miners in Colorado's mountain camps. He made his way on foot, as money was too dear to spend on luxuries such as a horse or wagon. He stopped wherever he could to preach and pass the hat to gatherings of settlers.

When Father Dyer neared Denver, it is rumored that someone stole his last $2; but he philosophized that he was no worse off than if someone had stolen his last $500.

If Father Dyer didn't have a building to speak in, he

Father Dyer

had the congregation sit outside on logs. He occasionally held services in saloons, requesting only that alcoholic beverages be removed from the shelves before the service began. Dyer's fire-and-brimstone approach to preaching appealed to the miners; he fired up his congregations with fear and wonderment.

Father Dyer found that donations were sometimes hard to come by. After one of his 500-mile, two-month-long treks, he collected a measly total of only $43. Although Dyer was prepared to be poor, since poverty went with preaching, he somehow had to keep himself alive while carrying forth the word. He fortified his existence by delivering mail, selling newspapers, and prospecting part-time.

Dyer was a tough man, not to be deterred from his calling by Colorado's severe winters. He made ski-snowshoes 11 feet long to enable him to trek with the mail across the snowdrifts. He became known as the Snowshoe Itinerant. Dyer nearly lost his life more than once from being caught in blizzards.

On one of his trips over Boreas Pass to Breckenridge in 1880, Father Dyer was looking downward rather than heavenward when he discovered gold. It made possible the first church in Breckenridge. Dyer built a cabin near the Warrior's Mark Mine, and the camp became known as Dyersville. Located at the top of Indiana Gulch, neither the camp of Dyersville nor the mine ever amounted to much. Father Dyer stayed in Dyersville for just a short time before moving back to Breckenridge, as by then he was nearly 70 and did not have the energy he once had.

John Evans

John Evans was born in Waynesville, Ohio, in 1814. He attended medical school at Cincinnati College and practiced medicine throughout the Midwest. Settling in Chicago, Evans helped found Mercy Hospital and the Illinois Medical Society. He also was one of the principal founders of Northwestern University in Evanstown, Illinois; the college town located north of Chicago is named in his honor.

Evans instructed at Rush Medical College in Chicago from 1845 to 1857 but made his fortune investing in Chicago real estate and railroads. His wealth also brought political influence. Gilpin sat on the Chicago City Council and was instrumental in founding the Illinois Republican Party, through which he met and became friends with Abraham Lincoln.

Lincoln appointed Evans governor of the Colorado Territory in

John Evans

1862. As governor, Evans was a great proponent of the railroads. During his term, the territorial legislature incorporated the Colorado & Pacific Wagon, Telegraph and Railroad Company in order to help attract investment funds to Colorado. With Governor Evans's support, Congress passed a revised Pacific Railroad Bill in 1864, which would create the first transcontinental railroad. This same year, Congress passed legislation providing for a Colorado state government. Evans oversaw the development of the constitution, but when it was put to a vote, the public decided against statehood.

Despite his achievements, Evans's tenure was tainted by scandal stemming from the massacre of Indians at Sand Creek in 1864. Although Evans was the superintendent of Indian affairs, it is argued that he sanctioned the attack by the Colorado militia on the peaceful Cheyenne at Sand Creek. The massacre prompted a congressional investigation and resulted in Evans losing his appointment as governor.

After his tenure as governor, Evans remained influential in the settlement and development of Denver. When the Union Pacific Railroad bypassed Denver for Cheyenne, Wyoming, Evans lobbied and helped raise money to build the Denver Pacific Railroad, which linked Denver to the transcontinental Union Pacific line. He also funded several other railroad lines, helping to make Denver a major railway hub in the West. Finally, he helped found the Colorado Seminary in 1864, which would later become the University of Denver.

In 1895, on Evans's 81st birthday, the Colorado Legislature named one of the 14,000-foot peaks on the Front Range "Mount Evans" in honor of the former governor. Established in 1867, the town of Evans, Colorado, also bears the name of the Colorado statesman and businessman. Evans died on July 7, 1897, and is buried in Denver's Riverside Cemetery.

Barney Ford

Although Barney Ford was born a slave on January 22, 1822, in Virginia, he would become an incredible success and notable Denver pioneer. He grew up working on a plantation in South Carolina but escaped north with help from the Underground Railroad. When he reached Chicago, he learned the barber's trade and helped other slaves escape through the Underground Railroad. In 1849, Barney married Julia Lyoni, who helped him choose his last name, as slaves usually had only the last name of their master. Barney chose the name Ford after the train the Lancelot Ford.

In 1851, the Fords left Chicago, hoping to strike gold in California. While en route, their ship stopped at the port of Greytown in Nicaragua, and they decided to stay. There they opened the United States Hotel but were forced to leave a few years later due to the threat of war. Ford's hotel gave him a taste of riches and he became determined to make his fortune in the West.

Ford arrived in Breckenridge, Colorado, in 1860 and attempted gold mining. As an African American, he could not stake his own claim. Resolved, he made an arrangement with a local lawyer to place a claim in the lawyer's name and share profits. The lawyer betrayed Ford who then lost his claim. Ford subsequently left Breckenridge and opened a barbershop in Denver, which burned down along with a large percentage of the city in the 1863 fire. Determined to succeed, Ford secured a loan from a local banker and built People's Restaurant. His restaurant was wildly successful; with the profits, he built the Inter Ocean Hotel in downtown Denver.

After the Civil War, Ford turned his attention to fighting for the rights of his fellow African Americans. Ford's success in business earned him a degree of political influence, which he used to convince Congress to reject Colorado's 1865 bid for statehood. Ford refused to support a state constitution that did not grant African Americans the right to vote. He helped ensure that Colorado would allow all males the right to vote.

Ford was also notable as the first African American to sit on a grand jury in Colorado. In addition to demanding political rights, Ford worked to help provide African Americans with practical tools for success. Ford had taught himself to read and write, and in Denver he started programs to educate freed slaves.

In 1880, after some financial difficulty, Ford moved back to Breckenridge, where he opened Ford's Chop House. He rebuilt his fortune through mining investments and his restaurants, Ford's Chop House and the Oyster Ocean, a Denver restaurant he had purchased. In 1882, Ford built a large home in downtown Breckenridge, which stands as a historical landmark today. Ford and his wife moved back to Denver in their old age, and Ford became one of the few African American millionaires of the time.

Ford died in 1902 a highly respected citizen and businessman. *The Denver Post* wrote of him, "Barney Ford was the most noted caterer and restaurateur in the Rocky Mountain region, respected by everyone and patronized by the best people." He earned the title the "Black Baron of Colorado."

William Gilpin

Born in 1815 to wealthy Quaker parents, William Gilpin was a visionary who believed in American expansion westward. Gilpin graduated from the University of Pennsylvania in 1833 and briefly attended West Point. During the Seminole War, Gilpin was sent to recruit troops in Missouri and there developed an interest in politics and the West.

Gilpin joined John Frémont on his western expedition of 1843, which he left to visit Fort Vancouver, Oregon. Gilpin helped settlers there establish a government and draft a petition to Congress for support. Reporting to Congress, Gilpin emphasized the need for western settlement and for a reliable means of transcontinental transportation. He became an adviser to the powerful statesmen Thomas Hart Benton, James Buchanan, and James Polk.

During the Mexican-American War in 1847, Major Gilpin organized a battalion of soldiers in the fight for New Mexico, leading American forces to a number of victories. When the Mexicans conceded defeat, Gilpin was discharged from the army and re-

William Gilpin

turned to Missouri. There he commanded a volunteer force organized to protect the Santa Fe Trail from Indian attacks.

Over the years, Gilpin frequently wrote and spoke about the West. He had a theory that the temperate zone surrounding the 40th parallel north nurtured civilizations and fostered wealth and progress. In 1859, he wrote a book entitled *The Central Gold Region*, in which he stated his belief that the Mississippi Valley would serve as the center of future civilization and that Denver would be the capital. His portrayals of the great abundance of the West drew many settlers to Colorado.

Because of his support for Abraham Lincoln and his familiarity with western affairs, the government appointed Gilpin governor of the Colorado Territory in 1861. His most important task was to ensure that Colorado remained loyal to the Union. In keeping with this goal, Gilpin built up the territory's military, forming the 1st Colorado Regiment of Volunteers. Although he recruited a number of talented officers, including Major John Chivington, Captain Edward Wynkoop, and Captain Samuel Cook, no federal money was forthcoming. To protect the Colorado Territory and surrounding locations from Confederate attacks, Gilpin decided to issue unauthorized drafts on the federal treasury to cover expenses.

When in 1862 Confederate troops threatened to invade New Mexico, Gilpin sent the Colorado Volunteers to help repel them. In the battle at Glorita Pass, the Volunteers won a significant victory against the Confederates. Although eventually honoring Gilpin's drafts on the treasury, the government initially refused to pay the debt and removed him as governor of the Colorado Territory in 1862.

After leaving office, Gilpin acquired a number of Mexican land grants. He made a considerable amount of money, but his business dealings tarnished his reputation. Gilpin remained interested in western development and railroads in particular. He wrote a book in 1890 called *The Cosmopolitan Railway: A Compacting and Fusing Together All the World's Continents*. In it he foresaw America as a world leader, connected by a system of rail lines.

Colorado's preeminent orator (or to some the preeminent windbag), William Gilpin died suddenly in 1894 in a carriage accident. He is buried in Wheat Ridge, at Mount Olivet Cemetery.

Alice Ivers aka "Poker Alice"

Born in England in 1851, Alice Ivers and her family moved to Virginia when Alice was in her late teens. The Ivers later moved to Colorado, where Alice married a mining engineer named Frank Duffield. The couple moved to Leadville where they would live for five years. During their marriage, Alice learned to play cards by observing Frank play card games with his friends. After a mine explosion killed Frank, Alice took up playing poker to earn money. She played well and soon earned the nickname "Poker Alice."

Alice moved frequently, stopping to play in the gambling halls of Colorado boomtowns such as Georgetown, Central City, and Creede. She was a fashionable and well-dressed woman, but she always kept her gun within reach. When she reputedly won big in Silver City, New Mexico, Alice traveled to New York City to spend her winnings. But she was soon

Poker Alice

lured back west by the siren song of the gambling tables.

In Deadwood, South Dakota, Alice worked as a dealer in the saloon Bedrock Tom. There she met Warren Tubbs who became her second husband. Together they had seven children, and for a time Alice stayed away from the gambling halls. After her husband died of pneumonia in 1910, Alice returned to gambling. She supposedly got back in the game in order to recover her wedding ring, which she had pawned to pay for her husband's funeral.

Not long after her husband's death, Alice married George Huckert who worked on her homestead while Alice gambled. At this time, Alice bought an old home on Bear Butte Creek near Sturgis, South Dakota, to use as a brothel and gambling house. The story goes that Alice asked the bank for a loan of $2,000, which she promised to repay in two years. When she returned a year later and paid the whole amount, she said: "Well, it's this way. I knew the Grand Army of the Republic was having an encampment here in Sturgis. And I knew that the state Elks convention would be here, too. But I plumb forgot about all those Methodist preachers coming to town for a conference."

Alice was never a prostitute herself, but because she operated a brothel, she was in and out of trouble with the law for the remainder of her life. In 1913, a serious incident occurred when Alice fired shots to quiet some unruly soldiers. In doing so she killed a man. At her trial she was acquitted of the crime, which was ruled an accidental death.

For the last 20 years of her life, Alice continued to gamble in the nearby town of Deadwood, with her signature cigar in her mouth. She died on February 27, 1930, from a gall bladder operation. A Sturgis businessman purchased her brothel and converted it into a bed-and-breakfast.

Nathan C. Meeker

Nathan C. Meeker was born on January 12, 1817, in Euclid, Ohio. In the 1860s, he served as the agricultural editor for the *New York Tribune*, which was published by Horace Greeley. In 1869, Meeker wrote an article that sought volunteers to move to the western frontier in the Colorado Territory to form a utopian community of "high moral standards." Although Meeker did not expect many replies, he received thousands. He selected about 700 people from the replies and offered them the opportunity to purchase shares in the venture. He used the capital he raised to buy land.

The group of settlers, known as the Union Colony, headed west in the spring of 1870 to begin their new community. They named their town Greeley, in honor of Meeker's former publisher, who had helped fund the experiment. The year

Meeker arrived, he started up a newspaper called *The Greeley Tribune*, which is still published today. The colony prospered and was influential in settling the region.

In 1878, the government appointed Meeker to serve as Indian agent for the White River Ute Reservation. Meeker did not have a great deal of experience dealing with Indians, and was convinced that the Ute should give up hunting for agriculture and the Christian religion. When Meeker plowed the grazing land used by Ute horses, a medicine man, Chief Johnson, attacked him. In response, federal officials sent troops to quell the Indians.

Despite warnings from the Ute to not enter their reservation land, the soldiers attacked. In what would become known as the Meeker Massacre of 1879, the Ute burned the Indian agency buildings, killed Meeker and the other white men, and took Meeker's daughters, his wife, and another woman into the mountains and held them captive for 23 days. Ute chief Ouray negotiated the release of the captives but could not prevent his people from losing their lands. The Indians were forced to withdraw to reservations in Utah and southwestern Colorado. The town of Meeker, Colorado, is named for the unfortunate Indian agent, and a historic marker just east of the town on Highway 64 marks the site of the massacre.

Chief Ouray

Chief Ouray was a peaceful man who led the Ute Indians during a time of great upheaval. He was born in Taos, New Mexico, in 1833. According to legend, meteors streaked across the sky on the night of his birth, a sign interpreted by the elders of good things to come. As a child he learned English and Spanish, and later in life the Ute and Apache languages.

When Ouray turned 18, he moved to Colorado to join his father, who was the leader of the Tabeguache Ute. Upon his father's death in 1860, Ouray became chief. He assumed the mantle at a time of increasing conflict between Indians and white settlers. Chief Ouray desired peace, and he became an effective negotiator by using his mastry of multiple languages.

Chief Ouray in 1877

In 1873, along with other Ute leaders, Ouray signed the Brunot Treaty with the U.S. government. The treaty, which the Ute signed under protest, required the Indians to relinquish part of the land they had received in an earlier treaty. When Colorado achieved statehood in 1876, the miners and settlers encroached further and sought to have the treaties renegotiated. The political slogan became "The Ute Must Go."

Chief Ouray recognized the futility of resisting white expansion but was unable to control all the bands of Ute.

The White River Ute especially resented the Brunot Treaty. Rebelling against Indian agent Nathan Meeker's attempts to convert the Indians into an agricultural people, the White River Ute attacked and killed a group of men including Meeker at the White River Indian Agency in 1879. The Indians also kidnapped Meeker's daughters and wife. The Meeker Massacre evolved into a full-blown conflict between the Ute and U.S. government soldiers.

Ouray acted swiftly to negotiate the release of the kidnapped women, but the political storm that developed could not save the Ute from losing more land. Weeks of testimony in Washington before congressional committees ensued, the result of which was the Washington Treaty, signed in 1880 by Chiefs Ouray, Shavano, and Antero, as well as other Indian leaders. It was necessary for three-quarters of all Ute males to sign this treaty for it to become effective. Before all the signatures were obtained, Ouray died in August 1880 at the age of 46. The town of Ouray, Colorado, is named in his honor.

Annabelle Stark

Annabelle Stark who grew up in Salida, Colorado, was a college-educated woman with beauty, charm, and a flair for fashion.

Annabelle's mother had been caring for Annabelle's two brothers in St. Elmo; after her mother's death, Annabelle moved there to cook and care for her brothers.

Annabelle was a kind woman who took care of others when they were sick or feeble. She became known as the "Queen of St. Elmo" and was popular throughout the community.

One winter, snow blocked the Alpine Tunnel to such an extent that supplies could not get through to the town. Annabelle took it upon herself to bake bread for 12 consecutive days so that the crews clearing the tracks could have something to eat.

As St. Elmo went into decline and the population moved away, Annabelle and her brother Tony (the other brother had passed away years before) stayed on. Tony ran the post office until it was closed in 1952. As St. Elmo's last two residents, Annabelle and Tony rented out cabins and ran a general store

Annabelle Stark's store today

Annabelle Stark's store, circa 1930

that catered to tourists during the summers. At all other times of the year, Tony and Annabelle were isolated from the rest of the world.

In 1958, Annabelle was injured, and her brother had to seek help to save her life. When help arrived, they discovered both Stark siblings suffering from malnutrition and living in filth. Annabelle's once lovely hair was so dirty that it had to be cut to remove an ingrown ribbon.

Hundreds of newspapers, bones, decayed food, and clothing were piled throughout their home. There were even bags full of silver dollars.

Both Annabelle and Tony were hospitalized in Salida; Tony died within a few weeks, but Annabelle lingered on for several years and died in a Salida nursing home.

American Indian Tribes of Colorado

Prehistoric Settlement

Evidence of the first humans to inhabit North America nearly 12,000 years ago has been discovered in Colorado. Most scientists believe the first inhabitants were hunters who followed herds of large game from Asia into Alaska by way of the Bering Strait. Gradually over generations, the hunters migrated south into the Great Plains, some eventually reaching as far as Cape Horn in South America. The first people who settled within the boundaries of present-day Colorado were nomadic hunters known as Paleo-Indians. Primitive weapons are the only evidence of their existence. The early hunters sharpened stones into projectile points and fastened them to spears made from straightened willow or other tree branches.

Clues to the existence of the earliest group of settlers in North America, the Clovis people, have been discovered at several sites, including the Lamb Springs site near Littleton and the Dent site near Greeley. Researchers found spear points, or Clovis points, among the bones of several mammoths—large Ice Age relatives of the elephant. The hunters attached sharp points of 4 or 5 inches in length to the ends of spears to penetrate the thick skin of the huge animals.

The next classification of early hunters, Folsom people, appeared an estimated 1,000 years after the Clovis people. These hunters adapted to the warming climate, causing many species of Ice Age mammals in North America to become extinct, including the camel, horse, saber-toothed tiger, dire wolf, and mammoth. Findings at the Lindenmeier site northeast of Fort Collins, as well as several other sites throughout the state, suggest the Folsom people may not have been as nomadic as their ancestors. Tools, weapons, and numerous animal bones were uncovered at the Folsom campsite, which may have served as a base camp that the hunters returned to year after year.

Roughly 10,000 years ago, the Plano culture emerged and endured nearly 3,000 years. This group continued to refine their hunting tools and techniques. Evidence dating back to this period has been recovered from sites throughout the state and reveals that groups of as many as 150 hunters coordinated efforts to kill herds of up to 300 bison at a time. It is believed the group's diet also included a wider variety of vegetation such as roots, nuts, and berries.

In the Archaic period, which began an estimated 7,000 years ago, bands of several nuclear families moved seasonally to follow their food source—a wider variety of small game and plants than their ancestors' diets. They moved with herds of bison, deer, antelope, bighorn sheep, and elk, but they also hunted fox, rabbits, squirrels, birds, and reptiles. Additionally, they gathered roots and plants, including wild mustard, onions, serviceberries, plums, rice grass, chokecherries, wild buckwheat, and prickly pear cactus. Pemmican, a preserved food made from powdered meat and berries combined with animal fat, might have been first made during this period.

The greatest cultural advancements came from the Anasazi Indians of southwestern Colorado. This group of Indians is also known as Ancestral Puebloan because the Pueblo Indians are likely descendents of the group. During the period of the Anasazi, true farming began, which was likely learned from the tribes of Indians in Mexico. Early Anasazi are known as Basketmakers for their intricately crafted baskets. Later they discovered pottery making, often placing coils of clay inside a basket then smoothing the surface with a stone. Early agriculture consisted mainly of planting corn and squash with the aid of sharpened sticks, but later beans were grown. This dependable and stationary food supply allowed them to settle for the first time in more permanent structures instead of following moving herds of big game.

Around A.D. 700, the Basketmakers began living in villages, abandoning their pithouses for small groups of pueblos situated on tops of mesas. These square or rectangular structures, sometimes multilevel, were originally made of posts and adobe and were situated side-by-side facing south. Later the Indians used masonry to construct the flat-topped dwellings. Small villages also had a ceremonial chamber called a kiva. Similar to a pithouse, these gathering places were 7 or 8 feet below ground, circular, and 12 to 14 feet in diameter but could be larger depending on the population of the village.

For reasons that are uncertain—possibly because of a growing population, a need to preserve resources, or from a new threat, such as hostile tribes—around A.D. 1050, some Anasazi left their successful pueblo farming villages and established expansive and elaborate multistoried structures, often protected by overhangs, on the sheer sides of canyon walls. One of the most amazing and well-preserved examples of such a settlement is Cliff Palace in Mesa Verde National Park in southwest Colorado. The Classic Pueblo, or Cliff Dwelling, period was the pinnacle of Anasazi culture, during which they elaborately constructed and painted the walls of their homes and used the most advanced farming techniques in existence at the time. Likely as a result of an extended drought, the Anasazi left the cliff dwellings after only about 200 years, probably moving south and west along the Colorado River in search of more fertile lands and other natural resources, completely abandoning the cliff structures by the turn of the thirteenth century.

Indians Prior to the Establishment of the Colorado Territory

Sent north from Mexico on horseback in search of gold, the Spanish expedition led by Francisco Vasquez de Coronado in 1541 was the first group of Europeans to encounter the Indians of the Southwest. Although the sight of light-skinned men who were "seemingly attached to huge dogs" stunned the Indians, they were eager to obtain the animals when the Indians learned of their strength and potential usefulness. As the Spanish settled into New Spain, now Mexico, they began to explore farther north with the intent to colonize. In 1598, the first such group settled in New Mexico among the Pueblo Indians, establishing firm control over the tribe, which had originally resisted Christianity and the new European way of life.

This settlement allowed Colorado Indians to obtain new tools such as steel knives and other metal objects and farming equipment. The Spanish settlers would not trade or sell their livestock, so Colorado Indian tribes obtained horses by raiding Spanish settlements or by trading with the northern Mexican Indian tribes. The New Mexican colonists also captured and enslaved members of the Colorado Apache, Navajo, and Ute tribes. Eventually conflict over Spanish treatment of the Pueblo escalated into a revolt in which the tribe drove the Spanish out of New Mexico with the aid of the Colorado Navajo and Apache.

News of French encroachment from the east spurred the Spanish to re-establish control in the Southwest, and Don Diego de Vargas traveled north into Colorado, coming in contact with the Ute in the late 1600s. In 1706, Captain Juan de Ulibarri traveled through Colorado to present-day Pueblo where he discovered that the French had begun trading guns with the Pawnee and Apache. By 1750, the French had explored the Colorado plains, meeting and trading with the tribes they encountered along the way. Despite the trouble the French caused the Spanish, the Ute and the Spanish formed an alliance in 1750. The Ute readily aided subsequent Spanish expeditions traveling farther north and west into North America. In 1779, Governor Juan Bautista de Anza almost achieved a historic peace between the warring Comanche and Ute tribes, although it was not maintained.

In the eighteenth century, the eastern plains of what was to become Colorado were controlled by the Kiowa-Apache and, south of the Arkansas River, the Comanche. The vast area west of the Front Range was almost entirely controlled by various bands of Ute, who had lived there for approximately 10,000 years, longer than any other tribe lived within the future boundaries of Colorado.

Several small areas were controlled by other tribes. The area north of the Green River, in the northwest corner of the state, was the southeastern border of the Northern Shoshone lands. The Pawnee had a presence in the Platte River area, in the northeast portion of the state. The Jicarilla Apache lands extended up from New Mexico into the San Luis Valley.

Ute domination of the entire area west of the eastern slope of the Rockies did not alter in the period leading up to the establishment of the Colorado Territory in 1861. However, there were many migrations occurring on the eastern plains.

As white settlement pushed the eastern tribes west, the Apache, the Comanche, and the Pawnee were gradually dislodged from Colorado land and replaced by the Arapaho and Cheyenne.

The Arapaho had originally come from the Great Lakes region. Sometime in the early 1800s, pressure from the Sioux, who were in turn under pressure from their traditional enemies the Chippewa, created a general migration west. Concurrently, the Cheyenne, who in the late 1700s had gained use of horses and had become nomadic buffalo hunters, were also being pushed west from the Great Lakes region.

In the 1830s, the Cheyenne split into two groups. One group became allies of their former enemies, the Sioux. The other, the Southern Cheyenne, migrated to eastern Colorado and made war against the Kiowa-Apache and Comanches. The Arapaho had also split into two groups during the early 1800s, and the Southern Arapaho formed a loose alliance with the Southern Cheyenne. These allied tribes took over most of the eastern plains of Colorado.

Then, in 1840, the Cheyenne and Arapaho made a peace settlement with the Kiowa-Apache and Comanche, which meant that the Kiowa-Apache and Comanche were able to retain a presence in the southeast corner of the state, south of the Arkansas River.

The Arapaho and Cheyenne tribes would occasionally venture into the mountains to collect poles for their teepees or lodges; when deer, elk,

and buffalo became scarce in the mountain parks, the Ute would descend to the plains in search of further herds to hunt. All these tribes were great warriors, and there was constant tension and intermittent warring between the Ute and the alliance of the Cheyenne and Arapaho.

Wars and Treaties

In 1859, the Pikes Peak gold rush erupted, and thousands of white prospectors and settlers poured across Cheyenne and Arapaho territory. From his appointment in 1862, Governor John Evans sought to open up eastern Colorado to these white settlers; but the two tribes refused to sell their lands and move to reservations. Evans decided to force the issue through what became known as the Cheyenne-Arapaho War, or the Colorado War, of 1864–65.

The first shot in the war came when territorial military commander Colonel John Chivington launched a surprise attack against the Arapaho and Cheyenne camped at Sand Creek. The ensuing battle, which came to be known as the Sand Creek Massacre, left 200 Indians dead and many others wounded and mutilated; many women were raped. Only 10 soldiers lost their lives. In response, the Indians raided white settlements and twice attacked Julesburg. These attacks further fueled public support for a policy of extermination. After many more encounters, a treaty was negotiated in 1865; but the last battle on the Colorado plains was not fought until 1869.

During this period, the Ute maintained an uneasy peace with the whites who were slowly encroaching on their lands. The initial fur trapping and prospecting had not greatly affected the Ute way of life, but numerous gold discoveries from 1858 to 1860 led to greater incursions of white settlers into Ute territory.

In 1868, in response to the influx of miners and continued pressure for land to settle, a treaty known as the Kit Carson Treaty was negotiated by Chief Ouray, whereby the Ute gave up their land in the central Rockies and San Luis Valley and agreed to be settled on 16 million acres of land in western Colorado. Two agencies, the White River Agency and the Los Piños Agency, were established in 1869 to maintain the reservation and to distribute the promised $50,000 worth of supplies to the Ute every year.

Early prospecting efforts into the San Juan Mountains, the heartland of the Uncompahgre Ute, were slowed not so much by the Kit Carson Treaty or the fearsome reputation of the Ute, but by the lack of early success in finding gold and the intrusion of the Civil War.

However, in the early 1870s, pressure from mining increased dramatically. Discoveries at Henson and in the Animas River Val-

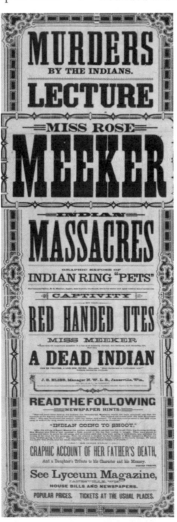

A poster advertising a lecture on the Meeker Massacre to be given by Rose Meeker, daughter of Nathan Meeker, circa 1880

A 1936 painting by Robert Lindneux depicting the Sand Creek Massacre

ley and prospecting in many other areas led to yet another treaty and further loss of land by the Ute. The Brunot Treaty, signed by Chief Ouray and other Ute chiefs in Washington in 1873, ceded the San Juan region to the U.S. government.

Indian Tribes

Ute

The longest permanent residents of Colorado, Ute bands have likely populated most of the mountainous area of the state for as long as 800 years. They generally occupied the region from the Front Range west to the Utah border and from the Yampa River in the north to the San Juan River in the south. The Grand River, Yampa, and Unitah bands inhabited the north of the future state of Colorado; the Tabeguache (Uncompahgre) in the central Western Slope; and the Capote, Mouache, and Weminuche in the southwestern territory. The Ute bands also lived in portions of western Utah and northern New Mexico. They might have migrated east from the deserts of California and Utah or from northern Mexico.

This group spoke a Uto-Aztecan language, similar to Aztec, Shoshone, and Comanche dialects. The eight major Ute bands lived as hunters and gatherers, rarely planting corn or beans. In the summers, they hunted bison, deer, elk, sheep, antelope, and jackrabbits with spears and the bow and arrow at higher

The two memorials placed at the site of the 1879 battle between the U.S. Army and the Ute after the Meeker Massacre honoring the soldiers and the Indians killed or injured

elevations. They gathered numerous varieties of plants including the yampa and the yucca, as well as seeds, berries, and nuts. In the winter they followed the animals south or into valleys. Deer meat was preferred, dried or freshly cooked, and the ribs were often roasted. Beaver tails, roasted in the ashes of cooking fires, were a delicacy. They also ate roasted, skinned rattlesnakes and sage hens and their eggs. Eagles, although not eaten, were valued for their feathers. The Ute lured the birds with deer meat to the top of a pit where the hunter was waiting to grab their legs, pluck their feathers, and set them free. Sometimes men were lowered by ropes to the nests to capture a baby eagle, which they would keep in a cage until it was large enough to harvest their feathers.

The early Ute lived in brush-covered structures but quickly began using the tepee, stick structures covered with treated leather that were more easily transported from place to place. They wore clothes made from the skins of the plentiful game in the Colorado Rockies and were known for making the softest buckskin in the surrounding region. Women generally wore a dress with knee-high leggings and moccasins and had two dresses, which they washed with soap rendered from the yucca plant. Men generally wore a breechcloth, leggings tied to a belt, moccasins, and a buckskin shirt. The shirts were tinted with smoke and often decorated with beads or enemy scalps. Children wore buckskin clothes in the fashion of the adults. Toddlers wore little clothing with the exception of a belt with a loop, which the women could grab in case of a sudden attack. Infants were swaddled in buckskin and laced into a cradleboard.

The Ute creation story recounts how Sinawaf, the Creator, put sticks in a bag, which Coyote, a trickster, opened and then people came out. People, all speaking different languages, came out wandering far and wide. Sinawaf had planned to distribute the people evenly so they wouldn't fight over land. The people who remained in the bag were the Ute, people superior to the ones who escaped. They believed that evil did not exist in the world, only conflict that could be overcome. Other beliefs included the curative value of hot springs and the religious properties of the dances such as the Bear Dance, a three- to four-day celebration of their survival of the harsh winter and a renewal of life.

After they acquired horses, nearly 30 years before other western Indian tribes, they became a fierce and much-feared tribe. They organized large bison hunting parties on the plains as well as raids, bringing back meat, stolen goods, and sometimes women of other tribes. These women taught them about the lifestyle of the Plains Indians. The tribe's access to horses, which allowed them more access to trade and speed and agility to raid other camps, along with the lush, native landscape, encouraged larger populations and a more structured social system than other tribes in the region.

Following the Meeker Massacre in 1879, 665 White River Ute were driven west to the Unitah Reservation in eastern Utah, and the government uprooted 1,360 Uncompahgre Ute and moved them to some acreage adjacent to the Unitah Reservation. The other bands, Mouache, Capote, and Weminuche, were moved to a strip of land on Colorado's southwestern border. Struggling to adapt to reservation life, several large groups of Ute fled the reservations to lands in western Colorado and South Dakota in an attempt to return to their previous hunting/herding way of life. Unsuccessful, they returned. Slowly reservation acreage dwindled due to the federal government's practice of allotment, and disease decimated the populations on each of the three Ute reservations. In more recent decades, the Ute have attempted numerous business ventures but have been unsuccessful. Currently the Ute derive minimal income from tourism and the energy industry through mineral extraction.

Apache

The term Apache refers to a large conglomerate of bands united by the Athapascan language. It is believed that this group migrated south from Canada, possibly sometime around 800 years ago. Some scholars believe part of the group migrated south along the west side of the Rocky Mountains and the other part on the east side of the range.

The bands that ranged over the territory of modern-day Colorado migrated south along the Front Range and include the Jicarilla Apache and the Kiowa Apache, both residents of Colorado Territory at one time. It is believed that for a time the Jicarilla Apache settled in the Platte and Arkansas River valleys in Colorado where they hunted game, gathered plants, and to a lesser extent farmed corn, squash, beans, and melons. While still preserving the fundamental culture of the Athapascan culture living in eastern Colorado Territory, they began to adopt some of the culture of the Plains Indians as well.

Early Spanish explorers were the first Europeans to come in contact with the Apache in the area of Colorado. In fact, the word Jicarilla is Spanish for "little basket," and the name was bestowed upon them for their superior basket-making techniques. As European exploration and settlement increased, the Apache acquired horses, becoming fierce hunters. When encroaching white settlement pushed eastern Indian tribes west, the Comanche defeated the Apache, forcing them south out of the present-day Colorado plains into present-day New Mexico. Arriving later than other Indian cultures in the area, they instantly gained a fearful reputation as fierce warriors and raiders.

The word Apache is itself derived from the Zuni word *apachu*, which means "enemy." The Apache call themselves N'de, Inde, or Dine, all of which translate to "the people." However, for a brief stint in U.S. history, the label Apache was used to describe almost any Indian who rode a horse, wore a breechcloth, and was hostile toward Americans. Apache raids struck terror in Pueblo Indians, such as the Zuni, and Europeans too would come to dread these deadly fighters. For centuries their presence constrained Spanish and Mexican expansion northward. European settlements would often be targeted for raids, and any punitive action attempted by organized armed forces was repulsed using guerrilla tactics.

Yet there was more to Apache culture than raiding and warfare. They developed well-defined social structures, with lineage traced through the mother, complete with musical entertainment and a complex mythology. The position of leadership in the tribes was not hereditary but rather determined by force of personality and experience. Customarily chiefs could compel their followers to action only in times of war.

The Apache were predominantly nonagricultural and relied on hunting (mainly deer and rabbit) and gathering for their subsistence, though some tribes did adopt seasonal farming practices. When food was scarce, as was often the case in the harsh climate of the American Southwest, bands resorted to raids on both European and neighboring Native American settlements.

Apache houses were usually domed huts known as wikiups. They consisted of pole frames covered with brush, grass, or reed mats, and often had a fire pit and smoke hole. The people generally dressed in deerskin, although they acquired cotton and wool clothes through trades and raids. Basket weaving among Apaches rose to quite an artful craft, producing various coiled shapes of intricate design. Interestingly, the Apache also invented a painted stringed instrument known as the Apache fiddle. Made from a yucca stalk, the sound box had a single string held onto a tuning fork that was played with a bow, not unlike that of a violin.

The Apache were also a deeply religious people. They believed in an array of gods, the most powerful being Ussen, the Giver of Life. Mountain spirits, or gaans, were also important, especially in the elaborate ceremonies presided over by shamans. The major ceremony of this tribal culture is the Sunrise Dance (Na'ii'es), held for Apache females in the summer months of the year following the girl's first menstruation. Attempts by Westerners to convert the Apache to Christianity have been largely unsuccessful.

The United States annexed Apache homelands in 1848 in accordance with the Treaty of Guadalupe Hidalgo and again through the Gadsden Purchase of 1853–54. Mistrust and betrayal between Indians and the hoards of white settlers following the allure of western mines soon sparked the Apache Wars. Apache chief Geronimo's uprising between 1881 and 1886 was the last sustained Indian resistance of its kind.

Today, the remaining Jicarilla Apache live in New Mexico on a reservation created by the U.S. government in 1887. They sell their native craft, in particular their handwoven baskets, to visitors. Although the Apache are widely known for their baskets, they also sell beadwork and clay pottery.

Portrait of a Jicarilla Apache man

Arapaho

Originally from the area of present-day northern Minnesota and members of the Algonquian Indians, the Arapaho tribe moved south in the early 1700s and settled areas in South Dakota, Nebraska, Wyoming, and Kansas. In the early 1800s, European settlement in the east began pushing Indian tribes west, and the Arapaho and Cheyenne drove the Apache, Comanche, and Pawnee off the plains of Colorado Territory.

The Arapaho had acquired horses from the neighboring Comanche and began to hunt buffalo. Living in easily transportable tepees made from buffalo hide to follow the hunt, they moved principally in bands that were flexible in composition. A hierarchy of men's lodges, or ceremonial societies, coordinated band cooperation, especially for military purposes. Men earned their way through seven lodges as they aged; members of the old men's lodge wielded the greatest authority.

The Arapaho refer to themselves as Inuna-ina, which translates to "our people." They believed in an overall creator known as Be He Teiht and used medicine bundles, such as special pipes or hoops, which they felt possessed magical or healing powers. The most sacred ceremony for the Arapaho was the Sun Dance, held each summer for about a week before the buffalo hunt. It was a time of sacrifice and thanksgiving, an event meant to emphasize the continuity between life and death and the interconnectedness of all things.

By the 1850s, the Arapaho bands had divided into two separate tribes: the Northern Arapaho who lived on the North Platte River in Wyoming, and the Southern Arapaho who lived on the South Platte River in Colorado. Around the same time, white settlers began to encroach upon Arapaho and Cheyenne land. The Arapaho, as well as the Cheyenne, signed the Treaty of Fort Laramie in 1851, in which the U.S. government designated the area between the North Platte and Arkansas Rivers in Colorado Arapaho and Cheyenne territory. The gold rush of 1859 soon brought prospectors into the area, disrupting the Arapaho way of life.

Several Arapaho and Cheyenne chiefs from the southern bands signed a treaty at Fort Wise, Kansas, in 1861, ceding the majority of Arapaho and Cheyenne lands to the U.S. government. Escalating tension between the Indians and American settlers resulted in the 1864 Sand Creek Massacre, during which peaceful Arapaho and Cheyenne were slaughtered on Sand Creek near Fort Lyon (about 20 miles northeast of the present-day town of Eads on Colorado's eastern plains). Following the massacre, infuriated Indians revolted against whites in the Cheyenne-Arapaho War of 1864–65. The Arapaho signed the Treaty of Medicine Lodge in 1867 and agreed to move to a new reservation between the Cimarron and Arkansas Rivers. Disagreeing with the settlement, Arapaho chiefs Tall Bull and Roman Nose and their followers joined with the Kiowa and Comanche on the warpath in 1868.

The Arapaho failed in their struggle for independence and in 1876 the Southern Arapaho, some 1,600 in all, settled in western Oklahoma on the Cheyenne-Arapaho Reservation. Today, approximately 7,000 Southern Arapaho live on the Cheyenne-Arapaho Reservation.

Comanche

Scholars believe that sometime during the 1600s the Comanche broke off from the Shoshone tribe in the area of what is today Wyoming and migrated south along the Front Range of the Colorado Rockies. Later during the 1600s, the tribe acquired the horse from the Spanish. The tribe hunted and raided on horseback over a sweeping territory that today includes northern Mexico, New Mexico, southeastern Colorado, southwestern Kansas, Oklahoma, and Texas.

Becoming skilled trainers and breeders after acquiring the horse, the Comanche developed techniques of communicating with their horses through touch and spoken commands. The tribe also realized the value of maintaining huge herds, which were frequently amassed by stealing horses in raids against settlers and other tribes. The tribe even tracked wild mustangs for use in developing their herds. In turn, they supplied horses to traders, settlers, and other Plains tribes throughout their huge territory, and this widespread practice provided the Comanche with a significant amount of wealth.

The Comanche name most likely derives from the Spanish corruption of the Ute word for Koh-mahts, translated as "enemy" or "those against us." The Comanche called themselves Nermernuh, meaning "the people." The Comanche did not have a single leader but a small council of leaders, which included a peace chief and a war chief. The war chief, who held authority only during times of conflict, was chosen for his bravery in combat. It is believed that the Comanche killed more whites than any other tribe in proportion to their numbers.

The tribe practiced polygamy, and men would commonly marry two or more sisters in a family. Men rode and hunted while women cooked meals, made tepees, and sewed clothing. Children were highly valued in Comanche society and were rarely punished. At the tender age of four or five years, Comanche boys and girls alike were taught to ride. Becoming skillful riders, young men learned horse-mounted warfare tactics such as pulling up a fallen compatriot while in motion, or leaning over to shoot arrows from beneath a horse's neck while at a full gallop. Girls even learned advanced riding skills and accompanied the men on antelope hunts. When ready to become a warrior, a young man would take part in an elaborate coming-of-age ceremony. Before a man could go on the warpath, he first

Arapaho lodge and squaws, circa 1870

Studio portrait of Comanche men, circa 1900

had to kill a buffalo on the hunt.

Buffalo were highly valued. On the Great Plains, the Comanche lived a nomadic, hunting lifestyle following buffalo herds great distances with the use of their horses. The meat constituted a large part of their diet, and skins from the animal were used to craft tepees and clothing. Additional products of the buffalo hunt were traded with neighboring tribes and, later, various European and American settlers. Settlers both valued the Comanche as traders and feared them as warriors.

In the early 1800s when Arapaho and Cheyenne were pushed into today's eastern Colorado, the Comanche migrated out of Colorado Territory to the southern plains and Texas. They fought aggressively to retain their independence throughout the 1800s, but the decimation of buffalo herds and encroachment of white settlers culminated in the Red River War of 1874–75 and the eventual surrender of the Comanche.

In 1906, the U.S. government allotted each Comanche 160 acres of land in eastern Oklahoma and opened remaining reservation lands to white settlement. The Comanche have managed to maintain a strong tribal identity and today number more than 10,000.

Shoshone

The Shoshone, or Shoshoni, tribe consisted of a number of groups united by a dialect of the Uto-Aztecan language. The tribe includes two distinct groups, the Western Shoshone and the Northern Shoshone. The western group ranged from what is today central Nevada east to northwestern Utah and north to central and western Idaho. The northern group inhabited areas of today's northwestern Colorado, western Wyoming, northeastern Utah, and eastern Idaho.

A nomadic people, the Shoshone moved from place to place, hunting buffalo. In the 1700s, they acquired horses from their relatives, the Comanche, making it much easier to track and hunt game. The tribe lived in tepees made of buffalo hides, which they could easily transport. Most of their clothing was made from hides, which the women would often decorate with beadwork, an art for which the Shoshone were well known.

Culturally and linguistically, the Shoshone were closely related to other tribes of the Great Basin, including the Western Shoshone, the Bannock Shoshone, the Ute, and the Paiute. Tribes extending from the Great Basin to Central Mexico used the same language. They also held similar religious beliefs and organizational structure to the tribes of the Great Basin. They shared the belief that the world is inhabited by benevolent spirits and treated with reverence their shamans, or medicine men. Tribes were typically arranged in bands around extended

Shoshone men, circa 1895

family, and these bands would come together at certain times, such as during winter and communal hunts.

The Shoshone maintained a friendly relationship with early settlers and explorers. Sacajawea, a Lamhi Shoshone woman, helped Meriwether Lewis and William Clark as an interpreter on their expedition through the Pacific Northwest around 1805. Shoshone chief Washakie was also regarded as helpful and a facilitator of peace by the U.S. government. Washakie signed two treaties with the government, in 1863 and in 1868, which set the boundaries of Shoshone land known today as the Wind River Reservation located in Wyoming. He was so respected by the U.S. government that at his death in 1900 he received a full military burial, the only known Native American to have received this honor.

The Shoshone managed to preserve most of their traditional lands and ceremonies. They continue to hold the annual Sun Dance on the Wind River Reservation, and each tribe hosts a powwow, featuring traditional dancing. Fort Washakie, earlier Camp Brown, serves as the headquarters for tribal government and is known as the final resting place for both Chief Washakie and Sacajawea. They share the Wind River Reservation with the Northern Arapaho.

Cheyenne

Originally from the area of the northern United States, what is present-day Minnesota, the Cheyenne moved southwest in the mid-eighteenth century after facing increasing territorial pressure from the neighboring Sioux tribe. By the mid-1800s, the Cheyenne had abandoned their agricultural and pottery traditions and adopted the nomadic culture of the Plains Indians. They replaced earth lodges with tepees and switched their diet from agricultural products to those that could be hunted and gathered. Their organizational structure differed from other Plains tribes in that the various Cheyenne bands were politically unified. They had a central governing body, the Council of Forty-Four, named for the number of chiefs on the council.

When the Cheyenne moved into the Black Hills of South Dakota, around the turn of the nineteenth century, they encountered the Arapaho tribe, who would become their close allies. When the two tribes moved together along the eastern

A Cheyenne man with his wife in 1905

had been guaranteed safety by the commander at the nearby Fort Cobb, but Custer attacked regardless, and the Cheyenne suffered more than 100 casualties. Although some of the more militant Cheyenne continued to fight, the resistance of the Southern Cheyenne largely crumbled after a number of united tribes lost the Red River War of 1874–1875.

The Southern Cheyenne live on a reservation in Oklahoma established in 1867. The Cheyenne were one of the last Native American nations to be subdued and placed on a reservation.

Kiowa

One of the most warlike of the Plains Indian tribes, the Kiowa migrated from the basin of the Missouri River to the Black Hills of South Dakota and Wyoming. Encounters with the Lakota Sioux and Cheyenne in this region forced the Kiowa farther south into the southern plains. In 1790, the Kiowa made an alliance and entered into a mutual defense pact with the Comanche, and later with the Plains Apache (also known as the Kiowa Apache). The groups roamed over the territory of today's southeastern Colorado.

The Kiowa were a nomadic tribe that hunted the buffalo. They organized themselves in extended family groups, or kindreds, and these extended families were further divided through a class system with ranks: rich, second best, poor, and worthless. Various kindreds would gather with lesser-ranked kindreds to form hunting bands, which would then be led by the most respected brother.

A very spiritual people, the Kiowa believed that a powerful, universal force was present in all things found in nature. The most powerful spirits were the sun, moon, stars, air, and buffalo. Few men could receive such power, but those who did became either great warriors or healers. Every year the Kiowa would hold the Sun Dance, a ceremony common among the Plains tribes.

The Kiowa fought alongside the Comanche, Cheyenne, and Arapaho against the white settlers in 1864 at Adobe Walls in Texas and the Red River War of 1874–1875 in Oklahoma, but were relocated to a reservation in southwestern Oklahoma by the Treaty of Medicine Lodge. They lived on this land with the Comanche until the Dawes Act of 1887, under which the U.S. government divided reservation land, allotting 160 acres to each Kiowa man. The population of Kiowa is currently around 10,000, and many still live on or near the old reservation land in Oklahoma. The Kiowa have a reputation for their fine artwork, and a number of tribal members continue to produce what is now referred to as Plains Indian ledger art.

Studio portrait of Kiowa men, circa 1900

slope of the Rocky Mountains, they created an alliance against the Kiowa and Comanche, although the two groups would later make a peace settlement in 1840.

The Cheyenne inhabited the territory of eastern Colorado until conflict with the encroaching white settlers and treaties with the U.S. government pushed them out. The increased traffic from white settlers was destroying their hunting grounds, but the Cheyenne, along with the Arapaho, agreed to the Fort Laramie Treaty of 1851 with the U.S. government, which designated certain lands to the Cheyenne. Not long after, gold was discovered and prospectors moved onto land that had been designated to the Cheyenne, which violated the treaty. Again in 1861 with the Treaty of Fort Wise, the Cheyenne agreed to move onto a small reservation between the Arkansas River and Sand Creek in the area of eastern Colorado. A number of warriors rejected the treaty, refusing to relinquish their traditional hunting grounds.

The relationship between Indians and settlers remained uneasy after the treaty. The Cheyenne-Arapaho War erupted in 1864–65 between the United States and a loose alliance of the Arapaho, Cheyenne, Kiowa, and Apache tribes. The Cheyenne bore the brunt of U.S. Army aggression during the war. In 1864, Colonel John Chivington, leading a division of the Colorado militia, attacked and destroyed the Cheyenne village on Sand Creek near Fort Lyon (about 20 miles northeast of the present-day town of Eads on Colorado's eastern plains), which was believed to be under Army protection. Between 150 and 200 Indians were killed and the event became known as the Sand Creek Massacre.

A similar incident occurred after the signing of the Medicine Lodge Treaty in 1867, in which the Cheyenne agreed to relocate to a reservation in Oklahoma. Again, certain members of the tribe continued to attack and raid. In retaliation, Colonel George Custer led the 7th Cavalry against Chief Black Kettle's encampment on the banks of the Washita River near present-day Cheyenne, Oklahoma, in 1868. This village

Events

Trapping, Trading, and the Mountain Men Era

Europeans dominated the North American fur trade well after the Revolutionary War ended in 1783. The British Hudson Bay Company controlled much of present-day Canada and the Pacific Northwest, while the Spanish operated in the modern-day South. Around the turn of the eighteenth century, Americans began to enter the fur trade in earnest. At the time, beaver was in the greatest demand because Europeans desired its fur for luxurious hats and coats.

Although individual trappers had ventured into the West before 1800, the fur trade did not penetrate west until the period around the 1803 Louisiana Purchase and the 1804–06 Lewis and Clark Expedition. Meriwether Lewis and William Clark's famous exploration of the West, which revealed faster and more profitable ways to transport furs overland, helped expand American interests in the fur trade while the British continued using waterways.

News of improved trade routes and discoveries of rich beaver country helped spark westward expansion. Men from the East started traveling west in hopes of making their fortune in the fur trade. American trading companies were also drawn to the wealth of the West. In 1807, Manuel Lisa built the first western trading post, Fort Raymond, in present-day Montana. The subsequent year, John Jacob Astor organized the powerful American Fur Company, which would come to dominate the fur trade. Because Astor wielded so much power, he was able to undermine the government-established factory system that helped regulate trade between Indian trappers and suppliers.

By 1810, competition for furs was increasing. Trappers hunted larger and larger territories for beaver, but trapping farther from supply centers and transportation lines increased the time to market. Expanding territories also meant that trappers crossed into hunting land unofficially occupied by rival companies or traditional Indian lands. Fur trapping and trading instigated the initial conflicts between Indians and Anglo-Americans. In addition to the increasing difficulty of trapping sought-after animals, the demand for furs dropped dramatically, as the Napoleonic wars destroyed much European wealth.

Despite the obstacles to trapping, a number of men still traveled westward to make their fortune in the fur business. One of the most prominent entrepreneurs was William H. Ashley. He became famous for popularizing the system of trade whereby trappers met annually at a "rendezvous," a designated location to trade their furs with suppliers. The first of these annual meetings took place on the Green River in 1825. The rendezvous system also helped to alleviate Indians' fear of losing their land, as trappers participating in this system were perpetually on the move.

Other trappers still profited from operating a trading post at a fixed location. The Bent Brothers operated Bent's Fort on the Arkansas River and built a strong trade network along the Santa Fe Trail. They maintained a virtual monopoly on the buffalo robe trade in the region. Antoine Robidoux built Fort Uncompahgre near present-day Delta, Colorado, and dominated trade in the Green River Valley.

A majority of mountain men who made their living trapping were explorers in their own right. They helped open the West and paved the way for settlement. Men like Jedediah Smith, John Frémont, Kit Carson, and James Bridger discovered useful trade and pioneer routes, as well as helped map the topography of the West.

Trappers often paved the way to settlement, which paradoxically made hunting for beaver more difficult. By the 1880s, beaver populations were on the decline and the fur trade slowly began to shift from beaver to buffalo. Although the fur trade was not a significant part of the American economy, it did have an influence on the emerging landscape of America by expanding settlement into the West. The monopolistic nature of the fur trade also foreshadowed the organization of other emerging American industries.

Colorado Territory/Statehood

Long occupied by Indian tribes such as the Ute, Arapaho, and Cheyenne, Colorado did not have permanent white settlement until around 1851 when New Mexico farmers moved north, settling in southeastern Colorado. White explorers had traveled through the region before this time. Zebulon Pike, for example, explored Colorado in 1806, and John Frémont extensively explored the area, creating maps that would later be used by thousands of settlers heading west. Traders and trappers also frequently roamed the region in search of beaver. Few of these people, however, settled permanently.

After initial settlement by New Mexican farmers, the population blossomed when the Pikes Peak gold rush brought tens of thousands of people to the goldfields of present-day Colorado. Far removed from the government of the Kansas and Nebraska territories, miners and settlers in the Pikes Peak area banded together to form their own government, which they called Jefferson Territory. This improvised government did not function well, but it was soon replaced in 1861 by an official, sanctioned government. Congress created the Colorado Territory, delineating it with the same borders Colorado has today. Congress fashioned the new territory from pieces of the Kansas, Utah, Nebraska, and New Mexico territories. Although Golden was named the original territorial capital, the phenomenal growth of Denver essentially made the city the de facto capital.

William Gilpin was appointed the first territorial governor. Gilpin's primary responsibility was to ensure that Colorado Territory remained in the Union, as the Civil War had recently erupted and Kansas had been deeply divided over the question of slavery. The Union also desired control of Colorado Territory so that mineral resources would benefit their cause. As a result, Gilpin formed a local volunteer military force to fight against the Confederates.

After the war, Union volunteers often served in state militias, which forced Indians from the territory. The second territorial governor, John Evans, was removed from his post because of his supposed endorsement of the Sand Creek Massacre, during which about 200 peaceful Cheyenne were murdered.

From the Civil War onward, Colorado's population greatly expanded, aided by improved transportation and the lure of gold and silver. However, the population could not agree on whether to become a state. The issue was debated for 15 years from the time Colorado became a territory. In 1864, national Republican leaders pushed the issue of statehood for Colorado, expecting to gain the newly formed state's electoral votes. Territorial voters turned down the offer of statehood.

Opinions began to change not long after when newspaperman William Newton Byers and politician Casimiro Barela made a convincing case for statehood. As a state, Colorado could receive government protection from Indians and more easily attract business to the state. By the time the settlers in the territory had organized their interests and applied for statehood in 1865, 1866, and 1868, the U.S. government was no longer interested.

National and local interests finally merged in 1876, and Colorado was granted statehood. Delegates began drafting a constitution in 1875. They failed to clarify the state's position on many divisive issues, including women's right to vote and government's role in business. The constitution's ambiguity made it more reasonable to voters, who overwhelmingly accepted it. President Ulysses S. Grant officially declared Colorado the 38th state in the Union on August 1, 1876. Although some Easterners resented the increasing prominence of the West, Coloradoans entered into statehood with a great deal of optimism, spurred by a booming economy and a burgeoning population.

The Mining Era

When news of gold discoveries in California spread throughout the nation in 1848–49 and caused a frenzied excitement over striking it rich, prospectors rushed west, some through the Rocky Mountains. Many who were unsuccessful in California remembered the rumors of gold in the Rockies and decided to test their luck in what would become Colorado Territory. William Green Russell was one such prospector whose miniscule gold-find in Dry Creek (in present-day Denver) prompted the Pikes Peak gold rush. News of this discovery spread, and by 1858 crowds of prospectors began arriving.

In 1859, rich gold strikes further west in the canyons and gulches around present-day Central City and Idaho Springs soon drained the newly settled towns on the plains as prospectors left to scour the mountains for gold. As miners flooded into Colorado Territory, so did support for the industry that helped develop long-term settlement. New communities that would become the cities of Loveland, Golden, Colorado Springs, and Cañon City sprang up with permanent buildings, schools, churches, newspapers, and even an organized baseball league.

As gold ore became increasingly more difficult to mine during the 1860s, silver began to gain prominence. News of silver discoveries was reported as early as 1859, and the ore

had been mined as a byproduct in the Central City area. Buzz over Nevada's Comstock Lode gave the idea of mining silver more relevance, but the lack of smelting methods made the process unprofitable. The lure of gold waiting to be found in the mountains was an idea too romantic for Colorado prospectors to abandon easily and the industry endured.

Through trial and error, practical smelting methods were developed and the silver boom arrived in Colorado in the 1870s. Initially, Georgetown was the center of silver mining, but Boulder County struck silver at the Caribou Mine near present-day Nederland. Leadville also became a hive of silver mining activity and eventually became the top producer of silver in the state.

Mining became the chief industry in Colorado late 1870s and 1880s. During this period, the Ute Indians were forced to move onto smaller and smaller reservations, and mining spread across the Continental Divide and into the San Juan Mountains in western Colorado. As the production from silver mines increased, the price of silver began to diminish. In 1892, silver began declining rapidly in value, which led to the silver panic of 1893.

The Silver Crash of 1893

In the eighteenth century, currencies were typically backed by one or more precious metals. All major countries chose either gold or silver, or a combination of the two, as the basis of their currency. At the time, it was a major political issue both in Europe and in the United States; most countries changed their policy more than once during the course of the 1700s and 1800s.

Adherents of the system believed that it stabilized not only the prices of gold and silver but also the value of all commodities, thereby simplifying foreign exchange. Most economists came to oppose the practice.

In 1792, Secretary of the Treasury Alexander Hamilton led the U.S. Congress to adopt a bimetallic monetary standard, meaning that both gold and silver were used to back the currency. Silver dollars contained 371.25 grains, and gold dollars 24.75 grains—a 15:1 ratio.

One of the difficulties of this system is that as the relative market value of gold or silver changes, one coin becomes more valuable than the other; the more-valuable coin's circulation decreases as people melt it down and sell the metal and use the less-valuable coin for commerce. A metal's market value can change because of major discoveries of one of the metals, or because of one nation's changing its policy about the value of a metal backing its currency.

In 1834, the United States was forced to change the gold content of its coins, because France changed its policy. The U.S. ratio of silver to gold was increased to 16:1.

The Californian and Australian gold rushes in 1849 and 1850 resulted in the relative price of gold declining. The value of the silver in silver dollars became greater than the face value of the coins, resulting in widespread melting down of silver dollars. During the course of the Civil War, silver dollars disappeared from circulation; and in 1873, the United States moved to a gold standard, eliminating the free coinage of silver.

Subsequently, the large discoveries of silver in Colorado led to the price of silver falling below the old mint price and created a political clamor for the government to revert to the old policy that supported the silver price. In 1878, Congress responded by reintroducing the minting of silver dollars but restricted silver purchases to between $2 million and $4 million per month. This was insufficient to quiet the clamor, and in 1890 Congress passed the Sherman Silver Purchase Act to provide for the purchase of $4.5 million per month. This resulted in the immediate increase in the price of silver from 84¢ to $1.50 per ounce, which had a dramatic effect on the silver miners in Colorado; times were booming.

However, the act caused the U.S. Treasury to start stocking silver bullion, since the value of silver decreased as increasing amounts were discovered. The government's stockpiling led to a lack of confidence in the currency and caused speculators to hoard gold, thus depleting U.S. reserves.

On August 7, 1893, President Grover Cleveland called an emergency session of Congress and repealed the Sherman Act. This reduced demand for silver by $4.5 million per month, and the price of silver crashed. Overnight, many Colorado mines became unprofitable and ceased operations. Populations moved, and many silver mining towns were doomed to become ghost towns.

In 1896, the presidential election was fought on the issue of gold versus silver. William Jennings Bryan supported silver, but William McKinley won. In 1900, McKinley succeeded in passing the Gold Standard Act, which led to further decline in the depressed silver price, more mine closures, and more ghost towns in the West.

In 1967, the United States eliminated the gold backing from the currency; by 1970, all silver content had been eliminated from U.S. coins, and the government sold the remaining silver reserves.

Mining Operations

Gold and silver deposits are frequently found together. They are formed when molten minerals are forced up from deep within the earth into the bedrock. Usually gold and silver also exist with other minerals such as pyrite (fool's gold) and galena (which has a silvery appearance). Commonly, the host rock is quartz.

Over time, erosion breaks down the rock deposits and the gold is freed and left in pure form. Water then disperses the free gold along streambeds. In its free form, gold exists in a variety of shapes: nuggets, scale, shot, grains, dust. These free deposits are known as "placers" when the gold is found in streambeds or along stream banks. A deposit of gold that is still contained in a rock formation is called a "lode."

Gold dredge #3 near Breckenridge

Placer Mining

Because placers are relatively easy to find, they are normally the first gold deposits discovered in any area. Miners typically follow the placers upstream to the mother lode.

Placer mining is the simplest form of mining operations, since it merely involves separating the free gold from the dirt, mud, or gravel with which it is mixed. The process takes a number of forms:

- simple panning
- sluicing to process a larger volume, using the same principle as panning
- dredging to process even larger volumes of rock (Dredge mining utilizes a power-driven chain of small buckets mounted on a barge, leaving in its wake squalid piles of washed rock to mark its course for decades to come. Processing tons of rock and soil quickly, dredges overcame the problem of large quantities of low-grade gravel. Dredges could move up to three-quarters of a million yards of earth per annum.)
- hydraulic mining (used where the ancient riverbeds had long since disappeared, leaving the gold on dry land and some

Panning for gold, circa 1895

Hydraulic mining

Typical Amalgamation/Concentration Mill

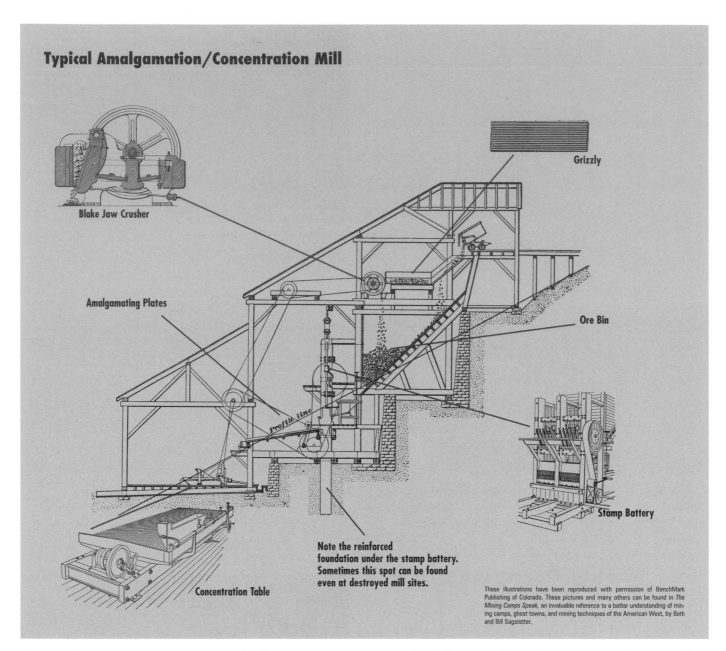

Blake Jaw Crusher

Grizzly

Amalgamating Plates

Ore Bin

Profile Line

Stamp Battery

Note the reinforced foundation under the stamp battery. Sometimes this spot can be found even at destroyed mill sites.

Concentration Table

These illustrations have been reproduced with permission of BenchMark Publishing of Colorado. These pictures and many others can be found in *The Mining Camps Speak,* an invaluable reference to a better understanding of mining camps, ghost towns, and mining techniques of the American West, by Beth and Bill Sagstetter.

distance from any existing stream. Hydraulic mining uses hoses to bring water from up to 3 miles away and wash away the extraneous material to recover the gold.)

Placer mining was known as "poor man's mining," because panning a creek could be done with very little capital. Colorado's placer production has been nearly all gold.

Hard-Rock Mining

Hard-rock mining involves digging ore out of the ground and recovering it from the quartz (or other minerals) surrounding it.

Hard-rock mining in its simplest form involves tunneling horizontally under the vein (either directly or from an initial vertical shaft), then digging out the ore into mine cars placed beneath it. In the 1800s, mining cars were pulled by mules along tracks laid in the mines. If the mine incorporated a vertical shaft, then a hoist would lift the ore to the surface. Dig-

ging the shafts was made much easier during the 1870s, when hand drilling techniques were made obsolete by machine drills and dynamite.

Once extracted from the mine, the gold had to be separated from the host rock. To do this economically in the latter half of the nineteenth century, mining companies made use of stamp mills. Large structures that processed the ore in stages, stamp mills required water and a downhill slope. Milling involved progressively crushing the ore, then processing it chemically to extract the precious metal. Mine workers brought the ore into the mill and fed it into a stamper, which weighed up to a ton. The stamper crushed the host rock; then a slurry of the crushed ore and water was fed over a series of mercury-coated amalgamation plates, which captured the precious metal.

Because hard-rock mining required substantial capital, only large mining corporations normally undertook hard-rock mining operations. The men who worked the mines were employees of the larger corporations.

Animals

Mammals

Bighorn Sheep

Bighorn sheep are grayish-brown with yellowish-white rump patches and short brown tails. Some have whitish fur around their muzzles, eyes, bellies, and calves. They have muscular bodies and thick necks. Ewes weigh around 150 pounds, and rams range from 150 to 250 pounds. Both the male and female have horns that grow continually and never molt. The male's are massive and coil up and back over his ears, down

Bighorn sheep

and forward in a "C" shape, up to 40 inches long. The ewe's horns are thin and only slightly curved—no more than a half curl.

Bighorn sheep are active by day, dwelling on cliffs, mountain slopes, and rolling foothills. They feed on a wide variety of grasses and shrubs.

Rams challenge each other by having butting contests in which they simultaneously charge each other. Their combined speed can be more than 40 miles per hour just before impact, and their foreheads meet with a crack that can be heard a mile away. These contests can last for as long as 20 hours. Horn size determines status among rams, but these ramming contests establish hierarchy among the rams with horns of similar size.

Many bighorns have died from diseases contracted from domestic livestock; the bighorn population has suffered greatly. Relocation programs and efforts to reduce competition with livestock have successfully recovered some of the herds.

Bison

The bison has an imposing appearance, with its dark brown shaggy hair, woolly mane, massive head, high shoulders, short legs, and long, tufted tail. Bison are the largest terrestrial animals in North America. Cows range in weight from 800 to 1,000 pounds, and bulls can weigh well over 2,000 pounds. Both sexes have short, black, sharply curved horns with pointy tips.

Bison are herd animals, grazing in groups of at least a dozen but also in massively larger herds. Grazing animals, bison feed

Bison

mainly on grasses and shrubs. In winter, they clear snow from vegetation with their hooves and heads. Most active in early morning and late afternoon, they rest in the midday heat, chewing cud or dust-bathing. Bison are good swimmers, so buoyant that their heads, humps, and tails remain above water.

When frightened, bison will stampede, galloping at high speeds. Because they are unpredictable at all times, do not approach bison too closely for any reason.

Males may battle each other in an attempt to mate with a cow. Fights can involve butting, horn locking, shoving, and hooking. When butting, males walk to within 20 feet of each other, raise their tails, and charge. Their foreheads collide with the force of freight trains and, without apparent injury, they continue charging until one animal gives up.

Once, the North American population of bison was estimated to be 70 million. However, a mass extermination by white men began around 1830, encouraged by the government in an attempt to subdue the Indians. Today's bison population is estimated at approximately 30,000. You are unlikely to encounter bison on the open range as you travel the routes in this book. They are only found in national parks, refuges, game farms, and the like.

Black Bear

Black bears can actually be black, brown, or cinnamon. Approximately 60 percent of the Colorado black bear population is brown. The bears' bodies are powerful and densely furred, with slight shoulder humps, small rounded ears, small eyes set close together, and five dark, strongly curved front claws on each foot. Females range in weight from 120 to 200 pounds, and males range from 200 to 400 pounds.

Nocturnal and solitary, black bears are fairly common in Colorado's high country. They stay in forested habitats throughout the year, although they can sometimes be seen on open slopes searching for fresh greens. They usually make their dens in tree cavities, under logs, in brush piles, or under buildings, lining them with leaves or grass. Black bears are omnivorous; they eat both plants and animals. They feast on

Black bear

grasses, sedges, berries, fruits, tree bark, insects, honey, eggs, fish, rodents, and even miscellaneous garbage. In the fall they go into a feeding frenzy to gain as much weight as possible to get them through their winter hibernation, often adding a four-inch layer of fat to keep them warm and nourished.

During hibernation, black bears crawl into their dens, and their bodies go dormant for the winter; they do not eat, drink, urinate, or defecate during their long sleep. Their kidneys continue to make urine, but it is reabsorbed into their bloodstream. They awaken by an internal clock in the spring and wander out in search of food.

The black bear has a lumbering walk but can actually travel up to 30 miles per hour in a bounding trot. Black bears are powerful swimmers, able fishers, and agile tree climbers.

Black bears breed in the summer; the females undergo a phenomenon in which the fertilized egg passes into the uterus but changes very little until late fall, when it implants and then begins to grow quickly. Females commonly give birth to a litter of one to five young in January or February.

Bobcat

Bobcats are a reddish-tawny color, with dark spots on their body and legs. Their ears are slightly tufted. Their bellies are usually buff and spotted. They have short, stubby tails with three horizontal, dark stripes. Females range in weight from 15 to 25 pounds, and males range from 20 to 35 pounds.

The most common wildcat, bobcats live in virtually every habitat in Colorado below 10,000 feet—from dry, rocky mountainsides to forests to rocky or brushy arid lands. Because of their secretive nature, bobcats are seldom seen.

Bobcats feast mostly on rabbits, ground squirrels, mice, birds, insects, lizards, and frogs. They are efficient predators who have keen eyes and ears to locate prey in poor light. They stalk and move at blinding speed for short distances to pounce and make the kill.

Solitary animals, the sexes come together only for mating. Litters of two or three kittens are born in April and May in maternity dens of dry leaves in hollow logs and under rock ledges or fallen trees. The bobcat population is currently stable, although trapping by humans once nearly decimated the species.

Bobcat

Cougar, Mountain Lion, Puma

These wildcats have grayish-, yellowish-, or reddish-brown fur, with buff areas on their bellies, necks, and faces. They are feline in appearance, with long, heavy legs; padded feet; retractable claws; black-tipped tails; small, round heads; short muzzles; small, rounded ears; supple bodies; strong legs; and long tails. The females range in weight from 80 to 150 pounds, and males range from 120 to 180 pounds. Cougars are good climbers and jumpers, able to leap more than 20 feet.

Elusive and rarely seen, cougars are territorial loners who live in the wilderness throughout the mountains, foothills, and canyons. Carnivorous eaters, they thrive on large mammals such as deer and elk as well as on porcupine, mice, rabbits, and grouse. They locate prey, slink forward close to the ground, then spring onto their victims' backs, holding and biting the

Cougar

neck. They may bury the "leftovers" of a large kill and return one or more times to eat.

The cougars breed in pairs, and females with young move together. Each has its home range and rarely ventures outside it. Cougars breed every other year, and although there is no fixed breeding season, it often occurs in winter or early spring. Their maternity dens are lined with vegetation and may be located in caves, in thickets, under rock ledges, or in similarly concealed, protected places. Two to four spotted kittens are born in maternity dens from May to July.

Coyote

The coyote is grayish-brown with rusty or tan fur on its legs, feet, and ears. Canine in appearance, with pointed muzzles and bushy tails, coyotes range in weight from 30 to 50 pounds. Their tracks appear much like those of a domestic dog but in a nearly straight line; hind feet usually come down in foreprints, with four toes per print.

Coyotes can be found in every type of habitat in Colorado—from the eastern plains to the slopes of the alpine tundra. Coyotes inhabit the deepest wilderness as well as the suburbs of Denver. Coyotes rarely seek shelter and remain in dens only when they have pups. They are both carnivores and scavengers with an opportunistic variety of diet including rabbits, mice, squirrels, birds, frogs, snakes, grasshoppers, fruits, berries, and sheep and other domestic livestock. In winter they often eat carrion from larger animals, especially deer, as an important food source.

Coyote

They are vocal animals whose call is commonly heard at dusk or dawn, consisting of a series of barks and yelps, followed by a prolonged howl and short yaps. Coyotes howl as a means of communicating with each other; one call usually prompts other coyotes to join in, resulting in a chorus audible for significant distances.

They are stealthy runners and can cruise at 25 to 35 miles per hour, making leaps as high as 14 feet. They hunt singly or in pairs, acting as a relay team to chase and tire their prey.

Coyotes are monogamous and often mate for life. Their maternal dens are usually found or dug by the female under large boulders, in caves, on hillsides, or along river embankments. The openings, or mouths, of these dens usually measure several feet wide and are often marked by a mound of earth and tracks. Unless disturbed, a coyote might use the same den from year to year. Coyotes breed in February, March, and April, and give birth to a litter of four or more pups by May.

The population of coyotes is flourishing, despite the popular demand for their fur in the 1970s and 1980s. Their main enemies are humans.

Elk

Elk are large deer with brown bodies, tawny-colored rumps, thick necks, and sturdy legs. Cows range in weight from 500 to 600 pounds, and bulls range from 600 to 1,000 pounds. Only the males have antlers, which they shed each year.

From the eastern foothills to the western border of Colorado, elk are often found in timberline or in grassy clearings just below timberline. They remain in herds throughout the year and feed on grasses, shrubs, and trees.

In the late summer and early fall, bulls display behavior caused by their high levels of testosterone: They begin thrashing bushes and "bugling"—making a sound that begins as a bellow, changes to a shrill whistle or scream, and ends with a series of grunts. This vocalization broadcasts a bull's presence to other bulls and functions as a call of domination to the cows. Bulls become territorial and make great efforts to keep the cows together

Elk

(a harem may consist of up to 60 cows), mating as they come into heat and keeping other bulls at distance. Bulls often clash antlers in mating jousts but are seldom hurt.

Calves are born in the late spring after a gestation period of about nine months.

Colorado has the largest elk population in the United States.

Fox

Four types of foxes live in Colorado: the swift fox, kit fox, red fox, and gray fox.

The *swift fox* has yellow eyes and buff yellow fur, with grayish areas above, and white chins, throats, and bellies. Most have a black tip on their tails. Swift foxes are the smallest of Colorado's foxes, weighing three to six pounds and measuring 15 to 20 inches long, with 10-inch tails. This fox is found primarily in eastern regions of Colorado in plains, short-grass prairies, and open desert areas. Swift foxes live in underground dens with several entrances and sometimes settle in old badger or marmot dens. They eat rodents and insects. In winter, they can catch food under the snow. Swift foxes can run up to 25 miles per hour, hence their name. Because they are trusting and easily killed, swift foxes are currently in danger of extinction. Trapping, shooting, poisoning, and automobiles are the major causes of mortality. Captive breeding programs are under way to re-establish the

Kit foxes

swift fox in portions of its historic range and its future depends on our ability to preserve its habitat.

The *kit fox* is very similar in appearance to the swift fox, except that it has a longer tail and larger, more closely set ears. Kit foxes live in the desert shrublands of western and southwestern Colorado.

Red foxes are rusty red in color, with white underparts, chins, and throats. Their tails are very bushy, long, and red, with white tips. Their lower legs and feet are black. The red fox weighs 8 to 12 pounds and measures about 2 feet long with a 15-inch tail. This animal is the most common fox in Colorado, partly because of its adaptability to a wide variety of habitats. They are found in all types of habitats, from alpine tundra to farmland to forests. Red foxes are primarily nocturnal, elusive animals, making them difficult to observe. Their favorite foods are voles and mice, followed by almost anything that is available—including rabbits, birds, reptiles, fruits, berries, eggs, insects, and carrion from larger animals. An adult red fox can eat up to 100 mice per week. Red foxes have keen hearing and can listen for burrowing or gnawing animals underground and then dig into the soil or snow to capture them. They continue to catch food even when they are full, burying the excess in the dirt or snow for later. For years, unregulated trapping took a heavy toll on the red fox population, but the collapse of the fur industry has improved matters. With poultry farms being made nearly predator-proof, farmers kill fewer foxes. The red fox's range is expanding, although competition with the coyote may have a restraining effect.

Red fox

The *gray fox* is recognizable by its salt-and-pepper gray coat, its rust-colored legs and feet, its white throat and belly, its black-tipped tail, and the dark streak down its spine. The gray fox weighs 7 to 13 pounds and is about 22 to 30 inches long with a 10- to 15-inch tail. This animal prefers heavier cover and is more nocturnal than the red fox, so it is rarely seen. It lives in wooded and brushy slopes in the valleys, north to the Wyoming border. The gray fox is the only fox that commonly climbs trees and has been known to rest, hide, or escape into them. Gray foxes sometimes raise their young in large, hollow trees, some

Gray fox

of which have entrance holes as high as 20 feet. More often, dens are located among rocks, in cliffsides, or in hollow trees or logs. Because the gray fox's pelt is undesirably bristly, it has never been heavily hunted or trapped for its fur. Like the other foxes, their worst enemies are humans.

Mountain Goat

Mountain goats have white shaggy hair all over their bodies, with longer hair under their chins to form a beard. They have black eyes, noses, hooves, and horns. Their bodies are compact, and their legs are short. Nannies weigh around 150 pounds, and billies weigh from 200 to 325 pounds. Both females and males have smooth, backward-curving horns, although the male's are much larger. Because horns grow continuously throughout the animal's lifetime and are never shed, the older males tend to have largest horns.

Mountain goat

Mountain goats are found in the highest, most inhospitable, remote places in Colorado. They are hardy animals who live throughout the year on alpine cliffs and meadows, even when temperatures drop far below zero, winds gust up to 100 miles per hour, and blizzards rage. Mountain goats feed on grasses, sedges, and other green plants.

Their hooves, with rubbery soles for traction, are well adapted for traversing rocky peaks. Their bodies are slender, so they can traverse narrow mountain ledges. Short legs and powerful shoulder muscles allow the goat to ascend steep, rugged terrain. Their shaggy outer layer of hair creates insulation from the extreme cold with protective, long hollow strands; while their inner layer of hair is more like a thick woolen sweater.

Mountain goats follow a social hierarchy. The older, stronger goats dominate, followed by aggressive adult females, followed by two-year-old males, two-year-old females, yearlings, and kids. Adult males are subordinate to other classes, except during rutting. In breeding season, rival billies threaten each other; but the threats do not always result in a fight.

The mountain goat is not native to the Rocky Mountains but was successfully introduced to the area by humans.

Mule Deer

Gray in winter, the mule deer's coat changes to reddish-brown in summer. Some have a whitish throat and rump patch. Their tails are either black-tipped or black on top. Mule deer have large, mulelike ears that move almost constantly. They are medium-sized deer with stocky bodies and long, slim, sturdy legs. Does range in weight from 100 to 180 pounds, and bucks range from 150 to 400 pounds. Only the buck has antlers; he sheds them in the winter and begins to grow another set in the spring.

The most common large mammal in Colorado, mule deer can be found in dense populations throughout the state, particularly in abundance in the San Juans, Rockies, and Sangre de Cristos. They tend to spend the summers on high mountain pastures, alpine meadows, and sometimes logged areas. The onset of winter snowstorms causes them to migrate to lower slopes, where food supplies are more abundant. Mule deer's summer forage includes grasses, sagebrush, serviceberry, and chokecherry. In winter they browse on twigs, shrubs, and acorns. They are most active in the mornings, evenings, and moonlit nights.

Mule deer

The mule deer's social group generally consists of the doe and her fawn or twins, while bucks are often solitary. In November, bucks become increasingly active and intolerant of each other, sometimes engaging in conflict or vigorous fights wherein each tries, with antlers enmeshed, to force down the other's head. Injuries are rare, and usually the loser withdraws.

Mule deer breed in mid-November; fawns usually arrive in June, July, and August, with spotted coats for camouflage. A doe giving birth for the first time normally produces a single fawn, whereas an older doe tends to have twins.

Pronghorn

Pronghorns are pale or reddish-tan in color on the upper body and outer legs, with two white bands across the throat, a white rump patch, white chest, white lower sides, and white inner legs. The buck has vertical black markings from eyes to snout and along the sides of the throat. Does range in weight from 75 to 110 pounds, and bulls range from 110 to 130 pounds. Both sexes have sets of horns; the doe's are seldom longer than three or four inches, but a buck's horns can grow as long as 20 inches, curving back and slightly inward.

Pronghorns are common and highly visible in open, rolling plains or grasslands. Active night and day, they alternate bits of sleep with watchful feeding. Pronghorns feed on grasses and forbs in summer and sagebrush and other shrubs in winter.

They are the fastest animal in the Western Hemisphere and have been clocked at 80 miles per hour, although 45 miles per hour is more usual. The pronghorns run with their mouths open, not from exhaustion but to gasp extra oxygen. When it senses danger, a pronghorn snorts and erects the white hairs on its rump (twice as long as the body hairs), which creates a flash of white as it flees and warns other pronghorn of danger. If a surprise attack forces a pronghorn to fight rather than flee, it uses its

Pronghorn

sharp hooves, which can effectively drive off a coyote.

Adult bucks establish territories in March and hold them through the September breeding season. Throughout the spring and summer, non-territorial bucks gather into bachelor herds, while the does and fawns drift on and off the territories. By late September, territorial bucks try to hold groups of does and fawns on their territories for breeding and keeping other bucks away. These territories are abandoned after the breeding season. Horns are shed, and all ages and both sexes congregate on the winter range. The young are usually born in April, May, and June.

Pronghorn populations were reduced to less than 25,000 in the mid-1920s due to the fencing of range land, which hampered migration and foraging (pronghorns cannot leap fences like deer—they crawl under them instead). With management and transplantation of herds by game departments, the pronghorn population is steadily increasing, and current estimates are at more than 500,000.

Raccoon

Raccoons have salt-and-pepper coloring with black masks across their eyes and black-and-white-ringed tails. Raccoons appear slightly hunchbacked. They are about two feet long, with a 10-inch tail. They range in weight from 10 to 25 pounds.

Raccoons are found near water, living in dens in hollow trees, logs, rock crevices, or ground burrows. They live in lower elevations throughout Colorado. They feed mostly along streams, lakes, or ponds; and their favorite foods include

Raccoon

fruits, nuts, grains, insects, eggs, and fish. They appear to wash their food before eating it but are actually feeling for the edible parts.

Raccoons do not hibernate but may sleep for several days during cold weather.

Raccoons give birth in April and May to litters of between two and seven young. Naturalists estimate that there are 15 to 20 times as many raccoons now than there were in the 1930s.

River Otter

Dark brown in color, with silvery fur on their underparts, river otters have long, cylindrical bodies; small, rounded ears; large noses; small, beady eyes; long whiskers; and thick, furry tails. River otters are about three feet long, with 10- to 18-inch tails; they range in weight from 10 to 25 pounds.

River otters live in large rivers, streams, or beaver ponds throughout Colorado, especially in the north. They enjoy a variety of food but feed primarily on fish, frogs, and aquatic invertebrates. River otters can stay under water for two to three minutes, because their pulse slows and skin flaps close over their ears and nostrils. They have powerful feet and webbed toes to propel them through the water. Stiff whiskers help them hunt by feel under water. Cold waters do not bother them, because

River otter

their dense fur and oily underfur does not allow water to reach their skin.

River otters tend to use beaver and muskrat burrows as their own. They are very playful animals who spend much time frolicking and chasing each other.

Pups are born in litters of one to four in March, April, and May—furry, blind, and helpless. River otters were reintroduced in several places in Colorado in 1976.

White-Tailed Deer

White-tailed deer are grayish-brown in winter and reddish-brown in summer. Their tails are white below and brown above. The white-tailed deer has small ears and a slim, graceful appearance. Does range in weight from 120 to 180 pounds, and bucks range from 150 to 400 pounds. Only the buck has antlers; he sheds them in the winter and begins to grow another set in the spring.

White-tailed deer are occasionally found in farmlands, but they prefer a somewhat denser woodland habitat in riparian areas. These deer are adaptable to live near human communities, but are timid and elusive—primarily nocturnal. White-tailed deer forage on a variety of foods—including shrubs, trees, acorns, or grass—according to what is in season. They also enjoy garden vegetables (corn, peas, lettuce, apples, herbs) and other agricultural items.

When nervous, the white-tailed deer snorts through its nose and stamps its hooves; when spooked, it raises its white tail, thus alerting other deer of danger. They are good swimmers, can run 30 to 40 miles per hour, and can jump 30 feet horizontally and over 8 feet vertically.

White-tailed deer breed in much the same manner as mule deer, except that buck fighting is less common. They are fewer in population than mule deer and are altogether absent from western Colorado.

White-tailed deer

Rodents

Although rodents are mammals, they have been categorized separately for ease of reference.

Beaver

Beavers are very large rodents with thick brown fur; chunky bodies; short legs; rounded heads; small, rounded ears; yel-

Beaver

lowish-orange front incisors; webbed hind feet; and flat, hairless, paddle-shaped tails. Their weight ranges from 30 to 60 pounds.

Throughout Colorado, beavers live in lakes, streams, ponds, and rivers from 4,000 feet to timberline. They eat bark and twigs. Since they do not hibernate, they collect large caches of twigs and branches to eat in their lodge during the winter.

Beavers have thick layers of fat and waterproof fur, so icy waters don't bother them. They have skin flaps that close over their ears and nostrils when submerged and webbed feet for swimming. Their eyes have a clear membrane cover that allows them to see in water and protects their eyes from floating debris. A beaver can remain submerged for up to 15 minutes before coming up for air.

A beaver's work in progress

Beavers build dams of sticks and mud across streams and slow rivers. They gnaw down trees, strip them, cut them into small sections, and weave them into the dam, holding the logs in place with mud. They also build lodges with one or more entrances below water and the living chamber well above waterline.

Beavers mate for life, which can be as long as 20 years. Furry beaver kits are born in the lodges in spring, with their eyes open.

The beaver population almost died out during the nineteenth century because of unregulated trapping for their fash-

Beaver lodges

ionable fur (used primarily for hats). However, due to fashion changes and the Colorado legislature placing the beaver on a list of protected animals, the beaver population has been re-established and is thriving.

Chipmunk

Several varieties of chipmunks in Colorado share similar characteristics and are not easily discerned from each other. Ranging in color from chestnut to yellowish-gray to light gray, chipmunks are small rodents with dark and light stripes on their face. Dark stripes line their backs from the neck to the base of the tail, with white stripes running parallel on the back

Chipmunk

portion only. The palest chipmunks tend to be found in arid environments. They measure about three to six inches long, with three- to four-inch tails, and weigh a mere one to four ounces.

Chipmunks are active during the day and hibernate in winter. They eat a variety of vegetation, including seeds, leaves, fruits, flower components, and other plants. They have large, fur-lined internal cheek pouches used for carrying food. Chipmunks stow away a great deal of their food; instead of relying on stored body fat to sustain them during hibernation, they awaken periodically throughout winter and early spring to eat from their caches.

They dig burrows and line them with grass underneath rocks, logs, and roots; these burrows become the nests where they have their young. Babies are born blind and naked after a gestation period of about 30 days.

Cottontail, Rabbit

One of the most abundant animals in nature, cottontails are very similar in appearance and behavior to hares (jackrabbits), except that they tend to be smaller and have shorter ears, smaller feet, and shorter hind legs. They do not turn white in winter. Of the several types of cottontail in Colorado, the *desert cottontail* is found in the southwest and the eastern plains; the *eastern cottontail* is found in woodlands in the east; and the most common cottontail found in the Rockies is the *mountain cottontail,* also called *Nuttall's cottontail.*

Mountain cottontail

Because of their vulnerability at birth, cottontails are born in maternal nests, which the pregnant female finds and prepares about a week before giving birth. She locates a suitable spot where brush or high grass provides protection and makes a saucer-like depression in the ground, lining it with her own downy fur, soft grasses, and leaves. Adults may have three or four litters per year in a good habitat. Unlike hares, cottontails are born naked, with their eyes closed.

Hare, Jackrabbit

Hares are very similar in appearance to cottontails (rabbits), but they tend to be larger and have longer ears, bigger feet, and longer back legs. It is suggested that hares got the name "jackrabbit" because their large ears resemble those of jackasses. Their fur is a mottled gray and brown in summer. It be-

Black-tailed jackrabbit

comes almost pure white in northern areas of the state in winter, while in the south it gets paler but still holds tinges of brown and gray. Does (females) are larger than bucks, which is unusual in mammals. Their weight varies from 3 to 10 pounds.

Colorado's three species of hare are the *white-tailed jackrabbit* (found in mountain parks and shortgrass prairies), the *black-tailed jackrabbit* (found in semi-desert country in western and southern Colorado, as well as eastern plains), and the *snowshoe hare* (found mainly in sub-alpine forests).

In summer, jackrabbits eat mostly green plants, such as clover and flowers. In winter, they rely more on shrubs. Their huge ears are so sensitive that they can detect the muted sound of a coyote as its fur brushes against the grass. When threatened, they first freeze, laying their ears back to be less conspicuous, their coat assisting with the camouflage. If this fails, they can move from a hiding place like lightning, at speeds up to 35 miles per hour, and change direction instantly.

Snowshoe hare

Unlike cottontails, young hares are born fully furred, with their eyes open. The female puts each young hare into an individual form, or depression, in the ground, thus decreasing a predator's chance of taking her entire litter. She keeps her distance by day and comes several times to nurse at night so that she attracts less attention.

Marmot, Rockchuck

Brown to yellowish-brown with yellowish bellies, marmots have heavy bodies with short legs, small ears, and bushy tails. Marmots range in weight from 5 to 10 pounds and measure one to two feet in length, with a five- to seven-inch tail. They are the largest ground-dwelling squirrels in the region.

Found living in colonies throughout rocky areas, their habitats vary from talus slopes to pastures with large boulders. They feed on grass and plants. Sunbathing on rocks is a favored pastime; while the group enjoys the activity, at least one marmot stands guard to warn the others of danger. When danger approaches, the sentry lets out high-pitched chirps so that the group can scurry to safety.

Marmot

These burrowing animals spend as much as eight months of the year underground and begin hibernation as early as September. In April and May, females give birth to three to six naked and blind young in their grass-lined dens.

Pika

These small rodents have short, dense, gray-brown fur; round bodies; short legs; large heads; short, rounded ears; and no visible tail. They are small and mouselike, about eight inches long and four to seven ounces in weight.

Pika

Pikas live in colonies found in rocky fields and talus slopes above 8,500 feet in alpine and subalpine meadows throughout Colorado. Pikas feed on a variety of grasses, sedges, and forbs. They spend most of the summer gathering great quantities of vegetation and storing it for winter. They clip off bits and carry it back to rock piles where they spread it out to dry in the sun. If rain threatens before the stacks are cured, the pika carries its harvest one mouthful at a time to the shelter of a rocky burrow. It is not uncommon for one pika to store as much as four bushels.

When not foraging, pikas like to find a safe perch near an escape route and keep an eye out for predators. Active during the day, pikas blend with the rocks, yet their characteristic squeak gives them away every time. You can often hear a pika before you see it, although it is usually difficult to tell the direction from which the sound comes. Uttered at the first sign of danger, the call is picked up by other pikas and echoed throughout the colony.

Instead of hibernating for winter, the pika is active all year, moving around beneath the rocks in tunnels dug through the snow. It lives off the caches of food gathered in the summer.

Pikas usually mate in the early spring, producing a litter in May or June; a second litter may be produced in late summer.

Porcupine

Porcupines are gray-brown, with chunky bodies, high arching backs, and short legs. Yellowish hair covers long quills all over their backs, rumps, and tails. These rodents measure up to two feet in length, with an eight-inch tail, and range in weight from 10 to 28 pounds. Next to the beaver, they are the largest rodents in Colorado.

Found in nearly all forested areas throughout the state, porcupines are active year-round. Porcupines feast on green plants, grass, and leaves in summer and tree bark in winter. They are slow-moving animals with poor eyesight, yet they are equipped with thousands of barbed quills for protection against predators. Contrary to popular belief, porcupines do not throw their quills; quills are released from the porcupine's body and penetrate the enemy's skin. Not only are quills hard to pull out, they readily work themselves in farther. This can produce painful and fatal results.

Porcupine

Porcupines are primarily nocturnal, but they can occasionally be seen resting in treetops during the day. They make their dens in logs or caves and use them for sleeping and birthing.

Kits are born in May and June, after a gestation period of seven months. They are born headfirst, with quills aimed backwards.

Prairie Dog

The prairie dog varieties described here are roughly the same size: one to two-and-a-half pounds, about one foot tall. Prairie dogs are active during daylight hours only, and they are most energetic at dawn and dusk. They feed on grass, plants, and insects, with a particular fondness for grasshoppers.

Prairie dog

Black-tailed prairie dogs, found in the grasslands of the eastern plains of Colorado, are the most common variety. They are brownish-yellow on the back and sides, with whitish bellies, small ears, and black-tipped tails. Black-tailed prairie dogs are social animals who live in colonies, or "prairie dog towns," composed of several families. On purely a friendly level, they approach each other and touch noses and incisors to "kiss." They communicate by barking a variety of different sounds and groom each other socially—not as an act of courtship.

Black-tailed prairie dogs retreat to their burrows for brief periods during warm summer days to escape the afternoon heat or for longer periods of time when the weather is severely cold. They do not hibernate but go dormant in bitter winter weather, arousing to feed during warm spells.

They give birth in their burrows to one litter of deaf, blind, and hairless pups in April, after a gestation period of about 30 days.

White-tailed prairie dogs are fawny-colored, sprinkled with black on the back and sides, with whitish bellies, small ears, and white-tipped tails. They are similar to black-tailed prairie dogs, except they are slightly smaller, less social, and they hibernate from fall to spring. They live at higher elevations on the plains in the northwestern portion of Colorado.

Their pups are born in April, after a gestation period of about 30 days. They vacate their burrows in May and June, and their dens are taken over by other animals.

Gunnison's prairie dogs are a yellowish color, mixed with black, with slightly paler bellies, and short, white-tipped tails. The smallest of the prairie dog species found in Colorado, they live in high mountain valleys and plateaus of the Rocky Mountains in southwestern and central Colorado at elevations of 6,000 to 12,000 feet.

Gunnison's prairie dogs are less social than the two types discussed above, with smaller communities that are considerably less developed. Their modes of communication include a distinctive danger call that is often repeated and gets louder as the urgency intensifies.

Females typically give birth to one litter in May, after a gestation period of 27 to 33 days.

Squirrel

The most abundant ground squirrel in Colorado, the *rock squirrel* is also the largest. Rock squirrels are mottled gray-brown in front and darker behind, with buff bellies. Their tails are long and bushy with sprinklings of brown and buff edges. True to its name, the rock squirrel dwells in rocky locales—such as cliffs, canyon walls, talus slopes, and boulder piles—and digs its den in the ground below.

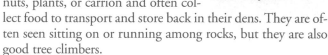
Abert's squirrel

Rock squirrels dine on berries, nuts, plants, or carrion and often collect food to transport and store back in their dens. They are often seen sitting on or running among rocks, but they are also good tree climbers.

Vocalizations include an alarm call, which is short and followed by a lower-pitched trill. They have a sharp, sometimes quavering whistle.

Females normally bear two litters during the year, one in late spring or early summer and the other in late summer or early fall.

Abert's squirrels (also called *tassel-eared squirrels*) have grizzled gray, black, or reddish sides and backs, with white or black bellies. They can also be solid black in Colorado.

The Abert's squirrel is a large tree squirrel with very distinctive tasseled ears (less tufted in summer). They live in ponderosa pine forests, feeding on pine cones, bark, buds, and twigs of the trees. They build nests of twigs in the trees, where they sleep at night, court, mate, and raise their young.

Abert's squirrels do not hibernate; they remain in their nests during cold weather and venture out to recover stored food below. Mating chases last all day in late winter, during which males frantically chase the females around. A litter of about four young is usually born in April or May, after a gestation period of about 46 days.

The *red squirrel* (also called *pine squirrel* or *chickaree*) is a small tree squirrel found in Colorado's forested habitats including suburbs with mature trees. Its coat is flecked rust-red in the summer and gray-red in the winter. Red squirrels are seven to eight inches long, with bushy four- to six-inch tails.

Red squirrel

The red squirrel is the smallest tree squirrel, yet the most common in Colorado's Rocky Mountains. They enjoy opportunistic varieties of nuts, seeds, eggs, pine cones, and fungi. They often have a preference for a favorite feeding stump or branch, where you might find piles of cones or seed pods. In the fall, they stow large quantities of food in caches in the ground, in hollow trees, and in other spots. They do not hibernate in winter. Red squirrels make nests of grass and shredded bark in tree cavities or branches. Litters of young are born in April and May, after a gestation period of 35 days; sometimes mothers bear a second litter in August or September.

Snakes

Bullsnake

Also called gopher snakes, bullsnakes are found throughout Colorado in a wide range of habitats below 8,500 feet. They tend to live in riparian areas, forests, canyons, and shrubby areas. Large snakes, they can grow to a length of 36 to 110 inches.

Bullsnakes are often mistaken for rattlesnakes because of their similarity in appearance and behavior. When cornered or disturbed, a bullsnake will often hiss and coil, shaking its tail like a rattlesnake, even striking. Yet the formidable-looking snake is harmless. Unlike the rattler, the bullsnake is a constrictor, wrapping its coils around its prey and squeezing it to death. Bullsnakes avoid the hottest hours of the day by staying in the shade and moving about early and late in

Bullsnake

the day. They hibernate from October to April in deep dens in cracks of rocks or in caves. Bullsnakes are known to share their dens with other snakes, such as rattlesnakes, milk snakes, and garter snakes.

Garter Snake

Four types of garter snake found in Colorado are the *black-neck, western terrestrial, plains,* and *common garter snake.* The most abundant species is the western terrestrial, which is distributed throughout most of Colorado but absent from the northeastern portion of the state. The moderately slender bod-

Garter snake

ies of adults range from 24 to 42 inches in length. Their coloring is brown to gray, with a gray and tan checkerboard pattern that darkens and becomes obscure with age. They have light stripes down the sides of their bodies, which become less prominent with age. There is also a distinctive light stripe down the back of some individuals. Western terrestrial garter snakes feed on snails, slugs, earthworms, fish, various small reptiles, and small rodents. When captured, they emit an unpleasant fluid from vent glands.

Milk Snake

Milk snakes have vivid buff, black, and red horizontal stripes around their bodies. Adults reach a maximum total length of about 36 inches. They are often confused with the deadly coral snake, a species not found in Colorado. Milk snakes are found in a wide range of habitats throughout most of the state. In southeastern Colorado, they are most likely

Milk snake

to be found at elevations below 8,000 feet and in western Colorado below 6,000 feet. A constrictor, the milk snake kills its prey by squeezing. Milk snakes are often lured to farms, ghost towns, and abandoned buildings by their favorite food, rodents.

Western Rattlesnake

Western rattlesnakes are found in virtually every terrestrial habitat throughout Colorado, from grasslands, sand hills, rocky areas, riparian vegetation, mountain and semidesert shrublands to open coniferous forests. Only perennially wet areas seem to be avoided. They live at maximum elevations of about 9,500 feet.

The western rattlesnake is typically greenish yellow with darker blotches (although individual colors will vary, depending

Western rattlesnake

on how long it has been since the last molt), triangular head, narrow neck, and ranges from 15 to 65 inches, including the obvious rattle on the end of its tail.

Western rattlesnakes live in prairie dog burrows or crevices during winter and emerge for spring-summer activities in May. In hot summer weather they usually prowl at dusk and at night. Pores in their heads pick up scents and heat to help detect prey. The snake kills its prey by injecting it with venom through hollow fangs that snap downward and forward as it strikes.

To human beings, a western rattler's bite is painful and can cause infection and illness, although there have been few fatalities documented among bitten adults. It is rare for people to die from snakebiktes. They are not aggressive snakes, although they usually rattle and assume a coiled, defensive posture when approached. If left alone, they normally crawl away and seek a hiding place. Exercise caution in tall grass, rocky areas, and around prairie dog towns, especially in the mornings and evenings and after summer thunderstorms.

Birds

Black-Billed Magpie

One of the most commonly seen birds in Colorado, the black-billed magpie has black and white coloration and a long tail, which make it easy to identify. It lives anywhere from cities to wilderness areas, and it eats almost anything, thriving by being adaptable. It is a big, flashy, boisterous, and loud bird, with a reputation for raiding the nests of other birds, picking sores of cattle, and attacking the eyes of injured animals. Magpies are found all over Colorado year-round, but mainly at elevations lower than 10,000 feet. Their sturdy

Black-billed magpie

nests, made of mud and reeds, are used from year to year; they also mate with the same partners from year to year.

Eagle

The two eagles in Colorado are the golden eagle and the bald eagle. The bald eagle is primarily a winter visitor, arriving around November. Eagles are noted for their strength and keen vision. They have large, heavy, hooked bills and strong, sharp claws called talons. They are usually brown, black, or gray, sometimes with markings on the head, neck, wings, or tail. The bald eagle is not really bald; it was named for its white head. The rest of its plumage is brown, except for its white tail. Eagles prey on small animals such as fish, rodents, birds, and snakes. They have very

Bald eagle

sharp eyesight and hunt while soaring high in the air or watching from a high perch, swooping down to make the kill with their powerful talons. The eagle makes its nest, or aerie, high in a tree or on a rocky ledge where it cannot be reached by other animals, since young eagles remain helpless for a long period. Each year the birds add new material to the nest. The largest known nest ever measured was 20 feet deep and nearly 10 feet wide.

Golden eagle

Great Horned Owl

The great horned owl is the largest, most commonly seen and widespread of the owl species in Colorado. It has been

Great horned owl

found throughout Colorado in areas ranging from cottonwood groves to coniferous forests below 10,000 feet. It has long ear tufts and yellow eyes. At night you can sometimes hear its deep, resonating hoots. They are skilled hunters, well equipped for killing their prey. They use their sharp talons to grip prey such as rabbits, weasels, squirrels, and birds in a deadly lock. The owls have a wide range of vision: Their necks can swivel nearly 180 degrees, and they can practically see in the dark.

Hummingbirds

The name hummingbird originates from the noise the wings of these birds make in flight. Hummingbirds are the smallest

Hummingbirds

of all birds and are only a few inches long. They feed on nectar, although they also regularly consume small insects. They obtain nectar by inserting their bills and tongues into a flower, thus accumulating pollen on their bills and heads; this pollen is then transferred from flower to flower. Hummingbirds are strong fliers and have exceptional flight characteristics for birds: They can hover and also fly backwards. The rate of their wing beats is extremely rapid, reaching as high as 80 beats per second. Some hummingbirds save energy on cool nights by lowering their usually high body temperature until they become sluggish and unresponsive, a condition termed torpor. In contrast, during daylight hours hummingbirds are often very active and can be highly aggressive, sometimes attacking much larger potential predators, such as hawks and owls.

Jays

The *gray jay* is 10 to 13 inches long, with gray and white plumage, and no crest on its head. Mainly found year-round in coniferous forests in the mountains from 8,500

Gray jay

feet to timberline, the gray jay is not very afraid of humans. This resourceful little bird has learned that people can mean food. It sometimes eats out of human hands, steals food, or even pries open containers. On their own, gray jays eat seeds, small birds, carrion, and insects.

Steller's jay

The gray jay is one of five jays found in Colorado. The others are the *Steller's jay* (dark crest, metallic blue, equally bold), *pinyon jay* (grayish-blue, timid, lives in pinyon pines), *blue jay* (deep blue, found in urban areas), and *scrub jay* (low elevations in oak stands).

Mountain Bluebird

These beautiful, sky-blue birds are primarily summer residents in western Colorado. Most arrive by mid-March. They normally take over nests abandoned by woodpeckers because their beaks are not strong enough to hollow out their own cavities. Their survival today is difficult, as the logging indus-

Mountain bluebird

try cuts down many standing dead trees that they would normally use as homes. They readily adapt to whatever homes they can find, including chipmunk burrows, abandoned car bumpers, and fence posts in open areas.

Mountain Chickadee

The mountain chickadee is a year-round resident in the Colorado mountains. It is a small, energetic bird that sings its name: "Chick-a-dee-dee-dee." It must consume nearly its body weight in seeds and insects each day just to stay alive because of its amazingly fast heart rate of 500 beats per minute. During cold Colorado weather, it puffs out its feathers so it resembles a fluffy ball with a beak.

Mountain chickadee

Northern Flicker

The northern flicker, a type of woodpecker, can be identified in flight by a flash of salmon-red color under its wings and tail. Viewed at rest, the northern flicker has a brown crown, a brownish body, and a red streak behind the bill. The birds are found mainly in coniferous forests and aspen stands. They have powerful beaks to make nesting holes in trees. They eat mostly insects, especially ants.

Northern flicker

Ptarmigan

Ptarmigans are stocky members of the grouse family that inhabit tundra, moors, and alpine areas. They have short, rounded white wings, extensively feathered toes, and upper tail coverts that extend to the tip of the tail. Males have red "combs" above their eyes. Ptarmigans undergo seasonal color changes: In winter their white plumage matches the snow, and in summer their mottled brown plumage blends with the vegetation. Their camouflage is a good thing for their protection, because their stubby wings prohibit them from flying very far. They eat berries, buds, and leaves and fall prey to hunters, foxes, and owls.

Ptarmigan

Red-Winged Blackbird

These birds are one of the most common breeding birds in Colorado, found at elevations to about 9,000 feet. They are about eight or nine inches long and black with crimson shoulder patches, bordered with yellow. The red coloration serves as a flag used in courtship and also in aggression. They enjoy marshes, wetlands, and open fields but migrate in late September to spend their winters in warmer areas, even as far south as Costa Rica.

Red-winged blackbird

Plants

Alpine Zones (above 11,500 feet)

Alpine plants grow in conditions that are so harsh even the trees cannot survive. They grow above timberline in a variety of habitats, ranging from the delicate sod of alpine meadows to boulder fields to talus slopes and mountain lakes and ponds.

Since the tundra receives very little precipitation, alpine plants have adapted with strong roots that reach deep down, allowing them to feed on the scarce nutrients and moisture in the soil. Their lengthy roots further assist to protect them against arctic winds, serving as an anchor. Short stems allow them to hug the ground and reduce wind resistance.

When alpine plants flower, their blooms are often full-sized with brilliant displays—typically during June or July when they receive maximum daylight. Most are perennials (which last from year to year); annuals simply do not have time to start from seeds and complete a full life cycle before the brief growing season comes to an end.

Marsh Marigold, Elk's Lips

Marsh marigolds are found high in the mountains in small pools or wet areas that are often the result of early spring runoff. These low plants each bear just one white flower one to two inches across, with many yellow stamens. The leaves are heart-shaped. Sometimes marsh marigolds push up through the snow and bloom very early in the season. Height: 3 to 10 inches.

Marsh marigolds

Moss Campion

Not truly a moss, this common mat-forming plant grows close to the ground and has many densely crowded, woody branches. Its many pink, rose, or white flowers do not bloom until the plant is about 10 years old. Moss campion spreads like blankets across rocky ridges and slopes. Height: less than 1 inch.

Moss campion

Sky Pilot, Skunkweed

These plants emit a skunklike odor that comes from the leaves and stems when they are crushed. The bluish-purple flowers actually have a sweet, pleasant smell. Bell-shaped flowers grow in crowded clusters around the head, blooming from June to August. They are often found growing on rocky slopes. Height: 4 to 12 inches.

Sky pilot

Subalpine Zones (to about 11,500 feet)

Subalpine plants are found midway between alpine regions and the mountain forests. They often have an even shorter growing period than alpine plants, since snow tends to stay longer in areas protected from wind and sun.

Dogtooth violet

Dogtooth Violet, Avalanche Lily, Glacier Lily

This is not a violet, but actually a lily that is found in moist meadows, growing in large patches near melting snowdrifts. It has one or more yellow blossoms that curve backward from the stem. The flowers appear very early, sometimes even pushing up through the snowbanks. This plant is edible and serves as food to many mountain animals, including bears. Height: 6 to 18 inches.

Globeflower

This plant resembles the marsh marigold and also grows in marshy areas and wet meadows. The easiest way to tell a globeflower plant from a marsh marigold is by the yellow color and its three jagged-edged leaves. Globeflowers bloom from May to August. Height: 10 to 18 inches.

Globeflower

Parry Lousewort

These unusual-looking plants have yellow blossoms atop a stalky stem with sharp-toothed leaves. If you use your imagination, the cluster of flowers somewhat resembles an ear of corn, interspersed with tiny green leaves between the kernels. The unusual name apparently comes from an early superstition that animals could acquire lice from eating the plant. Lousewort is found on open slopes and in meadows. Height: 4 to 12 inches.

Parry lousewort

Parry Primrose

The deep magenta flowers of this plant have yellow "eyes." They rest atop a vertical stem, with all the leaves sprouting from the base, rising nearly as tall as the flower and emitting an unpleasant odor. The height of Parry primrose is unusual, considering the elevation at which they grow. Found in rock crevices, meadows, bogs, and along streams and other moist areas, they bloom from July to August. Height: 10 to 24 inches.

Parry primrose

Purple Fringe

Purple fringe is a beautiful, dense spike of bluish-purple flowers. Plants have several stems, varying in height but rarely exceeding one foot. Purple fringe blooms early in the season and into the summer. It is common in rocky or gravely meadows and dry slopes. Height: 4 to 12 inches.

Purple fringe

Snowball Saxifrage

There are a number of saxifrage varieties that grow in Colorado. The snowball saxifrage has a cluster of white flowers atop a leafless vertical stem that, from a distance, resembles a ball of snow. It grows in the moist crevices of boulders and can actually break the rocks apart! It blooms in midsummer. Height: 2 to 12 inches.

Snowball saxifrage

Montane Zone (8,000–10,000 feet)

Plants in the montane (mountain) zone have a short growing season. They grow often on steep, rocky hillsides and have to compete with trees and shrubs for nutrients in the soil.

Colorado Columbine

Although red and yellow columbines also grow in the region, the Colorado columbine is the state flower. It has five bluish-lavender petals and five white ones. The blue is symbolic of Colorado's blue skies, and the white represents snow. Columbines like moist soil and are found in ravines, rocky slopes, aspen groves, and forest clearings. They bloom from early summer to midsummer. Height: 4 to 24 inches.

Colorado columbine

Monkshood

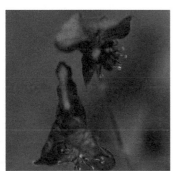

Monkshood

This creamy white and bluish-violet flower has two tiny petals under a hood. Monkshood is poisonous and was once used as a medicine to lower fevers. It grows in meadows and other moist sites and normally blooms in midsummer or late summer. Height: 24 to 72 inches.

Yellow Monkeyflower, Wild Lettuce

These low, creeping plants have bright yellow blooms and grow in masses. The petals have tiny orange or reddish-brown spots. This plant is also called wild lettuce because Native Americans and early settlers ate the bitter leaves. The blooming season is usually from May to August. Height: 4 to 18 inches.

Yellow monkeyflower

Foothills (5,500–8,000 feet)

Foothills are very hospitable areas for plants to grow for several reasons. They generally get plenty of water and nutrients due to snowmelt and rain runoff from the mountains. The mountains also provide them with extra protection from winds and storms.

Goldenrod, Yellowweed

Goldenrod is a genus in the sunflower family. It typically has a slender, unbranched stem with short-stalked or stalkless leaves and small, yellowish flower heads in complex clusters. It is one of the later-blooming plants, usually blooming around July to September. Height: 12 to 72 inches.

Goldenrod

Pasqueflower

This is a large, solitary, blue, white, or purple flower that measures two to two-and-a-half inches in diameter. Six petals curve up and around the greenish-yellow centers. The leaves

Pasqueflower

have a feathery appearance, but since the flower usually opens before the leaves, early in the season it can be mistaken for a globeflower. Pasqueflowers grow in meadows and hillsides in fairly deep soil. The blossoms may emerge from March to June. Height: 2 to 16 inches.

Rocky Mountain Phlox

Rocky Mountain phlox

These sweet-smelling plants have many little flowers, half an inch to one inch long, varying in color from white to pink, blue, or lavender. They grow on shrubby slopes; several stems spread around and over rocks and gravel to form a deep rooting system. They bloom from May to July. Height: 6 to 12 inches.

Shooting Star, Birdbill

The shooting star looks like a colorful rocket. It has backward-curving magenta petals with a yellow circle in the center, pointing down to form the nose. There is a rosette of leaves around the base of the stalk. Elk, deer, and cattle graze on the young shoots, which are found growing in rich soil and partial shade along streams and in wet meadows during June and July. Height: 6 to 16 inches.

Shooting star

Plains (below 5,500 feet)

Plants in this area have to survive drastic changes in weather, from cold winters to hot summers, with long periods of drought. They can be found in eastern Colorado and in some pockets of the western part of the state. Many of these plants have few leaves in order to conserve root moisture. Some protect themselves with thorny or tough leaves that animals won't eat.

Milkweed

Milkweed

Milkweeds have small but complex flowers in rounded clusters that vary from white or yellowish to red or purplish, with paired leaves and fruit pods filled with seeds. The sap has toxic properties, which are destroyed by boiling. Native Americans used to cook and eat the shoots, leaves, buds, flowers, and seed pods. Milkweeds are commonly found in clumps beside streams, ditches, and roadsides. Height: 18 to 72 inches.

Prickly Pear

Prickly pear

This cactus has round pads with prickly spines coming out of the body, which is covered with a thick layer of wax to prevent water evaporation. Its flowers may be red, purple, or yellow; the blooms appear from May to June and last only a few days. It has edible fruit, which is pear-shaped and spine-covered and has a sweet flesh. Height: 3 to 15 inches.

Salsify, Goat Dandelion

Salsify

This plant looks much like a tall, large dandelion after it goes to seed. Its yellow flowers bloom in the morning and close by noon. Salsify is not a plant native to Colorado—it was brought by European settlers as a garden vegetable. Height: 12 to 18 inches.

Multiple Life Zones

These plants can grow in a variety of situations and environments all around Colorado. They may vary in appearance slightly, depending on elevation, climate, rainfall, and exposure to sunshine.

Indian Paintbrush

Indian paintbrush

Indian paintbrush flowers are small, modified leaves called "bracts," which have colorful tips of fiery orange, pink, maroon, red, or yellow, giving the appearance of a dipped paintbrush. The roots of these plants steal food from other plants. Native to slopes and meadows, this plant blooms from May to September. Height: 12 to 36 inches.

Mountain Candytuft

Mountain candytuft

Candytuft is a small herb belonging to the mustard family. It has clusters of small, white, four-petaled flowers on top of the stems. Oval leaves surround the stem's base; and tiny, arrow-shaped leaves adorn the stem farther up. Candytufts are very common plants that are able to grow in thin soil or around rocks. Sometimes they bloom near snowbanks in alpine regions. Height: 1 to 5 inches.

Mountain Harebell

Harebell

The mountain harebell has violet-blue, bell-like flowers that hang downward to protect its pollen in the rain. It typically has round leaves (although the alpine variety can have heart-shaped or grasslike leaves) attached at the base of the stem. The stems support just one full-sized or oversized blossom. Mountain harebells are found from the foothills to timberline and their season and size varies, according to elevation and location. Height: 4 to 12 inches.

Shrubby Cinquefoil, Yellow Rose

Shrubby cinquefoil

These shrubs have yellow flowers that measure about one inch across, with five petals each. Cinquefoils keep their leaves in winter; big game animals eat them when food is scarce, although they don't enjoy the taste. Cinquefoils are found in open woods and meadows from June to August. Height: 12 to 36 inches.

Yarrow

Yarrow

Yarrow is an aromatic herb in the daisy family. The white flowers grow in flat clusters; the leaves are dissected into many fine segments, giving a feathery or fernlike appearance. Yarrow is commonly found in all zones. Height: 6 to 10 inches.

Trees

Aspen

Aspen trees, North America's widest-spread tree species, have smooth, cream-colored bark with green, heart-shaped, deciduous leaves that turn brilliant gold in the fall. Because of the wide, flat shape of aspen leaves, the breeze nearly constantly flutters the tree's foliage, giving them the nickname "quaking aspen."

Older trees are dark at the base. Aspen grow from 40 to 70 feet tall and 1 to 2 feet in diameter. They are normally found

Aspens with fall foliage

in montane and subalpine elevations up to timberline, in dry, cool places, often close to clean, flowing water. Often growing alongside Douglas firs, groves of aspen trees allow sunlight to penetrate to the forest floor, thus encouraging diverse plant growth and providing food and shelter for numerous wildlife species.

Green aspen foliage is preferred over the leaves of other trees by deer, cattle, sheep, and goats. The bark of the tree is a beaver's primary food source.

The pioneering species often quickly populates disaster-struck areas, such as after wildfires, landslides, mud slides, or avalanches. Colorado boasts the largest percentage of natural acreage of aspens in the world.

Blue Spruce

Blue spruce trees are sometimes confused with the Engelmann spruce, but are distinguished by having larger cones and growing at a lower elevation. Blue spruce trees are normally found

Blue spruce cones

at elevations below 9,000 feet. The pyramid shape characterizes them, as do stiff, blue-green-gray needles and scaly bark. Blue spruces produce pale brown cones, hanging in separate clusters on the same tree, mainly in the upper portion, up to four inches long. Many reach heights of over 100 feet. This is Colorado's state tree.

Blue spruce

Bristlecone Pine

Bristlecone pines are evergreens with short, green, needle-like leaves that grow in bundles of five. They are crowded in a long, dense mass curved against the twig, in a manner that resembles the tail of a fox. The trees have a clear, sticky resin on the

Bristlecone pine cones

cones and needles that becomes white with age. The cones are dark brown, from two to four inches long, cylindrical, and covered in spiny scales. They are usually found at elevations above 9,000 feet, on steep slopes and in areas with high winds and little rainfall. Bristlecone pines vary in height from 60 feet to as short as 3 feet at higher elevations. The stubby

Bristlecone pine

needles may be retained for 20 to 30 years before being replaced. Bristlecones grow slowly and can take up to 3,000 years to reach their full height. Some bristlecone pines are among the oldest trees in the world.

Cottonwood

Cottonwoods are deciduous members of the poplar family, with smooth, grayish-green bark that is often deeply furrowed on older trees. Their foliage is dark, shiny green above and paler below, turning dull yellow in the fall. Sometimes confused with aspen, the plains cottonwood is distinguished by larger, coarser, more deeply toothed, heart-shaped leaves; cottonwoods are also larger than aspens and have coarser bark, except when young. Narrowleaf cottonwood leaves are pointed at the tip, almost willowlike, with a long oval shape. Cottonwoods like moist soils and are often found near mountain streams and in coniferous forests. This handsome hardwood grows at elevations from 5,000 to 9,000 feet and usually reaches a height between 40 and 60 feet.

Cottonwood

Douglas Fir

The Douglas fir is a conical evergreen with thick, furrowed, corky, dark red-brown bark. It has flattened, needlelike leaves and red-brown oblong cones that have three-pronged tongues sticking out between the cone scales. At the end of the twig there is usually one, though sometimes more than one, cone-shaped, sharp-pointed bud, brownish-red in color.

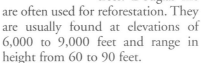
Douglas fir cones

These long-lived conifers grow in vast forests, often in pure stands, with well-drained soil. They are among the world's most important timber trees. Douglas firs are often used for reforestation. They are usually found at elevations of 6,000 to 9,000 feet and range in height from 60 to 90 feet.

Douglas fir

Engelmann Spruce

These evergreens are large trees with dark or blue-green needles and a dense, narrow, conical crown of branches in close rows. The branches are horizontal, often short, dense, and drooping, with cones less than two inches long. Straight, tall, and slender, Engelmann spruces are shaped vaguely like church spires—about 1 to 2.5 feet in diameter, growing upwards of 50 to 80 feet, in groves very close together. At high elevations, the Engelmann is dwarfed, straggling, and naked on the windward side; but when growing in the open, it retains its lower branches more completely and takes on more ample outlines. It is normally found between 9,000 feet and timberline. Its needles, twigs, and seeds provide food to a variety of wildlife.

Engelmann spruce cones

Engelmann spruce

Juniper

Juniper

Rocky Mountain junipers are also called mountain red cedars. They are stout, spreading, bushy trees with minute gray-green leaves that are blunt and grow close to the twig. Berries are blue in color, about a fourth of an inch in diameter, containing one or several seeds. Junipers range in height from 10 feet in exposed situations to as tall as 30 feet in sheltered canyons, where the limbs might tend to droop like those of a weeping willow. Junipers are often found growing near pinyon trees (the U.S. Forest Service refers to the two together as P & J). The berries serve as an important food source to some birds and small wildlife.

Lodgepole Pine

Lodgepole pines

The bark of lodgepole pine trees is thin and loosely scaly. The foliage is yellow-green. Trees have yellow-brown, egg-shaped cones that range in length from 0.75 to 2 inches. These resin-sealed cones remain on the trees for many years. In the event of a forest fire, the resin melts away causing the cones to open and distribute the seeds to regenerate the species. These trees vary enormously in size, from 15 to 80 feet high. They may be tall with a narrow, conical, dense crown or remain small with a broad, rounded crown. Stands of the taller trees look like fields of evenly spaced telephone poles, with little separating them but fallen needles. They are shorter at higher elevations, where winds twist them into gnarled, bent shapes. Lodgepole pines are found primarily from 8,000 to 11,000 feet.

Lodgepole pine cones

In recent years, an epidemic infestation of the mountain pine beetle, a type of bark beetle, infected virtually the entire population of lodgepole pine trees in Colorado, a total of more than 1.5 million acres. The infestation began in 1997 when drought conditions made the trees susceptible to the destructive, rice-sized beetle. Mountain pine beetles burrow beneath the tree's bark and lay eggs, often at the same time spreading a fungus that encourages death of the tree. Throughout the following decade, drought and warm winters combined with crowded growing conditions left the trees too weak to ward off attacks and encouraged widespread beetle infiltration. Colorado land management agencies report that millions of acres of trees have already died or will die, and it will take decades to reforest the affected land.

Pinyon Pine

Pinyons are small, bushy evergreen trees with short trunks and compact, rounded

Pinyon pine cone

crowns. The gray to red-brown bark is rough and scaly. Needles range from three-fourths inches to two inches long, usually two to a bundle, with blue-green foliage on the younger trees and dark, yellow-green foliage on more mature ones. Cones are one to two inches and have edible seeds that are eaten raw or roasted, known as Indian nuts or pine nuts. Pinyon pines range in height from 10 to 35 feet. They are usually found in open woodlands (often with juniper) in the foothills at elevations of 6,000 to 8,000 feet.

Pinyon pine

Ponderosa Pine

Also called western yellow pine, ponderosa pines have long needles (three to seven inches) that grow in clusters of two or three. The bark of young

Pondersoa pine cones

trees is dark brown and furrowed, while older trees develop orange, flaky bark. The cones are red-brown and spiky, about three to five inches long. The ponderosa pine grows 60 to 90 feet tall and is usually found at lower elevations of 6,000 to 8,500 feet.

Ponderosa pine

The Front Range Region

TRAILS IN THE FRONT RANGE REGION

- ■ 1   Sevenmile Creek Trail
- ■ 2   Old Flowers Road
- ■ 3   Moody Hill Trail
- ■ 4   Crystal Mountain Trail
- ■ 5   Storm Mountain Road
- ■ 6   Old Fall River Road
- ■ 7   Pole Hill Road
- ■ 8   Pierson Park Trail
- ■ 9   Bunce School Road
- ■ 10   Middle St. Vrain and Coney Creeks Trail
- ■ 11   Caribou Flats Trail
- ■ 12   Switzerland Trail
- ■ 13   Gross Reservoir Trail
- ■ 14   Rollins Pass Trail
- ■ 15   Central City to Rollinsville Trail
- ■ 16   Kingston Peak Trail
- ■ 17   Nevadaville Loop
- ■ 18   Oh My God Road
- ■ 19   La Salle Pass Trail
- ■ 20   Badger Mountain Road
- ■ 21   Rampart Range Road
- ■ 22   Watson Park Trail
- ■ 23   Dakan Mountain Road
- ■ 24   Long Hollow Road
- ■ 25   Winding Stairs to Ice Cave Creek Road
- ■ 26   Balanced Rock Road
- ■ 27   Schubarth Road
- ■ 28   Hell Creek Road
- ■ 29   Mount Herman Road
- ■ 30   Pikes Peak Highway
- ■ 31   Old Stage Road to Gold Camp Road
- ■ 32   Mount Baldy Trail
- ■ 33   Emerald Valley Trail
- ■ 34   Phantom Canyon Road
- ■ 35   The Shelf Road

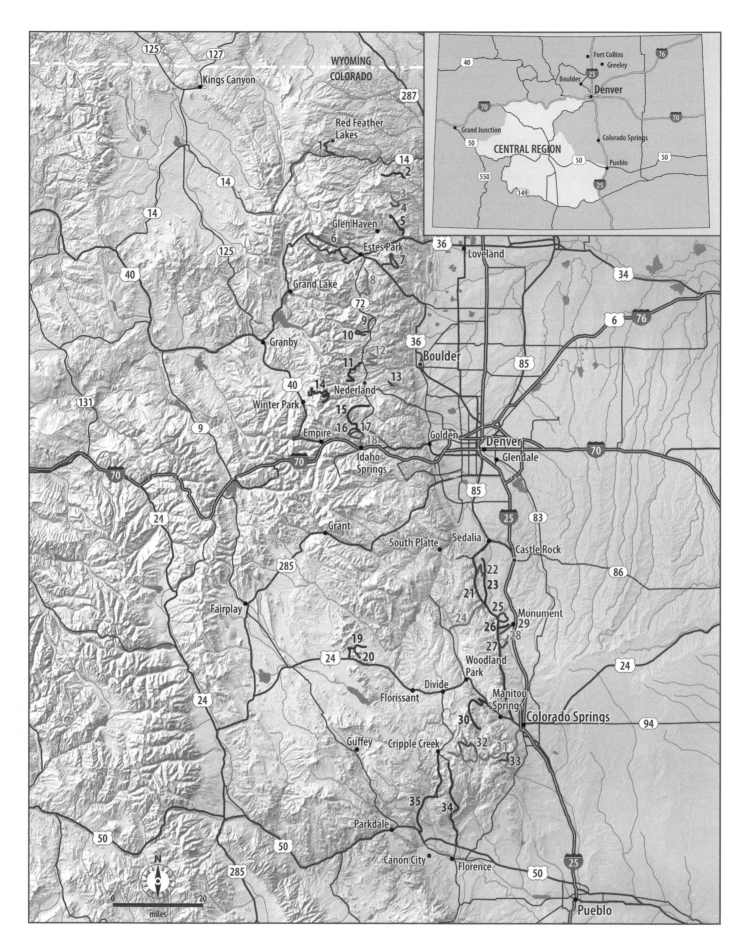

Sevenmile Creek Trail

Starting Point:	**Pingree Hill Road (CR 69), 0.3 miles**
	north of Colorado 14 and Rustic
Finishing Point:	**Manhattan Road (CR 162), 3.3 miles**
	south of Red Feather Lakes Road
	(CR 74E)
Total Mileage:	**8.5 miles**
Unpaved Mileage:	**8.5 miles**
Driving Time:	**1.5 hours**
Elevation Range:	**7,265 to 9,225 feet**
Usually Open:	**June to November**
Difficulty Rating:	**4**
Scenic Rating:	**8**

Special Attractions

■ Many small creek crossings.
■ Beautiful fall color.

Description

Sevenmile Creek Trail, which is actually longer than 7 miles, starts and ends on the road between Rustic and Red Feather Lakes. The trail loops to the west through Arapaho & Roosevelt National Forests, with basically two legs separated by a wide, open staging area. The first leg follows Sevenmile Creek into the forest and crosses through the creek many times. Not all the crossings are included in the directions below since they present no navigational difficulties. This southerly part of the trail is much more interesting than the latter section because it has numerous creek crossings, a fair bit of rock-crawling, a boggy stretch of mud (if you so desire), and a few mining ruins. The northerly part of the trail is mainly included for access to and from the area.

The trail starts opposite a staging area on Pingree Hill Road and heads northwest along a single-lane trail with ample passing places. The first 4 miles or so are a relatively straight shot

Sevenmile Creek crossing

to the northwest along the creek. This part of the trail makes for slow travel because of the abundance of medium-sized rocks that must be negotiated. The creek crossings can also be quite rocky, especially upon entry and departure. At the 4.1-mile point, the trail enters a clearing where a track on the left heads into a very muddy pit and continues farther along Sevenmile Creek. Here the main trail continues north, heading uphill past some unidentified mining remains.

The trail continues to climb away from Sevenmile Creek along a narrow track that becomes easier. The track eventually leads to a wide staging area of sorts, with tracks leaving from it in different directions. Both the far right track and the far left track end at Manhattan Road. However, the track on the left is the more interesting route and therefore is the one described below.

The final part of the trail is easier in standard but slightly more difficult to navigate. Many unmarked tracks can lead to confusion, but following the Route Directions you should have no problem.

This trail was researched in the fall and proved to have one of the most glorious displays of fall color of any trails in the vicinity. The aspens along Sevenmile Creek are the most brilliant.

View of trail winding through Sevenmile Creek Valley

View of trail through a stand of aspens

Current Road Information

Arapaho & Roosevelt National Forests
Canyon Lakes Ranger District
2150 Centre Avenue, Building E
Fort Collins, CO 80526
(970) 295-6700

Map References

USFS Arapaho & Roosevelt National Forests
Maptech CD:
  Denver/Steamboat Springs/North Central
Benchmark's *Colorado Road & Recreation Atlas*, p. 48
Colorado Atlas & Gazetteer, p. 19
The Roads of Colorado, p. 47
Trails Illustrated, #112

Route Directions

▼ 0.0		Trail starts on graded dirt Pingree Hill Road (CR 69) opposite an open staging area, 0.3 miles north of Colorado 14 and Rustic. Zero trip meter and turn northwest onto dirt road.
5.2 ▲		Trail ends back on graded dirt Pingree Hill Road (CR 69). Turn right for Colorado 14; turn left for Red Feather Lakes.
GPS: N40°42.23′ W105°35.11′		
▼ 0.2	SO	Seasonal closure gate and information board.
5.0 ▲	SO	Seasonal closure gate and information board.
▼ 0.3	SO	Cross through wash; then campsite on right.
4.9 ▲	SO	Campsite on left; then cross through wash.
▼ 1.1	BL	Track straight ahead; then cross through creek.
4.1 ▲	SO	Cross through creek; then track on sharp left.
GPS: N40°42.88′ W105°35.94′		
▼ 1.5	SO	Campsite on left and track on right.
3.7 ▲	SO	Campsite on right and track on left.
▼ 1.7	SO	Track on right.
3.5 ▲	SO	Track on left.
▼ 1.8	BL	Track on sharp left; then cross through creek.
3.4 ▲	BR	Cross through creek; then track on left.
▼ 2.8	SO	Track on right goes to campsite in 0.1 miles.
2.4 ▲	SO	Track on left goes to campsite in 0.1 miles.
GPS: N40°43.21′ W105°37.54′		
▼ 3.3	SO	Track on right climbs hill.
1.9 ▲	SO	Track on left climbs hill.
▼ 4.1	SO/BL	Track on left goes through mud pit and continues along Sevenmile Creek; then cabin

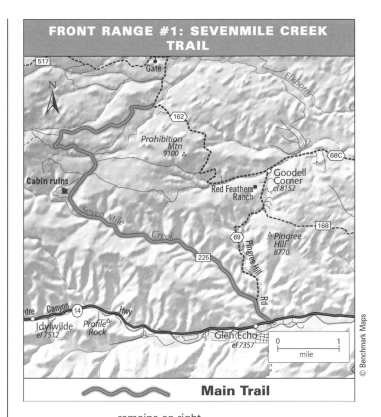

Main Trail

		remains on right.
1.1 ▲	BR	Cabin remains on left; then track on right goes through mud pit and continues along Sevenmile Creek.
GPS: N40°43.68′ W105°38.59′		
▼ 4.6	SO	Track on sharp left.
0.6 ▲	BL	Track on right.
▼ 4.7	SO	Track on sharp left.
0.5 ▲	BL	Track on right.
▼ 5.1	SO	Seasonal closure gate.
0.1 ▲	SO	Seasonal closure gate.
▼ 5.2	TL	Trail comes into a wide area that continues straight ahead. Make your first left and zero trip meter.
0.0 ▲		Continue to the southwest.
GPS: N40°44.06′ W105°38.21′		
▼ 0.0		Continue to the northwest.
3.3 ▲	TR	Trail comes into a wide area that continues straight ahead. Make your first right and zero

Optional side trail through a mud pit

Cabin alongside the trail

▼ 0.5		SO	Track on left to campsite.
	2.8 ▲	SO	Track on right to campsite.
▼ 1.0		TR	FR 871 on left.
	2.3 ▲	TL	FR 871 continues straight ahead.
		GPS: N40°44.46' W105°38.92'	
▼ 1.1		BR	Two entrances to track on left.
	2.2 ▲	BL	Two entrances to track on right.
▼ 1.8		BL	Two entrances to wide track on right.
	1.5 ▲	BR	Two entrances to wide track on sharp left.
		GPS: N40°44.36' W105°38.18'	
▼ 2.6		SO	Track on left.
	0.7 ▲	BL	Track on right.
▼ 3.0		SO	Track on left.
	0.3 ▲	SO	Track on right.
▼ 3.3			Two tracks on left; then trail ends on Manhattan Road (CR 162). Turn right for Colorado 14; turn left for Red Feather Lakes.
	0.0 ▲		Trail starts on Manhattan Road (CR 162), 3.3 miles south of Red Feather Lakes Road (CR 74E) and 6.6 miles north of Colorado 14. Zero trip meter and turn southwest onto FR 171.
		GPS: N40°45.08' W105°37.00'	

Old cabin at Lewis Ranch

only two students at Stove Prairie. The school closed for a year but soon reopened as new families moved into the area.

In 1964, a new classroom was added to the building, and more additions were made in 1974. The original schoolhouse still stands where it was first built.

Description

Old Flowers Road begins at the historic Stove Prairie Ranch and School and heads west through Arapaho & Roosevelt National Forests. The first 3.3 miles run through private property and over numerous cattle guards. The impressive stone buildings of the well-kept Stove Prairie Ranch stand out quite noticeably along this section of trail. Stay on the trail here and make sure you close the gate at the 3.3-mile mark after passing through.

The trail properly begins after the gate as it heads into Arapaho & Roosevelt National Forests. It winds through the foothills along an easy, formed dirt track. A few embedded rocks will remind you to keep your speed down if you get going too fast. Once in the National Forest, most of the trail runs through the trees, preventing any grand vistas. However, this in no way precludes this trail from being a peaceful wooded drive.

A couple miles into the National Forest, a few remains can be seen on either side of the trail. The remains include a cabin as well as some other more curious items. A little after the

---

FRONT RANGE REGION TRAIL #2

Old Flowers Road

Starting Point:	Stove Prairie Road (CR 27) at the Stove Prairie School
Finishing Point:	CR 63E, 7.9 miles south of Colorado 14
Total Mileage:	12 miles
Unpaved Mileage:	12 miles
Driving Time:	1.25 hours
Elevation Range:	7,330 to 8,650 feet
Usually Open:	June to November
Difficulty Rating:	3
Scenic Rating:	8

Special Attractions

■ Historic Stove Prairie Ranch and School.

■ Scenic, wooded drive with access to Cache La Poudre Wilderness.

History

Stove Prairie School sits at the crossroads of Old Flowers Road and CR 27. The building started as a one-room schoolhouse, built in 1896–97 by Emanuel Vannorsdel and Harlen Bosworth with the help of neighbors. The original structure included a belfry, but it was removed after the first year because it allowed snow to drift into the classroom.

Belle Thompson was the first teacher at the school. Thompson, like many other mountain schoolteachers, had to board with members of the community. By 1904, 37 students of varying ages, all taught by one teacher, attended the school. Soon after, three new schools opened in the district, leaving

Stove Prairie School at the beginning of the trail

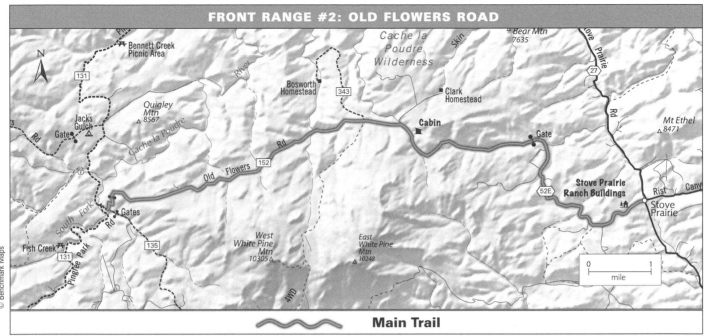

© Benchmark Maps

~~~~~~~~~~ **Main Trail**

remains is an excellent, private backcountry campsite in the Poverty Flats area. Just a bit after the campsite, FR 343 heads north toward the Cache La Poudre Wilderness. This is a less popular way into the wilderness than the trailheads off the main road through Poudre Canyon.

The forest finally opens up somewhat near the end, providing views to the north. Overall, the trail is not spectacular but an excellent outing nonetheless. Much of the scenery, especially the stone buildings of the Stove Prairie Ranch, gives the impression of the northeastern part of the country and is very quaint.

Current Road Information

Arapaho & Roosevelt National Forests
Canyon Lakes Ranger District
2150 Centre Avenue, Building E
Fort Collins, CO 80526
(970) 295-6700

Map References

USFS   Arapaho & Roosevelt National Forests
Maptech CD: Denver/Steamboat Springs/North Central
Benchmark's *Colorado Road & Recreation Atlas*, p. 48
Colorado Atlas & Gazetteer, p. 19
The Roads of Colorado, pp. 47, 48
Trails Illustrated, #112, #101

Route Directions

▼ 0.0			Trail starts on Stove Prairie Road (CR 27) at the Stove Prairie School, 19.9 miles north of US 34. Zero trip meter and head southwest on graded dirt road, signed FR 152.
	3.3 ▲		Trail ends on Stove Prairie Road (CR 27) at the Stove Prairie School. Turn right for US 34; turn left for Colorado 14; continue straight on Rist Canyon Road for US 287 and Fort Collins.

GPS: N40°37.15' W105°21.43'

▼ 0.7		BR	Cattle guard; then private road on left.
	2.6 ▲	SO	Private road on right; then cattle guard.
▼ 1.7		SO	Cattle guard.
	1.6 ▲	SO	Cattle guard.
▼ 1.8		SO	Cattle guard.
	1.5 ▲	SO	Cattle guard.
▼ 2.2		SO	Cattle guard.
	1.1 ▲	SO	Cattle guard.
▼ 2.8		SO	Cattle guard.
	0.5 ▲	SO	Cattle guard.
▼ 3.3		SO	Gate. Entering Arapaho & Roosevelt National Forests; then seasonal closure gate. Remain on FR 152. Zero trip meter.
	0.0 ▲		Continue to the east.

GPS: N40°37.95' W105°23.49'

▼ 0.0			Continue to the west.
	8.7 ▲	SO	Seasonal closure gate. Leaving Arapaho & Roosevelt National Forests; then gate. Zero trip meter.
▼ 0.2		SO	Cross through wash.
	8.5 ▲	SO	Cross through wash.
▼ 0.6		SO	Cross through wash.

Stove Prairie Ranch buildings

8.1 ▲	SO	Cross through wash.	
▼ 0.7	SO	Cross through wash.	
8.0 ▲	SO	Cross through wash.	
▼ 1.5	SO	FR 152B on right; then track on right.	
7.2 ▲	SO	Track on left; then FR 152B on left.	

GPS: N40°37.99' W105°25.08'

▼ 1.8	SO	Gate.	
6.9 ▲	SO	Gate.	
▼ 2.2	SO	Remains on both sides of trail.	
6.5 ▲	SO	Remains on both sides of trail.	

GPS: N40°37.92' W105°25.62'

▼ 2.6	BL	Great campsite ahead; then cross through wash.	
6.1 ▲	BR	Cross through wash; then campsite on left.	
▼ 3.3	SO	FR 343 on right; then FR 152C on left.	
5.4 ▲	SO	FR 152C on right; then FR 343 on left.	

GPS: N40°38.28' W105°26.57'

▼ 3.8	SO	Cross through wash.	
4.9 ▲	SO	Cross through wash.	
▼ 4.3	SO	Cross through wash.	
4.4 ▲	SO	Cross through wash.	
▼ 5.1	SO	FR 236 on right.	
3.6 ▲	SO	FR 236 on left.	

GPS: N40°37.75' W105°28.33'

▼ 6.6	BR	Track on left.	
2.1 ▲	SO	Track on right.	
▼ 6.9	BL	Track on right.	
1.8 ▲	BR	Track on left.	
▼ 7.8	SO	Cattle guard.	
0.9 ▲	SO	Cattle guard.	

Old machinery remains along the trail

▼ 8.4	BR	Campsite on left.	
0.3 ▲	BL	Campsite straight ahead.	
▼ 8.6	TR	Seasonal closure gate; then T-intersection with FR 135.	
0.1 ▲	TL	FR 135 continues straight ahead. Turn left onto FR 152 and pass through seasonal closure gate.	
▼ 8.7		Trail ends on wide, graded dirt CR 63E. Turn right for Colorado 14.	
0.0 ▲		Trail starts on CR 63E, 7.9 miles south of Colorado 14 and just south of a bridge over the South Fork Poudre River. Zero trip meter and turn east on narrow dirt road signed as Monument Gulch Road (FR 135).	

GPS: N40°37.07' W105°31.46'

FRONT RANGE REGION TRAIL #3

Moody Hill Trail

Starting Point:	Buckhorn Canyon Road (CR 44H), 1.5 miles west of Stove Prairie Road (CR 27)
Finishing Point:	Buckhorn Canyon Road (CR 44H), 8.5 miles from Stove Prairie Road (CR 27)
Total Mileage:	7.7 miles
Unpaved Mileage:	7.7 miles
Driving Time:	1 hour
Elevation Range:	6,590 to 8,545 feet
Usually Open:	June to November
Difficulty Rating:	4
Scenic Rating:	8

Special Attractions
■ Provides access to the more difficult Front Range #4: Crystal Mountain Trail.
■ Steep hill climb near the start.

Description
Moody Hill Trail starts and ends on graded dirt Buckhorn Canyon Road (CR 44H), west of paved Stove Prairie Road. The start of the trail is not especially well marked so keep an eye out to the south as you come within a mile and a half west of Stove Prairie Road. The trail immediately starts to climb a series of short pitches up Moody Hill. The trail surface is relatively flat with few imbedded rocks, making it an easy climb in low gear. Views are limited along this early section as the road is more or less closed in under the trees.

Coming out onto Moody Hill, the vegetation enclosing the trail opens up, revealing vistas to the south and west over Arapaho & Roosevelt National Forests. The route snakes along a ridge for a short stretch before coming into a very scenic meadow, complete with some cabin ruins and a couple of primitive campsites. The trail meanders through the meadow before reaching a T-intersection.

The trail continues along FR 132 through some areas that have been noticeably logged. Many of the trees toward the end

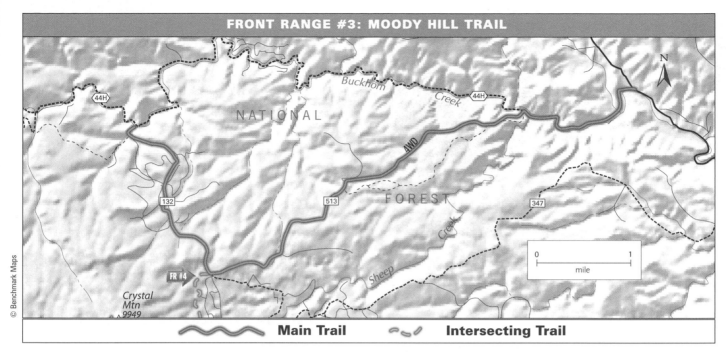

Main Trail   Intersecting Trail

of the trail are young. The 4WD section of the trail ends at the 4-way intersection near the end of the first leg. From this point, you can continue southwest along difficult Front Range #4: Crystal Mountain Trail or finish Moody Hill Trail by heading northwest down wide graded Crystal Mountain Road. If you decide to tackle Front Range #4: Crystal Mountain Trail, make sure you are ready to handle some tough rock-crawling that will challenge any stock 4WD.

Moody Hill Trail finishes by heading down a wide county road called Crystal Mountain Road. This part of the trail passes a lot of private property, so stay on the main road, which is used more as an access road than as part of the trail proper. If starting the trail in reverse, Crystal Mountain Road is marked as a private road; however, it is a public right-of-way.

Current Road Information

Arapaho & Roosevelt National Forests
Canyon Lakes Ranger District
2150 Centre Avenue, Building E
Fort Collins, CO 80526
(970) 295-6700

Map References

USFS   Arapaho & Roosevelt National Forests
Maptech CD:
        Denver/Steamboat Springs/North Central
Benchmark's *Colorado Road & Recreation Atlas*, p. 48
Colorado Atlas & Gazetteer, p. 19
The Roads of Colorado, p. 48
Trails Illustrated, #101

Route Directions

▼ 0.0   Trail begins on Buckhorn Canyon Road (CR 44H), 1.5 miles west of Stove Prairie Road (CR 27). Zero trip meter and proceed southwest up formed dirt road through seasonal closure gate. Trail is marked FR 513/344.

5.2 ▲		Trail ends on Buckhorn Canyon Road (CR 44H). Turn right for Stove Prairie Road (CR 27); turn left for a long drive out to Colorado 14.
		GPS: N40°34.26′ W105°20.90′
▼ 0.7	SO	Campsite on right.
4.5 ▲	SO	Campsite on left.
▼ 1.1	SO	FR 513A on right goes past a campsite.
4.1 ▲	SO	FR 513A on left goes past a campsite.
		GPS: N40°32.66′ W105°21.25′
▼ 1.6	SO	Track on left.
3.6 ▲	SO	Track on right.
▼ 2.3	SO	Track on left to campsite.
2.9 ▲	SO	Track on right to campsite.
▼ 2.6	TL	FR 513C on right; then T-intersection with FR 132.
2.6 ▲	TR	FR 132 continues straight ahead. Turn right onto FR 513; then FR 513C on left.
		GPS: N40°33.81′ W105°22.95′
▼ 3.0	BL	FR 132B on right.
2.2 ▲	BR	FR 132B on left.
▼ 3.9	SO	Seasonal closure gate.
1.3 ▲	SO	Seasonal closure gate.

The trail crossing through a meadow

Meadow with Moody Hill in the distance

▼ 4.2		SO	Seasonal closure gate.
1.0 ▲		SO	Seasonal closure gate.
▼ 4.4		SO	Private road on sharp left; then campsite on right.
0.8 ▲		BL	Campsite on left; then private road on right.
▼ 5.1		SO	FR 132D on right.
0.1 ▲		BR	FR 132D on left.

GPS: N40°32.77' W105°24.65'

| ▼ 5.2 | | TR | 4-way intersection. Road on left dead-ends at private property. Front Range #4: Crystal Mountain Trail is straight ahead. Zero trip meter and turn right onto graded dirt Crystal Mountain Road. |
| 0.0 ▲ | | | Continue to the east. |

GPS: N40°32.74' W105°24.79'

Cabin ruins beside the trail

▼ 0.0			Continue to the northwest.
2.5 ▲		TL	4-way intersection. Road straight ahead dead-ends at private property. Front Range #4: Crystal Mountain Trail is on the right. Zero trip meter and turn left onto graded dirt road.
▼ 0.1		SO	Campsite on right.
2.4 ▲		SO	Campsite on left.
▼ 2.5			Trail ends back on Buckhorn Canyon Road (CR 44H). Turn right for Stove Prairie Road (CR 27); turn left for a long drive out to Colorado 14.
0.0 ▲			Trail starts on Buckhorn Canyon Road (CR 44H), 7 miles from the eastern end of the trail and 8.5 miles from Stove Prairie Road (CR 27). Zero trip meter and head southwest on graded dirt road, signed to private property.

GPS: N40°34.17' W105°26.68'

FRONT RANGE REGION TRAIL #4

Crystal Mountain Trail

Starting Point:	Front Range #3: Moody Hill Trail, 5.2 miles from the eastern end
Finishing Point:	Summit of Crystal Mountain
Total Mileage:	4 miles
Unpaved Mileage:	4 miles
Driving Time:	2 hours
Elevation Range:	8,440 to 9,935 feet
Usually Open:	June to November
Difficulty Rating:	7
Scenic Rating:	10

Special Attractions
- Difficult rock-crawling.
- Spectacular view from the top of Crystal Mountain.
- Opportunity to collect crystals.

Description

Crystal Mountain Trail is one of those trails that will give any four-wheeler a number of war stories and maybe a couple of dings and scratches on their vehicle to go along with them. The first couple miles of the trail start out innocently enough, with beautiful views and no serious obstacles. This part of the trail is especially scenic during the fall, when the many aspens in the area turn brilliant yellow.

The 2.1-mile point signals the start of the rock-crawling. Past this point, long wheelbase vehicles will begin to have some problems. An unmodified high-clearance, short wheelbase 4WD with good tires can make it through; however, most of the vehicles that travel this route have at least a small lift and larger tires. One rocky obstacle in the trail will present a serious challenge to stock high-clearance 4WDs. However, this one has an optional loop to the left side that bypasses the challenge. Beyond the rock obstacle, the trail immediately enters a clearing with some difficult rocky climbs to the left and a mild alternate route to the right. Although the initial obsta-

Rocky obstacle with the side route around it

cles have easier alternative routes around them, the rest of the trail must be tackled more or less head-on.

Past the clearing, the trail climbs into the trees and the surface becomes more rocky and rutted with the occasional tree root extending into the trail. It is a good idea to run this trail with another vehicle or at the very least with another person to spot. The many rocky climbs often have only one reasonable line for unmodified rigs, and a spotter will help you stay on that line instead of bouncing all around and getting knocked back.

The trail standard stays relatively consistent until the 3.8-mile mark. At this point, the route continues straight ahead, but turn right instead to climb to the top of Crystal Mountain. This climb is very loose and can easily have vehicles fishtailing. Walk this final section before attempting it in your vehicle to make sure you are up for it. A track on the right in the middle of the ascent provides a spot to catch your breath and turn around if need be.

The view from the top of Crystal Mountain is well worth the effort required to get there.

View from summit of Crystal Mountain

Current Road Information

Arapaho & Roosevelt National Forests
Canyon Lakes Ranger District
2150 Centre Avenue, Building E
Fort Collins, CO 80526
(970) 295-6700

Map References

USFS   Arapaho & Roosevelt National Forests
Maptech CD:
          Denver/Steamboat Springs/North Central
Benchmark's *Colorado Road & Recreation Atlas,* p. 48
Colorado Atlas & Gazetteer, p. 19
Trails Illustrated, #101

Route Directions

▼ 0.0		Trail starts at 4-way intersection on Front Range #3: Moody Hill Trail, 5.2 miles from the eastern end and 2.5 miles from the western end. Zero trip meter and turn southwest on formed dirt FR 344.
	GPS: N40°32.73′ W105°24.80′	
▼ 0.1	SO	Seasonal closure gate.
▼ 0.7	SO	Track on right.
▼ 1.4	SO	Two entrances to track on left.
▼ 1.5	SO	Track on left through meadow.
▼ 1.8	BR	Track on left.

Beginning of the final climb to the summit

N

132

513

FR #3

Crystal
Mtn
△9949

Boiler Hill
△8863

0   1
mile

© Benchmark Maps

〰️ **Main Trail**   ᵔᵔᵕ **Adjacent Trail**

▼ 2.1	BL/BR	Track straight ahead is more difficult option; bear left and come into open area. Then bear right past tracks on left, which are more difficult routes that climb to the same point.
		GPS: N40°31.72' W105°24.90'
▼ 2.3	BL	Track on right.
▼ 2.6	BR	Track on left.
▼ 3.2	BR	Track on left.
		GPS: N40°32.11' W105°25.42'
▼ 3.5	BR	Track on left.
▼ 3.8	TR	Track straight ahead. Turn right and start the final climb to the top.
		GPS: N40°32.22' W105°26.03'
▼ 3.9	BL	Track on right in mid-climb.
▼ 4.0		Trail ends on top of Crystal Mountain.
		GPS: N40°32.33' W105°25.97'

Another rock obstacle in the trail

Storm Mountain Road

Starting Point:	Cedar Park Road (CR 43), 0.2 miles northwest of US 34
Finishing Point:	Viewpoint on Storm Mountain
Total Mileage:	9.3 miles
Unpaved Mileage:	7.7 miles
Driving Time:	1.5 hours
Elevation Range:	6,215 to 9,865 feet
Usually Open:	June to November
Difficulty Rating:	5
Scenic Rating:	10

Special Attractions

- Incredible views from Storm Mountain.
- Great backcountry campsites.

Description

Storm Mountain Road is only a proper 4WD trail for the final several miles. The first 7 miles of graded dirt road run mostly through private property with patches of forestland interspersed. The private driveways are noted in the Route Directions for ease of navigation.

The trail gets more interesting past the seasonal closure gate at 6.7 miles and the intersection at the 7-mile point. Heading past FR 153 into Galuchie Park, it narrows and becomes rougher. The park is a scenic open meadow with several great campsites as well as excellent aspen viewing in fall. The best campsite, a wide, flat area sheltered by a rock wall and the edge

The trail running through an aspen stand

View from the end of the trail with Longs Peak in the distance

of the forest, is off a side track to the right, 0.1 miles past the intersection with FR 153.

Past Galuchie Park, the trail turns back into the woods and starts a steep climb. Although the climb is steep, there are no serious obstacles in the trail. With a slow, steady pace using low range, most high-clearance 4WD vehicles will ascend the hill with no problems. Beyond the hill, the trail makes its way through the woods and into another clearing called Foggy Park. The route snakes up Foggy Park along a loose trail of dirt and rubble. Once you reach the upper part of Foggy Park, take a minute to look back to the south and southwest. The views are fabulous, and they only get better from here.

The trail runs back into the forest for the final half-mile climb to the top of Storm Mountain. Another excellent back-country campsite is located to the left of the trail approximately 2 miles after the intersection with FR 153. Tucked away in the woods, this campsite is more sheltered than the previous one, which clings to the edge of a meadow.

The trail ends at a wide overlook near the top of Storm Mountain. The view to the south, east, and west is unparalleled.

A trail to the left leads about a tenth of a mile up the hill to the summit of Storm Mountain. This track joins the track that leaves the main trail approximately 2.2 miles after the intersection with FR 153. They are both more difficult than the rest of the trail and should be scouted before any attempt is made to climb them. Likewise, the track that continues north from the overlook is also difficult and leads only about a tenth of a mile farther. This track ends at an old quarry and another overlook of the scenery to the northeast.

Current Road Information
Arapaho & Roosevelt National Forests
Canyon Lakes Ranger District
2150 Centre Avenue, Building E
Fort Collins, CO 80526
(970) 295-6700

Map References
USFS Arapaho & Roosevelt National Forests
Maptech CD:
Denver/Steamboat Springs/North Central
Benchmark's *Colorado Road & Recreation Atlas*, pp. 48, 62
Colorado Atlas & Gazetteer, p. 29
Trails Illustrated, #101

A difficult climb to the summit

View from the summit of Storm Mountain

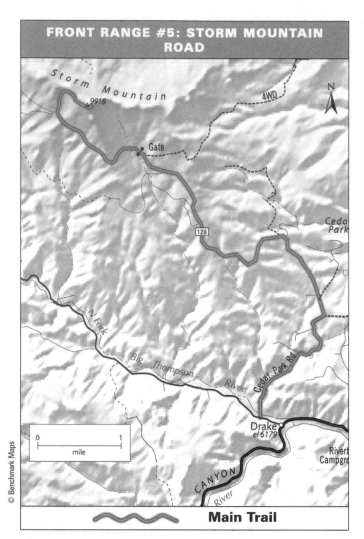

Storm Mountain
9918

Gate

128

Cedar Park

N Fork

Big Thompson River

Cedar Park Rd

Drake el 6179

Riverton Campground

CANYON River

0   mile   1

© Benchmark Maps

Main Trail

Route Directions

▼ 0.0		Trail starts on Cedar Park Road (CR 43), 0.2 miles northwest of US 34. Zero trip meter and turn right (north) onto unmarked road signed to forest access. Immediately, cross over North Fork Big Thompson River on bridge; then road turns to graded dirt. Road is marked FR 128.

GPS: N40°26.01' W105°20.74'

▼ 0.5	SO	Road becomes paved.
▼ 1.9	SO	Longs Peak Road on left.
▼ 2.1	TL	T-intersection. Palisade Mountain Drive on right. Turn left onto Storm Mountain Road (FR 128), following sign to forest access. Road turns back to graded dirt.

GPS: N40°27.00' 105°19.91'

▼ 2.4	SO	Lakeview Drive on right. Remain on FR 128, following sign to forest access; then Bob Cat Pace on right.
▼ 3.4	BL	Cedar Park Drive on right.
▼ 4.2	SO	Track on right.
▼ 5.0	SO	Track on left.
▼ 5.7	SO	Wide graded dirt track on left. Remain on Storm Mountain Road (FR 128).

GPS: N40°27.93' W105°21.58'

▼ 5.9	TR	Private drive ahead. Remain on FR 128.
▼ 6.0	BL	Track on right.
▼ 6.4	SO	Aspen Drive on right.
▼ 6.6	BR	Track on left. Remain on FR 128, following sign

▼ 6.7	SO	to forest access. Seasonal closure gate.
▼ 7.0	BL	FR 153 on right and small track straight ahead rejoins right away. Bear left onto FR 153 and zero trip meter.

GPS: N40°28.67' W105°22.37'

▼ 0.0		Continue to the west. Track rejoins on right.
▼ 0.1	BL	Track on right to campsite.
▼ 1.5	BR	Track on left. Entering Foggy Park.
▼ 2.0	BR	Great campsite on left.

GPS: N40°29.23' W105°23.32'

▼ 2.2	SO	Difficult track on left goes to top of Storm Mountain and rejoins in 0.1 miles.
▼ 2.3		Trail ends at view point on Storm Mountain. Track ahead goes 0.1 miles to another view point that looks to the northeast. Difficult track on left to the top of mountain.

GPS: N40°29.10' W105°23.10'

FRONT RANGE REGION TRAIL #6

Old Fall River Road

Starting Point:	Intersection of US 34 and Old Fall River Road
Finishing Point:	Alpine Visitors Center
Total Mileage:	10.6 miles (one-way)
Unpaved Mileage:	10.6 miles
Driving Time:	45 minutes (one-way)
Elevation Range:	8,523 to 11,907 feet
Usually Open:	July to mid-October
Difficulty Rating:	1
Scenic Rating:	8

Special Attractions

- Drive the first motor route across Rocky Mountain National Park.
- Chasm Falls.
- Scenic vistas of Rocky Mountain National Park.

History

Old Fall River Road travels a route once used by Indians to cross the Continental Divide. Called the Dog's Tail by the Arapaho, the passageway was frequently covered in deep snow, allowing dogs to more easily drag a travois, a V-shaped sled made from two poles lashed together with hide or blankets stretched between.

Construction on Old Fall River Road began in 1913 before the establishment of Rocky Mountain National Park. Convicts from the state penitentiary provided labor for the first stages of construction, and contractors finished the project in 1920. Old Fall River Road was dedicated on September 14, 1920, becoming the first road in northern Colorado to traverse the Rocky Mountains.

The unpaved road was a popular route, but difficult to navigate. Numerous tight switchbacks were built one above the

Fall River Valley

other up the mountain. The road was extremely narrow, rarely exceeding 14 feet in diameter, and few pullouts were provided. In 1932, Old Fall River Road was designated a one-way route, helping ease travel difficulties. Nothing could be done, however, about the steep grade of the road, which sometimes reached 16 percent. Some early vehicles had to climb up the mountain in reverse in order to make fuel systems powered by gravity work properly. Today visitors to Rocky Mountain National Park use Old Fall River Road as a scenic, historic route that is an alternative to the paved roads throughout the park.

Description

Old Fall River Road is located in Rocky Mountain National Park. You will need to pay the park entrance fee or use your National Parks and Federal Recreational Lands Annual Pass to access this trail. We recommend stopping at the Fall River Visitor Center and purchasing the booklet, *Guide to Old Fall River Road*, which details the scenery and history along the drive.

Use the Fall River Entrance Station on US 34 for the easiest access to the trail.

Approximately 2 miles beyond the Fall River Entrance Station, the trail begins at the intersection of Old Fall River Road and US 34. For the first 1.8 miles, the trail is a paved, two-lane road. Several hiking trailheads and a picnic area are located along this initial section of the trail. After approximately 1.8 miles, the road narrows into one-lane and the pavement ends. As the trail climbs, it becomes a shelf road in places, but it is not difficult. The well-maintained surface is wide and sound.

Navigating the remainder of the route is easy. Be aware that this road is extremely popular with park visitors, and traffic can be heavy. Because of the traffic, this is a one-way route and should only be undertaken from east to west following the directions given below. Also because of the traffic, along with the narrower width of the trail, opportunities to pull off the trail and stop to take photographs are drastically limited. To avoid traffic, it is best to travel this route early in the morning.

View near the end of the trail with Alpine Visitors Center on the hill in the distance

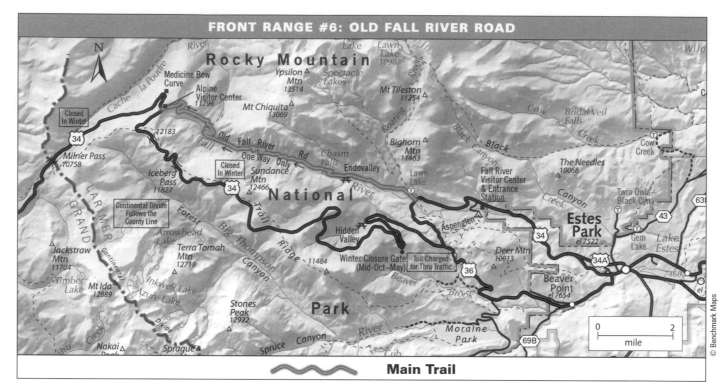

Main Trail

© Benchmark Maps

Current Road Information

Rocky Mountain National Park
1000 US 36
Estes Park, CO 80517
(970) 586-1206

Map References

Maptech CD:
      Denver/Steamboat Springs/North Central
Benchmark's *Colorado Road & Recreation Atlas*, p. 62
Colorado Atlas & Gazetteer, p. 29
The Roads of Colorado, p. 47
National Park Service Rocky Mountain National Park Map
(free with park admission)

Route Directions

▼ 0.0		Trail begins at the intersection with US 34 and Old Fall River Road. Proceed west on Old Fall River Road.
		GPS: N40°24.34' W105°37.52'
▼ 0.1	SO	Lawn Lake Trailhead on right.
▼ 0.4	SO	Parking lot on left.
▼ 0.5	SO	East Alluvial Fan Parking Area on right.
▼ 0.7	SO	Cross over creek.
▼ 0.8	SO	West Alluvial Fan Parking Area; then seasonal gate.
▼ 1.8	BR	Fork through seasonal gate; then pavement ends.
▼ 2.1	SO	Cross bridge over Chiquita Falls.
▼ 3.1	SO	Chasm Falls Trail on left.
▼ 10.6		Trail ends at Alpine Visitors Center.
		GPS: N40°26.49' W105°45.776'

Alpine meadow and pond near the end of the trail

Pole Hill Road

Starting Point:	US 36, 3.4 miles east of the intersection of Colorado 7 and US 36
Finishing Point:	US 36, 3.4 miles east of the intersection of Colorado 7 and US 36
Total Mileage:	6.6 miles
Unpaved Mileage:	6.6 miles
Driving Time:	1 hour
Elevation Range:	8,045 to 8,950 feet
Usually Open:	June to November
Difficulty Rating:	3
Scenic Rating:	8

Special Attractions

■ Excellent backcountry campsites.
■ Expansive views over Estes Park and the eastern side of Rocky Mountain National Park.

Description

Pole Hill Road provides wonderful views and camping opportunities to visitors to the Estes Park area. The driving is not difficult, but there are several places where you can choose more difficult lines for a challenge.

The trail starts 3.4 miles from Estes Park and immediately passes through a subdivision before coming to a gate marking the start of forest service land. Past the gate, backcountry campsites abound. Immediately on the left are some great sites that overlook Estes Park. The trail continues to an overlook called The Notch, which provides fantastic views over the town. The campsites on either side of The Notch are some of the best along the trail.

The trail surface is generally formed dirt with some ruts

The Notch

and some imbedded rocks. However, any stock SUV should be able to complete the trail without difficulty.

Past The Notch, the trail follows narrow Solitude Creek as it climbs east toward Panorama Peak. Although some maps still show a road going up to the peak, the track is now gated, and the only access to the top is by foot. The trail then loops west to finish back on FR 122.

Current Road Information

Arapaho & Roosevelt National Forests
Canyon Lakes Ranger District
2150 Centre Avenue, Building E
Fort Collins, CO 80526
(970) 295-6700

View over Estes Park to Rocky Mountain National Park

Many good backcountry campsites can be found along the trail

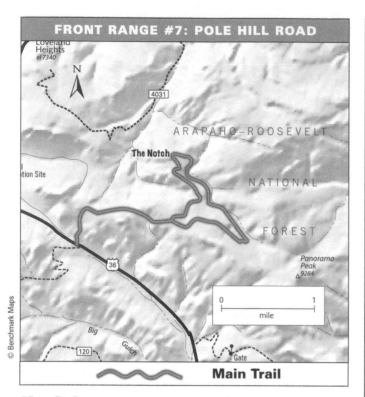

© Benchmark Maps

Loveland
Heights
el 7340

4031

ARAPAHO-ROOSEVELT

The Notch

NATIONAL

tion Site

FOREST

US 36

Panorama
Peak
△9284

0 ——————— 1
mile

Big
Gulch

120

Gate

~~~~~~~~ **Main Trail**

Map References

USFS   Arapaho & Roosevelt National Forests
Maptech CD:
          Denver/Steamboat Springs/North Central
Benchmark's *Colorado Road & Recreation Atlas*, p. 62
Colorado Atlas & Gazetteer, p. 29
The Roads of Colorado, p. 64
Trails Illustrated, #101

Route Directions

▼ 0.0		Trail starts on US 36, 3.4 miles east of the intersection of Colorado 7 and US 36 in Estes Park. Zero trip meter and turn north on graded dirt CR 122. Once on the road, there is a sign calling it Pole Hill Road.
	GPS: N40°21.39′ W105°27.26′	
▼ 0.1	SO	Meadow View Drive on right.
▼ 0.2	SO	Timber Lane on right.
▼ 0.6	SO	Pine Tree Drive on right.
▼ 0.8	SO	Private road on right. Proceed on FR 122, signed as forest access, and pass through seasonal closure gate.
	GPS: N40°21.70′ W105°26.98′	
▼ 1.2	SO	Campsites with great views on left.
	GPS: N40°21.73′ W105°26.60′	
▼ 1.6	SO	Cattle guard.
▼ 1.7	BL/SO	FR 247A continues straight ahead; then track on right and track on left.
	GPS: N40°21.02′ W105°26.11′	
▼ 1.8	SO	Track on left is FR 122B. Remain on FR 122.
	GPS: N40°21.07′ W105°26.02′	
▼ 2.2	SO	FR 122 continues to the right. Head north on unsigned FR 122A.
	GPS: N40°21.86′ W105°25.70′	
▼ 2.4	SO	Track on left and campsite on left.
▼ 2.7	SO	Viewing platform beside road on left at The

		Notch; then campsites on left around the bend.
	GPS: N40°22.10′ W105°26.06′	
▼ 2.9	BR	Track on left goes 0.1 miles to nice campsites and overlook.
▼ 3.7	TR	T-intersection with FR 122.
	GPS: N40°21.92′ W105°25.57′	
▼ 0.0		Continue to the southwest.
▼ 0.1	TL	T-intersection with FR 247D.
	GPS: N40°21.84′ W105°25.63′	
▼ 0.7	SO	Track on right.
▼ 1.1	BR	Closed road on left.
▼ 1.4	TR	Gated track on left at T-intersection. Turn right onto FR 247.
	GPS: N40°21.25′ W105°24.74′	
▼ 1.8	BL	FR 247 continues straight ahead. Proceed on FR 247A.
	GPS: N40°21.31′ W105°25.11′	
▼ 2.9		Trail ends back on FR 122. Track on right is FR 247A. Bear left and retrace your steps back to US 36.
	GPS: N40°21.02 W105°26.11′	

The trail at its most difficult

Pierson Park Trail

Starting Point:	**Colorado 7, 7.4 miles northwest of intersection with Colorado 72**
Finishing Point:	**Fish Creek Road, 2.7 miles from intersection with US 36**
Total Mileage:	**12.2 miles**
Unpaved Mileage:	**12.2 miles**
Driving Time:	**1.25 hours**
Elevation Range:	**7,740 to 9,315 feet**
Usually Open:	**June to November**
Difficulty Rating:	**3**
Scenic Rating:	**8**

Special Attractions

■ Scenic alternative to the Peak to Peak Highway.
■ Many wonderful campsites within easy range of Estes Park.

Description

Pierson Park Trail is a mild off-road trail that makes an excellent alternative to the Peak to Peak Highway (Colorado 7) heading in or out of Estes Park. The trail starts along the Peak to Peak Highway in Meeker Park, and for the first couple of miles it follows along the county road through private property. Stay on the main road through this area. Just after the trail turns onto FR 119, it passes through a gate marking the start of forest service land.

Once on forestland, the road becomes smaller and rockier; however, it is still a relatively easy drive. The many campsites along the southern part of the trail make perfect spots to car camp. One campsite that is particularly nice is in a clearing just west of House Rock, 3 miles north of the first zero point.

Past this site, the road climbs another 0.2 miles to a gate at the high point of the trail. Remember to close the gate behind you.

Past the gate, the road descends gently at first, then becomes steeper until the intersection at the second zero point. This is the most difficult part of the trail and the part where four-wheel drive is the most useful because it takes the load off the brakes. If driving the trail in reverse, this climb would push the difficulty rating up to a 4.

Pierson Park Trailhead sign

Eventually the route arrives at its namesake, Pierson Park, and the Pierson Park Hiking Trail. This area is more exposed with some nice rock outcrops to scramble up. A fabulous overlook of Estes Park and a campsite is located near the seasonal closure gate. Continue through the subdivision to the trail's end on Fish Creek Road just south of town.

This trail bypasses the trailhead for one of the most popular backcountry hikes in Colorado's Front Range, Longs Peak Trail. It leads west from the Peak to Peak Highway just a short distance north of the southern end of the Pierson Park Trail. This fantastic hike ascends to the summit of the 14,241-foot Longs Peak, located within Rocky Mountain National Park. If you intend to attempt this hike, contact the Rocky Mountain National Park service first for the necessary information and permits.

Current Road Information

Arapaho & Roosevelt National Forests
Canyon Lakes Ranger District
2150 Centre Avenue, Building E
Fort Collins, CO 80526
(970) 295-6700

The trail winding through Pierson Park

View of Rocky Mountain National Park from the trail

Map References

USFS   Arapaho & Roosevelt National Forests
Maptech CD:
        Denver/Steamboat Springs/North Central
Benchmark's *Colorado Road & Recreation Atlas*, p. 62
Colorado Atlas & Gazetteer, p. 29
The Roads of Colorado, p. 64
Trails Illustrated, #200

Route Directions

▼ 0.0			From the intersection of Colorado 72 and Colorado 7, head 7.4 miles northwest and turn right on Cabin Creek Road (CR 82). Zero trip meter and head north.
	2.0 ▲		Trail ends on Colorado 7. Turn right for Estes Park; turn left for Colorado 72.
		GPS: N40°14.24' W105°31.79'	
▼ 0.9		TR	T-intersection. Turn right on CR 82E; CR 82 continues on left.
	1.1 ▲	TL	CR 82 continues ahead. Turn left on CR 82.
		GPS: N40°14.54' W105°30.97'	
▼ 1.5		SO	Cattle guard and sign. Private property next 2 miles.
	0.5 ▲	SO	Cattle guard.
▼ 2.0		BL	Road continues ahead to Johnny Park. Bear left on FR 119 signed to Pierson Park and zero trip meter.
	0.0 ▲		Continue to the west.
		GPS: N40°14.11' W105°30.09'	
▼ 0.0			Head northeast on FR 119.
	4.9 ▲	TR	Turn right on unsigned CR 82E and zero trip meter.
▼ 0.1		SO	Entering National Forest; then pass through gate.
	4.8 ▲	SO	Pass through gate; then leaving National Forest.
▼ 0.4		SO	Hiking trail on left follows old 4x4 route.
	4.5 ▲	SO	Hiking trail on right follows old 4x4 route.
▼ 1.3		BR	Two entrances to FR 325 on left.
	3.6 ▲	BL	Two entrances to FR 325 on right.
		GPS: N40°14.88' W105°29.81'	
▼ 2.1		SO	Parking area and campsite on right.
	2.8 ▲	SO	Parking area and campsite on left.
▼ 3.0		SO	Campsite in clearing on left.
	1.9 ▲	SO	Campsite in clearing on right.
▼ 3.2		SO	Pass through gate and close behind you.
	1.7 ▲	SO	Pass through gate and close behind you.
▼ 4.3		SO	Cross through wash.
	0.6 ▲	SO	Cross through wash.
▼ 4.4		SO	Cross through wash; then track on left goes to campsite and continues past; then cross through second wash.
	0.5 ▲	SO	Cross through wash; then track on right goes to campsite and continues past; then cross through second wash.
		GPS: N40°16.78' W105°29.46'	
▼ 4.6		SO	Entering firewood area.
	0.3 ▲	SO	Leaving firewood area.
▼ 4.9		BL	Track straight on continues 0.2 miles to private property. Bear left following FR 119 and zero trip meter.
	0.0 ▲		Continue to the south.
		GPS: N40°16.99' W105°29.08'	
▼ 0.0		SO	Continue to the northwest.
	5.3 ▲	BR	Track on left goes 0.2 miles to private property.

			Bear right following FR 119 and zero trip meter.
▼ 0.1		SO	Cross through wash.
	5.2 ▲	SO	Cross through wash.
▼ 0.4		SO	Track on left; then leaving firewood area.
	4.9 ▲	SO	Entering firewood area; then track on right.
▼ 0.5		SO	Cross over wash.
	4.8 ▲	SO	Cross over wash.
▼ 0.7		SO	Closed road on right in clearing.
	4.6 ▲	SO	Closed road on left in clearing.
		GPS: N40°17.46' W105°29.46'	
▼ 0.9		SO	Track on right.
	4.4 ▲	SO	Track on left.
▼ 1.6		BR	Track on left to campsite in clearing; then FR 119D on left. Bear right following FR 199.
	3.7 ▲	BL	FR 119D on right. Bear left following FR 119; then track on right to campsite in clearing.
		GPS: N40°18.04' W105°29.42'	
▼ 1.7		SO	Track on right goes 0.1 miles to Pierson Park Trailhead.
	3.6 ▲	SO	Track on left goes 0.1 miles to Pierson Park Trailhead.
		GPS: N40°18.09' W105°29.37'	
▼ 1.8		SO	Track on right; then track on left.
	3.5 ▲	BR	Track on right; then track on left. Bear right at

Elk grazing near the trail

			second intersection.
▼ 2.3		SO	Gated track on right.
	3.0 ▲	BR	Gated track straight ahead.
▼ 2.4		SO	Hiking trail on left.
	2.9 ▲	SO	Hiking trail on right.
		GPS: N40°18.55′ W105°29.38′	
▼ 2.6		SO	FR 119D on left.
	2.7 ▲	BL	FR 119D on right.
		GPS: N40°18.75′ W105°29.39′	
▼ 3.1		SO	Pass through seasonal closure gate; then viewpoint on right.
	2.2 ▲	SO	Viewpoint on left; then pass through seasonal closure gate.
▼ 3.3		TR	T-intersection. Turn right on graded dirt Little Valley Drive (unsigned).
	2.0 ▲	TL	Turn left on FR 119 following sign for Pierson Park.
		GPS: N40°19.03′ W105°29.46′	
▼ 3.6		BR	Track on left. Remain on Little Valley Drive.
	1.7 ▲	TL	Track straight on. Remain on Little Valley Drive.
▼ 3.7		TL	Track on right. Remain on Little Valley Drive.
	1.6 ▲	BR	Track straight ahead. Remain on Little Valley Drive.
▼ 3.8		BR	Two tracks on left. Remain on Little Valley Drive.
	1.5 ▲	BL	Two tracks on right. Remain on Little Valley Drive.
▼ 4.2		SO	Leaving Little Valley neighborhood.
	1.1 ▲	SO	Entering Little Valley neighborhood.
▼ 4.5		SO	Graded dirt Saint Francis Way on left.
	0.8 ▲	SO	Graded dirt Saint Francis Way on right.
▼ 4.9		TL	T-intersection. Blue Valley Drive on right. Remain on Little Valley Drive.
	0.4 ▲	TR	Blue Valley Drive ahead. Remain on Little Valley Drive.
▼ 5.3			Trail ends on paved Fish Creek Road. Turn right for Estes Park and US 36.
	0.0 ▲		From US 36 on outskirts of Estes Park drive 2.7 miles south on Fish Creek Road. Turn left onto graded dirt Little Valley Drive. Zero trip meter and head south.
		GPS: N40°20.17′ W105°30.11′	

FRONT RANGE REGION TRAIL #9

Bunce School Road

Starting Point:	Peaceful Valley Campground, 0.4 miles west of Peak to Peak Highway
Finishing Point:	Peak to Peak Highway (Colorado 7), 0.6 miles northwest of intersection with Colorado 72
Total Mileage:	5.2 miles
Unpaved Mileage:	5.2 miles
Driving Time:	45 minutes
Elevation Range:	8,240 to 8,855 feet
Usually Open:	Mid-May to November
Difficulty Rating:	2
Scenic Rating:	8

The first switchback on the trail

Special Attractions

- Historic Bunce School.
- Rock climbing at the Ironclads.

History

Bunce School Road is just south of Allenspark. The town was first founded as Allen's Park in 1896. Many of the earliest residents hoped to strike veins of gold rumored to run all the way from the town of Ward, 8 miles to the south. An 1897 news report trumpeted the growth of Allen's Park, claiming there were 30 prospects, and the town was filled with stores and hotels. Some of the top-producing mines in the area were the Snowbank, the Tiger, the Bland, the Black Horse, and the Vulcan.

Residents hatched grand plans to build a mill and to build the town up into one of the largest in the state. Before these plans could be put into action, production at the mines steeply declined and the town was largely abandoned. Allenspark experienced a revival in the early 1900s as a tourist and outdoor recreation destination. Today the town has a population of about 500. The Allenspark area Hilltop Guild helps maintain the Bunce School House, which was built in 1888 and is listed on the National Register of Historic Places.

The trail passes near the Rock Creek ski area, which operated from 1947 into the early 1950s. Bill Hottel was the area's first manager. Hottel was a member of the U.S. Army's 10th

The Ironclads beside the trail

Mountain Division. The 10th Mountain Division trained principally at Camp Hale in Colorado, and many veterans of the division went on to develop the ski industry in the United States after World War II. A planned expansion for the 1951–52 ski season failed and the resort closed. Much of the area has since become overgrown, and it is difficult to delineate where runs were once located.

Description

This short, mellow trail provides a quiet and scenic alternate route to the Peak to Peak Highway near the intersection of Colorado 72 and Colorado 7. Much of the southern part of the trail passes through private property. With the exception of certain tracts of land that are fenced off, boundaries between private and public land are not well marked on the ground. Remain on the main trail until you are sure that you are on public land. When you begin to see a number of primitive campsites on either side of the trail, you are back on forest-land.

The trail starts out from the western side of the developed Peaceful Valley USFS Campground and immediately starts to switchback up the side of the hill. These switchbacks are the rockiest part of the trail, but they are easily negotiated by any high-clearance 4WD. Views of the Continental Divide get better and better as you climb above the campground.

Once you have completed the climb, the trail runs along a formed dirt trail that is more or less flat. After rain, water can stay on the trail in a number of places. The result is a series of mud pits that should be bypassed to avoid trail damage. The route progresses north toward the Ironclads, an impressive rock formation popular with climbers. This trail only offers a few glimpses of the Ironclads, the best of which comes when you crest a hill along the trail. About a mile before the trail's

Bunce School at the end of the trail

end, side trails head left toward the rocks themselves. The Ironclads offer a variety of challenges, from bouldering to multi pitch routes.

The trail continues through forest service land with numerous campsites on either side of it and finishes at the historic Bunce School. The trail is very popular with the full range of off-road enthusiasts. Be aware that you may encounter motorbikes and ATVs darting around blind corners.

Current Road Information

Arapaho & Roosevelt National Forests
Boulder Ranger District
2140 Yarmouth Avenue
Boulder, CO 80301
(303) 541-2500

Map References

USFS   Arapaho & Roosevelt National Forests
Maptech CD:
        Denver/Steamboat Springs/North Central
Benchmark's *Colorado Road & Recreation Atlas*, p. 62
Colorado Atlas & Gazetteer, p. 29
The Roads of Colorado, p. 64
Trails Illustrated, #102

Route Directions

▼ 0.0			From Peak to Peak Highway (Colorado 72), 17.8 miles north of Nederland and 4 miles south of the intersection with Colorado 7, turn west into Peaceful Valley Campground. Proceed 0.4 miles through the campground on paved road. On far side of campground, zero trip meter and turn sharp right onto FR 115.
	5.2 ▲		Trail ends on the west side of Peaceful Valley Campground. Turn right for more difficult Front Range #10: Middle St. Vrain and Coney Creeks Trail; turn left for Peak to Peak Highway.
		GPS: N40°07.91' W105°30.56'	
▼ 0.7		SO	Seasonal closure gate; then campsite on left is set back from the trail.
	4.5 ▲	SO	Campsite on right is set back from the trail; then seasonal closure gate.
▼ 0.8		SO	Narrow track on left.

The beginning of the trail

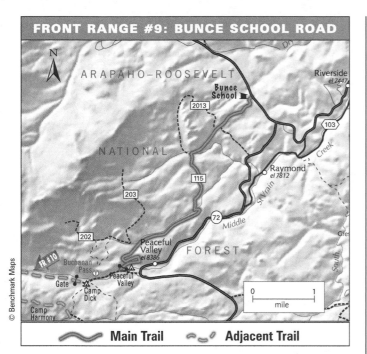

© Benchmark Maps

ARAPAHO–ROOSEVELT

Riverside
el 7447

Bunce
School

2013

103

NATIONAL

Raymond
el 7812

115

203

St. Vrain

72 Middle

Gres

202

Peaceful
Valley
el 8386

FOREST

FR #10

Buchanan
Pass

Gate

Peaceful
Valley

South

Camp
Dick

Camp
Harmony

0   mile   1

〜〜〜 **Main Trail**   〜〜 **Adjacent Trail**

4.4 ▲	SO	Narrow track on sharp right.	
▼ 0.9	SO	Track on left; then campsite on left. Remain on FR 115.	
4.3 ▲	SO	Campsite on right; then track on right. Remain on FR 115.	
		GPS: N40°08.17′ W105°30.30′	
▼ 1.6	SO	Track on right.	
3.6 ▲	SO	Track on left.	
▼ 2.3	SO	Track on right.	
2.9 ▲	SO	Track on left.	
▼ 3.6	SO	Two tracks on right cut off a right hand switchback.	
1.6 ▲	BR	Two tracks on left cut off a left-hand switchback.	
▼ 3.8	SO	Narrow track on left.	
1.4 ▲	SO	Narrow track on right.	
▼ 4.2	SO	Two tracks on left. Remain on FR 115.	
1.0 ▲	BL	Two tracks on right. Remain on FR 115.	
▼ 4.4	SO	FR 217 on sharp right; then two tracks on right.	
0.8 ▲	BR	Two tracks on left; then FR 217 on left.	
		GPS: N40°09.99′ W105°28.63′	
▼ 4.5	SO	Two tracks on right.	
0.7 ▲	SO	Two tracks on left.	
▼ 4.6	SO	Track on left.	
0.6 ▲	SO	Track on right.	
▼ 4.9	SO	Two tracks on left; then staging area on right and left.	
0.3 ▲	SO	Staging area on left and right; then two tracks on right.	
▼ 5.1	BR	Private track on left; then Bunce School on left.	
0.1 ▲	BL	Bunce School on right; then private track on right.	
		GPS: N40°10.36′ W105°28.15′	
▼ 5.2		Trail ends on Peak to Peak Highway (Colorado 7). Turn right for Colorado 72; turn left for Estes Park.	
0.0 ▲		Trail begins on Peak to Peak Highway (Colorado 7), 0.6 miles northwest of Colorado 72 and just past Kelly House. Zero trip meter and turn west onto Bunce School Road, following "Historic Bunce School—Built 1888" sign.	
		GPS: N40°10.44′ W105°28.09′	

Middle St. Vrain and Coney Creeks Trail

Starting Point:	Ranger station at the western end of Camp Dick, 1.2 miles west of Peak to Peak Highway
Finishing Point:	CR 96 opposite Beaver Reservoir, 2.7 miles west of Peak to Peak Highway
Total Mileage:	8.6 miles
Unpaved Mileage:	8.6 miles
Driving Time:	3.5 hours
Elevation Range:	8,735 to 9,860 feet
Usually Open:	Mid-June to mid-October
Difficulty Rating:	7
Scenic Rating:	9

Special Attractions

- Difficult rock-crawling perfect for more advanced drivers.
- Deep crossing of Coney Creek.
- Access to the Indian Peaks Wilderness.

Description

This loop trail off of the Peak to Peak Highway is a great ride for skilled drivers in high-clearance 4WD vehicles. This trail is one of the more difficult in the area and is best driven by those who are not phased by deep water crossings or technical rock-crawling. Skid plates are an advantage.

The trail starts out from the western end of Camp Dick USFS Campground, which is located just west of Peaceful Valley USFS Campground. Both of these sites make for great places to stay during any visit to the region. Pass through the seasonal closure gate and head west along Middle St. Vrain

Boulders on the north side of the trail

Creek. This first part of the trail has become popular with bouldering enthusiasts. One excellent boulder is within the first quarter mile of the trail, easily visible on the right.

The trail indicates what you are in for with a couple rocky sections early on. It is best to scout these sections on foot first to find the best line. Those driving longer wheelbase vehicles and vehicles with low-hanging sidesteps may find it difficult to negotiate these obstacles without scraping. If you do not like the start of the trail, be warned that it gets more difficult later on. The trail remains relatively flat for the stretch along Middle St. Vrain Creek. There are a couple of muddy water crossings along this stretch. In normal conditions, they are easy to negotiate. However, in the spring and after rainstorms, they could become impassable. About halfway through the trail, Coney Flat Road breaks off to the right. Continue another 0.1 miles to the hiking trailhead for access to the Indian Peaks Wilderness.

After turning onto Coney Flat Road, the trail starts to climb and immediately presents a few challenging rock-crawls. The rocks are about the size of those encountered earlier, but this time there is the added challenge of climbing a hill while driving over the rocks. In 0.7 miles is the deep crossing of Coney Creek. There is a boardwalk across the creek on the south side of the crossing. You may wish to check it out on foot before crossing. Again, spring runoff and summer rainstorms can make the crossing impassable.

Current Road Information

Arapaho & Roosevelt National Forests
Boulder Ranger District
2140 Yarmouth Avenue
Boulder, CO 80301
(303) 541-2500

Map References

USFS   Arapaho & Roosevelt National Forests
Maptech CD:
        Denver/Steamboat Springs/North Central
Benchmark's *Colorado Road & Recreation Atlas*, p. 62
Colorado Atlas & Gazetteer, p. 29
The Roads of Colorado, p. 63
Trails Illustrated, #102

A creek crossing along the trail

Route Directions

▼ 0.0			From Peak to Peak Highway (Colorado 72), 17.8 miles north of Nederland and 4 miles south of the intersection with Colorado 7, turn west into Peaceful Valley Campground. Proceed through the campground on paved road. Pass the start of Front Range #9: Bunce School Road and continue to the western end of Camp Dick, which is 1.2 miles from Peak to Peak Highway. Zero trip meter and head west on rocky FR 114. Pass through seasonal closure gate; then Buchanan Pass Hiking Trail on both sides of road.
	3.6 ▲		Buchanan Pass Hiking Trail on both sides of road; then pass through seasonal closure gate. Trail ends at the western end of Camp Dick. Continue 1.2 miles through campgrounds to Peak to Peak Highway (Colorado 72).
		GPS: N40°07.80′ W105°31.44′	
▼ 0.4		SO	Track on right.
	3.2 ▲	SO	Track on left.
▼ 0.6		SO	Dispersed camping permitted past this point.
	3.0 ▲	SO	Dispersed camping ends.
▼ 1.8		SO	Track on right to campsite.
	1.8 ▲	SO	Track on left to campsite.
		GPS: N40°08.15′ W105°33.29′	
▼ 2.5		SO	Cross through creek.
	1.1 ▲	SO	Cross through creek.
▼ 3.6		TL	Track continues 0.1 miles straight ahead to Buchanan Pass Trail. Turn left on FR 507, following sign for Coney Flat Road and Beaver Reservoir Road. Zero trip meter.
	0.0 ▲		Continue to the east.
		GPS: N40°08.18′ W105°34.99′	
▼ 0.0			Continue to the southeast.
	5.0 ▲	TR	Track continues 0.1 miles straight ahead to Buchanan Pass Trail. Turn right, following sign to Peaceful Valley.
▼ 0.5		SO	Trail forks and immediately rejoins.
	4.5 ▲	SO	Trail forks and immediately rejoins.
▼ 0.7		SO	Seasonal closure gate; then Beaver Creek Hiking Trail #911 on right; then cross through Coney Creek.
	4.3 ▲	SO	Cross through Coney Creek; then Beaver Creek Hiking Trail #911 on left; then seasonal closure gate.
		GPS: N40°07.83′ W105°34.62′	
▼ 0.9		SO	Cross through creek.
	4.1 ▲	SO	Cross through creek.
▼ 1.4		BR	Trail on left for hikers and skiers only.
	3.6 ▲	SO	Trail on right for hikers and skiers only.
▼ 1.6		BR	Track on left to campsite.
	3.4 ▲	BL	Track on right to campsite.
▼ 3.4		SO	Trail on left for hikers and skiers only.
	1.6 ▲	BL	Trail on right for hikers and skiers only.
▼ 3.6		SO	Good campsite on right.
	1.4 ▲	SO	Good campsite on left.
		GPS: N40°07.62′ W105°35.52′	
▼ 4.0		SO	Track on right.
	1.0 ▲	SO	Track on left.
▼ 4.3		SO	Track on right.
	0.7 ▲	SO	Track on left.
▼ 4.6		SO	Track on right.
	0.4 ▲	SO	Track on left.
▼ 4.7		SO	Hiking trail on left.
	0.3 ▲	SO	Hiking trail on right.

FRONT RANGE #10: MIDDLE ST. VRAIN AND CONEY CREEKS TRAIL

	Main Trail		Adjacent Trail

▼ 4.9	SO	Leaving Roosevelt National Forest. Beaver Reservoir Cutoff Hiking Trail #851 on left.
0.1 ▲	SO	Beaver Reservoir Cutoff Hiking Trail #851 on right. Entering Roosevelt National Forest.

▼ 5.0		Trail ends on wide graded dirt CR 96 in front of Beaver Reservoir. Turn left for Peak to Peak Highway (Colorado 72).
0.0 ▲		Trail starts on CR 96 opposite Beaver Reservoir, 2.7 miles west of Peak to Peak Highway (Colorado 72). Zero trip meter and turn northwest on rocky FR 507, signed to Coney Flats and Camp Dick.

GPS: N40°07.28′ W105°31.43′

Difficult spot at the beginning of the Coney Creek section of the trail

FRONT RANGE REGION TRAIL #11

Caribou Flats Trail

Starting Point:	**Peak to Peak Highway (Colorado 72), 7.1 miles north of Nederland**
Finishing Point:	**Eldorado Avenue in Eldora**
Total Mileage:	**13.3 miles**
Unpaved Mileage:	**13.3 miles**
Driving Time:	**2 hours**
Elevation Range:	**8,700 to 10,360 feet**
Usually Open:	**Mid-June to late October**
Difficulty Rating:	**5**
Scenic Rating:	**9**

Special Attractions

- Trail passes historic Caribou town site and Eldora.
- Moderately difficult trail with an exciting shelf road descent.
- Access to great backcountry campsites as well as a developed campground.

History

Caribou Flats Trail passes through a historic mining district that developed as a result of one man's lucky find. While on a hunting trip in 1860, Sam Conger discovered a peculiar type of rock on Caribou Hill, near Nederland, Colorado. Eight years later, while in Laramie, Wyoming, he noticed a similar type of rock loaded in one of the Union Pacific Railroad's cars. When he picked up a piece of the ore to further examine it, he was told by a guard to keep away from the car, which contained high-grade silver from the Comstock Mine in Nevada. Conger replied that he knew where there was a whole mountain of the stuff.

After realizing the value of his earlier discovery, Conger hurried back to Caribou Hill to retrieve a sample of the ore and have it assayed. When it proved to be quality silver, Conger took five partners and they stockpiled ore over the winter to be shipped to the smelters in the spring. They were unable

Meadow alongside Caribou Creek

to keep their strike a secret for long, and by the spring of 1870 hundreds of prospectors had joined them.

The town of Caribou was platted in 1870 and grew rapidly. A bakery, grocery stores, and several saloons and hotels served the residents. Although Caribou was one of the richest camps in northern Colorado, it was a difficult place to live. Located at an elevation of 10,000 feet, the town frequently faced bitter winds, with some gusts exceeding 100 miles per hour. Snow usually fell from mid-September until June, forcing many people to enter and exit their homes through the second-story window. School was held from May 1 until November 1, to avoid the worst of the snow and cold. One Caribou resident joked that he enjoyed summer . . . both days of it!

The fortunes of the town mirrored that of the nearby mines. In the 1870s, roughly 20 mines were making a profit, with the camp producing about $500,000 in gold and silver in 1875 alone. The Caribou Mine was the top producer in the area, generating between $6 million and $8 million in gold and silver over its span of operation. The mine changed hands multiple times after the rich silver lode was first discovered. In 1873, the Mining Company Nederland, which was formed in Holland, purchased the mine for $3 million. Poor management forced the company to sell to Coloradan Jerome Chaffee for back taxes. A display of silver from the Caribou Mine at the Philadelphia Centennial Celebration in 1876 drew investment to the area.

Caribou started to decline in the 1880s. A fire in 1879 destroyed much of the town, which was rebuilt on a smaller scale. Diphtheria and scarlet fever epidemics further diminished the local population. The silver crash of 1893 dealt a significant blow to Caribou's economy. The town also continually faced the problem of poor accessibility. The closest railroad station was in Cardinal, about 2 miles away, and ore had to be hauled by wagon along "coon trail," a dirt road following Coon Creek from Nederland to Caribou. Another devastating fire in 1900 wiped out the town, and it has been virtually deserted since. One man, "the hermit of Caribou," remained until his death in 1944.

In 1946, the Consolidated Caribou Silver Mining Company completed the 3,500-foot Idaho Tunnel, a project that had been abandoned about 50 years earlier. The president of the company ordered the final blast, opening the tunnel from his Rockefeller Center offices in New York City. The tunnel did not revive Caribou, however, and it remained deserted except for some sporadic lease mining activity.

Just south of Caribou lies the town of Eldora. The Grand Island Mining District was organized in 1861, but there was little mining activity until Sam Conger's discovery of the Caribou Mine. In 1891, a group of prospectors from Central City located the Happy Valley placer claim, and they formed a camp called Happy Valley. A rival company established a town by the same name nearby, so the original settlement renamed itself Eldorado Camp. Mail delivery was unreliable, as a mining town in California was also named Eldorado Camp. At one point, angry workers from the Terror Mine in Colorado

The main crossing of Caribou Creek

View of Caribou Mine from the trail

had to wait to receive their pay because payroll had accidentally been shipped to California. To avoid further incidents, the town dropped the last syllable of its name to become Eldora.

In 1892, numerous lode mines were discovered in the vicinity of Eldora, and the town prospered. It served as a supply center and railroad hub for other nearby mining camps. So many people flocked to Eldora, there were housing shortages. The large population supported a lively social scene. The Gold Miner Hotel held lavish dances for the Eldora elite, and numerous dance halls and gambling houses catered to the less wealthy. A number of young men patronized the Monte Carlo brothel supposedly to take "ballroom dancing lessons."

By the turn of the century, many of the mines surrounding Eldora were virtually exhausted. After the rich pockets of minerals on the surface were mined, most of the remaining ore was low quality. Only three mines were in operation in 1898. Promoters continued to hype the district, and people were swindled into buying worthless claims. Mining dried up around 1917, but the town has managed to survive as a summer getaway destination. The nearby Eldora ski area, established in the 1960s, continues to draw tourists to the area.

Description

Caribou Flats Trail is a backcountry adventure with numerous highlights and has the added advantage of being less than an hour's drive from Boulder. The beginning of the trail is an unpaved, wide county road that takes off from the Peak to Peak Highway and heads west. Right away, the route passes the Sourdough Trailhead, an excellent single-track trail for hikers, equestrians, and mountain bikers that heads north toward Brainard Lake and Peaceful Valley. There is ample parking opposite the trailhead for unloading your horses or bikes.

The trail eventually turns off the graded route and heads southwest toward the old mining town of Caribou on a small rocky trail. Remaining on the county road will take you to the developed Rainbow Lakes USFS Campground in less than a

mile. Hiking trails that lead off from the campground access the scenic Rainbow Lakes, Arapaho Glacier, and other points within the Indian Peaks Wilderness. The route to Caribou begins by passing a few dispersed camping areas before coming to a short, rutted descent. Two tracks make the descent, and the right-hand option is the easier of the two. The route then fords Caribou Creek. Here a number of possible crossings provide different levels of difficulty. Again, the right-hand main crossing is the easiest.

Once south of Caribou Creek, the trail continues to follow along the creek and a wide meadow. This section is very scenic, especially in the fall when the aspens are gold. Looking northwest above the meadow, treeless Bald Mountain dominates the scenery until the trail veers into the woods and views become limited. This stretch of trail is often muddy, and ruts quickly fill with standing water. Most of the water holes do not present a challenge, but a few hide embedded rocks, so be careful and scout ahead when unsure.

Difficult rutted spot early in the trail

Not much is left at the wide intersection where the town of Caribou was once located. A track on the sharp left heads west to some old mining remains but quickly becomes narrow and overgrown. The main road to the southwest runs out to Nederland and can be used to cut this trail in half if need be. Use caution when exploring the town site and the surrounding areas on foot; many mine adits and open discovery shafts dot the landscape and may be concealed. If the trail up to this point has proven too difficult, it only gets harder so consider heading into Nederland from here.

The trail turns north and back into the forest at this point. For the first mile, the trail climbs into subalpine vegetation with many open vistas. It tops out at a saddle between Caribou Hill and Klondike Mountain, with views straight ahead to the Eldora Ski Resort. From the saddle, it is all downhill to the town of Eldora. Traveling southwest along Mineral Mountain, the trail follows a single-lane shelf road full of embedded rock. Passing places are limited, and you may need to back up for approaching vehicles. Remember, vehicles traveling uphill have the right-of-way, but as always, common sense should prevail. This is the narrowest and most difficult part of the trail. The final switchback just above Eldora is probably the most difficult obstacle on the trail. It is a very tight switchback with rocks embedded on the inside just waiting to scratch up your vehicle's paint job. Longer wheelbase vehicles could have serious difficulty making the turn. The trail ends in the quiet town of Eldora.

Current Road Information
Arapaho & Roosevelt National Forests
Boulder Ranger District
2140 Yarmouth Avenue
Boulder, CO 80301
(303) 541-2500

Map References
USFS   Arapaho & Roosevelt National Forests
Maptech CD:
        Denver/Steamboat Springs/North Central
Benchmark's *Colorado Road & Recreation Atlas*, p. 62
Colorado Atlas & Gazetteer, pp. 29, 39
The Roads of Colorado, p. 63
Trails Illustrated, #102

Route Directions

▼ 0.0   Trail starts on Peak to Peak Highway (Colorado 72), 7.1 miles north of the roundabout in Nederland. Turn west on wide, graded dirt CR 116 (also marked FR 298), signed to University of Colorado Mountain Research Station. Zero trip meter.
  4.3 ▲ Trail ends on Peak to Peak Highway (Colorado 72). Turn right for Nederland; turn left for Ward.

GPS: N40°01.94' W105°31.29'

▼ 0.4   SO Sourdough Trailhead on right with parking area on left.
  3.9 ▲ SO Sourdough Trailhead on left with parking area on right.

GPS: N40°01.68' W105°31.49'

▼ 0.8   BL Track on right to Mountain Research Station.

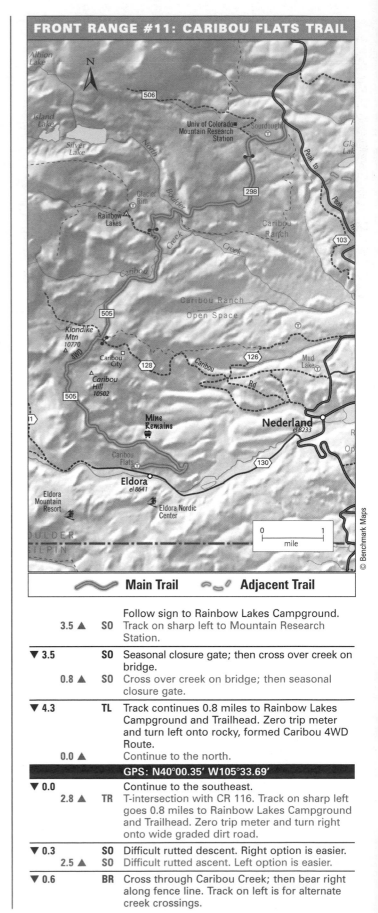

FRONT RANGE #11: CARIBOU FLATS TRAIL

〰 **Main Trail**   ⌇ **Adjacent Trail**

3.5 ▲	SO	Follow sign to Rainbow Lakes Campground. Track on sharp left to Mountain Research Station.
▼ 3.5	SO	Seasonal closure gate; then cross over creek on bridge.
0.8 ▲	SO	Cross over creek on bridge; then seasonal closure gate.
▼ 4.3	TL	Track continues 0.8 miles to Rainbow Lakes Campground and Trailhead. Zero trip meter and turn left onto rocky, formed Caribou 4WD Route.
0.0 ▲		Continue to the north.

GPS: N40°00.35' W105°33.69'

▼ 0.0		Continue to the southeast.
2.8 ▲	TR	T-intersection with CR 116. Track on sharp left goes 0.8 miles to Rainbow Lakes Campground and Trailhead. Zero trip meter and turn right onto wide graded dirt road.
▼ 0.3	SO	Difficult rutted descent. Right option is easier.
2.5 ▲	SO	Difficult rutted ascent. Left option is easier.
▼ 0.6	BR	Cross through Caribou Creek; then bear right along fence line. Track on left is for alternate creek crossings.

2.2 ▲	BL	Track ahead goes to alternate creek crossings. Bear left and cross through Caribou Creek.	

GPS: N40°00.05' W105°33.42'

▼ 1.2	SO	Unmarked track on left. Remain on FR 505.
1.6 ▲	SO	Unmarked track on right. Remain on FR 505.
▼ 1.5	SO	Track on right is closed to motor vehicles; then second track on right to designated campsites.
1.3 ▲	SO	Track on left to designated campsites; then second track on left is closed to motor vehicles.
▼ 2.1	BL	Track on right.
0.7 ▲	BR	Track on left.

GPS: N39°59.43' W105°34.54'

▼ 2.8	TR	5-way intersection. Turn first right, following to Eldora and Caribou 4WD Route. Second right goes to mine workings. First left goes 0.6 miles to tailings piles and mine workings. Second left is graded dirt Caribou Road, which goes to Nederland. Zero trip meter.
0.0 ▲		Continue to the northeast.

GPS: N39°58.86' W105°34.73'

▼ 0.0		Continue to the northwest on FR 505 and pass through seasonal closure gate.
6.2 ▲	TL	Seasonal closure gate; then 5-way intersection. Turn first left on Caribou 4WD Route (FR 505). Track on first right goes to mine workings. Straight ahead, graded dirt Caribou Road goes to Nederland. Second left goes 0.6 miles to tailings piles and mine workings. Zero trip meter.
▼ 0.5	SO	Track on right.
5.7 ▲	SO	Track on left.
▼ 0.9	SO	Track on left is closed to motorized vehicles and track on right.
5.3 ▲	SO	Track on right is closed to motorized vehicles and track on left.

GPS: N39°58.87' W105°35.48'

▼ 1.2	TL	T-intersection on saddle. Caribou Hill on left and Klondike Mountain on right.
5.0 ▲	TR	Track continues straight ahead toward Klondike Mountain. Caribou Hill is behind and to the right.

GPS: N39°58.65' W105°35.53'

▼ 1.7	SO	Track on right.
4.5 ▲	SO	Track on left.
▼ 1.8	SO	Track on left.
4.4 ▲	SO	Track on right.
▼ 3.1	SO	Mining remains and shaft on left.
3.1 ▲	SO	Mining remains and shaft on right.

GPS: N39°57.50' W105°34.67'

▼ 5.9	SO	Seasonal closure gate and information board.
0.3 ▲	SO	Seasonal closure gate and information board.
▼ 6.0	BL	Houses on left and right; then track continues straight ahead.
0.2 ▲	TR	T-intersection; then houses on left and right.

GPS: N39°57.03' W105°34.13'

▼ 6.1	TR	T-intersection with graded dirt road.
0.1 ▲	TL	Track ahead turns into gravel road.

GPS: N39°57.00' W105°34.14'

▼ 6.2		Trail ends on paved Eldorado Avenue in Eldora. Turn left for Nederland.
0.0 ▲		Trail starts at intersection of Eldorado Avenue and Sixth Avenue in Eldora, 3.3 miles west of Colorado 119/72 and 1.9 miles from the turnoff to Eldora Ski Resort. Turn north on graded dirt Sixth Avenue and zero trip meter. The turn from Colorado 119/72 is clearly signed to Eldora.

GPS: N39°56.97' W105°34.22'

Switzerland Trail

Starting Point:	Gold Hill Road (CR 52), 2.7 miles west of Gold Hill
Finishing Point:	Peak to Peak Highway (Colorado 72), 5.8 miles north of Nederland
Total Mileage:	14.3 miles
Unpaved Mileage:	14.3 miles
Driving Time:	1 hour
Elevation Range:	7,740 to 9,120 feet
Usually Open:	May to October
Difficulty Rating:	1
Scenic Rating:	9

Special Attractions

- Mount Alto Picnic Ground.
- Trail follows an old railroad grade.
- Trail is also a very popular mountain bike route.

History

Switzerland Trail begins approximately 2.7 miles west of the town of Gold Hill, the first mining town in Colorado. Perched on the divide between Four Mile Creek and Left Hand Creek, the town was established when rich gold ore was discovered in the vicinity. On January 15, 1859, a group of friends, includ-

Fireplace at Mount Alto Picnic Ground

Shelf road section with the trail below

Trail with Mount Alto Picnic Ground in the distance

ing Charles Clouser and James Aiken, was the first to find gold. Amazingly, the group panned in the neighborhood of $70,000 in gold within the next six months. The Horsfal Mine, one of the richest gold mines in the district, yielded more than $3 million of ore during its years of operation.

Learning a lesson from the Wild West California mining districts where claim jumping and other unscrupulous mining practices were rampant, early Gold Hill residents organized laws for the district as one of their first orders of business. Both men and women over the age of 16 could vote, and residency restrictions were minimal—requiring only that a person live in the district for 10 days! Elected officials registered claims and settled disputes. Such organization kept peace in town when prospectors flocked to the district after news spread of the rich discoveries of gold during 1859-60. Gold Hill boomed with 1,500 residents.

As soon as 1861, the easily accessible gold was virtually exhausted, and a number of miners left the region. During the Civil War, the value of gold was inflated, and eastern investors drove up the price of the mines in the district as they rushed to invest in the gold mining industry. Even after turning to hard rock mining, the gold mines around Gold Hill were largely tapped out by 1870.

Two years later, the discovery of tellurium revived the Gold Hill District. Tellerium contains both gold and silver, and the district's ore was found to be particularly rich with the element. A number of original claim holders returned to Gold Hill when news of the discovery spread. During the years of active mining between 1868 and 1909, the Gold Hill District managed to produce $12.5 million worth of gold. One mine, the Slide, produced more than $2 million worth of gold alone.

Like the majority of mining towns, Gold Hill faced a number of challenges to its survival. A forest fire swept the area in 1894 and would have entirely destroyed the town if a snowstorm had not quenched the flames. Transportation to and from the isolated mountain town was also difficult. Ore had to be carried by wagon down to Boulder. On the return trip,

heavy loads of mining equipment were hauled by up to 24 horses and took as long as a week to reach Gold Hill. The narrow gauge Colorado & Northwestern extended a line to just west of Gold Hill. For a time the line improved transportation, but ultimately it proved unprofitable. The line, also called "The Switzerland Trail," was abandoned in 1919.

The majority of the mines in the Gold Hill District closed in the 1930s. A few summer residents who enjoyed the cool mountain climate kept the town on the map. Today, many of the original buildings have been restored and are occupied. Blue Bird Casey's Table Inn, immortalized in writer Eugene Casey's poem, "Casey's Table d'Horte," is on the National Register of Historic Places.

About a mile along the trail is the Mount Alto Picnic Ground. Originally this site served as a stopover on the Switzerland Trail for tourists from Boulder taking the Colorado & Northwestern for a day trip in the mountains. Although the stone fireplace is all that remains today, the lodge, dance pavilion, and cabins that were located here were once the site of much merriment.

As the trail descends into Fourmile Canyon, it passes the old railroad and mining town of Sunset, which developed as

Sunset town site

an important junction for the Greeley, Salt Lake & Pacific Railroad. In 1894, a severe flood destroyed most of the line. Three years later, the Colorado & Northwestern built along a similar route on higher ground. Transporting ore alone, the railroad was unsustainable, so it began transporting tourists. The train would stop at Sunset, before visiting Mount Alto and Gold Hill. Visitors could stay at the Columbine Hotel for $5 a week and enjoy a home cooked meal of mountain-raised beef, vegetables, and fruit. Despite the influx of tourists, Sunset remained a small town, with 175 residents at its peak population in 1894.

Today, an old cemetery and a few cabins are all that remains, although a ghost reportedly haunts the town site. Local legend has it that a young man built a house on the hill between Sunset and Gold Hill as a wedding present for his bride-to-be. She died before the two were married, and now she supposedly returns to the "Honeymoon House" when the moon is full to whisper of her undying love.

Description

For its entire length, the Switzerland Trail follows a wide, graded dirt road through a mix of Roosevelt National Forest and private land. The trail is easy, and passenger cars could make the drive in good conditions, but a high-clearance vehicle would make the trip more pleasant. Before you start, a visit to the old mining town of Gold Hill is well worthwhile.

The trail begins on Gold Hill Road and heads south, passing the Mount Alto Picnic Ground. A two-story stone fireplace and chimney stands in the middle of the picnic grounds. Past the picnic grounds, the trail begins its long descent to the bottom of Fourmile Canyon, where it passes the town site of Sunset. An old ore cart with a plaque marks the spot, which is now private property.

From Fourmile Canyon Road, the trail begins a long climb up the south side of the canyon. It passes a few more-difficult tracks on the right that climb the canyon wall more directly. One of these is the somewhat rocky and overgrown trail along Pennsylvania Gulch, which passes some old mining remains.

The trail passes numerous cuttings for the railroad grades on its way to intersecting with Sugarloaf Road, which heads down to Boulder via Colorado 119. The main trail turns west onto this road and heads back to the Peak to Peak Highway.

Current Road Information

Arapaho & Roosevelt National Forests
Boulder Ranger District
2140 Yarmouth Avenue
Boulder, CO 80301
(303) 541-2500

Map References

USFS   Arapaho & Roosevelt National Forests
Maptech CD:
            Denver/Steamboat Springs/North Central
Benchmark's *Colorado Road & Recreation Atlas,* p. 62
Colorado Atlas & Gazetteer, p. 29
The Roads of Colorado, p. 64
Trails Illustrated, #102

Route Directions

▼ 0.0		Trail starts on Gold Hill Road (CR 52), 4.1 miles east of Peak to Peak Highway (Colorado 72) and 2.7 miles west of Gold Hill. Zero trip meter and turn south on graded dirt road, following sign for Switzerland Trail, Mt. Alto Picnic Ground, and Sunset town site. Hiking trail immediately on right.
4.6 ▲		Hiking trail on left; then trail ends on graded dirt Gold Hill Road (CR 52). Turn right for Gold Hill; turn left for the Peak to Peak Highway (Colorado 72).
GPS: N40°03.24′ W105°27.34′		
▼ 0.5	SO	Tracks on left climb hill.
4.1 ▲	SO	Tracks on right climb hill.
▼ 0.7	SO	Track on left; then two tracks on left climb hill.
3.9 ▲	SO	Two tracks on right climb hill; then track on right.
▼ 1.1	SO	Mount Alto Picnic Ground on left.
3.5 ▲	SO	Mount Alto Picnic Ground on right.
GPS: N40°02.83′ W105°26.53′		
▼ 1.5	SO	Track on left.
3.1 ▲	SO	Track on right.
▼ 1.8	SO	Campsite on right.
2.8 ▲	SO	Campsite on left.
▼ 4.6	SO	4-way intersection at Sunset town site (now private property). Road on left is Fourmile Canyon Road. Private road on right. Zero trip meter.
0.0 ▲		Continue to the southwest on FR 109.
GPS: N40°02.23′ W105°28.03′		
▼ 0.0		Continue to the northeast.
4.2 ▲	SO	4-way intersection at Sunset town site (now private property). Road on right is Fourmile Canyon Road. Private road on left. Zero trip meter.
▼ 0.2	BL	Track on right on left-hand switchback signed to Pennsylvania Gulch.
4.0 ▲	BR	Track on left on right-hand switchback signed to Pennsylvania Gulch.
GPS: N40°02.14′ W105°28.13′		
▼ 0.9	BL	Track on right on left-hand switchback goes up Bear Gulch.
3.3 ▲	BR	Track on left on right-hand switchback goes up Bear Gulch.
GPS: N40°01.97′ W105°27.79′		
▼ 1.2	BL	Track on right.
3.0 ▲	BR	Track on left.
▼ 2.7	BR	Two entrances to track on left to exposed campsites.
1.5 ▲	BL	Two entrances to track on right to exposed campsites.
▼ 3.6	SO	Track on left.
0.6 ▲	SO	Track on right.
▼ 3.7	SO	Track on right.
0.5 ▲	SO	Track on left.
▼ 4.1	SO	Entering wide parking area.
0.1 ▲	SO	Leaving wide parking area.
▼ 4.2	TR	T-intersection with Sugarloaf Road (CR 120). Left goes to Colorado 119 and Boulder. Zero trip meter.
0.0 ▲		Continue to the northwest.
GPS: N40°01.50′ W105°25.49′		
▼ 0.0		Continue to the south.
5.5 ▲	TL	Track continues straight ahead to Colorado 119 and Boulder. Zero trip meter and turn into wide parking area.

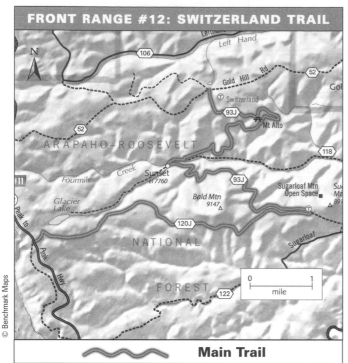

Main Trail

▼ 0.3		SO	Track on left.
5.2 ▲		SO	Track on right.
▼ 0.4		BR	Track on left.
5.1 ▲		SO	Track on right.
▼ 0.5		BL	Track on right.
5.0 ▲		SO	Track on left.
▼ 0.6		BR	Track on left.
4.9 ▲		SO	Track on right.
▼ 1.0		SO	Camping area on left.
4.5 ▲		SO	Camping area on right.

GPS: N40°01.35' W105°26.53'

▼ 2.4		SO	Two tracks on right—first is closed to motorized vehicles.
3.1 ▲		SO	Two tracks on left—second is closed to motorized vehicles.
▼ 3.7		SO	Track on left is FR 233C.
1.8 ▲		SO	Track on right is FR 233C.

GPS: N40°01.51' W105°28.91'

| ▼ 4.0 | | SO | Track on left is FR 233A. |
| 1.5 ▲ | | SO | Track on right is FR 233A. |

GPS: N40°01.44' W105°29.21'

▼ 4.1		SO	Track on right and left.
1.4 ▲		SO	Track on right and left.
▼ 4.3		SO	Leaving Roosevelt National Forest. Many tracks on left and right to private property for the next 1.2 miles.
1.2 ▲		SO	Entering Roosevelt National Forest.

GPS: N40°01.24' W105°29.40'

| ▼ 5.5 | | | Trail ends on Peak to Peak Highway (Colorado 72). Graded dirt road opposite. Turn right for Ward; turn left for Nederland. |
| 0.0 ▲ | | | Trail starts on Peak to Peak Highway (Colorado 72), 5.8 miles north of the roundabout in Nederland. Turn east on unsigned, graded dirt road and zero trip meter. Graded dirt road opposite. Many tracks on left and right to private property for the next 1.2 miles. |

GPS: N40°01.07' W105°30.55'

Gross Reservoir Trail

Starting Point:	**End of CR 68, 2 miles east of Magnolia Road**
Finishing Point:	**Gross Reservoir**
Total Mileage:	**2.7 miles (one-way)**
Unpaved Mileage:	**2.7 miles**
Driving Time:	**30 minutes (one-way)**
Elevation Range:	**7,315 to 7,825 feet**
Usually Open:	**Late May to late October**
Difficulty Rating:	**3**
Scenic Rating:	**8**

Special Attractions

- Gross Reservoir.
- Large network of trails for ATVs and motorbikes.
- Fishing, boating, and camping opportunities.

Description

This short trail is perfect for people living in or visiting the Denver/Boulder section of the Front Range. Just a quick drive up Magnolia Road, which makes a loop off of Boulder Canyon, a staging area at the end of CR 68 is where the trail starts. Many ATV and motorbike enthusiasts use the network of trails in this area, so it is not uncommon to see trucks and trailers unloading their vehicles.

Side trail to campsites

Gross Reservoir

This trail is a main backbone route through the area that follows well-signed FR 359. Numerous tracks of varying difficulties branch off to the right and left. Many are loops off the main trail or, as you approach the reservoir, are tracks that go out to campsites along the shore.

FR 359 is not very difficult in itself. Many high-clearance vehicles could drive it, but 4WD is preferred. If you are breaking off to explore the side trails, 4WD is highly recommended. One such trail breaks off to the right of the main route at 0.9 miles and heads down a hill to an excellent campsite. From the campsite, you can bear right down a very steep hill that has a solid surface. At the bottom of the hill, turning left takes you out to Gross Reservoir; turning right takes you upstream along Winiger Gulch.

The main trail continues toward the reservoir, passing numerous side trails. Arriving on the west side of Gross Reservoir, many of the campsites along the shore have fire pits and are managed by the U.S. Forest Service. Sea kayaks, canoes, and rowing skulls are allowed from Memorial Day through the end of September. Fishing is also allowed, and the Colorado Division of Wildlife stocks the reservoir.

Current Road Information

Arapaho & Roosevelt National Forests
Boulder Ranger District
2140 Yarmouth Avenue
Boulder, CO 80301
(303) 541-2500

Map References

USFS   Arapaho & Roosevelt National Forests
Maptech CD:
            Denver/Steamboat Springs/North Central
Benchmark's *Colorado Road & Recreation Atlas*, p. 62
Colorado Atlas & Gazetteer, p. 39
The Roads of Colorado, p. 64
Trails Illustrated, #102

Route Directions

▼ 0.0		Trail starts at the end of CR 68, 2 miles from Magnolia Road, where the road forks. CR 68 can be found on the right side of Magnolia Road, 5.5 miles east of the intersection of Colorado 119/72. Turn right through seasonal closure gate into a staging area and zero trip meter.
		GPS: N39°57.67' W105°23.78'
▼ 0.1	BR	Track on left to campsite.
▼ 0.3	BR	Track on left climbs hill to campsite. View straight ahead of Gross Reservoir.
▼ 0.5	BR	Track on left. Follow sign for FR 359.
		GPS: N39°57.42' W105°23.59'
▼ 0.6	BL	Track on right.
▼ 0.7	SO	Track on left. Follow sign for FR 359.
▼ 0.9	SO	Track on right goes to campsite and continues down to Winiger Gulch.
▼ 1.3	BL	Track on right.
▼ 1.4	SO	Track on right; then FR 359F on left. Remain on FR 359.
		GPS: N39°57.01' W105°23.11'
▼ 1.9	SO	FR 359F rejoins on left.

FRONT RANGE #13: GROSS RESERVOIR TRAIL

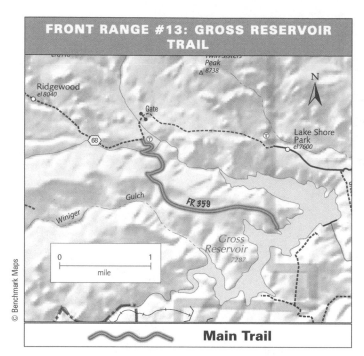

Main Trail

▼ 2.3	SO	Track on left goes 0.3 miles to campsites by Gross Reservoir.
	GPS: N39°57.01' W105°22.33'	
▼ 2.4	SO	Track on right; then track on left. Remain on FR 359.
▼ 2.5	BL	Road forks then rejoins. Remain on FR 359.
▼ 2.6	SO	Track on right; then track on left at bottom of hill.
▼ 2.7		Trail ends at campsites by Gross Reservoir.
	GPS: N39°56.80' W105°22.15'	

Difficult climb on the side trail

Rollins Pass Trail

Starting Point:	Rollins Pass Road (CR 16), 7 miles west of Rollinsville
Finishing Point:	Cutting where the road is blocked by boulders
Total Mileage:	11.9 miles (one-way)
Unpaved Mileage:	11.9 miles
Driving Time:	1 hour (one-way)
Elevation Range:	9,215 to 11,250 feet
Usually Open:	Mid-July to late October
Difficulty Rating:	2
Scenic Rating:	9

Special Attractions

- Chance to drive along a historically significant railroad route.
- Yankee Doodle Lake, Jenny Lake, and Forest Lakes.
- More difficult FR 502 offers a fun return loop.

History

Following the historic route of the Denver, Northwestern & Pacific (DNW&P), Rollins Pass Trail begins just east of the Moffat Tunnel, one of the most famous railway tunnels in the United States. The tunnel was the vision of Denver financier David H. Moffat. Moffat began construction on the DNW&P in 1901. The line was completed in 1909 and trav-

View of one of the trestles from above

Rock shelters with James Peak in the distance

eled over Rollins Pass. Heavy amounts of snow along the pass made operating the line expensive. The DNW&P had to designate about 40 percent of its operating budget just for snow removal.

Moffat hoped to drastically reduce costs by building a tunnel beneath the Continental Divide, thus avoiding Rollins Pass. Moffat, however, did not have the funds to move forward with the tunnel after building the railroad. Not giving up, he turned to the state to procure funding for the tunnel. Although Moffat died in 1911, pressure to build the tunnel remained, and in 1922 the Colorado legislature created the Moffat Tunnel Improvement District. On February 18, 1926, President Coolidge pressed a telegraph key in Washington, D.C., setting off the first blast of dynamite to begin construction on the tunnel. Although construction costs were originally estimated at about $6 million, these ballooned to roughly $18 million at the time of completion in 1928.

Moffat Tunnel is actually two tunnels. One is leased by the City of Denver to transport water from the Western Slope to the city. The other tunnel is used by railroads. Moffat's original DNW&P was reorganized as the Denver & Salt Lake Railroad (D&SL) in 1913, and the tunnel was turned over to the D&SL in 1928. The D&SL later merged with the Denver & Rio Grande Western Railroad (D&RGW) in 1947. Today, the Winter Park Ski Train from Denver runs through the Moffat Tunnel.

Climbing above the tunnel, the trail overlooks the remains of the town of Tolland. Originally called Mammoth, after nearby Mammoth Gulch, the town was renamed by Mrs. Charles B. Toll, the town's postmistress and operator of a large hotel. Tolland originally developed as a mining town, but gained importance as a stop along the DNW&P. The railroad was built through Tolland in 1904, bringing thousands of tourists from Denver to the town during the summer months. When a large railroad depot was built, a number of businesses sprang up to cater to the visitors.

After the Moffat Tunnel opened, tourist traffic to Tolland declined. Soon the railroad eliminated the Tolland stop, and the town's fortunes faded. Today, a number of buildings remain, many of which are private summer homes. The old schoolhouse still sits near the tracks and can be seen clearly from the trail.

The trail ends just before the summit of Rollins Pass, also known as Corona Pass. Rollins Pass was once an Indian trail and reportedly was the location Mormons used to cross the Continental Divide en route to Salt Lake City. In 1866, John Q. Rollins, for whom the pass is named, built a wagon road over the pass. Moffat built the DNW&P over the pass in 1901 at great expense. Before the Moffat Tunnel was constructed, a railroad station, hotel, and restaurant operated at the pass. A number of workers were stationed at the pass to help service the train. These workers named the pass Corona, as it was the crown of "the top of the world."

A short walk from the end of the trail is Needle Eye Tunnel. In 1979, vandals caused a rock slide, which closed the tunnel. Although it was repaired in 1987, another rock slide closed the tunnel in 1990. The tunnel has remained blocked since then.

Description

Rollins Pass Trail is an easy dirt road suitable for passenger vehicles as far as Yankee Doodle Lake. Past the lake, a high-clearance 2WD is all that is needed to get to the cutting where fallen boulders block the road.

The road starts out just east of the historic Moffat Tunnel and immediately begins its long gradual climb back over the South Boulder Creek Valley. The road climbs along the north side of the valley, offering better and better views to the south

View of Yankee Doodle Lake from Needle Eye Tunnel

Jenny Lake in the distance

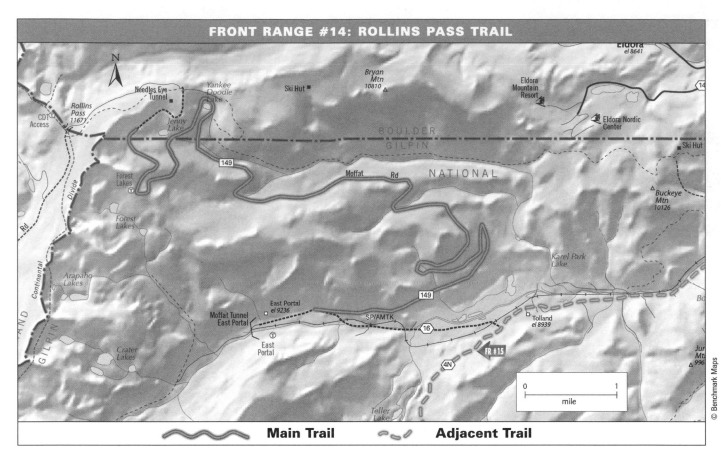

Main Trail   **Adjacent Trail**

and east. An old yellow schoolhouse, easily visible from the shelf road, marks the town site of Tolland.

A number of campsites can be seen along the beginning of the trail. The few sites within the first mile of the trail fall on National Forest land and are open to camping. The trail then passes through private property until around the intersection with FR 502 at the first zero point. Boundaries between private and public land are not well marked on this trail and are somewhat confusing on the National Forest map. If you want to camp off the side of the road, do so either within the first mile or wait until you reach the upper part of the trail near the lakes. Wherever you camp, do your best to make sure that it is on public land.

The trail continues to climb along a shelf road for some distance, slowly gaining elevation. The route passes many cuttings and crosses over many culverts, reminders of the days before the Moffat Tunnel when trains were the only vehicles climbing this trail. Once you reach Yankee Doodle Lake, a number of muddy tracks to the right filter down to the more difficult FR 502. The lake, set in a rocky basin, makes for a great stop along the trail. Anglers will enjoy trying to catch brook and rainbow trout in this lake as well as in Jenny Lake. The latter can be found by heading northwest on a side track encountered 0.7 miles farther up the trail.

The main trail continues to climb until it stops abruptly at some fallen boulders in an old cutting. From here, you can hike about a half mile to the old Needle Eye Tunnel. The hike provides spectacular views to the southeast over Jenny Lake. The Needle Eye Tunnel is now closed. You can scramble above the tunnel and continue along the old railroad bed. Some rock

hut foundations can be found above the tunnel; past it, you will reach some old railroad trestles and eventually Rollins Pass.

The popular trail is often used by snowmobilers and backcountry skiers in winter.

Current Road Information
Arapaho & Roosevelt National Forests
Boulder Ranger District
2140 Yarmouth Avenue
Boulder, CO 80301
(303) 541-2500

Map References
USFS   Arapaho & Roosevelt National Forests
Maptech CD:
Denver/Steamboat Springs/North Central
Benchmark's *Colorado Road & Recreation Atlas,* p. 62
Colorado Atlas & Gazetteer, p. 39
The Roads of Colorado, p. 63
Trails Illustrated, #102, #103

Route Directions

▼ 0.0   Trail starts on Rollins Pass Road (CR 16), 7 miles west of Rollinsville and Peak to Peak Highway (Colorado 119). Zero trip meter and turn right (northeast) on FR 149, following signs to Rollins Pass. Track straight ahead goes 0.5 miles to Moffat Tunnel.

GPS: N39°54.31' W105°37.83'

▼ 0.5   **SO**   Campsites on right.

		GPS: N39°54.54' W105°36.22'	
▼ 0.6	SO	Narrow track on left climbs hill.	
▼ 0.8	SO	Exposed campsite on right.	
		GPS: N39°54.70' W105°35.92'	
▼ 2.7	SO	Track on left.	
▼ 3.5	SO	Track on left.	
		GPS: N39°54.77' W105°36.55'	
▼ 4.1	SO	Narrow track on sharp left.	
▼ 5.2	SO	Track on left; then second entrance to track on left and track on right.	
		GPS: N39°55.28' W105°36.90'	
▼ 5.3	SO	Track on left and right.	
▼ 5.4	SO	Track on right rejoins and campsite on right; then FR 502 on right. Zero trip meter.	
		GPS: N39°55.36' W105°36.90'	
▼ 0.0	SO	Continue to the northeast on FR 149.	
▼ 0.2	SO	Track on right.	
▼ 0.3	SO	Track on right rejoins.	
▼ 2.2	SO	Track on left.	
▼ 2.3	SO	Second entrance to track on left goes to campsite in 0.2 miles; then campsite on right.	
		GPS: N39°55.41' W105°38.87'	
▼ 3.3	SO	Track on left to campsite.	
▼ 3.6	SO	Cross through wash.	
▼ 3.7	SO	Tracks on right.	
▼ 3.8	SO	FR 502 on right. Yankee Doodle Lake on left.	
		GPS: N39°56.27' W105°39.13'	
▼ 4.0	SO	Track on right.	
▼ 4.5	SO	FR 505 on right goes 0.3 miles to Jenny Lake.	
		GPS: N39°55.90' W105°39.66'	
▼ 5.2	SO	Two hiking trails on left.	
▼ 5.5	SO	Hiking and horse riding trail on left goes to Forest Lakes.	
		GPS: N39°55.43' W105°40.08'	
▼ 5.8	SO	Hiking trail on right.	
▼ 6.5		Trail ends at a cutting where the road is blocked by boulders. Park and hike along the old road to the collapsed Needle Eye Tunnel.	
		GPS: N39°56.05' W105°40.06'	

FRONT RANGE REGION TRAIL #15

Central City to Rollinsville Trail

Starting Point:	CR 3 and CR 2, 1.1 miles northwest of Central City
Finishing Point:	Colorado 119 in Rollinsville, approximately 13 miles north of Black Hawk
Total Mileage:	16.0 miles
Unpaved Mileage:	15.2 miles
Driving Time:	1 hour
Route Elevation:	8,600 to 10,600 feet
Usually Open:	June to October
Difficulty Rating:	3
Scenic Rating:	8

Rollinsville, circa 1920

Special Attractions
- Historic mining area.
- Access to a network of 4WD roads.

History

This trail passes the sites of a number of old mining towns. Apex, founded in 1891 and platted in 1895, was established to provide housing for the miners working the several good mines within a mile of town. The town reached its peak population around 1896. It had two hotels, a dance hall, several churches, a school, and a newspaper called *The Apex Pine Cone*. The post office opened in 1894 and closed in 1932.

The most productive mine was the Mackey, named for its original owner. After it changed hands a number of times, it came under the ownership of a man by the name of Mountz, who formed a partnership to develop it. After $30,000 worth of ore had been shipped, the partner stole all but $400 and disappeared. Convinced that there was a rich vein to be found, Mountz continued to operate the mine but soon exhausted his funds. Out of frustration, he set a charge with the last of his dynamite to collapse the mine. With this last desperate act, he uncovered the elusive main vein of ore. It was assayed at $1,800 per ton; he had finally struck it rich.

Nugget was a one-mine camp that thrived in the late 1890s. A post office was opened in 1895 but closed only six years later. The town soon faded because of its proximity to

Rollinsville train depot, circa 1915—this was also a Western Union telegraph office

Town of Apex today

A parade on main street of Apex, circa 1898

American City, only half a mile north. There was not enough activity to support both towns, and American City proved to be the more successful.

Tolland, first called Mammoth, was originally a mining town but became a stage way station between Rollinsville and Middle Park. In 1904, when the railroad came through on its way to Rollins Pass before the nearby Moffat Tunnel opened, the town became a railroad station. A post office opened at this time and remained in operation until 1944. The railroad relocated a large brick station from Denver and rebuilt it at Tolland. This substantial structure with its large, covered platform had lunchrooms and a souvenir shop for the thousands of tourists that used to make the journey from Denver to fish, hike, picnic, or just admire the summer wildflowers.

Rollinsville was established by General John Q. Rollins, a prominent man who had many interests in mining, cattle ranching, and hotels throughout the Midwest and Rocky Mountains. Rollins improved the old army road that crossed Rollins Pass, then called Boulder Pass. Before the army arrived, the route had been a favorite Indian trail and is also believed to have been the route taken by the Mormons on their way to Salt Lake City.

Rollins obtained a charter in 1866 to build a freight road over the pass as a toll road. The road opened in 1873, and to service the captive audience using his toll road he built the town of Rollinsville, which included a large hotel that he

named the Rollins House. He also owned the local stagecoach service and the lumber operation. When establishing the town, he outlawed saloons, dance halls, prostitution, and gambling. Rollins also operated a number of nearby mines, and he built a mill near the town to process the ore. However, even in the town's heyday, the population never exceeded 200. As the importance of the pass road and the mines waned, saloons were allowed to open in the town, but Rollins continued to decline.

Description

The road to Apex is a maintained county road through pleasant ranchland. From the town of Apex, the road gets bumpy but is still easy.

There is a great deal of historic mining activity still evident until the road passes the Nugget town site. From the ridge past the Elk Park area there are good views to the southwest to Kingston Peak and the surrounding area and northwest to the Rollins Pass area. As you continue toward Tolland, there are also good views ahead to South Boulder Creek Valley and, in fall, across large stands of wonderful golden aspens.

The most difficult section of road is the stretch between Nugget and Tolland. It can be rough and rutted, especially late in the season. Nonetheless, it remains relatively easy, and from the intersection with CR 16 to Front Range #14: Rollins Pass Trail the road is maintained by the county.

The Boodle Mill outside of Central City

Grave marker in cemetery along Upper Apex Road

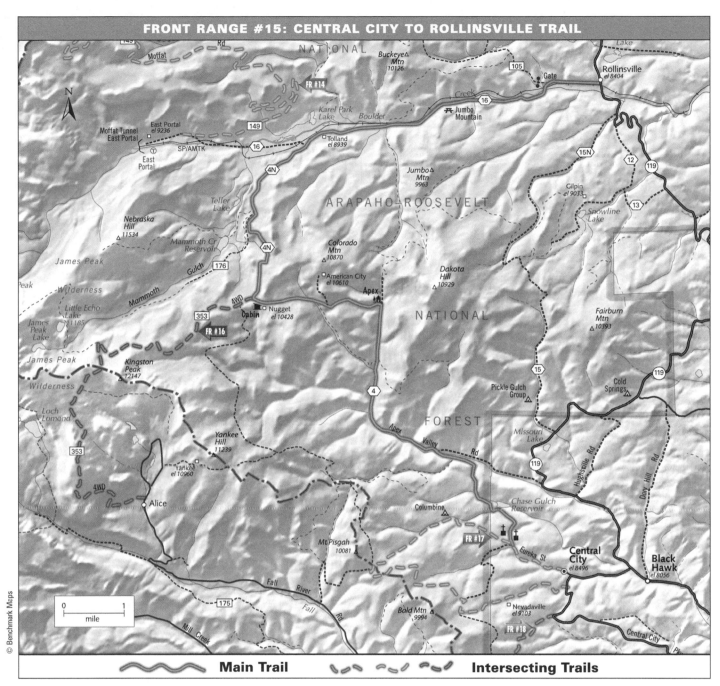

~~~~ **Main Trail**   ⌒⌒⌒ **Intersecting Trails**

Current Road Conditions

Arapaho & Roosevelt National Forests
Clear Creek Ranger District
101 Chicago Creek Road
Idaho Springs, CO 80452
(303) 567-3000

Map References

USFS   Arapaho & Roosevelt National Forests
Maptech CD:
       Denver/Steamboat Springs/North Central
Benchmark's *Colorado Road & Recreation Atlas*, pp. 62, 74
Colorado Atlas & Gazetteer, p. 39
The Roads of Colorado, p. 71
Trails Illustrated, #103

Route Directions

▼ 0.0		Begin at the intersection of Upper Apex Road (CR 3) and Bald Mountain Road, 1.1 miles northwest of Central City via Eureka Street. Zero trip meter and continue northwest along Upper Apex Road (CR 3).
5.3 ▲		End at the intersection of CR 3 and Bald Mountain Road, 1.1 miles northwest of Central City.
	GPS: N39°48.48' W105°31.78'	
▼ 0.1	SO	Cemetery grounds on left; Central City Cemetery on right.
5.2 ▲	SO	Cemeteries on left and right.
▼ 0.9	SO	Chase Gulch Reservoir on right.
4.4 ▲	SO	Chase Gulch Reservoir on left.
▼ 2.3	TL	Bridge over Clear Creek; then intersection with Apex Valley Road (CR 4 S) on left.

Along the trail toward Tolland

3.1 ▲		BR	Intersection with Upper Apex Rd (CR 3) on right.

GPS: N39°49.81' W105°33.16'

▼ 5.3		TL	Town of Apex. Intersection with Elk Park Road (CR 4 N) on left. Zero trip meter.
0.0 ▲			Continue along CR 4 S.

GPS: N39°51.93' W105°34.16'

▼ 0.0			Continue along Elk Park Road (CR 4 N).
2.2 ▲		TR	At town of Apex, turn onto Apex Valley Road (CR 4 S).
▼ 1.0		SO	Mining remains on left.
1.2 ▲		SO	Mining remains on right.
▼ 1.2		SO	Town site of Nugget with cabin on left. Cross through Elk Creek. Although there are a number of side roads, remain on main track.
1.0 ▲		SO	Town site of Nugget with cabin on right.

GPS: N39°51.96' W105°35.46'

▼ 2.1		SO	Enter Roosevelt National Forest and cross cattle guard. Then tracks on left.
0.1 ▲		SO	Tracks on right. Cross cattle guard and leave Roosevelt National Forest.
▼ 2.2		TR	Intersection with Front Range #16: Kingston Peak Trail (FR 353) on left. Zero trip meter.
0.0 ▲			Proceed east toward Apex.

GPS: N39°51.97' W105°36.61'

▼ 0.0			Follow signs to Rollinsville.
8.5 ▲		TL	Intersection with Front Range #16: Kingston Peak Trail on right and unmarked Elk Park Road on left. Zero trip meter.

Tolland

▼ 1.2		SO	FR 416 on right. Follow sign to FR 176.
7.3 ▲		SO	Follow sign marked FR 353.
▼ 1.8		SO	Tracks on left to Mammoth Basin and Old Reservoir site. Continue toward Rollinsville.
6.7 ▲		SO	Tracks on right to Mammoth Basin and Old Reservoir site. Continue toward Apex.
▼ 3.4		TR	Intersection with Rollins Pass Road (FR 149) on left. Moffat Tunnel is three miles to the left.
5.1 ▲		TL	Intersection with FR 176 signed to Mammoth Gulch Road on left.

GPS: N39°54.25' W105°35.47'

▼ 3.7		SO	Town of Tolland.
4.8 ▲		SO	Town of Tolland.
▼ 5.9		SO	Picnic area on left.
2.6 ▲		SO	Picnic area on right.
▼ 8.5			End at intersection with Colorado 119 in Rollinsville, approximately 13 miles north of Black Hawk.
0.0 ▲			From Colorado 119 in Rollinsville (just after bridge over railroad line if heading north), zero trip meter and turn onto FR 149 (CR 16) toward the Moffat Tunnel.

GPS: N39°55.03' W105°30.12'

FRONT RANGE REGION TRAIL #16

Kingston Peak Trail

Starting Point:	**Fall River Road in Alice**
Finishing Point:	**Front Range #15: Central City to**
	Rollinsville Trail, 8.5 miles from
	Rollinsville
Total Mileage:	**9.4 miles**
Unpaved Mileage:	**9.4 miles**
Driving Time:	**2 hours**
Elevation Range:	**10,065 to 12,030 feet**
Usually Open:	**June to September**
Difficulty Rating:	**5**
Scenic Rating:	**9**

View of Yankee Hill

Rock House near the trail

Expansive view from the trail just below Kingston Peak

Special Attractions
- Long stretch above treeline.
- Wonderful views over James Peak, as well as numerous lakes.
- The Rock House.

History

Kingston Peak Trail begins in the historic town of Alice, Colorado, which served as a stage stop on the route between Central City and Georgetown and grew to be the largest mining camp on Fall River. Gold was discovered on the Fall River in the early 1880s, and a number of people flocked to Alice. Within months, more than $50,000 had been taken from the Alice Mine using hydraulic giants that employed water pressure to dislodge the ore and carry it through a series of sluices where the gold was captured.

Along with this form of placer mining, lode mining also commenced. Lode mining involves the extraction of ore from the earth using tunnels and an extensive amount of manual labor. A stamp mill was also constructed at the mine, helping to crush the ore retrieved in the lode mining process. Much of the ore for the mill came from Alice's large glory hole, which measured 100 feet across and 50 feet deep. A glory hole is an open-pit mine. Ore is mined when rocks fall to the bottom of the pit and then are removed through tunnels at the pit floor. There was an extensive tunnel from Alice's glory hole to the mill where the ore was processed.

Mailbox beside the Rock House with Loch Lomond in the distance

In 1897, the Alice Mine was sold to a man from New York for $250,000. He poured thousands of dollars into further developing the mine, but production continued to decline. The quality of the ore decreased, and the stamp mill became unable to crush much of the harder pyritic rock being extracted. The Alice Mine closed in 1899 and quickly became deserted. The American Smelting and Refining Company purchased the Alice Mine in 1936 and resumed mining but soon after abandoned the project. Today, Alice hosts a large population of summer tourists. St. Mary's Glacier, on nearby Kingston Peak, provides summer skiing opportunities.

Description

Kingston Peak Trail provides an excellent route for drivers of high-clearance 4WDs who want to get from I-70 over to

View of Alice from the trail

Rollinsville or Central City on the Peak to Peak Highway. The trail starts out by taking a tour through the Alice subdivision. The subdivision is somewhat confusing to the newcomer, and streets are not always signed. Pay close attention to the route directions to make sure you stay on route.

Once out of town, the trail continues to climb along a well-defined, rocky route. You will have great views to the right over Alice, as well as Yankee Hill Road, which ascends the hill east of town. Then views to the left reveal numerous alpine lakes. The most prominent is Loch Lomond, nestled in the valley below James Peak. However, a keen eye will also spot Fall River Reservoir, Chinns Lake, and Sherwin Lake. The best view point over the lakes is at the Rock House, situated just above treeline. The Rock House no longer has a roof, just crumbling down walls and of all things a mailbox. If you plan to drive this trail, bring a rock from your part of the world and leave it on the pile for good luck. Rocks on the walls come from as far away as Sedona, Arizona. Also, don't forget to sign the register and leave your thoughts for future passersby.

The trail continues above treeline. Be sure to avoid straying from the trail; this alpine tundra is very fragile and takes years to recover from vehicle tracks. The trail is not difficult, and there is no need to cut a parallel track. Just before the high point of the trail, an old road on the left now serves as hiking access to James Peak. The trail then comes to a pass with the exposed Kingston Peak on the right. The northbound descent from the pass is probably the most difficult part of the trail, and if traveling in the opposite direction would increase the overall difficulty of the trail from a 5 to a 6. It is a very steep descent with a loose surface. Stock 4WDs should have no trouble descending it in low gears.

The trail follows a shelf road down to a parking area at the first switchback. There are great views from the shelf road over the Continental Divide and the South Boulder Creek Valley. From the switchback, an old road to the west is now the James Peak Lake Hiking Trail. You can see that lake as well as Little Echo Lake from the trailhead.

Continuing down the mountain, the trail comes back into subalpine vegetation. It passes a few more old roads, now closed to motorized vehicles, as well as some present-day trails such as FR 175. The area's rich mining history is evident in the number of roads as well as mining remains and tailings that

View of Loch Lomond in the distance

can be seen along the trail. The route finally ends on Front Range #15: Central City to Rollinsville Trail. The trail has some slightly technical spots and some steep shelf roads, but it has no specific obstacles that would require a great amount of skill. It should not be driven in rain or snow.

Current Road Information
Arapaho & Roosevelt National Forests
Clear Creek Ranger District
101 Chicago Creek Road
Idaho Springs, CO 80452
(303) 567-3000

Map References
USFS   Arapaho & Roosevelt National Forests
Maptech CD:
          Denver/Steamboat Springs/North Central
Benchmark's *Colorado Road & Recreation Atlas*, p. 74
Colorado Atlas & Gazetteer, p. 39
The Roads of Colorado, p. 79
Trails Illustrated, #103

Route Directions

▼ 0.0			Trail starts on Fall River Road in Alice. From I-70, take exit #238 and zero trip meter at the bottom of the exit ramp. Head north on Fall River Road for 8.3 miles. Zero trip meter and turn west on graded dirt Alice Road.
	5.5 ▲		Trail ends on paved Fall River Road (CR 275). Turn right for I-70.
		GPS: N39°49.15′ W105°38.56′	
▼ 0.1		TR	4-way intersection. Turn right on Silvercreek Road. Alice Roadl on left.
	5.4 ▲	TL	4-way intersection. Silvercreek Road continues straight ahead. Turn left onto Alice Road.
▼ 0.3		TL	Silvercreek Road continues straight ahead. Turn left onto Texas Drive.
	5.2 ▲	TR	T-intersection with Silvercreek Road.
▼ 1.0		TR	T-intersection. Turn right onto unsigned Nebraska Drive; then follow up left-hand switchback and right-hand switchback.
	4.5 ▲	TL	Come down switchbacks; then turn left onto Texas Drive.
		GPS: N39°49.07′ W105°39.23′	
▼ 1.2		TL	Nebraska Drive continues straight ahead. Turn left onto Hillside Road (sign says Glory Hole Road).
	4.3 ▲	TR	T-intersection with Nebraska Drive.
▼ 1.4		TR	Hillside Road continues straight ahead. Turn right onto unsigned Hilltop Road. Road narrows and becomes rougher as you leave Alice.
	4.1 ▲	TL	T-intersection with Hillside Road. Road widens as you enter Alice.
		GPS: N39°48.95′ W105°39.46′	
▼ 2.4		SO	Track on right to exposed campsite.
	3.1 ▲	SO	Track on left to exposed campsite.
▼ 2.9		TR	Track on left to overlook.
	2.6 ▲	TL	Track straight ahead to overlook.
		GPS: N39°49.25′ W105°39.93′	
▼ 3.6		SO	Rock House on left.
	1.9 ▲	SO	Rock House on right.
		GPS: N39°49.69′ W105°39.88′	
▼ 5.2		SO	Hiking trail toward James Peak follows old

FRONT RANGE #16: KINGSTON PEAK TRAIL

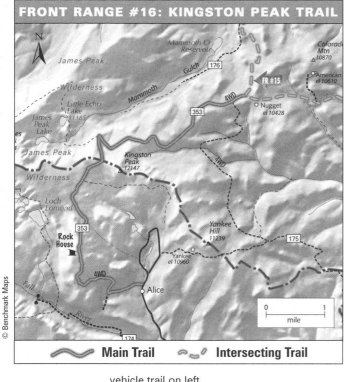

Main Trail   **Intersecting Trail**

			vehicle trail on left.
0.3 ▲	SO		Hiking trail toward James Peak follows old vehicle trail on right.
▼ 5.5	SO		Top of pass. Kingston Peak is to the right.
0.0 ▲			Continue to the west.
	GPS: N39°50.96′ W105°39.44′		
▼ 0.0			Continue to the east.
3.9 ▲	SO		Top of pass. Kingston Peak is to the left.

▼ 0.5	BR		Hiking trail to James Peak Lake follows old vehicle trail on left.
3.4 ▲	BL		Hiking trail to James Peak Lake follows old vehicle trail on right.
	GPS: N39°51.36′ W105°39.48′		
▼ 0.9	SO		Hiking trail on right goes to Kingston Peak.
3.0 ▲	SO		Hiking trail on left goes to Kingston Peak.
▼ 1.5	SO		Hiking trail on right.
2.4 ▲	SO		Hiking trail on left.
	GPS: N39°51.28′ W105°38.60′		
▼ 1.8	BR		Network of tracks on left. Remain on FR 353.
2.1 ▲	BL		Network of tracks on right. Remain on FR 353.
▼ 1.9	BL		Track on right leads to hiking trail in 0.1 miles.
2.0 ▲	BR		Track on left leads to hiking trail in 0.1 miles.
▼ 2.4	SO		Track on right is FR 175.
1.5 ▲	SO		Track on left is FR 175.
	GPS: N39°51.35′ W105°37.85′		
▼ 2.5	SO		Track on right. Remain on FR 353.
1.4 ▲	SO		Track on left. Remain on FR 353.
▼ 2.6	SO		Track on right is FR 175, signed to Pisgah Lake. Remain on FR 353, following sign to Apex.
1.3 ▲	SO		Track on left is FR 175, signed to Pisgah Lake.
▼ 2.8	SO		Track on left.
1.1 ▲	SO		Track on right.
▼ 2.9	SO		Cattle guard.
1.0 ▲	SO		Cattle guard.
▼ 3.9			Trail ends on Front Range #15: Central City to Rollinsville Trail. Turn right for Central City; turn left for Rollinsville.
0.0 ▲			Trail starts on Front Range #15: Central City to Rollinsville Trail, 8.5 miles from Rollinsville. Zero trip meter and turn west on FR 353, signed as Kingston 4WD Route.
	GPS: N39°51.97′ W105°36.61′		

James Peak, James Peak Lake, and Little Echo Lake

Nevadaville Loop

Starting Point:	Central City
Finishing Point:	Central City
Total Mileage:	11.1 miles
Unpaved Mileage:	9.7 miles
Driving Time:	30 minutes
Route Elevation:	8,600 to 9,500 feet
Usually Open:	June to October
Difficulty Rating:	3
Scenic Rating:	8

Special Attractions

- Historic mining district.
- Central City and Nevadaville ghost town.

History

Gold was discovered in Gregory Gulch on May 6, 1859, and within weeks the area was teeming with thousands of prospectors. Newspaperman Horace Greeley rushed to the area to witness the scene and widely reported the find, attracting people from all over the world. Mountain City was the name of the first settlement in the area, but Central City soon absorbed it and became the dominant town.

Nevadaville, which was established at the same time as Central City, was also known as Nevada and Nevada City. The

One of the many historic mining sites to see along Nevadaville Loop

post office was established using the name Nevad, but to avoid confusion with the California town, the name was changed to Bald Mountain. Although the post office used this name until it closed in 1921, the residents continued to use Nevadaville.

Within its first year Nevadaville had grown to more than 2,000 residents, which made it larger than Denver. In 1860, the fledgling town passed a resolution that "there be no Bawdy houses, Grog Shops, or Gambling Saloons." However, this resolution was either overturned or not enforced because reports indicate that later there were 13 saloons operating in the town.

Nevadaville, circa 1895

Bald Mountain Trading Post in Nevadaville

Old mining operation outside Nevadaville

The biggest problem was lack of a reliable water supply. Ditches were dug from both Peck Gulch and Fall River, but neither solved the shortage. The town suffered five devastating fires.

The Leadville boom in 1879 caused many residents to move on, and the town was nearly deserted in the wake of the 1893 silver panic. After the last fire in 1914, the town was not rebuilt. Nevadaville staged a few brief revivals, but by 1930 the population was two. Today, only a handful of structures remain.

Description

This is a reasonably simple loop to navigate with a number of side trails that can be explored. Mining activity abounds, especially from Central City until shortly past Nevadaville. The road is easy to Nevadaville; from there it gets a little rougher, but under dry conditions it is not difficult at any point.

If you like learning history from headstones, this route provides many opportunities. Shortly past Nevadaville is the Bald Mountain Cemetery and toward the end of the route are four Central City cemeteries clustered around the intersection where the Boodle Mill is located.

Current Road Conditions

Arapaho & Roosevelt National Forests
Clear Creek Ranger District
101 Chicago Creek Road
Idaho Springs, CO 80452
(303) 567-3000

Map References

USFS   Arapaho & Roosevelt National Forests
Maptech CD:
          Denver/Steamboat Springs/North Central
Benchmark's *Colorado Road & Recreation Atlas,* p. 74
Colorado Atlas & Gazetteer, p. 39
The Roads of Colorado, p. 71
Trails Illustrated, #103

Route Directions

▼ 0.0		Take Spring or Main Street to the intersection of Bridge and Nevada Streets. Zero trip meter and follow Nevada Street out of town to the southwest.
4.3 ▲		End at the intersection of Bridge and Nevada Streets in Central City.
GPS: N39°47.95′ W105°30.73′		
▼ 0.3	TR	Intersection with Nevadaville Road on right. Follow sign to Nevadaville.
4.0 ▲	TL	Intersection with Nevadaville Road on left.
GPS: N39°47.79′ W105°31.02′		
▼ 0.5	SO	Pavement ends.
3.8 ▲	SO	Pavement begins.
▼ 0.9	SO	Old mining operation on left.
3.4 ▲	SO	Old mining operation on right.
▼ 1.1	SO	Nevadaville.
3.2 ▲	SO	Nevadaville.
▼ 1.2	SO	Mining ruins on left.
3.1 ▲	SO	Mining ruins on right.
▼ 1.7	BL	Road becomes Bald Mountain Road.
3.1 ▲	BR	Road becomes Nevadaville Road.

▼ 2.3	TL	Intersection. Turn onto FR 273.2.	
2.0 ▲	TR	Onto road to Nevadaville.	

GPS: N39°47.72' W105°32.54'

▼ 2.6	SO	Bald Mountain (Nevadaville) Cemetery on right.
1.7 ▲	SO	Bald Mountain (Nevadaville) Cemetery on left.
▼ 3.5	SO	Small track on left.
0.7 ▲	SO	Small track on right.
▼ 4.2	BL	Fork in road. FR 401.1 is to the right. Follow FR 273.2.
0.1 ▲	SO	FR 401.1 enters on left.

GPS: N39°48.10' W105°34.01'

▼ 4.3	SO	Road on left is Alpine Way through a residential neighborhood.
4.0 ▲	SO	Road on right is Alpine Way through a residential neighborhood.

GPS: N39°48.05' W105°34.14'

▼ 4.4	TR	Intersection with FR 175.1 on right and FR 277.3 on left. Straight ahead is FR 273.1 to Hamlin Gulch. Zero trip meter.
0.0 ▲		Proceed southeast on FR 273.2.

GPS: N39°48.04' W105°34.18'

▼ 0.0		Proceed northwest on FR 175.1 toward Central City.
3.9 ▲	TL	Intersection with FR 273.2 on left and and FR 277.3 on right. Zero trip meter.

Stands of aspen along the trail

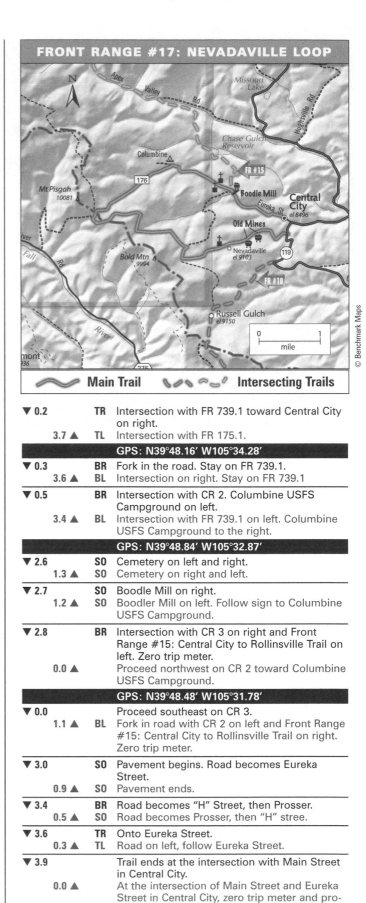

FRONT RANGE #17: NEVADAVILLE LOOP

© Benchmark Maps

〜 Main Trail **〰 〜 Intersecting Trails**

▼ 0.2	TR	Intersection with FR 739.1 toward Central City on right.
3.7 ▲	TL	Intersection with FR 175.1.

GPS: N39°48.16' W105°34.28'

▼ 0.3	BR	Fork in the road. Stay on FR 739.1.
3.6 ▲	BL	Intersection on right. Stay on FR 739.1
▼ 0.5	BR	Intersection with CR 2. Columbine USFS Campground on left.
3.4 ▲	BL	Intersection with FR 739.1 on left. Columbine USFS Campground to the right.

GPS: N39°48.84' W105°32.87'

▼ 2.6	SO	Cemetery on left and right.
1.3 ▲	SO	Cemetery on right and left.
▼ 2.7	SO	Boodle Mill on right.
1.2 ▲	SO	Boodler Mill on left. Follow sign to Columbine USFS Campground.
▼ 2.8	BR	Intersection with CR 3 on right and Front Range #15: Central City to Rollinsville Trail on left. Zero trip meter.
0.0 ▲		Proceed northwest on CR 2 toward Columbine USFS Campground.

GPS: N39°48.48' W105°31.78'

▼ 0.0		Proceed southeast on CR 3.
1.1 ▲	BL	Fork in road with CR 2 on left and Front Range #15: Central City to Rollinsville Trail on right. Zero trip meter.
▼ 3.0	SO	Pavement begins. Road becomes Eureka Street.
0.9 ▲	SO	Pavement ends.
▼ 3.4	BR	Road becomes "H" Street, then Prosser.
0.5 ▲	SO	Road becomes Prosser, then "H" stree.
▼ 3.6	TR	Onto Eureka Street.
0.3 ▲	TL	Road on left, follow Eureka Street.
▼ 3.9		Trail ends at the intersection with Main Street in Central City.
0.0 ▲		At the intersection of Main Street and Eureka Street in Central City, zero trip meter and proceed northwest out of town on Eureka.

GPS: N 39°48.05' W 105°30.75'

Oh My God Road

Starting Point:	**Idaho Springs**
Finishing Point:	**Central City**
Total Mileage:	**8.5 miles**
Unpaved Mileage:	**5.9 miles**
Driving Time:	**45 minutes**
Elevation Range:	**7,560 to 9,360 feet**
Usually Open:	**May to October**
Difficulty Rating:	**1**
Scenic Rating:	**8**

Special Attractions

- Old mines and mining equipment along the way.
- Expansive views from high elevation.
- Russell Gulch ghost town.

History

Russell Gulch was an important pioneer settlement in Colorado. In 1859, W. G. Russell made the first gold strike, and soon more than 1,000 prospectors flocked to the area. By the end of 1860, the number of people living in Russell Gulch increased to 2,500. The town had a school with more than a

Colorful house in Russell Gulch

dozen students and a church with Sunday services. The mining heyday of Russell Gulch was short-lived, and ore played out within about four years. By 1887, the population had dropped to only about 200. Some mining continued into the twentieth century, however. Subsequently, during the 1920s, Russell Gulch became a hive of activity for bootlegging during prohibition.

Description

Oh My God Road (sometimes referred to as Oh My Gawd Road) is a scenic and steep but easy drive from Idaho Springs to Central City. Portions of the road have been paved, but mostly it is a dirt road. The condition of the road surface is

One of many mining ruins to see along Oh My God Road

Mine adit alongside the road

Russell Gulch Schoolhouse is surprisingly well preserved

bumpy at times and is best avoided when wet. Depending on how recently the road has been graded, it may be heavily corrugated.

The trail begins in Idaho Springs, where it follows Colorado Boulevard to the turnoff signed to Virginia Canyon, Central City, and Blackhawk. Following the sign to Virginia Canyon, you will first pass through a quiet neighborhood of historic homes where the road is paved. After about half a mile, the pavement ends and the road begins its gentle, graded ascent. Along the trail you will see numerous abandoned mine workings and endless mounds of tailings piles. A few of the old structures are in remarkably good shape and make for excellent photo opportunities.

Navigation of this route is straightforward. After approximately 3.5 miles, the trail passes through the historic mining community of Russell Gulch. You will see a mixture of stone foundations and some well-preserved buildings. Once past the Glory Hole Mine, it is only about a mile to the trail's end in Central City.

Russell Gulch structures

Current Road Information

Idaho Springs Visitors Center
1416 Miner Street
Idaho Springs, CO 80452
(303) 567-4382

Map References

USFS   Arapaho & Roosevelt National Forests
Maptech CD:
             Denver/Steamboat Springs/North Central
Benchmark's *Colorado Road & Recreation Atlas*, p. 74
Colorado Atlas & Gazetteer, p. 39
The Roads of Colorado, p. 123

Route Directions

▼ 0.0		From I-70 take exit 140 in Idaho Springs. Proceed north along 13th Avenue. Turn right at Colorado Boulevard and drive for about 0.25 miles. Bear left at sign for Virginia Canyon and zero trip meter.
2.4 ▲		Trail ends at intersection with Colorado Boulevard in Idaho Springs.
	GPS: N39°44.57' W105°30.88'	
▼ 70 yds	TL	Canyon Street on left. Follow sign toward Russell Gulch.
2.4 ▲	TR	Intersection with signed Placer Street.
▼ 0.5	BR	Pavement ends. Follow sign to Central City.
1.9 ▲	BL	Track on right; then pavement begins.
	GPS: N39°45.00' W105°30.93'	
▼ 2.0	SO	Ore bin remaining from mill on right.
0.4 ▲	SO	Mine/mill ruins on left.
	GPS: N39°45.37' W105°31.36'	
▼ 2.4	TR	Intersection with unmarked CR 281 (Two Brothers Road). Zero trip meter.
0.0 ▲		Proceed southeast on CR 279.
	GPS: N39°45.47' W105°31.75'	
▼ 0.0		Continue to the north on CR 279.
6.1 ▲	TL	Intersection with unmarked CR 281. Zero trip

Glory Hole Gold Mine

FRONT RANGE #18: OH MY GOD ROAD

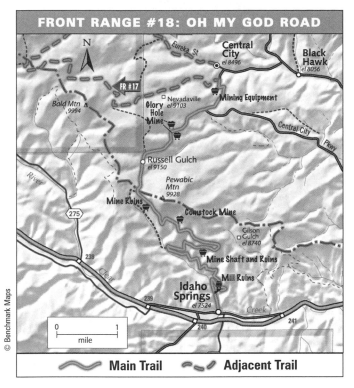

Main Trail 〰️   Adjacent Trail ◦〰️

© Benchmark Maps

			meter.
▼ 0.5		SO	Mine ruins on left uphill through the trees.
5.6 ▲		SO	Mine ruins on right through the trees.
▼ 1.1		BL	Tracks on left and track on right. Old mine shaft and ruins to the right on the hillside below road. Follow sign to Central City.
5.0 ▲		SO	Tracks on left and right.

GPS: N39°45.45' W105°31.05'

▼ 2.0		SO	Pavement begins. Comstock Mine comes into view.
4.1 ▲		SO	Pavement ends.

GPS: N39°45.72' W105°31.56'

▼ 2.1		SO	Comstock Mine on right.
4.0 ▲		SO	Comstock Mine on left.

GPS: N39°45.80' W105°31.50'

▼ 2.8		SO	Mine ruins on left.
3.3 ▲		SO	Mine ruins on right.

GPS: N39°46.10' W105°32.09'

▼ 3.2		SO	Pavement ends. Continue along Virginia Canyon Road.
2.9 ▲		SO	Pavement begins. Continue along Virginia Canyon Road.

GPS: N39°46.34' W105°32.26'

▼ 3.5		SO	Pass through the old mining town of Russell Gulch.
2.6 ▲		SO	Pass through historic Russell Gulch, an old mining town.

GPS: N39°46.67' W105°32.21'

▼ 3.7		SO	Upper Russell Gulch Road on right.
2.4 ▲		TR	Upper Russell Gulch Road on left.

GPS: N39°46.80' W105°32.18'

▼ 3.9		SO	Old schoolhouse on right.
2.2 ▲		SO	Old schoolhouse on left.

▼ 4.8		SO	Upper Russell Gulch Road on right.
1.3 ▲		BR	Upper Russell Gulch Road on left.

GPS: N39°47.26' W105°31.34'

▼ 4.9		SO	Glory Hole Mine on left and right. Cross under mine chute.

1.2 ▲		SO	Glory Hole Mine on right and left. Cross under mine chute.

GPS: N39°47.35' W105°31.34'

▼ 5.2		SO	Pavement begins.
0.9 ▲		SO	Pavement ends.

GPS: N39°47.44' W105°31.06'

▼ 5.3		SO	CR 6 on right. Continue on CR 279.
0.8 ▲		SO	CR 6 on left. Follow sign for Idaho Springs.

▼ 5.6		SO	Mining equipment on left.
0.5 ▲		SO	Mining equipment on right.

▼ 6.1			Trail ends at stop sign at intersection of Bridge and Spring in Central City. Start of Front Range #17: Nevadaville Loop on left.
0.0 ▲			Trail starts in Central City at intersection of Bridge and Spring. Zero trip meter and follow sign for Virginia Canyon Road ("Oh My God Road").

GPS: N39°47.96' W105°30.76'

La Salle Pass Trail

Starting Point:	Intersection of CR 31 and FR 44, south of Tarryall
Finishing Point:	CR 23-A and US 24
Total Mileage:	9.4 miles
Unpaved Mileage:	9.4 miles
Driving Time:	30 minutes
Elevation Range:	8,814 to 9,753 feet
Usually Open:	June to October
Difficulty Rating:	2
Scenic Rating:	8

Special Attractions

- Accessible trail to beginning 4-wheel drivers.
- Expansive views along trail.
- Good aspen viewing in fall.
- Network of forest roads to explore.

Road sign near La Salle Pass

An open section of the trail with Badger Mountain in the background

History

La Salle Pass, which divides the waters of the South Platte River to the west and Marksbury Gulch to the east, was named for Samuel La Salle, who had a mining claim on Tarryall Creek. A group of miners led by La Salle built a wagon road over the pass, which became the main thoroughfare through the Puma Hills and into South Park.

Description

La Salle Pass is a wide one-lane road with plenty of pullouts for passing oncoming vehicles. At first the trail runs alongside private land on the left and open range on the right as it gently ascends toward La Salle Pass. Although rabbit brush and evergreens mixed with aspens dot the landscape, views of the surrounding rolling hills are open at the beginning of the trail.

Not frequently maintained, the road's surface is bumpy from embedded rocks, erosion, and water bars, but the drive does not pose difficulty for any stock 4WD. Soon the trail gains elevation and runs through forestland where the trail becomes increasingly eroded. Along this section, the ruins of two old log cabins and a barn remain under the canopy of trees. Level clearings shaded by the trees would make good backcountry campsites.

Beyond the intersection with Front Range #20: Badger Mountain Road, the road is well maintained, and the ride is considerably less bumpy. The trail leaves the forest and arrives in open range with a few small stands of aspen and expansive views up to Badger Mountain and of the surrounding landscape. As the trail ends at the intersection with US 24, it becomes a wide, graded gravel road. This pleasant drive is situated among a network of forest roads that offer further opportunities for exploration.

Current Road Information

Pike & San Isabel National Forests
South Park Ranger District
320 US 285
Fairplay, CO 80440
(719) 836-2031

Map References

USFS   Pike National Forest
Maptech CD: Colorado Springs/Ski Areas/Central
Benchmark's *Colorado Road & Recreation Atlas*, p. 88
Colorado Atlas & Gazetteer, p. 49
The Roads of Colorado, pp. 95, 96
Trails Illustrated, #137 (incomplete)

Route Directions

▼ 0.0		Trail begins at intersection of CR 31 and FR 44. Proceed west/southwest on FR 44.
	4.1 ▲	Trail ends at intersection with CR 31. Turn right for US 24; turn left for Tarryall.
GPS: N39°05.39' W105°29.42'		
▼ 1.0	BL	Intersection with two roads on right.
	3.1 ▲	SO	Intersection with two roads on left.
GPS: N39°05.52' W105°30.47'		
▼ 2.0	SO	Cattle guard.
	2.1 ▲	SO	Cattle guard.
▼ 2.3	SO	Building ruins on left.
	1.8 ▲	SO	Building ruins on right.
GPS: N39°05.17' W105°31.55'		
▼ 3.1	SO	Cattle guard; then signed entrance to Pike National Forest.
	1.0 ▲	SO	Signed entrance to Pike National Forest; then cattle guard.

The road traveling through dense forest

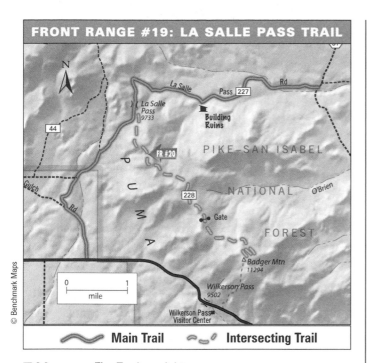

© Benchmark Maps

| | 0 | 1 |
| mile | | |

〜〜 **Main Trail**   〜・〜 **Intersecting Trail**

▼ 3.6		TL	Track on right.
	0.5 ▲	TR	Track on left.
▼ 4.1		SO	Track on left is Front Range #20: Badger Mountain Road (FR 228). Zero trip meter.
	0.0 ▲		Proceed north on FR 44.

GPS: N39°05.09' W105°32.18'

▼ 0.0			Proceed south following signs for FR 442.
	5.3 ▲	SO	Track on right is Front Range #20: Badger Mountain Road (FR 228). Zero trip meter.
▼ 0.4		BR	Road forks with FR 226 on left and FR 442 on right. Sign posted to US 24 and Tarryall Reservoir.
	4.9 ▲	BL	Road forks. FR 226 on right; FR 442 on left. Sign posted to US 24 and Tarryall Reservoir.
▼ 0.8		BL	Road forks with FR 229 on right.
	4.5 ▲	BR	Road forks with FR 229 on left.
▼ 1.1		BL	Track on right is FR 442A; then track on left is FR 442A. Follow sign to LaSalle Pass.
	4.2 ▲	BR	Track on right is FR 442A; then track on left is FR 442A. Follow sign to LaSalle Pass.

GPS: N39°04.98' W105°33.67'

▼ 1.5		SO	Track on right is FR 442D.
	3.8 ▲	BR	Track on left is FR 442D.
▼ 1.7		BL	Track on right.
	3.6 ▲	BR	Track on left.
▼ 1.8		SO	Track on right.
	3.5 ▲	SO	Track on left.
▼ 1.9		BL	FR 44B on right.
	3.4 ▲	BR	FR 44B on left.

GPS: N39°04.79' W105°34.38'

▼ 2.5		SO	Track on left.
	2.8 ▲	BR	Track on right.
▼ 2.7		SO	Seasonal gate; then leave Pike National Forest.
	2.6 ▲	SO	Seasonal gate; then enter Pike National Forest.
▼ 2.8		TR	Intersection with unmarked road on left.
	2.5 ▲	TL	Intersection with unmarked road on right.
▼ 3.2		TL	Intersection. Turn left for US 24. Turn sharp right for Tarryall Reservoir.
	2.1 ▲	TR	Intersection. Turn left for US 24. Turn sharp left for Tarryall Reservoir.

GPS: N39°04.06' W105°35.12'

▼ 3.7		SO	Intersection with Larimer Road.
	1.6 ▲	SO	Intersection with Larimer Road.
▼ 4.2		SO	Intersection with Jackson Road.
	1.1 ▲	SO	Intersection with Jackson Road.
▼ 4.6		SO	Track on left.
	0.7 ▲	SO	Track on right.
▼ 5.2		SO	Track on right.
	0.1 ▲	SO	Track on left.
▼ 5.3			Cattle guard; then trail ends at T-intersection with US 24. Turn right for Lake George; turn left for US 285.
	0.0 ▲		Trail begins at intersection with US 24 and CR 23-A. Proceed north on CR 23-A toward LaSalle Pass Road.

GPS: N39°02.88' W105°33.68'

FRONT RANGE REGION TRAIL #20

Badger Mountain Road

Starting Point:	Intersection with Front Range #19: La Salle Pass Trail, FR 44 and FR 228
Finishing Point:	Summit of Badger Mountain
Total Mileage:	4.3 miles (one-way)
Unpaved Mileage:	4.3 miles
Driving Time:	30 minutes (one-way)
Elevation Range:	9,738 to 11,269 feet
Usually Open:	May to October
Difficulty Rating:	3
Scenic Rating:	9

Special Attractions

- Expansive views of the landscape from overlooks along trail.
- Beautiful fall color.

Expansive view from along the trail to Badger Mountain summit

View from the overlook before reaching the end of the trail

Description

Badger Mountain Road begins on Front Range #19: La Salle Pass Trail near the pass. It follows FR 228, climbing to the summit of Badger Mountain and ending at a cluster of communications towers and equipment. Maintenance vehicles that service the equipment at the top of the mountain frequently use this road, so be aware you will likely encounter an oncoming vehicle.

Immediately gaining elevation, this narrow, one-lane forest road travels through dense stands of aspen and evergreen trees. The standard is numerous embedded rocks and considerable erosion, making for a bumpy ride. However, there are no obstacles that would present difficulty for a stock, high-clearance 4WD. For most of the trail's length, there are plenty of pull-outs for passing. Short sections of the route are shelf road, and the trail can also be steep in places.

As the trail climbs, breaks in the trees reveal glimpses of the surrounding landscape and hint at the sweeping views near the summit. At approximately 2.3 miles, an overlook to the southwest provides the best views of the surrounding landscape, including the South Fork of the Platte River, Spinney Mountain Reservoir, and Elevenmile Reservoir.

The trail continues to climb and the aspen stands disappear as you reach the summit at approximately 11,300 feet. A few

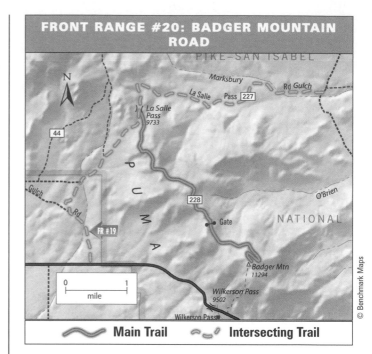

FRONT RANGE #20: BADGER MOUNTAIN ROAD

© Benchmark Maps

~~~ **Main Trail**   ~~~ **Intersecting Trail**

trees and the numerous radio towers on the summit obscure views, but a trip to the top is worth the effort. The towers and equipment clustered at the summit appear to be the center of Park County communications with towers owned by several private companies as well as county, state, and other government agencies.

Current Road Information

Pike & San Isabel National Forests
South Park Ranger District
320 US 285
Fairplay, CO 80440
(719) 836-2031

Map References

USFS   Pike National Forest
Maptech CD: Colorado Springs/Ski Areas/Central
Benchmark's *Colorado Road & Recreation Atlas,* p. 88

Communications towers at the end of the trail

The trail near the summit

Colorado Atlas & Gazetteer, p. 49
The Roads of Colorado, p. 95
Trails Illustrated, #137 (incomplete)

Route Directions

▼ 0.0		Trail begins at intersection with Trail#19: LaSalle Pass Trail (FR 44) and FR 228. Proceed east on FR 228, following sign to Badger Mountain.
	GPS: N39°05.09' W105°32.18'	
▼ 2.3	SO	Scenic overlook to the southwest and pullout on right.
	GPS: N39°03.68' W105°31.75'	
▼ 2.4	SO	Track on right.
▼ 4.3		Trail ends at radio towers at top of mountain.
	GPS: N39°03.02' W105°30.85'	

FRONT RANGE REGION TRAIL #21

Rampart Range Road

Starting Point:	**Sedalia**
Finishing Point:	**Garden of the Gods in Colorado Springs**
Total Mileage:	**65.3 miles**
Unpaved Mileage:	**55.6 miles**
Driving Time:	**3.5 hours**
Elevation Range:	**5,800 to 9,370 feet**
Usually Open:	**May to November**
Difficulty Rating:	**1**
Scenic Rating:	**6**

Special Attractions

- Access to a network of 4WD trails.
- Easy access from Denver or Colorado Springs.
- Red rock formations and the Garden of the Gods.
- Numerous ATV, trail bike, and hiking trails near the trail.
- Numerous picnic spots.

View of Rampart Range Road near Devil's Head in the mid-1920s

More interesting rock formations along the trail

History

The Civilian Conservation Corps (CCC) constructed Rampart Range Road as a public works project during the Great Depression. A number of the trails that intersect with Rampart Range Road were originally stagecoach roads or stock and game trails. There is also a local legend that a buried treasure is waiting to be discovered somewhere between Devil's Head Peak and Deckers. Apparently, train robbers made off with $60,000 after stopping the Denver & Rio Grande Railroad and buried their treasure to escape from pursuing law enforcement. They marked the location of the stolen gold on a tree, but a forest fire destroyed their markings. The treasure, which is said to be worth millions today, is supposedly still buried in the Rampart Range area.

At Devil's Head Campground along Rampart Range Road, there is a 1.4-mile hiking trail to Devil's Head Fire Lookout. Devil's Head was chosen as the location for the lookout because visibility extends 100 miles in every direction, making it easy to locate signs of a forest fire over great distances. The forest service built the first lookout tower at this location in 1907.

In 1919, Helen Dowe became the first woman lookout employed by the forest service and worked at Devil's Head Fire

Spectacular red rocks

Lookout for two years. She lived in a small cabin at the base of the tower, and each day she climbed a series of wooden ladders 200 feet to the top. Using 72 pack mules to transport equipment, the Army Corps of Engineers reconstructed the original tower in 1951. In 1991, the Devil's Head Fire Lookout was the only remaining lookout tower on the Front Range, and it was placed on the National Register of Historic Places. To this day, the tower is staffed from mid-May to mid-September.

In the mid-1940s, local residents began exploring Rampart Range Road on their Harley Davidson motorcycles and in their Triumphs. In the late 1960s, dirt bikes became more affordable, and more people began exploring the network of forest roads. Rampart Range has hosted numerous dirt bike races, including the difficult Bear Track Enduro in the early 1970s. Today, 4WDs, ATVs, as well as dirt bikes ride Rampart Range's trails, which are maintained by the forest service.

Description

This is a wide, well-maintained dirt road that can easily be driven by a passenger vehicle in good conditions, although 4WD will make the ride more enjoyable. The road can be eroded in places, especially early in spring when snowmelt makes the trail extremely muddy. It can also become quite corrugated.

While the trail does not present 4WD challenges, it is a very scenic drive with numerous places to picnic or camp. Many of the numerous intersecting forest roads are more difficult and present 4WD challenges. The route travels past many large, interesting rock formations and through pine forest mixed with occasional aspen groves. Near the route's end, the rocks become red with a similar appearance to the 250-million-year-old sedimentary rock formations found within Garden of the Gods at the end of the trail.

This route commences in Sedalia and heads southwest on Colorado 67 toward Deckers before turning south onto Rampart Range Road at the 9.7-mile point. Approximately 13

View of Rampart Range Road with interesting rock formations in the background

Spectacular view of the trail and Colorado Springs in the distance

miles after turning onto Rampart Range Road, Front Range #22: Watson Park Trail (FR 502) intersects the route on the left. In approximately 2.5 miles, Front Range #24: Long Hollow Road (FR 348) intersects with the main trail. This road provides another side road opportunity that also can loop back to Rampart Range Road. This trail serves as a backbone road to a number of other trails that are also included in this book.

As you approach Colorado Springs, the road starts to switchback as it descends from Rampart Range, and there are some excellent views across to the plains of eastern Colorado. The road ends at the Garden of the Gods.

If you are beginning this trail from the Garden of the Gods, finding the start of Rampart Range Road can be a little tricky. From I-25 take exit 146 and zero your trip meter. Proceed west on Garden of the Gods Road. After 2.2 miles, turn left onto 30th Street and follow the sign to Garden of the Gods. At the 3.5-mile point, the Garden of the Gods Visitors Center is on the left. Then at the 3.6-mile point, turn right into the Garden of the Gods. At the 4.1-mile point turn right onto Juniper Way Loop. There are three intersections along this road before you reach Rampart Range Road. At the intersection at 5.0 miles, bear right; at 5.7 miles, bear right; and at 5.9 miles, bear left. At the 6.2-mile point, turn right onto Rampart Range Road. This is where the trail begins.

Current Road Information

Pike & San Isabel National Forests
Pikes Peak Ranger District
601 South Weber Street
Colorado Springs, CO 80903
(719) 636-1602

Map References

USFS   Pike National Forest
Maptech CD:
        Colorado Springs/Ski Areas/Central
Benchmark's *Colorado Road & Recreation Atlas*, pp. 75, 89
Colorado Atlas & Gazetteer, pp. 50, 62

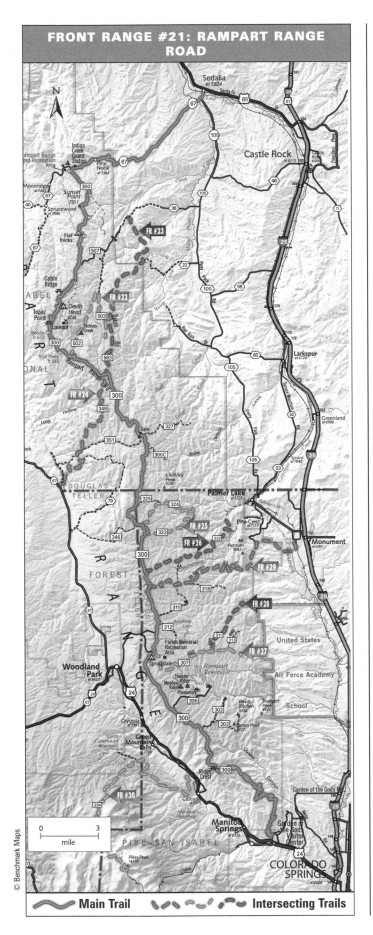

FRONT RANGE #21: RAMPART RANGE ROAD

Main Trail ~~~ ~~~ **Intersecting Trails**

© Benchmark Maps

The Roads of Colorado, pp. 72, 73, 88, 89
Trails Illustrated, #135, #137

Route Directions

▼ 0.0 In Sedalia, at the intersection of US 85 (Santa Fe) and Colorado 67, zero trip meter and proceed southwest toward Deckers.

9.7 ▲ End at intersection with US 85 in Sedalia.

GPS: N 39°26.34' W 104°57.68'

▼ 9.7 TL Intersection with Rampart Range Road (FR 300). Zero trip meter.

0.0 ▲ Continue on Colorado 67 toward Sedalia.

GPS: N 39°22.67' W 105°05.60'

▼ 0.0 Continue along Rampart Range Road toward Devil's Head.

8.8 ▲ TR Intersection with Colorado 67. Zero trip meter.

▼ 0.1 SO Seasonal gate.
8.7 ▲ SO Seasonal gate.

▼ 2.9 SO Restrooms and parking area on left.
5.9 ▲ SO Restrooms and parking area on right.

▼ 4.5 SO USFS Flat Rocks Campground on right.
4.3 ▲ SO USFS Flat Rocks Campground on left.

▼ 4.6 SO Flat Rocks scenic overlook on left; then campsites.
4.2 ▲ SO Campsites; then Flat Rocks scenic overlook on right.

▼ 6.3 SO FR 507 on left toward Jackson Creek Road.
2.5 ▲ SO FR 507 on right toward Jackson Creek Road.

GPS: N 39°18.23' W 105°05.26'

▼ 7.3 SO Dutch Fred Trailhead and restrooms on left.
1.5 ▲ SO Dutch Fred Trailhead and restrooms on right.

GPS: N 39°20.809' W 105°05109'

▼ 8.4 SO USFS Cabin Ridge picnic ground on right in 0.2 miles.
0.4 ▲ SO USFS Cabin Ridge picnic ground on left in 0.2 miles.

GPS: N 39°16.77' W 105°06.30'

▼ 8.8 BR Intersection. Devil's Head Campground and hiking trail to fire lookout is straight ahead in 0.5 miles. Zero trip meter.
0.0 ▲ Continue north on Rampart Range Road.

GPS: N 39°16.54' W 105°06.43'

▼ 0.0 Continue south on Rampart Range Road.
4.6 ▲ BL Intersection. Devil's Head Campground and hiking trail to fire lookout on right in 0.5 mile. Zero trip meter.

▼ 2.0 SO USFS Topaz Point picnic area on right.
2.6 ▲ SO USFS Topaz Point picnic area on left.

▼ 4.6 SO Front Range #22: Watson Park Trail (FR 502) to Jackson Creek Campground on left. Zero trip meter.
0.0 ▲ Continue north on Rampart Range Road (FR 300).

GPS: N 39°13.99' W 105°05.76'

▼ 0.0 Continue south on Rampart Range Road (FR 300).
2.5 ▲ SO Front Range #22: Watson Park Trail (FR 502) to Jackson Creek Campground on right. Zero trip meter.

▼ 2.5 SO Front Range #24: Long Hollow Road (FR 348) to Fern Creek, Colorado 67, Woodland Park, and Colorado Springs on right. Zero trip meter.
0.0 ▲ Continue north on Rampart Range Road (FR 300).

GPS: N 39°13.15' W 105°03.87'

▼ 0.0 Continue south on Rampart Range Road (FR 300).
0.1 ▲ SO Front Range #24: Long Hollow Road (FR 348)

		to Fern Creek, Colorado 67, Woodland Park, and Colorado Springs on left.
▼ 0.1	SO	Front Range #23: Dakan Mountain Road (FR 563) on left. Zero trip meter.
0.0 ▲		Continue north on Rampart Range Road (FR 300).

GPS: N 39°13.19' W 105°03.70'

▼ 0.0		Continue south on Rampart Range Road (FR 300).
11.9 ▲	SO	Front Range #23: Dakan Mountain Road (FR 563) on right.

GPS: N 39°13.19' W 105°03.68'

▼ 4.6	SO	Gate. Track on right goes to radio towers.
7.3 ▲	SO	Track on left goes to radio towers. Gate.
▼ 5.0	SO	FR 351 (Fern Creek Road) on right. FR 327 on left.
6.9 ▲	SO	FR 327 on right. FR 351 (Fern Creek Road) on left.

GPS: N 39°10.40' W 105°01.50'

▼ 9.6	SO	Saylor Park. FR 325 on left.
2.3 ▲	SO	Saylor Park. FR 325 on right.

GPS: N 39°06.97' W 105°02.04'

▼ 11.0	SO	FR 346 (Hotel Gulch Road) on right toward Mt. Deception.
0.9 ▲	SO	FR 346 (Hotel Gulch Road) on left toward Mt. Deception.
▼ 11.3	SO	FR 324 (Ice Cave Creek Road) on left.
0.6 ▲	SO	FR 324 (Ice Cave Creek Road) on right.
▼ 11.9	SO	Front Range #25: Winding Stairs to Ice Cave Creek Road (FR 323) on left. Zero trip meter.
0.0 ▲		Continue north on Rampart Range Road (FR 300).

GPS: N 39°05.82' W 105°01.28'

▼ 0.0		Continue south on Rampart Range Road (FR 300).
2.4 ▲	SO	Front Range #25: Winding Stairs to Ice Cave Creek Road (FR 323) on right. Zero trip meter.
▼ 2.4	SO	Front Range #26: Balanced Rock Road (FR 322) on left. Zero trip meter.
0.0 ▲		Continue north on Rampart Range Road (FR 300).

GPS: N 39°04.00' W 105°01.39'

▼ 0.0		Proceed south on Rampart Range Road (FR 300).
1.0 ▲		Front Range #26: Balanced Rock Road (FR 322) on right. Zero trip meter.
▼ 1.0	BR	Front Range #29: Mount Herman Road (FR 320) on left. Zero trip meter.
0.0 ▲		Continue north on Rampart Range Road (FR 300).

GPS: N 39°03.36' W 105°01.10'

▼ 0.0		Continue south on Rampart Range Road (FR 300).
4.0 ▲	BL	Front Range #29: Mount Herman Road (FR 320) on right. Zero trip meter.
▼ 1.9	SO	FR 315 (Beaver Creek Road) on left.
2.1 ▲	SO	FR 315 (Beaver Creek Road) on right.
▼ 2.3	SO	FR 312 (Ensign Gulch Road) to Carrol Lakes on left.
1.7 ▲	SO	FR 312 (Ensign Gulch Road) to Carrol Lakes on right.
▼ 2.5	BL	Intersection with FR 393 toward Woodland Park on right. Proceed toward Rampart Reservoir.
1.5 ▲	BR	Intersection with FR 393 toward Woodland Park on left.

GPS: N 39°01.48' W 105°00.70'

▼ 3.8	SO	FR 309 to Farish Recreation Area on left; then exit Pike National Forest.
0.2 ▲	SO	Entering Pike National Forest; then FR 300 to

		Farish Recreation Area on right.
▼ 4.0	SO	Stop sign. Intersection with Front Range #27: Shubarth Road to the left. Woodland Park and Loy Gulch to the right. Follow sign to Rampart Reservoir. Sign prohibits target shooting for next 17.5 miles. Zero trip meter.
0.0 ▲		Continue north on Rampart Range Road (FR 300).

GPS: N 39°.00.27' W 105°00.94'

▼ 0.0		Continue south on Rampart Range Road (FR 300).
14.7 ▲	SO	Intersection with Front Range #27: Shubarth Road to the right. Woodland Park and Loy Gulch to the left. Zero trip meter.
▼ 0.8	SO	USFS Springdale Campground on left.
13.9 ▲	SO	USFS Springdale Campground on right.
▼ 2.4	SO	Rainbow Gulch Trailhead (to reservoir) on left.
12.3 ▲	SO	Rainbow Gulch Trailhead (to reservoir) on right.
▼ 3.8	SO	FR 306 on left to Rampart Reservoir.
10.9 ▲	SO	FR 306 on right to Rampart Reservoir.

GPS: N 38°57.70' W 104°59.72'

▼ 5.9	BR	FR 303 (Northfield Road) on left.
8.8 ▲	SO	FR 303 (Northfield Road) on right.
▼ 8.9	SO	Ridge Crest Scenic Overlook on right.
5.8 ▲	SO	Ridge Crest Scenic Overlook on left.
▼ 14.7	SO	USFS Rampart Shooting Range on right. Zero trip meter.
0.0 ▲		Proceed north on Rampart Range Road.

GPS: N 38°53.86' W 104°54.68'

▼ 0.0		Proceed south on Rampart Range Road.
5.6 ▲	SO	USFS Rampart Shooting Range on left. Zero trip meter.
▼ 5.3	SO	Rock formations—part of Garden of the Gods.
0.3 ▲	SO	Rock formations—part of Garden of the Gods.
▼ 5.6		Trail ends at Garden of the Gods.
0.0 ▲		At the Garden of the Gods, turn onto Rampart Range Road (FR 300) and zero trip meter.

GPS: N 38°51.97' W 104°53.79'

FRONT RANGE REGION TRAIL #22

Watson Park Trail

Starting Point:	Intersection of Front Range #21: Rampart Range Road and FR 502, 13 miles from the north end of Rampart Range Road
Finishing Point:	T-intersection with Front Range #23: Dakan Mountain Road (FR 563)
Total Mileage:	5.9 miles, plus 0.8-mile spur
Unpaved Mileage:	6.7 miles, plus 0.8-mile spur
Driving Time:	45 minutes
Elevation Range:	7,751 to 8,617 feet
Usually Open:	May to November
Difficulty Rating:	3
Scenic Rating:	9

Interesting rock formations near the beginning of the trail

Special Attractions

- Spectacular fall aspen viewing.
- Exploring Watson Park.
- Numerous backcountry campsites.

Description

Watson Park Trail begins at the intersection of Front Range #21: Rampart Range Road (FR 300) and FR 502. This trail is popular with motorbike and ATV riders, and campers can choose from numerous undeveloped sites with fire rings. Aspen and pine trees flank the trail, and interesting rock formations vary the scenery. Where a creek beside the road flows into a boggy area full of huge boulders, numerous colorful wildflowers and thistle grow in the moist ground. Wildlife also thickly populates the area, and mule deer, elk, and ptarmigans are frequently seen. Although the trail is just off the busy Rampart Range Road, the scenery lends a more remote character to the route.

Starting out, the trail is a wide, graded dirt road that is narrower than Rampart Range. After the first mile, which passes through a section of fenced private land with a few residences, the trail becomes more difficult. Negotiating the potholes and embedded rocks without damage requires a high-clearance 4WD. At the intersection with FR 503, the trail becomes nar-

row enough to make passing oncoming vehicles somewhat of a challenge. This track, which is rated a 3 for difficulty, begins to climb and becomes a bumpy shelf road with very few pullouts, making passing another vehicle even more of a challenge.

The shelf road's loose and uneven surface makes having off-road tires an asset, and the steep drop-off from the road makes the drive exciting. It is necessary to pick a line through some of the rougher spots to avoid damage to the underbody of a stock, high-clearance vehicle. Avoid this trail in wet conditions when steep sections would be nearly impassable. Some of the narrowest sections of this trail would require significant amounts of difficult reversing in order to pass another vehicle.

The spur, which is located near the end of the main trail, is a narrow gravel road lined with aspen trees and rocks that leads to scenic Watson Park. As the road descends into the park, erosion and a large, creek-fed water crossing make a high-clearance 4WD preferable. Dirt bikes and ATVs have created numerous tracks around the park, some of which are challenging and fun for 4WD vehicles. Campers have choices of many undeveloped sites within the wide clearing, and a number of

A blind corner on the trail

Boulders beside the trail

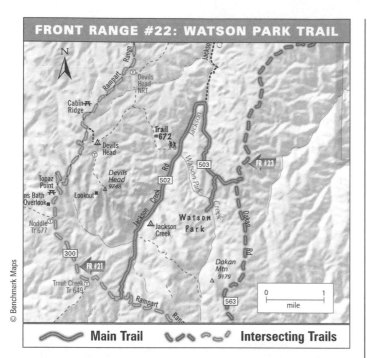

FRONT RANGE #22: WATSON PARK TRAIL

Main Trail ~~~ Intersecting Trails

© Benchmark Maps

trailheads for hikers and mountain bikers take off from the edges of the park. Because of snowmelt in the early spring or after periods of rain, the creek may be too deep to cross, and the ground can be extremely muddy in wet conditions. This scenic spur following Jackson Creek is rated a 3 for difficulty.

Current Road Information
Pike & San Isabel National Forests
South Platte Ranger District
19316 Goddard Ranch Court
Morrison, CO 80465
(303) 275-5610

Map References
USFS   Pike National Forest
Maptech CD:
        Colorado Springs/Ski Areas/Central
Benchmark's *Colorado Road & Recreation Atlas*, p. 75
Colorado Atlas & Gazetteer, p. 50
Trails Illustrated, #135

Rough, steep section of trail

Route Directions

| ▼ 0.0 | | Trail begins just beyond 13 miles from the start of Front Range #21: Rampart Range Road at the intersection with FR 502. |
| 3.9 ▲ | | Trail ends at T-intersection of FR 502 and Front Range #21: Rampart Range Road. |

GPS: N39°13.99' W105°05.76'

| ▼ 0.5 | BL | Track on right to undeveloped campsite. |
| 3.4 ▲ | BR | Track on left to undeveloped campsite. |

GPS: N39°14.38' W105°05.64'

| ▼ 0.8 | BL | Gated track on right. |
| 3.1 ▲ | BR | Gated track on left. |

GPS: N39°14.62' W105°05.50'

| ▼ 0.9 | SO | Pond on left. |
| 3.0 ▲ | SO | Pond on right. |

| ▼ 1.5 | SO | Jackson Creek USFS Campground is fee area on right. |
| 2.4 ▲ | SO | Jackson Creek USFS Campground is fee area on left. |

GPS: N39°15.16' W105°05.29'

| ▼ 1.9 | BL | Gated track on right. |
| 2.0 ▲ | BR | Gated track on left. |

GPS: N39°15.43' W105°05.01'

| ▼ 2.3 | SO | Campsite on left. |
| 1.6 ▲ | SO | Campsite on right. |

GPS: N39°15.73' W105°04.92'

| ▼ 2.7 | SO | Trail #672 for mountain biking, hiking, and ATVs on right; then left. |
| 1.2 ▲ | SO | Trail #672 for mountain biking, hiking, and ATVs on right; then left. |

GPS: N39°16.03' W105°04.76'

| ▼ 2.8 | SO | Trail #679 for mountain biking, hiking, and ATVs on left. |
| 1.1 ▲ | SO | Trail #679 for mountain biking, hiking, and ATVs on right. |

GPS: N39°16.13' W105°04.66'

| ▼ 3.7 | SO | Track on left to campsite. |

More interesting rock formations alongside the trail

0.2 ▲	BL	Track on right to campsite.
		GPS: N39°16.82' W105°04.34'
▼ 3.9	BR	FR 502 ends and FR 503 begins. Zero trip meter.
0.0 ▲		Continue northwest on FR 502.
		GPS: N39°16.91' W105°04.14'
▼ 0.0		Continue southeast on FR 503; then cross over creek and track on left to campsite.
1.5 ▲	BL	Cross over creek and track on right to campsite; then FR 503 ends and FR 502 begins. Zero trip meter.
▼ 1.2	SO	Track on left to campsite with large boulder.
0.3 ▲	SO	Track on right to campsite with large boulder.
		GPS: N39°15.95' W105°04.10'
▼ 1.5	TL	Intersection with spur on left. Zero trip meter.
0.0 ▲		Continue northwest on FR 503.
		GPS: N39°15.79' W105°03.90'

Spur to Watson Park

▼ 0.0		Zero trip meter and proceed southwest toward Watson Park.
▼ 0.1	SO	Track on left.
▼ 0.5	SO	Creek crossing into Watson Park.
		GPS: N39°15.42' W105°04.02'
▼ 0.8	SO	Spur ends in Watson Park with tracks and trailheads at numerous locations throughout the park.
		GPS: N39°15.23' W105°04.17'

Continuation of Main Trail

▼ 0.0		Continue southeast on FR 503.
0.5 ▲	TR	Intersection with spur on right. Zero trip meter.
▼ 0.4	BR	Road forks at triangle intersection is cut through to Front Range #23: Dakan Mountain Road (FR 563); signed right for Front Range #21: Rampart Range Road or left for Sedalia.
0.1 ▲	SO	Track on right is cut through to Front Range #23: Dakan Mountain Road.
▼ 0.5		Trail ends at intersection with Front Range #23: Dakan Mountain Road (FR 563).
0.0 ▲		Trail begins at intersection of Front Range #23: Dakan Mountain Road (FR 563) and FR 503.
		GPS: N39°15.73' W105°03.49'

FRONT RANGE REGION TRAIL #23

Dakan Mountain Road

Starting Point:	**Intersection of FR 563 and Front Range #21: Rampart Range Road**
Finishing Point:	**Intersection of Jackson Creek Road (CR 38) and Hidden Valley Road**
Total Mileage:	**11.5 miles**
Unpaved Mileage:	**11.5 miles**
Driving Time:	**45 minutes**
Elevation Range:	**6,437 to 9,021 feet**
Usually Open:	**May to November**
Difficulty Rating:	**3**
Scenic Rating:	**7**

Slickrock section of the trail

Special Attractions
- Good undeveloped campsites and picnic areas.
- Interesting large boulders.
- Brilliant yellow aspen stands in fall.

Description
This is another of the narrower and rougher forest roads that intersect Front Range #21: Rampart Range Road. This trail enjoyably twists and turns through the forest, maneuvering around huge boulders and through intricate rock formations. Alternately the road runs through a burn restoration area and stands of aspen and evergreen trees. Although trees run along both sides of the road, they don't obscure the nice view of the surrounding scenic peaks and rock formations. Numerous ideal spots to stop and picnic or camp can be found along this route.

Although the track is one-lane, there are plenty of pullouts for passing oncoming vehicles. The trail's surface, formed of dirt and gravel, is eroded and embedded with rocks. Large humps and dips in the road for drainage make a high-clearance vehicle preferable. The road also has short, steep sections with loose, gravelly surfaces that make using aggressively tread-

Huge boulder beside the trail

ed tires an advantage. Otherwise, momentum will help propel your vehicle over the hills. The roughest sections give the road a rating of 3 for difficulty.

Current Road Information
Pike & San Isabel National Forests
South Platte Ranger District
19316 Goddard Ranch Court
Morrison, CO 80465
(303) 275-5610

Map References
USFS   Pike National Forest
Maptech CD:
           Colorado Springs/Ski Areas/Central
Benchmark's *Colorado Road & Recreation Atlas,* pp. 75, 89
Colorado Atlas & Gazetteer, p. 50
The Roads of Colorado, p. 50
Trails Illustrated, #135

Climbing the slickrock on the trail

Route Directions

▼ 0.0		Trail begins at intersection of Front Range #21: Rampart Range Road and FR 563.
3.6 ▲		Trail ends at intersection with Front Range #21: Rampart Range Road and FR 563. Turn right for Sedalia. Turn left for Colorado Springs.

GPS: N39°13.19' W105°03.70'

▼ 3.6	BR	Intersection with Front Range #22: Watson Park Trail (FR 503) on left. Zero trip meter.
0.0 ▲		Continue south on Dakan Mountain Road (FR 563).

GPS: N39°15.76' W105°03.47'

▼ 0.0		Continue northeast on Dakan Mountain Road (FR 563).
4.1 ▲	BL	Intersection with Front Range #22: Watson Park Trail (FR 503) on right. Zero trip meter.

▼ 0.1	BR	Track on left to Front Range #22: Watson Park Trail (FR 503). Follow signs to FR 563; then cross over slick rock.
4.0 ▲	SO	Cross over slick rock; then track on right to Front Range #22: Watson Park Trail (FR 503). Follow sign to FR 563.

GPS: N39°15.76' W105°03.47'

▼ 0.3	SO	Campsite on left.

Rough section of the trail

Erosion in Watson Park

3.8 ▲	SO	Campsite on right.	
▼ 1.1	SO	Track on right.	
3.0 ▲	SO	Track on left.	
		GPS: N39°16.53' W105°03.29'	
▼ 2.3	BR	Road on left.	
1.8 ▲	BL	Road on right.	
		GPS: N39°17.46' W105°03.01'	
▼ 2.9	SO	Campsite on left.	
1.2 ▲	SO	Campsite on right.	
		GPS: N39°17.27' W105°2.47'	
▼ 4.1	SO	Seasonal closure gate. Zero trip meter.	
0.0 ▲		Continue south on FR 563.	
		GPS: N39°18.24' W105°01.95'	
▼ 0.0	BR	Tracks on left and right; continue north on FR 563.	
0.4 ▲	BL	Road forks; then pass through seasonal closure gate. Zero trip meter.	
▼ 0.4	SO	Seasonal closure gate; then unmarked road on left. Zero trip meter.	
0.0 ▲		Continue west on FR 563 toward Front Range #21: Rampart Range Road.	
		GPS: N39°18.55' W105°01.87'	
▼ 0.0		Continue east on FR 563 toward Gott Mountain.	
3.4 ▲	SO	Zero trip meter at unmarked road on right; then pass through seasonal closure gate.	
▼ 1.8	SO	Seasonal closure gate.	
1.6 ▲	SO	Seasonal closure gate.	

Watson Park Creek crossing near the end of the spur

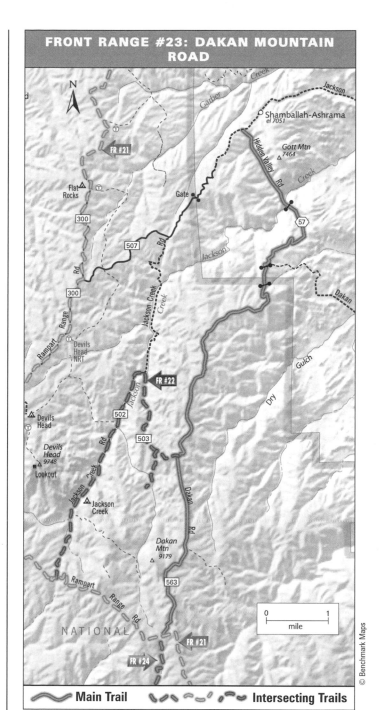

FRONT RANGE #23: DAKAN MOUNTAIN ROAD

Main Trail   Intersecting Trails

		GPS: N39°19.26' W105°01.47'	
▼ 1.9	BL	Signed public crossing; then cross through creek.	
1.5 ▲	BR	Cross through creek; then signed public crossing.	
▼ 3.4		Trail ends at intersection signed Jackson Creek Road (CR 38) and Hidden Valley Road. Make a sharp left for Front Range #21: Rampart Range Road. Turn right for Colorado 105 and Castle Rock.	
0.0 ▲		Trail begins at intersection signed Jackson Creek Road (CR 38) and Hidden Valley Road. Follow Hidden Valley Road southwest into Pike National Forest.	
		GPS: N39°20.39' W105°02.35'	

Long Hollow Road

Starting Point:	**Intersection of FR 348 and Front Range #21: Rampart Range Road**
Finishing Point:	**Intersection of Colorado 67 and FR 350/CR 49, 10 miles north of Woodland Park**
Total Mileage:	**9.5 miles**
Unpaved Mileage:	**9.4 miles**
Driving Time:	**1 hour**
Elevation Range:	**7,539 to 8,840 feet**
Usually Open:	**May to November**
Difficulty Rating:	**3**
Scenic Rating:	**8**

Special Attractions

- Long, scenic, remote-feeling trail.
- Views of Pikes Peak to the south.
- Meadows blanketed with wildflowers in the spring.

Description

Long Hollow Road winds its way south from Front Range #21: Rampart Range Road through Pike National Forest, presenting impressive views of Colorado's famous fourteener, Pikes Peak. The trail starts out as a wide, graded dirt road but becomes bumpy from erosion and sections of embedded and loose rocks. These sections are rough enough to make a high-clearance 4WD preferable and give the trail its difficulty rating of 3. In general, the road can be bumpy, but it is not very difficult for most stock 4WDs. The road climbs switchbacks with intermittent drop-offs, but there is plenty of room to pass oncoming vehicles.

Dense evergreen forest mixed with stands of aspen alternate with open meadows and parks filled with spring wildflowers, such as purple daisies, red trumpet, mullein, thistle, and numerous others. Predominantly formed of red dirt and rock, one section of trail is littered with white rocks from a deposit of marble just off the trail. Another section of trail runs through a rock garden of large, interesting boulders.

The forest limits views for the majority of the drive, but one particularly open section provides spectacular views of the mountains to the south. Numerous undeveloped campsites surround the trail, and ATV and dirt bike tracks leave the main trail in several locations. It is not uncommon to see a herd of elk grazing in the open meadows nearby. The trail ends after a section of fenced private property at a T-intersection with Colorado 67, approximately 10 miles north of Woodland Park.

Current Road Information

Pike & San Isabel National Forests
South Platte Ranger District
19316 Goddard Ranch Road
Morrison, CO 80465
(303) 275-5610

Pike & San Isabel National Forests
Pikes Peak Ranger District
601 South Weber Street
Colorado Springs, CO 80903
(719) 636-1602

Map References

USFS   Pike National Forest
Maptech CD:
           Colorado Springs/Ski Areas/Central
Benchmark's *Colorado Road & Recreation Atlas*, p. 89
Colorado Atlas & Gazetteer, p. 50
The Roads of Colorado, p. 96
Trails Illustrated, #135

Route Directions

▼ 0.0			Trail begins at intersection of Front Range #21: Rampart Range Road and FR 348.
	5.5 ▲		Trail ends at intersection of Front Range #21: Rampart Range Road and FR 348.
		GPS: N39°13.15' W105°03.87'	
▼ 0.6		SO	Track on right.

The trail travels through evergreen forest

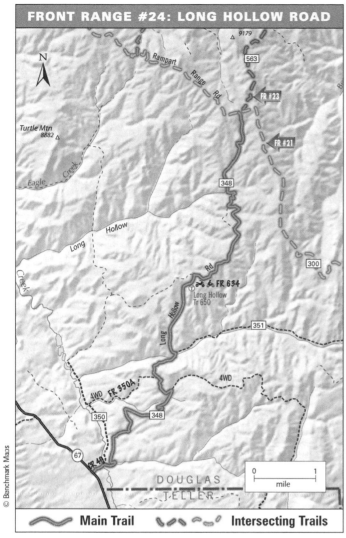

FRONT RANGE #24: LONG HOLLOW ROAD

Main Trail ~~~ **Intersecting Trails**

	4.9 ▲	SO	Track on left.
▼ 0.7		SO	Track on left to pond and campsite.
	4.8 ▲	SO	Track on right to pond and campsite.
▼ 0.8		BL	Track on right.
	4.6 ▲	BR	Track on left.
▼ 1.1		SO	Track on right.
	4.4 ▲	BR	Track on left.
	GPS: N39°12.32' W105°04.13'		
▼ 1.4		BL	Track on right.
	3.0 ▲	SO	Track on left.
▼ 2.1		BR	Track on left.
	3.4 ▲	BL	Track on right.
	GPS: N39°11.74' W105°03.88'		
▼ 2.2		BR	Track on left.
	3.3 ▲	BL	Track on right.
▼ 2.8		SO	Track on left.
	2.7 ▲	BL	Track on right.
▼ 3.7		SO	Campsite on left.
	1.8 ▲	SO	Campsite on right.
	GPS: N39°10.81' W105°04.47'		
▼ 3.8		SO	FR 634 for dirt bikes and ATVs on left.
	1.7 ▲	SO	FR 634 for dirt bikes and ATVs on right.
▼ 4.0		BL	FR 650 for dirt bikes and ATVs on right.
	1.5 ▲	BR	FR 650 for dirt bikes and ATVs on left.
▼ 5.0		SO	Seasonal closure gate.

	0.5 ▲	SO	Seasonal closure gate.
▼ 5.5		SO/TR	Pass FR 348F on right then FR 351 on left. Turn right to continue on FR 348. Zero trip meter.
	0.0 ▲		Continue north on FR 348.
	GPS: N39°10.71' W105°05.08'		
▼ 0.0			Continue south on FR 348.
	3.9 ▲	SO	Zero trip meter. FR 348F on left; then FR 351 on right.
▼ 0.6		TL	FR 348E and FR 350A on right. Turn left to continue on FR 348.
	3.3 ▲	TR	Turn right on FR 348 then pass FR 350A and FR 348E on left.
	GPS: N39°09.46' W105°05.47'		
▼ 1.1		BL	FR 348D signed dead end on right.
	2.8 ▲	BR	FR 348D signed dead end on left.
▼ 1.2		BR	FR 347 on left.
	2.7 ▲	BL	FR 347 on right.
▼ 1.3		SO	FR 348C on left.
	2.6 ▲	SO	FR 348C on right.
▼ 1.8		SO	FR 348B on left.
	2.1 ▲	BL	FR 348B on right.
▼ 2.8		SO	Gated track on left.
	1.1 ▲	SO	Gated track on right.
▼ 3.4		SO	Track on left.
	0.5 ▲	SO	Track on right.
	GPS: N39°08.31' W105°06.23'		
▼ 3.5		SO	FR 344 on left.
	0.4 ▲	SO	FR 344 on right.
▼ 3.9		BL	Stop sign at intersection with FR 350 and CR 49. Zero trip meter.
	0.0 ▲		Proceed northeast on FR 348.
▼ 0.0			Proceed southwest on CR 49.
	0.06 ▲	BR	Intersection with FR 350 on left and FR 348 on right. Zero trip meter.
	GPS: N39°08.16' W105°06.39'		
▼ 0.1			Trail ends at T-intersection with Colorado 67. Turn left for Woodland Park; turn right for Deckers.
	0.0 ▲		Trail begins at intersection of Colorado 67 and CR 49, approximately 10 miles north of Woodland Park. Proceed northeast on CR 49.
	GPS: N39°08.04' W105°06.53'		

Boulders alongside the trail

Winding Stairs to Ice Cave Creek Road

Starting Point:	Intersection of Front Range #21:
	Rampart Range Road and FR 323
Finishing Point:	Intersection of Front Range #21:
	Rampart Range Road and FR 324
Total Mileage:	7.7 miles
Unpaved Mileage:	7.7 miles
Driving Time:	30 minutes
Elevation Range:	8,686 to 9,310 feet
Usually Open:	May to November
Difficulty Rating:	2
Scenic Rating:	8

Special Attractions

- Winding, backcountry road that is well maintained and accessible to passenger vehicles in good conditions.
- Old marble mine.

Description

This pleasant trail begins at the intersection of Front Range #21: Rampart Range Road and FR 323 and winds through the forest, connecting with FR 324, and exiting several miles north of the starting point on Rampart Range Road. Along the beginning of FR 323, the aspen and evergreen trees are shorter and allow for expansive views in all directions. At the 1.8-mile point, there is a particularly stunning view to the south of America's Mountain, Pikes Peak.

The easygoing trail, which is a wide, well-maintained dirt road, gradually heads downhill into a thick forested area passing several good backcountry campsites along the way. Before the intersection with FR 324, the road becomes narrower and is eroded in places, and some of the trees grow quite close to

Old quarry near the trail

the trail. There are also interesting boulders alongside the road.

Proceeding onto FR 324, the road is well-maintained but still narrow with trees growing close to the trail and overhanging the trail in places. It is possible the tree branches could scratch a vehicle's paint job. This forest road has short sections that are eroded and embedded with rocks, but they would not present too much of an obstacle for a passenger vehicle in dry conditions. The trail will become muddy during early spring from snowmelt and after rain.

The trail gently climbs back uphill past an old marble quarry and ends at the intersection with Rampart Range Road.

Current Road Information

Pike & San Isabel National Forests
Pikes Peak Ranger District
601 South Weber Street
Colorado Springs, CO 80903
(719) 636-1602

Erosion on the trail

The trail is closeted by thick pine forest

Map References

USFS   Pike National Forest
Maptech CD:
      Colorado Springs/Ski Areas/Central
Benchmark's *Colorado Road & Recreation Atlas*, p. 89
Colorado Atlas & Gazetteer, p. 50
The Roads of Colorado, p. 97
Trails Illustrated, #137

Route Directions

▼ 0.0			Trail begins at intersection with Front Range #21: Rampart Range Road and FR 323.
	2.6 ▲		Trail ends at intersection with Front Range #21: Rampart Range Road and FR 323.
			GPS: N39°05.82' W105°01.28'
▼ 0.3		SO	Track on right; then track on left.
	2.3 ▲	SO	Track on left; then track on right.
▼ 0.6		SO	Track on right.
	2.1 ▲	SO	Track on left.
▼ 0.8		SO	Track on right.
	1.8 ▲	SO	Track on left.
▼ 1.1		SO	Track on right.
	1.5 ▲	SO	Track on left.
▼ 2.2		SO	Track on right.
	0.5 ▲	SO	Track on left.
			GPS: N39°06.06' W104°59.33'
▼ 2.6		TL	Road forks with FR 323 on right and FR 324 on left. Zero trip meter.
	0.0 ▲		Proceed south on FR 323.

Easygoing section of trail

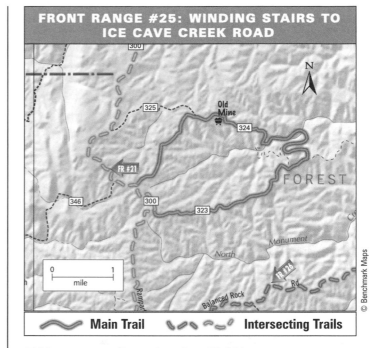

© Benchmark Maps

〰️ **Main Trail**   〰️〰️ **Intersecting Trails**

▼ 0.0			Proceed north on FR 324.
	3.5 ▲	TR	Intersection with FR 323. Zero trip meter.
			GPS: N39°06.27' W104°59.03'
▼ 1.0		BL	Track on right.
	2.5 ▲	SO	Track on left.
▼ 2.8		SO	Marble mine on left.
	0.6 ▲	SO	Marble mine on right.
			GPS: N39°07.18' W105°00.06'
▼ 2.9		SO	Track on left to old marble mine.
	0.5 ▲	BL	Track on right to old marble mine.
			GPS: N39°07.19' W105°00.14'

Close-up of rocks in the old quarry

▼ 3.0		SO	FR 324B on right.
	0.5 ▲	BR	FR 324B on left.
▼ 3.5		BL	Road forks with FR 324A on right. Zero trip meter.
	0.0 ▲		Proceed east on FR 324.
▼ 0.0			Proceed west on FR 324.
	1.7 ▲	SO	FR 324A on left. Zero trip meter.

GPS: N39°06.27' W105°00.67'

▼ 0.8		BL	Track on right.
	1.0 ▲	BR	Track on left.
▼ 1.7			Trail ends at intersection with Front Range #21: Rampart Range Road.
	0.0 ▲		Trail begins where FR 324 leaves Front Range #21: Rampart Range Road.

GPS: N39°06.18' W105°01.56'

Lovely stands of aspen along Balanced Rock Road

FRONT RANGE REGION TRAIL # 26

Balanced Rock Road

Starting Point:	**Intersection of Front Range #21: Rampart Range Road and Balanced Rock Road (FR 322)**
Finishing Point:	**Campsite above Upper Reservoir**
Total Mileage:	**7.4 miles (one-way)**
Unpaved Mileage:	**7.4 miles**
Driving Time:	**1 hour (one-way)**
Elevation Range:	**7,790 to 9,385 feet**
Usually Open:	**May to November**
Difficulty Rating:	**3**
Scenic Rating:	**7**

Special Attractions

- Scenic picnic spots.
- Interesting rock formations along trail.

Description

This relatively narrow road has a number of deep ruts that can be up to a foot deep. Although these obstacles are mostly avoidable by picking a good line between them, a stock high-clearance 4WD vehicle is recommended in case a wheel should slip into one of these ditches. The road is also suitable for ATVs.

The trail starts off as an easygoing forest road off of Front Range #21: Rampart Range Road but becomes steeper and narrower after approximately 2 miles. There are a number of rock formations along the trail, which are frequently scattered among the stands of aspen. Scenic picnic spots can be found along the many side roads. Trail #715, Raspberry-Chautauqua Mountain Trail, for hikers and mountain bikers takes off from just before a narrow switchback near the end of the trail.

The trail dead-ends at a gate and small camping area above Upper Reservoir. There are no through roads at the end of the trail, so return to Rampart Range Road the way you came.

Rock formation along the road

Another rock formation

Current Road Information
Pike & San Isabel National Forests
Pikes Peak Ranger District
601 South Weber Street
Colorado Springs, CO 80903
(719) 636-1602

Map References
USFS Pike National Forest
Maptech CD:
    Colorado Springs/Ski Areas/Central
Benchmark's *Colorado Road & Recreation Atlas*, p. 89
Colorado Atlas & Gazetteer, p. 50
Trails Illustrated, #137

Route Directions

▼ 0.0		At the intersection of Front Range#21: Rampart Range Road and Balanced Rock Road (FR 322) zero trip meter and proceed northeast onto FR 322.
		GPS: N 39°04.00′ W 105°01.39′
▼ 0.1	BL	Track on right.
▼ 0.7	SO	Track on right.
▼ 1.0	SO	Track on left.
▼ 1.5	SO	Track on right.
▼ 2.6	BR	Track on left.
▼ 3.1	BR	Fork in road; track on left rejoins main trail in a short distance.
		GPS: N 39°04.77 W 104°58.67′
▼ 3.4	SO	Track on right.

Portions of the road are rutted

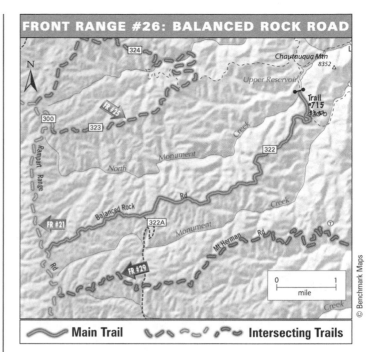

FRONT RANGE #26: BALANCED ROCK ROAD

© Benchmark Maps

〰️ **Main Trail**　　⌇⌇⌇ **Intersecting Trails**

▼ 4.4	BL	Fork in road. Short track (0.4 miles) on right leads to picnic spot and scenic overlook.
		GPS: N 39°04.97′ W 104°57.51′
▼ 4.9	SO	Track on left to campsite with views.
		GPS: N 39°05.22′ W 104°57.27′
▼ 5.8	BL	Fork in road; track on right rejoins main trail in a short distance.
▼ 5.9	BR	Track on left.
▼ 6.5	BR	Fork in road; track on left rejoins main trail in a short distance.
		GPS: N 39°05.98′ W 104°56.48′
▼ 6.7	SO	Trail #715 on right for hikers and mountain bikers.
▼ 6.9	TR	Tight switchback.
▼ 7.2	SO	Track on left.
▼ 7.4	BR	Track on left goes to campsite. Trail ends at gate.
		GPS: N 39°06.44′ W 104°56.47′

FRONT RANGE REGION TRAIL #27

Schubarth Road

Starting Point:	Intersection of Front Range #21:
	Rampart Range Road and Loy Creek
	Road
Finishing Point:	Dead end
Total Mileage:	7.5 (one-way)
Unpaved Mileage:	7.5
Driving Time:	1 hour (one-way)
Elevation Range:	9,130 to 9,340 feet
Usually Open:	May to November
Difficulty Rating:	4
Scenic Rating:	8

The trail runs through an open meadow at the beginning

Special Attractions

- Remote-feeling, fun trail.
- Access to several hiking and mountain biking trails.
- Excellent backcountry campsites.
- Brilliant golden aspen stands in fall.

Description

Schubarth Road begins at the intersection of Front Range #21: Rampart Range Road and Loy Creek Road and starts off by traveling through private property. Help keep trails open by staying on the trail through this section. Rolling along through wide-open grazing land, a few aspens and evergreens dot the pasture. Along this open section, there are wonderful views to the south of Pikes Peak jutting skyward from the surrounding landscape. After the cattle guard at the 0.4-mile point, the trail enters dense forest. A sign posted near this point indicates that some of the surrounding land is owned by the United States Air Force Academy and requests travelers refrain from hunting in the vicinity. Beyond this point, sections of the trail are eroded, steep, and bumpy from embedded rocks.

In places the trail is flanked by dense forest, and it travels through a beautiful grove of aspens at mile 2.5. Large boulders, some even bigger than a Chevrolet Suburban, vary the scenery. Hiking Trail #721, Schubarth Trail, briefly joins the main road and then sets off to the south where it intersects with a network of hiking trails that lead to either Rampart Reservoir or to the Air Force Academy campus. Mountain bikers also ride FR 307 and are also able to explore its hiking trails or other unmarked side trails. Numerous spots adjacent to the trail are perfect for secluded backcountry camping or picnicking. At mile 2.9, a good view of Rampart Reservoir opens up to the south. Wildlife such as ptarmigans and deer are also abundant in the area. This route has very little traffic compared to Rampart Range or some of its other popular side trails. All of these characteristics give this trail a remote and tranquil character.

The trail is narrow and passing may be difficult, especially in locations where trees grow right along the edges of the narrow trail. Along these sections, it is likely that branches will scrape the paintwork of full-sized vehicles. Embedded roots make the trail bumpy and slow going. Mud or all-terrain tires are useful on this trail, where wet sections stay muddy due to the dense canopy of vegetation shading the road. An unmarked track at the end of the trail creates a small loop, intersecting again with the main trail in a short distance. Head back along the main road for about a mile, and you will reach Front Range #28: Hell Creek Road (FR 311) to continue to explore. You will need to retrace your tracks back to Front Range #21: Rampart Range Road to exit the area because there are no through roads connected to this trail.

Current Road Information

Pike & San Isabel National Forests
Pikes Peak Ranger District
601 South Weber Street
Colorado Springs, CO 80903
(719) 636-1602

Map References

USFS   Pike National Forest
Maptech CD:
          Colorado Springs/Ski Areas/Central
Benchmark's *Colorado Road & Recreation Atlas*, p. 89
Colorado Atlas & Gazetteer, pp. 50, 62
The Roads of Colorado, p. 97
Trails Illustrated, #137

Route Directions

▼ 0.0   Schubarth Road begins at a stop sign at the intersection of Front Range #21: Rampart Range Road and Loy Creek Road. Turn left and proceed east on Loy Creek Road toward Schubarth Road (FR 307).

Aspen stands alongside the trail

FRONT RANGE #27: SCHUBARTH ROAD

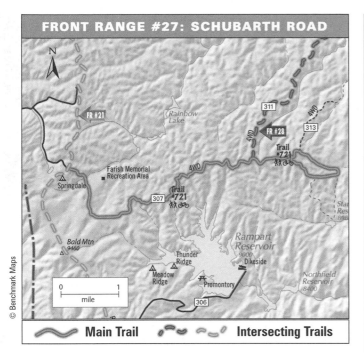

| | | Main Trail | | | Intersecting Trails |

		GPS: N39°00.26' W105°00.94'	
▼ 0.35	BR	Private drives on right and left. Bear right onto public road that continues on between private drives.	
▼ 0.4	TR	Follow sign for Schubarth Trail.	
		GPS: N39°00.11' W105°00.57'	
▼ 0.6	SO	Cattle guard.	
▼ 0.7	SO	Cattle guard. Zero trip meter.	
		GPS: N38°59.86' W105°00.53'	
▼ 0.0		Continue south on FR 307.	
▼ 1.0	SO	Private drive on right.	
▼ 1.3	SO	Cattle guard.	
▼ 1.9	SO	Track on right.	
▼ 2.0	SO	Track on right.	
▼ 2.2	BL	Track on right.	
		GPS: N38°59.86' W104°58.93'	
▼ 2.6	SO	Tracks on right; then Trail #721 for hikers and mountain bikers joins FR 307.	
▼ 3.3	SO	FR 307A on left. Zero trip meter.	
		GPS: N39°00.35' W104°58.26'	
▼ 0.0		Continue east on FR 307.	
▼ 1.1	BR	Road forks with Front Range #28: Hell Creek Road (FR 311) on left and FR 307 on right. Zero trip meter.	
		GPS: N39°00.43' W104°57.36'	
▼ 0.0		Continue east on FR 307.	
▼ 0.8	SO	Trail #721 exits FR 307 to the right.	
▼ 1.2	SO	FR 313 on left. Zero trip meter.	
		GPS: N39°00.47' W104°56.32'	
▼ 0.0		Continue east on FR 307.	
▼ 0.8	TL	Track on left. Zero trip meter.	
		GPS: N39°00.38' W104°55.60'	
▼ 1.1	BL	Road forks. Unmarked track on right.	
▼ 2.3		Trail rejoins FR 307 at signed intersection with FR 313. Turn right for Front Range #21: Rampart Range Road and Front Range #28: Hell Creek Road.	
		GPS: N39°00.47' W104°56.32'	

Hell Creek Road

Starting Point:	Intersection of Front Range #27: Schubarth Road (FR 307) and FR 311
Finishing Point:	Dead end
Total Mileage:	3.7 miles (one-way)
Unpaved Mileage:	3.7 miles
Driving Time:	45 minutes (one-way)
Elevation Range:	8,488 to 9,288 feet
Usually Open:	May to November
Difficulty Rating:	4
Scenic Rating:	9

Special Attractions

- Charming trail with remote feel.
- Numerous boulder gardens for climbing and exploring.
- Good backcountry campsites.
- Short spur to camping area with 180-degree views over Colorado Springs.

Description

Hell Creek Road (FR 311) begins about a mile from the end of Front Range #27: Schubarth Road (FR 307). Traveling northward, the trail follows a narrow corridor through dense forest of evergreen and some stands of aspen trees. The bumpy road is eroded and has many wheel ruts, potholes, and em-

Steep section of the trail

bedded tree roots. The trees that grow close to the narrow trail make passing oncoming vehicles difficult in places, and backing up may be necessary. The branches of these trees will likely scratch the paintwork of full-sized vehicles.

Some sections of the trail are steep and may have loose, rocky, or eroded surfaces. Other sections can be boggy. Using mud or all-terrain tires is an advantage on this trail because they provide better traction. Rotted and uprooted trees have collapsed over the trail in places. Huge rocks and rock formations near the trail are fun to explore and would be excellent for climbing or bouldering.

Although the trail travels through dense forest with no views at first, gradually the trees thin, and there are limited views of the surrounding scenery through the trees. The trail then begins to follow a ridgeline where the trees continue to recede. Views are not dramatic at this point because the surrounding landscape is flat. As the trail approaches a bluff, Colorado Springs and the eastern plains are visible through the trees. The Air Force Academy campus is also visible from the ridgeline near the end of the trail. In fall, large stands of brilliant yellow aspen in the gulches below the trail contrast dramatically with the dark evergreens.

Trees grow close to the trail

Boulders beside the road

In places, huge boulders and trees are so close to the trail that they must be carefully negotiated so as not to scratch or scrape your vehicle. Near the end, the trail becomes a very narrow shelf road on which most vehicles will get scratched by tree branches. The trail dead-ends at the edge of a clearing where there is plenty of room to turn around.

The spur near the end of the trail travels about a tenth of a mile to a good backcountry campsite with an impressive 180-degree panorama of Colorado Springs and the eastern plains. The track to the campsite is very narrow with overgrown trees and grass. If scratching paintwork is a concern, it is best to walk the short track to see the view.

Although relatively short, this trail is a favorite. It has varied scenery and is fun to drive along with the added bonus of little traffic. The unbelievably huge boulders make this trail especially interesting. Under one cluster of boulders in particular, the overhang has been carefully sheltered with logs, forming an enclosure that makes an excellent campsite.

Current Road Information
Pike & San Isabel National Forests
Pikes Peak Ranger District
601 South Weber Street
Colorado Springs, CO 80903
(719) 636-1602

Map References
USFS   Pike National Forest
Maptech CD:
        Colorado Springs/Ski Areas/Central
Benchmark's *Colorado Road & Recreation Atlas*, p. 89
Colorado Atlas & Gazetteer, p. 50
The Roads of Colorado, p. 97
Trails Illustrated, #137

Route Directions

▼ 0.0		Proceed northeast off Front Range #27: Schubarth Road at intersection with FR 311.
		GPS: N39°00.43' W104°57.36'
▼ 2.3	SO	FR 311A on right. Zero trip meter.
		GPS: N39°01.92' W104°56.35'
▼ 0.0		Continue east on FR 311.

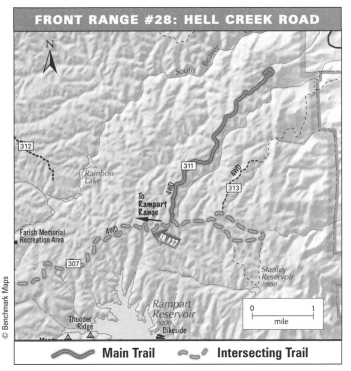

N

312

Rainbow
Lake

311

4WD

313

To
Rampart
Range

4WD

FR #27

Farish Memorial
Recreation Area

4WD

307

Stanley
Reservoir
8980

Rampart
Reservoir
9000

Thunder
Ridge

Dikeside

South Beaver

© Benchmark Maps

0   1
mile

〰️ **Main Trail**   ᵔᵔᵔ **Intersecting Trail**

▼ 0.9	SO	Sheltered campsite under boulder.
		GPS: N39°02.40' W104°55.69'
▼ 1.2	TL	Track on right goes 0.1 miles to campsite with 180-degree views east over Colorado Springs.
		GPS: N39°02.53' W104°55.52'
▼ 1.4		Trail ends at dead end.
		GPS: N39°02.54' W104°55.68'

FRONT RANGE REGION TRAIL #29

Mount Herman Road

Starting Point:	Intersection of Second Street and Beacon Lite Road in Monument
Finishing Point:	Intersection with Front Range #21: Rampart Range Road
Total Mileage:	13.8 miles
Unpaved Mileage:	11.3 miles
Driving Time:	1 hour
Elevation Range:	6,871 to 9,416 feet
Usually Open:	May to November
Difficulty Rating:	2
Scenic Rating:	8

Special Attractions

- Interstate access to Pike National Forest and Rampart Range.
- Easy shelf road with expansive views over Monument and Colorado Springs.
- Beautiful rock formations.

Description

Mount Herman Road begins in the town of Monument not far from the I-25 overpass. It provides good highway access to Pike National Forest and Rampart Range and its network of forest roads. Proceed west from I-25 at the intersection of US 105 and Second Street in Monument. Zero your trip meter at the intersection of Second Street and Beacon Lite Road and follow the directions given below to navigate through the Monument suburbs for access to Pike National Forest. The trail is easy to navigate after it begins traveling west on Mount Herman Road.

Soon after turning onto Mount Herman Road, the paved road enters Pike National Forest. The pavement ends approximately 2.5 miles from the beginning of the trail, and the road becomes a graded gravel road that is wide and well maintained. After approximately 3.8 miles, the trail begins its gentle ascent toward the foothills, and its surface becomes bumpy with wheel ruts, potholes, and embedded rocks. These few small obstacles can make the ride rough and give the trail its difficulty rating of 2, but they do not pose a difficulty to stock 4WDs.

During the trail's ascent to Rampart Range, it narrows and becomes enclosed by oak scrub on either side. Then the road begins to alternate between sections of winding shelf road and more-level sections running through a corridor of trees. This trail sees a lot of traffic, so be aware it may be difficult to see oncoming vehicles just around any of the blind corners along the road. Also along shelf sections, there are some steep drop-offs and places where the road has eroded, making it quite narrow. These locations are usually marked with hazard signs. A few other obstacles you may need to watch out for are rock slides and downed trees across the road.

Balanced rock beside the trail

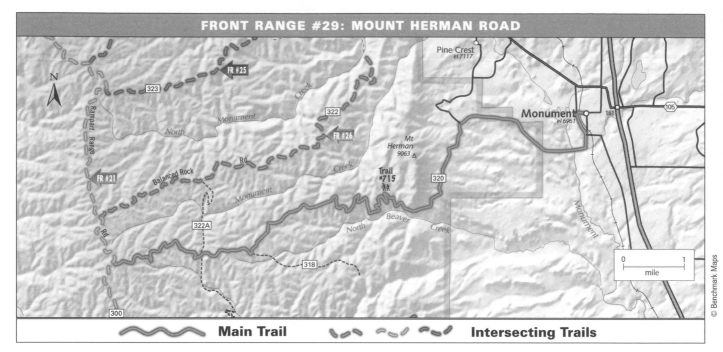

Main Trail   Intersecting Trails

Climbing approximately 2,500 feet in total, there are overlooks along the road with expansive views over Colorado's eastern plains, the Air Force Academy campus, and Pikes Peak. Many interesting rock formations are also found along this trail. One in particular near Rampart Range is a large boulder balanced on top of a smaller rock.

Near where the trail ends at the intersection with Rampart Range Road, it passes several clearings that would be good for parking to unload mountain bikes, dirt bikes, or ATVs or for camping. Becoming wider and smoother, the road ends approximately 24 miles north of the Garden of the Gods on Front Range #21: Rampart Range Road.

Current Road Information

Pike & San Isabel National Forests
Pikes Peak Ranger District
601 South Weber Street
Colorado Springs, CO 80903
(719) 636-1602

Map References

USFS   Pike National Forest
Maptech CD:
       Colorado Springs/Ski Areas/Central
Benchmark's *Colorado Road & Recreation Atlas*, p. 89

View of Monument from the trail

Colorado Atlas & Gazetteer, p. 50
Trails Illustrated, #137

Route Directions

▼ 0.0	TR	Trail begins at the intersection of Second Street and Beacon Lite Road in Monument. Zero trip meter and proceed west on Second Street.
1.0 ▲	TL	The trail ends at the intersection of Second Street and Beacon Lite Road in Monument.

GPS: N39°05.48' W104°52.09'

▼ 0.3	SO	Railroad crossing.
0.7 ▲	SO	Railroad crossing.
▼ 0.4	TL	Intersection of Second Street and Mitchell Avenue to Mt. Herman Road on left.
0.6 ▲	TR	Intersection of Mitchell Avenue and Second Street.

GPS: N39°05.49' W104°52.51'

▼ 1.0	TR	Intersection of Mitchell Avenue and Mt. Herman Road. Zero trip meter.
0.0 ▲		Proceed north on Mitchell Avenue.
▼ 0.0		Proceed west on Mt. Herman Road following sign to Mt. Herman and FR 320.
9.1 ▲	TL	Intersection of Mt. Herman Road and Mitchell Avenue. Zero trip meter.

GPS: N39°04.98' W104°52.39'

▼ 0.8	SO	Enter Pike National Forest.
8.3 ▲	SO	Leave Pike National Forest.
▼ 1.5	SO	Pavement ends.
7.6 ▲	SO	Pavement begins.

GPS: N39°05.40' W104°53.77'

▼ 2.3	SO	Red Rocks Drive on right.
6.8 ▲	SO	Red Rocks Drive on left.
▼ 5.1	SO	Trail #715 on right.
4.0 ▲	SO	Trail #715 on left.

GPS: N39°04.31' W104°56.07'

▼ 7.6	BL	Track on right.
1.5 ▲	BR	Track on left.
▼ 8.1	BL	Campsite on right.
1.0 ▲	BR	Campsite on left.

GPS: N39°04.16' W104°57.63'

▼ 8.4	BL	Track on right.
0.7 ▲	BR	Track on left.
▼ 9.1	SO	Two tracks on left; second is FR 320C. Zero trip meter.
0.0 ▲		Continue northeast on Mt. Herman Road.

GPS: N39°03.79' W104°58.25'

▼ 0.0		Continue southwest on Mt. Herman Road.
3.7 ▲	SO	Two tracks on right; first is FR 320C. Zero trip meter.
▼ 0.8	SO	Overlook on left.
2.9 ▲	SO	Overlook on right.

GPS: N39°03.52' W104°58.80'

▼ 1.0	SO	FR 318 on left is a dead end.
2.7 ▲	SO	FR 318 on right is a dead end.
▼ 1.5	SO	Track on right; and FR 315 on left.
2.2 ▲	SO	Track on left; and FR 315 on right.
▼ 3.7		Trail ends at intersection with Front Range #21: Rampart Range Road. Turn right for Sedalia and Denver; turn left for Woodland Park and Colorado Springs.
0.0 ▲		Trail begins at intersection with Front Range #21: Rampart Range Road. Proceed southeast on Mt. Herman Road.

GPS: N39°03.36' W104°01.10'

Pikes Peak Highway

Starting Point:	**Intersection of US 24 and Pikes Peak Highway**
Finishing Point:	**Pikes Peak summit**
Total Mileage:	**19.0 miles (one-way)**
Unpaved Mileage:	**11.5 miles**
Driving Time:	**1 hour (one-way)**
Elevation Range:	**7,384 to 14,110 feet**
Usually Open:	**April to October**
Difficulty Rating:	**1**
Scenic Rating:	**10**

Special Attractions

■ Drive to the summit of Colorado's most famous fourteener.

■ Impressive 360-degree views from 14,110 feet.

■ Camping, fishing, hiking, and biking around the various reservoirs and in the recreation areas along the trail.

■ View wildlife in all five life zones.

History

Ute Indians, who inhabited southern Colorado in the 1700s, followed trails along Pikes Peak's slopes during their hunting and gathering migrations. At 14,110 feet, Pikes Peak, the 31st highest peak in Colorado, is one of the state's 54 peaks that exceeds 14,000 feet, also know as the fourteeners. The well-known mountain is the farthest east of the fourteeners.

Crystal Creek Reservoir

Glen Cove gift shop and restaurant

View of Pikes Peak Highway from Rampart Range Road

Spanish explorer Juan Bautista de Anza also left a record of crossing the slopes of Pikes Peak in the 1700s. Zebulon Pike named the mountain in 1806 when he and his party of explorers attempted to climb the towering peak. Heavy snow stopped the group more than 4,000 feet short of the summit. Finally, in 1820, geologist Edwin James, historian of Major Stephen Long's expedition, became the first to successfully climb to the summit in recorded history. The mountain became an icon of the West in the 1850s when gold was discovered in the Rocky Mountains; the resulting influx of gold seekers became known as the Pikes Peak gold rush.

Development on the mountain quickly followed. To report weather conditions, the Signal Corps of the U.S. Army con-structed the first manned building on the summit, a telegraph station, in 1873. A guard was also stationed in Manitou Springs to charge a fee to hikers using the trail to the peak. One summit guard, Sergeant John O'Keefe, caused a national scandal in 1876 by reporting that giant rats had eaten his young daughter.

In 1888, a carriage road from Cascade, Colorado, to the top of Pikes Peak opened. Passengers traveled halfway up the mountain in horse-drawn carriages and finished their journey riding sure-footed mules. One carriage passenger, Katherine Lee Bates, penned the words to "America the Beautiful" after witnessing the awe-inspiring panorama from the mountaintop in 1893. Another traveler, Zalmon Simmons, founder of Sim-

Trail winding up to the summit of Pikes Peak

mons Mattress Company, was also so inspired by the views but got so sore and exhausted from riding a mule that he established the Manitou & Pikes Peak Cog Railway, which was completed in 1890.

Although the carriage road fell into disuse after the opening of the railroad, the first automobile traversed the route on August 12, 1901. Driven by C. A. Yount and W. B. Felker, the vehicle was a two-cylinder Locomobile Steamer. In 1915, Spencer Penrose, owner of the Broadmoor Hotel, bought the old road to equip it for automobile travel and reopened it. Penrose also established the second-oldest auto race in the country, the Pikes Peak Hill Climb, to publicize the new road. (The Indy 500 is the oldest auto race.) Between 1916 and 1936, the toll road, which charged $2 per person, operated at a loss because of the expense of snow removal. Finally in 1936, it was turned over to the U.S. Forest Service, which for the next 12 years managed the road and allowed visitors to summit the peak at no charge. With no funding, the road deteriorated drastically.

Around the time Spencer Penrose was revitalizing the automobile, Fred Barr was working on building his own route to the summit, a hiking trail. He completed surveying his chosen route in 1918, and under his supervision construction was completed in 1921. The 12.6-mile trail is noteworthy because its 7,500 feet of elevation gain is the greatest of any of Col-

Old cog railway station

orado's fourteeners. Today the famous route is known as the Barr Trail. At about the time of the trail's completion, Barr built a cabin at an elevation of 10,200 feet to serve as a halfway-point camp. To this day, hikers and climbers use Barr Camp as an overnight rest stop. The cabin is also staffed for search-and-rescue operations of which there are at least 30 each year.

Pike National Forest encompasses Pikes Peak, but the forest service leases the Pikes Peak Highway to the City of Colorado Springs for its administration. The city charges a per-person fee for vehicles to drive to the top of the mountain. Currently, more than half a million visitors summit Pikes Peak each year, either via Pikes Peak Highway, the Barr Trail, or the Pikes Peak Cog Railway. The iconic peak has the distinction of being the most-visited mountain in North America as well as the second most visited in the world behind Japan's Mount Fuji.

Description

To access this trail, each vehicle must stop at the toll gate and pay an entry fee. Navigation of the route is easy, and there are many points of interest on this trail to stop and see. The road starts off as a paved road and alternates between blacktop and graded dirt for its entire length. Almost immediately the road begins to climb, and you will ascend approximately 6,610 feet by the time you reach the summit of Pikes Peak. The elevation gain yields scenic vistas of the surrounding landscape, Colorado Springs, and the eastern plains for most of the length of the trail. Vegetation including evergreens, aspens, scrub oak, and wildflowers add color to the scenery, and wildlife including deer, marmots, many species of birds and near the summit mountain goats and bighorn sheep are commonly seen near the trail.

The road twists and turns to the summit becoming a two-lane shelf road and passing numerous scenic overlooks, picnic areas, trailheads, reservoirs, and other points of interest. The road is well maintained with some corrugations, but it is accessible to passenger vehicles. To prevent your engine from overheating on the way up, shift into lower gears to help maintain speed and engine cooling. Also on the way down it is a good idea to use a low gear to maintain speed, causing the en-

Cog railway track and view of Reservoir #7 and Reservoir #8

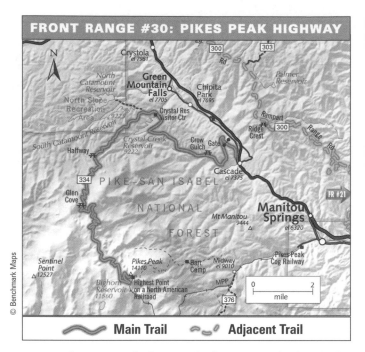

© Benchmark Maps

~~~ Main Trail   ~~~ Adjacent Trail

gine to slow your vehicle instead of using your brakes to descend. This will prevent your brakes from overheating and potentially failing. If your engine does overheat, there are water stations at miles 3, 10, 11, and 13 beyond the toll gate.

Be aware that this road is very popular, and traffic can be heavy. If you have several vehicles behind you, be considerate of other travelers by pulling over and allowing them to pass. If you wish to stop, do so in designated pullouts and parking areas that are well out of the way of other vehicles.

Current Road Information

Pike & San Isabel National Forests
Pikes Peak Ranger District
601 South Weber Street
Colorado Springs, CO 80903
(719) 636-1602

Map References

USFS   Pike National Forest
Maptech CD:
          Colorado Springs/Ski Areas/Central
Benchmark's *Colorado Road & Recreation Atlas*, p. 89
Colorado Atlas & Gazetteer, p. 62
The Roads of Colorado, pp. 112, 113
Trails Illustrated, #137

Route Directions

▼ 0.0		Proceed northwest at the intersection of US 24 and Pikes Peak Highway.
GPS: N38°53.83' W104°58.31'		
▼ 0.3	BL	Road forks.
GPS: N38°54.08' W104°58.39'		
▼ 0.7	SO	Stop at pay station. Zero trip meter.
▼ 0.0		Continue northwest on Pikes Peak Highway.
GPS: N38°54.50' W104°58.94'		
▼ 1.5	SO	Overlook on left.
▼ 1.9	SO	Crow Gulch Picnic Area on right.

GPS: N38°54.03' W104°59.51'		
▼ 5.0	SO	Pikes Peak North Slope Recreation Area on left.
▼ 5.8	SO	Catamount Reservoir on right.
▼ 6.8	SO	Pavement ends.
▼ 8.4	SO	Halfway Picnic Ground on right.
GPS: N38°54.09' W105°03.90'		
▼ 9.5	SO	Overlook on left and right.
GPS: N38°53.55' W105°04.12'		
▼ 11.5	SO	Glen Cove Inn & Check Station on left. Zero trip meter.
▼ 0.0		Proceed south on Pikes Peak Highway.
GPS: N38°52.55' W105°04.41'		
▼ 6.8		Trail ends at the summit of Pikes Peak.
GPS: N38°50.43' W105°02.54'		

FRONT RANGE REGION TRAIL #31

Old Stage Road to Gold Camp Road

Starting Point:	Broadmoor Hotel in Colorado Springs
Finishing Point:	T-intersection with CR 81 and CR 8
Total Mileage:	27.8 miles
Unpaved Mileage:	25.7 miles
Driving Time:	2 hours
Elevation Range:	6,910 to 10,199 feet
Usually Open:	Mid-April to October
Difficulty Rating:	1
Scenic Rating:	8

Special Attractions

- Follows gold mining era railroad grade.
- Expansive views over Colorado Springs.
- Numerous hiking, biking, and ATV trails intersecting the main trail.
- Excellent rock climbing.

4-way intersection a mile beyond the trail's starting point at the Broadmoor

History

Old Stage Road was originally a stage route linking the Cripple Creek Mining District to the city of Colorado Springs during peak gold and silver mining years. The trail originates in a residential area of Colorado Springs near the Broadmoor Resort, itself a historic attraction.

On July 1, 1891, the Broadmoor opened as a casino to which a small hotel was later added. In 1897, the building changed hands and became a girls' school and boardinghouse. Spencer Penrose, also the creator of Front Range #30: Pikes Peak Highway, bought the complex in 1916 with the vision of transforming it into the most beautiful resort in the world. Two years later the opulent, pink stucco hotel, patterned after architecture the Penroses had seen during their extensive international travels, opened with four wings and a golf course. The hotel immediately became popular with domestic and international vacationers and businesspeople, and today continues to host guests from around the world. Along Old Stage Road you also pass the Broadmoor Stables.

Nearly 5 miles beyond the stables, Old Stage Road meets Gold Camp Road, originally the grade of the Colorado Springs & Cripple Creek District Railway, also called the Short Line. After Bob Womack discovered gold in Cripple Creek in 1890, the mines in and around Cripple Creek began to produce so much gold that three railroads were constructed connecting the mining district to larger cities. The Cripple Creek area became the largest gold-producing district in the world during its peak years, yielding more than $400 million in gold.

As the mines decreased production, the railway collapsed under financial strain. W. D. Corley bought the line at a public auction in 1924 and removed the rails. He transformed the route into the Corley Mountain Highway, a toll road for automobiles, which were gaining popularity at the time. Corley's road also failed, and in 1939 the government purchased the road for public use and placed the newly dubbed Gold Camp Road under the management of the U.S. Forest Service.

The poorly maintained road was open to the public only in the summer, and in August 1988 the ceiling of tunnel #3 collapsed, closing an 8-mile segment of the route. Although the forest service still tentatively plans to repair the bridge and re-open the road in its entirety, Gold Camp Road currently can only be accessed by vehicle from Colorado Springs via Old Stage Road. The closed portion of the trail has become popular with hikers and mountain bikers.

Description

The beginning of Old Stage Road to Gold Camp Road travels through a suburban Colorado Springs neighborhood near the Broadmoor Resort. To reach the start of the trail, take exit 138 off of I-25 and turn onto Circle Drive. Proceed west on Circle Drive, which becomes Lake Avenue, for approximately 2.5 miles to the main entrance of the Broadmoor Hotel. Zero your trip meter and proceed south through the roundabout on Lake Circle.

After navigating through the residential area, the pavement ends and the trail begins in earnest at a small parking area and a switchback where it immediately begins to ascend, revealing a spectacular view over Colorado Springs. At this point, the road is wide, well maintained, and formed of graded dirt and gravel. As the road climbs, it becomes a shelf road, hugging the sheer red rock wall with steep drop-offs on one side. Passing is easy except at blind corners, which are frequent for the first several miles after the pavement ends. Also along this section, private land surrounds the road. Please respect private property and stay on the main trail. Unlicensed vehicles such as dirt bikes and ATVs will be ticketed on this trail.

Old Stage and Gold Camp Roads are mainly surrounded by evergreens and aspens, which frequently open up to reveal spectacular views of the surrounding slopes. Corrugation and potholes are the only obstacles on this easygoing trail, making it easy enough for 2WD passenger vehicles. Cars should avoid traveling this route in wet conditions to avoid sliding off the trail, damaging it, or getting stuck.

After twisting and turning up to the entrance of Pike National Forest, the trail begins to travel through dense forest, no longer a shelf road. Although the grade narrows, passing an oncoming vehicle is still not a problem. It is worth stopping at the overlook at mile 7 for the incredible view to the northeast over Colorado Springs. The St. Peters Dome Trailhead (Trail #621) is accessible from this point as well. Frequently the trail passes through narrow rock cuttings and sections of interest-

Rosemont Reservoir from the trail

Abandoned mill at the end of the trail in the town of Victor

ing rock formations and slick rock. The gentle banking and level grade of the route conjures up images of the days trains once billowed black smoke while making their way along this route into Colorado Springs loaded with gold ore from the Cripple Creek Mines. On one particularly interesting section of the old railroad grade, both sides of the trail fall away with nearly a 100-foot drop on both sides.

Wildlife is abundant around the trail. In fall, brilliantly colored aspens contrast with the dark evergreens, and the road is blanketed in golden coin-shaped leaves. Near the end of the dirt section of trail there are many lakes, ponds, and private residences. The trail ends in the quaint town of Victor where evidence of the peak gold mining days is still visible.

Current Road Information

Pike & San Isabel National Forests
Pikes Peak Ranger District
601 South Weber Street
Colorado Springs, CO 80903
719-636-1602

Map References

USFS Pike National Forest
Maptech CD:
    Colorado Springs/Ski Areas/Central
Benchmark's *Colorado Road & Recreation Atlas*, p. 89
Colorado Atlas & Gazetteer, p. 62
The Roads of Colorado, pp. 112, 113
Trails Illustrated, #137

Route Directions

▼ 0.0		The trail begins at the main entrance to the Broadmoor Hotel. Zero trip meter and proceed south through the roundabout on Lake Circle, which becomes Pourtales Road.
1.3 ▲		Trail ends at the main entrance of the Broadmoor Hotel.

GPS: N38°47.50' W104°50.94'

▼ 0.3	BR	Road becomes Mirada Road.
1.0 ▲	BL	Road becomes Pourtales Road.

▼ 0.7	BR	Road becomes Cheyenne Mountain Boulevard.
0.6 ▲	BL	Road becomes Mirada Road.

▼ 1.3	SO	Intersection with Penrose Boulevard on right, Cheyenne Mountain Zoo Road on left, and Old Stage Road straight ahead. Zero trip meter.
0.0 ▲		Proceed northeast on Cheyenne Mountain Boulevard.

GPS: N38°46.73' W104°51.30'

▼ 0.0		Proceed southwest on paved Old Stage Road through residential neighborhood.
0.8 ▲	SO	Intersection with Penrose Boulevard on left, Cheyenne Mountain Zoo Road on right, and Cheyenne Mountain Boulevard straight ahead. Zero trip meter.

▼ 0.8	UTR	Pavement ends at end of residential area.
0.0 ▲		U-turn to the left and proceed south on Old Stage Road.

GPS: N38°46.61' W104°51.83'

▼ 4.1	SO	Enter Pike National Forest.
18.1 ▲	SO	Leave Pike National Forest.

GPS: N38°45.20' W104°53.27'

▼ 5.7	SO	FR 369 and entrance to Broadmoor Stables on

The road was formerly a narrow gauge railroad route

One of the tunnels along the route

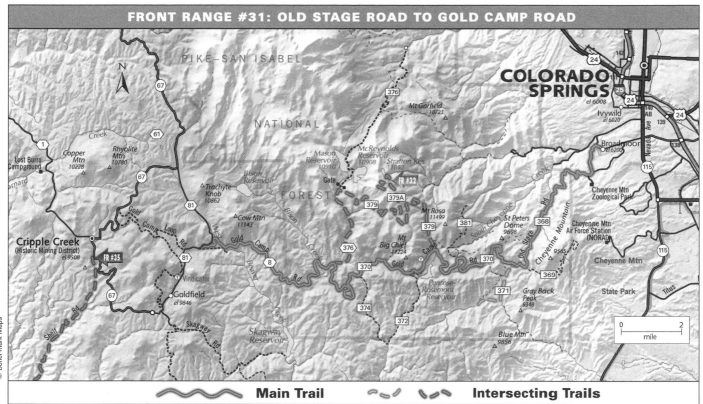

| | | Main Trail | | | | Intersecting Trails |

		left.	
16.5 ▲	SO	FR 369 and entrance to Broadmoor Stables on right.	

GPS: N38°44.02' W104°53.77'

▼ 6.2	SO	Front Range #33: Emerald Valley Trail (FR 371) on left and signed entrance to Hidden Valley Ranch. Zero trip meter.
0.0 ▲		Proceed southeast on Gold Camp Road.

GPS: N38°44.01' W104°54.21'

▼ 0.0		Proceed northwest on Gold Camp Road.
6.1 ▲	SO	Front Range #33: Emerald Valley Trail (FR 371) on right and signed entrance to Hidden Valley Ranch. Zero trip meter.

▼ 0.7	SO	Dead-end track on right.
5.4 ▲	BR	Dead-end track on left.

▼ 1.3	BR	Road on left.
4.8 ▲	BL	Road on right.

▼ 1.5	SO	Scenic overlook and St. Peters Dome Trailhead (Trail #621) on right.
4.6 ▲	SO	Scenic overlook and St. Peters Dome Trailhead (Trail #621) on left.

GPS: N38°44.55' W104°54.77'

▼ 4.0	SO	FR 381 and old railroad grade on right.
2.1 ▲	SO	FR 381 and old railroad grade on left.

GPS: N38°44.22' W104°56.37'

▼ 4.5	SO	Track on right.
1.6 ▲	SO	Track on left.

▼ 5.0	SO	Rosemont Reservoir Trailhead on left.
1.1 ▲	SO	Rosemont Reservoir Trailhead on right.

▼ 5.3	SO	Track on right.
0.8 ▲	SO	Track on left.

▼ 6.1	SO	Front Range #32: Mount Baldy Trail (FR 379) on right. Zero trip meter.
0.0 ▲		Proceed northeast on Gold Camp Road.

GPS: N38°44.44' W104°57.38'

▼ 0.0	SO	Proceed southwest on Gold Camp Road.
9.8 ▲	SO	Front Range #32: Mount Baldy Trail (FR 379) on left. Zero trip meter.

▼ 0.7	SO	FR 372 on left, signed dead end.
9.1 ▲	SO	FR 372 on right, signed dead end.

▼ 1.8	SO	Cattle guard
8.0 ▲	SO	Cattle guard.

▼ 2.3	SO	FR 370C on right.
7.5 ▲	SO	FR 370C on left.

▼ 2.6	SO	Track on right.
7.2 ▲	SO	Track on left.

▼ 3.9	SO	FR 374 on left.
5.9 ▲	SO	FR 374 on right.

GPS: N38°43.74' W105°00.54'

▼ 7.0	SO	FR 376 on right is Front Range #32: Mount Baldy Trail. Zero trip meter.
0.0 ▲		Proceed south on Gold Camp Road.

GPS: N38°43.98' W105°01.19'

▼ 0.0		Proceed northwest on Gold Camp Road past pond and private residence on right.
7.2 ▲	SO	Private residence and pond on left; then FR 376 on left is Front Range #32: Mount Baldy Trail.

▼ 0.3	SO	Cattle guard; then pass through tunnel.
6.9 ▲	SO	Pass through tunnel; then cattle guard.

▼ 2.8	SO	Leaving Pike National Forest.
4.4 ▲	SO	Entering Pike National Forest.

GPS: N38°43.50' W105°03.06'

▼ 6.8	SO	Cattle guard.
0.4 ▲	SO	Cattle guard.

▼ 7.2		Trail ends at intersection of CR 8 and CR 81. Turn right for Gillett; turn left for Victor.
0.0 ▲		Trail begins at intersection of CR 8 and CR 81. Proceed east on CR 8.

GPS: N38°44.64' W105°06.06'

Mount Baldy Trail

Starting Point:	**Front Range #31: Old Stage Road to Gold Camp Road**
Finishing Point:	**Front Range #31: Old Stage Road to Gold Camp Road**
Total Mileage:	**10.9 miles, plus 1.7-mile spur to Stratton Reservoir**
Unpaved Mileage:	**10.9 miles, plus 1.7-mile spur**
Driving Time:	**2 hours**
Elevation Range:	**9,449 to 11,294 feet**
Usually Open:	**Mid-April to October**
Difficulty Rating:	**7**
Scenic Rating:	**9**

Special Attractions

- High-elevation trail close to Colorado Springs.
- Bristlecone pines on spur trail.
- Challenging and scenic trail.
- Interesting Stratton Reservoir at end of spur trail.

Rocky section of the trail

Description

Mount Baldy Trail begins by traveling north from Front Range # 31: Old Stage Road to Gold Camp Road. This trail is also good for mountain bikes, dirt bikes, and ATVs. Beginning as an easy one-lane road with enough room to pass, the trail consistently and steadily climbs away from Old Stage Road. Although the trail is easy, it is eroded with wheel ruts and loose and embedded rocks. The dense evergreen forest encloses the trail with some clearings for backcountry camping. As the trail progresses, it gradually gets rougher and more difficult from more rocks and erosion. One sandy creek crossing not far from the beginning of the trail is just about a foot deep, but snowmelt in spring and after rains could cause the crossing to become impassable. After fording the creek, the road gets rougher again with more embedded and loose rocks. As the trail continues to climb, the trees grow closer to the trail, which causes passing to be more of a challenge.

The vegetation clears away briefly when crossing through Frosty Park and Deer Park, and the track becomes a shelf road for short sections. Drainage humps have also been constructed in the trail to prevent excessive water damage. At mile 2.3 in the middle of a switchback, the trees open up to an expansive overlook of Colorado Springs. It is also around this point where several clearings that would make nice backcountry campsites are located.

On the main trail beyond the turnoff to the spur trail, FR 379A, the road becomes even more difficult, and the vegetation closes in so close to the trail that it may scrape the sides of full-sizeed 4WDs. Rocks embedded in the trail along this segment can be sharp. Pick a good line to avoid puncturing a tire. Erosion along this section can also be severe. At mile 4.8, the road earns a difficulty rating of 6 due to the challenging location of numerous embedded and loose rocks. Near timberline, the trees grow shorter and more dispersed, and a wonderful view of the summit of Mount Baldy presents itself. Mile 6.5 is where the most difficult portion of the trail begins. A steep, off-camber climb up a low traction hill and the following steep and extremely low-traction descent down a loose dirt and gravel slope tops the difficulty level out at 7. A shorter-

Narrow shelf section of the spur trail

View of Colorado Springs from the spur trail

wheel base vehicle would be an advantage on this difficult section, although this trail was researched in a Chevrolet Suburban.

FR 379A is the spur trail up to the summit of Mount Baldy. It is not difficult to navigate, so it is not included in the Route Directions. This 3-rated track consistently climbs, becoming a shelf road from which there are spectacular views to the northeast. Since the road is so narrow and has a soft edge, passing is difficult and may require reversing into a safe spot. Remember that vehicles traveling uphill have the right-of-way. At some points trees obscure the views, but they get shorter and more dispersed as the trail gains elevation. Climbing, the road continues to narrow, pushing vehicles close to the dramatic drop-off.

Ancient bristlecone pine trees appear near timberline, quite a unique feature of this trail. As you approach a steep, loose climb at around mile 1.7, a closure gate may be locked, stopping progress. If the gate is open, the trail continues for another mile up to Mount Baldy summit and communications towers. Stratton Reservoir and dam are also located here. From near the summit, there are spectacular views over Colorado Springs and the eastern plains, and the landscape is rugged and exposed above tree line, making this exciting side track a highlight of the trail.

Current Road Information
Pike & San Isabel National Forests
Pikes Peak Ranger District
601 South Weber
Colorado Springs, CO 80903
(719) 636-1602

Map References
USFS   Pike National Forest
Maptech CD:
        Colorado Springs/Ski Areas/Central
Benchmark's *Colorado Road & Recreation Atlas,* p. 89

Stratton Reservoir at the end of the spur

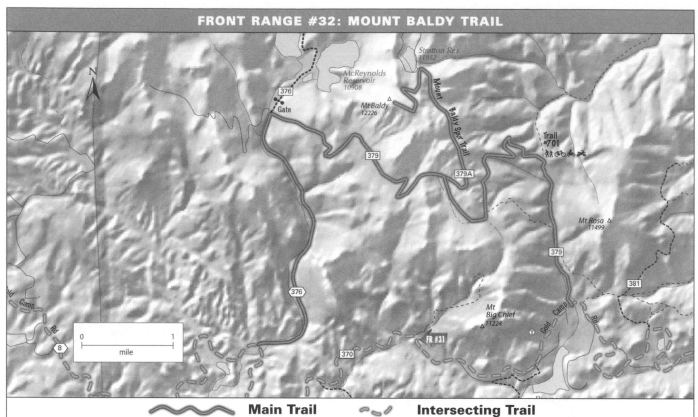

~~~~ Main Trail   **~◡◡ Intersecting Trail**

Colorado Atlas & Gazetteer, p. 62
The Roads of Colorado, p. 113
Trails Illustrated, #137

Route Directions

▼ 0.0   Trail begins at the intersection with Front
               Range #31: Old Stage Road to Gold Camp
               Road and FR 379. Zero trip meter and proceed
               northwest on FR 379.
   6.5 ▲   Trail ends at the intersection of FR 379 and
               Front Range #31: Old Stage Road to Gold
               Camp Road. Turn left for Colorado Springs.

               Turn right for Cripple Creek.

GPS: N38°44.44' W104°57.38'		
▼ 0.3	SO	Cross through Beaver Creek.
6.2 ▲	SO	Cross through Beaver Creek.

GPS: N38°44.71' W104°57.47'		
▼ 1.7	SO	TR #701, Captain Jack's multiuse trail system on right.
4.8 ▲	SO	TR #701, Captain Jack's multiuse trail system on left.

GPS: N38°45.78' W104°57.72'		
▼ 3.9	SO	FR 307C on left.
2.7 ▲	SO	FR 307C on right.

Another rocky section of the main trail

Trail running through a meadow before the difficult section begins

		GPS: N38°45.29' W104°58.72'
▼ 4.4	SO	FR 379A on right is spur to summit of Mount Baldy.
2.2 ▲	SO	FR 379A on left is spur to summit of Mount Baldy.
		GPS: N38°45.66' W104°58.98'
▼ 6.5	SO	Trail becomes a loose, rocky, steep ascent rated 7 for difficulty. Zero trip meter.
0.0 ▲		Continue east on FR 379.
		GPS: N38°45.91' W105°00.21'
▼ 0.0		Continue up loose, rocky, steep ascent.
1.2 ▲	SO	End of loose, rocky, steep descent. Standard of trail improves. Zero trip meter.
▼ 1.2	TL	FR 376 on left. Zero trip meter.
0.0 ▲		Proceed east on FR 376.
		GPS: N38°46.23' W105°01.10'
▼ 0.0		Proceed south on FR 376.
3.2 ▲	TR	FR 376 on right. Zero trip meter.
▼ 1.5	SO	Cattle guard.
1.7 ▲	SO	Cattle guard.
▼ 3.2		Trail ends at Front Range #31: Old Stage Road to Gold Camp Road. Turn left for Colorado Springs; turn right for Cripple Creek.
0.0 ▲		Trail begins on Front Range #31: Old Stage Road to Gold Camp Road.
		GPS: N38°43.98' W105°01.19'

FRONT RANGE REGION TRAIL #33

Emerald Valley Trail

Starting Point:	**Intersection of FR 371 and Front Range #31: Old Stage Road to Gold Camp Road**
Finishing Point:	**Backcountry campsite**
Total Mileage:	**4.2 miles (one-way)**
Unpaved Mileage:	**4.2 miles**
Driving Time:	**45 minutes (one-way)**
Elevation Range:	**8,148 to 9,038 feet**
Usually Open:	**Mid-April to October**
Difficulty Rating:	**5**
Scenic Rating:	**8**

Special Attractions

- Technical trail through beautiful aspen groves.
- Numerous creek crossings.
- Good for mountain bikes, dirt bikes, and ATVs.

Description

This narrow, dirt trail is not frequently maintained and is just wide enough for two vehicles to pass. The first mile and a half follows power lines, and erosion and loose rocks create an increasingly rough, bumpy ride as the trail progresses. After passing Cather Springs Ranch and Emerald Valley Ranch, the trail visibly increases in difficulty. The obstacles you see beyond mile 1.5 are the standard for the remainder of this out-and-back trail. The entrance to Emerald Valley Ranch is the easiest

One of the many creek crossings on the trail

place to turn around if you do not like what you see. Beyond this point, the trail has a difficulty rating of 5.

Both embedded and loose rocks create obstacles through which a good line should be chosen in order to avoid underbody damage. Technically challenging spots include embedded tree roots, off-camber sections with embedded roots and rocks, severe erosion, navigating underwater obstacles, and consistent rock-crawling. The road also narrows, making passing a challenge.

Emerald Valley Trail follows Fountain Creek and crosses it many times. An advantage of the numerous rocks and roots in the trail is that the crossings don't get boggy. The deepest of the crossings was just over a foot deep, but snowmelt in early spring or just after periods of rain means the crossings could be much deeper. A beaver pond near one of the crossings could also become a problem to ford in very wet conditions. Along one part, the trail and creek join, and you drive through the creek for a short distance.

Aside from the excitement of fording Fountain Creek, many good undeveloped campsites and hiking trails leave the road in several locations. Some interesting cabin remains are

Rocky section on the trail

located at mile 2.5. Another point of interest is seeing the underground aqueduct to Rosemont Reservoir peeking aboveground on various spots along the trail. Some evergreens and large stands of aspen trees densely flank both sides of the trail, making this a spectacular fall aspen viewing area. Although there is not much opportunity for views, the trail follows along the base of several towering peaks that are visible at most points and make an impressive background for the lush vegetation. Mountain bike and ATV riders and dirt bikers commonly ride this wet trail.

The road dead-ends at a shaded clearing with room for several backcountry campsites and plenty of room to turn around. No motor vehicles are permitted beyond here, but a faint trail continues beyond this point.

Current Road Information
Pike & San Isabel National Forests
Pikes Peak Ranger District
601 South Weber
Colorado Springs, CO 80903
(719) 636-1602

Map References
USFS   Pike National Forest
Maptech CD:
            Colorado Springs/Ski Areas/Central
Benchmark's *Colorado Road & Recreation Atlas,* pp. 89, 101
Colorado Atlas & Gazetteer, p. 62
The Roads of Colorado, pp. 112, 113

Route Directions

▼ 0.0		Trail begins at intersection of Front Range #31: Old Stage Road to Gold Camp Road and FR 371 at sign to Emerald Valley Ranch.
	GPS: N38°44.00' W104°54.21'	
▼ 0.3	SO	Track on left; sign posted no vehicles.
▼ 0.6	SO	Entrance to Cather Spring Ranch. Private property; no trespassing.
▼ 1.5	BR	Entrance to Emerald Valley Ranch. Zero trip meter.
▼ 0.0		Proceed south east on FR 371.

Stands of aspens along the trail

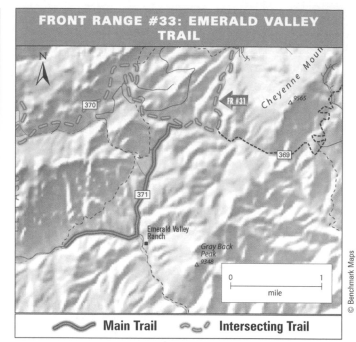

FRONT RANGE #33: EMERALD VALLEY TRAIL

〰️ **Main Trail**   ⌒〰️ **Intersecting Trail**

	GPS: N38°42.94' W104°54.74'	
▼ 1.5	SO	Difficult, rocky crossing through creek.
▼ 1.7	SO	Cross through creek.
	GPS: N38°42.69' W104°56.38'	
▼ 1.9	SO	Cross through creek.
▼ 2.0	SO	Cross through creek.
▼ 2.2	SO	Cross through creek.
▼ 2.4	SO	Cross through creek.
▼ 2.5	SO	Cross through creek.
▼ 2.7		Trail ends at backcountry campsite.
	GPS: N38°42.27' W104°57.35'	

FRONT RANGE REGION TRAIL #34

Phantom Canyon Road

Starting Point:	Intersection of CR 81 and CR 86, east of Victor
Finishing Point:	CR 67 and US 50, east of Cañon City
Total Mileage:	29.3 miles
Unpaved Mileage:	24.4 miles
Driving Time:	2 hours
Elevation Range:	5,465 to 9,732 feet
Usually Open:	May to October
Difficulty Rating:	1
Scenic Rating:	8

Special Attractions
- Follows gold-mining-era railroad grade.
- Opportunity to drive through old train tunnels blasted through the rock walls.
- Sheer canyon walls and interesting rock formations.
- Excellent for camping, biking, and picnicking.

Battle Mountain information board where the trail starts outside Victor

History

Phantom Canyon Road follows the route of the Florence & Cripple Creek narrow gauge railroad. The first of three railroads that would connect the Cripple Creek Mining District to surrounding cities, the route supplied the boomtown with coal and other goods and transported gold ore for processing out of the mineral-rich town. Twelve stations along the route helped to service the trains.

The railroad first reached Cripple Creek on July 1, 1894. With the exception of storm damage that occurred and was repaired in 1895, the road operated successfully for 16 years. In 1897, the railroad reached its peak, transporting 239,469 passengers and 208,411 tons of freight, garnering $218,926 in profits. On July 21, 1912, a storm damaged the line between Victor and Florence. Beyond repair, the line was abandoned by the railroad company, which in 1915 sold locomotives and rolling stock to the Nevada-California-Oregon Railroad. Today the grade has been transformed into a road, which is part of the Gold Belt Tour National Scenic Byway.

At the end of the line, the town of Florence processed and shipped Cripple Creek's gold ore. Florence also mined its own resources, coal and oil. The West's first oil well, located just north of Cañon City, led to the discovery of large amounts of oil in Florence.

Description

Phantom Canyon Road, part of the Gold Belt Tour National Scenic Byway, begins at the intersection of CR 81 and CR 86 near the Battle Mountain historical marker in the town of Victor. It is a two-lane, graded dirt road that is well maintained but can be very slippery and muddy in wet conditions. Evergreens with patches of aspens blanket the rolling hills and are a nice backdrop for this scenic railroad grade. Navigation of the route is straightforward.

At mile 5, the trail narrows and becomes a shelf road in sections. Some embedded rocks make the ride bumpy but do not increase the difficulty. The trail descends into Phantom Canyon and winds down to its floor. In several places along the descent, there are nice views into the canyon. Although the road continues to narrow, oncoming vehicles can still pass one another easily. Be aware of cattle ranging in canyon. Cows may be walking on the road. Traveling along the bottom of the canyon, be aware that the area is subject to flash floods in the summer months.

Vegetation includes sunflowers, mullein, evergreen trees, and cottonwood trees on the banks of Eightmile Creek. Rock slides can occur, falling from the tall, sheer rock walls that form the canyon enclosing the trail. In places, the rock walls have been blasted through to create tunnels the perfect size and shape for the trains that used to run along the grade. This road is popular with mountain bikers, and developed picnic sites and backcountry campsites are abundant along this route. At mile 24.5 the road becomes paved, and the surrounding vegetation becomes more desertlike. Several varieties of cactus and sunflowers grow along this section of the trail. Phantom Canyon Road ends at the intersection of CR 67 and US 50 just east of Cañon City.

Current Road Information

Bureau of Land Management
Royal Gorge Field Office
3170 East Main Street
Cañon City, CO 81212
(719) 269-8500

Map References

BLM   Royal Gorge
Maptech CD:
　　　Colorado Springs/Ski Areas/Central;
　　　Alamosa/Pueblo/South Central
Benchmark's *Colorado Road & Recreation Atlas,* p. 101
Colorado Atlas & Gazetteer, pp. 62, 72
The Roads of Colorado, p. 112
Trails Illustrated, #137

Route Directions

▼ 0.0　　　Trail begins at intersection of CR 81 and CR 86 outside the town of Victor. Proceed southeast on CR 86.

This was the route of the Florence & Cripple Creek Railroad

27.8 ▲			Trail ends at intersection of CR 81 and CR 86 outside the town of Victor. Turn right for Goldfield; turn left for Victor.
			GPS: N38°42.63' W105°07.99'
▼ 0.1		SO	Pavement ends.
27.7 ▲		SO	Pavement begins.
▼ 0.8		BR	CR 861 to Skaguay Reservoir on left.
27.0 ▲		SO	CR 861 to Skaguay Reservoir on right.
			GPS: N38°42.18' W105°07.51'
▼ 8.8		SO	Cattle guard.
19.0 ▲		SO	Cattle guard.
▼ 10.9		SO	Rest stop.
16.9 ▲		SO	Rest stop.
▼ 11.1		SO	Cattle guard.
16.7 ▲		SO	Cattle guard.
▼ 18.9		SO	Tunnel.
8.9 ▲		SO	Tunnel.
▼ 21.5		SO	Rest stop.
6.3 ▲		SO	Rest stop.
▼ 22.2		SO	Tunnel; then bridge crossing.
5.6 ▲		SO	Bridge crossing; then tunnel.
▼ 23.6		SO	Cattle guard.
4.2 ▲		SO	Cattle guard.
▼ 24.5		SO	Pavement resumes.
3.3 ▲		SO	Pavement resumes.
▼ 27.8		SO	Intersection of CR 67 and CR 123. Zero trip meter.
0.0 ▲			Continue north on CR 67.
			GPS: N38°27.68' W105°06.80'
▼ 0.0			Continue south on CR 67.

Tunnel along the trail

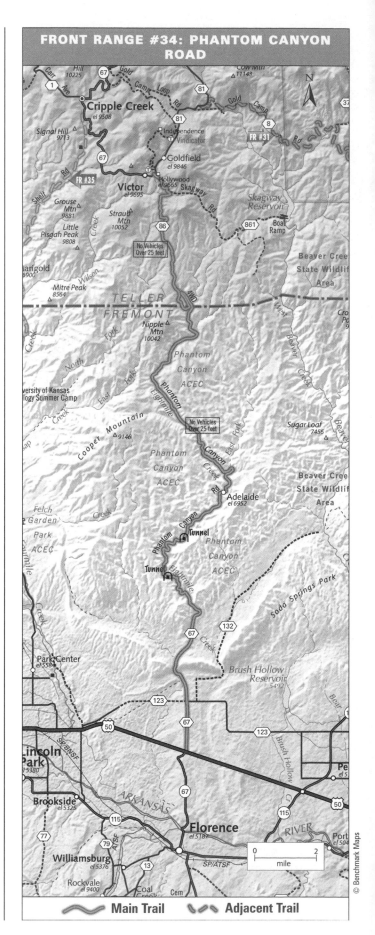

FRONT RANGE #34: PHANTOM CANYON ROAD

∿ **Main Trail**   ⌒⌒ **Adjacent Trail**

© Benchmark Maps

GPS: N38°26.25' W105°06.82'

FRONT RANGE REGION TRAIL #35

The Shelf Road

Starting Point:	Intersection of CR 69 and US 50, approximately 3 miles northwest of Cañon City
Finishing Point:	Intersection of US 67 and CR 1 in Cripple Creek
Total Mileage:	28.1 miles
Unpaved Mileage:	26.5 miles
Driving Time:	2 hours
Elevation Range:	5,745 to 9,397 feet
Usually Open:	April to October
Difficulty Rating:	4
Scenic Rating:	10

Special Attractions

- Network of challenging 4WD trails not on maps.
- Good backcountry campsites.
- Dramatic rock formations of Red Canyon Park.
- World-renowned rock climbing along the northern section of the Shelf Road.
- Hiking, camping, and picnicking in Red Canyon Park.
- Impressive sheer canyon walls.

History

Red Canyon Park was land once occupied by the Ute Indians. The Ute were forced off this land and onto reservations predominantly in Utah through various treaties with the U.S.

Rock obstacle along the trail

government. Congress granted the 600-acre Red Canyon Park to Cañon City, Colorado, on March 2, 1923. The park is free to the public and has well-maintained facilities including restrooms, picnic tables, hiking trails, and camping areas. The park includes numerous rock formations, some with spires towering over 100 feet.

The spires are the result of a series of geological processes that occurred over millions of years. In the Pennsylvanian period, between 286 and 320 million years ago, two land masses, the Uncompahgria and Front Range, rose upward. As they rose, they shed red, sandy sediment that was deposited in nearby basins. Along the east slope of the Front Range, the Fountain Formation developed from this sediment. Erosion of the Fountain Formation has created the pillars now exposed in Red Canyon Park. Today the park is known for its world-class rock climbing opportunities.

A few miles north of Cañon City, to the east of Red Canyon Park Road, lies Garden Park Dinosaur Monument. In 1877, Jurassic dinosaur bones were discovered near Cañon City in the Morrison Formation, a sequence of sedimentary rock that has yielded the greatest number of dinosaur fossil discoveries in the United States. The 1877 discovery drew two prominent paleontologists, Edward Drinker Cope and Othniel Charles Marsh, out west. In Garden Park, they continued the so-called Bone Wars, competing with each other to find the greatest number of new dinosaur species.

Section of trail that becomes boggy in wet conditions

Old stone building ruins beside the trail

View from the trail before it descends into Red Canyon Park

Their rivalry was not always friendly, as the two men threw various accusations at one another, including spying, stealing fossils, and bribery. The competition to find more fossils became so intense that both men spent their personal fortunes and had to appeal to government and academic institutions to continue their work. At his death, Cope issued the final challenge to Marsh by donating his skull to science. He hoped that his brain measurement would be larger than his adversary's because, at the turn of the century, brain size was considered a measure of intelligence.

Today, Cañon City hosts the Dinosaur Depot Museum. The museum's collection includes the world's most complete stegosaurus, discovered in Garden Park in 1992. The Garden Park Fossil Area is also open to visitors, with exhibits and self-guided tours.

To the north of Red Canyon Park and Garden Park Dinosaur Monument is the upper portion of the Shelf Road. Cañon City constructed this road in 1892 as a stage and wagon road into the Cripple Creek Mining District. Tolls to travel along the road varied from 30 cents for a horse and rider to $1.75 for a stagecoach. One of the toll keepers lived in a cabin at the bottom of the canyon, still visible today, and would climb up the hill to collect the necessary tolls. The narrow Shelf Road is preserved today as part of the Gold Belt Tour National Scenic Byway. The road remains in much the same condition as travelers experienced it in the 1900s.

Description

The Shelf Road is one of three roads that comprise the Gold Belt Tour National Scenic Byway, which extends from Florence and Cañon City in the south to Florissant in the north. The other two roads included in the Gold Belt Tour are High Park Road, a paved two-lane road west of the Shelf Road, and Front Range #34: Phantom Canyon Road.

The initial section of this trail that begins approximately 3 miles northwest of Cañon City at the intersection of US 50 and CR 69 is not part of the Gold Belt Tour and is not recommended for inexperienced four-wheel drivers. Although the road begins as a wide, well-maintained dirt road passing through a residential area, the difficulty increases once past the suburban neighborhoods. After approximately 5 miles, the road narrows and becomes bumpy with embedded rocks. Formed primarily of dirt, the trail can be very muddy after snowmelt or rain. The low, desertlike vegetation surrounding the trail includes pinyon and juniper pines, prickly pear cacti,

The shelf section of the trail

rabbitbrush, cottonwood trees, sunflowers, and thistle, and allows for open views of the surrounding arid foothills. This stretch of trail is quite scenic.

After approximately 7 miles, the difficulty rating of the trail jumps to a 4 because the one-lane track is quite eroded and has many ruts. Embedded in the surface are rocks as large as 8 inches in diameter. These obstacles require drivers to pick a good line through them in order to avoid damaging their vehicle. Avoid this trail in wet conditions; the mud would be impassible. Although the road along this section is a one-lane track, there are plenty of turnouts for passing oncoming vehicles. As the trail proceeds, its surface alternates between these more difficult sections and smoother stretches.

Next the trail enters a scenic clearing with some old stone building ruins nearby. This park would make a nice setting for camping and picnicking. There is also ample room for parking to unload mountain bikes, dirt bikes, or ATVs for exploring the network of unmarked trails in the vicinity. These trails are not marked on maps, and many appear to be more challenging than the main trail. Beyond the clearing, the trail gains enough elevation so that there are views to the north of the scenic red sandstone formations in Red Canyon Park.

The trail leaves CR 69 at the intersection with CR F24 and enters Red Canyon Park. The trail, which can be rutted and eroded in places, winds down some switchbacks into the park. Within Red Canyon Park are dramatically beautiful red sandstone formations, picnic areas, restroom facilities, and hiking trails. A well-maintained dirt road that is accessible to passenger vehicles loops around the park. Exit the park and head

Window Rock above the trail

north toward Cripple Creek on CR 9, which is paved for approximately 1.6 miles.

This intersection marks the beginning of the section of this trail that is part of the Gold Belt Tour. After the pavement ends, the road is wide, well maintained, and formed of gravel and dirt. The Shelf Road Recreation Area and the Bank Campground, which is a fee area, can also be accessed near this point in the trail. The recreation area with its 500 established routes is well known for its world-class rock climbing. Many of the routes that scale the limestone canyon walls are quite challenging. Within the recreation area there are also opportunities for hiking and mountain biking.

Near the sign indicating the upcoming shelf road (about 3 miles after exiting Red Canyon Park), the road becomes nar-

The Shelf Road with the toll keepers cabin in the valley

row and starts gaining elevation. Soon there is a sheer drop-off from the road to Fourmile Creek below. The shelf section is about a mile in total. Drop-offs from the shelf road are exciting, but the drive is not difficult. In places the road can be bumpy from erosion and embedded rocks or steep in short sections, but these elements do not present a challenge to stock 4WD vehicles. From time to time the road is narrow, but there are plenty of pullouts for passing oncoming vehicles.

Along this 1-mile stretch, Window Rock is visible atop the canyon's limestone walls. This formation is a naturally occurring hole through the rock precipice. Pinyon and juniper pines and rabbit brush adorn the trail. Sometimes bighorn sheep can be spotted roaming near the creek. Cows also range through the ravine. Keep an eye out for the toll keeper's cabin (described above) also located in the canyon below. The cabin is on private property, so please enjoy the historic building from the road.

The trail continues to gain elevation as it climbs north toward Cripple Creek. Climbing from an elevation of approximately 5,700 feet in the Plains Life Zone with its desertlike vegetation, it runs through the Foothills Life Zone and into the Montane Life Zone up to approximately 9,400 feet.

Red rock formations in Red Canyon Park

Throughout the drive, a visible transition occurs in the vegetation surrounding the trail. Nearing the elevation of 8,000 feet, you will begin to see more greenery, such as blue spruce and other evergreens, aspen trees, wildflowers, and grasses. Along with the interest of the changing flora, expansive views open of the mountains to the south.

Approaching Cripple Creek, more evidence of the region's historic mining days remains in old buildings and mine workings. You will also see the large, current mining operations of the Cripple Creek & Victor Gold Mining Company. The mine you see is called the Cresson Project, which has been active since 1995. This company has conducted mining operations in the Cripple Creek Mining District since 1976. The mining company estimates that more than 23 million troy ounces of gold and silver have been extracted from this district since the first mining began in the 1890s.

Current Road Information

Bureau of Land Management
Royal Gorge Field Office
3170 East Main Street
Cañon City, CO 81212
(719) 269-8500

Map References

BLM   Royal Gorge
Maptech CD-ROM:
        Colorado Springs/Ski Areas/Central
Benchmark's *Colorado Road & Recreation Atlas*, pp. 89, 100, 101
Colorado Atlas & Gazetteer, pp. 62, 72
The Roads of Colorado, p. 112
Trails Illustrated, #137

Route Directions

▼ 0.0		The trail begins at the intersection of CR 69 and US 50, approximately 3 miles northwest of Cañon City. Zero trip meter and proceed northeast on CR 69.
7.2 ▲		The trail ends at the intersection of CR 69 and US 50, approximately 3 miles northwest of Cañon City. Turn left for Cañon City; turn right for Parkdale.
		GPS: N38°28.82' W105°15.82'
▼ 1.2	SO	Cattle guard.
6.0 ▲	SO	Cattle guard.
▼ 3.0	SO	Cattle guard.
4.2 ▲	SO	Cattle guard.
▼ 3.6	SO	Cattle guard.
3.6 ▲	SO	Cattle guard.
▼ 4.2	SO	Cattle guard.
3.0 ▲	SO	Cattle guard.
▼ 5.6	SO	Cattle guard.
1.6 ▲	SO	Cattle guard.
▼ 6.2	SO	Track on right.
1.0 ▲	SO	Track on left.
		GPS: N38°33.40' W105°16.30'
▼ 6.4	SO	Track on left; then cross through creek bed.
0.8 ▲	SO	Cross through creek bed; then track on right.
		GPS: N38°33.47' W105°16.42'
▼ 7.2	SO	Track on left. Zero trip meter.

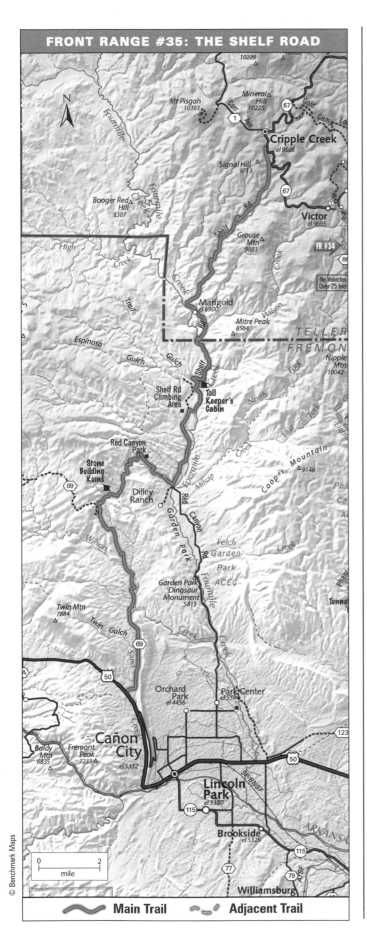

Main Trail Adjacent Trail

© Benchmark Maps

	0.0 ▲		Proceed south on CR 69.
▼ 0.0			Continue north on CR F25.
	1.3 ▲	SO	Track on right. Zero trip meter.
			GPS: N38°34.01' W105°16.79'
▼ 0.2		SO	Cross through creek bed.
	1.1 ▲	SO	Cross through creek bed.
			GPS: N38°34.23' W105°16.85'
▼ 0.3		SO	Old building ruin on left and road splits for 0.1 miles.
	1.0 ▲	SO	Road splits for 0.1 miles; then old building ruin on right.
			GPS: N38°34.19' W105°16.79'
▼ 1.0		SO	Track on right.
	0.3 ▲	SO	Track on left.
▼ 1.1		SO	Track on right.
	0.2 ▲	SO	Track on left.
▼ 1.2		SO	Track on left.
	0.1 ▲	SO	Track on right.
▼ 1.3		BL	Road forks. Zero trip meter.
	0.0 ▲		Proceed southwest on CR F25.
▼ 0.0			Proceed northeast on CR F24.
	2.0 ▲	SO	Road forks. Zero trip meter.
			GPS: N38°34.57' W105°16.00'
▼ 1.1		SO	Entering Red Canyon Park.

Window Rock

0.9 ▲	SO	Leaving Red Canyon Park.

GPS: N35°35.19' W105°15.81'

▼ 2.0	TL	Picnic area on right; then T-intersection with loop through park. Zero trip meter.
0.0 ▲		Proceed to the south on CR F25.
▼ 0.0		Proceed to the north through the park.
1.9 ▲	SO	Intersection with road that loops through park; then picnic area on left. Zero trip meter.

GPS: N38°35.54' W105°15.36'

▼ 0.3	SO	Picnic area and restrooms on left.
1.6 ▲	SO	Picnic area and restrooms on right.

GPS: N38°35.54' W105°15.21'

▼ 1.0	TL	Picnic area on right; then ford through usually dry creek and T-intersection with road that loops through park.
0.9 ▲	TR	Intersection with road that loops through park; then picnic area on left and ford usually dry creek.
▼ 1.9	TL	Ford usually dry creek; then cattle guard at intersection with CR 9. Zero trip meter.
0.0 ▲		Proceed northwest on unpaved CR F24; then cattle guard and ford usually dry creek.

GPS: N38°34.76' W105°14.17'

▼ 0.0		Proceed northeast on paved CR 9 toward Cripple Creek.
14.3 ▲	TR	Intersection of CR 9 and CR F24 at entrance to Red Canyon Park. Zero trip meter.

GPS: N38°34.76' W105°14.17'

▼ 1.6	SO	Pavement ends.
12.7 ▲	SO	Pavement begins.
▼ 2.8	BR	Road to Sand Gulch and access to the Shelf Road Recreation Area on left; then the Bank Campground (fee area) on left. Follow sign to Cripple Creek.
13.5 ▲	BL	The Bank Campground (fee area) on right; then road to Sand Gulch and access to the Shelf Road Recreation Area on right.

GPS: N38°36.88' W105°13.49'

▼ 4.4	BR	Track on left.
9.9 ▲	BL	Track on right.
▼ 7.1	SO	Cattle guard.
7.2 ▲	SO	Cattle guard.
▼ 8.1	SO	Cattle guard.
6.2 ▲	SO	Cattle guard.
▼ 9.3	SO	Bridge over creek.
5.0 ▲	SO	Bridge over creek.

GPS: N38°40.65' W105°12.75'

▼ 12.0	SO	Cattle guard.
2.3 ▲	SO	Cattle guard.
▼ 13.8	SO	Cattle guard.
0.5 ▲	SO	Cattle guard.
▼ 14.3	SO	Intersection of CR 88 and CR 881. Zero trip meter.
0.0 ▲		Proceed southwest on CR 88.
▼ 0.0		Continue northeast on CR 88.
1.4 ▲	SO	Intersection of CR 88 and CR 881. Zero trip meter.

GPS: N38°43.42' W105°10.56'

▼ 1.4		Trail ends at intersection of CR 88 and US 67 in Cripple Creek. Turn right for Victor.
0.0 ▲		Trail begins at the intersection of CR 88 and US 67. Zero trip meter and proceed southwest on CR 88.

GPS: N38°44.56' W105°10.58'

The Northern Region

TRAILS IN THE NORTHERN REGION

- 1   Echo Park and Yampa Bench Trail
- 2   Cathedral Bluffs Trail
- 3   Baxter Pass Trail
- 4   Little Bookcliffs Wild Horse Trail
- 5   Rattlesnake Canyon Trail
- 6   Land's End Road
- 7   Granby Lakes Trail
- 8   Bar HL to Rifle Gap Trail
- 9   Buford Road
- 10   Sleepy Cat and Thornburgh Battle Trail
- 11   Flat Tops Trail
- 12   Coffee Pot Road
- 13   Red Dirt Creek and Derby Mesa Trail
- 14   Red and White Mountain Trail
- 15   Blacktail Road
- 16   Buffalo Pass Trail
- 17   Ellis Jeep Trail
- 18   Elkhorn Mountain and Stock Driveway
- 19   Farwell Mountain Trail
- 20   Muddy Creek Trail
- 21   Stillwater Pass Trail

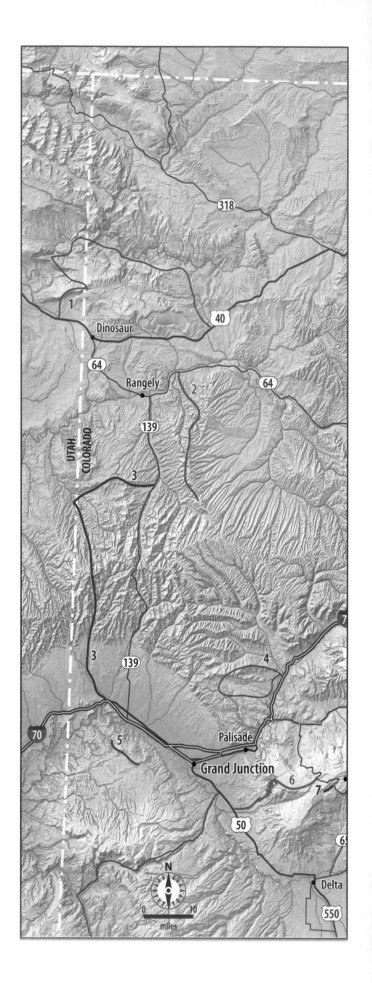

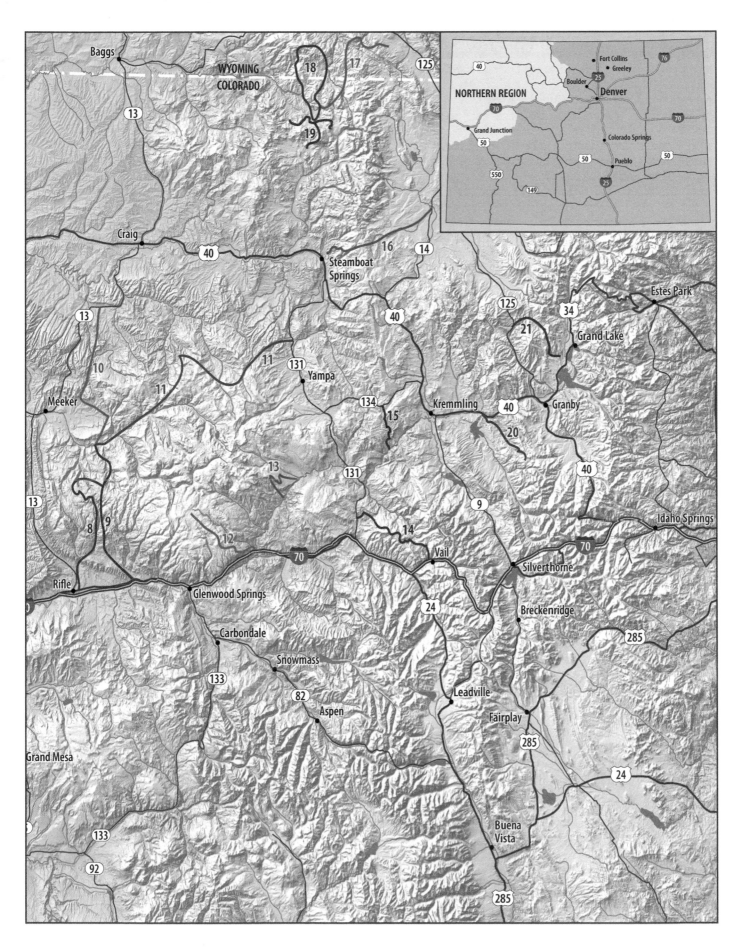

Echo Park and Yampa Bench Trail

Starting Point:	US 40 in Utah, 12.3 miles east of Jensen
Finishing Point:	US 40 in Colorado, 28.5 miles east of Utah state line
Total Mileage:	81.4 miles
Unpaved Mileage:	68.2 miles
Driving Time:	4 hours
Elevation Range:	5,200–8,100 feet
Usually Open:	May to November
Difficulty Rating:	2
Scenic Rating:	10

Special Attractions

- Travel through part of Dinosaur National Monument.
- Petroglyphs by the Fremont Indians.
- Spectacular views overlooking the Yampa River.
- Sand Canyon and Echo Park.
- Chew Ranch and Baker cabin.

History

The earliest known white men to pass through Echo Park were fur trappers (William H. Ashley, for example, came through in the 19th century) but the rock art displayed along the canyon walls shows that the region was inhabited by Indians at least 600 years earlier. Echo Park was named during John Wesley Powell's 1869 expedition of the Colorado Plateau, and in 1883, Patrick Lynch was the first man to homestead in the canyon.

Just before the trail passes the panel of petroglyphs, it comes to the remains of the old Chew Ranch. Born in England, Jack Chew moved to America with his family and grew up in south-ern Utah. Around the age of 12, Chew ran away from home and met up with the McCarty gang. A band of notorious outlaws and cattle rustlers, the McCarty gang demonstrated an unexpected soft side when they allowed Jack to live with them for the next 10 years, during which Jack learned about horses, cattle, and life in the Utah wilderness. He eventually started his own family and settled down in northeastern Utah on what is now known as the Chew Ranch.

By 1912, the Chews had left their ranch and moved across to Pats Hole in Colorado. Pats Hole sits at the meeting of the Yampa and Green Rivers. In the days of the Outlaw Trail, members of the Wild Bunch found this place to be the best river crossing on their way in and out of Brown's Park to the north.

The Baker cabin is another historic site along the trail and is located about 150 yards off the main trail along a disused vehicle track. The cabin, stables, and corral were built in 1918 and abandoned in the 1930s.

Description

On US 40, about 12 miles east of Jensen and 1.2 miles east of Utah 45, turn north onto CR 16S (Blue Mountain Road) and head toward Dinosaur National Monument. The first section of the trail follows a graded county road that soon turns east and travels through dense pinyon and juniper about a mile south of the 2,000-foot cliffs that rise up to the Yampa Plateau. The trail then briefly crosses into Colorado, returns to Utah, and then returns to Colorado for the rest of the trail.

After 11.7 miles, you reach the national monument information center; turn north here onto paved Harpers Corner Drive. About 7.4 miles along Harpers Corner Drive, Canyon Overlook is to the right. The land here drops away quickly along the faultline between the Yampa and Red Rocks continental plates. Over millions of years, one of the Weber sandstone plates fell away from the other and was then carved out even further by the Yampa River. The result is this narrow river canyon 2,600 feet below the overlook.

About 5.5 miles farther up the road there is an overlook into the valley where three faults come together. Shortly thereafter, turn east onto Echo Park Road and begin the descent into the iron-red valley. Originally used by the Chew family, this steep road had no switchbacks, forcing the homesteaders to hitch horses to the rear of their wagons to act as brakes. The road is not as difficult to negotiate these days and can be driven by passenger cars as well as SUVs; however, it should not be driven by large vehicles or ones towing trailers. Avoid the road when it is wet; the red clay becomes thick and greasy and is impassable.

About 5 miles from the turn onto Echo Park Road, the red scenery gives way to buff-colored sandstone as you enter Sand Canyon. The road surface in the canyon becomes sandy, but remains easy to drive. After 7.4 miles along Echo Park Road, a 3.8-mile spur trail leads down another beautiful sandstone canyon to the 800-foot Steamboat Rock at the confluence of the Green and Yampa Rivers. This Echo Park landmark stands at the old outlaw river crossing known as Pats Hole.

Along the spur to Pats Hole and Echo Park is the Chew Ranch and the Fremont Indian petroglyphs. At the end, there is a developed campground and a boat launch for white-water raft-

View from Echo Park Road

The Green River from Harding Hole Overlook

ing on the Green River. Fees and noncommercial river permits are required for rafting; for information, call (970) 374-2468.

After returning to the main trail, you begin a 1,000-foot ascent onto Yampa Bench, which winds through a number of canyons and draws. Even though the road here is periodically graded, it does have a few washouts and occasional rough spots. This section of the route is more remote, and the scenery, though somewhat varied, consists mostly of sagebrush, pinyon, and juniper. The highlights along the Yampa Bench are the high overlooks above the twisting canyons of the Yampa River. The old Baker cabin sits about 150 yards off the main road up an old, abandoned vehicle track that still serves as a walking path.

Although the drive along the Echo Park and Yampa Bench Trail takes about four hours nonstop, you could easily spend a few days exploring the side canyons, camping along the river, and relaxing at some of the many overlooks. The trail eventually ends at US 40 in Colorado.

The Chew Ranch

Baker Cabin

Current Road Information

Dinosaur National Monument
4545 E. Highway 40
Dinosaur, CO 81610-9724
(970) 374-3000

Map References

BLM Vernal, Rangely, Dutch John, Canyon of Lodore
Maptech CD ROM: Craig/Meeker/Northwest Colorado
Benchmark's *Colorado Road & Recreation Atlas*, pp. 56, 42
Benchmark's *Utah Road & Recreation Atlas*, p. 55
Colorado Atlas & Gazetteer, pp. 22, 23, 32, 33
Utah Atlas & Gazetteer, p. 57
The Roads of Colorado, pp. 57, 73
Trails Illustrated, #220 (incompete)

Route Directions

▼ 0.0			On US 40, about 12.3 miles east of Jensen, zero trip meter and turn north onto CR 16S (Blue Mountain Road).
11.7 ▲			Trail ends at US 40; turn right for Jensen, left

Site of petroglyphs near Chew Ranch

			for Colorado.
GPS: N 40°17.25′ W 109°08.40′			
▼ 1.0		SO	Track on right. Then cross over Cliff Creek.
	10.7 ▲	SO	Cross over Cliff Creek. Then track on left.
▼ 1.7		SO	Track on left.
	10.0 ▲	SO	Track on right.
▼ 4.0		SO	Corral on left. Then cross Miners Draw.
	7.7 ▲	SO	Cross Miners Draw. Then corral on right.
▼ 7.3		SO	Cattle guard.
	4.4 ▲	SO	Cattle guard.
▼ 11.7		TL	Cattle guard, then turn left onto paved Harpers Corner Drive and zero trip meter. Dinosaur National Monument information center is to the left.
	0.0 ▲		Continue along unpaved road.
GPS: N 40°21.76′ W 108°58.97′			
▼ 0.0			Continue along paved road.
	13.2 ▲	TR	Turn right onto CR 16S (Blue Mountain Road). Zero trip meter.
▼ 0.6		SO	Cattle guard.
	12.6 ▲	SO	Cattle guard.
▼ 0.7		SO	Seasonal gate.
	12.5 ▲	SO	Seasonal gate.
▼ 2.0		SO	Marker #12 for Wolf Creek Fault.
	11.2 ▲	SO	Marker #12 for Wolf Creek Fault.
▼ 2.3		SO	Marker for good wildlife viewing area.
	10.9 ▲	SO	Marker for good wildlife viewing area.
▼ 4.2		SO	Marker #14 notes that this is highest point along Harpers Corner Drive.
	9.0 ▲	SO	Marker #14 notes that this is highest point along Harpers Corner Drive.
▼ 4.6		SO	Cattle guard.
	8.6 ▲	SO	Cattle guard.
▼ 7.4		SO	Canyon Overlook on right. Picnic area and nature trail.
	5.8 ▲	SO	Canyon Overlook on left. Picnic area and nature trail.
▼ 9.3		SO	Cross state line into Utah.
	3.9 ▲	SO	Cross state line into Colorado.
▼ 11.7		SO	View right of Douglas Mountain and Zenobia Peak (9,006 feet).
	1.5 ▲	SO	View left of Douglas Mountain and Zenobia Peak (9,006 feet).
▼ 12.0		SO	Corral on left; used in spring and fall for cattle and sheep.
	1.2 ▲	SO	Corral on right; used in spring and fall for cattle and sheep.
▼ 12.9		SO	Marker notes meeting point of Yampa, Red

Wash on Yampa Bench Road

0.3 ▲	**SO**	Rock, and Mitten Park Faults. From overlook you can see Echo Park Road. Parking area and view back onto Echo Park Road.	
▼ 13.2	**TR**	Turn right onto Echo Park Road. Then cross cattle guard. Zero trip meter.	
0.0 ▲		Continue along main road.	

GPS: N 40°28.62' W 109°05.84'

▼ 0.0		Descend into canyon.
7.4 ▲	**TL**	Turn left onto paved Harpers Corner Drive. Zero trip meter.
▼ 3.2	**SO**	Cross cattle guard.
4.2 ▲	**SO**	Cross cattle guard.
▼ 4.9	**SO**	Entering Sand Canyon.
2.5 ▲	**SO**	Leaving Sand Canyon.
▼ 7.4	**SO**	Straight is spur trail to Pats Hole and Echo Park. Main trail continues right on Yampa Bench Road. Zero trip meter. You will return to this intersection.
0.0 ▲		Continue along route.

GPS: N 40°29.38' W 108°59.37'

Spur Trail to Pats Hole

▼ 0.0		Proceed north toward Pats Hole.
7.6 ▲	**SO**	At intersection of Yampa Bench Road and

		Echo Park Road, zero trip meter and continue straight ahead.
▼ 1.2	**SO**	Chew Ranch buildings on right and left.
6.4 ▲	**SO**	Chew Ranch buildings on right and left.

GPS: N 40°29.97' W 109°00.47'

▼ 1.3	**SO**	Cross Pool Creek ford.
6.2 ▲	**SO**	Cross Pool Creek ford.
▼ 1.7	**SO**	Log structure on left.
5.9 ▲	**SO**	Log structure on right.
▼ 2.7	**SO**	Ford.
4.9 ▲	**SO**	Ford.

GPS: N 40°30.68' W 108°59.33'

▼ 2.8	**SO**	Petroglyphs about 35 feet above creek on left. Pullover area on right.
4.8 ▲	**SO**	Petroglyphs about 35 feet above creek on right. Pullover area on left.
▼ 3.2	**SO**	Whispering Cave on right.
4.4 ▲	**SO**	Whispering Cave on left.
▼ 3.3	**SO**	Ford.
4.2 ▲	**SO**	Ford.
▼ 3.4	**SO**	Ford.
4.2 ▲	**SO**	Ford.
▼ 3.6	**SO**	Road on left.

Yampa River in Echo Park Hole

Main Trail

	4.0 ▲	SO	Road on right.
▼ 3.7		SO	Ford.
	3.9 ▲	SO	Ford.
▼ 3.8		UT	Pats Hole and Echo Park. Boat launch area, public toilets, and camping. Return to previous intersection where you zeroed trip meter.
	3.8 ▲	UT	Pats Hole and Echo Park. Boat launch area, public toilets, and camping. Return to previous intersection where you zeroed trip meter.

GPS: N 40°31.19' W 108°59.39'

▼ 7.6		TL	At intersection of Yampa Bench Road and Echo Park Road, zero trip meter and turn left onto Yampa Bench Road (CR 14N).
	0.0 ▲		Continue toward Pats Hole.

GPS: N 40°29.38' W 108°59.37'

Continuation of Main Trail

▼ 0.0			Continue along Yampa Bench Road.
	6.4 ▲	TR	Turn right for spur trail to Pats Hole and Echo Park. Main trail continues left on Echo Park Road. Zero trip meter. You will return to this intersection.
▼ 1.0		SO	Cross through wash.
	5.4 ▲	SO	Cross through wash.
▼ 2.7		SO	Cattle guard.
	3.7 ▲	SO	Cattle guard.
▼ 3.8		SO	Track on right.
	2.6 ▲	SO	Track on left.
▼ 5.7		SO	Cross through wash.
	0.7 ▲	SO	Cross through wash.

Main Trail

▼ 5.9		SO	Cross through wash.
	0.5 ▲	SO	Cross through wash.

GPS: N 40°28.13′ W 108°54.62′

▼ 6.3		SO	Cross through wash.
	0.1 ▲	SO	Cross through wash.
▼ 6.4		SO	Castle Park Overlook on left. Zero trip meter.
	0.0 ▲		Continue toward Echo Park Road.

GPS: N 40°28.01′ W 108°54.13′

▼ 0.0			Continue along Yampa Bench Road.
	2.7 ▲	SO	Castle Park Overlook on right. Zero trip meter.
▼ 0.9		SO	Cattle guard.
	1.8 ▲	SO	Cattle guard.
▼ 1.1		BR	Road forks. Left is private road to Mantle Ranch. Then cross through wash.

	1.6 ▲	BL	Cross through wash. Then road forks. Right is private road to Mantle Ranch.

GPS: N 40°27.50′ W 108°53.33′

▼ 2.7		SO	Track on left to Harding Hole Overlook. Zero trip meter.
	0.0 ▲		Continue along main trail.

GPS: N 40°27.73′ W 108°51.73′

▼ 0.0			Continue along main trail.
	1.2 ▲	SO	Track on right to Harding Hole Overlook. Zero trip meter.
▼ 1.2		SO	Wagon Wheel Point Overlook on left. For best views, walk about 250 yards. Zero trip meter.
	0.0 ▲		Continue along trail.

GPS: N 40°27.59′ W 108°50.64′

▼ 0.0			Continue along trail.
	15.2 ▲	SO	Wagon Wheel Point Overlook on right. For best views, walk about 250 yards. Zero trip meter.
▼ 1.6		SO	Cross through wash.
	13.6 ▲	SO	Cross through wash.
▼ 4.5		SO	Closed track on right to Baker cabin, stables, and corrals.
	10.7 ▲	SO	Closed track on left to Baker cabin, stables, and corrals.

GPS: N 40°27.04′ W 108°47.60′

▼ 7.2		SO	Track on left.
	8.0 ▲	SO	Track on right.
▼ 8.5		SO	Track on left.
	6.7 ▲	SO	Track on right.
▼ 12.1		SO	Cattle guard.
	3.1 ▲	SO	Cattle guard.
▼ 15.2		SO	Cattle guard. Leave Dinosaur National Monument. Zero trip meter.
	0.0 ▲		Continue along main trail.

GPS: N 40°25.69′ W 108°39.36′

▼ 0.0			Continue along main trail.

An old wood stove near Baker cabin

15.9 ▲	SO	Enter Dinosaur National Monument and cross cattle guard. Zero trip meter.	
▼ 0.1	BR	Bear right onto CR 95. CR 14N continues straight.	
15.8 ▲	BL	Bear left onto CR 14N.	

GPS: N 40°25.65' W 108°39.30'

▼ 1.2	TR	T-intersection.
14.7 ▲	TL	Road on left.

GPS: N 40°24.87' W 108°39.73'

▼ 1.3	BL	Road on right is CR 14. Continue on CR 95.
14.6 ▲	BR	Road on left is CR 14. Continue along CR 95.
▼ 6.3	SO	Cattle guard.
9.6 ▲	SO	Cattle guard.
▼ 6.5	TL	Turn left onto CR 16, Wolf Creek Road.
9.4 ▲	TR	Turn right onto CR 95.

GPS: N 40°21.65' W 108°40.06'

▼ 6.7	SO	Cattle guard.
9.2 ▲	SO	Cattle guard.
▼ 9.8	SO	Road on left.
6.1 ▲	SO	Road on right.
▼ 15.9		Cattle guard. Trail ends at US 40. Turn right for Utah and Jensen.
0.0 ▲		On US 40, about 28.5 miles east of the Utah/Colorado state line, zero trip meter and turn north onto CR 16.

GPS: N 40°16.67' W 108°33.54'

Baker cabin

Cathedral Bluffs Trail

Starting Point:	Intersection of Colorado 64 and CR 122
Finishing Point:	Locked gate
Total Mileage:	49.9 miles (one-way)
Unpaved Mileage:	49.9 miles
Driving Time:	3 hours (one-way)
Elevation Range:	5,375 to 8,878 feet
Usually Open:	May to October
Difficulty Rating:	3
Scenic Rating:	10

Special Attractions

- Picturesque Cathedral Bluffs.
- Expansive 360-degree views.

History

During the Eocene epoch, around 40 million years ago, the rising Rocky and Uintah mountain ranges began to block the proper flow of rivers and streams, creating the massive Lake Uintah. This lake covered much of present-day western Colorado, eastern Utah, and southern Wyoming. Sediments washed down from the mountains and settled at the bottom of the lake over millions of years.

Much of the sediment deposited was composed of organic matter that became sealed in an amalgam of limestone and dolomite mixed with clay. Over time, much of the organic matter has developed into kerogen, a crude, immature form of oil. The oil shale deposits in the states formerly covered by Lake Uintah measure in the trillions of barrels. However, the oil is expensive and environmentally damaging to mine.

Uplifting and erosion have shaped the Cathedral Bluffs over many years. Numerous fossils can be found in the bluffs,

The trail runs along Calamity Ridge

Views from Calamity Ridge are expansive on clear days

as the thin layers of sediment, like those deposited on the bottom of Lake Uintah, preserve impressions of plant and animal remains well.

This trail also skirts and briefly enters the BLM Piceance Basin–East Douglas Wild Horse Management Area. The wild horses roaming this remote area are descended from horses brought to America by Spanish explorers. As early as 1882, settlers passing through the region reportedly viewed bands of wild horses in the region. Herds grew during the drought and depression of the 1930s as ranchers abandoned their homesteads. Horses within this management area currently number from 90 to 145 and primarily include bays, blacks, sorrels, and browns.

Description

This long, scenic out-and-back trail begins approximately 10 miles northeast of Rangely at the intersection of Colorado 64 and CR 122. In total the trip is nearly 100 miles, so it pays to be prepared before setting out on this remote backcountry adventure. Make sure to fill up your gas tank and have a spare tire that is inflated and in good condition. Avoid the trail if it has recently rained and be sure to take plenty of water and

The trail making its way over flat ground to the ridgeline

Communications towers just off the main trail

emergency supplies. Stay alert while driving this trail to avoid preventable accidents. Please leave all gates, whether they are open or closed, as you found them.

The trail runs south along Calamity Ridge above Cathedral Bluffs and enters the BLM Piceance Basin–East Douglas Wild Horse Management Area. Summer is the best time to view the wild horse herds here. In addition to the wild horses, other wildlife, including porcupine, deer, antelope, elk, eagles, hawks, coyotes, and sage grouse, are abundant. Pick a clear day to drive this trail in order to best appreciate the amazingly expansive views from high points along the way. The scenery is also varied and interesting with the opportunity of viewing the Cathedral Bluffs close up as well as from a distance and the diverse range of vegetation surrounding the trail. Several other 4WD roads that are interesting to explore intersect with the

Memorial at the Cathedral Bluffs overlook

main trail, and many good backcountry campsites are located nearby.

For the first 14 miles, the road is a wide, maintained gravel road. At the turnoff onto CR 103, the road narrows into one lane with plenty of room for passing and is formed primarily of dirt. Here the road can be slick in wet conditions and is rutted in a few places. The trail climbs to the ridge above Cathedral Bluffs and undulates along the hilltop, alternately dipping into patches of Douglas fir and small aspen stands and then rising above the trees onto the windswept bluff with panoramic views in all directions. On a clear day you can see as far as the La Sal Mountains near Moab, Utah, to the southwest, the Flat Tops Wilderness to the east, and into Wyoming to the north. Most of the trail runs along the exposed ridgeline with the minimal vegetation of oak shrub and some sagebrush.

The trail runs very close to the edge of Cathedral Bluffs at one point, making it possible to closely examine the multicolored layers of rock that form the scenic precipice. The bluffs are quite scenic and can be viewed at a distance from several locations along the trail, especially toward the end. Approximately 10 miles from the trail's end near the turnoff onto CR 26, the surface of the road changes again. It becomes a one-lane road formed of soft, dark soil that becomes boggy and impassible in wet conditions. This stretch is extremely rutted and eroded and gives the trail its difficulty rating of 3. Running through open range populated with herds of cattle, the trail ends at a locked gate. The views from this point are also quite expansive.

Current Road Information

Colorado Bureau of Land Management
White River Field Office
220 East Market Street
Meeker, CO 91641
(970) 878-3800

Map References

BLM　White River
Maptech CD: Craig/Meeker/Northwest
Benchmark's *Colorado Road & Recreation Atlas,* pp. 56, 68
Colorado Atlas & Gazetteer, pp. 22, 23, 32, 33
The Roads of Colorado, pp. 57, 73

Route Directions

▼ 0.0		Trail begins at the intersection of Colorado 64 and CR 122. Zero your trip meter and proceed south on CR 122, signed Calamity Ridge, 14 miles; Yellow Creek, 29 miles; and Piceance Creek, 35 miles.
		GPS: N40°09.58′ W108°40.13′
▼ 0.1	SO	Cattle guard.
▼ 6.2	SO	Cattle guard; then corral on right.
▼ 6.4	SO	Road on right.
▼ 9.9	SO	Corral on right.
▼ 11.4	SO	Cattle guard.
▼ 14.0	TR	Intersection with CR 103 on right and CR 1036 on left. Zero trip meter.
		GPS: N40°02.16′ W108°33.19′
▼ 0.0		Proceed southeast on CR 103.

View of the Cathedral Bluffs above Spring Creek Valley from the overlook

▼ 4.4	SO	Cattle guard.
▼ 7.3	SO	Cattle guard.
▼ 10.6	SO	Road on right is access to communications towers. Zero trip meter.
▼ 0.0		Proceed southwest on CR 103.

GPS: N39°55.31′ W108°37.40′

▼ 0.3	SO	Road on right.
▼ 1.1	BR/SO	Fork with CR 80 on left and CR 103 on right; then cattle guard.

GPS: N39°54.67′ W108°36.99′

▼ 3.5	SO	Bike trail on left.

▼ 4.2	SO	Road on left.
▼ 7.3	SO	Road on left and cross natural gas pipeline.

GPS: N39°50.31′ W108°35.66′

▼ 7.4	SO/BR	Fence line; then bear right at intersection with CR 70 on left.

GPS: N39°50.21′ W108°35.57′

▼ 7.5	SO	Track on right to Cathedral Bluffs overlook. Zero trip meter.

GPS: N39°50.18′ W108°35.58′

▼ 0.0		Proceed southeast on CR 103.
▼ 3.6	TR	Cattle guard and T-intersection with CR 68 on

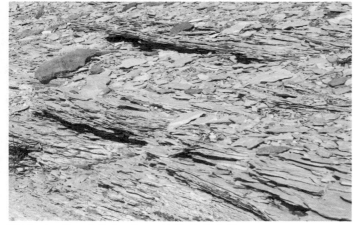

The layers of rock that make up Cathedral Bluffs

Close-up of the different types of rock that form the layers of Cathedral Bluffs

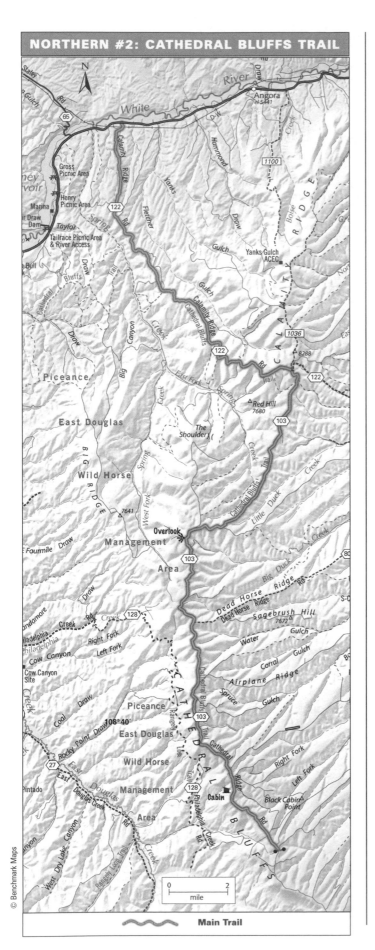

~~~ **Main Trail**

			left and CR 103 on right.
		GPS: N39°47.83′ W108°33.70′	
▼ 4.5	SO	Gate.	
▼ 6.7	SO	Gate.	
▼ 7.5	SO	Cathedral Bluffs can be examined up close on right.	
		GPS: N39°45.46′ W108°31.52′	
▼ 7.8	BR	Road on left is CR 144.	
		GPS: N39°45.20′ W108°31.30′	
▼ 8.6	SO	CR 144 on left.	
▼ 8.7	TR	Intersection with CR 26 on left and right; CR 26A straight ahead. Zero trip meter.	
		GPS: N39°44.62′ W108°31.00′	
▼ 0.0		Proceed southwest on CR 26.	
▼ 2.3	SO	Gate.	
▼ 2.4	SO	Gate; then enter state wildlife area and Square S Summer Range.	
▼ 3.3	SO	Cattle guard.	
▼ 5.3	SO	Road on left to cow camp.	
▼ 5.6	TL	Fork.	
		GPS: N39°41.11′ W108°33.64′	
▼ 6.3	SO	Old cabin on right.	
		GPS: N39°40.52′ W108°33.45′	
▼ 7.8	SO	Gate.	
▼ 9.1	SO	Trail ends at locked gate.	
		GPS: N39°38.81′ W108°32.23′	

Deep wheel rut in the last few miles of trail

Baxter Pass Trail

Starting Point:	Mack
Finishing Point:	Intersection of CR 116 and
	Colorado 139
Total Mileage:	80.2 miles
Unpaved Mileage:	72.2 miles
Driving Time:	4 hours
Elevation Range:	4,457 to 8436 feet
Usually Open:	Early June to mid-October
Difficulty Rating:	4
Scenic Rating:	8

Special Attractions

- Remote, scenic location.
- Landscape that is unique in Colorado.
- Access to a network of 4WD trails.

History

This pass was originally an old Ute Indian trail that provided access between the Gunnison area and the White River and Green River regions of western Colorado and eastern Utah.

Albert "Bert" Carlton, who had made a fortune in Cripple Creek, decided to shift his attention to copper mining in Utah. To transport the ore, he established the 72-mile Uintah Railway in 1905, which traveled from Mack, Colorado, to Watson, Utah.

The route went up and over Baxter Pass, which created a huge obstacle with some of the hardest grades any railroad had attempted to climb. The route was dangerous, and auxiliary steam engines were required to make the ascent to the pass.

The Watson area was found to be very rich in uintaite (also known as Gilsonite, a natural asphalt, petroleum-based resource). The Gilsonite mines, most of them near Dragon, Utah, were developed by the Barber Asphalt Company of St. Louis. Baxter Pass was actually named for C. O. Baxter of the Barber Asphalt Company.

The "Gilsonite Road" railway looped and turned to climb over Baxter Pass until 1939. The railway ceased operations when it became cheaper to pipe the Gilsonite over the pass to Mack.

Description

This route provides the opportunity to travel through some of the most remote country in Colorado with scenery much different than that along any of the other trails in this book.

Eight miles from exit 11 on I-70, on CR 8, the pavement ends, but the road is still a wide, maintained, rural road suitable for 2WD vehicles. The road deteriorates slowly as you travel toward the pass and becomes quite rutted in spots as it

An old cabin beside the trail

traverses the barren sage plateau. After heavy rain, it is very boggy and can become impassable. In muddy conditions, the difficulty rating for this road could increase to 5 or higher.

There are numerous side roads, many of which are used for natural gas mining operations and pipeline maintenance and are not open to the public. If they are open, nearly all are definitely dry-weather options. Proceed with caution, however, because nearly all of this backcountry is privately owned. The side roads provide an occasional challenge to navigation. Some are used nearly as frequently as the "main" road, making it difficult to discern which is the main road and which is the side road.

As the road approaches Baxter Pass, it alternates between a single track with turnouts and a two-lane track. The last mile to the pass is reasonably steep as it switchbacks to the summit, and the road is quite eroded in parts. The sections of shelf road are not intimidating.

From the summit of the pass, there are scenic, expansive views on both sides.

On the descent, the road travels through stands of aspens interspersed in the pine forest. There are a couple of short sections that may be boggy, even when the rest of the track is dry. After about 4 miles, there is a scenic view of McAndrews Lake. Farther along the route, the road winds through beautiful canyon country and across numerous creek beds or washes (most of them dry).

A section of mud that is typical of conditions after rain

Current Road Information

Colorado Bureau of Land Management
Grand Junction Field Office
2815 H Road
Grand Junction, CO
(970) 244-3000

White River Field Office
220 East Market Street
Meeker, CO 81641
(970) 878-3800

Map References

BLM   Grand Junction; White River
Maptech CD: Grand Junction/Western Slope
Benchmark's *Colorado Road & Recreation Atlas*, pp. 82, 68
The Roads of Colorado, pp. 48, 64, 80
Colorado Atlas & Gazetteer, pp. 32, 42

Route Directions

▼ 0.0		Take I-70 west of Grand Junction to exit 11 into the town of Mack. Zero trip meter at the stop sign and turn left.
35.3 ▲		End at junction to I-70.
	GPS: N 39°13.36′ W 108°51.74′	
▼ 2.3	TR	Onto CR 8 (8 Road).
32.9 ▲	TL	Onto CR 80 (US 6).
▼ 5.1	TL	Onto S Road, also CR 4. Straight ahead will dead-end.
30.2 ▲	TR	Onto CR 8 (8 Road).
	GPS: N 39°16.97′ W 108°54.05′	
▼ 8.0	SO	Cattle guard. Unpaved road.
27.3 ▲	SO	Paved. Cattle guard.
▼ 10.3	SO	Bridge over creek.
25.0 ▲	SO	Bridge over creek.
▼ 10.8	SO	Bridge over creek.
24.4 ▲	SO	Bridge over creek.
▼ 10.9	BR	Fork in the road. Left goes to Prairie Canyon. Follow CR 4.
24.3 ▲	SO	Track on right goes to Prairie Canyon. Remain

An old sign on the Colorado/Utah border

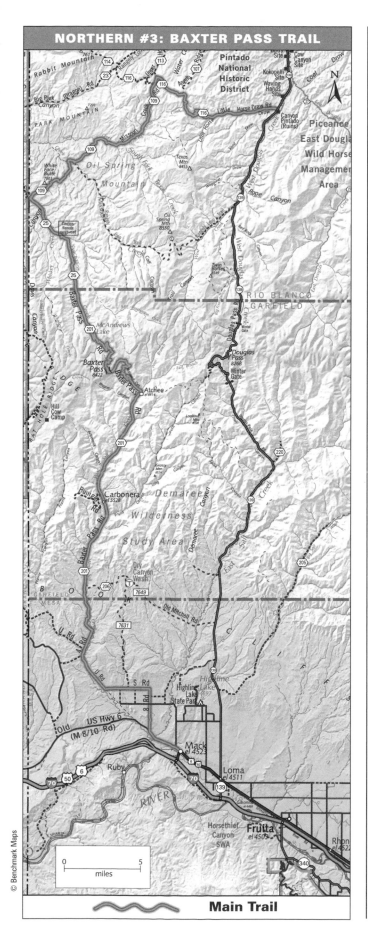

Main Trail

© Benchmark Maps

The old railroad grade ascending the pass

			on CR 4.
▼ 11.8		SO	Cattle guard.
	23.4 ▲	SO	Cattle guard.
▼ 15.0		SO	Cattle yards on right. Approximately here, road name changes from Mesa CR 4 to Garfield CR 201.
	20.2 ▲	SO	Cattle yards on left. Approximately here, road name changes from Garfield CR 201 to Mesa CR 4.
▼ 16.0		SO	Cattle guard.
	19.3 ▲	SO	Cattle guard.
▼ 20.6		SO	Cattle guard.
	14.6 ▲	SO	Cattle guard.
▼ 21.8		SO	Bridge.
	13.5 ▲	SO	Bridge.
▼ 22.8		SO	Cattle guard and cattle yards on right.
	12.4 ▲	SO	Cattle yards on right. Cattle guard.
▼ 23.1		SO	Track on left.
	12.2 ▲	SO	Track on right.
▼ 24.3		SO	Track on right.
	11.0 ▲	SO	Track on left.
▼ 24.4		SO	Track on left.
	10.9 ▲	SO	Track on right.
▼ 25.4		SO	Track on left into West Canyon.
	9.9 ▲	SO	Track on right into West Canyon.

The one old building remaining at Atchee

▼ 25.5		SO	Cattle guard.
	9.8 ▲	SO	Cattle guard.
▼ 27.6		BL	Fork in road.
	7.7 ▲	SO	Fork in road.

GPS: N 39°32.19' W 108°55.30'

▼ 27.7		SO	Cattle guard.
	7.5 ▲	SO	Cattle guard.
▼ 29.6		SO	Fork in road. Old town site of Atchee on right with one remaining building.
	5.7 ▲	SO	Old town site of Atchee on left with one remaining building.

GPS: N 39°33.81' W 108°54.74'

▼ 30.8		SO	Cattle guard.
	4.5 ▲	SO	Cattle guard.
▼ 31.1		SO	Bridge over creek.
	4.2 ▲	SO	Bridge over creek.
▼ 33.2		BL	Track on right.
	2.0 ▲	BR	Track on left.
▼ 33.6		SO	Track on right.
	1.7 ▲	SO	Track on left.
▼ 35.3		SO	Cattle guard and Baxter Pass. Tracks on left and right are jeep trails. Zero trip meter.
	0.0 ▲		Continue on CR 201.

GPS: N 39°34.96' W 108°57.14'

▼ 0.0			Continue on CR 201.
	15.8 ▲	SO	Baxter Pass. Cattle guard. Tracks on left and right are jeep trails. Zero trip meter.
▼ 3.1		SO	Shack on left.
	12.7 ▲	SO	Shack on right.
▼ 4.5		SO	Old shack on left and McAndrews Lake.
	11.3 ▲	SO	Old shack on right and McAndrews Lake.
▼ 6.0		SO	Gate—leave it as you find it.
	9.8 ▲	SO	Gate—leave it as you find it.
▼ 6.6		SO	Gate. Ranch on right.
	9.2 ▲	SO	Ranch on left. Gate.
▼ 8.3		SO	Cattle guard. Approximately here, road name changes from Garfield CR 201 to Rio Blanco CR 25.
	7.5 ▲	SO	Cattle guard. Approximately here, road name changes from Rio Blanco CR 25 to Garfield CR 201.
▼ 9.0		SO	Cattle guard.
	6.8 ▲	SO	Cattle guard.
▼ 10.2		SO	Cabin ruins on left.
	5.6 ▲	SO	Cabin ruins on right.
▼ 10.4		SO	Gate and cattle yard. Cross creek.
	5.4 ▲	SO	Cross creek. Cattle yard and gate.
▼ 12.1		SO	Cross over creek.
	3.7 ▲	SO	Cross over creek.
▼ 13.4		SO	Road on left to Whiskey Creek and Gentry Ranch.
	2.4 ▲	SO	Road on right to Whiskey Creek and Gentry Ranch.

GPS: N 39°43.12' W 109°01.44'

▼ 14.6		SO	Track on left to Davis Canyon.
	1.2 ▲	SO	Track on right to Davis Canyon.
▼ 15.8		TR	Intersection. You are almost on the Utah border. Bearing left leads toward Bonanza, Utah. Turn right to Rangely, Colorado. Zero trip meter.
	0.0 ▲		Proceed toward Baxter Pass on CR 25.

GPS: N 39°44.83' W 109°02.92'

▼ 0.0			Proceed toward Rangely on CR 109.
	4.6 ▲	TL	Intersection. You are almost on the Utah border. Zero trip meter.
▼ 0.1		SO	Cross through Evacuation Creek.
	4.4 ▲	SO	Cross through Evacuation Creek.

▼ 2.1		BR	Track on left.
	2.4 ▲	BL	Track on right.
▼ 2.6		BL	Track on right to network of trails.
	1.9 ▲	BR	Track on left to network of trails.
▼ 3.0		SO	Private mining track on right.
	1.5 ▲	SO	Private mining track on left.
▼ 3.7		SO	Cross through wash.
	0.9 ▲	SO	Cross through wash.
▼ 4.4		BL	Track on right. Then cross through wash.
	0.2 ▲	BR	Cross through wash. Road forks.
▼ 4.6		BR	Fork in road. Old cabin on left. Zero trip meter.
	0.0 ▲		Continue on CR 109.

GPS: N 39°46.90' W 108°59.67'

▼ 0.0			Continue on CR 109.
	24.5 ▲	BL	Old cabin on right. Road forks. Zero trip meter.
▼ 4.1		SO	Cross through wash.
	20.4 ▲	SO	Cross through wash.
▼ 4.3		SO	Cross through wash.
	20.2 ▲	SO	Cross through wash.
▼ 5.5		SO	Cross through wash.
	19.0 ▲	SO	Cross through wash.
▼ 7.0		BL	Track on right.
	17.5 ▲	BR	Fork in road.
▼ 7.9		SO	Track on left.
	16.6 ▲	SO	Track on right.
▼ 8.0		SO	Track on right.
	16.5 ▲	SO	Track on left.
▼ 8.8		TL	T-intersection. To the right dead-ends.
	15.7 ▲	TR	Intersection. Straight on dead-ends.

GPS: N 39°50.62' W 108°53.71'

▼ 9.2		SO	Intersection. Tracks on left and right.
	15.3 ▲	SO	Intersection. Tracks on left and right.
▼ 9.4		BL	Fork in the road. Follow CR 109.
	15.1 ▲	BR	Road on left.
▼ 9.8		SO	Oil well on left.
	14.7 ▲	SO	Oil well on right.
▼ 10.1		SO	Track on right.
	14.4 ▲	SO	Track on left.
▼ 10.3		SO	Track on left.
	14.2 ▲	SO	Track on right.
▼ 10.6		SO	Track on left.
	13.9 ▲	SO	Track on right.
▼ 11.0		TR	T-intersection.
	13.5 ▲	TL	Road on left.

GPS: N 39°51.79' W 108°54.30'

▼ 12.9		BL	CR 111 on right.
	11.6 ▲	BR	CR 111 on left.
▼ 13.3		SO	CR 113 on left.
	11.2 ▲	SO	CR 113 on right.
▼ 15.2		SO	CR 107 on left.
	9.3 ▲	SO	CR 107 on right.
▼ 20.0		SO	Track on right.
	4.5 ▲	BL	Fork in road. Follow Little Horse Draw.
▼ 21.0		SO	Conoco Natural Gas plant on right.
	3.5 ▲	SO	Conoco Natural Gas plant on left.
▼ 22.1		SO	Conoco Natural Gas plant.
	2.4 ▲	SO	Conoco Natural Gas plant.
▼ 24.5			End at intersection of CR 116 with Colorado 139.
	0.0 ▲		At intersection of Colorado 139 and CR 116 (also signposted as "Little Horse Draw"), zero trip meter and proceed west along CR 116.

GPS: N 39°49.91' W 108°44.62'

Little Bookcliffs Wild Horse Trail

Starting Point:	Intersection of 4th Street and CR 45 in De Beque
Finishing Point:	Intersection of South Dry Fork Road (CR X.5) and CR 45, approximately 3 miles northwest of De Beque
Total Mileage:	46.0 miles
Unpaved Mileage:	45.4 miles
Driving Time:	3 hours, excluding spurs
Elevation Range:	4,870 to 7,085 feet
Usually Open:	April to November
Difficulty Rating:	2
Scenic Rating:	8

Special Attractions
- Wild horse viewing.
- Views of the Grand Valley.
- Scenic sandstone rock formations.
- Network of spurs within the horse range to explore.

History
This trail passes through the BLM Little Bookcliffs Wild Horse Management Area. Within the management area, a monument was erected in memory of one Nevada native who was critical to the survival of America's wild horses and burros. Velma B. Johnston, also known as Wild Horse Annie, was instrumental in the passage of legislation protecting wild horses and burros as well as the resulting establishment of this management area and others like it.

On her way to work one day in 1950, Johnston noticed a truck that was dripping with blood from the back. Following

The trail winds through Main Canyon

the truck, she found out it was carrying wild horses that had been rounded up for slaughter. Troubled by how cruelly the animals were treated, she began a vigorous campaign involving schoolchildren to raise the public's awareness to the plight of the dwindling herds. Her difficult campaign realized partial success in the passage of the Wild Horse Annie Act in September 1959. This act made the use of motorized vehicles to capture wild horses or burros illegal. Because the act did not include measures for the protection of the animals, she continued her tireless advocacy for the cause. Finally, on June 19, 1971, the Senate unanimously passed the Wild Free-Roaming Horse and Burro Act of 1971 that federally protects the wild herds.

As a result of Wild Horse Annie's efforts, the act dictates, "...Wild free-roaming horses and burros are living symbols of the historic and pioneer spirit of the West; that they contribute to the diversity of life forms within the Nation and enrich the lives of the American people." Today the Colorado Bureau of Land Management operates four wild horse management areas including Little Bookcliffs. The other three, which are also located in western Colorado, are Piceance Basin–East Douglas Creek (see Northern #2: Cathedral Bluffs Trail, p. 220), east of Rangely; Spring Creek, southwest of Montrose; and Sandwash Basin situated in the northwestern corner of Colorado.

The ancestry of the horses roaming the Little Bookcliffs area can be traced back to the horses that were once owned by local miners, ranchers, and migrating farmers. A few of the horses are descendants of Indian ponies, and fewer still can be linked back to the horses of Spanish explorers. The herd numbers from 110 to 120 horses, the majority of which are bays, blacks, and sorrels.

Description
The trail begins in De Beque and heads south to Wagon Truck Ridge, which runs west through Winter Flats into the Little Bookcliffs Wild Horse Management Area. The trail then winds back to the east and follows South Dry Fork Creek Road, ending just 3 miles northwest of De Beque. Plenty of opportunities to view wild horses in their protected habitat along with plentiful other wildlife exist along this route. Keep an eye out for the interesting sandstone rock formations; one in particular is noted on many maps as "The Goblins." This lightly traveled trail also presents some good, private backcountry campsites.

Starting out, follow the route directions closely or use a GPS because navigating the unmarked roads out of town can be confusing. The trail begins as a gravel road traveling through private grazing land on both sides. The surrounding landscape is flat at first, and there are views of the sandstone Little Bookcliffs in the distance. The desertlike vegetation is mainly pinyon and juniper pines with rabbitbrush and sagebrush. Progressing, the road is formed mainly of dirt that becomes very boggy when wet. Wheel ruts remain from vehicles traveling along the road when it was muddy. Avoid this trail in wet conditions.

After approximately 3 miles, a sign indicates you are heading toward the wild horse area and on BLM land. The dirt road with very few embedded rocks begins to travel alternately through small ravines and canyons and open areas past a number of natural gas and oil wells, working its way toward the sandstone cliffs. Winding through the lowlands, numerous washes cut across the road from water draining to lower ground. Major washes are noted in the route directions, but there are too many to include them all. Be aware that summer thunderstorms can cause flash floods.

The dry soil can produce clouds of dust during periods of high wind. Hoofprints on the dusty trail compel travelers to keep a sharp eye out for the horses and other wildlife. At points the trail climbs to higher ground, revealing views down into canyons and over the Grand Valley. From Winter Flats, the road turns to the northeast to join South Dry Fork Road, and navigating the numerous unmarked intersections with roads that look similar to the main trail can be tricky. The road is alternately smooth and maintained in places and eroded with a few potholes and wheel ruts in others, but none of these elements would present a challenge to stock 4WD vehicles in dry conditions. These features give the trail its difficulty rating of 2.

The arid landscape combined with the feeling of remoteness makes this trip seem similar to an outback safari along some stretches. Wildlife is abundant, and some you are likely to see include wild horses, chipmunks, deer, elk, rabbits, eagles, and falcons. Others that travelers are less likely to see include mountain lions, bobcats, and coyotes.

South Dry Fork Road (CR X.5) is a wide, well-maintained dirt road that runs through a flat, open area with much more greenery. Approaching the trail's end at the intersection with CR 45, the surrounding land is private property.

Spurs to Indian Park, Main Canyon, and North Soda within the management area intersect with the main trail in several locations. Be aware that these roads can be more eroded than the main trail and possibly present more 4WD chal-

lenges. Since none of these spurs are through roads, plan to add about an extra hour of out-and-back travel time for each spur you plan to drive, plus extra time for stops. The best times to see the horses are in the mornings and evenings when they roam through the low-lying sagebrush parks throughout the horse range.

Current Road Information

Colorado Bureau of Land Management
Grand Junction Field Office
2815 H Road
Grand Junction, CO 81506
(970) 244-3000

Map References

BLM   Grand Junction
Maptech CD: Grand Junction/Western Slope
Benchmark's *Colorado Road & Recreation Atlas,* pp. 69, 83
Colorado Atlas & Gazetteer, p. 43
The Roads of Colorado, pp. 73, 74, 89, 90
Little Book Cliffs Wild Horse Range, Free BLM Brochure

Route Directions

▼ 0.0		Trail begins at the intersection of Fourth Street and 45 Road in De Beque, signed 23 miles to Little Bookliffs Wild Horse Area. De Beque is located off I-70 between the Parachute and Palisade exits.
4.1 ▲		Trail ends at the intersection of Fourth Street and 45 Road in De Beque. Turn right for I-70. Turn left for end of trail and CO 139.
GPS: N39°20.01' W108°12.60'		
▼ 0.2	TL	Head south on Minter Street.
3.9 ▲	TR	Continue east on Fourth Street.
▼ 0.3	SO	Cross Third Street.
3.9 ▲	SO	Cross Third Street.
▼ 0.3	BR	Continue west on Second Street.

Herd of wild horses at the beginning on the Indian Park spur

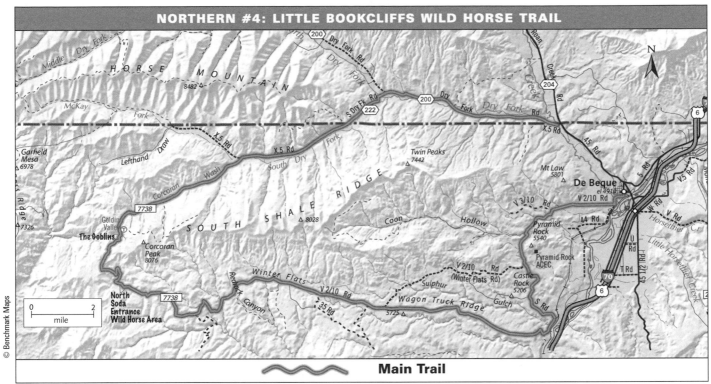

Main Trail

3.8 ▲	BL	Proceed north on Minter Street.	
▼ 0.5	SO	Cross Denver Street.	
3.7 ▲	SO	Cross Denver Street.	
▼ 0.6	SO	Cross bridge over Roan Creek.	
3.6 ▲	SO	Cross bridge over Road Creek.	
▼ 0.7	SO	Pavement ends.	
3.5 ▲	SO	Pavement begins.	
▼ 0.8	TR	Continue west on Road Y 2/10.	
3.3 ▲	TL	Proceed north on 44 Road.	

GPS: N39º19.66' W108º13.16'

▼ 1.9	SO	Cross over irrigation ditch.
2.2 ▲	SO	Cross over irrigation ditch.
▼ 2.1	SO	Cattle guard.
2.0 ▲	SO	Cattle guard.
▼ 2.9	BL	Road forks. Follow sign to Wild Horse Area.
1.2 ▲	BR	Road forks. Follow sign to Wild Horse Area.

GPS: N39º19.50' W108º15.46'

▼ 3.2	SO	Cross through wash.
0.9 ▲	SO	Cross through wash.
▼ 3.3	SO	Track on left.
0.8 ▲	SO	Track on right.
▼ 3.7	SO	Track on right.
0.4 ▲	SO	Track on left.
▼ 4.1	BL	Track on right signed to Coon Hollow. Zero trip meter.
0.0 ▲		Continue north on main trail.

GPS: N39º18.99' W108º16.36'

▼ 0.0		Continue south on main trail.
4.8 ▲	SO	Track on left signed to Coon Hollow. Zero trip meter.
▼ 0.3	SO	Cross through wash.
4.6 ▲	SO	Cross through wash.
▼ 0.6	SO	Cattle guard.
4.2 ▲	SO	Cattle guard.
▼ 0.8	SO	Cross through wash.
4.0 ▲	SO	Cross through wash.

▼ 1.0	SO	Oil well on right.
3.9 ▲	SO	Oil well on left.
▼ 1.2	BL	Cross through wash; then road forks. Continue southeast on main trail.
3.7 ▲	BR	Road forks; then cross through wash. Continue northwest on main trail.

GPS: N39º18.11' W108º16.50'

▼ 1.3	SO	Cross through 7 washes.
3.6 ▲	SO	Cross through 7 washes.
▼ 1.7	BL	Track on right.
3.2 ▲	SO	Track on left.
▼ 1.9	SO	Track on left.
3.0 ▲	SO	Track on right.
▼ 2.2	SO	Cross through wash.
2.6 ▲	SO	Cross through wash.
▼ 2.8	SO	Track on right, signed Short Cut.
2.0 ▲	SO	Track on left, signed Short Cut.

GPS: N39º17.06' W108º16.27'

▼ 2.9	BR	Track on left.
1.9 ▲	BL	Track on right.
▼ 3.0	SO	Track on right.
1.8 ▲	SO	Track on left.
▼ 3.1	BL	Track on right.
1.7 ▲	SO	Track on left.
▼ 3.9	TR	Intersection with unmarked roads.
0.9 ▲	TL	Unmarked intersection.

GPS: N39º16.59' W108º15.49'

▼ 4.1	BR	Road on left.
0.7 ▲	BL	Road forks.

GPS: N39º16.44' W108º15.36'

▼ 4.2	SO	Cross through fence.
0.6 ▲	SO	Cross through fence.
▼ 4.5	SO	Cross through wash; then cross over wash.
0.3 ▲	SO	Cross over wash; then cross through wash.
▼ 4.8	TR	Unmarked intersection. Zero trip meter.
0.0 ▲		Continue east on main trail.

			GPS: N39°16.02' W108°15.76'
▼ 0.0			Continue west on main trail.
	5.9 ▲	TL	Unmarked intersection. Zero trip meter.
▼ 0.2		TL	Track on right to natural gas mine.
	5.7 ▲	TR	Track on left to natural gas mine.
▼ 0.6		SO	Track on left.
	5.3 ▲	SO	Track on right.
▼ 0.9		BL	Intersection.
	5.0 ▲	BR	Intersection.
▼ 1.9		SO	Track on left.
	4.1 ▲	SO	Track on right.
▼ 2.2		SO	Track on right.
	3.7 ▲	SO	Track on left.
			GPS: N39°16.33' W108°17.81'
▼ 3.0		SO	Cattle guard.
	2.9 ▲	SO	Cattle guard.
▼ 4.8		SO	Track on right.
	1.2 ▲	SO	Track on left.
			GPS: N39°16.75' W108°20.36'
▼ 5.8		SO	Cattle guard.
	0.1 ▲	SO	Cattle guard.
▼ 5.9		SO	Intersection with road on right. Signposted to Wild Horse Area. Zero trip meter.
	0.0 ▲		Proceed east on main trail.
			GPS: N39°16.76' W108°21.61'
▼ 0.0			Continue west on main trail.
	7.6 ▲	SO	Intersection with road on left. Zero trip meter.
▼ 0.5		SO	Road forks. Signed 10 miles to Wild Horse area straight on, and 5 miles to Deer Park on left.
	7.1 ▲	SO	Road on right signed to Deer Park.
			GPS: N39°16.81' W108°22.15'
▼ 2.2		SO	Cattle guard.
	5.5 ▲	SO	Cattle guard.
▼ 2.3		SO	Cross Winter Flats Area.
	5.4 ▲	SO	Cross Winter Flats Area.
▼ 2.4		SO	Road on left signed to Wild Horse Area.
	5.3 ▲	SO	Road on right signed to Wild Horse Area.
			GPS: N39°17.21' W108°24.14'
▼ 2.9		SO	Cross through wash.
	4.8 ▲	SO	Cross through wash.
▼ 3.6		SO	Track on left.
	4.0 ▲	SO	Track on right.
			GPS: N39°17.49' W108°25.47'
▼ 4.2		SO	Cattle guard; then cross through wash.
	3.5 ▲	SO	Cross through wash; then cattle guard.
▼ 5.4		SO	Track on right dead-ends.
	2.2 ▲	SO	Track on left dead-ends.
▼ 5.5		SO	Old corral on left; then stock pond; then track on left.
	2.1 ▲	SO	Track on right; then stock pond; then old corral on right.
			GPS: N39°17.18' W108°27.19'
▼ 6.1		SO	Cross through wash.
	1.5 ▲	SO	Cross through wash.
▼ 7.0		SO	Cattle guard.
	0.6 ▲	SO	Cattle guard.
▼ 7.2		SO	Cross over wash.
	0.4 ▲	SO	Cross over wash.
▼ 7.6		SO	Intersection signed Wild Horse Area North Soda Entrance, 5 miles straight ahead and Wild Horse Area Indian Park Entrance, 5 miles to left. Zero trip meter.
	0.0 ▲		Proceed northeast on main trail.

			GPS: N39°16.62' W108°28.47
▼ 0.0			Continue west on main trail.
	3.0 ▲	SO	Road on right. Zero trip meter.
▼ 0.9		SO	Road on left.
	2.2 ▲	SO	Road on right signed to Wild Horse Area North Soda Entrance, 5 miles straight ahead and Wild Horse Area Indian Park Entrance, 5 miles to the right.
▼ 2.1		TL	Two roads on right.
	0.9 ▲	TR	Two road on left.
			GPS: N39°17.21' W108°30.20'
▼ 2.6		SO	Cross through wash.
	0.4 ▲	SO	Cross through wash.
▼ 3.0		BL	Track on right to natural gas well. Zero trip meter.
	0.0 ▲		Continue southeast on main trail.
			GPS: N39°17.33' W108°30.96'
▼ 0.0			Continue northwest on main trail.
	0.5 ▲	SO	Track on left to gas well. Zero trip meter.
▼ 0.2		BR	Intersection signed Wild Horse Area North Soda Entrance, 2 miles.
	0.3 ▲	SO	Intersection with track on right signed Wild Horse Area North Soda Entrance, 2 miles.
			GPS: N39°17.36' W108°31.19'
▼ 0.5		SO	Intersection with track on left. Signed 21 miles to Roan Creek Hwy. Zero trip meter.
	0.0 ▲		Proceed southeast on main trail.
			GPS: N39°17.48' W108°31.45'
▼ 0.0			Proceed through cattle guard and continue west on main trail.
	6.5 ▲	SO	Cattle guard; then track on right signed 8 miles to Wild Horse Area Indian Park Entrance, and 2 miles to Wild Horse Area Soda Springs Entrance. Zero trip meter.
▼ 1.5		TR	T-intersection.
	4.9 ▲	TL	Track on left.
			GPS: N39°17.86' W108°32.07'
▼ 1.7		SO	Stock pond on left and overlook on right.
	4.8 ▲	SO	Stock pond on right and overlook on left.
▼ 1.9		SO	Gate.
	4.6 ▲	SO	Gate.
▼ 2.2		SO	Stock ponds on right.
	4.3 ▲	SO	Stock ponds on left.
▼ 2.5		SO	"The Goblins" rock formations on left and right.

The Goblins

4.0 ▲	SO	"The Goblins" rock formations on right and left.
▼ 3.0	SO	Cattle guard.
3.4 ▲	SO	Cattle guard.
▼ 3.5	SO	Stock pond on right.
3.0 ▲	SO	Stock pond on left.
▼ 3.7	SO	Stock pond on right.
2.8 ▲	SO	Stock pond on left.
▼ 4.7	SO	Stock ponds on right.
1.8 ▲	SO	Stock ponds on left.
▼ 4.8	SO	Stock pond on left.
1.7 ▲	SO	Stock pond on right.
▼ 5.3	SO	Track on right.
1.2 ▲	SO	Track on left.

GPS: N39°19.82' W108°29.74'

▼ 5.4	SO	Cattle guard.
1.0 ▲	SO	Cattle guard.
▼ 6.5	BL	Road on right. Zero trip meter.
0.0 ▲		Continue west on main trail.

GPS: N39°20.24' W108°28.59'

▼ 0.0		Continue east on main trail.
13.5 ▲	BR	Road on left. Zero trip meter.
▼ 0.5	SO	Stock pond on right.
13.1 ▲	SO	Stock pond on left.
▼ 0.9	SO	Pond on left and track on right.
12.6 ▲	SO	Track on left and pond on right.

GPS: N39°20.51' W108°27.69'

▼ 1.3	SO	Pond on left.
12.2 ▲	SO	Pond on right.
▼ 1.5	SO	Cross over creek.
11.6 ▲	SO	Cross over creek.
▼ 1.7	SO	Corral on left.
11.8 ▲	SO	Corral on right.
▼ 2.0	TR	Cattle guard; then T-intersection with Road X 5/10.
11.5 ▲	TL	Intersection with road signed to Wild Horse Mesa.

GPS: N39°21.04' W108°26.75'

▼ 3.4	SO	Cattle guard.
10.1 ▲	SO	Cattle guard.
▼ 5.8	SO	Cattle guard.
7.7 ▲	SO	Cattle guard.
▼ 7.2	SO	Cross over bridge.
6.3 ▲	SO	Cross over bridge.
▼ 7.4	SO	S Dry Fork Road on left.
6.1 ▲	BL	S Dry Fork Road on right.

GPS: N39°22.87' W108°21.58'

▼ 7.9	SO	Cattle guard.
5.6 ▲	SO	Cattle guard.
▼ 10.7	SO	Cattle guard.
2.8 ▲	SO	Cattle guard.
▼ 13.2	SO	Cattle guard.
0.3 ▲	SO	Cattle guard.
▼ 13.4	SO	Cross over bridge; then pavement begins and trail ends at mile 13.5 at intersection with South Dry Fork Road (CR X.5) and CR 45. Turn right for De Beque and I-70; turn left for Colorado 139.
0.0 ▲		Trail begins at intersection of CR 45 and South Dry Fork Road (CR X.5 Road). Proceed east on South Dry Fork Road.

GPS: N39°21.95' W108°15.09'

Rattlesnake Canyon Trail

Starting Point:	Intersection of Rim Rock Road and CR 16.5
Finishing Point:	Rattlesnake Arches Trailhead
Total Mileage:	11.2 miles (one-way)
Unpaved Mileage:	11.1 miles
Driving Time:	1.5 hours (one-way)
Elevation Range:	5,856 to 7,000 feet
Usually Open:	Lower Road, August 15 to February 15; Upper Road, April 15 to August 15; closed February 15 to April 15.
Difficulty Rating:	2 (4 for the last 2 miles)
Scenic Rating:	10

Special Attractions

■ Overlook of red sandstone Rattlesnake Canyon.
■ Scenic drive through Colorado National Monument to access the trail.
■ Hiking trails to natural arches.

Rock obstacles embedded in the trail

Rattlesnake Canyon from the overlook

History

John Otto, "the hermit of Monument Canyon," settled in the Grand Junction area in the early 1900s and started constructing trails through the nearby canyons. Appreciating the beauty of the area, a number of Grand Junction residents joined Otto in petitioning the federal government to make the area a national park. On May 24, 1911, President William H. Taft

Sign near the beginning of the trail

established the area as Colorado National Monument. Otto was a strong proponent of building a road that would span the length of the entire monument.

The Serpent's Trail first opened up the monument to automobiles in 1921, but Otto's vision of a road traversing the length of the monument did not come to fruition until 1950. Construction for what would become known as Rim Rock Road began as early as 1931. Workers from the Civilian Conservation Corps, the depression-era agency established by Franklin Delano Roosevelt, helped greatly in building the road.

On December 12, 1933, a disastrous accident occurred during construction, when a group of workers accidentally brought down part of the cliff on fellow workers operating lower down the canyon. Nine men died. The attack on Pearl Harbor in 1941 and the country's subsequent entry into World War II virtually brought a halt to public work on the road project, as men were required for the war effort. With the end of the war, construction started again in 1949, and the road was completed the following year.

Rattlesnake Canyon, managed by the Colorado Bureau of Land Management, is located in the Black Ridge Canyons Wilderness, just outside Colorado National Monument. In 2000, President William Clinton signed into law the Colorado Canyons National Conservation Area and Black Ridge

Rocky section of the trail

Red standstone formation beside the trail

Canyons Wilderness Act, which protects 122,300 acres of land along a 24-mile stretch of the Colorado River. The name Colorado Canyons National Conservation Area was changed to McInnis Canyons National Conservation Area on January 1, 2005, in honor of former U.S. representative Scott McInnis.

Rattlesnake Canyon boasts nine natural arches, a number second only to Arches National Park near Moab, Utah. Some of the most notable are named Cedar Tree Arch (also known as Rainbow Arch), East Rim Arch (also known as Akiti Arch or Centennial Arch), and Bridge Arch (also known as Hole-in-the-Bridge Arch). These arches have a span measuring from 40 to 76 feet and a height ranging from 30 to 120 feet.

A natural arch, such as those found in Rattlesnake Canyon, is a rock exposure that has had a hole completely worn through it, leaving an intact frame. Erosion is the principal factor in the formation of arches. Although some argue that wind erosion creates arches, wind only polishes and shapes what other erosive forces have formed. These other erosion processes are numerous and include tectonic movement, glaciation, water flow, and rock expansion and contraction, among others.

Description

Access this trail by entering the Colorado National Monument through the west entrance, located south of Fruita off of Colorado 340. The drive through the monument takes about 25 minutes and is very scenic. The intersection of Rim Rock Road and CR 16.5, which is signed 5 miles to Glad Park Store, is the turnoff that marks the start of the trail.

Soon after the trail begins, it leaves the national monument and enters McInnis Canyons National Conservation Area. The road climbs to the intersection of Upper and Lower Roads. Which road you take will be determined by what time of year you are traveling. The Upper Road is open from April 15 to August 15, and the Lower Road is open from August 15 to February 15. Both roads are closed from February 15 through April 15. The directions below follow the Lower

Section of trail that can become washed out

The smooth beginning of Rattlesnake Canyon Trail

Road. The Upper Road is similar in character to the Lower Road.

Traveling along Black Ridge, the trail is one lane with plenty of room for passing oncoming vehicles. Primarily formed of dirt, this road is best avoided in wet conditions when it becomes slick with mud. Along this section, the trail is mainly smooth with a few widely dispersed embedded rocks and potholes and passes several dispersed camping areas. Pinyon and juniper pines, sagebrush, and rabbitbrush surround the trail and shelter the campsites. The low-growing vegetation allows for views over the Colorado River, the Grand Valley, and the red sandstone canyons within the Colorado National Monument. The difficulty rating is a 2 until the trail meets up with the Upper Road again after approximately 9 miles.

After the Upper and Lower Roads intersect at the Mee Canyon Overflow Parking Area, the trail enters a day use area. Camping is not allowed beyond this point, and the difficulty rating gradually increases as the trail progresses. The obstacles will vary depending upon the time of year you travel and when the road has last been repaired. Throughout the season draining water and wind can wash out sections of the trail, making travel more difficult. Plan on encountering large embedded rocks that create ledges and other obstacles through which drivers must pick a line in order to avoid damaging their vehicles. The difficulty rating increases to a 4 along the last couple of miles of the trail, and a high clearance 4WD is required.

For the last several miles, the trail parallels Rattlesnake Canyon to the west, and a good overlook is located at the 10.5-mile point. It is worth the time to stop and photograph the striking red sandstone canyon. Another overlook is located near the Rattlesnake Arches Trailhead, a short walk from the end of the trail. The scenery from that vantage point is also dramatic with expansive views of the Colorado River to the north running through red rock canyons.

Current Road Information

Colorado Bureau of Land Management
Grand Junction Field Office
2815 H Road
Grand Junction, CO 81506
(970) 244-3000

Map References

BLM Grand Junction
Maptech CD: Grand Junction/Western Slope
Benchmark's *Colorado Road & Recreation Atlas*, p. 82
Colorado Atlas & Gazetteer, p. 42
The Roads of Colorado, pp. 88, 89

Route Directions

▼ 0.0   Trail begins at the intersection of Rim Rock Road and CR 16.5, signed 5 miles to Glade Park Store. Zero trip meter and proceed west on paved CR 16.5.

GPS: N39°03.32′ W108°44.49′

▼ 0.1 SO Cattle guard; leave Colorado National Monument; pavement ends.
▼ 0.2 TR/SO Black Ridge Road on right; then seasonal gate; then enter McInnis Canyons National Conservation Area.

GPS: N39°03.29′ W108°44.68′

▼ 0.5 SO Cross through wash.
▼ 0.8 SO Cross through wash.
▼ 1.5 TR Lower Road on right and Upper Bench Road on left.

GPS: N39°03.66′ W108°45.66′

▼ 1.8 SO Track on right.
▼ 1.9 TL Road on right is short track to communications towers access and good overlook. Campsite on left. Turn left; then pass through seasonal closure gate.

Overlooking Colorado National Monument from the trail

© Benchmark Maps

0 ——— 2
mile

Main Trail

GPS: N39°03.89' W108°45.37'		
▼ 3.2	SO	Fence line.
▼ 3.9	SO	Campsite on right.
▼ 4.6	SO	Campsite on right.
▼ 4.7	SO	Cattle guard.
▼ 5.1	SO	Campsite on right.
▼ 8.6	SO	Cattle guard.
▼ 8.7	TR	Upper Bench Road and Mee Canyon Overflow Parking Area on left. Signposted trail beyond this point is day use only.
GPS: N39°06.44' W108°50.36'		
▼ 9.8	SO	Cross through wash area.
▼ 10.5	SO	Rattlesnake Canyon overlook on left.
GPS: N39°07.72' W108°50.18'		
▼ 11.2		Trail ends at Rattlesnake Arches Trailhead.
GPS: N39°08.22' W108°50.01'		

Caves and arches in the wall of Rattlesnake Canyone

Land's End Road

Starting Point:	**Intersection of US 50 and Kannah Creek Road**
Finishing Point:	**Intersection of Colorado 65 and Land's End Road (CR 100)**
Total Mileage:	**37.8 miles**
Unpaved Mileage:	**25.1 miles**
Driving Time:	**1.5 hours**
Elevation Range:	**4,843 to 10,658 feet**
Usually Open:	**July to October**
Difficulty Rating:	**1**
Scenic Rating:	**10**

Special Attractions

■ Dramatic shelf road climbing up to Grand Mesa.
■ Network of 4WD trails to explore.
■ Snowmobile and cross-country skiing trail in winter.

History

Sometime around a hundred million years ago a series of geological events began that would form the flat-topped mountain now known as Grand Mesa. At that time it is believed this area was on the boggy shoreline of a lake. Over time the sea dried up, and uplift caused the ground to rise. Volcanoes began to erupt, and lava flows covered the land, cooling to form Grand Mesa's flat surface. Sometime around 15 million years ago, glaciers moved across the lava rock surface, scooping out the large shallow depressions that have become the numerous lakes on Grand Mesa today.

Although the top of Grand Mesa ranges in elevation from approximately 10,000 to 11,000 feet, it is cloaked in lush vegetation such as Engelmann spruce and subalpine fir mixed

Land's End Road as it climbs to the top of Grand Mesa

THE NORTHERN REGION   237

with stands of aspen trees, grassy meadows filled with wild-flowers, and abundant wildlife. Archeological evidence recovered on Grand Mesa places human inhabitants on the mountain as early as 10,000 years ago. The first documented European exploration of Grand Mesa took place during the Dominguez-Escalante expedition in 1776 when the local Ute Indians guided the Spanish explorers over the mesa.

Farmers and ranchers settled the valley below Grand Mesa in the early 1880s. President Benjamin Harrison created what we know today as the Grand Mesa National Forest in 1892 to settle range wars between rival livestock operations. Originally named the Battlement Mesa Timberland Reserve, in 1924 it was renamed and placed under the administration of the U.S. Forest Service. The country's first forest ranger, William Kreutzer, lived in Cedaredge and managed the Grand Mesa.

Outdoor recreation has always been popular on Grand Mesa. The first resort community, Mesa Resort Company, was established in 1893. Promoting fishing on the large number of lakes on the mesa, the company constructed several lodges and more than 300 summer homes. Skiing is also a popular recreation activity on Grand Mesa. Dating back to 1939, Mesa Creek Ski Area was the first to establish organized ski runs. It relocated in 1964 and continues to operate today as the Powderhorn of the Grand Mesa Ski Area on the northern slopes of the mountain.

Scenic touring of Grand Mesa has also been a popular pursuit as early as the days of horse-drawn carriages. In those days Grand Mesa was remote and rugged, and carriage trips lasted several days. In 1895, the first road was constructed through Plateau Canyon and improved accessibility. Regular traffic including freight wagons and a stage route traversed the road. Again in 1911 the road was improved with the use of convict labor, and the route became part of the Pikes Peak Ocean-to-Ocean Highway, which was largely abandoned with the development of the federal highway system in the 1920s.

The Civilian Conservation Corps (CCC) constructed a second road to the summit of Grand Mesa in 1933. Originally known as the Veteran Road, the winding route was renamed Land's End Road and is now part of the Grand Mesa Scenic Byway. The CCC also constructed the stone building that is now home to the Land's End Observatory where visitors can overlook the Gunnison River Valley and the Colorado Plateau and see as far as the La Sal Mountains near Moab, Utah, and central Colorado on a clear day.

Description

This winding, scenic road is an exciting drive that is accessible to passenger vehicles in dry conditions. It begins as a paved two-lane county road at the intersection of US 50 and Kannah Creek Road, signed National Forest Access to Grand Mesa. Zero your trip meter and head east on Kannah Creek Road while enjoying the view of Grand Mesa rising up in the distance ahead. The road forks after approximately 3 miles, and you follow Land's End Road to the northeast.

After approximately 9.2 miles, the road enters the Grand Mesa National Forest, and the pavement ends. Here the road becomes wide, well maintained, and formed of dirt and gravel. It immediately begins to climb the western slopes of Grand Mesa, and passengers begin to see down into the surrounding canyons covered with pinyon and juniper pines, rabbitbrush, and sagebrush. The road progresses through a corridor of oak scrub brush and past pull-offs for camping, parking, and corrals for equestrians. Next the road begins to switchback, revealing expansive views back over the Juanita and Hallenback Reservoirs to the Gunnison River Valley and toward Grand Junction and the Uncompaghre Plateau.

Aggressively gaining elevation, the exciting shelf road clings to the mountain with significant drop-offs on its western edge. The drive is not difficult, and the few corrugations on the

A switchback near the end of the climb

Land's End Observatory

road's wide, sound surface do not present an obstacle to most vehicles. About a mile beyond the first overlook, the vegetation surrounding the trail begins to change because of the different atmospheric conditions at the higher elevation. Stands of aspen are mixed with oak scrub bushes, and conifers are more frequently mixed into the variety of trees growing alongside the trail. After approximately 14.5 miles, you will come to the Wild Rose USFS Picnic Area, which has a small parking area, picnic tables, corrals, and restroom facilities.

Beyond the seasonal closure gate past the picnic area, the road becomes increasingly narrow with plenty of room to pass oncoming vehicles, but the switchbacks create blind curves around which it is difficult to see oncoming traffic. Stay alert and drive carefully as the road climbs. Near the top of Grand Mesa, the switchbacks run through a rocky talus slide area with significant drop-offs. The road is narrowest at this point, and the turnouts should be used for passing oncoming traffic with care. Along with the interest of the changing scenery as the road climbs, views become more and more spectacular and expansive.

Land's End Observatory is located on the rim of Grand Mesa at the end of the climb up Land's End Road. It has the best vantage point from which to stop and admire the view. The observatory also has information boards on the history of Land's End Road and Grand Mesa. During business hours (daily 9:30 A.M. to 4:30 P.M. from July 1 to Labor Day and weekends in September), information, books, and maps are available in the gift shop. Interestingly, the observatory is built from the basalt rock that is commonly found on Grand Mesa.

At this point the road becomes paved and follows the southeast rim of the mesa. Along this section of road there are a few overlooks of the Kannah Creek Valley cloaked with its numerous stands of aspens, but they can be extremely rocky. Douglas fir and Engelmann spruce trees surround the open grassy, rocky meadows. Beyond the observatory, the road again becomes unpaved for a short distance, but it is a wide, graded road. Leaving the rim of Grand Mesa, the trail passes Raber Historic Cow Camp with two preserved cabins, interpretive signs, and a walking trail. The site is a replica of a summer camp that ranchers during the 1940s and 1950s would have established for the cowboys tending their herds of cattle grazing on the mesa. Not far beyond the Raber Camp, Land's End Road ends at the intersection with Colorado 65.

Current Road Information

Grand Mesa, Uncompahgre, & Gunnison National Forests
Grand Valley Ranger District
2777 Crossroads Boulevard, Suite 1
Grand Junction, CO 81506
(970) 242-8211

Grand Mesa Visitor Center
Located on US-65 at Cobbett Lake in Cedaredge
(970) 856-4153

Map References

USFS   Grand Mesa National Forest
Maptech CD: Grand Junction/Western Slope
Benchmark's *Colorado Road & Recreation Atlas*, p. 83
Colorado Atlas & Gazetteer, pp. 43, 44, 55
The Roads of Colorado, pp. 89, 90
Trails Illustrated, #136 (incomplete)

Route Directions

▼ 0.0	Trail begins at intersection of Colorado 50 and Kannah Creek Road signed National Forest Access, Grand Mesa, Land's End. Zero trip meter and proceed east on Kannah Creek Road.
9.2 ▲	Trail ends at intersection of Colorado 50. Turn right for Grand Mesa; turn left for Delta.

Carson Lake, one of the many scenic lakes near the trail

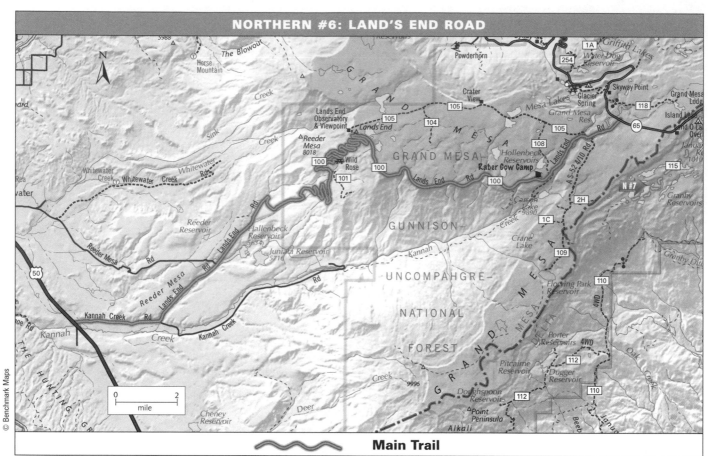

Main Trail

		GPS: N38°56.14' W108°23.78'	
▼ 2.9		BL	Road forks. Follow sign to Grand Mesa/Land's End.
	6.3 ▲	SO	Road on left. Proceed west on Land's End Road.
▼ 5.7		SO	Cattle guard.
	3.5 ▲	SO	Cattle guard.
▼ 6.3		SO	Cattle guard.
	2.9 ▲	SO	Cattle guard.
▼ 7.8		SO	Seasonal closure gate.
	1.5 ▲	SO	Seasonal closure gate.
▼ 9.2		SO	Cattle guard, pavement ends, and enter Grand Mesa National Forest. Zero trip meter.
	0.0 ▲		Continue traveling west on Land's End Road.
		GPS: N38°59.45' W108°16.24'	
▼ 0.0			Continue east on Land's End Road.
	3.9 ▲	SO	Exit Grand Mesa National Forest, cattle guard, and road becomes paved. Zero trip meter.
▼ 3.9		SO	Overlook on right. Zero trip meter.
	0.0 ▲		Continue descending switchbacks down Land's End Road.
		GPS: N38°59.53' W108°14.40'	
▼ 0.0			Continue ascending switchbacks up Land's End Road.
	7.9 ▲	SO	Overlook on left. Zero trip meter.
▼ 2.5		SO	Wild Rose National Forest Picnic Area on right.
	5.3 ▲	SO	Wild Rose National Forest Picnic Area on left.
		GPS: N39°00.74' W108°14.12'	
▼ 2.8		SO	Seasonal closure gate.
	5.1 ▲	SO	Seasonal closure gate.
▼ 4.7		SO	Overlook on left.
	3.2 ▲	SO	Overlook on right.

▼ 7.7		TL	Intersection signed Land's End Observatory to left, 0.25-mile and Colorado 65 to the right, 12 miles. Road becomes paved. Follow sign to Land's End Observatory.
	0.1 ▲	TR	Intersection with Land's End Road on right.
		GPS: N39°01.47' W108°13.34'	
▼ 7.9		TL	Enter Land's End Observatory parking lot. Zero trip meter at exit.
	0.0 ▲		Exit observatory parking lot, zeroing tip meter. Turn right onto paved road and proceed southeast.
		GPS: N39°01.55' W108°13.42'	
▼ 0.0			Exit observatory parking lot, zeroing trip meter. Turn right onto paved road and proceed southeast.
	1.8 ▲	TL	Enter Land's End Observatory parking lot. Zero trip meter at exit.
▼ 0.1		BL	Intersection with road on right. Signposted "Beginning of Grand Mesa Scenic Byway."
	1.7 ▲	SO	Intersection with road on left. Follow signs to Land's End Overlook.
▼ 0.7		SO	Cattle guard.
	1.1 ▲	SO	Cattle guard.
▼ 1.0		SO	Scenic overlook with good views on right.
	0.8 ▲	SO	Scenic overlook with good views on left.
▼ 1.8		SO	FR 100 3C to Coal Creek Overlook on right. Do not attempt in a passenger vehicle. Zero trip meter.
	0.0 ▲		Proceed northwest on CR 100, Land's End Road.
		GPS: N39°00.39' W108°12.32'	
▼ 0.0			Proceed southeast on CR 100, Grand Mesa Scenic Byway.
	6.5 ▲	SO	FR 100 3C to Coal Creek Overlook on left. Do not attempt in a passenger vehicle. Zero trip

© Benchmark Maps

		meter.
▼ 1.7	SO	Cattle guard and pavement ends.
4.8 ▲	SO	Pavement begins and cattle guard.
▼ 4.0	SO	Cattle guard.
2.5 ▲	SO	Cattle guard.
▼ 4.6	SO	Raber Cow Camp Historic Site on left and Deep Creek Trailhead #709 for hikers, horseback riders, and mountain bikers on right and left.
1.9 ▲	SO	Raber Cow Camp Historic Site on right and Deep Creek Trailhead #709 for hikers, horseback riders, and mountain bikers on left and right.
	GPS: N39°00.13' W108°07.93'	
▼ 6.5	SO	Intersection with FR 108 on left and right. Zero trip meter.
0.0 ▲		Proceed southwest on Land's End Road.
	GPS: N39°00.32' W108°06.22'	
▼ 0.0		Proceed northeast on Land's End Road.
1.9 ▲	SO	Intersection with FR 108 on right and left. Zero trip meter.
▼ 0.2	SO	Cattle guard.
1.7 ▲	SO	Cattle guard.
▼ 1.9	SO	Intersection with FR 105 on left. Zero trip meter.
0.0 ▲		Proceed west on Land's End Road.
	GPS: N39°01.48' W108°04.93'	
▼ 0.0		Continue east on Land's End Road.
1.4 ▲	SO	Intersection with FR 105 on right. Zero trip meter.
▼ 0.2	SO	Intersection with FR 109 on right.
1.3 ▲	SO	Intersection with FR 109 on left.
	GPS: N39°01.44' W108°04.72'	
▼ 1.1	SO	Reservoir #6 on left.
0.3 ▲	SO	Reservoir #6 on right.
	GPS: N39°01.74' W108°03.77'	
▼ 1.3	SO	Seasonal closure gate.
0.1 ▲	SO	Seasonal closure gate.
▼ 1.4		Restrooms on right and trail ends at intersection with Colorado 65. Turn left for Grand Junction (52 miles); turn right for Delta (35 miles).
0.0 ▲		Trail begins at intersection with Colorado 65 and Land's End Road (CR 100). Zero trip meter and proceed southwest on Land's End Road.
	GPS: N39°01.94' W108°03.52'	

Raber Historic Cow Camp

Granby Lakes Trail

Starting Point:	**Intersection of Colorado 65 and Island Lake Road**
Finishing Point:	**Shore of Big Battlement Lake**
Total Mileage:	**4.1 miles**
Unpaved Mileage:	**4.1 miles**
Driving Time:	**1 hour**
Elevation Range:	**9,960 to 10,460 feet**
Usually Open:	**July to October**
Difficulty Rating:	**5**
Scenic Rating:	**9**

Special Attractions

- Fall aspen viewing.
- Numerous lakes for fishing.
- Rocky, technical trail.

Description

This short, out-and-back trail begins as a paved road at the turnoff to Island Lake. Although it is only 4 miles, the ride is very rocky and slow going. The numerous scenic lakes and large aspen stands make the effort worthwhile, especially for drivers looking for an additional 4WD challenge. Proceed through the Island Lake USFS Campground where the paved road that loops through the campground intersects with FR 115. The campground is a fee area with nice, shady spots and

One of the many lakes beside the trail

Small pond near the beginning of the trail

A short smooth section of the trail

electrical hookups. Proceeding through the campground, you will arrive at a parking lot on the left and FR 115 on the right, where the trail really gets started.

This forest road is a narrow, rocky, one-lane track that is popular with dirt bike and ATV riders. A high clearance 4WD is required to travel this road, which is an infrequently maintained dirt road with a lot of embedded rocks, some of which are quite large. The basalt rocks embedded in the road protrude from the surface as much as 5 inches and can be quite sharp. A combination of careful wheel placement and the use of off-road tires will help prevent punctures.

The road follows a corridor through the conifer forest. Although the road is rocky, it can be quite muddy in wet conditions and can stay muddy for long periods after rain because the trees shade the road. In places, finding a good line through the large rocks can be difficult, especially within the first half mile of the trail. The numerous rocks make turning around almost impossible, so if you do not like the look of the begin-

The trail ends on the shoreline of Big Battlement Lake

View of Reservoir #7 from the trail

Private cabins near the end of the trail

ning of FR 115, do not attempt it. It is more difficult than it looks at the start of the forest road. As the trail progresses, the difficulty rating remains a consistent 5.

The forest that forms a canopy over the road becomes mixed with stands of aspen, and where the trees open up there are rock gardens and views of many lakes in the distance. Granby Reservoir #11 is located at the 2.5-mile point, and lakes surround the trail after traveling 3 miles.

Near the end, the trail passes two log cabins on private property, and the nearby lakes are surrounded by stands of aspen that glow a brilliant golden yellow in the fall. Passing Reservoir #7, the trail ends at the shore of Big Battlement Lake. Some backcountry campsites can be found around the lakes, and wildlife is also abundant in the vicinity.

Current Road Information

Grand Mesa, Uncompahgre, & Gunnison National Forests
Grand Valley Ranger District
2777 Crossroads Boulevard, Suite 1
Grand Junction, CO 81506
(970) 242-8211

Grand Mesa Visitor Center
Located on US 65 at Cobbett Lake in Cedaredge
(970) 856-4153

Map References

USFS   Grand Mesa National Forest
Maptech CD: Grand Junction/Western Slope
Benchmark's *Colorado Road & Recreation Atlas*, p. 83
Colorado Atlas & Gazetteer, pp. 44, 56
The Roads of Colorado, p. 90
Trails Illustrated, #136

Route Directions

▼ 0.0		Trail begins at Colorado 65 and Island Lake Road, signed to Island Lake.
	GPS: N39°02.34' W108°00.37'	
▼ 0.1	SO	Road on left.
	GPS: N39°02.30' W108°00.34'	
▼ 0.2	SO	Island Lake on left.
▼ 0.6	TR	Island Lake Campground on right. Zero trip meter.

	GPS: N39°01.89' W108°00.51'	
▼ 0.0		Proceed southwest into Island Lake Campground.
▼ 0.3	TR	Leave campground; then intersection with FR 115. Proceed southwest on FR 115.
	GPS: N39°01.70' W108°00.57'	
▼ 0.5	SO	Pond on left.
▼ 0.7	SO	Track on left.
	GPS: N39°01.48' W108°00.80'	
▼ 1.4	SO	Track on left.

The trail is rocky for its entire length

NORTHERN #7: GRANBY LAKES TRAIL

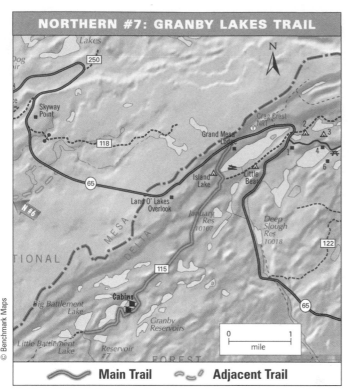

© Benchmark Maps

~~~ **Main Trail**   ~~~ **Adjacent Trail**

GPS: N39°00.92' W108°01.04'		
▼ 2.6	SO	Granby Reservoir #11 on left.
GPS: N39°00.28' W108°02.01'		
▼ 3.1	SO	Old corral on right.
▼ 3.5	BR	Intersection with several tracks. Track on left ends in 0.3 miles at Granby Reservoir #7. Zero trip meter.
GPS: N38°59.72' W108°02.48'		
▼ 0.0		Proceed west, taking the uphill trail.
▼ 0.3	SO	Ponds on right.
▼ 0.5	SO	Track on right.
▼ 0.6	SO	Big Battlement Lake on right.
▼ 0.7		Trail ends on shore of Big Battlement Lake.
GPS: N38°59.70' W108°03.40'		

NORTHERN REGION TRAIL #8

Bar HL to Rifle Gap Trail

Starting Point:	**Intersection of Northern #9: Buford Road and FR 211**
Finishing Point:	**Intersection of Colorado 325 and Colorado 13 in Rifle**
Total Mileage:	**41.3 miles**
Unpaved Mileage:	**30 miles**
Driving Time:	**3 hours**
Elevation Range:	**5,543 to 9,580 feet**
Usually Open:	**Late May to October**
Difficulty Rating:	**4**
Scenic Rating:	**10**

Stock pond beside the trail

Special Attractions

- Scenic, varied trail with good aspen fall color viewing.
- Spruce USFS Picnic Ground.
- Scenic Rifle Creek Canyon.
- A large network of forest roads to explore.
- Numerous backcountry and developed camping areas.
- Snowmobile and snowshoeing trails in winter.

History

Bar HL to Rifle Gap Trail begins by traveling over the rolling hills of the White River National Forest through territory that has been used for cattle grazing and ranching since the 1800s. In the area around the trail, the Elk Ranch is still run by the original owners, the Dodo family. The East Elk Ranch, the Puma Paw Ranch, and the Coulter Lake Guest Ranch operate year-round. The Guest Ranch rents cabins and provides numerous activities for its guests.

Rifle Mountain Park is one of three parks along the route. A special act of Congress, passed on June 7, 1910, allowed a number of municipalities throughout the country to claim land for the establishment of parks. Rifle claimed what would become Rifle Mountain Park. President Warren G. Harding made the park official on October 21, 1921. Today the park is renowned for its rock climbing.

Forest service signs direct travelers through the network of roads in the vicinity

After leaving Rifle Mountain Park, the trail passes by Rifle Falls State Park, well known for the triple waterfall Rifle Falls. Tourists have been visiting the falls since 1883. A grotto, formed by mist from the falls, continues to draw artists to the park.

Finally, the trail winds through Rifle Gap State Park. In 1967, Rifle Gap Reservoir, located in the park, was completed. The reservoir stores water from Rifle Creek, while a pumping plant distributes water from the Colorado River for irrigation purposes. Although a number of settlers initially came to the area as prospectors, many turned to farming and ranching after their attempts at mining failed. The reservoir helps sustain the agricultural industry in the region, which remains strong to this day.

The town of Rifle was established in 1882. It is named after nearby Rifle Creek, which is so called because around 1880, a soldier, placing mileposts between the Colorado and White Rivers, left his rifle alongside the creek. When he returned and found the rifle, he named the creek after his weapon.

More recently, Rifle has received some publicity from various art projects staged in and around the town. In 1972, artist Christo, known for his large-scale outdoor art installations, suspended his Valley Curtain across Rifle Gap. The Valley Curtain project took 28 months to complete but had to be re-moved after only 28 hours due to winds in excess of 60 mph. Rifle also served as the backdrop for part of the 1971 movie *Vanishing Point*.

Description

This scenic trail is a true backcountry adventure. Starting out, it winds through the rolling open pastures within the White River National Forest, traveling alternately through spruce, fir, and aspen stands. Then the scenery changes dramatically when the trail becomes a shelf road that switchbacks through an aspen forest down into the incredibly scenic Rifle Creek Canyon. This road, which is also a snowmobile trail in winter, can be extremely muddy in wet conditions and can become impassable. It is best to avoid the road in early spring when snowmelt saturates the ground or after recent periods of rain. Many forest roads, which are interesting to explore, intersect with the main trail throughout its entire length.

At the intersection of Northern #9: Buford Road (FR 245) and FR 211, the trail takes off on FR 211, heading northwest as a wide one-lane dirt road that is bumpy with potholes and embedded rocks. Rolling along through the hills of the open range, the trail is rutted in places, making a high-clearance 4WD preferable. After about 13 miles, the composition of the trail changes, and it becomes formed of a dark, soft soil with very few embedded rocks. This section of the trail is excep-

One of the many stands of aspen along the trail

View from the shelf section into Rifle Creek Valley

tionally mud-prone and becomes impassable when wet. Also embedded in this stretch of road are wheel ruts of up to a foot deep that have been created by vehicles traversing the road when it is boggy. These deep ruts must be negotiated even when the road is dry and will remain until the road is repaired or graded. Because a high-clearance 4WD vehicle is required to navigate the ruts without high centering, this section gives the trail its difficulty rating of 4.

The standard of the road improves over the next 2 miles as you approach the Rifle Creek Cow Camp with its old cabin alongside the trail. Beyond the gate at the cow camp, the road changes into a shelf road that descends for about 1.5 miles

This forest road is also a snowmobile route in the winter

through a large stand of aspen trees. Beyond the section of shelf road, the trail exits onto pastureland with good backcountry campsites. Views from the road on clear days can be quite scenic and expansive, especially in the fall when the aspen stands glow golden yellow. Cattle roam this section, and you are likely to encounter cows on the road.

About 2 miles beyond Orphan Spring, the trail comes to a cattle guard and an overlook of the Coulter Lake Guest Ranch deep within Rifle Creek Valley below. Here the scenery changes again as the trail becomes a shelf road that begins to switchback down into the valley through thick stands of aspen, Engelmann spruce, and blue spruce trees. Winding down into the canyon, the trail sheds 1,200 feet of elevation in approximately 3.5 miles.

At the bottom of the canyon, the trail becomes a wide, maintained dirt road traveling south along Rifle Creek through the forest of Engelmann spruce, blue spruce, and a few aspens. The scenic Spruce USFS Picnic Ground (fee area) is beside the creek at this location and is the perfect place to stop and take a break. Beyond the picnic ground, the trail leaves White River National Forest and enters Rifle Mountain Park (fee area) where dirt bikes and ATVs are prohibited. The park has scenic campsites with picnic tables and fire rings right on the creek. The walls of the canyon close in, and the road travels right beside Rifle Creek, winding through the narrow, very scenic ravine. Cottonwoods with yellow foliage in the fall grow along the creek, and there are established rock climbing routes on the canyon walls. Leaving Rifle Mountain Park, the trail becomes paved and runs through Rifle Falls State Park where the numerous waterfalls and limestone caves attract many visitors each year.

Beyond the Rifle Falls Fish Hatchery, the road becomes a major paved county road (CR 325), and the trail travels south on main roads through Rifle Gap State Park and past Rifle Gap Reservoir to its end in Rifle. Rifle Gap State Park has numerous facilities, including picnic tables, a campground, fishing, and boating access. After the trail crosses the Rifle Gap Dam, it ends about 3 miles farther south in the town of Rifle.

Current Road Information

White River National Forest
Blanco Ranger District
220 East Market Street
Meeker, CO 81641
(970) 878-4039

Rifle Falls State Park
5775 US 325
Rifle, CO 81650
(970) 625-1607

Rifle Gap State Park
5775 US 325
Rifle, CO 81650
(970) 625-1607

Map References

USFS   White River National Forest
Maptech CD: Craig/Meeker/Northwest
Benchmark's *Colorado Road & Recreation Atlas*, p. 70
Colorado Atlas & Gazetteer, pp. 34, 35
The Roads of Colorado, p. 75
Trails Illustrated, #125 (incomplete)

Spruce USFS Picnic Ground

Route Directions

▼ 0.0			Trail begins at the intersection of Northern #9: Buford Road and FR 211. Proceed southwest on FR 211.
	9.3 ▲		Trail ends at the intersection of Northern #9: Buford Road and FR 211.
		GPS: N39°48.18' W107°37.94'	
▼ 0.4		SO	Intersection with FR 825 on left signed to Little Box Canyon.
	8.9 ▲	SO	Intersection with FR 825 on right signed to Little Box Canyon.
▼ 1.4		SO	Tracks on left and right; then corral on left.
	7.9 ▲	SO	Corral on right; then tracks on left and right.
▼ 1.7		SO	FR 210 on right.
	7.6 ▲	SO	FR 210 on left.
		GPS: N39°48.60' W107°39.34'	

Rifle Creek Cow Camp

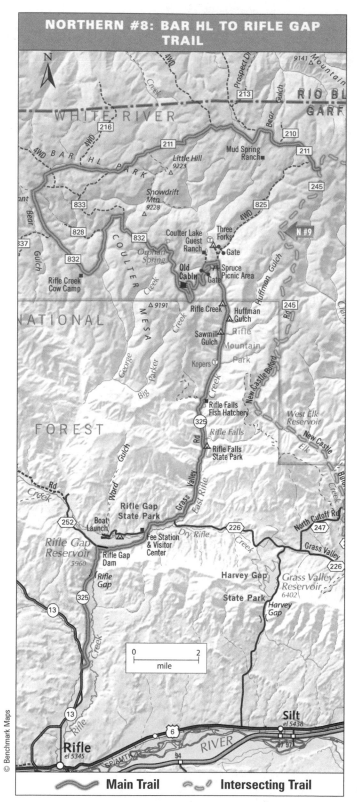

Main Trail   Intersecting Trail

▼ 2.7		BL	FR 212 on right.
	6.6 ▲	SO	FR 212 on left.

GPS: N39°49.03' W107°40.06'

▼ 4.0		SO	FR 214 on right signed Four Mile Road, 6 miles to East Miller Creek.
	5.3 ▲	SO	FR 214 on left signed Four Mile Road, 6 miles to East Miller Creek.
▼ 5.9		SO	Cattle guard.

© Benchmark Maps

	3.4 ▲	SO	Cattle guard.
▼ 7.0		SO	Trailhead and parking area on left.
	2.3 ▲	SO	Trailhead and parking area on right.

GPS: N39°48.34' W107°44.15'

▼ 8.0		SO	Bar HL Cow Camp on left.
	1.3 ▲	SO	Bar HL Cow camp on right.
▼ 9.3		SO	FR 216 on right. Zero trip meter.
	0.0 ▲		Proceed east on FR 211.

GPS: N39°47.93' W107°46.31'

▼ 0.0			Proceed west on FR 211.
	16.0 ▲	SO	FR 216 on left. Zero trip meter.
▼ 1.0		SO	Cattle guard.
	14.9 ▲	SO	Cattle guard.
▼ 1.2		SO	Intersection with FR 217 on right and left.
	14.8 ▲	SO	Intersection with FR 217 on right and left.

GPS: N39°47.79' W107°47.54'

▼ 1.4		SO	Cattle guard.
	14.6 ▲	SO	Cattle guard.
▼ 1.7		SO	FR 833 on left.
	14.3 ▲	SO	FR 833 on right.
▼ 2.1		SO	FR 211.2A on right.
	13.9 ▲	SO	FR 211.2A on left.
▼ 3.5		SO	FR 837 on right. Proceed southeast on FR 832.
	12.4 ▲	SO	FR 837 on left. Proceed northwest on FR 832.

GPS: N39°46.156' W107°47.45'

▼ 5.0		SO	Gate—leave it as you found it.
	10.9 ▲	SO	Gate—leave it as you found it.
▼ 5.2		SO	Rifle Creek Cow Camp on right.
	10.8 ▲	SO	Rifle Creek Cow Camp on left.
▼ 5.3		SO	Gate—leave it as you found it.
	10.7 ▲	SO	Gate—leave it as you found it.

Wheel ruts show the trail gets very muddy in wet conditions

▼ 6.8	SO	Cattle guard.
9.1 ▲	SO	Cattle guard.
▼ 7.4	SO	Old cabin in valley on right.
8.55 ▲	SO	Old cabin in valley on left.
▼ 7.5	SO	Cattle guard.
8.4 ▲	SO	Cattle guard.
▼ 8.1	SO	Intersection with FR 832 straight on and FR 833 on left.
7.9 ▲	BL	Intersection with FR 833 on right. Proceed to the left on FR 832.

GPS: N39°46.60' W107°44.91'

| ▼ 8.8 | SO | Pond on left. |
| 7.2 ▲ | SO | Pond on right. |

GPS: N39°46.20' W107°44.67'

▼ 9.2	SO	Road on right.
6.8 ▲	SO	Road on left.
▼ 10.1	SO	Orphan Spring on left.
5.9 ▲	SO	Orphan Spring on right.

GPS: N39°45.79' W107°43.56'

▼ 11.1	SO	FR 835 on right.
4.9 ▲	SO	FR 835 on left.
▼ 12.1	SO	Cattle guard.
3.9 ▲	SO	Cattle guard.
▼ 13.8	SO	N221 Road on left.
2.2 ▲	SO	N221 Road on right.

GPS: N39°45.25' W107°42.00'

▼ 15.4	SO	Seasonal closure gate; then road on left signed to Coulter Lake Guest Ranch.
0.6 ▲	SO	Road on right signed to Coulter Lake Guest Ranch; then seasonal closure gate.
▼ 16.0	TR	T-intersection with FR 825 to the left. FR 832 to the right signed to CR 325 and 15 miles to

The trail in Rifle Mountain Park

| | | Rifle. Zero trip meter. |
| 0.0 ▲ | | Proceed northwest on FR 832. |

GPS: N39°45.47' W107°41.54'

▼ 0.0		Proceed southeast on FR 832 toward Colorado 325 and Rifle.
16.1 ▲	TL	T-intersection with FR 825 to the right. FR 832 to the left. Zero trip meter.
▼ 0.2	SO	Spruce USFS Picnic Ground on right.
15.9 ▲	SO	Spruce USFS Picnic Ground on left.

GPS: N39°45.26' W107°41.50'

▼ 1.3	SO	Exit White River National Forest and enter Rifle Mountain Park (fee area). Road becomes CR 217. Information board on left; then cattle guard.
14.8 ▲	SO	Cattle guard; then information board on right. Leave Rifle Mountain Park (fee area) and enter White River National Forest and road becomes FR 832.
▼ 2.0	SO	Campground on left.

Old cow camp beside the trail

Mud Spring Ranch alongside FR 211

14.1 ▲	SO	Campground on right.	
▼ 2.3	SO	Campground on right.	
13.8 ▲	SO	Campground on left.	
▼ 2.7	SO	Bridge over creek.	
13.4 ▲	SO	Bridge over creek.	
▼ 3.8	SO	Cross over creek.	
12.3 ▲	SO	Cross over creek.	

▼ 4.2	SO	Exit Rifle Mountain Park and information board on left.	
12.0 ▲	SO	Information board on right and enter Rifle Mountain Park.	
▼ 4.8	SO	Road becomes Colorado 325 and pavement begins.	
11.3 ▲	SO	Pavement ends and road becomes CR 217.	
		GPS: N39°41.77′ W107°41.98′	
▼ 4.9	SO	Rifle Falls Fish Hatchery on left and parking area on right.	
11.2 ▲	SO	Parking area on left and Rifle Falls Fish Hatchery on right.	
▼ 6.5	SO	Rifle Falls State Park on left.	
9.6 ▲	SO	Rifle Falls State Park on right.	
▼ 10.5	SO	Enter Rifle Gap State Park.	
5.6 ▲	SO	Leave Rifle Gap State Park.	
▼ 11.6	SO	Rifle Gap Reservoir on right.	
4.5 ▲	SO	Rifle Gap Reservoir on left.	
▼ 11.8	SO	Rifle Gap Reservoir and Dam.	
4.3 ▲	SO	Rifle Gap Reservoir and Dam.	
▼ 13.2	SO	Golf course.	
2.9 ▲	SO	Golf course.	
▼ 16.1		Trail ends at the intersection with Colorado 13 in Rifle.	
0.0 ▲		Trail begins at intersection of Colorado 13 and Colorado 325 in Rifle. Zero trip meter and proceed north on Colorado 325.	
		GPS: N39°34.47′ W107°46.27′	

Scenic, narrow Rifle Creek Canyon in Rifle Mountain Park

Buford Road

Starting Point:	**Intersection of 7th Street and Main Street in New Castle**
Finishing Point:	**General Store in Buford**
Total Mileage:	**49.7 miles, including spur**
Unpaved Mileage:	**40.6 miles**
Driving Time:	**3 hours**
Elevation Range:	**5,561 to 10,098 feet**
Usually Open:	**Early June to November**
Difficulty Rating:	**2**
Scenic Rating:	**9**

Special Attractions

- Easygoing, scenic forest road.
- Outstanding aspen viewing in the fall.
- Network of forest roads to explore.

History

This road travels north from the town of New Castle to Buford along a scenic forest road. In the early 1880s, settlers in the town of New Castle, Colorado, discovered rich coal deposits in the region. Although the town was first known as Grand Buttes and later Chapman, it was incorporated as New Castle on February 2, 1888, after the English mining center of Newcastle-upon-Tyne. New Castle claimed two of the best-producing coal mines in the county, the Consolidated Mine on Ward's Peak and the Vulcan Mine on Roderick's Ridge.

Once mined, the coal was taken by rail to Aspen and Leadville to power their smelters. Two train depots for the Denver & Rio Grande Railroad and the Colorado Midland Railway could be found in New Castle, making relatively fast transportation of coal and supplies among population centers possible.

With the mining boom of the 1890s, New Castle's population grew rapidly, fluctuating between 1,500 and 2,500 peo-

The trail runs through large aspen stands

ple. A number of businesses sprung up to meet the needs of the new town, and by 1889 the Colorado Business Directory listed 50 businesses in New Castle, 10 of which were saloons.

On February 18, 1896, disaster struck New Castle when the Vulcan Mine exploded, killing 49 men. Other mines in the area had high levels of methane gas, which made for unstable conditions. By 1899, both the Vulcan and the Consolidated Mines were closed, and the population had dipped to 431. Despite the explosion—which had occurred just a little more than a decade earlier—a mining company began operations in 1910, just 200 yards from the site of the original Vulcan Mine. On December 16, 1913, this mine exploded, taking the lives of 37 miners.

After this explosion, mining activity in the area declined. New Castle maintained a steady population of about 700 residents. Today a memorial statue, erected in 2004, rests in Burning Mountain Park, honoring the lives of the miners lost to the blasts. In the nearby closed mines, steam still spurts out on occasion.

Description

This easygoing, scenic drive, which is accessible to passenger vehicles in dry conditions, travels out of the sleepy town of New Castle north through the White River National Forest to the town of Buford. For its entire length, this trail is a well-maintained, two-lane dirt road that may develop some corru-

Restroom at the edge of a wide clearing beside the trail

Bridge at the south end of Meadow Lake near the end of the spur

Meadow Lake

gations and potholes between maintenance. The road can be boggy in sections and is best avoided when wet. Navigation is not difficult with the exception of residential New Castle. Sticking to the main roads heading northwest out of town will take you to the Buford Road Forest Access.

Traveling through a corridor of trees for most of its length, numerous stands of aspen are mixed into the evergreen forest, making for truly outstanding fall aspen viewing. Hundreds of good, level, shady backcountry campsites are located near the trail, and the Meadow Lake USFS Campground (fee area) is at the end of the spur to the scenic Meadow Lake. A boat ramp at the lake is for boats with electric motors only. Restroom facilities are also located at the lake.

In sections that are not densely forested, the road travels through rolling idyllic pastureland. From the main trail near the spur to Meadow Lake, views into the South Fork Canyon are also visible through the trees. Lake Avery State Wildlife Area with a picnic area overlooking the scenic lake is also located at the north end of the trail.

Current Road Information

White River National Forest
Blanco Ranger District
220 East Market Street
Meeker, CO 81641
(970) 878-4039

White River National Forest
Rifle Ranger District
0094 CR 244
Rifle, CO 81650
(970) 625-2371

Map References

USFS   White River National Forest
Maptech CD: Criag/Meeker/Northwest
Benchmark's *Colorado Road & Recreation Atlas*, pp. 58, 70

Colorado Atlas & Gazetteer, pp. 34, 35
The Roads of Colorado, pp. 59, 75
Trails Illustrated, #124, #125 (incomplete)

Route Directions

▼ 0.0		Trail begins at the intersection of 7th Street and Main Street in New Castle. Zero trip meter and proceed north on 7th Street through a residential area; then the road becomes Rio Grande Avenue.
9.1 ▲		Trail ends at the intersection of 7th Street and Main Street in New Castle.
		GPS: N39°34.30' W107°32.24'
▼ 0.6	SO	Intersection with 2nd Street.
8.6 ▲	SO	Intersection with 2nd Street.
▼ 0.7	BL	Road on right.
8.4 ▲	BR	Road on left.
▼ 1.4	BL	Fork with unpaved road straight ahead. Proceed northwest on Castle Valley Boulevard.
7.7 ▲	SO	Proceed south on Rio Grande Avenue.
▼ 1.9	BL	Fork.
7.2 ▲	SO	Road on right.
▼ 4.8	TR	Intersection with CR 245 on right, signed National Forest Access to Buford.
4.3 ▲	TL	Intersection with CR 245 and Buford Road.
		GPS: N39°36.64' W107°36.26'
▼ 9.1	SO	Cattle guard, pavement ends, and enter White River National Forest. Zero trip meter.
0.0 ▲		Proceed southeast on wide, maintained dirt road.
		GPS: N39°39.90' W107°37.53'
▼ 0.0		Proceed northwest on wide, maintained dirt road.
13.5 ▲	SO	Leave White River National Forest. Pavement begins; then cattle guard. Zero trip meter.
▼ 0.5	SO	White River National Forest information board on right.
13.1 ▲	SO	White River National Forest information board on left.
▼ 1.0	SO	Trail #2256, Fowler Creek Hiking Trail on right.
12.5 ▲	SO	Trail #2256, Fowler Creek Hiking Trail on left.

▼ 1.9		**SO**	Pond on left.
	11.6 ▲	**SO**	Pond on right.
▼ 2.3		**SO**	Cattle guard.
	11.2 ▲	**SO**	Cattle guard.
▼ 7.5		**SO**	Triangle Park. Parking area and restrooms on left.
	6.0 ▲	**SO**	Triangle Park. Parking area and restrooms on right.

GPS: N39°43.94' W107°38.86'

▼ 7.7		**SO**	FR 820 on right.
	5.8 ▲	**SO**	FR 820 on left.

GPS: N39°44.09' W107°38.84'

▼ 8.3		**SO**	Cattle guard; then seasonal closure gate.
	5.2 ▲	**SO**	Seasonal closure gate; then cattle guard.
▼ 9.8		**SO**	Seasonal closure gate.
	3.7 ▲	**SO**	Seasonal closure gate.
▼ 10.7		**SO**	FR 860 on left.
	2.8 ▲	**SO**	FR 860 on right.

GPS: N39°46.13' W107°39.22'

▼ 12.7		**SO**	Seasonal closure gate.
	0.8 ▲	**SO**	Seasonal closure gate.
▼ 13.1		**SO**	FR 830 on right.
	0.4 ▲	**SO**	FR 830 on left.

GPS: N39°47.68' W107°37.88'

▼ 13.5		**SO**	Northern #8: Bar HL to Rifle Gap Trail on left, signed 5 miles to Rifle Creek and 7 miles to Bar HL Park. Zero trip meter.
	0.0 ▲		Proceed south on FR 245 toward New Castle.

GPS: N39°48.01' W107°37.94'

▼ 0.0			Proceed north on FR 245 toward Buford.
	6.3 ▲	**SO**	Northern #8: Bar HL to Rifle Gap Trail on right, signed 5 miles to Rifle Creek and 7 miles to Bar HL Park. Zero trip meter.

▼ 1.6		**SO**	Cattle guard.
	4.7 ▲	**SO**	Cattle guard.
▼ 1.8		**SO**	Middle Mountain Road (FR 248) on left.
	4.5 ▲	**SO**	Middle Mountain Road (FR 248) on right.

GPS: N39°48.44' W107°36.52'

▼ 2.9		**SO**	Cattle guard.
	3.4 ▲	**SO**	Cattle guard.
▼ 3.1		**SO**	FR 822 on right signed to Clark Ridge and 17 miles to Buford.
	3.2 ▲	**SO**	FR 822 on left signed to Clark Ridge and 32 miles to New Castle.

GPS: N39°48.35' W107°35.42'

▼ 4.6		**SO**	FR 248 on left.
	1.7 ▲	**SO**	FR 248 on right.
▼ 6.3		**SO**	FR 601 on right. Zero trip meter.
	0.0 ▲		Proceed south on FR 245.

GPS: N39°50.73' W107°34.74'

Spur to Meadow Lake

▼ 0.0		**TR**	Leave main trail and proceed southeast on FR 601 toward Meadow Lake.
▼ 2.4		**SO**	Trail #1831 on left.
▼ 2.5		**SO**	Hiking trail to Cliff Lakes on left.
▼ 3.1		**SO**	FR 601.4D on right.
▼ 3.5		**TR**	Intersection with FR 601 straight ahead continuing to Cow Lake and Blair Mountain. Proceed south on FR 823 toward Meadow Lake.

GPS: N39°49.86' W107°32.55'

▼ 5.4		**TR**	Intersection with FR 821 straight ahead. Remain on FR 823 to Meadow Lake.
▼ 5.7		**BL**	Meadow Lake USFS Campground on right. Continue toward Meadow Lake.
▼ 5.9		**SO**	Boat ramp and restroom facilities on left.
▼ 6.1			Spur ends at Meadow Lake parking area.

Golden aspens along the trail in the fall

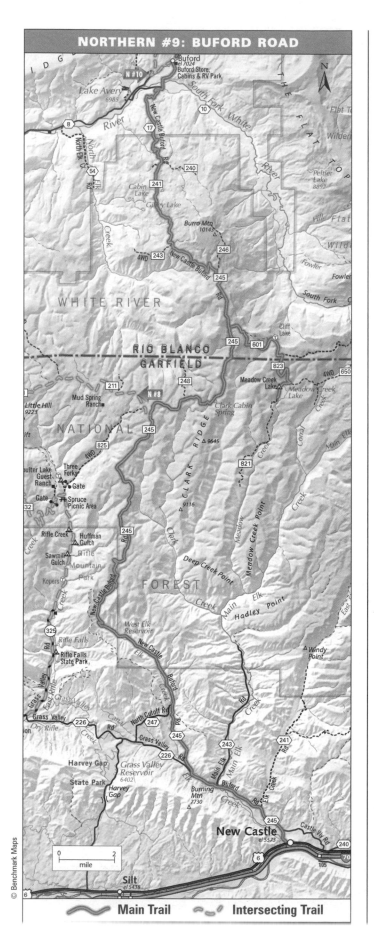

Main Trail ～～ **Intersecting Trail** ～～

Continuation of Main Trail

▼ 0.0			Proceed north on FR 245 toward Buford.
	14.5 ▲	SO	FR 601 on left. Zero trip meter.

GPS: N39°50.73' W107°34.74'

▼ 2.2		SO	FR 246 on right.
	12.3 ▲	SO	FR 246 on left.

▼ 4.9		SO	FR 243 on left.
	9.6 ▲	SO	FR 243 on right.

▼ 7.1		SO	Trail #1833 for hiking and horseback riding on left.
	7.4 ▲	SO	Trail #1833 for hiking and horseback riding on right.

▼ 7.4		SO	Cattle guard.
	7.1 ▲	SO	Cattle guard.

▼ 7.5		SO	Cattle guard.
	7.0 ▲	SO	Cattle guard.

▼ 8.0		SO	Cattle guard.
	6.5 ▲	SO	Cattle guard.

▼ 8.4		SO	FR 241 on left.
	6.1 ▲	SO	FR 241 on right.

▼ 9.6		SO	USFS information board on left.
	4.9 ▲	SO	USFS information board on right.

▼ 9.9		SO	Cattle guard.
	4.6 ▲	SO	Cattle guard.

▼ 13.1		SO	Intersection with CR 10 on left and track on right.
	1.4 ▲	BR	CR 17 on right and track on left.

GPS: N39°58.34' W107°37.46'

▼ 13.2		SO	South Fork Road on right signed National Forest Access; then cross bridge over the North Fork of the White River.
	1.3 ▲	SO	Cross bridge over North Fork of the White River; then South Fork Road on left.

▼ 14.4		TR	T-intersection with CR 8.
	0.1 ▲	TL	Intersection with Buford Road (CR 17) on left.

▼ 14.5			Trail ends at the General Store in the town of Buford and the intersection of Northern #10: Sleepy Cat and Thornburgh Battle Trail and Northern #11: Flat Tops Trail.
	0.0 ▲		Trail begins at the General Store in the town of Buford and the intersection of Northern #10: Sleepy Cat and Thornburgh Battle Trail and Northern #11: Flat Tops Trail. Zero trip meter and proceed southwest on CR 8.

GPS: N39°59.25' W107°36.99'

Buford General Store

Sleepy Cat and Thornburgh Battle Trail

Starting Point:	General Store on CR 8 in Buford
Finishing Point:	Intersection of Colorado 13 and CR 45
	30 miles northeast of Meeker
Total Mileage:	41.5 miles
Unpaved Mileage:	40.2 miles
Driving Time:	3.5 hours
Elevation Range:	6,341 to 9,539 feet
Usually Open:	Mid-May to early November
Difficulty Rating:	3
Scenic Rating:	9

Special Attractions

- Scenic trail with some 4WD challenges.
- Thornburgh Indian Battle Site.
- Network of forest roads to explore.
- Good backcountry campsites.

History

Once a Ute trail, this route follows part of what used to be a government road running from Meeker, Colorado, to Rawlins, Wyoming. The newly formed Colorado Territory granted a charter in 1861 to the Colorado and Pacific Wagon, Telegraph and Railroad Company, allowing the company to cross Yellow Jacket Pass. Three years later, the territory issued a similar charter to the Pacific Wagon Road Company, which operated the Berthoud Salt Lake Wagon Road.

During Ferdinand V. Hayden's survey of Colorado, he mapped the Yellow Jacket Pass area. By 1876, the pass appeared on maps and was a frequently used travel route.

In 1879, Ute Indians attacked Major Thomas Thornburgh and his cavalry unit along the trail. Major Thornburgh was killed along with 13 of his men. The unit had been called to the area at the request of Indian agent Nathan Meeker, who

The road can be boggy in wet conditions

believed troops were necessary to "civilize" the uncooperative Ute. Before the attack, Thornburgh met with some Ute tribal leaders who expressed their mistrust of Meeker and the soldiers.

Due to the volatility of the situation, Thornburgh decided he would enter Ute Reservation lands with only a small party of men in order to avoid immediate conflict. He was unable to act on this plan, however, because the Ute attacked the party near the reservation border. When more troops later arrived in support, the Ute raised the flag of surrender but not before they had killed Meeker and 11 men at the Indian agency in what would become known as the Meeker Massacre. A sign just north of the pass commemorates the attack by the Ute on Major Thornburgh.

Description

This trail begins at the General Store in Buford and travels a short distance southwest on CR 8 to the intersection with CR 115, signed National Forest Access to Sleepy Cat. This intersection is less than 1.5 miles from the store.

At the beginning, the trail climbs past the turnoff to Avery Lake State Wildlife Area (fee area) and a private residence before entering White River National Forest where the road be-

Avery Lake State Wildlife Area

One of the many forest service signs directing travelers through the network of roads

Intersection of several forest roads not far from Yellow Jacket Pass

out to the northeast after approximately 13 miles for the rocky peak that resembles a cat curled up sleeping. Beyond this point, the trail begins to descend toward Yellow Jacket Pass at the intersection of FR 250 and CR 15.

The trail leaves the forest, crosses Yellow Jacket Pass, and begins traveling northeast on CR 15. The county road is wide, maintained, and formed of dirt and gravel. This section of the trail is accessible to passenger vehicles in good conditions. After about 4.7 miles, you will arrive at the historical markers for the Thornburgh Indian Battle of 1879 on the west side of the trail. One monument commemorates the U.S. Army soldiers lost in the battle, and the other is a memorial to the Indian warriors lost in the fight. Beyond the battle site, the road becomes CR 45, and it travels through open ranchland until its end just beyond the interesting rock formation, Monument Butte, at the intersection with Colorado 13.

Current Road Information

White River National Forest
Blanco Ranger District
220 East Market Street
Meeker, CO 81641
(970) 878-4039

Map References

USFS   White River National Forest
Maptech CD: Craig/Meeker/Northwest
Benchmark's *Colorado Road & Recreation Atlas,* p. 58
Colorado Atlas & Gazetteer, pp. 24, 25
The Roads of Colorado, p. 59
Trails Illustrated, #124 (incomplete)

comes FR 250. For most of its length this forest road travels through dense oak scrub, aspen, and conifer forest. Obstacles include a long creek crossing, erosion, ruts, and embedded rocks. These elements give the trail its difficulty rating of 3. They should not present an obstacle to high-clearance stock 4WD vehicles and mainly serve to make the trail bumpy and slow going. It is best to avoid this road in wet conditions because it can become muddy and impassible.

This trail is a typical narrow forest road. It is one-lane, but there are plenty of pullouts for passing oncoming vehicles. Climbing to its high point near Sleepy Cat Peak, after which the trail is named, it can be steep in short sections. Keep an eye

The narrow forest road runs through large aspen stands

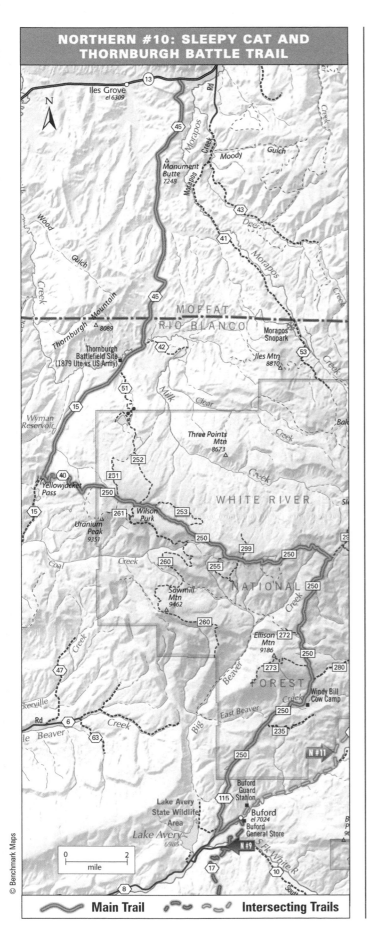

NORTHERN #10: SLEEPY CAT AND THORNBURGH BATTLE TRAIL

〜〜 **Main Trail**   ⌁ ⌁ ⌁ **Intersecting Trails**

© Benchmark Maps

Route Directions

▼ 0.0		Trail begins at the General Store in Buford at the intersection of Northern #9: Buford Road and Northern #11: Flat Tops Trail on CR 8. Zero trip meter and proceed southwest on CR 8.
8.6 ▲		Trail ends at the General Store in Buford.

GPS: N39°59.25' W107°37.00'

▼ 1.3	TR	Road on right is signed National Forest Access to Sleepy Cat. Pavement ends.
7.3 ▲	TL	Pavement begins at the intersection with CR 8.

GPS: N39°58.58' W107°38.13'

▼ 1.6	SO	Cattle guard.
7.0 ▲	SO	Cattle guard.
▼ 1.7	BR	Road straight ahead dead-ends in 0.8 miles at Avery Lake Picnic Area and overlook.
6.9 ▲	SO	Road on right dead-ends in 0.8 miles at Avery Lake Picnic Area and overlook.
▼ 2.3	BR	Camping area on left. Signposted to East Beaver, 5 miles.
6.4 ▲	BL	Camping area on right. Signposted to East Beaver, 5 miles.
▼ 2.5	SO	Cattle guard.
6.2 ▲	SO	Cattle guard.
▼ 3.6	SO	Enter White River National Forest. Trail becomes FR 250; then seasonal closure gate.
5.1 ▲	SO	Seasonal closure gate; then exit White River National Forest.

Monument to the U.S. Army soldiers lost in the Thornburgh Battle

▼ 3.9		SO	Pond on left.
	4.7 ▲	SO	Pond on right.
▼ 4.2		SO	White River National Forest information board on right.
	4.5 ▲	SO	White River National Forest information board on left.
▼ 5.1		SO	Cattle guard.
	3.6 ▲	SO	Cattle guard.
▼ 5.8		SO	Road on right; then cattle guard.
	2.8 ▲	SO	Cattle guard; then road on left.
		GPS: N40°01.80′ W107°36.22′	
▼ 6.7		SO	Cross through East Beaver Creek; then track on left.
	2.0 ▲	SO	Track on right; then cross through East Beaver Creek.
		GPS: N40°02.22′ W107°35.62′	
▼ 8.1		SO	Track on left.
	0.5 ▲	SO	Track on right.
▼ 8.4		SO	FR 289 on right.
	0.3 ▲	SO	FR 289 on left.
		GPS: N40°02.93′ W107°34.44′	
▼ 8.6		SO	FR 280 on right. Zero trip meter.
	0.0 ▲		Proceed south on FR 250.
		GPS: N40°03.142′ W107°34.39′	

▼ 0.0			Proceed north on FR 250.
	5.0 ▲	SO	FR 280 on left. Zero trip meter.
▼ 0.4		SO	FR 273 on left.
	4.6 ▲	SO	FR 273 on right.
▼ 1.6		SO	FR 272 on left.
	3.4 ▲	SO	FR 272 on right.
▼ 2.1		SO	Road on right.
	2.9 ▲	BR	Road on left.
		GPS: N40°04.65′ W107°34.88′	
▼ 2.6		SO	Road on right.
	2.4 ▲	BR	Road on left.
		GPS: N40°04.97′ W107°34.71′	
▼ 3.5		SO	FR 270 on right.
	1.5 ▲	SO	FR 270 on left.
▼ 5.0		TL	Intersection with FR 290 on right. Signposted Yellow Jacket 10 miles to the left, and Little Lost Park 5 miles to the right. Zero trip meter.
	0.0 ▲		Proceed southwest on FR 250.
		GPS: N40°03.142′ W107°34.39′	
▼ 0.0			Proceed north on FR 250.
	8.1 ▲	TR	Intersection with FR 290 on left. Zero trip meter.
▼ 1.3		SO	Cross through creek.
	6.8 ▲	SO	Cross through creek.
		GPS: N40°06.893′ W107°34.83′	

Wide crossing of East Beaver Creek

▼ 1.7		SO	Cross through creek.
	6.4 ▲	SO	Cross through creek.
▼ 2.0		SO	Cross through creek.
	6.1 ▲	SO	Cross through creek.
▼ 2.9		SO	FR 258 on left.
	5.2 ▲	BL	FR 258 on right.
▼ 4.8		SO	FR 255 on left.
	3.3 ▲	SO	FR 255 on right.
▼ 6.1		BL	FR 254 on right.
	2.0 ▲	BR	FR 254 on left.
	GPS: N40°07.47′ W107°39.02′		
▼ 7.4		SO	Road on right.
	0.7 ▲	SO	Road on left.
	GPS: N40°07.99′ W107°40.21′		
▼ 7.8		SO	Two roads on left.
	0.3 ▲	SO	Two roads on right.
	GPS: N40°08.04′ W107°40.64′		
▼ 8.0		SO	FR 252 on right, signed 4 miles to Aldrich Lakes.
	50 yds ▲	BR	FR 252 on left, signed 4 miles to Aldrich Lakes.
▼ 8.1		SO	FR 260 on left. Zero trip meter.
	0.0 ▲		Proceed southeast on FR 250.
	GPS: N40°08.09′ W107°40.92′		
▼ 0.0			Proceed northwest on FR 250.
	4.3 ▲	SO	FR 260 on right. Zero trip meter.
▼ 0.7		SO	FR 251 on right.
	3.6 ▲	SO	FR 251 on left.
▼ 1.5		SO	White River National Forest information board on right.
	2.8 ▲	SO	White River National Forest information board on left.
▼ 1.7		SO	Cattle guard.
	2.6 ▲	SO	Cattle guard.
▼ 4.3		TR	Cattle guard; then seasonal closure gate at intersection with CR 15 at Yellow Jacket Pass. Zero trip meter.
	0.0 ▲		Proceed southwest on FR 250 through cattle guard.
	GPS: N40°08.88′ W107°44.40′		
▼ 0.0			Proceed northeast on CR 15 toward Thornburgh Battle Site.
	15.5 ▲	TL	Seasonal closure gate at intersection with CR 15 at Yellow Jacket Pass. Zero trip meter.
▼ 4.6		SO	CR 51 on right.
	10.9 ▲	SO	CR 51 on left.
▼ 4.7		SO	Thornburgh Battle Site with 2 monuments on left.
	10.8 ▲	SO	Thornburgh Battle Site with 2 monuments on right.
▼ 5.8		TL	CR 42 straight ahead is a dead end. Follow CR 45 northwest.
	9.7 ▲	TR	Stop sign at T-intersection with CR 15 on right and CR 42 on left.
▼ 6.4		SO	Cattle guard.
	9.1 ▲	SO	Cattle guard.
▼ 7.1		SO	Enter Moffat County.
	8.5 ▲	SO	Enter Rio Blanco County.
▼ 12.8		SO	Monument Butte on right.
	2.7 ▲	SO	Monument Butte on left.
▼ 15.5			Trail ends at stop sign at intersection with Colorado 13. Turn left for Meeker.
	0.0 ▲		Trail begins at the intersection of Colorado 13 and CR 45. Zero trip meter and proceed south on CR 45.
	GPS: N40°20.25′ W107°39.26′		

Flat Tops Trail

Starting Point:	Intersection of Northern #9: Buford Road, Northern #10: Sleepy Cat and Thornburgh Battle Trail, and CR 8 in Buford
Finishing Point:	T-intersection with Colorado 131 in Yampa
Total Mileage:	67.6, including spur
Unpaved Mileage:	52.4 miles
Driving Time:	3.5 hours, including spur
Elevation Range:	7,044 to 10,333 feet
Usually Open:	Late May to November
Difficulty Rating:	1
Scenic Rating:	9

Special Attractions

- Scenic views of the Flat Tops Range.
- Aspen fall color viewing.
- Network of forest roads to explore.
- Snowmobile trail in winter.

History

Flat Tops Trail Scenic Byway begins near the town of Meeker, named after the slain Indian agent Nathan Meeker. In 1878, Meeker arrived at the White River Ute Reservation determined to convert the Ute into God-fearing farmers. Meeker's unwanted changes and unfulfilled promises angered the Ute who attacked and killed Meeker and 11 other men in what became known as the Meeker Massacre. In response, the army established a post on the White River. When the army left in 1883, they sold the buildings and land to settlers who named the town Meeker.

Farther east, Flat Tops Trail crosses through land that was originally part of the White River Plateau Timberland Reserve, now called the White River National Forest. This reserve, which set aside public land that had been public domain, was created in October 1891 by executive order of President Benjamin Harrison. The reserve was the first of its kind in Colorado and second in the nation.

The Flat Tops, known to the Ute as the "Shining Mountains," are on the northern end of the White River Plateau. About 52 million years ago, the plateau was uplifted to roughly 10,500 feet. Thick flows of basaltic lava covered the uplifted area during three periods of volcanic activity, which occurred between 2.4 and 7.5 million years ago. The lava flows gave the mountains the appearance of being "flat topped." During the Ice Age, melted water from the glaciers covering the Flat Tops eroded areas of the hardened lava and formed numerous lakes. In the nineteenth century, wildfires cleared large stands of forest where today aspen trees flourish.

When President Theodore Roosevelt traveled through the Flat Tops area on a hunting trip around the turn of the nineteenth century, he learned of the public's adverse sentiment about "locking up" of the land. The 1897 Organic Act specified the purpose of the forest reserves and allowed for the harvesting and use of resources from the forests with permission from the secretary of the Interior. Signs of mining, ranching, and lumber-producing activities can be found along Flat Tops Trail today.

Even with the passage of the Organic Act, there remained a number of proponents for complete preservation, and the land surrounding the Flat Tops Trail provided inspiration for and gave birth to the wilderness movement. When U.S. Forest Service official Arthur Carhart visited Trappers Lake, he petitioned for the area to become a wilderness preserve. Trappers Lake gained the nickname "Cradle of Wilderness," as Carhart's preservation movement led to the passage of the Wilderness Act in 1964. Currently, the Flat Tops Wilderness is the second-largest wilderness area in Colorado, after the Weiminuche Wilderness area in southwest Colorado.

In 2002, two wildfires ripped through the forests surrounding Trappers Lake, East Lost Lake, and West Lost Lake. The Big Fish Fire, sparked by lightning, burned some 17,000 acres. The forest service deliberately let the fire burn in order to clear up "old and decadent" forest. The blaze spread faster than predicted, however, and the forest service was unable to prevent it from destroying the historic main lodge of Trappers Lake Lodge and Resort, which had been built in 1918. That same year, the Lost Lakes Fire, also started by lightning, destroyed an additional 5,500 acres of forest. Today the destruction from the fire is still clearly evident, although new growth is emerging.

Description

This trail, part of the Flat Tops Trail Scenic Byway, begins at the Buford General Store and travels northeast on maintained county roads through Medicine Bow & Routt National Forests. From most places on the road, there are scenic views of the surrounding landscape, including the Flat Tops Wilderness and numerous large stands of aspen and cottonwoods that glow golden yellow in fall. The trail makes its way over Ripple Creek Pass, Egry Mesa, the Dunckley Flat Tops, and Dunckley Pass, ending in the town of Yampa. Navigation is not difficult.

Many good backcountry campsites as well as numerous developed forest service campgrounds are located along this lengthy trail. This road is accessible to passenger vehicles in good conditions. For most of its length, the road is smooth with some corrugations and widely dispersed potholes and wheel ruts. The road can become muddy, and it is best to avoid it in wet conditions. ATVs and unlicensed dirt bikes are prohibited on this trail, but horseback riding is allowed. This is a major snowmobile route in the winter.

The trail starts on a paved road that follows the scenic North Fork of the White River, which has cottonwood trees growing in the grassy meadows surrounding its banks. The pavement ends after nearly 10 miles, and the road becomes wide, maintained, and formed of dirt and gravel. After ap-

North Fork of the White River beside the trail

proximately 18 miles, the spur to Trappers Lake leaves the main trail and sets off to the southeast toward the Flat Tops Wilderness. The spur trail makes its way past numerous alpine lakes and follows the North Fork of the White River to the edge of the Flat Tops Wilderness. Passing the historic Trappers Lake Lodge, numerous developed USFS campgrounds are located at the end of the spur near Trappers Lake. It is a short walk to the scenic overlook of the lake. The spur road is not difficult, but it is bumpier than the main trail from the increased number of ruts and potholes.

Beyond the spur, the main trail climbs several switchbacks as it makes its way to Ripple Creek Pass at 10,343 feet. Several scenic overlooks with picnic tables, restroom facilities, and information boards describing the region's scenery and wildlife are located along this section of the trail. The evergreen and aspen trees enclose the trail, which passes numerous hiking trailheads as it winds east toward Dunckley Pass. Beyond the pass, the road descends and exits the national forest where it becomes paved. The land surrounding the trail is private ranchland covered with sagebrush and a few cottonwood trees. The trail ends in the town of Yampa.

Current Road Information

Medicine Bow & Routt National Forests
Yampa Ranger District
300 Roselawn Avenue
Yampa, CO 80483
(970) 638-4516

White River National Forest
Blanco Ranger District
220 East Market Street
Meeker, CO 81641
(970) 878-4039

Map References

USFS   White River National Forest; Routt National Forest
Maptech CD: Craig/Meeker/Northwest;
        Denver/Steamboat Springs/North Central
Benchmark's *Colorado Road & Recreation Atlas*, pp. 58, 59
Colorado Atlas & Gazetteer, pp. 24, 25, 26, 34, 35
The Roads of Colorado, pp. 58, 59, 60, 61
Trails Illustrated, #119, #122, #124 (incomplete)

Route Directions

▼ 0.0		Trail commences at the intersection of Northern #9: Buford Road, Northern #10: Sleepy Cat and Thornburgh Battle Trail, and CR 8 at the Buford General Store. Zero trip meter and proceed east on paved CR 8, designated Flat Tops Trail Scenic Byway.
18.3 ▲		Trail ends at the intersection of Northern #9: Buford Road, Northern #10: Sleepy Cat and Thornburgh Battle Trail, and CR 8 at the Buford General Store.
	GPS: N39°59.25′ W107°36.99′	
▼ 9.8	SO	Pavement ends; then White River National Forest Guard Station.

View of the Flat Tops Wilderness from the trail

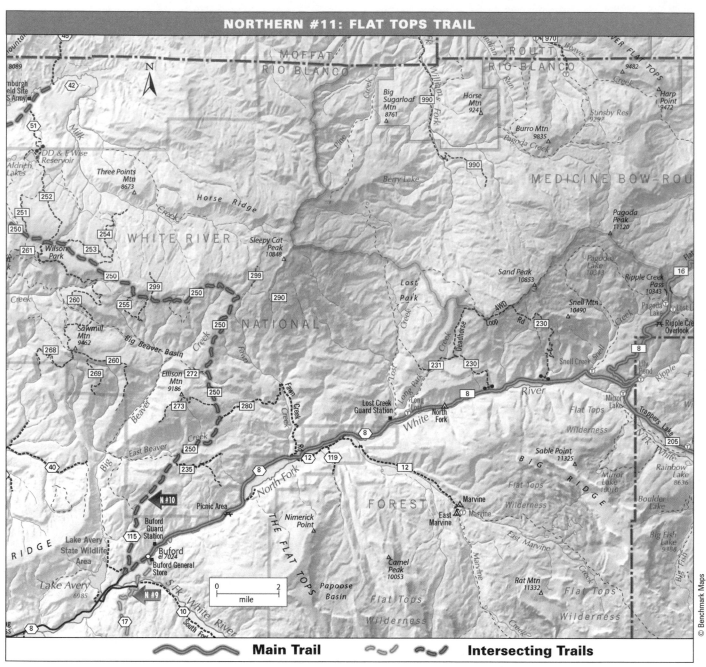

Benchmark Maps

~~~~ **Main Trail**   ~~/ ~~ **Intersecting Trails**

8.5 ▲	SO	White River National Forest Guard Station; then pavement begins.	
▼ 10.2	SO	Long Lost Trailhead on left.	
8.1 ▲	SO	Long Lost Trailhead on right.	
▼ 10.8	SO	Enter White River National Forest and information board on right.	
7.5 ▲	SO	Leave White River National Forest.	
▼ 11.7	SO	North Fork USFS Campground on left.	
6.6 ▲	SO	North Fork USFS Campground on right.	
▼ 13.3	SO	Dead Horse Loop Road (FR 230) on left signposted to Long Park.	
5.0 ▲	SO	Dead Horse Loop Road (FR 230) on right signposted to Long Park.	
▼ 13.9	SO	Track on left; then cross over Missouri Creek.	
4.4 ▲	SO	Cross over Missouri Creek; then track on right.	
▼ 15.1	SO	Dead Horse Loop Road (FR 230) on left signposted to Sand Peak.	

3.2 ▲	SO	Dead Horse Loop Road (FR 230) on right signposted to Sand Peak.	
▼ 16.6	SO	Cattle guard; then cross over Snell Creek; then road on left is FR 203.	
1.7 ▲	SO	Road on right is FR 203; then cross over Snell Creek; then cattle guard.	
▼ 16.8	SO	Pagoda Lake and Pagoda Peak Hiking Trail on left.	
1.5 ▲	SO	Pagoda Lake and Pagoda Peak Hiking Trail on right.	
▼ 18.3	SO	FR 205 to Trappers Lake on right. Zero trip meter.	
0.0 ▲		Proceed southwest on CR 8.	

GPS: N40°04.14' W107°19.17'

Spur to Trappers Lake

▼ 0.0	TR	Turn off of main trail onto FR 205 then cross over Ripple Creek.	
▼ 0.3	SO	Mirror Lake Trail (FR 206) on right.	
▼ 2.3	SO	Cross over Beaver Creek.	

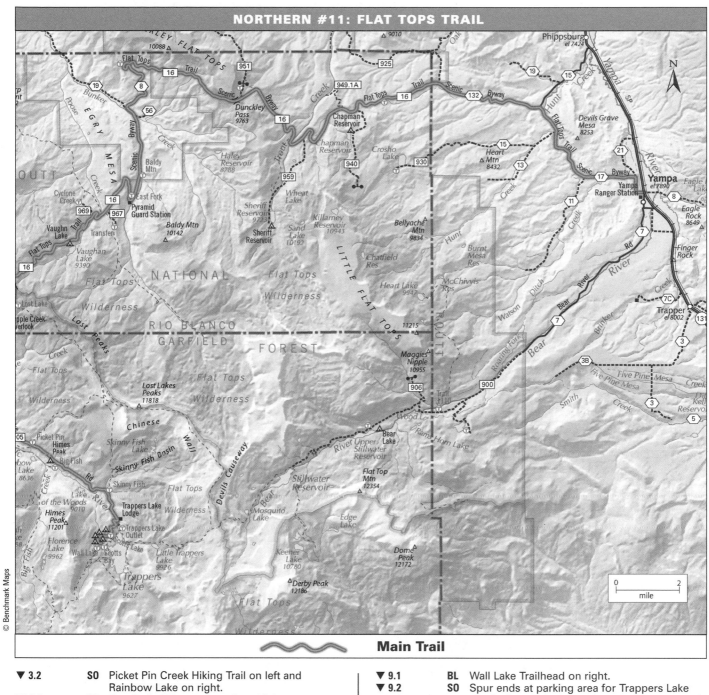

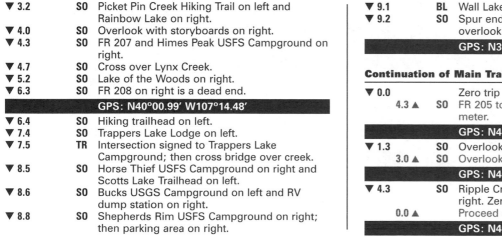

Main Trail

▼ 3.2	**SO**	Picket Pin Creek Hiking Trail on left and Rainbow Lake on right.
▼ 4.0	**SO**	Overlook with storyboards on right.
▼ 4.3	**SO**	FR 207 and Himes Peak USFS Campground on right.
▼ 4.7	**SO**	Cross over Lynx Creek.
▼ 5.2	**SO**	Lake of the Woods on right.
▼ 6.3	**SO**	FR 208 on right is a dead end.

GPS: N40°00.99′ W107°14.48′

▼ 6.4	**SO**	Hiking trailhead on left.
▼ 7.4	**SO**	Trappers Lake Lodge on left.
▼ 7.5	**TR**	Intersection signed to Trappers Lake Campground; then cross bridge over creek.
▼ 8.5	**SO**	Horse Thief USFS Campground on right and Scotts Lake Trailhead on left.
▼ 8.6	**SO**	Bucks USGS Campground on left and RV dump station on right.
▼ 8.8	**SO**	Shepherds Rim USFS Campground on right; then parking area on right.

▼ 9.1	**BL**	Wall Lake Trailhead on right.
▼ 9.2	**SO**	Spur ends at parking area for Trappers Lake overlook and picnic area.

GPS: N39°59.44′ W107°14.451′

Continuation of Main Trail

▼ 0.0		Zero trip meter and proceed northeast on CR 8.
4.3 ▲	**SO**	FR 205 to Trappers Lake on left. Zero trip meter.

GPS: N40°04.14′ W107°19.17′

▼ 1.3	**SO**	Overlook with storyboards on left.
3.0 ▲	**SO**	Overlook with storyboards on right.

GPS: N40°04.39′ W107°19.79′

▼ 4.3	**SO**	Ripple Creek overlook and picnic area on right. Zero trip meter.
0.0 ▲		Proceed southwest on CR 8.

GPS: N40°05.80′ W107°18.50′

▼ 0.0			Proceed northeast on CR 8.
	9.6 ▲	SO	Ripple Creek overlook and picnic area on left. Zero trip meter.
▼ 1.0		SO	Corral on right and staging area on left.
	8.6 ▲	SO	Corral on left and staging area on right.
▼ 4.2		SO	Vaughn Lake USFS Campground and Vaughn Lake on right.
	5.4 ▲	SO	Vaughn Lake USFS Campground and Vaughn Lake on left.
▼ 5.9		SO	Track on left to Cyclone Creek Hiking Trailhead.
	3.7 ▲	SO	Track on right to Cyclone Creek Hiking Trailhead.
▼ 6.6		SO	Track on right to Transfer Hiking Trailhead.
	3.0 ▲	SO	Track on left to Transfer Hiking Trailhead.
▼ 8.7		SO	Pyramid Ranger Station and East Fork Hiking Trailhead on right.
	0.9 ▲	SO	Pyramid Ranger Station and East Fork Hiking Trailhead on left.
▼ 8.9		SO	Exit Routt National Forest.
	0.7 ▲	SO	Enter Routt National Forest.
▼ 9.6		SO	Baldy USFS Hiking and Equestrian Trailhead on right. Intersection with CR 56 on left. Zero trip meter.
	0.0 ▲		Proceed southeast on CR 16 following Flat Tops Trail Scenic Byway.

GPS: N40°11.63' W107°13.28'

▼ 0.0			Proceed northwest on CR 16 following Flat Tops Trail Scenic Byway.
	7.2 ▲	SO	Baldy USFS Hiking and Equestrian Trailhead on left. Intersection with CR 56 on right. Zero trip meter.
▼ 0.4		SO	Cattle guard.
	6.8 ▲	SO	Cattle guard.
▼ 3.9		SO	Cattle guard.
	3.3 ▲	SO	Cattle guard.
▼ 4.1		SO	Enter Routt National Forest.
	3.1 ▲	SO	Leave Routt National Forest.
▼ 7.2		SO	Dunkley Pass overlook and Fish Creek Hiking Trail on right. Zero trip meter.
	0.0 ▲		Proceed southwest on CR 16.

GPS: N40°12.11' W107°09.48'

▼ 0.0			Proceed northeast on CR 16 past FR 951 on left.
	10.0 ▲	SO	Dunkley Pass overlook and Fish Creek Hiking Trail on left. Zero trip meter.
▼ 4.5		SO	Road on right.

	5.5 ▲	SO	Road on left.
▼ 5.0		SO	Cattle guard.
	5.0 ▲	SO	Cattle guard.
▼ 7.0		SO	FR 940 to Chapman Reservoir on right.
	3.0 ▲	SO	FR 940 to Chapman Reservoir on left.

GPS: N40°11.97' W107°05.05'

▼ 7.1		SO	Road on left.
	2.9 ▲	SO	Road on right.
▼ 7.9		SO	USFS information board on left.
	2.1 ▲	SO	USFS information board on right.
▼ 8.0		SO	Roads on left and right; then cattle guard.
	2.0 ▲	SO	Cattle guard; then roads on left and right.
▼ 9.9		SO	Leaving Routt National Forest.
	0.1 ▲	SO	Entering Routt National Forest.
▼ 10.0		SO	CR 25 on left. Zero trip meter.
	0.0 ▲		Proceed northwest on CR 16.

GPS: N40°12.60' W107°01.98'

▼ 0.0			Proceed southeast on CR 16.
	9.1 ▲	SO	CR 25 on right. Zero trip meter.
▼ 0.6		SO	Cattle guard.
	8.5 ▲	SO	Cattle guard.
▼ 2.1		SO	Cattle guard.
	7.0 ▲	SO	Cattle guard.
▼ 3.6		BR	Fork.
	5.5 ▲	BL	Fork.

GPS: N40°11.90' W106°58.38'

▼ 3.7		TR	Intersection with CR 15. Road becomes paved; then road becomes CR 17.
	5.4 ▲	TL	Pavement ends. Intersection with CR 15 on right and CR 16 on left.

GPS: N40°11.90' W106°58.29'

▼ 8.4		TR	Intersection with CR 21 on left and CR 17 continues on right.
	0.7 ▲	TL	Intersection with CR 21 straight ahead and CR 17 continues on left.
▼ 9.0		SO	Intersection with CR 17.
	0.1 ▲	SO	Intersection with CR 17.
▼ 9.1			Trail ends at T-intersection with Colorado 131 in Yampa. Turn right for I-70; turn left for Steamboat Springs.
	0.0 ▲		Trail begins at T-intersection of Colorado 131 and CR 17 in Yampa. Proceed west on CR 17.

GPS: N40°09.46' W106°54.53'

Numerous stands of aspen flank the trail

Coffee Pot Road

Starting Point:	Exit #133 off of I-70
Finishing Point:	Bison Lake
Total Mileage:	33.7 miles, including spur (one-way)
Unpaved Mileage:	30.8 miles
Driving Time:	2 hours, including spur (one-way)
Elevation Range:	6,154 to 10,797 feet
Usually Open:	July to September
Difficulty Rating:	1
Scenic Rating:	8

Special Attractions

- Expansive views over Vail Valley.
- Fishing in the numerous scenic alpine lakes.
- A network of forest roads to explore.
- Several scenic USFS campgrounds and good backcountry camping.
- Accessible to snowmobiles in winter.

History

The town of Dotsero, located at the beginning of Coffee Pot Road, was established in 1880. It sits at the southern end of the Dotsero Cutoff of the Denver & Rio Grande Railroad. The town at the other end of the cutoff is named Orestod

Expansive view over Vail Valley from the trail

(Dotsero spelled backward). The name "Dotsero" may have come from a shortening of "Dot Zero," as surveyors for the Denver & Rio Grande Railroad found the town registered as .0 on the plats. Other sources claim that Dotsero is a Ute name or that it was a station name on the standard gauge railroad line to Glenwood Springs.

Dotsero was built at the base of the Dotsero volcano. An eruption in about 2200 B.C. produced the large explosion crater seen today near the junction of the Colorado and Eagle Rivers west of the Gore Range. Lava flows helped shape the area around Dotsero. The eruption was Colorado's most recent. One of the main industries in Dotsero over the years has been making cinder blocks from the cone debris of the volcano.

View of Deep Creek Canyon from the scenic overlook

Farther along Coffee Pot Road, the trail passes by Deep Lake. The Ute used to make their hunting camps alongside the lake in the early 1800s. In 1905, President Theodore Roosevelt camped in the area while on his Flat Tops hunting trip. The Flat Tops wagon road went from Dotsero to Meeker, and Deep Lake served as a stopover for travelers. A day hotel was built in 1890 but was destroyed by fire 16 years later. The Engelmann spruce trees surrounding the lake suffered from a bark beetle epidemic in 1947–49, though a new forest has since been established.

Description

This scenic backroad begins off of I-70 exit #133 near the town of Dotsero. The road climbs deep into the forest to the edge of the pristine Flat Tops Wilderness and ends at a cluster of scenic alpine lakes. This smooth trail has some corrugations and a few potholes but is accessible to passenger vehicles in dry conditions.

The trail really gets started after following the meandering Deep Creek through the Deep Creek Recreation Area into White River National Forest. Several scenic dispersed campsites are located beside Deep Creek along this section of the trail. Beyond the restroom and information board after about 6.4 miles, the road begins to switchback up the canyon and becomes a wide shelf road with plenty of room for passing oncoming vehicles. Climbing higher and higher, the views of the Vail Valley become more and more expansive and are second to none.

Take an interesting detour off the main road to the Deep Creek overlook, where views into the bottomless Deep Creek Canyon are impressive, and information boards tell the story behind rugged and striking landscape. Winding through the alpine meadows and past several scenic forest service campgrounds, the trail arrives at Deep Lake, a picture-perfect setting for a picnic or simply a place to stop and stretch your legs. The trail ends a short distance beyond Deep Lake and past Heart Lake near the shores of the crystal clear Bison Lake.

Current Road Information

White River National Forest
Eagle Ranger District
125 West 5th Street
Eagle, CO 81631
(970) 328-6388

Map References

USFS White River National Forest
Maptech CD: Craig/Meeker/Northwest
Benchmark's *Colorado Road & Recreation Atlas*, p. 71
Colorado Atlas & Gazetteer, pp. 35, 36
The Roads of Colorado, p. 76
Trails Illustrated, #123

Deep Creek near the beginning of the trail

Expansive views over the rolling alpine meadows and lakes surrounding the trail

Route Directions

▼ 0.0		Leave I-70 at exit #133 near the town of Dotsero. Zero trip meter at the end of the exit ramp at the intersection with Frontage Road (US 6). Turn right and proceed along Frontage Road (US 6) to the north; then west toward Dotsero.
	GPS: N39°38.95′ W107°03.18′	
▼ 0.4	SO	Cottonwood Lane on right.
▼ 0.6	SO	Bridge over Colorado River.
▼ 0.7	TR	T-intersection with Colorado River Road.
	GPS: N39°38.95′ W107°03.96′	

▼ 2.4	TL	Coffee Pot Road on left, signed National Forest Access. Zero trip meter.
	GPS: N39°40.13′ W107°04.08′	
▼ 0.0		Proceed northwest on Coffee Pot Road.
▼ 0.5	BL	Road on right; then pavement ends.
▼ 1.0	SO	Cattle guard.
▼ 1.1	SO	Cross over Deep Creek.
▼ 1.9	SO	Information board and restroom on left.
▼ 6.5	SO	Track on right.
▼ 7.2	SO	Enter Garfield County.
▼ 7.4	SO	Cattle guard.
▼ 8.4	SO	Cattle guard.
▼ 12.5	SO	Cattle guard and enter White River National

Camp site in Deep Creek Recreation Area

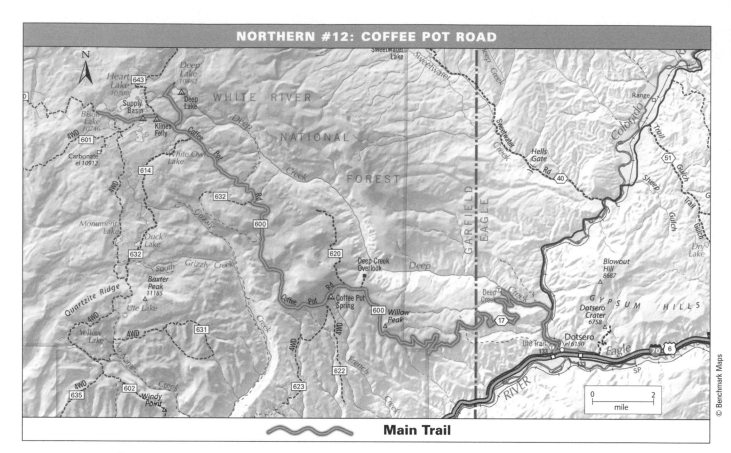

Main Trail

▼ 12.9	SO	Forest. FR 603 on right.
		GPS: N39°39.41' W107°09.91'
▼ 13.0	BR	Road on left.
▼ 13.8	SO	FR 603 on right.
▼ 15.0	SO	FR 603 on right.
▼ 15.2	SO	Road on right goes 0.4 miles to Deep Creek overlook. Zero trip meter.
		GPS: N39°40.76' W107°11.08'
▼ 0.0		Proceed west on Coffee Pot Road (FR 600).
▼ 0.2	SO	FR 604 on left.
▼ 0.4	SO	FR 620 on right.
▼ 0.8	SO	Road on right.

▼ 1.2	SO	Coffee Pot USFS Campground on left.
▼ 1.5	SO	Roads on left signed FR 622 to Dead Horse Road, and FR 623 to Wagon Gulch Road.
		GPS: N39°40.39' W107°12.42'
▼ 3.5	SO	Hiking trails on left and track on right.
▼ 4.1	SO	Cross over creek and track on right.
		GPS: N39°41.21' W107°14.02'
▼ 5.3	SO	FR 621 on right.
▼ 5.5	SO	Enter Crane Park.
▼ 5.9	SO	Pond on left.
▼ 6.6	SO	Road on right.
▼ 6.9	SO	Road on right.
▼ 7.5	BR	FR 632 on left signed 4 miles to Grizzly Cow

The trail rolls through open, alpine meadows

Rock formation near the beginning of the trail

Deep Lake Day Use Area

Camp and 10 miles to Transfer Trail.

GPS: N39°43.17' W107°15.12'		
▼ 7.9	SO	Road on left.
▼ 8.6	SO	FR 633 on right.
▼ 9.6	SO	Track on right.
▼ 10.8	SO	FR 634 on right.
▼ 11.2	SO	FR 614 on left signed 1 mile to White Owl Lake, 5 miles to Duck Lake, 8 miles to Buck Lake and track on right. Zero trip meter.
GPS: N39°45.05' W107°17.33'		
▼ 0.0		Proceed southeast on FR 600.
▼ 0.3	SO	Track on right; then pond on left.
▼ 0.8	TL	Intersection with FR 601 on left and FR 600 on right. Zero trip meter.
GPS: N39°45.38' W107°18.03'		

Spur to Deep Lake

▼ 0.0	TR	Leave main trail and proceed northeast on FR 600 toward Deep Lake.
▼ 1.0	BL	Fork with road on right to campground and road on left to Deep Lake Day Use Area.
GPS: N39°46.07' W107°18.09'		
▼ 1.2	BR	Fork with road on right to Deep Lake Day Use Area. Road on left signed 6 miles to Indian

Camp, 8 miles to South Fork Meadows, and 9 miles to Budges White River Resort.

▼ 1.4		Trail ends at Deep Lake Day Use Area.
GPS: N39°46.31' W107°18.167'		

Continuation of Main Trail

▼ 0.0		Proceed northwest on FR 601.
GPS: N39°45.38' W107°18.03'		
▼ 0.5	SO	Pond on left.
▼ 0.6	BL	Fork with road to Bison Lake on left and road to Heart Lake on right; then track on left.
▼ 1.2	SO	Supply Basin USFS Campground on left.
GPS: N39°45.61' W107°19.29'		
▼ 1.3	SO	Lake on left.
▼ 1.4	SO	Intersection with FR 601 on left and FR 640 straight on. Signed Bison Lake 1 mile straight ahead, Adams Lake 9 miles to the right, and Blair Mountain 11 miles to the right.
GPS: N39°45.57' W107°19.50'		
▼ 1.9	SO	Track on right.
▼ 2.4	SO	Cross through creek.
▼ 2.7		Track on right and trail ends at Bison Lake.
GPS: N39°45.73' W107°20.75'		

Bison Lake at the end of the trail

Red Dirt Creek and Derby Mesa Trail

Starting Point:	**Dotsero**
Finishing Point:	**Derby Junction at the intersection of**
	CR 39 and CR 301
Total Mileage:	**31.7 miles**
Unpaved Mileage:	**16.8 miles**
Driving Time:	**2 1/4 hours**
Elevation Range:	**6,339 to 9,000 feet**
Usually Open:	**Mid-June to late October**
Difficulty Rating:	**3**
Scenic Rating:	**8**

Special Attractions
- Moderately easy 4WD route.
- Varied scenery, including the red-walled canyon along Red Dirt Creek.

Description
The route begins at Dotsero and travels north on CR 301, a scenic road traveling along the raging Colorado River. The first turnoff onto FR 611 is unmarked but is easy to find, immediately after a one-lane bridge over the Colorado River where the road returns to the west side of the river. Immediately after the intersection, FR 611 squeezes back between the river and the valley wall.

The road follows the course of Red Dirt Creek along the scenic, red-walled, wooded canyon. The road is narrow but has adequate pull-offs for passing.

As the road departs the creek, the scenery changes to oak brush and sagebrush, and the ascent to Derby Mesa commences. About 2.4 miles after leaving the creek, there is a short, steep section with a large rock to be negotiated in the middle of the road.

The road continues though open country before the final reasonably steep and narrow switchback onto the mesa.

From the intersection with CR 39, it is a straightforward, 5-mile journey to Derby Junction, 1 mile south of the Burns post office and 6.25 miles north of the intersection of FR 611, where the route initially turned off CR 39.

Current Road Conditions
White River National Forest
Eagle Ranger District
125 West 5th Street
Eagle, CO 81631
(970) 328-6388

Map References
USFS   White River National Forest
Maptech CD: Central Colorado/Colorado Springs/Ski Areas
Benchmark's *Colorado Road & Recreation Atlas*, p. 71
The Roads of Colorado, pp. 52, 53, 68
Colorado Atlas & Gazetteer, p. 36
Trails Illustrated, #120, #122

The start of the trail as it squeezes between the rock wall and the Colorado River

NORTHERN #13: RED DIRT CREEK AND DERBY MESA TRAIL

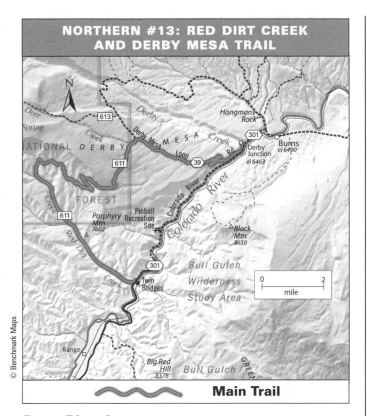

Main Trail

© Benchmark Maps

Route Directions

▼ 0.0		Take Exit #133 north from I-70 into Dotsero. Zero trip meter at the intersection of Frontage Road and CR 301. Proceed north on CR 301.
14.9 ▲		End at the intersection of Frontage Road and CR 301 in Dotsero.

GPS: N 39°38.97' W 107°03.93'

▼ 14.9	TL	After a one-lane bridge, there is an unmarked track, CR 39 (FR 611) on the left along the canyon wall. Zero trip meter.
0.0 ▲		Proceed south on CR 301.

GPS: N 39°48.28' W 106°58.27'

▼ 0.0		Proceed along FR 611.
11.8 ▲	TR	Onto CR 301. Zero trip meter.
▼ 0.1	BR/BR	Fork in road. Then track on left.
11.7 ▲	BL/BL	Track on right. Then fork in road.
▼ 0.4	SO	Track on left.
11.4 ▲	SO	Track on right.
▼ 0.6	SO	Fence and gate.
11.2 ▲	SO	Fence and gate.
▼ 1.5	SO	Fence and gate.
10.3 ▲	SO	Fence and gate.
▼ 2.1	BL	Private driveway on right.
9.7 ▲	BR	Private driveway on left.
▼ 2.7	BL	Two small tracks on right.
9.1 ▲	BR	Two small tracks on left.
▼ 2.8	SO	Small track on right at bend in the road.
9.0 ▲	SO	Small track on left at bend in the road.
▼ 3.1	SO	Old cabin on left. Then cattle guard and enter the National Forest.
8.7 ▲	SO	Cattle guard. Leave the National Forest. Old cabin on right.
▼ 4.8	SO	Cattle guard.
7.0 ▲	SO	Cattle guard.
▼ 5.2	TR	Fork in road. Straight will dead-end in a short distance.

6.6 ▲	BL	Track on right dead-ends.

GPS: N 39°51.24' W 107°02.06'

▼ 5.7	SO	Water trough on left.
6.1 ▲	SO	Water trough on right.
▼ 6.0	SO	Gate. Cross through and leave it as you found it.
5.8 ▲	SO	Gate. Cross through and leave it as you found it.
▼ 7.6	SO	Short, steep uphill section.
4.2 ▲	SO	Short, steep descent.
▼ 9.4	SO	Gate. Cross through and leave it as you found it.
2.4 ▲	SO	Gate. Cross through and leave it as you found it.
▼ 9.7	SO	Track on right.
2.1 ▲	SO	Track on left.
▼ 10.5	SO	Cross over creek.
1.3 ▲	SO	Cross over creek.
▼ 11.1	SO	Track on right.
0.7 ▲	SO	Track on left.

GPS: N 39°51.82' W 106°58.61'

▼ 11.5	SO	Leave White River National Forest. Cross through gate and leave it as you found it.
0.3 ▲	SO	Enter White River National Forest. Cross through gate and leave it as you found it.
▼ 11.8	SO	Cross over creek. Then cattle guard and intersection. Zero trip meter.
0.0 ▲		Continue on FR 611 toward White River National Forest. Then cross over creek.

GPS: N 39°52.34' W 106°58.16'

▼ 0.0		Continue along road toward Derby Junction.
5.0 ▲	TL	Intersection. Zero trip meter. Sign: Red Dirt Road 611 to Red Dirt Creek and Colorado River Road. Cross cattle guard.
▼ 5.0		End at the stop sign at intersection with CR 301, Derby Junction.
0.0 ▲		On CR 301 in Derby Junction, turn at National Forest Access sign and Conoco sign, and zero trip meter. This intersection is further marked with eight cabins on the left.

GPS: N 39°52.16' W 106°54.28'

NORTHERN REGION TRAIL #14

Red and White Mountain Trail

Starting Point:	**North roundabout at the end of ramp**
	off I-70 exit 176 in Vail
Finishing Point:	**Intersection of CR 131 and CR 6**
	(Muddy Creek Road)
Total Mileage:	**36.7 miles, including spur**
Unpaved Mileage:	**35.1 miles**
Driving Time:	**2 hours, including spur**
Elevation Range:	**7,124 to 10,675 feet**
Usually Open:	**June to early November**
Difficulty Rating:	**2**
Scenic Rating:	**8**

Piney River along the spur to Piney Lake

Boggy section of the trail beside the South Fork of Dickson Creek

Special Attractions

- Scenic views of the Gore Mountain Range and Red and White Mountain.
- Good backcountry camping.
- Accessible to snowmobiles in winter.

History

After winding through the densely vegetated aspen and conifer stands of the White River National Forest northwest of Vail, the Red and White Mountain Trail crosses Muddy Pass shortly before exiting the forest. The pass is named after Muddy Creek, an offshoot of the Colorado River. In 1844, with his guide Kit Carson, Captain John Frémont traveled over Muddy Pass. Frémont greatly appreciated the views and wrote, "We fell into a broad and excellent trail, made by buffalo, where a wagon would pass with ease."

Later, railroad surveyors would express a similar sentiment, calling Muddy Pass an ideal rail route. Although the Denver, Utah & Pacific Railroad surveyed the pass for a rail line in 1881, construction never took place. The pass received national attention in 1879 when it was mentioned in multiple articles that appeared in *Forest & Stream* magazine. A noted anthropologist and naturalist, George Bird Grinnell, penned the articles.

Near the end of the Red and White Mountain Trail, the town of Wolcott (previously named Brussels) once served as an important stop along multiple stage and mail routes in the late 1800s. Wolcott was the last stop for the Steamboat Springs stage mail route and was also a supply point for Routt and Grand Counties. The town was established in 1889 and named after the Colorado state senator Edward O. Wolcott.

Just northeast of Wolcott, a short way off the trail, lies Tracy's Hideout. Harry Tracy along with his partner, David Lant, used an old house in the area as a hideout after escaping from a Utah penitentiary. Also in the vicinity is the site where the

The trail near the entrance to the National Forest

Expansive view from the trail as it exits the National Forest

The trail travels through open range near the end

prehistoric three-toed horse was discovered in 1934. Today the fossils are on display at the Denver Museum of Nature & Science.

Red and White Mountain, for which the trail is named, is a laccolith, an intrusive dome of solidified magma that has pushed the rock layers above it upward but has not broken the surface. On Red and White Mountain, the overlying layers of rock have largely been eroded, exposing the igneous rock of the laccolith.

Description

Showcasing the jagged peaks of the Gore Mountain Range, Red and White Mountain Trail starts in Vail and winds through the aspen stands and pine groves of White River National Forest and along the edge of Vail Valley to the town of Wolcott. Numerous good backcountry campsites are located along most of the route, and the road is popular with hikers,

mountain bikers, and dirt bike and ATV riders as well as Jeeps. A number of more challenging 4WD trails also intersect with the main trail.

This scenic backcountry trail begins as a paved road at exit 176 off of I-70. The pavement ends at the forest service access point after about 1.7 miles. Nice views of Vail are visible from this beginning section of the trail. Traveling along Red Sandstone Road (FR 700), a number of hiking trails snake off the road and provide an opportunity to explore the pristine Eagles Nest Wilderness. The road is bumpy with corrugations, potholes, and wheel ruts, which give the trail its difficulty rating of 2, but do not present an obstacle to most stock 4WDs. The trail can become muddy and should be avoided in wet conditions.

The crimson dirt road continues through the forest, and from time to time overlooks between the trees reveal spectacular vistas of the rugged landscape of red sandstone buttes and

View of the rugged Gore Range from the trail

the craggy mountains. Divert from the main trail onto FR 701 for a pleasant trip alongside the Piney River to Piney Lake. Numerous picture-perfect picnic spots and backcountry campsites can be found nestled in the trees on the road to Piney Lake.

On the horizon farther along the main road, you will see Red and White Mountain, the trail's namesake. The bands of different colors on the slopes were created by a geological process over thousands of years. Essentially, layers of rock have been pushed upward and eroded, exposing layers of colorful solidified volcanic rock beneath.

Just before the trail leaves the forest there is a short rocky section. After exiting the forest, the road crosses Muddy Pass. The trail becomes a wide, maintained gravel road before it ends just north of Wolcott.

Current Road Information

White River National Forest
Holy Cross Ranger District
24747 US 24
Minturn, CO 81645
(970) 827-5715

Map References

USFS   White River National Forest
Maptech CD: Colorado Springs/Ski Areas/Central
   Colorado
Benchmark's *Colorado Road & Recreation Atlas*, p. 72
Colorado Atlas & Gazetteer, p. 37
The Roads of Colorado, pp. 77, 78
Trails Illustrated, #108, #120, #121

A section typical of the trail

Route Directions

| ▼ 0.0 | | Trail begins at the north roundabout off the westbound exit 176 off of I-70 in Vail. Zero trip meter at the end of exit ramp and proceed through the roundabout to travel west on North Frontage Road. |
| 1.7 ▲ | SO | Trail ends at the north roundabout at exit 176 off of I-70 in Vail. |

GPS: N39°38.70′ W106°22.66′

| ▼ 1.0 | TR | Red Sandstone Road on right. |
| 0.7 ▲ | TL | T-intersection with North Frontage Road. |

| ▼ 1.3 | SO | Trailhead parking. |
| 0.3 ▲ | SO | Trailhead parking. |

| ▼ 1.7 | SO | Pavement ends and the road becomes FR 700; then closure gate. Zero trip meter. |
| 0.0 ▲ | | Proceed southeast on Red Sandstone Road. |

GPS: N39°38.84′ W106°23.58′

| ▼ 0.0 | | Proceed northwest on FR 700. |
| 2.6 ▲ | SO | Closure gate; then road becomes Red Sandstone Road. Pavement begins. Zero trip meter. |

| ▼ 0.6 | SO | Hiking trail on right; then USFS information boards on right. |
| 2.0 ▲ | SO | USFS information boards on left; then hiking trail on left. |

| ▼ 2.6 | SO | Road on right to Lost Lake (Lost Lake Road). Zero trip meter. |
| 0.0 ▲ | | Proceed southeast on FR 700. |

GPS: N39°40.40′ W106°23.93′

| ▼ 0.0 | | Proceed northwest on FR 700. |
| 3.9 ▲ | SO | Road on left to Lost Lake (Lost Lake Road). Zero trip meter. |

| ▼ 1.0 | SO | Cross over creek. |
| 2.9 ▲ | SO | Cross over creek. |

| ▼ 2.7 | SO | FR 720 on right is gated. |
| 1.2 ▲ | SO | FR 720 on left is gated. |

GPS: N39°41.45′ W106°25.41′

| ▼ 3.4 | SO | Hiking trail on left. |
| 0.5 ▲ | SO | Hiking trail on right. |

| ▼ 3.8 | SO | Intersection with FR 734 on left. |
| 0.1 ▲ | SO | Intersection with FR 734 on right. |

GPS: N39°41.83′ W106°26.13′

| ▼ 3.9 | TL | Fork with FR 701 on left and spur to Piney Lake to the right. Zero trip meter. |
| 0.0 ▲ | | Proceed southwest on FR 701 through seasonal gate. |

GPS: N39°41.87′ W106°26.25′

Spur to Piney Lake

▼ 0.0		Zero trip meter and proceed west toward Piney Lake.
▼ 1.4	SO	Track on left to backcountry campsite and picnic spot.
▼ 2.4	SO	Backcountry camping spots on left and right; then cross bridge over creek.
▼ 2.5	TR	Parking area on right for Piney River Hiking Trail.
▼ 2.9	SO	Track on right to backcountry campsite.
▼ 3.9		Spur ends at parking area and entrance to Piney River Ranch.

GPS: N39°43.23′ W106°24.30′

Continuation of Main Trail

| ▼ 0.0 | | Proceed northeast on FR 701 through seasonal gate. |
| 8.0 ▲ | BR | Fork with FR 701 on right and the spur to Piney Lake to the left. Zero trip meter. |

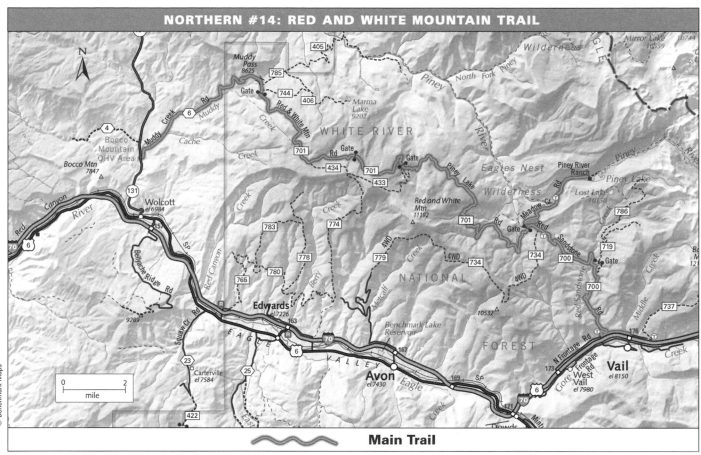

Main Trail

▼ 2.3	SO	FR 700.2 on right.
5.7 ▲	SO	FR 700.2 on left.

▼ 3.6	SO	Cross through creek.
4.4 ▲	SO	Cross through creek.

▼ 8.0	SO	FR 730 on right. Zero trip meter.
0.0 ▲		Proceed south on FR 701.

GPS: N39°43.60' W106°29.73'

▼ 0.0		Proceed north on FR 701.
10.2 ▲	SO	FR 730 on left. Zero trip meter.

▼ 1.1	SO	Cross over creek.
9.1 ▲	SO	Cross over creek.

▼ 1.4	SO	Cabin ruins on right.
8.8 ▲	SO	Cabin ruins on left.

GPS: N39°43.55' W106°30.74'

▼ 1.7	SO	FR 433 on left.
8.5 ▲	SO	FR 433 on right.

GPS: N39°43.66' W106°30.96'

▼ 6.3	SO	FR 434 on left; then FR 734 on left.
3.9 ▲	SO	FR 734 on right; then FR 434 on right.

GPS: N39°43.64' W106°34.43'

▼ 7.6	SO	Cattle guard.
2.6 ▲	SO	Cattle guard.

▼ 8.9	SO	Cattle guard.
1.3 ▲	SO	Cattle guard.

▼ 10.0	SO	Seasonal closure gate.
0.2 ▲	SO	Seasonal closure gate.

▼ 10.2	SO	FR 744 on right. Zero trip meter.
0.0 ▲		Proceed south on FR 701 across Muddy Pass.

GPS: N39°45.92' W106°36.21'

▼ 0.0		Proceed north on FR 701 across Muddy Pass. The road becomes CR 6.

6.5 ▲	SO	FR 744 on left. Signed Piney Station 5 miles to the left, Red and White Mountain 6 miles to the right, and June Creek 8 miles to the right. Zero trip meter.

▼ 0.4	SO	FR 405 on right.
6.1 ▲	SO	FR 405 on left.

GPS: N39°46.04' W106°36.30'

▼ 2.2	SO	Cattle guard.
4.2 ▲	SO	Cattle guard.

▼ 6.5		Forest service information board; then trail ends at intersection of CR 131.
0.0 ▲		Trail begins at intersection of CR 131 and CR 6 (Muddy Creek Road). Proceed northeast on CR 6.

GPS: N39°43.76' W106°40.71'

Short, rocky section of the trail

Blacktail Road

Starting Point:	**Trough Road (CR 1), at the intersection with CR 11**
Finishing Point:	**Colorado 134, 0.5 miles west of Blacktail Picnic Grounds**
Total Mileage:	**14.6 miles**
Unpaved Mileage:	**14.6 miles**
Driving Time:	**1 hour**
Elevation Range:	**6,880 to 9,110 feet**
Usually Open:	**June to December**
Difficulty Rating:	**2**
Scenic Rating:	**9**

Special Attractions
- Radium Hot Springs.
- Choice of a couple developed campgrounds.

Description
Blacktail Road is not really a 4WD route; rather, it is a pleasant, scenic drive through some beautiful and varied country with a few special attractions. The route starts out southwest of Kremmling by heading northwest along a wide, graded county road. The first (and most wonderful) highlight of the trail is located near the O. C. Mugrage Campground. Park at the campground, which is equipped with restroom facilities, and cross the road to a hiking trail that ascends a steep hill. This is the start of the hiking trail to Radium Hot Springs. The hiking trail climbs the hill and then levels out on the bench. The hike can be confusing because it is an old 4WD route, and a few other hiking trails crisscross the same area. The trail is about half a mile long and heads north at the start,

Colorado River at Radium Hot Springs

then loops around to the northwest, and finally makes a short northeasterly descent to the springs.

The hot springs, adjacent to the Colorado River, are magnificent. The only thing that disrupts this serene experience is the occasional freight train running along the opposite side of the river. Water seeps out of a rock wall and collects in a makeshift rock pool beside the river. The springs are hot but not uncomfortably so, making for a perfect stop almost all year round. In summer, most people access the springs via rafting trips along the Colorado River.

Past the campground, the road crosses the Colorado River and continues into the town of Radium, which currently consists of a handful of houses. Past Radium, the road becomes smaller and begins to climb above the river, providing some excellent views of the waterway's wide basin. The road remains graded dirt as it travels through the Radium State Wildlife Area. It passes the entrance to the Walt Woodward Wildlife Viewing Area, with a hiking trail that heads west alongside the creek.

The trail then heads into the southern reaches of Medicine Bow & Routt National Forests, where its designation changes from CR 11 to FR 212. The trail travels past numerous backcountry campsites in the forest. It also passes some very scenic aspen-fringed meadows before ending on Colorado 134, just west of Gore Pass.

Current Road Information
Medicine Bow & Routt National Forests
Yampa Ranger District
300 Roselawn Avenue
Yampa, CO 80483
(970) 638-4516

Map References
USFS   Routt National Forest
Maptech CD:
        Denver/Steamboat Springs/North Central;
        Colorado Springs/Ski Areas/Central
Benchmark's *Colorado Road & Recreation Atlas*, p. 60
Colorado Atlas & Gazetteer, pp. 27, 37
The Roads of Colorado, p. 61
Trails Illustrated, #119, #120

Route Directions

▼ 0.0		From the intersection of US 40 and Colorado 9 in Kremmling, head south on Colorado 9 for 2.3 miles. Turn right onto Trough Road (CR 1), just after a large cutting and proceed 14.7 miles to the southwest. Trail starts on Trough Road (CR 1), at the intersection with CR 11. Zero trip meter and turn sharp right (northwest) onto wide, graded CR 11, following sign to Radium.
	2.5 ▲	Trail ends on Trough Road (CR 1). Turn right for Colorado 131; turn left for Colorado 9 and Kremmling.
		GPS: N39°56.08' W106°31.69'
▼ 1.4	SO	O. C. Mugrage Campground on left; then hiking trail on right goes to Radium Hot Springs.
	1.1 ▲	SO	Hiking trail on left goes to Radium Hot Springs; then O. C. Mugrage Campground on right.

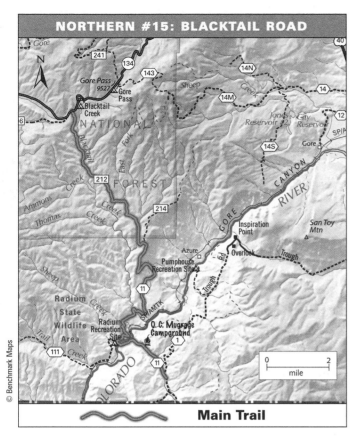

Main Trail

GPS: N39°57.08' W106°32.54'		
▼ 1.9	SO	Cross over creek on bridge.
0.6 ▲	SO	Cross over creek on bridge.
▼ 2.3	BR	Radium BLM Recreation Area on left—fee area.
0.2 ▲	BL	Radium BLM Recreation Area on right—fee area.
GPS: N39°57.09' W106°33.36'		
▼ 2.4	SO	Cross over Colorado River on bridge.
0.1 ▲	SO	Cross over Colorado River on bridge.
▼ 2.5	BR	Entering Radium. Cross over railroad tracks; then bear right onto CR 11, following sign to

The Colorado River

Meadow near the northern end of the trail

			Blacktail. Track to the left is CR 111. Zero trip meter.
0.0 ▲			Continue to the south, leaving Radium.
GPS: N39°57.22' W106°33.50'			
▼ 0.0			Continue to the northeast, leaving Radium.
5.7 ▲	BL		Entering Radium. CR 111 on right. Bear left onto CR 11 and zero trip meter. Cross over railroad tracks.
▼ 1.0	SO		Cattle guard. Entering Radium State Wildlife Area.
4.7 ▲	SO		Cattle guard. Leaving Radium State Wildlife Area.
▼ 1.3	BR		CR 113 on left is a dead end. Remain on CR 11.
4.4 ▲	SO		CR 113 on sharp right is a dead end. Remain on CR 11.
▼ 1.7	SO		Track on sharp right.
4.0 ▲	SO		Track on left.
▼ 1.8	BR		Turnout on left to Walt Woodward Wildlife Viewing Area—information boards and hiking trail.
3.9 ▲	SO		Turnout on right to Walt Woodward Wildlife Viewing Area—information boards and hiking trail.
GPS: N39°58.11' W106°32.89'			
▼ 2.7	SO		Cattle guard.
3.0 ▲	SO		Cattle guard.
▼ 3.9	BL		CR 114 on right—no river access. Remain on CR 11, now called Blacktail Road.
1.8 ▲	SO		CR 114 on sharp left—no river access. Remain on CR 11.
▼ 5.7	BL		FR 214 on right. Zero trip meter.
0.0 ▲			Continue to the south.
GPS: N39°59.84' W106°32.46'			
▼ 0.0			Continue to the north.
6.4 ▲	SO		FR 214 on sharp left. Zero trip meter.
▼ 0.6	SO		Cattle guard. Entering Medicine Bow & Routt National Forests. Road is now FR 212.
5.8 ▲	SO		Cattle guard. Leaving Medicine Bow & Routt National Forests. Road is now CR 11.
▼ 1.4	SO		Track on left.
5.0 ▲	SO		Track on right.
▼ 1.6	SO		Cross over creek; then track on left.
4.8 ▲	SO		Track on right; then cross over creek.
▼ 2.4	SO		Track on left.
4.0 ▲	SO		Track on right.

▼ 3.0		SO	Cattle guard.
	3.4 ▲	SO	Cattle guard.
▼ 3.6		SO	Hiking trail on right.
	2.8 ▲	SO	Hiking trail on left.
▼ 3.9		BR	FR 218 on left.
	2.5 ▲	SO	FR 218 on right.
		GPS: N40°01.93′ W106°34.46′	
▼ 5.8		SO	Cattle guard.
	0.6 ▲	SO	Cattle guard.
▼ 6.4			Trail ends on Colorado 134. Turn right for US 40; turn left for Colorado 131.
	0.0 ▲		Trail starts on paved Colorado 134, 13.3 miles west of US 40 and 0.5 miles west of Blacktail Picnic Grounds. Zero trip meter and turn south onto graded dirt FR 212, following sign to French Creek, Colorado River, and Radium.
		GPS: N40°03.78′ W106°35.18′	

View over the basin west of Steamboat Springs

NORTHERN REGION TRAIL #16

Buffalo Pass Trail

Starting Point:	**CR 36, 2.5 miles north of US 40**
Finishing Point:	**Colorado 14 at the site of Hebron**
Total Mileage:	**31.7 miles**
Unpaved Mileage:	**24 miles**
Driving Time:	**1.5 hours**
Elevation Range:	**6,995 to 10,410 feet**
Usually Open:	**July to mid-October**
Difficulty Rating:	**1**
Scenic Rating:	**8**

Special Attractions

- Historic pass route.
- Numerous recreation opportunities at Buffalo Pass.

History

Buffalo Pass was once used by the Ute Indians to ambush buffalo migrating between the Yampa Valley and North Park. When the Ute inhabited the area, North Park was teeming with herds of deer, antelope, and buffalo. Buffalo were so prevalent that the Ute gave North Park the name "Bull Pen." The Utes' hunt on the pass provided the tribe with meat for the winter.

The route over Buffalo Pass did not come into regular use until 1865. As the buffalo before them, travelers used the trail as the principal passage between North Park and Steamboat Springs. The highway built over Rabbit Ears Pass in 1959 drew much of the traffic away from the Buffalo Pass route.

Around the turn of the twentieth century, drivers of early models of automobiles would challenge their cars by driving them over Buffalo Pass. In the 1930s there was a proposal to build a major highway over Buffalo Pass, but nothing ever came of it. The U.S. Forest Service made improvements on the road in 1959 and again in 1965 to accommodate modern vehicles.

Description

Buffalo Pass Trail is a very easy but scenic route that takes you from Steamboat Springs over the Park Range to Colorado 14. Passenger vehicles can drive the route in good weather since the entire dirt road is well graded. The trail starts on CR 36, south of the Strawberry Park Hot Springs.

The first part of the trail offers some good camping opportunities at the developed Dry Lake Campground, as well as at numerous backcountry campsites along the way. The route is very winding and often provides great views back toward Steamboat Springs.

The trail continues its gentle climb to Buffalo Pass. The first thing you encounter is the Wyoming Hiking Trail that heads north into the Mount Zirkel Wilderness. Next is a track to the very scenic and developed Summit Lake Campground. The campground is perched above a lake of the same name. After the campground, a parking area is located at Buffalo Pass. Beyond the pass, a track leads off to the right to Fish Creek Reservoir.

On the east side of the Park Range, the trail passes numerous tracks that have been gated by the forest service. The backcountry part of the trail ends when you leave the National Forest; however, the remaining stretch of county road out to Colorado 14 has been included for ease of navigation.

View of Summit Lake from Summit Lake Campground

Main Trail

Current Road Information

Medicine Bow & Routt National Forests
Hahns Peak/Bears Ears Ranger District
925 Weiss Drive
Steamboat Springs, CO 80487
(970) 879-1870

Medicine Bow & Routt National Forests
Parks Ranger District
100 Main Street
Walden, CO 80480
(970) 723-8204

Map References

USFS Routt National Forest
Maptech CD: Denver/Steamboat Springs/
 North Central Colorado
Benchmark's *Colorado Road & Recreation Atlas*, p. 46
Colorado Atlas & Gazetteer, pp. 16, 17
The Roads of Colorado, pp. 45, 46
Trails Illustrated, #114, #117

Route Directions

▼ 0.0			Trail starts on CR 36, 2.5 miles north of US 40. To get to the start of the trail from US 40, turn northeast on 7th Avenue and follow signs for Hot Springs and Buffalo Pass. Zero trip meter and turn east onto paved FR 60, following sign to Dry Lake Campground, Buffalo Pass, Fish Creek Reservoir, and Colorado 14.
	3.3 ▲		Trail ends on CR 36, just outside of Steamboat Springs. Turn right for Strawberry Park Hot Springs; turn left for Steamboat Springs.
		GPS: N40°30.80′ W106°49.39′	
▼ 0.2		SO	CR 38A on left.
	3.1 ▲	SO	CR 38A on right.
▼ 0.4		SO	Pavement ends.
	2.9 ▲	SO	Pavement begins.
▼ 1.7		SO	Entering Medicine Bow & Routt National Forests.
	1.6 ▲	SO	Leaving Medicine Bow & Routt National Forests.
▼ 3.3		SO	Dry Lake Campground on left and parking area for Buffalo Pass Recreation Area on right. Spring Creek Hiking Trail leaves the parking area to the right. Zero trip meter.
	0.0 ▲		Continue to the northwest.
		GPS: N40°32.08′ W106°47.05′	
▼ 0.0			Continue to the southeast.
	7.7 ▲	SO	Dry Lake Campground on right and parking area for Buffalo Pass Recreation Area on left. Spring Creek Hiking Trail leaves the parking area to the left. Zero trip meter.
▼ 0.1		SO	Seasonal closure gate.
	7.6 ▲	SO	Seasonal closure gate.
▼ 2.9		SO	Campsite on right offers great views.
	4.8 ▲	SO	Campsite on left offers great views.
▼ 3.3		SO	Small track on left.
	4.4 ▲	SO	Small track on right.
▼ 3.6		SO	Seasonal closure gate.
	4.1 ▲	SO	Seasonal closure gate.
▼ 3.9		SO	FR 309 on right.
	3.8 ▲	SO	FR 309 on left.
		GPS: N40°31.57′ W106°44.71′	
▼ 4.4		SO	Track on left goes to exposed campsite.

View of Summit Lake from the trail

3.3 ▲		SO	Track on right goes to exposed campsite.
▼ 5.4		SO	Track on right.
	2.3 ▲	SO	Track on left.
▼ 6.6		SO	FR 306 on right.
	1.1 ▲	SO	FR 306 on left.

GPS: N40°32.11' W106°42.06'

▼ 7.4		SO	Cross over wash.
	0.3 ▲	SO	Cross over wash.
▼ 7.7		SO	Wyoming Hiking Trail #1101 on left; then cross over creek; then FR 60A on left goes to Summit Lake Campground. This is Buffalo Pass. Zero trip meter and remain on FR 60.
	0.0 ▲		Continue to the northwest.

GPS: N40°32.67' W106°41.10'

▼ 0.0			Continue to the southeast past FR 310 on the right.
	9.4 ▲	SO	FR 310 on left to Fish Creek Reservoir. This is Buffalo Pass. FR 60A on right goes to Summit Lake Campground; then cross over creek; then Wyoming Hiking Trail #1101 on right. Zero trip meter and remain on FR 60.
▼ 0.5		SO	Small pond on right.
	8.9 ▲	SO	Small pond on left.
▼ 6.6		SO	Seasonal closure gate.
	2.8 ▲	SO	Seasonal closure gate.
▼ 6.7		BL	FR 620 on right goes to Sawmill Creek.
	2.7 ▲	BR	FR 620 on left goes to Sawmill Creek.

GPS: N40°32.26' W106°37.88'

▼ 8.1		SO	Camping area on right.
	1.3 ▲	SO	Camping area on left.
▼ 8.5		SO	FR 20 on right goes to Hidden Lakes Campground.
	0.9 ▲	SO	FR 20 on left goes to Hidden Lakes Campground.

GPS: N40°33.36' W106°36.93'

▼ 9.1		SO	Faint track on right.
	0.3 ▲	SO	Faint track on left.
▼ 9.4		SO	Private road on left; then FR 615 on left goes to Teal Lake Campground, Tiago Lake, and Trail #1126; then Grizzly Creek Campground on left. Zero trip meter.
	0.0 ▲		Continue to the east past a private road on right.

GPS: N40°33.40' W106°36.01'

▼ 0.0			Continue to the west.
	11.3 ▲	SO	Grizzly Creek Campground on right; then FR 615 on right goes to Teal Lake Campground, Tiago Lake, and Trail #1126. Zero trip meter.
▼ 0.2		SO	Grizzly Creek Guard Station on right. Leaving Medicine Bow & Routt National Forests over cattle guard.
	11.1 ▲	SO	Entering Medicine Bow & Routt National Forests over cattle guard. Grizzly Creek Guard Station on left.
▼ 1.7		SO	CR 1 on sharp right.
	9.6 ▲	BR	CR 1 on left.
▼ 4.0		SO	CR 5 on sharp left; then pavement begins.
	7.3 ▲	BL	Pavement ends; then CR 5 on right.
▼ 8.7		SO	CR 26 on right.
	2.6 ▲	SO	CR 26 on left.
▼ 11.3			Trail ends on Colorado 14 at the site of Hebron. Turn right for US 40; turn left for Walden.
	0.0 ▲		Trail starts on Colorado 14 at the site of Hebron, 11.5 miles south of the intersection with Colorado 125. Zero trip meter and turn west on paved CR 24.

GPS: N40°35.81' W106°24.42'

Ellis Jeep Trail

Starting Point:	**Intersection of FR 550 and FR 500**
Finishing Point:	**Cowdrey**
Total Mileage:	**50.6 miles**
Unpaved Mileage:	**45.6 miles**
Driving Time:	**3 1/2 hours**
Elevation Range:	**7,883 to 9,739 feet**
Usually Open:	**Mid-June to mid-September**
Difficulty Rating:	**6**
Scenic Rating:	**9**

Special Attractions

- Challenging, remote 4WD trail.
- Elk viewing.
- Forms a 4WD loop route when combined with Northern #18: Elkhorn Mountain and Stock Driveway.

History

Jack Ellis, an Elk River cattleman, built the Ellis Jeep Trail in 1888 to supply lumbermen in the Hog Park area with beef and supplies. The trail ran from the Elk River to Hahns Peak and Hog Park and on to the Encampment River. It was the main supply route between the towns of Hahns Peak and Commissary on the Colorado/Wyoming border just north of the Hog Park Guard Station. The supply wagons and sleds were pulled by as many as eight, and seldom less than four, horses.

Description

You will definitely need a 4WD vehicle to cross the extremely boggy sections of this trail in the meadows along the South Fork of Hog Park Creek. The difficulty rating for this trail is based on its state under the driest conditions; in other conditions, the route is impassable, and many vehicles get bogged each year.

Crossing these meadows requires careful investigation on foot to locate the driest route. As this is a very remote area of Colorado, you will be wise to take the trail in more than one vehicle or bring a winch (and extension straps) if you do not want to risk a long walk. Such precautions will also help avoid damage to the trail.

The route involves several creek crossings, some of which have narrow clearance between the trees and deep wheel ruts and potholes. Some lower-clearance 4WD vehicles and those fitted with side steps may have difficulties at these crossings.

The route travels through lodgepole pine forest interspersed with open meadows. Elk and mule deer are frequently viewed in the early morning or late afternoon.

The route starts at the intersection of FR 550 and FR 500, 3.6 miles after turning off CR 129 and some 34 miles north of Steamboat Springs. The boggiest section of the trail is encountered at the 9.5-mile point.

Before crossing the creek it is advisable to walk ahead for the next mile or so to check conditions. The creek crossing can itself be boggy, but the more difficult sections come after it. Shortly after crossing the creek, the trail turns right and descends down an open meadow. It then turns left into the trees, crosses the creek again, and emerges into another meadow. This is the boggiest section of the trail; if you cannot get through, you will have a very hard time getting back out.

From this point, there are a few tricky creek crossings where the surrounding area can be rutted and boggy and clearance between the trees tight. But if you've made it this far, these crossings should seem easy!

The route continues uneventfully to Hog Park Guard Station and the Wyoming border, then continues east to Cowdrey on a well-maintained, unpaved road; but you may also choose to loop around to the west and then south back to Steamboat Springs, by way of either Elkhorn Mountain and Stock Driveway (Northern #18) or the well-maintained FR 550. From Hog Park USFS Picnic Ground to the intersection of FR 550 and FR 508 (to connect with Northern #18) is 8.6 miles.

Backcountry campsites are plentiful along the trail, and water is readily available.

Current Road Conditions

Routt National Forest
Hahns Peak Ranger District
925 Weiss Drive
Steamboat Springs, CO 80487
(970) 879-1870

Exploring the forest near the trail

Map References

USFS   Routt National Forest
Maptech CD: Denver/Steamboat Springs/North Central
Benchmark's *Colorado Road & Recreation Atlas*, pp. 45, 46
The Roads of Colorado, pp. 20, 22
Colorado Atlas & Gazetteer, pp. 16, 17
Trails Illustrated, #113, #116

Route Directions

▼ 0.0		At intersection of FR 550 and FR 500, zero trip meter and proceed east along FR 500 toward Big Red Park.
7.5 ▲		End at intersection with FR 550.
GPS: N 40°53.46′ W 106°54.93′		
▼ 0.1	SO	FR 506 on left.
7.4 ▲	SO	FR 506 on right.
▼ 1.0	SO	500.1D on left.
6.5 ▲	SO	500.1D on right.
▼ 1.1	SO	FR 509 on left.
6.4 ▲	SO	FR 509 on right.
▼ 1.6	SO	FR 402 on right. Cross over King Solomon Creek.
5.9 ▲	SO	Cross over King Solomon Creek. FR 402 on left.
▼ 2.4	SO	FR 505 on right.
5.1 ▲	SO	FR 505 on left.
▼ 4.2	SO	Cross over Middle Fork of the Little Snake River.
3.3 ▲	SO	Cross over Middle Fork of the Little Snake River.
▼ 4.6	SO	500.1A on right.
2.9 ▲	SO	500.1A on left.
▼ 5.1	SO	Track on right.
2.3 ▲	SO	Track on left.
▼ 5.5	SO	Cross over creek and track on left.
2.0 ▲	SO	Track on right. Cross over creek.
▼ 6.6	SO	Faint track on left.
0.9 ▲	SO	Faint track on right.
▼ 7.2	SO	Track on right.
0.3 ▲	SO	Track on left.
▼ 7.3	SO	FR 499 south is a sharp right (becomes Wyoming Trail walking track).
0.1 ▲	SO	FR 499 south on left (becomes Wyoming Trail walking track).
▼ 7.5	TR	Onto FR 499. Zero trip meter.
0.0 ▲		Continue along FR 500.
GPS: N 40°56.59′ W 106°51.70′		
▼ 0.0		Continue along FR 499.
2.6 ▲	TL	Onto FR 500. Zero trip meter.
▼ 0.2	SO	Cabin ruins on right.
2.4 ▲	SO	Cabin ruins on left.
▼ 2.0	SO	Cross through the South Fork of Hog Park Creek.
0.6 ▲	SO	Cross through the South Fork of Hog Park Creek.
GPS: N 40°57.77′ W 106°50.89′		
▼ 2.1	BR	Descend down a boggy meadow.
0.5 ▲	BL	Ascend another boggy meadow; then bear left.
▼ 2.3	BL	Cross through creek and enter second meadow with some potentially very boggy sections.
0.3 ▲	BR	Cross boggy meadow. Cross through creek; then bear right.
▼ 2.6	SO	Creek crossing. Zero trip meter.
0.0 ▲		Continue along FR 499.
GPS: N 40°58.34′ W 106°50.22′		
▼ 0.0		Continue along FR 499.
3.3 ▲	SO	Creek crossing. Zero trip meter.

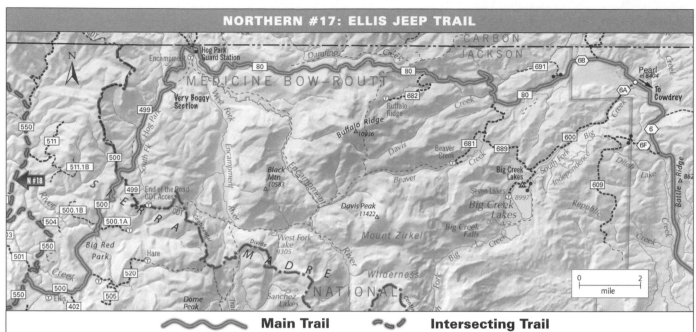

⌇⌇⌇ **Main Trail**   ⌇⌇ **Intersecting Trail**

▼ 1.0	BL	Intersection of FR 499 and FR 82. Proceed along FR 82.
2.3 ▲	BR	Intersection of FR 499 and FR 82. Proceed along FR 499.

GPS: N 40°58.96' W 106°49.61'

▼ 2.9	BL	Proceed through gate; then intersection with FR 82.1A. Remain on FR 82.
0.4 ▲	BR	Intersection with FR 82.1A; then gate. Remain on FR 82.

GPS: N 41°00.00' W 106°49.23'

▼ 3.3	TR	Intersection with CR 6B (also posted as FR 496, but the FR label will change to FR 80 shortly). Zero trip meter.
0.0 ▲		Proceed along CR 6B west.

GPS: N 41°00.27' W 106°49.04'

▼ 0.0		Proceed along CR 6B east.
37.2 ▲	TL	Intersection with CR 6B. Zero trip meter.
▼ 0.2	SO	Encampment trailhead; then bridge over Encampment River. Road on left (FR 496) to Encampment, Wyoming. Remain on FR 80 east.
37.0 ▲	SO	FR 496 on right to Encampment, Wyoming. Bridge over Encampment River.
▼ 2.0	SO	Gated track on left.
35.2 ▲	SO	Gated track on right.
▼ 2.4	SO	Cross through Ryan Park.
34.8 ▲	SO	Cross through Ryan Park.
▼ 4.1	SO	Gated track on left.
33.1 ▲	SO	Gated track on right.
▼ 4.4	SO	Gated track on left.
32.8 ▲	SO	Gated track on right.
▼ 6.7	SO	Track on right.
30.5 ▲	SO	Track on left.
▼ 8.7	SO	Gated track on right.
28.5 ▲	SO	Gated track on left.
▼ 9.0	SO	Gated track on left.
28.2 ▲	SO	Gated track on right.
▼ 9.6	SO	Track on right is FR 682, through Buffalo Park to Buffalo Ridge trailhead.
27.6 ▲	SO	Track on left is FR 682, through Buffalo Park to Buffalo Ridge trailhead.
▼ 10.4	SO	Track on left.

26.8 ▲	SO	Track on right.
▼ 13.2	SO	FR 690 on right.
24.0 ▲	SO	FR 690 on left.
▼ 13.5	SO	FR 681 to Big Creek Lake on right.
23.7 ▲	SO	FR 681 to Big Creek Lake on left.
▼ 15.6	SO	Track on right.
21.6 ▲	SO	Track on left.
▼ 15.7	SO	FR 691 on left.
21.5 ▲	SO	FR 691 on right.
▼ 16.0	SO	Cattle guard. Entering private land.
21.2 ▲	SO	Cattle guard.
▼ 17.4	BR	Road on left.
19.8 ▲	BL	Road on right.

GPS: N 40°59.76' W 106°33.81'

▼ 19.0	SO	Town of Pearl. Bear Creek Road (FR 600) on right.
18.2 ▲	SO	Bear Creek Road (FR 600) on left. Town of Pearl.
▼ 19.5	SO	Bridge over South Fork of Big Creek.
17.7 ▲	SO	Bridge over South Fork of Big Creek.
▼ 22.1	SO	FR 609 on right.
15.1 ▲	SO	FR 609 on left.
▼ 29.4	SO	CR 7 on right.
7.8 ▲	SO	CR 7 on left.
▼ 30.6	SO	Road on right.
6.6 ▲	SO	Road on left.
▼ 32.1	SO	CR 35 on left.
5.1 ▲	SO	CR 35 on right.
▼ 32.2	SO	Paved.
5.0 ▲	SO	Unpaved.
▼ 35.2	SO	Bridge over North Platte River.
2.0 ▲	SO	Bridge over North Platte River.
▼ 36.0	SO	Cross over bridge.
1.2 ▲	SO	Cross over bridge.
▼ 37.2		End at intersection of CR 6W and CR 125 beside Cowdry General Store.
0.0 ▲		In Cowdry at intersection of CR 6W and CR 125 (beside Cowdry General Store), zero trip meter and proceed west on CR 6W.

GPS: N 40°51.58' W 106°18.76'

Elkhorn Mountain and Stock Driveway

Starting Point:	**Intersection of CR 129 and FR 550**
Finishing Point:	**Intersection of CR 129 and FR 550**
Total Mileage:	**33.5 miles**
Unpaved Mileage:	**33.5 miles**
Driving Time:	**2.5 hours**
Elevation Range:	**7,030 to 9407 feet**
Usually Open:	**Mid-June to late September**
Difficulty Rating:	**4**
Scenic Rating:	**8**

Special Attractions

- Remote 4WD trail.
- Varied scenery, with wonderful aspen viewing in the fall.
- Forms a 4WD loop route when combined with Northern #17: Ellis Jeep Trail.

History

Basque shepherds developed this route in the late 1800s. The carvings on the aspens date from that time.

Description

This route commences along FR 550, a well-maintained gravel road that intersects with CR 129 about 30 miles north of Steamboat Springs.

About 2 miles after the turnoff onto FR 508, the road becomes 4WD. Shortly after passing the Elkhorn Mine, the road

The trees grow close to the trail in sections

starts the first of two rather steep sections as it ascends Elkhorn Mountain. After leveling off for about half a mile, the road descends the west side of Elkhorn Mountain. The track is rocky and eroded in places but in dry conditions should not pose any problems other than a bumpy ride.

The road travels through some magnificent stands of aspen, with the clearance between the trees being a squeeze for a full-sized vehicle. In fall, the aspen leaves radiate a yellow glow that casts a luminous effect over the entire area.

The route continues through a couple of areas that are likely to be boggy and rutted after rain. The base is reasonably firm, so these sections should not pose too much of an obstacle if you have high clearance and maintain a steady momentum.

At CR 129, the road returns to well-maintained 2WD conditions and proceeds south to rejoin FR 550, where this route commenced.

Current Road Conditions

Medicine Bow & Routt National Forest
Hahns Peak Ranger District
925 Weiss Drive
Steamboat Springs, CO 80487
(970) 879-1870

Map References

USFS Medicine Bow & Routt National Forest
Maptech CD: Denver/Steamboat Springs/North Central;
         Craig/Meeker/Northwest
Benchmark's *Colorado Road & Recreation Atlas*, p. 45
The Roads of Colorado, pp. 20, 21
Colorado Atlas & Gazetteer, p. 16
Trails Illustrated, #116

Route Directions

▼ 0.0			At intersection of CR 129 and FR 550, just north of Columbine, zero trip meter, turn onto Whiskey Park Road (FR 550), and proceed northeast.
	11.5 ▲		End at intersection of CR 129 and FR 550.
		GPS: N 40°51.65' W 106°57.63'	
▼ 0.1		SO	Seasonal gate.
	11.4 ▲	SO	Seasonal gate.
▼ 3.6		SO	Road on right to Big Red Park is FR 500, turnoff for Northern #17: Ellis Jeep Trail.
	7.9 ▲	SO	Road on left to Big Red Park is FR 500, turnoff for Northern #17: Ellis Jeep Trail.
		GPS: N 40°53.46' W 106°54.93'	
▼ 3.7		SO	FR 501 on left.
	7.8 ▲	SO	FR 501 on right.
▼ 4.2		SO	Cross over King Solomon Creek.
	7.3 ▲	SO	Cross over King Solomon Creek.
▼ 6.1		SO	Duncan Road (FR 504) on right.
	5.4 ▲	SO	Duncan Road (FR 504) on left.
▼ 7.5		SO	FR 503 on left to King Solomon Creek and Slater. Then cattle guard.
	3.9 ▲	SO	Cattle guard. FR 503 on right to King Solomon Creek and Slater.
▼ 8.4		SO	Cross over Middle Fork of the Little Snake River.
	3.1 ▲	SO	Cross over Middle Fork of the Little Snake River.
▼ 9.2		SO	FR 502.1A on left. FR 553 on right.

2.3 ▲	SO	FR 553 on left. FR 502.1A on right.
▼ 9.5	SO	Cross over Middle Fork of Snake River.
2.0 ▲	SO	Cross over Middle Fork of Snake River.
▼ 9.8	SO	FR 511 on right.
1.7 ▲	SO	FR 511 on left.
▼ 10.5	SO	Enter Whiskey Park.
0.9 ▲	SO	Leave Whiskey Park.
▼ 10.7	SO	Cross over Whiskey Park Creek.
0.8 ▲	SO	Cross over Whiskey Park Creek.
▼ 11.4	SO	Leave Whiskey Park.
0.1 ▲	SO	Enter Whiskey Park.
▼ 11.5	TL	Onto Elkhorn Mountain Road (FR 508). Zero trip meter.
0.0 ▲		Continue along FR 550.

GPS: N 40°58.36' W 106°54.95'

▼ 0.0		Proceed along FR 508.
8.8 ▲	TR	Onto FR 550. Zero trip meter.
▼ 0.6	SO	FR 508B on left.
8.2 ▲	SO	FR 508B on right.
▼ 1.1	SO	Track on right.
7.7 ▲	SO	Track on left.
▼ 1.2	BR	Fork in the road. Follow FR 508.
7.6 ▲	BL	Fork in the road. Follow FR 508.
▼ 1.6	SO	Whiskey Park Trailhead. Cross over creek.
7.2 ▲	SO	Cross over creek. Whiskey Park Trailhead.
▼ 2.4	SO	Elkhorn Mine building ruins on left.
6.4 ▲	SO	Elkhorn Mine building ruins on right.
▼ 2.5	SO	Track to Elkhorn Mine on left.
6.3 ▲	SO	Track to Elkhorn Mine on right.
▼ 2.6	BR	Fork in the road. Follow FR 508. 508F is straight ahead.
6.2 ▲	BL	Follow FR 508.
▼ 2.7	BR	Fork in the road. Follow FR 508.
6.1 ▲	BL	Track on right.
▼ 4.0	BR	Walking track 1149 on left.
4.8 ▲	SO	Walking track 1149 on right.
▼ 4.7	BL	Fork in the road. FR 1149 on right.
4.0 ▲	BR	Fork in the road. FR 1149 on left.

GPS: N 40°59.45' W 106°59.02'

▼ 5.1	SO	Stock trough on right.
3.6 ▲	SO	Stock trough on left.

GPS: N 40°59.23' W 106°59.33'

▼ 5.3	SO	Cross through small creek.
3.4 ▲	SO	Cross through small creek.
▼ 5.5	SO	508H on left.
3.2 ▲	SO	508H on right.
▼ 5.6	SO	Track on left.
3.2 ▲	SO	Track on right.
▼ 7.6	SO	Cross over creek.
1.1 ▲	SO	Cross over creek.
▼ 8.7	SO	Cattle guard. Leaving Routt National Forest; entering Three Forks Ranch.
0.1 ▲	SO	Leaving Three Forks Ranch; entering Routt National Forest. Cattle guard.

GPS: N 40°59.98' W 107°01.84'

▼ 8.8	TL	T-intersection with FR 551. Zero trip meter.
0.0 ▲		Continue on FR 508.

GPS: N 40°59.95' W 107°01.96'

▼ 0.0		Continue on FR 551.

An old water trough along the stock driveway

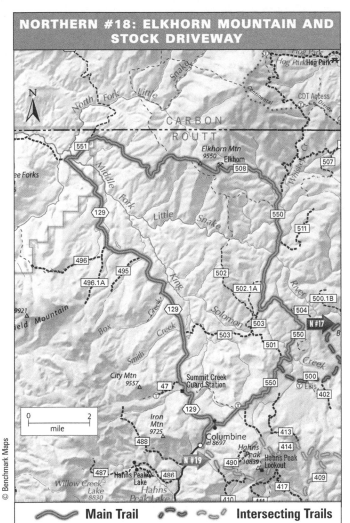

© Benchmark Maps

Main Trail ～ ～ **Intersecting Trails**

13.2 ▲	TR	Intersection with FR 508. Zero trip meter.	
▼ 0.8	SO	Cross bridge.	
12.4 ▲	SO	Cross bridge.	
▼ 1.1	TL	T-intersection. U-turn left onto FR 129.	
12.1 ▲	TR	Onto FR 551.	

GPS: N 40°59.38' W 107°02.91'

▼ 2.3	SO	Cattle guard. Three Forks Ranch entrance.
10.9 ▲	SO	Three Forks Ranch entrance. Cattle guard.
▼ 2.7	SO	Cattle guard.
10.5 ▲	SO	Cattle guard.
▼ 3.3	SO	FR 407 on left.
9.9 ▲	SO	FR 407 on right.
▼ 6.6	SO	Cattle guard.
6.6 ▲	SO	Cattle guard.
▼ 8.1	SO	Cattle guard.
5.1 ▲	SO	Cattle guard.
▼ 9.3	BR	FR 503 on left. Follow FR 129 toward Columbine.
3.9 ▲	SO	FR 503 on right.
▼ 11.9	SO	FR 129.1A on left.
1.3 ▲	SO	FR 129.1A on right.
▼ 13.2		End at intersection with FR 550.
0.0 ▲		At intersection of FR 550 and FR 129 above Columbine, zero trip meter and proceed along FR 129.

GPS: N 40°51.65' W 106°57.63'

Farwell Mountain Trail

Starting Point:	**CR 129 in the town of Hahns Peak**
Finishing Point:	**CR 129 in Columbine**
Total Mileage:	**11.7 miles, plus 3.9-mile spur to Farwell**
	Mountain and 0.9-mile spur to Hahns
	Peak
Unpaved Mileage:	**11.7 miles, plus spurs**
Driving Time:	**3.5 hours, including spurs**
Elevation Range:	**8,120 to 10,185 feet**
Usually Open:	**June to October**
Difficulty Rating:	**5**
Scenic Rating:	**10**

Special Attractions

■ Two excellent spurs take you to excellent view points.

■ Many side tracks for ATV and motorbike enthusiasts.

■ Accessible for snowmobiles in winter.

Description

Farwell Mountain Trail arcs to the east of CR 129, making an exciting alternate route between the towns of Hahns Peak and Columbine. The trail begins by heading through Hahns Peak. The first of the trail's challenges comes at the 1.1-mile mark: A 10-yard stretch of mud, which appears to be boggy all the time, is located just out of town. When conditions are dry, it is much easier to negotiate.

The trail then heads northeast through a wide meadow above Ways Gulch. Be sure to stay on the trail at this point, avoiding the temptation to cut a new track. The trail is not difficult at this point, but it is rough enough to keep your speed in check. The trail steadily climbs up the spur to Farwell Mountain, passing through the meadow and into a more sheltered area.

The trail can become very boggy

Farwell Mountain

The spur to Farwell Mountain is probably the most difficult part of this trail, but it remains a 4-rated track with a couple spots that would become a 5 if conditions were less than ideal. The spur climbs the entire way along a loose, rubbly surface. It winds through the forest and eventually comes to an intersection before a near-treeless area that looks like it has suffered the ravages of wildfire in the past. The track on the left at this intersection is open; however, due to forest service closures, it does not continue all the way to FR 400. The trail climbs the last few pitches to the communications towers at the top of Farwell Mountain. The views from the top are breathtaking. If you walk a short distance to the south, there is an overlook of Pearl and Steamboat Lakes. Hahns Peak is also visible from the summit.

The main trail continues past the spur to Farwell Mountain, climbing steadily along a shelf road to another spur to Hahns Peak. This short spur is essentially one steep climb that switchbacks its way just below the peak. The surface is some-

Alpine meadow surrounded by aspen stands

what loose, so use a slow, steady pace. The spur ends at a wide parking area before a road closure sign. Views from this point are excellent, but the hike up to the summit is well worth the effort. Back on the main trail, it is a relatively easy drive back to CR 129 at Columbine.

This trail has many side tracks and makes an excellent starting point from which to explore the area. This network of trails is quite popular with ATV and motorbike enthusiasts.

Current Road Information
Medicine Bow & Routt National Forests
Hahns Peak/Bears Ears Ranger District
925 Weiss Drive
Steamboat Springs, CO 80487
(970) 879-1870

Map References
USFS   Routt National Forest
Maptech CD: Denver/Steamboat Springs/
  North Central
Benchmark's *Colorado Road & Recreation Atlas*, pp. 45, 46
Colorado Atlas & Gazetteer, p. 16
The Roads of Colorado, pp. 28, 29, 44, 45
Trails Illustrated, #116

Route Directions

▼ 0.0			Trail starts on CR 129 in the town of Hahns Peak. Zero trip meter. Turn north onto Main Street and proceed through town.
	5.8 ▲		Trail ends on CR 129 in the town of Hahns Peak. Turn left for Steamboat Springs; turn right for Columbine.
			GPS: N40°48.34′ W106°56.65′
▼ 0.6		SO	FR 40 on left.
	5.2 ▲	BL	FR 40 on right.
▼ 0.8		SO	Track on left; then track on right.
	5.0 ▲	SO	Track on right; then track on left.
▼ 1.1		SO	Muddy section on trail.
	4.7 ▲	SO	Muddy section on trail.
▼ 1.8		BR	FR 411 on left.
	4.0 ▲	SO	FR 411 on sharp right.
			GPS: N40°48.58′ W106°55.25′
▼ 2.4		SO	Entering Medicine Bow & Routt National Forests through seasonal closure gate.
	3.4 ▲	SO	Leaving Medicine Bow & Routt National Forests through seasonal closure gate.
▼ 2.7		BR	FR 417A on left.
	3.1 ▲	SO	FR 417A on sharp right.
▼ 3.0		BR	FR 409D on left.
	2.8 ▲	BL	FR 409D on right.
▼ 3.6		SO	FR 417 on left.
	2.2 ▲	SO	FR 417 on right.
			GPS: N40°49.56′ W106°54.03′
▼ 3.7		SO	Track on right.
	2.1 ▲	BR	Track on left.
▼ 4.5		SO	Cross through wash.
	1.3 ▲	SO	Cross through wash.
▼ 5.1		SO	Cross through creek.
	0.7 ▲	SO	Cross through creek.
▼ 5.3		TL	T-intersection with unmarked road.
	0.5 ▲	TR	Unmarked road continues straight ahead.

NORTHERN #19: FARWELL MOUNTAIN TRAIL

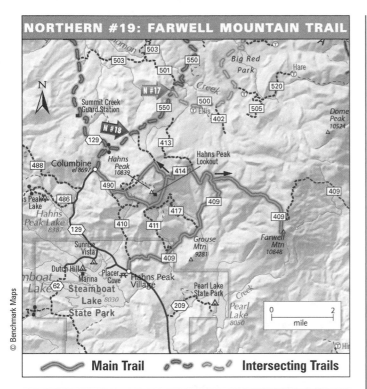

Main Trail ~~~ **Intersecting Trails** ~~~

GPS: N40°50.59' W106°53.34'

| ▼ 5.7 | BR | Track on left is first entrance to FR 414. |
| 0.1 ▲ | SO | Track on sharp right goes back up to FR 414. |

| ▼ 5.8 | TL | Track on right is spur to Farwell Mountain (FR 409). Zero trip meter and turn left onto FR 414. |
| 0.0 ▲ | | Continue to the southwest on FR 409. |

GPS: N40°50.92' W106°53.60'

Spur to Farwell Mountain

| ▼ 0.0 | | Proceed northeast on FR 409. |
| ▼ 0.4 | BL | Track straight ahead. Remain on main trail. |

Communications towers at the summit of Farwell Mountain

| ▼ 3.2 | BR | Track on left. Bear right onto FR 409B. |
| ▼ 3.9 | | Trail ends at radio towers on Farwell Mountain. |

GPS: N40°49.41' W106°51.08'

Continuation of Main Trail

| ▼ 0.0 | | Continue to the west on FR 414. |
| 2.9 ▲ | TR | Track straight ahead is spur to Farwell Mountain. Zero trip meter and turn sharp right onto FR 409. |

GPS: N40°50.92' W106°53.60'

| ▼ 0.8 | SO | Track on right and track on left. |
| 2.1 ▲ | SO | Track on right and track on left. |

| ▼ 2.2 | BL | Track straight ahead is FR 414. |
| 0.7 ▲ | BR | Track straight ahead is FR 414. |

GPS: N40°51.03' W106°55.27'

| ▼ 2.5 | SO | Cross through wash. |
| 0.4 ▲ | SO | Cross through wash. |

| ▼ 2.9 | BL | Track on sharp right is spur to Hahns Peak. Zero trip meter and proceed past second track on right. |
| 0.0 ▲ | | Continue to the north. |

GPS: N40°50.55' W106°55.47'

Spur to Hahns Peak

Beginning of final climb up Farwell spur

View of Pearl Lake from the trail

▼ 0.0		Proceed north up the shelf road.
▼ 0.9		Spur ends below Hahns Peak where the road is blocked. From here, you can park and hike the final distance up to Hahns Peak.

GPS: N40°50.75′ W106°55.74′

Continuation of Main Trail

▼ 0.0		Continue to the southeast.
	3.0 ▲	Track on sharp left; then second track on left is spur to Hahns Peak. Zero trip meter.

GPS: N40°50.55′ W106°55.47′

▼ 0.3	SO	Track on sharp left.
	2.7 ▲ BL	Track on right.
▼ 0.5	SO	FR 409B on sharp left.
	2.5 ▲ SO	FR 409B on right.
▼ 0.7	BL	FR 417 on sharp left; then track on right.
	2.3 ▲ BL	Track on sharp left; then FR 417 on right.

GPS: N40°50.24′ W106°55.88′

▼ 0.9	SO	FR 410B on sharp left.
	2.1 ▲ BL	FR 410B on right.
▼ 1.0	BL	Track on right.
	2.0 ▲ SO	Track on left.
▼ 1.2	BL	Track on right.
	1.8 ▲ SO	Track on left.
▼ 1.4	SO	Track on left goes to campsite in 0.1 miles.
	1.6 ▲ SO	Track on right goes to campsite in 0.1 miles.
▼ 1.5	SO	Cross through creek.
	1.5 ▲ SO	Cross through creek.
▼ 1.7	BL	FR 418 on right, signed to Hahns Peak and Trail No. 1158.
	1.3 ▲ BR	FR 418 on left, signed to Hahns Peak and Trail No. 1158.

GPS: N40°50.56′ W106°56.86′

▼ 2.1	SO	FR 410 on left is for motorbikes only.
	0.9 ▲ SO	FR 410 on right is for motorbikes only.
▼ 3.0		Trail ends on CR 129 in Columbine. Turn left for the town of Hahns Peak and Steamboat Springs.
	0.0 ▲	Trail starts on CR 129 in Columbine, 4.7 miles from the southern end of the trail in Hahns Peak. Zero trip meter and head northwest on narrow, rough FR 490.

GPS: N40°51.21′ W106°57.91′

Muddy Creek Trail

Starting Point:	Intersection of Crooked Creek Road (FR 139) and FR 134
Finishing Point:	Intersection of CR 3 and US 40 near Parshall
Total Mileage:	17.8 miles
Unpaved Mileage:	15.8 miles
Driving Time:	1.25 hours
Elevation Range:	7,600 to 9,900 feet
Usually Open:	Late May to late November
Difficulty Rating:	3
Scenic Rating:	8

Special Attractions

■ Scenic road through Arapaho National Forest that can be used to form a loop.
■ Side road to FR 139.
■ The challenge of negotiating numerous mud holes.

Description

This 4WD trail is another side road to FR 139. It is a scenic road that is usually more challenging than many of the others in the area. We have rated the trail based on dry conditions, when the greatest problem you may face is negotiating the many rutted mud holes. However, if the conditions are adverse, the trail can be impassable to stock vehicles. These conditions are especially likely during fall hunting season when the trail is heavily used. At such times, the rating would be either 6 or 7. One fairly steep downhill section is extremely slippery when wet, which makes traveling in the southerly, or reverse, direction even more difficult. We recommend mud tires and/or chains if the weather conditions make mud likely. At times the clearance is tight as you pass between the trees, but overall the route offers little difficulty unless the road is muddy.

The route is more scenic than many in the area. There are panoramic views from the higher sections, and the forest includes some sizable stands of aspen, which in combination with the attractive open meadows provide welcome variety to the scenery. As you exit the forest, the route travels through rolling rangeland before offering a good view of Williams Fork Reservoir.

Current Road Conditions

Arapaho & Roosevelt National Forests
Sulphur Ranger District
9 Ten Mile Drive, Granby, CO 80446
(970) 887-4100

Map References

USFS Arapaho & Roosevelt National Forests
Maptech CD: Colorado Springs/Ski Areas/Central

NORTHERN #20: MUDDY CREEK TRAIL

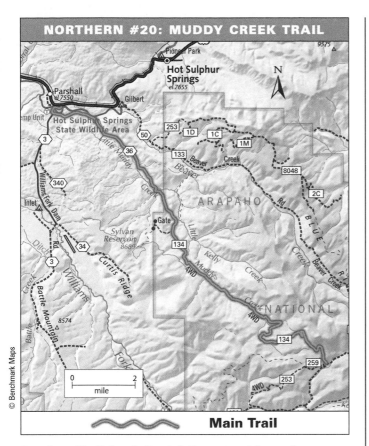

Main Trail

© Benchmark Maps

Benchmark's *Colorado Road & Recreation Atlas*, p. 61
Colorado Atlas & Gazetteer, pp. 28, 38
The Roads of Colorado, p. 54
Trails Illustrated, #106, #107

Route Directions

▼ 0.0			From FR 139, zero trip meter and turn onto Muddy Creek Road (FR 134).
	10.7 ▲		End at the intersection with FR 139.
		GPS: N 39°55.68′ W 106°00.21′	
▼ 0.1		SO	Cook Creek Road (FR 253) on left.
	10.6 ▲	SO	Cook Creek Road (FR 253) on right.
▼ 0.8		SO	Track on left.
	9.9 ▲	SO	Track on right.
▼ 1.0		SO	Track on left.
	9.7 ▲	SO	Track on right.
▼ 2.9		SO	Track on left.
	7.8 ▲	SO	Track on right.
▼ 4.5		BL	Two tracks on right; then cross over Muddy Creek.
	6.1 ▲	BR	Cross over Muddy Creek; then two tracks on left.
		GPS: N 39°56.87′ W 106°01.95′	
▼ 5.4		SO	Cross through gate (leave it as you find it).
	5.3 ▲	SO	Cross through gate (leave it as you find it).
▼ 6.1		SO	Track on right.
	4.6 ▲	SO	Track on left.
▼ 7.0		SO	Cross bridge over creek; then track on left.
	3.7 ▲	SO	Track on right; then cross bridge over creek.
		GPS: N 39°57.75′ W 106°04.16′	
▼ 7.0		SO	Cross through gate (leave it as you find it).
	3.6 ▲	SO	Cross through gate (leave it as you find it).

▼ 7.4		SO	Track on right.
	3.3 ▲	SO	Track on left.
▼ 7.6		SO	Track on left.
	3.0 ▲	SO	Track on right.
▼ 7.8-8.0		SO	A potentially very boggy section.
	2.6-2.8 ▲	SO	A potentially very boggy section.
▼ 8.2		SO	Tracks on left and right; then cross over creek.
	2.4 ▲	SO	Cross over creek; then tracks on left and right.
▼ 9.5		SO	Track on right.
	1.1 ▲	SO	Track on left.
		GPS: N 39°59.17′ W 106°05.76′	
▼ 9.9		SO	Track on right.
	0.8 ▲	SO	Track on left.
▼ 10.2		SO	Track on left.
	0.4 ▲	BL	Track on right.
▼ 10.7		SO	Leave Arapaho National Forest and cross cattle guard. Name of road changes to CR 340. Zero trip meter.
	0.0 ▲		Continue along route.
		GPS: N 39°59.66′ W 106°06.69′	
▼ 0.0			Continue along route.
	7.1 ▲	SO	Cross cattle guard and enter Arapaho National Forest. Name of road changes to FR 134. Zero trip meter.
▼ 0.5		SO	Cattle guard.
	6.6 ▲	SO	Cattle guard.
▼ 0.8		SO	Cattle guard.
	6.3 ▲	SO	Cattle guard.
▼ 2.0		SO	Cattle guard.

A section of the trail showing how muddy it can become, especially during hunting season

5.1 ▲	SO	Cattle guard.	
▼ 3.1	SO	Cattle guard.	
4.0 ▲	SO	Cattle guard.	
▼ 5.1	TR	Intersection with CR 3.	
2.0 ▲	BL	Onto CR 340.	
		GPS: N 40°01.76' W 106°10.86'	
▼ 6.8	BR	Cross creek.	
0.3 ▲	BL	Cross creek.	
▼ 7.1		End at intersection with US 40.	
0.0 ▲		At the intersection of US 40 and CR 3 near Parshall, zero trip meter and proceed along CR 3.	
		GPS: N 40°03.10' W 106°09.91'	

NORTHERN REGION TRAIL #21

Stillwater Pass Trail

Starting Point:	**Intersection of FR 120 (Kawuneeche Road) and FR 123**
Finishing Point:	**Intersection of Stillwater Pass Road and Colorado 125**
Total Mileage:	**19.6 miles**
Unpaved Mileage:	**19.6 miles**
Driving Time:	**1.25 hours**
Elevation Range:	**8,646 to 10,624 feet**
Usually Open:	**June to mid-November**
Difficulty Rating:	**2**
Scenic Rating:	**8**

Special Attractions

- Easygoing, scenic drive through Arapaho & Roosevelt National Forests.
- Good backcountry camping opportunities.
- A network of forest roads to explore.
- A network of multiuse trails for dirt bikes, ATVs, and snowmobiles in winter.

History

Stillwater Pass Road skirts the Bowen Gulch Protection Area to the west. The area was first established in 1993 and helps to preserve one of Colorado's largest and most outstanding old-growth spruce-fir forests. Some of the trees are more than 400 years old and measure about 4 feet in diameter, uncommon at such a high elevation (10,500 feet).

In 1988, the U.S. Forest Service sold logging rights to the Louisiana-Pacific Corporation. This decision enraged a number of environmental activists, who chained themselves to trees in order to stop the logging operations. Their protest met with success, as the U.S. government granted protection status to the area in 1993.

Although there are no roads through the area, visitors can explore it on foot. The Bowen Gulch Interpretive Trail, constructed in 1993 by the forest service, the Colorado Division of Wildlife, and the Colorado Mountain Club Foundation,

travels through the old-growth forest in the protection area. A number of species not normally found this far south can be spotted here. These include wood frogs, pygmy shrews, and even a wolverine on occasion.

Just north of Stillwater Pass Road is Willow Creek Pass, named for one of the streams that originate nearby. The pass was first noted as Good Pass in the federally commissioned 1873 Hayden Survey, although there is no record of why it was so named. The route over the pass began as an Indian trail and was developed in 1902, much later than similar pass roads. A stage line provided transport between the towns of Granby and Walden in the early twentieth century. Passengers could stop for a meal at the Willow Lodge roadhouse, located at the top of the pass. Today the pass sits along the Continental Divide Trail.

Description

This scenic trail begins heading west from Kawuneeche Road (FR 120). For most of its length, it is a wide, well-maintained forest road along which navigation is not difficult. There is a network of forest roads in the area for further exploring, and the extensive multiuse trail system crisscrossing the road is

View of Shadow Mountain Lake from the trail

Willow Creek runs beside the trail

popular with motorbikes, ATVs, and snowmobiles in the winter. A large staging area for unloading motorbikes, ATVs, and snowmobiles is located at the beginning of the trail.

Numerous good backcountry campsites are located along this trail, which travels through pine and aspen stands. Especially on the east side of the pass, stands of aspens glow golden yellow in fall. Climbing through the forest to the northwest toward the pass, the road narrows into one-lane with plenty of pullouts for passing. A few potholes, some erosion, and embedded rocks on the climb to the summit give the trail its difficulty rating of 2. These elements do not present difficulties to most stock 4WD vehicles.

Beyond the pass, the road descends to follow the scenic Willow Creek. Although views from the trail are limited, at points there are overlooks of Shadow Mountain Lake, the Indian Peaks, and Rocky Mountain National Park.

Current Road Information
Arapaho & Roosevelt National Forests
Sulpher Ranger District
9 Ten Mile Drive
Granby, CO 80446
(970) 887-4100

Map References
USFS   Arapaho & Roosevelt National Forests
Maptech CD: Denver/Steamboat Springs/
   North Central
Benchmark's *Colorado Road & Recreation Atlas*, p. 61
Colorado Atlas & Gazetteer, p. 28
The Roads of Colorado, pp. 62, 63
Trails Illustrated, #115, #200

Route Directions

▼ 0.0			Trail begins at the intersection of Kawuneeche Road (FR 120) and FR 123. Zero trip meter and proceed west on FR 123.
	7.8 ▲		Trail ends at T-intersection with Kawuneeche Road (FR 120).
		GPS: N40°13.54′ W105°53.42′	
▼ 0.1		SO	Idelglen OHV Staging Area with restrooms and parking area. Hiking trailhead on right.
	7.7 ▲	SO	Hiking trailhead on left. Idelglen OHV Staging Area, restrooms, and parking area.
▼ 0.2		SO	Seasonal closure gate.
	7.7 ▲	SO	Seasonal closure gate
▼ 1.2		SO	FR 835.2 on left.
	6.6 ▲	SO	FR 835.2 on right.
▼ 1.5		SO	FR 835.3A on left.
	6.4 ▲	SO	FR 835.3A.
▼ 1.9		SO	FR 835.3 on right.
	5.9 ▲	SO	FR 835.3 on left.
▼ 2.6		SO	Bull Mountain Trail on left for hiking, horseback riding, mountain biking, snowmobiling, and dirt biking.
	5.3 ▲	SO	Bull Mountain Trail on right.
▼ 2.9		SO	Bull Mountain Trail on left for hiking, horseback riding, mountain biking, snowmobiling, and dirt biking.
	5.0 ▲	SO	Bull Mountain Trail on right.
▼ 3.7		SO	Hiking trail on left.
	4.1 ▲	SO	Hiking trail on right.
▼ 3.8		SO	FR 116.2 on left.
	4.1 ▲	SO	FR 116.2 on right.
▼ 4.5		SO	Hiking trail on left and right.
	3.4 ▲	SO	Hiking trail on left and right.
▼ 5.5		SO	Intersection. FR 190 on left.
	2.3 ▲	SO	Intersection. FR 190 on right.

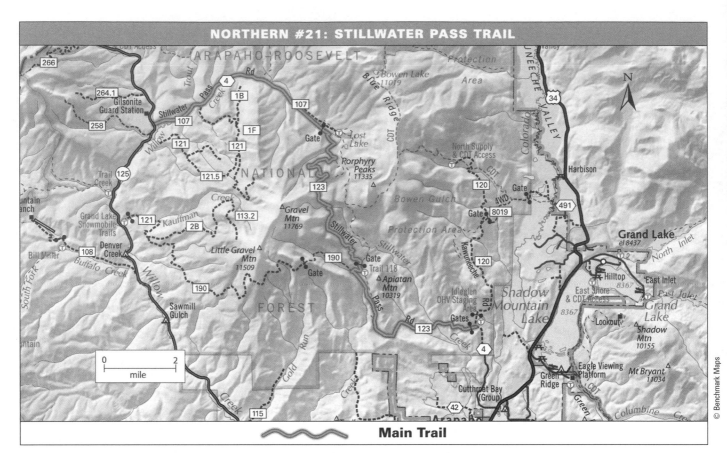

~~~ **Main Trail**

		GPS: N40°14.90' W105°57.47'				
▼ 5.6	SO	Little Gravel Spur Road (FR 816.1) on left.
2.3 ▲	SO	Little Gravel Spur Road (FR 816.1) on right.
▼ 5.7	SO	Seasonal closure gate.
2.2 ▲	SO	Seasonal closure gate.
▼ 5.9	BL	FR 123.2 on right.
1.9 ▲	BR	FR 123.2 on left.
		GPS: N40°14.90' W105°57.18'

▼ 6.1	SO	Cross over creek.
1.7 ▲	SO	Cross over creek.
▼ 6.2	SO	FR 123.2A and Gilsonite Hiking Trail on right.
1.6 ▲	SO	FR 123.2A and Gilsonite Hiking Trail on left.
▼ 7.0	SO	Pony Park on right.
0.8 ▲	SO	Pony Park on left.
▼ 7.8	TR	Intersection with FR 815.2 straight on and FR 123 on right. Zero trip meter.

One of the narrower sections of the trail

0.0 ▲		Continue south on FR 123.
	GPS: N40°15.91' W105°58.22'	
▼ 0.0		Continue north on FR 123.
11.8 ▲	TL	Intersection with FR 815.2 straight on and FR 123 on left. Zero trip meter.
▼ 0.8	SO	Cross over creek.
11.1 ▲	SO	Cross over creek
▼ 1.2	TR	FR 815.2 on left.
10.6 ▲	TL	FR 815.2 on right.
	GPS: N40°16.66' W105°58.57'	
▼ 1.3	SO	FR 815.1 on right.
10.5 ▲	SO	FR 815.1 on left.
▼ 2.2	SO	FR 814.1 on right.
9.6 ▲	BR	FR 814.1 on left.
▼ 4.1	SO	Hiking trail on right.
7.7 ▲	SO	Hiking trail on left.
▼ 4.5	SO	Cross over creek.
7.3 ▲	SO	Cross over creek.
▼ 4.6	SO	Multiuse trail on left.
7.2 ▲	SO	Multiuse trail on right.
▼ 5.9	SO	Trailhead and parking area on left; then cross over creek.
5.9 ▲	SO	Cross over creek; then trailhead and parking area on right.
▼ 6.0	SO	Seasonal closure gate.
5.8 ▲	SO	Seasonal closure gate.
▼ 6.1	SO	Road on right is FR 123.3 to Lost Lake.

5.7 ▲	BR	Road on left is FR 123.3 to Lost Lake.
	GPS: N40°18.70' W105°58.65'	
▼ 6.2	SO	FR 812.1 on right.
5.6 ▲	SO	FR 812.1 on left.
▼ 7.1	SO	Cross over creek.
4.8 ▲	SO	Cross over creek.
▼ 7.5	SO	Hiking trail on left.
4.4 ▲	SO	Hiking trail on right.
▼ 8.4	SO	Seasonal closure gate; then FR 123.4A on right.
3.4 ▲	BR	FR 123.4A on left; then seasonal closure gate.
	GPS: N40°19.72' W106°00.69'	
▼ 8.8	SO	Illinois Pass Trailhead on right.
3.0 ▲	SO	Illinois Pass Trailhead on left.
▼ 10.2	SO	Kauffman Creek Trail, FR 121 on left.
1.6 ▲	SO	Kauffman Creek Trail, FR 121 on right.
	GPS: N40°19.02' W106°02.36'	
▼ 11.7	SO	Bridge over creek; then forest service information board on right.
0.1 ▲	SO	Forest service information board on left; then bridge over creek.
▼ 11.8		Trail ends at the intersection with Colorado 125. Turn left for Granby.
0.0 ▲		Trail begins at the intersection of Colorado 125 and Stillwater Pass Road (CR 4). Proceed east on Stillwater Pass Road.
	GPS: N40°18.48' W106°03.82'	

Aspen stands mixed into the evergreen forest surrounding the trail

The Central Region

TRAILS IN THE CENTRAL REGION

- ■ 1   Saxon Mountain Road
- ■ 2   Guanella Pass Trail
- ■ 3   Waldorf and Santiago Ghost Town Trail
- ■ 4   Peru Creek Trail
- ■ 5   Handcart Gulch Trail
- ■ 6   Red Cone Peak Trail
- ■ 7   Webster Pass Trail
- ■ 8   Santa Fe Peak Trail
- ■ 9   Deer Creek Trail
- ■ 10   Radical Hill Trail
- ■ 11   Saints John and Glacier Ridge Trail
- ■ 12   Middle Fork of the Swan Trail
- ■ 13   North Fork of the Swan
       and Wise Mountain Trail
- ■ 14   Georgia Pass Trail
- ■ 15   Glacier Peak Trail
- ■ 16   Boreas Pass Trail
- ■ 17   Shrine Pass Trail
- ■ 18   Ptarmigan Pass
       and McAllister Gulch Loop
- ■ 19   Weston Pass Trail
- ■ 20   Breakneck Pass
       and Browns Pass Trail
- ■ 21   Mosquito Pass Trail
- ■ 22   Hagerman Pass Trail
- ■ 23   Lincoln Creek Trail
- ■ 24   Aspen Mountain Trail
- ■ 25   Midnight Mine and Little Annie Trail
- ■ 26   Taylor Pass Trail
- ■ 27   Reno Divide Trail
- ■ 28   Schofield Pass
       and Devils Punchbowl Trail
- ■ 29   Lead King Basin Trail
- ■ 30   Old Monarch Pass Road
- ■ 31   Black Sage Pass Road
- ■ 32   Waunita Pass Road
- ■ 33   Hancock Pass Trail
- ■ 34   Tomichi Pass Trail
- ■ 35   Cumberland Pass Trail
- ■ 36   Alpine Tunnel Road
- ■ 37   Tincup Pass Trail
- ■ 38   Mount Antero Trail
- ■ 39   Browns Lake Trail
- ■ 40   Baldwin Lakes Trail
- ■ 41   Boulder Mountain Trail
- ■ 42   Pomeroy Lakes
       and Mary Murphy Mine Trail
- ■ 43   Marshall Pass Poncha Creek Trail
- ■ 44   Marshall Pass Railway Grade Road
- ■ 45   Hayden Pass Trail
- ■ 46   Medano Pass
       and Great Sand Dunes Trail

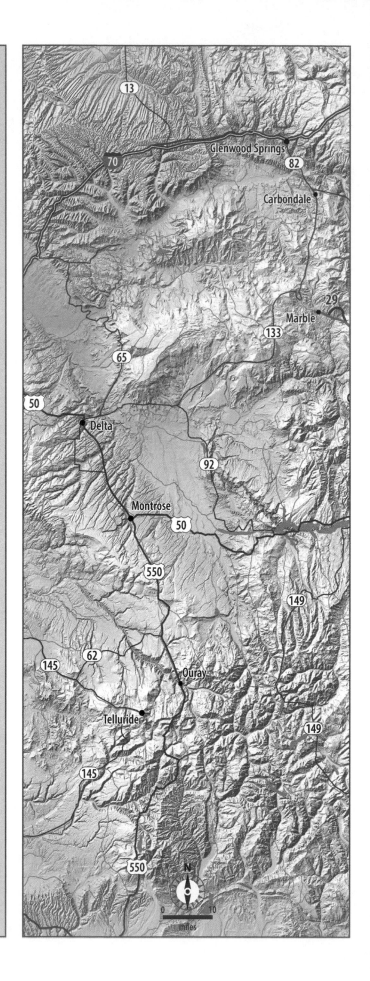

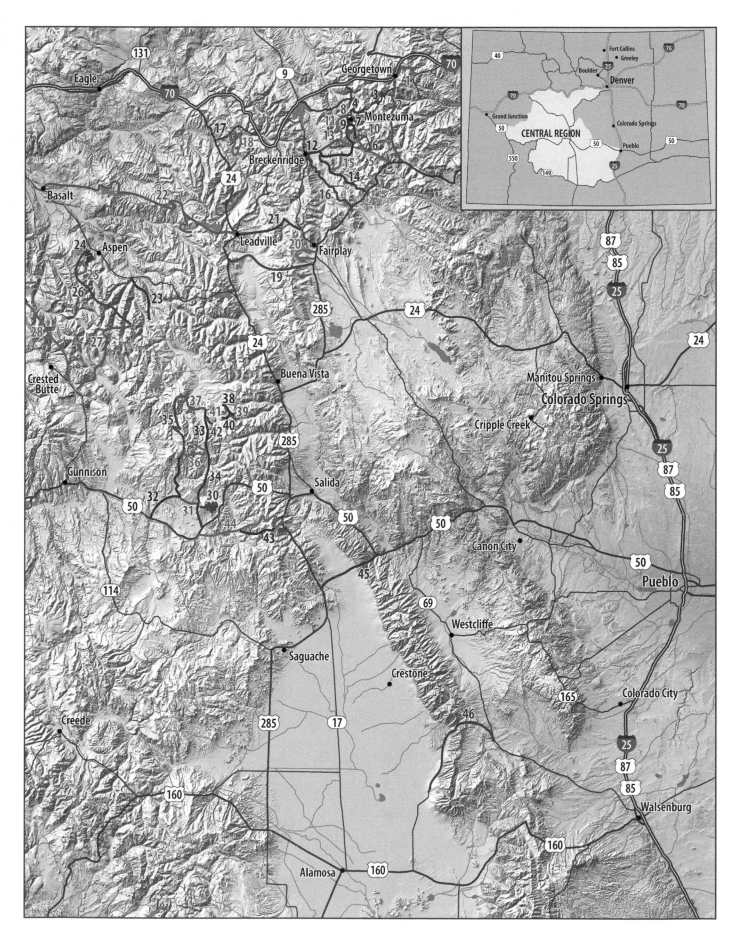

Saxon Mountain Road

Starting Point:	Clear Creek Road, 1.4 miles from I-70
Finishing Point:	Colorado 103, 4.9 miles south of I-70
Total Mileage:	13.1 miles
Unpaved Mileage:	13.1 miles
Driving Time:	2 hours
Route Elevation:	8,405 to 11,140 feet
Usually Open:	Late May to October
Difficulty Rating:	4
Scenic Rating:	8

Special Attractions

- Excellent views over Georgetown and Georgetown Lake.
- Trail links with a large network of side roads.
- Area is rich in mining history.
- Accessible to snowmobiles in winter.

History

Mining began in the area of Lamartine around 1887. Four men from Idaho Springs, Colorado, discovered a large vein of silver while following Trail Creek. Together, the four staked a claim and named it Lamartine. When one of the partners died not long after staking the claim, Peter Himrod bought a quarter interest in the claim from the partner's widow for $250. When none of the remaining partners seemed interested in developing the claim, he bought them out.

The Lamartine was first seriously worked in 1887. Although Himrod poured thousands of dollars into the mine, he received little return on his investment. When Himrod died, he passed the mine on to his son, who continued to finance its development. Himrod's son became frustrated with the lack of results and sold the mine for $360. The new owners quickly found the rich ore sought after by Himrod and his son.

With this discovery in the late 1880s, the town of Lamartine was established. The town flourished in the 1890s and early 1900s, as the Lamartine Mine produced millions of dol-

One of the trail's many switchbacks

View back down over the trail's switchbacks with Georgetown below

lars' worth of gold, silver, and lead. Yet even at the peak of the town's mining production, the population of Lamartine never exceeded 500. In 1905, the Lamartine Mine was leased out and eventually abandoned.

A couple of miles down the mountain from Lamartine was the town of Freeland. The town was established around 1880 and grew rapidly after the discovery of the Freeland lode in 1877. In 1878, a reporter from the *Georgetown Miner* wrote that 17 houses had been built in Freeland in the prior year. Just a week later, another reporter claimed that 34 houses were occupied in the town. Undisputedly, a number of businesses were flourishing in Freeland.

The town boasted a meat market, grocery store, assay office, and blacksmith shop. A post office, as well as a public school, opened in 1879. A teacher at the school, Bernice Poppen, reported that many of the pupils were older than herself. That same year the town blacksmith helped organize a Presbyterian church. He was described by a fellow resident as one who "points out the error of their ways to perishing sinners on Sundays." Freeland had a reputation of being a severely moral town, with little of the rough activities typical of many western mining towns. A visitor to the town reported that one could hear "no enticing jingle of beer glasses at Freeland."

The prosperity of the town was largely dependent upon the production of the Freeland Mine. The Freeland turned out large quantities of ore, which contained mainly silver as well as some gold and copper. The mine had its own sawmill to provide lumber for homes, heating, and supports within the mines. At the time of the mine's peak production, the majority of trees surrounding Freeland were cut.

Freeland was a bustling place during the boom years and even merited inclusion in the Colorado Business Directory from 1893 to 1905. Around the turn of the century, however, production at the Freeland Mine began to decline, and the town's fortunes followed. By 1901, only 100 people resided in Freeland. The post office closed in 1908, and the town became abandoned.

Description

Saxon Mountain Road begins on the northeastern edge of Georgetown and immediately begins its long ascent up a shelf road along the northwestern flank of Saxon Mountain. The road switchbacks a number of times during the climb, revealing better and better views over Georgetown and Georgetown

Lake. The road surface is very rocky; however, the rocks are small and easily negotiated by high-clearance vehicles. The surface is loose enough to make four-wheel drive preferable but not absolutely necessary.

The road flattens out and enters the forest on top of the mountain. At the first zero point, FR 712.2C continues ahead and climbs toward the top of Saxon Mountain. Navigation thus far has been very simple. However, once on the mountain, numerous side roads (marked and unmarked) can easily lead to confusion. The main trail is not always the correct one as far as the route described below goes. A GPS unit is a big help in staying on track. Although the many side tracks make for difficult navigation, they are also a lot of fun to explore.

The trail standard remains relatively consistent for the entire trip. There are many rocks scattered about the trail; a few ruts also make the driving more interesting.

The trail passes a few indications of the region's mining history. A few crumbling cabins can be found along the trail. Additional remains can be found along trails branching off of the main route. The trail also passes right through the bustling town of Lamartine, now little more than an empty lot. At press time, the forest service reports that a condominium complex may be built in the vicinity of Lamartine. Currently, only some land has been cleared. Finally, there are some large tailings piles passed along the trail, as well as an old boiler that was shipped all the way across the country from Coatesville, Pennsylvania.

The trail widens as it joins graded dirt Ute Creek Road. The final descent along Ute Creek passes private property. Stay on the main trail here and do not explore the private side roads. The trail ends on Colorado 103, a few miles south of Idaho Springs. A good side trip from the end of the trail is to take Colorado 103 south to the Mount Evans Scenic Byway, a paved road that takes you to the top of the 14,264-foot mountain.

Current Road Information

Arapaho & Roosevelt National Forests
Clear Creek Ranger District
101 Chicago Creek Road
Idaho Springs, CO 80452
(303) 567-3000

Old cabin and campsite beside the trail

Map References

USFS Arapaho & Roosevelt National Forests
Maptech CD:
      Denver/Steamboat Springs/North Central
Benchmark's *Colorado Road & Recreation Atlas*, p. 74
Colorado Atlas & Gazetteer, p. 39
The Roads of Colorado, p. 79
Trails Illustrated, #104

Route Directions

▼ 0.0   From the Georgetown exit (#238) of I-70, zero trip meter and head east toward town. At 0.1 miles, make your first right onto Argentine Road. At 0.8 miles, turn right onto 22nd Street. At 0.9 miles, turn right onto Clear Creek Road. At 1.4 miles, zero trip meter and turn right (east) onto Saxon Mountain Road (not labeled at time of research).

5.8 ▲   Trail ends on Clear Creek Road. Turn right and follow above directions in reverse for I-70 and Georgetown.

GPS: N39°43.15' W105°41.44'

▼ 0.2   BR   Private driveways on left and old building on right. Follow sign to Saxon Mountain summit.
5.6 ▲   SO   Private driveways on right and old building on left.

▼ 1.0   SO   Seasonal closure gate.
4.8 ▲   SO   Seasonal closure gate.

▼ 1.4   SO   Track on left.
4.4 ▲   SO   Track on sharp right rejoins.

▼ 1.5   SO   Track on left rejoins.
4.3 ▲   SO   Track on right.

▼ 1.8   SO   Cabin remains on right; then campsite on left.
4.0 ▲   BR   Campsite on right; then cabin remains on left.

GPS: N39°43.51' W105°40.99'

▼ 2.1   BR   Track down hill on left.
3.7 ▲   SO   Track on sharp right.

GPS: N39°43.72' W105°40.94'

▼ 2.5   SO   Track on left on right-hand switchback.
3.3 ▲   BL   Track straight ahead on left-hand switchback.

▼ 2.7   BR   Track on left on right-hand switchback goes past campsite to mining remains.
3.1 ▲   BL   Track on straight ahead on left-hand switchback goes past campsite to mining remains.

GPS: N39°43.68' W105°40.80'

▼ 3.5   SO   Cabin remains on right.
2.3 ▲   SO   Cabin remains on left.

▼ 4.3   BR   Track on left.
1.5 ▲   SO   Track on sharp right.

GPS: N39°43.78' W105°40.36'

▼ 5.0   SO   Cabin remains and campsite on right.
0.8 ▲   SO   Cabin remains and campsite on left.

▼ 5.8   TL   FR 712.2C continues straight ahead. Turn left onto FR 712.2, following sign to Cascade Creek. Zero trip meter.
0.0 ▲   Continue to the north.

GPS: N39°43.67' W105°39.36'

▼ 0.0   Continue to the east.
3.3 ▲   TR   T-intersection. Track on left is FR 712.2C. Remain on FR 712.2, following sign to Georgetown. Zero trip meter.

▼ 0.1   BR/TL   At fork in road, bear right onto FR 710.1, following sign to Griffith Mountain. FR 712.2 is on left. Then 4-way intersection. FR 710.1 on right is signed to Highland Park. Also track

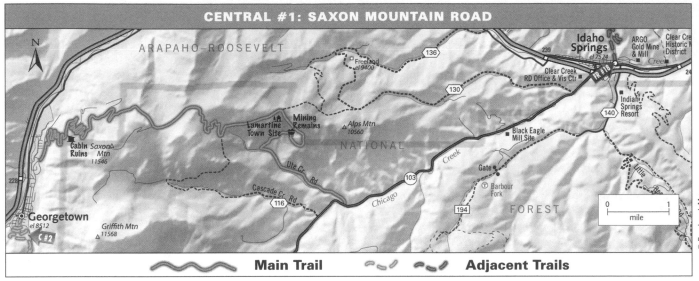

Main Trail ~~~ / ~~~ / **Adjacent Trails**

© Benchmark Maps

straight ahead. Turn left onto FR 712.2, following sign to Lamartine.

▲ 3.2	TR	4-way intersection. Track on left. Track straight ahead and to the right is FR 710.1. Turn right onto FR 710.1, following sign to Georgetown. Then track on sharp right is FR 712.2 rejoining.

GPS: N39°43.63' W105°39.30'

▼ 0.2	SO	Narrow track on sharp left is FR 712.2 rejoining.
3.1 ▲	BL	Track on right is FR 712.2.

▼ 0.7	SO	Track on right; then track on left.
2.6 ▲	SO	Track on right; then track on left.

▼ 1.0	SO	Track on left; then faint track on right.
2.3 ▲	SO	Faint track on left; then track on right.

GPS: N39°43.92' W105°38.49'

▼ 1.5	SO	Track on right is FR 712.21.
1.8 ▲	BR	Track straight ahead is FR 712.21.

GPS: N39°43.59' W105°38.37'

▼ 1.8	TR	4-way intersection. FR 712.2G on left. Unmarked track ahead goes to cabin remains.
1.5 ▲	TL	4-way intersection. FR 712.2G on straight ahead. Unmarked track on right goes to cabin remains.

GPS: N39°43.75' W105°38.20'

Difficult section near the top of the switchbacks

▼ 2.2	SO	Track on sharp right is FR 712.2B.
1.1 ▲	BR	Track on left is FR 712.2B.

▼ 2.4	SO	Track on sharp left is FR 712.2F.
0.9 ▲	BL	Track on right is FR 712.2F.

▼ 2.9	SO	Track on right goes to camping area.
0.4 ▲	SO	Track on left goes to camping area.

▼ 3.2	SO	Track on left is FR 712.2E.
0.1 ▲	SO	Track on right is FR 712.2E.

▼ 3.3	TR	Track on left is FR 727.1B; then Lamartine town site. Camping area on left. Track straight ahead is FR 712.1. Zero trip meter.
0.0 ▲		Continue to the west on FR 712.2.

GPS: N39°43.90' W105°37.07'

▼ 0.0		Continue to the southeast on FR 712.2A, following sign to Ute Creek. Track on right is FR 727.1B.
4.0 ▲	TL	T-intersection at Lamartine town site. Camping area straight ahead. Track on right is FR 712.1. Zero trip meter.

▼ 0.5	SO	Private property on left. Many tracks on right and left lead to private property for the next 3.5 miles.
3.5 ▲	SO	Private property on right.

▼ 1.1	SO	Tailings piles and mining remains on left and right; then track on left and campsite and pylon on right.
2.9 ▲	SO	Campsite and pylon on left and track on right; then tailings piles and mining remains on left and right.

GPS: N39°43.55' W105°36.84'

▼ 1.7	TL	T-intersection. Track on right is private. Turn left onto FR 118.0.
2.3 ▲	TR	Track ahead is private. Follow homemade sign for Lamartine and Cascade.

GPS: N39°43.33' W105°37.39'

▼ 4.0		Trail ends at T-intersection with Colorado 103. Turn left for Idaho Springs; turn right for Mount Evans.
0.0 ▲		Trail starts on Colorado 103, 4.9 miles south of I-70, just south of mile marker 5. Turn north onto graded dirt Ute Creek Road and zero trip meter. Many tracks on right and left lead to private property for the next 3.5 miles.

GPS: N39°42.52' W105°35.83'

Guanella Pass Trail

Starting Point:	Grant, at intersection of US 285 and CR 62
Finishing Point:	Georgetown, at Old Georgetown Railway Station
Total Mileage:	24.2 miles
Unpaved Mileage:	10.5 miles
Driving Time:	1 hour
Route Elevation:	8,600 to 11,669 feet
Usually Open:	Year-round
Difficulty Rating:	1
Scenic Rating:	9

Special Attractions

- Attractive scenery with expansive views from the pass.
- An accessible backcountry route, which can be undertaken by passenger vehicles.
- Fall viewing of the aspens.
- Abundant wildlife.

History

This pass is named for Byron Guanella, a Clear Creek commissioner who was a supporter of building a road over the pass.

Buffalo used to graze their way across this pass, and the Indians used the pass as they followed the migration of the buffalo herds. Early prospectors seeking to use the pass were always on guard against being attacked by the Indians. In 1861, Captain Edward Berthoud and Jim Bridger crossed the pass when surveying potential routes for a railroad west.

The route starts in the town of Grant, which was established in 1870 and originally named Grantville, in honor of President Ulysses S. Grant. Its population peaked at about 200 in 1887.

The route ends in Georgetown, which began as a gold settlement in 1859, when George Griffith from Kentucky found

Clear Lake USFS Campground

gold there. He brought his wife, his brother, their father, and a couple of prospectors to the area. They called it George's Town, in honor of George Griffith. The group worked hard to live on the modest amounts of gold they found despite the large amounts of seemingly worthless silver-bearing ore in their lode.

In 1864, plentiful veins of quartz were discovered, creating a boom that brought prospectors pouring into the area. The resulting settlement was called Elizabethtown in honor of George's wife, Elizabeth. Before long, George's Town and Elizabethtown combined under the name Georgetown, and a post office was established in 1866.

The following year brought the silver explosion. Houses and businesses were erected at a dizzying rate, the streets buzzed with activity, merchants did brisk business, and lots of people were on the verge of becoming very wealthy. Georgetown was known as the Silver Queen of the Rockies. As it grew, the town acquired an attractive mix of Victorian cottages and a substantial brick business district. Georgetown became the home of many rich men with rich tastes. Large, ornate residences grew in size and ostentation as their owners prospered.

Although Georgetown had a wild side—with more than thirty saloons and plenty of red-light houses and gambling dens—it was also a mining town with culture and refinement. Citizens enjoyed two opera houses, met in public halls and a Masonic lodge, and attended society events. In contrast to most other mining camps, families were an integral part of Georgetown. Schools and churches were constructed from the early days, and homes were built with an air of permanence.

Georgetown is home to many interesting old and historic buildings. The Hotel de Paris (now a museum

View of the northern end of the trail

Grant in 1938, shortly before the tracks were removed

operated by the National Society of Colonial Dames) was a luxurious French inn of outstanding quality that used to accommodate businessmen from the East and Europe while they speculated over mining investments. President Ulysses S. Grant stayed there and was very fond of it. The Hotel de Paris was richly furnished and served exotic foods. The owners bottled their own wine and kept an extensive wine cellar. Fish were kept in an indoor fountain so they could be selected by and prepared for the guests. The Hammill House (now a museum at Argentine and Third Streets) was once a modest home built by mining investor and politician William A. Hammill. As Hammill grew wealthier, his house became more opulent. He added bay windows, a solarium with curved glass panels, a stable, an office, and a six-seat outhouse (with three walnut seats for the family and three pine ones for the servants). The Maxwell House is another immaculately kept Victorian home that was quite modest in its original state and took on a much more lavish appearance as the owner prospered.

In 1884, railroad workers accomplished a true feat of engineering when they completed the Georgetown Loop narrow gauge between Georgetown and Silver Plume (2 miles west of

Commemorative plaque at the pass

Georgetown). A series of curves constructed in a spiral fashion helped trains gain momentum for the steep grades on the straightaways; in one spot, the railroad actually crossed over itself on a 300-foot trestle. The journey, popular with tourists who wanted to observe the beautiful scenery and experience the thrill, was similar to a roller-coaster ride.

After the silver crash of 1893, Georgetown became a sleepy mountain town, although it continued to produce gold and other metals. The railroad was abandoned in 1939; the trestle was dismantled, and the rails were scrapped. However, the entire narrow gauge railway route between Georgetown and Silver Plume has been reconstructed. During Colorado's milder months, thousands of tourists ride the Georgetown Loop Railroad across the 95-foot Devil's Gate High Bridge between Silver Plume and Georgetown.

Georgetown today is a charming community with interesting architecture and a fascinating history. The town has been a National Historic Landmark since 1966. In 1970, residents formed the Georgetown Society, which has made an ongoing effort to restore and preserve many of Georgetown's Victorian buildings (including the Hammill House) to their original states.

Description
Today, this very popular route is used year-round for picnicking, camping, and cross-country skiing. The easy 2WD route is very scenic and provides good fall viewing of the aspens.

Guanella Pass summit

The route starts at the tiny township of Grant and heads north on FR 118 beside Geneva Creek, traveling through a wooded valley with scenic rock formations along the road. The land surrounding the road alternates between private property and national forest.

After about 4 miles, the road starts its climb toward the pass and leaves the creek behind. It continues above the timberline, with the scenery becoming considerably more rugged. The summit offers expansive views of Mount Bierstadt, Mount Evans, and the Sawtooth Range to the east and the Continental Divide to the west.

The descent to Georgetown follows Clear Creek past a number of lakes and reservoirs, as well as the Cabin Creek hydroelectric plant. The paved road switchbacks down into the town of Georgetown.

The route offers access to four forest service campgrounds and numerous hiking trails. It is especially scenic in fall when the vast aspen stands turn bright yellow and blanket the surrounding mountains.

Current Road Information
Arapaho & Roosevelt National Forests
Clear Creek Ranger District
101 Chicago Creek Road
Idaho Springs, CO 80452
(303) 567-3000

Georgetown Visitor Information Center
1491 Argentine
Georgetown, CO 80444
(303) 569-2405

Map References
USFS Arapaho & Roosevelt National Forests
Maptech CD:
        Colorado Springs/Ski Areas/Central;
        Denver/Steamboat Springs/North Central
Benchmark's *Colorado Road & Recreation Atlas*, p. 74
Colorado Atlas & Gazetteer, pp. 39, 49
The Roads of Colorado, p. 79
Trails Illustrated, #104 (incomplete)

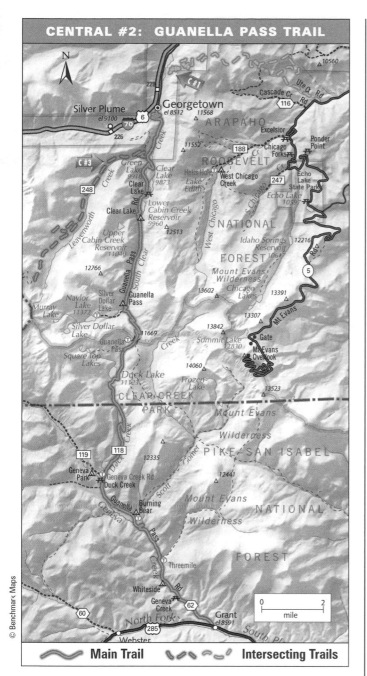

CENTRAL #2: GUANELLA PASS TRAIL

Main Trail — **Intersecting Trails**

© Benchmark Maps

Route Directions

| ▼ 0.0 | | At intersection of US 285 and CR 62 in Grant, zero trip meter and turn onto Guanella Pass Road toward Georgetown. |
| 12.9 ▲ | | End at intersection with US 285 in Grant. |

GPS: N 39°27.61' W 105°39.75'

▼ 0.4	SO	Unpaved.
12.5 ▲	SO	Paved.
▼ 1.5	SO	Enter National Forest.
11.4 ▲	SO	Leave National Forest.
▼ 1.7	SO	Geneva Creek Picnic Grounds.
11.2 ▲	SO	Geneva Creek Picnic Grounds.
▼ 2.3	SO	USFS Whiteside Campground.
10.6 ▲	SO	USFS Whiteside Campground.
▼ 4.0	SO	Pavement begins.
8.9 ▲	SO	Pavement ends.
▼ 5.0	SO	Burning Bear Trailhead on left.

7.9 ▲	SO	Burning Bear Trailhead on right.
▼ 5.1	SO	Cattle guard.
7.8 ▲	SO	Cattle guard.
▼ 5.2	SO	USFS Burning Bear Campground.
7.6 ▲	SO	USFS Burning Bear Campground.
▼ 6.8	SO	Track to Geneva City town site at Duck Creek Picnic Ground on left.
6.1 ▲	SO	Track to Geneva City town site at Duck Creek Picnic Ground on right.
▼ 10.4	SO	Track on left to Geneva Creek (FR 119).
2.5 ▲	SO	Track on right to Geneva Creek (FR 119).
▼ 11.2	SO	Unpaved.
1.7 ▲	SO	Paved.
▼ 12.9	SO	Summit of Guanella Pass. Zero trip meter.
0.0 ▲		Continue toward Grant.

GPS: N 39°35.72' W 105°42.61'

▼ 0.0		Continue toward Georgetown.
8.1 ▲	SO	Summit of Guanella Pass. Zero trip meter.
▼ 1.9	SO	Silver Dollar Lake Trail (1 mile) on left.
6.2 ▲	SO	Silver Dollar Lake Trail (1 mile) on right.
▼ 2.1	SO	USFS Guanella Campground on left.
6.0 ▲	SO	USFS Guanella Campground on right.
▼ 4.2	SO	Cross over South Clear Creek.
3.9 ▲	SO	Cross over South Clear Creek.

Geneva Creek alongside Guanella Pass Trail

▼ 5.0		SO	USFS Clear Lake Campground on left.
	3.1 ▲	SO	USFS Clear Lake Campground on right.
▼ 5.2		SO	Paved.
	2.9 ▲	SO	Unpaved.
▼ 6.2		SO	Road to Clear Lake on right.
	1.9 ▲	SO	Road to Clear Lake on left.
▼ 6.9		SO	Green Lake on right.
	1.2 ▲	SO	Green Lake on left.
▼ 8.1		SO	Intersection with Central #3: Waldorf and Santiago Ghost Town Trail (FR 248.1) on left. Zero trip meter.
	0.0 ▲		Proceed south on Guanella Pass Road.
			GPS: N39°40.99′ W105°42.17′
▼ 0.0			Proceed north on Guanella Pass Road.
	3.2 ▲	SO	Intersection with Central #3: Waldorf and Santiago Ghost Town Trail (FR 248.1) on right. Zero trip meter.
▼ 0.8		SO	Georgetown water supply reservoir on right.
	2.4 ▲	SO	Georgetown water supply reservoir on left.
▼ 2.5		SO	Enter Georgetown, remaining on the paved road. As it comes into town, the name becomes Rose Street.
	0.8 ▲	SO	Leave Georgetown on Guanella Pass Road toward Guanella Pass.
▼ 3.2			End at Royal Gorge Route Railroad offices on the corner of Rose and 11th Streets.
	0.0 ▲		From the Royal Gorge Route Railroad offices at the corner of Rose and 11th Streets in Georgetown, zero trip meter and proceed south along Rose Street.
			GPS: N 39°42.69′ W 105°41.69′

Leavenworth Creek near the beginning of the trail

CENTRAL REGION TRAIL #3

Waldorf and Santiago Ghost Town Trail

Starting Point:	**Central #2: Guanella Pass Trail, 2.5 miles south of Georgetown**
Finishing Point:	**Argentine Pass**
Total Mileage:	**13.6 miles, including spur**
Unpaved Mileage:	**13.6 miles, including spur**
Driving Time:	**2 hours, including spur (one-way)**
Route Elevation:	**9,580 to 13,265 feet**
Usually Open:	**June to September**
Difficulty Rating:	**5**
Scenic Rating:	**10**

Special Attractions

■ Waldorf town site and Santiago ghost town.
■ Rocky climb up to Argentine Pass.
■ Excellent side route from any trip over Guanella Pass.

History

Part of the East Argentine Mining District, the Waldorf mines were discovered and worked early in Colorado mining histo-ry. A large silver deposit was discovered in 1864, and the town of Waldorf was established three years later. Methodist minister Edward John Wilcox encouraged the development of the Waldorf mines, founding the Waldorf Milling and Mining Company and investing money in building the Argentine Central Railroad.

The Argentine Central originated in Silver Plume, traveled through Waldorf, and ended at the summit of Mount Mc-Clellan. When the railroad line was completed in 1906, it was the highest steam railroad route in the world. In addition to hauling ore, the railroad transported tourists to Waldorf and Mount McClellan. Soon revenue from tourists outnumbered that from transporting freight roughly 10:1. Of great interest to sightseers was the Ice Palace, an old mine covered in ice formations. The building of a tunnel allowing the Argentine Central to travel under the Continental Divide was attempted but abandoned during construction due to lack of funds.

The town of Waldorf was relatively small, with a peak population of 300. The town had a large mill, a boardinghouse, a small store, a machine shop, and a power house. A post office

An old hoist at Waldorf town site

Old living quarters at Santiago

opened in 1906. Located at 11,666 feet, it registered as the highest post office in the nation. The Argentine Central went bankrupt in 1912. After the rail line's brief revival as the Argentine and Grays Peak Railway, the tracks were removed in 1920 and the roadbed turned into an automobile road. Over the life of the mines, about $4 million in silver and gold was produced.

The ghost town of Santiago was located just above Waldorf. William Rogers first discovered ore at the Santiago Mine in 1898. The name of the mine likely comes from the town of Santiago, Cuba, as around the time of the mine's discovery the United States was engaged in the Spanish-American War and had just taken Santiago.

Like a number of other mines in Clear Creek County, the Santiago Mine was worked seasonally. The years of peak production for the Santiago occurred around the turn of the nineteenth century. A railroad spur off the Argentine Central Railroad was built in 1909–10 to help transport ore. A tramway built between Santiago and Waldorf in 1913 made transportation between the two towns easier. Little is known about when the town was abandoned.

Santiago mine adit and ore cart tracks

The nearby Argentine Pass, previously named Sanderson Pass and Snake River Pass, once marked the divide between Spanish and French territory in North America. During the gold rush, the pass connected Georgetown to the rich mining districts above Peru Creek and the Snake River basin. Although Argentine Pass was close to the Peru Mining District, it was not named after the neighboring South American country Argentina. Rather, the name was derived from the Latin word "argentine," meaning "silver."

In 1869, Commodore Stephen Decatur and the Georgetown and Snake River Wagon Road Company built a toll road over the pass, the highest pass road over the Continental Divide during its years of operation. The road was not a commercial success because travelers increasingly found alternate routes over the divide in order to avoid the steep slopes of the frighteningly narrow road. The famous survey party led by Ferdinand V. Hayden crossed Argentine Pass in 1873. Photographer William H. Jackson, accompanying Hayden's party, took many photographs of the area. Argentine Pass is no longer accessible to motor vehicles, as numerous rock slides over the years have made the route impassable.

Extensive mill remains at Santiago

Santiago ghost town

Description

Waldorf and Santigo Ghost Town Trail branches off of Central #2: Guanella Pass Trail and immediately climbs several switchbacks. Embedded rock makes the drive slow going. For much of its length, the road is narrow enough to require using a pullout or backing up for a short distance if you meet an oncoming vehicle.

Aggressively gaining elevation, the trail climbs more than 1,000 feet in about a mile. Below timberline, views are limited as it mostly follows a corridor through the trees. The stands of aspen trees here have brilliant yellow leaves in fall.

Most of the section of trail that runs above Leavenworth Creek is a shelf road, climbing higher and higher up the side of the valley until it reaches the town site of Waldorf. Above tree line, views of the surrounding peaks and alpine meadows, which bloom with wildflowers in spring, are expansive. There are also several good campsites along the section of trail up to Waldorf.

The most notable thing about the site of Waldorf is the abundance of tailings piles. Other than that, there are a few buildings left as well as a Quonset hut. A couple of tracks make their way around the few remaining structures and continue up the steep side of McClellan Mountain to additional mining remains and past a cluster of bristlecone pines. Branching off the track to McClellan Mountain is the spur to Santiago ghost town.

A cluster of bristlecone pines beside the trail

View to the west from Argentine Pass and what remains of the old vehicle trail

A rocky and eroded section of the trail

Set among the rugged and exposed mountain peaks, the remains of the old mining camp of Santiago are interesting to explore. Many well-preserved buildings and much mining equipment are left at Santiago. The buildings, including a large mill and a small cabin that served as living quarters, are clustered around the prominent mine adit. Sections of track for the ore carts that transported earth from inside the mine to the mill still remain.

Past Waldorf, the trail starts to climb again along FR 248.1V. This part of the trail is much looser and rockier than before but still well within the capabilities of a stock high-clearance 4WD. These last couple miles make for slow travel; however, the views back down the Leavenworth Creek Valley as well as the views of Argentine Peak and Mount Wilcox just keep getting better. Once on the pass, you can see the old vehicle route (now a hiking trail) that descends the other side toward Central #4: Peru Creek Trail. Many peaks are visible, but Mount Edwards, Grays Peak, and Ruby Mountain are the most prominent.

Current Road Information

Arapaho & Roosevelt National Forests
Clear Creek Ranger District
101 Chicago Creek Road
Idaho Springs, CO 80452
(303) 567-3000

Map References

USFS Arapaho & Roosevelt National Forests
Maptech CD:
      Denver/Steamboat Springs/North Central
Benchmark's *Colorado Road & Recreation Atlas*, p. 74
Colorado Atlas & Gazetteer, p. 39
The Roads of Colorado, p. 79
Trails Illustrated, #104

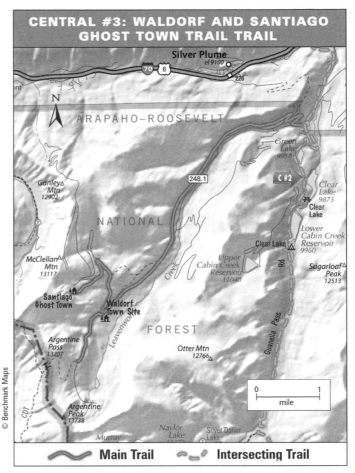

CENTRAL #3: WALDORF AND SANTIAGO GHOST TOWN TRAIL TRAIL

© Benchmark Maps

〰️ **Main Trail** ⌁ **Intersecting Trail**

Route Directions

▼ 0.0		From Georgetown, take Central #2: Guanella Pass Trail 2.5 miles; make a right on a sharp curve. Zero trip meter and head south on dirt road (FR 248.1), following signs for Waldorf.
		GPS: N39°40.99' W105°42.13'
▼ 0.2	SO	Track on left.
▼ 0.4	SO/BR	Cross over Leavenworth Creek; then two tracks on right lead to campsites; bear right on right-hand switchback; track on left is narrow and overgrown and climbs hill.
▼ 0.6	SO	Track on right leads to campsite.
▼ 0.9	TR	Turn sharp right; track FR 248.1B continues ahead, leading to mine remains and many campsites.
		GPS: N39°40.99' W105°42.53'
▼ 1.1	TL	FR 248.1Q (dead end) straight ahead; turn left on left-hand switchback.
▼ 2.3	SO	Cross through wash; then track on left.
▼ 2.7	SO	Narrow crossing over wash.
▼ 3.4	BR	Fork in road. Zero trip meter.
		GPS: N39°39.99' W105°44.38'
▼ 0.0		Proceed southwest up the hill.
▼ 0.2	SO	Cross over creek.
▼ 0.7	SO	Track on sharp right; then cross through wash.
		GPS: N39°39.46' W105°44.62'
▼ 1.2	SO	FR 248.1A on left; then right.
▼ 1.8	SO	Track on left to campsite.
▼ 1.9	SO	Cross through wash.
▼ 5.9	SO	Enter Waldorf town site; track on sharp right is 248.1; mill and mine remains on left; Quonset hut on right up hill. Zero trip meter.
		GPS: N39°38.27' W105°45.87'

▼ 0.0		Proceed northeast on FR 248.1.
▼ 0.6	SO	Track on left; then track on right.
▼ 0.7	SO	Track on left and right (FR 248.1N).
▼ 1.0	UTL	Track straight on goes up to McClellan Mountain; track on sharp left proceeds to Santiago ghost town.

GPS: N39°39.05′ W105°45.98′

▼ 1.4	BL	Intersection with FR 248.1N to the left and right.
▼ 1.6	SO	Gate.
▼ 1.7	SO	Track on left; then grave on left and foundations on right.
▼ 1.8		Spur ends at Santiago Mine and ghost town.

GPS: N39°38.59′ W105°46.30′

Continuation of Main Trail

▼ 0.0		Continue to the west; then pass two tracks on right through Waldorf.
▼ 0.1	SO	Continue on FR 248.1V.
▼ 0.3	SO	Cross through wash; then track on left goes to mine.
▼ 0.5	BL	Track on right; then cross through wash; then bear left when trail forks.
▼ 0.6	SO	Track on right rejoins.
▼ 0.8	SO	Trail forks then immediately rejoins.
▼ 0.9	BR	FR 248.1U continues ahead. Bear right following FR 248.1V.

GPS: N39°37.62′ W105°46.25′

| ▼ 2.5 | | Trail ends at Argentine Pass. |

GPS: N39°37.53′ W105°46.90′

CENTRAL REGION TRAIL #4

Peru Creek Trail

Starting Point:	**Intersection of CR 5 (Montezuma Road) and FR 260**
Finishing Point:	**Gate at Shoe Basin Mine ore bin**
Total Mileage:	**4.7 miles (one-way)**
Unpaved Mileage:	**4.7 miles**
Driving Time:	**1 hour (one-way)**
Route Elevation:	**10,007 to 11,149 feet**
Usually Open:	**Late May to October**
Difficulty Rating:	**2**
Scenic Rating:	**10**

Special Attractions

- The substantial Pennsylvania Mine and Mill.
- Abundant mining remains along the entire the length of the trail.
- Popular ATV, dirt bike, and mountain bike trail.
- Rugged, above-timberline scenery of Peru Creek Valley.
- Spring wildflowers and large beaver dams in Peru Creek.
- Numerous hiking trailheads.
- Good backcountry campsites and picnic spots.
- Snowmobile trail in winter.

Old abandoned cabin in Peru Creek Valley

History

In 1865, newspaperman D. C. Collier and future Colorado senator H. M. Teller were among the first men to arrive in the valley just south of the site where silver ore was reportedly first discovered in Colorado Territory. It was Collier who suggested that the town be named for the Aztec emperor Montezuma. The town grew quickly and by 1868 rivaled Breckenridge as one of Summit County's largest towns.

Transportation proved problematic for Montezuma as it was for many other mining towns. However, the population

Pennsylvania Mill tipple

Inside the Pennsylvania Mill

Tramhouse perched on the hill above the Pennsylvania Mill

escalated with the development of multiple wagon routes in the district. By 1880, more than 800 people lived in Montezuma, and the town boasted a schoolhouse, post office, three hotels, a steam sawmill, a smelting furnace, and concentration works. A larger schoolhouse even had to be built in 1884 to accommodate the growing number of students.

Montezuma was well known as a social and hospitable town, famous for its poker playing. It was said the game never stopped, as there was always someone willing to take the place of anyone who dropped out. Like many other mining towns, Montezuma had a red-light district. One "soiled dove" in particular, Dixie, was recognized throughout the town, as she would go to local baseball games to support the home team. She also fed all of the town's stray animals, buying cans of milk and beef by the caseload.

A fire ravaged the town in 1915, and the population continued to dwindle until it numbered about a dozen in 1956. In the 1950s, the Roberts Tunnel project, built to carry water from Lake Dillon to Denver via an underground tunnel, brought about a small revival, as construction workers moved into town. An-

Peru Creek runs alongside the trail

other fire, however, destroyed half the homes in town in 1958. Today there are a few remaining residents in Montezuma, although the town is much diminished from its mining heyday.

Farther up Peru Creek is the ghost town of Argentine. First established in 1868 as Decatur, the town took off upon J. W. Hall's 1879 discovery of silver at the Pennsylvania Mine, one of the best producers in the area. Production declined at the Pennsylvania in the 1890s, and the silver crash of 1893 forced most of the silver mines in the area to close. However, the

View of the west side of Argentine Pass from the trail

Ruins at the Pennsylvania Mill

Pennsylvania managed to remain in operation throughout the silver crash, and in 1893 the town was revived with the new name of Rathbone. From 1893 to 1898, the Pennsylvania not only survived but prospered, producing over $3 million in earnings during this period. An avalanche in the winter of 1898 destroyed most of the town.

New silver discoveries in 1902 drew prospectors to the region, and the town experienced a final rebirth as Argentine. The Decatur Mining Syndicate sold the Pennsylvania Mine to the Ohio Mines Company in 1902. The Rothschild Company later purchased the mine, which continued to function into the 1940s.

Description
This backcountry adventure begins less than a mile north of Montezuma in a parking area at the intersection of CR 5 and FR 260. Starting off as an easygoing drive through pine forest, the wide, gravel road (which is well maintained for its entire length) gradually gains elevation. The trail crosses Peru Creek and proceeds past several hiking trailheads and many good backcountry campsites. For the first several miles, views are limited because the road follows Peru Creek through the trees. Also along this section, several forest roads branch off the main trail, and old cabins and other aban-

donded mining equipment remain among the trees.

In around 3.5 miles, the trail reaches timberline and the trees thin out, revealing expansive views of Peru Creek Valley. Rugged peaks enclose the valley's alpine meadows. The Pennsylvania Mine and Mill ruins appear on the south side of the valley. The wooden mill building is collapsing around the old ore processing equipment that remains inside. An old tramhouse is also perched on the hillside above the mill, and there are several more interesting buildings to explore on the maze of tracks just off the main trail in Cinnamon Gulch. The remains of the mine are well worth the diversion to explore.

Beyond the Pennsylvania Mine complex, the trail continues alongside Peru Creek through alpine meadows, which are blanketed with wildflowers in spring. There are several more old cabins and some more mining equipment scattered throughout the valley. Numerous beaver ponds and dams are another point of interest in Peru Creek. The patient observer is likely to spot a beaver in the clear creek waters.

About a mile beyond Cinnamon Gulch, the trail ends at a gate and an ore bin from the nearby Shoe Basin Mine. Hikers can proceed beyond the gate to the Argentine Pass Trailhead, a strenuous 2-mile climb to Argentine Pass and the Continental Divide.

A beaver lodge, dam, and pond in Peru Creek

One of the many good backcountry campsites near the trail

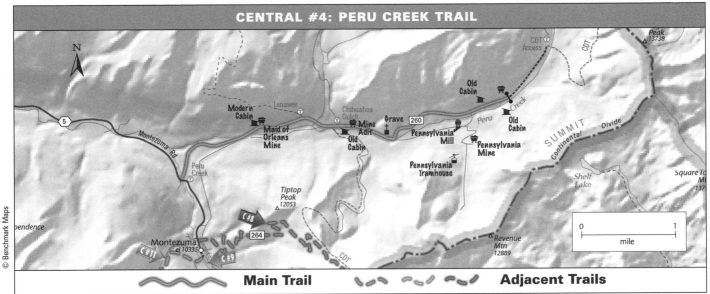

Main Trail   Adjacent Trails

Current Road Information

White River National Forest
Dillon Ranger District
680 Blue River Parkway
Silverthorne, CO 80498
(970) 468-5400

Map References

USFS White River National Forest
Maptech CD.
     Denver/Steamboat Springs/North Central
Benchmark's *Colorado Road & Recreation Atlas*, p. 73
Colorado Atlas & Gazetteer, p. 38
The Roads of Colorado, p. 79
Trails Illustrated, #104

Route Directions

▼ 0.0		Trail begins at intersection of Montezuma Road (CR 5) and FR 260. Zero trip meter and proceed northeast on FR 260 through seasonal gate.
GPS: N39°35.53′ W105°52.25′		
▼ 1.0	BL	Track on right.
GPS: N39°35.92′ W105°51.46′		
▼ 1.1	SO	Cross over Peru Creek.
▼ 1.4	SO	Cabin with mine loader on left and sheds on right.
▼ 1.6	SO	Lenawee Hiking Trailhead on left.
▼ 1.9	SO	Cross over creek.
▼ 2.1	SO	Track on right is FR 265, signed Warden Gulch and Morgan Creek to the right and Argentine Pass Trailhead straight ahead.
▼ 2.2	SO	FR 263 on right; then track on left signed to Chihuahua Gulch Road and Chihuahua Lake Trailhead.
GPS: N39°36.03′ W105°50.29′		
▼ 2.3	SO	Old cabin on right; then old mine adit on left.
▼ 2.4	SO	Grave on left.
▼ 2.8	SO	Picnic area on left.
▼ 3.3	SO	Cabin remains on right.
▼ 3.7	SO	Road on right ends in 0.2 miles at Pennsylvania Mine and Mill ruins in Cinnamon Gulch. Zero trip meter.

GPS: N39°36.16′ W105°48.79′		
▼ 0.0		Proceed east on FR 260.
▼ 0.4	SO	Old cabin on left.
GPS: N39°36.25′ W105°48.34′		
▼ 0.8	SO	Parking lot on left.
▼ 0.9	SO	Cabin on right.
▼ 1.0		Trail ends near Shoe Basin Mine ore bin at gate.
GPS: N39°36.59′ W105°47.92′		

Boilers and shaft at the Pennsylvania Mine

Handcart Gulch Trail

Starting Point:	Intersection of US 285 and CR 60
	(FR 120) at the town site of Webster
Finishing Point:	Webster Pass
Total Mileage:	9.6 miles
Unpaved Mileage:	9.6 miles
Driving Time:	1.75 hours
Route Elevation:	9,200 to 12,096 feet
Usually Open:	Mid-August to late September
Difficulty Rating:	6
Scenic Rating:	9

Special Attractions

- Varied four-wheel driving challenges, including an extremely narrow shelf road.
- Spectacular views, particularly of Red Cone Peak.
- Access to an extensive network of 4WD trails.

History

The area is named for two prospectors who in 1860 brought their handcart loaded with supplies up the valley and made the area's first gold discovery while panning the creek.

Towns that developed in the vicinity included Webster, Hall Valley, and Handcart Gulch. Webster was a staging point for passengers and freight headed across Webster Pass. For a time in the 1870s it was the end of the line for the Denver, South Park & Pacific Railroad. It was known as a wild town where gunplay was common; traffic was heavy to the boot hill cemetery north of town. As the railroad was extended and bet-

North Fork of the South Platte River near the beginning of the trail

The intersection of Handcart Gulch Trail and Red Cone Peak Trail

ter pass routes were opened, Webster went into decline. Its post office closed in 1909.

The town of Hall Valley, also known as Hall's Gulch, Hallville, and Hall City, was centered on the fortunes of the Whale Mine. At the town's peak, around 1876–77, the population reached about 500. Hall Valley was renowned as a very rowdy place where the saloons were open all day and all night. When two of the mine foremen who had earned the wrath of the miners for their bullying management were in town, the miners lynched them both!

It is not clear if Col. J. W. Hall was the owner or the manager of the Whale Mine, but it is clear that both he and the English company that operated it subsequently were incompetent, and as the fortunes of the mine declined, so did the town.

The town of Handcart Gulch, located a short distance farther up the valley, was also short-lived, and its prosperity mirrored that of Hall Valley.

Description

The route starts at the town site of Webster (nothing remains of the town) at the intersection of US 285 and CR 60 (FR 120), 3.2 miles west of Grant.

Initially, this is the same route that leads to Webster Pass by way of Red Cone Peak. The well-maintained 2WD road travels along Hall Valley beside the headwaters of the North Fork of the South Platte River though pine and aspen groves.

After the intersection with Red Cone Peak Trail 5 miles along the route, the road soon becomes rough and rocky. Large rocks in the road make selecting the correct line important. There is a boggy spot

Lower section of the trail

Rocky, difficult section of the trail

The narrow shelf section of Handcart Gulch Trail descending from Webster Pass before switchbacking into the valley

that has been repaired by the Colorado Association of 4 Wheel Drive Clubs just in front of a cabin 1.7 miles after the turnoff to Red Cone. Be aware that logs used to repair this muddy section may have become dislodged, uncovering sharp stakes. Remain on the trail through this section to prevent further damage to the ground around the trail, or worst of all, trail closure.

The road continues through two manageable creek crossings and then commences its final assault on the pass. The ascent begins with a number of switchbacks and culminates in a long, very narrow, off-camber rough shelf cut into the steep talus mountainside. This stretch of road is frequently obstructed by rocks that you must clear in order to pass; it is only just wide enough for a full-sized vehicle to squeeze through. The last hundred feet are usually blocked by a snowdrift until late into summer.

The view from the pass is wonderful: To the east is the one-way (downhill only) road off Red Cone Peak, southeast is the west face of Red Cone, north is the Snake River Valley, and southwest is the shelf road you have just ascended.

Narrow shelf road near Webster Pass

Current Road Information

Pike National Forest
South Platte Ranger District
19316 Goddard Ranch Court
Morrison, CO 80465
(303) 275-5610

Map References

USFS Pike National Forest
Maptech CD:
    Colorado Springs/Ski Areas/Central;
    Denver/Steamboat Springs/North Central
Benchmark's *Colorado Road & Recreation Atlas*, p. 73
Colorado Atlas & Gazetteer, pp. 38, 48
The Roads of Colorado, p. 79
Trails Illustrated, #104 (incomplete)

Route Directions

▼ 0.0		From intersection of US 285 and CR 60 (FR 120) at the site of Webster, zero trip meter. Proceed west on unpaved road marked with sign to Red Cone Road and Handcart Gulch.
5.0 ▲		End at intersection with US 285 at the site of Webster.
GPS: N 39°27.46′ W 105°43.27′		
▼ 0.9	SO	Enter Pike National Forest.
4.1 ▲	SO	Leave Pike National Forest.
▼ 1.7	SO	Track on left with campsite. Cattle guard.
3.3 ▲	SO	Cattle guard. Track on right with campsite.
▼ 2.9	SO	Burning Bear hiking trail on right. Town site of Hall Valley.
2.1 ▲	SO	Burning Bear hiking trail on left. Town site of Hall Valley.
GPS: N 39°28.46′ W 105°45.70′		
▼ 3.1	SO	Road on left to Beaver Creek (FR 123).
1.9 ▲	SO	Road on right to Beaver Creek (FR 123).
▼ 4.6	SO	USFS Handcart Campground and FR 120A on left.
0.3 ▲	SO	USFS Handcart Campground and FR 120A on right.
▼ 4.9	SO	Hall Valley Campground and Gibson Lake

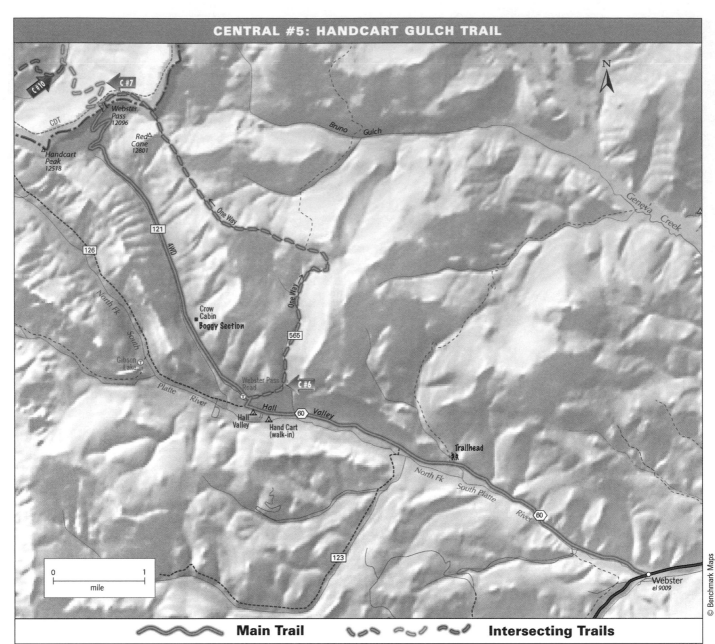

		Main Trail			**Intersecting Trails**

		Trailhead (FR 120B) to the left. Town site of Handcart Gulch.	
0.1 ▲	SO	Hall Valley Campground and Gibson Lake Trailhead (FR 120B) to the right. Town site of Handcart Gulch.	

GPS: N 39°28.98' W 105°48.20'

▼ 5.0	TL	T-intersection. Turn left onto road to Handcart Gulch (FR 121). Track on right is Central #6: Red Cone Peak Trail, which also leads to Webster Pass. Zero trip meter.
0.0 ▲		Proceed along Handcart Gulch road (FR 120).

GPS: N 39°29.02' W 105°48.27'

▼ 0.0		Proceed along Handcart Gulch road.
4.6 ▲	BR	Intersection. Left goes to Central #6: Red Cone Peak and loops back to Webster Pass. Right leads to US 285. Zero trip meter.

▼ 0.1	SO	Track on right.
4.5 ▲	BR	Track on left.

▼ 0.4	BL	Intersection. FR 5652 on right.

4.1 ▲	BR	Intersection. FR 5652 on left.

▼ 0.5	SO	Track on right to walking trail.
4.0 ▲	SO	Track on left to walking trail.

▼ 1.7	SO	Building on right. Potentially very boggy and rutted section of the track.
2.9 ▲	SO	Building on left. Potentially very boggy and rutted section of the track.

▼ 2.8	SO	Cross through creek.
1.8 ▲	SO	Cross through creek.

▼ 3.1	SO	Cross through creek.
1.5 ▲	SO	Cross through creek.

GPS: N 39°31.31' W 105°49.89'

▼ 4.2-4.6	SO	Travel along a very narrow shelf.
0.0-0.4 ▲	SO	Travel along a very narrow shelf.

▼ 4.6		End at Webster Pass.
0.0 ▲		From the summit of Webster Pass, zero trip meter and proceed south on Handcart Gulch road (FR 120) along a narrow shelf.

GPS: N 39°31.86' W 105°49.92'

Red Cone Peak Trail

Starting Point:	Intersection of US 285 and Park CR 60
	(FR 120), at the town site of Webster
Finishing Point:	Webster Pass
Total Mileage:	11.2 miles (one-way)
Unpaved Mileage:	11.2 miles
Driving Time:	2 hours (one-way)
Route Elevation:	9,200 to 12,600 feet
Usually Open:	Early July to late September
Difficulty Rating:	7
Scenic Rating:	10

Special Attractions

- Spectacular alpine views.
- The adventure of tackling a very challenging 4WD trail.
- Access to an extensive network of 4WD trails.

Special Note on the Difficulty of This Road

This trail is one of the most difficult included in this book. We have limited the scope of this book primarily to trails with difficulty ratings up to a maximum of 5. So why include one rated 7? First, the views are fabulous. Second, it provides a route for those four-wheelers who want to test their skills on a truly demanding road. However, be warned. Some experienced four-wheel drivers consider this the most dangerous 4WD trail in the state.

The route offers a range of challenges. Clearance is very tight between the trees in the early part of the trail. There are also a number of very tight switchbacks, severely eroded sections, and quite large (and not always embedded) rocks. However, these obstacles by themselves would warrant a difficulty rating of only 5.

By far the most challenging and potentially dangerous obstacle is the very steep downhill section of loose talus at the end of the trail. It is because of this section that the U.S. Forest Service has banned travel on this road from the Webster Pass direction, making the road one-way only. If you do not handle your vehicle properly when descending the talus slope, the rear of the vehicle is likely to swing around, causing it to roll. The floor of Handcart Gulch is about 1,500 feet below—and that is where you will stop!

However, there is a safe way to make the descent: Select first gear in low range and go down slowly. You must exercise particular care if you use the brakes because if the wheels lock up, the rear of the vehicle will swing around. If the back of the vehicle starts to come around, the only way to straighten it is to accelerate. In the heat of a crisis, however, many drivers will find the need to accelerate the opposite of their instincts. If you need to employ this technique, be careful not to overdo it. This steeply descending section of road is bumpy because of broad corrugations caused by vehicles sliding on the talus; if you have to accelerate, be prepared to bounce all over the place.

Description

This trail commences at the intersection of Central #5: Handcart Gulch Trail, 5 miles from US 285. Navigating this trail is easy, as there are no other side roads.

The start of Red Cone Peak Trail is quite rocky. The road travels through pine and aspen forest that becomes just pine as the road ascends. The clearance between the trees is just wide enough for a full-sized vehicle. The road crosses a creek bed that is often heavily eroded. Along the way, you will also encounter a number of switchbacks and rocks. A couple of uphill sections (although short) are quite challenging because of large rocks and a loose, eroded surface.

Steep section of Red Cone Peak Trail

After emerging from timberline, the road travels along a lengthy, open tundra ridge before making its final, sharp ascent to a narrow perch above the steep, dangerous descent to Webster Pass. This is a good place to stop and admire one of the most breathtaking views in Colorado while gathering yourself for the last section, now in clear view.

The distance from the summit of Red Cone Peak to Webster Pass is about three-quarters of a mile and is broken into three short, steep sections, with the first being the hardest.

From Webster Pass, you get to look back on the slope you have just negotiated and across to the vivid red surface of Red Cone Peak.

Current Road Information
Pike & San Isabel National Forests
South Platte Ranger District
19316 Goddard Ranch Court
Morrison, CO 80465
(303) 275-5610

Map References
USFS   Pike National Forest
Maptech CD:
      Colorado Springs/Ski Areas/Central;
      Denver/Steamboat Springs/North Central

Heading down the steep section of the Red Cone Peak Trail

The trail climbs Red Cone Peak before descending to Webster Pass and Radical Hill Trail in the distance on the left

Benchmark's *Colorado Road & Recreation Atlas*, pp. 73, 74
Colorado Atlas & Gazetteer, pp. 39, 48, 49
The Roads of Colorado, p. 79
Trails Illustrated, #104 (incomplete)

Route Directions

▼ 0.0		From intersection of US 285 and CR 60 (FR 120) at the site of Webster, zero trip meter. Proceed northwest on unpaved road marked with sign to Red Cone Road and Handcart Gulch.
	GPS: N 39°27.46′ W 105°43.27′	
▼ 0.9	SO	Enter Pike National Forest.
▼ 1.7	SO	Track on left with campsite. Cattle guard.
▼ 2.9	SO	Burning Bear walking trail on right.
▼ 3.1	SO	Road on left to Beaver Creek (FR 123).
▼ 4.6	SO	USFS Handcart Campground.
▼ 4.9	SO	Hall Valley Campground and Gibson Lake Trailhead (FR 120B) to the left.
	GPS: N 39°28.98′ W 105°48.20′	
▼ 5.0	TR	T-intersection. Road on left is Central #5: Handcart Gulch Trail (FR 121), which also leads to Webster Pass. Zero trip meter and proceed

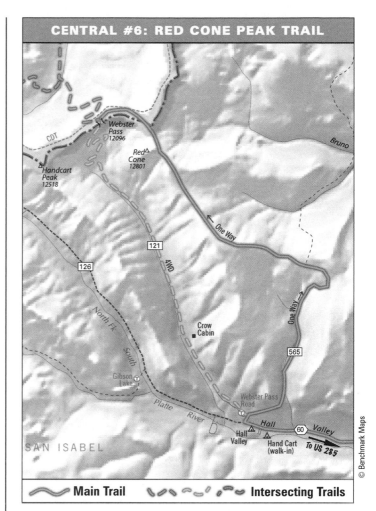

CENTRAL #6: RED CONE PEAK TRAIL

〜〜 **Main Trail**   〜〜 **Intersecting Trails**

© Benchmark Maps

along Red Cone Peak Trail (FR 565).

	GPS: N 39°29.02′ W 105°48.27′	
▼ 0.1	TR	Sign for Webster Pass.
▼ 1.0	SO	Cross through creek.
▼ 3.6	BL	Fork in road.
▼ 5.5	SO	First steep descent.
▼ 6.2		End at Webster Pass crossing.
	GPS: N 39°31.90′ W 105°49.92′	

Looking across Hall Valley to Red Cone Peak Trail as it descends to Webster Pass (marked)

Looking up at Red Cone Peak

Webster Pass Trail

Starting Point:	Webster Pass, at the intersection of FR 285, Central #5: Handcart Gulch Trail (FR 121) and Central #6: Red Cone Peak Trail
Finishing Point:	Intersection with Central #11: Saints John and Glacier Mountain Trail (FR 275)
Total Mileage:	5.1 miles
Unpaved Mileage:	5.1 miles
Driving Time:	45 minutes
Route Elevation:	10,300 to 12,096 feet
Usually Open:	Early July to late September
Difficulty Rating:	3
Scenic Rating:	9

Special Attractions

■ Views from the summit.
■ Access to an extensive network of 4WD trails.
■ Attractive Snake River Valley.

History

Native Americans used Webster Pass for many years before the arrival of the white man. Prospectors first traveled the pass in the 1860s, and in 1878 a partnership of the Webster brothers and the Montezuma Silver Mining Company built a wagon road over the crossing. The route was the main freight route to the Snake River Mining District. The itinerant Father Dyer traveled across the route regularly to deliver the mail and conduct his far-flung ministry. In the early 1890s, David Moffat, the president of the Denver & Rio Grande Railroad, surveyed the crossing at Webster Pass as a possible rail route. The road

Webster Pass Trail follows the Snake River through the valley

fell into disuse and was reopened in 1971 through the efforts of 4WD clubs.

Description

This route takes you from Webster Pass, where it intersects the roads over Red Cone Peak and through Handcart Gulch, down the Snake River Valley and into the township of Montezuma. From the pass, there is a magnificent view of the Handcart Gulch area to the southeast and the Snake River Valley to the northwest. The road up Red Cone Peak is one-way and cannot be entered from Webster Pass. A snowdrift usually blocks the alternative road into Handcart Gulch until late in summer.

The route remains above timberline as it switchbacks down from Webster Pass on a reasonably wide road that has a sound surface. Passing other vehicles is easy at the switchbacks. As you reach the valley floor, you will cross the headwaters of the Snake River and pass the road toward Radical Hill, which departs to the left.

This route is simple to navigate.

One of the tight switchbacks near the end of the trail at Webster Pass

Fording the Snake River

Mountain goats grazing near Webster Pass

Current Road Information

White River National Forest
Dillon Ranger District
680 Blue River Parkway
Silverthorne, CO 80498
(970) 468-5400

Map References

USFS White River National Forest
Maptech CD:
      Denver/Steamboat Springs/North Central
Benchmark's *Colorado Road & Recreation Atlas,* p. 73
Colorado Atlas & Gazetteer, p. 38
The Roads of Colorado, p. 79
Trails Illustrated, #104

Route Directions

▼ 0.0		From the summit of Webster Pass, zero trip meter and proceed down FR 285.
1.5 ▲		End at intersection with Central #6: Red Cone Peak Trail straight ahead (a one-way road with no entry from this point) and Central #5:

Webster Pass viewed from Radical Hill Trail

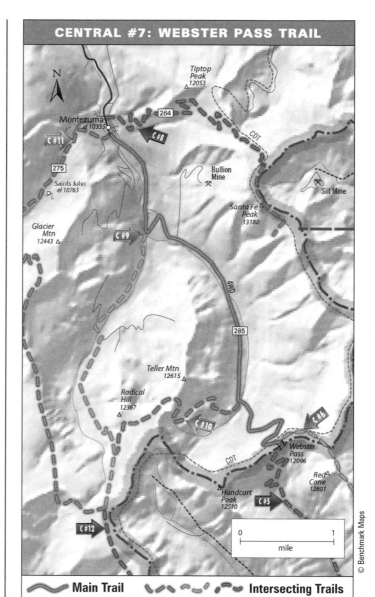

© Benchmark Maps

~~~ **Main Trail**   ~~~ **Intersecting Trails**

		Handcart Gulch Trail to the right.
GPS: N 39°31.90' W 105°49.92'		
▼ 1.5	SO	Intersection with Central #10: Radical Hill Trail on left. Zero trip meter.
0.0 ▲		Proceed southeast on FR 285.
GPS: N 39°32.29' W 105°50.50'		
▼ 0.0		Proceed north on FR 285.
2.6 ▲	BL	Intersection with Central #10: Radical Hill Trail on right. Zero trip meter.
▼ 1.2	SO/TL	Cross through Snake River; then intersection.
1.4 ▲	TR	Intersection; then cross through Snake River.
GPS: N 39°33.31' W 105°50.65'		
▼ 1.4	SO	Track on right; then cross through creek.
1.2 ▲	SO	Cross through creek; then track on left.
▼ 1.9	SO	Seasonal closure gate.
0.7 ▲	SO	Seasonal closure gate.
▼ 2.2	SO	Private Bullion Mine Road on right.
0.4 ▲	SO	Private Bullion Mine Road on left.
▼ 2.6	TR	Intersection of Webster Pass Trail and Central #9: Deer Creek Trail (CR 5/FR 5). Zero trip meter.

View to the north from Webster Pass

0.0 ▲			Proceed along Webster Pass Trail (FR 285).
			GPS: N 39º34.10' W 105º51.57'
▼ 0.0			Proceed north along CR 5.
1.0 ▲		TL	Intersection of Central #9: Deer Creek Trail (CR 5/FR 5) and Webster Pass Road. Zero trip meter.
▼ 0.3		SO	Ruins of mine and log buildings.
0.7 ▲		SO	Ruins of mine and log buildings.
▼ 1.0			End at the intersection with Central #11: Saints John and Glacier Mountain Trail (FR 275).
0.0 ▲			From the intersection of Central #11: Saints John and Glacier Mountain Trail (FR 275), zero trip meter and proceed south on CR 5 (FR 5).
			GPS: N 39º34.80' W 105º52.05'

CENTRAL REGION TRAIL #8

Santa Fe Peak Trail

Starting Point:	**Montezuma**
Finishing Point:	**Santa Fe Peak near the Silver Wave**
	Mine, at the end of a dead-end road
	(FR 264)
Total Mileage:	**5.2 miles (one-way)**
Unpaved Mileage:	**5.2 miles**
Driving Time:	**1.5 hours (one-way)**
Route Elevation:	**10,300 to 12,800 feet**
Usually Open:	**Early June to early October**
Difficulty Rating:	**5**
Scenic Rating:	**9**

Special Attractions

■ Spectacular, panoramic alpine views.
■ Shelf road with some very challenging sections.
■ Many other 4WD trails in the vicinity.

A view of Santa Fe Peak Trail crossing a ridgeline

Description

This route commences at the first intersection on the left as you drive into Montezuma from Keystone (or, coming from the fire station, the last intersection on the right). The unpaved route heads uphill through the homes within the town limits. At this point, there are a number of side roads, but stay on the main road and proceed up a series of mild switchbacks. As the road ascends from timberline, it begins a tighter series of switchbacks.

Once you are out of town, navigation becomes fairly straightforward. The road levels out as it travels along an open ridge that provides some wonderful views. It then commences another series of short switchbacks before leveling off at an open, rocky meadow that offers spectacular 360-degree views.

As you leave this meadow, the road becomes significantly more difficult—especially if you are in a full-sized vehicle. It narrows, becomes rougher, and has a looser surface. As you proceed, the road starts to descend gently around a rocky, narrow shelf with a steep drop-off along the west side of Santa Fe Peak. We recommend that from this point you park your vehicle in an out-of-the-way spot and walk down to the Silver Wave Mine, as there is no place to turn around at the mine.

Looking across toward Radical Hill from the trail

CENTRAL #8: SANTA FE PEAK TRAIL

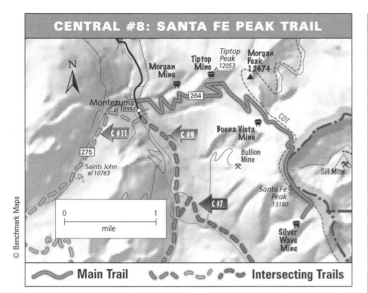

© Benchmark Maps

Morgan Mine · Morgan Peak 12474 · Tiptop Mine · Tiptop Peak 12053 · 264 · Montezuma el 10335 · C #11 · 275 · C #9 · Buena Vista Mine · Bullion Mine · Saints John el 10763 · Sill Mine · Santa Fe Peak 13180 · C #7 · Silver Wave Mine · CDT

N

0 —————— 1
mile

〜〜 **Main Trail**   ໐໐໐〜໐໐ **Intersecting Trails**

You may park along a ridge just under half a mile from the mine or at the last switchback, about 150 yards before the mine. The ridge provides a great view of Geneva Creek Valley to the east, the Snake River Valley to the southwest, and Red Cone Peak and Webster Pass to the south.

Current Road Information

White River National Forest
Dillon Ranger District
680 Blue River Parkway
Silverthorne, CO 80498
(970) 468-5400

Map References

USFS White River National Forest
Maptech CD:
      Denver/Steamboat Springs/North Central
Benchmark's *Colorado Road & Recreation Atlas*, p. 73
Colorado Atlas & Gazetteer, p. 38
The Roads of Colorado, p. 79
Trails Illustrated, #104

A narrow rough section of the trail

Route Directions

▼ 0.0 From the Montezuma Snake River Fire Station, zero trip meter and proceed north on CR 5 (FR 5).

GPS: N 39°34.85' W 105°52.03'

▼ 0.1 TR Intersection with Santa Fe Peak Road (FR 264).
▼ 0.2 SO Enter National Forest.

GPS: N 39°34.96' W 105°51.92'

▼ 0.9 SO Track on left—closed.
▼ 1.3 SO Mine ruins on right (private property).
▼ 1.4 SO Track to cabin (private property) on right; then mine ruins on right.
▼ 1.7 SO Track to mine on right (private property).
▼ 1.9 SO Mine on right.
▼ 2.6 SO Track on right. Stay on FR 264.
▼ 2.7 SO Timberline.
▼ 3.0 SO Quail Mine on right.

GPS: N 39°34.83' W 105°50.72'

▼ 3.3 SO View down onto Montezuma and Snake River Valley.
▼ 3.8 SO Intersection. Track on right goes to Buena Vista Mine. Remain on FR 264.

GPS: N 39°34.67' W 105°50.33'

▼ 4.1 SO Enter large plateau with spectacular 360-degree views.
▼ 4.6 SO Turn-around and parking opportunity prior to shelf road.
▼ 4.8 SO Ridge. Full-sized vehicles should stop at this point. Last good spot for turning around.

GPS: N 39°34.09' W 105°50.08'

▼ 5.1 BR Last switchback.
▼ 5.2 End at Silver Wave Mine.

GPS: N 39°34.02' W 105°50.11'

CENTRAL REGION TRAIL #9

Deer Creek Trail

Starting Point:	**Intersection with Central #11: Saints John and Glacier Mountain Trail (FR 275)**
Finishing Point:	**Three-way intersection with Central #12: Middle Fork of the Swan Trail and Central #11: Saints John and Glacier Mountain Trail**
Total Mileage:	**5.0 miles**
Unpaved Mileage:	**5.0 miles**
Driving Time:	**45 minutes**
Route Elevation:	**10,300 to 12,400 feet**
Usually Open:	**Mid-June to late September**
Difficulty Rating:	**4**
Scenic Rating:	**8**

Special Attractions

- Provides access to an extensive network of 4WD trails.
- A relatively easy road that provides a good introduction to roads in the area.

A lower section of Deer Creek Trail

Looking into the beautiful Deer Creek Valley

History

Montezuma, a silver camp named after the last Aztec emperor of Mexico, was founded in the 1860s. Henry Teller, who went on to serve as a U.S. senator for 29 years, was possibly one of the first to locate silver in the area. The camp grew slowly, mainly because silver rather than gold was found and because of its inaccessibility. Ore shipments had to be made via the newly opened but difficult route across Argentine Pass, which led to high transportation costs.

Sign at the end of the trail

When the Loveland and Webster Passes were built in the late 1870s and silver mining was booming, Montezuma began to flourish. A regular stage traveled across both passes. Soon Montezuma was the focal point for the many mining camps in the district, offering supplies, a school, and entertainment such as dance halls, saloons, and poker games—which are said to have gone on 24 hours a day. Montezuma reached its peak population of about 800 residents around 1880, and the following year the city was incorporated. In 1882, Montezuma's new trustees set about cleaning up the town, establishing fines for drunkenness and outlawing gambling and prostitution.

Montezuma suffered greatly from the silver crash of 1893, although it never did become a ghost town. In 1958, a fire started at the Summit House hotel and blazed through town, completely destroying the hotel, the town hall, houses, garages, and other buildings. Almost half of the 75 residents were rendered homeless—a week before Christmas. In 1972, it lost its post office. Today, the town is a mixture of old and new buildings. The one-room schoolhouse, which operated from 1884 to 1958, still stands on a slope east of Main Street.

View from the end of Deer Creek Trail

Franklin was the site of the headquarters of the Montezuma Silver Mining Company. It was deliberately located an appropriate distance from the jarring activity of the company's mines and was intended to become an elite community of the company's management. The first building was a large two-story house built for the mine superintendent. It was the showpiece of the town and was used to entertain visiting dignitaries. Today the foundations of the house are all that remain. At some point, a sawmill was also built at the site. Little else was ever built and the community was short-lived.

Description

Deer Creek Trail serves as the backbone for an extensive network of 4WD roads branching in all directions. Many of the roads are poorly marked, and navigation can be difficult. We strongly recommend that you use a copy of the *Trails Illustrated* map for the area. It is not entirely accurate but is more detailed than most of the alternative maps.

The trail climbing above timberline

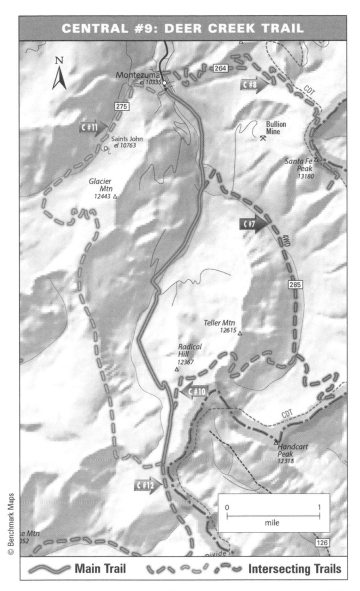

CENTRAL #9: DEER CREEK TRAIL

Main Trail ~~~ **Intersecting Trails**

© Benchmark Maps

Route Directions

▼ 0.0		From the intersection with Central #11: Saints John and Glacier Mountain Trail (FR 275), zero trip meter and proceed south on CR 5 (FR 5).
1.0 ▲		End at the intersection with Central #11: Saints John and Glacier Mountain Trail (FR 275).
GPS: N 39°34.80′ W 105°52.05′		
▼ 0.7	SO	Ruins of mine and log buildings.
0.3 ▲	SO	Ruins of mine and log buildings.
▼ 1.0	SO	Track on left is Central #7: Webster Pass Trail. Town site of Franklin. Zero trip meter.
0.0 ▲		Continue along CR 5/FR 5.
GPS: N 39°34.08′ W 105°51.57′		
▼ 0.0		Continue on CR 5/FR 5.
4.0 ▲	SO	Track on right is Central #7: Webster Pass

Deer Creek

Other than navigation, this route presents no major difficulties. The road is bumpy and includes some easy switchbacks, but the surface is sound.

Franklin is located just north of the intersection with Central #7: Webster Pass Trail. It is private property.

Current Road Information

White River National Forest
Dillon Ranger District
680 Blue River Parkway
Silverthorne, CO 80498
(970) 468-5400

Map References

USFS White River National Forest
Maptech CD:
    Denver/Steamboat Springs/North Central
Benchmark's *Colorado Road & Recreation Atlas*, p. 73
Colorado Atlas & Gazetteer, p. 38
The Roads of Colorado, p. 79
Trails Illustrated, #104

▼ 0.3	SO	Parking area. Cross over creek.
3.7 ▲	SO	Cross over creek. Parking area.
▼ 0.6	SO	Gated track on right.
3.4 ▲	SO	Gated track on left.
▼ 0.9	SO	Track on right dead-ends at mines.
3.1 ▲	SO	Track on left dead-ends at mines.
▼ 1.0	SO	Arapaho National Forest information board. Seasonal closure gate.
3.0 ▲	SO	Seasonal closure gate. Arapaho National Forest information board.
▼ 1.5	SO	Track to the right goes to mines.
2.4 ▲	SO	Track to the left goes to mines.
▼ 1.6	SO	Cross over Deer Creek. Track on the left.
2.4 ▲	SO	Track on right. Cross over Deer Creek.
▼ 1.7	SO	Track on left goes to numerous mines.
2.3 ▲	SO	Track on right goes to numerous mines.
▼ 2.0	SO	Short track to the right.
2.0 ▲	SO	Short track to the left.
▼ 2.2	BL	Track on the right.
1.8 ▲	BR	Track on the left.
▼ 3.4	BR	Track on left is first turnoff to Central #10: Radical Hill Trail (FR 286).
0.6 ▲	BL	Track on right is second turnoff to Radical Hill.
▼ 3.5	SO	Track on left is second turnoff to Radical Hill.
0.5 ▲	SO	Track on right is first turnoff to Central #10: Radical Hill Trail (FR 286).
▼ 4.0		End at 3-way intersection signpost that points to the Middle Fork of the Swan to the south and to Glacier Mountain, the North Fork of the Swan, and Saints John to the west.
0.0 ▲		Begin at 3-way intersection signpost that points to the Middle Fork of the Swan to the south and to Glacier Mountain, the North Fork of the Swan, and Saints John to the west.

GPS: N 39°31.24' W 105°52.09'

CENTRAL REGION TRAIL #10

Radical Hill Trail

Starting Point:	**Intersection of Central #9: Deer Creek Trail and FR 286**
Finishing Point:	**Central #7: Webster Pass Trail (FR 285)**
Total Mileage:	**2.5 miles**
Unpaved Mileage:	**2.5 miles**
Driving Time:	**45 minutes**
Route Elevation:	**11,400 to 12,600 feet**
Usually Open:	**Mid-June to late September**
Difficulty Rating:	**6**
Scenic Rating:	**10**

Special Attractions

- Very challenging 4WD trail.
- Interconnects with a network of other 4WD trails.
- Wonderful alpine scenery.

A rocky section close to the intersection with Webster Pass Trail

Description

This is a short, challenging road with a steep, loose, and very narrow shelf section. If you start at Deer Creek Trail, the difficult section is downhill. This route is the easier way of tackling it.

From Deer Creek Trail, the route commences a gentle ascent through a broad expanse of alpine tundra across the top of Radical Hill and over to Teller Mountain. After only about the first mile of the route, from the top of Teller Mountain, there is a particularly good view down into the Snake River Valley.

As you proceed from this point, the road turns, descends sharply, and switchbacks onto a very narrow shelf cut into the face of the mountain. The road is significantly eroded in spots as well as being off-camber and having a loose surface. As it curves around the mountain, it levels off and becomes wide enough to accommodate two vehicles when passing is necessary.

The balance of this short trail is a rough, rocky ride, but the worst is definitely over.

Current Road Information

White River National Forest
Dillon Ranger District
680 Blue River Parkway
Silverthorne, CO 80498
(970) 468-5400

Map References

USFS White River National Forest
Maptech CD:
     Denver/Steamboat Springs/North Central

A view across Teller Mountain

CENTRAL #10: RADICAL HILL TRAIL

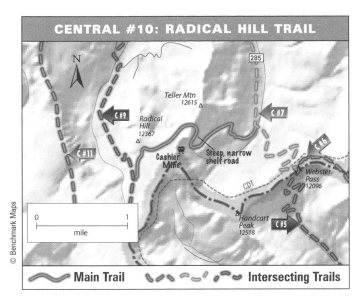

© Benchmark Maps

Main Trail 〜〜 ⌒ ⌒ ⌒ **Intersecting Trails**

Benchmark's *Colorado Road & Recreation Atlas*, p. 73
Colorado Atlas & Gazetteer, p. 38
The Roads of Colorado, p. 79
Trails Illustrated, #104

Route Directions

▼ 0.0		From intersection of Central #9: Deer Creek Trail (FR 5) and FR 286, zero trip meter and turn onto FR 286.
2.5 ▲		End at intersection with Central #9: Deer Creek Trail (FR 5).
GPS: N 39°31.66' W 105°51.91'		
▼ 0.1	SO	Track on right is alternative track to Deer Creek Trail.
2.4 ▲	BL	Track on left is alternative track to Deer Creek Trail.
▼ 0.9	SO	Scenic overlook and start of steep, narrow descent.
1.6 ▲	SO	Scenic overlook.

The trail where it switchbacks down into the Swan River Valley

Another view of the narrow, dangerous shelf road at the end of the trail

▼ 1.4	SO	Track on right to cabin.
1.1 ▲	SO	Track on left to cabin.
GPS: N 39°32.05' W 105°51.18'		
▼ 2.5	BL	Track on right; then end at intersection with Central #7: Webster Pass Trail.
0.0 ▲		At intersection of Central #7: Webster Pass Trail and Radical Hill Trail (FR 286), zero trip meter and proceed along FR 286.
GPS: N 39°32.29' W 105°50.46'		

CENTRAL REGION TRAIL #11

Saints John and Glacier Mountain Trail

Starting Point:	**Intersection of CR 5 and FR 275**
Finishing Point:	**Three-way intersection with Central**
	#9: Deer Creek Trail and with Central
	#12: Middle Fork of the Swan Trail
Total Mileage:	**7.2 miles**
Unpaved Mileage:	**7.2 miles**
Driving Time:	**1.5 hours**
Route Elevation:	**10,300 to 12,200 feet**
Usually Open:	**Mid-July to late September**
Difficulty Rating:	**4**
Scenic Rating:	**8**

Special Attractions

■ Moderately challenging 4WD trail that offers a mix of historic sites, varied trail conditions, and excellent scenery.
■ Access to a network of 4WD trails.

THE CENTRAL REGION **325**

Saints John in the 1870s

History

Saints John was originally named Coleyville, after John Coley, who located the first ore in 1863. Legend has it that hunters in the area in 1861 ran out of bullets and resorted to using pieces of rock in their guns. Two years later, they were in Nevada and noticed a great similarity between the rich ore they saw there and the rocks that they had used as ammunition. They contacted Coley, who set up camp in the area and subsequently located silver ore.

A prospector named Bob Epsey is also celebrated for an unusual strike. Suffering from a hangover one day, Epsey lay down to sleep it off under a shady tree. When he awoke, he steadied himself by grasping a rock as he stood. When the rock broke off in Epsey's hand, he discovered in it a big chunk of solid ore.

The town was renamed Saints John by Freemasons who gave it the biblical name after John the Baptist and John the Evangelist. Saints John became a company town when it was taken over by the Boston Silver Mining Association, an East Coast company, in 1872. At great expense, the company erected a sophisticated milling and smelter work, complete with bricks imported from Europe. A few years later it was taken over by the Boston Mining Company. For such a remote mining town, Saints John had a 350-volume library (complete with regularly stocked newspapers from Boston and Europe), a boardinghouse, a dining hall, a company store, an assay office, various cabins, and a beautiful superintendent's house with elegant furnishings from Europe and the eastern United States. However, the mining companies did not allow a saloon, so the miners regularly traveled down the mountain to Montezuma, where they indulged to their hearts' content in brothels, saloons, and poker dens.

Poor access, harsh winters, and waning silver finds caused the decline of Saints John. Argentine and Webster Passes were impassable because of snow in the winter and at other times from rock slides. The post office was closed by 1881, and the town was deserted by the 1890s.

The Wild Irishman Mine was discovered by a New York City policeman named Michael Dulhaney, who came to Colorado and struck it rich in the late 1870s. It operated throughout the 1880s but remained just a camp and was never formally incorporated as a town. The camp had no church or school. Several cabins were situated around the mine so that the miners could be close to their work. The Wild Irishman camp is typical of a number of camps where men and their families worked during the mining boom. The ruins of the mine and the miners' cabins are still evident in a beautiful timberline meadow.

Description

This route offers a variety of attractions: the historic mining town of Saints John, old mines, creek crossings, and stunning alpine views.

As the roads in the area are frequently unmarked, we recommend that you take a copy of the *Trails Illustrated* map #104. It is not completely accurate but is more detailed than most of the alternatives and will prove helpful.

The road is rough in sections but sound. Some sections are steep but should prove well within the capability of a 4WD vehicle.

The road starts in Montezuma and ascends some switchbacks to the Saints John town site. It passes by the Wild Irishman Mine before switchbacking a steep slope onto the exposed Glacier Mountain. It then winds along the narrow ridge past the General Teller Mine and ends at the three-way intersection with Central #9: Deer Creek Trail and the Central #12: Middle Fork of the Swan Trail.

The Wild Irishman Mine and site of the 1880s town

Current Road Information

White River National Forest
Dillon Ranger District
680 Blue River Parkway
Silverthorne, CO 80498
(970) 468-5400

Map References

USFS White River National Forest
Maptech CD:
    Denver/Steamboat Springs/North Central
Benchmark's *Colorado Road & Recreation Atlas*, p. 73
Colorado Atlas & Gazetteer, p. 38
The Roads of Colorado, p. 79
Trails Illustrated, #104 (minor inaccuracies)

Route Directions

▼ 0.0			At the intersection of CR 5 and FR 275 in Montezuma, zero trip meter and proceed onto FR 275 toward Saints John.
	7.2 ▲		End at intersection of CR 5 and FR 275 in Montezuma.

GPS: N 39°34.80' W 105°52.05'

▼ 0.2		SO	Track on left goes to the Equity Mine with old buildings in 0.2 miles.
	7.0 ▲	SO	Track on right goes to the Equity Mine with old buildings.
▼ 0.5		SO	Enter Arapaho National Forest.
	6.7 ▲	SO	Leave Arapaho National Forest.
▼ 0.6		SO	Track on right crosses Saints John Creek and leads to Grizzly Gulch.
	6.6 ▲	SO	Track on left crosses Saints John Creek and leads to Grizzly Gulch.
▼ 1.3		SO	Town site of Saints John.
	5.9 ▲	SO	Town site of Saints John.

GPS: N 39°34.33' W 105°52.85'

▼ 1.4		TR	Follow Jeep trail sign. Cross Saints John Creek. Track on left.
	5.8 ▲	TL	Track on right. Cross Saints John Creek.
▼ 1.8		SO	Cross Saints John Creek. Arapaho National Forest information board. Seasonal closure gate.
	5.4 ▲	SO	Seasonal closure gate. Cross Saints John Creek.

GPS: N 39°34.00' W 105°53.23'

▼ 2.3		TL	T-Intersection. Right goes to camping possibilities. Cross creek.
	4.9 ▲	TR	Cross creek. Track on left goes to camping possibilities.
▼ 2.5		SO	Creek crossing.
	4.7 ▲	SO	Creek crossing.
▼ 2.8		SO	Wild Irishman Mine is approximately 100 yards off the road on left.
	4.4 ▲	SO	Wild Irishman Mine is approximately 100 yards off the road on right.
▼ 2.9		SO	Wild Irishman Mine tailings.
	4.3 ▲	SO	Wild Irishman Mine tailings.
▼ 3.0		TR	Trail on left goes to Wild Irishman Mine.
	4.2 ▲	TL	Trail on right goes to Wild Irishman Mine.
▼ 3.5		SO	Short trail on left.
	3.7 ▲	SO	Short trail on right.
▼ 3.7		SO	Trail on left.
	3.5 ▲	SO	Trail on right.

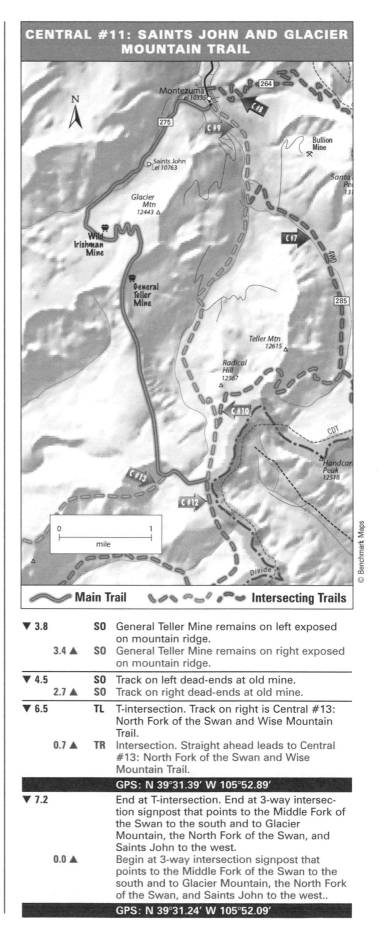

CENTRAL #11: SAINTS JOHN AND GLACIER MOUNTAIN TRAIL

Main Trail   Intersecting Trails

© Benchmark Maps

▼ 3.8		SO	General Teller Mine remains on left exposed on mountain ridge.
	3.4 ▲	SO	General Teller Mine remains on right exposed on mountain ridge.
▼ 4.5		SO	Track on left dead-ends at old mine.
	2.7 ▲	SO	Track on right dead-ends at old mine.
▼ 6.5		TL	T-intersection. Track on right is Central #13: North Fork of the Swan and Wise Mountain Trail.
	0.7 ▲	TR	Intersection. Straight ahead leads to Central #13: North Fork of the Swan and Wise Mountain Trail.

GPS: N 39°31.39' W 105°52.89'

▼ 7.2			End at T-intersection. End at 3-way intersection signpost that points to the Middle Fork of the Swan to the south and to Glacier Mountain, the North Fork of the Swan, and Saints John to the west.
	0.0 ▲		Begin at 3-way intersection signpost that points to the Middle Fork of the Swan to the south and to Glacier Mountain, the North Fork of the Swan, and Saints John to the west..

GPS: N 39°31.24' W 105°52.09'

Middle Fork of the Swan Trail

Starting Point:	Three-way intersection with Central #9: Deer Creek Trail and with Central #11: Saints John and Glacier Mountain Trail
Finishing Point:	Breckenridge at intersection of Colorado 9 and Tiger Road
Total Mileage:	12.2 miles
Unpaved Mileage:	9.6 miles
Driving Time:	1 hour
Route Elevation:	9,250 to 12,200 feet
Usually Open:	Mid-June to early October
Difficulty Rating:	5
Scenic Rating:	8

Special Attractions

■ Interesting, though unsightly, remains of extensive placer mining by dredge boats.
■ Beautiful, wooded valley along the upper reaches of the Middle Fork of the Swan River.
■ Challenging uphill section.
■ Access to a network of 4WD trails.

History

Towns along this route were Swandyke, Tiger, Swan City, Delaware Flats, and Braddocks.

Swandyke boomed briefly in the late 1890s, considerably later than most other Colorado mining camps. The gold camp was divided into two sections called Swandyke and Upper Swandyke, about a mile apart. Stagecoach service connected

Tiger township, circa 1940

the camp to Breckenridge and over Webster Pass to Jefferson; and from there, railroad service ran regularly to Denver. Swandyke's population peaked at about 500 in 1899, when the post office was set up. Few of the miners remained through the winter. During the camp's first winter, in 1898–99, extremely heavy snowfalls led to a number of snow slides, which destroyed most of the buildings in the new town. One avalanche carried Swandyke's mill down one side of the mountain and across a deep gulch, leaving the wreckage on the opposite mountainside. Swandyke was a ghost town by 1902, although the post office was not officially closed until 1910.

Tiger, another mining camp, was established following discovery of the Tiger Lode in 1864. Soon additional discoveries were made in the area. Shortly after the turn of the century, the Royal Tiger Mining Company was formed and bought up most of the mines. It established the company town of Tiger and provided well for the miners. They had free electricity, steam heat, and a school for the children; the company even held regular dances and free movie shows. The mine closed in 1940 and Tiger quickly became a ghost town. Because the town was much younger than most ghost towns, the buildings remained in good condition, and in the 1960s the town was

One of the many panoramic views afforded by this trail

The trail following alongside the Middle Fork of the Swan River

The benign-looking uphill section that can become impassable in wet conditions

Loose, steep, and rocky section of the trail

reoccupied as a hippy commune. However, authorities responded by burning it to the ground in 1973.

About a half mile past the site of Tiger, Swan City sprang to life in May 1880, and within three months it had a post office, a general store, a saloon, and a hotel, but within ten years the gold mines were no longer profitable and the town was deserted. Although mining in the area was revitalized with the arrival of dredge boats, Swan City was obliterated—buried beneath tons of rubble left by the dredges.

Delaware Flats was established in 1860 during the initial gold rush to the area. This was eight years prior to the Kit Carson Treaty, when the district was ceded by the Ute. Within a year, the town had a post office and several hundred prospectors. In 1875, the name of the town was changed to Preston. The post office closed in 1880, and twenty years later the dredge boats completely buried the site. Today, the golf course is on the western end of the reclaimed town site.

Braddocks, at the intersection of Tiger Road and Colorado 9, was founded by Dave Braddocks who operated the local stage line and livery stable. In 1884, the Denver, South Park & Pacific Railroad built a station at the location.

Description

This route commences at the three-way intersection at the end of Deer Creek Trail and travels along an alpine ridge toward the headwaters of the Middle Fork of the Swan River.

At the 0.8-mile point, there is a sign to Hall Valley. This road does not go through to Hall Valley but goes to an overlook of the valley. It is a worthwhile side trip that not only provides a wonderful view down into the valley but also offers a spectacular panoramic view across the top of Handcart Gulch to Red Cone Peak and the trail descending from it (Central #7) to Webster Pass. The shelf road from Webster Pass that leads down into Handcart Gulch (Central #5) is also clearly visible from this vantage point.

Shortly after, the road travels along the side of the mountain before beginning the steep descent down to the valley floor. The surface during the descent is quite loose in sections and can be considerably looser if wet. Traveling uphill under such conditions in a stock vehicle can be nearly impossible. It is for this short section of road that the route warrants its difficulty rating; otherwise a rating of 4 would be more appropriate. The road continues along the extremely attractive Mid-

View over Hall Valley from the overlook

An old cabin near the trail

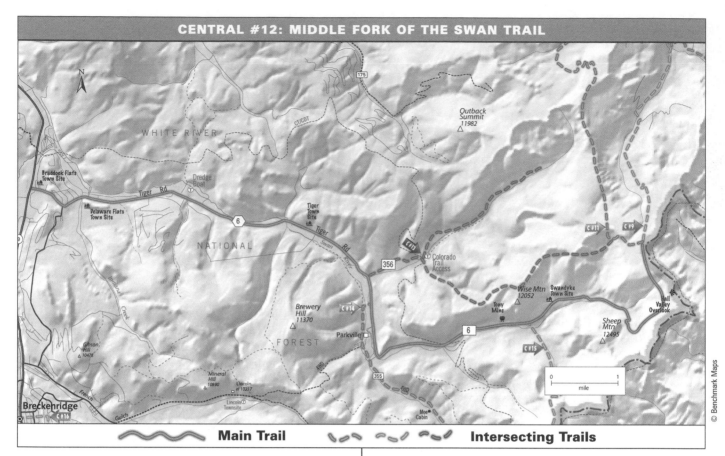

Main Trail   **Intersecting Trails**

© Benchmark Maps

dle Fork of the Swan River before intersecting with Central #14: Georgia Pass Trail.

From this point, the road is easily accessible to 2WD vehicles as it threads a path through an almost continual line of huge tailings dumps from the dredge mining in the early 1900s. At the 3.6-mile point from the intersection with Georgia Pass Trail, in a pond among tailings, lie the remains of the mining boat Tiger Dredge #1.

The route ends at the intersection of Colorado 9 and Tiger Road (at the Highlands at Breckenridge public golf course). This intersection was the site of the towns of Delaware Flats and Braddocks, named for the Denver, South Park & Pacific Railroad station that was located there.

Current Road Information

White River National Forest
Dillon Ranger District
680 Blue River Parkway
Silverthorne, CO 80498
(970) 468-5400

Map References

USFS   White River National Forest
Maptech CD: Colorado Springs/Ski Areas/Central;
        Denver/Steamboat Springs/North Central
Benchmark's *Colorado Road & Recreation Atlas*, p. 73
Colorado Atlas & Gazetteer, p. 38
The Roads of Colorado, pp. 78, 79
Trails Illustrated, #104 (minor inaccuracies), #109

Route Directions

▼ 0.0   Begin at 3-way intersection signpost that points to the Middle Fork of the Swan to the south and to Glacier Mountain, the North Fork of the Swan, and Saints John to the west.

6.1 ▲   End at 3-way intersection signpost that points to the Middle Fork of the Swan to the south and to Glacier Mountain, the North Fork of the Swan, and Saints John to the west..

Remains of Tiger Dredge #1 boat near the Breckenridge end of the trail

		GPS: N 39°31.24' W 105°52.09'
▼ 0.7	TR	T-intersection. Straight ahead to Hall Valley overlook (this side road ends at a scenic overlook in 0.8 miles). Proceed toward Middle Fork of the Swan on FR 220.
5.4 ▲	TL	T-intersection. Hall Valley scenic overlook is to the right. Follow sign to Montezuma. Then pass a small track on right.
		GPS: N 39°30.83' W 105°51.74'
▼ 1.5	SO	Track on left.
4.7 ▲	SO	Track on right.
▼ 2.2	SO	Cross through creek.
3.7 ▲	SO	Cross through creek.
▼ 2.4	SO	Track on right is Trail #62.
3.5 ▲	SO	Track on left is Trail #62.
▼ 2.8	SO	Deserted log cabin on right. Site of Swandyke.
3.3 ▲	SO	Deserted log cabin on left. Site of Swandyke.
		GPS: N 39°30.49' W 105°53.50'
▼ 3.0	SO	Cross through creek; then track on right.
3.1 ▲	SO	Track on left; then cross through creek.
▼ 3.2	SO	Cabin ruins on right.
2.9 ▲	SO	Cabin ruins on left.
▼ 3.3	BL	Track on right.
2.8 ▲	SO	Track on left.
▼ 3.4	SO	Private track to the Tony Mine on right.
2.7 ▲	SO	Private track to the Tony Mine on left.
		GPS: N 39°30.14' W 105°54.71'
▼ 3.5	SO	Track on left.
2.6 ▲	SO	Track on right.
▼ 3.7	SO	Track on left.
2.4 ▲	BR	Fork.
▼ 5.3	SO	Seasonal gate and exit White River National Forest.
0.8 ▲	SO	Seasonal gate and enter White River National Forest.
▼ 6.1	SO	Road on left goes to Central #14: Georgia Pass Trail. Zero trip meter.
0.0 ▲		Continue straight on.
		GPS: N 39°30.39' W 105°56.71'
▼ 0.0		Continue straight ahead on CR 6 (Tiger Road) toward Breckenridge.
6.1 ▲	SO	Road on right is Central #14: Georgia Pass Trail. Signed to Middle Fork straight ahead and South Fork (Georgia Pass) to the right. Zero trip meter.
▼ 0.4	BL	Intersection with Central #13: North Fork of the Swan and Wise Mountain Trail on right.
5.7 ▲	BR	Intersection with Central #13: North Fork of the Swan and Wise Mountain Trail on left.
▼ 1.4	SO	Road on left. Tiger town site on right.
4.7 ▲	SO	Road on right. Tiger town site on left.
		GPS: N 39°31.37' W 105°57.69'
▼ 3.5	SO	Pavement begins; then parking area for viewing historic dredge boat on right.
2.6 ▲	SO	Parking area for viewing historic dredge boat on left; then pavement ends.
▼ 6.1		End at intersection with Colorado 9. Breckenridge is to the left.
0.0 ▲		At intersection of Colorado 9 and CR 6 (Tiger Road), 3.2 miles north of Breckenridge Visitor Center, zero trip meter and proceed east along Tiger Road. This intersection is marked with a sign for the Breckenridge Public Golf Course.
		GPS: N 39°31.95' W 106°02.58'

North Fork of the Swan and Wise Mountain Trail

Starting Point:	Intersection of Central #12: Middle Fork of the Swan Trail and FR 354
Finishing Point:	Intersection of Central #11: Saints John and Glacier Mountain Trail and FR 356
Total Mileage:	9.6 miles
Unpaved Mileage:	9.6 miles
Driving Time:	1.5 hours
Route Elevation:	10,000 to 12,400 feet
Usually Open:	Early July to early October
Difficulty Rating:	6 (5 traveling the reverse direction)
Scenic Rating:	9

Special Attractions

- Spectacular, expansive views.
- Town site of Rexford and views of mine and cabin ruins.
- Challenging, short, steep section along the trail.
- Access to a network of 4WD roads.

History

In 1880, Daniel Patrick discovered the Rochester lode. Two mines, the Rochester King and the Rochester Queen, were developed the following year by the Rexford Mining Corporation. To enable development of the mines in this remote location, the company also built the town of Rexford on land it owned. A mill was built near the mines to process the ore before shipment to a smelter in Denver. Within two years, declining production and high costs closed the mine, and the town was deserted.

Rexford had a post office from 1882 until the following year as well as a general store, a saloon, a boardinghouse for the miners, and several cabins. At its peak, the town had twice-weekly mail service from Montezuma. Several buildings are

The remains of Rexford in 1961

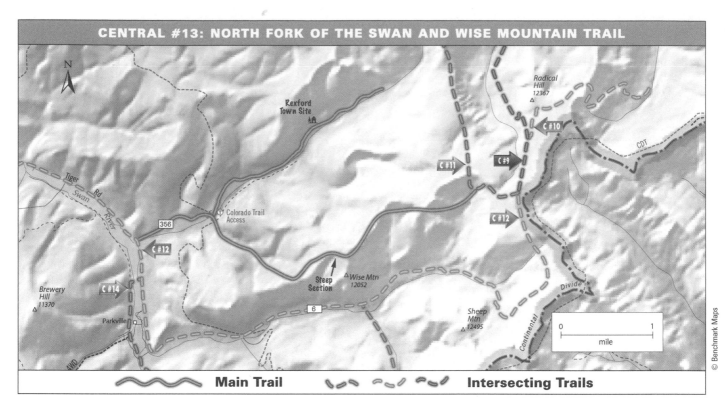

N

Radical Hill 12367 △

C #10

C #11   C #9

CDT

Rexford Town Site

C #12

Tiger Rd

Swan River

356

Colorado Trail Access

Continental Divide

C #12

Steep Section

△ Wise Mtn 12052

C #14

Brewery Hill 11370 △

Parkville

6

Sheep Mtn △ 12495

0   1
mile

4WD

© Benchmark Maps

〜〜〜 **Main Trail**   〜〜〜 **Intersecting Trails**

still evident at Rexford but all have, at least partially, collapsed. About three-quarters of a mile before Rexford, two buildings that were used by loggers when they were working the area are still standing. They were built after the demise of Rexford.

Description

The road commences at the intersection with Central #12: Middle Fork of the Swan Trail. Initially, the road is graded but becomes rough after a mile of so. Nonetheless, it remains easy for the first 2.2 miles; good backcountry camping sites exist along this section. However, after the turnoff for Rexford, water crossings, short sections that can be muddy, and progressively steeper sections make a 4WD necessary.

After returning from the side road to Rexford, the main trail climbs above timberline and goes past a mine before in-

tersecting a trail to a small cabin perched atop Wise Mountain, which, although very exposed to the elements, is still used. Turning to the left, the trail crosses the treeless ridgeline for about half a mile before encountering the most difficult section of the route: a very steep, loose section that transitions be-

Sign to Wise Mountain with old miners' cabin in the background

Creek crossing

tween two ridgelines. Until this point, the trail would have only been rated a 5 for difficulty, but this section increases the rating to a 6. (Going downhill, the rating remains a 5.)

From Wise Mountain, there are sweeping views in all directions. In particular, spectacular views are afforded down into the Middle Fork of the Swan River Valley and north toward Saints John.

The road ends at the intersection with Central #11: Saints John and Glacier Mountain Trail. From this point, you can select from a number of routes leading to Montezuma or Breckenridge.

Current Road Information

White River National Forest
Dillon Ranger District
680 Blue River Parkway
Silverthorne, CO 80498
(970) 468-5400

Map References

USFS White River National Forest
Maptech CD:
    Denver/Steamboat Springs/North Central
Colorado Atlas & Gazetteer, p. 38
The Roads of Colorado, p. 79
Trails Illustrated, #104

Route Directions

▼ 0.0   From Central #12: Middle Fork of the Swan Trail (CR 6/Tiger Road), zero trip meter and proceed along FR 354, following sign to North Fork.
2.2 ▲   End at intersection with Tiger Road, which is also Central #12: Middle Fork of the Swan Trail. Right goes toward Breckenridge, and left continues the Middle Fork Trail and also goes toward Georgia Pass.

GPS: N 39°30.80' W 105°56.79'

▼ 0.5   SO   Track on left.
1.7 ▲   SO   Track on right.

▼ 0.6   SO   Seasonal gate.
1.6 ▲   SO   Seasonal gate.

▼ 0.9   SO   Gated track on right.
1.2 ▲   SO   Gated track on left.

▼ 1.6   SO   Cross over North Fork River.
0.6 ▲   SO   Cross over North Fork River.

▼ 1.7   SO   Road on left.
0.4 ▲   SO   Road on right.

GPS: N 39°31.43' W 105°55.23'

▼ 2.2   BL   Fork in road. Remains of two cabins from a logging camp. Zero trip meter.
0.0 ▲   Continue along track toward the Middle Fork of the Swan River.

GPS: N 39°31.65' W 105°54.75'

▼ 0.0   Proceed along side road toward Rexford. (This road dead-ends, so you will have to return to this spot.)
4.4 ▲   SO   After returning to the intersection beside the two logging cabins, proceed straight on. Track on the left toward Wise Mountain. Zero trip meter.

▼ 0.4   SO   Cabin on left.

4.0 ▲   SO   Cabin on right.

GPS: N 39°31.90' W 105°54.54'

▼ 0.7   SO   Site of Rexford. Numerous cabin ruins on left and right.
3.7 ▲   SO   Rexford town site.

GPS: N 39°32.04' W 105°54.25'

▼ 1.8   SO   Cabin ruins on right.
2.6 ▲   SO   Cabin ruins on left.

GPS: N 39°32.48' W 105°53.35'

▼ 1.9   BR   Track on left. Cross through creek.
2.5 ▲   BL   Cross through creek. Track on right.

▼ 2.0   BL   Fork in the road.
2.4 ▲   BR   Fork in the road.

GPS: N 39°32.49' W 105°53.18'

▼ 2.2   UT   End of track at mine.
2.2 ▲   UT   End of track at mine.

GPS: N 39°32.40' W 105°53.18'

▼ 2.4   BR   Fork in the road.
2.0 ▲   BL   Fork in the road.

▼ 2.5   BL   Cross through creek. Track on right.
1.9 ▲   BR   Track on left. Cross through creek.

▼ 2.6   SO   Cabin ruins on left.
1.8 ▲   SO   Cabin ruins on right.

GPS: N 39°32.48' W 105°53.35'

▼ 3.7   SO   Rexford town site.
0.7 ▲   SO   Site of Rexford. Numerous cabin ruins on left and right.

▼ 4.0   SO   Cabin on right.
0.4 ▲   SO   Cabin on left.

▼ 4.4   TL   Upon returning to the intersection beside the two old logging cabins, zero trip meter and turn left.
0.0 ▲   Turn right and proceed along the side road to Rexford. (This road dead-ends, so you will have to return to this spot.)

GPS: N 39°31.65' W 105°54.75'

▼ 0.0   Cross through the North Fork of the Swan and proceed toward Wise Mountain.
1.3 ▲   TR   Cross through the North Fork of the Swan. Intersection and the remains of two logging cabins. Zero trip meter.

▼ 0.1   SO   Cross through creek.
1.2 ▲   SO   Cross through creek.

▼ 0.3   SO   Cabin on right.
1.1 ▲   SO   Cabin on left.

▼ 1.3   SO   Mine on left.
0.1 ▲   SO   Mine on right.

GPS: N 39°30.87' W 105°54.17'

▼ 1.4   TL   Intersection. Mine on Wise Mountain and cabin are 0.1 miles to the right. Deer Creek is to the left. Zero trip meter.
0.0 ▲   Proceed toward North Fork.

GPS: N 39°30.80' W 105°54.13'

▼ 0.0   Proceed toward Deer Creek.
1.6 ▲   TR   Intersection. Mine on Wise Mountain and cabin are 0.1 miles straight ahead. North Fork is to the right. Zero trip meter.

▼ 1.6   SO   End at intersection with Central #11: Saints John and Glacier Mountain Trail on left.
0.0 ▲   From Central #11: Saints John and Glacier Mountain Trail, zero trip meter and proceed south on FR 356 toward North Fork and Wise Mountain.

GPS: N 39°31.39' W 105°52.89'

Georgia Pass Trail

Starting Point:	**Central #12: Middle Fork of the Swan Trail and FR 355**
Finishing Point:	**Intersection of US 285 and CR 35 in Jefferson**
Total Mileage:	**16.2 miles**
Unpaved Mileage:	**16.2 miles**
Driving Time:	**1.5 hours**
Route Elevation:	**9,500 to 11,585 feet**
Usually Open:	**Mid-June to late September**
Difficulty Rating:	**4**
Scenic Rating:	**7**

Special Attractions

- Historic route and mining sites.
- Parkville Cemetery.
- Can be combined with Central #7: Webster Pass Trail to form a loop.

History

Before the establishment of the Colorado Territory in 1861, Georgia Pass traversed the boundary of the Utah and Kansas Territories.

Georgia Pass summit

Crossing over the Continental Divide, the pass was traveled heavily by both the Ute, and after their migration south from Montana and Wyoming in the early 1800s, the Arapaho. The Arapaho were the more hostile of the two tribes. Many early prospectors and settlers avoided the pass when they were in the vicinity. John Frémont visited the area in 1844, but he chose to detour to Hoosier Pass to steer clear of the Arapaho.

Despite the threat of attack by the Arapaho, many early prospectors braved the route. It was heavily used in the 1859 gold rush to the Blue River diggings, which included the mining camps of Breckenridge, Lincoln City, and Frisco on the Blue River; Tiger and Parkville on the Swan River; and Montezuma, Saints John, and Argentine in the Snake River area.

Breckenridge produced Colorado's largest gold nugget, the 14-pound "Tom's Baby,"

A monument in the Parkville Cemetery

Michigan Creek flowing over the road

which disappeared a few years after it was discovered and was presumed stolen to be broken down or melted. But in 1971, officials of the Denver Museum of Natural History found it in a box that was thought to contain dinosaur bones. The nugget is now on exhibit at the museum.

The first recorded wagon crossing over Georgia Pass was in November 1861; later that year, approval for a toll road was granted. A stagecoach service operated across the pass between Swandyke and Jefferson.

Description

The route commences at the intersection with Central #12: Middle Fork of the Swan Trail. Initially, the road is easily accessible to 2WD vehicles but gradually becomes more difficult.

Soon after the start, the route passes the town site of Parkville, the main mining camp in Summit County during

Old log cabin beside the trail

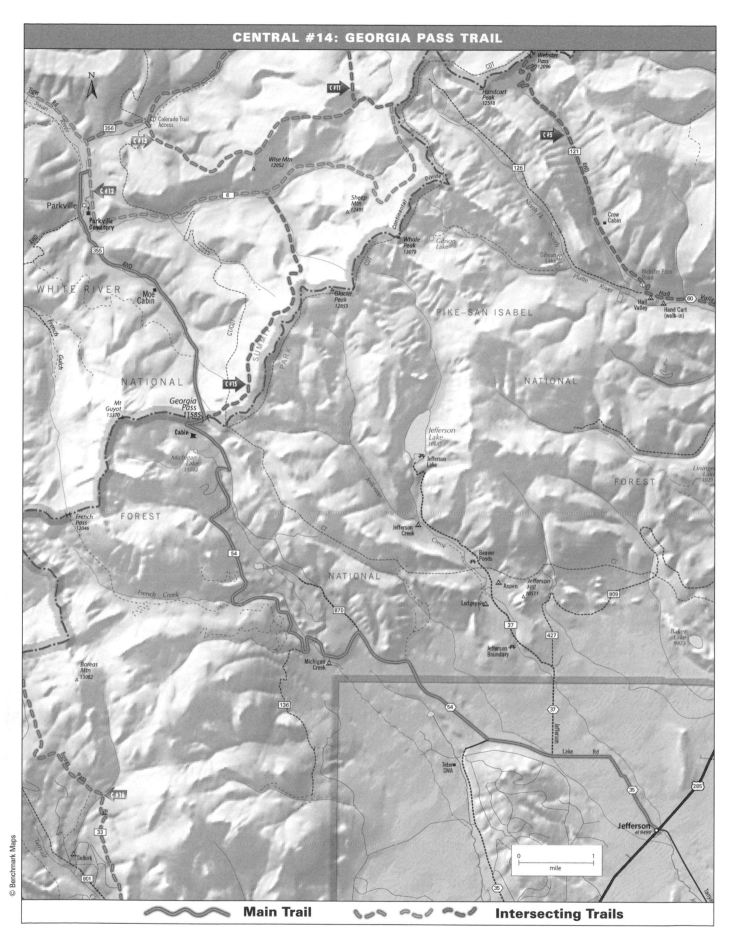

Main Trail ~~~~~ **Intersecting Trails**

ATVs on Georgia Pass Trail

the gold rush of the 1860s. All that remains of the once bustling town of 10,000 is the cemetery, which can be reached via a short walking track.

After Parkville, the road forks. This route follows the left fork; the right fork turns toward Georgia Gulch and leads to Breckenridge via Georgia Gulch, American Gulch, French's Gulch, and the town site of Lincoln City.

From here to the summit, stay on the main road rather than follow any of the intersecting roads—most are dead ends. The summit is an open, grassy saddle with good views of Mount Guyot to the west.

The south side of the pass down to Jefferson is narrow initially but much easier than the north side. From Jefferson, it is 16 miles southwest to Fairplay, 23 miles east to Bailey, and 8.4 miles northeast to the turnoff for Central #5: Handcart Gulch Trail.

Current Road Information
White River National Forest
Dillon Ranger District
680 Blue River Parkway
Silverthorne, CO 80498
(970) 468-5400

Pike & San Isabel National Forests
South Park Ranger District
320 US 285
Fairplay, CO 80440
(719) 836-2031

Map References
USFS   White River National Forest; Pike National Forest
Maptech CD:
          Colorado Springs/Ski Areas/Central;

Denver/Steamboat Springs/North Central
Benchmark's *Colorado Road & Recreation Atlas*, p. 73
Colorado Atlas & Gazetteer, p. 48
The Roads of Colorado, p. 79
Trails Illustrated, #104, #105, #109

Route Directions

▼ 0.0			Begin at intersection of CR 6/Tiger Road (Central #12: Middle Fork of the Swan Trail) and FR 355. Zero trip meter and proceed toward Georgia Pass on FR 355.
	4.5 ▲		End at intersection of CR 6 (Tiger Road). This is Central #12: Middle Fork of the Swan Trail.
		GPS: N 39°30.37′ W 105°56.73′	
▼ 0.6		SO	Cross through creek bed. Town site of Parkville on right.
	3.9 ▲	SO	Cross through creek bed. Town site of Parkville on left.
▼ 0.8		SO	Walking track on left. Parkville Cemetery and Masonic marker are about 150 yards down the trail.
	3.7 ▲	SO	Walking track on right. Parkville Cemetery and Masonic marker are about 150 yards down the trail.
▼ 0.9		BL	Fork in the road. Track on right goes to Georgia Gulch. Cross bridge; then track on left.
	3.6 ▲	BR	Track on right; then cross bridge to intersection. Track on the left goes to Georgia Gulch.
		GPS: N 39°27.70′ W 105°56.82′	
▼ 1.6		SO	Log cabin ruins on left.
	2.9 ▲	SO	Log cabin ruins on right.
▼ 2.3		SO	White cabin (private property) on right.
	2.2 ▲	SO	White cabin (private property) on left.
▼ 2.8		BL	Follow FR 355. Track on right crosses through creek.
	1.7 ▲	BR	Track on left crosses through creek.
		GPS: N 39°28.73′ W 105°55.33′	

Loose, rocky descent from Georgia Pass

▼ 2.9		BL	Cross through creek.
	1.6 ▲	BR	Cross through creek.
▼ 3.0		BR	Fork in road. Take right fork and cross through creek.
	1.5 ▲	BL	Cross through creek. Track on right.
▼ 3.1		BR	Fork in road. Track on left.
	1.4 ▲	SO	Track on right.
▼ 3.2		BR	Track on left.
	1.3 ▲	BL	Track on right.
▼ 3.4		SO	Seasonal closure gate.
	1.1 ▲	SO	Seasonal closure gate.

GPS: N 39°28.31' W 105°55.08'

▼ 3.6		TL	Intersection.
	0.9 ▲	TR	Intersection.

GPS: N 39°28.15' W 105°55.18'

▼ 3.7		SO	Cross over creek.
	0.8 ▲	SO	Cross over creek.
▼ 4.4		SO	Intersection. Proceed up hill.
	0.1 ▲	SO	Intersection.
▼ 4.5		SO	Summit of Georgia Pass. Central #15: Glacier Peak Trail is to the left. Zero trip meter at the summit marker.
	0.0 ▲		Continue along Georgia Pass Road.

GPS: N 39°27.50' W 105°54.98'

▼ 0.0			Continue toward Jefferson and Michigan Creek Campground on FR 54.
	12.2 ▲	SO	Summit of Georgia Pass. Central #15: Glacier Peak Trail is to the left. Zero trip meter at the summit marker.
▼ 0.3		SO	Track on right is FR 541.
	11.9 ▲	BR	Track on left is FR 541.
▼ 0.4		SO	Track on right is FR 545.
	11.8 ▲	SO	Track on left Is FR 545.
▼ 0.7		SO	Cabin on right.
	11.5 ▲	SO	Cabin on left.
▼ 2.5		SO	Cross over creek.
	9.7 ▲	SO	Cross over creek.
▼ 3.9		SO	Track on left to camping spots; then cross over creek.
	8.3 ▲	SO	Cross over creek; then track on righ to campsites.
▼ 5.6		SO	FR 136 on right.
	6.6 ▲	SO	FR 136 on left.
▼ 6.3		SO	USFS Michigan Creek Campground on right.
	5.9 ▲	SO	USFS Michigan Creek Campground on left.

GPS: N 39°24.68' W 105°53.01'

▼ 6.9		TR	Intersection.
	5.3 ▲	TL	Intersection.
▼ 7.2		SO	Leave Pike National Forest.
	5.0 ▲	SO	Enter Pike National Forest.
▼ 9.3		BL	Intersection.
	2.9 ▲	BR	Intersection.
▼ 10.2		SO	Pavement ends; then road on left to Jefferson Lake
	2.0 ▲	SO	Road on right to Jefferson Lake; then pavement ends.
▼ 11.7			Trail ends at the intersection of US 285 and CR 35 in Jefferson.
	0.0 ▲		At intersection of US 285 and CR 35 in Jefferson, zero trip meter and proceed along CR 35 toward Georgia Pass. This intersection is marked with a National Forest sign to Jefferson Lake Road and Michigan Creek Road.

GPS: N 39°22.67' W 105°48.01'

Glacier Peak Trail

Starting Point:	Summit of Central #14: Georgia Pass Trail
Finishing Point:	S.O.B. Hill
Total Mileage:	4.2 miles (one-way)
Unpaved Mileage:	4.2 miles
Driving Time:	1 hour
Route Elevation:	11,000 to 11,585 feet
Usually Open:	Mid-July to mid-September
Difficulty Rating:	5
Scenic Rating:	8

Special Attractions

- Short side road from Georgia Pass.
- Great scenery, particularly the view of Mount Guyot.

Description

This trail is an interesting side road from Georgia Pass. At the summit of the pass there are a number of trails, and it can be difficult to distinguish one from another. The Glacier Peak Trail departs to the northeast, heading directly away from the face of the information board at the summit.

Initially, it is rough but not difficult. A little more than half a mile from the summit two 4WD roads intersect to the right. The road to the right is easy and offers a mile or so of scenic alpine meadow to explore. The center, shorter road climbs the hill and provides a very good view of the area. It is more difficult than the other side road.

A pickup truck (circled) that has crashed down the mountain

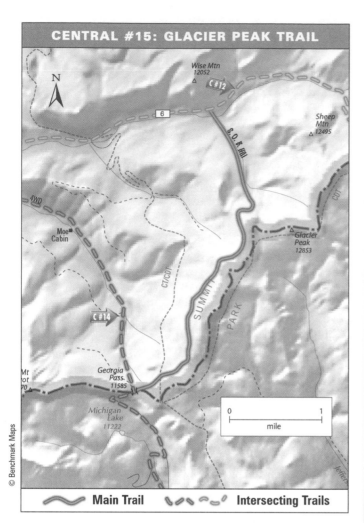

CENTRAL #15: GLACIER PEAK TRAIL

Main Trail   Intersecting Trails

© Benchmark Maps

The main route continues to the left. As you continue along this rough, off-camber, narrow shelf road, there is a great view across to Mount Guyot. The ski runs of Breckenridge and Dillon Reservoir can also be sighted in the distance. Although rough, the surface of the road is mostly embedded rock and is generally sound.

As you continue, the road descends back below timberline. At one point, as you travel along a narrow shelf road, you can look across the valley and glimpse (between the trees on the left-hand side of the road) a turquoise pickup that has crashed down the slope and landed near the bottom of the valley.

Toward the end of the route, after you pass some alpine meadows, there is a creek crossing with a short, steep descent and an even steeper ascent. This is the most difficult section. At this point we end the directions because the road deteriorates dramatically as it descends the aptly named S.O.B. Hill, which has a difficulty rating of 8. This is an extremely challenging, steep slope interspersed with many large boulders. To proceed further would certainly risk damage to any larger stock vehicle.

If you proceed despite the risk, you will come out close to an intersection with Central #12: Middle Fork of the Swan Trail. Once down S.O.B. Hill, the road crosses through the Middle Fork of the Swan River and then, almost immediately, intersects the trail between the Tony Mine and Swandyke town site.

Current Road Information

White River National Forest
Dillon Ranger District
680 Blue River Parkway
Silverthorne, CO 80498
(970) 468-5400

Map References

USFS   White River National Forest
Maptech CD:
　　　　Colorado Springs/Ski Areas/Central;
　　　　Denver/Steamboat Springs/North Central
Benchmark's *Colorado Road & Recreation Atlas*, p. 73
The Roads of Colorado, p. 79
Trails Illustrated, #109

Route Directions

▼ 0.0		From the summit marker on Central #14: Georgia Pass Trail, zero trip meter and proceed toward sign for Glacier Ridge and Colorado Trail on FR 268.
		GPS: N39°27.50' W105°54.98'
▼ 0.4	SO	Colorado Trail hiking trail crosses track.
▼ 0.7	BL	Intersection with FR 268.1 and 268.2.
▼ 2.4	SO	Short track on right to a scenic view down into Missouri Gulch. Zero trip meter.
		GPS: N39°29.14' W105°53.81'
▼ 0.0		Continue along track.
▼ 1.1	SO	On mountainside to the left, you can see a turquoise-colored car that has crashed down the slope.
▼ 1.2	SO	Cross through creek.
▼ 1.4	SO	Several cabin ruins on left.
▼ 1.6	SO	Cross through creek and cabin ruins on left. Then cross through another creek.
▼ 1.7	SO	Cross through creek and climb steep embankment.
▼ 1.8	SO	End here unless you want to venture down S.O.B. Hill. The road continues to the right but is not passable at the level of this book.
		GPS: N39°29.75' W105°53.68'

CENTRAL REGION TRAIL #16

Boreas Pass Trail

Starting Point:	Breckenridge Welcome Center
Finishing Point:	Como at the intersection of US 285 and
	CR/FR 33
Total Mileage:	31.9 miles
Unpaved Mileage:	27.0 miles
Driving Time:	1.25 hours
Route Elevation:	9,600 to 11,481 feet
Usually Open:	Late May to mid-October
Difficulty Rating:	1
Scenic Rating:	8

Denver, South Park & Pacific roundhouse in Como at the beginning of Boreas Pass Trail

Special Attractions
- Travel the route of a famous old narrow gauge railway, which in its time was the highest in the United States.
- Narrow railway cuttings, fine views, and the sites of many old mining camps.
- In fall, excellent views of the changing aspens.

History
This pass was called by many names—Ute, Hamilton, Tarryall, and Breckenridge—before receiving its present name in the late 1880s. Boreas, the Greek god of the north wind, is an appropriate namesake for this gusty mountain route.

The Ute crossed the pass going south to spend their winters in warmer regions. In 1839, Thomas Farnham, a Vermont lawyer, traveled the pass on his trek across Colorado. In the late 1850s, prospectors poured over the pass from South Park to reach the gold discoveries in the Blue River District. At this time, the crossing was nothing more than a burro trail, but miners braved the winter snow to walk the pass on snowshoes.

In the 1860s, the road was upgraded, and a daily stage traveled across Boreas Pass. In 1884, the Denver, South Park & Pacific Railroad laid narrow gauge tracks over the pass. For a time, the line was the highest in the United States and required over a dozen snowsheds. Steep grades of more than 4 percent made the route difficult for trains pulling heavy loads.

Bakers Tank

The grades were such a problem that when P. T. Barnum's circus came to Breckenridge, it had to unload the elephants to help pull the train the last 3 miles to the summit. The railroad continued to operate until 1937.

In 1952, the U.S. Army Corps of Engineers converted the old railroad grade for automobile use but bypassed the most dangerous potion near Windy Point.

Description
This scenic and extremely popular route is suitable for passenger vehicles, although it is unpaved and frequently scarred by numerous potholes.

The route starts in Breckenridge and joins Boreas Pass Road a short distance south of town. Windy Point, identifiable by a large rock outcropping, lies about a half mile from the turnoff onto Boreas Pass Road. The route continues past the restored Bakers Tank.

The summit of Boreas Pass was the site of a Denver, South Park & Pacific Railroad station. The station house, which has been restored as an interpretative center, is only one of the buildings that was located at the site. There was also a two-room telegraph house and a storehouse, as well as a wye in the tracks to allow the trains to turn around. Today, several cabins and a train car are located at the summit, information boards tell the history of the site.

At Como, the stone roundhouse still stands, but the wooden portion of the roundhouse and the 43-room Pacific Hotel were destroyed by fire. The roundhouse is being restored.

Current Road Information
White River National Forest
Dillon Ranger District
680 Blue River Parkway
Silverthorne, CO 80498
(970) 468-5400

Pike & San Isabel National Forests
South Park Ranger District
320 US 285
Fairplay, CO 80440
(719) 836-2031

Tailings piles in Tarryall Creek

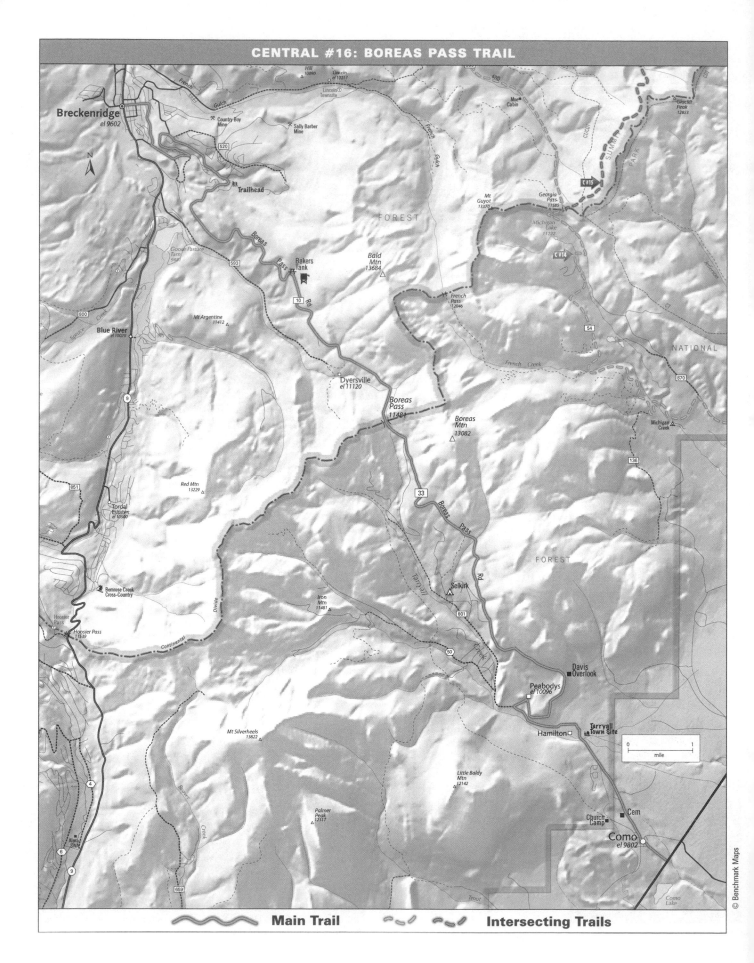

Main Trail ~~~~ Intersecting Trails

© Benchmark Maps

A cutting in the rock made for the railroad

Map References

USFS White River National Forest; Pike National Forest
Maptech CD:
      Colorado Springs/Ski Areas/Central
Benchmark's *Colorado Road & Recreation Atlas*, p. 73
Colorado Atlas & Gazetteer, p. 48
The Roads of Colorado, pp. 78, 79, 95
Trails Illustrated, #109

Route Directions

▼ 0.0		Outside Breckenridge Welcome Center at 203 South Main Street, zero trip meter and proceed south.
10.5 ▲		End at Breckenridge Welcome Center at 203 South Main Street.

GPS: N 39°28.82' W 106°02.76'

▼ 0.5	TL	Onto Boreas Pass Road (CR 33/FR 33).
10.0 ▲	TR	T-intersection with Colorado 9.
▼ 4.0	SO	Pavement ends.
6.5 ▲	SO	Road becomes paved.
▼ 4.1	SO	Cross through gate.
6.4 ▲	SO	Cross through gate.
▼ 5.6	SO	Walking track on left.
4.9 ▲	SO	Walking track on right.
▼ 7.1	SO	Bakers Tank on left with walking track behind it.
3.4 ▲	SO	Bakers Tank on right with walking track behind it.
▼ 7.7	SO	Track on left.
2.8 ▲	SO	Track on right.
▼ 8.0	SO	Track on left.
2.5 ▲	SO	Track on right.

▼ 9.0	SO	Site of Farnham Station, post office, and store on left. On right is a walking track to Dyersville site, about 0.5 miles from road.
1.5 ▲	SO	Site of Farnham Station, post office, and store on right. On left is a walking track to Dyersville site, about 0.5 miles from road.

GPS: N 39°25.50' W 105°58.88'

▼ 10.6	SO	Exit Pike National Forest and cross through seasonal closure gate; then summit of Boreas Pass and historic buildings. Zero trip meter.
0.0 ▲		Proceed northwest on Boreas Pass Road; then cross through seasonal closure gate and enter Pike National Forest.

GPS: N 39°24.64' W 105°58.07'

▼ 0.0		Proceed southeast on Boreas Pass Road.
11.0 ▲	SO	Summit of Boreas Pass and historic buildings. Zero trip meter.
▼ 13.2	SO	Cross over Selkirk Gulch Creek.
8.3 ▲	SO	Cross over Selkirk Gulch Creek.
▼ 14.4	SO	Track on right goes to Upper Tarryall Road and access to Selkirk Campground.
7.1 ▲	BR	Track on left goes to Upper Tarryall Road and access to Selkirk Campground.
▼ 15.2	SO	Cross over Halfway Gulch Creek.
6.3 ▲	SO	Cross over Halfway Gulch Creek.
▼ 17.5	SO	Seasonal gate.
4.0 ▲	SO	Seasonal gate.
▼ 17.7	TL	Intersection of CR 50 and CR33.
3.8 ▲	TR	Intersection of CR 50 and CR 33
▼ 18.4	SO	Site of Tarryall City mining camp.
2.9 ▲	SO	Site of Tarryall City mining camp.
▼ 18.8	SO	Cross Tarryall Creek. Mining ruins on right.
2.5 ▲	SO	Mining ruins on left. Cross Tarryall Creek.
▼ 20.0	SO	Site of Hamilton mining camp.
2.3 ▲	SO	Site of Hamilton mining camp.
▼ 20.4	SO	Road becomes paved.
0.9 ▲	SO	Pavement ends.
▼ 20.5	SO	Town of Como.
0.8 ▲	SO	Leaving Como.
▼ 20.7	TL	Intersection.
0.6 ▲	TR	Intersection.
▼ 20.8	SO	Old stone roundhouse on left.
0.5 ▲	SO	Old stone roundhouse on right.
▼ 21.3		Cattle guard. End at intersection with US 285.
0.0 ▲		At intersection of Boreas Pass Road (CR 33/FR 33) and US 285 in Como, zero trip meter and proceed along CR 33 toward Boreas Pass.

GPS: N 39°18.64' W 105°53.15'

Overlook from along Boreas Pass Trail

Visitors center at Boreas Pass

Shrine Pass Trail

Starting Point:	**Redcliff**
Finishing Point:	**Interstate 70, at exit 190 near Vail Pass**
Total Mileage:	**10.8 miles**
Unpaved Mileage:	**10.7 miles**
Driving Time:	**45 minutes**
Route Elevation:	**8,800 to 11,089 feet**
Usually Open:	**Mid-June to late September**
Difficulty Rating:	**2**
Scenic Rating:	**8**

Special Attractions

- Spectacular views of the Mount of the Holy Cross.
- Fall viewing of the aspens.
- Summer wildflowers.

History

Shrine Pass is so named because it overlooks and provides a wonderful view of the Mount of the Holy Cross, a famous 14,000-foot peak. The route was an Indian trail. It rose to prominence in the 1920s when Orion W. Daggett, a Redcliff newspaper publisher, proposed a shrine be built there. His amazing plans included not only viewing facilities but also an airport and a golf course. In 1931, he opened the road that he intended to use for this project, attracting a crowd of hundreds to the event. The project was never undertaken, but proponents continued to raise it periodically for some years. Before 1940, the pass road served as the main route between Denver and Grand Junction.

The Mount of the Holy Cross was declared a national monument by President Herbert Hoover, but it lost its status in 1950 due to the deterioration of the right arm of the cross.

Log cabin remains along the trail

CENTRAL #17: SHRINE PASS TRAIL

© Benchmark Maps

〰️ **Main Trail**   〰️ **Intersecting Trail**

Description

The route leaves Redcliff and travels initially beside Turkey Creek through the narrow, wooded valley. As the route gains altitude, there are a number of viewing spots along the way that provide distant but spectacular views of the Mount of the Holy Cross to the southwest. Closer to the broad, open pass are alpine meadows that are famous for their vivid wildflower displays in summer. The huge stands of aspens also attract many sightseers in the fall. In winter, the area is very popular for cross-country skiing.

The road is easy and accessible to 2WD vehicles the entire distance.

Current Road Information

White River National Forest
Holy Cross Ranger District
24747 US 24
Minturn, CO 81645
(970) 827-5715

Map References

USFS   White River National Forest
Maptech CD:
　　　　Colorado Springs/Ski Areas/Central
Benchmark's *Colorado Road & Recreation Atlas*, pp. 72, 73
Colorado Atlas & Gazetteer, p. 37
The Roads of Colorado, p. 78
Trails Illustrated, #108

Route Directions

▼ 0.0			At intersection of US 24 and FR 709 in Redcliff, zero trip meter and proceed east, following sign to Shrine Pass (FR 709).
	2.4 ▲		End at intersection with US 24 in Redcliff.
			GPS: N 39°30.78' W 106°22.03'
▼ 0.1		SO	Cross bridge; then pavement ends.
	2.3 ▲	SO	Pavement begins; then cross bridge.
▼ 1.9		SO	Seasonal gate. FR 745 on left.
	0.5 ▲	SO	FR 745 on right. Seasonal gate.

Hikers at Shrine Ridge Trailhead

▼ 2.4	SO	Track on right over bridge is Central #18: Ptarmigan Pass and McAllister Gulch Loop. Zero trip meter.
0.0 ▲		Continue along FR 709 toward Redcliff.

GPS: N 39°31.39' W 106°19.49'

▼ 0.0		Continue along FR 709 toward Shrine Pass.
8.4 ▲	SO	Track on left over bridge is Central #18: Ptarmigan Pass and McAllister Gulch Loop. Zero trip meter.
▼ 1.6	SO	FR 758 on right. Cabins.
6.8 ▲	SO	Cabins. FR 758 on left.
▼ 1.7	SO	Cross over Turkey Creek.
6.7 ▲	SO	Cross over Turkey Creek.
▼ 3.2	SO	Cross over creek.
5.2 ▲	SO	Cross over creek.
▼ 3.4	SO	Track on right.
5.0 ▲	SO	Track on left.
▼ 4.0	TL	FR 713 on right.
4.4 ▲	TR	FR 713 on left.

GPS: N 39°33.41' W 106°16.07'

▼ 4.7	BR	Lime Creek Road (FR 728) on left.
3.7 ▲	BL	Lime Creek Road (FR 728) on right.
▼ 4.9	SO	Sign for Mount Holy Cross overlook. Public restrooms, parking lot, and walking track on right.
3.5 ▲	SO	Sign for Mount Holy Cross overlook. Public restrooms, parking lot, and walking track on left.
▼ 5.3	SO	Track on right.
3.1 ▲	SO	Track on left.
▼ 6.2	SO	Summit of Shrine Pass. Hiking trail and public restrooms on right.
2.2 ▲	SO	Hiking trail and public restrooms on right.

Even the most straightforward trail requires care especially when passing

Aspen stands along the trail

		Summit of Shrine Pass.

GPS: N 39°32.72' W 106°14.45'

▼ 8.4		Seasonal gate; then stop sign and pavement begins. The trail ends I-70.
0.0 ▲		The intersection for Shrine Pass is on I-70 at exit 190, approximately 1 mile east of Vail Pass summit. Zero trip meter where the side road ends.

GPS: N 39°31.74' W 106°13.06'

CENTRAL REGION TRAIL #18

Ptarmigan Pass and McAllister Gulch Loop

Starting Point:	Intersection of Central #17: Shrine Pass Trail (FR 709) and FR 747
Finishing Point:	Intersection of Central #17: Shrine Pass Trail (FR 709) and FR 747
Total Mileage:	21.4 miles
Unpaved Mileage:	21.4 miles
Driving Time:	3 hours
Route Elevation:	9,200 to 11,765 feet
Usually Open:	Mid-June to late September
Difficulty Rating:	4
Scenic Rating:	9

Special Attractions

- Panoramic views of the Mount of the Holy Cross, a 14,000-foot peak.
- Numerous creek crossings.
- Historic site of the Camp Hale Army Base.
- Interesting loop route that is only moderately difficult.

History

During World War II, this area was used as a training ground for the 10th Mountain Division of the U.S. Army, based at the now decommissioned Camp Hale Army Base. The base was the only facility that offered training in mountain and

A section of trail typical of this route

The trail crossing the beautiful alpine meadow on Hornsilver Mountain

winter warfare. The division fought with distinction, and after the war a number of the veterans from the 10th Mountain Division were instrumental in establishing Colorado's ski industry.

Description

This route is a side road of Central #17: Shrine Pass Trail. Initially, it travels through a very scenic, narrow canyon with barely enough room at its base for the road and Wearyman Creek. The road crosses through the shallow creek a number of times before reaching FR 708 in less than a mile.

FR 708 immediately starts to climb steeply and continues through the dense forest with numerous switchbacks, where passing oncoming vehicles is possible. The road rises above timberline into a broad alpine meadow and continues to the top of Hornsilver Mountain, from which point there is a spectacular 360-degree view; to the southwest is the Holy Cross Wilderness Area and the Mount of the Holy Cross, a famous 14,000-foot peak. This mountain was declared a national monument by President Herbert Hoover, but it lost its status in 1950 due to the deterioration of the right arm of the cross.

The route continues across a fairly level ridge to Resolution Mountain. At around the 6-mile point, the road commences a steep descent for about half a mile. As you turn onto FR 702 (Resolution Road), a right turn takes you to the old Camp Hale Army Base and US 24. The route continues to the left toward Ptarmigan Pass. The road to the pass is wide and well maintained.

The descent from the pass via FR 747 (Wearyman Road) heads back below timberline and is rough, narrow, and often boggy. There is also another short section of shelf road. You will have to cross the creek several times before returning to the intersection with Shrine Pass Road.

We highly recommend the *Trails Illustrated* maps listed below to assist with navigation of this route.

Current Road Information

White River National Forest
Holy Cross Ranger District
24747 US 24
Minturn, CO 81645
(970) 827-5715

Map References

USFS   White River National Forest
Maptech CD:
    Colorado Springs/Ski Areas/Central
Benchmark's *Colorado Road & Recreation Atlas*, p. 73
Colorado Atlas & Gazetteer, pp. 37, 47
The Roads of Colorado, p. 78
Trails Illustrated, #108, #109

Camp Hale Army Base in the 1940s

Main Trail ~ *Intersecting Trail*

© Benchmark Maps

Route Directions

▼	▲		
0.0			From intersection of Central #17: Shrine Pass Trail (FR 709) and FR 747, zero trip meter at Wearyman Creek bridge and proceed toward Ptarmigan Pass and McAllister Gulch.
	0.7		Cross bridge and end at Central #17: Shrine Pass Trail (FR 709).

GPS: N 39°31.39' W 106°19.49'

▼	▲		
0.2		SO	Cross through creek; then 100 yards farther, cross through creek again.
	0.5	SO	Cross through creek; then 100 yards farther, cross through creek again.
0.3		SO	Cross through creek.
	0.4	SO	Cross through creek.
0.4		SO	Cross through creek.
	0.3	SO	Cross through creek.
0.7		TR	Cross through creek. Intersection with McAllister Gulch Road (FR 708). Zero trip meter.
	0.0		Proceed along FR 747.

GPS: N 39°31.20' W 106°18.87'

▼	▲		
0.0			Proceed along FR 708.
	10.0	TL	Intersection with Wearyman Road (FR 747) Cross through creek. Zero trip meter.
1.1		BR	Fork in road.
	8.9	BL	Fork in road.
2.1		BL	Track on right.
	7.9	BR	Track on left.
2.2		BL	Track on right.
	7.8	BR	Track on left.
2.9		BL	Intersection. Spot on right with broad, panoramic views of Eagle River Valley to the southwest and northwest.
	7.0	BR	Intersection. Spot on left with broad, panoramic views of Eagle River Valley to the southwest and northwest.

GPS: N 39°29.98' W 106°19.88'

▼	▲		
3.6		SO	Meadow at top of Hornsilver Mountain with 360-degree views.
	6.4	SO	Meadow at top of Hornsilver Mountain with 360-degree views.

GPS: N 39°29.86' W 106°19.41'

▼	▲		
4.3		BR	Intersection.
	5.6	BL	Intersection.

GPS: N 39°29.27' W 106°17.82'

▼	▲		
8.4		SO	Private cabin on right. National Forest boundary.
	1.6	SO	National Forest boundary. Private cabin on left.
8.8		TL	Intersection. Track on right dead-ends.
	1.2	TR	Intersection. Sign to McAllister Gulch. Dead end is straight ahead.

GPS: N 39°27.76' W 106°19.76'

▼	▲		
9.2		TL	Intersection. Follow Ptarmigan Pass sign to the left.
	0.8	TR	Intersection.
10.0		TL	Intersection with Resolution Road (FR 702). Road on right connects with US 24 in 1.1 miles and site of old Camp Hale U.S. Army Base. Zero trip meter.
	0.0		Continue along FR 708.

GPS: N 39°26.90' W 106°19.12'

▼	▲		
0.0			Continue along FR 702.
	5.3	TR	Onto FR 708. Zero trip meter
0.2		SO	Seasonal gate.
	5.1	SO	Seasonal gate.
1.3		SO	Track on right dead-ends. Remain on Resolution Road (FR 702).
	4.0	SO	Track on left dead-ends.
4.8		TR	Intersection with FR 751.
	0.5	TL	Intersection with Resolution Road (FR 702).
5.3		SO	Summit of Ptarmigan Pass. Road becomes FR 747. Zero trip meter.
	0.0		Continue along FR 702.

GPS: N 39°29.59' W 106°15.14'

▼	▲		
0.0			Continue along FR 747.
	5.4	SO	Summit of Ptarmigan Pass. Road becomes FR 702. Zero trip meter.
1.4		SO	Cross through creek.
	4.0	SO	Cross through creek.
2.1		SO	Cross through creek.
	3.2	SO	Cross through creek.
3.1		SO	Cross through creek.
	2.3	SO	Cross through creek.
4.6		SO	Cross through creek.
	0.8	SO	Cross through creek.
4.7		SO	Intersection with FR 708 to McAllister Gulch on left. Cross through creek.
	0.7	SO	Cross through creek. Intersection with FR 708 to McAllister Gulch on right.

GPS: N 39°31.20' W 106°18.87'

▼	▲		
5.0		SO	Cross through creek.
	0.4	SO	Cross through creek.
5.1		SO	Cross through creek.
	0.3	SO	Cross through creek.
5.2		SO	Cross through creek.
	0.2	SO	Cross through creek.
5.3		SO	Cross through creek.
	0.1	SO	Cross through creek.
5.4			Cross bridge and end at Shrine Pass Trail (FR 709).
	0.0		From intersection of Central #17: Shrine Pass Trail (FR 709) and FR 747, zero trip meter at Wearyman Creek bridge and proceed toward Ptarmigan Pass and McAllister Gulch.

GPS: N 39°31.39' W 106°19.49'

Weston Pass Trail

Starting Point:	**Intersection of US 24 and CR 7, 5.1 miles south of Leadville Airport**
Finishing Point:	**Intersection of Park CR 5 and US 285**
Total Mileage:	**25.7 miles**
Unpaved Mileage:	**23.4 miles**
Driving Time:	**1.5 hours**
Route Elevation:	**9,400 to 11,921 feet**
Usually Open:	**Late June to late September**
Difficulty Rating:	**2**
Scenic Rating:	**7**

A section of trail typical of this route

Special Attractions

■ Attractive scenery along an easy 4WD trail.
■ Access to a network of 4WD trails.

History

Like so many passes in the Colorado Rockies, Weston Pass was a Ute trail before being developed as a wagon road. In 1860, during the first gold boom in the Leadville area, the new wagon road was known as the Ute Trail. The stagecoach way station on the eastern side of the pass grew into the town of Weston. Father Dyer made early use of the pass and in 1861 was caught in a blizzard and nearly perished.

Four freight and passenger service companies sprang up to meet the enormous demand. One, the Wall & Witter Stage Company, maintained 400 horses, 11 freight wagons, and 7 stagecoaches to service its operations. In 1873, the Hayden survey party found a good wagon road over Weston Pass at a time when there was barely a burro trail over Mosquito Pass.

The Denver, South Park & Pacific Railroad reached Weston in 1879, adding new impetus to the town's growth. In that year, the Wall & Witter Stage Company collected $1.5 million in fares; on just one day in September, 225 teams were count-

ed as they crossed the pass, pulling either wagons or stagecoaches. As proof that traveling the pass road was thirsty work, Park County issued no fewer than eight new liquor licenses in 1879 to establishments between the town and the top of the pass.

However, in 1881, the railroad made it into Leadville, sending Weston Pass into rapid decline.

In the 1950s, the pass road was renovated and has been well maintained ever since as a recreational road.

Description

The route commences at the intersection of US 24 and CR 7, 5.1 miles south of the Leadville Airport entrance on the left as you leave Leadville.

Navigation along the Weston Pass route is a simple matter, and the road is suitable for cars—except for a couple of miles on the west side of the summit, where high clearance is preferable.

The road travels beside Union Creek on the west side and along the South Fork of the South Platte River on the east side. Both offer numerous, good backcountry camping sites. Additionally, on the west side there is a U.S. Forest Service campground.

Current Road Information

Pike & San Isabel National Forests
Leadville Ranger District
810 Front Street
Leadville, CO 80461
(719) 486-0749

Map References

USFS Pike National Forest; San Isabel National Forest
Maptech CD:
      Colorado Springs/Ski Areas/Central
Benchmark's *Colorado Road & Recreation Atlas*, p. 87
Colorado Atlas & Gazetteer, pp. 47, 48
The Roads of Colorado, p. 94
Trails Illustrated, #110

A view of one of the stands of aspens along the Weston Pass route

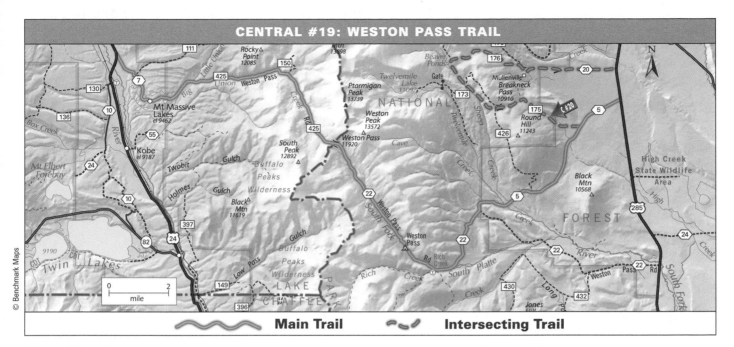

Main Trail ~~~   **Intersecting Trail** ~~~

Route Directions

▼ 0.0		At intersection of US 24 and CR 7, zero trip meter and proceed southeast along CR 7 (FR 425) toward Weston Pass. There is a sign for Massive Lakes.
10.5 ▲		End at intersection with US 24.

GPS: N 39°10.58' W 106°19.27'

▼ 3.0	SO	Cattle guard.
7.5 ▲	SO	Cattle guard.
▼ 7.1	SO	Cross over creek.
3.4 ▲	SO	Cross over creek.
▼ 7.5	SO	Track on left.
3.0 ▲	SO	Track on right.
▼ 8.4	SO	Track on left.
2.1 ▲	SO	Track on right.
▼ 8.7	SO	Cabin ruins on right.
1.8 ▲	SO	Cabin ruins on left.
▼ 8.8	SO	Track on left.
1.7 ▲	SO	Track on right.
▼ 9.3	SO	Cabin ruins below shelf road.
1.2 ▲	SO	Cabin ruins below shelf road.
▼ 10.4	SO	Track on right.
0.1 ▲	SO	Track on left.
▼ 10.5	SO	Summit of Weston Pass. Zero trip meter.
0.0 ▲		Continue along FR 425.

GPS: N 39°07.88' W 106°10.88'

▼ 0.0		Continue along FR 425.
8.4 ▲	SO	Summit of Weston Pass. Zero trip meter.
▼ 0.1	SO	Cabin ruins on the left and right. Track on left to small lake.
8.3 ▲	SO	Track on right to small lake. Cabin ruins on the left and right.
▼ 0.2	SO	Site of the Ruby Mine.
8.2 ▲	SO	Site of the Ruby Mine.
▼ 0.8	SO	Track on left.
7.6 ▲	SO	Track on right.
▼ 1.7	SO	Track on left.
6.7 ▲	SO	Track on right.
▼ 1.9	SO	Site of Park Place roadside restaurant on left.
6.5 ▲	SO	Site of Park Place roadside restaurant on right.
▼ 4.5	SO	Road on right to USFS Weston Pass Campground.
3.9 ▲	SO	Road on left to USFS Weston Pass Campground.

GPS: N 39°04.63' W 106°07.99'

▼ 5.6	SO	Rich Creek Trailhead on right and cattle guard. Leave the National Forest.
2.8 ▲	SO	Leave the National Forest. Cattle guard; then Rich Creek Trailhead on left.
▼ 6.8	BL	Road on right goes to a private ranch.
1.6 ▲	CR	Road on left goes to a private ranch.
▼ 7.5	SO	Cattle guard.
0.9 ▲	SO	Cattle guard.
▼ 7.9	SO	Road on left.
0.5 ▲	SO	Road on right.
▼ 8.4	TL	FR 425 ends at fork in the road. Left fork goes to US 285 via CR 5. Right fork goes to US 285 via CR 22. Both alternatives reach the highway in 7 miles. Zero trip meter.
0.0 ▲		Proceed along FR 425.

GPS: N 39°05.85' W 106°05.28'

▼ 0.0		Proceed along CR 5.
6.8 ▲	BR	Onto FR 425. Zero trip meter.
▼ 1.6	SO	Cattle guard.
5.2 ▲	SO	Cattle guard.
▼ 1.9	BR	Road on left.
4.9 ▲	BL	Road on right.
▼ 2.2	SO	Cattle guard.
4.6 ▲	SO	Cattle guard.
▼ 3.6	SO	Cattle guard.
3.2 ▲	SO	Cattle guard.
▼ 5.2	SO	Central #20: Breakneck Pass and Browns Pass Trail on left. Cattle guard.
1.6 ▲	SO	Cattle guard. Central #20: Breakneck Pass and Brown Pass Trail on right.

GPS: N 39°08.39' W 106°01.42'

▼ 6.8		Cattle guard; then end at intersection with US 285.
0.0 ▲		At intersection of US 285 and Park CR 5, zero trip meter and proceed west on Weston Pass Road, CR 5. Cross cattle grid and follow sign to Weston Pass.

GPS: N 39°09.20' W 105°59.93'

Breakneck Pass and Browns Pass Trail

Starting Point:	**Intersection of US 285 and Park CR 5**
Finishing Point:	**Intersection of CR 20 and US 285**
Total Mileage:	**13.9 miles**
Unpaved Mileage:	**11.8 miles**
Driving Time:	**1.5 hours**
Route Elevation:	**9,600 to 11,372 feet**
Usually Open:	**Early June to early October**
Difficulty Rating:	**3**
Scenic Rating:	**7**

Special Attractions

- Access to a network of 4WD trails.
- Fairly easy 4WD trail that travels under the canopy of the dense forest.
- Aspen viewing in the fall.

History

Little is known about the history of these two pass roads, but it is likely that they were built, or at least improved, in the early 1900s to open access to the mines in the Sheep Park area.

Description

The route commences at the intersection of US 285 and Central #19: Weston Pass Trail (CR 5) about 4.5 miles south of Fairplay and travels through attractive ranchland for 1.6 miles before turning onto Breakneck Pass Road (FR 175).

Proceeding from the intersection, the road is fairly steep and rocky in sections. It might also be boggy if it has rained recently. The clearance between the trees is tight in spots, especially for full-sized vehicles. Nonetheless, although the road becomes rough and narrow, it is not difficult.

The unmarked Breakneck Pass is at the intersection with FR 426, at which point the main road proceeds straight on, the road on the left is closed, and FR 426 (to the right) takes you on an alternative loop past ruins of a mine and a cabin. FR 426 is a more interesting route than FR 175 from this point and rejoins

A stand of aspens envelops the road near Breakneck Pass

the main road at the start of Sheep Park. The route directions for FR 426 are provided below.

As you travel through Sheep Park, Browns Pass Road (FR 176) turns off to the right. The track climbs uphill steeply for about three-tenths of a mile and can be quite difficult if it is wet (under which circumstances the road's difficulty rating would be higher than 3). After this initial ascent, the road levels out and is easy except for some tight clearance between the trees. Browns Pass is marked with a rough sign.

This little-used route lacks the drama of many 4WD roads in Colorado but offers a variety of scenery from the tranquil meadows of Sheep Park to dense forests with thick stands of aspen that cover the road in gold during fall. Some higher sections of the route also provide good views of the Mosquito Range to the west.

Current Road Information

Pike & San Isabel National Forests
South Park Ranger District
320 US 285
Fairplay, CO 80440
(719) 836-2031

Map References

USFS Pike National Forest
Maptech CD:
      Colorado Springs/Ski Areas/Central
Benchmark's *Colorado Road & Recreation Atlas*, p. 87
Colorado Atlas & Gazetteer, p. 48
The Roads of Colorado, p. 94
Trails Illustrated, #110

Route Directions

▼ 0.0			At intersection of US 285 and Park CR 5, zero trip meter and proceed west on Weston Pass Road, CR 5. Cross cattle grid and follow sign to Weston Pass.
	5.0 ▲		End at intersection with US 285.
			GPS: N 39°09.20' W 105°59.93'
▼ 1.6		TR	Cross cattle guard. Turn onto Breakneck Pass Road (FR 175).
	3.4 ▲	TL	Turn onto CR 5. Cross cattle guard.
			GPS: N 39°08.39' W 106°01.42'
▼ 3.2		SO	Cattle guard. Enter Pike National Forest.
	1.8 ▲	SO	Leave Pike National Forest. Cattle guard.
▼ 3.5		SO	Track on left to camping.
	1.5 ▲	SO	Track on right to camping.
▼ 5.0		TR	Intersection with Round Hill Road (FR 426) on right. To the left, FR 426 is closed a little farther on. Zero trip meter.
	0.0 ▲		Continue along FR 175.
			GPS: N 39°08.91' W 106°04.65'
▼ 0.0			Proceed along FR 426.
	2.8 ▲	TL	Intersection with Breakneck Pass Road (FR 175). Zero trip meter.
▼ 1.4		BL	Track on right. Cabin ruins and mine.
	1.4 ▲	BR	Track on left. Cabin ruins and mine.
▼ 1.6		SO	Cabin ruins on right.
	1.2 ▲	SO	Cabin ruins on left.
▼ 2.0		TR	Intersection to rejoin FR 175.
	0.8 ▲	TL	Intersection with FR 426, a faint trail to the left

near the end of Sheep Park.

| ▼ 2.8 | BR | Onto Browns Pass Road (FR 176). Zero trip meter. |
| 0.0 ▲ | | Proceed along FR 175. |

GPS: N 39°10.35′ W 106°06.42′

| ▼ 0.0 | | Proceed along FR 176. |
| 6.1 ▲ | BL | Onto FR 175. Zero trip meter. |

| ▼ 0.5 | SO | Several cabin ruins on right. |
| 5.6 ▲ | SO | Several cabin ruins on left. |

| ▼ 0.6 | SO | Summit of Browns Pass. FR 1761 track on the left. |
| 5.5 ▲ | SO | Summit of Browns Pass. FR 1761 track on the right. |

GPS: N 39°10.47′ W 106°05.77′

| ▼ 1.1 | SO | Cabin ruins on right. |
| 5.0 ▲ | SO | Cabin ruins on left. |

| ▼ 1.4 | BR | Track on left. |
| 4.7 ▲ | BL | Track on right. |

| ▼ 2.8 | SO | Cross through creek. |
| 3.3 ▲ | SO | Cross through creek. |

| ▼ 2.9 | BR | Track on left (FR 179). Remain on FR 176. |
| 3.2 ▲ | BL | Track on right (FR 179). Remain on FR 176. |

GPS: N 39°10.17′ W 106°03.53′

| ▼ 3.2 | SO | FR 178 on left. |
| 2.9 ▲ | SO | FR 178 on right. |

| ▼ 3.4 | SO | Leaving Pike National Forest. Gate (leave it as you find it). |
| 2.7 ▲ | SO | Gate (leave it as you find it). Entering Pike National Forest. |

| ▼ 3.6 | SO | Gravel road. |
| 2.5 ▲ | SO | Gravel road. |

| ▼ 4.0 | TL | Intersection with CR 20. |

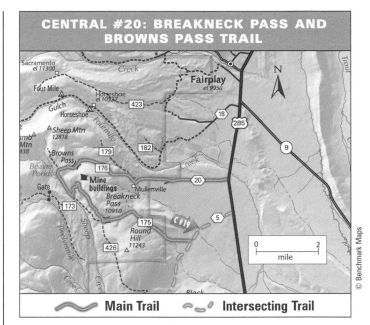

CENTRAL #20: BREAKNECK PASS AND BROWNS PASS TRAIL

∿∿ **Main Trail** ⌢⌣⌐ **Intersecting Trail**

| 2.1 ▲ | TR | Turn from CR 20 onto FR 176. Signs read: "Browns Pass, Fourmile Road, National Forest Access." |

GPS: N 39°09.99′ W 106°02.45′

| ▼ 4.5 | SO | Cattle guard. |
| 1.6 ▲ | SO | Cattle guard. |

| ▼ 6.1 | | Cattle guard. End at intersection with US 285. |
| 0.0 ▲ | | At intersection of CR 20 and US 285 (there is a sign for National Forest access and Browns Pass), zero trip meter and proceed along CR 20. |

GPS: N 39°10.14′ W 106°00.06′

The remains of a miners' cabin near Breakneck Pass

Mosquito Pass Trail

Starting Point:	Colorado 9 and Mosquito Pass Road (CR 12) at Alma Junction
Finishing Point:	Leadville
Total Mileage:	16.7 miles
Unpaved Mileage:	15.2 miles
Driving Time:	2 hours
Route Elevation:	10,200 to 13,186 feet
Usually Open:	Early August to mid-September
Difficulty Rating:	6
Scenic Rating:	10

Special Attractions

- The highest pass road in America.
- Great historic significance.
- Wonderful alpine views.

History

According to legend, this pass got its name in 1861 at a meeting of local residents who gathered to try to choose one of the many names proposed at their previous, inconclusive meeting. When they opened the minutes from that meeting, they found that a mosquito had been squashed in the middle of their list of proposed names. The new name was approved by acclamation!

The Indians used the pass, but the first white men recorded to have crossed it were Thomas Farnham and his party in their exploratory journey across Colorado in 1839. In 1861, the Mosquito gold mining camp was established to the east of the pass.

From 1864, the pass was used by the itinerant Methodist preacher Father Dyer, who carried the mail across the pass for pay of $18 per week. In winter, he traveled on snowshoes at

A scenic alpine lake near the trail

night when the surface of the snow was harder. A small memorial to him stands at the summit of the pass.

Horace A. W. Tabor crossed the pass with Augusta, his wife, on horseback in 1870 but noted that a road barely existed. In 1873, Hayden's survey team crossed the pass and noted only a well-used burro trail.

Western Union built a telegraph line over the pass in 1878. Later that year, Horace Tabor and other investors formed the Mosquito Pass Wagon Road Company to construct a toll road over the pass. This wagon road was completed the following year, when freight wagons and stagecoaches were among the 150 vehicles crossing the pass each day. The pass became known as the "highway of frozen death" because of the many travelers who froze to death while walking across the pass road in winter to avoid paying the stagecoach fare.

In 1880, both the Denver, South Park & Pacific Railroad and the Denver & Rio Grande Railroad commenced service to Leadville, ringing the death knell for the pass road. The road fell into disuse and was closed from 1910 until 1949, when local residents restored it to hold the first Get Your Ass Over the Pass burro race. The race is now a well-established event, held every July.

Old miners' cabins near the beginning of Mosquito Pass Trail

Switchbacks where the trail begins to climb steeply

Remains of the North London Mill

A hoist at the North London Mill site

The town of Alma Junction is located at the intersection of Mosquito Pass Road and the road between Alma and Fairplay. It was also called London Junction and Alma Station, and although it was never incorporated, 150 people lived there in 1884. At its peak, the population reached 300. The town served as a stop for travelers to and from Leadville and Fairplay as well as a home to those who worked in the nearby London Mines. The McLaughlin stagecoach line ran between Alma and Fairplay, providing transfers at London Junction for travelers heading west across the pass.

In 1882, a spur of the London, South Park & Leadville Railroad was completed—a 6-mile segment leading from London Junction, through Park City, to the London Mountain mining area. Used for hauling ore from the London Mines, the spur was abandoned two years later when the mines closed down.

The London Mines were established in the 1870s, and small settlements grew up in the area to house the miners. A concentration works was constructed at London Junction in 1883 to process ore. The South London Mine, which opened

in 1874, lies on the eastern slope of Mosquito Pass. It was the terminus of the London, South Park & Leadville spur up Mosquito Gulch. The North London Mine was high on London Mountain (12,280 feet). The mine had its own boardinghouses and an aerial tram, with wooden tram towers that are still visible among the trees. The tram was constructed to span the 3,300-foot distance between the North London Mine and its mill because a conventional chute was not sufficient. Ruins of cabins and the bunkhouse can be seen at the site.

The North London and South London Mines merge via a tunnel beneath them that goes through the mountain. In total, more than 100 miles of tunnels burrow through London Mountain in all directions and have yielded millions of dollars' worth of ore.

Description

The route commences at Alma Junction, the intersection of Colorado 9 and Mosquito Pass Road (CR 12), which was the junction of the railway spur to the London Mill and the main line.

Mosquito Creek runs beside the American Mill

American Mill with tram remains perched on the hill above

The easy 2WD road continues past the town of Park City, an old stagecoach stop, and then past the Orphan Boy Mine, which operated well into the twentieth century, at the 3.3-mile point. At the 4.4-mile point, the route continues past the intersection of FR 696 on the left, which travels around the south of London Mountain and reconnects with the pass road but is usually closed to through traffic. A couple of miles farther, FR 12 turns left, crosses Mosquito Creek, and commences the ascent toward the pass, providing scenic views of the valley.

The side road to Cooney Lake has several creek crossings and passes through the water at the bottom tip of the lake. The water at these crossings can be more than 18 inches deep, and the road can be very rutted and boggy in places. It is an interesting 4WD road but considerably more challenging than the main pass road.

At the summit, the view is spectacular: South Park spreads out to the east, and to the west is Leadville, Turquoise Lake, and the massive Sawatch Range with its 15 fourteeners, including the three highest peaks in the Rockies.

The road descending toward Leadville, although it begins steeply, is generally easier than the road on the east side. About 1.5 miles from the summit, a track to Birdseye Gulch intersects on the right. This road heads north toward Colorado 91 but has some extremely boggy sections at about the 1.5-mile point. To avoid damage to the terrain, do not attempt this trail without a winch (and a long winch extension strap to reach the sometimes distant winching points).

The main road from this point affords a straightforward drive into Leadville, past Horace Tabor's Matchless Mine.

Mosquito Pass is the highest pass road open to automobiles in the United States

Current Road Information

Pike & San Isabel National Forests
Leadville Ranger District
810 Front Street
Leadville, CO 80461
(719) 486-0749

Map References

USFS Pike National Forest; San Isabel National Forest
Maptech CD:
          Colorado Springs/Ski Areas/Central
Benchmark's *Colorado Road & Recreation Atlas*, p. 87
Colorado Atlas & Gazetteer, pp. 47, 48
The Roads of Colorado, p. 94
Trails Illustrated, #109

Narrow, rocky, and eroded section of shelf road on Mosquito Pass Trail

Father Dyer memorial at the summit of Mosquito Pass

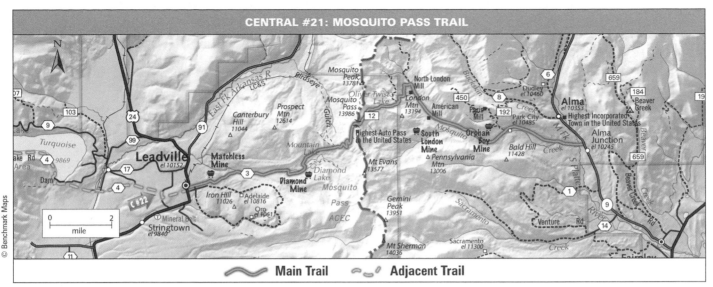

~~~ **Main Trail**   ~ ~ ◡ **Adjacent Trail**

Route Directions

▼ 0.0		Start at Alma Junction, which is the intersection of Colorado 9 and CR/FR 12, 1.3 miles south of Alma. Turn onto CR 12, zero trip meter, and proceed west along Mosquito Pass Road. Sign points toward Mosquito Gulch.
7.8 ▲		End at intersection with Colorado 9.

GPS: N 39°16.23′ W 106°02.83′

▼ 0.2	SO	Site of cabins and other buildings that were part of Alma Junction. Grade of old railroad wye is visible between the river and the highway.
7.6 ▲	SO	Site of cabins and other buildings that were part of Alma Junction. Grade of old railroad wye is visible between the river and the highway.

▼ 2.4	SO	Road on right to Park City.
5.4 ▲	SO	Road on left to Park City.

▼ 2.5	SO	Site of Park City, a stage stop that grew into a town.
5.3 ▲	SO	Site of Park City, a stage stop that grew into a town.

▼ 3.4	SO	Orphan Boy Mine.
4.4 ▲	SO	Orphan Boy Mine.

▼ 4.5	BR	Intersection. Remain on FR 12. South London Mine ruins are to the left along FR 696.
3.3 ▲	SO	Intersection. Remain on FR 12. South London Mine ruins are to the right along FR 696.

GPS: N 39°16.72′ W 106°07.29′

▼ 5.4	SO	View of wooden tram towers in trees on slope to the left.
2.4 ▲	SO	View of wooden tram towers in trees on slope to the right.

▼ 6.2	SO	Track on left to North London Mill and tailings dump.
1.6 ▲	SO	Track on right to North London Mill and tailings dump.

▼ 6.7	TL	Intersection. Turn left, remaining on FR 12. On the right is FR 856. Then cross creek.
1.1 ▲	TR	Cross creek. Intersection. On the left is FR 856.

▼ 7.4	SO	Track on right to Champaign Mine.
0.4 ▲	SO	Track on left to Champaign Mine.

▼ 7.5	SO	Cross through creek.
0.3 ▲	SO	Cross through creek.

▼ 7.8	TL	Intersection. Road on right goes to Cooney Lake. Zero trip meter.
0.0 ▲		Continue along FR 12.

GPS: N 39°17.46′ W 106°09.67′

The view to the west over Leadville from Mosquito Pass

Mosquito Creek has washed out a section of the trail

▼ 0.0			Continue along FR 12.
	1.7 ▲	BR	Intersection. Side road to Cooney Lake. Zero trip meter.
▼ 0.1		SO	North London Mine on left.
	1.6 ▲	SO	North London Mine on right.
▼ 0.2		SO	Track on right and mining machinery on left.
	1.5 ▲	SO	Mining machinery on right and track on left.
▼ 0.7		SO	Track on left (FR 696) is gated farther on.
	1.0 ▲	SO	Track on right dead-ends.
▼ 1.7		SO	Tracks on the left and right. Then summit of Mosquito Pass. Zero trip meter.
	0.0 ▲		Proceed toward Leadville. Mosquito Pass Road changes to FR 12 on this side.

GPS: N 39°16.86′ W 106°11.12′

▼ 0.0			Proceed toward Leadville. Mosquito Pass Road changes to FR 438 on this side.
	7.2 ▲	SO	Summit of Mosquito Pass. Tracks on the left and right. Zero trip meter.
▼ 0.3		BL	Bypass trail on right is one-way downhill and rejoins at 0.8 miles.
	6.9 ▲	SO	Track from 6.4-mile point rejoins on left.
▼ 0.4		SO	Track on left.
	6.8 ▲	SO	Track on right.
▼ 0.8		SO	Track from 0.3-mile point rejoins on right.
	6.4 ▲	BR	Track on left (no entry—one-way).
▼ 1.4		SO	Track to Birdseye Gulch on right. Stay on main road toward Leadville.
	5.8 ▲	SO	Track on left to Birdseye Gulch. Stay on main road toward Mosquito Pass.

GPS: N 39°16.15′ W 106°11.74′

▼ 2.8		TL	Road forks. Stay to the left.
	4.4 ▲	BR	Road forks. Stay to the right.

GPS: N 39°15.69′ W 106°13.15′

▼ 3.0		SO	Cross over creek. Then gate to Diamond Mine on left. Follow main road.
	4.2 ▲	SO	Gate to Diamond Mine on right. Cross over creek.

GPS: N 39°15.57′ W 106°13.06′

▼ 3.2		TR	Intersection.
	4.0 ▲	TL	Intersection.
▼ 3.3		SO	Mine structure on right.
	3.9 ▲	SO	Mine structure on left.
▼ 3.6		SO	Cross over creek.
	3.6 ▲	SO	Cross over creek.
▼ 3.8		SO	Mine on right and left.
	3.4 ▲	SO	Mine on right and left.
▼ 4.6		SO	Road on left.
	2.6 ▲	SO	Road on right.
▼ 5.4		SO	Intersection. Road on right.
	1.8 ▲	SO	Intersection. Road on left.
▼ 5.6		SO	Road on left.
	1.6 ▲	SO	Road on right.
▼ 6.0		SO	Matchless Mine on right.
	1.2 ▲	SO	Matchless Mine on left.
▼ 6.9		SO	Leadville, Colorado & Southern Railway station on right.
	0.3 ▲	SO	Leadville, Colorado & Southern Railway station on left.
▼ 7.2			End at intersection of 7th Street and Harrison Avenue in Leadville.
	0.0 ▲		At the intersection of Harrison Avenue and 7th Street in Leadville, zero trip meter and proceed east along 7th Street.

GPS: N 39°14.99′ W 106°17.47′

Hagerman Pass Trail

Starting Point:	Leadville
Finishing Point:	Basalt
Total Mileage:	62.5 miles, plus 5.9-mile spur to Hagerman Tunnel
Unpaved Mileage:	22.0 miles, plus 5.9-mile spur to Hagerman Tunnel
Driving Time:	3 hours, plus 1 hour for spur
Route Elevation:	6,600 to 11,982 feet
Usually Open:	Mid-July to late September
Difficulty Rating:	3, 4 for spur
Scenic Rating:	9

Special Attractions

- Historic railroad route.
- Network of 4WD trails to explore.
- Excellent fall aspen viewing.
- Fishing, boating, and camping at Turquoise Lake.
- Good for ATVs, motorbikes, and mountain bikes.
- Snowmobiling and cross-country skiing in winter.

History

Hagerman Pass Road is the product of one of the great railroad stories of the 1880s, the golden period of railroad expansion in Colorado. The pass was named for James J. Hagerman, the president of the Colorado Midland Railroad. Previously it had been known as Cooke Pass, and before that the Hayden survey party had called it Frying Pan Pass in 1873.

East portal of Carlton Tunnel

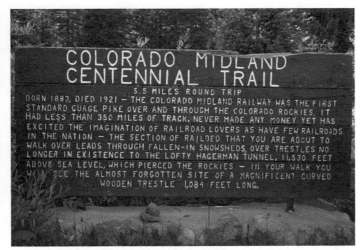
Sign at the trailhead to the site of Douglass City

A small lake near the summit of Hagerman Pass

In 1885, the Colorado Midland Railway began construction on a railway running from Aspen to Leadville. The railway was remarkable at that time because it was a standard gauge track rather than the prevalent narrow gauge. To enable trains to cross the Continental Divide, the company commenced construction of the Hagerman Tunnel in 1885, completing the project the following year. It was 2,164 feet long and located only 450 feet from the pass's summit at 11,528 feet, the highest standard gauge railroad in the United States at the time. To reach the tunnel, the tracks made three horseshoe turns at a grade of 1.5 percent. One of the turns was made with the help of an enormous 1,084-foot curved trestle bridge.

On the east side of the tunnel was Douglass City, a notorious mining camp that boasted six saloons and a brothel. The camp was home to the railroad construction workers as well as to miners.

The railroad opened in 1887 but faced financial difficulties right from the start. The operating costs were prohibitive. Six locomotives had to operate full-time to clear the rails in the winter, embankments collapsed from water damage, and the trestle bridge required constant upkeep. In 1893, the rail line was closed, and the train was rerouted to the new Busk-Ivanhoe Tunnel that had been constructed 600 feet lower. The new tunnel had proved much more difficult to build than anticipated because of liquid mud floods. When completed, it was nearly 2 miles long, 15 feet wide, and 21 feet high. Construction had taken three years, claimed 20 lives, and cost three times the budget of $1 million.

In 1897, after suffering continuous financial troubles since its formation, the Colorado Midland Railway was sold at a foreclosure. The new owners initially reverted to using the Hagerman Tunnel but went back to the Busk-Ivanhoe Tunnel in 1899. From 1922 until 1943, after the tracks had been torn

Crooked Creek Reservoir

The embankments of the spur to Hagerman Tunnel are reminiscent of the original railroad grade

The collapsed west end of Hagerman Tunnel

up, the Busk-Ivanhoe Tunnel was known as the Carlton Tunnel and used as State Highway 104. As it was only wide enough for a single lane of motor vehicles, an alternating system of traffic control was used. A water pipeline laid through the tunnel to transfer water from the Western Slope to the east is still in use today.

In the 1960s, a new tunnel was built to divert additional water to the Eastern Slope as part of the multimillion-dollar Fryingpan-Arkansas Project, which provides electricity to many Front Range cities. This lower 4-mile-long tunnel is known as the Charles H. Bousted Tunnel.

Description

The Hagerman Pass turnoff is 2.2 miles past the Turquoise Lake dam wall. The road is not difficult, but high clearance is recommended for the embedded rock and erosion. In the nar-

rower sections, adequate pull-offs facilitate passing. Below timberline, the road travels through pine and aspen forest.

The east entrance to the Carlton (Busk-Ivanhoe) Tunnel is about 3.5 miles along Hagerman Pass Road. A mile farther on is a hiking trail that leads to the remains of Douglass City, the site of the trestle bridge, Hagerman Lake, and the east entrance of the Hagerman Tunnel. It is an easy walk along the old railway grade that takes about 2 hours and 30 minutes.

The road continues through the pine forest that opens before the summit to an impressive view. Also evident is the high-voltage line between Denver and Grand Junction; the Hagerman Pass Road was used in the construction of the line.

On the west side of the pass, a spur provides an opportunity to visit Ivanhoe Lake and the west side of the Carlton (Busk-Ivanhoe) Tunnel. By driving the entire 6 miles of the spur, you will reach the western entrance of the Hagerman

View of Ivanhoe Lake with the old railroad embankment crossing the lake toward the Carlton Tunnel western entrance

The western end of the Carlton Tunnel is now collapsed

Tunnel, which is now collapsed. The scenic drive over this abandoned section of the original railroad grade is well worth the extra time.

Beyond the spur, Hell Gate gauging station is ahead on the left, a scenic stop on the Colorado Midland Railroad. This section of the trail is a wide shelf road traveling high above Ivanhoe Creek. Driving through the large cuttings that were originally made for the railroad is evocative of the days when trains carried their loads over this route.

The road, which continues past the open expanse of Sellar Park, becomes an easy 2WD road before returning to pavement about 14 miles from the summit.

Current Road Information

San Isabel National Forest
Leadville Ranger District
810 Front Street
Leadville, CO 80461
(719) 486-0749

Map References

USFS   San Isabel National Forest; White River National
           Forest
Maptech CD:
           Colorado Springs/Ski Areas/Central
Benchmark's *Colorado Road & Recreation Atlas*,
           pp. 71, 72, 86
Colorado Atlas & Gazetteer, pp. 46, 47
The Roads of Colorado, pp. 76, 77, 93, 94
Trails Illustrated, #109, #110, #126, #127

Route Directions

▼ 0.0		In Leadville, from the intersection of West 6th Street and Harrison Avenue, zero trip meter and proceed west from the traffic light toward Turquoise Lake.
7.5 ▲		End at intersection with Harrison Avenue in Leadville.
GPS: N 39°14.93' W 106°17.49'		
▼ 0.8	TR	Stop sign.
6.7 ▲	TL	Stop sign.

Coke ovens beside the trail

Hagerman Pass Trail travels along the old railroad grade through rock cuttings and aspen stands

▼ 3.0	SO	Cross railway line.
4.5 ▲	SO	Cross railway line.
▼ 3.4	BR	Fork in road.
4.1 ▲	BL	Road on right.
▼ 4.1	SO	Road on right.
3.4 ▲	SO	Road on left.
▼ 4.3	SO	Dam wall—Turquoise Lake.
3.2 ▲	SO	Dam wall—Turquoise Lake.
▼ 5.6	SO	Road on right.
1.9 ▲	SO	Road on left.
▼ 7.5	BL	Onto Hagerman Pass Road (FR 105). Zero trip meter.
0.0 ▲		Proceed along Turquoise Lake Road.
GPS: N 39°16.12' W 106°25.00'		
▼ 0.0		Proceed along unpaved FR 105.
7.6 ▲	TR	Onto paved Turquoise Lake Road. Zero trip meter.
▼ 1.7	SO	Track on left is Sugarloaf Mountain Road (FR 105.1A).

Summit of Hagerman Pass

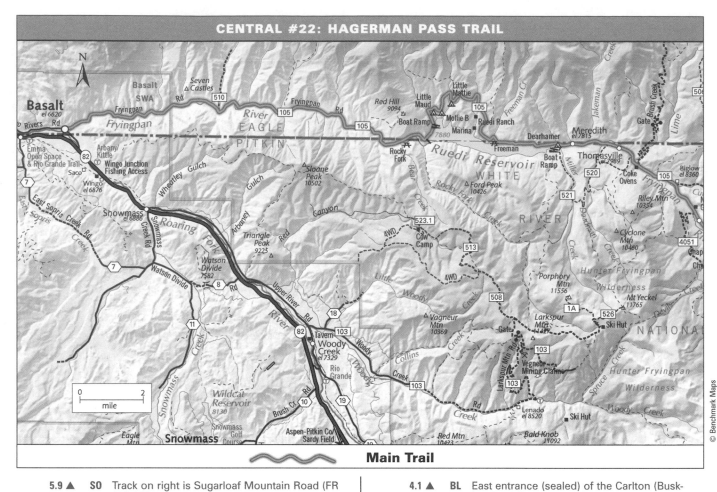

© Benchmark Maps

≈≈≈≈≈≈ **Main Trail**

5.9 ▲	**SO**	Track on right is Sugarloaf Mountain Road (FR 105.1A).	

▼ 3.4	**SO**	Cross over Busk Creek.
4.2 ▲	**SO**	Cross over Busk Creek.

▼ 3.5	**BR**	East entrance (sealed) of the Carlton (Busk-Ivanhoe) Tunnel on left.

Sections of Hagerman Pass Trail are shelf road traveling high above the Fryingpan River

4.1 ▲	**BL**	East entrance (sealed) of the Carlton (Busk-Ivanhoe) Tunnel on right.

▼ 4.5	**SO**	Colorado Midland Centennial Trail marker on left. Walking trail to trestle, tunnel, and Hagerman Lake via TR 1491.
3.1 ▲	**SO**	Colorado Midland Centennial Trail marker on right. Walking trail to trestle, tunnel, and Hagerman Lake via TR 1491.

GPS: N 39°15.56' W 106°27.51'

▼ 6.4	**SO**	Track on right to Skinner Hut.
1.2 ▲	**SO**	Track on left to Skinner Hut.

▼ 7.1	**SO**	Seasonal closure gate.
0.5 ▲	**SO**	Seasonal closure gate.

▼ 7.6	**SO**	Hagerman Pass summit. Zero trip meter.
0.0 ▲		Continue along FR 105.

GPS: N 39°15.80' W 106°28.83'

▼ 0.0		Continue along FR 105.
3.7 ▲	**SO**	Hagerman Pass summit. Zero trip meter.

▼ 3.6	**SO**	Seasonal gate.
0.1 ▲	**SO**	Seasonal gate.

▼ 3.7	**SO**	Intersection with FR 532 on the right and FR 527 (to Ivanhoe Lake) on the left. Zero trip meter.
0.0 ▲	**SO**	Remain on 105 and follow sign to Hagerman Pass.

GPS: N 39°17.53' W 106°31.67'

Spur to Hagerman Tunnel

▼ 0.0		Proceed south on FR 527 signed to Ivanhoe Lake; then seasonal closure gate and cross over creek.
▼ 1.0	**SO**	Track on left.

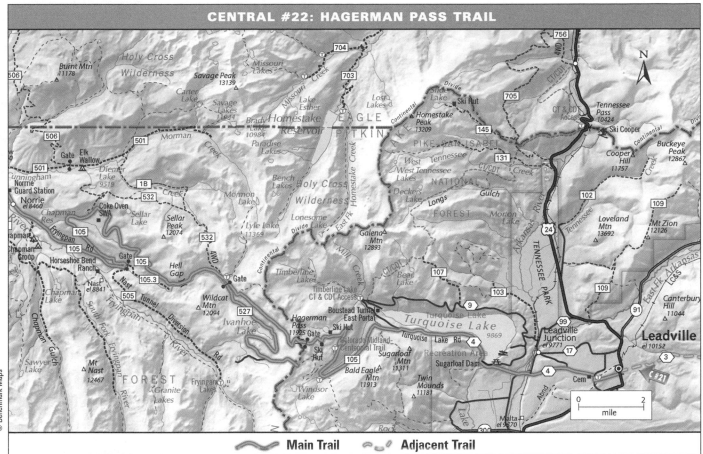

❯❯❯❯❯ Main Trail   ❯❯❯❯ Adjacent Trail

▼ 1.7	SO	Dam wall and Ivanhoe Lake on right.
▼ 2.5	SO	Gated track on right.
▼ 3.0	SO	Cross through creek.
▼ 3.1	SO	Cross through creek.
▼ 5.2	SO	Track on right goes to Lily Lake.

GPS: N 39°15.35' W 106°30.68'

| ▼ 5.7 | SO | Cross through creek. |
| ▼ 5.9 | SO | Spur ends at collapsed entry to Hagerman Tunnel. Return to main trail. |

GPS: N 39°15.33' W 106°29.44'

Continuation of Main Trail

| ▼ 0.0 | | Remain on FR 105 and follow sign to Ruedi Reservoir. |
| 3.7 ▲ | SO | Intersection with FR 532 on the left and FR 527 (to Ivanhoe Lake) on the right. Zero trip meter. |

| ▼ 1.2 | SO | Track on right. |
| 9.1 ▲ | SO | Track on left. |

| ▼ 1.6 | SO | Hell Gate scenic overlook and gauging station in the valley on left among trees. |
| 8.7 ▲ | SO | Hell Gate scenic overlook and gauging station in the valley on right among trees. |

| ▼ 7.4 | SO | Sellar Park on left. Track on right goes to Sellar Lake and Diemer Lake and up to North Fork Road. |
| 3.1 ▲ | SO | Sellar Park on right. Track on left goes to Diemer Lake and up to North Fork Road. |

GPS: N 39°19.21' W 106°36.63'

| ▼ 10.7 | BR | Intersection with road on left. Proceed onto paved Fryingpan Road. Zero trip meter. |
| 0.0 ▲ | | Continue along main road. |

GPS: N 39°17.89' W 106°35.21'

| ▼ 0.0 | | Continue along main road. |
| 33.0 ▲ | BL | Intersection. Continue toward Hagerman Pass on unpaved FR 105. Zero trip meter. |

| ▼ 0.1 | SO | Road on left to Fryingpan Lakes Trailhead. |
| 32.9 ▲ | SO | Road on right to Fryingpan Lakes Trailhead. |

| ▼ 3.4 | SO | USFS Chapman Dam Campground. |
| 29.6 ▲ | SO | USFS Chapman Dam Campground. |

| ▼ 3.7 | SO | USFS Chapman Dam Campground. |
| 29.3 ▲ | SO | USFS Chapman Dam Campground. |

| ▼ 6.9 | SO | Road on right is FR 400, Brush Creek Road. It goes to Eagle. |
| 26.1 ▲ | SO | Road on left is FR 400, Brush Creek Road. It goes to Eagle. |

GPS: N 39°21.10' W 106°41.30'

| ▼ 8.2 | SO | Thomasville. |
| 24.8 ▲ | SO | Thomasville. |

| ▼ 9.6 | SO | Meredith. |
| 23.6 ▲ | SO | Meredith. |

| ▼ 10.0 | SO | Ruedi Reservoir on left. |
| 23.0 ▲ | SO | Ruedi Reservoir on right. |

| ▼ 30.7 | SO | Basalt. |
| 2.3 ▲ | SO | Leaving Basalt. |

| ▼ 30.9 | TR | Intersection with Midland and Two Rivers Road (Business Route 82). |
| 2.1 ▲ | TL | Intersection with Fryingpan Road. |

| ▼ 33.0 | | End at intersection with 82 in Basalt. |
| 0.0 ▲ | | From traffic light at intersection of Colorado 82 and Business Route 82 (Two Rivers Road), zero trip meter and proceed along Business Route 82 toward Basalt. |

GPS: N 39°22.27' W 107°04.23'

Lincoln Creek Trail

Starting Point:	FR 106 off of Colorado 82
Finishing Point:	Collapsed mine portal
Total Mileage:	11.0 miles (one-way)
Unpaved Mileage:	11.0 miles
Driving Time:	2 hours (one-way)
Route Elevation:	9,639 to 11,897 feet
Usually Open:	Late May to September
Difficulty Rating:	4 to Ruby, 5 beyond
Scenic Rating:	10

Special Attractions

- Interesting remains in Ruby ghost town and the Lincoln Creek Mining District.
- Varied scenery along Lincoln Creek.
- Good camping opportunities.
- Access to hiking, mountain biking, fishing, picnicking, and swimming.
- Snowmobiling, cross-country skiing, and snowshoeing in winter.

History

In 1880, several miners from Independence, Colorado, discovered silver on the South Fork of the Roaring Fork River. Several mining camps were established, the largest of which was called South Independence. That same year, the men decided to shorten the name of the South Fork of the Roaring Fork to Lincoln Creek, after the newly established Lincoln Creek Mining District.

At the turn of the nineteenth century, the Ruby Mining and Development Company began operating the silver mines in the valley. The town changed its name to Ruby, either after the company or because of the "ruby" silver ore found in the vicinity. The company brought some development to the town, building a large two-story boardinghouse and several other log structures.

View of Lincoln Creek from the trail

Grizzly Reservoir

Transportation was a significant problem for the town, as ore had to be moved by pack train to Leadville. In 1906, a wagon road was built to reach Independence Pass Road so that ore could be hauled to Aspen. Ruby Mining and Development Company built a 50-ton concentrating plant to help reduce the amount of ore headed to Aspen.

Although tons of ore were transported to Aspen, mining activity largely stopped in 1912. Some prospectors continued on, leasing the mines until the 1950s. Many local geographical landmarks are named after Rudy's early prospectors, including Larson Peak (named after John Larson) and Anderson Lake (named after "Rattle Snake" Bill Anderson). Anderson is said to have kept the U.S. Forest Service out of the Anderson Lake area until the 1940s by force of his personality. Larson Peak stands at 12,900 feet and can be viewed to the west before reaching Ruby. Anderson Lake is located just west of Ruby and is accessible by a hiking trail.

Log cabin at Ruby ghost town

Today a number of the mine properties are still owned by descendants of original settlers. A sign on one of the cabins reads that John A. Nichols founded his claim during June 1903. He worked the claim for the next 30 years in summer, walking from Twin Lakes to Lincoln Gulch. In 1921, John, his son, and grandson were the first to drive a car, a Model T Ford, into Lincoln Gulch. To travel from Twin Lakes over Independence Pass took one day, and another day was required to drive 11 miles up Lincoln Gulch.

Description

Lincoln Creek Trail begins approximately 10 miles southeast of Aspen off of Colorado 82 at the intersection with FR 106. The trail follows FR 106, a vehicle corridor through the Collegiate Peaks Wilderness. Although the drive is bumpy and slow going for its entire length, the trail is one of our favorites and well worth spending the time to explore.

The trail winds through the forest and enters Lincoln Creek Mining District

Frenchman's cabin

The first several miles of the trail are heavily used because the area is popular for outdoor recreation, including hiking, mountain biking, fishing, picnicking, and swimming. The forest service also maintains a number of popular dispersed campsites adjacent to the scenic Lincoln Creek. Camping is not allowed outside of the designated sites for the first 6 miles of the trail, and all the campsites are located within the initial 2.5 miles.

At first the road follows alongside Lincoln Creek through pine and aspen forest, and views are limited. This section of trail is generally well maintained with a few potholes and is as an easy although bumpy drive. Where the creek runs close to the road, keep an eye out for the remarkable rock formations that have been created over time by the rushing waters of Lincoln Creek. To get the best view, pull off the trail and park in an out-of-the-way location that does not block other travelers.

Interesting rock formation in Lincoln Creek

The rushing waters of Lincoln Creek

View of Lincoln Creek Valley from the Ruby Mine

Section of rocky, eroded trail enclosed by low shrubs

It is a short walk to the bank of the creek and good view of the formations.

The Grizzly Reservoir and the Portal USFS Campground are located just beyond the halfway point. Rainbow trout are abundant in the reservoir, and the shady campground provides facilities, including picnic tables, vault toilets, fire grates, and trash disposal.

The difficulty rating increases to 4 beyond the Grizzly Reservoir. Since the trail beyond the reservoir is not frequently maintained, erosion has caused deeper potholes and corrugations around larger embedded rocks. The trees also begin to diminish at this point, revealing views of the Lincoln Creek Valley and the rugged peaks enclosing it. Although the taller trees start to recede, low oak scrub grows close to the trail. While not close enough to scratch the sides of your vehicle, the brush may complicate passing oncoming vehicles.

The trail climbs gradually through Lincoln Creek Mining District revealing wider and more expansive views and crossing through a number of drainage streams and washes. You will come across an old abandoned miners' cabin, among other evidence of the mining era, and finally arrive at Ruby ghost town near the end of the trail. There are several old structures that have collapsed at Ruby, and information boards have been posted to explain some of the local history. There is also a modern cabin that appears to be frequently used at the town site.

Past Ruby the difficulty rating becomes a 5 for the additional complications of large rocks embedded in the road's surface. By picking a sensible line and careful wheel placement through the obstacles, you will not damage you stock high-clearance 4WD. This rating is also for the narrow, loose, and off-camber shelf road that leads up the abandoned mine workings. The trail ends at the remnants of the Ruby Mine. The mine portals have collapsed, but the roads that branch off and climb the slopes of Red Mountain around the old mine workings are fun to explore.

Current Road Information
White River National Forest
Aspen Ranger District
806 West Hallam
Aspen, CO 81611
(970) 925-3445

Collapsed adit and old ore cart tacks of the Ruby Mine

Aspen stands on the mountain slopes above Grizzly Reservoir

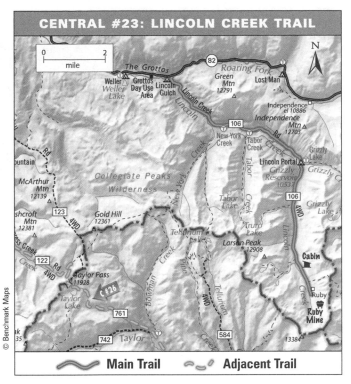

CENTRAL #23: LINCOLN CREEK TRAIL

Main Trail   Adjacent Trail

Map References

USFS   White River National Forest
Maptech CD:
    Colorado Springs/Ski Areas/Central
Benchmark's *Colorado Road & Recreation Atlas*, p. 86
Colorado Atlas & Gazetteer, p. 47
The Roads of Colorado, p. 93
Trails Illustrated, #127 (incomplete)

Route Directions

▼ 0.0   Zero trip meter and proceed south on FR 106 from Colorado 182, 10 miles southeast of Aspen, through seasonal gate and over bridge over the Roaring Fork River.

GPS: N39°07.17′ W106°41.31′

▼ 0.4   SO   Lincoln Gulch USFS Campground on right.
▼ 3.1   SO   New York Creek Trail on right.

GPS: N39°05.69′ W106°39.61′

▼ 4.1   SO   Tabor Creek Trail on right.

GPS: N39°05.55′ W106°38.66′

▼ 4.6   SO   Track on left.
▼ 6.0   SO   Maintenance Road, signposted Authorized Vehicles Only, on left and right; then Grizzly Reservoir on right.
▼ 6.1   BR   Proceed on FR 106 toward Ruby ghost town, Grizzly hiking trail, and Portal Campground. Zero trip meter.

GPS: N39°04.77′ W106°36.81′

▼ 0.0   Proceed uphill.
▼ 0.2   SO   Hiking Grizzly Lake trailhead on left; then track on left.
▼ 0.25   SO   Cross over creek.
▼ 0.3   SO   Portal Campground on right; then seasonal closure gate.

GPS: N39°04.55′ W106°36.75′

▼ 0.9   SO   Cross through creek.
▼ 2.0   SO   Cross through creek.

The end of the trail travels through fragile alpine tundra

▼ 2.8   SO   Cross through creek.
▼ 3.2   SO   Frenchman's cabin on left.

GPS: N39°02.17′ W106°37.04′

▼ 3.3   SO   Enter Lincoln Creek Mining District.
▼ 3.7   BL   Road on right to Petroleum and Anderson Lake hiking trail and old cabin. Zero trip meter.

GPS: N39°01.86′ W106°36.92′

▼ 0.0   Proceed southeast on FR 106.
▼ 0.4   SO   Old cabin on left.
▼ 0.5   SO   Track on right to cabin remains (on private property).
▼ 0.6   SO   Old cabin on right.

GPS: N39°01.39′ W106°36.62′

▼ 0.7   SO   Cross through creek.
▼ 0.8   SO   Modern cabin on left; then town site of Ruby.

GPS: N39°01.25′ W106°36.55′

▼ 1.0   TL   Road on left. Proceed up narrow, loose switchback.
▼ 1.2   Trail ends at collapsed mine portal.

GPS: N39°01.10′ W106°36.15′

Portal USFS Campground beside Grizzly Reservoir

Aspen Mountain Trail

Starting Point:	**Intersection of South Original Street and South Ute Avenue in Aspen**
Finishing Point:	**Sundeck complex and gondola lift station**
Total Mileage:	**4.7 miles**
Unpaved Mileage:	**4.6 miles**
Driving Time:	**1 hour**
Route Elevation:	**7,946 to 11,210 feet**
Usually Open:	**Mid-May to September**
Difficulty Rating:	**2**
Scenic Rating:	**10**

Special Attractions

- Spectacular views from high on Aspen Mountain of the town of Aspen and the Roaring Fork Valley.
- Chance to explore the famous Aspen Mountain ski slopes in summer.
- Short, interesting trail that begins in downtown Aspen.
- Good trail for hiking, mountain biking, riding ATVs and motorbikes, and frisbee golf.

History

Aspen Mountain Trail begins downtown and climbs Aspen Mountain traversing its world-famous ski slopes. Although today the town is a destination for the rich and famous, it was originally established in 1879 as a remote mountain mining camp named Ute City. At the peak of its silver production in the late 1880s, Aspen was considered one of the richest centers of silver production in the world. Although the silver crash of 1893 dealt a hard blow to Aspen's silver production, the industry managed to survive. It was during World War I and the 1920s when the town's mining activity declined significantly.

ATV on Aspen Mountain Trail

Although Aspen seemed as though it would fall into obscurity, the ski industry revived the town.

The 1928 Olympic gold medal winner in bobsledding, Billy Fiske, discussed popularizing the predominantly European sport of downhill skiing in 1936 with two friends, Thomas and Edward Flynn. The three formed a company and began developing ski facilities in Highland, near Aspen. The first ski run was cleared in 1937, and Aspen held its first official race in 1939. World War II derailed the group's plans when Fiske died fighting in the British Royal Air Force. The Flynns subsequently abandoned the project.

During the war, the U.S. Army's 10th Mountain Division trained as ski troopers at Colorado's Camp Hale, near Leadville, Colorado. After the war, Friedl Pfeifer, a member of the 10th Mountain Division, returned to Aspen, determined to shape it into a top-notch ski resort. Pfeifer founded Aspen's first ski school and helped convince Chicago financier Walter Paepcke to invest in Aspen's first chairlift. The lift officially opened on January 12, 1947, with the distinction of being the longest chairlift in the world with the greatest vertical rise. The ski trails were named after the mining areas they crossed—

Chairlift above the switchbacks of Aspen Mountain Trail

View of Aspen from the trail

A fence made from old skis on one of the trail's switchbacks

Smugglers, Tourtellotte Park, Little Nell—as an acknowledgment of the town's roots.

Aspen ski resort continued to expand after Aspen Mountain opened in 1947. Three more mountains—Buttermilk (1958), Aspen Highlands (1958), and Snowmass (1968)—helped enhance Aspen's reputation as a premier resort. With further help from Paepcke, the town also developed as a cultural center, attracting tourists year-round.

Description

The entrance to Aspen Mountain Trail is not immediately evident, so be prepared when navigating to the starting point by using a GPS, reading the route directions carefully in advance, or having a passenger navigate. The trail begins at the inter-

A ski lift on Aspen Mountain sits motionless during summer

section of South Original Street and South Ute Avenue in downtown Aspen. Proceed southwest through the intersection and take the narrow alleyway that swings around behind a cluster of condominiums. Proceed through the gate at the base of the mountain, and the trail immediately begins climbing the ski slopes. This trail, also known as Aspen Mountain Summer Road, is closed temporarily from time to time for maintenance to the ski runs.

The road climbs steeply, but it is an easy drive. Its surface is wide and well maintained with little or no loose or embedded rock depending upon how recently the road has been graded. The water bars across the road in places help prevent erosion, but their deep trenches make high clearance preferred (difficulty rating of 2). Although there are sections of shelf road that can be narrow, passing oncoming vehicles is not an issue because of the numerous pullouts.

Higher and higher the switchbacks ascend the ski hill beneath numerous lifts and the Silver Queen Gondola revealing

Frisbee golf course on Aspen Mountain

The Sundeck at the end of the trail

expansive views over Aspen and the Roaring Fork Valley. Stands of aspens on the slopes of Aspen Mountain make this a scenic and exciting fall color viewing drive. Popular for a multitude of outdoor recreation activities, including hiking, mountain biking, and riding ATVs and motorbikes, the road is heavily used when it is open for use in summer and fall. Near the trail's end, you will also pass through a frisbee golf course.

The trail concludes at the Sundeck and Silver Queen Gondola Station and the intersection with Central #25: Midnight Mine and Little Annie Trail. The experience of traversing the ski slopes of Aspen Mountain in summer along with the one-of-a-kind views are sure to make this trail a favorite.

Current Road Information

White River National Forest
Aspen Ranger District
806 West Hallam
Aspen, CO 81611
(970) 925-3445

Intersection showing the entrance to the trail

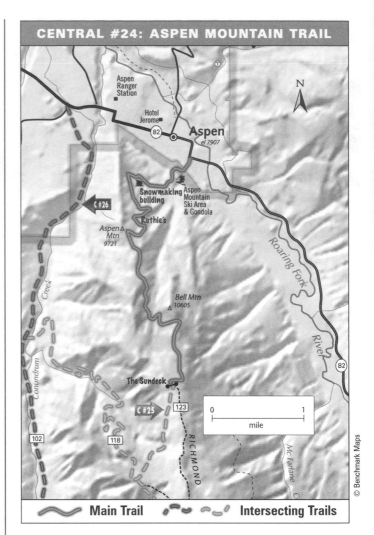

Map References

USFS White River National Forest
Maptech CD:
      Colorado Springs/Ski Areas/Central
Benchmark's *Colorado Road & Recreation Atlas*, p. 86
Colorado Atlas & Gazetteer, p. 46
The Roads of Colorado, p. 93
Trails Illustrated, #127

Route Directions

▼ 0.0		From the intersection of South Original Street and South Ute Avenue in Aspen, zero trip meter and proceed southwest through the intersection and into the narrow alleyway between condominium blocks. Proceed up the hill behind buildings.
	0.1 ▲	Trail ends at the intersection of South Original Street and South Ute Avenue in Aspen.
		GPS: N39°11.13' W106°48.98'
▼ 0.1	SO	Pavement ends. Seasonal gate at gondola. Zero trip meter.
	0.0 ▲	Proceed down the hill behind the block of condominiums.
		GPS: N39°11.11' W106°49.06'
▼ 0.0		Proceed south on Aspen Mountain Summer Road.
	4.6 ▲	Seasonal gate at gondola; then pavement

			begins. Zero trip meter.
▼ 0.2		SO	Aspen Hiking Trail on left.
	4.4 ▲	SO	Aspen Hiking Trail on right.
▼ 0.4		BL	Track on right; then proceed straight on past road on left.
	4.2 ▲	BL	Road on right; then proceed straight on past track on left.
▼ 0.8		SO	Aspen Mountain snowmaking building on left.
	3.8 ▲	SO	Aspen Mountain snowmaking building on right.
		GPS: N39°11.05′ W106°49.59′	
▼ 1.0		SO	Short track on left.
	3.6 ▲	SO	Short track on right.
▼ 1.7		SO	Track on right to ski lift; then Ruthie's on left.
	2.9 ▲	BR	Track on left to ski lift; then Ruthie's on right.
		GPS: N39°10.61′ W106°49.58′	
▼ 1.8		SO	Ski lift on left.
	2.8 ▲	SO	Ski lift on right.
▼ 2.3		SO	Gated track on right.
	2.3 ▲	SO	Gated track on left.
▼ 3.0		SO	Old cabin ruins on right.
	1.6 ▲	SO	Old cabin ruins on left.
▼ 3.3		TL	Track on right to Bonnie's restaurant.
	1.3 ▲	TR	Track on left to Bonnie's restaurant.
▼ 3.4		SO	Track on left to ski lift.
	1.2 ▲	SO	Track on right to ski lift.
▼ 4.5		SO	Track on left to snow equipment building.
	0.1 ▲	SO	Track on right to snow equipment building.
▼ 4.6			Trail ends at Sundeck complex, gondola lift station, and intersection with Central #25: Midnight Mine and Little Annie Trail.
	0.0 ▲		Trail begins at the intersection with Central #25: Midnight Mine and Little Annie Trail at the Sundeck complex and gondola lift station. Zero trip meter and proceed east on Aspen Mountain Summer Road.
		GPS: N39°09.11′ W106°49.15′	

CENTRAL REGION TRAIL #25

Midnight Mine and Little Annie Trail

Starting Point:	Summit of Aspen Mountain at the intersection of Central #24: Aspen Mountain Trail and FR 118
Finishing Point:	Intersection with Central #26: Taylor Pass Trail (Castle Creek Road or CR 15)
Total Mileage:	5.6 miles, plus 3.1-mile spur
Unpaved Mileage:	5.6 miles, plus 3.1-mile spur
Driving Time:	45 minutes
Route Elevation:	8,960 to 11,211 feet
Usually Open:	Mid-May to October
Difficulty Rating:	2 for main trail, 1 for spur
Scenic Rating:	8

View from the trail across Castle Creek Valley

Special Attractions

■ Popular trail for hiking, mountain biking, and riding ATVs and dirt bikes.
■ Good snowmobile trail in winter.
■ Numerous stands of aspen with spectacular fall color.

History

Midnight Mine and Little Annie Trail passes through a historic mining district that proved less sustainable than the mines north of Aspen Mountain. The area first saw prospectors when a group moved south from Aspen after failing to find silver. They founded the nearby town of Highland, which was located just east of the junction of Castle Creek and Conundrum Creek about midway between the end of the main trail (Midnight Mine Road, FR 118) and the end of the Little Annie Spur on Castle Creek Road (CR 15).

Some good strikes in 1879 drew more prospectors to the town. From a peak of 500 residents, the population of Highland leveled off at about 300 by 1880. Little gold was discovered, although other metals, as well as minerals, were found including galena, silver, copper, lead, carbonates, and iron.

By 1881, Highland's boom years were over, although the

The trail runs through aspen stands

town experienced periods of revival in 1889 and 1890. The Hope Mining, Milling, and Leasing Company attempted to reach the Little Annie Mine with an ambitious tunnel project in 1910. The company managed to bore for roughly 3 miles, but the ore found was of inferior quality. The project was halted in the early 1920s.

The first ski run in the Aspen area was opened in Highland through the efforts of Billy Fiske and brothers Thomas and Edward Flynn. Fiske died while flying for the British Royal Air Force during World War II, and the ski experiment was abandoned until Friedl Pfeifer helped open the first chairlift on nearby Aspen Mountain on January 12, 1947.

Description

Midnight Mine and Little Annie Trail begins at the intersection of Central #24: Aspen Mountain Trail and FR 118 at the summit of Aspen Mountain. Bear right at the summit near the gondola station and gate onto FR 118 (FR 123 branches off to the left).

The main trail, Midnight Mine Road (FR 118), is rated a 2 for difficulty because sections of the road are not frequently

Castle Creek

maintained. For the first halfmile, the trail is narrow and descends through a corridor of trees. Along this short section before reaching the Hidden Treasure Hiking Trailhead, there is little room for passing oncoming vehicles. Along the remainder of the length of Midnight Mine Trail, sections of shelf road can be narrow, but passing oncoming vehicles is not an issue because there are plenty of pullouts.

The road descends steeply in sections and switchbacks down the northwest face of Aspen Mountain. Although the trail mostly travels through stands of evergreen and aspen trees, which are quite scenic in

A steep switchback with Aspen Highlands ski runs in the distance

fall, breaks in the trees reveal views west across Castle Creek Valley to the impressively steep Aspen Highlands ski runs on the slopes of Lodge Peak.

After about a mile and a half, the Little Annie Spur diverges from the main trail and descends the south slope of Aspen Mountain. The spur is a wide and well-maintained road that switchbacks down into Castle Creek Valley past several tailings piles and old mining claims and ends at the intersection with Central #26: Taylor Pass Trail (Castle Creek Road or CR 15), approximately 4 miles north of Ashcroft ghost town.

Be aware that both the main trail and spur are heavily used for all sorts of outdoor recreation, including mountain biking, hiking, as well as riding dirt bikes and ATVs. The route is also a popular snowmobiling trail in winter with a large parking and staging area located near the lower end of FR 118, less than a mile from the intersection of Central #26: Taylor Pass Trail (Castle Creek Road or CR 15).

Current Road Information

White River National Forest
Aspen Ranger District
806 West Hallam
Aspen, CO 81611
(970) 925-3445

Map References

USFS White River National Forest
Maptech CD:
    Colorado Springs/Ski Areas/Central
Benchmark's *Colorado Road & Recreation Atlas*, p. 86
Colorado Atlas & Gazetteer, p. 46
The Roads of Colorado, p. 93
Trails Illustrated, #127

Route Directions

▼ 0.0   At the summit of Aspen Mountain and the
         intersection with Central #24: Aspen Mountain

CENTRAL #25: MIDNIGHT MINE AND LITTLE ANNIE TRAIL

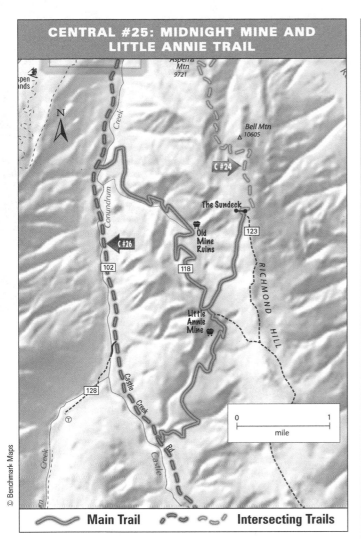

© Benchmark Maps

Main Trail ～～ **Intersecting Trails** ⌒ ⌒ ⌒

View of Little Annie Spur Trail

0.0 ▲		Taylor Pass Trail (Castle Creek Road or CR 15). Spur begins at intersection with Central #26: Taylor Pass Trail (Castle Creek Road or CR 15), approximately 4 miles north of Ashcroft ghost town. Zero trip meter and proceed northeast on the Little Annie Spur of Central #25: Midnight Mine and Little Annie Trail.

GPS: N39°06.41′ W106°49.88′

Continuation of Main Trail

▼ 0.0		Proceed west on FR 118.
4.2 ▲		Little Annie Spur on right. Zero trip meter.

GPS: N39°08.08′ W106°49.57′

▼ 0.1	SO	Track on right is a cut through to Central #24: Aspen Mountain Trail. Proceed north on FR 118.
4.1 ▲	SO	Track on right is a cut through to Central #24: Aspen Mountain Trail.

GPS: N39°08.17′ W106°49.66′

▼ 1.8	SO	Tailings piles and old mine workings on left and right.
2.4 ▲	SO	Tailings piles and old mine workings on left and right.

GPS: N39°08.89′ W106°49.80′

▼ 3.4	SO	Driveway on right.
0.8 ▲	SO	Driveway on left.

▼ 4.0	SO	Cross over Castle Creek.
0.2 ▲	SO	Cross over Castle Creek.

▼ 4.2		Trail ends at intersection with Central #26: Taylor Pass Trail, approximately 2.7 miles south of Colorado 82 on Castle Creek Road (CR 15). Midnight Mine signed Rd 15-A.
0.0 ▲		Trail begins at the intersection with Central #26: Taylor Pass Trail, approximately 2.7 miles south of Colorado 82 on Castle Creek Road (CR 15). Zero trip meter and proceed southeast on Midnight Mine Road (FR 118), signed Rd 15-A.

GPS: N39°09.63′ W106°50.89′

Trail, zero trip meter and proceed southwest past gondola station through gate and bear right past FR 123 onto FR 118.

1.4 ▲		Trail ends at summit of Aspen Mountain and intersection with Central #24: Aspen Mountain Trail.

GPS: N39°09.11′ W106°49.15′

▼ 0.5	SO	Hidden Treasure Hiking Trail on right.
0.9 ▲	SO	Hidden Treasure Hiking Trail on left.

▼ 1.2	BL	Road on right.
0.2 ▲	BR	Road on left.

▼ 1.3	TR	T-intersection.
0.1 ▲	TL	Road on left.

GPS: N39°08.14′ W106°49.57′

▼ 1.4		Little Annie Spur on left. Zero trip meter.
0.0 ▲		Proceed northeast on FR 118.

GPS: N39°08.08′ W106°49.57′

Little Annie Spur

▼ 0.0	TL	Proceed southeast on Little Annie Road.
3.1 ▲	TL	Spur ends at main trail. Zero trip meter and proceed west on FR 118.

▼ 1.7	BR	Intersection signed Lower Hurricane Road (dead end) on left.
1.4 ▲	BL	Intersection signed Lower Hurricane Road (dead end) on right.

▼ 3.1		Spur ends at intersection with Central #26:

Taylor Pass Trail

Starting Point:	Intersection of Central #27: Reno Divide Trail (FR 759) and Taylor River Road (CR/FR 742)
Finishing Point:	Aspen
Total Mileage:	25.5 miles
Unpaved Mileage:	15 miles
Driving Time:	2.5 hours
Route Elevation:	7,800 to 11,928 feet
Usually Open:	Early July to late September
Difficulty Rating:	6
Scenic Rating:	9

Special Attractions

■ Very challenging 4WD trail.
■ Taylor Lake, an attractive alpine lake near the summit.
■ A challenging creek crossing.
■ Spectacular summit views.
■ Aspen viewing in the fall.

History

Taylor Pass was officially named in 1940 for mining pioneer Jim Taylor, who prospected the area as early as 1860. The pass road was instrumental in making Ashcroft, where the first ore discoveries in the Roaring Fork Valley had been made in 1879, an important early supply center for mining in the area. The road is one of three formed in the wake of the major ore discoveries in the inaccessible Roaring Fork Valley in 1879 and 1880, as interests in Buena Vista, Crested Butte, and Leadville vied for access to the new area.

In 1880, Taylor Pass Road was built by Stevens and Company, owned by H. B. Gillespie, to haul freight into the area from Taylor Park and Buena Vista. Subsequently, the same company ran stagecoaches along the route. In 1881, a telegraph line was run over the pass.

The trail where it enters White River National Forest

Bridge over Castle Creek near Ashcroft ghost town

Although the Taylor Pass route to Crested Butte was easier than the Pearl Pass route, which opened in 1882, neither were satisfactory, as freight wagons had to be "snubbed" (that is, taken apart and hauled over in pieces) to cross the pass.

When rich ore was discovered in Aspen in 1880, it became apparent that Aspen was likely to eclipse Ashcroft as the center of the mining activity in the valley. Local business interests were quick to organize the Twin Lakes and Roaring Fork Toll Company to construct a road over what is now known as Independence Pass to the smelters and railhead at Leadville. This road opened in 1881 and proved by far the most successful of the three. The need for all of the roads passed in 1887, when the Denver & Rio Grande Railroad reached Aspen, followed by the Colorado Midland Railroad the following year.

The township of Dorchester was established well after the initial flurry of activity that resulted from the discoveries in the Roaring Fork Valley. In 1900, gold was discovered in the Italian Mountains, and Dorchester became the main mining camp in the area. Despite initial optimism that swelled the population to more than 1,000, the mines were never very successful. The harsh winters made operating the mines difficult and costly. Nonetheless, some of the mines were operated year-round despite the ever-present danger of snow slides. On one occasion, 15 were reported in a single day. Activity lingered on until World War I, helped by production of lead and zinc, but shortly afterward the mines were closed and the remaining residents moved away.

Ashcroft was settled shortly after silver strikes in 1879. Initially, the town was known as Castle Forks but was soon renamed Ashcroft. In its early days the town served as the gateway to Aspen for travelers coming over Taylor Pass or Cottonwood Pass. Established at about the same period as Aspen, Ashcroft seemed likely to become the more successful of the two. The Ashcroft post office was established in 1880. The town had five hotels, a newspaper, a school, a jail, a doctor, a bowling alley, several stores, and many saloons.

Two factors led to the decline of Ashcroft. One was the

Summit of Taylor Pass

The rocky section on the southern end of the trail

tion of the rocky streambed in water up to bumper level. However, the forest service rerouted the creek and leveled the road somewhat. This section had been the most difficult part of the road, particularly when water obscured large boulders.

A couple of miles farther on, after reaching timberline, the road splits into a number of alternative routes past Taylor Lake and up the final ascent to the summit. The one detailed in the directions below is the easiest and most scenic. It proceeds around the southern and western sides of Taylor Lake.

From the summit of the pass, you enter the White River National Forest. Two roads lead down to Aspen: Express Creek Road and Richmond Hill Road (FR 123). The directions follow the quicker and easier Express Creek Road via the ghost town of Ashcroft.

The initial descent is a steep, very narrow shelf road, and the gravel road surface can be loose and slippery. We recommend that you engage first or second gear in low range to avoid locking the brakes and proceed slowly. The steep descent, in two stages, lasts for about half a mile. The views from the summit and during the descent along Express Creek are magnificent. At timberline, the road enters a dense aspen forest as it continues to descend to Castle Creek Road, about one-quarter of a mile north of the ghost town of Ashcroft.

In 1974, the Aspen Historical Society leased Ashcroft's town site from the U.S. Forest Service in order to preserve the historic remains. Although some of the buildings you see there

completion of Independence Pass, which opened accessibility to nearby Aspen. Then, in 1887, the Denver & Rio Grande completed a railway line into Aspen, which encouraged Ashcroft's residents to migrate to Aspen.

Description

The start of this 4WD route can be reached either from Crested Butte by way of the Reno Divide Trail (Central #27) or from Tincup or Buena Vista by connecting with Taylor River Road (CR 742) at Taylor Park Reservoir.

The route commences heading west on CR 742, a well-maintained passenger vehicle road. The turnoff to Taylor Pass (FR 761) is a little more than 2 miles after the town site of Dorchester. From this point, the road is 4WD, although initially it is just a bumpy road through the forest.

At the 1.6-mile point in from CR 742, the trail formerly ran in the creek for about a hundred yards, requiring negotia-

A view of Taylor Lake from the pass

The refreshing waters of Taylor Lake in midsummer

Narrow, steep shelf section near the pass

today are original, others were brought in to replace deteriorated ones so that tourists can safely explore the resurrected ghost town.

From this point, the road is paved all the way into Aspen.

Current Road Information
Grand Mesa, Uncompahgre & Gunnison National Forests
Gunnison Ranger District
216 North Colorado
Gunnison, CO 81230
(970) 641-0471

Map References
USFS   Gunnison National Forest; White River National
       Forest
Maptech CD:
       Colorado Springs/Ski Areas/Central
Benchmark's *Colorado Road & Recreation Atlas*, p. 86
Colorado Atlas & Gazetteer, pp. 46, 59
The Roads of Colorado, p. 93
Trails Illustrated, #127, #131

Route Directions

▼ 0.0		At intersection of Central #27: Reno Divide Trail (FR 759) and Taylor River Road (CR/FR 742), zero trip meter and proceed northwest. This intersection is 11 miles north of Taylor Park Reservoir. Note: Sign here reads "Dead end."
5.6 ▲		End at intersection with Central #27: Reno Divide Trail (FR 759).
GPS: N 38°57.24' W 106°37.26'		
▼ 1.8	SO	Tellurium Creek Road on right.
3.8 ▲	SO	Tellurium Creek Road on left.
▼ 2.4	SO	Track on left to Old Dorchester Guard Station.
3.2 ▲	SO	Track on right to Old Dorchester Guard Station.
▼ 2.6	SO	USFS Dorchester Campground turnoff on left.
3.0 ▲	SO	USFS Dorchester Campground turnoff on right.
▼ 2.9	SO	Fishing Access Road on left.
2.7 ▲	SO	Fishing Access Road on right.
▼ 5.5	SO	Cattle guard.
0.1 ▲	SO	Cattle guard.
▼ 5.6	TR	Onto Taylor Pass Road (FR 761). Zero trip meter.
0.0 ▲		Proceed on FR 742.
GPS: N 38°59.73' W 106°42.17'		
▼ 0.0		Proceed onto FR 761.

Narrow, rocky section of trail climbing to Taylor Pass from the north

CENTRAL #26: TAYLOR PASS TRAIL

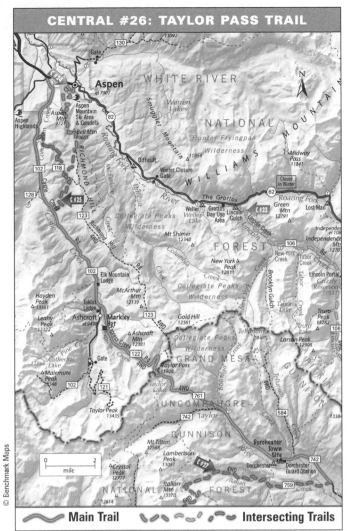

© Benchmark Maps

〰〰 **Main Trail**   ⌇⌇⌇ ⌢⌣⌢ ⟋⟍ **Intersecting Trails**

3.4 ▲	TL	Intersection: FR 761 and Taylor River Road (FR 742). Zero trip meter.

▼ 1.4		SO	Cross through creek.
	2.0 ▲	SO	Cross through creek.
▼ 1.5		BR	Fork in road.
	1.9 ▲	BL	Fork in road.
▼ 1.6		SO	Road follows the path of the old creek bed. Note: In the summer of 1997, the creek was diverted from this section to the east side of the road.
	1.8 ▲	SO	Road follows the path of the old creek bed.
▼ 2.9		SO	Cross through creek.
	0.5 ▲	SO	Cross through creek.
▼ 3.4		TL	Fork in road with sign to Taylor Pass Divide Road. 761.1A on left; FR 761.1 to the right. Zero trip meter.
	0.0 ▲		Proceed on FR 761.

GPS: N 39°01.04' W 106°44.92'

▼ 0.0			Proceed along 761.1A.
	1.4 ▲	TR	Fork in road. Zero trip meter.
▼ 0.1		SO	Taylor Lake on right.
	1.3 ▲	SO	Taylor Lake on left.
▼ 0.5		SO	Ponds on left.
	0.9 ▲	SO	Ponds on right.
▼ 0.6		BR	Fork in road. Follow sign to Taylor Pass.
	0.8 ▲	SO	Follow sign to "Taylor Pass Road #761, 1 mile."

GPS: N 39°00.71' W 106°45.42'

▼ 0.7		SO	Cross through creek.
	0.7 ▲	SO	Cross through creek.
▼ 1.4		BL	Taylor Pass. Zero trip meter.
	0.0 ▲	BR	Proceed from summit on the track to the southwest, which descends from the left-hand side of the "Taylor Pass" sign, entering Gunnison National Forest.

GPS: N 39°01.21' W 106°45.32'

▼ 0.0		BL	Proceed on the track (FR 122) that descends from the right-hand side of the "Taylor Pass" sign, entering White River National Forest. Follow Express Creek Road (FR 122) toward Ashcroft.
	4.6 ▲	BR	Taylor Pass. Zero trip meter.
▼ 0.6		SO	Bridge over Express Creek.
	4.0 ▲	SO	Bridge over Express Creek.
▼ 2.2		SO	Cross through creek.
	2.4 ▲	SO	Cross through creek.
▼ 2.7		SO	Track on left to Markley Hut.
	1.8 ▲	SO	Track on right to Markley Hut.

GPS: N 39°02.21' W 106°47.26'

▼ 4.0		SO	Cross through creek.
	0.6 ▲	SO	Cross through creek.
▼ 4.2		SO	Private track on left.
	0.4 ▲	SO	Private track on right.
▼ 4.4		SO	Bridge over Castle Creek.
	0.2 ▲	SO	Bridge over Castle Creek.
▼ 4.6		TR	Intersection with Castle Creek Road. The restored ghost town of Ashcroft is just to the left. Zero trip meter.
	0.0 ▲		Continue toward Taylor Pass on Express Creek Road.

GPS: N 39°03.63' W 106°48.03'

▼ 0.0			Proceed north along Castle Creek Road toward Aspen.
	3.8 ▲	TL	Intersection: Castle Creek Road (FR 102) and Express Creek Road (CR 15C). The restored ghost town of Ashcroft is 0.4 miles south. Zero trip meter.
▼ 3.8		SO	Central #25: Midnight Mine and Little Annie Trail spur on right. Zero trip meter.
	0.0 ▲	SO	Proceed south on Castle Creek Road.

GPS: N39°06.41' W106°49.88'

▼ 0.0		SO	Proceed north on Castle Creek Road toward Aspen.
	4.0 ▲	SO	Central #25: Midnight Mine and Little Annie Trail spur on left. Zero trip meter.
▼ 4.0		SO	Central #25: Midnight Mine and Little Annie Trail on right. Zero trip meter.
	0.0 ▲	SO	Proceed south on Castle Creek Road.

GPS: N39°09.63' W106°50.89'

▼ 0.0			Proceed north on Castle Creek Road toward Aspen.
	2.7 ▲	SO	Central #25: Midinight Mine and Little Annie Trail on left. Zero trip meter.
▼ 2.7		TR	Intersection with CR 13. Then almost immediately is the intersection with Colorado 82. Aspen is to the right. End of trail.
	0.0 ▲		At the intersection of Colorado 82 and CR 13 in Aspen, zero trip meter and proceed southwest. Almost immediately turn left onto Castle Creek Road.

GPS: N 39°11.74' W 106°50.39'

Reno Divide Trail

Starting Point:	Intersection of Colorado 135 and Cement Creek Road (FR 740)
Finishing Point:	Intersection of Central #26: Taylor Pass Trail (CR/FR 742) and Italian Creek Road (FR 759)
Total Mileage:	26.3 miles
Unpaved Mileage:	25.8 miles
Driving Time:	4 hours
Route Elevation:	8,595 to 12,015 feet
Usually Open:	Mid-June to mid-October
Difficulty Rating:	4
Scenic Rating:	8

Special Attractions

- Very scenic, varied, and moderately difficult 4WD trail.
- Access from Crested Butte to Taylor Pass.
- Good backcountry camping sites.

History

In 1879, prospectors crossed Pearl Pass into the Roaring Fork Valley and discovered ore near Ashcroft. In the following year, more rich ore was discovered near Aspen. By this time, the area was teeming with miners.

In 1880, a company was formed to build a road over Independence Pass from Leadville to Aspen in order to provide access to Leadville's railhead and smelters. At the same time, the pack trail over Taylor Pass, which had been used by prospectors since the previous year, was upgraded to a wagon road to provide access from Taylor Park and Buena Vista. The opening of Taylor Pass Road spurred the desire of those in Crested Butte to gain access to the new mining area. The road over

Reno Divide was built to forge a stage route connection to Taylor Pass Road.

The Denver & Rio Grande Railroad spur reached Crested Butte from Gunnison in 1881. By that time, Aspen was the center of a silver boom, following the first rich ore discoveries in the Roaring Fork Valley in 1879 and the further major discoveries the following year. Crested Butte was only 24 miles from Aspen and 16 miles from Ashcroft, and the railroad was determined to expand access to its new railhead from the Roaring Fork Valley. This prompted the development of Pearl Pass Road in 1882. Al-

Italian Creek Road

though more direct, this route was extremely difficult, requiring wagons to be snubbed over the pass (that is, taken apart and hauled over in pieces). Pearl Pass Road operated for only three years.

The toll road over Independence Pass from Leadville opened in 1881 and proved to be far more successful than either of the southern routes. With the arrival in Aspen of the Denver & Rio Grande Railroad in 1887 and the Colorado Midland Railroad in 1888, the two southern roads became obsolete.

Description

This route provides access from Crested Butte to Taylor Pass Road, which leads across the Continental Divide into Aspen. It provides an alternative 4WD route to the more difficult Pearl Pass.

The route starts at the intersection of Colorado 135 and Cement Creek Road (FR 740), about 7 miles south of Crested Butte. For the first 9 miles of the route, Cement Creek

Aspens along an easy section of road near the beginning of the trail

The trail following beside Cement Creek

Creek crossing near Stewart Mine

Road travels alongside the creek in a very picturesque setting. The valley alternates between very wide sections and very narrow sections: The walls close in to form a canyon just wide enough for the creek and the road to squeeze through and then open up to panoramic views. The road through this section is easily traveled by a 2WD vehicle.

Immediately after the turn onto FR 759, the road starts to climb. Although there are some sections of shelf road, they are lined with trees and are not intimidating. The surface of the road is sound and is maintained by the Gunnison 4-Wheelers Club.

After passing through the gate at the 3.6-mile point on FR 759, the road begins to deteriorate. For about the next 4 miles, the road is rough and can be very muddy after rain. Even under normal conditions, the road has muddy sections scarred with potholes, but it should not present too great an obstacle for a 4WD vehicle. This is the most difficult part of the journey.

Shortly after passing above timberline, you will encounter a steep-sided but narrow, small creek crossing along an off-camber section of the track. Having negotiated this crossing in a Suburban, we can attest to it being passable in a full size SUV.

The road flattens out and travels along an open alpine ridge past the Stewart and Star Mines. The views of the Italian Creek Valley and the Taylor River Valley are spectacular.

As the road descends, it is a bit rough, rocky, and muddy in sections, but the surface is generally sound and should not pose any problems under normal conditions.

From the gate just after the Lilly Pond Trailhead, the road (in dry conditions) is easily navigable in a car. However, after rain it can be very muddy. There are numerous backcountry camping spots along this section.

Current Road Information

Grand Mesa, Uncompahgre & Gunnison National Forests
Gunnison Ranger District
216 North Colorado
Gunnison, CO 81230
(970) 641-0471

Map References

USFS   Gunnison National Forest
Maptech CD:
      Colorado Springs/Ski Areas/Central
Benchmark's *Colorado Road & Recreation Atlas*, p. 86
Colorado Atlas & Gazetteer, pp. 58, 59
The Roads of Colorado, pp. 93, 109
Trails Illustrated, #131

Route Directions

▼ 0.0			At intersection of Colorado 135 and Cement Creek Road (FR 740), zero trip meter and proceed east.
	8.8 ▲		End at intersection with Colorado 135.
		GPS: N 38°48.27′ W 106°53.39′	
▼ 0.2		SO	Cross bridge.
	8.6 ▲	SO	Cross bridge.
▼ 0.5		SO	Unpaved.
	8.3 ▲	SO	Paved.
▼ 1.7		SO	Farris Creek Trailhead on left.
	7.1 ▲	SO	Farris Creek Trailhead on right.
▼ 3.2		SO	Track to USFS Summer Home Group on right.
	5.6 ▲	SO	Track to USFS Summer Home Group on left.
▼ 3.5		SO	USFS Cement Creek Campground.
	5.3 ▲	SO	USFS Cement Creek Campground.
▼ 4.5		SO	Seasonal closure gate.
	4.3 ▲	SO	Seasonal closure gate.
▼ 7.7		SO	Bridge.
	1.1 ▲	SO	Bridge.
▼ 7.9		SO	Cross over Cement Creek.
	0.9 ▲	SO	Cross over Cement Creek.
▼ 8.6		SO	Cross through small creek.
	0.2 ▲	SO	Cross through small creek.
▼ 8.8		BR	Intersection on right with FR 759 (Italian Creek Road) toward Reno Divide. Cement Creek Road continues straight ahead. Zero trip meter.
	0.0 ▲		Proceed south along Cement Creek Road.
		GPS: N 38°53.07′ W 106°47.42′	
▼ 0.0			Proceed along FR 759.
	9.2 ▲	TL	Intersection. Italian Creek Road and Cement Creek Road.
▼ 1.3		SO	Cabin ruins on left.
	7.9 ▲	SO	Cabin ruins on right.

A rustic signpost and cabin in the distance

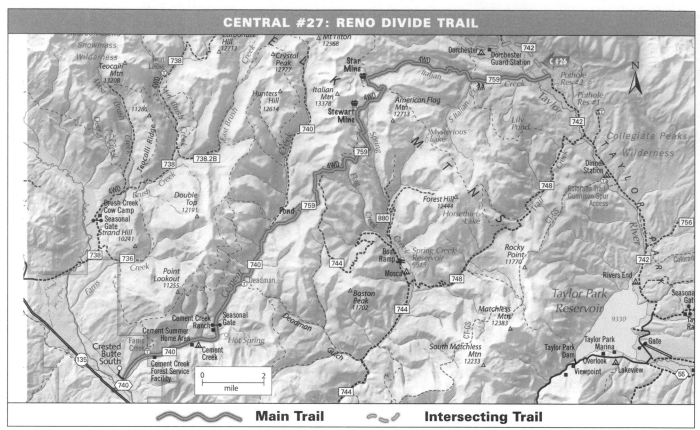

〰〰〰 **Main Trail**　　⌒⌒ **Intersecting Trail**

▼ 3.6　SO　Track on right. Gate. Track on left. Proceed through gate (leaving it as you found it). Follow FR 759.

　5.6 ▲　SO　Track on right. Proceed through gate (leaving it as you found it). Follow FR 759. Track on left.

GPS: N 38°54.46' W 106°45.76'

▼ 5.4　SO　Cross through small, muddy creek.

　3.8 ▲　SO　Cross through small, muddy creek.

▼ 5.7　SO　Cross through small creek.

　3.5 ▲　SO　Cross through small creek.

▼ 6.5　SO　Pond on left and track on right (closed to motorized vehicles).

　2.7 ▲　SO　Track on left (closed to motorized vehicles). Pond on right.

▼ 6.9　SO　Cross through creek.

　2.3 ▲　SO　Cross through creek.

▼ 7.5　BR　Track on left.

　1.6 ▲　BL　Track on the right is a difficult alternative track that rejoins the road at the gate at mileage point 5.6 ahead.

GPS: N 38°55.97 W 106°44.36'

▼ 7.7　SO　Cross through creek with steep sides.

　1.5 ▲　SO　Cross through creek with steep sides.

▼ 7.8　SO　Cross through small creek.

　1.3 ▲　SO　Cross through small creek.

▼ 8.1　SO　Stewart Mine and track to it on left.

　1.1 ▲　SO　Stewart Mine and track to it on right.

▼ 8.4　SO　Stewart Mine cabin ruins on right.

　0.8 ▲　SO　Stewart Mine cabin ruins on left.

▼ 8.8　BL　Track on right.

　0.4 ▲　BR　Track on left.

GPS: N 38°56.54' W 106°43.59'

▼ 8.9　BL　Fork in road. Right fork leads to overlook and returns to main

road in short distance.

　0.3 ▲　BR　Fork in road. Left fork leads to overlook and returns to main road in short distance.

▼ 9.2　BL　Fork in road. Star Trailhead on the right. Zero trip meter at sign.

　0.0 ▲　　　Continue along main track.

GPS: N 38°56.87' W 106°43.41'

▼ 0.0　　　Proceed toward Taylor Road.

　8.3 ▲　BR　Fork in road. Star Trailhead on the left. Zero trip meter at sign.

▼ 0.8　SO　Track on right.

　7.4 ▲　SO　Track on left.

▼ 1.0　SO/BL　Cabin ruins on left. Cross through small creek; then bear left past a track on the right.

　7.3 ▲　BR/SO　Track on the left. Cross through a small creek; then cabin ruins on right.

▼ 1.1　SO　Cross through two small creeks.

　7.2 ▲　SO　Cross through two small creeks.

▼ 1.2　BL　Mine ruins on right on private property. Follow sign toward Taylor Park.

　7.1 ▲　BR　Mine ruins on left. Follow sign to Cement Creek.

▼ 1.4　TR　Intersection. Private road on the left.

　6.9 ▲　TL　Private road is straight ahead.

▼ 2.0　SO　Track on right. Follow sign to Taylor Park.

　6.2 ▲　SO　Follow sign to Cement Creek.

▼ 2.7　SO　Cross through creek.

　5.5 ▲　SO　Cross through creek.

▼ 4.6　SO　Cross through creek.

　3.7 ▲　SO　Cross through creek.

▼ 5.3　SO　Dorchester walking trail on left.

　3.0 ▲　SO　Dorchester walking trail on right.

▼ 5.5　SO　Lilly Pond walking trail on right.

　2.8 ▲　SO　Lilly Pond walking trail on left.

GPS: N 38°57.20' W 106°40.17'		
▼ 5.6	SO	Gate.
2.6 ▲	SO	Gate.
▼ 7.8	SO	Cross bridge over Taylor River.
0.4 ▲	SO	Cross bridge over Taylor River.
▼ 8.3		End at intersection with Taylor River Road (CR/FR 742). Taylor Reservoir is to the right and Central #26: Taylor Pass Trail is to the left.
0.0 ▲		At intersection of Taylor River Road (CR/FR 742) and Italian Creek Road (FR 759), zero trip meter and proceed west along Italian Creek Road.
GPS: N 38°57.24' W 106°37.26'		

CENTRAL REGION TRAIL #28

Schofield Pass and Devil's Punchbowl Trail

Starting Point:	Mount Crested Butte
Finishing Point:	Marble
Total Mileage:	21.2 miles
Unpaved Mileage:	20.1 miles
Driving Time:	3.5 hours
Route Elevation:	8,000 to 10,707 feet
Usually Open:	Late July to mid-September
Difficulty Rating:	6
Scenic Rating:	10

Special Attractions

- Famous and dangerous 4WD trail along an old stagecoach route.
- Historic mill on Crystal River.
- Ghost towns of Gothic and Crystal and town site of Schofield.
- Can be combined with Kebler Pass Road (CR 12) to form a loop.

Emerald Lake

History

Schofield Pass was named for Judge B. F. Schofield, who founded the town of Schofield. Ute Indians used the pass, and they led the first white men across it. Prospectors traveled the pass frequently during the 1870s, although the first big strikes in the area did not occur until around 1880. In the mid-1870s, the Hayden survey party crossed Schofield Pass and plotted it on its map.

By the early 1880s, the cities of Marble, Crystal, Schofield, and Gothic were all at their peak. The pass road was heavily used but was never improved beyond a rough, narrow wagon road. Nonetheless, a stage ran from Crested Butte to Crystal for a number of years. This small road's political apogee came when it was traveled by President Ulysses S. Grant during his visit to many of the mining camps in the area, accompanied by John Routt, the last appointed governor of the territory and the first elected governor of the state.

The township of Gothic was established in 1879 with the discovery of gold and silver ores in the area. Within four months, nearly 200 buildings had been erected, including a hotel, three stores, a butcher shop, a barbershop, and a saloon. Millions of dollars' worth of gold and silver ores were extracted from the hills. At its peak, the bustling mining city had a population of around 8,000.

Gothic gained a reputation as a very wild town with lots of drinking, gambling, and prostitution. When, on his trip through the area in 1880, Ulysses S. Grant asked to see a wild mining town, he was shown Gothic. He reportedly drove his own stage into town and arrived to a riotous celebration.

Gothic's first mayor was elected by a roll of dice between two men. The winner was Garwood Judd, one of the town's saloon keepers. After gold and silver played out, fortunes receded quickly; by 1884, most of the residents had left town. Garwood Judd remained there by himself until his death in 1930, earning himself the reputation of "the man who stayed." He was proud of his title and even nailed a plaque engraved with the phrase over his door. His ashes were scattered around the town.

Schofield was platted in August 1879 by B. F. Schofield and his party. Prospectors discovered silver in the area as early as 1872, but their fear of Indians deferred permanent settle-

Waterfall near Schofield town site

Gothic

Crossing Crystal River above the treacherous section of the trail

ment for several years. A smelter was built in 1880 and a mill in 1881. By 1882, the town had a population of about 400 and the usual amenities of a hotel, a restaurant (whose staff had trouble boiling water because of the altitude), a general store, a blacksmith shop, and a barbershop.

When former president Ulysses S. Grant and former governor Routt visited Schofield, the residents of Schofield thought that if they could sell shares in one of the local mines to Grant, they could boast that the president owned a mine in Schofield. When that failed, they tried to unsuccessfully "lose" shares to Grant in a poker game—to no avail. Finally, they brought out a big barrel of whiskey, hoping to get Grant drunk and just give him the mining shares! Needless to say, Grant was impressed with Schofield's hospitality, but it is unclear whether he ended up with any claim.

Unfortunately, the ore found around Schofield was poor in quality. Although miners did find some good galena, the inaccessible location and high transportation costs drained off their profits. These factors, coupled with the immense problems of eight-month winters dumping as much as 40 feet of

snow, led to the demise of Schofield. The post office closed in 1885.

Crystal began as a silver mining camp in 1880. Early prospectors named the town after the crystal-like quartz they found along the creek. In the mid-1880s, Crystal had a population of about 500, a newspaper, a general store, many private homes, several saloons, and the Crystal Club (a men's club), which still stands in town.

The trail to Crystal was arduous, leading from Crested Butte over Schofield Pass. The difficulty of traversing this trail made it economically impossible to transport anything but the richest ores in or out of Crystal. Eventually, a better road was constructed, connecting the town with Carbondale.

Although Crystal survived the silver crash of 1893, its population was reduced to a small number of residents. The much-photographed Crystal Mill remains standing on the outskirts of town along the Crystal River. The mill was built by G. C. Eaton and supplied power to the local mines. A waterwheel turned an air compressor to supply air for drilling and power for a stamp mill and sawmill.

A useful reminder to check your brakes

An emedded rock that makes the road even more hazardous

The start of the infamous section above the Crystal River

Special Note on the Difficulty of This Road

The road through Crystal River Canyon down to the area known as the Devil's Punchbowl is known as one of the most dangerous 4WD roads in Colorado. The road's reputation is well deserved in light of the alarming number of fatalities that have occurred on it. The most tragic was in 1970, when seven members of one family perished when their Suburban plunged from the shelf road down a 200-foot drop-off and into the river. Many accidents have taken additional lives in the years since. Seven vehicles slipped off the road in the summer of 1997, and at least one of these accidents resulted in fatalities.

It is hard to dispute statistics like these, but most experienced four-wheelers will be puzzled by such a record. Certainly the road is very narrow and drops off precipitously into the river, but the surface is sound, and the road is no narrower, nor the drop more frightening, than that of many other 4WD roads in the state. Undoubtedly most accidents here must be caused by a combination of factors: the driver's inexperience, the onset of fear when committed beyond the point of turn-ing back, and perhaps even carelessness or a failure to appreciate the very small margin for error.

Another potential hazard is caused by having to cross the river immediately before starting down the canyon. Even in late summer, the water is likely to be bumper deep and will thoroughly soak your brakes. Therefore, follow the recommendation of the large sign erected by the forest service and check that your brakes are working properly before proceeding down the canyon. Also, do not be tempted to get out of your vehicle halfway down the canyon to take a photo and leave your vehicle reliant on the Park gear position.

As is the case with all the more difficult roads in this book, you should not attempt this route until you have traveled many other less difficult roads and are certain that you will not become flustered by the steep drop-off only a foot or so from your wheels. Less experienced drivers are well advised not to attempt this route in a full-sized vehicle.

In spite of the risk it involves, this is a very rewarding trail. If you decide to give it a go, remember to take it very slowly and carefully.

Description

The route starts in the ski resort of Mount Crested Butte. It follows a well-maintained gravel road to Gothic, now the home of the Rocky Mountain Biological Survey, which studies the wide variety of regional flora and fauna. A few well-preserved old buildings still stand. Set in a beautiful area, the town is experiencing a revival as a summer tourist and residential area.

Lizard Lake

Dead Horse Mill on the Crystal River

The summit of Schofield Pass lies beyond Emerald Lake. The low, wooded summit does not offer the views that are associated with most pass summits. The road to the pass is suitable for a passenger car. From that point on until about 2 miles out of Marble, stream crossings and rocky sections necessitate a high-clearance vehicle.

About a mile after the summit, the town site of Schofield lies in an open meadow beside the South Fork of the Crystal River. About a mile farther, you cross through a wide section of the South Fork of the Crystal River. In the later part of summer, this is unlikely to be more than bumper deep, but the streambed contains some large rocks.

Upon exiting the river, the road curves and immediately starts the narrow, steep descent down Crystal River Canyon. Shortly after commencing the downhill run, you are confronted with a large, embedded rock in the center of the road. You have the choice of squeezing past on the side of the rock wall or on the side of the drop-off. The road suffers from snow and rock slides, and it is not unusual to find it impassable—or at least requiring some clearance work.

At the bottom of the canyon are the Devil's Punchbowl and, fewer than 2 miles farther, the township of Crystal. The powerhouse overhanging the Crystal River, called the Dead Horse Mill or the Crystal Mill, is about a quarter of a mile past Crystal on the left. The road continues past the very scenic Beaver Lake and on into Marble.

Although most years this road is open for about eight weeks, sometimes the snow does not melt and the road is closed all summer.

Current Road Information

White River National Forest
Sopris Ranger District
620 Main Street
Carbondale, CO 81623
(970) 963-2266

Map References

USFS Gunnison National Forest; White River National Forest
Maptech CD:
      Colorado Springs/Ski Areas/Central;
      Grand Junction/Western Slope
Benchmark's *Colorado Road & Recreation Atlas*, p. 85
Colorado Atlas & Gazetteer, pp. 45, 46, 58
The Roads of Colorado, p. 92
Trails Illustrated, #128, #131, #133

Route Directions

▼	▲		
0.0			In Mt. Crested Butte, where the Grand Butte Hotel walkway crosses over Gothic Road, zero trip meter and proceed north along Gothic Road.
	10.6		End in Mt. Crested Butte town center.
		GPS: N 38°53.97′ W 106°57.97′	
1.1		SO	End of pavement. Follow main road.
	9.5	SO	Paved. Follow main road.
		GPS: N 38°54.77′ W 106°57.74′	
1.7		SO	Cattle guard. Enter National Forest
			(FR 317) and proceed toward Gothic.
	8.9	SO	Leave National Forest and proceed toward Crested Butte. Cattle guard.
3.3		SO	Cattle guard.
	7.3	SO	Cattle guard.
4.7		SO	Bridge over East River.
	5.9	SO	Bridge over East River.
5.0		SO	Bridge.
	5.6	SO	Bridge.
5.1		SO	Gothic ghost town: general store and visitor center.
	5.4	SO	Gothic ghost town.
5.7		SO	Track on right to Judd Falls, Trailriders, and Cooper Creek trailheads.
	4.9	SO	Track on left to Judd Falls, Trailriders, and Cooper Creek trailheads.
6.5		SO	Turnoff to USFS Avery Peak picnic grounds on right.
	4.1	SO	Turnoff to USFS Avery Peak picnic grounds on left.
6.7		SO	Seasonal gate and bridge.
	3.9	SO	Bridge and seasonal gate.
7.0		SO	USFS Gothic Campground on left. Then track to Wash Gulch on left.
	3.6	SO	Track to Wash Gulch. Then USFS Gothic Campground on right.
7.6		SO	Track to Rustler Gulch on right.
	3.0	SO	Track to Rustler Gulch on left.
8.0		SO	Track on left.
	2.6	SO	Track on right.
8.8		SO	Track on left.
	1.8	SO	Track on right.
9.8		SO	Track on left to Emerald Lake.
	0.8	SO	Track on right to Emerald Lake.
10.6		SO	Schofield Pass summit. Paradise Basin track on left; trailhead to Gothic on right. Zero trip meter.
	0.0		Continue on main road toward Gothic and Crested Butte. Leaving White River National Forest and entering Gunnison National Forest on FR 317.
		GPS: N 39°00.93′ W 107°02.80′	
0.0			Continue straight ahead toward Marble. Leaving Gunnison National Forest and entering White River National Forest.
	4.4	SO	Schofield Pass summit. Paradise Basin track on right; trailhead to Gothic on left. Zero trip meter.
0.7		SO	Baroni Mine portal on right. Then cross through creek.
	3.7	SO	Cross through creek. Baroni Mine portal on left.
1.1		SO	Track on left to North Pole Basin.
	3.3	SO	Track on right to North Pole Basin.
1.5		SO	Bridge over South Fork of Crystal River.
	2.9	SO	Bridge over South Fork of Crystal River.
1.7		SO	Tracks on right.
	2.7	SO	Tracks on left.
2.3		SO	Track on left to waterfall just off the road. Cross bridge with waterfall on right.
	2.1	SO	Waterfall on left; cross bridge. Track on right to waterfall just off the road.
2.5		SO	Cross over river.
	1.9	SO	Cross over river.
2.7		SO	Cross through wide creek.
	1.7	SO	Cross through wide creek.

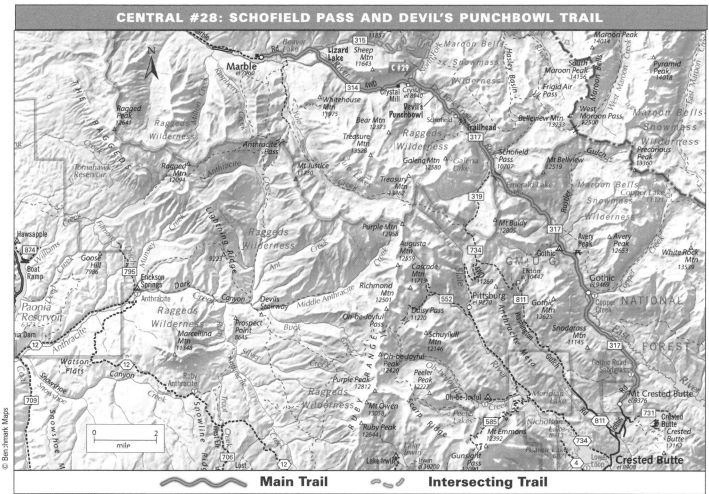

| Main Trail | | Intersecting Trail |

GPS: N 39°02.70' W 107°04.36'		
▼ 2.8	SO	Tight squeeze past one large rock.
1.6 ▲	SO	Tight squeeze past one large rock.
▼ 2.8-3.2	SO	Very narrow and rocky descent.
1.2-1.6 ▲	SO	Very narrow and rocky ascent.
▼ 3.2	SO	Narrow bridge over Crystal River.
1.2 ▲	SO	Narrow bridge over Crystal River.
GPS: N 39°02.99' W 107°04.67'		
▼ 4.4	BL	Intersection. Right goes to Central #29: Lead King Basin Trail. Zero trip meter.
0.0 ▲		Continue on main track toward Schofield Pass, Gothic, and Crested Butte.
GPS: N 39°03.56' W 107°05.77'		
▼ 0.0		Continue toward Crystal on FR 314.
4.3 ▲	BR	Intersection. Left goes to Central #29: Lead King Basin Trail. Zero trip meter.
▼ 0.5	SO	Crystal township.
3.8 ▲	SO	Crystal township.
▼ 0.6	SO	Cross over Crystal River.
3.7 ▲	SO	Cross over Crystal River.
▼ 0.7	SO	Crystal Mill on left.
3.6 ▲	SO	Crystal Mill on right.
GPS: N 39°03.56' W 107°06.22'		
▼ 2.9	SO	Track on left.
1.5 ▲	SO	Track on right.
▼ 3.9	SO	Lizard Lake on right.
0.4 ▲	SO	Lizard Lake on left.
GPS: N 39°04.19' W 107°09.21'		

▼ 4.2	SO	Bridge over Lost Trail Creek.
0.1 ▲	SO	Bridge over Lost Trail Creek.
▼ 4.3	BL	Intersection with Central #29: Lead King Basin Trail (FR 315) on right. Left to Marble. Zero trip meter.
0.0 ▲		Continue along main road.
GPS: N 39°04.49' W 107°09.50'		
▼ 0.0		Proceed toward Marble.
1.9 ▲	BR	Intersection with Central #29: Lead King Basin Trail (FR 315) on left. Zero trip meter.
▼ 0.6	SO	Road on right.
1.3 ▲	SO	Road on left.
▼ 1.2	SO	Beaver Lake on left.
0.7 ▲	SO	Beaver Lake on right.
▼ 1.5	TL	Stop sign.
0.4 ▲	TR	Stop sign.
▼ 1.6	TR	Intersection.
0.3 ▲	TL	Intersection.
▼ 1.7	SO	Bridge.
0.1 ▲	SO	Bridge.
▼ 1.8	TL/TR	Onto 1st Street; then right onto State Street.
0.1 ▲	TL/TR	Onto 1st Street; then right onto Main Street (CR 3/FR 315).
▼ 1.9		End in front of Marble Community Church on State Street.
0.0 ▲		On State Street in Marble, go to the Marble Community Church. Zero trip meter and proceed east.
GPS: N 39°04.25' W 107°11.30'		

Lead King Basin Trail

Starting Point:	**Intersection of Central #28: Schofield Pass and Devil's Punchbowl Trail (FR 314) and FR 315**
Finishing Point:	**Intersection of FR 315 and FR 314**
Total Mileage:	**7.7 miles**
Unpaved Mileage:	**7.7 miles**
Driving Time:	**1.75 hours**
Route Elevation:	**8,592 to 10,800 feet**
Usually Open:	**Late July to mid-September**
Difficulty Rating:	**5**
Scenic Rating:	**8**

Special Attractions

■ Abundant wildflowers in early summer.
■ The challenging, narrow, and rocky section at the east end of the route.

Description

This trail is a side road of Schofield Pass Road. It commences 3.7 miles west of Crystal township and 1.9 miles east of Marble and finishes 0.5 miles east of Crystal township.

Initially, FR 315 ascends from the road running alongside the Crystal River (FR 314) through pine and aspen forest. The road is bumpy with embedded rock and drainage channels cut across it but is not difficult in dry conditions. Sections of black soil can become very boggy after rain.

A series of switchbacks is encountered in an uphill section, but the surface is firm, and the only difficulty is caused by wheel ruts worn by other vehicles.

At about the 7-mile point the road gets considerably more difficult, especially in a full-size vehicle, as you follow the creek cascading down into the valley. Clearances between trees and rocks are tight. The route is more difficult if attempted from east to west rather than in the direction we have described.

The area is justly famous for the wildflowers that carpet the basin in July and August, and numerous aspen provide color later in the season.

Current Road Information

White River National Forest
Sopris Ranger District
620 Main Street
Carbondale, CO 81623
(970) 963-2266

Map References

USFS   White River National Forest
Maptech CD:
      Colorado Springs/Ski Areas/Central
Benchmark's *Colorado Road & Recreation Atlas*, p. 85
Colorado Atlas & Gazetteer, p. 46
The Roads of Colorado, p. 92
Trails Illustrated, #128

Route Directions

▼ 0.0			At the intersection of FR 314 and FR 315 between Marble and Crystal, zero trip meter and follow sign toward Lead King Basin.
	7.7 ▲		End at intersection with Central #28: Schofield Pass and Devil's Punchbowl Trail (FR 314) between Marble and Crystal.
		GPS: N 39°04.49' W 107°09.50'	
▼ 0.4		SO	Private track on left to Colorado Outward Bound School.
	7.3 ▲	SO	Private track on right to Colorado Outward Bound School.
▼ 0.7		SO	North Lost Creek Trailhead on left. Cross through North Lost Creek.
	7.0 ▲	SO	Cross through North Lost Creek. North Lost Creek Trailhead on right.
▼ 1.8		SO	Cross over creek.
	5.9 ▲	SO	Cross over creek.
▼ 2.0		BL	Fork in road. Continue on FR 315.
	5.7 ▲	BR	Fork in road. Continue on FR 315.

A gentle, scenic section surrounded by aspen stands and pine trees

As the trail ascends it gets rougher and more eroded

CENTRAL #29: LEAD KING BASIN TRAIL

Main Trail ~~~ **Intersecting Trail** ~~~

			GPS: N 39°04.68' W 107°07.46'
▼ 2.3		SO	Cross through creek.
5.4 ▲		SO	Cross through creek.
▼ 3.7		BR	Track on left.
4.0 ▲		BL	Track on right.
▼ 4.0		SO	Cross through creek. Then track on left.

3.7 ▲		SO	Track on right. Cross through creek.
▼ 4.1		SO	Track on left.
3.6 ▲		SO	Track on right.
▼ 6.1		SO	Cross through creek.
1.6 ▲		SO	Cross through creek.
▼ 6.2		SO	Cross through creek.
1.5 ▲		SO	Cross through creek.
▼ 6.3		SO	Trailhead parking area on left.
1.4 ▲		SO	Trailhead parking area on right.
▼ 6.5		SO	Track on left crosses through creek.
1.2 ▲		SO	Track on right crosses through creek.
▼ 6.6		BR	Cross bridge over creek. Bear right at each of two intersections.
1.1 ▲		BL	Bear left at each of two intersections. Cross bridge over creek.
▼ 6.7		SO	Cross through creek.
1.0 ▲		SO	Cross through creek.
▼ 7.7			End at intersection with FR 314. Marble and Crystal to the right. Schofield Pass, Crested Butte, and Gothic to the left.
0.0 ▲			At intersection of Central #28: Schofield Pass and Devil's Punchbowl Trail (FR 314) and FR 315, zero trip meter and proceed along FR 315.
			GPS: N 39°03.56' W 107°05.77'

Lost Lake

Old Monarch Pass Road

Starting Point:	**Intersection of US 50 and FR 237 (1 mile east of Monarch Pass)**
Finishing Point:	**Intersection of Central #34: Tomichi Pass Trail (FR 888) and FR 237**
Total Mileage:	**10.3 miles**
Unpaved Mileage:	**10.3 miles**
Driving Time:	**30 minutes**
Route Elevation:	**8,900 to 11,375 feet**
Usually Open:	**Early June to November**
Difficulty Rating:	**1**
Scenic Rating:	**7**

Special Attractions

■ Access to a network of 4WD trails.

■ An alternative to the main highway, US 50.

History

In 1878, 11 years before finding gold near Wagon Wheel Gap and establishing the town that was to bear his name, Nicholas Creede found silver on the east side of Monarch Pass; within months, 3,000 prospectors had arrived. The discovery led to the establishment of several towns in the area, including Maysville, Garfield (originally called Junction City), and Monarch (called Chaffee City until 1884). In the same year,

View to the southeast of the Monarch Crest Tram on top of Monarch Mountain

View from above the summit of Old Monarch Pass

silver, gold, and lead were discovered in the Tomichi Valley on the west side of Monarch Pass.

In 1880, the Denver & Rio Grande Railroad built a spur line from Salida to Monarch, which continued to operate in summers until 1982. Also in 1880, a wagon road was built to serve as a stage route. This route travels from the ski area and connects with Old Monarch Pass Road. Today it is sometimes referred to as the Old, Old Monarch Pass Road. It had been open as a 4WD road but has now been closed by the forest service.

In the 1920s, Old Monarch Pass Road was opened, crossing the pass about 1 mile south of the original route. Although it was designed as a motor vehicle road, it was never paved but is still well maintained.

Following much debate about whether Marshall Pass or Monarch Pass should be used as the route for US 50, the present Monarch Pass Road was constructed in 1939. The ski area opened in the same year. When it opened, Charles Vail, the state highway engineer, named the pass after himself and had "Vail Pass" signs placed at the summit. Local residents expressed their objections to this unilateral decision by obliterating the signs with black paint. Many years later, his wish was more permanently granted along I-70.

Description

Old Monarch Pass Road (FR 237) provides a good alternative route between US 50 from the east of Monarch Pass through to the 4WD roads in the Tomichi Valley. It commences 1 mile east of the present summit, and the entrance is well marked. The road is graded, wide, and easy for a passenger vehicle to negotiate. There are some sections with steep drop-offs, but in dry conditions these do not pose any serious problems.

The route follows a high-voltage power line through dense pine forest with only occasional stands of aspens and few expansive mountain views. It is not an unusually scenic route, and the best views are at the highest point, near the main pass.

CENTRAL #30: OLD MONARCH PASS TRAIL

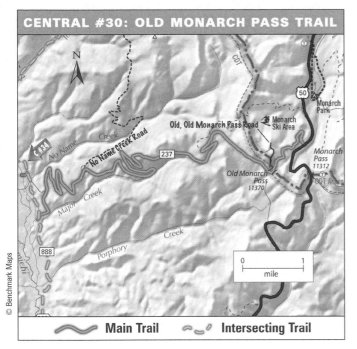

© Benchmark Maps

〰️ **Main Trail** 〰️ **Intersecting Trail**

Current Road Information

Grand Mesa, Uncompahgre, & Gunnison National Forests
Gunnison Ranger District
216 North Colorado
Gunnison, CO 81230
(970) 641-0471

Map References

USFS Gunnison National Forest
Maptech CD:
      Colorado Springs/Ski Areas/Central;
      Alamosa/Pueblo/South Central
Benchmark's *Colorado Road & Recreation Atlas*, p. 98
Colorado Atlas & Gazetteer, pp. 59, 69
The Roads of Colorado, p. 110
Trails Illustrated, #130 (incomplete), #139

Route Directions

▼ 0.0   From US 50, turn onto Monarch Pass Road (FR 237). Zero trip meter and proceed west.
10.3 ▲   End at intersection with US 50.

GPS: N 38°30.27' W 106°19.65'

▼ 0.2   **SO**   Road on right dead-ends in 0.3 miles.
10.1 ▲   **SO**   Road on left dead-ends in 0.3 miles.

▼ 1.1   **SO**   Track on right.
9.2 ▲   **SO**   Track on left.

▼ 1.3   **SO**   Monarch Pass summit. Vandals had removed the plaque from the summit marker when we were there.
9.0 ▲   **SO**   Monarch Pass summit.

GPS: N 38°29.90' W 106°20.25'

▼ 2.8   **SO**   Campsites on left.
7.5 ▲   **SO**   Campsites on right.

▼ 3.3   **SO**   Campsites on left.
7.0 ▲   **SO**   Campsites on right.

▼ 4.6   **SO**   Track on left.
5.7 ▲   **SO**   Track on right.

▼ 7.6   **SO**   Track marked to Galena Gulch and No Name

Good backcountry campsite with a creek near the trail

     Creek on right. Note: This trail is gated about 3 miles in at GPS: N 38°30.84' W 106°23.09'. There are ruins of an old mine where the track is blocked.

2.7 ▲   **SO**   Track marked to Galena Gulch and No Name Creek on left.

GPS: N 38°29.88' W 106°23.76'

▼ 8.8   **SO**   Short track on left to campsites with attractive views.
1.5 ▲   **SO**   Short track on right to campsites with attractive views.

▼ 10.3   End at intersection with Central #34: Tomichi Pass Trail (FR 888).
0.0 ▲   At intersection of Central #34: Tomichi Pass Trail (FR 888) and FR 237, zero trip meter and proceed along FR 237 toward Old Monarch Pass.

GPS: N 38°29.16' W 106°24.58'

Sign marking the summit of Old Monarch Pass

Black Sage Pass Road

Starting Point:	Intersection of Central #34: Tomichi Pass Trail (FR 888) and FR 887
Finishing Point:	Intersection of Central #32: Waunita Pass Road (FR 763) and FR 887
Total Mileage:	7.0 miles
Unpaved Mileage:	7.0 miles
Driving Time:	30 minutes
Route Elevation:	8,970 to 9,745 feet
Usually Open:	Early July to late October
Difficulty Rating:	1
Scenic Rating:	7

Special Attractions

■ Easy road through gentle, attractive countryside.
■ Access to a network of 4WD trails.

History

The Hayden survey party traveled this route between Pitkin and Whitepine. When silver was discovered near Pitkin in the late 1870s, this route provided a lower, more undulating, albeit longer, entryway to the area. By 1880, a stagecoach and numerous freight wagons were using this road daily.

In 1882, the Denver, South Park & Pacific Railroad opened the line to Pitkin through the Alpine Tunnel. The route remained in use to deliver freight from Pitkin. By this time, the resort of Waunita Hot Springs was very popular and also needed stagecoaches and freight wagons to ferry tourists and supplies.

Subsequently, the pass was used principally for access between Whitepine and Gunnison. The stage way station at the summit of the pass continued to operate into the late 1890s.

Description

The road is accessible to passenger cars under dry conditions. It provides an easy drive through attractive ranchland and a gentle ascent to a forested summit before the scenery widens out into an open valley.

The route connects with a number of other routes in this book. To the east is Old Monarch Pass Road, and to the north are Tomichi Pass, Hancock Pass, and the Alpine Tunnel.

Current Road Information

Grand Mesa, Uncompahgre & Gunnison National Forests
Gunnison Ranger District
216 North Colorado
Gunnison, CO 81230
(970) 641-0471

Map References

USFS   Gunnison National Forest
Maptech CD:
     Colorado Springs/Ski Areas/Central;
     Alamosa/Pueblo/South Central
Benchmark's *Colorado Road & Recreation Atlas*, p. 98
Colorado Atlas & Gazetteer, pp. 59, 69
The Roads of Colorado, p. 109
Trails Illustrated, #139

Route Directions

▼ 0.0			At intersection of Central #34: Tomichi Pass Trail (FR 888) and FR 887, zero trip meter and proceed west along FR 887 toward Waunita Hot Springs.
	3.5 ▲		End at intersection with Central #34: Tomichi Pass Trail (FR 888).
		GPS: N 38°30.10' W 106°25.26'	
▼ 1.1		SO	Cattle guard.
	2.4 ▲	SO	Cattle guard.
▼ 1.5		SO	Track on left to campsites.
	2.0 ▲	SO	Track on right to campsites.
▼ 2.2		SO	Track on right.
	1.3 ▲	SO	Track on left.
▼ 3.5		SO	Summit of Black Sage Pass. Zero trip meter. Cross cattle guard. Short side road on left

View from the summit of Black Sage Pass

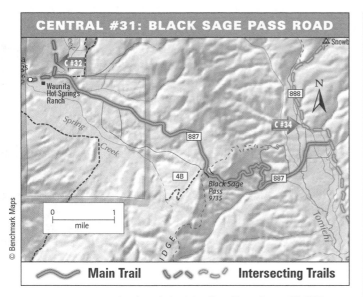

CENTRAL #31: BLACK SAGE PASS ROAD

Main Trail

Intersecting Trails

© Benchmark Maps

		dead-ends in 1.2 miles. Remain on FR 887.
0.0 ▲		Continue along FR 887.

GPS: N 38°29.46′ W 106°27.11′

▼ 0.0		Continue toward Waunita Hot Springs and Pitkin.
3.5 ▲	SO	Track on right. Cross cattle guard. Summit of Black Sage Pass. Zero trip meter.

▼ 1.7	SO	Cattle guard.
1.8 ▲	SO	Cattle guard.

Summit of Black Sage Pass

▼ 3.3	TL	Intersection with FR 774 on right.
0.2 ▲	TR	Intersection with FR 774 straight on. Remain on FR 887.

GPS: N 38°30.81′ W 106°29.61′

▼ 3.5		End at intersection with Central #32: Waunita Pass Road.
0.0 ▲		At intersection of FR 887 and FR 763, zero trip meter and proceed east on FR 887.

GPS: N38°30.82′ W106°29.90′

Dirt bikes on the western end of Black Sage Pass Road

Waunita Pass Road

Starting Point:	Pitkin
Finishing Point:	Intersection of CR/FR 887 and US 50
Total Mileage:	19.0 miles
Unpaved Mileage:	19.0 miles
Driving Time:	1 hour
Route Elevation:	9,190 to 10,303 feet
Usually Open:	Year-round
Difficulty Rating:	1
Scenic Rating:	6

Special Attractions
- Easy road through gentle, attractive countryside.
- Access to a network of 4WD trails.

History
With the rich ore discoveries in the Monarch Pass area and on through the Tomichi Valley in 1878, stages and freight operations made regular journeys between Salida and Pitkin across Monarch, Black Sage, and Waunita Passes.

In 1880, the Denver & Rio Grande Railroad built a spur line from Salida to Monarch; and in 1882, the Alpine Tunnel railroad was opened by the Denver, South Park & Pacific Railroad, providing a railroad to Pitkin.

Waunita Pass Road continued to be used for freight to the Tomichi Valley silver mining area. The route also provided access between Pitkin and the resort facilities at Waunita Hot Springs. However, the road was in decline from the time of the railroad.

The road passes the site of Bowerman where in 1903 J. C. Bowerman struck gold at the Independent Mine and started a rush into the area. Although newspapers heavily promoted the strike, it is doubtful that the coverage was justified by the true extent of the discovery.

A sketch of Waunita Hot Springs Resort in 1916 showing hotel, cottages, post office, tennis courts, and bathhouses

Bowerman told people that his find was so rich that even a single blast could yield thousands of dollars. However, the first shipment from the Bowerman mine was postponed many times, and he became secretive about the true assay of his mine and even fenced off the property. In the end, it took more than a year for him to make the first shipment, by which time a boomtown had been incorporated. By then, however, the initial enthusiasm was already on the wane.

Description
The route is generally accessible to passenger vehicles, passing through gentle valley scenery along Hot Springs Creek, then through pine and aspen forest before reaching the pass and dropping down into Pitkin.

The town site of Bowerman is on private property.

Current Road Information
Grand Mesa, Uncompahgre & Gunnison National Forests
Gunnison Ranger District
216 North Colorado
Gunnison, CO 81230
(970) 641-0471

View of the rolling hills surrounding Waunita Pass Road

Waunita Hot Springs Reservoir

Map References

USFS   Gunnison National Forest
Maptech CD:
           Colorado Springs/Ski Areas/Central;
           Alamosa/Pueblo/South Central
Benchmark's *Colorado Road & Recreation Atlas*, p. 98
Colorado Atlas & Gazetteer, pp. 59, 69
The Roads of Colorado, p. 109
Trails Illustrated, #139

Route Directions

▼ 0.0		From the Pitkin City Hall building at Main and 4th Streets in Pitkin, zero trip meter and proceed southwest.
10.7 ▲		End at the Pitkin City Hall building at Main and 4th Streets in Pitkin.
GPS: N 38°36.48' W 106°31.15'		
▼ 0.1	TL	Intersection with 2nd Street on left.
10.6 ▲	TR	Onto Main Street.
▼ 0.2	TR	Onto State Street.
10.5 ▲	TL	Onto 2nd Street.
▼ 0.3	TL	Onto 1st Street.
10.4 ▲	TR	Onto State Street.
▼ 0.4	BR	Fork with FR 763 on right.
10.3 ▲	BL	Fork with 1st Street on left.
▼ 0.6	SO	Bridge over Quartz Creek.
10.1 ▲	SO	Bridge over Quartz Creek.
▼ 1.5	SO	Cattle guard; then Gunnison National Forest sign.
9.2 ▲	SO	Cattle guard.
▼ 3.4	SO	Track on right.
7.3 ▲	SO	Track on left.
▼ 3.8	SO	Track on left.
6.9 ▲	SO	Track on right.
▼ 4.8	SO	Summit of Waunita Pass. Road to Wiley Gulch on left and FR 698 on right.
5.9 ▲	SO	FR 698 on left and Wiley Gulch road on right. Summit of Waunita Pass.

GPS: N 38°34.68' W 106°30.56'		
▼ 6.6	SO	Two small tracks on left.
4.1 ▲	SO	Two small tracks on right.
▼ 6.9	SO	Site of Bowerman (private property).
3.8 ▲	SO	Site of Bowerman (private property).
GPS: N 38°33.75' W 106°30.69'		
▼ 8.6	SO	Wiley Gulch on left.
2.1 ▲	SO	Wiley Gulch on right.
▼ 10.7	TR	Intersection. Track on the left is Central #31: Black Sage Pass Road. Zero trip meter.
0.0 ▲		Proceed toward Pitkin on FR 763.
GPS: N 38°30.82' W 106°29.90'		
▼ 0.0		Proceed toward Waunita Hot Springs on FR 887.
8.3 ▲	TL	T-intersection. Straight on is Central #31: Black Sage Pass Road. Zero trip meter.
▼ 0.2	SO	Cattle guard.

Waunita Hot Springs Resort today

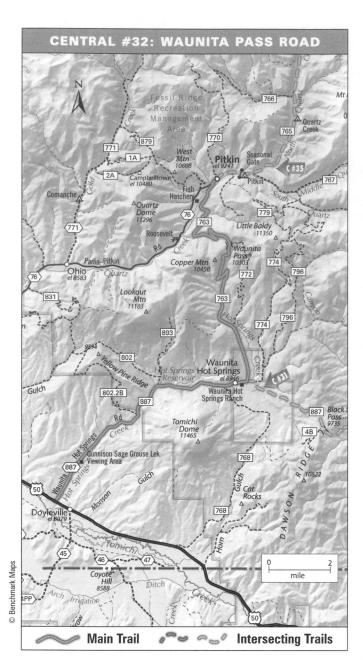

© Benchmark Maps

~ **Main Trail**   ~ ~ ~   **Intersecting Trails**

8.1 ▲	SO	Cattle guard.
▼ 0.5	SO	Waunita Hot Springs Ranch Resort on right.
7.8 ▲	SO	Waunita Hot Springs Ranch Resort on left.
▼ 2.4	SO	Track to Waunita Hot Springs Reservoir on right.
5.9 ▲	SO	Track to Waunita Hot Springs Reservoir on left.
▼ 2.5	SO	Track on right.
5.8 ▲	SO	Track on left.
▼ 2.6	SO	Great Horse Gulch track on right.
5.7 ▲	SO	Great Horse Gulch track on left.
▼ 2.9	SO	Short track on left.
5.4 ▲	SO	Short track on right.
▼ 3.5	SO	Bridge over Hot Springs Creek.
4.8 ▲	SO	Bridge over Hot Springs Creek.
▼ 8.3		Cattle guard and end at intersection with US 50.
0.0 ▲		At intersection of US 50 and CR/FR 887, zero trip meter and proceed north on 887.

GPS: N 38°27.39' W 106°37.02'

Hancock Pass Trail

Starting Point:	St. Elmo
Finishing Point:	Intersection with Central #36: Alpine Tunnel Road (FR 839) and FR 888
Total Mileage:	9.3 miles
Unpaved Mileage:	9.3 miles
Driving Time:	1.25 hours
Route Elevation:	9,980 to 12,250 feet
Usually Open:	Early July to October
Difficulty Rating:	4 (5 if traveling toward St. Elmo)
Scenic Rating:	9

Special Attractions

- St. Elmo township and the sites of Hancock and Romley.
- Spectacular summit views of Brittle Silver Basin.
- Hiking trail to the east portal of the Alpine Tunnel.
- Moderately difficult 4WD route.
- Access to a network of 4WD trails.

History

The history of the Hancock Pass crossing is poorly documented, perhaps because of the confusion between this pass and Williams Pass, which is located a couple of miles farther north. Hancock Pass was used as a mining route in the 1880s but has never been an important commercial route. It was not officially named until 1962. Much of the route on the east side of the pass follows the old Denver, South Park & Pacific railway grade toward the Alpine Tunnel.

This trip originates at one of the most photographed and best-preserved ghost towns in Colorado: St. Elmo (see box).

Old log cabin remains on Hancock Pass Trail

A rock has crashed into one of the cabins near the Allie Belle Mine

Above: the Allie Belle Mine building in 1950
Below: the precarious position of the building today

The route passes the town site of Romley founded in the late 1870s for the workers of the nearby Mary Murphy and Pat Murphy Mines.

The Mary Murphy Mine was by far the biggest mine in the Alpine District. It is said to be named after a kind nurse in Denver who once cared for the prospector who discovered the mine. The Mary Murphy grew so large that it supported Romley, St. Elmo, and Hancock, making the region quite prosperous.

When the Denver, South Park & Pacific Railroad came through Romley in 1881, a 5,000-foot tramway was built to transfer ore to the railroad cars. In 1908, tragedy struck when sparks from a train engine kindled a fire that reduced most of Romley to ashes. When the town was rebuilt, the buildings were painted bright red with white trim, although nobody knows why!

The Mary Murphy Mine, which continued to operate until 1926, is located on the road to Pomeroy Lakes (Central #42). In 1982, the mining company destroyed the buildings

Hancock Lakes

that remained in the deserted town.

The Denver, South Park & Pacific Railroad established the town of Hancock in 1880 to support the construction of the Alpine Tunnel. It was named for the Hancock Placer, the first claim in the area. Most of the hundreds of workers employed to build the tunnel lived in Hancock. With five general stores, a hotel, several saloons and restaurants, and two sawmills cutting lumber for the tunnel and railroad, the town supported a population of close to 1,000.

After the Alpine Tunnel was completed in 1881, Hancock became a station on the line to Pitkin. Main Street faced the railroad tracks. The population declined substantially when the tunnel was completed, but many workers were still needed to keep the tracks clear of heavy snow. Large crews labored constantly throughout winter months.

Hancock's population continued to dwindle when many of the area mines closed down, but the big decline occurred after 1910 when the Alpine Tunnel caved in. Hancock became a true ghost town. All the buildings have now collapsed, although the structures and foundations are clearly visible in the meadow. The last to fall away was a saloon, and the remains of it and other buildings are still evident.

Description

Romley is located about 2.5 miles from St. Elmo. Shortly past Romley is the turnoff for the road to Pomeroy Lakes, which goes past the Mary Murphy Mine.

At the 4.8-mile point is one of the most precarious-looking structures you are likely to see. The building, which looks as though it will slide into the middle of the road at any moment, once stored ore produced by the Allie Belle Mine while it was waiting to be loaded into rail trucks. Despite appearances, the building has been cantilevered this way for years and is presumably quite sound. A number of other mine buildings are located above this structure. A huge rock has rolled down the hill and crashed through the back wall of a miners' cabin—we hope not while he was in residence!

Not far past the leaning storage shed lies the town site of Hancock.

Just past Hancock, there is a parking lot at the start of the hiking trail to the Atlantic railway station, which was located at the eastern end of the Alpine Tunnel. Before 1992, this road was open to vehicles, but a landslide blocked it that year, leaving as the only access a 2.5-mile hike along the old railway grade.

Shortly after the parking lot there is an intersection. Turn right and continue on the trail to Hancock Pass. Bear left to a 1.4-mile road to Hancock Lakes Trailhead (GPS coordinates: N 38°37.18′ W 106°21.29′). A half-mile walk from the trailhead are the picturesque Hancock Lakes.

Until this intersection, the route is an easy 2WD road and suitable for passenger vehicles. However, from this point on, the road becomes progressively tougher and is rated 4WD.

The summit of the pass provides a spectacular view of Brittle Silver Basin and the ridge of 13,000-foot peaks beyond. The Tomichi Pass shelf road is clearly visible, clinging to the southern ridge surrounding the basin.

From the summit, the remaining mile of road descends steeply into Brittle Silver Basin. For the last hundred yards, loose rocks make getting traction a little difficult, especially if you are going uphill toward the pass.

The descent from Hancock Pass looking toward Tomichi Pass

Current Road Information

Grand Mesa, Uncompahgre & Gunnison National Forests
Gunnison Ranger District
216 North Colorado
Gunnison, CO 81230
(970) 641-0471

Map References

USFS   Gunnison National Forest; San Isabel National Forest

Maptech CD:
   Colorado Springs/Ski Areas/Central

Benchmark's *Colorado Road & Recreation Atlas*, p. 98

Colorado Atlas & Gazetteer, p. 59

The Roads of Colorado, p. 110

Trails Illustrated, #130

Route Directions

▼ 0.0			At Miner's Exchange general store in St. Elmo, zero trip meter and proceed east out of St. Elmo on CR 162.
	5.7 ▲		End at Miner's Exchange general store in St. Elmo.
		GPS: N 38°42.23′ W 106°20.65′	
▼ 0.3		TR	Onto CR/FR 295 toward Hancock.
	5.4 ▲	TL	Onto CR 162 toward St. Elmo.
▼ 0.8		SO	San Isabel National Forest Service board sign on right.
	4.9 ▲	SO	San Isabel National Forest Service board sign on left.
▼ 2.4		SO	Cross through creek.
	3.3 ▲	SO	Cross through creek.
▼ 2.5		SO	Romley on right.
	3.2 ▲	SO	Romley on left.
▼ 3.1		BR	Road forks.
	2.6 ▲	SO	Track on right.
▼ 3.3		SO	Central #42: Pomeroy Lakes and Mary Murphy Mine Trail is on left.
	2.4 ▲	SO	Track on right to Pomeroy Lakes and Mary Murphy Mine.
		GPS: N 38°40.38′ W 106°21.95′	
▼ 4.8		SO	Old ore storage house for the Allie Belle Mine on left, a precariously perched building overhanging the road.
	0.9 ▲	SO	Ore storage house for the Allie Belle Mine on right.
		GPS: N 38°39.08′ W 106°22.07′	
▼ 5.5		SO	Hancock town site.
	0.2 ▲	SO	Hancock town site.
		GPS: N 38°38.40′ W 106°21.64′	
▼ 5.6		BL	Cross over creek; then fork in road. Follow sign to Hancock Pass and Hancock Lakes. Track on right is parking for walking track to the Alpine Tunnel east portal.
	0.1 ▲	BR	Left is parking area. Bear right toward Hancock; then cross over creek.
▼ 5.7		TR	U-turn onto FR 299 toward Hancock Pass. (SO goes to Hancock Lakes Trailhead.) Zero trip meter.
	0.0 ▲		Proceed toward Hancock.
		GPS: N 38°38.27′ W 106°21.63′	
▼ 0.0			Proceed along FR 299.
	3.6 ▲	TL	U-turn left goes to Hancock. Right goes to Hancock Lakes. Zero trip meter.

CENTRAL #33: HANCOCK PASS TRAIL

(map)

Main Trail   Intersecting Trails

© Benchmark Maps

▼ 1.5		SO	Track on right to mine.
	2.1 ▲	SO	Track on left to mine.
▼ 1.9-2.0		SO	Mine portals on right along the road.
	1.6-1.7 ▲	SO	Mine portals on left along the road.
▼ 2.0		SO	Hancock Pass sign is slightly before the summit. After crest, road is now named FR 266.
	1.6 ▲	SO	Hancock Pass sign is slightly past the summit. After crest, road is now named FR 299.

GPS: N 38°37.31′ W 106°22.44′

▼ 2.9		SO	Rough and rocky shallow crossing through creek. Remains of old cabin on right.
	0.7 ▲	SO	Remains of old cabin on left. Cross through creek.
▼ 3.0		TR	Intersection. Left to Tomichi Pass (FR 888) and right to Pitkin.
	0.6 ▲	BL	Intersection. FR 888 continues to Tomichi Pass. Follow road to Hancock Pass (FR 266).

GPS: N 38°36.69′ W 106°22.69′

| ▼ 3.6 | | | End at intersection with Central #36: Alpine Tunnel Road (FR 839). |
| | 0.0 ▲ | | At intersection of Central #36: Alpine Tunnel Road (FR 839) and FR 888, zero trip meter and proceed along FR 888. |

GPS: N 38°36.83′ W 106°23.37′

Tomichi Pass Trail

Starting Point:	Intersection of Central #33: Hancock Pass Trail (FR 266) and FR 888
Finishing Point:	Intersection of FR 888 and US 50
Total Mileage:	15.9 miles
Unpaved Mileage:	12.1 miles
Driving Time:	2 hours
Route Elevation:	8,600 to 12,020 feet
Usually Open:	Early July to October
Difficulty Rating:	5
Scenic Rating:	9

Special Attractions

- A challenging 4WD trail.
- Wonderful summit views of Brittle Silver Basin and Hancock Pass Trail.
- Town sites of Tomichi and Whitepine.
- Access to a network of 4WD trails.

History

"Tomichi" is the Ute word for hot water, a reference to the many hot springs in the area.

The main access to the mining areas of Tomichi and Whitepine was southeast to Monarch via Old Monarch Pass or west to Gunnison via Black Sage Pass. From the late 1870s, this entire area was teeming with miners, and Tomichi Pass Road was built to provide access north from the mining settlements of Tomichi and Whitepine to the Denver, South Park & Pacific Railroad and the towns of Pitkin and, via Hancock Pass, St. Elmo. However, the route was too high and difficult to be developed much beyond a pack trail, although wagons did use it when road and weather conditions allowed.

Whitepine Cemetery

Akron Mine remains

A log bridge over a muddy section of Tomichi Pass Trail

Tomichi was laid out because of silver finds in the area in 1880. Before long, the town's population swelled to nearly 1,500. A smelter was constructed to serve the Magna Charta Tunnel, the best producing silver mine in the area, and the other local mines. Unfortunately, it was destroyed by fire in 1883. The silver crash in 1893 drastically reduced the town's population. All the nearby mines were closed except the Eureka, which operated until 1895. In 1899, a huge avalanche struck the town, destroying all the buildings and mine machinery. Five or six people were killed, and all survivors abandoned the site.

Prospectors began arriving in Whitepine in 1879, and the town was founded in 1880 and thrived throughout the 1880s. Its population reached about 3,000, but despite high expectations, none of the area mines produced much, and with the silver crash of 1893, the town was doomed. By the following year, Whitepine was virtually deserted.

The town saw a brief resurgence of activity in 1901 and staged a more lasting comeback when lead, zinc, and copper were mined during World Wars I and II, mainly at the Akron Mine. The Akron Mine hit a high point in 1948, when it reached production of 100 tons per day. In 1946, Whitepine opened a ski area with an 1,800-foot rope tow, but after just two years the tow was dismantled and moved. Whitepine is now primarily a summer residence, with many reconstructed miners' cabins.

The Whitepine and Tomichi stage line serviced the two towns with regular stages to Sargents from 1881. At Sargents, passengers could connect with the Denver & Rio Grande Railroad, which reached town that year following the completion of the line across Marshall Pass.

Description

Tomichi Pass Trail remains one of the more difficult roads in the area. On the north side of the pass, the road crosses a plank bridge over boggy ground before climbing a very narrow shelf that can be blocked by talus slides. It may be necessary to clear the road in order to pass safely. The road is certainly better suited to a smaller 4WD vehicle, but we have traveled it both ways in a Suburban, so it is possible to safely negotiate it in a full-sized vehicle. The wrecked 4WD vehicle below the road serves as a cautionary billboard for the reckless.

The summit provides a wonderful view back to Hancock Pass Trail. On the south side of the pass, the road begins a long, fairly gentle descent, with narrow sections where passing another vehicle is difficult. The road surface is rough but is mainly embedded rock and provides a sound footing. People who are afraid of heights will be pleased to know that drop-offs along this road are mostly restricted to the immediate vicinity of the summit of the pass.

Sign near the cemetery hints of the rough ascent to Tomichi Pass

Only a few headstones remain at Tomichi Cemetery

View of the Tomichi Pass Trail from Hancock Pass

Once the road descends below timberline, it becomes smoother and easier. About 3 miles after the pass, the road goes through the old Tomichi Cemetery. This heavily forested site is all that remains of the Tomichi township.

From Whitepine, the road may be negotiated in a car.

Current Road Information
Grand Mesa, Uncompahgre & Gunnison National Forests
Gunnison Ranger District
216 North Colorado
Gunnison, CO 81230
(970) 641-0471

Map References
USFS Gunnison National Forest
Maptech CD:
      Colorado Springs/Ski Areas/Central;
      Alamosa/Pueblo/South Central
Benchmark's *Colorado Road & Recreation Atlas*, p. 98
Colorado Atlas & Gazetteer, pp. 59, 69
The Roads of Colorado, p. 110
Trails Illustrated, #130, #139

Route Directions

▼ 0.0			From intersection of FR 266 and FR 888, zero trip meter and proceed along FR 888 toward Tomichi.
	15.9 ▲		End at intersection with Central #33: Hancock Pass Trail (FR 266). Straight ahead leads to Central #36: Alpine Tunnel Road.
		GPS: N 38°36.69' W 106°22.69'	
▼ 0.3		SO	Interesting mine with several old buildings, an old boiler, and open portal.
	15.6 ▲	SO	Interesting mine with several old buildings, an old boiler, and open portal.
		GPS: N 38°36.62' W 106°22.46'	
▼ 0.8		SO	Plank bridge over boggy area.
	15.1 ▲	SO	Plank bridge over boggy area.
▼ 1.1		SO	Summit of Tomichi Pass.
	14.8 ▲	SO	Summit of Tomichi Pass.
		GPS: N 38°36.20' W 106°22.95'	
▼ 1.3		SO	Walking trail on right to Canyon Creek, South Quartz, Horseshoe Creek.

14.6 ▲		SO	Walking trail on left to Canyon Creek, South Quartz, Horseshoe Creek.
▼ 1.9		SO	Cross through creek.
	14.0 ▲	SO	Cross through creek.
▼ 2.0		SO	Cross through creek.
	13.9 ▲	SO	Cross through creek.
▼ 2.4		SO	Cross through creek.
	13.5 ▲	SO	Cross through creek.
▼ 2.6		SO	Cross through creek.
	13.3 ▲	SO	Cross through creek.
▼ 2.9		SO	Cross through creek.
	13.0 ▲	SO	Cross through creek.
▼ 3.4		SO	Cross through creek.
	12.5 ▲	SO	Cross through creek.
▼ 4.0		SO	Tomichi Cemetery on left. Bear right at intersection with FR 888.1C.
	11.9 ▲	SO	Tomichi Cemetery on right. Bear left at FR 888.1C.
		GPS: N 38°34.26' W 106°22.19'	
▼ 4.1		SO	Cross through creek.
	11.8 ▲	SO	Cross through creek.
▼ 4.2		SO	Track on left.
	11.7 ▲	SO	Track on right.
▼ 4.3		SO	Track on left.
	11.6 ▲	SO	Track on right.
▼ 4.4		TL	Track on right is a dead end. Turn toward Whitepine.
	11.5 ▲	TR	Track on left is a dead end. Turn toward Tomichi Pass.
		GPS: N 38°34.06' W 106°22.44'	
▼ 6.1		SO	Bridge over Tomichi Creek.
	9.8 ▲	SO	Bridge over Tomichi Creek.
▼ 6.5		SO	Town of Whitepine.
	9.4 ▲	SO	Town of Whitepine.
		GPS: N 38°32.59' W 106°23.57'	
▼ 6.8		SO	Mine and mill on left.
	9.1 ▲	SO	Mine and mill on right.
▼ 8.4		SO	USFS Snowblind Campground on left.

Rocky intersection of Tomichi Pass Trail and Hancock Pass Trail

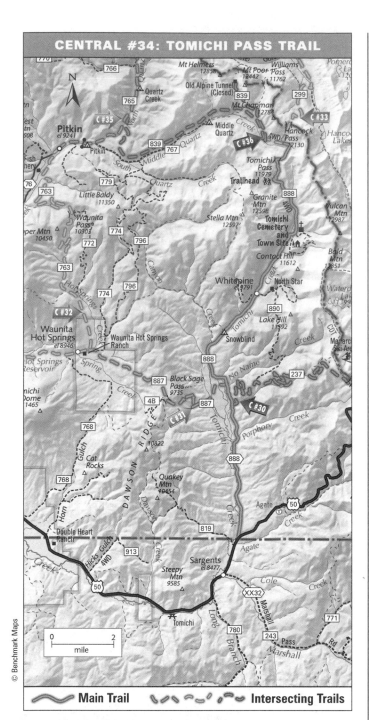

~~~ Main Trail **Intersecting Trails**

7.5 ▲	SO	USFS Snowblind Campground on right.	
▼ 10.0	SO	Intersection with Central #31: Black Sage Pass Road (FR 887) to the right.	
5.9 ▲	SO	Intersection with Central #31: Black Sage Pass Road (FR 887) to the left.	
GPS: N 38°30.11' W 106°25.25'			
▼ 11.4	SO	Central #30: Old Monarch Pass Road on left.	
4.5 ▲	SO	Central #30: Old Monarch Pass Road on right.	
▼ 12.1	SO	Road becomes paved.	
3.8 ▲	SO	Pavement ends.	
▼ 15.9		End at intersection with US 50.	
0.0 ▲		At intersection of US 50 and FR 888, zero trip meter and proceed along FR 888 toward Whitepine.	
GPS: N 38°25.40 W 106°24.36'			

Cumberland Pass Trail

Starting Point:	Tincup
Finishing Point:	Pitkin
Total Mileage:	15.7 miles
Unpaved Mileage:	15.2 miles
Driving Time:	1.5 hours
Route Elevation:	9,190 to 12,015 feet
Usually Open:	Early July to late September
Difficulty Rating:	3
Scenic Rating:	10

Special Attractions

- The historic and attractive town of Tincup, one of the wildest towns of the old West.
- Tincup Cemetery.
- Access to a multitude of side roads near the summit.
- Spectacular, panoramic summit views.
- Bon Ton Mine, with its deserted cabins and mine buildings.

History

The main road was built in 1882, upgrading an earlier pack trail. Until this time, Tincup had received the majority of its supplies across the gentler slopes of Cottonwood Pass. However, when the Denver, South Park & Pacific Railroad reached Pitkin in 1882, it became necessary to have a good freight route from Tincup to Quartz, the major depot established by the railroad 2.5 miles north of Pitkin.

Description

The main road over Cumberland Pass is one of the highest 2WD roads in the United States. This 4WD road takes an alternative, more direct, but slower route from Tincup to the north side of the pass.

The route leaves Tincup and travels past the old cemetery, which consists of four grassy knolls. One was for Catholics, one for Protestants, and another for Jews; the fourth—and

Boot Hill section of Tincup Cemetery

The panoramic view afforded as the trail croosses a meadow near the summit

Log cabin ruins near the Bon Ton Mine

largest—is the Boot Hill section, which was reserved as the final resting place for those who died with their boots on and guns blazing. The size of Boot Hill is a reflection of Tincup's notoriety as one of the wildest towns of the old West.

This route turns off from the main Cumberland Pass road at the 0.3-mile point. The turnoff is unmarked and not easily noticed. As it climbs toward the pass, the road passes numerous abandoned mines, rusting mining machinery, and decaying cabins as it winds through the pine trees. Although it is narrow in sections and has some loose surfaces, the road provides no particular difficulty in dry conditions.

As the road ascends above timberline, magnificent panoramic views open up, and numerous 4WD trails crisscross the area. Staying on the correct trail can be tricky in this section; fortunately, the summit is visible, and most trails allow you to head in that direction. Because so many people use these roads, it is especially important to Tread Lightly! and remain on the trails open to 4WD vehicles.

At the summit, the high peaks of the Sawatch Range dominate the skyline to the east, the Elk Mountains are in the distance to the west, and the Willow Creek Valley is to the north, with the main 2WD road to Tincup visible as it descends into the valley.

The descent toward Pitkin is along a well-maintained 2WD road. It passes through the remains of the Bon Ton Mine, which has numerous old cabins. The mine commenced

A footbridge to the Protestant knoll of Tincup Cemetery

operations around 1910 but found its greatest success when it switched to molybdenum production.

Five miles past the Bon Ton is the turnoff for the Alpine Tunnel and Tomichi and Hancock Passes.

Current Road Information

Grand Mesa, Uncompahgre & Gunnison National Forests
Gunnison Ranger District
216 North Colorado
Gunnison, CO 81230
(970) 641-0471

Map References

USFS Gunnison National Forest
Maptech CD:
        Colorado Springs/Ski Areas/Central
Benchmark's *Colorado Road & Recreation Atlas*, pp. 86, 98
Colorado Atlas & Gazetteer, p. 59
The Roads of Colorado, p. 109
Trails Illustrated, #130

Route Directions

▼ 0.0			Start at intersection of Mirror Lake Road (FR 267) and Cumberland Pass Road (FR 765) in Tincup. Zero trip meter and proceed south.
	4.9 ▲		End at intersection with Mirror Lake Road (FR 267), which is also Central #37: Tincup Pass Trail.
			GPS: N 38°45.27' W 106°28.77'
▼ 0.1		**SO**	Cross bridge.
	4.8 ▲	**SO**	Cross bridge.
▼ 0.2		**SO**	FR 765.2A to Tincup Cemetery on left.
	4.7 ▲	**SO**	FR 765.2A to Tincup Cemetery on right.
▼ 0.3		**TL**	Turn onto unmarked turnoff on left, FR 765.2B.
	4.6 ▲	**TR**	Turn onto FR 765 toward Tincup.
			GPS: N 38°44.98' W 106°28.83'
▼ 2.1		**TL**	Intersection.
	2.8 ▲	**TR**	Intersection.
			GPS: N 38°43.57' W 106°28.73'
▼ 2.3		**SO**	Private cottages on left.
	2.6 ▲	**SO**	Private cottages on right.
			GPS: N 38°43.37' W 106°28.78'

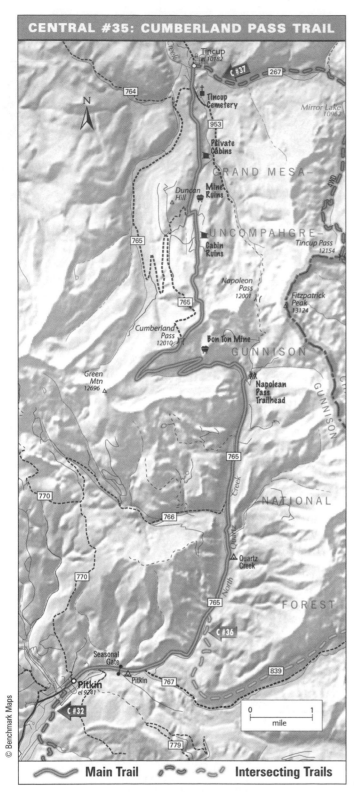

Main Trail   Intersecting Trails

▼ 2.5		BL	Track on right.
2.4 ▲		BR	Track on left.

GPS: N 38°43.19' W 106°28.70'

▼ 2.6	SO	Mine on left, building ruins, and tailings dump. Then bear right at track on left. Then turn left and right through an S-turn.
2.2 ▲	TR/TL	S-turn. Then bear left at track on right. Then continue past mine on right, building ruins and tailings dump.

The summit of Cumberland Pass

GPS: N 38°43.12' W 106°28.70'

▼ 2.7		SO	Track on left. Abandoned mine machinery.
2.1 ▲		SO	Track on right. Abandoned mine machinery.

GPS: N 38°43.04' W 106°28.71'

▼ 2.9		BL	Fork in road.
2.0 ▲		BR	Track on left.

GPS: N 38°42.87' W 106°28.68'

▼ 3.0		BL	Fork in road.
1.9 ▲		BR	Fork in road.
▼ 3.1		SO/BR	Track on right to several cabin ruins. Then bear right at fork in road.
1.8 ▲		BL/BR	Track on right. Track on left to cabin ruins.

GPS: N 38°42.75' W 106°28.65'

▼ 3.2		SO	Track on right. Track on left.
1.7 ▲		SO	Track on left. Track on right.
▼ 3.4		BR	Fork in road. Then continue straight on past track on right.
1.5 ▲		SO	Track on left. Then bear left at fork in road.

GPS: N 38°42.47 W 106°28.70'

▼ 3.5		BL	Track on right.
1.4 ▲		BR	Track on left.
▼ 4.1		BR	Fork in road.
0.8 ▲		BL	Fork in road.
▼ 4.5		BR	Fork in road.
30 yds ▲		BL	Fork in road.
▼ 30 yds		BL	Fork in road.
0.4 ▲		BR	Fork in road.
▼ 4.9		TL	Cumberland Pass summit and intersection with Cumberland Pass Road. Zero trip meter at summit marker.
0.0 ▲			Proceed along 765.2B.

GPS: N 38°41.37' W 106°29.03'

▼ 0.0			Continue south on FR 765 toward Pitkin.
7.9 ▲		TR	Cumberland Pass summit. Zero trip meter at summit marker and shortly after turn right onto 4WD track (FR 765.2B).
▼ 0.6		SO	4WD track on right.
7.3 ▲		SO	4WD track on left.
▼ 0.9		SO	4WD track on right.
7.0 ▲		SO	4WD track on left.
▼ 1.0		UT	Track on right.
6.9 ▲		UT	Track on left.
▼ 1.3		SO	4WD track on left.
6.6 ▲		SO	4WD track on right.

© Benchmark Maps

▼ 2.8	SO	Bon Ton Mine on left and cluster of old mine buildings.
5.2 ▲	SO	Bon Ton Mine on right and cluster of old mine buildings.
		GPS: N 38°40.97′ W 106°28.80′
▼ 4.0	SO	Track on left leads to Napoleon Pass Trailhead.
3.8 ▲	SO	Track on right leads to Napoleon Pass Trailhead.
▼ 4.9	SO	Tracks on right and left.
2.9 ▲	SO	Tracks on left and right.
▼ 5.3	SO	Cross North Quartz Creek.
2.5 ▲	SO	Cross North Quartz Creek.
▼ 5.5	SO	Track on right.
2.3 ▲	SO	Track on left.
▼ 5.9	SO	FR 766 to Hall's Gulch on right.
1.9 ▲	SO	FR 766 to Hall's Gulch on left.
		GPS: N 38°39.07′ W 106°28.15′
▼ 6.6	SO	Track on left to Mosquito Creek.
1.3 ▲	SO	Track on right to Mosquito Creek.
▼ 6.9	SO	USFS Quartz Campground on left.
1.0 ▲	SO	USFS Quartz Campground on right.
▼ 7.9	SO	Town site of Quartz. Central #36: Alpine Tunnel Road (FR 839) on left. Zero trip meter.
0.0 ▲		Proceed along FR 765 toward Cumberland Pass.
		GPS: N 38°37.49′ W 106°28.52′
▼ 0.0		Proceed along FR 765 toward Pitkin.
2.9 ▲	SO	Town site of Quartz. Central #36: Alpine Tunnel Road (FR 839) on right. Zero trip meter.
▼ 1.5	SO	FR 767 on left.
1.4 ▲	SO	FR 767 on right.
▼ 1.9	SO	Seasonal gate; then USFS Pitkin Campground on left.
1.0 ▲	SO	USFS Pitkin Campground on right; then seasonal gate.
▼ 2.4	TR	Stop sign at intersection of State and 9th Streets in Pitkin. Silver Plume General Store.
0.5 ▲	TL	Onto FR 765.
▼ 2.5	TL	Onto Main Street.
0.4 ▲	TR	Onto 9th Street.
▼ 2.9		End at Pitkin City Hall at intersection of Main Street (CR 76) and 4th Street.
0.0 ▲		In front of the Pitkin City Hall at the intersection of Main Street (CR 76) and 4th Street, zero trip meter and proceed northeast along Main Street.
		GPS: N 38°36.50′ W 106°31.14′

Sign at the summit of Cumberland Pass

Alpine Tunnel Road

Starting Point:	Intersection of Alpine Tunnel Road (FR 839) and Central #35: Cumberland Pass Trail (FR 765) at Quartz town site
Finishing Point:	Alpine Station
Total Mileage:	9.5 miles
Unpaved Mileage:	9.5 miles
Driving Time:	45 minutes (one-way)
Route Elevation:	11,180 to 11,597 feet
Usually Open:	Early July to September
Difficulty Rating:	1
Scenic Rating:	10

Special Attractions

- The restored Alpine Station.
- The Palisades section of the old railroad grade.
- Railroad water tanks.
- Town sites of Quartz and Woodstock and the site of the Sherrod Loop.

History

Two railroads waged a battle to be the first to connect the Gunnison area to Denver. The Denver & Rio Grande Railroad chose Marshall Pass as its route, so the owner of the Denver, South Park & Pacific Railroad, former governor John Evans, financed a project to tunnel through the Sawatch Range.

Crossing the Palisades

Alpine Tunnel Station

A tunnel through the Continental Divide seemed a shorter and more strategic route. Bids were opened to build the Alpine Tunnel in 1879. The bore through the mountain was to be 1,800 feet long. However, the railroad underestimated the severity of the weather, the geologic rock formations at the site, and the difficulty of working at the 11,600-foot altitude, with wind gusts to 50 miles per hour and temperatures at 40 degrees below zero.

In 1880, work began, and 500 laborers worked day and night. Work camps were established at each end of the tunnel. Severe weather conditions and poor working conditions created and exacerbated gigantic labor problems. Workers walked off the site in droves when they experienced the high winds and freezing temperatures they were expected to endure. The railroad recruited workers from the East and Midwest by offering free transportation to Colorado. More than 100,000 men were employed, and many worked only a day or two before leaving. Sometimes the entire crew threatened to quit en masse.

The tunnel was bored by July 1881, almost a year behind schedule (which had allowed only six months to complete the project). When the competing Denver & Rio Grande reached Gunnison in early August, the discouraged Denver, South Park & Pacific Railroad company halted the Alpine Tunnel project for about six months. Finally, work continued, and the first train passed through the tunnel in December 1881.

Tunnel Gulch water tank

The Alpine Station was developed at the west, or Pacific, end of the tunnel, with a bunkhouse where track workers lived, a storehouse, and a section house. The section house included a kitchen, a dining room, a pantry, and several bedrooms. A large stone engine house was built at the station in 1881. Aside from holding six engines, the engine house also contained a large coal bin and a water tank with a 9,516-gallon capacity, a turntable, and a locomotive service area. In 1883, a telegraph office was constructed.

Snowsheds were erected at each end of the tunnel bore to protect the rails. The shed on the Atlantic side was 150 feet in length, and the one on the Pacific side was 650 feet.

Train service through the Alpine Tunnel began in June 1882. The completed project was considered an engineering marvel. At 16 places on the western descent, walls were laid to provide a shelf for rail construction. The most spectacular shelf is at the Palisades, a mile below the tunnel, where a stone wall 450 feet long, 30 feet high, and 2 feet thick was built from hand-cut stones without mortar. You can see this wall along the drive to the Alpine Tunnel. Over 500,000 feet of California redwood were used to reinforce the tunnel, as workers found loose rock and decomposed granite instead of self-supporting granite. The total cost of the tunnel was more than $250,000.

The remains of the stone engine house

The railroad embankment leading to the collapsed southern end of the Alpine Tunnel

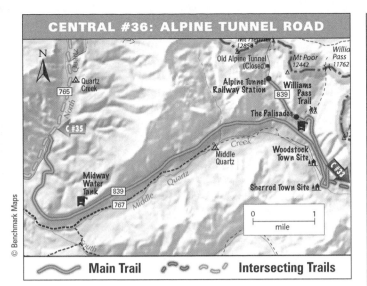

CENTRAL #36: ALPINE TUNNEL ROAD

Many problems plagued the Alpine Tunnel during its period of operation. In March 1884, a train whistle caused a severe snow slide that swept away the town of Woodstock and killed 13 of its residents. The town was not rebuilt. In 1906, a fire destroyed the wood buildings at Alpine Station; even the stone buildings were demolished when they collapsed from the intense heat of the blaze. In 1910, several people lost their lives when the tunnel caved in. The tunnel was never reopened. Rails were first removed in November 1918; however, the rails in the tunnel itself remain in place. Eventually the railroad property was sold.

Description

This historic route is an easy 2WD road that is popular with tourists and has plenty of pull-offs to enable passing where the road is narrow. The only concern is that it has very steep drop-offs in some sections.

This route starts at the town site of Quartz, approximately 3 miles northeast of Pitkin on Cumberland Pass Road (FR 765) at the Alpine Tunnel Road turnoff (FR 839). The town was originally founded in 1879 as a mining camp, but it was the arrival of the Denver, South Park & Pacific Railroad in 1882 that spurred its development. It was a major service depot for the railroad.

The remnants of the Midway water tank lie nearly 3 miles along the route. The tank was so named because it is at the halfway point between Pitkin and the Alpine Tunnel. The tank, which collapsed and has been removed from the base structure, used to hold 47,500 gallons.

A little more than 2 miles farther is the Tunnel Gulch water tank, which has been restored by the Mile High Jeep Club. This 30,000-gallon tank replaced the Woodstock tank. The route continues past the town site of Woodstock. The stone base of the old Woodstock railway water tank is all that remains.

The Sherrod Loop is marked by an information board. The loop was a horseshoe section of track that enabled the trains to turn 228 degrees to remain on the sunnier south side of the valley. The snow on the north slope was 10 to 20 feet deep and typically did not melt until the summer.

About 1.25 miles after the turnoff to Hancock Pass, you drive across the Palisades, which clings to the cliff face.

The route finishes at a parking area, a short walk from Alpine Station. The telegraph station has been restored, and you can see the ruins of the stone engine house and section house. Volunteers have reconstructed the station platform and relaid 120 feet of the original Denver, South Park & Pacific rails. A further short walk takes you to the tunnel entrance, which is completely blocked by a rock slide.

Current Road Information

Grand Mesa, Uncompahgre & Gunnison National Forests
Gunnison Ranger District
216 North Colorado
Gunnison, CO 81230
(970) 641-0471

Map References

USFS   Gunnison National Forest
Maptech CD:
      Colorado Springs/Ski Areas/Central
Benchmark's *Colorado Road & Recreation Atlas*, p. 98
Colorado Atlas & Gazetteer, p. 59
The Roads of Colorado, pp. 109, 110
Trails Illustrated, #130

Route Directions

▼ 0.0			From the T-intersection of Alpine Tunnel Road (FR 839) and Central #35: Cumberland Pass Trail (FR 765) at the site of Quartz, zero trip meter and proceed east toward the Alpine Tunnel.
7.3 ▲			End at intersection with Central #35: Cumberland Pass Trail.
		GPS: N 38°37.47' W 106°28.52'	
▼ 3.2		SO	Remains of Midway water tank on left. Only base is left standing.
4.1 ▲		SO	Remains of Midway water tank on right.
▼ 6.4		SO	Tunnel Gulch water tank on left.
0.9 ▲		SO	Tunnel Gulch water tank on right.
▼ 7.0		SO	Town site of Woodstock on right.
0.3 ▲		SO	Town site of Woodstock on left.
▼ 7.2		SO	Town site of Sherrod and Sherrod Loop on right.
0.1 ▲		SO	Town site of Sherrod and Sherrod Loop on left.
▼ 7.3		TL	Intersection with FR 888 (Central #33: Hancock Pass Trail). Zero trip meter.
0.0 ▲			At intersection of FR 888 (Central #33: Hancock Pass Trail) with FR 839 (Alpine Tunnel Road), zero trip meter and proceed toward Quartz and Pitkin on FR 839.
		GPS: N 38°36.83' W 106°23.36'	
▼ 0.0			Continue on FR 839 toward Alpine Station.
▼ 0.1		SO	South Park Railroad marker on right and Gunnison National Forest.
▼ 0.2		SO	Track on left to private cabin.
▼ 0.9		SO	Williams Pass Road sign on right.
▼ 1.3		SO	Palisades marker on left. Elevation 11,300 feet.
▼ 2.2			Public toilets, picnic tables, and gate. It is a short walk to the Alpine Station buildings beyond the gate.
		GPS: N 38°38.29' W 106°24.45'	

Tincup Pass Trail

Starting Point:	St. Elmo
Finishing Point:	Tincup
Total Mileage:	12.4 miles
Unpaved Mileage:	12.4 miles
Driving Time:	1.25 hours
Route Elevation:	9,980 to 12,154 feet
Usually Open:	Early July to October
Difficulty Rating:	3
Scenic Rating:	8

Special Attractions

- The historic and attractive towns of St. Elmo and Tincup.
- Very attractive scenery, including the summit views and Mirror Lake.
- Access to a network of 4WD trails.
- Excellent backcountry campsites.

History

Tincup Pass was first used by the Indians and then as a pack trail. A wagon road was built following the flood of silver prospectors into the area in 1879. By 1880, the pass was an established freight route, with wagon service run by Witowski and Dunbar's Hack Line. In 1881, it was developed further and became a toll road; soon three stage lines were running daily stages over the pass. The route was surveyed for a number of railroads, and a tunnel was even started under the pass, but the project was soon abandoned. The pass road was used during World War I to train the cavalry. In 1954, prison laborers upgraded the road.

Tincup was established after the Gold Cup Mine was discovered in 1879; the town was first named Virginia City but its name was changed in 1882. People flooded into Tincup, which in its heyday became the second largest town in Gunnison County. It was notorious as one of the wildest and roughest mining camps in Colorado. Its saloons and gambling parlors operated night and day. Drunkenness and shootings were casual occurrences.

Tincup was ruled by the underworld with organized crime in control of all city offices, many saloons, gaming halls, and the brothels, which seemed to flourish in the early mining camps. When the first marshal started work in 1880, he was told to see nothing, do nothing, and hear nothing; his first arrest would be his last. He lasted only a few months; when he was not paid, he quit. The second marshal occasionally rounded up a few drunks, put them in jail, and then released them. The third marshal decided to harass a saloon owner one night and didn't live long enough to regret it. The fourth marshal went insane and killed himself. The fifth marshal was shot and killed.

Tincup managed to survive through the silver crash of 1893 with its gold and silver production. The town continued into the twentieth century only to end dramatically in a fire that burned it to the ground in 1906. The fire started in a store that sold kerosene. As the flames spread, they destroyed everything in one city block. The town was rebuilt, but it never fully recovered. In 1913, a second fire severely damaged several other buildings.

After the Gold Cup Mine closed in 1917, Tincup declined rapidly, and in 1918 the post office closed.

Description

The route starts from the western edge of St. Elmo, a famous ghost town that looks as if it were created by Hollywood, and immediately starts the climb toward the pass. Initially, the road follows the North Fork of Chalk Creek, passing numerous backcountry campsites.

The road is reasonably wide but quite rough, although the surface is sound. As the road progresses, it becomes rockier, but the rocks are embedded, so the surface remains solid. The road travels through pine and spruce forest.

Mirror Lake

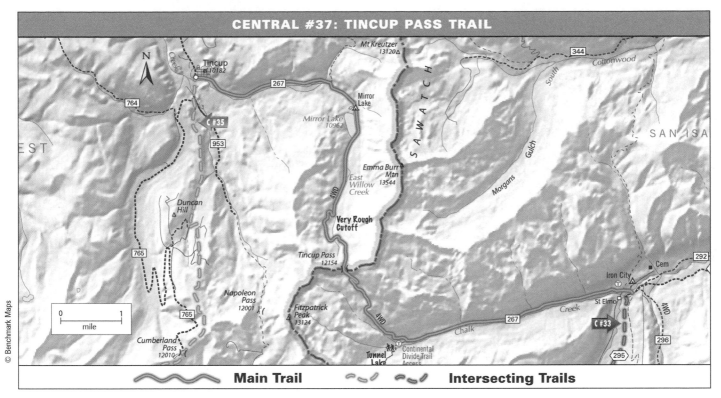

Main Trail   **Intersecting Trails**

The summit offers beautiful views of the Arkansas River Valley and the Taylor Park area. Mirror Lake can be glimpsed in the foreground as you look west toward Tincup.

About 3 miles west of the summit, the road travels along the edge of Mirror Lake, a popular fishing spot. Nearby, there is a U.S. Forest Service campground. There are also numerous very good backcountry campsites between Mirror Lake and Tincup.

From Mirror Lake, the road is easily negotiated by car.

Current Road Information

Grand Mesa, Uncompahgre & Gunnison National Forests
Gunnison Ranger District
216 North Colorado
Gunnison, CO 81230
(970) 641-0471

The trail near the summit of Tincup Pass

Map References

USFS Gunnison National Forest; San Isabel National Forest

Maptech CD:
   Colorado Springs/Ski Areas/Central

Benchmark's *Colorado Road & Recreation Atlas*, p. 86
Colorado Atlas & Gazetteer, p. 59
The Roads of Colorado, pp. 109, 110
Trails Illustrated, #129, #130

Route Directions

▼ 0.0		In front of the Miner's Exchange in St. Elmo, zero trip meter and proceed west.
9.3 ▲		End in front of the Miner's Exchange in St. Elmo.
	GPS: N 38°42.23' W 106°20.65'	
▼ 0.1	TR	At Tincup sign; then cross bridge over North Fork of Chalk Creek.
9.2 ▲	TL	Onto St. Elmo's main street.
▼ 0.2	BR	Fork in road.
9.1 ▲	BL	Track on right.
▼ 0.4	SO	Poplar Gulch Trailhead on right.
8.9 ▲	SO	Poplar Gulch Trailhead on left.
▼ 0.8	SO	Cattle guard.
8.5 ▲	SO	Cattle guard.
▼ 1.8	SO	Cross over creek.
7.5 ▲	SO	Cross over creek.
▼ 3.0	SO	Track on right.
6.3 ▲	SO	Track on left.
▼ 3.9	SO	Tunnel Lake walking trail on left.
5.4 ▲	SO	Tunnel Lake walking trail on right.
	GPS: N 38°41.54' W 106°24.80'	
▼ 4.6	SO	Cross through creek.
4.7 ▲	SO	Cross through creek.
▼ 6.1	SO	Tincup Pass summit. Enter Gunnison National

Tincup

		Forest.
3.2 ▲	SO	Tincup Pass summit. Enter San Isabel National Forest.

GPS: N 38°42.57' W 106°26.00'

▼ 6.1	SO	Cattle guard.
3.2 ▲	SO	Cattle guard.
▼ 6.7	BL	Old alternative route is straight ahead.
2.6 ▲	BR	More difficult alternative route rejoins on left.
▼ 7.5	SO	More difficult alternative route rejoins on right.
1.8 ▲	BR	More difficult alternative route on left.
▼ 8.8	SO	Cross through creek at head of Mirror Lake.
0.5 ▲	SO	Cross through creek at head of Mirror Lake.
▼ 9.3	SO	Tincup side of Mirror Lake and angler parking on left. Zero trip meter.
0.0 ▲	BL	Follow track around the left side of Mirror Lake toward Tincup Pass.

GPS: N 38°44.78' W 106°25.81'

▼ 0.0		Proceed along Mirror Lake Road (FR 267).
3.1 ▲	BL	Mirror Lake and angler parking on right. Zero trip meter.
▼ 0.1	SO	Track to USFS Mirror Lake Campground on left.
3.0 ▲	SO	Track to USFS Mirror Lake Campground on right.
▼ 0.4	SO	Timberline Trailhead on right.
2.7 ▲	SO	Timberline Trailhead on left.
▼ 0.9	SO	Cross over East Willow Creek.
2.2 ▲	SO	Cross over East Willow Creek.
▼ 2.9	BL	Fork in road. Entering Tincup.
0.2 ▲	BR	Leaving Tincup.
▼ 3.1		End in Tincup at intersection with Cumberland Pass Road (FR 765).
0.0 ▲		At intersection of Mirror Lake Road (FR 267) and Cumberland Pass Road (FR 765) in Tincup, zero trip meter and proceed toward Mirror Lake.

GPS: N 38°45.27' W 106°28.77'

Mount Antero Trail

Starting Point:	Intersection of CR 162 and Baldwin Creek Road (FR 277)
Finishing Point:	Mount Antero
Total Mileage:	Approximately 6.5 miles (one-way)
Unpaved Mileage:	Approximately 6.5 miles
Driving Time:	1.75 hours (one-way)
Route Elevation:	9,400 to 14,269 feet
Usually Open:	Mid-June to late September
Difficulty Rating:	5
Scenic Rating:	9

Special Attractions

- A very challenging and famous 4WD trail.
- Wonderful alpine scenery.
- Access to a network of 4WD trails.

History

Mount Antero is named for Chief "Graceful Walker" Antero of the Uintah band of the Ute Indians. Antero was one of the signatories to the Washington Treaty of 1880, which revised the terms of the Brunot Treaty signed seven years earlier and led to the Ute losing nearly all their land. Antero was a force for peace during the period of very problematic relations between the Ute and the whites in the late 1860s and 1870s. In 1869, John Wesley Powell spent the winter with Antero and Chief Douglas (who was later held responsible for the Meeker Massacre) and learned to speak the Ute language.

While Mount Antero was doubtless examined by prospectors in the late 1870s as silver was being discovered all around, it proved to have little silver to offer. In fact, not a single claim

The trail climbing Mount Antero above timberline

The narrow, loose descent

Parked near Mount White with Mount Antero in the background

was staked. What the prospectors did not notice, or failed to appreciate, was that Mount Antero offered a fortune in gemstones.

In 1884, a prospector named Nathaniel D. Wanemaker discovered a number of blue aquamarines in the area. He constructed a small stone cabin high on the south side of the mountain. It is said that he discovered $600 worth of gems in his first summer and continued to prospect for gems for many years.

Mount Antero has proved extraordinarily rich in aquamarines, topaz, and clear and smoky quartz crystals. The aquamarines range in color from pale blue-green to deep blue. Some of the clear crystals from Mount Antero are huge; a 7-inch specimen is on display at the Harvard Mineralogical Museum and another was cut into a 6-inch-diameter sphere and displayed at the 1893 Columbian Exposition. The more common smoky quartz crystals weigh as much as 50 pounds.

The most recent mining on Mount Antero has been for beryllium, a lightweight, corrosion-resistant, rigid, steel gray metallic element that melts only at extremely high temperatures. Beryllium is a prized aerospace structural material, as a moderator and reflector in nuclear reactors, and in a copper al-

loy used for springs, electrical contacts, and non-sparking tools. In the 1950s, the access road on the mountain's south shoulder was constructed by the company mining the beryllium.

Description

The Mount Antero route starts at the intersection of the road between Nathrop and St. Elmo (CR 162) and FR 277. The turnoff is 12 miles west of US 285 along CR 162 and 3.3 miles east of St. Elmo.

FR 277 ascends steeply right from the point of departure from CR 162. It is a rough, rocky shelf road through the pine and aspen forest but offers some very good views back into the valley and the township of Alpine. The track is narrow and has some very steep drop-offs. Pull-offs for passing other vehicles are only just adequate in some sections. High clearance is definitely required, but if you carefully select your line, the rocks are not large enough to cause vehicle damage.

Some good news: Once you have completed the first 2 miles, you are past the most difficult section of the route.

At the 2.7-mile point, you cross through Baldwin Creek, which has a firm base and is usually only about a foot deep.

The trail switchbacking to the summit of Mount Antero

Crossing a talus bed

The trail swichbacks above treeline

From the creek crossing, the road again climbs a couple of loose talus slopes before emerging above timberline. The road then commences a series of narrow switchbacks before winding around the south face and continuing up the east face. Passing opportunities are limited in this section, so it pays to watch for oncoming vehicles and plan ahead.

At the 3.8-mile point, there is an intersection. The track on the right leads to a dead end. This is the last chance to turn around before the end of the road, and the next section is more difficult than anything encountered until this point. (Note: The difficulty rating for this route is based on stopping here.) We recommend that if you wish to see the last half mile of the road, you walk it.

Current Road Information

Pike & San Isabel National Forests
Salida Ranger District
325 West Rainbow Boulevard
Salida, CO 81201
(719) 539-3591

Crossing Baldwin Creek

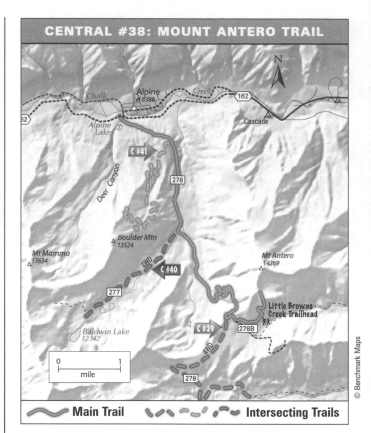

CENTRAL #38: MOUNT ANTERO TRAIL

© Benchmark Maps

〜〜 **Main Trail**   〜〜〜〜 **Intersecting Trails**

Map References

USFS   San Isabel National Forest
Maptech CD:
         Colorado Springs/Ski Areas/Central
Benchmark's *Colorado Road & Recreation Atlas*, p. 99
Colorado Atlas & Gazetteer, p. 59
The Roads of Colorado, p. 110
Trails Illustrated, #130

Route Directions

▼ 0.0		From CR 162 (3.3 miles east of St. Elmo), turn onto Baldwin Creek Road (FR 277) toward Mt. Antero and zero trip meter.
		GPS: N 38°42.60' W 106°17.46'
▼ 1.1	SO	Track on right is Central #41: Boulder Mountain Trail.
▼ 2.7	TL	Central #40: Baldwin Lakes Trail is straight ahead (FR 277.2). Zero trip meter.
		GPS: N 38°40.99' W 106°16.32'
▼ 0.0		Cross through Baldwin Creek and continue on FR 278 toward Mt. Antero.
▼ 0.2	SO	Cross through creek.
▼ 0.3	SO	Track on left.
▼ 1.5	SO	Cross through creek.
▼ 3.3	BL	Central #39: Browns Lake Trail (278.2) on right. Remain on 278.A.
		GPS: N 38°39.70' W 106°15.43'
▼ 3.4	SO	Intersection with 278.B on right, which climbs Mt. White, providing spectacular views all around, especially looking back at Mt. Antero and into the valley to the south.
▼ 3.8	BL	Track on right. Park and walk remaining section.
		GPS: N 38°39.74' W 106°14.94'

Browns Lake Trail

Starting Point:	Intersection of Central #38: Mount Antero Trail (FR 278A) and FR 278.2
Finishing Point:	Browns Creek Trailhead
Total Mileage:	3.3 miles (one-way)
Unpaved Mileage:	3.3 miles
Driving Time:	45 minutes (one-way)
Route Elevation:	2,800 to 11,400 feet
Usually Open:	Mid-June to late September
Difficulty Rating:	4
Scenic Rating:	10

Special Attractions

- The extremely scenic Browns Lake.
- Part of a network of 4WD trails near the summit of Mount Antero.

Description

The 4WD trail to Browns Lake, a side road from the Mount Antero road, sees much less traffic than that more famous route.

After turning off the Mount Antero road, you cross an alpine meadow before commencing the rocky descent down into Browns Creek Valley. The road enters the timberline and wends its way through the pine forest with rather tight clearance between the trees.

The trail proceeds past the remains of a mining camp, including the ruins of a miners' cabin. Proceeding toward the trailhead and the end of the 4WD road, you'll enjoy picture-postcard views of Browns Lake, located in the valley at an altitude of 11,286 feet.

The trail approaching Browns Lake

The road is moderately difficult, with sections of narrow switchbacks, loose surface rock, and some tight clearances, but the solitude and the scenery make it all worthwhile.

Current Road Information

Pike & San Isabel National Forests
Salida Ranger District
325 West Rainbow Boulevard
Salida, CO 81201
(719) 539-3591

Map References

USFS   San Isabel National Forest
Maptech CD:
      Colorado Springs/Ski Areas/Central
Benchmark's *Colorado Road & Recreation Atlas*, p. 99
Colorado Atlas & Gazetteer, p. 60
The Roads of Colorado, p. 110
Trails Illustrated, #130

Browns Lake

Beautiful Browns Lake in the distance

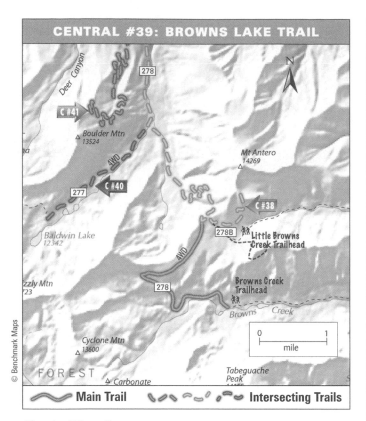

278

Deer Canyon

C #41

Boulder Mtn
13524

4WD

Mt Antero
14269

277

C #40

C #38

Baldwin Lake
12342

278B

Little Browns
Creek Trailhead

4WD

zzly Mtn
23

278

Browns Creek
Trailhead

Browns Creek

0   1
mile

Cyclone Mtn
13600

FOREST

Carbonate

Tabeguache
Peak

© Benchmark Maps

〜〜〜 **Main Trail**   ⟋⟋⟋⟍ ⌒⟋ ⟍⟋⟍ **Intersecting Trails**

Route Directions

▼ 0.0		At intersection of Mt. Antero Trail (FR 278.A) and trail to Browns Lake (FR 278.2), zero trip meter and proceed along FR 278.2 into the valley.
	GPS: N 38°39.70′ W 106°15.43′	
▼ 1.9	SO	Cabin ruins on right.
▼ 2.0	SO	Cabin ruins on left.
▼ 2.5	SO	Cross through creek.
▼ 3.3		Track ends at Browns Creek Trailhead.
	GPS: N 38°38.63′ W 106°14.70′	

CENTRAL REGION TRAIL #40

Baldwin Lakes Trail

Starting Point:	Intersection of Central #38: Mount Antero Trail (FR 278) and Baldwin Creek Road (FR 277)
Finishing Point:	Parking area at Baldwin Lakes
Total Mileage:	2.9 miles (one-way)
Unpaved Mileage:	2.9 miles
Driving Time:	1 hour (one-way)
Route Elevation:	10,880 to 12,200 feet
Usually Open:	Mid-June to late September
Difficulty Rating:	5
Scenic Rating:	7

A rough, loose section of the trail

Special Attractions

■ Challenging 4WD trail.
■ Scenic views of Baldwin Lakes.

Description

The Baldwin Lakes route is a very rough and rocky side road to the Mount Antero road. The talus roadbed is slippery, and sharp rocks make a flat tire a continual threat.

Baldwin Lakes

Baldwin Lakes

The first section of road travels along the creek, past open meadows and many backcountry camping spots. As it continues up to the first lake, you travel through the pine forest, emerging to cross huge talus rock slides and then re-entering the forest. About 2 miles along the road, the surface rock becomes mostly embedded in the soil and more stable. There is a fairly steep section where the melting snow drains across the trail, making it boggy and somewhat slippery when you are going uphill. The last section of the road has large embedded rocks to negotiate before you reach the small parking area.

Views of Baldwin Creek Valley, the high alpine bowl encircled by steep valley walls, and the lakes cradled in its base combine to make the journey very scenic.

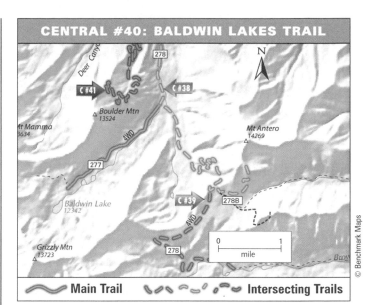

Current Road Information

Pike & San Isabel National Forests
Salida Ranger District
325 West Rainbow Boulevard
Salida, CO 81201
(719) 539-3591

Map References

USFS   San Isabel National Forest
Maptech CD:
    Colorado Springs/Ski Areas/Central
Benchmark's *Colorado Road & Recreation Atlas*, p. 99
Colorado Atlas & Gazetteer, p. 59
The Roads of Colorado, p. 110
Trails Illustrated, #130

The scenic Baldwin Creek Valley

Route Directions

▼ 0.0		From the intersection of FR 278 and FR 277.2, at the small parking area beside Baldwin Creek crossing, zero trip meter and proceed toward Baldwin Lakes.
		GPS: N 38°40.97' W 106°16.34'
▼ 0.2	SO	Remains of log cabin.
▼ 0.9	BR	Fork in road.
▼ 1.5	BL	Fork in road. Follow lower track (FR 277). Track on right goes to old mine farther up the mountain.
		GPS: N 38°40.14' W 106°17.45'
▼ 2.2	BR	Small parking area on left with view of the lakes and a walking track.
		GPS: N 38°39.69' W 106°18.10'
▼ 2.9		Small parking/turnaround area. From this point, the track becomes more difficult than our rating indicates. Large embedded rocks make impact with the underside of the vehicle likely.
		GPS: N 38°39.95' W 106°18.36'

CENTRAL REGION TRAIL #41

Boulder Mountain Trail

Starting Point:	Intersection of Central #40: Baldwin Lakes Trail (FR 277) and Boulder Mountain Road
Finishing Point:	Mine shaft and cabin ruins near the top of the mountain
Total Mileage:	4.8 miles (one-way)
Unpaved Mileage:	4.8 miles
Driving Time:	1.25 hours (one-way)
Route Elevation:	9,950 to 12,800 feet
Usually Open:	Mid-June to late September
Difficulty Rating:	5
Scenic Rating:	8

Special Attractions

■ Challenging 4WD trail.
■ Spectacular alpine views.

Description

This route, another side road to the Mount Antero Trail, is also rough and rocky but less so than the Mount Antero road. The challenge of this road is that it is narrow with very high drop-offs. To make matters more interesting, especially if you have a full-sized vehicle, small pine trees grow on the inside edge of the track, pushing you perilously close to the edge. To add to the excitement, sections of the road are significantly off-camber!

The road carries less traffic than others in the area, which is fortunate because there are sections where the only way to get around an oncoming vehicle is for one vehicle to reverse a

A switchback on Boulder Mountain Trail

good distance. Remember that the vehicle going uphill has the right-of-way, but common sense should always prevail. Because of the steep talus slopes, you have to stop often and clear rubble off the road.

On the way up, the route affords some wonderful, panoramic views across to the Mount Antero road and the adjoining mountain peaks, but when you reach the mine at the top, the view is truly spectacular—across the Chalk Creek Valley, Alpine Lake, and the township of Alpine.

A relatively easy section of Boulder Mountain Trail

The mine at the end of the trail

At the end of the trail are the windswept ruins of an old mine cabin and an open mine portal set into the bare talus slope.

Current Road Information
Pike & San Isabel National Forests
Salida Ranger District
325 West Rainbow Boulevard
Salida, CO 81201
(719) 539-3591

Map References
USFS San Isabel National Forest
Maptech CD:
      Colorado Springs/Ski Areas/Central
Benchmark's *Colorado Road & Recreation Atlas*, p. 99

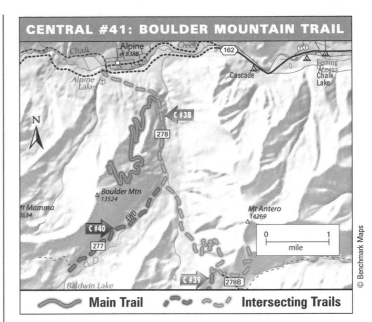

CENTRAL #41: BOULDER MOUNTAIN TRAIL

© Benchmark Maps

Colorado Atlas & Gazetteer, p. 59
The Roads of Colorado, p. 110
Trails Illustrated, #130

Route Directions

▼ 0.0		From the 1.1-mile mark on Mt. Antero Trail (Baldwin Creek Road), zero trip meter and make a sharp right turn onto an unmarked, rocky track.
		GPS: N 38°42.21' W 106°16.47'
▼ 0.9	SO	Campsites off to the left and right. Then cabin ruins and track on left.
▼ 4.8		Top of track. Mine shaft and ruins.
		GPS: N 38°41.20' W 106°17.32'

Mining ruins at the end of the trail

Pomeroy Lakes and Mary Murphy Mine Trail

Starting Point:	**Intersection of Central #33: Hancock Pass Trail (FR 295) and FR 297.1**
Finishing Point:	**Parking area at Pomeroy Lakes**
Total Mileage:	**2.7 miles (one-way)**
Unpaved Mileage:	**2.7 miles**
Driving Time:	**1 hour (one-way)**
Route Elevation:	**10,500 to 12,035 feet**
Usually Open:	**Mid-June to late September**
Difficulty Rating:	**5**
Scenic Rating:	**7**

Special Attractions

■ Remains of the Mary Murphy Mine.
■ A varied, challenging, short 4WD trail.
■ Pomeroy Lakes in their barren, scenic, alpine setting.

History

According to legend, Dr. A. E. Wright, who discovered the Mary Murphy Mine in the mid-1870s, named it after a nurse who cared for him when he was taken to the hospital in Denver. If Mary was a nurse with whom Wright was smitten, it is not clear who the adjoining Pat Murphy Mine was named af-

Mary Murphy Mine tram support

ter. One thing is certain: The Mary Murphy Mine was enormously successful and was the main engine of the local economy. It supported the towns of St. Elmo, Romley, and Hancock. When the mine closed in 1926, it spelled the end for these towns and also for the remaining section of the old Alpine Tunnel railroad. The tracks were torn up within the year.

Description

This route starts along the road to Hancock that follows the Alpine Tunnel railroad grade.

Mill remains

After turning onto FR 297, the road passes many remains of the Mary Murphy Mine, located high above the road on the mountainside. Towers used by the tramway, which extended over 2 miles into Pomeroy Gulch from the railway grade, are still clearly evident as you drive along the initial section of the road. There are also a number of buildings where the tramway deposited the ore that it carried down from the top of the mountain.

Until this point the road is suitable for 2WD vehicles, but as the route proceeds along FR 297.2, the road becomes high-clearance 4WD only.

Continuing toward the lake, you pass a number of good backcountry camping sites and a grave on the side of the road that dates back to 1884.

The road gets progressively rockier and more rutted and eroded before reaching the parking area near the lakes, merely 2.7 miles from the start.

Current Road Information
Pike & San Isabel National Forests
Salida Ranger District
325 West Rainbow Boulevard
Salida, CO 81201
(719) 539-3591

Map References
USFS   San Isabel National Forest
Maptech CD:
          Colorado Springs/Ski Areas/Central
Benchmark's *Colorado Road & Recreation Atlas*, pp. 98, 99
Colorado Atlas & Gazetteer, p. 59
The Roads of Colorado, p. 110
Trails Illustrated, #130

Route Directions

▼ 0.0		At the intersection of Central #33: Hancock Pass Trail (FR 295) with sign to Mary Murphy Mine and Pomeroy Lakes, zero trip meter and proceed along FR 297.1.
GPS: N 38°40.38' W 106°21.95'		
▼ 0.2	SO	Rocky ascent. Mine ruins on right.
▼ 0.3	SO	Cabin on left. Cross over creek.
▼ 0.6	SO	Track on left.
▼ 0.7	SO	Mary Murphy Mine headquarters on right. Mine and tailings on left.
▼ 0.8	SO	Tracks on left.
▼ 0.9	SO	Gated track on left goes to Mary Murphy Mine ruins. Zero trip meter.
GPS: N 38°39.95' W 106°21.34'		

Looking across Chalk Creek at log cabin ruins

Pomeroy Lake

CENTRAL #42: POMEROY LAKES AND MARY MURPHY MINE TRAIL

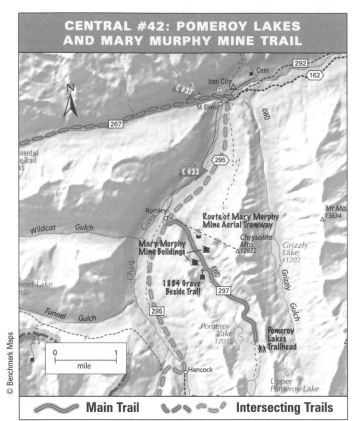

▼ 0.0	BR	Continue on FR 297.2 to Pomeroy Lakes.
▼ 0.2	SO	Track on right.
▼ 0.5	SO	Short track on left to mine ruins up the hill. Cross through creek.
▼ 0.7	SO	Grave on right (date: 1857-1884).
▼ 0.8	SO	Track on left.
▼ 1.0	TL	Track on right and straight ahead to campsites.
▼ 1.2	SO	Cross through creek.
▼ 1.8		End at Pomeroy Lakes and parking area.

GPS: N 38°38.90′ W 106°20.34′

CENTRAL REGION TRAIL #43

Marshall Pass Poncha Creek Trail

Starting Point:	**Intersection of Central #44: Marshall Pass Railway Grade Road and FR 203**
Finishing Point:	**Marshall Pass**
Total Mileage:	**8.1 miles**
Unpaved Mileage:	**8.1 miles**
Driving Time:	**1.25 hours**
Route Elevation:	**8,595 to 10,846 feet**
Usually Open:	**Mid-June to late September**
Difficulty Rating:	**3**
Scenic Rating:	**8**

The foundations of one of Mears's old railroad bridges

Special Attractions

- 4WD alternative to the railroad grade route to Marshall Pass.
- Very good views, especially near the summit.
- Access to good backcountry campsites, fishing, and many hiking trails.

Description

This route is narrower, rougher, and scenically more varied than the main road to Marshall Pass, which follows the old railroad grade (Central #44). However, while not suitable for passenger vehicles, it offers little difficulty to a 4WD vehicle.

The trail begins at the intersection of Central #44: Marshall Pass Railway Grade Road and FR 203.

A beaver dam that has created a pool beside the trail

Old railway bridge over Poncha Creek

FR 203 gets progressively narrower and rougher, although it remains suitable for passenger vehicles in dry conditions. After Starvation Creek, creek crossings and the rougher road make a high-clearance vehicle necessary.

FR 203 offers numerous undeveloped campsites beside Poncha Creek for the first 6 miles after its intersection with CR/FR 200. From this point, the trail starts its ascent toward the pass, and camping possibilities become scarce. Eventually, the road departs from the creek to make the final climb through a series of alpine meadows, offering spectacular views before reaching the pass.

There are some very good backcountry campsites and numerous fishing spots beside Poncha Creek. For those who prefer more of the comforts of home, the particularly scenic O'Haver Lake offers a developed U.S. Forest Service campground with access for RVs and camper trailers. A number of hiking trails run through the area, including the Colorado Trail and the Continental Divide Trail.

Current Road Information
Pike & San Isabel National Forests
Salida Ranger District
325 West Rainbow Boulevard
Salida, CO 81201
(719) 539-3591

Map References
USFS   Gunnison National Forest
Maptech CD:
      Alamosa/Pueblo/South Central
Benchmark's *Colorado Road & Recreation Atlas*, p. 99
Colorado Atlas & Gazetteer, p. 70
The Roads of Colorado, p. 110
Trails Illustrated, #139

Rocky section of the trail

ATV on Marshall Pass Poncha Creek Trail

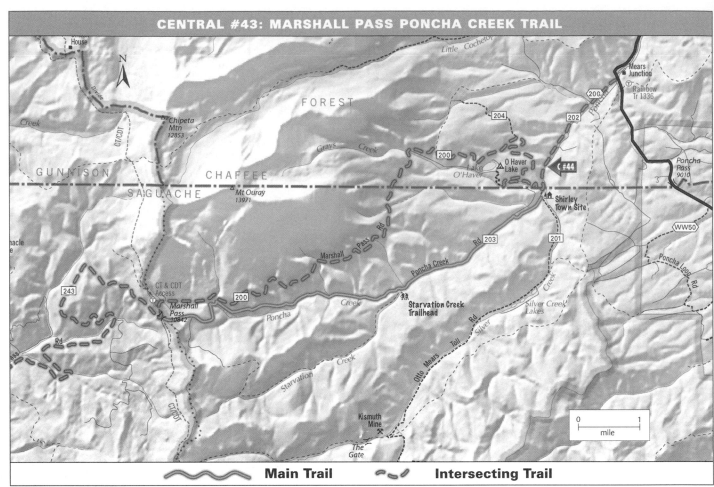

Main Trail   **Intersecting Trail**

Route Directions

▼ 0.0   Trail begins at the intersection of Central #44: Marshall Pass Railway Grade Road (FR 200) and FR 203. Zero trip meter and proceed toward Poncha Creek on FR 203.

    8.1 ▲   TR   Trail ends at the intersection with Central #44: Marshall Pass Railway Grade.

> **GPS: N 38°25.37′ W 106°08.45′**

▼ 0.8   SO   Track on right. Beaver Creek sign.

    7.3 ▲   SO   Track on left. Beaver Creek sign.

▼ 1.0   BR   Signpost reads "Via Poncha Creek 7– FR 203." Intersection. Numerous good backcountry camping spots are found all along Poncha Creek.

    7.1 ▲   BL   Intersection.

> **GPS: N 38°24.92′ W 106°08.31′**

▼ 3.4   SO   Trailhead for Starvation Creek walking trail.

    4.7 ▲   SO   Trailhead for Starvation Creek walking trail.

▼ 3.6   SO   Track on right is 0.25 miles in length with additional camping spots.

    4.5 ▲   SO   Track on left.

▼ 4.6   SO   Cross over Tent Creek.

    3.5 ▲   SO   Cross over Tent Creek.

▼ 5.1   SO   Track on left down to Poncha Creek and numerous campsites down below the road.

    3.0 ▲   SO   Track on right.

▼ 5.5   SO   Cross over creek. Slightly farther, there's a short track on the right and four campsites.

    2.6 ▲   SO   Track on left; then cross over creek.

> **GPS: N 38°23.70′ W106°12.50**

▼ 6.8   SO   Cross over Ouray Creek

    1.3 ▲   SO   Cross over Ouray Creek.

▼ 6.9   SO   Camping on right and left in grassy areas; then cross over Poncha Creek.

    1.2 ▲   SO   Cross over Poncha Creek.

▼ 7.0   SO   Open meadow on left with scenic views of valley and Sangre de Cristo mountain range to the east. No vehicle access.

    1.1 ▲   SO   Open meadow on right with scenic views.

▼ 7.1   SO   Track on left to campsite.

    1.0 ▲   SO   Track on right to campsite.

▼ 7.5   SO   4WD track on left (203.1A) to Starvation Creek walking trail. This side trip leads 1.6 miles to TR 1408, which loops back to Marshall Pass after 6.6 miles. At the 1.8-mile point there is a scenic overlook. GPS: N 38°22.96′ W 106°13.19′.

    0.6 ▲   SO   Track on right to scenic overlooks.

> **GPS: N 38°23.53′ W 106°14.22′**

▼ 8.0   TL   Intersection with Central #44: Marshall Pass Railway Grade Road (FR 200). Track on left is the Colorado Trail.

    0.1 ▲   TR   FR 200 continues straight ahead.

> **GPS: N 38°23.50′ W 106°14.75′**

▼ 8.1   Summit of Marshall Pass. Central #44: Marshall Pass Railway Grade Road (FR 200) continues to Sargents.

    0.0 ▲   Summit of Marshall Pass. Zero trip meter.

> **GPS: N 38°23.50′ W 106°14.85′**

Marshall Pass Railway Grade Road

Starting Point:	Mears Junction at US 285 and FR 200, 5 miles south of Poncha Springs
Finishing Point:	Sargents
Total Mileage:	29.7 miles
Unpaved Mileage:	29.7 miles
Driving Time:	1.25 hours
Route Elevation:	8,420 to 10,846 feet
Usually Open:	Late May to mid-October
Difficulty Rating:	1
Scenic Rating:	7

Special Attractions

- Easy, scenic road along a historic railroad grade.
- Developed campground and good fishing at picturesque O'Haver Lake.
- Provides a loop route between Marshall Pass and Mears Junction, when combined with Central #43: Marshall Pass Poncha Creek Trail.
- Steam train water tank in Sargents.

History

This pass is named for Lieutenant William L. Marshall, who discovered it while on the Wheeler survey expedition in 1873. Reportedly, he was suffering from a toothache and sought a quicker route back to Denver and relief from a dentist!

In 1877, Otto Mears constructed a wagon road to Gunnison across the pass from his Poncha Pass toll road. It served as

Aspens beside the old rairoad grade in early fall

a stagecoach route until the opening of the railroad and was used by President Grant in 1880. Mears sold the road to the Denver & Rio Grande Railroad. The Denver & Rio Grande was embroiled in a classic railroad battle during the early 1880s in its race to be first to link the Arkansas Valley and the Gunnison Basin area. The Denver, South Park & Pacific Railroad chose a route that necessitated the construction of the famous Alpine Tunnel (Central #36).

With the aid of 23 snowsheds to protect it from the elements, a Denver & Rio Grande narrow gauge railway won the battle by using the Marshall Pass route. Operations commenced in 1881 and continued until 1953. The tracks were dismantled in 1955. A post office, located at the station at the top of the pass, continued to operate until 1952. President William H. Taft was probably the most famous passenger to cross the pass by train.

Located on the western end of the trail is Sargents. The town was established in the late 1870s and was named for

Denver & Rio Grande train climbing the grade to Marshall Pass in 1900

An old railroad cutting

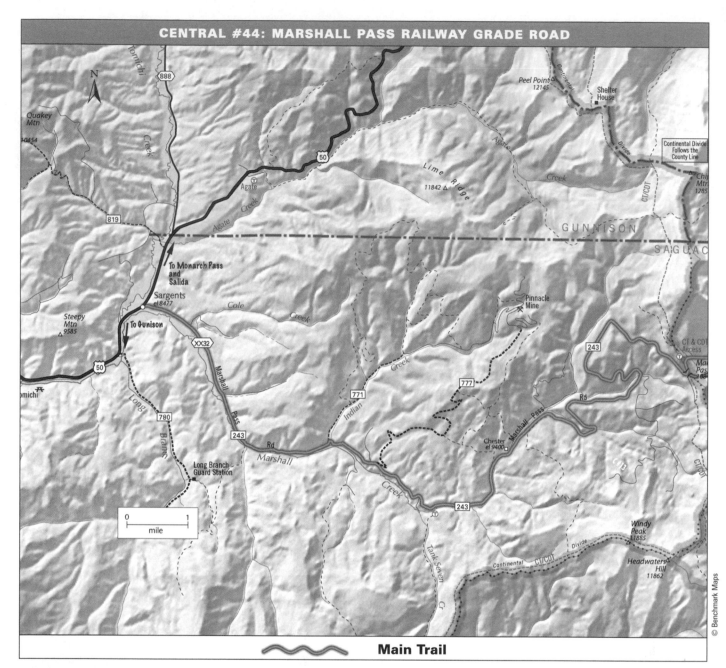

Main Trail

© Benchmark Maps

Joseph Sargent who had been employed at the Los Piños Indian Agency and had established a ranch in the area in 1879. Initially the settlement was known as Marshalltown, but the name was changed in 1882. The town never grew very large and in the late 1880s had a population of only about 150.

Description

This route follows the old railroad grade and is easier than the alternative route via Poncha Creek (Central #43). The route is unpaved but wide and well graded. It is suitable for RVs and trailers making their way to the campground at O'Haver Lake or across Marshall Pass on CR 200.

O'Haver Lake offers good fishing and a developed forest service campground with access for RVs and camper trailers. A number of hiking trails run through the area, including the Colorado Trail and the Continental Divide Trail.

The trail starts at Mears Junction, which is the intersection of US 285 and CR/FR 200. Once the junction of two of Otto Mears's toll roads, the intersection is located about 5 miles south of Poncha Springs and 2.4 miles north of Poncha Pass. West of the pass, the journey runs through gentle, rolling countryside and ranchland with many stands of aspens adding color in fall. At Sargents, there is an old wooden water tank that used to service the steam locomotives that chugged up Marshall Pass from 1881 to 1953.

Current Road Information

Pike & San Isabel National Forests
Salida Ranger District
325 West Rainbow Boulevard
Salida, CO 81201
(719) 539-3591

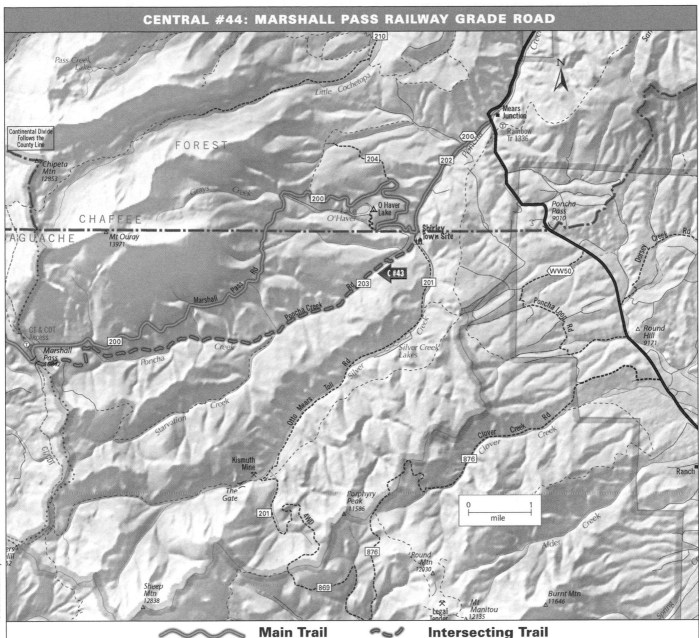

~~~~~ **Main Trail**   ⌒⌒⌒ **Intersecting Trail**

Map References

USFS Gunnison National Forest; San Isabel National
Forest
Maptech CD:
Alamosa/Pueblo/South Central
Benchmark's *Colorado Road & Recreation Atlas*, p. 99
Colorado Atlas & Gazetteer, pp. 69, 70
The Roads of Colorado, p. 102
Trails Illustrated, #139

Route Directions

▼ 0.0		At Mears Junction, zero trip meter and turn from US 285 onto CR/FR 200 heading west across cattle guard.
3.1 ▲		Cross cattle guard and end at intersection with US 285.

GPS: N 38°26.89′ W 106°06.40′

▼ 1.3	SO	Cattle guard.
1.8 ▲	TL	Cattle guard.
▼ 2.2	TR	Shirley town site. Public toilets on left. Turn right onto CR/FR 202.
0.9 ▲	TL	Turn left onto CR/FR 200. Shirley town site and public toilets on right.
▼ 3.1	TR	Intersection with CR/FR 200. O'Haver Lake is straight ahead, with fishing access and developed camping. Central #43: Marshall Pass Poncha Creek Trail to the left. Zero trip meter.
0.0 ▲		Proceed east on FR 202 toward Mears Junction.

GPS: N 38°25.37′ W 106°08.45′

▼ 0.0		Proceed northeast on FR 200.
10.3 ▲	TL	Intersection with FR 202. O'Haver Lake is to the right. Central #43: Marshall Pass Poncha Creek Trail is straight ahead. Zero trip meter.
▼ 1.7	SO	Track on right is CR 204.

Another of the many stands of aspen along the route

8.6 ▲		SO	Track on left is CR 204.
▼ 2.4		SO	O'Haver Lake on left below road.
7.9 ▲		SO	O'Haver Lake on right below road.
▼ 3.9		SO	Cross over Gray's Creek.
6.4 ▲		SO	Cross over Gray's Creek.
▼ 6.8		SO	Cross over Tent Creek.
3.5 ▲		SO	Cross over Tent Creek.
▼ 7.2		SO	Track on right.
3.1 ▲		SO	Track on left.
▼ 9.0		SO	Old railway embankment across Ouray Creek.
1.3 ▲		SO	Old railway embankment across Ouray Creek.
▼ 9.9		SO	Hiking trail on right.
0.4 ▲		SO	Hiking trail on left.
▼ 10.0		SO	Marshall Pass Trailhead sign and public toilets on left.
0.3 ▲		SO	Marshall Pass Trailhead sign and public toilets on right.
▼ 10.2		SO	Road on left is Central #43: Marshall Pass Poncha Creek Trail. Track on left is the Colorado Trail. Zero trip meter.
0.0			Proceed north on FR 200.

GPS: N 38°25.37' W 106°08.45'

▼ 0.0			Proceed northeast on FR 200.
16.4 ▲		BL	Track on right is the Colorado Trail; then Central #43: Marshall Pass Poncha Creek Trail on right. Zero trip meter.
▼ 0.1			Summit of Marshall Pass.
16.3 ▲		SO	Track on left; then enter San Isabel National Forest; then cattle guard. Summit of Marshall Pass. Proceed west across cattle guard onto FR 243; then track on right.

GPS: N 38°23.50' W 106°14.85'

▼ 0.2		SO	Seasonal gate.
16.2 ▲		SO	Seasonal gate.
▼ 1.0		SO	Track on left.
15.4 ▲		SO	Track on right.
▼ 1.3		SO	Track on left.
15.1 ▲		SO	Track on right.
▼ 3.9		SO	Track on left for hiking, horses, and snowmobiles.
12.5 ▲		SO	Track on right for nonmotorized vehicles.
▼ 4.3		SO	Cattle guard.
12.1 ▲		SO	Cattle guard.
▼ 6.0		SO	Cross Millswitch Creek. Two tracks (closed) on left.
10.4 ▲		SO	Two tracks (closed) on right. Cross Millswitch Creek.
▼ 8.2		SO	Track on right to site of Chester.
8.2 ▲		SO	Track on left to site of Chester.

GPS: N 38°22.28' W 106°18.45'

▼ 11.0		TL	Seasonal gate. Intersection with road on right.
5.4 ▲		TR	Intersection and seasonal gate. Take FR 243 toward Marshall Pass.

GPS: N 38°22.20' W 106°20.62'

▼ 11.5		SO	Cattle guard.
4.9 ▲		SO	Cattle guard. Entering National Forest sign.
▼ 12.0		SO	Sign: "Indian Creek." Road on right is CR 35 W. (You are on CR XX 32.)
4.4 ▲		SO	CR 35 W on left goes to a network of 4WD tracks and the Pinnacle Mine.
▼ 16.4			End at intersection with US 50 in Sargents.
0.0 ▲			At intersection of US 50 and CR XX 32 (FR 243) in Sargents, zero trip meter and proceed along the county road toward Marshall Pass.

GPS: N 38°24.46' W 106°24.90'

O'Haver Lake

A small pond beside the trail

Hayden Pass Trail

Starting Point:	Villa Grove
Finishing Point:	Intersection of Hayden Creek Road (CR 6) and US 50
Total Mileage:	15.8 miles
Unpaved Mileage:	14.4 miles
Driving Time:	1.5 hours
Route Elevation:	6,590 to 10,870 feet
Usually Open:	Early July to mid-October
Difficulty Rating:	3
Scenic Rating:	7

Special Attractions

- One of the few 4WD trails in the Sangre de Cristo range.
- Varied 4WD route with good views, particularly of the San Luis Valley.
- Can be combined with Central #46 across Medano Pass to form a loop.

History

This pass was another used by the Ute to cross between the San Luis Valley and the Arkansas River to the northeast. In 1874, a wagon road was built across the pass, and Ferdinand Hayden noted this road when his survey party crossed it in 1875. The pass is officially named for an early settler of the Wet Mountain Valley, Lewis Hayden.

By the late 1870s, Hayden Pass was a popular route to Villa Grove—an important supply center at that time to the main route west via Cochetopa Pass and to the mining area of Bonanza, some 17 miles northwest. It connected to the network of toll roads built by Otto Mears over the Cochetopa, Los Piños, and Poncha Passes. Mears built one of his first toll roads between Villa Grove and Bonanza, alongside Kerber Creek.

The road on the east side of Hayden Pass

Villa Grove, established in 1870 as Garibaldi, was nestled in a grove of trees. In 1872, the name was changed to Villa-grove, which was subsequently broken into two words. A narrow gauge spur line of the Denver & Rio Grande Railroad terminated at Villa Grove prior to being extended to Alamosa in 1890.

Description

The route heads east from Villa Grove, but the turnoff is unmarked except for a "Villa Grove Common" sign. The road initially travels through the ranchland of the San Luis Valley before starting its ascent toward the pass.

The route is easy to navigate but has a few sections, mainly on the east side, that are steep and quite rough and require high clearance. It travels through pine forest most of the way but provides some good views along the route, particularly the sweeping views back across the San Luis Valley.

The route passes Rainbow Trail, a 55-mile hiking trail, and two U.S. Forest Service campgrounds before reaching US 50 at Coaldale, 4.1 miles west of Cotopaxi and 20 miles south of Salida.

The trail as it starts the ascent to the pass

Looking toward Coaldale from near the summit

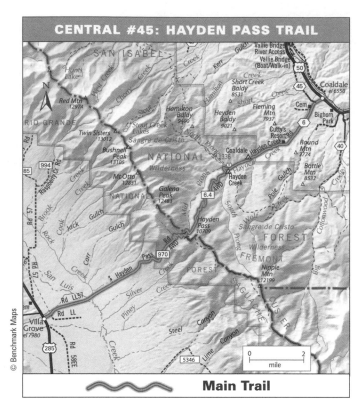

CENTRAL #45: HAYDEN PASS TRAIL

~~~~~ **Main Trail**

Current Road Information
Pike & San Isabel National Forests
Salida Ranger District
325 West Rainbow Boulevard
Salida, CO 81201
(719) 539-3591

Map References
USFS Rio Grande National Forest; San Isabel National
Forest
Maptech CD:
Alamosa/Pueblo/South Central
Benchmark's *Colorado Road & Recreation Atlas*, pp. 99, 100
Colorado Atlas & Gazetteer, pp. 70, 71
The Roads of Colorado, p. 127

Route Directions

| ▼ 0.0 | | | At intersection of US 285 and CR LL 57 (FR 970) in Villa Grove, zero trip meter and proceed east along LL 57. |
| 6.9 ▲ | | | End at intersection with US 285 in Villa Grove. |

GPS: N 38°14.96' W 105°56.92'

▼ 0.1		SO	Cattle guard and sign to Hayden Pass.
6.8 ▲		SO	Cattle guard.
▼ 1.6		SO	Cross over San Luis Creek.
5.3 ▲		SO	Cross over San Luis Creek.
▼ 2.7		SO	Cattle guard. CR 60 MM on left.
4.2 ▲		SO	CR 60 MM on right. Cattle guard.
▼ 2.8		SO	Track on right.
4.1 ▲		SO	Track on left.
▼ 4.1		SO	Track on left.
2.8 ▲		SO	Track on right.
▼ 4.2		SO	Track on right.
2.7 ▲		SO	Track on left.

| ▼ 4.6 | | SO | Enter Rio Grande National Forest. |
| 2.3 ▲ | | SO | Leave Rio Grande National Forest. |

GPS: N 38°16.84' W 105°52.30'

| ▼ 6.9 | | SO | Summit of Hayden Pass. Zero trip meter. |
| 0.0 ▲ | | | Continue. Enter Rio Grande National Forest. Name of road changes to FR 970. |

GPS: N 38°17.60' W 105°50.95'

▼ 0.0			Continue. Enter San Isabel National Forest. Name of road changes to FR 64.
8.9 ▲		SO	Summit of Hayden Pass. Zero trip meter.
▼ 1.1		SO	Track on left.
7.8 ▲		SO	Track on right.
▼ 1.5		SO	Cabin on right.
7.4 ▲		SO	Cabin on left.
▼ 1.9		SO	Track on left.
7.0 ▲		SO	Track on right.
▼ 2.0		SO	Track on left.
6.9 ▲		SO	Track on right.
▼ 2.8		SO	Track on left.
6.1 ▲		SO	Track on right.
▼ 4.1		TR	Intersection. San Isabel National Forest Campground entrance and Rainbow Trail walking track straight ahead. Turn onto CR 6 (FR 006) toward Coaldale.
4.8 ▲		TL	Intersection. San Isabel National Forest Campground entrance and Rainbow Trail walking track. Turn onto FR 64.

GPS: N 38°19.79' W 105°49.36'

▼ 5.4		SO	USFS Coaldale Campground on right.
3.5 ▲		SO	USFS Coaldale Campground on left.
▼ 8.6		SO	Paved road on left.
0.3 ▲		SO	Paved road on right.
▼ 8.9			End at intersection with US 50.
0.0 ▲			Intersection: US 50 and CR 6, at Coaldale. Sign: "NF Access Hayden Creek." Zero trip meter and proceed south along CR 6 (FR 006), also called Hayden Creek Road.

GPS: N 38°22.06' W 105°45.11'

An expansive view on the east side of the pass

Medano Pass and Great Sand Dunes Trail

Starting Point:	**Intersection of Colorado 69 and FR 559**
Finishing Point:	**Tollbooth for Great Sand Dunes**
	National Monument on Colorado 150
Total Mileage:	**21.6 miles**
Unpaved Mileage:	**20.1 miles**
Driving Time:	**2 hours**
Route Elevation:	**7,706 to 9,940 feet**
Usually Open:	**Late May to late October**
Difficulty Rating:	**4**
Scenic Rating:	**10**

Special Attractions

- The spectacular Great Sand Dunes National Park & Preserve with much more scenic access than the paved roads.
- Four-wheel driving through sand and numerous creek crossings.
- Historic pass route that can be combined with Central #45 across Hayden Pass to form a loop.

History

Medano means "sand hill" in Spanish, and the pass was also known as Sandhill Pass.

In 1807, Zebulon Pike crossed the pass after his famous attempt to climb the 14,000-foot peak that bears his name. By the 1850s, the pass was much used by fur traders and the mountain men heading for the San Juan region of Colorado. Captain John Gunnison even considered using it as a railroad route as early as 1853. In that same year, the Frémont expedi-

Sandy trail with the massive sand dunes in the distance

tion party crossed the pass but viewed the sand as too great an obstacle for a successful wagon route.

In 1866, a band of Ute attacked and killed settlers near La Veta, a small settlement 35 miles southeast of Medano Pass. They retreated over the pass but were captured by Kit Carson and Chief Ouray.

The route has never been developed for use by wagons or as a railroad and remains much as it has always been.

Description

This route commences at the intersection of Colorado 69 and FR 559, 23 miles south of Westcliffe and 9 miles west of Gardener. For nearly the first 7 miles, the road is 2WD as it travels through the Wolf Springs Ranch.

From the intersection with FR 412, it becomes a 4WD road and begins to switchback its way toward the pass. It is narrow and rough but presents no great problem as the surface is sound. The forest service has cut numerous channels across the road to protect it from erosion.

A section of trail alongside the towering sand dunes

Medano Creek crossing

From the summit, the scenery on the descent changes, with interesting rock formations and numerous creek crossings. These are shallow enough (12 to 18 inches) that they should not pose any problem for a 4WD vehicle; rather, they add some variety to the trail. Use caution if it has rained recently, as the road can become boggy.

Increasing patches of sand herald the Great Sand Dunes National Monument, one of Colorado's natural wonders. Before entering the monument, the main route is intersected by a number of side roads, along many of which the sand can be a greater obstacle than it is on this section of the main road.

After entering the Great Sand Dunes National Monument, the road travels beside the towering sand dunes, providing a much better view of them than that from the paved roads most visitors use. In places, the sand dunes are as close as 75 yards from the trail. There are a number of pull-offs, but be careful as the sand can be treacherous. It is a short walk to the creek and across to the face of the dunes.

A warning sign with the massive sand dunes soaring in the background

As the road travels deeper into the monument, the sand gets progressively worse, and you may need to deflate your tires to about 20 pounds. You may reinflate your tires at an air compressor station, which is open during the peak season months. At other times, or if it is not available, inquire at the Visitor Center for assistance.

Signs warn you of the most difficult section, where the sand is deep and loose, and steady momentum is required to avoid getting stuck. Shortly after this, you encounter the paved road (Colorado 150) that carries most visitors to the national monument.

Current Road Information
Great Sand Dunes National Park and Preserve
11999 US 50
Mosca, CO 81146
(719) 378-6300

Map References
USFS   San Isabel National Forest
Maptech CD:
        Alamosa/Pueblo/South Central
Benchmark's *Colorado Road & Recreation Atlas*, p. 114
Colorado Atlas & Gazetteer, p. 81
The Roads of Colorado, pp. 143, 144

Route Directions

▼ 0.0			At the intersection of Colorado 69 and FR 559, zero trip meter and turn onto FR 559 at sign marked "National Forest Access, Medano Pass."
	9.3 ▲		End at intersection with Colorado 69.
		GPS: N 37°50.19' W 105°18.44'	
▼ 0.3		SO	Cross over Muddy Creek.
	9.0 ▲	SO	Cross over Muddy Creek.
▼ 6.8		SO	Cattle guard. Enter San Isabel National Forest.
	2.5 ▲	SO	Cattle guard. Leave San Isabel National Forest.
		GPS: N 37°51.66' W 105°24.09'	
▼ 7.2		SO	Track on left.
	2.1 ▲	SO	Track on right.
▼ 7.3		SO	Track on right.
	2.0 ▲	SO	Track on left.
▼ 7.4		SO	FR 412 on right to South Muddy Creek.
	1.9 ▲	SO	FR 412 on left to South Muddy Creek.
▼ 9.3		SO	Medano Pass. Leaving San Isabel National Forest and entering Great Sand Dunes National Preserve. Track on right; then gate. Zero trip meter.
	0.0 ▲		Continue on main trail, now designated FR 559.
		GPS: N 37°51.37' W 105°25.91'	
▼ 0.0			Continue on main trail, now designated FR 235.
	6.0 ▲	SO	Gate and track on left; then Medano Pass. Leave Great Sand Dunes National Preserve and enter San Isabel National Forest. Zero trip meter.
▼ 0.2		SO	Bridge over creek.
	5.8 ▲	SO	Bridge over creek.
▼ 0.5		BL	Fork in track. Remain on 235. Turn right for some attractive backcountry campsites.
	5.5 ▲	BR	Fork in track. Remain on 235. Turn left for

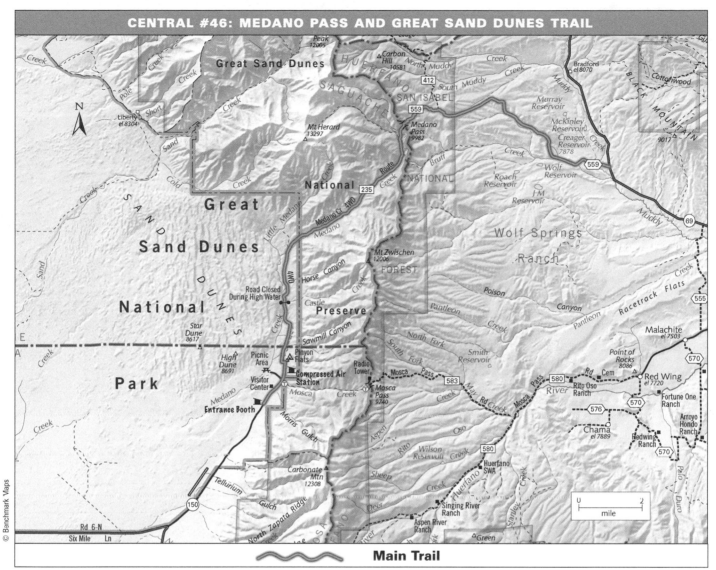

Main Trail

some attractive backcountry campsites.

▼ 1.4		SO	Cross through creek.
	4.6 ▲	SO	Cross through creek.
▼ 1.6		SO	Cross through creek.
	4.4 ▲	SO	Cross through creek.
▼ 1.9		SO	Track on right to cabin ruins. Then cross through creek.
	4.1 ▲	SO	Cross through creek. Track on left to cabin ruins.
▼ 2.2		SO	Cluster of cabin ruins.
	3.8 ▲	SO	Cluster of cabin ruins.
GPS: N 37°49.85' W 105°26.76'			
▼ 2.6		SO	Cross through creek.
	3.4 ▲	SO	Cross through creek.
▼ 3.3		SO	Cross through creek.
	2.7 ▲	SO	Cross through creek.
▼ 3.6		SO	Small track on right.
	2.4 ▲	BR	Small track on left.
▼ 3.7		SO	Cross through creek twice.
	2.3 ▲	SO	Cross through creek twice.
▼ 4.4		SO	Cross through creek.
	1.6 ▲	SO	Cross through creek.
▼ 4.9		SO	Cross through creek.

	1.1 ▲	SO	Cross through creek.
▼ 5.1		SO	Ruins (chimney) of old building.
	0.9 ▲	SO	Ruins (chimney) of old building.
GPS: N 37°48.47' W 105°28.99'			
▼ 5.2		SO	Cross through creek.
	0.8 ▲	SO	Cross through creek.
▼ 5.6		SO	Cross through large creek.
	0.4 ▲	SO	Cross through large creek.
▼ 5.8-5.9		SO	Tracks on left.
	0.1-0.2 ▲	SO	Tracks on right.
▼ 6.0		SO	Leave Great Sand Dunes National Preserve and enter Great Sand Dunes National Park. Zero trip meter.
	0.0 ▲		Cross through gate and proceed along FR 235.
GPS: N 37°48.10' W 105°29.85'			
▼ 0.0			Cross through gate and proceed along FR 235.
	4.8 ▲	SO	Leave Great Sand Dunes National Park and enter Great Sand Dunes National Preserve. Zero trip meter.
▼ 0.1		SO	Sand Creek Trail on right. Little Medano Trail on left.
	4.7 ▲	SO	Little Medano Trail on right. Sand Creek Trail on left.
▼ 0.6		SO	Cross through creek. Then picnic area, park-

Sand Creek meandering through the dunes

			ing, and cabins.
4.2 ▲		SO	Cabins, parking, and picnic areas. Then cross through creek.
▼ 2.4		SO	Gate and picnic spots.
	2.4 ▲	SO	Picnic spots and gate.
▼ 4.8		TR	Pavement. Intersection with Colorado 150. (Note: Compressed air is available across the road.) Zero trip meter.
	0.0 ▲		Proceed on Medano Pass Road (FR 235). Sign reads "Medano Pass Primitive Road."

GPS: N 37°44.66' W 105°30.39'

▼ 0.0			Proceed along Colorado 150.
	1.5 ▲	TL	Opposite the National Parks building marked "private residence" and tire air station on right.

			Zero trip meter.
▼ 0.5		SO	Road on right to sand dunes and picnic area.
	1.0 ▲	SO	Road on left to sand dunes and picnic area.
▼ 0.7		SO	Nature trail on left.
	0.8 ▲	SO	Nature trail on right.
▼ 0.9		SO	Intersection. Visitor Center on the right.
	0.6 ▲	SO	Visitor Center on the left. Intersection.
▼ 1.5			End at the tollbooth for Sand Dunes National Park.
	0.0 ▲		At the tollbooth for Sand Dunes National Park, zero trip meter and proceed toward the dunes.

GPS: N 37°43.50' W 105°31.12'

The Southwest Region

TRAILS IN THE SOUTHWEST REGION

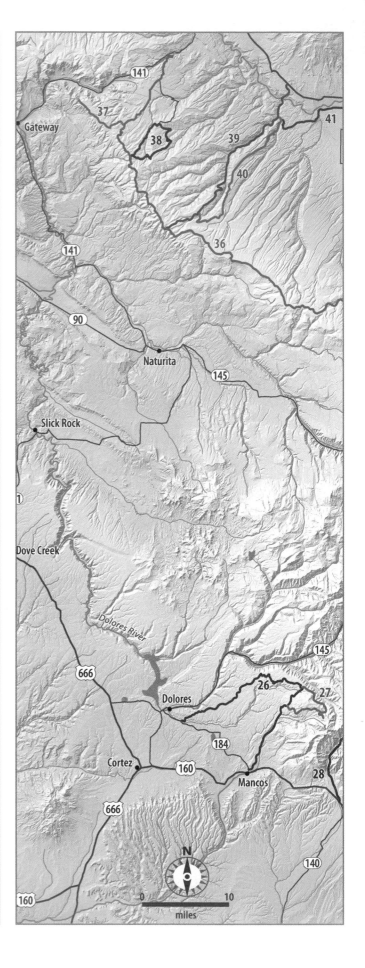

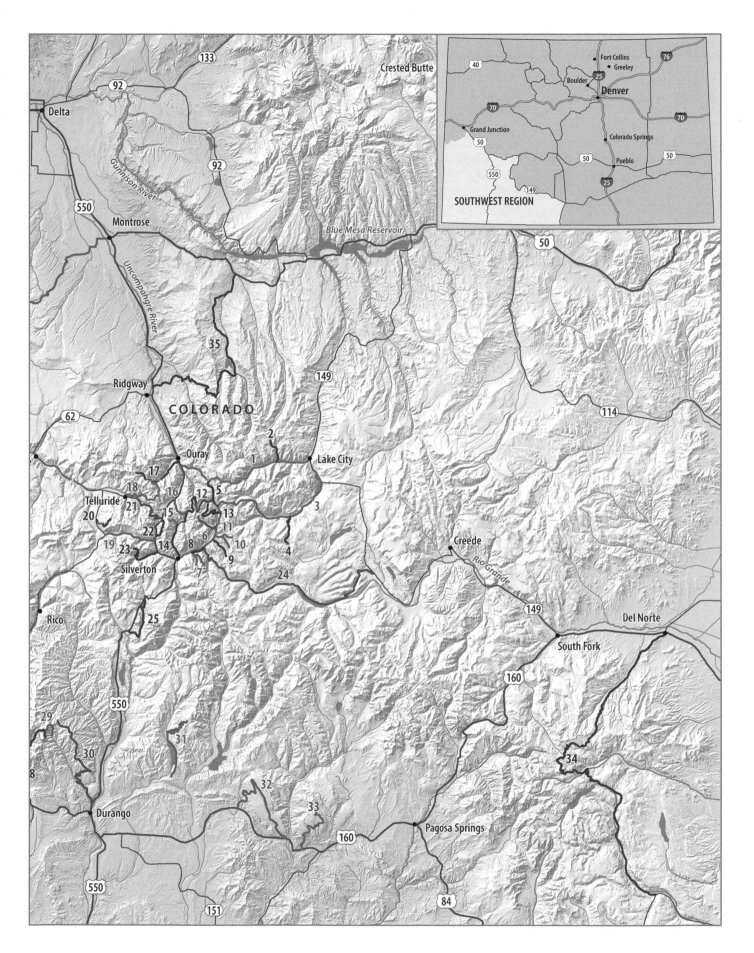

Engineer Pass Trail

Starting Point:	Ouray
Finishing Point:	Lake City—Intersection with Southwest #3: Cinnamon Pass Trail
Total Mileage:	31.0 miles
Unpaved Mileage:	27.3 miles
Driving Time:	3 hours
Route Elevation:	8,932 to 12,800 feet
Usually Open:	Mid-June to early October
Difficulty Rating:	4
Scenic Rating:	10

Special Attractions

- Part of the historic Alpine Loop, the location of many of Colorado's famous mining sites.
- Driving through the 20-foot deep channel in the snow early in the season.
- Spectacular Rocky Mountain scenery.
- Whitmore Falls.

History

Six years before building the Million Dollar Highway between Ouray and Silverton, Otto Mears extended his toll road from Saguache to Lake City and through to Animas Forks, via Engineer Pass. Mears's network of toll roads continued south to Eureka and Silverton and north to Mineral Point, Poughkeepsie, and Ouray.

From its completion in August 1877, this road was an important stagecoach route and the principal freight route for the wagons and mule trains that hauled supplies and ore between

The Empire Chief Mine adit

all the main mining camps in the area and Saguache, which was the closest major supply center. Within three years, the route had daily stages run by the Rocky Mountain Stage and Express Company.

The Engineer Pass 4WD trail passes the sites of some of the major mining camps that were established in the area. The turnoff to the first, Poughkeepsie, is located 2.5 miles from the start of the trail. This town was perched at an elevation of 11,650 feet and about 7 miles south of Ouray; its remote location and the poor quality of access roads hindered its development. The winters were so long and harsh that miners could work only two or three months of the year. Despite the hardships Poughkeepsie residents had to endure, the town was surprisingly well planned. It had a post office established in 1880, a newspaper called the *Poughkeepsie Telegraph*, stores, restaurants, saloons, and other businesses. Miners usually sent ore to Lake City or Silverton by burro via rough roads. Transporting the ore in this manner was so difficult and expensive that eventually mine owners decided the expense wasn't worth it and ceased operations. No buildings from the town remain.

Mineral Point mining camp was located about 1.75 miles southwest of Engineer Pass, at an elevation of 11,500 feet. Prospectors Abe Burrows and Charles McIntyre founded the camp in

Engineer Pass

1873. To generate interest in the camp and to raise capital, promoters of Mineral Point circulated far-fetched advertisements with unrealistic pictures and claims. One advertisement depicted a steamship running up the Animas River and streetcars running from Mineral Point to Animas Forks!

In truth, only very mediocre transportation was available, and miners had to use cumbersome wagons or burros to transport their ore. Most was sent either to Silverton via Animas Forks or to Lake City. Because of the inhospitable winters, the lack of transportation, and the silver crash of 1893, by the mid-1890s Mineral Point was on its way to becoming a ghost camp.

Just beyond Engineer Pass is the site of Engineer City, established around 1874 when H. A. Woods staked the first claim in the area and named it the Annie Woods Lode. By 1875, the population of prospectors grew to about 400. For a short time, Engineer City prided itself on being the largest city in the state without a saloon. The prospectors were simply too busy looking for silver to spend time in a bar. In 1882, the Frank Hough Mine was discovered. A camp of about 50 men operated the mine, located in American Flats on the eastern side of Engineer Mountain. Operations ceased in 1900, and the ruins of the mine remain.

Rose's Cabin was once a lively inn offering food, lodging, and entertainment to miners and travelers. Corydon Rose was one of the first pioneers to explore the San Juans after a treaty was signed with the Utes in 1873. Rose decided to build an inn to serve the area, locating it about halfway between Ouray and Lake City to provide a convenient stopover for travelers along the route.

The area around the cabin began to grow in population as miners settled there. They built cabins nearby and worked mines in the surrounding hills. It is estimated that about 50 people settled in the vicinity. Rose's Cabin served the community as its local bar, restaurant, hotel, general store, and post office. Rose kept 60 burros in a stable to ship supplies to the miners and carry their ore down to his cabin. The cabin was the hive of activity in the region. Only a few traces of the cabin remain. The structure still standing is the old stable; the cabin was situated to the left.

Capitol City was established about 10 miles west of Lake City after rich silver discoveries in 1877 brought prospectors to the area. The town of Galena City began as a tent city, but the tents were soon replaced by more permanent structures. George S. Lee, a miner with grand plans, had the town's name changed to Capitol City because he was certain that Colorado would move its capital to the San Juan Mountains and he would live in the governor's mansion. To aid in the construction of Capitol City, Lee built a sawmill and planing mill. He also erected the Henson Creek Smelter 1 mile below the town to process ore from the many mines nearby.

A town site of 200 acres was laid out; a schoolhouse was built, although the population never exceeded 400 and there were only a handful of students. Lee built himself a large and elegant house at the edge of town to be the governor's mansion, where he and his wife entertained lavishly. Their home even had a ballroom and orchestra pit. Bricks imported from Pueblo were estimated to have cost a dollar apiece! However,

Lee's efforts did not bear fruit: Capitol City never even became the county seat.

About 4 miles before reaching Lake City the road passes through the town of Henson, a mining camp that grew up around the Ute-Ulay Mine. In 1871, Henry Henson discovered the mine, but the land belonged to the Indians, who did not take kindly to white trespassers. Henson was unable to develop the property until well after the Brunot Treaty of 1873, because violence with the Indians continued for several years. White settlers clashed with the native Indians near Lake City as late as 1879.

There was also a long, bitter, and violent miners strike in Henson. Reportedly, the strike started because the mine owners insisted that all single men board at the company boardinghouse. To protest, miners went on strike. When the owners hired non-union labor to replace the striking miners, fights erupted and some scabs were run out of town. The volatility of the situation prompted the governor of Colorado to send four companies of cavalry and two companies of infantry to

Empire Chief Mill

Henson Creek runs alongside the trail

settle the dispute. The dispute eventually went to trial, and all the miners were forced to leave camp.

Henson's post office, established in May 1883, was closed in November 1913. The buildings still standing in Henson are privately owned, and many are still in use.

Description

This route commences south of Ouray on the Million Dollar Highway, US 550.

If you wish to avoid the hardest section of the Engineer Pass Trail, the route can be commenced at Silverton by taking Southwest #6: Silverton to Animas Forks Ghost Town and then Southwest #5: North Fork Cutoff to connect with Engineer Pass Trail.

The turnoff from US 550 onto Engineer Pass Trail is well marked with a national forest access sign. This 4WD track gets straight down to business. In fact, the next 5 miles are the hardest of the entire trip. Sections of the road are steep and rough. It is also narrow with sheer drop-offs. Although it may appear threatening at first, it is readily passable for 4WD vehicles if taken slowly and carefully.

A tip for those who are nervous about driving shelf roads and encountering oncoming vehicles: Leave early. This road is popular, and oncoming 4WD vehicles will be encountered frequently later in the day, as those traveling from Lake City are descending. Pull-offs are reasonably frequent.

At the 1.6-mile point, you pass the Mickey Breene Mine, which was discovered in 1890. The mine yielded high-grade ore and produced copper and silver.

About 2.5 miles from US 550, the road intersects with the Poughkeepsie 4WD road. This road is difficult and should be taken only by those willing to risk vehicle damage.

From the Mineral Point turnoff, the terrain starts to clear, with numerous open, although boggy meadows. The climb continues to Engineer Pass at 12,800 feet.

From the summit, the road descends through the southern edge of American Flats and past the site of Engineer City.

From this point, the road follows the path of Henson Creek all the way to Lake City.

About 2 miles after the summit, there is a scenic old cabin beside the creek at Palmetto Gulch; shortly after that, a bridge crosses the creek at what was the site of the Palmetto Gulch Mill. From this point, the road is passable by passenger vehicles.

The road passes close by Rose's Cabin, which was an important way station on the stage route. The remains of the buildings can still be seen. Less than a mile farther is the Empire Chief Mill that was worked from January to March 1929, when an avalanche killed four men and destroyed most of the buildings.

A few miles on, a sign marks a short walking trail down to beautiful Whitmore Falls. Though short, the hike back up is strenuous.

The original Capitol City, with its grand aspirations to be the state capital, is now reduced to the remains of the post office. However, the town site is on private land, and new homes continue to be built there.

The route continues to Henson and then through Henson Creek Canyon to Lake City.

Bulldozers plow portions of Engineer Pass, which is usually opened around mid-June. When the road crews get through, they leave in their wake a narrow channel through the snow, with walls of snow up to 20 feet high on either side.

Current Road Information

San Juan Mountains Center
Joint Forest Service/BLM office
PO Box 709
1246 Blair Street
Silverton, CO 81433
(970) 387-5530
Closed in Winter

Lake City Chamber of Commerce
800 Gunnison Avenue
Lake City, CO 81235
(970) 944-2527

Silverton Chamber of Commerce
414 Greene Street
Silverton, CO 81433
(970) 387-5654

Map References

USFS   Uncompahgre National Forest; Gunnison National Forest
Maptech CD: Southwest/Durango/Telluride
Benchmark's *Colorado Road & Recreation Atlas*, pp. 110, 111
Colorado Atlas & Gazetteer, pp. 66, 67, 76, 77
The Roads of Colorado, pp. 123, 124
Trails Illustrated, #141

Route Directions

▼ 0.0		In front of Beaumont Hotel at 5th and Main in Ouray, zero trip meter and proceed south out of town, remaining on US 550.
3.7 ▲		End in front of Beaumont Hotel at 5th and Main in Ouray.
GPS: N38°01.30′ W107°40.29′		

The trail being bulldozed in early summer

▼ 3.7	TL	National forest access sign on right. Engineer Mountain and Alpine Loop signs are at the dirt track entrance. Zero trip meter.
0.0 ▲		Proceed on US 550 toward Ouray. Paved road.
GPS: N37°59.26′ W107°39.01′		
▼ 0.0		Proceed along jeep trail.
7.0 ▲	TR	Intersection with US 550. Zero trip meter.
▼ 1.6	SO	Mickey Breene Mine ruins on left.
5.4 ▲	SO	Mickey Breene Mine ruins on right.
▼ 1.7	SO	Private road on left.
5.3 ▲	SO	Private road on right.
▼ 2.0	SO	Diamond Creek crossing. Track on right to backcountry campsites.
5.0 ▲	SO	Track on left to backcountry campsites. Diamond Creek crossing.
▼ 2.4	TL	Poughkeepsie Gulch 4WD trail to the right.

Wildflowers blooming in early summer near the turnoff to Mineral Point

4.6 ▲	BR	Intersection with Poughkeepsie Gulch 4WD trail on the left.	

GPS: N37°58.01′ W107°37.60′

▼ 3.4	SO	Track on left.	
3.6 ▲	SO	Track on right.	
▼ 3.7	SO	Track on right to backcountry campsites.	
3.3 ▲	SO	Track on left to backcountry campsites.	
▼ 4.2	SO	Miner's cabin on left. Tracks on left to Des Ouray Mine.	
2.8 ▲	SO	Tracks on right to Des Ouray Mine. Cabin on right.	
▼ 4.4	SO	Track on right. Stay on main road.	
2.6 ▲	SO	Track on left. Stay on main road.	
▼ 4.6	SO	Track on right to backcountry campsites.	
2.4 ▲	SO	Track on left to backcountry campsites.	
▼ 5.0	SO	Track on right to backcountry campsites.	
2.0 ▲	SO	Track on left to backcountry campsites.	
▼ 5.1	TL	Intersection: Signpost to Mineral Point. Follow sign to Engineer Mountain.	
1.9 ▲	BR	Intersection.	

GPS: N37°57.72′ W107°35.71′

▼ 5.2	SO	View across the valley to San Juan Chief Mill.	
1.8 ▲	SO	View across the valley to San Juan Chief Mill.	
▼ 5.8	SO	Public restrooms on right.	
1.2 ▲	SO	Public restrooms on left.	
▼ 6.1	SO	Tracks on right lead to series of open mine portals.	
0.9 ▲	SO	Tracks on left lead to series of open mine portals.	

▼ 7.0	TL	Intersection with Southwest #5: North Fork Cutoff. Signs indicate Silverton and Animas Forks to the right; Lake City via Engineer Pass to the left. Zero trip meter.	
0.0 ▲		Continue toward Ouray.	

GPS: N37°57.42′ W107°34.47′

▼ 0.0		Continue on main road toward Engineer Pass.	
6.1 ▲	TR	Three-way intersection. Straight ahead is Southwest #5: North Fork Cutoff, which leads to Animas Forks and Silverton. Zero trip meter.	
▼ 0.8	UT	Follow sign to Engineer Pass. An unmarked track is straight ahead.	
5.3 ▲	UT	Unmarked track is straight ahead.	
▼ 1.9	SO	Road on left to Oh! Point.	
4.2 ▲	SO	Road on right to Oh! Point.	
▼ 2.3	BR	Summit of Engineer Pass. Two walking track trailheads are at summit: Bear Creek and Ridge Stock Driveway. Follow sign to Lake City.	
3.8 ▲	BL	Summit of Engineer Pass. Two walking track trailheads are at summit: Bear Creek and Ridge Stock Driveway.	

GPS: N37°58.46′ W107°35.08′

▼ 2.5	SO	Frank Hough Mine remains and American Flats.	
3.6 ▲	SO	Frank Hough Mine remains and American Flats.	
▼ 2.8	SO	Site of Engineer City.	
3.3 ▲	SO	Site of Engineer City.	
▼ 3.2	SO	Horsethief Trail walking track on left.	

Palmetto Gulch Cabin

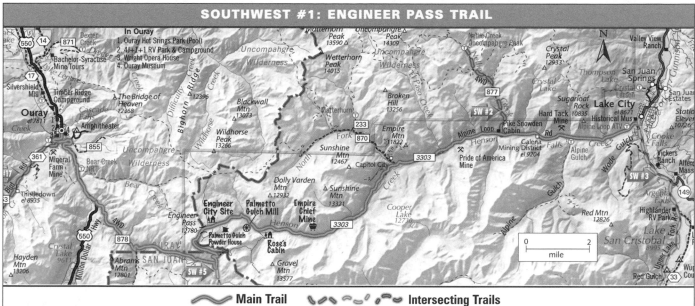

~~~ **Main Trail** ~~~ **Intersecting Trails**

2.9 ▲		SO	Horsethief Trail walking track on right.
▼ 3.4		SO	Palmetto Gulch powderhouse and mine remains on right. Track on right to open mine shaft.
	2.7 ▲	SO	Track on left to open mine portal. Palmetto Gulch powderhouse and mine remains on left.
▼ 4.4		SO	Palmetto Gulch cabin.
	1.7 ▲	SO	Palmetto Gulch cabin.
▼ 4.6		SO	Thoreau's Cabin on left.
	1.5 ▲	SO	Thoreau's Cabin on right.
▼ 4.8		SO	Bridge and Palmetto Gulch mill remains. 2WD vehicles sufficient beyond this point.
	1.3 ▲	SO	Palmetto Gulch mill remains and bridge. 4WD vehicles recommended beyond this point.
▼ 5.1		SO	Track on right to backcountry campsites along Henson Creek. Track networks with next two entries.
	1.0 ▲	SO	Track on left to backcountry campsites along Henson Creek.
▼ 5.4		SO	Track on right goes to same vicinity as previous. Also goes across creek to Hurricane Basin and past a mine.
	0.7 ▲	SO	Track on left to backcountry campsites along Henson Creek.
▼ 6.1		BL	Road to Rose's Cabin site on right. Zero trip meter.
	0.0 ▲		Continue along main road toward Engineer Pass.

GPS: N37°58.58' W107°32.20'

▼ 0.0		SO	Continue along main road toward Lake City.
	9.0 ▲	BR	Road to Rose's Cabin site on left. Zero trip meter.
▼ 0.1		SO	Public restrooms on right.
	8.9 ▲	SO	Public restrooms on left.
▼ 0.8		SO	Empire Chief Mine and Mill on left.
	8.2 ▲	SO	Empire Chief Mine and Mill on right.
▼ 1.2		SO	Waterfall on right.
	7.8 ▲	SO	Waterfall on left.
▼ 2.4		SO	Smelter chimney on right from the Lee Mining and Smelter Company.
	6.6 ▲	SO	Smelter chimney on left from the Lee Mining and Smelter Company.
▼ 3.4		SO	Whitmore Falls walking track on right.

5.6 ▲		SO	Whitmore Falls walking track on left.
▼ 4.5		SO	Corral on right.
	4.5 ▲	SO	Corral on left.
▼ 5.0		SO	Capitol City town site. Private land and new homes.
	4.0 ▲	SO	Capitol City town site.

GPS: N38°00.35' W107°28.05'

▼ 5.1		BR	Bridge; then signpost on left indicating road to N. Henson Road via Matterhorn Creek and Uncompahgre Peak.
	3.9 ▲	BL	Walking trails on right; then bridge.
▼ 7.1		SO	Bridge and track on right.
	1.9 ▲	SO	Bridge and track on left.
▼ 8.6		SO	Open mine portal on left along road.
	0.4 ▲	SO	Open mine portal on right along road.
▼ 8.9		SO	Public restrooms on left.
	0.4 ▲	SO	Public restrooms on right.
▼ 9.0		SO	Track on left is Southwest #2: Nellie Creek Trail. Zero trip meter.
	0.0 ▲	SO	Continue on main road toward Engineer Pass.

GPS: N38°01.22' W107°23.97'

▼ 0.0			Continue on main road toward Lake City.
	5.1 ▲	SO	Track on right is Southwest #2: Nellie Creek Trail. Zero trip meter.
▼ 1.3		SO	Town of Henson.
	3.7 ▲	SO	Town of Henson.
▼ 1.7		SO	Open mine portal on left along road.
	3.4 ▲	SO	Open mine portal on right along road.
▼ 2.5		SO	Alpine Gulch Trailhead on right.
	2.6 ▲	SO	Alpine Gulch Trailhead on left.
▼ 4.0		SO	Ruins of old mill on left.
	1.2 ▲	SO	Ruins of old mill on right.
▼ 5.1		TR	Stop sign in Lake City. SO at next intersection, Silver Street.
	0.1 ▲	BL	Proceed along CR 20.
▼ 5.2			Trail ends at the intersection of 1st Street and Gunnison Avenue (Colorado 149).
	0.0 ▲		At the intersection of 1st Street and Gunnison Avenue (Colorado 149), zero trip meter and proceed northwest along 1st Street. SO across Silver Street.

GPS: N38°01.58' W107°19.03'

Nellie Creek Trail

Starting Point:	**Intersection of Southwest #1: Engineer Pass Trail and FR 877**
Finishing Point:	**Uncompahgre Peak Trailhead**
Total Mileage:	**4.0 miles (one-way)**
Unpaved Mileage:	**4.0 miles (one-way)**
Driving Time:	**45 minutes**
Route Elevation:	**9,400 to 11,500 feet**
Usually Open:	**Mid-June to early October**
Difficulty Rating:	**4**
Scenic Rating:	**8**

Special Attractions

- Interesting side road from Engineer Pass Trail.
- Scenery ranging from waterfalls to spectacular Uncompahgre Peak.
- Access to Uncompahgre Trailhead and the numerous hiking trails of the Uncompahgre Wilderness.

History

From much of the higher section of this trail you view the towering Uncompahgre Peak. At 14,309 feet, it is the highest mountain in the San Juans and the sixth highest in Colorado. The Hayden Survey Party made the first recorded ascent in 1874 and Lt. William Marshall of the later Wheeler Survey also climbed it. Prior to these times, the Ute used the peak as a lookout.

The mountain became notorious for its large population of grizzly bears, which was mentioned by both of the survey parties. However, evidently not everyone was deterred by their presence because in the late 1800s, the peak became a popular excursion for parties of hikers from the nearby mining towns of Capitol City and Lake City. Hikers find the north face treacherous to climb, but access from the southwest and southeast is relatively easy.

No major mines were ever found on the mountain itself.

Description

The initial section of this road is a gentle climb through the forest, following the course of Nellie Creek. This lower section of the creek and the nearby forest show the signs of many industrious beavers' labor. The trail is rough with occasional loose boulders, but generally they are embedded, so the trail is not difficult to drive in a high-clearance vehicle. The biggest problem you are likely to have is passing vehicles you encounter traveling the other way, as some sections are too narrow to pass without one driver reversing to a suitable spot.

There are numerous aspen trees at the lower reaches that add color in the fall to the already very attractive scenery provided by Nellie Creek, which flows beside the trail for much of the route, and a waterfall located at the 0.7-mile point.

After about 0.75 miles, there is a section of shelf road upon which you continue the climb. The road levels off after a little more than 1.5 miles and you get a good view of Uncompahgre Peak. After you cross a shallow creek, the climb through the forest continues. The trail switchbacks up to an-

An early section of the trail that travels beside Nellie Creek

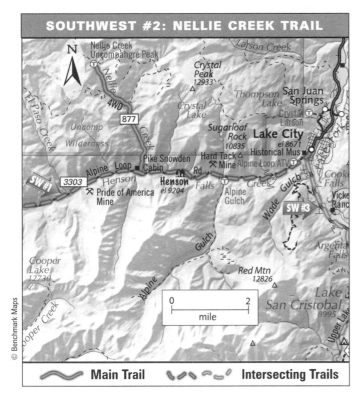

Main Trail — Intersecting Trails

© Benchmark Maps

other relatively level segment that can become quite boggy in wet weather conditions. The trail becomes rougher at this time and there are a number of shallow creek crossings. This section is the most difficult part of the trail but under dry conditions it just warrants a difficulty rating of 4.

After about 3 miles, the trail levels off and enters an alpine meadow. A mile farther, the trail ends at the parking area for the Uncompahgre Peak Trailhead.

Current Road Information

Grand Mesa, Uncompahgre and Gunnison National Forests
Gunnison Ranger District
216 North Colorado
Gunnison, CO 81230
(970) 641-0471

Lake City Chamber of Commerce
800 Gunnison Avenue
Lake City, CO 81235
(970) 944-2527

Map References

USFS   Gunnison National Forest; Uncompahgre National Forest
Maptech CD: Southwest/Durango/Telluride
Benchmark's *Colorado Road & Recreation Atlas*, p. 111
Colorado Atlas & Gazetteer, p. 67
The Roads of Colorado, p. 123
Trails Illustrated, #141

Route Directions

▼ 0.0   From Southwest #1: Engineer Pass Trail (5.1 miles from Lake City), zero trip meter and proceed

along the 4WD track with sign to Nellie Creek Trailhead and Uncompahgre Peak Trail (FR 877).

GPS: N38°01.22' W107°23.97'		
▼ 0.7	SO	Waterfall in trees on left.
▼ 1.6	SO	Beaver lodge on right.
▼ 1.7	SO	Great view of rugged Uncompahgre Peak.
▼ 1.8	SO	Cross through Nellie Creek.
GPS: N38°02.58' W107°24.23'		
▼ 2.2	SO	Ruins of two log buildings across creek.
▼ 2.3	UT	Short track on right.
▼ 2.6	SO	Cross through creek.
▼ 3.4	SO	Cross through creek.
▼ 4.0		Public restrooms; then end of track at trailhead and parking area.
GPS: N38°03.74' W107°25.32'		

SOUTHWEST REGION TRAIL #3

Cinnamon Pass Trail

Starting Point:	Lake City at intersection with
	Southwest #1: Engineer Pass Trail
Finishing Point:	Animas Forks
Total Mileage:	26.6 miles
Unpaved Mileage:	20.4 miles
Driving Time:	2 hours
Route Elevation:	8,932 to 12,620 feet
Usually Open:	Late May to late October
Difficulty Rating:	3
Scenic Rating:	9

Cinnamon Pass

Special Attractions

- Animas Forks ghost town.
- Part of the Alpine Loop, the location of many historic mining towns.
- Moderately easy 4WD trail opened by snowplow early in the season.
- Wonderful, varied scenery.

History

The Ute used this pass road before white exploration of the area. Then, in the early 1860s, Charles Baker used the pass on his journey into the San Juan Mountains when he reported finding gold, triggering a minor gold rush. In 1873, Albert Burrows further explored the area, and in the following year, the Hayden Survey Party crossed the pass.

In the mid-1870s, Washington bureaucrats came to the conclusion that because the pass was not on the Continental Divide, the mail service should be able to cross it all year long; they awarded a contract on just that basis, despite the impossibility of the task.

In 1877, Enos Hotchkiss constructed the first wagon road over the pass. It was an important freight road for a period but was not maintained after the ore in the area declined.

The route starts at the still active town of Lake City. It was established following the discovery of the Golden Fleece Mine in 1874, originally named the Hotchkiss Mine, which became the best ore producer in the area, although many other strikes followed.

In 1875, Lake City, named for nearby Lake San Cristobal, was registered and stagecoaches began making three trips a week to Saguache. That same year, Harry M. Woods published Lake City's first newspaper, *The Silver World*. The post office opened when the stagecoach service was extended to include a mail stage to Del Norte.

Lake City was one of the first towns in Colorado to have telephone service. In 1876, Western Union initiated telephone service, and by 1881, service had been extended to Silverton, Ouray, Capitol City, Rose's Cabin, Mineral Point, and Animas Forks. Musicians utilized the telephone service to perform popular telephone concerts for listeners along the various lines!

At its high point, Lake City had around 2,500 residents. Since the town was platted at the junction of two toll roads—Saguache to Silverton and Antelope Springs to Lake City—hundreds of people passed through the community each week. Stagecoaches continued to stop in the city daily. The Denver & Rio Grande Railroad arrived in 1889. There were two trains daily in the 1890s, and ore shipments left aboard these trains regularly.

The wild red-light district on the west of town was known as Hell's Acres. Gambling dens and dance halls were interspersed among the many brothels. Lake City had its rough side: Many of its residents were killed in mine accidents, snow slides, and shoot-outs.

Lake City experienced a series of economic fluctuations. It suffered greatly after the silver crash of 1893 and went into a

View of Animas Valley from Cinnamon Pass Trail in spring before the snow has melted

American Basin

long decline, relieved only by subsequent gold and lead production.

After the turn of the century, Lake City was on the decline; but camping, fishing, and hunting helped revive it as a summer community. In 1933, the railroad tracks were sold for scrap. Lake City never became a ghost town, although its population dwindled and it is currently a sleepy little community. Many original buildings were made of stone and still survive. The large stone schoolhouse was built in 1882. The courthouse where Alferd Packer was tried was built in 1877 and is still used.

From Lake City, the paved road extends past Lake San Cristobal, which was initially formed in about A.D. 1270 by the Slumgullion Slide, a huge mud and rock slide. A second major slide about 350 years ago completed the formation of Lake San Cristobal, the second largest natural lake in Colorado.

The route passes the turnoff to Sherman town site that was originally founded in 1877 and named for an early pioneer. The town grew slowly at first and then expanded quickly in the 1880s. Although several mines in the area yielded large amounts of gold, silver, copper, and lead, the principal mine was the Black Wonder. Located on the north side of town, the Black Wonder produced primarily silver, and most of the mine's ore was transported to the smelters in Lake City. Sherman's population and prosperity fluctuated with the fortunes of the Black Wonder Mine, which continued to produce ore into the early 1900s. The town of Sherman peaked in the mid-1880s, when one summer the population reached about 300.

Sherman was a convenient stagecoach stop since it was located halfway between Animas Forks and Lake City. To travel on the toll road between Sherman and Lake City cost $2.50, and the cost to travel between Sherman and Animas Forks was $2.00 in either direction.

Around 1900, a 150-foot dam was constructed upstream of Sherman, but only a few days after the dam's completion, runoff from torrential rains flooded the mountainside, ripped the dam to pieces, and swept away much of the town of Sherman. The silver crash three years later ended Sherman's hopes for recovery, although the town was not completely deserted until the 1920s.

A cluster of mining camps sprouted up in the alpine meadow of Burrows Park between 1877 and 1880. The park was 5 miles long and 0.5-miles wide. The exact locations of the camps are disputed, but the general area is about 10 miles southwest of Lake City, at the western end of the valley.

Burrows Park

Burrows Park was the name of one of the camps, which was founded in 1877. About a mile south of Burrows Park, there was a community named Tellurium. This tiny camp had only about a dozen people, who hoped to find tellurium there. The highly optimistic group built an expensive mill. Unfortunately, Tellurium never became prosperous, and it was soon deserted. Another camp named Sterling was located a short distance beyond Tellurium, toward Animas Forks. Nearer the Continental Divide toward Cinnamon Pass, Whitecross was the largest of the settlements and served as the center of activity for the other camps. Whitecross's post office, established in 1880, was first called Burrows Park, after the region. Two years later it was renamed Whitecross.

Many men who lived in this area worked at the Tabasco Mine and Mill, which operated from 1901 to 1904 and was one of the first mines to use electric alternating current. Tabasco, the Louisiana hot sauce manufacturing company, owned both the mine and the mill. Ruins of the mine are scattered around the summit of Cinnamon Pass.

Description

Today Cinnamon Pass Trail is a seasonal, moderately easy 4WD road. It is part of the historic and majestic Alpine Loop. The other half of the loop is Southwest #1: Engineer Pass Trail. These two roads form the backbone of a network of roads throughout the region. Cinnamon Pass Trail is the easier of the two, but in the peak summer months both are extremely popular 4WD routes.

The scenery varies from the rugged alpine environment of year-round snow and barren talus slopes near the summit to the wildflower-covered valleys and rushing streams draining the melting snow. At either end of the route are wonderful historic towns, one a ghost town, the other a hive of activity.

Initially, the gravel road is an easy, maintained road. After entering the Gunnison National Forest, the road intersects Southwest #4: Carson Ghost Town Trail on the left. The trail crosses Wager Gulch and passes the historic ghost town of Carson and continues over the Continental Divide.

Three miles farther along CR 30 is the intersection with CR 35—a short side road leading to the site of Sherman. While the remains of the town are clearly visible, the forest has reclaimed the entire area.

After the Sherman turnoff, the road narrows into a shelf road overlooking the canyon. However, it remains comfortably wide even for full-sized 4WD vehicles, with a sufficient number of pull-offs available to facilitate passing.

A short distance farther, the road enters Burrows Park Basin—the region of Whitecross, Burrows Park, Tellurium, and Sterling townships. The road passes the two remaining buildings of Burrows Park and a public restroom.

About 3.5 miles farther, after passing the turnoff to the American Basin, which is renowned for its spring wildflowers, the road becomes more difficult as it ascends above timberline into alpine tundra. At this point, the views become expansive. From the summit of Cinnamon Pass, the road descends into the picturesque ghost town of Animas Forks, an amazingly well-preserved ghost town where numerous buildings remain.

Bulldozers clear the snow on Cinnamon Pass, usually opening it by Memorial Day.

Current Road Information

San Juan Mountains Center
Joint Forest Service/BLM office
PO Box 709
1246 Blair Street
Silverton, CO 81433
(970) 387-5530
Closed in Winter

Lake City Chamber of Commerce
800 Gunnison Avenue
Lake City, CO 81235
(970) 944-2527

Silverton Chamber of Commerce
414 Greene Street
Silverton, CO 81433
(970) 387-5654

Map References

USFS   Uncompahgre National Forest; Gunnison National Forest
Maptech CD: Southwest/Durango/Telluride
Benchmark's *Colorado Road & Recreation Atlas*, pp. 110, 111
Colorado Atlas & Gazetteer, pp. 67, 77
The Roads of Colorado, pp. 123, 124
Trails Illustrated, #141

Route Directions

▼0.0		At the intersection of Gunnison Avenue (Colorado 149) and 1st Street, zero trip meter and proceed south on Colorado 149.
14.0 ▲		End at intersection of Gunnison Avenue (Colorado 149) and 1st Street.

GPS: N38°01.58′ W107°19.03′

▼ 2.2	TR	Follow Alpine Loop Drive sign.
11.8 ▲	TL	Onto Colorado 149.

▼ 6.2	BR	Before bridge. Follow Alpine Loop sign onto unpaved road.
7.8 ▲	BL	Bridge on right. Turn onto paved road.

▼ 8.9	SO	USFS Williams Creek Campground on right.
5.1 ▲	SO	USFS Williams Creek Campground on left.

▼ 11.1	SO	Southwest #4: Carson Ghost Town Trail on left.
2.9 ▲	SO	Southwest #4: Carson Ghost Town Trail on right.

GPS: N37°54.39′ W107°21.60′

▼ 11.3	SO	Cross over bridge.
2.7 ▲	SO	Cross over bridge.

▼ 12.3	SO	Public toilets on left.
1.7 ▲	SO	Public toilets on right.

▼ 12.9	SO	Mill Creek BLM campground on left.
1.1 ▲	SO	Mill Creek BLM campground on right.

▼ 14.0	BR	Intersection with CR 35 on left to Sherman town site. Follow sign to Cinnamon Pass and Silverton. Zero trip meter.
0.0 ▲		Continue on main road toward Lake City.

GPS: N37°54.21′ W107°24.68′

▼ 0.0		Continue on main road toward Cinnamon Pass.
7.5 ▲	SO	Intersection with CR 35 to Sherman town site on right. Zero trip meter.

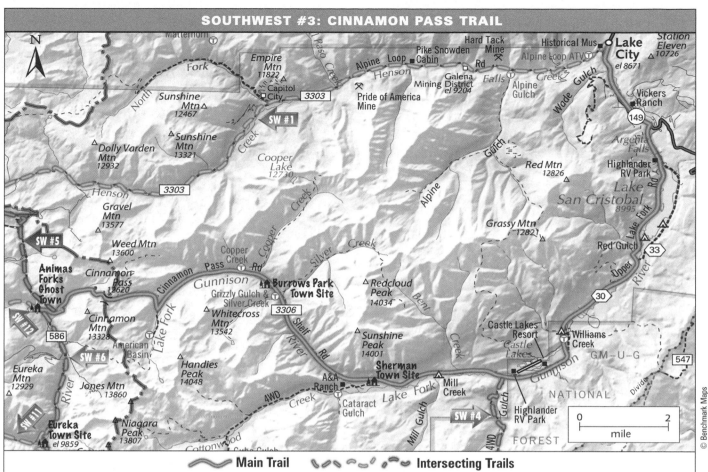

~ **Main Trail**   ~ **Intersecting Trails**

▼ 0.5	SO	Cross bridge.
7.0 ▲	SO	Cross bridge.
▼ 3.9	SO	Cross over Silver Creek.
3.7 ▲	SO	Cross over Silver Creek.
▼ 4.0	SO	Burrows Park town site. Grizzly Gulch (left) and Silver Creek (right) Trailheads. Public toilets.
3.5 ▲	SO	Burrows Park town site. Grizzly Gulch (right) and Silver Creek (left) Trailheads. Public toilets.
		GPS: N37°56.24′ W107°27.63′
▼ 5.5	SO	Mine on right.
2.0 ▲	SO	Mine on left.
▼ 6.3	SO	Cattle guard.
1.3 ▲	SO	Cattle guard.
▼ 6.4	SO	Creek crossing.
1.1 ▲	SO	Creek crossing.
▼ 7.1	SO	Track on left leads to mines.
0.4 ▲	SO	Track on right leads to mines.
▼ 7.4	SO	Creek cascade on right flows underneath road.
0.2 ▲	SO	Creek cascade on left flows underneath road.
▼ 7.6	BR	Intersection. Posted sign reads "4WD recommended past this point." American Basin on left. Zero trip meter.
0.0 ▲		Continue on main road toward Lake City.
		GPS: N37°55.87′ W107°30.80′
▼ 0.0		Continue on main road toward Cinnamon Pass.
2.2 ▲	BL	Intersection. American Basin on right. Zero trip meter.
▼ 0.4	SO	Cross over creek.
1.8 ▲	SO	Cross over creek.

▼ 0.5	SO	Deserted cabin on right; then Tabasco Mill ruins.
1.6 ▲	SO	Tabasco Mill ruins; then deserted cabin on left.
▼ 2.2	SO	Summit of Cinnamon Pass. Zero trip meter.
0.0 ▲		Continue on main road toward Lake City.
		GPS: N37°56.03′ W107°32.25′
▼ 0.0		Continue on main road toward Animas Forks.
2.8 ▲	SO	Summit of Cinnamon Pass. Zero trip meter.
▼ 0.1	BL	Track on right.
2.7 ▲	BR	Track on left.
▼ 0.7	SO	Cross over Cinnamon Creek.
2.1 ▲	SO	Cross over Cinnamon Creek.
▼ 2.1	UT	Track straight ahead is Southwest #5: North Fork Cutoff. Continue on main road.
0.7 ▲	UT	Follow switchback toward Cinnamon Pass. Straight ahead is Southwest #5: North Fork Cutoff.
▼ 2.5	UT	Intersection. Go toward Animas Forks. Silverton is straight ahead.
0.3 ▲	UT	Intersection. Follow switchback toward Cinnamon Pass. Silverton is straight ahead.
		GPS: N37°55.78′ W107°33.90′
▼ 2.8		Cross bridge into Animas Forks and end at intersection. Southwest #6 to Silverton is to the left; Southwest #12: California Gulch Trail is to the right.
0.0 ▲		At three-way intersection in Animas Forks, zero trip meter and proceed across bridge toward Cinnamon Pass.
		GPS: N37°55.89′ W107°34.22′

Carson Ghost Town Trail

Starting Point:	Intersection of Southwest #3:
	Cinnamon Pass Trail and FR 568
Finishing Point:	Carson ghost town
Total Mileage:	3.7 miles (one-way)
Unpaved Mileage:	3.7 miles
Driving Time:	30 minutes
Route Elevation:	9,400 to 12,350 feet
Usually Open:	Mid-June to late September
Difficulty Rating:	4
Scenic Rating:	9

Special Attractions

- Well-preserved ghost town of Carson.
- Views from the Continental Divide.

History

Following the discovery of silver at Carson in 1881, a wagon road was built to service the mines, leading from the Gunnison River to Lake City. Carson was very close to the Continental Divide and was one of the most remote mining camps in Colorado. The silver crash of 1893 led to its demise, and no buildings remain standing.

In 1896, prospectors discovered gold in the area, and a new town was built at a lower elevation than the original. It is this second town of Carson that remains today as a ghost town. It was abandoned in 1903; the road that serviced it also fell into disuse.

Description

This short side trip from Cinnamon Pass Trail is well worth the time and effort of crossing a section of very slippery mud that exists on the trail most years. The rewards are exploring the well-preserved ghost town and spectacular panoramic views from the crest of the Continental Divide.

Stalls in the Carson ghost town stables

The route commences from Southwest #3: Cinnamon Pass Trail, 15.4 miles from Animas Forks and 11.3 miles from Lake City. A sign that reads "Wager Gulch/Carson" marks the turnoff.

The road is initially fairly steep but reasonably wide and has an adequate number of pull-offs. Occasional embedded rocks and erosion can require care in selecting the right line, but the road should not be too rough for a normal 4WD vehicle.

The most difficult problem can be mud. The first 2 miles of this trail are usually spotted with muddy sections. The sur-

A view of Carson ghost town today

A group of trail riders visiting Carson ghost town

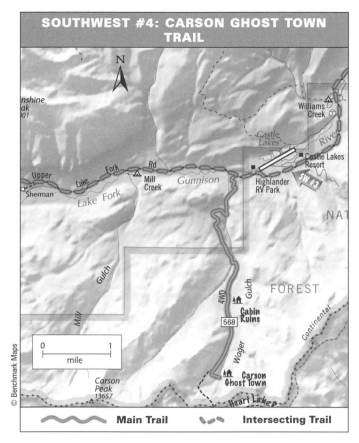

SOUTHWEST #4: CARSON GHOST TOWN TRAIL

Main Trail ~~~~~   Intersecting Trail

Current Road Information

Grand Mesa, Uncompahgre and Gunnison National Forests
Gunnison Ranger District
216 N. Colorado
Gunnison, CO 81230
(970) 641-0471

Map References

USFS   Uncompahgre National Forest; Gunnison National
Forest
Maptech CD: Southwest/Durango/Telluride
Benchmark's *Colorado Road & Recreation Atlas*, p. 111
Colorado Atlas & Gazetteer, p. 77
The Roads of Colorado, pp. 123, 139
Trails Illustrated, #141

Route Directions

▼ 0.0   From intersection of Southwest #3:
               Cinnamon Pass Trail and FR 568, zero
               trip meter and proceed toward Carson

Carson ghost town, nestled in Wager Gulch

face is firm but it can be very slippery and wheel-rutted, and because the forest shelters the road, the mud is slow to dry.

Getting adequate traction depends on the weight of your vehicle, the state of the road on the day you attempt it, and, most importantly, the tires you are using. Exercise care in order to avoid oncoming vehicles that can have difficulty steering or stopping on the downhill slope.

Once you pass the mud, this road is straightforward. Exploring Carson and witnessing the views from the Continental Divide are well worthwhile.

The Continental Divide is just over a mile past the creek crossing at Carson. From the Continental Divide, the route deteriorates into walking trails, so you'll need to retrace your tracks and return to Cinnamon Pass Trail.

One of the larger buildings still standing in Carson ghost town

on FR 568. This intersection is 11.3 miles from Lake City.

		GPS: N37°54.39′ W107°21.60′	
▼ 0.1	BL	Series of private driveways.	
▼ 0.7	SO	Creek crossing.	
▼ 1.7	BR	Fork in road. Continue uphill.	
▼ 2.2	SO	Creek crossing.	
▼ 2.8	SO	Cabin ruins on left.	
▼ 3.5	BL	Fork in road. Turn toward Carson ghost town. Straight ahead will lead across the Continental Divide and to the site of Old Carson.	
▼ 3.6	SO	Cross through creek.	
▼ 3.7	BL	Carson town site with many well-preserved structures.	
		GPS: N37°52.13′ W107°21.72′	

SOUTHWEST REGION TRAIL #5

North Fork Cutoff

Starting Point:	**Intersection with Southwest #3: Cinnamon Pass Trail**
Finishing Point:	**Intersection with Southwest #1: Engineer Pass Trail**
Total Mileage:	**2 miles**
Unpaved Mileage:	**2 miles**
Driving Time:	**20 minutes**
Route Elevation:	**11,489 to 12,169 feet**
Usually Open:	**Late May to late October**
Difficulty Rating:	**4**
Scenic Rating:	**9**

Description

This route is straightforward and is included in this book to allow more flexibility in traveling the Alpine Loop, which primarily consists of Southwest #1: Engineer Pass Trail and Southwest #3: Cinnamon Pass Trail. By linking these two roads, the Alpine Loop can be started or finished from any of three towns: Lake City, Ouray, or Silverton.

The North Fork Cutoff usually opens before the summit of Engineer Pass is cleared, allowing access to the western end of Engineer Pass Trail, which can be used as a route between Ouray and Animas Forks.

Although the route includes sections of shelf road, it is not very narrow and has a reasonable number of pull-offs. However, it is sufficiently rough to require a high-clearance vehicle.

Current Road Information

San Juan Mountains Center
Joint Forest Service/BLM office
PO Box 709
1246 Blair Street
Silverton, CO 81433
(970) 387-5530
Closed in Winter

Map References

USFS Uncompahgre National Forest; Gunnison National Forest
Maptech CD: Southwest/Durango/Telluride
Benchmark's *Colorado Road & Recreation Atlas*, p. 110
Colorado Atlas & Gazetteer, p. 77
The Roads of Colorado, p. 123
Trails Illustrated, #141

Route Directions

▼ 0.0		At the intersection of Southwest #3: Cinnamon Pass Trail and Southwest #5: North Fork Cutoff, 0.7 miles from Animas Forks, zero trip meter and proceed north.	
	2.0 ▲	End at intersection with Cinnamon Pass Trail. Bear left to Lake City. Bear right to Animas Forks.	
		GPS: N37°56.02′ W107°34.10′	
▼ 0.3		SO	Mine on left.
	1.7 ▲	SO	Mine on right.

Denver Lake and open mine portals along the North Fork Cutoff

SOUTHWEST #5: NORTH FORK CUTOFF

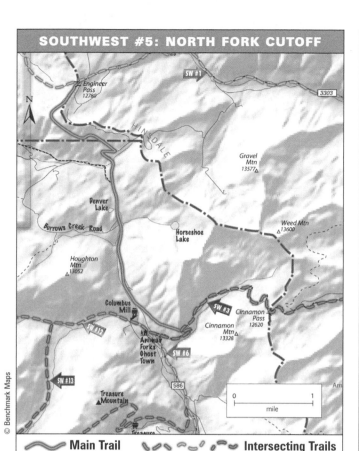

Main Trail ~ Intersecting Trails

▼ 0.4		SO	Tram cables overhead.
1.6 ▲		SO	Tram cables overhead.
▼ 0.6		SO	Track on right.
1.4 ▲		SO	Track on left.
▼ 0.9		SO	Open mine portal in mountainside on the left.
1.1 ▲		SO	Open mine portal in mountainside on the right.
▼ 1.0		SO	Cross over creek.
1.0 ▲		SO	Cross over creek.
▼ 1.2		SO	Cross over creek.
0.8 ▲		SO	Cross over creek.
▼ 1.4		BR	Open mine portal on left. Track on left leads to mines along Burrows Creek and dead-ends in approximately 2 miles. Follow sign to Engineer Pass and Alpine Loop.
0.6 ▲		BL	Track on right leads to mines along Burrows Creek and dead-ends. Open mine portal on right.

GPS: N37°56.91' W107°34.53'

▼ 1.6		SO	Track on left to Denver Lake, cabin, and mine. Cross over creek. Track on right.
0.4 ▲		SO	Track on left. Cross over creek. Track on right to Denver Lake, cabin, and mine.
▼ 1.7		SO	Mine ruins on right.
0.3 ▲		SO	Mine ruins on left.
▼ 2.0			End at intersection with Southwest #1: Engineer Pass Trail. Left goes to Ouray. Right goes to Engineer Pass and Lake City.
0.0 ▲			At the intersection of Southwest #1: Engineer Pass Trail and North Fork Cutoff, zero trip meter and proceed south along North Fork Cutoff toward Animas Forks.

GPS: N37°57.41' W107°34.48'

Silverton to Animas Forks Ghost Town

Starting Point:	**Silverton**
Finishing Point:	**Animas Forks**
Total Mileage:	**12.1 miles**
Unpaved Mileage:	**10.0 miles**
Driving Time:	**45 minutes**
Route Elevation:	**9,400 to 11,370 feet**
Usually Open:	**Mid-May to late October**
Difficulty Rating:	**1**
Scenic Rating:	**8**

Special Attractions

- Animas Forks, one of Colorado's best ghost towns.
- The extremely historic road following part of the old railway grade, with innumerable points of historic interest.

History

This route commences in Silverton, a well-preserved historic mining town that was founded in 1873. It is the terminus for the famed Durango and Silverton Narrow Gauge Railroad, which is a popular tourist destination in the summer months.

From Silverton, the route follows the Animas River as it passes numerous mines that dot the area known as Bakers Park, which extends all the way to Eureka. The park was named after Charles Baker, one of the first explorers in the

A snow bridge across the Animas River in late spring

A view of Animas Forks today

gone by was Saguache Street and led into the center of town. The square building is the restored water tank; the room below was used as the town jail. The foundations of several other buildings are evident.

The massive foundations that rise up the mountainside on the other side of the Animas River are the remains of the Sunnyside Mill. The Sunnyside Mine, located in Eureka Gulch behind the mill, was discovered in 1873. By 1910, it consisted of 10 miles of tunnel and employed 300 miners. The first wooden mill opened in 1899 and is located to the left of the existing foundations, which belong to the second Sunnyside Mill (which started production in 1918). The second mill incorporated much of the dismantled Gold Prince Mill, relocated from Animas Forks.

About half a mile from Eureka, the ruins of a boardinghouse and a bridge across the Animas River can be seen on the right. The boardinghouse was built in 1907 to house the workers from the Tom Moore Mine.

The road at this point follows the old Silverton Northern Railroad line, built by Otto Mears in 1903–1904. Four hundred men worked on this section of the railroad line; it had an average grade of seven percent, which resulted in the train having an average speed of only 4 miles per hour. Going up, the train could only pull a coal car and one empty car, and on the downhill, it was limited to a maximum of three ore cars.

The other natural obstacle that challenged the railroad was snow. On the left of the road can be seen the remnants of one of the snowsheds built by Otto Mears to protect the railroad

area, who triggered a minor gold rush into territory still occupied by the Ute in the early 1860s.

At the 6-mile point is the town site of Middleton, a small mining camp in the late 1800s, of which nothing remains. At the 7.7-mile point is the town site of Eureka. At the southern end of the town site is a turnoff on the right, which in days

A view of Animas Forks nestled in the valley with the road continuing beyond toward California Gulch

from snow slides, which are prevalent in the area. Despite Mears's best endeavors, nature proved too strong an adversary, and the snowsheds were destroyed in the first winter. High operating costs and declining mineral production led to the closure of the railroad in 1916.

Across the river from the snowshed can be seen the remnants of the last toll road built by Otto Mears in the mid-1880s—the only one he lost money on.

As you cross the Animas River on the entry into Animas Forks ghost town, the foundations on the right are the remains of the Gold Prince Mill, the largest concentrating mill in Colorado when it was built in 1904. On the left is the location of the railroad turntable used to turn around the steam engine of the Silverton Northern Railroad for the return to Silverton.

Farther into Animas Forks, a number of buildings remain to the left of the road. The most famous of these is the two-story Walsh House with the front bay window. This was the home of William Duncan and was constructed in 1879. It has been speculated that Thomas Walsh's daughter stayed there when writing her father's biography and also that Walsh rented a room there in his younger (and poorer) days. It is extremely unlikely that either story is true. The buildings across the Animas River as you leave town are the Columbus Mine and Mill, built in about 1880. This mill ceased operations in 1948.

Description

The entire route is an easy, well-maintained, gravel road suitable for passenger vehicles under good weather conditions.

Current Road Information

San Juan Mountains Center
Joint Forest Service/BLM office
PO Box 709
1246 Blair Street
Silverton, CO 81433
(970) 387-5530
Closed in Winter

Another well-preserved cabin in Animas Forks

The Columbus Mill in Animas Forks

Silverton Chamber of Commerce
414 Greene Street
Silverton, CO 81433
(970) 387-5654

Map References

USFS Uncompahgre National Forest; San Juan National Forest
Maptech CD: Southwest/Durango/Telluride
Benchmark's *Colorado Road & Recreation Atlas*, p. 110
Colorado Atlas & Gazetteer, p. 77
The Roads of Colorado, p. 123
Trails Illustrated, #141

Route Directions

▼ 0.0		From the Silverton City Hall at Greene (main) Street and 14th Street, zero trip meter and proceed northeast out of town.
7.8 ▲		End in front of the Silverton City Hall at Greene and 14th Streets.
	GPS: N37°48.79′ W107°39.72′	
▼ 0.2	BR	Road forks. Bear right onto Colorado 110. Remain on paved road.
7.6 ▲	BL	Road forks. Bear left and remain on paved road.
▼ 0.4	SO	Campground on the right.
7.4 ▲	SO	Campground on the left.
▼ 0.5	SO	Lackawanna Mill on right across the river. Hillside Cemetery on left.

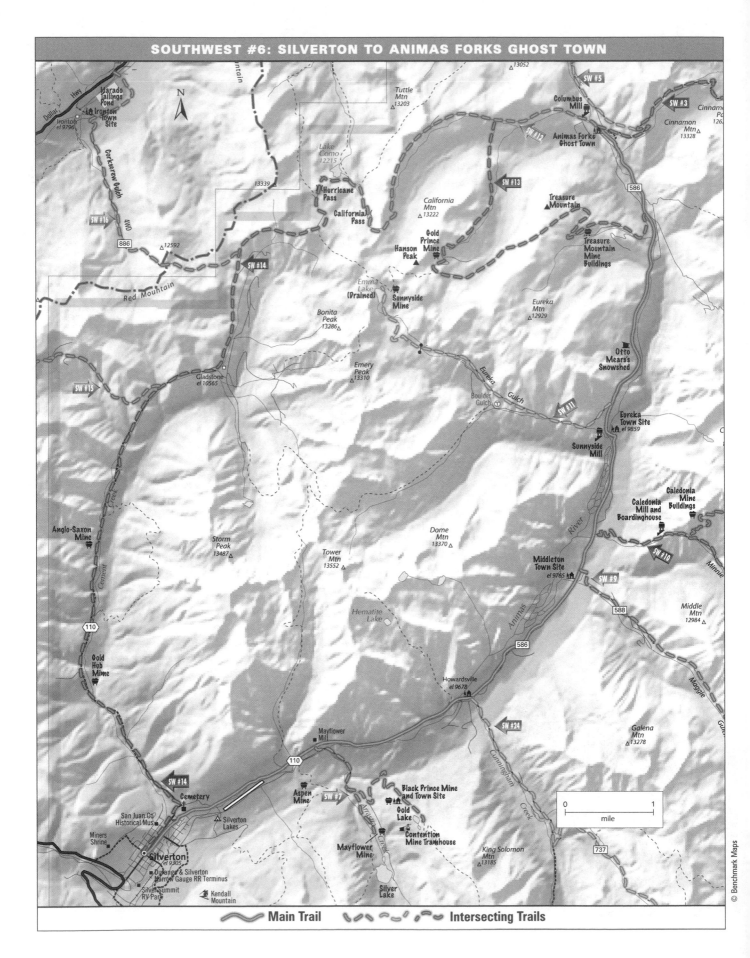

N

SW #5

SW #3

Cinnamon Pa...

△ 13052

Tuttle Mtn
13203

Columbus Mill

Cinnamon Mtn
13328 △

SW #12

Animas Forks Ghost Town

586

Idarado Tailings Pond

Ironton Town Site

Dollar... Hwy

Ironton
el 9796

Corkscrew Gulch

SW #16

886

△ 12592

4WD

13339

Hurricane Pass

California Pass

California Pass

California Mtn
13222 △

SW #13

Treasure Mountain

SW #14

Red Mountain

Hanson Peak

Gold Prince Mine

Treasure Mountain Mine Buildings

Emma Lake (Drained)

Sunnyside Mine

Eureka Mtn
12929 △

Otto Mears's Snowshed

Bonita Peak
13286 △

SW #15

Gladstone
el 10565

Emery Peak
13310 △

Eureka Gulch

Boulder Gulch

SW #11

Eureka Town Site
el 9859

Sunnyside Mill

Caledonia Mine Buildings

Caledonia Mill and Boardinghouse

Anglo-Saxon Mine

Storm Peak
13487 △

Tower Mtn
13552 △

Dome Mtn
13370 △

River

SW #10

Minnie

Cement Creek

Middleton Town Site
el 9765

SW #9

588

Middle Mtn
12984 △

110

Hematite Lake

Animas

586

Gold Hub Mine

Howardsville
el 9678

Maggie Gulc...

SW #24

Galena Mtn
13278 △

Mayflower Mill

SW #14

110

Cemetery

San Juan Co Historical Mus.

Miners Shrine

Silverton Lakes

Aspen Mine

SW #7

Black Prince Mine and Town Site

Gold Lake

Cunningham Creek

King Solomon Mtn
13185 △

737

Silverton
el 9305

Durango & Silverton Narrow Gauge RR Terminus

Silver Summit RV Park

Kendall Mountain

Mayflower Mine

Contention Mine Tramhouse

Arrastra Creek

Silver Lake

0 ——— 1
mile

© Benchmark Maps

〰 **Main Trail**   ◦◦◦ ◦ ◦ **Intersecting Trails**

7.3 ▲	SO	Hillside Cemetery on right. Lackawanna Mill on left across the river.	

▼ 0.7	BR	Road fork entering on left.
7.0 ▲	BL	Road fork entering on right.

▼ 1.6	SO	Aspen Mine ruins on right across the river.
6.2 ▲	SO	Aspen Mine ruins on left across the river.

▼ 1.7	SO	On the right side of the road, in the distance about 3 miles east, the tramhouse and boarding house of the Old Hundred Mine are evident about three-quarters of the way up Galena Mountain.
6.1 ▲	SO	The tramhouse and boardinghouse of the Old Hundred Mine are evident on the left, in the distance about 3 miles southeast, three-quarters of the way up Galena Mountain.

▼ 2.0	SO	Silver Lake Mill on right.
5.8 ▲	SO	Silver Lake Mill on left.

▼ 2.1	SO	Southwest #7: Arrastra Gulch Trail and Southwest #8: Silverton Northern Railroad Grade on right.
5.7 ▲	SO	Southwest #7: Arrastra Gulch Trail and Southwest #8: Silverton Northern Railroad Grade on left.

▼ 2.2	SO	Mayflower Mill and tram on left.
5.6 ▲	SO	Mayflower Mill and tram on right.

▼ 3.8	SO	Little Nation Mine on right, halfway up the mountainside.
4.0 ▲	SO	Little Nation Mine on left, halfway up the mountainside.

▼ 4.0	SO	Bridge across the Animas River.
3.8 ▲	SO	Bridge across the Animas River.

▼ 4.2	SO	Bridge across Cunningham Creek; then turnoff for Southwest #24: Cunningham Gulch and Stony Pass Trail on the right. Town site of Howardsville. Little Nations Mill.
3.6 ▲	SO	Little Nations Mill. Town site of Howardsville. Turnoff for Southwest #24: Cunningham Gulch and Stony Pass Trail on the left; then bridge across Cunningham Creek.

GPS: N37°50.06' W107°35.68'

▼ 6.0	SO	Southwest #9: Maggie Gulch Trail on right. Town site of Middleton.
1.8 ▲	SO	Town site of Middleton. Southwest #9: Maggie Gulch Trail on left.

▼ 6.6	SO	Cross over creek. Southwest #10: Minnie Gulch Trail on right.

The much-photographed Walsh House in Animas Forks

	1.2 ▲	SO	Southwest #10: Minnie Gulch Trail on left. Cross over creek.
▼ 6.7		SO	Track to campsites on right.
	1.1 ▲	SO	Track to campsites on left.
▼ 7.7		BL	Entry to Eureka town site on right. Campsites.
	0.1 ▲	BR	Entry to Eureka town site on left. Campsites.
▼ 7.8		SO	Bridge over Animas River. Zero trip meter.
	0.0 ▲		Continue along main road.

GPS: N37°52.76' W107°33.92'

▼ 0.0			Continue along main road.
	4.3 ▲	SO	Bridge over Animas River. Zero trip meter.
▼ 0.1		BR	Sunnyside Mill on left.
	4.2 ▲	BL	Sunnyside Mill on right.
▼ 0.3		SO	Southwest #11: Eureka Gulch Trail on left.
	4.0 ▲	SO	Southwest #11: Eureka Gulch Trail on right.
▼ 0.5		SO	Historic boardinghouse for mine workers on right.
	3.7 ▲	SO	Historic boardinghouse for mine workers on left.
▼ 1.0		SO	Log remains of a snowshed built by Otto Mears on left.
	3.3 ▲	SO	Log remains of a snowshed built by Otto Mears on right.
▼ 1.8		SO	Silver Wing Mine on right.
	2.5 ▲	SO	Silver Wing Mine on left.
▼ 2.7		SO	Remains of dam used to feed the Silver Wing Mine.
	1.6 ▲	SO	Remains of dam used to feed the Silver Wing Mine.
▼ 2.8		SO	Southwest #13: Picayne Gulch and Placer Gulch Trail on left. Track on right crosses Animas River and joins the road to Burns Gulch.
	1.5 ▲	SO	Southwest #13: Picayne Gulch and Placer Gulch Trail on right. Track on left crosses Animas River and joins the road to Burns Gulch.
▼ 2.9		SO	Track on left. Cross over Animas River. Turnoff to Burns Gulch on right.
	1.4 ▲	SO	Turnoff to Burns Gulch on left. Cross over Animas River. Track on right.
▼ 3.5		SO	Cross over Cinnamon Creek.
	0.8 ▲	SO	Cross over Cinnamon Creek.
▼ 3.6		BL	Proceed toward Animas Forks. Cutoff to Cinnamon Pass Trail on right. Public restrooms on left.
	0.7 ▲	BR	Public restrooms on right. Cutoff to Cinnamon Pass Trail on left. Proceed on main road toward Silverton.
▼ 3.9		SO	Cross over Animas River. Gold Prince Mill ruins on right.
	0.4 ▲	SO	Gold Prince Mill ruins on left. Cross over Animas River.
▼ 4.1		SO	Public restrooms on right. Animas Forks jailhouse site behind the restrooms.
	0.2 ▲	SO	Animas Forks jailhouse site behind the public restrooms on left.
▼ 4.3			Animas Forks ghost town. Bridge across Animas River is on the right, leading to Southwest #3: Cinnamon Pass and Southwest #1: Engineer Pass. The Columbus Mill is straight ahead.
	0.0 ▲		At the bridge over the Animas Forks River at the north end of Animas Forks, zero trip meter and proceed south toward Silverton.

GPS: N37°55.89' W107°34.22'

Arrastra Gulch Trail

Starting Point:	Intersection with Southwest #6: Silverton to Animas Forks Ghost Town
Finishing Point:	Gold Lake in Little Giant Basin
Total Mileage:	6.1 miles
Unpaved Mileage:	6.1 miles
Driving Time:	1 hour (one-way)
Route Elevation:	9,850 to 12,200 feet
Usually Open:	Mid-June to early October
Difficulty Rating:	5
Scenic Rating:	10

Special Attractions

- Picturesque Gold Lake.
- Black Prince mining camp.
- Numerous other old mining remains.

History

The historic interest of this 4WD trail centers on the numerous mines that were located in the area. Many of the mining operations built mills to process their ore and tramways to transport the ore from the mines to the mills.

The first historic site is the Whale Mill, which was an early water-powered mill erected in about 1888 that was eventually incorporated into the Silver Lake Mill operation.

The shelf road cut into the talus rock above Arrastra Creek

Gold Lake

The Mayflower Mine was discovered in the late 1880s. Following the construction of Mayflower Mill in 1929, ore from the mine was carried nearly 2 miles by a steel tramway down to the mill for processing.

The Contention Mine tramway carried ore 1.25 miles from the Big Giant and Black Prince Mines to Contention Mill, located on the north side of the Animas River, beside the railroad. Near the Black Prince Mine is a mining camp that still contains a number of long-deserted buildings. The mining company constructed them in 1915 to house its workers.

Near the end of the route is the Big Giant Mine, which was discovered in the 1870s but was only a marginal operation. After the mine was bought by the Contention Mining Company, its tramway was used to carry ore to the Contention Mill for processing.

Description

This route is another side road of Colorado 110, Southwest #6: Silverton to Animas Forks Ghost Town. It starts at the unmarked turnoff to Arrastra Gulch. Shortly after the start, the trail crosses a bridge over the Animas River, and then a shelf road that climbs toward Arrastra Gulch commences. Progressing along this road, there is a good view of the creek and valley below. The road is sound and reasonably wide.

At the 0.8-mile point the road forks. The route directions follow the right-hand fork first and then return to explore the other fork. The right-hand section follows the gulch to end just below the Mayflower Mine, at which point the road gets much narrower and is washed out a short distance ahead.

The left-hand fork is the harder of the two roads. It leads to the Black Prince Mine and the buildings that have survived from the mining camp. From there, the road climbs to the majestic surrounds of Gold Lake, nestled in Little Giant Basin. This fork of the route starts by ascending a narrow shelf that has limited opportunity for passing. It is rough and rocky but not extremely difficult because the surface is fairly sound. The rocks on the trail are not large enough to pose clearance problems for a 4WD vehicle, but some are sharp. From the Black Prince mining camp the road gets narrower with a very steep drop-off. The scenic location of Gold Lake makes the journey well worthwhile.

Most of this trail rates a 3 for difficulty. The latter section, exploring the left-hand fork, rates a 4 until the Black Prince mining camp, and then the trail becomes rated 5 for the last short section to Gold Lake. The trail is particularly scenic, especially along the upper reaches and in the vicinity of Gold Lake. There are numerous aspens to provide autumn color in the lower section of the trail.

Current Road Information

Silverton Chamber of Commerce
414 Greene Street
Silverton, CO 81433
(970) 387-5654

A pond with the Black Prince mining camp in the background

Map References

Contention Mine tramhouse

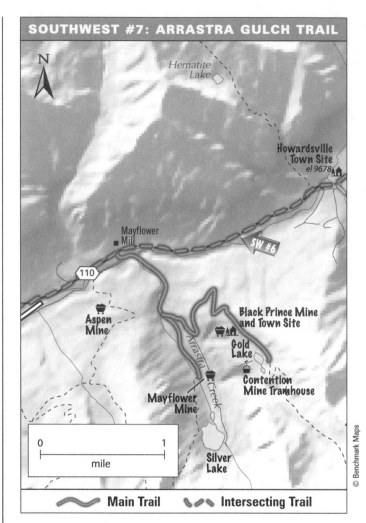

SOUTHWEST #7: ARRASTRA GULCH TRAIL

Main Trail — *Intersecting Trail*

© Benchmark Maps

Route Directions

▼ 0.0   From Southwest #6: Silverton to Animas Forks Ghost Town (CR 110) opposite the Mayflower Mill, zero trip meter and proceed downhill on the Arrastra Gulch road toward the river. This intersection is 2.1 miles from Silverton City Hall.

     GPS: N37°49.62' W107°37.77'

▼ 0.2   **SO**   Track on the left and right is Southwest #8: Silverton Northern Railroad Grade; then cross Arrastra Creek.

▼ 0.3   **SO**   Cross under Mayflower Mill tram. Track on right goes to up Arrastra Gulch to the Silver Lake Mine.

▼ 0.5   **SO**   Ruins of dam in creek on right.

▼ 0.7   **SO**   Whale Mill ruins down at the creek on the other side. Level with the road, across the steam, are the ruins of a wooden support for the Silver Lake tram.

▼ 0.8   **BL/BR**   Fork with track straight ahead into meadow; then fork with track on left to Contention Mine and Mill. Zero trip meter. (You will return to this point to explore the left-hand fork.)

     GPS: N37°49.21' W107°37.23'

▼ 0.0   Cross under tram line.

▼ 0.2   **SO**   Wooden tram structure on right.

▼ 0.3   **SO**   Track on left.

▼ 0.6   **SO**   Track on left to Mayflower Mine and tram station.

▼ 0.7   **SO**   Cross under tram line. Tram towers on the right.

▼ 1.0   **SO**   Road deteriorates.

▼ 1.2	UT	Trail washed out at head of gulch. Mayflower Mine on hill to the left. Turn around and return to the fork where you last reset the trip meter.
	GPS: N37°48.33' W107°36.69'	
▼ 2.4	TR	Intersection. Zero trip meter.
	GPS: N37°49.21' W107°37.23'	
▼ 0.0		Proceed along left-hand fork toward the Contention Mine and Mill.
▼ 0.1	SO	Pass under tram cable.
▼ 0.3	SO	Both wooden and steel tram supports on right.
▼ 0.4	TL	Turn sharply onto the road to Little Giant Basin.
	GPS: N37°49.06' W107°36.99'	
▼ 0.9	SO	Pass under tram cables for the Contention tram.
▼ 1.0	SO	Pass under tram cables.
▼ 1.3	SO	Pass under tram cables.
▼ 1.5	SO	Pass under tram cables.
▼ 2.1	BL	Black Prince mining camp.
	GPS: N37°48.35' W107°36.29'	
▼ 2.4	SO	King Solomon Mine portal on left.
▼ 2.7	SO	Big Giant/Contention Mine and Mill on right.
▼ 2.9		End at beautiful Gold Lake.
	GPS: N37°48.39' W107°35.96'	

![A view of the Black Prince mining camp](...)

A view of the Black Prince mining camp

Silverton Northern Railroad Grade

Starting Point:	Intersection with Southwest #7:
	Arrastra Gulch Trail
Finishing Point:	Intersection with Southwest #6:
	Silverton to Animas Forks Ghost Town,
	near Howardsville
Total Mileage:	2.6 miles
Unpaved Mileage:	2.6 miles
Driving Time:	30 minutes
Route Elevation:	9,550 to 10,250 feet
Usually Open:	Mid-May to October
Difficulty Rating:	2
Scenic Rating:	8

Special Attractions

- Historic Silverton Northern Railroad grade.
- Remains of the Silver Lake Mill.
- Numerous additional mining sites.

History

Otto Mears incorporated the Silverton Northern Railroad in November 1895 to connect Silverton to Animas Forks, located 14 miles apart. His original plan was to continue the tracks beyond Animas Forks all the way to Lake City. The first section of railway to Howardsville and Eureka opened in June 1896. The second section to Animas Forks opened in 1903, with an average grade of seven percent. The line above Eureka

Howardsville

The Silver Lake Mill, circa 1890

was removed in 1920, and the lower section ceased operations in 1939; the tracks were removed in 1942. This route follows the old railroad grade from just below Arrastra Gulch to Howardsville.

The foundations of the Silver Lake Mill are a prominent feature along this route. Ore had been discovered at the Silver Lake Mine in about 1890, and the mine was greatly developed by the incorporation of further claims. The original claim was located at an elevation of 12,275 feet beside Silver Lake at the top of Arrastra Gulch. Two mills were built to process ore from this mine. The first was located at the mine. The second and more substantial mill was built in the late 1890s. This mill is still evident beside the Animas River and the Silverton Northern Railroad grade.

A tramway was constructed to carry ore over 2.5 miles from the mine to the new mill. The Silver Lake operation processed more than $7 million worth of ore before being bought by the Guggenheim empire in 1901 for $1.25 million. In 1906, the

The site of the Silver Lake Mill today

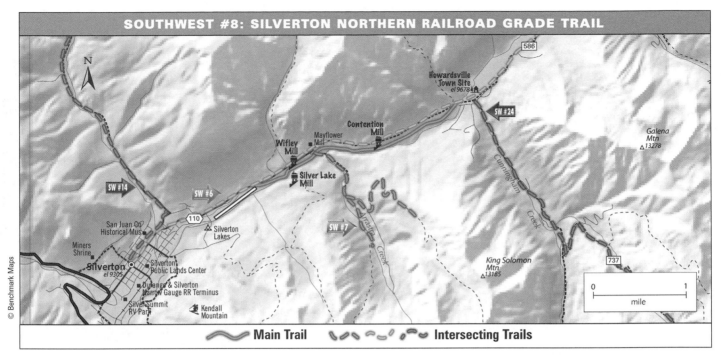

~~~ Main Trail   **◗◗◖ ~◡◗ ◗◖ ◖ Intersecting Trails**

© Benchmark Maps

---

mill burned down. It was rebuilt but ceased operations in 1914. It burned down again in 1949 and what remained was sold for scrap.

The route also passes the site of the Wifley Mill. From 1913 to 1919, Otto Mears and Arthur Wifley leased the Silver Lake Mine and chose to process the ore, which they mainly recovered from the tailing dumps at the Wifley Mill, which was located on the north side of the Animas River at the bottom of Arrastra Gulch.

Description

The route starts a short distance along Southwest #7: Arrastra Gulch Trail. Initially, it heads southwest to the location of the Silver Lake Mill. This section dead-ends after a short distance, at which point the route returns to the Arrastra Gulch road, crosses it, and continues along the old railway grade all the way to Howardsville.

This trail, which is easy the entire length, is a very interesting short side route because of its mining and railroad history. It travels closely beside the scenic Animas River.

Current Road Information

Silverton Chamber of Commerce
414 Greene Street
Silverton, CO 81433
(970) 387-5654

Map References

Maptech CD: Southwest/Durango/Telluride
Benchmark's *Colorado Road & Recreation Atlas*, p. 110
Trails Illustrated, #141 (incomplete)

Route Directions

▼ 0.0		From the 0.1-mile point along Southwest #7: Arrastra Gulch Trail, zero trip meter and turn right onto track that was once the Silverton

Northern Railroad grade. This intersection is before Southwest #7 crosses the river.

1.0 ▲		End at intersection with Southwest #7: Arrastra Gulch Trail.

GPS: N37°49.66′ W107°37.63′

▼ 0.1	SO	Site of the Wifley Mill on hillside to the right.
0.5 ▲	UT	Fork in the road. Left crosses through creek. Right is closed. Turn around and retrace tracks.
▼ 0.2	SO	Silver Lake Mill ruins across the Animas River on left.
0.2 ▲	SO	Silver Lake Mill ruins across the Animas River on right.
▼ 0.5	UT	Fork in the road. Left crosses through creek. Right closed. Turn around and retrace tracks.
0.1 ▲	SO	Site of the Wifley Mill site on hillside to the right.
▼ 1.0	SO	Cross Southwest #7: Arrastra Gulch Trail. Pass under the Mayflower tram lines. Zero trip meter.
0.0 ▲		Proceed along the river road on the south side of Arrastra Gulch Trail.

GPS: N37°49.65′ W107°37.55′

▼ 0.0		Continue along the river road on the north side of Arrastra Gulch Trail.
1.6 ▲	SO	Pass under the Mayflower tram lines; then cross Southwest #7: Arrastra Gulch Trail. Zero trip meter.
▼ 0.4	SO	Ruins of tram stands are visible on the moutainside across the river. Foundation and timbers on the left are from the Contention Mill.
1.2 ▲	SO	Foundation and timbers from the Contention Mill on right. Then tram stand ruins are on mountainside across the river.
▼ 0.5	SO	Remains of a swing bridge (cables and occasional timbers) cross overhead; then timbers and a decaying structure are evident high on the valley wall, which were part of a wooden flume.
1.1 ▲	SO	Timbers and a decaying structure are part of a wooden flume across the river, high on the valley wall; then remains of a swing bridge (cables and occasional timbers) cross overhead.
▼ 1.6		End at intersection with Southwest #6:

0.0 ▲

Silverton to Animas Forks Ghost Town
(CR 110), just south of Howardsville.
From Southwest #6: Silverton to Animas
Forks Ghost Town at the southern side of
Howardsville, zero trip meter at the bridge
over the Animas River and turn onto a small
trail marked "Private Property—stay on road"
and proceed south.

GPS: N37°50.08' W107°35.95'

SOUTHWEST REGION TRAIL #9

Maggie Gulch Trail

Starting Point:	**Intersection of Southwest #6: Silverton to Animas Forks Ghost Town and FR 588 at Middleton town site**
Finishing Point:	**Intersection Mill**
Total Mileage:	**4.1 miles (one-way)**
Unpaved Mileage:	**4.1 miles**
Driving Time:	**1 hour**
Route Elevation:	**9,800 to 11,900 feet**
Usually Open:	**June to October**
Difficulty Rating:	**3**
Scenic Rating:	**8**

Special Attractions

■ Varied, easy, and scenic side road.
■ Numerous mining remains.

History

At the beginning of this trail is the town site of Middleton. The town was named for Middle Mountain, which in turn got its name because it was located midway between Howardsville and Eureka. There were as many as a hundred claims being worked in the area in the 1890s. The town was formed in 1894, the year after the first mine was discovered. The town never amounted to much, and many of the residents relocated to Howardsville or Eureka.

The remains of the Intersection Mill

The trail above Maggie Creek

Maggie Gulch still contains plenty of evidence of early mining activity. The structures from the Ridgway tramway were used to transport ore from the Ridgway Mine located some 2,000 feet higher. It carried the ore nearly a mile to the floor of the gulch for carting to the railroad.

Farther along, above and to the left of the road, is the Little Maud Mine, which was worked from the 1890s with intermittent success. The washed-out road that crosses Maggie Creek leads to the Empire Mine, a product of mining activity in recent times.

The Intersection Mine and Mill date back to around 1900. Much of the mill machinery is still located at the site. The mines above this site, along the hiking trail, were also part of this operation.

Description

This trail starts at the town site of Middleton. Nothing remains today, but a public toilet is located at the site. The road forks almost immediately, and you bear left up a straightforward shelf road that switchbacks up the mountain. The right-hand fork is a short road that leads to several backcountry camping spots.

As the road climbs, it affords a good view through the gulch. The track travels along a fairly wide shelf that is lined with pine and aspen. At this point, the route is easy, with a smooth, sound surface and adequate places to pass any oncoming vehicles.

In less than a mile, the trail climbs almost 1,000 feet and the scenery changes dramatically as it emerges above the timberline and crosses an expansive talus slope. The aspens in the gulch below provide a particularly scenic view in the fall. The Ridgway Mine tram is also evident in the valley below.

The route then crosses a short, narrow section of shelf road as it passes a scenic waterfall at the top of the gulch. Entering a broad alpine basin, the scenery changes again as the trail pro-

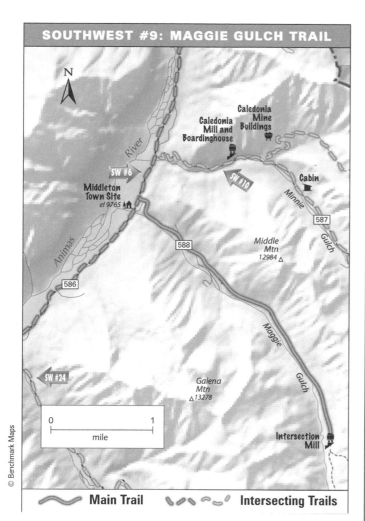

N

SW #6

SW #10

SW #24

Caledonia
Mine
Buildings

Caledonia
Mill and
Boardinghouse

Middleton
Town Site
el 9765

Cabin

587

Minnie

Gulch

Middle
Mtn
12984 △

588

586

River

Animas

Maggie

Gulch

Galena
Mtn
△13278

Intersection
Mill

0   mile   1

© Benchmark Maps

〰 **Main Trail**   〰 **Intersecting Trails**

ceeds along the last section of the journey, which ends at the Intersection Mill. There are extensive ruins of the mill and its machinery that operated in the early 1900s. At this point, the road contracts into a hiking trail, which continues to the Continental Divide, crossing it about 0.75 miles northeast of Stony Pass.

Current Road Information

Silverton Chamber of Commerce
414 Greene Street
Silverton, CO 81433
(970) 387-5654

Map References

USFS Uncompahgre National Forest; San Juan National Forest
Maptech CD: Southwest/Durango/Telluride
Benchmark's *Colorado Road & Recreation Atlas*, p. 110
Colorado Atlas & Gazetteer, p. 77
The Roads of Colorado, p. 139
Trails Illustrated, #141

Route Directions

▼ 0.0   From Southwest #6: Silverton to Animas Forks Ghost Town in Middleton, zero trip meter and proceed east on FR 588 toward

The trail crosses a talus slope

Maggie Gulch. The road immediately forks, so bear left and proceed up hill.

		GPS: N37°51.30' W107°34.30'
▼ 0.9	SO	Track on left.
▼ 1.1	SO	Attractive view of waterfall at head of gulch.
▼ 1.2	BL	Track on the right goes across the gulch to the Ruby Mine.
▼ 1.6	SO	Track enters on left.
▼ 3.0	SO	Track on left to the Little Maud Mine.
▼ 3.7	BL	Road forks. To the right it crosses Maggie Creek and leads to the Empire Mine, but the bridge has been washed out.
		GPS: N37°49.14' W107°32.12'
▼ 3.9	SO	Cross through creek.
▼ 4.1	SO	Cross through creek. Then end at Intersection Mill with plenty of room to turn around.
		GPS: N37°48.85' W107°32.14'

SOUTHWEST REGION TRAIL #10

Minnie Gulch Trail

Starting Point:	Intersection with Southwest #6:
	Silverton to Animas Forks Ghost Town
	and FR 587
Finishing Point:	Kittimac Mine
Total Mileage:	5.1 miles (one-way)
Unpaved Mileage:	5.1 miles
Driving Time:	1 hour
Route Elevation:	9,800 to 11,800 feet
Usually Open:	June to October
Difficulty Rating:	4
Scenic Rating:	8

Special Attractions

■ Historic mining district with well-preserved buildings.
■ Moderately difficult trail with good scenery.

The Caledonia Mill boardinghouse

History

Caledonia Mine was established in 1872, and the Caledonia Mill was built in the early 1900s to treat ore extracted from the Caledonia Mine. The mill is located 0.5 miles northeast and 1,200 feet above the mill. Stone foundations of the mill are clearly visible stretching up the hillside. Remains of the tram that transported ore down from the mine are also visible above the mill. Shortly past the mill are remains of three buildings. On the right-hand side of the road is the mill superintendent's house, and on the left, the larger building is the boardinghouse for mill workers. Both of these buildings are well preserved.

Near the end of this trail is the Kittimac Mine, which may have been part of the same discovery as the Caledonia Mine in 1872. A tramway was constructed around 1900 to carry ore from the mine to the new Kittimac Mill, which was built beside the Silverton Northern Railroad tracks next to the Animas River. The tramway was nearly 2 miles long and descended nearly 2,000 feet.

The Esmerelda Mine operated at its peak in the early 1900s and continued to operate for many years. Its longevity was due to high assays of both the mine's silver and gold ore.

Description

This route heads east from Southwest #6: Silverton to Animas Forks Ghost Town road, initially traveling through the forest beside Minnie Creek. A little over a mile from the start is the site of the Caledonia Mill on the left, across Minnie Creek.

Continuing along the route you come to a fork in the road; both legs of this fork are included in this route. The left-hand fork is described first. This road switchbacks up the mountain and although it is narrow, the surface is sound. The trail passes a tram support for the Kittimac Mine that transported ore to the Kittimac Mill located on the Animas River, just south of the start of this 4WD trail.

Farther along is the Caledonia Mine boardinghouse and stables. The boardinghouse is leaning at a precarious angle, only saved from collapse by the supports that have been put in place. The road continues to the Caledonia and Kittimac Mines. As it does, it gets narrower and steeper. Turn around at an appropriate place and head back down to the fork in the road to explore the other leg of the fork, which leads to the Esmerelda Mine.

Once on the right-hand fork, the road heads farther up Minnie Gulch, traveling above the creek. It passes two cabins, a waterfall from a side creek, and another cabin with a stone foundation—all on the left side of the road. The road gets more difficult as you travel along this last section, so turn around whenever you think conditions warrant and return to the beginning of the trail.

The difficulty rating for this trail reflects conditions at the upper reaches of both forks. The earlier stages are quite easy. The varied scenery and the numerous mining remains make this short trail well worth doing.

Current Road Information

Silverton Chamber of Commerce
414 Greene Street
Silverton, CO 81433
(970) 387-5654

Map References

USFS Uncompahgre National Forest; San Juan National Forest
Maptech CD: Southwest/Durango/Telluride
Benchmark's *Colorado Road & Recreation Atlas*, p. 110
Colorado Atlas & Gazetteer, p. 77
The Roads of Colorado, pp. 123, 139
Trails Illustrated, #141

Route Directions

▼ 0.0		From Southwest #6: Silverton to Animas Forks Ghost Town (CR 110), zero trip meter and proceed east along FR 587 toward Minnie Gulch. This intersection is about 6.6 miles from Silverton City Hall.
		GPS: N37°51.77' W107°34.07'
▼ 1.0	SO	Cross over Minnie Creek.
▼ 1.1	SO	Stone foundation from the Caledonia Mill on left across the creek.
▼ 1.2	SO	Building on the right; then two on the left. The large, well-preserved structure on the left was the Caledonia Mill boardinghouse.
		GPS: N37°51.48' W107°33.06'
▼ 1.4	BL	Cross over creek; then zero trip meter and bear left at the intersection. This route will

The Caledonia Mine boardinghouse and stables

later return to explore the track on the right, which goes to the Esmerelda Mine.

GPS: N37°51.27′ W107°32.27′		
▼ 0.0		Proceed uphill.
▼ 0.2	SO	Kittimac Mine tram structure on left.
▼ 0.7	SO	At switchback, proceed toward the well-preserved Caledonia Mine boardinghouse and ruins of a stable. From these buildings, turn around and continue up the mountain.
▼ 0.9	SO	Caledonia Mine on left.
▼ 1.0	BR	Track on left; then end at the Kittimac Mine a short distance farther. From here, the route directions will return to complete the fork that was passed earlier.
GPS: N37°51.93′ W107°32.22′		

Continuation from the fork in the road

▼ 0.0		Zero trip meter at fork in the road. Turn left to continue along the other leg toward the Esmerelda Mine.
GPS: N37°51.27′ W107°32.27′		
▼ 1.6	SO	Two cabins on left.
▼ 2.2	SO	Cross through creek with waterfall on left.
GPS: N37°51.26′ W107°32.26′		
▼ 2.6	SO	Cabin ruins with stone foundation on left.
▼ 2.7	SO	Esmerelda Mine tramway ruins on right. End of trail.
GPS: N37°50.90′ W107°31.94′		

Remains of the Caledonia Mill in Minnie Gulch

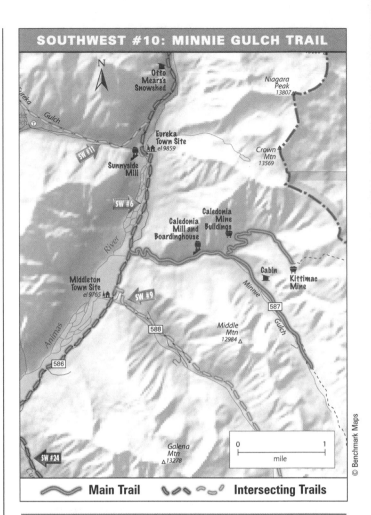

SOUTHWEST #10: MINNIE GULCH TRAIL

～～～ **Main Trail**   ◟◞◠◡◞ **Intersecting Trails**

© Benchmark Maps

SOUTHWEST REGION TRAIL #11

Eureka Gulch Trail

Starting Point:	**Intersection with Southwest #6:**
	Silverton to Animas Forks Ghost Town
Finishing Point:	**Sunnyside Mine at Lake Emma**
	(drained)
Total Mileage:	**3.6 miles (one-way)**
Unpaved Mileage:	**3.6 miles**
Driving Time:	**30 minutes**
Route Elevation:	**10,000 to 12,100 feet**
Usually Open:	**June to October**
Difficulty Rating:	**3**
Scenic Rating:	**7**

Special Attractions
■ Visiting the location of the historic Sunnyside Mine.
■ Lake Emma, accidentally drained in 1978.

History
This trail starts at the Sunnyside Mill at the town site of Eureka and finishes at the Sunnyside Mine, which once provid-

ed the main economic support for the area. The Sunnyside Mine, established in 1873, became one of the best producers in the area. It operated continuously until 1931, when it shut down for a few years and then reopened in 1937. Two years later the miners went on strike; because an agreement could not be reached, the mine was shut down again.

The first of the two Sunnyside Mills to be built in Eureka opened in 1899, with a 3-mile cable tramway connecting it to the mine. The second Sunnyside Mill, which incorporated much of the machinery from the Gold Prince Mill that had operated at Animas Forks, began operations in 1918. It was built on the north side of the old mill. Eureka's mills also served the Toltec, the Golden Fleece, the Tom Moore, the Silver Wing, and the Sound Democrat Mines. Finally, the mill was dismantled and sold for salvage in 1948.

Eureka, which had been founded in the early 1870s, flourished. The population reached 2,000, and the town had many stores, meat markets, saloons, and a restaurant. It was incorporated in 1883, making it one of only two incorporated towns in San Juan County (Silverton was the other). Eureka had its own post office, and a monthly newspaper, *The San Juan Expositor*, was published there. Otto Mears routed the Silverton Northern Railroad through the town in 1896, further strengthening the town's economy.

Toward the end of its operation, the Silverton Northern Railroad's steam engines were replaced by a combination of auto and locomotive parts called the Casey Jones, which could speed down the tracks between Silverton and Eureka in just 20 minutes. To clear snow off the tracks, the Casey Jones carried brooms strapped behind its cowcatcher. Service between Silverton and Eureka ended in 1939, and the railroad was sold and junked in 1942.

In 1976, the state of Colorado declared Eureka formally abandoned because it had not had a municipal government for the previous five years. Today, only a reconstructed two-story building stands on what was Eureka's flat town site. You also can still see the enormous skeleton of the second Sunnyside Mill.

Eureka town site viewed from near the start of the trail

The Sunnyside Mine buildings beside Lake Emma in 1929

As you drive up Eureka Gulch, there is much evidence of the mining activity that once existed. The Midway Mill, named for its location between the Sunnyside Mine and Eureka township, was constructed in 1890 and was connected to the Sunnyside Mine by a tramway. At the turn of the century, this tramway was extended to Eureka when the first Sunnyside Mill opened. A second tramway was constructed in 1917 to service the new mill. The new tram incorporated some of the upper section of the old tramway, which brought its total length to 3 miles.

Continuing up Eureka Gulch, you pass a closed track on the left, which leads to the mile-long Terry Tunnel. Constructed in 1906, the tunnel was bored into the mountainside to connect with the Sunnyside vein.

One-half mile farther up the gulch is a large portal from the Ben Franklin Mine, which dates from the early 1870s.

Many remnants of the Sunnyside tramway can be seen in the vicinity of the Sunnyside Mine. In 1888, a mill was built at the site of the mine but proved too expensive to operate. In the early 1900s, as many as 200 men were employed at the mine. The Sunnyside Mine continued to operate on and off until 1991. In the 1960s, it was still producing 600 tons of ore per day. The foundations of many of the buildings remain. Extensive reclamation work was undertaken in the area in the 1990s.

The Sunnyside Mine buildings were clustered along the shore of Lake Emma. On Sunday, June 4, 1978, a tunnel that was being excavated about 70 feet under Lake Emma collapsed and completely drained the lake. Thousands of gallons of water and millions of tons of mud and rocks drained into the American Tunnel before exiting at Gladstone, some 2 miles away and 1,500 feet lower. The Terry Tunnel was also filled. The cleanup took more than two years to complete. Because the disaster occurred on a Sunday, the miners were not working, and fortunately no one was killed.

Description
The route starts with a climb along a shelf road that is well maintained and reasonably wide, with plenty of opportunities for passing. After about 0.5 miles, the road levels off and continues along the wall of the gulch.

The route is simple to navigate and easy to drive. The scenery is attractive, but the real attraction of the trail is its historical significance, evidence of which is abundant.

Current Road Information
Silverton Chamber of Commerce
414 Greene Street
Silverton, CO 81433
(970) 387-5654

Map References
USFS   Uncompahgre National Forest; San Juan National Forest
Maptech CD: Southwest/Durango/Telluride
Benchmark's *Colorado Road & Recreation Atlas*, p. 110
Colorado Atlas & Gazetteer, p. 77
The Roads of Colorado, p. 123
Trails Illustrated, #141

SOUTHWEST #11: EUREKA GULCH TRAIL

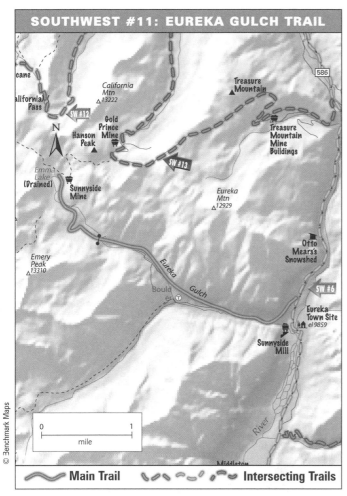

Main Trail ～～～ ～～～ Intersecting Trails

© Benchmark Maps

Route Directions

▼ 0.0		From Southwest #6: Silverton to Animas Forks Ghost Town (about 0.3 miles north of Eureka), zero trip meter and turn onto Eureka Gulch Trail. Proceed up the hill.
		GPS: N37°53.09' W107°33.82'
▼ 0.4	SO	Ruins of the second Sunnyside Mill are on left directly below road. On right is a tram structure that carried ore from the mine to the mill, almost 3 miles.
▼ 0.7	BR	Fork in road.
▼ 0.9	SO	Snowslide defense structure beside the road on left and a private cabin on left across Eureka Creek.
▼ 1.0	SO	Track on left to Midway Mill in the South Fork of Eureka Gulch.
▼ 1.8	SO	Johnson Tower on left across the valley, halfway up mountain.
▼ 2.1	SO	Cross over Parson's Creek with waterfall on right.
▼ 2.3	SO	Tram tension station on left across valley on the mountain slope.
▼ 2.4	SO	Track on left is gated and goes to the next entry.
▼ 2.5	SO	Reclamation ponds on left for the Terry Tunnel.
▼ 2.7	SO	Cross over Eureka Creek.
▼ 2.8	SO	Large portal beside the road is from the Ben Franklin Mine.
▼ 2.9	BR	Fork in the road.
▼ 3.0	BR	Road joins on left.
▼ 3.3	SO	Sunnyside Mine tram station on right.
▼ 3.4–3.6	SO	Remains of mine buildings.
▼ 3.6	SO	End at site of drained Lake Emma.
		GPS: N37°54.17' W107°36.86'

A tram angle station for the cable tramway that ran from the Sunnyside Mine to the Midway and Sunnyside Mills

A close-up of the tramway angle station

California Gulch Trail

Starting Point:	**Animas Forks**
Finishing Point:	**Intersection with Southwest #14:**
	Silverton to Lake Como Trail
Total Mileage:	**4.2 miles**
Unpaved Mileage:	**4.2 miles**
Driving Time:	**1 hour**
Route Elevation:	**11,400 to 12,930 feet**
Usually Open:	**June to late October**
Difficulty Rating:	**4**
Scenic Rating:	**9**

Special Attractions

- Spectacular scenery, especially the expansive view from California Pass.
- Many historic mining sites and structures.
- A short, moderately easy 4WD trail.
- Part of a large network of 4WD trails.

History

Numerous mines and mills operated in California Gulch, and plenty of evidence of this activity remains today.

The Columbus Mine, located at the northern edge of Animas Forks, was discovered in the early 1880s. The mine yielded a large tonnage of ore, but it was low-grade, and high transportation costs meant that the mine was barely economical. As a producer of zinc, it had some of its best years during World War II. The mill, located at the mine, was built in 1927. The whole operation closed in 1948.

The Columbus Mine and Mill

The Bagley Mill, built in 1912 to treat ore from Frisco Tunnel, was regarded as one of the best mills in the area; it had a capacity of 150 tons of ore a day. Construction on Frisco Tunnel, which burrows over a mile into Houghton Mountain, began in 1904 and took four years to complete. The mining operations ceased in about 1915.

About a mile farther is Vermilion Mine, which started operations in the early 1900s, with the mill being constructed in 1909.

Close to the pass as you climb out of the gulch is the Mountain Queen Mine, which was discovered in 1877 and operated until the 1940s. Rasmus Hanson owned the mine, and it has been speculated that Thomas Walsh managed it before he made his fortune from Camp Bird Mine.

Description

This route departs to the northwest of Animas Forks and is clearly marked to California Gulch. Traveling along California Gulch above timberline, the trail is relatively easy, with numerous mine remains and open mine portals along the way.

The road ascends to California Pass from which there is a spectacular 180° view. From the pass, you look down onto Lake Como and Poughkeepsie Gulch, the road back to Animas Forks, and across to Hurricane Pass and Hurricane Peak.

The section of the road descending from California Pass is the harder part of this route and traverses quite different terrain. There is a series of tight switchbacks along a narrow shelf

The Bagley Mill

road. At times, the road is steep, and passing other vehicles can be difficult.

The road is usually open from mid-June to late October, but snow often remains alongside the road throughout the summer. This trail is likely to be muddy early in the season.

The Columbus Mill standing beside the West Fork of the Animas River

The steep slope at the end of California Gulch that the trail climbs

Lake Como

Current Road Information

San Juan Mountains Center
Joint Forest Service/BLM office
PO Box 709
1246 Blair Street
Silverton, CO 81433
(970) 387-5530
Closed in Winter

Silverton Chamber of Commerce
414 Greene Street
Silverton, CO 81433
(970) 387-5654

Map References

USFS Uncompahgre National Forest; Gunnison National
Forest
Maptech CD: Southwest/Durango/Telluride
Benchmark's *Colorado Road & Recreation Atlas,* p. 110
Colorado Atlas & Gazetteer, p. 77
The Roads of Colorado, p. 123
Trails Illustrated, #141

Route Directions

▼ 0.0   At the north end of Animas Forks, zero trip
meter beside the bridge over the Animas River
and proceed northwest (do not cross bridge),
following signs to California Gulch. Cross over

SOUTHWEST #12: CALIFORNIA GULCH TRAIL

N

Houghton Mtn △13052

SW #5

Columbus Mill

Tuttle Mtn △13203

Animas Forks Ghost Town

SW #3

Lake Como △12215

SW #13

SW #6

586

Hurricane Pass

California Pass

California Mtn △13222

Treasure Mountain ▲

SW #14

Gold Prince Mine

Hanson Peak ▲

Treasure Mountain Mine Buildings

© Benchmark Maps

Emma Lake (Drained)

Sunnyside Mine

0 — mile — 1

〰️ **Main Trail**   ᷍᷍᷍᷍ **Intersecting Trails**

		the West Fork of the Animas River; pass the Columbus Mine and Mill on the right.
▼ 4.2 ▲		End at bridge in Animas Forks.
	GPS: N37°55.89' W107°34.22'	
▼ 0.5	SO	Bagley Mill and Frisco Tunnel on right.
3.6 ▲	SO	Bagley Mill and Frisco Tunnel on left.
▼ 0.7	BL	Track to Bagley Mill on right.
3.5 ▲	BR	Track to Bagley Mill on left.
▼ 1.0	BR	Southwest #13: Picayne Gulch and Placer Gulch Trail on left.
3.2 ▲	BL	Southwest #13: Picayne Gulch and Placer Gulch Trail on right.
▼ 1.1	BR	Track on left to cabin.
3.1 ▲	BL	Track on right to cabin.
▼ 1.5	SO	Vermilion Mine and Mill ruins on right.
2.7 ▲	SO	Vermilion Mine and Mill ruins on left.
▼ 1.7	SO	Burrows Mine ruins on right.
2.4 ▲	SO	Burrows Mine ruins on left.
▼ 2.9	SO	Cross over creek.
1.3 ▲	SO	Cross over creek.
▼ 3.0	SO	Open mine portal on right side of road.
1.2 ▲	SO	Open mine portal on left side of road.
▼ 3.4	UT	Intersection.
0.8 ▲	UT	Intersection.
▼ 3.5	SO	Road on left.
0.7 ▲	BL	Fork in the road.
▼ 3.6	SO	Mountain Queen Mine on right.
0.6 ▲	SO	Mountain Queen Mine on left.
▼ 3.8	UT	Summit of California Pass. The lake you look down upon is Lake Como.
0.4 ▲	UT	Summit of California Pass.
	GPS: N37°55.02' W107°36.91'	
▼ 4.2		End at intersection with Southwest #14: Silverton to Lake Como Trail to the left. Corkscrew Gulch, Poughkeepsie Gulch, and Lake Como are 0.3 miles ahead.
0.0 ▲		The trail begins at the intersection with Southwest #14: Silverton to Lake Como Trail at California Pass. Zero trip meter and proceed downhill toward California Gulch.
	GPS: N37°55.26' W107°37.26'	

SOUTHWEST REGION TRAIL #13

Picayne Gulch and Placer Gulch Trail

Starting Point:	Intersection with Southwest #12: California Gulch Trail
Finishing Point:	Intersection with Southwest #6: Silverton to Animas Forks Ghost Town
Total Mileage:	6.2 miles
Unpaved Mileage:	6.2 miles
Driving Time:	1 hour
Route Elevation:	10,500 to 13,000 feet
Usually Open:	June to October
Difficulty Rating:	4
Scenic Rating:	8

Special Attractions

- Varied, scenic trail.
- Many interesting mining buildings and other mining structures.
- Abundant wildflowers in early summer.

The deep snow that must be bulldozed in the spring

The Treasure Mountain Mill and other buildings

Hanson built the Hanson Mill in 1889 to process the ore. The mine was still being worked in the 1950s.

In the early 1900s, Treasure Mountain Gold Mining Company built the cluster of buildings that the trail passes in Picayne Gulch, which include a substantial boardinghouse. This mining company consolidated and worked some 30 claims in the area including the Golden Fleece, the Scotia, and the San Juan Queen. The tunnel near the buildings is the Santiago Tunnel, built in 1937.

Description

At the start of this route, the road immediately crosses the West Fork of the Animas River. The road continues into the gulch and travels above Placer Creek. The scenery in the gulch is treeless alpine tundra. The beauty of the open countryside is enhanced in the early summer by massive displays of wildflowers. Placer Gulch still holds much evidence of the mines, mills, and tramways that turned it into a hive of activity long ago.

The road to the Gold Prince Mine located at the top of the gulch is the easier part of the trail and only rates a 3 for difficulty. From the Gold Prince, the road switchbacks up to the ridge and crosses into Picayne Gulch. This segment is fairly

History

At the start of the trail, remains of the Gold Prince Mine tramway are visible on the face of Treasure Mountain to the left. Built in 1905, the tramway ran 1.5 miles from the mine at the top of the gulch down to the angle station at Treasure Mountain and then another 0.75 miles to the Gold Prince Mill in Animas Forks. The tram transported 50 tons of ore each hour.

About a mile farther are the concrete foundations of the Mastodon Mill, which was constructed in the mid-1880s and treated ore from both the Mastodon and the Silver Queen Mines.

The Sound Democrat Mine was established in 1899. Initially ore had to be transported to the mill constructed at the Sunnyside Mine. In 1906, the Sound Democrat Mill began operations and continued until 1914.

At the top of the gulch is the Gold Prince Mine, which had been known previously as the Sunnyside Extension and the Mountain Pride. Nearby is the concrete foundation of the boardinghouse that once housed 150 miners. Beside it is the tram tower used to unload supplies for the boardinghouse. The Gold Prince began ore production in 1874 and worked the same veins as the Sunnyside Mine, located less than a mile to the southwest on the other side of Hanson Peak. Reamus

A view of the road behind the buildings remaining from Treasure Mountain Gold Mining Company

The Treasure Mountain boardinghouse

steep but is quite wide; there are plenty of opportunities to pass oncoming vehicles. Once into Picayne Gulch, the route travels through broad open meadows where flocks of sheep are left to graze in the summer. This section of road is cleared by snowplow at the start of the season and can be quite muddy when wet.

The road re-enters the forest and passes the cluster of buildings constructed by the Treasure Mountain Gold Mining Company. Among these is a substantial boardinghouse that had an adjoining bathroom with bath, toilet, and hot and cold running water. The bathroom was connected to the boardinghouse by an enclosed corridor.

The last section of the trail is a narrow shelf road that descends to intersect with Southwest #6: Silverton to Animas Forks Ghost Town. Passing opportunities are limited on this short section, but the surface is sound and it is not difficult.

Current Road Information

Silverton Chamber of Commerce
414 Greene Street
Silverton, CO 81433
(970) 387-5654

Map References

USFS Uncompahgre National Forest; San Juan National Forest
Maptech CD: Southwest/Durango/Telluride
Benchmark's *Colorado Road & Recreation Atlas*, p. 110
Colorado Atlas & Gazetteer, p. 77
The Roads of Colorado, p. 123
Trails Illustrated, #141

Route Directions

▼ 0.0			From Southwest #12: California Gulch Trail (approximately 1 mile northwest of Animas Forks), zero trip meter at sign to Placer Gulch and proceed south toward Placer Gulch. Cross over the West Fork of the Animas River.
	6.2 ▲		Cross over the West Fork of the Animas River and end at intersection with Southwest #12: California Gulch Trail. Animas Forks is approximately 1 mile to the right.
			GPS: N37°48.79′ W107°39.72′
▼ 0.1		SO	Mine ruins on left directly below road.
	6.1 ▲	SO	Mine ruins on right directly below road.
▼ 1.1		SO	Concrete foundations of Mastodon Mill on left.
	5.1 ▲	SO	Concrete foundations of Mastodon Mill on right.
▼ 1.3		SO	Red-roofed mill on left across river is the Sound Democrat Mill.
	4.9 ▲	SO	Red-roofed mill on right across river is the Sound Democrat Mill.
▼ 1.5		SO	Two standing tram supports on left.
	4.7 ▲	SO	Two standing tram supports on right.
▼ 1.6		SO	Concrete foundation for Gold Prince boardinghouse on left with tram tower beside it. Mine building on right.
	4.6 ▲	SO	Concrete foundation for Gold Prince boardinghouse on right with tram tower beside it. Mine building on left.
▼ 1.7		SO	Track on left; then cross creek. Shortly after, ruins of the Sunnyside Mine Extension/Gold Prince Mine structure on right.
	4.5 ▲	SO	Mine ruins of the Sunnyside Mine Extension/Gold Prince Mine structure on left. Cross creek; then track on right.
▼ 1.8		UT	Track on left to Hidden Treasure, Silver Queen, and Sound Democrat Mines.

4.4 ▲	UT	Track on right to Hidden Treasure, Silver Queen, and Sound Democrat Mines.	
▼ 2.7	BL	Tracks on right to scenic overlook.	
3.5 ▲	SO	Tracks on left to scenic overlook.	
▼ 2.9	SO	View to the Sound Democrat Mill in the gulch below on left.	
3.3 ▲	SO	View to the Sound Democrat Mill in the gulch below on right.	
▼ 3.8	SO	Faint track on right.	
2.4 ▲	SO	Faint track on left.	
▼ 4.1	SO	Short access track on left to ruins from Golden Fleece and Scotia Mines.	
2.1 ▲	SO	Short access track on right to ruins from Golden Fleece and Scotia Mines.	
▼ 4.3	SO	Open mine portal on left.	

A view across Picayne Gulch

SOUTHWEST #13: PICAYNE GULCH AND PLACER GULCH TRAIL

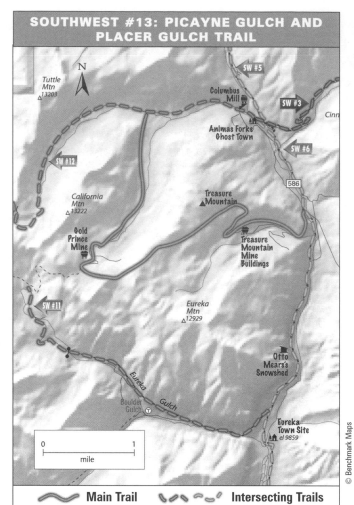

© Benchmark Maps

〰 **Main Trail**   ᵥᵥᵥ ᵔᵥ⌐ **Intersecting Trails**

1.9 ▲	SO	Open mine portal on right.	
▼ 4.5	SO	View across the valley to the southeast is Burns Gulch Trail.	
1.7 ▲	SO	View across the valley behind you to the southeast is Burns Gulch Trail.	
▼ 4.9	SO	Treasure Mountain Gold Mining Company buildings and mine on right; then track on right goes into Upper Picayne Basin.	
1.3 ▲	SO	Track on left goes into Upper Picayne Basin; then Treasure Mountain Gold Mining Company buildings and mine on left.	
▼ 5.0	SO	Open mine portals on right.	
1.2 ▲	SO	Open mine portals on left.	
▼ 5.2	SO	Treasure Mountain Gold Mining Company buildings on right.	
1.0 ▲	BR	Treasure Mountain Gold Mining Company buildings on left.	
▼ 5.8	SO	Track on right to the Toltec Mine.	
0.4 ▲	BR	Track on left to the Toltec Mine.	
▼ 6.0	SO	Open mine portal on left.	
0.2 ▲	SO	Open mine portal on right.	
▼ 6.2		End at intersection with Southwest #6: Silverton to Animas Forks Ghost Town.	
0.0 ▲		From Southwest #6: Silverton to Animas Forks Ghost Town ((approximately 1.5 miles south of Animas Forks and 2.8 miles north of Eureka), zero trip meter and turn onto track to Picayune Gulch.	

GPS: N37°54.99′ W107°33.45′

Silverton to Lake Como Trail

Starting Point:	**Silverton**
Finishing Point:	**Intersection with Southwest #12:**
	California Gulch Trail near Lake Como
Total Mileage:	**10.3 miles**
Unpaved Mileage:	**10.3 miles**
Driving Time:	**1 hour**
Route Elevation:	**9,200 to 12,407 feet**
Usually Open:	**Silverton to Gladstone: year-round;**
	Gladstone to Lake Como: June to
	October
Difficulty Rating:	**4**
Scenic Rating:	**10**

Special Attractions

- Spectacular, rugged scenery.
- Beautiful Lake Como encircled by mountains.
- Numerous mining sites.
- Access to a network of other 4WD trails.

History

From Silverton to Gladstone, this route closely parallels the tracks laid by the Silverton, Gladstone & Northerly Railroad. In April 1899, the Gold King Mining Company established the railroad to reduce its freight costs to the new mill it was constructing in Gladstone. The train commenced operations on August 4 of that year. Then in 1910, Otto Mears leased the Gold King Mine and Mill operations and with it the Silverton, Gladstone & Northerly Railroad. In 1915, he purchased the railroad from the mine owners. The railway continued to operate until 1924 and was officially abandoned in 1937. The last of the tracks were torn up and sold for scrap during World War II.

About halfway along Cement Creek Valley (on the other side of the creek) is the site of the Boston and Silverton Mill, which had an output of 100 tons per day when it was built in the 1890s, making it one of the larger mining operations in the valley. A newer mill is on the site of the first mill. The Gold Hub Mining Company acquired the whole operation in the late 1930s. The Yukon Tunnel located just behind the mill continued to operate until the 1980s.

The Hurricane Pass summit

The Gold King Mining Company bought the Anglo-Saxon Mine, which had been discovered in the late 1890s; it produced tungsten used in the manufacture of bulletproof steel during World War II.

On the left shortly after the road crosses to the east side of the creek is the Elk Mountain Mine, which operated for about 20 years before closing in the 1920s.

On the western edge of the town of Gladstone stand the foundations of the Mogul Mill, which was constructed in 1906 to treat ore from the Mogul Mine. The mill was connected to the Mogul Mine by a 2-mile-long tramway.

An old boiler located below Hurricane Pass

Description

Navigating the route from Silverton to Gladstone, a well-maintained gravel road, is straightforward.

From the turnoff to Lake Como, just past the Mogul Mill foundations in Gladstone, the road becomes much narrower and travels along a shelf above the North Fork of Cement Creek for about 2.5 miles. Although this section is much more difficult than the road between Silverton and Gladstone, the

Looking down the Gold King Tramway to Gladstone, circa 1906

surface is quite sound, albeit bumpy, and the only real difficulty is negotiating your way past oncoming vehicles.

As you travel along this shelf section, the 4WD trail to Mogul Mine can be seen to the east across the creek.

As you continue, you quickly climb above timberline; the scenery becomes much more rugged and offers some spectacular mountain views. There is a wonderful view of Lake Como and Poughkeepsie Gulch from nearby Hurricane Pass. Signs of mining activity abound along this route.

Current Road Information

Silverton Chamber of Commerce
414 Greene Street
Silverton, CO 81433
(970) 387-5654

Map References

USFS Uncompahgre National Forest
Maptech CD: Southwest/Durango/Telluride
Benchmark's *Colorado Road & Recreation Atlas*, p. 110
Colorado Atlas & Gazetteer, pp. 76, 77
The Roads of Colorado, pp. 123, 139
Trails Illustrated, #141

Route Directions

▼ 0.0			From the Silverton City Hall at Greene (main) Street and 14th Street, zero trip meter and proceed northeast out of town.
	6.5 ▲		End in front of the Silverton City Hall at Greene Street and 14th Street.
		GPS: N37°48.79′ W107°39.72′	
▼ 0.2		SO	Follow CR 110 straight ahead. CR 110 also turns to the right.
	6.3 ▲	BR	Proceed toward Silverton.
▼ 0.4		BL	Hillside Cemetery is straight ahead.
	6.1 ▲	BR	Hillside Cemetery is to the left.
▼ 0.7		BR	Track on left; then cross over creek.
	5.8 ▲	BL	Cross over creek; then track on right.
▼ 1.0		SO	Unpaved.
	5.5 ▲	SO	Paved.
▼ 2.5		SO	Bridge over Cement Creek and track on left.
	4.0 ▲	SO	Track on right and bridge over Cement Creek.
▼ 3.1		SO	Boston and Silverton Mill site on the right. Newer buildings are part of the Gold Hub Mining Company.
	3.4 ▲	SO	Boston and Silverton Mill site on the left. Newer buildings are part of the Gold Hub Mining Company.
▼ 3.5		SO	Track on left.

A view of Lake Como with Poughkeepsie Gulch in the background

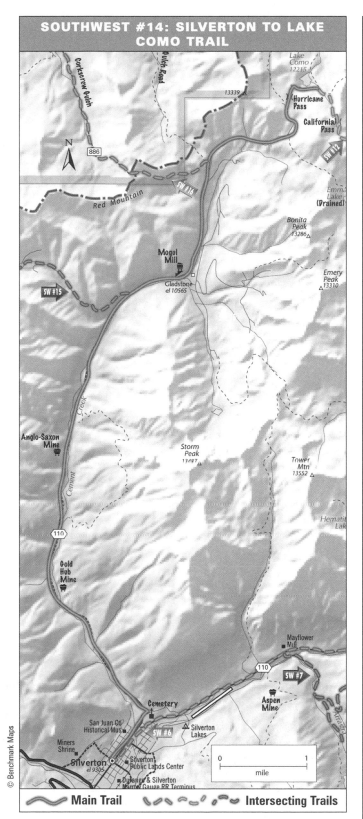

SOUTHWEST #14: SILVERTON TO LAKE COMO TRAIL

Main Trail ~~~ **Intersecting Trails**

© Benchmark Maps

3.0 ▲	SO	Track on right.	
▼ 3.8	SO	Logs and building behind it on left are remnants of the Anglo-Saxon Mine.	
2.7 ▲	SO	Logs and building behind it on right are remnants of the Anglo-Saxon Mine.	
▼ 4.1	SO	Bridge over Cement Creek.	
2.3 ▲	SO	Bridge over Cement Creek.	

The Mogul Mill ruins located in Gladstone

▼ 4.6	SO	Cabin on left is part of the Elk Mountain Mine.
1.9 ▲	SO	Cabin on right is part of the Elk Mountain Mine.
▼ 5.0	SO	Cross over creek and railroad bed. Track on left goes through Georgia Gulch to the Kansas City Mine.
1.5 ▲	BL	Track on right goes through Georgia Gulch to the Kansas City Mine. Cross over creek.
▼ 6.0	SO	Southwest #15: Prospect Gulch Trail (CR 35) on left
0.5 ▲	SO	Road on right is Southwest #15: Prospect Gulch Trail (CR 35).
GPS: N37°53.31′ W107°39.66′		
▼ 6.5	SO	Site of the Mogul Mill on left. Town site of

The Mogul Mill and the town of Gladstone, circa 1940

0.0 ▲			Gladstone existed in the flat area to the right. Zero trip meter at the mill. Continue along track toward Silverton.
		GPS: N37°53.44′ W107°39.10′	
▼ 0.0			Continue along main road.
	1.5 ▲	SO	Site of the Mogul Mill on right. Town site of Gladstone existed in the flat area to the left. Zero trip meter at the mill.
▼ 0.1		BL	Turn onto CR 10 toward Hurricane Pass, California Pass, and Corkscrew Gulch on left.
	1.4 ▲	BR	Onto Cement Creek Road.
		GPS: N37°53.46′ W107°38.99′	
▼ 0.7		SO	Track from the road to Mogul Mine joins in on right.
	0.8 ▲	BR	Road forks.
▼ 0.9		SO	Track on right is private property to a modern cabin.
	0.6 ▲	SO	Track on left is private property to a modern cabin.
▼ 1.5		SO	Southwest #16: Corkscrew Gulch Trail (CR 11) on left goes to US 550. The road you can see in valley on right is Mogul Mine Road. Zero trip meter.
	0.0 ▲		Proceed along CR 10 toward Gladstone.
		GPS: N37°54.61′ W107°38.68′	
▼ 0.0			Proceed toward Hurricane Pass.
	2.3 ▲	BL	Southwest #16: Corkscrew Gulch Trail on right. Zero trip meter.
▼ 1.1		SO	Lower Queen Anne Mine ruins on left.
	1.2 ▲	SO	Lower Queen Anne Mine ruins on right.
▼ 1.2		SO	Track on right.
	1.1 ▲	SO	Track on left.
▼ 1.4		SO	Mine on right is the Upper Queen Anne Mine.
	0.9 ▲	SO	Mine on left is the Upper Queen Anne Mine.
▼ 1.6		SO	Open mine portal on left.
	0.7 ▲	SO	Open mine portal on right.
▼ 1.8		SO	Hurricane Pass summit with a viewpoint on left down to Lake Como.
	0.5 ▲	SO	Summit of Hurricane Pass.
		GPS: N37°55.19′ W107°37.56′	
▼ 2.3			End at intersection with Southwest #12: California Gulch Trail. Lake Como and Poughkeepsie Gulch are 0.3 miles to the left at GPS: N 37°55.41′ W 107°37.38′.
	0.0 ▲		From Southwest #12: California Gulch Trail near Lake Como, zero trip meter at sign to Silverton and Corkscrew Gulch and proceed in that direction toward Hurricane Pass.
		GPS: N37°55.26′ W107°37.26′	

Assorted mining remains before the ascent to Hurricane Pass

Prospect Gulch Trail

Starting Point:	Intersection of Southwest #14: Silverton to Lake Como Trail and CR 35
Finishing Point:	Galena Queen Mine
Total Mileage:	1.9 miles (one-way)
Unpaved Mileage:	1.9 miles
Driving Time:	30 minutes (one-way)
Route Elevation:	10,600 to 11,900 feet
Usually Open:	June to October
Difficulty Rating:	3
Scenic Rating:	8

Special Attractions

■ Numerous old mines.

■ The remaining buildings and equipment at the Galena Queen Mine.

History

Prospect Gulch contains many mines dating back to the early 1880s. The first major operation that you will see evidence of is the Henrietta Mine, where deposits were discovered in the 1890s. Initially, ore produced at the mine was treated at the Fisher Mill in Gladstone. In the early 1900s, a mile-long tramway was built to transport the ore to the Silverton, Gladstone & Northerly Railroad, which passed the entrance to this route as it headed up Cement Creek Valley. The railroad took the ore back down to Silverton for treatment.

At the top of the gulch is the Galena Queen Mine, established around 1890. It was only a small mining operation but continued production into the early 1900s; much of the old machinery is still located at the site. Reclamation works are being undertaken in the vicinity.

A boiler from the Galena Queen Mine

Machinery once used by the Galena Queen Mine

Description

This route commences at the intersection of Southwest #14: Silverton to Lake Como Trail and CR 35, about 0.5 miles east of Gladstone. The entrance to this road is at the bottom of Dry Gulch. The road wraps around the southwest portion of the mountain before entering Prospect Gulch; from there, it parallels the creek to the head of the gulch.

From the start of this route, the road ascends through the forest. The graded gravel surface is wide. The route is fairly easy to drive and very easy to navigate for the 1.9-mile route we have described. From there the road becomes much more difficult as it continues to climb Red Mountain; it is steep and narrow, and the surface is loose. Although we have not driven to the end of the road, we believe that the road does not go through.

Current Road Information

Silverton Chamber of Commerce
414 Greene Street
Silverton, CO 81433
(970) 387-5654

Map References

USFS Uncompahgre National Forest; San Juan National Forest
Maptech CD: Southwest/Durango/Telluride
Benchmark's *Colorado Road & Recreation Atlas*, p. 110
Colorado Atlas & Gazetteer, p. 77
The Roads of Colorado, p. 123
Trails Illustrated, #141

Route Directions

▼ 0.0   From Southwest #14: Silverton to Lake Como Trail (Cement Creek Road), zero trip meter at sign for CR 35 and proceed uphill toward Prospect Gulch. This turnoff is about 6 miles north of Silverton and 0.5 miles south of Gladstone.

GPS: N37°53.31' W107°39.66'

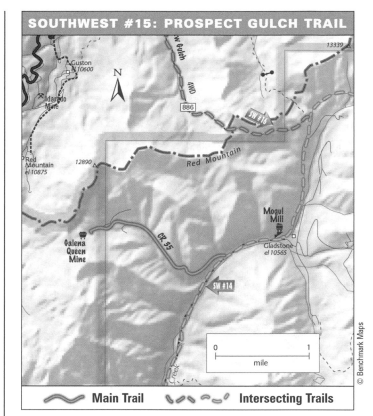

SOUTHWEST #15: PROSPECT GULCH TRAIL

© Benchmark Maps

〜 **Main Trail**   ⌇⌇ ⌢ ⌣' **Intersecting Trails**

▼ 0.7	SO	Old tram tower that serviced the Henrietta Mine on left.
▼ 1.0	SO	Track on left to the Henrietta Mine.
▼ 1.1	SO	Cabin on right.
▼ 1.2	SO	Modern mine building on right.
▼ 1.3	BR	Road forks. Left goes to the Crown Prince Mine.
▼ 1.4	SO	John and Joe Mine and mine buildings on right.
▼ 1.7	BR	Fork in the road. Left goes to the Henrietta Mine. Track on right goes up Red Mountain.

GPS: N37°53.46' W107°41.13'

▼ 1.9		End at the Galena Queen Mine.

GPS: N37°53.52' W107°41.35'

SOUTHWEST REGION TRAIL #16

Corkscrew Gulch Trail

Starting Point:	Intersection of US 550 and FR 886
Finishing Point:	Intersection with Southwest #14:
	Silverton to Lake Como Trail
Total Mileage:	4.8 miles
Unpaved Mileage:	4.8 miles
Driving Time:	30 minutes
Route Elevation:	9,800 to 12,600 feet
Usually Open:	Mid-June to late October
Difficulty Rating:	4
Scenic Rating:	9

View of abandoned mine buildings and tailings piles in Ironton, circa 1941

Special Attractions
■ Exceptional scenery, with panoramic views of the Red Mountain Peaks and the more distant mountains both west and east of the trail.
■ Provides access to a large network of 4WD trails.

History
This route commences near the town site of Ironton, which was located at the southern end of the old tailings pond. The town was formed in 1883 as a tent colony following the mining craze around Red Mountain four years earlier. Ironton developed into a somewhat refined town. Some merchants of the better stores in Ouray and Silverton opened branches in Ironton. Ironton served as the residential center for workers in the nearby mines, such as the Yankee Girl and the Guston.

The town also served as an important stage and supply center for the region. Wagons arrived at regular intervals, and ore wagons left from the city continuously. When Otto Mears opened the Rainbow Route, extending his railroad from Silverton, over Red Mountain Pass, through to Ironton in 1889, the town had a grand welcoming celebration.

Prospectors found gold in nearby mountains, which helped create another rush. New mine shafts were drilled deeper into the mountains. The digging of deep mine shafts resulted in the discovery of underground water; unfortunately, the water was found to contain deadly sulfuric acid, which often ate through machinery, making equipment maintenance a constant and expensive endeavor.

The modest success of the gold mines was not sufficient for the town to survive the impact of the silver crash of 1893, and most of Ironton's residents moved on to other areas. A few hardy residents remained until the early 1930s. Some old buildings are left in the area.

Description
This route is moderately difficult to drive because some sections of the road are rough, steep, and narrow, and there are several sharp switchbacks to negotiate. However, other than locating the start of the trail, which is unmarked, navigation is straightforward.

The route commences at the Idarado Mine tailings pond on US 550. Initially the road, which is unmarked but designated FR 886, travels through the forest as it starts the ascent into Corkscrew Gulch. Sections of the road surface are clay and become very boggy in wet conditions. After crossing a couple of shallow creeks, you encounter several switchbacks as the road climbs out of the gulch.

Once above timberline, you have a panoramic view of adjoining mountains and valleys, including the three Red Mountains. As the road starts to descend, it re-enters the forest. From the turnoff to Gray Copper Gulch, the road is quite steep immediately prior to coming to an end at the intersection with Southwest #14: Silverton to Lake Como Trail.

Current Road Information
Grand Mesa, Uncompahgre and Gunnison National Forests
Ouray Ranger District
2505 South Townsend Avenue
Montrose, CO 81401
(970) 240-5300

Map References
USFS Uncompahgre National Forest
Maptech CD: Southwest/Durango/Telluride
Benchmark's *Colorado Road & Recreation Atlas*, p. 110
Colorado Atlas & Gazetteer, pp. 76, 77
The Roads of Colorado, p. 123
Trails Illustrated, #141

The unmarked entrance to Corkscrew Gulch Trail along US 550

SOUTHWEST #16: CORKSCREW GULCH TRAIL

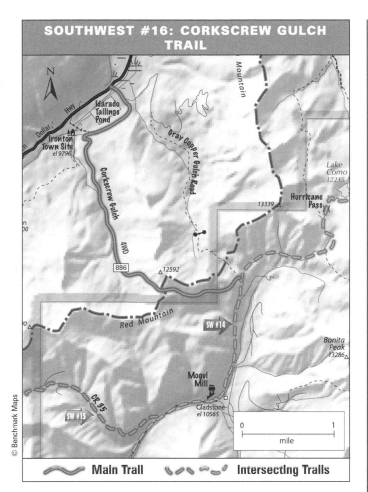

Main Trail   Intersecting Trails

© Benchmark Maps

Route Directions

▼ 0.0		Begin at the sign for the Idarado Mine and its tailings on US 550. Zero trip meter and proceed east onto FR 886, crossing over plank bridge. This intersection is about 15 miles from Silverton and 7.7 miles from Ouray.
4.8 ▲		Cross plank bridge and end at US 550. Ouray is to the right and Silverton is to the left.
	GPS: N37°56.33′ W107°40.27′	
▼ 0.2	BR	Sign indicates Brown Mountain left; Corkscrew Gulch right.
4.6 ▲	BL	Continue on trail.
▼ 0.3	SO	Sign reads "Corkscrew Gulch 4x4 only."
4.5 ▲	SO	Continue on trail.
▼ 0.6	SO	Track on right is the North Pipeline Trailhead.
4.2 ▲	SO	Track on left is the North Pipeline Trailhead.
▼ 1.1	SO	Track on left.
3.7 ▲	SO	Track on right.
▼ 1.5	SO	Track on left.
3.3 ▲	SO	Track on right.
▼ 1.6	SO	Cross through creek.
3.2 ▲	SO	Cross through creek.
▼ 2.0	SO	Cross through creek.
2.8 ▲	SO	Cross through creek.
▼ 2.7	BL	Cabin on right.
2.1 ▲	BR	Cabin on left.
▼ 2.8	SO	Sign to Gladstone and Silverton.
2.0 ▲	SO	Sign to US 550.
▼ 3.6	SO	Pond on left.
1.2 ▲	SO	Pond on right.

▼ 3.7	SO	Intersection.
1.1 ▲	SO	Intersection.
▼ 4.7	SO	Track on left to Gray Copper Gulch.
0.1 ▲	SO	Track on right to Gray Copper Gulch.
▼ 4.8		End at intersection with Southwest #14: Silverton to Lake Como Trail.
0.0 ▲		From Southwest #14: Silverton to Lake Como Trail (1.5 miles from Gladstone), zero trip meter and turn onto CR 11 toward Corkscrew Gulch.
	GPS: N37°54.61′ W107°38.68′	

Yankee Boy Basin Trail

Starting Point:	Ouray
Finishing Point:	Yankee Boy Basin
Total Mileage:	9.1 miles
Unpaved Mileage:	8.6 miles
Driving Time:	1 hour
Route Elevation:	7,800 to 11,850 feet
Usually Open:	Mid-June to early October
Difficulty Rating:	3
Scenic Rating:	8

Special Attractions

- Historic mines and old mining camps.
- Canyon Creek shelf road.
- Abundant wildflowers in Yankee Boy Basin.

History

On the way to Yankee Boy Basin you pass the famous Camp Bird Mine. In 1896, Thomas Walsh, an Irishman, discovered very rich gold in Imogene Basin. He immediately purchased more than 100 claims in the area and consolidated them under the name Camp Bird.

Waterfalls along Sneffels Creek in Yankee Boy Basin

Camp Bird shelf road with Canyon Creek below

Camp Bird, a company town that grew up around the Camp Bird Mine, soon became the second largest gold producer in Colorado, turning out ore that was worth more than $1 million per year. The camp had its own post office, which was established in 1898 and discontinued in 1918.

Walsh furnished a boardinghouse for his employees with marble-topped lavatories, electric lights, steam heat, and even a piano. Meals were deliciously prepared and served on china plates.

Winter and snow were always problems for the community. The men often had to tunnel out of their quarters to reach the mine. Avalanches killed several men over the years. It was necessary to construct a 2-mile aerial tramway from the mines to the mill. Underground tunnels linked the Camp Bird and the Tomboy Mines.

Six years after establishing the prosperous mine, millionaire Walsh sold the properties to an English company for $3.5 million cash, a half million in shares of stock, and royalties on future profits. Upon selling the mine, Walsh showed his appreciation to his employees by issuing bonus checks of up to $5,000.

With profits from Camp Bird, Walsh bought a mansion in Washington, D.C., and his wife and daughter hobnobbed with international society. They became the "jet-setters" of their era. Walsh's daughter, Evalyn, married Edward B. McLean, whose family owned the *Washington Post*. For wedding gifts, each family gave the couple $100,000, which they supposedly spent before the honeymoon was over. Evalyn Walsh McLean later purchased the famed Hope Diamond, which is now on display at the Smithsonian Institution.

The first cabin in Yankee Boy Basin was built during the winter of 1874–75 when several prospectors endured the harsh, snowy winter. As the snow thawed, it was clear they had chosen a very successful locale for mining; they discovered both gold and silver and founded a mining camp called Porters. This was before Ouray was established and several years prior to the first strikes at Camp Bird.

During the peak production years of this mining district as many as 3,000 men worked the silver and gold mines in Yankee Boy Basin. Sneffels served as the headquarters for local mines, although some smaller camps were situated around the more distant mines. Some of the profitable mines included the Yankee Boy, the Ruby Trust, the Wheel of Fortune, and the best producer of all, the Virginius Mine. In 1884, the Revenue Tunnel was constructed to intercept the Virginius at a cost of $600,000. The Virginius-Revenue project was so successful it paid for itself almost immediately and then many times over.

A shelf road was cut into the mountain to Ouray, passing the future site of Camp Bird. The narrow ledges and steep grades were dangerous; rock and snow slides were frequent.

Although the silver crash of 1893 saw the closure of some local mines, rich ore and good management kept the Virginius open. Prospectors discovered additional gold veins. Opera-

A cutting along the Camp Bird shelf road

The trail is short, varied, and is a good introduction to four-wheel driving. Attractions include historic mines, deserted town sites, rugged mountain scenery, and wonderful natural beauty, including alpine meadows that are covered with wildflowers in the late spring. About 5 miles from Ouray, the route traverses a spectacular shelf road perched above Canyon Creek. The road is well maintained and relatively wide.

From Camp Bird, the route takes you through a fairly wide, flat valley to the Revenue Mine and Mill and the old mining town of Sneffels, which can be viewed from the road but is on private property.

About 0.5 miles farther, the road forks, with the road to Governor Basin to the left and the road to Yankee Boy Basin to the right. Until this point, the road is negotiable by passenger vehicles; farther on, high-clearance 4WD vehicles have an advantage.

The Governor Basin 4WD trail is a narrow shelf road that is much more difficult than the Yankee Boy road. Passing is challenging in many sections, and snow can block the road late into summer, necessitating the sometimes-difficult job of turning around. Nonetheless, for those with the experience and nerve, the Governor Basin road offers some majestic scenery and historic mines (difficulty rating: 5).

The road into Yankee Boy Basin passes Twin Falls and numerous mines as it follows alongside Sneffels Creek to the end

Sneffels town site

Camp Bird Mine

tions were suspended in 1905 for some improvements to the mining works, but in 1906, a fire badly damaged the mine.

In 1909, operations resumed as normal, but the activity was short-lived. When miners began sending their ore to the more economical Tomboy Mill on Imogene Pass, the Revenue Mill ceased operations. Ten years later, the mill was destroyed by fire.

The Sneffels post office closed down in 1930. The town experienced a brief revival during the late 1940s when some enterprising folks rehabilitated several of the town's buildings and attempted to get the Revenue Tunnel operating again, but the town was never the same. The Revenue-Virginius properties later became the property of Camp Bird.

Description

Yankee Boy Basin is a very popular location during the peak summer months for both sightseers and hikers. To help alleviate traffic jams, accidents that can be fatal, and ultimately trail closures, please refer back to the Before You Go chapter at the beginning of the book and follow our 4WD Road Rules (page 11). Being courteous and following proper trail etiquette makes the journey more enjoyable for everyone.

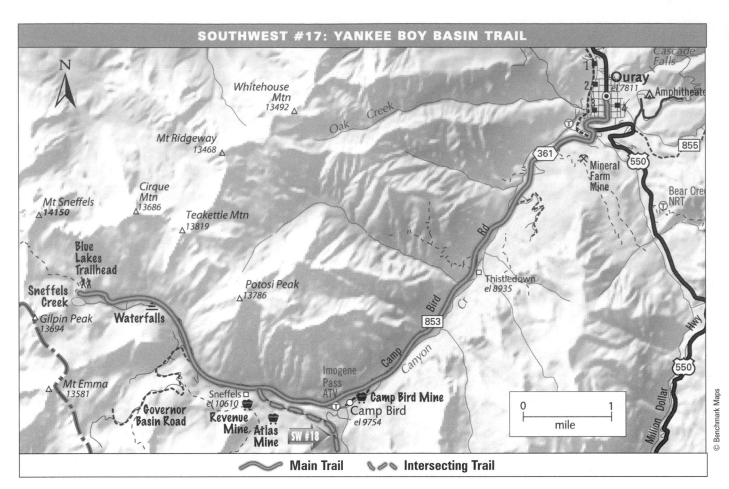

Main Trail 〰️ ⚬⚬⚬ Intersecting Trail

of the trail, some 2 miles farther. Towering peaks including Stony Mountain (12,698 feet) and Mount Sneffels (14,150 feet) surround the basin. The abundant spring wildflowers include columbine, bluebells, and Indian paintbrush.

Numerous backcountry camping sites are located near the trail, but camping is not permitted within 0.25 miles of Sneffels Creek in Yankee Boy Basin or the tributary creek from Governor Basin. Also, camping is not allowed on private lands without written permission. Firewood is scarce in the basin, so if you are planning to camp, we recommend that you either bring wood with you or use a gas stove according to local fire regulations.

Current Road Information

Grand Mesa, Uncompahgre and Gunnison National Forests
Ouray Ranger District
2505 South Townsend Avenue
Montrose, CO 81401
(970) 240-5300

Map References

USFS Uncompahgre National Forest
Maptech CD: Southwest/Durango/Telluride
Benchmark's *Colorado Road & Recreation Atlas*, p. 110
Colorado Atlas & Gazetteer, pp. 66, 76
The Roads of Colorado, pp. 122, 123
Trails Illustrated, #141

Route Directions

| ▼ 0.0 | | In front of Beaumont Hotel at 5th Avenue and Main Street in Ouray, zero trip meter and proceed south out of town, remaining on US 550. |
| 6.4 ▲ | | End at Beaumont Hotel in Ouray at 5th Avenue and Main Street. |

GPS: N38°01.30' W107°40.29'

| ▼ 0.5 | TR | Toward Box Canyon Falls on Camp Bird Road, CR 361. |
| 5.9 ▲ | TL | On US 550 toward Ouray. |

| ▼ 0.6 | BL | Box Canyon Falls on right. |
| 5.8 ▲ | BR | Box Canyon Falls on left. |

| ▼ 2.4 | SO | Bridge over Canyon Creek. Campsites. |
| 4.0 ▲ | SO | Campsites. Bridge over Canyon Creek. |

| ▼ 3.1 | SO | Camping on the left and right. |
| 3.3 ▲ | SO | Camping on the left and right. |

GPS: N38°59.61' W107°42.02'

| ▼ 3.3 | SO | Bridge over Weehawken Creek. |
| 3.1 ▲ | SO | Bridge over Weehawken Creek. |

| ▼ 5.0 | SO | Camping on the left and right. |
| 1.4 ▲ | SO | Camping on the left and right. |

| ▼ 5.1 | SO | Camp Bird Mine turnoff to the left. |
| 1.3 ▲ | SO | Camp Bird Mine turnoff to the right. |

| ▼ 5.7 | SO | Canyon wall dramatically overhangs the road. |
| 0.7 ▲ | SO | Canyon wall dramatically overhangs the road. |

| ▼ 6.2 | SO | Track on right. |
| 0.2 ▲ | SO | Track on left. |

| ▼ 6.4 | SO | Intersection. Southwest #18: Imogene Pass Trail on left. Track on right. Zero trip meter. |
| 0.0 ▲ | | At intersection of Southwest #18: Imogene Pass Trail and Yankee Boy Basin Trail, zero trip |

meter and proceed northeast toward Ouray and US 550.

		GPS: N37°58.53' W107°44.70'
▼ 0.0		Continue along road toward Yankee Boy Basin.
▼ 0.1	SO	Road on right.
▼ 0.3	SO	Revenue Mine and Sneffels site on left. Track on right.
▼ 0.5	SO	Road on right.
▼ 0.7	BR	Numerous campsites on left and right. Atlas Mine ruins on left across the river. Go past the information board.
		GPS: N37°58.67' W107°45.36'
▼ 0.9	BR	Road forks. Governor Basin road is to the left.
		GPS: N37°58.73' W107°45.52'
▼ 1.2	SO	Closed track on left.
▼ 1.3	SO	Dual waterfall view on left.
▼ 1.5	SO	Private road on left. Walker Ruby Mining.
▼ 1.6	SO	Public restrooms on left.
▼ 1.7	SO	Short road on left goes to a mine portal and then rejoins the main track.
▼ 1.9	SO	Cross through creek. Yankee Boy Mine and tailings dump on right. Track on left rejoins from previous entry.
▼ 2.1	SO	Tracks on left and right.
▼ 2.7		End of track.
		GPS: N37°59.45' W107°46.76'

Yankee Boy Basin

Imogene Pass Trail

Starting Point:	Intersection with Southwest #17: Yankee Boy Basin Trail
Finishing Point:	Telluride
Total Mileage:	12.8 miles
Unpaved Mileage:	12.2 miles
Driving Time:	2.5 hours
Route Elevation:	9,000 to 13,114 feet
Usually Open:	Late June to late September
Difficulty Rating:	4
Scenic Rating:	10

Special Attractions

- The highest pass road in the San Juan Mountains, with spectacular scenery and a wealth of historical interest.
- The ghost town of Tomboy.
- Views of Bridal Veil Falls and the switchbacks of Southwest #21: Black Bear Pass Trail.

History

The Imogene Pass road was built in 1880 for access to Ouray from the Tomboy Mine. It was named for Imogene Richardson, the wife of one of Thomas Walsh's partners in the Camp Bird Mine. Wires carrying the first commercial transmission of alternating current electricity were strung across this pass in the 1890s. The power was generated in Ames and transmitted to Ouray.

The Tomboy Mine, located in 1880 by Otis C. Thomas, was situated high above Telluride. Tomboy was Thomas's nickname. For several years there was little activity at Tomboy be-

Crossing through Imogene Creek during the spring runoff

A view of the trail on the east side of Imogene Pass

cause it was so difficult to reach. However, after the silver crash in 1893, prospectors struck gold at the Tomboy, and the mine began to produce handsomely. At its peak, the mining camp supported about 900 people.

In 1901, the Western Federation of Miners called their first strike in the Telluride area. This strike was successful, and non-union laborers were chased out of Tomboy over Imogene Pass. In 1903, the Tomboy Mill again began to use non-union labor, and a second strike was called. The mine owners asked Governor James Peabody to call up the state militia, and the governor, in turn, called on President Theodore Roosevelt to send federal troops. The U.S. Army stayed away, but when 500 state troopers arrived, the violence escalated.

The union even brought in a hired gun, Harry Orchard, whom they had previously commissioned to assassinate the governor of Idaho. On union orders, he attempted to murder Governor Peabody, but the plot failed. With the area under military rule, the union and the strike were broken. The union

labor was run out of town but set up camp at Red Mountain and plotted to recapture Tomboy and Telluride. Fort Peabody was constructed at the top of the pass in 1903 to protect against such an attack. The attack never occurred.

Although Tomboy's residents relied on Telluride for supplies, they did not necessarily turn to Telluride for entertainment. About halfway between the Tomboy and the Smuggler Mines was a renegade district called The Jungle, offering a mix of brothels, poker dens, and saloons.

The Tomboy Mine was sold for $2 million to the Rothschilds of London in 1897 and continued to operate until 1927.

This route was reopened as a 4WD road in 1966, following the efforts of various 4WD clubs.

Description

Imogene Pass is a very popular 4WD trail during the peak summer months. To help alleviate traffic jams, accidents that can be fatal, and ultimately trail closures, please refer back to the Before You Go chapter at the beginning of the book and follow our 4WD Road Rules (page 11). Being courteous and following proper trail etiquette makes the journey more enjoyable for everyone.

Imogene Pass is the second highest pass road in the United States and provides a wonderfully scenic route through the San Juan Mountains. The route passes two major mining camps: Camp Bird and Tomboy.

From the Yankee Boy Basin turnoff, the standard of the road deteriorates and high-clearance and 4WD become necessary. The track travels through the forest and Imogene Creek Valley. There are a number of creek crossings as the track proceeds toward the pass, although none should prove to be any problem for a high clearance 4WD vehicle. The road narrows for the final ascent to the pass, but there are adequate pull-offs available for passing.

About 2 miles from the pass, the track enters the ghost town of Tomboy, 2,880 feet above Telluride and 3 miles distant. The town site has numerous historic remains. Although the buildings of Tomboy continue to deteriorate from the on-

Mill foundations at Tomboy

Social Tunnel

The trail heading to Telluride with Tomboy in the foreground

slaught of harsh weather, Tomboy remains one of the better ghost towns to explore; many of the foundations and some of the structures are clearly evident.

Some 2 miles past Tomboy, the road passes through Social Tunnel, a short passage through a rock outcrop that provides a popular photo opportunity. This location on the trail is also a spectacular overlook with views of the switchbacks of Southwest #21: Black Bear Pass Trail as well as both Ingram Falls and Bridal Veil Falls.

Current Road Information

Grand Mesa, Uncompahgre and Gunnison National Forests
Norwood Ranger District
PO Box 388
1150 Forest Street
Norwood, CO 81423
(970) 327-4261

A storm closing in across mining debris at Tomboy

An information board at Tomboy

Map References

USFS Uncompahgre National Forest
Maptech CD: Southwest/Durango/Telluride
Benchmark's *Colorado Road & Recreation Atlas*, p. 110
Colorado Atlas & Gazetteer, p. 76
The Roads of Colorado, pp. 122, 123
Trails Illustrated, #141

Route Directions

▼ 0.0		At intersection with Southwest #17: Yankee Boy Basin Trail and Imogene Pass Trail (FR 869), zero trip meter and proceed across bridge over Sneffels Creek. Track on right; then bear left.
5.3 ▲		Track on left. Cross bridge over Sneffels Creek. End at intersection with Southwest #17: Yankee Boy Basin Trail.
	GPS: N37°58.53′ W107°44.70′	
▼ 0.2	SO	Track on right—no access.

Imogene Pass summit

A view of Bridal Veil Falls and powerplant from Imogene Pass Trail

5.1 ▲	SO	Track on left—no access.	
▼ 0.4	SO	Creek crossing.	
4.9 ▲	SO	Creek crossing.	
▼ 0.8	SO	Old cabin on left.	
4.5 ▲	SO	Old cabin on right.	
▼ 1.2	BR	Private road to Camp Bird Mine on left.	
4.1 ▲	BL	Private road to Camp Bird Mine on right.	
▼ 1.5	SO	Imogene Creek cascading down through the valley on left.	
3.8 ▲	SO	Imogene Creek cascading down through the valley on right.	
▼ 1.9	SO	Track on right. Old sign to Imogene Pass. Cross through Imogene Creek with cascade on left. Another track on right goes to an old log building and mine.	
3.4 ▲	SO	Track on left goes to an old log building and mine. Cross through Imogene Creek. Track on left.	
▼ 2.0	SO	Spectacular view of Imogene Creek cascading into valley.	
3.3 ▲	SO	Spectacular view of Imogene Creek cascading into valley.	
▼ 2.3	SO	Cross bridge over Imogene Creek. Track on left to Richmond Basin.	
3.0 ▲	SO	Track on right to Richmond Basin. Cross bridge over Imogene Creek.	

GPS: N37°57.22′ W107°43.45′

▼ 2.7	SO	Track on right to buildings and mine. Cross through creek.	
2.6 ▲	SO	Cross through creek. Track on left to buildings and mine.	
▼ 2.9	SO	Track on right. Follow Imogene Pass sign.	
2.4 ▲	SO	Track on left.	

Tomboy Mill ruins

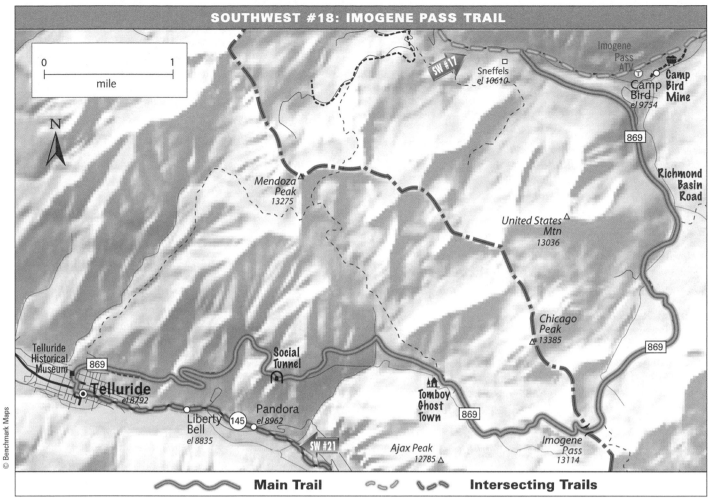

Telluride Historical Museum

Telluride
el 8792

Liberty Bell
el 8835

Pandora
el 8962

Social Tunnel

Mendoza Peak
13275

Sneffels
el 10610

SW #17

Imogene Pass ATV

Camp Bird
el 9754

Camp Bird Mine

Richmond Basin Road

United States Mtn
13036

Chicago Peak
13385

Tomboy Ghost Town

Ajax Peak
12785

Imogene Pass
13114

SW #21

869   145   869

0 —— 1 mile

N

© Benchmark Maps

~~~ **Main Trail**   **Intersecting Trails**

▼ 3.0	BR	Series of tracks; continue to the right.
2.3 ▲	SO	Roads rejoin on the right.
▼ 3.1	SO	Roads rejoin on the left.
2.2 ▲	BL	Roads on the right.
▼ 4.1	SO	Cross through creek.
1.2 ▲	SO	Cross through creek.
▼ 4.4	SO	Cross through creek.
0.9 ▲	SO	Cross through creek.
▼ 5.2	BR	Track on left to Ptarmigan Lake.
0.1 ▲	BL	Track on right to Ptarmigan Lake.
▼ 5.3	SO	Summit of Imogene Pass. Zero trip meter.
0.0 ▲		Continue along main road.

GPS: N37°55.88' W107°44.07'

▼ 0.0		Stay on main road and proceed downhill.
7.5 ▲	SO	Summit of Imogene Pass. Zero trip meter.
▼ 1.2	SO	Track on left. Stay on main road.
6.3 ▲	SO	Track on right. Stay on main road.
▼ 1.4	SO	Cross over drainage.
6.1 ▲	SO	Cross over drainage.
▼ 1.5	SO	Tracks on right.
6.0 ▲	SO	Tracks on left.
▼ 1.7	SO	Stone building remains on left.
5.8 ▲	SO	Stone building remains on right.
▼ 1.8	UT	Overlook of Tomboy mining township.
5.7 ▲	UT	Overlook of Tomboy mining township.
▼ 2.1	SO	Tomboy site.
5.4 ▲	SO	Tomboy site.

GPS: N37°56.18' W107°45.23'

▼ 2.4	SO	Mill; then bridge over creek.
5.1 ▲	SO	Bridge over creek; then mill.
▼ 2.5	SO	Track on right.
5.0 ▲	SO	Track on left.
▼ 3.0	BR	Track on left.
4.5 ▲	BL	Track on right.
▼ 3.1	SO	Bridges over two creeks.
4.4 ▲	SO	Bridges over two creeks.
▼ 3.3	SO	Tomboy Mine remains.
4.2 ▲	SO	Tomboy Mine remains.
▼ 3.8	SO	Colorful mine buildings.
3.7 ▲	SO	Colorful mine buildings.
▼ 4.3	SO	Social Tunnel.
3.2 ▲	SO	Social Tunnel.
▼ 6.6	SO	Seasonal closure gate.
0.9 ▲	SO	Seasonal closure gate.
▼ 6.9	UT	Onto Gregory Avenue at intersection with North Oak. Then turn right onto North Fir.
0.5 ▲	TL	Onto Gregory Avenue. Then U-turn to the right at North Oak.
▼ 7.1	TR	Intersection of N. Fir and W. Colorado.
0.4 ▲	TL	Intersection of N. Fir and W. Colorado.
▼ 7.5		End at Visitor Information Center on West Colorado in Telluride.
0.0 ▲		From Visitor Information Center on West Colorado in Telluride, zero trip meter and proceed east on W. Colorado (main street).

GPS: N37°56.37' W107°49.15'

Ophir Pass Trail

Starting Point:	**Intersection of Colorado 145 and FR 630 south of Telluride**
Finishing Point:	**Intersection of FR 679 and US 550 between Ouray and Silverton**
Total Mileage:	**9.8 miles**
Unpaved Mileage:	**9.8 miles**
Driving Time:	**1.75 hours**
Route Elevation:	**9,500 to 11,789 feet**
Usually Open:	**Mid-June to October**
Difficulty Rating:	**3**
Scenic Rating:	**9**

Special Attractions

- Driving through the 20-foot-high channel in the snow early in the season.
- The long, narrow shelf road set into the talus slope on the west side of the pass.
- Varied scenery, with exceptional views from near the summit.

History

This route was originally called the Navajo Trail and was a well-used Indian hunting trail. The remains of an Indian camp were still visible near the pass in the 1880s.

Trappers were the first white men to use the pass. Explorers and prospectors followed in the 1860s, and the road across the pass became a recognized pass route. In the mid-1870s after the Brunot Treaty opened the region, a wagon road was built across the pass. The wagon road was converted into a toll road in 1880. When Otto Mears built his railroad through the area in 1891, the need for the pass road declined.

Throughout the mining period, the name Ophir referred to two towns: Old Ophir and Ophir Loop. Located at the foot of Ophir Pass, Old Ophir, or just Ophir, was established in 1870, shortly before Ophir Loop. Early settlers named the towns after an Old Testament reference to a region rich in gold in hopes that the nearby mines would bring similar fortunes. The first claims were staked in 1875, after which time prospectors worked the area sporadically.

By 1885, the population of Ophir grew to 200. In three years, it blossomed to 500. Ophir had five saloons, several churches, a school, and its own electricity and waterworks.

The town was often snowbound because of avalanches. In December 1883, a mail carrier named Swen Nilson left Silverton to deliver 60 pounds of Christmas packages and letters to Ophir and was never seen or heard from again. Although some people believed he had stolen the mail and fled the country, Swen's brother set out to search for him. After two years, he finally discovered Swen's skeleton with the mail sack still around his neck.

New Ophir, or Ophir Loop, was founded in the mid-1870s, just 2 miles from Ophir. Although a railway in this area seemed inconceivable, Otto Mears did not know the word impossible. Getting trains started up the steep grade to Lizard Head Pass was a true feat of railroad engineering. Mears oversaw the construction of three tiers of tracks with loops crossing above and below each other and trestles as high as 100 feet. Over this incredible structure, the railroad ran from Telluride to Durango. Two cars of ore were shipped from Ophir Loop

A packtrain of mules on the old Ophir Pass toll road, circa 1920

The railroad track on the Ophir Pass route in 1951

The channel cut through the snow near Ophir Pass in late spring each year

each day, and the town accumulated a small population as a few of Ophir's residents moved closer to the railroad.

The population of Ophir dwindled after the turn of the twentieth century, and the area was close to being a ghost town by 1929. In 1960, it was listed as one of four incorporated towns in the United States with no residents. However, the town is now home to a number of summer residents.

The current 4WD road was opened in 1953.

Description

The trail commences at the turnoff from Colorado 145 at the site of the Ophir Loop; but it is not well marked, so we rec-

ommend that you measure the distance from Telluride on your odometer. Those with GPS receivers will be glad to have the benefit of modern technology to easily locate the trail.

Across the highway from the start of this trail is a short road to the township of Ames, the site of the first commercial alternating current electricity generating plant in the United States.

As you leave the old township of Ophir, the road starts to ascend immediately through a scenic wooded area and aspen stands. As the ascent continues, the road rises above timberline and becomes a narrow shelf road cut into the talus slope with some tight switchbacks and high, sheer drop-offs. This section

Talus mounds beside the road at the Ophir Pass summit

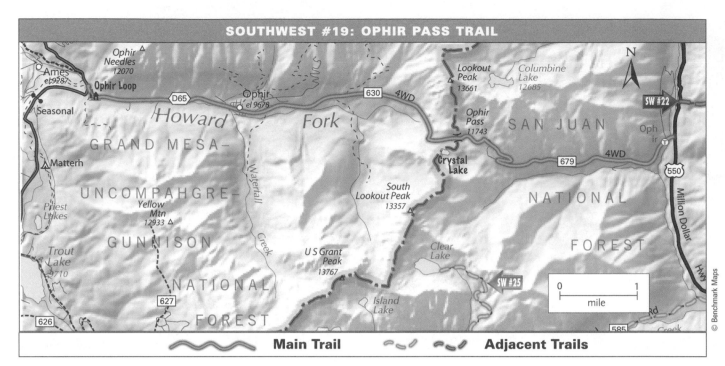

	Main Trail			Adjacent Trails

is the most difficult part of the route. For a short stretch, passing requires careful negotiation. Traveling slowly and carefully, moderately experienced drivers should not have any difficulty. The road is certainly easier than Southwest #21: Black Bear Pass Trail, but those who are tempted to take the route too lightly should heed the lesson offered by the remains of a wrecked vehicle that rolled off the road near this location.

From the summit of the pass to US 550, the route is much easier. Although the road is wider and the surface more sound, it remains a shelf road for much of the balance of the journey.

The varied scenery offers particularly sweeping views on the west side of the pass. The east side is more heavily wooded than the west side, and the wildflowers in the valley add vivid color in season.

The trail intersects with FR 820 and the forest road is an alternative route to US 550. The road, about 1.5 miles long, provides a challenging crossing through Mineral Creek when water levels are high. FR 820 joins US 550, 0.7 miles north of where the main route

Ophir Pass

intersects. Ouray is about 18 miles north of the intersection with US 550 and Silverton is 5 miles south of it.

The road opens in early to mid-June each year. The snow-plow clears only the east side of the pass to the summit. When the road first opens, the plow leaves a narrow channel through the snow—the sides can be up to 20 feet high.

Current Road Information

San Juan National Forest
Columbine Ranger District
PO Box 439
367 South Pearl Street
Bayfield, CO 81122
(970) 884-2512

Map References

USFS Uncompahgre National Forest; San Juan National Forest
Maptech CD: Southwest/Durango/Telluride
Benchmark's *Colorado Road & Recreation Atlas*, p. 110
Colorado Atlas & Gazetteer, p. 76
The Roads of Colorado, pp. 122, 138, 139
Trails Illustrated, #141

Route Directions

▼ 0.0		At intersection of Colorado 145 and FR 630 at Ophir Loop (no signpost, but opposite the Ames turnoff), zero trip meter and turn onto FR 630 heading east toward Ophir. This is 10 miles from the Telluride Visitor Center.
5.7 ▲		End at intersection of Colorado 145 and FR 630 at Ophir Loop.
		GPS: N37°51.74' W107°52.11'
▼ 0.6	SO	Seasonal gate.
5.1 ▲	SO	Seasonal gate.
▼ 2.0	SO	Seasonal gate. Enter town of Ophir. Follow sign to Ophir Pass.

3.7 ▲	SO	Leave Ophir. Seasonal gate.
▼ 2.1	BR	Road forks; then Ophir Pass sign.
3.6 ▲	BL	Road forks.
▼ 2.6	BL/TR	Stay on main road.
3.1 ▲	TL/BR	Stay on main road.
▼ 2.7	SO	Leaving town on Ophir Pass Trail.
3.0 ▲	SO	Enter Ophir town limits.
▼ 3.2	SO	Track on right.
2.4 ▲	SO	Track on left.
▼ 3.7	SO	Two tracks on left.
2.0 ▲	SO	Two tracks on right.
▼ 3.8	SO	Track on left.
1.9 ▲	SO	Track on right.
▼ 4.1	SO	Track on left.
1.6 ▲	SO	Track on right.
▼ 4.2	SO	Tracks on left and right. Track on right goes to the lake and campsites.
1.5 ▲	SO	Track on left goes to the lake and campsites. Tracks on right.
▼ 5.7	SO	Summit of Ophir Pass. Zero trip meter.
0.0 ▲		Continue along main track toward Ophir.

GPS: N37°51.00' W107°46.72'

▼ 0.0		Continue along main track.
4.1 ▲	SO	Summit of Ophir Pass. Zero trip meter.
▼ 0.5	SO	Tracks on left.
3.6 ▲	SO	Tracks on right.
▼ 1.0	UT	Track on left.
3.1 ▲	BL	Track on right.
▼ 3.2	SO	Track on right.
0.9 ▲	SO	Track on left.
▼ 3.7	SO	Columbine Lake Trail on left (FR 820).
0.4 ▲	SO	Columbine Lake Trail on right (FR 820).
▼ 3.9	SO	Cross bridge.
0.2 ▲	SO	Cross bridge.
▼ 4.1		End at intersection with US 550.
0.0 ▲		From intersection of US 550 and San Juan CR 8 (FR 679), zero trip meter and proceed along CR 8 toward Ophir.

GPS: N37°50.84' W107°43.44'

SOUTHWEST REGION TRAIL #20

Alta Ghost Town Trail

Starting Point:	**Telluride**
Finishing Point:	**Alta Lakes**
Total Mileage:	**12.4 miles (one-way)**
Unpaved Mileage:	**4.2 miles**
Driving Time:	**1 hour (one-way)**
Route Elevation:	**9,700 to 11,100 feet**
Usually Open:	**Mid-June to October**
Difficulty Rating:	**2**
Scenic Rating:	**8**

Special Attractions

■ Alta, a well-preserved ghost town.
■ The picturesque Alta Lakes.

History

Alta was the company town for the Gold King Mine, where ore deposits were discovered in 1878. The mine operated as recently as the 1940s. Gold, silver, copper, and lead were mined and transported in aerial tramcars from the Gold King and other mines to Ophir Loop, 2 miles farther down the mountain.

Alta's Gold King was a very rich mine, but it was expensive to operate because of its high elevation. Fortunately, L. L. Nunn found a way to reduce expenses by running electrical power to the mine. In 1881, he organized a contract with the Westinghouse company to construct an electrical plant in Ames, less than 3 miles away.

A makeshift sign along the trail

George Westinghouse was a supporter of alternating current electricity against the strong opposition of Thomas Edison.

The plant harnessed the power of the San Miguel River, transmitting 3,000 volts of alternating current back up to the Gold King Mine. Encouraged by the success of this first alternating current power transmission plant in America, Nunn expanded his venture to supply the city of Telluride, as well as many nearby mines, and installed transmission lines across Imogene Pass. Subsequently, alternating current electricity became widely used in Colorado and the world.

There were three mills at Alta, all of which have burned down. The last one burned in 1945 while seven men were

The boardinghouse at the Gold King Mine

underground. The superintendent ordered the portal to be dynamited in order to cut off the draft that was feeding the fire even though his son was one of the men inside.

Due to the longevity of the Gold King Mine, Alta thrived longer than most high-country mining towns. Visitors can still see quite a few well-preserved historic buildings, including a boardinghouse, cabins, and some more substantial homes. Alta never had a church or a post office.

Description

FR 632 is a well-maintained, unpaved road that leaves Colorado 145 and proceeds east to the township of Alta. In good weather conditions, passenger vehicles can easily traverse the road.

FR 632 leaves Colorado 145, 1.7 miles north of the intersection with the start of Southwest #19: Ophir Pass Trail. On the west side of Colorado 145 at the Ophir Pass turnoff is the road to the township of Ames, where the electricity for Alta was generated from the power station built in 1881.

The very scenic Alta Lakes are located at timberline, a short distance above Alta ghost town. The lakes have good picnic facilities and public toilets.

The road to the lakes is also easy, but the road that encircles the lakes can be extremely rutted and muddy. This section of road would have a difficulty rating of 5.

A number of maps suggest that there is a road from the Alta Lakes to the Telluride ski area. However, when we were last there, this road had been blocked off. We were not able to confirm that this road would be reopened.

Current Road Information

Grand Mesa, Uncompahgre and Gunnison National Forests
Norwood Ranger District
PO Box 388
Norwood, CO 81423
(970) 327-4261

Alta Lakes

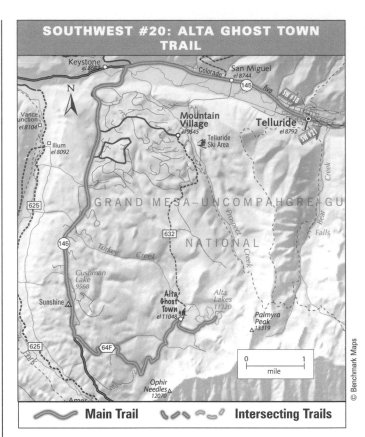

© Benchmark Maps

〜〜 **Main Trail**　　♭♭♭ ⌒♭⌒ **Intersecting Trails**

Map References

USFS Uncompahgre National Forest
Maptech CD: Southwest/Durango/Telluride
Benchmark's *Colorado Road & Recreation Atlas*, p. 110
Colorado Atlas & Gazetteer, p. 76
The Roads of Colorado, p. 122
Trails Illustrated, #141

Route Directions

▼ 0.0		In front of the Telluride Visitor Information Center on W. Colorado in Telluride, zero trip meter and proceed west out of town.
		GPS: N37°56.37' W107°49.15'
▼ 3.1	TL	Follow Colorado 145 south toward Ophir.
▼ 7.8	SO	Sunshine Campground on right.
▼ 8.2	TL	National forest access sign on right (FR 632) toward Alta and Alta Lakes. Unpaved. Zero trip meter.
		GPS: N37°53.02' W107°53.25'
▼ 0.0		Proceed toward Alta on FR 632.
▼ 2.9	SO	Track on right.
▼ 3.0	SO	Track on left with private property sign. Gate. Sign to stay on designated roads.
▼ 3.1	SO	Track on right.
▼ 3.4	SO	Private track on left. Private track on right.
▼ 3.7	BR	Ghost town of Alta. Zero trip meter at small sign for Alta Lakes.
		GPS: N37°53.13' W107°51.28'
▼ 0.0		Follow track on right toward Alta Lakes.
▼ 0.3	BL	Road forks.
▼ 0.5		Road forks. End at Alta Lakes. There are numerous spots for picnics and tracks winding around the lakes.
		GPS: N37°52.83' W107°50.87'

Black Bear Pass Trail

Starting Point:	Ouray
Finishing Point:	Telluride
Total Mileage:	25.2 miles (one-way)
Unpaved Mileage:	10.1 miles
Driving Time:	2.5 hours (one-way)
Route Elevation:	9,000 to 12,840 feet
Usually Open:	Mid-July to late September
Difficulty Rating:	6
Scenic Rating:	10

Special Attractions

- Expansive views of Telluride, nestled in the valley 4,000 feet below.
- Ingram Falls and Bridal Veil Falls, the highest waterfall in Colorado.
- The challenge of completing a difficult 4WD trail.

History

Black Bear Pass has also been known as Ingram Pass, after J. Ingram, who established the Smuggler-Union Mine in 1876. Although Black Bear Pass is now the name commonly used, the U.S. Geological Survey Board on Geographical Names has not accepted it.

Black Bear Pass Trail was developed in the late 1800s to provide access to the Black Bear Mine. In the early 1900s, it fell into disrepair and was reopened as a 4WD road in 1959 through the efforts of the Telluride Jeep Club.

At 365 feet, Bridal Veil Falls is the highest waterfall in Colorado. On the canyon rim above the falls is a restored hydroelectric plant, built in 1904. Now a National Historic Landmark, it once generated power for nearby mines.

Description

The one-way Black Bear Pass Trail is one of the more difficult 4WD trails included in this book. It can be dangerous and has claimed many lives during the past 30 years. Just how difficult you will find it depends on your vehicle, your 4WD experience, and current road conditions. We have included it here for drivers who wish to try a more demanding road and because it is justly famous for its scenery.

The trail is not suitable for a full-sized vehicle due to the very tight switchbacks on the steep western side of the pass. It

A view from Imogene Pass Trail of Ingram Falls and Bridal Veil Falls with Black Bear Pass Trail switchbacking between them

Mining debris alongside Ingram Creek, which cascades down from Black Bear Pass

is the only trail in this region that we have never traveled in our Suburban. Taken slowly and carefully in a small vehicle, this pass should not be beyond the abilities of any driver who has comfortably undertaken a broad selection of the easier trails included in this book.

The portion of the trail that earns its difficulty rating stretches from the summit of the pass to the U-turn at the entrance to the power station at Bridal Veil Falls, about 4 miles below. This section is one-way and can only be traveled from east to west.

From the Million Dollar Highway (US 550) the road starts its climb toward the pass. About a mile before the summit of the pass, the road flattens out, leading through lovely meadows with alpine lakes and waterfalls in beautiful alpine tundra countryside.

At the summit, a network of tracks provides a multitude of panoramic views. The abundance of tracks makes it difficult to identify the main track down to the west side; but by looking down into the valley (to the northwest of the summit), you can easily see the road you need to take.

A view descending from Black Bear Pass toward Telluride

An alpine meadow near Black Bear Pass

Bridal Veil Falls and the power station built to generate power for the Smuggler-Union Mine

Dropping down from the pass, the road heads into a treeless alpine valley but remains quite easy. The water crossings may be of concern to some drivers, but the base of the road is sound and should pose little problem when taken carefully. Some slipping on the talus surface must be anticipated. Up to this point, the degree of difficulty would be rated only 3. As you will have noticed, though, the spectacular views are already evident.

The road continues to get rougher and more difficult as you descend. Obstacles that may prove too challenging for inexperienced four-wheelers include tight, off-camber switchbacks, loose talus, and narrow shelf roads with thousand-foot-plus drop-offs. Because of the difficulty of this section of road, local 4WD rental businesses do not permit their vehicles to cross this pass.

The very tight switchbacks commence about 2 miles below the summit. The road has a formidable reputation, and when you arrive at this series of switchbacks, it is easy to see why. One switchback is particularly notorious and is justly considered impassable for full-sized vehicles. A short distance farther, the road crosses the creek directly above Ingram Falls.

Many scenic views of Bridal Veil Falls and the historic hydroelectric power station are visible from the route. Numerous mines and tramways are evident during the journey down into Telluride.

We think this is one of the great 4WD roads of Colorado. Although experienced four-wheelers may not find it as difficult as it is reputed to be, we are sure they will consider it a great drive.

Current Road Information

Grand Mesa, Uncompahgre and Gunnison National Forests
Norwood Ranger District
PO Box 388
1150 Forest Street
Norwood, CO 81423
(970) 327-4261

Map References

USFS   Uncompahgre National Forest; San Juan National
         Forest
Maptech CD: Southwest/Durango/Telluride
Benchmark's *Colorado Road & Recreation Atlas,* p. 110
Colorado Atlas & Gazetteer, p. 76
The Roads of Colorado, pp. 122, 123
Trails Illustrated, #141

Route Directions

▼ 0.0		In front of Beaumont Hotel at 5th and Main in Ouray, zero trip meter and proceed south out of town, remaining on US 550.
		GPS: N38°01.30′ W107°40.29′
▼ 12.9	TR	Onto Black Bear Pass Trail (FR 823), just beyond the summit marker of Red Mountain. Only a small brown 4WD signpost marks the track. Zero trip meter.
		GPS: N37°53.81′ W107°42.78′
▼ 0.0		Proceed along on FR 823
▼ 0.1	SO	Mine remains.
▼ 1.0	BR	Road forks. To the left is FR 822.
▼ 1.2	BR	Track on left. Waterfall on right.
▼ 1.3	SO	Track on right.
▼ 2.9	BL	Road forks.
▼ 3.2	SO	Summit of Black Bear Pass. Zero trip meter.
		GPS: N37°53.99′ W107°44.52′
▼ 0.0		Proceed from the summit on main track, heading northwest down the hill.
▼ 1.6	SO	Track on left to Ingram Lake.
▼ 1.8	SO	Spectacular view of Telluride on left.

Telluride from the trail

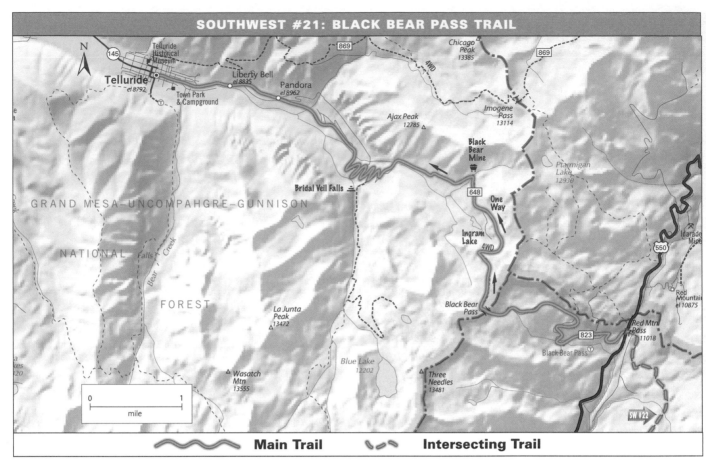

Main Trail · · · **Intersecting Trail**

▼ 2.1 BL Track on right goes to Black Bear Mine. Cross through creek.

▼ 2.6 SO Very tight downhill switchback.

▼ 2.8 SO Mine portal on the right side of road.

▼ 3.2 SO Mine on left.

▼ 3.3 SO Cross through Ingram Creek at Ingram Falls. Mine ruins.

GPS: N37°55.34′ W107°45.60′

▼ 4.1 UT One-way sign. End of difficult section. Closed driveway to old power station on left.

▼ 4.7 SO Mine entrance (closed) on right.

▼ 5.0 SO Parking at Bridal Veil Falls.

▼ 5.5 SO Cross Ingram Falls runoff.

▼ 5.8 SO Cross over creek.

▼ 6.4 SO Tracks on left and right.

▼ 6.5 BL Entrance to Pandora Mill on right (no access).

▼ 6.6 SO Tailing ponds on left and Pandora Mill on right.

GPS: N37°55.84′ W107°46.70′

▼ 6.9 SO Road changes from dirt to paved surface.

▼ 8.0 SO Telluride Cemetery on right.

▼ 8.4 SO Enter Telluride's main street (W. Colorado).

▼ 9.1 End at Visitor Information Center on W. Colorado (main street) in Telluride.

GPS: N37°56.37′ W107°49.15′

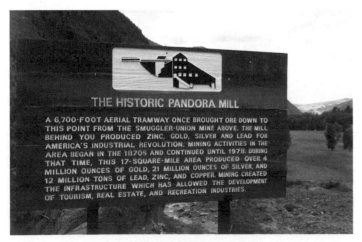

An information board at the Pandora Mill near Telluride

Pack train on Black Bear Pass Trail, circa 1908

Brown's Gulch Trail

Starting Point:	Intersection with US 550, 0.2 miles south of Red Mountain Pass
Finishing Point:	Intersection with US 550, 0.7 miles north of turnoff to Southwest #19: Ophir Pass Trail
Total Mileage:	5.8 miles
Unpaved Mileage:	5.8 miles
Driving Time:	1 hour
Route Elevation:	10,200 to 12,100 feet
Usually Open:	June to October
Difficulty Rating:	3
Scenic Rating:	8

Special Attractions

- Great views of U.S. Basin and the surrounding mountains.
- Historic mining area.
- Located near many other trails.

Description

The entrance to this trail is unmarked. It is located opposite the entrance to Southwest #21: Black Bear Pass Trail. There are some old buildings that were part of the Longfellow Mine on the left of the entrance to the trail. Although long since deserted, they are in good condition.

The trail climbs through the forest after leaving US 550. It is narrow, but passing oncoming vehicles is not a problem. Af-ter about 2 miles, the trail rises above timberline and views are expansive. Initially, there is a good view to the west of Red Mountain in the foreground and beyond it to the row of mountain peaks from Ophir Pass to Black Bear Pass. A short distance farther, as you travel just below the ridgeline, walk the short distance to a wonderful overlook into U.S. Basin and across to McMillan Peak to the east.

Continuing, the trail descends back into the forest. The road travels through some recent mining operations before it proceeds to switchback down the mountain and then to rejoin US 550.

The road is reasonably steep in places and can become muddy. However, in good weather conditions the surface is sound and should not pose problems. Only a few short sections of shelf road, all of which are low on the "white knuckle" rating, are encountered along this route.

Current Road Information

San Juan National Forest
Columbine Ranger District
PO Box 439
367 South Pearl Street
Bayfield, CO 81122
(970) 884-2512

Map References

USFS San Juan National Forest; Uncompahgre National Forest
Maptech CD: Southwest/Durango/Telluride
Benchmark's *Colorado Road & Recreation Atlas*, p. 110
Colorado Atlas & Gazetteer, p. 76
The Roads of Colorado, p. 123
Trails Illustrated, #141

A view of the trail near an overlook into U.S. Basin

Old buildings from the Longfellow Mine

Route Directions

▼ 0.0			From the top of Red Mountain Pass on US 550, proceed east onto the unmarked track beside old buildings from the Longfellow Mine and zero trip meter. This turn is approximately opposite Southwest #21: Black Bear Pass Trail.
	5.8 ▲		End at intersection with US 550 at Red Mountain Pass.
		GPS: N37°53.76' W107°42.79'	
▼ 0.1		BR	Fork with FR 825 on right. Follow sign to U.S. Basin (FR 825).
	5.7 ▲	BL	Track on right.
▼ 0.2		SO	Track on right.
	5.6 ▲	SO	Track on left.
▼ 0.7		BR	Track on left; then cross over creek.
	5.1 ▲	BL	Cross over creek; then track on right.
▼ 0.8		BL	Fork in road. Track on right goes to private property.
	5.0 ▲	SO	Entrance to private property is on left.
▼ 0.9		SO	Cross over creek.
	4.9 ▲	SO	Cross over creek.
▼ 1.0		BR	Track on left.
	4.8 ▲	BL	Track on right.
▼ 1.3		SO	Cross through creek.
	4.5 ▲	SO	Cross through creek.
▼ 2.8		SO	Faint track on left to a scenic overlook of mountains and basin; a cabin is visible on mountain across the valley.
	3.0 ▲	SO	Faint track on right to an overlook; a cabin is visible on mountain across the valley.
		GPS: N37°52.98' W107°42.33'	
▼ 3.6		SO	Track on right.
	2.2 ▲	SO	Track on left.
▼ 3.7		BL	Track on right; then bear right at the fork in road.
	2.1 ▲	BR	Continue past track entering on right; then bear right at the next fork.
▼ 3.8		SO	Road enters on left. Pass through mining area.
	1.9 ▲	BL	Mining operations area. Fork in road.
▼ 3.9		SO	Mine portal on left.
	1.8 ▲	SO	Mine portal on right.
▼ 4.1		SO	Cross over creek.

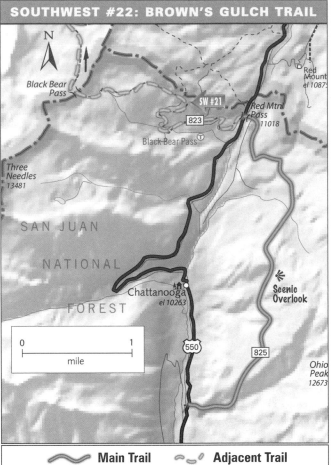

SOUTHWEST #22: BROWN'S GULCH TRAIL

~~~ **Main Trail**   ～～ **Adjacent Trail**

© Benchmark Maps

	1.7 ▲	SO	Cross over creek.
▼ 5.8			End at intersection with US 550.
	0.0 ▲		From US 550 (about 0.7 miles north of Southwest #19: Ophir Pass Trail), zero trip meter and proceed east along FR 82—-an unmarked dirt track.
		GPS: N37°51.50' W107°43.40'	

SOUTHWEST REGION TRAIL #23

Bandora Mine and Clear Lake Trail

Starting Point:	**Intersection of US 550 and CR 7/FR 585**
Finishing Point:	**Clear Lake**
Total Mileage:	**14.5 miles**
Unpaved Mileage:	**14.5 miles**
Driving Time:	**1 hour**
Route Elevation:	**9,600 to 12,300 feet**
Usually Open:	**June to October**
Difficulty Rating:	**3**
Scenic Rating:	**9**

The abandoned Bandora Mine and Mill, circa 1950

Special Attractions
- Scenic, particularly the picturesque setting of Clear Lake.
- Good camping, both developed and backcountry.

History
Silver was first discovered near Mineral Creek in 1882, and several rich strikes followed. The Bandora Mine was acquired by the Blanco Mining Company in 1940 and worked into the 1950s. By that time there were no accommodations for the miners at the mine, and most commuted from Silverton.

Description
To start this trail, turn off US 550 onto CR 7, a maintained gravel road, and proceed toward Mineral Creek Campground. The road travels beside South Mineral Creek, along which you can see numerous ponds and lodges created by ever-industrious beavers.

The route directions first guide you to Bandora Mine and then to Clear Lake. At the 3.7-mile point, you pass the turnoff for the lake on the right-hand side, which is worth noting as you pass. After traveling to the Bandora Mine and South Park, the route directions will direct you back to this point to visit Clear Lake.

Shortly after this intersection, you pass the USFS Mineral Creek Campground on the left. Many good backcountry camping opportunities are also located along this trail. After passing the campground, the road becomes rougher but it is not difficult. After traveling through a short section of dense forest, then through open scrub country, the trail passes below Bandora Mine and enters a large, level meadow known as South Park. This segment of the route ends at an old cabin on the far side of the park.

Returning to the turnoff to Clear Lake, zero your trip meter and turn left, proceeding toward Clear Lake. Immediately starting to ascend, you travel through pine and spruce forest. Although this part of the route is along a shelf, it is not difficult, and there are plenty of passing spots. The segment to Clear Lake is a little rough and rocky, but the surface is sound.

An old cabin at the end of the trail

The road proceeds to switchback up the mountain, climbing above timberline and providing a couple of good observation points for the waterfalls created by Clear Creek. Finally, the road levels off as you enter the very picturesque basin that cradles Clear Lake.

A camping site with Bandora Mine in the backgound

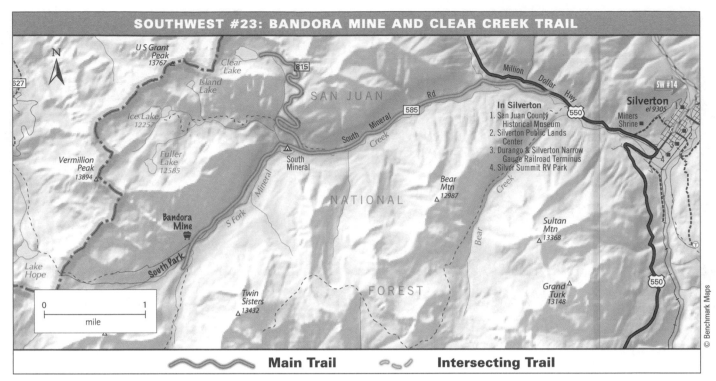

SOUTHWEST #23: BANDORA MINE AND CLEAR CREEK TRAIL

Main Trail ⌇⌇⌇   **Intersecting Trail** ⌇⌇

© Benchmark Maps

Current Road Information
San Juan National Forest
Columbine Ranger District
PO Box 439
367 South Pearl Street
Bayfield, CO 81122
(970) 884-2512

Map References
USFS San Juan National Forest; Uncompahgre National
    Forest
Maptech CD: Southwest/Durango/Telluride
Benchmark's *Colorado Road & Recreation Atlas,* p. 110
Colorado Atlas & Gazetteer, p. 76
The Roads of Colorado, pp. 138, 139
Trails Illustrated, #141

Clear Lake

Route Directions

▼ 0.0		From US 550, zero trip meter and turn onto CR 7/FR 585, signed national forest access to South Mineral Campground.
	GPS: N37°49.11′ W107°42.10′	
▼ 1.0	SO	Cross over bridge.
▼ 1.6	SO	Track on right.
▼ 2.3	SO	Cross over creek.
▼ 3.7	BL	Fork in road. Turning right goes to Clear Lake (you will return to this intersection later). Continue toward USFS Mineral Campground, remaining on main road.
	GPS: N37°48.32′ W107°45.74′	
▼ 4.3	SO	USFS South Mineral Campground on left. Parking on right. Continue straight ahead.
	GPS: N37°48.29′ W107°46.31′	
▼ 4.5	SO	Cross over creek with Rico-Silverton Trailhead and waterfall on the right.
▼ 6.3	SO	Cross through creek.
▼ 6.4	SO	Bandora Mine and Mill ruins on the right.
	GPS: N37°47.20′ W107°47.99′	
▼ 6.6	SO	Track on left goes to a cabin.
▼ 6.7	SO	Cross though creek.
▼ 6.9		End of track. A mining cabin is across the creek.
	GPS: N37°46.80′ W107°48.11′	

Continuation from Clear Lake turnoff

▼ 0.0		From CR 7 (South Mineral Creek Campground access road), zero trip meter and proceed up the hill.
	GPS: N37°48.32′ W107°45.74′	
▼ 2.8	SO	Closure gate.
▼ 3.3	SO	Waterfall on left.
	GPS: N37°49.22′ W107°46.46′	
▼ 3.5	SO	Mine straight ahead at switchback. Proceed up hill.
	GPS: N37°49.17′ W107°46.33′	
▼ 4.1	BR	Track on left goes on up the mountain.
▼ 4.4		End of trail at beautiful Clear Lake.
	GPS: N37°49.58′ W107°46.90′	

A section of the trail as it switchbacks up to Clear Lake

Cunningham Gulch and Stony Pass Trail

Starting Point:	**Howardsville from Southwest #6: Silverton to Animas Forks Ghost Town**
Finishing Point:	**Intersection of FR 520 and Colorado 149, between Lake City and Creede**
Total Mileage:	**37.7 miles**
Unpaved Mileage:	**37.2 miles**
Driving Time:	**3.25 hours**
Route Elevation:	**9,200 to 12,588 feet**
Usually Open:	**Mid-June to late October**
Difficulty Rating:	**5**
Scenic Rating:	**9**

Special Attractions

- A varied and scenic 4WD trail.
- A challenging stream crossing.
- Relative solitude; this trail has less traffic than many others in the peak summer months.

History

Cunningham Gulch is named for Major W. H. Cunningham, who brought a party of mining investors from Chicago through the area. Stony Pass got its name because of its rocky terrain. It was also known as Hamilton Pass (after the builder of the first wagon road over the pass) and as Rio Grande Pass.

The Stony Pass crossing holds a great deal of historic interest. The Ute used the trail for centuries, and Spanish artifacts have also been found in the area. It is believed that Charles Baker discovered the pass in 1860. Baker led a party of prospectors to the area well before the Brunot Treaty officially opened the territory to white settlers in 1873.

Cunningham Gulch

Major E. M. Hamilton built a wagon road along the route in 1872, which was improved seven years later. During this period, the road was heavily used as a stage route and a major supply line for the 4,000 miners working claims in the area.

When the railroad reached Silverton in 1882, the pass was less frequently used. However, the route remained open and was classified as a state highway at one point in the early 1900s. Eventually, it was completely abandoned until the forest service reopened it in the 1950s as a 4WD recreational route.

This trail starts in the town of Howardsville, originally named Bullion City for the Bullion City Company, which laid out the town as a promotional settlement in late 1872. However, the following year the residents changed the name to Howardsville, for the individual who built the first cabin on the site.

Because Howardsville was growing at the same time as nearby Silverton, the two towns became rivals. Howardsville was named the first county seat in Colorado in 1874, but the following year voters moved the county seat to Silverton. Howardsville consisted of about 30 buildings and at its peak had about 150 residents. The post office that served Howardsville was claimed to have been the first in western Colorado; it operated from 1874 to 1939.

Two brothers who headed west from New York to seek their fortunes in silver, established Highland Mary, a town near the Highland Mary Mill and Highland Mary Mine at the top of Cunningham Gulch. The enterprising Ennis brothers took the rather eccentric step of consulting a fortune-teller to decide where they should begin prospecting. The fortune-teller reportedly pointed to an area on the map where the two would find treasure.

The brothers named the area Highland Mary and continued to visit the spiritualist for advice. Her instructions regarding where and how to find ore led the brothers on a peculiar search through the mountains, during which they unknow-

ingly crossed over some rich gold veins. Occasionally they made some lucky discoveries. By 1885, the Ennis brothers had invested about a million dollars in the mine and had paid the spiritualist another $50,000. The pair ended up bankrupt; they sold the mine and their nearby elaborate house and returned to New York.

The new owners of the mine prospected by more conventional methods, and Highland Mary immediately began to pay off. It became one of the best producing mines in Cunningham Gulch and operated sporadically through the years until 1952. All that remains today are the ruins of the mill.

On the eastern side of the pass, near where Pole Creek flows into the Rio Grande River, is the site that was proposed for Junction City. The town was platted after ore was found in 1894, but the ore soon ran out and most of the miners left before any construction occurred.

Description

The route is a long 4WD trail with varied scenery. It is lightly used compared to other, better-known routes in the San Juan Mountains during summer. It is usually open by the middle of June.

The trail begins in Howardsville, between Silverton and Animas Forks, as an attractive 2WD road, running alongside Cunningham Creek and up Cunningham Gulch. Within a couple of miles it becomes steeper, narrower, and rougher as it climbs up a ledge overlooking the gulch. It soon narrows to the width of one vehicle with occasional pull-offs for passing.

As the road approaches the summit of Stony Pass, it levels out into a beautiful alpine valley with typical vegetation and many wildflowers. Open portals of mines and decaying cabins remain.

From the pass, the road tracks along the edge of the Weminuche Wilderness Area and follows the headwaters of the Rio Grande River. At around the 10-mile point, the road reveals great access to some quiet and scenic fishing spots.

The road from the summit has a relatively gentle grade. The biggest potential problems in the first 10 miles of the descent are mud and occasional shallow creek crossings. The few rough stretches are relatively short.

At the 11.8-mile point is the Pole Creek crossing, which is the deepest of all of the stream crossings included in this book. If you are traveling early in the season, we advise you to start this trail in the morning because snowmelt causes the creek to rise significantly throughout the day. Later in the day, this crossing could be impassable or cause vehicle damage. Later in the season, the creek can still be two feet deep, but the creek bed is sound. With good tires and a slow, steady pace, high-clearance 4WD vehicles should have no problem crossing.

The degree of difficulty of the next few miles is a matter of how long it has been since the last rain. When wet, the road can be very muddy. Assess the situation and proceed cautiously when crossing the creeks; sharp approach and departure angles at these crossings can hang up your vehicle. The trail winds through forest in this section, so once it gets muddy, it can stay that way for some time. Clearance between the trees is narrow at times, and the road has a couple of short, rocky sections.

Old, lonely miners' cabin and some of the many mines near the summit of Stony Pass

Current Road Information

San Juan Public Lands Center
Joint Forest Service/BLM Office
15 Burnett Court
Durango, CO 81301
(970) 247-4874
Closed in winter

Rio Grande National Forest
Divide Ranger District (Creede)
Third and Creede Avenue
Creede, CO 81130
(719) 658-2556

Map References

USFS Uncompahgre National Forest; Rio Grande National
Forest
Maptech CD: Southwest/Durango/Telluride
Benchmark's *Colorado Road & Recreation Atlas*, pp. 110, 111
The Roads of Colorado, pp. 139, 140
Colorado Atlas & Gazetteer, pp. 77, 78
Trails Illustrated, #140, #141

Route Directions

▼ 0.0		At intersection of Southwest #6: Siverton to Animas Forks Ghost Town and the turnoff to Cunningham Gulch in Howardsville, zero trip meter and proceed toward Cunningham Gulch and Stony Pass.
5.8 ▲		End at intersection with Southwest #6: Silverton to Animas Forks Ghost Town.

GPS: N37°50.12' W107°35.69'

▼ 0.2	BR	Fork in road. Left goes to Old Hundred Mine.
5.6 ▲	SO	Road on right to Old Hundred Mine.
▼ 1.0	SO	Old Hundred Mine and Mill on left.
4.8 ▲	SO	Old Hundred Mine and Mill on right.

▼ 1.3	SO	Site of Green Mountain Mill on right.
4.5 ▲	SO	Site of Green Mountain Mill on left.
▼ 1.5	SO	Buffalo Boy Mine tramhouse and tram on left.
4.3 ▲	SO	Buffalo Boy Mine tramhouse and tram on right.
▼ 1.7	BR/BL	Follow sign to Creede via Stony Pass on CR 3. Road enters on left and goes back to Old Hundred Mine; then road forks and the track on right goes to the town site of Highland Mary in 3.4 miles.
4.1 ▲	BL/BR	Intersection. Roads enter on left and right. Continue on middle road.
▼ 2.5	SO	Cross through creek.
3.3 ▲	SO	Cross through creek.
▼ 3.2	BR	Short track on left.
2.6 ▲	BL	Short track on right.
▼ 3.3	BR	Track on left.
2.5 ▲	BL	Track on right.
▼ 3.5	BL	Cross under tramway. Track entering on right.
2.3 ▲	BR	Track entering on left. Cross under tramway.
▼ 3.7	SO	Small bridge over creek.
2.1 ▲	SO	Small bridge over creek.
▼ 4.0	SO	Cross over creek. Small track on right.
1.8 ▲	SO	Small track on left. Cross over creek.
▼ 4.7	SO	Small track on right.
1.1 ▲	SO	Small track on left.
▼ 5.8	SO	Summit of Stony Pass. Zero trip meter.
0.0 ▲		Continue along road.

GPS: N37°47.75' W107°32.93'

▼ 0.0		Continue along road.
6.2 ▲	SO	Summit of Stony Pass. Zero trip meter.
▼ 0.2	SO	Cabin and mine tracks on right.
6.0 ▲	SO	Cabin and mine tracks on left.
▼ 1.0	SO	West Ute Creek and Ute Creek trails.
5.2 ▲	SO	West Ute Creek and Ute Creek trails.
▼ 1.3	SO	Cross over creek.
4.9 ▲	SO	Cross over creek.
▼ 3.6	SO	Cross over creek.
2.6 ▲	SO	Cross over creek.

The trail crossing Pole Creek

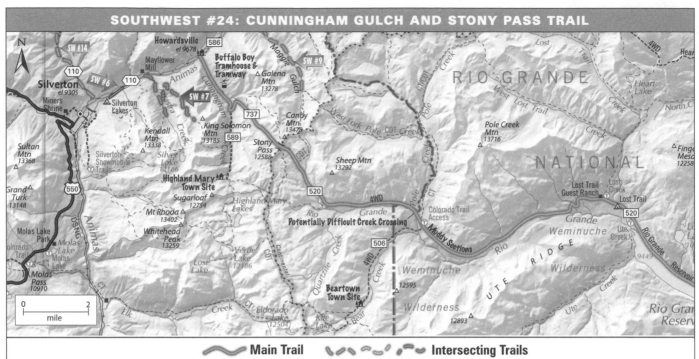

~~~ **Main Trail**   ~~~ **Intersecting Trails**

▼ 5.3   SO   Track to river on right.
   0.9 ▲   SO   Track to river on left.

▼ 5.4   SO   Pass through fence line.
   0.8 ▲   SO   Pass through fence line.

▼ 6.0   SO   Cross through Pole Creek. Beware that this crossing may be deep.
   0.2 ▲   SO   Cross through Pole Creek. Beware that this crossing may be deep.

GPS: N37°45.86' W107°28.00'

▼ 6.2   BL   Intersection. FR 506 on right goes to Beartown site and Kite Lake. Town site of Junction City. Zero trip meter.
   0.0 ▲   Continue toward Stony Pass and Silverton.

GPS: N37°45.72' W107°27.97'

▼ 0.0   Continue toward Rio Grande Reservoir and Creede. Pole Creek Trail is on left.
   16.2 ▲   SO   Pole Creek Trail on right. Intersection. FR 506 on left goes to Beartown site and Kite Lake. Town site of Junction City. Zero trip meter.

▼ 0.7   SO   Cross through creek.
   15.5 ▲   SO   Cross through creek.

▼ 1.0   SO   Gate.
   15.2 ▲   SO   Gate.

▼ 2.1   SO   Cross through Sweetwater Creek.
   14.1 ▲   SO   Cross through Sweetwater Creek.

▼ 2.3   SO   Beaver ponds and dams on right.
   13.7 ▲   SO   Beaver ponds and dams on left.

▼ 2.9   SO   Cross through creek.
   13.3 ▲   SO   Cross through creek.

▼ 3.0   SO   Water crossing. This one can be deep.
   13.2 ▲   SO   Water crossing. This one can be deep.

▼ 3.2   SO   Cross through creek.
   13.0 ▲   SO   Cross through creek.

▼ 3.5   SO   Cross through creek.
   12.7 ▲   SO   Cross through creek.

▼ 4.3   SO   Cross through creek.
   11.9 ▲   SO   Cross through creek.

▼ 4.4   SO   Series of water crossings. None difficult.
   11.4 ▲   SO   Series of water crossings. None difficult.

▼ 5.0   SO   Cattle guard. Cross through creek.
   11.2 ▲   SO   Cross through creek. Cattle guard. Sign reads "Brewster Park."

▼ 5.7   SO   Track on right to river.
   10.5 ▲   SO   Track on left to river.

▼ 6.5   BR   Track on left. Cross through creek.
   9.7 ▲   SO   Cross through creek. Track on right.

▼ 6.7   SO   Track to campsites on right.
   9.5 ▲   SO   Track to campsites on left.

▼ 7.1   SO   Track on right.
   9.1 ▲   SO   Track on left.

▼ 7.9   SO   Lost Trail Creek Trailhead on left. Cattle guard.
   8.3 ▲   SO   Cattle guard. Lost Trail Creek Trailhead on right.

▼ 8.3   SO   Bridge over creek. Lost Trail Campground on right.
   7.9 ▲   SO   Lost Trail Campground on left. Bridge over creek.

▼ 9.1   SO   Ute Creek Trailhead on right. Public restrooms.
   7.1 ▲   SO   Public restrooms. Ute Creek Trailhead on left.

▼ 10.1   SO   Cattle guard. Overlook to Rio Grande Reservoir.
   6.1 ▲   SO   Overlook to Rio Grande Reservoir. Cattle guard.

GPS: N37°44.99' W107°19.87'

▼ 13.2   SO   Track on right to reservoir. Public restrooms available.
   3.0 ▲   SO   Track on left to reservoir. Public restrooms available.

▼ 14.2   SO   Seasonal closure gate. Track on right to Rio Grande Reservoir (no access).
   2.0 ▲   SO   Track on left to Rio Grande Reservoir (no access). Seasonal closure gate.

GPS: N37°43.35' W107°16.00'

▼ 14.8   SO   Turnoff on right to USFS Thirtymile Campground, Weminuche Trailhead, Thirtymile

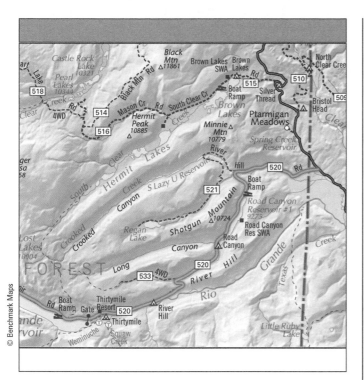

		Resort, and Squaw Creek Trailhead.
1.4 ▲	SO	Turnoff on left to USFS Thirtymile Campground, Weminuche Trailhead, Thirtymile Resort, and Squaw Creek Trailhead.
▼ 16.2	SO	USFS River Hill Campground. Zero trip meter.
0.0 ▲		Continue along main road toward Stony Pass.

GPS: N37°43.81′ W107°13.86′

▼ 0.0		Continue along main road.
9.5 ▲	SO	USFS River Hill Campground. Zero trip meter.
▼ 1.2	SO	Cattle guard. Road on left to Sawmill Canyon.
8.3 ▲	SO	Road on right to Sawmill Canyon. Cattle guard.
▼ 2.9	SO	Road Canyon Reservoirs #2 on right.
6.6▲	SO	Road Canyon Reservoir #2 on left.
▼ 3.3	SO	USFS campground.
6.2 ▲	SO	USFS campground.
▼ 3.6	SO	Seasonal gate.
5.9 ▲	SO	Seasonal gate.
▼ 4.2	SO	Road Canyon Reservoir #1 on right.
5.3 ▲	SO	Road Canyon Reservoir #1 on left.
▼ 4.4	SO	Public toilets.
5.1 ▲	SO	Public toilets.
▼ 5.1	SO	Public toilets.
4.4 ▲	SO	Public toilets.
▼ 6.2	BR	Fork in the road.
3.3 ▲	BL	Track on right.
▼ 6.8	SO	Cattle guard.
2.7 ▲	SO	Cattle guard.
▼ 9.0	SO	Pavement begins.
0.5 ▲	SO	Unpaved road.
▼ 9.5		Cattle guard. Stop sign. End at intersection with Colorado 149. Lake City is approximately 32 miles to the left; Creede is approximately 20 miles to the right.
0.0 ▲		At intersection of Colorado 149 with FR 520, zero trip meter and proceed onto FR 520. Creede is approximately 20 miles east.

GPS: N37°47.41′ W107°07.71′

Old Lime Creek Road

Starting Point:	Intersection of US 550 and south end of FR 591
Finishing Point:	Intersection of US 550 and north end of FR 591
Total Mileage:	11.2 miles
Unpaved Mileage:	11.2 miles
Driving Time:	1.5 hours
Elevation Range:	8,757 to 9,810 feet
Usually Open:	Year-round
Difficulty Rating:	2
Scenic Rating:	10

Special Attractions

- Amazing views of Lime Creek, Twilight Peak, and Weminuche Wilderness across Lime Creek Valley from an exciting shelf road.
- Shady backcountry or developed campsites and scenic picnic areas on Lime Creek.
- Scenic lake with beaver dams and lily pads.
- Aspen fall color viewing.
- Snowmobile trail in winter.
- Scenic, leisurely side trip off US 550.
- Interesting, historic original route of US 550.

History

The Ute Indians, who lived in this area as early as the fourteenth and fifteenth centuries, first used this track for hunting. Game, fowl, and wild vegetation were plentiful, allowing the Ute to live prosperously.

Things began changing when Spanish explorers, who ventured into the rugged San Juans searching for silver, first visited the area in 1765 and then again in 1776. Although the

Lime Creek Valley

Fording Lime Creek on the short spur at the end of the trail

Spanish were unsuccessful extracting silver from the San Juans, in the mid-1800s white settlers from the east came to the San Juans to test their own silver and gold thumbs. Indian hunting trails helped prospectors penetrate the rugged wilderness.

At first ore-seekers attempted to extract silver, but a discovery of gold near Denver in 1858 caused gold miners to flock to this area as well. Supplies were brought in and ore was initially shipped out using burros over the primitive animal and Indian hunting trails, but as the size and weight of the loads increased, wider roads were needed for freight wagons. Teams of oxen and horses were needed to power these loads over the steep terrain.

Sturdy roadbeds began being constructed for these freight wagons. Work to develop a viable freight route between Durango and Silverton began in earnest in the early 1900s after the federal government passed road legislation and the state of Colorado instituted a highway department. The introduction of the automobile, and along with it the tourism industry, necessitated even more road improvements, including the elimination of steep grades and sharp turns where possible.

Many of the original wagon roads were abandoned in favor of an easier route, which would become the highway we know today as US 550, the Million Dollar Highway. Construction was completed on the highway in July 1924, when the road was dedicated on Red Mountain Pass.

This road was originally part of the highway, when in 1918 construction began to upgrade the wagon roads. This section of road was constructed as part of the highway in order to avoid Coal Bank Hill and Potato Mountain. With advancements in road building technology and the debris clearing from the 26,000-acre Lime Creek wildfire (1879), the road took its current route along the shale slopes of Engineer Mountain and over Coal Bank Pass. The San Juan National Forest now maintains this beautiful and historic section of the original Million Dollar Highway.

Description
The trail, FR 591, begins off of US 550, approximately 3 miles north of Purgatory Ski Area and 20 miles south of Silverton. It starts out as a wide, maintained dirt road with plenty of room for two oncoming cars to pass. Beginning to gain elevation almost immediately, the trail alternately travels through large, open meadows and thick forest of aspens and conifer trees.

At mile 2.8, you arrive at Scout Lake. An attractive spot for landscape painters, in summer the lake is thick with blooming lily pads. The lake is also home to abundant wildlife, including geese, ducks, and beaver and their lodges. In fact, if you stay on the lookout for wildlife along the entire length of the trail, you will more than likely be rewarded. The area is home to an abundance of deer and other wildlife.

Past Scout Lake, the road becomes a wide shelf road with scenic views down into Lime Creek Valley below. Rocks embedded in the shelf section of this road give this trail its difficulty rating of 2, no obstacle for a high-clearance 4WD vehicle. The track continues to climb and is corrugated in sections. As the ascent levels off, the road becomes a narrow, very high shelf with sheer drop-offs. Although the trail is narrow, there are plenty of pullouts for passing oncoming vehicles. High above Lime Creek, views along this section of the trail are quite spectacular, especially in fall when brilliant yellow aspens blanket the valley. Also along this section of the trail, worthy of note are the intricate, stone "road guards" constructed by the Civilian Conservation Corps in the 1930s.

An old car that may have fallen from US 550

Intricate stone workings added by the Civilian Conservation Corps in the 1930s

Gradually the trail descends into the valley and follows alongside Lime Creek, a wide meandering creek. As the trail follows the creek over a talus slide, the trail becomes quite rocky. On Lime Creek, a pleasant USFS campground (East Lime Creek USFS Campground) has well-shaded spots with picnic tables, fire grates, and a pit toilet. The site is also a pristine fishing spot. If you plan to camp at this idyllic location in the summer months, remember to bring the bug spray for mosquitoes.

Beyond the campground, the trail begins to climb again away from creek. In general the trail evens out and becomes a smooth dirt road at its north end as it winds through stands of aspen. In some sections, the road is still a shelf, although it is wider and the drop-off less severe than along previous sections of the trail.

Just beyond the historical marker and before the trail ends, a track to the right follows the old route of US 550 just less than a mile to the north of the main trail. This dead-end sidetrack has a fun crossing through Lime Creek and is interesting to explore. The original route of US 550 is still quite evident, and even some pavement from the original road remains. The track also passes a few old wrecked cars that appear to have fallen from US 550 above. The track dead-ends after 0.7 miles. Both this sidetrack and the track off the main trail to the south (a left turn off the main trail) have some nicely shaded backcountry campsites.

The trail ends at the intersection with US 550, 11 miles south of Silverton and 12 miles north of Purgatory Ski Area. This route is a scenic and exciting snowmobile trail in winter months.

Current Road Information

San Juan National Forest
Columbine Ranger District
PO Box 439
367 South Pearl Street
Bayfield, CO 81122
(970) 884-2512

Map References

USFS   San Juan National Forest
Maptech CD: Southwest/Durango/Telluride
Benchmark's *Colorado Road & Recreation Atlas*, p. 110
Colorado Atlas & Gazetteer, p. 76
The Roads of Colorado, pp. 38, 39
Trails Illustrated, #140
Other: *Jeep Trails of the San Juans*

Route Directions

▼ 0.0			Trail begins at intersection of US 550 and FR 591, signed National Forest Access Old Lime Creek Road, approximately 3 miles north of Purgatory Ski Area and 20 miles south of Silverton. Turn onto unpaved road and head south.
	2.8 ▲	SO	Trail ends at intersection with US 550 at south end at FR 591, Old Lime Creek Road.
			GPS: N37°39.51′ W107°48.56′
▼ 0.1		SO	Cattle guard.
	2.7 ▲	SO	Cattle guard.
▼ 0.4		SO	Undeveloped camping area on right.
	2.4 ▲	SO	Undeveloped camping area on left.
▼ 0.8		SO	Private road on left.
	2.0 ▲	SO	Private road on right.
			GPS: N37°39.44′ W107°47.88′
▼ 1.0		SO	Private road on left.
	1.8 ▲	SO	Private road on right.
			GPS: N37°39.59′ W107°47.73′
▼ 1.2		SO	Private driveway on left and track on right.
	1.6 ▲	SO	Private driveway on right and track on left.
▼ 1.3		SO	Private driveway on left.

Lime Creek flows beside Lime Creek USFS Campground

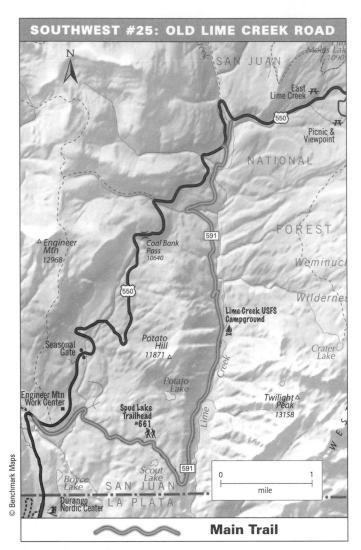

Main Trail

© Benchmark Maps

1.5 ▲	SO	Private driveway on right.	
GPS: N37°39.51' W107°47.66'			
▼ 2.8	SO	Pond on right. Zero trip meter.	
0.0 ▲		Continue southwest on FR 591.	
GPS: N37°39.12' W107°46.45'			
▼ 0.0		Continue northeast on FR 591.	
3.0 ▲	SO	Pond on left. Zero trip meter.	
▼ 0.1	SO	Trailhead on left is #661 to Potato Lake.	
2.9 ▲	SO	Trailhead on right is #661 to Potato Lake.	
▼ 0.5	SO	Track on left.	
2.5 ▲	SO	Track on right.	
GPS: N37°38.96' W107°46.12'			
▼ 1.1	SO	Trailhead on right.	
2.0 ▲	SO	Trailhead on left.	
▼ 3.0	SO	USFS East Lime Creek Campground on right. Zero trip meter.	
0.0 ▲		Continue south on FR 591, Old Lime Creek Road.	
GPS: N37°40.00' W107°45.26'			
▼ 0.0		Continue north on FR 591, Old Lime Creek Road.	
5.4 ▲	SO	USFS East Lime Creek Campground on left. Zero trip meter.	
▼ 0.4	SO	Track on right to undeveloped campsites.	
5.0 ▲	SO	Track on left to undeveloped campsites.	
GPS: N37°40.34' W107°45.12'			

▼ 1.8	SO	Track on right to overlook of creek.	
3.6 ▲	SO	Track on left to overlook of creek.	
▼ 2.8	SO	Campsite on right.	
2.6 ▲	SO	Campsite on left.	
▼ 3.5	SO	Cross over creek.	
1.9 ▲	SO	Cross over creek.	
GPS: N37°42.37' W107°45.68'			
▼ 3.7	SO	Track on left.	
1.7 ▲	SO	Track on right.	
▼ 4.1	SO	Track on right.	
1.3 ▲	SO	Track on left.	
▼ 4.8	SO	Cross over creek.	
0.6 ▲	SO	Cross over creek.	
▼ 5.2	SO	Track on right and historical marker on left.	
0.2 ▲	SO	Track on left and historical marker on right.	
GPS: N37°43.27' W107°44.94'			
▼ 5.3	SO	Track on left to undeveloped campsites and track on right follows old US 550 north 0.7 miles.	
0.1 ▲	SO	Track on right to undeveloped campsites and track on left follows old US 550 north 0.7 miles.	
▼ 5.4		Trail ends at intersection with US 550, signed National Forest Access Old Lime Creek Road, approximately 11 miles south of Silverton and 12 miles north of Purgatory Ski Area.	
0.0 ▲		Trail begins at intersection of US 550 and the north end of FR 591 signed National Forest Access Old Lime Creek Road.	
GPS: N37°43.27' W107°45.01'			

SOUTHWEST REGION TRAIL #26

Jersey Jim Lookout Loop

Starting Point:	**Highways 160 and Colorado 184 in Mancos**
Finishing Point:	**3.6 miles southeast of Dolores on Colorado 184**
Total Mileage:	**41.5 miles**
Unpaved Mileage:	**40.0 miles**
Driving Time:	**2 hours**
Elevation Range:	**7,031 to 10,103 feet**
Usually Open:	**Mid-April to mid-October**
Difficulty Rating:	**1**
Scenic Rating:	**9**

Special Attractions

- Multitude of aspen stands with amazing fall color.
- Historic Jersey Jim Fire Lookout that can be rented for overnight stays.
- Large network of 4WD trails.
- Shady backcountry campsites as well as developed Transfer USFS Campground.
- Access to numerous hiking, mountain biking, ATV, motorbike, and equestrian trails.

History

Among the first humans to populate the area include the Anasazi, or Ancestral Puebloans, the constructors of Mesa Verde National Park's amazing cliff dwellings. While the civilization's disappearance is a mystery, some believe these people migrated to Arizona and New Mexico where they still reside.

Sometime in the fourteenth or fifteenth century, Navajo and Ute Indians settled in the area. They farmed and hunted and continue to live in the area today. In the late 1700s, Spanish explorers blazed the Spanish Trail through the area.

In more recent years, farmers worked the fertile lands to grow important resources for the mines in the San Juan Mountains. Timber was harvested from the Dolores area, cattle ranchers in the Mancos Valley supplied meat, while produce and other agricultural products were grown in the fertile, lower-elevation fields around Cortez. Then the products were sent into the mines.

As the ore disappeared near the turn of the twentieth century, agriculture and tourism took over as the main industry driving the local economy, as it does today. The mining and agricultural history is evident in the San Juan National Forest, a haven for outdoor recreation. Miners accessing mining claims in the La Platas and loggers supplying the mines with timber created many of the current forest roads.

The Jersey Jim Fire Lookout, which towers 55 feet above the surrounding terrain, was used by the forest service from the 1940s to the 1970s to spot forest fires. The tower was named after an early-day rancher who grazed Jersey cattle in the area. Under permit, cattle still graze the forestlands today.

The tower would have been demolished in 1991 except for the efforts of the Jersey Jim Foundation, a volunteer organization that renovated the cabin and now operates it under permit from the forest service. The cabin is available for one- or two-night stays from late May to mid-October. Rental fees go toward the maintenance of the landmark. The one-room cab is furnished with its original fixtures and propane heating and lighting. No water is available in the tower. Starting in March, call (970) 533-7060 for more information.

The Aspen Guard Station is another structure of historical interest. The Civilian Conservation Corps built the structure, which was originally used as the district office for forest rangers in the 1930s. Later fire crews and seasonal forest employees lived in the cottage.

Jersey Jim Lookout is available for overnight rentals from late May through mid-October

In fall aspens turn brilliant yellow before dropping their leaves

The cabin fell into disuse for decades until 1994 when an artist-in-residence program began. Writers, painters, sculptors, musicians, photographers, dancers, performers, poets, and other artists have been selected to stay at the cabin for one or two weeks where they can practice their art in a beautiful, secluded setting. Oftentimes, participants donate a piece of artwork that represents their experience at the cabin. They also take part in open houses for the public and attend an annual art show each fall after their residency.

Description
This trail begins as a paved road in the city of Mancos, just less than 30 miles west of Durango on US 160. Begin by traveling north from Mancos on Colorado 184, then turn east on FR 561 (W. Mancos Road) after about 0.25 miles, following signs to Jackson Lake and Mancos State Park. After about 1.5 miles, the pavement ends and the road becomes a wide, well-maintained dirt road through private land. Vegetation around the trail mostly consists of low oak scrub and pinyon and juniper pines over which there are good views to the east of the La Plata Mountains.

The road gains elevation and narrows slightly after entering San Juan National Forest, but passing is not an issue. Heavy corrugations can develop along this section depending on how recently repairs to the road have been made. Within the boundaries of San Jan National Forest, abundant, shady backcountry campsites are available. At the 10-mile point, Transfer USFS Campground has facilities that include grills, picnic tables, and restrooms. The campground also has five sites adjacent to corrals for equestrian recreation.

West Mancos Overlook is also located at the campground, with views over Crystal Creek Ditch, the Mancos River, and Hesperus Mountain, as well as a number of other 13,000-foot-plus peaks in the La Plata Mountains. The West Fork of the Mancos River is also visible from the overlook. Aspens dominate the vegetation in this area and are brilliant yellow in fall, creating an impressive scene. The dense aspen growth along the entire length of the trail makes for some of the best fall aspen viewing in Colorado.

Continue north on FR 561 past the intersections and forks, following the signs to Jersey Jim Lookout. Beyond the fork with FR 560 on the left, the trail narrows, but the drive is still easy, with ample room for passing. Avoid using this trail in wet conditions, as travel through mud could damage the road or strand vehicles. Along this section, many hiking trails crisscross the road, making their way into the wilderness in all directions. Also along this section, the shady backcountry campsites are popular with hunters in fall.

At mile 11.6, the trail passes the Aspen Guard Station. Just beyond the guard station, continue on FR 561 past the intersection with the end of Southwest #27: Gold Run Loop (FR 350). Just past the intersection with FR 352 is the historic Jersey Jim Fire Lookout at the 13.6-mile point.

Beyond the tower at mile 16.5 is the intersection with the beginning of Southwest #27: Gold Run Loop on the right. Continuing on FR 556, or Rock Springs Road, the trail is a similarly wide and well-maintained dirt and gravel road. Other than corrugated sections, the drive is easy and is passable by passenger vehicle in good conditions.

As is evident from the corrals and cattle guards, the cattle grazed under permit in this area are trucked in and out from

The trail winds through dense aspen forest

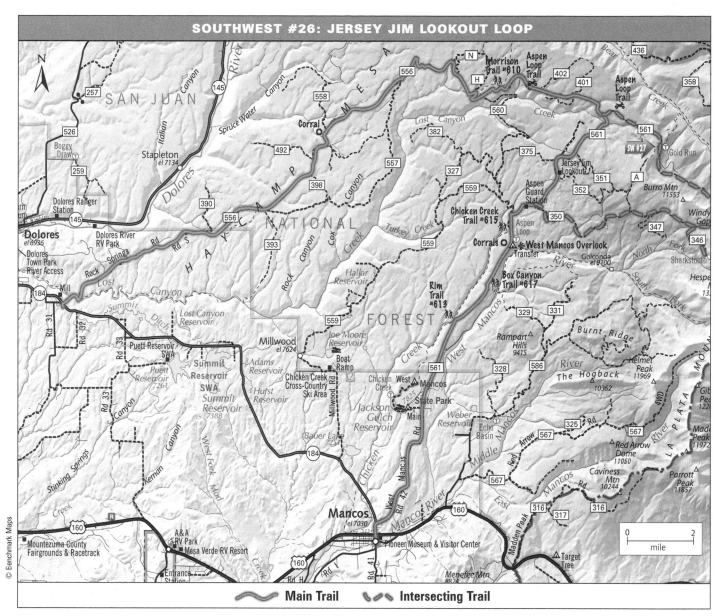

~~~ **Main Trail**   ⌇⌇⌇ **Intersecting Trail**

the substantial stock facilities here. The trail begins descending in this section and is a wide, maintained gravel road.

Toward the end of the trail around the 34-mile point, the trail leaves the boundaries of the San Juan National Forest and travels through private land. Stay on the road and respect private property owners. The road continues to descend to lower elevations, where aspens give way to ponderosa pine trees and oak scrub.

The forest roads that make up the first section of this trail are good snowmobiling, snowshoeing, and cross-country skiing trails in the winter months. The trail ends at the intersection with Colorado 184, 3.6 miles east of Dolores.

Current Road Information

San Juan National Forest
Dolores Ranger District
100 North Sixth
PO Box 210
Dolores, CO 81323
(970) 882-7296

Map References

USFS San Juan National Forest
Maptech CD: Southwest/Durango/Telluride
Benchmark's *Colorado Road & Recreation Atlas*, p. 121
Colorado Atlas & Gazetteer, pp. 75, 85
The Roads of Colorado, pp. 137, 138

Route Directions

▼ 0.0			Trail begins at the intersection of US 160 and Colorado 184 in the town of Mancos. Proceed north on US 184.
	10.0 ▲		Trail ends at US 160 in the town of Mancos. Turn left for Durango. Turn right for Cortez.
		GPS: N37°20.84′ W108°17.34′	
▼ 0.4		TR	Road 42 on right signposted to Jackson Lake, Mancos State Park, and FR 561.
	9.7 ▲	TL	T-intersection with Colorado 184.
		GPS: N37°21.15′ W108°17.34′	
▼ 1.5		SO	Pavement ends.
	8.5 ▲	SO	Pavement begins.

▼	▲		Notes
			GPS: N37°21.83' W108°16.56'
4.4	5.6	SO	Road to Mancos State Park on left. / Road to Mancos State Park on right.
5.6	4.4	SO	Cattle guard; then road becomes West Mancos Road, FR 561 entering San Juan National Forest. / Leave San Juan National Forest.
			GPS: N37°24.85' W108°15.29'
5.9	4.1	SO	Seasonal closure gate. / Seasonal closure gate.
6.2	3.8	SO	Cattle guard. / Cattle guard.
			GPS: N37°25.33' W108°15.05'
7.6	2.4	SO	Track on right; then cattle guard. / Cattle guard; then track on left.
			GPS: N37°26.32' W108°14.23'
7.9	2.1	SO	Corral; then track on left. / Track on right; then corral.
			GPS: N37°26.44' W108°13.96'
8.9	1.1	SO	Cattle guard; then Rim Trail Road on right. / Rim Trail Road on left; then cattle guard.
			GPS: N37°27.10' W108°13.36'
9.3	0.7	SO	Trail on right to Box Canyon. / Trail on left to Box Canyon.
			GPS: N37°27.38' W108°13.14'
10.0	0.0	SO	Intersection with FR 358 on right. Transfer Campground, West Mancos Overlook, and corral also on right. Zero trip meter. / Proceed south on FR 561.
0.0	2.1	SO	Proceed north on FR 561. Signposted to Gold Run Trailhead and Sharkstooth Trail. / Intersection with FR 358 on left. Transfer Campground, West Mancos Overlook, and corral also on left. Zero trip meter.
			GPS: N37°27.97' W108°12.66'
0.2	1.9	SO	TR 615, Chicken Creek Trail on left. / TR 615, Chicken Creek Trail on right.
			GPS: N37°28.18' W108°12.61'
0.9	1.2	BR / SO	Road forks with FR 560 on left. Continue on FR 561 following signs to Jersey Jim Lookout. / FR 560 U-turn to the right.
			GPS: N37°28.70' W108°12.65'
1.2	0.9	SO	Cross over Chicken Creek; then cattle guard. / Cattle guard; then cross over Chicken Creek.
			GPS: N37°28.97' W108°12.30'
1.5	0.6	SO	Cross over Rush Reservoir Ditch. / Cross over Rush Reservoir Ditch.
1.6	0.5	SO	Aspen Guard Station on right. / Aspen Guard Station on left.
			GPS: N37°29.00' W108°12.12'
2.0	0.1	SO	Cattle guard. / Cattle guard.
2.1	0.0	BL	Trail forks; the end of Southwest #27: Gold Run Loop (FR 350) to the right. Zero trip meter. / Continue southwest on FR 561.
0.0	4.5	BR	Continue northeast on FR 561. / Intersection with Southwest #27: Gold Run Loop to the left. Zero trip meter.
			GPS: N37°28.94' W108°11.71'
0.8	3.7	SO	Track on right. / Track on left.
			GPS: N37°29.35' W108°11.28'
1.4		SO	FR 352 on right.
3.1		SO	FR 352 on left.
			GPS: N37°29.73' W108°11.02'
1.5	3.0	SO	Jersey Jim Lookout on right. / Jersey Jim Lookout on left.
			GPS: N37°29.84' W108°11.06'
1.6	2.9	SO	Cattle guard. / Cattle guard.
2.1	2.3	SO	FR 372 on left. / FR 372 on right.
			GPS: N37°30.29' W108°10.82'
2.7	1.7	SO	Road on right. / Road on left.
			GPS: N37°30.39' W108°10.40'
4.1	0.4	SO	Cross over Turkey Creek Ditch. / Cross over Turkey Creek Ditch.
4.2	0.3	SO	Cross over Lost Canyon Creek. / Cross over Lost Canyon Creek.
			GPS: N37°31.03' W108°09.26'
4.5	0.0	BL	Intersection with Southwest #27: Gold Run Loop (FR 561) on right and FR 556 on left. Zero trip meter. / Continue northeast on FR 556.
0.0	5.6	BR	Continue northwest on FR 556, signposted Rock Springs Road. / Intersection with Southwest #27: Gold Run Loop on left (FR 561) and FR 556 on right. Zero trip meter.
			GPS: N37°31.26' W108°09.41'
1.6	4.1	SO	FR 556R on left. / FR 556R on right.
			GPS: N37°31.64' W108°10.50'
1.7	4.0	SO	FR 401 on right. / FR 401 on left.
			GPS: N37°31.65' W108°10.59'
2.0	3.6	SO	Cattle guard. / Cattle guard.
2.8	2.8	SO	FR 402 on right. / FR 402 on left.
			GPS: N37°31.89' W108°11.62'
3.5	2.1	SO	Aspen Loop Trail on right. / Aspen Loop Trail on left.
			GPS: N37°32.12' W108°12.18'
3.6	2.0	SO	Pond on left. / Pond on right.
3.7	1.9	SO	Aspen Loop Trail on left. / Aspen Loop Trail on right.
			GPS: N37°32.24' W108°12.22'
4.0	1.6	SO	Aspen Loop Trail on right. / Aspen Loop Trail on left.
			GPS: N37°32.26' W108°12.44'
4.6	1.0	SO	Cattle guard. / Cattle guard.
4.8	0.9	SO	Morris Trail on right and left. / Morris Trail on left and right.
			GPS: N37°32.01' W108°12.97'
5.6	0.0	SO	Intersection with FR 352 on left and Aspen Loop Trail on left and right. Zero trip meter. / Continue northeast on FR 556.
0.0	7.8	SO	Continue southwest on FR 556. / Intersection with FR 352 on right and Aspen Loop Trail on right and left. Zero trip meter.
			GPS: N37°31.77' W108°13.69'
0.3	7.5	SO	FR 556K on left. / FR 556K on right.

		GPS: N37°31.67' W108°14.00'	
▼ 0.6	BL	FR 556H on right; then cross over Morgan Gulch.	
7.2 ▲	BR	Cross over Morgan Gulch; then FR 556H on left.	
		GPS: N37°32.30' W108°14.48'	
▼ 1.6	SO	FR 556N on right.	
6.2 ▲	SO	FR 556N on left.	
		GPS: N37°32.30' W108°14.48'	
▼ 1.9	SO	Cattle guard.	
5.9 ▲	SO	Cattle guard.	
▼ 2.5	SO	Track on right.	
5.3 ▲	SO	Track on left.	
		GPS: N37°32.50' W108°14.86'	
▼ 2.6	SO	FR 556M on left.	
5.2 ▲	SO	FR 556M on right.	
		GPS: N37°32.39' W108°14.93'	
▼ 4.2	SO	Road on right.	
3.6 ▲	SO	Road on left.	
		GPS: N37°32.50' W108°16.14'	
▼ 4.8	SO	Cattle guard and corral on right.	
3.0 ▲	SO	Corral on left and cattle guard.	
▼ 5.0	SO	Track on right.	
2.8 ▲	SO	Track on left.	
		GPS: N37°32.06' W108°16.67'	
▼ 7.1	SO	Cattle guard.	
0.7 ▲	SO	Cattle guard.	
▼ 7.8	SO	FR 558 on right to Haycamp Point. Zero trip meter.	
0.0 ▲		Continue northeast on FR 556.	
▼ 0.0		Continue southwest on FR 556.	
11.5 ▲	SO	FR 558 on left to Haycamp Point. Zero trip meter.	
		GPS: N37°30.85' W108°19.12'	
▼ 0.3	SO	Cattle guard and private corral on right and left.	
11.2 ▲	SO	Private corral on right and left and cattle guard.	
		GPS: N37°30.58' W108°19.08'	
▼ 1.4	SO	Cattle guard.	
10.1 ▲	SO	Cattle guard.	
		GPS: N37°29.96' W108°19.57'	
▼ 3.6	SO	FR 557 and FR 393 on left.	
7.9 ▲	SO	FR 557 and FR 393 on right.	
		GPS: N37°28.88' W108°21.32'	
▼ 5.2	SO	Cattle guard; then private property of Lost Canyon Ranch on left.	
6.3 ▲	SO	Private property signed Lost Canyon Ranch on right; then cattle guard.	
		GPS: N37°28.37' W108°22.82'	
▼ 7.3	SO	Cattle guard.	
4.3 ▲	SO	Cattle guard.	
		GPS: N37°27.99' W108°24.84'	
▼ 8.2	SO	Cattle guard.	
3.3 ▲	SO	Cattle guard.	
		GPS: N37°27.82' W108°25.66'	
▼ 8.8	SO	Cattle guard.	
2.8 ▲	SO	Cattle guard.	
		GPS: N37°27.67' W108°26.22'	
▼ 9.6	SO	Stop sign at unmarked intersection.	
1.9 ▲	BR	Unmarked intersection.	
		GPS: N37°27.30' W108°26.92'	
▼ 10.0	SO	Cattle guard.	
1.5 ▲	SO	Cattle guard.	
		GPS: N37°27.15' W108°27.57'	
▼ 10.4	SO	Cattle guard.	

1.1 ▲	SO	Cattle guard.	
		GPS: N37°27.01' W108°27.70'	
▼ 11.1	SO	Cross bridge over Lost Canyon Creek.	
0.4 ▲	SO	Cross bridge over Lost Canyon Creek.	
▼ 11.5		Cattle guard; then trail ends at intersection with Colorado 184. Turn left for Durango and right for Dolores.	
0.0 ▲		Trail begins 3.6 miles east of Dolores on Colorado 184. Zero trip meter.	
		GPS: N37°26.60' W108°28.45'	

SOUTHWEST REGION TRAIL #27

Gold Run Loop

Starting Point:	Intersection with Southwest #26: Jersey Jim Lookout Loop and FR 561
Finishing Point:	Intersection with Southwest #26: Jersey Jim Lookout Loop and FR 350
Total Mileage:	15.8 miles, including spur one-way
Unpaved Mileage:	15.8 miles
Driving Time:	1.5 hours, including spur
Elevation Range:	8,972 to 10,994 feet
Usually Open:	Year-round
Difficulty Rating:	2
Scenic Rating:	8

Special Attractions

- Numerous hiking, mountain biking, horseback riding, ATV, and motorbike trailheads.
- Scenic, shady backcountry campsites.
- Views of Sharkstooth Mountain.

Description

At the intersection of Southwest #26: Jersey Jim Lookout Loop (FR 556) and FR 561, travel east on the wide one-lane, dirt road. Avoid this road in wet conditions and use caution if it has recently rained or snowed. As is evident from the deep ruts in this road, vehicles will easily become bogged.

Engelmann spruce trees mixed with a few aspens shade the trail in summer. In spring, abundant wildflowers blanket the surrounding terrain. In the warmer months, hike, mountain bike, or ride your horse, ATV, or motorbike from any of the numerous trailheads. The trail is also excellent for snowmobiling, cross-country skiing, or snowshoeing in winter, and in the fall the area is a popular base for hunters.

The trail becomes a wide shelf road descending into Bear Creek Canyon. Although the trail is a shelf road, the drop-offs are not sheer and the main obstacle drivers must contend with are the ruts, some of which are quite deep. Picking a good line will get you through them easily. Along the shelf section, there are beautiful overlooks of the valley below.

At the 2.3-mile point, the trail passes the Gold Run Trailhead, which has a corral, restrooms, and a parking lot. Beyond the trailhead, the trail is lightly used and backcountry camp-

Twin Lakes and Sharkstooth Mountain

sites are abundant. These scenic, quiet spots are also great for picnicking or wildlife viewing.

The trail crosses short sections of steep talus slopes, which appear to be the remains of significant rock slides. The road across the slides is wide and sound, and the slides are not an obstacle, but are scenic. Travelers crossing the slides will hear the warning cries of the rock-dwelling pikas.

At the 5.5-mile point, the trail intersects with FR 346, a 3-rated spur to Sharkstooth Trailhead. An unmaintained 4WD road, the spur is narrow, very rocky, and deeply rutted, but not overly challenging for a high-clearance 4WD vehicle. Depending on the time of year and recent precipitation, you may also encounter pools of standing water on the trail. Avoid the spur in wet conditions, as vehicles could easily get bogged.

The spur climbs steadily over flat terrain and yields fabulous views of Sharkstooth Mountain. Gradually the 1.5-mile trail winds its way in and out of forests and through meadows, ending at Sharkstooth Trailhead at the foot of Hesperus Mountain. The non-motorized Sharkstooth Trail accesses the Colorado Trail, Centennial Peak (13,062 feet), La Plata Canyon, and Windy Gap.

Beyond Sharkstooth spur, the main trail widens and becomes smooth and maintained with good views of Sharkstooth Mountain to the south. The end of the trail winds through dense stands of aspen, a canopy of yellow in the fall, and ends at the intersection with Southwest #26: Jersey Jim Lookout Loop (FR 561).

Current Road Information

San Juan National Forest
Dolores Ranger District
100 North Sixth
PO Box 210
Dolores, CO 81323
(970) 882-7296

Map References

USFS   San Juan National Forest
Maptech CD: Southwest/Durango/Telluride
Benchmark's *Colorado Road and Recreation Atlas,* p. 121
Colorado Atlas & Gazetteer, pp. 85, 86
The Roads of Colorado, p. 138

Route Directions

▼ 0.0		Trail begins at intersection of Southwest #26: Jersey Jim Lookout Loop (FR 556) and FR 561. Zero trip meter and proceed east on FR 561.
2.3 ▲		Trail ends at intersection with Southwest #26: Jersey Jim Lookout Loop (FR 556).
		GPS: N37°31.26′ W108°09.40′
▼ 0.4	SO	Aspen Loop Trailhead on left.
2.0 ▲	SO	Aspen Loop Trailhead on right.
		GPS: N37°31.35′ W108°09.04′
▼ 2.3	SO	Gold Run Trailhead with corral on left. Zero trip meter.
0.0 ▲		Proceed northwest on FR 561.
		GPS: N37°30.53′ W108°07.43′
▼ 0.0		Proceed southeast on FR 561.
5.6 ▲	SO	Gold Run Trailhead with corral on right. Zero trip meter.
▼ 0.6	SO	Track on right.
5.0 ▲	SO	Track on left.
▼ 4.7	BR	Tracks on left and FR 358 is gated.
0.8 ▲	BL	FR 358 is gated and tracks on right.
▼ 5.6	SO	Intersection with FR 350 straight on and FR 346 to Sharkstooth Trailhead on left. Zero trip meter.
0.0 ▲		Proceed east on FR 561.
		GPS: N37°28.54′ W108°06.37′

Spur to Sharkstooth Trailhead

▼ 0.0		Proceed southwest on FR 346.
		GPS: N37°28.54′ W108°06.37′
▼ 0.8	SO	Twin Lakes on left.
		GPS: N37°28.11′ W108°06.14′

SOUTHWEST #27: GOLD RUN LOOP

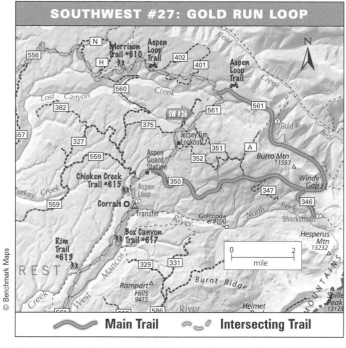

▼ 0.9		SO	Aspen Loop Trail on left for ATVs, hikers, bikers, and horses.

GPS: N37°28.07' W108°06.04'

▼ 1.5			Trail ends at trailheads for Sharkstooth Trail and Highline Loop National Recreation Trail.

GPS: N37°27.72' W108°05.70'

Continuation of main trail

▼ 0.0			Continue northwest on FR 350.

6.4 ▲		BL	Intersection with spur trail to Sharkstooth Trailhead, FR 346, on right and FR 561 straight on. Zero trip meter.

GPS: N37°28.54' W108°06.37'

▼ 2.1		SO	Cattle guard on one side of road.
	4.3 ▲	SO	Cattle guard on one side of road.

▼ 2.5		SO	Intersection with FR 351 on right and track on right to Jersey Jim Lookout.
	3.9 ▲	SO	Intersection with FR 351 on left and track on left to Jersey Jim Lookout.

GPS: N37°28.88' W108°08.60'

▼ 3.5		BL	Track on right; then cattle guard.
	2.9 ▲	BR	Cattle guard; then track on left.

GPS: N37°28.72' W108°09.36'

▼ 3.7		SO	Pond on left and undeveloped campsites on right and left.
	2.7 ▲	SO	Undeveloped campsites on left and right and pond on right.

▼ 4.3		SO	Track on left.
	2.1 ▲	SO	Track on right.

▼ 4.6		SO	Cross over Crystal Creek.
	1.8 ▲	SO	Cross over Crystal Creek.

GPS: N37°28.51' W108°10.20'

▼ 4.7		SO	Cattle guard.
	1.6 ▲	SO	Cattle guard.

▼ 5.3		SO	Tracks on right.
	1.1 ▲	SO	Tracks on left.

▼ 6.3		SO	Cross over Chicken Creek.
	0.1 ▲	SO	Cross over Chicken Creek.

▼ 6.4			Trail ends at intersection with Southwest #26: Jersey Jim Lookout Loop.
	0.0 ▲		Trail begins at the intersection of Southwest #26: Jersey Jim Lookout Loop and FR 350. Zero trip meter and proceed southeast on FR 350.

GPS: N37°28.94' W108°11.71'

The pleasant, lightly used Gold Run Loop

Columbus Mine Trail

Starting Point:	Intersection of CR 124 off US 160 in Hesperus
Finishing Point:	Closure gate a short hike from mine adit
Total Mileage:	14.2 miles (one-way)
Unpaved Mileage:	9.6 miles
Driving Time:	1 hour
Elevation Range:	8,166 to 11,647 miles
Usually Open:	May through mid-October
Difficulty Rating:	4
Scenic Rating:	10

Special Attractions

■ Much remaining evidence of historic mining activity.
■ Exciting shelf road.
■ Terrific photo opportunities.
■ Remote-feeling, high-elevation trail close to Durango.
■ Developed and dispersed USFS campgrounds.

History

Named after the Spanish word for silver, the La Plata Mountains have drawn silver and gold seekers since the 1700s, and were one of the first places to be prospected in southwestern Colorado. The search for precious metals created a thriving mining industry, and settlements within the La Platas developed, supported by some of the richest mines in the state.

Juan Maria de Rivera, the leader of a Spanish expedition through the area, is believed to have made the first gold discovery in these hills in 1765. It wasn't until roughly a century later that the first town site, Parrott City, was located in La Plata County. Nothing remains of the site, which is now located on private property.

A successful prospector, John Moss, planned the settlement after leading a small expedition into the La Plata Valley in 1873. Upon discovering veins of gold and quartz, Moss established with Chief Ignacio, the leader of the Southern Ute, a private treaty for mining and farming rights on 36 square miles of land. Moss then returned to his hometown in California to secure financial backing.

In his absence, the Brunot Treaty of 1873, in which the Ute relinquished 4 million acres of mineral rights within the San Juan Mountains, was signed. Word spread east about gold strikes in the vicinity and people flocked to the La Plata area, as well as Silverton, among other locations in the mineral-rich San Juans. Tensions between the Ute and white settlers were still high after the treaty was signed, but Moss maintained diplomatic relations while building Parrott City, named for his investor, Tiburcio Parrott of San Francisco.

Eventually Parrott City included a courthouse, a jail, a two-story hotel, two stores, several cabins, and even a weekly newspaper (1876–77) called *The Gazette*. In 1876, Parrott City became the official seat of La Plata County, and the population grew, some speculate, to as many as 1,000 residents. During the town's heyday, residents apparently had a habit of carrying whiskey around town in a communal water bucket, and a visitor remarked that the atmosphere was of a continual celebration. The ringleader, John Moss, kept a tapped barrel of whiskey in his office that visitors were welcome to sample at any time, as many times as they wished.

Parrott City's prospects soon began to wane, first when Tiburcio Parrott withdrew funding, and then again when the builders of the Denver & Rio Grande Railroad laid tracks south of Parrott City to the new town of Durango. The railroad gave Durango a strategic advantage over the less accessible mountain towns, and by 1881 the county seat relocated

La Plata City, circa 1894

La Plata River and Campground at La Plata City town site

The spectacular shelf road switchbacks up Lewis Mountain

there. The founding of La Plata City 3 miles to the north and nearer to the main mining activity further diminished Parrott City. The town was mostly abandoned by 1883.

Farther to the north, the town of La Plata City was established on the site of early Spanish explorers' first gold discoveries. By 1882, when the town gained a post office, La Plata City's population was roughly 200. By 1889, La Plata City was becoming crowded with rowdy, gold-seeking miners migrating from Parrott City and other dying towns in the area. Records approximate the town's residents at nearly 500.

During La Plata City's prime, one of the town's brothels became known as both "The Convent" and "Jesse's Convent,"

and subsequent histories recount that the town was so pious it was even home to a convent of nuns. Also officially named "La Plata" and "LaPlata," the locality maintained a post office until 1934, even though miners largely deserted the short-lived settlement around the turn of the twentieth century.

The fortunes of the area's mining communities rose and fell with the mines. Despite the initial promise of mines in the area, the ore was often scattered in small amounts rather than concentrated in large veins. Between John Moss's discovery in 1873 and the turn of the twentieth century, many mines opened in the area, but overall production did not meet expectations. The Comstock Mine near La Plata City, for exam-

Remains of the Columbus Mine near the end of Columbus Mine Trail

Old mine adit from the Bessie G Mine

ple, yielded only somewhere between $15,000 and $75,000 in total.

While many of the mines yielded little, there were some notable exceptions. The two mines just north of Parrott City, the May Day and the Idaho, produced more than half of the $6 million, which totaled the district's mining productivity from the years 1873 to 1943.

The May Day Mine proved so successful that in 1905 the May Day Gold Mining and Milling Company paid the construction costs to run a short branch from the Rio Grande Railroad to the mine. The spur operated until 1926. One gold nugget discovered there was valued at roughly $4,000. During its 40 years of operation, the May Day Mine yielded a total of 75,000 ounces of gold and 759,000 ounces of silver and supported the nearby town of Mayday.

The town of Hesperus, where the trail begins, sprung up after investor John Porter opened the Hesperus Coal Mine in 1882. The town's post office was established in 1891. The Porter Fuel Company eventually produced 150,000 tons of coal annually and employed 175 men. Also serving as a supply point and railroad stop for the gold mining activities in the La Plata Mountains, the Rio Grande Southern Railroad chose the name Hesperus for the tallest nearby mountain, Hesperus Peak (13,225 feet).

Although the town grew quiet along with the La Plata mines, it is still an active coal mining location. Today investors also hope to revive gold and silver mining in La Plata Canyon. The May Day Mine along with the Idaho Mine and Idaho Mill (located just north of the May Day Mine) are part of a 141-acre parcel that the Wildcat Mining Corporation of San Diego is leasing to restore mining operations.

New activity, possibly prompted by the 30-year-high prices of precious metals, is unusual, with only a few other active mines on record in the area, including the Mason Mine, the Incas Mine, and the Neglected Mine. Not without controversy, local residents are resisting the establishment of corporate mining operations in tranquil La Plata Canyon. Wildcat has been tied up for years in the process of permit approvals from numerous state, local, and regional governing agencies.

Description

This scenic and historic trail begins at the intersection of US 160 and CR 124 in the town of Hesperus, 11 miles west of Durango. Enjoy the impressive scenery of rugged peaks jutting above timberline and cloaked with aspen while traveling north on paved CR 124 for approximately 4.6 miles. Along this section, the trail runs through private land, so please respect private property owners and stay on the road.

At first the trail runs through flat, open land. Where the pavement ends, the road enters the San Juan National Forest, and nearby is the historic town site of Mayday. About a mile beyond that is the Snowslide USFS Campground.

The two forest service campgrounds along this trail have fire rings, picnic tables, and pit toilets. Water is available at Kroeger USFS Campground, located about 0.5 miles north of Snowslide. These campgrounds are fee areas. The camp-

grounds are generally open for use from Memorial Day through Labor Day, and a host is on site. The sites at these campgrounds are first come, first served.

Two other camping options are available at Miners Cabin and Madden Dispersed USFS Camping Areas. Camping is not allowed near this trail other than in these designated areas. There is no fee to camp in the dispersed sites.

After the pavement ends, the ride becomes bumpy due to the trail's embedded and loose rock surface, but the road is not difficult for high-clearance 4WD vehicles. The scenery is magnificent as the trail travels alongside the La Plata River through mixed forest of aspens, cottonwoods, Engelmann spruce, and other conifers. The trail is spectacular for wildlife viewing, and elk, deer, and blue birds among other animals are commonly sighted.

At the 7.7-mile point is the La Plata City town site. Very little remains in the clearing where the town was once located, but story boards commemorate the short-lived settlement.

Gradually the road becomes a wide shelf road with sheer, high drop-offs to the La Plata River below. The road begins to climb and is quite steep in sections. Several waterfalls are visible along this section of trail. The scenery is quite dramatic, with amazing views of the surrounding peaks jutting above timberline.

The trail's difficulty increases as it climbs. Embedded rocks can be very large, and erosion to the road adds to the obstacles over which the driver must navigate. These sections and the shelf sections give the trail its difficulty rating of 4. This trail and its side tracks are also popular for ATV and motorbike riders. High-clearance is required and 4WD is recommended for vehicles traveling this trail.

Near the intersection with Southwest #29: Kennebec Pass Trail (FR 571) at approximately the 12-mile point, the road starts to climb more aggressively and begins to switchback.

As the trail makes its way above timberline and enters Columbus Basin, the scenery changes dramatically. The floor of the basin is a beautiful alpine meadow with a creek flowing through it. Wildflowers abound in spring. The shelf road narrows and switchbacks up the steep talus slopes of Lewis Mountain, and there are substantially high drop-offs along this section of shelf.

After about 14 miles, the trail ends at a gate. Beyond the gate is an adit of the Bessie G Mine, a high-grade gold telluride deposit. More interesting old mine remains from the Columbus Mine are located just to the east beside the trail. Among the numerous remains are an old mine shaft, boiler, portable hoist, and a stove.

Current Road Information

San Juan National Forest
Columbine Ranger District
PO Box 439
367 South Pearl Street
Bayfield, CO 81122
(970) 884-2512

Map References

USFS   San Juan National Forest
Maptech CD: Southwest/Durango/Telluride
Benchmark's *Colorado Road and Recreation Atlas,* p. 121
Colorado Atlas & Gazetteer, p. 86
The Roads of Colorado, pp. 138, 154

Route Directions

▼ 0.0		Trail begins at the intersection of US 160 and CR 124 in Hesperus.
		GPS: N37°17.63' W108°02.08'
▼ 4.6	SO	Pavement ends. Mayday town site on right.
		GPS: N37°21.24' W108°04.68'
▼ 5.8	SO	Snowslide USFS Campground on right. Zero trip meter.
		GPS: N37°22.20' W108°04.69'
▼ 0.0		Continue northeast on CR 124.
▼ 0.4	SO	Kroeger Campground on left.
▼ 1.0	SO	Track on left.
▼ 1.2	SO	Madden Campground on right.
▼ 1.7	SO	FR 344 on left.
		GPS: N37°23.50' W108°04.29'
▼ 2.0	SO	La Plata City site on right.
		GPS: N37°23.70' W108°04.15'
▼ 2.5	SO	Cross Boren Creek.
▼ 3.5	SO	Private drive on right.
		GPS: N37°24.68' W108°03.16'
▼ 3.9	SO	Lewis Creek Campground. Zero trip meter.
		GPS: N37°24.90' W108°03.08'
▼ 0.0		Continue north on CR 124.
▼ 0.6	SO	Cross over Basin Creek.
▼ 0.9	SO	Track on left to old foundations and undeveloped campsites.
		GPS: N37°25.49' W108°02.61'
▼ 2.3	SO	Intersection with Southwest #29: Kennebec Pass Trail (FR 571) on left and FR 498 to Columbus Basin on right. Zero trip meter.
		GPS: N37°26.53' W108°01.90'
▼ 0.0		Continue northeast on FR 498.
▼ 0.6	SO	Cross over Columbus Creek.
▼ 0.9	SO	Old cabin on right.
		GPS: N37°26.28' W108°01.84'
▼ 1.0	SO	Track on left is steep 0.4-mile climb to old mine ruins.
		GPS: N37°26.17' W108°01.22'
▼ 2.1	SO	Short walk to the right to old mine remains.
▼ 2.2	SO	Trail ends at gate.
		GPS: N37°25.78' W108°00.99'

Kennebec Pass Trail

Starting Point:	Intersection Southwest #28: Columbus Mine Trail and FR 571
Finishing Point:	Kennebec Pass
Total Mileage:	2.9 miles (one-way)
Unpaved Mileage:	2.9 miles
Driving Time:	35 minutes (one-way)
Elevation Range:	10,477 to 11,999 feet
Usually Open:	May through mid-October
Difficulty Rating:	5
Scenic Rating:	10

Special Attractions

■ Mine and mill ruins.
■ Spectacular high-elevation shelf road.
■ Interesting historic pass road.
■ Access to the Colorado Trail.

History

High atop the La Plata Mountains near Kennebec Pass are a number of abandoned gold and silver mines that first began operating in the 1870s. John Moss, on a prospecting mission in 1873, discovered gold and quartz roughly 5 miles south of Kennebec Pass. A year later he founded Parrott City and mining began in earnest.

The mines directly along this trail did not prove particularly profitable. Well over half of all the money from mining in the area came from the May Day and Idaho Mines. Four other mines—the Neglected, the Incas, the Gold King, and the Red Arrow—produced over $1 million in metals.

Just as the mines near Kennebec Pass failed to meet expectations during the height of the gold rush, much more recently, a number of investors found themselves deceived as to the wealth of mining claims in the vicinity. An unscrupulous California telemarketing company promised a 10 to 1 return from stock investments in a company opening a mine near Kennebec Pass called the Tippecanoe Mine. In 1997, the courts ruled the company pay $2.4 million in damages.

This trail also provides an access point to the Colorado Trail, a continuous 468-mile recreational trail from Denver to Durango. The Colorado Trail is administered jointly by the U.S. Forest Service and the Colorado Trail Foundation; the forest service first proposed the idea in 1973. This hiking trail, which can also be used by mountain bikers and horseback rid-

Sections of the trail are rocky and eroded

ers in sections, traverses seven national forests, six wilderness areas, five major river complexes, and accesses eight of Colorado's mountain ranges. Thousands of volunteers helped complete the trail in 1987.

The last leg of the 468-mile trail follows Junction Creek Canyon into Durango and is also the most difficult. This segment negotiates rugged terrain with nearly 6,000 feet of elevation change.

Kennebec Pass Trail winds up to the shelf road that ends at the notch in the ridge between Cumberland Mountain and Snowstorm Peak

The last section of the trail is a narrow shelf road that ends at the notch on the slopes of Cumberland Mountain

Cumberland Mill remains

Description

This short, exciting trail begins at the intersection of Southwest #28: Columbus Mine Trail and FR 571. It is also quite a scenic trail through grassy meadows filled with wildflowers in spring; also surrounding the trail are Engelmann spruce, other conifers, aspens, and historic mining remains.

From its beginning the trail has a higher difficulty rating due to the large, loose, and embedded rocks, and steep, narrow shelf road with high drop-offs. At the 0.5 mile point, the trail crosses through the La Plata River and again at approximately mile 1.4. In general, the trail climbs steeply, gaining 1,523 feet in its short 2.9-mile length.

Above timberline, open views of the rugged surrounding terrain are amazing, and you catch your first glimpse of the incredible man-made notch carved into the ridge between Snowstorm Peak and Cumberland Mountain on the horizon. The last section of shelf road leading to the "pass" clings dramatically to the rocky slope of Columbus Mountain.

The trail travels through a short section of flat alpine meadow with numerous old mine adits and other relics. Beyond the mine ruins, the trail leaves the basin and begins climbing again up toward Kennebec Pass. At the 2-mile point there is a parking area at a scenic overlook and access to the Colorado Trail. Views of the Needles Range to the northeast are impressive. The true Kennebec Pass is accessed from this point by hiking southeast along the Colorado Trail about 0.5 miles.

Before attempting to drive the final stretch of shelf road, you should wait for any vehicles already on the road to return to the overlook area. This section is narrow, and passing another vehicle on the shelf would be impossible. The surface of the spectacular shelf road is sound, but the track is narrow and the drop-off is sheer and high, more than 300 feet.

The trail ends at the 12,000-foot man-made pass, which was carved into the ridge in order to connect the area's mines. It is worth the extra effort to drive to the last section of the trail for the fabulous views on both sides of the pass.

Spectacular view from the end of Kennebec Pass Trail

© Benchmark Maps

〜〜 **Main Trail** 〜◡◜ **Intersecting Trail**

Current Road Information

San Juan National Forest
Columbine Ranger District
PO Box 439
367 South Pearl Street
Bayfield, CO 81122
(970) 884-2512

Map References

USFS San Juan National Forest
Maptech CD: Southwest/Durango/Telluride
Benchmark's *Colorado Road and Recreation Atlas,* p. 121
Colorado Atlas & Gazetteer, p. 86
The Roads of Colorado, p. 138

Route Directions

▼ 0.0		Trail begins off Southwest #28: Columbus Mine Trail at intersection of FR 498 and FR 571. Proceed northeast on FR 571.
		GPS: N37°26.54' W108°01.89'
▼ 0.3	SO	Hiking trail on left.
		GPS: N37°26.67' W108°01.67'
▼ 0.6	SO	Cross through the La Plata River.
		GPS: N37°26.80' W108°01.39'
▼ 1.4	SO	Cross through La Plata River.
▼ 1.6	BL	Track on right and old mine remains. Zero trip meter.
		GPS: N37°26.79' W108°00.77'
▼ 0.0		Continue northeast on FR 571 to Kennebec Pass.
▼ 0.2	SO	ATV track on right.
▼ 0.4	BR	Scenic overlook and intersection with Colorado Trail on left.
		GPS: N37°27.10' W108°00.68'
▼ 1.3		Trail ends at a notch in the ridge between Cumberland Mountain (12,388 feet) and Snowstorm Peak (12,511 feet).
		GPS: N37°26.48' W108°00.48'

Junction Creek Trail

Starting Point:	Intersection of Main Avenue and Junction Road (25th Street) in Durango
Finishing Point:	Dead end
Total Mileage:	23.3 miles (one-way)
Unpaved Mileage:	19.8 miles
Driving Time:	1.25 hours
Elevation Range:	6,567 to 10,669 feet
Usually Open:	Year-round
Difficulty Rating:	1
Scenic Rating:	10

Special Attractions

- Numerous campsites, multi-use trailheads, and river access right in Durango.
- Easy, scenic drive starting in Durango.
- Animas Overlook.
- Colorado Trail access.

History

Junction Creek, located in the La Plata Mountains, was once an active part of the La Plata Mining District, one of the first areas to be prospected in southwest Colorado. The Neglected Mine, just off Junction Creek Trail, was established in 1895 and became one of the highest producing mines in the region. From 1895 to 1901, the claim was worked on a small scale until the discovery of rich veins of gold and silver telluride ores.

Junction Creek Trail gains elevation as it leaves Durango

View over Animas Valley from Animas Overlook

After intensive development, the mine reached peak production between 1902 and 1904, yielding 7,000 ounces of silver and 13,000 ounces of gold with an estimated value of $270,000. With ore exhausted, the mine ceased operations in 1905. Optimistic investors, who hoped to discover new gold or silver tellurides, re-established operations in 1911 and 1912, but yields totaled a disappointing $10,000 in ore. In the 1930s, another outfit called the Colorado Juno Mining Company revisited the mine but abandoned it after tests revealed more lackluster results.

During peak production years in the La Plata District, Durango's famous female pioneer and cowgirl amazingly began running supplies by mule train for the Neglected Mine and most other mines in the La Platas. The story goes that in the early 1900s during an especially harsh winter, Frank Rivers, who operated the Rivers and the Gorman Ruby Mine, could not find anyone to pack supplies to his men at the mines. He asked one of Durango's best-known cowhands, the 26-year-old Olga Schaaf, to make a one-time run.

At a time when trails to the mines were narrow, underdeveloped foot paths on the sheer slopes of the rugged La Plata Mountains and covered in feet of snow, she successfully led a train of burros loaded with supplies up to the remote mines. Subsequently she was contracted by the owner of the Neglected Mine to pack supplies to the mine for three years.

Famously, she packed supplies in the worst of conditions, using trains of as many as 35 burros. She provided custom saddles for each pack animal and knew each by name. Her pack teams transported tons of equipment, including food, coal, rails, timber, 25-foot coils, and once the corpse of a miner. Incredibly, one story recounts how, becoming stranded by a severe snowstorm at the Neglected Mine, she led 18 miners and 25 burros through drifts as high as 10 feet in well-below-freezing temperatures back to safety.

Other mines she serviced in the La Plata District included the May Day, the Durango Girl, the Bessie G, the Monarch,

the Lucky Moon, and the Gold King. After she retired in the 1940s, she ranched cattle on her homestead near Mayday.

Miners and settlers both braved the rugged terrain and harsh elements to settle the Animas Valley, an incredible view of which can be seen from the Animas Overlook on Junction Creek Trail. In fact, settlers established two towns of the same name, Animas City, in the valley visible from the overlook.

Charles Baker helped established the first Animas City, which was located about 15 miles farther north, near Rockwood. The would-be gold baron convinced hundreds of men, women, and children from Denver that the Animas River at Baker Park flowed over nuggets of gold. The Baker Expedition embarked on their arduous journey west in December 1860. Arriving at the Animas River in March 1861, the party constructed a substantial bridge that became known as Baker's Bridge. After crossing the river and advancing to Bakers Park, the party discovered little if any gold, but stranded with winter setting in, they constructed cabins for shelter from the elements. The following spring, the "settlement" was abandoned and the party disbanded.

Although the settlement failed, Baker's Bridge became a toll station and the bridge was used for decades until a flood in 1911 washed it away. In more recent times the location made history again when Robert Redford and Paul Newman

Junction Creek Trail winds through the La Plata Mountains

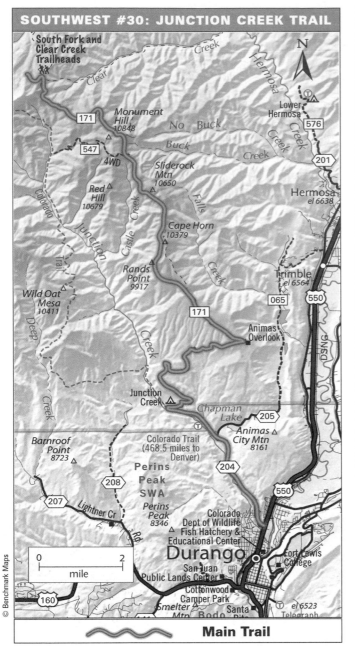

SOUTHWEST #30: JUNCTION CREEK TRAIL

Main Trail

wiped out the town. Through the sympathies of the bar patrons, he was rewarded with free drinks, which encouraged him to spread the fictional story from town to town.

The tall tale spread by the thirsty messenger may have caused the abandonment of several of the smaller camps and settlements in the area—at least until the cavalry arrived in Animas City. Stationed at Fort Flagler, the troops remained until the scare passed.

By 1880, the town had as many as 50 structures, including residences, a school, and a small business district of several stores, and a newspaper, *The Southwest*. At the time, Animas City was the largest town in southwest Colorado and eagerly anticipated the arrival of the Denver & Rio Grande Railroad. When the railroad made demands on the city that it refused to meet, the D&RG ran its line right past Animas City, 2 miles south to Durango. Almost overnight Durango became the center of commerce in southwest Colorado. Eventually what remained of Animas City became a northern suburb of the railroad hub, Durango.

Description

Junction Creek Trail begins in the outskirts of Durango at the intersection of Main Avenue (US 550) and Junction Road (25th Street). Traveling west on paved Junction Road through a residential area, follow the signs to Junction Creek Campground in San Juan National Forest. After 3.5 miles, the pavement ends after crossing a cattle guard. Here the trail enters the national forest and the road becomes FR 171.

Within the forest, the trail is a wide, maintained dirt road through ponderosa pine and scrub oak forest, which later becomes a wide shelf road. The easygoing road is passable by passenger vehicles in good conditions. Approximately 5 miles from the start of the trail, you will pass Junction Creek USFS Campground where facilities are available. The campground is a fee area.

About 5 miles farther, more points of interest are located at the turnoff to Animas Overlook, an interpretive trail and picnic area. The scenic view over Animas Valley against the backdrop of the skyscraping peaks of the San Juan Mountains to the north is worth the stop. At the overlook, the pleasant 0.6-mile interpretive trail, with opportunities for wildlife viewing, sweeping vistas, and information boards about the geology of the Animas Valley, is a good opportunity to stretch your legs.

Gaining elevation beyond the overlook, the road follows Junction Creek Canyon on its western side. The canyon is scenic with views down to Junction Creek and interesting rock formations on the opposite canyon wall.

Past the overlook, backcountry camping is allowed adjacent to the trail. At its upper reaches, the shelf road runs high above Junction Creek, and scenic and expansive views open up through breaks in the ponderosa pine, juniper, and aspen forest. The drop-off is significant, but the trail remains an easygoing and wide one-lane road, although sections that are quite corrugated will make the ride bumpy.

After traveling approximately 21 miles, a 3-rated, 1.6-mile spur trail heads off to the left and ends at a good clearing for backcountry camping and a hiking trailhead accessing the Colorado Trail. Along this spur is where the profitable Neg-

jumped from this spot into the Animas River while filming a scene of the movie *Butch Cassidy and the Sundance Kid* (1969).

The second and more successful Animas City, part of which is visible from Animas Overlook, was settled as a farming community sometime around 1874. The Animas City post office opened in 1877. Finding ample market in the mining camps for its agricultural products grown on the fertile banks of the Animas River, the town slowly grew, and the 1880 census reported a population of 286 residents.

The town grew slowly in part because of its constant fear of attacks from the Ute, who relinquished their lands to the U.S. government under conditions that were never met. So great was the town's fear of retribution from the tribe, on one occasion they sent a messenger north to bring back protection for the settlement.

The winded rider made a stop at a Howardsville bar where he announced that the Indians had burned Animas City and

lected Mine was once located. For a trail so close to the city, this track has quite a remote feel, a nice escape from the traffic and buzz of Durango. Beyond the spur about 2 miles farther, the main trail ends at a dead end.

Overall, the drive is worth the trip for the wildlife viewing and scenic overlooks that are enhanced by brilliant yellow aspens in fall. Located within Durango, this trail is a haven for all types of outdoor recreation, including fishing, white-water sports, mountain biking, camping, hiking, horseback riding, 4-wheeling, hunting, and ATV and motorbike trail riding.

Current Road Information

San Juan National Forest
Columbine Ranger District
PO Box 439
367 South Pearl Street
Bayfield, CO 81122
(970) 884-2512

Map References

USFS San Juan National Forest
Maptech CD: Southwest/Durango/Telluride
Benchmark's *Colorado Road and Recreation Atlas,* p. 122
Colorado Atlas & Gazetteer, p. 86
The Roads of Colorado, pp. 138, 154

Route Directions

▼ 0.0		Trail begins at intersection of Main Street (US 550) and Junction Road (25th Street) in Durango.
		GPS: N37°17.47' W107°52.50'
▼ 0.8	SO	Road becomes CR 204.
▼ 2.9	SO	Intersection with CR 205 to the right. Follow signs to Colorado Trail and Junction Creek Campground.
		GPS: N37°19.47' W107°53.77'
▼ 3.5	SO	Cattle guard and pavement ends; then enter San Juan National Forest.
		GPS: N37°19.88' W107°54.15'
▼ 4.9	SO	Junction Creek USFS Campground on left. Zero trip meter.
		GPS: N37°20.24' W107°54.86'
▼ 0.0		Continue northeast on FR 171.
▼ 2.3	SO	Seasonal closure gate.
		GPS: N37°21.16' W107°55.04'
▼ 2.9	SO	Track on right.
▼ 5.6	BL	Animas Overlook and interpretive trail on right. Zero trip meter.
		GPS: N37°21.77' W107°52.97'
▼ 0.0		Proceed northwest on FR 171.
▼ 4.7	SO	Track on left.
		GPS: N37°24.36' W107°55.17'
▼ 5.2	SO	Track on right to undeveloped campsite.
		GPS: N37°'24.72 W107°55.17'
▼ 6.8	SO	Track on left.
		GPS: N37°25.77' W107°55.96'
▼ 7.5	SO	Track on right is narrow 0.5-mile trail to campsite with expansive views.
		GPS: N37°26.27' W107°56.26'
▼ 8.4	SO	Track on left.

		GPS: N37°26.70' W107°56.77'
▼ 10.6	SO	Road on right is 1.6-mile spur trail rated a 3 for difficulty. Zero trip meter.
		GPS: N37°27.20' W107°58.38'
▼ 0.0		Continue northwest on FR 171.
▼ 0.9	BL	Hiking trails, gated road, and parking area on right.
		GPS: N37°27.81' W107°58.48'
▼ 2.2		Trail ends at turnaround.
		GPS: N37°27.93' W107°59.34'

SOUTHWEST REGION TRAIL #31

Transfer Park Road

Starting Point:	Intersection of CR 240 (Florida Road)
	and CR 243, 14 miles north of Durango
Finishing Point:	Weminuche Wilderness Boundary at
	Endlich Mesa Trailhead
Total Mileage:	17.5 miles (one-way)
Unpaved Mileage:	15.9 miles
Driving Time:	1.5 hours (one-way)
Elevation Range:	7,794 to 11,269 feet
Usually Open:	May through October
Difficulty Rating:	2, 3 for the spur
Scenic Rating:	9

Special Attractions

■ Scenic and historic trail ending at boundary of Weminuche Wilderness.

■ Low-use Miller Creek, Florida, and Transfer Park USFS Campgrounds.

■ Scenic, shady developed campsites on Florida River.

■ Fishing, boating, and other water recreation on Lemon Reservoir.

■ Mountain biking, ATV riding, hiking, horseback riding, fishing, and hunting access.

■ Network of 4WD tracks to explore near the boundary of the Weminuche Wilderness.

Lemon Reservoir

The trail is rocky, making for a rough ride

History

Among the initial undertakings of the Colorado River Storage Project, the Lemon Dam and Reservoir were designed to store the waters of the 68-mile drainage area that originates on the slopes of the 13,000-foot Needle Mountains and converges in the Florida River.

At a half mile wide and 3 miles long, Lemon Reservoir's storage capacity is 40,146 acre-feet of which 39,030 acre-feet is designated for active conservation. State lawmakers originally approved the water storage project in April 1956. The project was conceived for water conservation and to provide ample water for farmers and ranchers during the short growing season on the Florida Mesa, where agriculture by white settlers developed after the Ute were relocated to reservations in 1899.

The rest of the water flowing through the Lemon Reservoir complex is designated for irrigation, and the annual irrigation supply averages 25,740 acre-feet of water. Crops are grown on a total of 14,259 acres of the Florida Mesa and include corn, oats, wheat, alfalfa and other kinds of hay, as well as irrigated pastureland for livestock.

Named for the landowner of the site at the time of the dam's construction, Charles H. Lemon, the dam and reservoir along with its irrigation facilities were completed in December 1963 at a total cost of $11.1 million.

The National Park Service also recognized the recreation value of the reservoir and in 1964 invested more than $100,000 on camping areas, roads, parking lots, and a boat launch. Overwhelmed with campers, picnickers, and other visitors after opening for public use, the area added sanitation facilities in 1967. In July of the same year, the U.S. Forest Service began supervising the public facilities and lands in the vicinity of Lemon Reservoir.

Not surprisingly, the scenic banks of the Florida River, which can easily be explored north of the Lemon Reservoir, were used for thousands of years before the campers, picnickers, and 4-wheelers of today. It is believed the Anasazi roamed southwest Colorado, where they farmed corn and squash, hunted, and gathered wild plants, seeds, and berries more than 10,000 years ago.

When the group mysteriously disappeared, the Ute Indians lived off the land in much the same way. Historians date the first contact between the Ute and Spanish explorers to as early as 1640 when the Ute first obtained horses from the encounters. A Spanish expedition in the early 1760s led by Juan de Rivera is credited as being the first European exploration in the vicinity. On this journey, de Rivera named the Florida River and the La Plata Mountains, along with most of the other peaks and rivers in what is today La Plata County. Florida is Spanish for "flowery" and La Plata means "silver" in English.

Gold fever brought the first white settlers to the area as early as the 1860s. White settlement expanded with the increase of mining in the mountains, spurring the removal of the Ute from their land. The controversial process began in the 1860s and was complete by the turn of the twentieth century.

During the mining boom in the late 1880s, the banks of the Florida River, and the park where the Transfer Park USFS Campground is located today, were used as transfer sites where mining equipment and supplies were unloaded from wagons onto pack animals and transported to the mines near the head of the Florida drainage.

Local history recounts that Logtown was one of the isolated towns to which supplies were carried from Transfer Park.

Florida River near Florida USFS Campground

However, the town was so named in the late 1950s by back-packers who discovered the abandoned settlement that was located about 40 miles northeast of Durango. At that time 20 to 30 log cabins were still standing and an extensive amount of old mining equipment littered the area.

Although the true name of the town is unknown, one well-known mine, the Pittsburg, located in this inaccessible area, produced more than $1 million in bullion in the 1880s and 1890s. Today nothing much is left at the site, which is only accessible via a strenuous 8.5-mile hike beyond City Reservoir within the Weminuche Wilderness. The forest service trail is #542, City Reservoir Trail via Lime Mesa.

Description

This trail follows the length of Lemon Reservoir and climbs Miller Mountain (11,740 feet) to Endlich Mesa. Beginning at the intersection of CR 240, Florida Road, and CR 243, zero your trip meter and proceed north on CR 243. The pavement ends at the 1.6-mile point, and Lemon Dam is on the left side of the road immediately after the pavement ends. Lemon Reservoir comes into view as you proceed north along the main trail. You will also notice barren trees on the surrounding slopes, remains of the Missionary Ridge Wildfire in June 2002.

The road becomes a wide, maintained gravel road that is passable by passenger vehicle in good conditions. Potholes are the only hindrance to a smooth ride. The first section of the road travels beside private property (please do not trespass), and you soon arrive at Miller Creek USFS Campground on the banks of Lemon Reservoir. The campground has well-maintained facilities, including picnic tables, 12 camping spots, flush toilets, and fireplaces. Another advantage of the campgrounds on this trail is that they are frequently vacant.

Beyond Miller Creek Campground at the north end of the reservoir is Upper Lemon Day Use Area, featuring a concrete boat launch, fishing access, and restroom facilities. Fishermen who cast a line are frequently successful because the reservoir is stocked with kokonee salmon and trout. The road narrows slightly and begins gaining elevation just beyond the day use area. Ample shade is provided by the surrounding forest of blue spruce, Douglas fir, and aspen.

After approximately 7 miles, you will arrive at the intersection of FR 597 and FR 597A. FR 597A is a 1.5-mile, two-lane gravel road that travels beside the Florida River to the Florida and Transfer Park USFS Campgrounds. Smooth and maintained, the easy track has a few potholes, corrugations, and widely disbursed embedded rock but is passable by passenger vehicle. At 0.2 miles is the large Florida USFS Campground and picnic area with shady spots right on the banks of the Florida River.

Beyond the Florida Campground, the road travels over the flat forest floor. Transfer Park USFS Campground has two campsite loops and well-maintained facilities, including grill grates and picnic tables. Both campgrounds are lightly used. Transfer Park also has ample parking for a popular hiking trailhead, Burnt Timber Trail, which accesses the Weminuche Wilderness and proceeds to Lime Mesa, Mountain View Crest, the scenic City Reservoir, and historic Logtown town site.

Fishing access at Upper Lemon Day Use Area

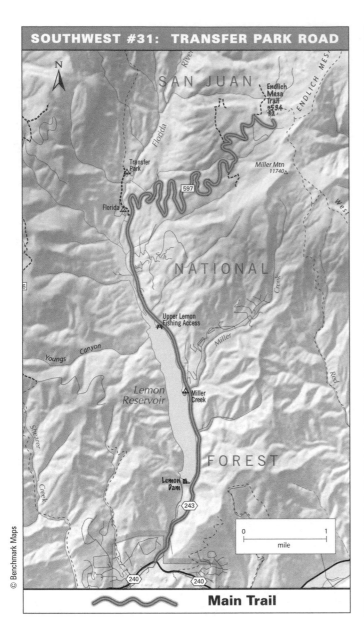

© Benchmark Maps

Main Trail

Proceeding north on the main trail (FR 597), the road narrows, becomes eroded and rocky, and travels through forested land with limited views of the surrounding San Juan Mountains. Although the road narrows, passing oncoming vehicles is not an obstacle. Since the surrounding terrain is flat, there are plenty of pullouts and there are also plenty of good backcountry campsites that are especially popular with hunters in fall. The ride is bumpy from embedded rock, loose rock, and erosion, giving the trail its difficulty rating of 2. For 4WD vehicles, the trail is easy, although still a rough ride.

As the trail continues to climb, it becomes an easy shelf road that gently slopes on the drop-off edge. The track is consistently rough as it switchbacks up the mountain. From the higher reaches of the trail, overlooks present the scenic Florida River Canyon and the slopes of Lime Mesa blanketed with aspens, a brilliant yellow display in fall.

The turnoff to FR 597C is located after traveling approximately 8 miles. This track is just under a mile in length and is a 3-rated spur off the main trail. The road is narrow and very

eroded, but its end provides a scenic overlook of Lime Mesa and the Florida River Canyon to the west.

The main trail proceeds about 1.5 miles to another turnoff onto FR 597D. The short track dead-ends after 0.75 miles. Proceed on the main trail a short distance (0.75 miles) beyond the last turnoff to its end at the Endlich Mesa Trailhead and boundary of the Weminuche Wilderness. The trailhead has hitching rails and loading chutes for horses. The view here (above 11,000 feet) is open and expansive, with Endlich Mesa to the northeast, Miller Mountain to the south, and the Florida River Canyon and Lime Mesa to the west. In spring, the colorful wildflowers in the meadow at the trail's end are a must-see.

Current Road Information

San Juan National Forest
Columbine Ranger District
PO Box 439
367 South Pearl Street
Bayfield, CO 81122
(970) 884-2512

Map References

USFS San Juan National Forest
Maptech CD: Southwest/Durango/Telluride
Benchmark's *Colorado Road and Recreation Atlas*, p. 122
Colorado Atlas & Gazetteer, pp. 86, 87
The Roads of Colorado, pp. 139, 155
Trails Illustrated, #140 (incomplete)

Route Directions

▼ 0.0		Trail begins at the intersection of CR 240 (Florida Road) and CR 243, 14 miles north of Durango.
		GPS: N37°21.66' W107°40.28'
▼ 1.6	SO	Pavement ends and Lemon Dam on left.
▼ 3.4	SO	Miller Creek Campground and boat launch on left.
		GPS: N37°24.37' W107°39.64'
▼ 4.8	SO	Upper Lemon Day Use Area on left.
		GPS: N37°25.41' W107°40.21'
▼ 5.2	SO	Cattle guard.
		GPS: N37°25.62' W107°40.47'
▼ 6.9	SO	Cattle guard; then intersection with FR 597A to Florida Transfer Park USFS Campgrounds to the left. Zero trip meter.
▼ 0.0		Proceed north on FR 597.
		GPS: N37°27.10' W107°40.70'
▼ 7.1	SO	Cattle guard.
		GPS: N37°27.86' W107°38.78'
▼ 8.1	TR	Intersection with FR 597C straight ahead and FR 597 to the right. Zero trip meter.
		GPS: N37°28.22' W107°38.88'
▼ 0.0		Continue east on FR 597.
▼ 1.7	TR	Intersection with FR 597D straight ahead and FR 597 to the right. Zero trip meter.
		GPS: N37°28.69' W107°38.26'
▼ 0.0		Proceed southeast on FR 597.
▼ 0.8		Trail ends at border of Weminuche Wilderness and trailhead.
		GPS: N37°28.69' W107°37.95'

First Notch Trail

Starting Point:	Intersection of US 160 and First Notch Road, 23 miles west of Pagosa Springs
Finishing Point:	Intersection of US 160 and CR 135, 32 miles west of Pagosa Springs
Total Mileage:	20.8 miles
Unpaved Mileage:	20.8 miles
Driving Time:	1.5 hours
Elevation Range:	6,671 to 9,610 feet
Usually Open:	April through October
Difficulty Rating:	4
Scenic Rating:	9

Special Attractions

- Trail within a network of 4WD roads.
- Spectacular fall aspen viewing.
- Access to trails for ATVs, motorbikes, and snowmobiles.
- Shady and private backcountry camping sites.
- Popular with hunters in fall season.

Description

West of Pagosa Springs 23 miles, the trail begins at the intersection of US 160 and First Notch Road (FR 620). Crossing a cattle guard, proceed north on First Notch Road, a wide, maintained, smooth dirt and gravel road.

Initially the trail crosses through forest of low oak and willow scrub, ponderosa pine, Engelmann spruce, cottonwood, and aspen trees that block views of the surrounding terrain. The forest recedes in sections, revealing grassy parks and shady clearings for backcountry camping and picnicking.

Sign at turnaround area before the trail becomes difficult

The easygoing road passes gated tracks and grazing cattle, following power lines generally to the northwest. The smooth surface ends at a turnaround area after which the road becomes FR 620, a narrow one-lane 4WD trail. The rock-embedded, eroded track runs through a dense stand of aspen trees that are close to the road, making passing along this section impossible without backing up. The difficulty rating increases from 1 to 4 on this section due to the large embedded rock, uneven surface, and narrow width of the trail.

The embedded rock and eroded surface make this section slow going. In wet conditions, this drive can be muddy and slippery, creating the likelihood of puncturing a tire or getting stuck in the mud. If you drive this trail in wet conditions, mud tires are highly recommended.

After about 8 miles, bear left at a fork in the road. This portion of trail has less embedded rock, but the rough ride continues due to potholes and ruts.

While the trail gains elevation, there are few views because of the generally dense vegetation bordering the road. When rare views present themselves, they are particularly scenic in the fall months due to the large number of aspens growing in the vicinity.

After traveling 11.5 miles, FR 620 intersects with CR 135. Turn left and head south on the wide, maintained dirt road. If scenery is your thing, take note of the broad, expansive views of the Grassy Mountains to the northwest, Indian Mountain (10,477 feet) to the north, Wickenson Mountain (8,792 feet), Severn Peak (8,178 feet), and Shaefer Mountain (8,646 feet) to the west.

Along CR 135, the difficulty rating drops back down to a 1, with more difficulty in wet and muddy conditions. Traveling 9.2 more miles, the trail ends at the intersection with US 160, approximately 32 miles west of Pagosa Springs and 27 miles east of Durango.

Muddy, rocky, and eroded FR 620, part of the First Notch Road

Current Road Information
San Juan National Forest
Columbine Ranger District
PO Box 439
367 South Pearl Street
Bayfield, CO 81122
(970) 884-2512

Map References
USFS San Juan National Forest
Maptech CD: Southwest/Durango/Telluride
Benchmark's *Colorado Road and Recreation Atlas*, pp. 122, 123
Colorado Atlas & Gazetteer, p. 87
The Roads of Colorado, p. 155

Route Directions

▼ 0.0　　SO　This trail begins 23 miles west of Pagosa Springs, at the intersection of US 160 and First Notch Road (FR 620). Zero trip meter and proceed north across cattle guard on FR 620.

　7.0 ▲　SO　Cattle guard; then trail ends at the intersection of First Notch Road (FR 620) and US 160 between Durango and Pagosa Springs.

GPS: N37°13.74' W107°21.46'

▼ 0.2　　SO　Cattle guard; then seasonal closure gate.

　6.8 ▲　SO　Seasonal closure gate; then cattle guard.

GPS: N37°13.90' W107°21.46'

▼ 2.6　　SO　Cattle guard.

　4.4 ▲　SO　Cattle guard.

GPS: N37°15.21' W107°23.23'

▼ 5.3　　SO　FR 133 on left.

　1.6 ▲　SO　FR 133 on right.

GPS: N37°16.60' W107°24.11'

▼ 6.2　　SO　Cattle guard.

　0.7 ▲　SO　Cattle guard.

GPS: N37°17.27' W107°24.50'

▼ 7.0　　TR　Turnaround area with FR 620 on right. Zero trip meter.

　0.0 ▲　　　Proceed southwest on First Notch Road (not marked).

GPS: N37°17.72' W107°24.97'

▼ 0.0　　　　Proceed northwest on FR 620 signed Moonlick Park Road.

　4.6 ▲　TL　Enter turnaround area with trail on left. Zero trip meter.

▼ 1.2　　SO　Pass through gate.

　3.5 ▲　SO　Pass through gate.

GPS: N37°18.70' W107°25.18'

▼ 1.3　　BL　Road forks with unmarked track on right.

　3.3 ▲　SO　Unmarked track on left.

GPS: N37°18.81' W107°25.24'

▼ 2.7　　SO　Seasonal gate; then trail on right to numerous springs, open to snowmobiles, ATVs, and dirt bikes.

　2.0 ▲　SO　Trail on left to numerous springs, open to snowmobiles, ATVs, and dirt bikes; then seasonal gate.

GPS: N37°19.73' W107°26.22'

▼ 4.6　　TL　Cattle guard; then T-intersection with CR 135. Zero trip meter.

　0.0 ▲　　　Proceed northeast on FR 620; then cattle guard.

GPS: N37°21.00' W107°27.51'

▼ 0.0　　　　Proceed southwest on CR 135; then cattle guard.

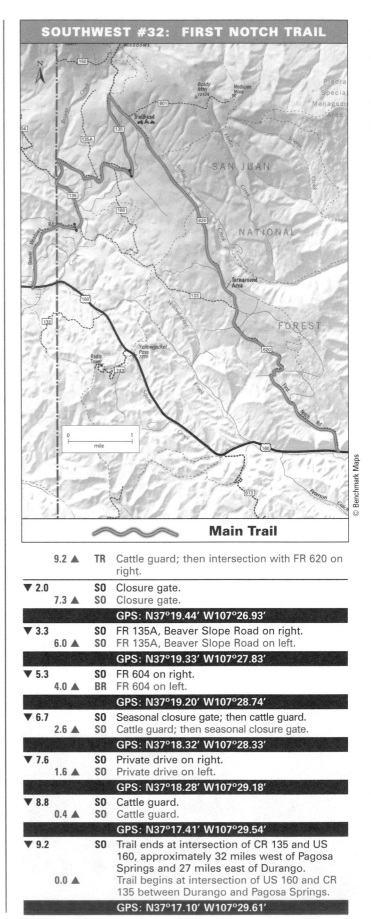

SOUTHWEST #32:　FIRST NOTCH TRAIL

~~~~~~~~　**Main Trail**

　9.2 ▲　TR　Cattle guard; then intersection with FR 620 on right.

▼ 2.0　　SO　Closure gate.

　7.3 ▲　SO　Closure gate.

GPS: N37°19.44' W107°26.93'

▼ 3.3　　SO　FR 135A, Beaver Slope Road on right.

　6.0 ▲　SO　FR 135A, Beaver Slope Road on left.

GPS: N37°19.33' W107°27.83'

▼ 5.3　　SO　FR 604 on right.

　4.0 ▲　BR　FR 604 on left.

GPS: N37°19.20' W107°28.74'

▼ 6.7　　SO　Seasonal closure gate; then cattle guard.

　2.6 ▲　SO　Cattle guard; then seasonal closure gate.

GPS: N37°18.32' W107°28.33'

▼ 7.6　　SO　Private drive on right.

　1.6 ▲　SO　Private drive on left.

GPS: N37°18.28' W107°29.18'

▼ 8.8　　SO　Cattle guard.

　0.4 ▲　SO　Cattle guard.

GPS: N37°17.41' W107°29.54'

▼ 9.2　　SO　Trail ends at intersection of CR 135 and US 160, approximately 32 miles west of Pagosa Springs and 27 miles east of Durango.

　0.0 ▲　　　Trail begins at intersection of US 160 and CR 135 between Durango and Pagosa Springs.

GPS: N37°17.10' W107°29.61'

Devil Mountain Trail

Starting Point:	Intersection of US 160 and FR 626, 20 miles west of Pagosa Springs
Finishing Point:	Summit of Devil Mountain
Total Mileage:	11.3 miles, including spur (one-way)
Unpaved Mileage:	11.3 miles, including spur
Driving Time:	1.75 hours (one-way)
Elevation Range:	6,532 to 9,957 feet
Usually Open:	April through October
Difficulty Rating:	2, 4 for the spur
Scenic Rating:	8

Special Attractions

- Site of Devil Mountain Fire Lookout.
- Sweeping panoramas from the summit of Devil Mountain.
- Shady, private backcountry campsites.
- Wildlife viewing.
- Views of Chimney Rock and the adjacent Chimney Rock Archeological Area.

History

Originally built in 1955 to assume primary lookout duties for the region, the steel-framed Devil Mountain Fire Lookout replaced the nearby Chimney Rock Fire Lookout, which is still located within the Chimney Rock Archeological Area just south of the start of Devil Mountain Trail (FR 626).

Devil Mountain Fire Lookout was sold to the Jicarilla tribe in the 1990s and relocated from the summit of Devil Mountain to a spot on their land in New Mexico. The lookout is now known as Atole. The footings that remain at the summit of Devil Mountain are now used for radio equipment and a few other small structures.

USGS marker on Devil Mountain Trail

The old Chimney Rock Fire Lookout can be visited from mid-May through September by guided tour. A fee is charged for access to the Chimney Rock Archeological Area. The lookout was originally built in 1940 on the site of an ancient fire pit, probably used by Chacoan Indians, who lived primarily in Chaco Canyon, 90 miles south, in what is today New Mexico.

When the Chimney Rock Lookout was decommissioned, the upper story was removed. In 1988, the structure was modified again to be used by the Chimney Rock Interpretive Association. From October to February, when the archeological area is closed for winter, the lookout can be viewed by walking 3 miles south from US 160. From March 1 to May 15, the area is closed for falcon nesting.

Located due south of Devil Mountain Trail, the geological formation known as Chimney Rock includes the two rock "towers" that stand 300 feet above the surrounding terrain. Spanish explorers referred to the formations as La Piedra Parada, or standing rock, and later American settlers dubbed the formation Chimney Rock. It wasn't until the 1920s that researcher Jean Jeançon named the smaller of the two rock towers Companion Rock.

Jeançon is also credited with the discovery of the ancient structures at the base of Chimney Rock. Finally in the 1970s, archeologists excavated and reinforced the 16 structures, which include the Great Kiva, a pit house, the Ridge House, and the Great House. All these historic sites can be explored on a guided tour in the Chimney Rock Archeological Area, 4,100 acres of San Juan National Forest established in 1970.

Chocoan Indians are thought to have built these ancient structures near Chimney Rock sometime around A.D. 1000. Historians believe Chimney Rock was sacred to the group. Suggestions of the rock's significance and function include a religious shrine, a lunar observatory, or a timber-harvesting

Rocky sections on Devil Mountain Trail

Radio equipment at the site of Devil Mountain Fire Lookout

site. Research shows the short-lived settlement burned and was abandoned around A.D. 1100.

In more recent times, Chimney Rock and Companion Rock have been a refuge of a different sort. Companion Rock in particular is a popular nesting site for the peregrine falcon. After the use of DDT became widespread in the 1930s and 1940s, populations of the falcon in the eastern United States became completely extinct and populations in the West were reduced 80 to 90 percent by the mid-1960s.

In 1970, the falcon was placed on the endangered species list. Through the efforts of reintroduction programs and the ban on the use of DDT, the U.S. Fish and Wildlife Service reclassified the status of the falcon as threatened in 1984. Falcon populations have increased and stabilized so much that the falcon was removed from both the endangered and threatened species list in August 1999. Keen wildlife observers may spot the falcon from any of the trails in the vicinity.

Description

FR 626, or Devil Mountain Trail, begins traveling north from US 160, 20 miles west of Pagosa Springs, 21 miles east of Bayfield, and approximately 40 miles east of Durango. The unmaintained dirt road is a wide one-lane trail with room to pass oncoming vehicles. Embedded rocks and ruts make the drive rough, and the trail is best driven in dry conditions to avoid damaging the road or getting bogged. Although the ride is rough, the main trail is not difficult.

Initially the road travels through forest of scrub oak and evergreens, predominantly ponderosa and lodgepole pines. Also along the first half a mile, the track follows alongside private land. Please stay on the trail and respect private property.

Consistently rocky, the track continues to climb, snaking toward the summit of Devil Mountain (9,922 feet); overlooks

Old outhouse at the summit of Devil Mountain

Only footings of Devil Mountain Fire Lookout remain at the summit of Devil Mountain, but there are still beautiful views over Devil Creek Canyon

from the trail become increasingly expansive through the trees. There are particularly scenic views to the south of Chimney Rock in the Chimney Rock Archeological Area. Aspen and cottonwood trees along with pinyon and juniper begin to appear in the forest surrounding the trail.

At 4.2 miles on the odometer, the trail forks and the main trail, FR 626, continues and becomes a shelf road with overlooks of aspen stands below in Devil Creek Canyon. Around this point on the trail are some clearings for shady backcountry campsites, picnic spots, or wildlife viewing locations. Elk and mule deer, along with a variety of other wildlife, are commonly seen in the vicinity.

Past the short section of shelf road, just over 10 miles into the trip, the Mesa Spring Hunter's Campground is located beside the trail, not far from the summit of Devil Mountain. The dispersed camping area has grill grates, a pit toilet, and a fresh water spring. As the trail travels through dense stands of aspen, other clearings near the trail make ideal backcountry campsites.

About 1 mile farther, the trail crosses over a section of slickrock, where it forks. The remaining section of the trail is the right-hand spur to the summit of Devil Mountain and the site of Devil Mountain Fire Lookout. The spur has a difficulty rating of 4, and this point makes a convenient turnaround for travelers not wanting the extra challenge. The rough, rocky 0.3-mile trip is worth the effort for the sweeping 360° panoramas at the summit of Devil Mountain. Radio equipment and an old outhouse are all that remain at the summit.

Current Road Information

San Juan National Forest
Pagosa Ranger District
180 Second Street
PO Box 310
Pagosa Springs, CO 81147
(970) 264-2268

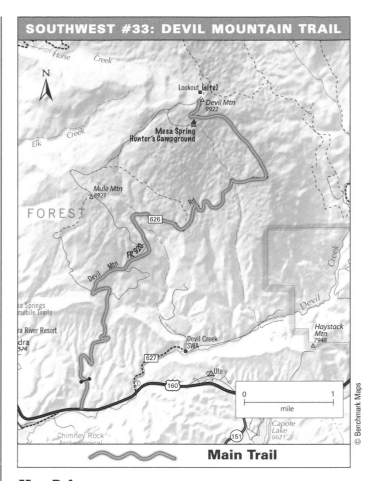

SOUTHWEST #33: DEVIL MOUNTAIN TRAIL

© Benchmark Maps

Main Trail

Map References

USFS San Juan National Forest
Maptech CD: Southwest/Durango/Telluride
Benchmark's *Colorado Road and Recreation Atlas,* p. 123
Colorado Atlas & Gazetteer, p. 87
The Roads of Colorado, pp. 155, 156

Route Directions

▼ 0.0		Trail begins at intersection of US 160 and FR 626 between Durango and Pagosa Springs.
		GPS: N37°12.41' W107°18.89'
▼ 0.5	SO	Seasonal closure gate.
		GPS: N37°12.88' W107°18.81'
▼ 2.2	SO	Cattle guard.
		GPS: N37°13.69' W107°18.46'
▼ 4.2	BR	Road forks with FR 920 on left. Zero trip meter.
▼ 0.0		Proceed east on FR 626.
		GPS: N37°14.63' W107°17.94'
▼ 0.5	SO	Cattle guard.
		GPS: N37°14.86' W107°17.59'
▼ 6.6	SO	Mesa Spring Hunter's Campground on left.
		GPS: N37°16.81' W107°16.68'
▼ 6.8	BR	Road forks in wide solid rock clearing. Zero trip meter.
▼ 0.0		Proceed northeast toward lookout area.
		GPS: N37°16.82' W107°16.78'
▼ 0.3		Trail ends at site of lookout tower.
		GPS: N37°17.06' W107°16.57'

Summitville Ghost Town Trail

Starting Point:	Intersection of Colorado 17 and FR 250
Finishing Point:	Del Norte
Total Mileage:	68.8 miles
Unpaved Mileage:	57.9 miles
Driving Time:	4 hours
Route Elevation:	8,000 to 11,900 feet
Usually Open:	Early July to late October
Difficulty Rating:	2
Scenic Rating:	6

Special Attractions

- The well-preserved ghost town of Summitville.
- An easy 4WD trail that is not heavily used.

History

This route crosses Stunner Pass and skirts Elwood Pass, both of which were part of two early access roads through the area. In 1884, the LeDuc and Sanchez Toll Road Company constructed the first road over Stunner Pass as a freight route to service mines that had started activity in the early 1880s. Mining activity here was short-lived, and by the early 1890s, the area was almost deserted. However, the route has been maintained for recreational access to the area.

The U.S. Army constructed a road across Elwood Pass in 1878 to connect Fort Garland and Fort Harris in Pagosa Springs. In the 1880s, mining began in the area, and significant deposits of gold and silver were found. Summitville ghost town is the best preserved of the mining camps from this period; numerous buildings still stand.

Gold was discovered in the Summitville area in 1870, and hundreds of prospectors rushed to the site. At its peak, the town had a population of more than 600, and 2,500 mining claims were staked. Summitville boomed during the 1880s and produced a fortune for Tom Bowen, who became a leading figure in Colorado politics and a great rival of Horace Tabor. The town was in decline by 1890 and deserted by 1893.

Shortly before the halfway point of the trail, you pass the township of Platoro, which was established after ore was discovered in 1882. It was named for the Spanish words plata and oro meaning silver and gold. Because of Platoro's inaccessibility, burros were the only means of transporting ore and supplies. In 1888, the wagon road to Summitville was completed and the town grew to a population of 300 by 1890. However, the ore in the area was of indifferent quality and the miners drifted away.

Although little is known about the township of Stunner, located a short distance northwest of Platoro, it is suspected that the first construction occurred in 1882. Both gold and silver were mined in the vicinity, but the remoteness of the camp prevented proper development. No railroad came through Stunner, but the LeDuc and Sanchez Toll Road Company built a road to the area.

Between 100 and 150 people lived in Stunner in its best days. A post office was established in 1890, but the town lasted only a few more years. Stunner's decline began because of the high costs of transporting ore from the area's mines and was speeded by the lack of good ores to justify these costs. Because nearby Summitville (on the other side of the range) offered better ore and lower transportation costs, Stunner's population began to dwindle. There is nothing left of Stunner. A U.S. Forest Service ranger station and the Stunner Campground are on the site of the old town.

Summitville, on South Mountain, at 11,200 feet, was once the highest of Colorado's major gold camps. In 1870, miner John Esmund discovered rich ore in abundance near the area that would, years later, become the Summitville mining camp. After Esmund's initial discovery, he returned to the location

The trail beside the Conejos River near Platoro

Chandler Mine boardinghouse, circa 1935

Chandler Mine boardinghouse at Summitville ghost town today

several times to extract ore, during which time he failed to file proper paperwork to become legal owner of the claim. When he showed up at the site in 1873, he found that someone else had established a mine on his spot. The mine, the Little Annie, became the best gold-producing mine in the district.

By 1882, Summitville had boomed to a population of more than 1,500; the town was made up of several hotels, *The Summitville Nugget* newspaper, saloons, stores, and nine mills at which ore from the nearby mines was processed. One of the mining companies set up a pool hall to entertain the men during their free time, especially over the long winter months. The hall attracted pool sharks who came to match skills with the miners from all over the state.

Del Norte, about 24 miles northeast of Summitville, was an important shipping point, supply center, and stagecoach junction. One of its residents, Tom Bowen, struck it rich with his Little Ida Mine in Summitville. Suave and colorful, Bowen wore many hats; and his skill and luck were legendary. Over the course of his life, Bowen was a judge, an entrepreneur, a lawyer, governor of Idaho Territory, brigadier general for the

Union Army, a U.S. senator, and a very big gambler. Bowen once lost shares of a mining company in a poker game, only to have the winner decide he didn't want the shares. Bowen redeemed the stock for a nominal purchase; and the mine, the Little Ida, later made him very rich. He purchased many other mining properties, including the Little Annie.

In 1885, some of the nearby mines began having financial difficulties and even the Little Annie could not pay workers' salaries. Other mines were playing out, so the population of Summitville rapidly declined. By 1889, only about 25 residents remained in town.

There were a few short revivals in mining: one in the late 1890s and another in the late 1930s. In recent years, Galactic Resources Ltd. reopened operations, but they suffered heavy losses through 1991 and sold the balance of their mining interests. In 1993, Galactic filed for bankruptcy.

Although some of the ghost town's buildings have been torn down to make room for modern-day mining, a number of well-preserved buildings still stand in Summitville. It is an interesting ghost town to explore and photograph.

Summitville ghost town

Description

The first section of this route, FR 250 over Stunner Pass, is a well-maintained dirt road. The pass stretches between the Alamosa River to the north and the Conejos River to the south.

It offers a peaceful journey through gentle rolling hills, interspersed with rock formations and overlooks that provide wonderful views along the valley and across the mountains. Abundant aspen groves spangle the hillsides in gold during the fall. The area also offers many accessible campsites and hiking trails.

In good weather conditions, the Stunner Pass section (FR 250) of this route warrants a difficulty rating of only 1. The Elwood Pass section (FR 380) is more difficult and causes this route to be rated at 2; although FR 380 is higher, narrower, and rougher than FR 250, it is a relatively easy route and should provide no obstacles for a 4WD vehicle.

An extensive network of 4WD and hiking trails are located near the trail. Mining activity has continued in the Summitville area until recent times, although now operations are restricted to an Environmental Protection Agency-mandated cleanup of the mine remains.

Current Road Information

Rio Grande National Forest
Divide Ranger District
13308 West Hwy 160
Del Norte, CO 81132
(719) 657-3321

Rio Grande National Forest
Conejos Peak Ranger District
15571 CR T.5
LaJara, CO 81140
(719) 274-8971

Map References

USFS   Rio Grande National Forest
Maptech CD: Southwest/Durango/Telluride
Benchmark's *Colorado Road and Recreation Atlas,* pp. 112, 124
Colorado Atlas & Gazetteer, pp. 79, 80, 89, 90
The Roads of Colorado, pp. 141, 142, 157, 158
Trails Illustrated, #142

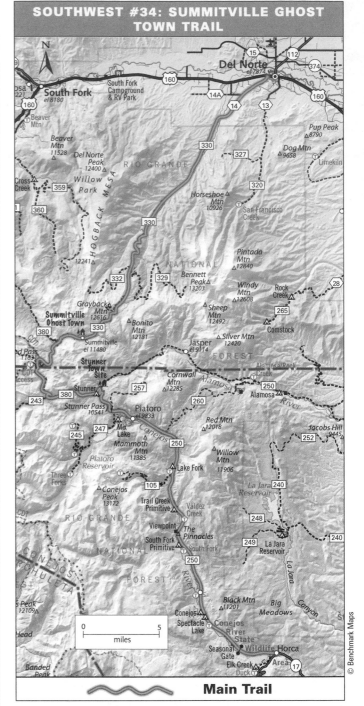

Main Trail

Route Directions

▼ 0.0			At intersection of Colorado 17 and FR 250, zero trip meter. There is a signpost for Platoro. Turn onto the unpaved road.
	16.1 ▲		End at intersection of Colorado 17 and FR 250.
		GPS: N37°07.98′ W106°21.01′	
▼ 6.0		SO	Cattle guard. USFS Spectacle Lake Campground.
	10.1 ▲	SO	USFS Spectacle Lake Campground. Cattle guard.
▼ 6.3		SO	USFS Conejos Campground.
	9.8 ▲	SO	USFS Conejos Campground.
▼ 7.4		SO	Intersection. FR 855 on left goes to Rybold Lake and No Name Lake.
	8.7 ▲	SO	Intersection. FR 855 on right goes to Rybold Lake and No Name Lake.
▼ 8.8		SO	Cattle guard.
	7.3 ▲	SO	Cattle guard.
▼ 10.8		SO	Southfork Trailhead.
	5.3 ▲	SO	Southfork Trailhead.
▼ 11.1		SO	Intersection. Track on left for fishing access. Public restrooms.
	5.0 ▲	SO	Intersection. Track on right for fishing access. Public restrooms.
▼ 11.8		SO	Cattle guard.
	4.3 ▲	SO	Cattle guard.
▼ 13.2		SO	Valdez Creek Campground.
	2.9 ▲	SO	Valdez Creek Campground.

▼ 13.8   **SO**   Trail Creek backcountry camping area.
2.3 ▲   **SO**   Trail Creek backcountry camping area.

▼ 13.9   **SO**   Track on right.
2.2 ▲   **SO**   Track on left.

▼ 14.2   **SO**   Cattle guard.
1.9 ▲   **SO**   Cattle guard.

▼ 16.1   **SO**   Track on left is FR 100 to Lake Fork Ranch. Zero trip meter.
0.0 ▲   Proceed along main road.

GPS: N37°17.87' W106°28.63'

▼ 0.0   Proceed along main road.
12.0 ▲   **SO**   Track on right is FR 100 to Lake Fork Ranch. Zero trip meter.

▼ 0.6   **SO**   Cattle guard.
11.4 ▲   **SO**   Cattle guard.

▼ 0.8   **SO**   USFS Lake Fork Campground.
11.2 ▲   **SO**   USFS Lake Fork Campground.

▼ 1.6   **SO**   Beaver Lake Trailhead.
10.4 ▲   **SO**   Beaver Lake Trailhead.

▼ 3.5   **SO**   Fisher Gulch.
8.5 ▲   **SO**   Fisher Gulch.

▼ 4.1   **SO**   Track on right is FR 260 to Robinson Gulch.
7.9 ▲   **SO**   Track on left is FR 260 to Robinson Gulch.

▼ 4.7   **SO**   Cattle guard.
7.3 ▲   **SO**   Cattle guard.

▼ 6.1   **SO**   Intersection. Platoro on left.
5.9 ▲   **SO**   Intersection. Platoro on right.

GPS: N37°21.25' W106°31.72'

▼ 6.5   **SO**   Track on left to Mix Lake Campground.
5.5 ▲   **SO**   Track on right to Mix Lake Campground.

▼ 7.6   **TR**   T-intersection. Left goes to Mix Lake and Platoro Reservoir.
4.4 ▲   **TL**   Intersection.

▼ 8.6   **BL**   Stunner Pass (unmarked). FR 257 on right goes to Lily Pond and Kerr Lake.
3.4 ▲   **BR**   FR 257 on left goes to Lily Pond and Kerr Lake. Stunner Pass (unmarked).

GPS: N37°21.73' W106°33.44'

▼ 11.7   **SO**   Bridge over Alamosa River. Campsites.
0.3 ▲   **SO**   Campsites. Bridge over Alamosa River.

▼ 12.0   **UT**   Intersection. Straight on goes to Monte Vista. Zero trip meter.
0.0 ▲   Continue on FR 380.

GPS: N37°23.04' W106°33.95'

▼ 0.0   Continue on FR 380.
11.7 ▲   **UT**   Intersection. Straight on goes to Monte Vista. Zero trip meter.

▼ 0.3   **SO**   USFS Stunner Campground on left. Old cabin on right is part of Stunner town site.
11.4 ▲   **SO**   Old cabin on left is part of Stunner town site. USFS Stunner Campground on right.

GPS: N37°22.88' W106°34.21'

▼ 0.9   **SO**   Cattle guard.
10.8 ▲   **SO**   Cattle guard.

▼ 1.1   **SO**   Drainage ford.
10.6 ▲   **SO**   Drainage ford.

▼ 2.1   **SO**   Track on right.
9.6 ▲   **SO**   Track on left.

▼ 2.4   **SO**   Track on right.
9.3 ▲   **SO**   Track on left.

▼ 4.0   **SO**   Lake DeNelda on left (private property).
7.7 ▲   **SO**   Lake DeNelda on right (private property).

▼ 4.1   **BR**   Intersection. Dolores Canyon Road, Treasure Creek Road, and Lake Annella are straight ahead. Turn toward Summitville and US 160.
7.6 ▲   **TL**   Intersection. Dolores Canyon Road and Treasure Creek Road are to the right. Proceed toward Platoro.

▼ 4.6   **SO**   Cattle guard.
7.1 ▲   **SO**   Cattle guard.

▼ 6.5   **SO**   Track on right.
5.2 ▲   **SO**   Track on left.

▼ 7.7   **SO**   Crater Lake hiking trail on left.
4.0 ▲   **SO**   Crater Lake hiking trail on right.

▼ 8.4   **SO**   Intersection. Track and Continental Divide Trail on left. Elwood Pass is a short distance along it. Straight ahead is South Fork sign.
3.3 ▲   **SO**   Intersection. Track and Continental Divide Trail on right. Elwood Pass is a short distance along it.

▼ 8.7   **SO**   Elwood Cabin on right. Track FR 3802A on left.
3.0 ▲   **SO**   Elwood Cabin on left. Track FR 3802A on right.

▼ 9.6   **SO**   Track on right.
2.1 ▲   **SO**   Track on left.

▼ 9.8   **SO**   Cattle guard.
1.9 ▲   **SO**   Cattle guard.

▼ 11.7   **TR**   Intersection. Summitville ghost town to the right. Southfork to the left. Zero trip meter.
0.0 ▲   Proceed toward Platoro.

GPS: N37°25.75' W106°37.70'

▼ 0.0   Proceed toward Summitville.
2.5 ▲   **TL**   Intersection. Southfork to the right. Platoro to the left. Zero trip meter.

▼ 2.0   **SO**   Summitville Historic Mining Town sign.
0.5 ▲   **SO**   Summitville Historic Mining Town sign.

▼ 2.5   **BL**   Summitville visitor information board. Zero trip motor.
0.0 ▲   Continue on route.

GPS: N37°25.93' W106°35.94'

▼ 0.0   Continue on route.
26.5 ▲   **BR**   Summitville visitor information board. Zero trip meter.

▼ 0.1   **TL**   Turn onto FR 330.
26.4 ▲   **TR**   Intersection with FR 244.

▼ 0.3   **SO**   Intersection. Go toward Del Norte. Wightman Fork is to the right and forks off from the mining entrance.
26.2 ▲   **SO**   Intersection.

▼ 0.6   **SO**   Track on right.
25.9 ▲   **SO**   Track on left.

▼ 1.7   **SO**   Track on left.
24.8 ▲   **SO**   Track on right.

▼ 2.7   **SO**   Track on left.
23.8 ▲   **SO**   Track on right.

▼ 7.8   **TR**   Intersection. Crystal Lakes and South Fork to the left. Follow toward Del Norte.
18.7 ▲   **BL**   Intersection. Crystal Lakes and South Fork to the right.

GPS: N37°29.31' W106°32.81'

▼ 9.3   **TL**   Cattle guard. Intersection. Fuches Reservoir and Blowout Pass to the right. Follow road to Del Norte (FR 14).
17.2 ▲   **TR**   Intersection. Fuches Reservoir and Blowout Pass straight on. Follow FR 330. Cattle guard.

▼ 11.0   **SO**   Road on left.
15.5 ▲   **SO**   Road on right.

▼ 11.2   **SO**   Cattle guard.
15.3 ▲   **SO**   Cattle guard.

▼ 12.3   **SO**   Track on right to campsite.

14.2 ▲	SO	Track on left to campsite.
▼ 13.0	SO	Track on left is FR 331 to Bear Creek.
13.5 ▲	SO	Track on right is FR 331 to Bear Creek.
▼ 14.0	SO	Track on right.
12.5 ▲	SO	Track on left.
▼ 14.3	SO	Track on right.
12.2 ▲	SO	Track on left.
▼ 14.4	SO	Track on right.
12.1 ▲	SO	Track on left.
▼ 15.1	SO	Seasonal gate.
11.4 ▲	SO	Seasonal gate.
▼ 15.2	SO	Cattle guard.
11.3 ▲	SO	Cattle guard.
▼ 15.6	SO	Pavement begins. Bridge.
10.9 ▲	SO	Bridge. Unpaved.
▼ 24.4	SO	Road 14A forks off on left.
2.1 ▲	SO	Road 14A on right.
▼ 26.5		End at intersection of FR 14 and US 160 in Del Norte.
0.0 ▲		At intersection of FR 14 and US 160 in Del Norte, zero trip meter and proceed along FR 14, signed National Forest Access, Pinos Creek Rd, Summitville.

GPS: N37°40.75′ W106°21.66′

SOUTHWEST REGION TRAIL #35

Owl Creek and Chimney Rock Trail

Starting Point:	**Intersection US 550 and CR 10 near Ridgway**
Finishing Point:	**Intersection CR 858 and US 50**
Total Mileage:	**40.9 miles**
Unpaved Mileage:	**40.9 miles**
Driving Time:	**2 hours**
Route Elevation:	**7,000 to 10,200 feet**
Usually Open:	**May to November**
Difficulty Rating:	**1**
Scenic Rating:	**8**

Special Attractions

- An easy trail that provides a more interesting, alternate route to the paved road between Ouray and Gunnison.
- Views of Chimney Peak and Courthouse Mountain.
- Scenic Silver Jack Reservoir.
- Access to good hiking, fishing, and backcountry camping.

Description

This route, on maintained gravel roads across mainly gentle grades, starts just north of Ridgway at the intersection of US 550 and CR 10. Initially, the road travels through ranch land before crossing Cimarron Ridge at Owl Creek Pass, and then it continues through Uncompahgre National Forest.

The route offers many good views of the conspicuous rock peaks known as Chimney Rock and Courthouse Mountain.

Many large stands of aspen line the route, providing wonderful fall scenery for photographers or for those who just enjoy the bright yellow panorama typical of fall in Colorado.

The road continues its gentle course past Silver Jack Reservoir and onto US 50.

Current Road Information

Grand Mesa, Uncompahgre and Gunnison National Forests
Ouray Ranger District
2505 South Townsend Avenue
Montrose, CO 81401
(970) 240-5300

Map References

USFS Uncompahgre National Forest
Maptech CD: Grand Junction/Western Slope
Benchmark's *Colorado Road and Recreation Atlas*, p. 96
The Roads of Colorado, pp. 107, 123
Colorado Atlas & Gazetteer, pp. 66, 67
Trails Illustrated, #141 (incomplete)

Easygoing trail through aspen forest

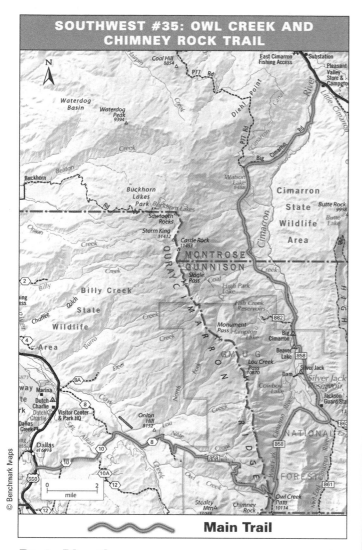

Main Trail

Route Directions

▼ 0.0			From US 550 (1.7 miles north of the junction with Colorado 62 in Ridgway and approximately 26 miles south of Montrose), zero trip meter and proceed east along CR 10. This turnoff is marked with a national forest access sign to Owl Creek Pass.
	8.6 ▲		End at intersection with US 550, about 12 miles north of Ouray.

GPS: N38°10.44′ W107°44.47′

▼ 0.8		BL	Road forks.
	7.7 ▲	BR	Intersection.
▼ 2.5		BL	Cow Creek goes to the right.
	6.1 ▲	BR	Cow Creek goes to the left.
▼ 3.9		BR	CR 8 enters on left.
	4.7 ▲	BL	Remain on CR 10 toward Ridgway and US 550.
▼ 4.9		SO	Bridge over creek.
	3.7 ▲	SO	Bridge over creek.
▼ 5.3		BL	Road forks. Turn onto CR 8 toward Owl Creek Pass.
	3.3 ▲	BR	Onto CR 10.
▼ 5.6		SO	Cattle guard.
	3.0 ▲	SO	Cattle guard.
▼ 6.1		SO	Cattle guard.
	2.5 ▲	SO	Cattle guard.

Chimney Rock

▼ 6.8		SO	Cattle guard. Road narrows.
	1.8 ▲	SO	Cattle guard.
▼ 7.7		SO	Cattle guard. Enter Uncompahgre National Forest. Name of road becomes FR 858.
	0.9 ▲	SO	Leave Uncompahgre National Forest; then cross cattle guard.
▼ 8.6		BL	Vista Point scenic overlook on right. Zero trip meter.
	0.0 ▲		Continue toward Ridgway.

GPS: N38°11.21′ W107°37.74′

▼ 0.0			Continue toward Owl Creek Pass.
	6.6 ▲	BR	Vista Point scenic overlook on left. Zero trip meter.
▼ 0.3		SO	Road on right.
	6.3 ▲	SO	Road on left.
▼ 2.7		SO	Track on left.
	3.8 ▲	SO	Track on right.
▼ 3.4		SO	Cattle guard.
	3.2 ▲	SO	Cattle guard.
▼ 4.0		BL	Track on right dead-ends in short distance.
	2.5 ▲	BR	Track on left dead-ends in short distance.
▼ 5.9		SO	Cross over Nate Creek Ditch.
	0.6 ▲	SO	Cross over Nate Creek Ditch.
▼ 6.6		SO	Cattle guard; then Owl Creek Pass. Track on left goes to parking bay. Zero trip meter at summit.
	0.0 ▲		Continue along main road toward Ridgway.

GPS: N38°09.45′ W107°33.71′

▼ 0.0			Continue along FR 858.
	6.6 ▲	SO	Owl Creek Pass. Track on right goes to a small parking area. Zero trip meter at the summit and

A stand of aspen and a rock outcrop near Silver Jack Reservoir

▼	▲		
			cross over cattle guard.
▼ 0.3		BL	Track on right is FR 860, which offers several viewing areas for Chimney Rock.
	6.3 ▲	BR	Track on left is FR 860. Remain on FR 858 toward Owl Creek Pass.
▼ 0.8		SO	Cattle guard.
	5.8 ▲	SO	Cattle guard.
▼ 2.9		SO	Cross over bridge.
	3.7 ▲	SO	Cross over bridge.
▼ 5.0		SO	Cattle guard.
	0.6 ▲	SO	Cattle guard.
▼ 6.3		SO	Cimarron Fork track on left.
	0.3 ▲	SO	Track to Cimarron Fork on right.
▼ 6.4		SO	Cross over bridge.
	0.2 ▲	SO	Cross over bridge.
▼ 6.5		SO	Track on right to Middle Fork (FR 861.1) Trailhead. Cross over bridge.
	0.1 ▲	SO	Cross over bridge. Track on left goes to Middle Fork Trailhead.
▼ 6.6		TL	Follow FR 858 toward Cimarron and Silver Jack Reservoir. Right goes to East Fork Trailhead. Zero trip meter.
	0.0 ▲		Continue toward Owl Creek Pass.

GPS: N38°12.32' W107°30.92'

▼	▲		
▼ 0.0			Continue along FR 858.
	19.1 ▲	TR	Straight goes to East Fork Trailhead. Zero trip meter.
▼ 0.8		SO	Cross cattle guard with fishing access on left.
	18.3 ▲	SO	Fishing access on right. Cross cattle guard.
▼ 1.7		SO	Alpine Trailhead on right.
	17.4 ▲	SO	Alpine Trailhead on left.
▼ 2.3		SO	FR 838 on right and Silver Jack Reservoir overlook on left.
	16.8 ▲	SO	Overlook to Silver Jack Reservoir on right and FR 838 on left.
▼ 2.6		SO	USFS Silver Jack Campground on left.
	16.5 ▲	SO	USFS Silver Jack Campground on right.
▼ 3.9		SO	USFS Beaver Lake Campground on left.
	15.2 ▲	SO	USFS Beaver Lake Campground on right.
▼ 4.6		SO	USFS Big Cimarron Campground on left. Paddock on right; then cattle guard. Cross bridge and leave the Uncompahgre National Forest. Road is now CR 858.
	14.5 ▲	SO	Enter Uncompahgre National Forest and road becomes FR 858. Cross bridge and cattle guard. USFS Big Cimarron Campground on right.
▼ 5.4		SO	Cross over bridge.
	13.7 ▲	SO	Cross over bridge.
▼ 9.0		SO	Cross over bridge.
	10.1 ▲	SO	Cross over bridge.
▼ 10.7		SO	Cross over bridge.
	8.4 ▲	SO	Cross over bridge.
▼ 11.4		SO	Cross over bridge.
	7.7 ▲	SO	Cross over bridge.
▼ 13.4		SO	CR P77 on left.
	5.7 ▲	SO	CR P77 on right.
▼ 17.2		SO	Cross over bridge.
	1.9 ▲	SO	Cross over bridge.
▼ 19.1			End at intersection with US 50.
	0.0 ▲		From US 50 (approximately 40 miles west of Gunnison) at the national forest access sign to Cimarron Road and Silver Jack Reservoir, zero trip meter and proceed southbound along Cimarron Road (CR 858).

GPS: N38°24.86' W107°31.57'

Uncompahgre Plateau Trail

Starting Point:	**Intersection of US 550 and Jay Jay Road, north of Montrose**
Finishing Point:	**Intersection of Colorado 141 and CR 26.10 (FR 402)**
Total Mileage:	**90.3 miles**
Unpaved Mileage:	**85.6 miles**
Driving Time:	**4 hours**
Route Elevation:	**5,597 to 9,120 feet**
Usually Open:	**Mid-June to late November**
Difficulty Rating:	**2**
Scenic Rating:	**7**

Special Attractions

■ Expansive views from the Uncompahgre Plateau, particularly from Windy Point.
■ An extensive network of 4WD trails.
■ Good backcountry camping.

History

Columbine Pass was named for Colorado's state flower, which once grew in abundance here. The pass is located on Uncompahgre Plateau. The Hayden Survey expedition noted and used the pass in the mid-1870s. The plateau was also an important summer hunting ground for the Ute for thousands of years prior to the Washington Treaty of 1880, in which they ceded the entire area and were relocated to reservations.

View from Rim Road into Dry Creek Basin

Description

This route starts at the intersection of US 550 and Jay Jay Road, 4.7 miles northwest of the national rorest office in Montrose (2505 S. Townsend). The next 5 miles involve a considerable number of intersections, so care is necessary to navigate correctly. At the end of this section of the route, you should turn onto Rim Road. There are more direct routes from Montrose, but this route offers the more varied and interesting views.

Initially, Rim Road is a well-maintained, wide 2WD road with some good views over the local ranch land and the San Juan Mountains in the distance to the south. There are also numerous small side roads: Stay on the main road in each case. Farther along the road, there are some sections that are rocky, but they will not pose any problems. The road travels along the rim of a canyon and provides good views of the terrain below.

After turning onto FR 402 (Divide Road), you will pass numerous campsites, which are heavily used in hunting season, and an extensive network of 4WD side roads, many of which can be very muddy. FR 402 is wide and well maintained and suitable for passenger vehicles in dry conditions. The views to the west, down into the valley below, are particularly scenic.

As you descend from Uncompahgre Plateau, the scenery transforms over to the red rock walls of Jacks Canyon before connecting with Colorado 141 in the vast Unaweep Canyon. From here, the road travels along the path of East Creek before crossing the Gunnison River and joining US 50. Gunnison is approximately 24 miles from the intersection with Colorado 141, at the start of the paved road.

Current Road Information

Grand Mesa, Uncompahgre and Gunnison National Forests
Grand Valley Ranger District
2777 Crossroads Boulevard, Suite 1
Grand Junction, CO 81506
(970) 242-8211

Colorado Bureau of Land Management
Uncompahgre Field Office
2465 South Townsend Avenue
Montrose, CO 81401
(970) 240-5300

Map References

BLM Montrose, Nucla, Delta
USFS Uncompahgre National Forest
Maptech CD: Grand Junction/Western Slope
Benchmark's *Colorado Road and Recreation Atlas*, pp. 82, 94, 95
Colorado Atlas & Gazetteer, pp. 54, 55, 65, 66
The Roads of Colorado, pp. 105, 106, 122

Route Directions

| ▼ 0.0 | | At intersection of US 550 and Jay Jay Road, turn west (left, if coming from Montrose). |
| 5.0 ▲ | | End at intersection with US 550. |

Red rock of Jacks Canyon

		GPS: N38°31.91' W107°56.19'	
▼ 0.1	SO	Cross railroad tracks. Name of road changes to Menoken Road.
4.9 ▲	SO	Cross railroad tracks.
▼ 1.4	SO	Cross over bridge and then a second bridge.
3.6 ▲	SO	Cross over two bridges.
▼ 1.6	BL	Fork in road; go left onto South River Road.
3.4 ▲	BR	At fork in the road.
▼ 2.0	BR	CR 5975 is on the left.
3.0 ▲	BL	CR 5975 is on the right.
▼ 2.9	BL	Intersection. Remain on paved road.
2.1 ▲	BR	Intersection.
▼ 3.5	TL	Stop sign at intersection. Turn onto CR 5850.
1.5 ▲	TR	Intersection. Turn onto South River Road.
		GPS: N38°31.56' W107°59.68'	
▼ 3.9	TR	Onto Kiowa Road.
1.1 ▲	TL	Onto CR 5850.
▼ 4.7	BL	Bear left; then cross bridge. Bear left again onto unpaved road named Shavano Valley Road.
0.2 ▲	BR	Onto Kiowa Road; then cross bridge and bear right again.
▼ 5.0	TR	Onto Rim Road. Zero trip meter.
0.0 ▲		Continue to the left.
		GPS: N38°30.92' W108°00.54'	
▼ 0.0		Proceed along Rim Road.
13.1 ▲	TL	Intersection. Zero trip meter.
▼ 1.7	SO	Track crosses road.
11.4 ▲	SO	Track crosses road.
▼ 2.2	SO	Track on right.
10.9 ▲	SO	Track on left.
▼ 2.5	SO	Track on right. Note: From this point, there will be numerous side tracks, but remain on Rim Road.
10.7 ▲	SO	Track on left.
▼ 3.0	SO	Track on right goes into canyon.
10.2 ▲	SO	Track on left goes into canyon. Note: From this point, there will be numerous side tracks, but remain on Rim Road.
		GPS: N38°29.14' W108°02.50'	
▼ 5.7	SO	Cross under high-voltage wires; then cross

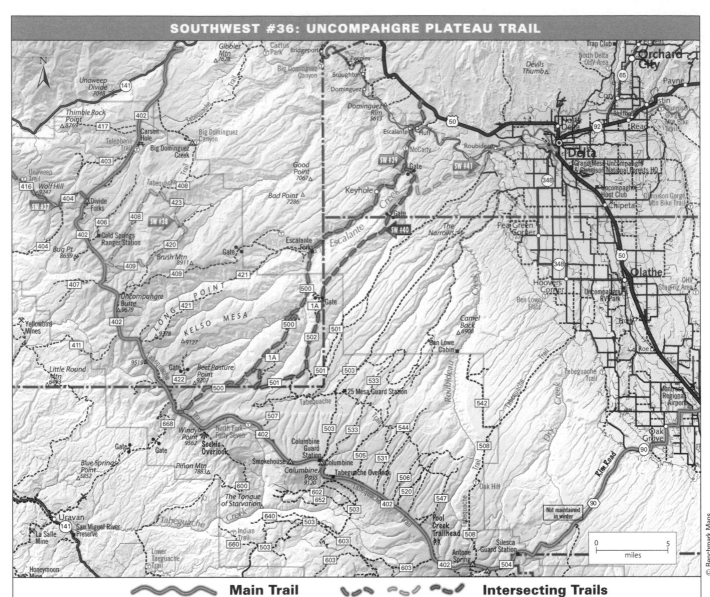

Main Trail ~~~~~ **Intersecting Trails**

© Benchmark Maps

			cattle guard.
7.5 ▲		SO	Cattle guard. Cross under high-voltage wires.
▼ 9.7		BL	Cattleyards on left; then fork in road.
3.5 ▲		BR	Fork in the road; then cattleyards on right.
▼ 12.2		SO	Cattleyards on left; then cattle guard.
0.9 ▲		SO	Cattle guard; then cattleyards on right.

GPS: N38°24.43' W108°04.21'			
▼ 13.1		TR	T-intersection with Old Highway 90. Turn right and go through seasonal closure gate. Zero trip meter.
0.0 ▲			Turn onto Rim Road.

GPS: N38°21.79' W108°02.94'			
▼ 0.0			Proceed along Old Highway 90.
23.6 ▲		TL	Intersection. Zero trip meter.
▼ 0.4		SO	Cross over East Fork of Dry Creek.
23.2 ▲		SO	Cross over East Fork of Dry Creek.
▼ 5.8		SO	USFS Silesca Ranger Station on left.
17.8 ▲		SO	USFS Silesca Ranger Station on right.
▼ 7.9		SO	FR 402 on left (Dave Wood Road and Norwood).
15.7 ▲		SO	FR 402 on right.

GPS: N38°19.02' W108°09.21'			
▼ 8.3		SO	USFS Iron Springs Campground on left.
15.2 ▲		SO	USFS Iron Springs Campground on right.
▼ 8.5		BR	Old Highway 90 turns left.
15.0 ▲		BL	Intersection: Old Highway 90.
▼ 8.8		SO	FR 527 on right.
14.7 ▲		SO	FR 527 on left.
▼ 9.5		SO	Road on right is Transfer Road/FR 508 to Olathe.
14.0 ▲		SO	FR 508 on left.
▼ 10.9		SO	West Antone Spring on left.
12.7 ▲		SO	West Antone Spring on right.
▼ 11.9		SO	Road to Pool Creek on right.
11.6 ▲		SO	Road to Pool Creek on left.
▼ 13.7		SO	Pool Creek Trailhead on right.
9.9 ▲		SO	Pool Creek Trailhead on left.
▼ 14.0		SO	West Pool Creek on right.
9.5 ▲		SO	West Pool Creek on left.
▼ 15.2		SO	FR 546 on right.
8.3 ▲		SO	FR 546 on left.
▼ 16.3		SO	FR 545 on right.

▼ 7.3 ▲	SO	FR 545 on left.	
▼ 17.5	SO	FR 520 on right to Long Creek.	
6.0 ▲	SO	FR 520 on left to Long Creek.	
▼ 18.2	SO	FR 506 on right to Payne Mesa.	
5.4 ▲	SO	FR 506 on left to Payne Mesa.	
▼ 18.7	SO	Cattleyards on left. FR 534 on right.	
4.9 ▲	SO	FR 534 on left. Cattleyards on right.	
▼ 19.7	SO	FR 531 to Moore Mesa on right.	
3.9 ▲	SO	FR 531 to Moore Mesa on left.	
▼ 21.2	SO	FR 505 on right.	
2.4 ▲	SO	FR 505 on left.	
▼ 22.8	SO	USFS Tabeguache scenic overlook on left.	
0.7 ▲	SO	USFS Tabeguache scenic overlook on right.	
▼ 23.6	BR	Columbine Pass. FR 503 and cattleyards on left. Zero trip meter.	
0.0 ▲		Continue on FR 402 to the left.	

GPS: N38°25.00' W108°22.86'

▼ 0.0		Continue on FR 402 to the right.	
33.6 ▲	BL	Columbine Pass. FR 503 and cattleyards on left. Zero trip meter.	
▼ 0.3	SO	FR 533 to Monitor Mesa on the right.	
33.2 ▲	SO	FR 533 to Monitor Mesa on the left.	
▼ 0.7	SO	USFS Columbine Campground on left.	
32.9 ▲	SO	USFS Columbine Campground on right.	
▼ 0.9	TL	Cattle guard; then cross through creek to intersection. Follow FR 402 toward Windy Point. To the right is FR 503, Delta-Nucla Road.	
32.7 ▲	TR	Intersection. FR 503 to Delta-Nucla is to the left. Turn right toward Columbine Pass. Cross creek; then cattle guard.	

GPS: N38°25.70' W108°22.89'

▼ 2.4	SO	Track on right.	
31.1 ▲	SO	Track on left.	
▼ 3.1	SO	FR 529 to Sawmill Mesa on right.	
30.5 ▲	SO	FR 529 to Sawmill Mesa on left.	
▼ 6.5	SO	FR 507, Lockhart on right.	
27.1 ▲	SO	FR 507, Lockhart on left.	
▼ 10.9	SO	FR 600 on left.	
22.7 ▲	SO	FR 600 on right.	
▼ 11.1	SO	Windy Point (great views!) on left.	
22.5 ▲	SO	Windy Point (great views!) on right.	
▼ 13.3	SO	FR 500 on right.	
20.3 ▲	SO	FR 500 on left.	
▼ 14.3	SO	Cattleyards on right.	
19.3 ▲	SO	Cattleyards on left.	
▼ 16.4	SO	Track on left.	
17.2 ▲	SO	Track on right.	
▼ 17.8	SO	Monument Hill on right.	
15.7 ▲	SO	Monument Hill on left.	
▼ 19.5	SO	Long Point and FR 421 on right.	
14.0 ▲	SO	Long Point and FR 421 on left.	
▼ 21.3	SO	FR 411 on left; then cattle guard.	
12.3 ▲	SO	Cattle guard; then FR 411 on right.	
▼ 21.6	SO	Short track on right.	
12.0 ▲	SO	Short track on left.	
▼ 23.0	SO	Uncompahgre Butte on right.	
10.5 ▲	SO	Uncompahgre Butte on left.	
▼ 24.2	SO	Track on right.	
9.3 ▲	SO	Track on left.	
▼ 25.0	SO	3 H on left.	
8.6 ▲	SO	3 H on right.	
▼ 25.8	SO	Mesa Creek FR 407 on left.	
7.8 ▲	SO	Mesa Creek FR 407 on right.	

▼ 27.3	SO	FR 408 on right.	
6.3 ▲	SO	FR 408 on left.	
▼ 28.2	SO	3 J on right dead-ends.	
5.4 ▲	SO	3 J on left dead-ends.	
▼ 29.2	SO	FR 410 on left dead-ends.	
4.4 ▲	SO	FR 410 on right dead-ends.	
▼ 29.4	SO	Track on right to USFS Cold Springs Work Center.	
4.2 ▲	SO	Track on left to USFS Cold Springs Work Center.	
▼ 31.0	SO	Track and cattleyards on left.	
2.5 ▲	SO	Cattleyards and track on right.	
▼ 33.4	SO	USFS Divide Forks Campground on left.	
0.2 ▲	SO	USFS Divide Forks Campground on right.	
▼ 33.6	SO	FR 404 Uranium Road on left. Zero trip meter.	
0.0 ▲		Continue along FR 402.	

GPS: N38°41.21' W108°41.18'

▼ 0.0		Continue along FR 402.	
15.0 ▲	SO	FR 404 Uranium Road on right. Zero trip meter.	
▼ 2.9	SO	Cattle guard.	
12.1 ▲	SO	Cattle guard.	
▼ 5.4	SO	FR 403 to Big Creek Reservoir on left.	
9.6 ▲	SO	FR 403 to Big Creek Reservoir on right.	
▼ 7.0	SO	Cattle guard.	
8.0 ▲	SO	Cattle guard.	
▼ 8.8	SO	USFS Uncompahgre information board, seasonal closure gate, and cattle guard.	
6.2 ▲	SO	Cattle guard. Seasonal closure gate and USFS Uncompahgre information board.	
▼ 9.2	SO	Dominquez State Wildlife area on right and road to Dominquez BLM campground.	
5.8 ▲	SO	Dominquez State Wildlife area on left and road to Dominquez BLM campground.	
▼ 12.9	SO	Cattle guard.	
2.1 ▲	SO	Cattle guard.	
▼ 15.0		Cattle guard. End at intersection with Colorado 141.	
0.0 ▲		At intersection of CR 90 and Colorado 141, zero trip meter and proceed along CR 90. Cross cattle guard.	

GPS: N38°50.26' W108°34.45'

SOUTHWEST REGION TRAIL #37

Far Pond Trail

Starting Point:	**Intersection of Southwest #36:**
	Uncompahgre Plateau Trail (FR 402)
	and FR 404
Finishing Point:	**Overlook of Unaweep Canyon**
Total Mileage:	**9.2 miles (one-way)**
Unpaved Mileage:	**9.2 miles**
Driving Time:	**1.25 hours (one-way)**
Elevation Range:	**8,706 to 9,429 feet**
Usually Open:	**Year-round**
Difficulty Rating:	**5**
Scenic Rating:	**8**

Special Attractions

- Fun, remote-feeling 4WD trail.
- Access to Divide Forks ATV Complex, a network of trails for ATVs, motorbikes, and mountain bikes, as well as access to trailheads for hikers and horseback riders only.
- Spectacular fall color aspen viewing.
- Wildlife viewing.

Description

Toward the north end of Southwest #36: Uncompahgre Plateau Trail is the intersection with FR 404. Zero your trip meter and proceed southwest on FR 404 toward Divide Forks USFS Campground to begin the trail. The wide one-lane dirt trail begins as a well-maintained road traveling along the aspen, ponderosa pine, and evergreen forest floor. In fall, most of the length of this trail is shaded by a beautiful yellow canopy of aspen foliage.

Divide Forks Campground is a no-fee dispersed camping area with fire grates and picnic tables. No water or toilet facilities are available at the site and there is no trash pickup.

Proceed on FR 404 until the intersection with FR 416 at 2.8 miles on the odometer. After turning right onto FR 416, you will see a sign for the Divide Forks ATV Complex. In this vicinity is a shady picnic area and a sign showing a map of all the trails within the ATV complex. The network contains as many as 15 trails, several of which intersect with the main trail.

At this point the road narrows and becomes more challenging due to both embedded and loose rock. The difficulty rating of the trail is a 5 for the track after the turnoff onto FR 416. Do not attempt this drive in wet conditions. The trail's surface is composed almost exclusively of dirt, making it a certainty vehicles will get stuck in the mud when the road is wet. Other obstacles to consider before navigating the remainder of the trail include large rocks, large ruts, downed trees, and sections of slickrock.

Clearings in the forest near the trail make for shady backcountry campsites, picnic sites, or wildlife viewing locations. Readily spotted wildlife include mule deer, elk, and ducks, among other flora and fauna. In sections the aspens grow quite close to the trail, minimizing passing ability. The track alternately travels over short sections of solid rock, forest, and grassy meadows.

At approximately 5.5 miles, cross through a gate making sure to leave it in the state you found it. Beyond the gate there are a series of ponds, Big Pond, Rim Pond, Middle Pond, and Far Pond. Approximately 0.5 miles past Far Pond, the trail ends at a picturesque overlook of Unaweep Canyon near some radio equipment.

Current Road Information

Grand Mesa, Uncompahgre and Gunnison National Forests
Grand Valley Ranger District
2777 Crossroads Boulevard, Suite 1
Grand Junction, CO 81506
(970) 242-8211

Map References

USFS Uncompahgre National Forest
Maptech CD: Grand Junction/Western Slope
Benchmark's *Colorado Road and Recreation Atlas*, pp. 82, 94
Colorado Atlas & Gazetteer, p. 54
The Roads of Colorado, pp. 104, 105

Route Directions

▼ 0.0		Trail begins at the intersection of Southwest #36: Uncompahgre Plateau Trail (FR 402) and FR 404. Proceed southwest on FR 404.
	GPS: N38°41.21′ W108°41.22′	
▼ 1.2	SO	FR 637 on right, open for all uses.
▼ 2.6	SO	FR 404 1A on right; then cattle guard.
	GPS: N38°40.95′ W108°43.54′	

Section of slickrock on Far Pond Trail

One in a series of ponds toward the end of Far Pond Trail

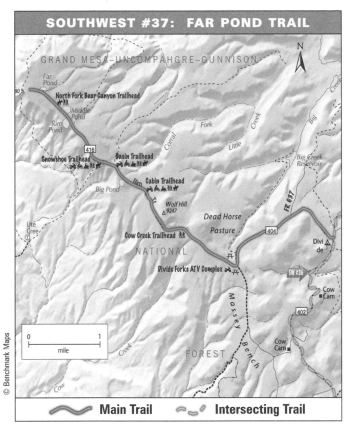

© Benchmark Maps

〜 **Main Trail**   〜〜 **Intersecting Trail**

▼ 2.8	TR	FR 416 on right, signed to Wolf Hill and Big Pond. Zero trip meter.
		GPS: N38°40.71' W108°43.50'
▼ 0.0		Continue west on FR 416.
▼ 1.0	SO	FR 416 1A on left.
		GPS: N38°41.08' W108°44.43'
▼ 1.3	SO	Cow Creek Trail #611 on left for hiking and horseback riding only; then pond on right.
		GPS: N38°41.30' W108°44.74'
▼ 1.7	SO	Fence line on left and right.
▼ 2.7	TL	Gate.
		GPS: N38°41.91' W108°45.67'
▼ 3.3	SO	Big Pond on left.
		GPS: N38°' W108°46.27'
▼ 3.7	BL	Gate; then intersection with Basin Trail #603, open for all uses.
		GPS: N38°42.36' W108°46.58'
▼ 3.8	SO	Snowshoe Trail #607 on left, open for all uses except 4WD vehicles.
▼ 4.5	SO	Pond on left.
		GPS: N38°42.77' W108°47.19'
▼ 5.0	TR	Follow track around to the right of Rim Pond on left.
		GPS: N38°43.00' W108°47.59'
▼ 5.3	SO	Mid Pond on right.
		GPS: N38°43.22' W108°47.67'
▼ 5.5	SO	North Fork Bear Canyon Trail #653 on right for hikers and horseback riders only.
▼ 5.9	BL	Far Pond on right.
		GPS: N38°43.52' W108°48.10'
▼ 6.4		Trail ends at communications equipment and overlook of Unaweep Canyon.
		GPS: N38°43.50' W108°48.58'

Dominguez Ridge Loop

Starting Point:	Intersection of Southwest #36:
	Uncompahgre Plateau Trail and FR 408
Finishing Point:	Intersection of Southwest #36:
	Uncompahgre Plateau Trail and FR 408
Total Mileage:	21.4 miles
Unpaved Mileage:	21.4 miles
Driving Time:	1.75 hours
Elevation Range:	7,840 to 9,069 feet
Usually Open:	Year-round
Difficulty Rating:	2
Scenic Rating:	7

Special Attractions

- Expansive views of Grand Mesa.
- Remote, low-traffic trail.
- Backcountry camping opportunities.

Description

The trail begins in a wide open meadow at the intersection of Southwest #36: Uncompahgre Plateau Trail and FR 408. Zero your trip meter and proceed east on FR 408. For nearly a mile after the trail commences, it travels through private ranch land. The high-elevation (more than 9,000 feet) open range is clearly a prime location for grazing cattle, so be alert for cows in the road. The trail also crosses a number of cattle guards and near several corrals.

With few trees near the trail, expansive views of Grand Mesa to the northeast are common. Scenic in the fall when the

Narrow section of Dominguez Ridge Loop

Easygoing Dominguez Ridge Loop

few aspens glow yellow, the low pinyon and juniper pines and sagebrush growing on the undulating landscape give the feeling of being a cowboy on the open range before the West was won. The trail is dusty in dry conditions and can be quite muddy when wet.

At the intersection of FR 408 and FR 423, turn right onto FR 423. The trail becomes narrow and rutted due to erosion. This section gives the trail its difficulty rating of 2, although the majority is an easygoing difficulty rating of 1.

The pleasant trail undulates over Dominguez Ridge, following both Keith Creek and Dominguez Creek at different points. At the intersection with FR 420, leave FR 423 and proceed on FR 420 for just under 4.9 miles. Traveling over the open range and alternately through scrub oak and stands of aspens, there are many good backcountry camping opportunities along the entire length of this trail.

The last leg of the trail is a 3.7-mile section of FR 409 (Brush Ridge Trail), which completes the loop back to FR 408 near where the trail began.

Current Road Information

Grand Mesa, Uncompahgre and Gunnison National Forests
Grand Valley Ranger District
2777 Crossroads Boulevard, Suite 1
Grand Junction, CO 81506
(970) 242-8211

Map References

USFS Uncompahgre National Forest
Maptech CD: Grand Junction/Western Slope
Benchmark's *Colorado Road and Recreation Atlas,* p. 94
Colorado Atlas & Gazetteer, pp. 54, 55
The Roads of Colorado, p. 105

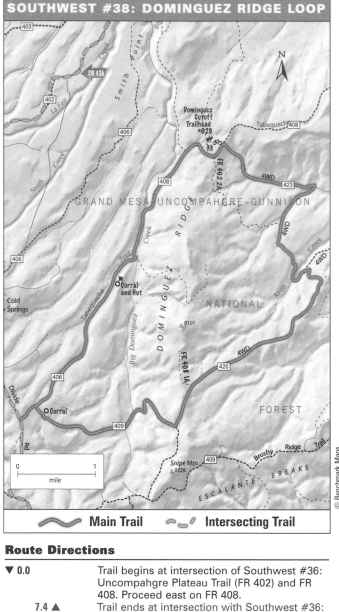

SOUTHWEST #38: DOMINGUEZ RIDGE LOOP

© Benchmark Maps

╌╌ **Main Trail**   ╌╌ **Intersecting Trail**

Route Directions

▼ 0.0			Trail begins at intersection of Southwest #36: Uncompahgre Plateau Trail (FR 402) and FR 408. Proceed east on FR 408.
	7.4 ▲		Trail ends at intersection with Southwest #36: Uncompahgre Plateau Trail (FR 402).
		GPS: N38°37.24' W108°40.02'	
▼ 0.4		SO	FR 409 on right; then cattle guard.
	7.0 ▲	SO	Cattle guard; then FR 409 on left.
		GPS: N38°37.48' W108°39.73'	
▼ 1.0		SO	Closed track on right; then cattle guard. Enter private property for the next 0.75 miles.
	6.4 ▲	SO	Cattle guard and exit private property; then track on left.
▼ 1.2		SO	Corral and hut on right on private property.
	6.2 ▲	SO	Corral and hut on left on private property.
		GPS: N38°38.00' W108°39.15'	
▼ 1.3		SO	Private road on right.
	6.1 ▲	SO	Private road on left.
▼ 1.4		SO	Stock pond on left.
	6.0 ▲	SO	Stock pond on right.
▼ 1.9		SO	Cattle guard and old zigzag-pattern fence line.
	5.5 ▲	SO	Old zigzag fence line and cattle guard.
		GPS: N38°38.44' W108°38.61'	
▼ 4.0		SO	Road on right.

3.4 ▲	SO	Road on left.

GPS: N38°39.82′ W108°37.52′

▼ 4.1	SO	Cross through wash.
3.3 ▲	SO	Cross through wash.
▼ 4.9	SO	Cross through creek.
2.5 ▲	SO	Cross through creek.

GPS: N38°40.54′ W108°37.33′

▼ 5.8	SO	Gate.
1.6 ▲	SO	Gate.

GPS: N38°41.09′ W108°36.81′

▼ 6.3	SO	FR 418 on right.
1.1 ▲	SO	FR 418 on left.

GPS: N38°41.50′ W108°36.45′

▼ 6.7	SO	FR 629, Dominguez Cutoff, on left for hikers, horseback riders, and mountain bikers only.
0.7 ▲	SO	FR 629, Dominguez Cutoff, on right for hikers, horseback riders, and mountain bikers only.

GPS: N38°41.56′ W108°36.11′

▼ 7.0	BL	FR 408 2A on right.
0.4 ▲	BR	FR 408 2A on left.

GPS: N38°41.38′ W108°35.83′

▼ 7.4	TR	FR 423 on right. Zero trip meter.
0.0 ▲		Proceed southwest on FR 423.

GPS: N38°41.65′ W108°35.61′

▼ 0.0		Proceed southeast on FR 423.
5.0 ▲	TL	FR 423 on left. Zero trip meter.
▼ 0.7	SO	Stock pond on left.
4.3 ▲	SO	Stock pond on right.
▼ 0.8	SO	Stock pond on left.
4.1 ▲	SO	Stock pond on right.
▼ 2.0	SO	Gate.
2.9 ▲	SO	Gate.

GPS: N38°40.95′ W108°33.92′

▼ 2.3	TR	FR 635, Bad Land, on left for hikers and horseback riders only. Stock pond on right. Proceed across dam.
2.7 ▲	TL	Cross dam and stock pond on left. FR 635, Bad Land, on right for hikers and horseback riders only.

GPS: N38°40.98′ W108°33.60′

▼ 2.4	SO	Gate.
2.6 ▲	SO	Gate.
▼ 3.4	SO	FR 408 2A on right.
1.6 ▲	SO	FR 408 2A on left.

GPS: N38°40.34′ W108°34.35′

▼ 5.0	SO	Intersection with FR 420. Zero trip meter.
0.0 ▲		Proceed southwest on FR 423.

GPS: N38°39.56′ W108°33.92′

▼ 0.0		Proceed northeast on FR 42.
4.9 ▲	SO	Intersection with FR 423. Zero trip meter.
▼ 0.6	BR	Track on left.
3.3 ▲	BL	Track on right.

GPS: N38°39.46′ W108°33.45′

▼ 1.9	SO	Gate.
3.0 ▲	SO	Gate.

GPS: N38°38.63′ W108°34.16′

▼ 3.9	TL/SO	Road on left and gate. Proceed through gate; then track on left. Continue straight on FR 420.
1.0 ▲	SO/TR	Pass track on right; then proceed through gate and turn right on road on right.

GPS: N38°37.92′ W108°36.15′

▼ 4.1	BL	FR 408 1A on right.
0.8 ▲	BR	FR 408 1A on left.

GPS: N38°37.77′ W108°36.32′

▼ 4.6	BR	Track on left.
0.3 ▲	BL	Track on right.
▼ 4.9	TR	Intersection with FR 409. Zero trip meter.
0.0 ▲		Proceed west on FR 409.

GPS: N38°37.21′ W108°36.67′

▼ 0.0		Proceed northwest on FR 409.
3.7 ▲	TL	FR 420 on left and FR 409 straight on. Zero trip meter.
▼ 0.2	BL	Track on right.
3.5 ▲	SO	Track on left.
▼ 0.4	SO	Cattle guard.
3.3 ▲	SO	Cattle guard.
▼ 0.9	SO	Track on right.
2.9 ▲	SO	Track on left.

GPS: N38°37.61′ W108°37.30′

▼ 1.1	SO	Cross through wash.
2.6 ▲	SO	Cross through wash.
▼ 2.5	SO	Private access road to cabin on right.
1.2 ▲	BL	Private access road to cabin on left.
▼ 3.3	SO	Corral on right; then cattle guard.
0.4 ▲	SO	Cattle guard; then corral on left.

GPS: N38°37.25′ W108°39.41′

▼ 3.7	TL	T-intersection with FR 408. Zero trip meter.
0.0 ▲		Proceed southeast on FR 409.

GPS: N38°37.48′ W108°39.73′

▼ 0.0		Proceed southwest on FR 408.
0.4 ▲	TR	FR 409 on right. Zero trip meter.
▼ 0.4	SO	Trail ends at intersection with Southwest #36: Uncompahgre Plateau Trail.
0.0 ▲		Trail begins at intersection with Southwest #36: Uncompahgre Plateau Trail and FR 408.

GPS: N38°37.24′ W108°40.02′

Dominguez Ridge Loop with Grand Mesa in the background

Escalante Canyon Road

Starting Point:	Intersection of US 50 and Road 650
	(Escalante Canyon Road), 12 miles
	northwest of Delta
Finishing Point:	Intersection of Southwest #36:
	Uncompahgre Plateau Trail
Total Mileage:	38.4 miles
Unpaved Mileage:	35.7 miles
Driving Time:	2.5 hours
Elevation Range:	4,809 to 9,665 feet
Usually Open:	Year-round
Difficulty Rating:	2
Scenic Rating:	8

Special Attractions

- Historic trail through a scenic red rock canyon.
- Walker Cabin and Palmer Smith Cabin.
- Gunnison River boat and raft launch.
- Access to a network of 4WD trails.

Fording Escalante Creek

Walker Cabin

History

Escalante Canyon gradually formed over 600 million years as Escalante Creek carved the 1,300-foot-deep gorge. Named for the two Spanish priests, Escalante and Dominguez, who explored the region in 1776 (though never set foot in the actual canyon), Escalante Canyon has a long history of human occupation. The Ute Indians for years had made the North Fork of the Escalante River their winter home. Early settlers, attracted by the yearlong water supply and sheltering cliffs, soon pushed the Indians off the land.

Many cattle outfits began using the canyon as their winter quarters. In 1886, John Musser took up residence in one of the first homesteads in the canyon, where he operated the Musser Cattle Company. Over the years the company has acquired ranch after ranch so that now most of the grazing paddocks along the canyon's entire length are consolidated under Musser Cattle. Not only is the cattle company the oldest and the largest in the area, it still uses some of its original ranching techniques, moving cattle on horseback.

John Musser chose Escalante Forks as the site of his original homestead. Where the branches of the Escalante join, this strategic location gave his cattle ready access to various grazing pastures.

The infamous Colorado Sheep War centered around cattlemen protecting their grazing land from flocks of hungry sheep. In the early 1900s, an unwritten code existed that relegated sheep to one side of the Gunnison River. When Howard Lathrop hung a swinging bridge across the river and brought his sheep to graze on "cattle" land, the cattlemen retaliated by shooting hundreds of his sheep under the cover of darkness. Eventually Lathrop fled unscathed with the rest of his sheep back across the divide. Two residents of the canyon, Cash Sampson and Ben Lowe, however, died in a shoot-out supposedly instigated by a quarrel stemming from the Sheep War.

Most people in the canyon managed to live peaceably with one another. One man, Henry Walker, and his large family lived in Escalante Canyon where his skillfully crafted brick cabin still stands. Built in 1911, the structure is a testament to Walker's bricklaying ability. The family was unable to afford cement for the mortar between the bricks, so Henry and his four sons laid the bricks using mud dug from a hole in the yard. The cement that exists on the cabin today is a thin coating applied later, after the family earned enough money to buy the materials. The Colorado Division of Wildlife owns the building today, and visitors are welcome to explore the cabin.

Another resident, Captain Henry A. Smith, was particularly sociable. When Smith was 65, the small but spunky man packed up and left his lifelong home of Joliet, Indiana, to serve in the Civil War. Though he served only a month in the war as acting captain, he became "Captain" for life.

A tombstone carver by trade, Cap, as he was known, laid three rock walls against an upright stone slab and hollowed a bed alcove and gun niche for himself out of the stone. Reportedly he intended the hollowed-out bed alcove to be his crypt after his death. Ironically, he died while on a trip to California where he was buried instead.

Above the stone house, high on the cliff, he inscribed his initials as well as the name of a friend, R. Bowen, who was a blacksmith in Delta. The two played cards during their visits. Located beneath Bowen's name is the symbol of his blacksmith shop, carved by the talented Captain Smith. Cemeteries throughout western Colorado once had sandstone tombstones Cap had adorned with beautiful, sentimental messages, roses, leaf arrangements, and ivy. Sadly, over time the elements have worn away his etchings.

The house was a convenient stopover between the mountain and town, and fellow area residents often stopped to visit over dinner or even stay overnight. To accommodate all his visitors, Cap later built a second rock house for all of his guests, complete with beds below and in the loft. The back wall of his cabin has a set of hinged shelves, concealing the secret room where he supposedly used to hide his meat supply. The house is now state owned but remains open to visitors. The Colorado Division of Wildlife maintains the site and has added a picnic table and fire grate—perhaps carrying on Cap's tradition of the stone cabin as being the most visited location in Escalante Canyon.

Escalante Creek flowing through Escalante Canyon

Cottonwoods growing on the banks of Escalante Creek

Description

Escalante Canyon Trail commences at the intersection of US 50 and Road 650 (Escalante Canyon Road). The intersection is 12 miles northwest of Delta and is easily identified by the Escalante Canyon historical marker and rest area.

Zeroing your trip meter, proceed southwest on the wide, graded gravel road. The road is flat and easygoing and surrounded by desert vegetation of pinyon and juniper, thistle, rabbitbrush, and various cacti. Winding down into Escalante Canyon, the road follows a dry creek bed. The canyon begins to take shape as scenic rock buttes rise up from the rocky landscape. Red rock formations adjacent to the road create a maze of nooks and crannies that are interesting to explore.

At approximately 2.6 miles on the odometer, the road briefly becomes paved as it crosses Southern Pacific railroad tracks and the Gunnison River. Large cottonwood trees with colorful fall foliage grow on the banks of the river, and a boat launch that is frequently used for rafting trips is situated at the crossing.

At the river crossing and beyond, the road travels through private property. Please be respectful and stay on the trail. The trail follows alongside Escalante Creek after crossing the Gunnison River, and the next major point of interest, old Walker Cabin, is located beside the road. Henry Walker's well-crafted cabin makes a great place to stop and take photos. Beyond the cabin, the red rock canyon walls rise higher above the trail. The creek below is an oasis where wildlife is abundant among the rocky terrain.

The tombstone engraver carved his initials in the stone rock wall near his cabins

Palmer Smith cabin is located 3.8 miles farther along the trail. It is worth exploring, as several structures remain at the site where Captain Smith carved his initials on the face of the red rock canyon wall. Please be respectful of the historical sites in the vicinity and leave them as you found them for future generations to enjoy.

Along the trail are sites for backcountry camping. Low vegetation provides some privacy, but sites within the canyon will have little if any shade. Be sure you are not on private property before setting up camp.

Along the section of trail between Palmer Canyon and Escalante Forks, the canyon widens, allowing more trees to grow around the trail. On this section of the trail is the Escalante Potholes Recreation Area. You will also cross numerous wash-

Captain Smith's cabins in Escalante Canyon

Cap's bed alcove and gun niche inside the main cabin

es on the trail (not all are noted in the Route Directions). Some corrugations are the only obstacles to a smooth drive, and most of the length of the trail is graded and well maintained.

Passing several tracks off the main trail and privately owned grazing paddocks, Escalante Forks is located 16.7 miles into the trail. About a mile farther there is a shallow ford through the North Fork of Escalante Creek.

Beyond the ford, the road becomes rougher with some embedded rock and erosion, but the difficulty rating does not increase. Use caution in this area in wet conditions as the road can become boggy.

After entering Uncompahgre National Forest the trail becomes signed FR 500. Beyond another creek crossing, the road traverses the canyon and switchbacks up the canyon wall onto Love Mesa. The short section of shelf road that climbs steeply out of the canyon provides dramatic overlooks of Escalante Canyon. For a short time the road rides along the rim of the canyon, delivering more sweeping vistas of the surrounding terrain.

The road follows the desertlike Love Mesa over open range. Use caution, as cattle pay little attention to where they graze (in the road). As you gradually gain elevation and travel through canopies of aspen and ponderosa pine, private and shady backcountry campsites are more readily located.

Many of the tracks and side roads off the main trail are not marked on the forest service map, so stay on the main trail and follow the route directions carefully to avoid going off track. On the last several miles of this trail, high clearance is preferred to best navigate the rocky and eroded sections, which increase the trail's difficulty rating to a 2. Through breaks in the aspen and conifer forest along the higher reaches of the trail near its end, expansive views over Uncompahgre Plateau are worth commemorating with a photograph, especially in the fall before the aspens lose their bright yellow leaves.

Current Road Information

Colorado Bureau of Land Management
Uncompahgre Field Office
2465 South Townsend Avenue
Montrose, CO 81401
(970) 240-5300

Grand Mesa, Uncompahgre and Gunnison National Forests
Grand Valley Ranger District
2777 Crossroads Boulevard, Suite 1
Grand Junction, CO 81506
(970) 242-8211

Map References

BLM Delta
USFS Uncompahgre National Forest
Maptech CD: Grand Junction/Western Slope
Benchmark's *Colorado Road and Recreation Atlas,* pp. 83, 94, 95
Colorado Atlas & Gazetteer, p. 55
The Roads of Colorado, pp. 105, 106

Route Directions

▼ 0.0   Trail begins at intersection of US 50 and Road 650, 12 miles northwest of Delta. Rest area and historical marker on left; then proceed southwest on Road 650.

2.7 ▲   Trail ends at intersection with US 650 at rest area and historical marker. Turn right for Delta and left for Grand Junction.

GPS: N38°47.08′ W108°14.81′

▼ 0.5   **SO**   Tracks on right and left.

Colorful rock formations in Escalante Canyon

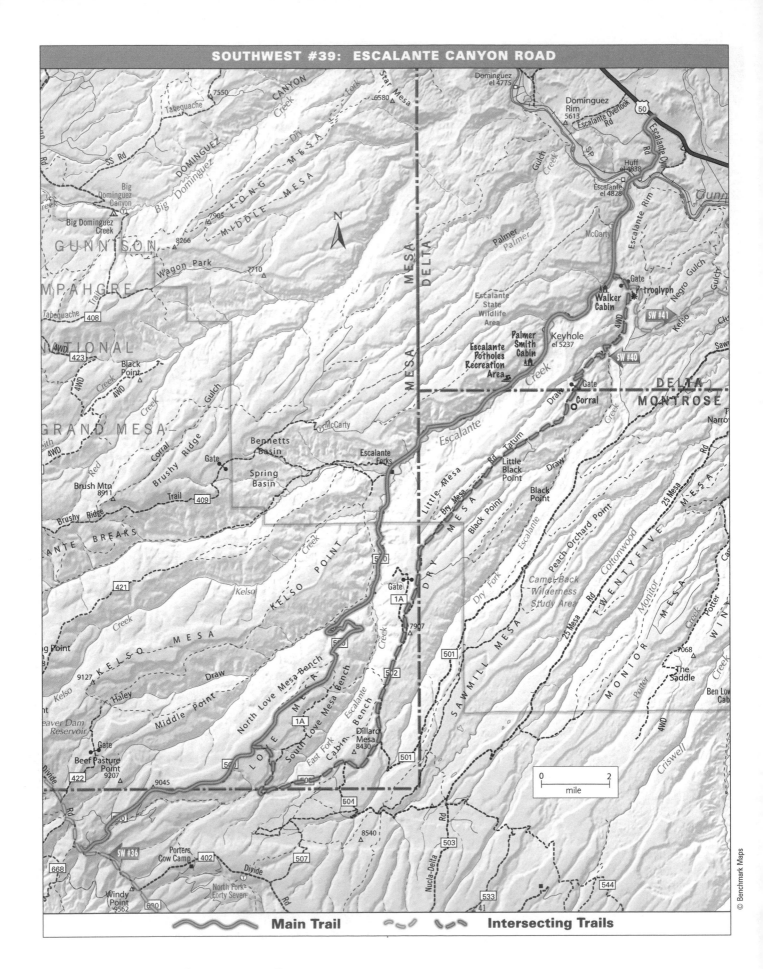

Main Trail ~~~~~   Intersecting Trails

The trail winds through scenic Escalante Canyon

	2.2 ▲	SO	Tracks on left and right.
▼ 0.6		SO	Cross over creek.
	2.1 ▲	SO	Cross over creek.
▼ 1.1		SO	Two tracks on right.
	1.6 ▲	SO	Two tracks on left.
▼ 2.6		SO	Pavement begins.
	0.1 ▲	SO	Pavement ends.
▼ 2.7		SO	Cross railroad tracks; then boat launch on right and cross bridge over Gunnison River. Pavement ends. Zero trip meter.
	0.0 ▲		Continue northeast on Road 650.
		GPS: N38°45.49′ W108°15.44′	
▼ 0.0			Proceed southwest on Road 650.
	3.6 ▲	SO	Pavement begins. Cross bridge over Gunnison River; then boat launch on left and cross railroad tracks. Zero trip meter.
▼ 0.1		SO	Cattle guard; then cross one-lane bridge over creek.
	3.4 ▲	SO	Cross one-lane bridge over creek; then cattle guard.
▼ 0.3		BL	Private driveway on right.
	3.3 ▲	BR	Private driveway on left.
▼ 2.1		SO	McCarty Trail for hikers only on right.
	1.5 ▲	SO	McCarty Trail for hikers only on left.
		GPS: N38°44.24′ W108°16.05′	
▼ 2.6		SO	Cattle guard.
	1.0S	SO	Cattle guard.
▼ 3.6		SO	Intersection Southwest #40: Dry Mesa Jeep Road (Road E23) on left. Signed to Escalante Rim Road and Dry Mesa Road and straight on to Escalante Forks and Palmer Gulch Road. Zero trip meter.
	0.0 ▲		Continue northeast on Road 650.
		GPS: N38°43.06′ W108°16.15′	
▼ 0.0			Continue southwest on Road 650.
	12.2 ▲	SO	Intersection with Southwest #40: Dry Mesa Jeep Road (Road E23) on right. Zero trip meter.
▼ 0.4		SO	Cross through wash.
	11.8 ▲	SO	Cross through wash.
		GPS: N38°42.81′ W108°16.42′	
▼ 0.5		SO	Walker Cabin on left.
	11.7 ▲	SO	Walker Cabin on right.
		GPS: N38°42.71′ W108°16.48′	
▼ 0.6		SO	Pavement begins.
	11.6 ▲	SO	Pavement ends.

▼ 0.7		SO	Pavement ends.
	11.5 ▲	SO	Pavement begins.
▼ 3.2		SO	Cabin and corral on right on private property.
	9.0 ▲	SO	Cabin and corral on left on private property.
▼ 4.3		SO	Palmer Smith Cabin and picnic area on right; then cross through wash.
	7.9 ▲	SO	Cross through wash; then Palmer Smith Cabin and picnic area on left.
		GPS: N38°40.83′ W108°18.73′	
▼ 4.6		SO	Cattle guard.
	7.6 ▲	SO	Cattle guard.
▼ 5.2		SO	Cross through wash.
	7.0 ▲	SO	Cross through wash.
▼ 5.5		SO	Road on left to parking area for Escalante Potholes Recreation Area.
	6.7 ▲	SO	Road on right to parking area for Escalante Potholes Recreation Area.
▼ 5.8		SO	Enter Montrose County; leave Delta County.
	6.4 ▲	SO	Enter Delta County; leave Montrose County.
▼ 6.2		SO	Cross through wash.
	6.0 ▲	SO	Cross through wash.
▼ 7.1		SO	Cross through wash.
	5.1 ▲	SO	Cross through wash.
▼ 7.4		SO	Track on left.
	4.8 ▲	SO	Track on right.
		GPS: N38°39.39′ W108°21.27′	
▼ 8.5		SO	Cross over creek.
	3.7 ▲	SO	Cross over creek.
		GPS: N38°39.22′ W108°22.25′	
▼ 9.1		SO	Cross over creek.
	3.2 ▲	SO	Cross over creek.
▼ 9.2		SO	Enter Mesa County; leave Montrose County.
	3.1 ▲	SO	Enter Montrose County; leave Mesa County.
▼ 9.4		SO	Track on right.
	2.8 ▲	SO	Track on left.
		GPS: N38°38.62′ W108°22.80′	
▼ 10.3		SO	Cattle guard.
	1.9 ▲	SO	Cattle guard.
▼ 10.5		SO	Escalante Forks; then bridge over creek.
	1.7 ▲	SO	Bridge over creek; then Escalante Forks.
		GPS: N38°38.02′ W108°23.68′	
▼ 10.8		SO	Cattle guard.
	1.4 ▲	SO	Cattle guard.
▼ 11.0		SO	Ford through creek.
	1.2 ▲	SO	Ford through creek.
		GPS: N38°37.61′ W108°23.75′	
▼ 11.2		SO	Cross through large wash.
	1.0 ▲	SO	Cross through large wash.
▼ 11.5		SO	Cattle guard.
	0.7 ▲	SO	Cattle guard.
▼ 11.9		SO	Cross through washes.
	0.3 ▲	SO	Cross through washes.
▼ 12.2		BL	Intersection with FR 421 on right and FR 500 to left, signed to Love Mesa and Divide Road. Zero trip meter.
	0.0 ▲		Continue north on Road 650.
		GPS: N38°36.73′ W108°24.00′	
▼ 0.0			Continue south on FR 500.
	8.6 ▲	BR	Intersection with FR 421 to left and FR 500 on right. Zero trip meter.
▼ 0.4		SO	Cross through wash.
	8.2 ▲	SO	Cross through wash.
▼ 1.1		SO	Cross through wash.
	7.5 ▲	SO	Cross through wash.

▼ 2.7		SO	Cattle guard; then enter state land.
	5.9 ▲	SO	Exit state land; then cattle guard.
▼ 2.9		SO	Cross through creek.
	5.7 ▲	SO	Cross through creek.
		GPS: N38°34.86' W108°24.30'	
▼ 3.2		BR	Road on left.
	5.4 ▲	BL	Road on right.
		GPS: N38°34.73' W108°24.43'	
▼ 3.6		SO	Cattle guard and exit state land.
	5.0 ▲	SO	Cattle guard and enter state land.
▼ 4.2		BL	Road on right to undeveloped campsites.
	4.4 ▲	SO	Road on left to undeveloped campsites.
		GPS: N38°34.32' W108°24.43'	
▼ 5.6		SO	Gate.
	3.0 ▲	SO	Gate.
▼ 8.3		BL	Track on right.
	0.3 ▲	BR	Track on left.
		GPS: N38°33.29' W108°25.55'	
▼ 8.5		SO	Track on left.
	0.1 ▲	BL	Track on right.
		GPS: N38°33.11' W108°25.59'	
▼ 8.6		SO	Intersection of FR 500 and FR 501 1A. Zero trip meter.
	0.0 ▲		Continue northeast on FR 500.
		GPS: N38°33.07' W108°25.62'	
▼ 0.0			Continue southwest on FR 500.
	3.6 ▲	SO	Intersection with FR 501 1A. Zero trip meter.
▼ 1.6		SO	Cattle guard.
	2.0 ▲	SO	Cattle guard.
▼ 2.5		SO	Track on left.
	1.1 ▲	SO	Track on right.
▼ 2.8		SO	Track on right.
	0.8 ▲	SO	Track on left.
		GPS: N38°31.55' W108°27.74'	
▼ 3.6		SO	Intersection with Southwest #40: Dry Mesa Jeep Road (FR 501). Zero trip meter.
	0.0 ▲	SO	Continue north on FR 500.
		GPS: N38°31.05' W108°28.26'	
▼ 0.0			Continue south on FR 500.
	4.6 ▲	SO	Intersection with Southwest #40: Dry Mesa Jeep Road (FR 501). Zero trip meter.
▼ 1.1		SO	Unmarked road on left and right; then road on right.
	3.5 ▲	SO	Road on left; then unmarked road on left and right.
		GPS: N38°30.62' W108°28.99'	
▼ 3.5		SO	Cattle guard.
	1.1 ▲	SO	Cattle guard.
▼ 4.6		SO	Road on left is FR 500 1A. Zero trip meter.
	0.0 ▲		Proceed southwest on FR 500.
		GPS: N38°29.74' W108°32.11'	
▼ 0.0			Continue northeast on FR 500.
	3.1 ▲	SO	FR 500 1A on right. Zero trip meter.
▼ 2.5		SO	Cattle guard.
	0.6 ▲	SO	Cattle guard.
▼ 2.9		SO	Cattle guard.
	0.2 ▲	SO	Cattle guard.
▼ 3.1			Trail ends at intersection with Southwest #36: Uncompahgre Plateau Trail (FR 402).
	0.0 ▲		Trail commences at intersection of Southwest #36: Uncompahgre Plateau (FR 402) and FR 500. Proceed north on FR 500.
		GPS: N38°28.53' W108°34.14'	

Dry Mesa Jeep Road

Starting Point:	Intersection with Southwest #39: Escalante Canyon Road and FR 501
Finishing Point:	Intersection with Southwest #39: Escalante Canyon Road and FR 501
Total Mileage:	25.5 miles
Unpaved Mileage:	25.5 miles
Driving Time:	1.75 hours
Elevation Range:	5,031 to 8,606 feet
Usually Open:	Year-round
Difficulty Rating:	4
Scenic Rating:	8

Special Attractions

■ Ute petroglyphs.

■ Exciting, rocky descent into Escalante Canyon.

■ One in a large network of 4WD trails.

History

Humans have occupied the Escalante Canyon as early as 12,000 years ago during the Paleo-Indian era, which is generally defined as the period from which the first signs of human presence can be found until the time agriculture and other signs of permanent settlement were detected.

As a result, researchers have found hundreds of unique sites that are evidence of the earliest inhabitants of the Escalante Canyon and the Uncompahgre Plateau. Particularly striking are the carvings in the stone canyon walls, or petroglyph sites. Ranging in age from 7000 B.C. to as recent as the 1800s, these historical records are believed to depict maps, hunting stories, histories, clan information, religious ceremonies, and shamanic themes.

Signs that the early inhabitants began farming and living off the land have also been located in Escalante Canyon and on Uncompahgre Plateau in the stone structures and caves

Loose, rocky switchback section of Dry Mesa Jeep Road

Dry Mesa Jeep Road in Escalante Canyon

The trail descends steeply into Escalante Canyon

they bore into the plateau slopes and canyon walls. It has not yet been established that these early artifacts can be linked to the amazing Anasazi cliff dwellings in Mesa Verde National Park, but no doubt historians will continue their fieldwork to determine the origins.

However, evidence can be directly linked to the subsequent Native American inhabitants, the Ute, who left behind scarred trees, Bear Dance rock art, teepee rings, and wickiups. The Tabeguache and Uncompahgre bands of Ute lived here from approximately the fifteenth century until their forcible relocation by white settlers in 1881.

The Spanish explored the area in the 1600s and 1700s. Their explorations provided the origins of many of the names of geographical features in the area, such as Escalante, who was a Spanish priest that passed near the area in 1776. By 1828, many fur traders had passed through the area, and Antoine Robidoux constructed Fort Uncompahgre on the Gunnison River as a trading post in what is today the city of Delta. In the following years miners, farmers, ranchers, and loggers arrived, and they all left their mark on the land.

In fact, on the land managed by the Uncompahgre Field Office of the Bureau of Land Management, more than 4,600 sites with artifacts have been recorded to date. Undoubtedly thousands more remain to be discovered because only 17 percent of this land has been formally surveyed for artifacts.

Dry Mesa Jeep Road itself is a part of the history of settlement in the canyon. It was constructed in 1926 as an improvement to the original road into Escalante Canyon. The road was extremely narrow and steep, with large rocks making travel over it treacherous for the horse-pulled buggies and wagons entering and exiting the canyon. Apparently it took four horses to pull one buggy and six horses to pull a wagon up the road.

Although Dry Mesa Jeep Road made canyon access easier, it also had a negative effect. The road's proximity to the Indian petroglyph made it readily accessible to vandals. Originally the petroglyph depicted chiefs riding horses, which were acquired after the Pueblo uprisings in 1680, but graffiti has all but decimated the original inscriptions. Viewing these historic artifacts is an amazing opportunity, so please treat all sites with respect so we can preserve this history for future generations.

Arid Dry Mesa

Description

This historic trail runs from the aspen and conifer forests of the Uncompahgre Plateau and along Dry Mesa and descends the colorful eastern rock wall of Escalante Canyon. At the intersection of Southwest #39: Escalante Canyon Road (FR 500), approximately 7.5 miles northeast of Southwest #36: Uncompahgre Plateau Trail, zero your trip meter and proceed east on FR 501, a wide dirt road with some embedded rock in sections. Initially traveling through aspen, ponderosa pine, and scrub oak forest, this section has beautiful fall color aspen viewing. Between breaks in the forest vegetation are overlooks of extensive aspen stands.

At the intersection with FR 501 1A, the surface of the road becomes gravel, and the track runs through sections of open meadows with good views of Escalante Canyon to the north. Beyond the intersection with FR 504, the road widens, and a lot of backcountry camping opportunities exist near the trail. Such sites are popular with hunters in the fall.

After approximately 2.7 miles, the road's gravel surface becomes primarily dirt, and it is rutted and eroded in places. Past the Dinosaur Quarry, the trail crosses through gates. Be sure to leave the gates as you found them, closing them if you had to open them to pass through.

Running alternately along the edge and the middle of Dry Mesa, the trail is a wide shelf road at times. It is recommended to avoid this trail when it is wet. The six- and seven-inch-deep wheel ruts that remain imprinted on the road's dry surface are a testament to how muddy the road can be, and how easily vehicles can get bogged. Also on this part of the trail, a few sections of slickrock create a stair effect that makes for a bumpy ride.

After approximately 10 miles, the trail begins to steeply descend the eastern wall of Escalante Canyon, and a sign warns of a section of rough 4WD road ahead. This exciting section of the narrow shelf trail, which switchbacks over a rocky surface into the canyon, increases the difficulty rating from a 2 to a 4, mainly for its steep aspect. This section may be more difficult or the road may even become impassible due to rock slides and washouts. In addition to being exciting, the descent is also quite scenic as the trail progresses through a rock garden of boulders, some of which are larger than a jeep!

After descending into Escalante Canyon, the trail travels toward Escalante Creek then follows it for a time, crossing through it numerous times. The crossings are most exciting in wet months. The road through this narrow and very scenic section of the canyon is rocky and lined with cottonwoods and sage.

Just before the intersection with Southwest #41: Escalante Rim Trail, you can walk over to view what remains of the Indian petroglyphs that date back to as early as the 1680s. The artifacts have been extensively vandalized, making it difficult to locate the original inscriptions. Please respect historic sites to preserve them for future generations. The trail ends just under a mile beyond the petroglyph site at the intersection with Southwest #39: Escalante Canyon Road approximately 3.5 miles south of US 50.

Current Road Information

Colorado Bureau of Land Management
Uncompahgre Field Office
2465 South Townsend Avenue
Montrose, CO 81401
(970) 240-5300

Grand Mesa, Uncompahgre and Gunnison National Forests
Grand Valley Ranger District
2777 Crossroads Boulevard, Suite 1
Grand Junction, CO 81506
(970) 242-8211

Map References

BLM Delta
USFS Uncompahgre National Forest
Maptech CD: Grand Junction/Western Slope
Benchmark's *Colorado Road and Recreation Atlas,* p. 95
Colorado Atlas & Gazetteer, p. 55
The Roads of Colorado, pp. 105, 106

Route Directions

▼ 0.0			Trail begins at the intersection of Southwest #39: Escalante Canyon Road and FR 501. Proceed east on FR 501.
	1.2 ▲		Trail ends at intersection with Southwest #39: Escalante Canyon Road (FR 500.)
		GPS: N38°31.05' W108°28.26'	
▼ 0.6		SO	Cattle guard.
	0.6 ▲	SO	Cattle guard.
▼ 1.2		BR	Intersection of FR 501 1A on left. Zero trip meter.
	0.0 ▲		Continue north on FR 501.
		GPS: N38°30.48' W108°27.61'	
▼ 0.0			Continue south on FR 501.
	3.7 ▲	BL	Intersection with FR 501 1A on right. Zero trip meter.
▼ 0.4		SO	Track on right.
	3.3 ▲	SO	Track on left.
		GPS: N38°30.17' W108°27.80'	
▼ 0.6		SO	Cattle guard.
	3.2 ▲	SO	Cattle guard.
▼ 0.7		SO	Track on right.
	3.0 ▲	SO	Track on left.
		GPS: N38°29.97' W108°28.06'	
▼ 0.8		SO	Cross over creek.
	2.9 ▲	SO	Cross over creek.
		GPS: N38°29.95' W108°28.12'	
▼ 1.1		SO	Cattle guard.
	2.6 ▲	SO	Cattle guard.
▼ 2.1		SO	Cross over creek.
	1.6 ▲	SO	Cross over creek.
▼ 3.7		TL	Cattle guard; then intersection with FR 501 to the left and FR 504 to the right. Zero trip meter.
	0.0 ▲		Continue southwest on FR 501.
		GPS: N38°30.64' W108°25.42'	
▼ 0.0			Continue northeast on FR 501.
	1.8 ▲	TR	Intersection with FR 501 to the right and FR 504 to the left; then cattle guard. Zero trip meter.
▼ 0.1		BR	Track on left.
	1.7 ▲	SO	Track on right.

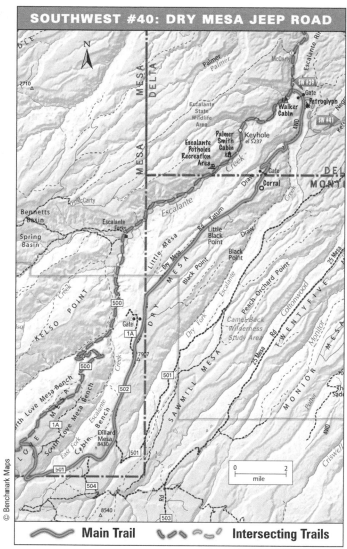

N

© Benchmark Maps

| | ~ Main Trail | | ꙮ ꙮ ꙮ ꙮ Intersecting Trails |

			GPS: N38°30.66' W108°25.30'
▼ 1.1		SO	Cattle guard.
0.7 ▲		SO	Cattle guard.
▼ 1.8		TL	Intersection with FR 502 on left. Zero trip meter.
0.0 ▲			Continue south on FR 501.

			GPS: N38°31.18' W108°23.96'
▼ 0.0			Continue north on FR 502.
3.4 ▲		TR	Intersection with FR 501 on right. Zero trip meter.
▼ 0.2		SO	Cross over creek.
3.2 ▲		SO	Cross over creek.
▼ 1.5		SO	Track on left; then cattle guard.
1.9 ▲		SO	Cattle guard; then track on right.
▼ 2.7		SO	Track on right.
0.7 ▲		SO	Track on left.

			GPS: N38°33.27' W108°23.51'
▼ 3.3		SO	Gate.
0.1 ▲		SO	Gate.

			GPS: N38°33.77' W108°23.18'
▼ 3.4		BR	Intersection with FR 502 1A on left to Dinosaur Quarry. Zero trip meter.
0.0 ▲			Continue south on FR 502.

| | | | GPS: N38°33.95' W108°23.16' |

▼ 0.0			Continue north on FR 502 toward Dry Mesa.
10.2 ▲		BL	Intersection with FR 502 1A on right to Dinosaur Quarry. Zero trip meter.
▼ 1.0		SO	Track on right.
9.2 ▲		SO	Track on left.

			GPS: N38°34.55' W108°22.99'
▼ 1.9		SO	Track on right.
8.3 ▲		SO	Track on left.
▼ 3.9		SO	Cattle guard; then road on left.
6.3 ▲		SO	Road on right; then cattle guard.

			GPS: N38°36.76' W108°21.92'
▼ 5.7		SO	Old corral on right.
4.6 ▲		SO	Old corral on left.
▼ 5.9		SO	BLM water catchment and tanks on left; then gate.
4.3 ▲		SO	Gate; then BLM water catchment and tanks on right.
▼ 7.5		SO	Track on left.
2.7 ▲		SO	Track on right.
▼ 8.5		SO	Track on right.
1.7 ▲		SO	Track on left.

			GPS: N38°39.23' W108°18.10'
▼ 9.0		SO	Old corral on right.
1.3 ▲		SO	Old corral on left.
▼ 10.0		SO	Advisory sign posted. Steep rough trail ahead. 4WD suggested.
0.2 ▲		SO	Sign. Standard of road improves.
▼ 10.2		SO	Gate. Zero trip meter.
0.0 ▲			Continue southwest on FR 502.

			GPS: N38°40.23' W108°17.39'
▼ 0.0			Continue northeast on FR 502; then stock pond on right
5.2 ▲		SO	Stock pond on left; then gate. Zero trip meter.
▼ 2.3		SO	Cross through rocky wash; then another wash.
2.9 ▲		SO	Cross through wash; then another rocky wash.

			GPS: N38°41.17' W108°16.28'
▼ 2.4		SO	Cross through wash.
2.8 ▲		SO	Cross through wash.
▼ 2.7		SO	Cross through wash.
2.6 ▲		SO	Cross through wash.

			GPS: N38°41.35' W108°16.07'
▼ 2.8		SO	Gate; then cross through creek.
2.4 ▲		SO	Cross through creek; then gate.

			GPS: N38°41.46' W108°15.96'
▼ 2.9		SO	Cross through creek.
2.3 ▲		SO	Cross through creek.

Indian petroglyphs near Dry Mesa Jeep Road

▼ 3.0		SO	Cross through creek.
	2.2 ▲	SO	Cross through creek.
▼ 3.4		SO	Cross through muddy section of creek.
	1.8 ▲	SO	Cross through muddy section of creek.
	GPS: N38º41.87′ W108º15.76′		
▼ 3.5		SO	Cross through creek.
	1.8 ▲	SO	Cross through creek.
▼ 3.6		SO	Cross through creek.
	1.7 ▲	SO	Cross through creek.
▼ 3.7		SO	Cross through creek.
	1.4 ▲	SO	Cross through creek.
▼ 3.9		SO	Gate; then cross through creek.
	1.4 ▲	SO	Cross through creek; then gate.
▼ 4.0		SO	Cross through creek.
	1.3 ▲	SO	Cross through creek.
▼ 4.1		SO	Cross through creek.
	1.1 ▲	SO	Cross through creek.
	GPS: N38º42.41′ W108º15.48′		
▼ 4.2		SO	Cross through creek.
	1.0 ▲	SO	Cross through creek.
▼ 4.4		SO	Indian petroglyphs on left; then cross through creek.
	0.8 ▲	SO	Cross through creek; then Indian petroglyphs on right.
	GPS: N38º42.62′ W108º15.53′		
▼ 4.7		SO	Intersection with Southwest #41: Escalante Rim Trail on right.; then cattle guard and cross through creek.
	0.6 ▲	BR	Cross through creek and cattle guard; then Intersection with Southwest #41: Escalante Rim Trail on left.
	GPS: N38º42.77′ W108º15.72′		
▼ 4.9		SO	Cross through creek.
	0.3 ▲	SO	Cross through creek.
▼ 5.2			Cross through creek; then trail ends at the intersection with FR 500 Southwest #39: Escalante Canyon Road.
	0.0 ▲		Trail begins at the intersection of FR 500 Southwest #39: Escalante Canyon Road and FR 502. Zero trip meter; then cross through creek.
	GPS: N38º43.05′ W108º16.15′		

Cottonwoods line Escalante Creek

Special Attractions

- Scenic shelf road along Escalante Canyon rim.
- Trail begins in downtown Delta.
- Town site of Roubideau.

History

After the Spanish explored the area in the 1600s and 1700s, many white European fur traders passed through the area on alternate routes off of the California and Santa Fe Trails. The enterprising French fur trader Antoine Roubidoux established trade lines through the area and constructed a permanent outpost nearby in 1828. In all likelihood, the Ute helped him locate the strategic position for his trading post, Fort Uncompahgre, on the Gunnison River in what is today the city of Delta.

In the following years miners, farmers, ranchers, loggers, and eventually the railroad arrived and settled the region. The town of Roubideau, named for the colorful French fur trader, was established by the Denver & Rio Grande Railroad sometime in 1881 after Indians were relocated to reservations. After the D&RG arrived in the Uncompahgre Valley and established the end of its line at Roubideau, the settlement

---

SOUTHWEST REGION TRAIL #41

Escalante Rim Trail

Starting Point:	**Intersection of 6th and Main Streets in downtown Delta**
Finishing Point:	**Southwest #40: Dry Mesa Jeep Road**
Total Mileage:	**14.3 miles**
Unpaved Mileage:	**14.3 miles**
Driving Time:	**1 hour**
Elevation Range:	**4,876 to 5,855 feet**
Usually Open:	**Year-round**
Difficulty Rating:	**3**
Scenic Rating:	**9**

Expansive view of Escalante Canyon from the trail

developed as a prime ranching location, and cowboys and cattle quickly flooded the area.

Not surprisingly, the cattle town's main structures included unloading ramps, loading chutes, corrals, and stockyards, although one resident recalls as many as five houses, a post office, a schoolhouse, a general store, and a dance hall. The dance hall and the saloons occupied the numerous cowboys during their time off—and probably accounts for why the schoolhouse was located on a hillside well away from the main street.

Gradually the numbers of incoming livestock dwindled as herds living on the surrounding plateaus and mesas multiplied. Most of the activity became rounding up cattle and shipping them off from Roubideau. Today the railroad spur that created the town still exists as a Southern Pacific line, but all that remains to commemorate the existence of the town is an information board at the site.

Description
Beginning in downtown Delta, this incredibly scenic trail passes the town site of Roubideau and descends into Escalante Canyon, traveling along its rim and providing fantastic views.

At the intersection of West 6th Street and Main Street, signed Public Lands Access Uncompahgre Plateau, proceed east on West 6th Street. As you navigate the city streets heading west out of town, the trail crosses the railroad tracks and the Uncompahgre River before arriving at what remains of the town of Roubideau.

The trail runs out a paved two-lane road to the intersection with dirt E23 Road, a wide, graded gravel road with a few characteristics of a 4WD road. Proceeding west on E23 Road the trail becomes rocky with some embedded rocks and crosses through a canyon and under power lines. The surrounding desertlike landscape is barren and rocky with sparse, low vegetation of cacti, rabbitbrush, scrub grass, and pinyon and juniper pines.

As the road climbs approaching the Escalante Canyon, there are 360° views of the surrounding countryside. Numerous tracks head off from the main trail in all directions with too many to note in the Route Directions below. Navigation is easy, though, proceeding east on the wide, maintained dirt road.

Suddenly Escalante Canyon opens up before you and the trail begins to navigate down the canyon wall. The trail becomes a shelf road from which you can see down into the canyon and easily locate Escalante Creek, lined with cottonwoods and other vegetation. Views of the rocky surroundings are spectacular. In addition to the sheer drop-offs, the shelf is steep and narrow in sections, with a moderately loose surface—all features that give the trail a 3 rating for difficulty. It is no obstacle for a high-clearance 4WD. The trail ends after a short but scenic 14 miles at the intersection with Southwest #40: Dry Mesa Jeep Road (FR 502).

Current Road Information
Colorado Bureau of Land Management
Uncompahgre Field Office
2465 South Townsend Avenue
Montrose, CO 81401
(970) 240-5300

Escalante Rim Trail is a shelf carved in the wall of Escalante Canyon

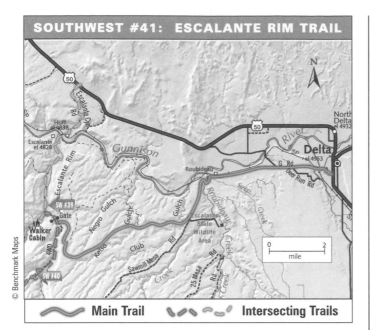

SOUTHWEST #41: ESCALANTE RIM TRAIL

| Main Trail | Intersecting Trails |

© Benchmark Maps

Map References

BLM Delta
Maptech CD: Grand Junction/Western Slope
Benchmark's *Colorado Road and Recreation Atlas,* pp. 83, 95
Colorado Atlas & Gazetteer, pp. 55, 56
The Roads of Colorado, p. 106

Route Directions

▼ 0.0			Trail begins at intersection of 6th and Main Streets in Delta, signed Public Lands Access to Uncompahgre Plateau. Proceed west down West 6th Street.
	6.6 ▲		Trail ends at intersection with Main Street in downtown Delta.
		GPS: N38°44.35' W108°04.26'	
▼ 0.1		TR	Intersection with Dodge Street.
	6.5 ▲	TL	Intersection with 6th Street.
▼ 0.2		TL	Intersection with 5th Street.
	6.4 ▲	TR	Intersection with Dodge Street.
▼ 0.4		SO	Cross railroad tracks; then cross bridge over Uncompahgre River.
	6.1 ▲	SO	Cross bridge over Uncompahgre River; then cross railroad tracks.
		GPS: N38°44.43' W108°04.84'	
▼ 0.7		SO	Cross railroad tracks.
	5.9 ▲	SO	Cross railroad tracks.
▼ 4.3		SO	Historical marker for town of Roubideau on right.
	2.3 ▲	SO	Historical marker for town of Roubideau on left.
▼ 5.1		SO	Cross bridge over Roubideau Creek.
	1.6 ▲	SO	Cross bridge over Roubideau Creek.
▼ 6.6		BR	Pavement ends and intersection with Road E23 and G Roads. Zero trip meter.
	0.0 ▲		Continue northeast on G Road.
		GPS: N38°42.83' W108°10.17'	
▼ 0.0			Continue southwest on Road E23.
	6.1 ▲	BL	Pavement begins and Road E23 intersects with G Road. Zero trip meter.
▼ 0.3		SO	Fence line on left and right.
	5.8 ▲	SO	Fence line on left and right.

▼ 0.4		SO	Cross through wash.
	5.7 ▲	SO	Cross through wash.
▼ 1.0		SO	Cattle guard.
	5.1 ▲	SO	Cattle guard.
▼ 1.6		BL	Track on right.
	4.5 ▲	BR	Track on left.
▼ 1.7		BR	Track on left.
	4.4 ▲	BL	Track on right.
		GPS: N38°42.63' W108°11.74'	
▼ 2.4		SO	Cross through wash.
	3.7 ▲	SO	Cross through wash.
▼ 2.5		SO	Track on left.
	3.5 ▲	SO	Track on right.
▼ 2.8		SO	Track on left.
	3.2 ▲	BL	Track on right.
		GPS: N38°42.60' W108°12.76'	
▼ 3.4		SO	Track on left; then track on right.
	2.6 ▲	BL	Track on left; then track on right.
▼ 4.0		SO	Short section of pavement crosses rocky area; then road on left.
	2.1 ▲	SO	Road on right; then short section of pavement crosses rocky area.
▼ 6.1		BL	Cattle guard; then track on right. Zero trip meter.
	0.0 ▲		Continue southeast on Escalante Rim Road (Road E23).
		GPS: N38°42.04' W108°15.31'	
▼ 0.0			Continue northwest on Escalante Rim Road (Road E23).
	1.6 ▲	BR	Track on left; then cattle guard.
▼ 1.6			Trail ends at intersection with Southwest #40: Dry Mesa Jeep Road (FR 502).
	0.0 ▲		Trail begins at intersection of Southwest #40: Dry Mesa Jeep Road (FR 502) and Road E23 or Escalante Rim Road.
		GPS: N38°42.77' W108°15.71'	

ATV riders on Escalante Rim Trail

Selected
Further Reading

Abbott, Carl, Stephen J. Leonard, and David McComb. *Colorado: A History of the Centennial State*. Niwot, Colo.: University Press of Colorado, 1994.

Aldrich, John K. *Ghosts of Chaffee County*. Lakewood, Colo.: Centennial Graphics, 1992.

———. *Ghosts of Park County*. Lakewood, Colo.: Centennial Graphics, 1994.

———. *Ghosts of Pitkin County*. Lakewood, Colo.: Centennial Graphics, 1992.

———. *Ghosts of Summit County*. Lakewood, Colo.: Centennial Graphics, 1997.

———. *Ghosts of the Eastern San Juans*. Lakewood, Colo.: Centennial Graphics, 1987.

———. *Ghosts of the Western San Juans*. Vols. 1 and 2. Lakewood, Colo.: Centennial Graphics, 1991.

Ayer, Eleanor. *Colorado Wildflowers*. Frederick, Colo.: Renaissance House, 1987.

Bancroft, Caroline. *Colorful Colorado*. Boulder, Colo.: Johnson Books, 1987.

———. *Unique Ghost Towns and Mountain Spots*. Boulder, Colo.: Johnson Books, 1961.

Bauer, Carolyn. *Colorado Ghost Towns—Colorado Traveler Guidebooks*. Frederick, Colo.: Renaissance House, 1987.

Beckner, Raymond M. *Along the Colorado Trail*. Pueblo, Colo.: O'Brien Printing & Stationery, 1975.

Benham, Jack. *Ouray*. Ouray, Colo.: Bear Creek Publishing, 1976.

Boyd, Leanne C. and H. Glenn Carson. *Atlas of Colorado Ghost Towns*. Vols. 1 and 2. Deming, N.M.: Carson Enterprises, Ltd., 1984.

Bright, William. *Colorado Place Names*. Boulder, Colo.: Johnson Books, 1993.

Brown, Robert L. *Colorado Ghost Towns Past & Present*. Caldwell, Idaho: Caxton Printers, Ltd., 1972.

———. *Ghost Towns of the Colorado Rockies*. Caldwell, Idaho: Caxton Printers, Ltd., 1990.

———. *Jeep Trails to Colorado Ghost Towns*. Caldwell, Idaho: Caxton Printers, Ltd., 1995.

Bueler, Gladys R. *Colorado's Colorful Characters*. Boulder, Colo.: Pruett Publishing, 1981.

Burt, William H., and Richard P. Grossenheider. *Peterson Field Guides: Mammals*. New York: Houghton Mifflin, 1980.

Carver, Jack, Jerry Vondergeest, Dallas Boyd, and Tom Pade. *Land of Legend*. Denver, Colo.: Caravon Press, 1959.

Coombes, Allen J. *Eyewitness Handbooks: Trees*. New York: Dorling Kindersley, 1992.

Crofutt, George A. *Crofutt's Grip-Sack Guide of Colorado*. Omaha: Overland Publishing, 1885. Reprinted, Boulder, Colo.: Johnson Books, 1981.

Cromie, Alice. *A Tour Guide to the Old West*. Nashville, Tenn.: Rutledge Hill Press, 1990.

Crutchfield, James A. *It Happened in Colorado*. Helena & Billings, Mo.: Falcon Press Publishing, 1993.

Dallas, Sandra. *Colorado Ghost Towns and Mining Camps*. Norman, Okla.: University of Oklahoma Press, 1985.

DeLong, Brad. *4-Wheel Freedom*. Boulder, Colo.: Paladin Press, 1996.

Dorset, Phyllis Flanders. *The New Eldorado: The Story of Colorado's Gold & Silver Rushes*. New York: Macmillan, 1970.

Eberhart, Perry. *Guide to the Colorado Ghost Towns and Mining Camps*. Chicago.: Swallow Press, 1995.

Edrinn, Roger. *Colorado Scenic Wildflowers*. Fort Collins, Colo.: Above the Timber, 1997.

Fisher, Vardis, and Opal Laurel Holmes. *Gold Rushes and Mining Camps of the Early American West*. Caldwell, Idaho: Caxton Printers, Ltd., 1968.

Florin, Lambert. *Ghost Towns of the West*. New York: Promontory Press, 1993.

Folzenlogen, Robert. *Colorado's Year: A Guide to Nature's Highlights*. Littleton, Colo.: Willow Press, 1996.

Foster, Mike. *Strange Genius: The Life of Ferdinand Vandeveer Hayden*. Niwot, Colo.: Roberts Rinehart Publishers, 1994.

Fothergill, Chuck, and Bob Sterling. *The Colorado Angling Guide*. Woody Creek, Colo.: Stream Stalker, 1989.

Gray, Mary Taylor. *Colorado Wildlife Viewing Guide*. Helena, Mont.: Falcon Press, 1992.

Green, Stewart M. *Bureau of Land Management Back Country Byways*. Helena, Mont.: Falcon Press, 1995.

Gregory, Lee. *Colorado Scenic Guide: Northern Region*. Boulder, Colo.: Johnson Books, 1990.

———. *Colorado Scenic Guide: Southern Region*. Boulder, Colo.: Johnson Books, 1990.

Griffin, Wayne W. *Central Colorado 4-Wheeling Guidebook*. Aspen, Colo.: Who Press, 1994.

Heck, Larry E. *4-Wheel Drive Roads & Ghost Towns of the San Juans*. Aurora, Colo.: Pass Patrol, 1995.

———. *4-Wheel Drive Roads to Outback Colorado*. Aurora, Colo.: Pass Patrol, 1995.

———. *4-Wheel Drive Trails & Ghost Towns of Colorado*. Aurora, Colo.: Pass Patrol, 1995.

Helmuth, Ed, and Gloria Helmuth. *The Passes of Colorado*. Boulder, Colo.: Pruett, 1994.

Hilton, George W. *American Narrow Gauge Railroads*. Stanford: Stanford University Press, 1990.

Hoxie, Frederick E., ed. *Encyclopedia of North American Indians*. Boston: Houghton Mifflin Company, 1996.

Jessen, Kennrth. *Colorado Gunsmoke: True Stories of Outlaws and Lawmen on the Colorado Frontier*. Loveland, Colo.: J. V. Publications, 1986.

———. *Ghost Towns Colorado Style*. Vol. 1. Loveland, Colo.: J.V. Publications, 1998.

———. *Ghost Towns Colorado Style*. Vol 2. Loveland, Colo.: J.V. Publications, 1999.

Jones, Charlotte Foltz. *Colorado Wildflowers*. Helena, Mont.: Falcon Press, 1994.

Koch, Don. *The Colorado Pass Book*. Boulder, Colo.: Pruett, 1992.

Kruger, Frances, and Carron A. Meany. *Explore Colorado: A Naturalist's Notebook*. Englewood, Colo.: Westcliffe, 1995.

Lamar, Howard R., ed. *The New Encyclopedia of the American West*. New Haven and London: Yale University Press, 1998.

Little, Elbert L. *Audubon Society Field Guide to North American Trees: Western Region*. New York: Alfred A. Knopf, 1980.

Litvak, Dianna. *Colorado Travel Smart Trip Planner*. Santa Fe, N.M.: John Muir, 1996.

McLean, Evalyn Walsh. *Father Struck it Rich*. Fort Collins, Colo.: FirstLight, 1996.

McTighe, James. *Roadside History of Colorado*. Boulder, Colo.: Johnson Books, 1984.

Mehls, Steven F. *The Valley of Opportunity: A History of West-Central Colorado*. Denver, Colo.: Bureau of Land Management, 1982.

Noel, Thomas J., Paul F. Mahoney, and Richard E. Stevens. *Historical Atlas of Colorado*. Norman, Okla.: University of Oklahoma Press, 1994.

Norton, Boyd, and Barbara Norton. *Backroads of Colorado*. Stillwater, Minn: Voyageur Press, 1995.

Ormes, Robert M. *Railroads and the Rockies*. Denver, Colo.: Sage Books, 1963.

———. *Tracking Ghost Railroads in Colorado*. Colorado Springs, Colo.: Green Light Graphics, 1992.

O'Rourke, Paul M. *Frontier in Transition: A History of Southwestern Colorado*. Denver, Colo.: Bureau of Land Management, 1980.

Parker, Ben H., Jr. *Gold Panning and Placering in Colorado*. Denver, Colo.: U.S. Geological Survey, Department of Natural Resources, 1992.

Peattie, Donald Culross. *A Natural History of Western Trees*. Boston, Mass.: Houghton Mifflin: 1950.

Pettem, Silvia. *Colorado Mountains & Passes—Colorado Traveler Guidebooks*. Frederick, Colo.: Renaissance House, 1991.

Pettit, Jan. *Utes: The Mountain People*. Boulder, Colo.: Johnson Books, 1994.

Pritchard, Sandra F. *Men, Mining & Machines*. Dillon, Colo.: Summit County Historical Society, 1996.

Reidhead, Darlene A. *Tour the San Juans*. Vols. 1 and 2. Cortez, Colo.: Southwest Printing, 1994.

Rennicke, Jeff. *Colorado Wildlife*. Helena, Mo.: Falcon Press, 1996.

Roberts, Harold D. *Mountain Wildflowers of Colorado*. Denver, Colo.: W. H. Kistler Stationery, 1957.

Roberts, Harold, and Rhoda Roberts. *Colorado Wildflowers*. Denver, Colo.: Bradford-Robinson, 1953.

Russo, Ron. *Mountain State Mammals*. Rochester, N.Y.: Nature Study Guild, 1991.

Rye, David. *Colorado's Guide to Hunting*. Glenwood Springs, Colo.: Mountain Peaks, 1992.

Sinnotte, Barbara. *Colorado: A Guide to the State & National Parks*. Edison, N.J.: Hunter, 1996.

Smith, Duane A. *Colorado Mining: A Photographic History*. Albuquerque, N.M.: University of New Mexico Press, 1977.

Southworth, Dave. *Colorado Mining Camps*. Round Rock, Tx.: Wild Horse, 1997.

———. *Gunfighters of the Old West*. Round Rock, Tx.: Wild Horse, 1997.

Strickler, Dr. Dee. *Alpine Wildflowers*. Columbia Falls, Mo.: The Flower Press, 1990.

———. *Forest Wildflowers*. Columbia Falls, Mo.: The Flower Press, 1988.

Swift, Kim. *Heart of the Rockies: A History of the Salida Area*. Boulder, Colo.: Johnson Books, 1996.

Taylor, Colin F. *The Plains Indians*. New York: Barnes & Noble Books and Salamander Books, 1997.

Ubbelohde, Carl, Maxine Benson, and Duane A. Smith. *A Colorado History*. Boulder, Colo.: Pruett Publishing, 1995.

Von Bamford, Lawrence, and Kenneth R. Tremblay, Jr. *Leadville Architecture*. Estes Park, Colo.: Architecture Research Press, 1996.

Waldman, Carl. *Encyclopedia of Native American Tribes*. New York: Facts on File, 1988.

Wassink, Jan L. *Mammals of the Central Rockies*. Missoula, Mont.: Mountain Press, 1993.

Wilkins, Tivis E. *Colorado Railroads Chronological Development*. Boulder, Colo.: Pruett Publishing, 1974.

Wilson, Ray D. *Colorado Historical Tour Guide*. Carpentersville, Ill.: Crossroads Communications, 1990.

Wolle, Muriel Sibelle. *The Bonanza Trail*. Chicago: The Swallow Press, 1953.

———. *Stampede to Timberline: The Ghost Towns and Mining Camps of Colorado*. Chicago.: Swallow Press and Ohio University Press, 1974.

Zim, Herbert S., Ph.D., and Alexander C. Martin, Ph.D. *Trees: A Guide to Familiar American Trees*. New York: Golden Press, 1964.

Zim, Herbert S., Ph.D., Sc.D., and Hobart M. Smith, Ph.D. *Reptiles and Amphibians (A Golden Guide)*. Racine, Wis.: Western, 1987.

Selected Internet sources

Animas Museum, http://animasmuseum.org

Aspen Historical Society, http://aspenhistoricalsociety.com

Buffalo Bill Museum and Grave, http://www.buffalobill.org

Chimney Rock Archeological Area, http://chimneyrockco.org

Colorado Byways, http://www.coloradobyways.org

Colorado Historical Society, http://www.coloradohistory.org

Colorado Ski History, http://www.coloradoskihistory.com

Colorado State Archives: State Penitentiary Records, http://www.colorado.gov/dpa/doit/archives/pen/history.htm

Colorado State Parks, http://parks.state.co.us

Durango Telegraph, http://durangotelegraph.com

Forest Fire Lookout Association, Colorado and Utah Chapter, http://coloradolookouts.com

Fort Collins Public Library, http://history.fcgov.com/local_history/Topics/nutshell.htm

Fort Lewis College, Center of Southwest Studies, http://swcenter.fortlewis.edu

GORP.com, http://gorp.away.com

La Plata County, http://co.laplata.co.us

Minerology Database, http://mindat.org

Mining Foundation of the Southwest, http://www.miningfoundationsw.org

Molly Brown House Museum, http://www.mollybrown.org

Mountain Studies Institute, http://mountainstudies.org

Myron Stratton Home, http://www.myronstratton.org/history.html

National Center for Disease Control: Hantavirus Pulmonary Syndrome, http://cdc.gov/ncidad/diseases/hanta/hps/

San Juan Public Lands Center, http://fs.fed.us/r2/sanjuan or http://co.blm.gov/sjra/index.htm

U.S. Bureau of Land Management, Colorado, http://blm.gov/co

U.S. Department of the Interior, Bureau of Reclamation, http://usbr.gov

U.S. Fish & Wildlife Service, http://fws.gov

U.S. Forest Service, http://www.fs.fed.us/r5/forests.html

White Water Rafting in North America, http://e-raft.com/regions/Colorado/colorado.asp

Index

About the Authors

Peter Massey grew up in the outback of Australia. After retiring from a career in investment banking at the age of thirty five, he served as a director of a number of companies in the United States, the United Kingdom and Australia. He moved to Colorado in 1993.

Jeanne Wilson was born and grew up in Maryland. After moving to New York City in 1980, she worked in advertising and public relations before moving to Colorado in 1993.

After traveling extensively in Australia, Europe, Asia, and Africa, the authors covered more than 80,000 miles touring the United States and the Australian Outback between 1993 and 1997. This experience became the basis for creating the *Backcountry Adventures* and *Trails* guidebook series.

Angela Titus was born in Missouri and grew up in Virginia, where she attended the University of Virginia. She traveled extensively throughout the western states, pursuing her interests in four-wheeling, hiking, and mountain biking. She moved to Alabama and worked for *Southern Living Magazine* traveling, photographing, and writing about the southeastern U.S. She moved to Colorado to join the Adler Publishing team in 2002.

Since research for the *Backcountry Adventures* and *Trails* books began, Peter, Jeanne, and Angela have traveled more than 100,000 miles throughout the western states.

Photograph Credits

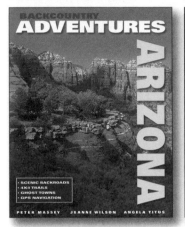

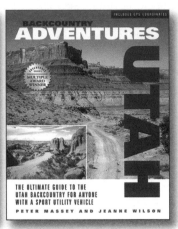
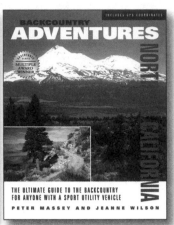